THE PAPERS OF
FREDERICK LAW OLMSTED

EDITORIAL STAFF

Charles E. Beveridge
Series Editor

Tina Hummel
Research Associate and Production Editor

ADVISORY BOARD

Charles Capen McLaughlin, Chair
Gunther Barth
Richard D. Breitman
Roger H. Brown
Jane Turner Censer
Alan M. Kraut
David Schuyler

THE PAPERS OF
FREDERICK LAW OLMSTED

VOLUME VII
PARKS, POLITICS, AND PATRONAGE

1874–1882

CHARLES E. BEVERIDGE

CAROLYN F. HOFFMAN

KENNETH HAWKINS
Editors

TINA HUMMEL
Assistant Editor

THE JOHNS HOPKINS UNIVERSITY PRESS
Baltimore

© 2007 The Johns Hopkins University Press
All rights reserved. Published 2007
Printed in the United States of America on acid-free paper
9 8 7 6 5 4 3 2 1

The Johns Hopkins University Press
2715 North Charles Street
Baltimore, Maryland 21218-4363
www.press.jhu.edu

Library of Congress Cataloging-in-Publication Data
(Revised for vol. 7)

Olmsted, Frederick Law, 1822–1903.
  The papers of Frederick Law Olmsted.

  Includes bibliographical references and indexes.
  Contents: v. 1. The formative years, 1822–1852 — v. 2. Slavery and the South, 1852–1857 — v. 3. Creating Central Part, 1857–1861 — v. 4. Defending the Union, 1861–1863 — v. 5. The California frontier, 1863–1865 — v. 6. The years of Olmsted, Vaux & Company, 1865–1874.
  1. Olmsted, Frederick, 1822–1903. 2. Landscape architects—United States—Correspondence. 3. Landscape architects—United States—Biography. I. McLaughlin, Charles Capen. II. Beveridge, Charles E. III. Title.
SB470.O5A2 1977   712   77-741
ISBN 0-8018-1798-6 (v. 1)   ISBN 0-8018-3885-1 (v. 5)
ISBN 0-8018-2242-4 (v. 2)   ISBN 0-8018-4198-4 (v. 6)
ISBN 0-8018-2751-5 (v. 3)   ISBN 0-8018-8336-9 (v. 7)
ISBN 0-8018-3067-2 (v. 4)

CONTENTS

ILLUSTRATIONS	xv
ACKNOWLEDGMENTS	xxiii
INTRODUCTION	1
EDITORIAL POLICY	24
SHORT TITLES USED IN CITATIONS	28
Chapter I JANUARY 1874–AUGUST 1874	33
"Country Living," *Nation*, January 22, 1874	34
To Justin Smith Morrill, January 22, 1874	36
To Salem H. Wales, March 4, 1874	43
To William Hammond Hall, March 23, 1874	50
To William Hammond Hall, March 28, 1874	53
To Seymour Ainsworth, Hiram Tompkins, and John L. Perry, April 21, 1874	55

CONTENTS

To Montgomery Cunningham Meigs, May 14, 1874	59
To Justin Smith Morrill and James Henry Platt, Jr., June 9, 1874	64
To Charles Sprague Sargent, July 8, 1874	68
To Justin Smith Morrill, August 16, 1874	69

Chapter II AUGUST 1874–JANUARY 1875 — 74

To Henry G. Stebbins, August 27, 1874	74
To Albert Gallatin Browne, November 12, 1874	82
To the Commissioners of Mount-Royal Park, November 21, 1874	84
To Whitelaw Reid, November 26, 1874	92
"The National Capitol," December 5, 1874	93
To the Buffalo Park Commission, December 15, 1874	99
To Montgomery Cunningham Meigs, January 15, 1875	103
To Henry G. Stebbins, January 15, 1875	108
To Frederick William Poppey, January 21, 1875	115
To the Board of Commissioners of the Department of Public Parks, c. January–February 1875	117

Chapter III FEBRUARY 1875–FEBRUARY 1876 — 123

To the Board of Commissioners of the Department of Public Parks, March 1, 1875	124
To Thomas Pynchon, c. March 10, 1875	129
To William L. Fischer, March 14, 1875	133
To William Robinson, c. March 20–30, 1875	135
To Frederick Law Olmsted, Jr., May 13, 1875	138
To Henry G. Stebbins, May 18, 1875	139

CONTENTS

To Montgomery Cunningham Meigs, June 1, 1875	144
To John A. Partridge, September 9, 1875	146
To William Hammond Hall, September 13, 1875	149
To Walter L. Sessions, October 9, 1875	151
To Horatio Admiral Nelson, October 11, 1875	156
To Thomas Hill, November 3, 1875	158
To George Jones, November 19, 1875	160
To Henry G. Stebbins, December 3, 1875	164
To Dennis Bowen, January 1, 1876	168
To Henry G. Stebbins, February 1, 1876	174
To Rev. J. H. Miller, February 28, 1876	179
Chapter IV April 1876–December 1876	183
To William Edward Dorsheimer, April 2, 1876	184
To Charles Eliot Norton, April 2, 1876	188
To Horatio Admiral Nelson, April 4, 1876	191
To Charles Henry Dalton, April 8, 1876	192
To Charles Eliot Norton, April 22, 1876	199
To Horatio Admiral Nelson, June 6, 1876	201
To Charles Eliot Norton, June 7, 1876	204
To Horatio Admiral Nelson, July 26, 1876	206
To William Runyon Martin, August 9, 1876	210
"Mr. Olmsted on Landscape Gardening," *The Garden*, August 12, 1876	223
To William McMillan, September 10, 1876	229
To Dennis Bowen, September 10, 1876	231
To William McMillan, September 11, 1876	233
To Horatio Admiral Nelson, September 28, 1876	235
To Frederick Law Olmsted, Jr., October 1, 1876	237

CONTENTS

"Preliminary Report of the Landscape Architect and the Civil and Topographical Engineer, upon the Laying Out of the Twenty-Third And Twenty-Fourth Wards," November 15, 1876 — 242

"Report of the Landscape Architect and the Civil and Topographical Engineer, Accompanying a Plan for Laying Out that Part of the Twenty-Fourth Ward Lying West of the Riverdale Road," November 21, 1876 — 251

To Thomas M. Lanahan, December 23, 1876 — 266

To Charles Eliot Norton, December 27, 1876 — 277

Chapter V JANUARY 1877–OCTOBER 1877 — 282

Memorandum on New York Capitol Patronage, 1877 — 283

To Charles Eliot Norton, February 15, 1877 — 284

To Whitelaw Reid, March 2, 1877 — 286

New York State Capitol Testimony, March 6, 1877 — 288

To William McMillan, March 16, 1877 — 304

To William Runyon Martin, March 20, 1877 — 306

To Horatio Admiral Nelson, March 26, 1877 — 313

"To the Public," March 26, 1877 — 315

To the Mount Royal Park Commission, April 28, 1877 — 317

To William Runyon Martin, May 16, 1877 — 318

"The Central Park," May 19, 1877: *American Architect and Building News*, June 2, 1877 — 324

To Horatio Admiral Nelson, July 24, 1877 — 328

To Mary Perkins Olmsted, July 24, 1877 — 329

To Mary Perkins Olmsted, July 25, 1877 — 330

To Mary Perkins Olmsted, August 10, 1877 — 331

To John Charles Olmsted, October 7, 1877 — 333

CONTENTS

CHAPTER VI   OCTOBER 1877–JULY 1878   339

   To William Runyon Martin, October 31, 1877   340

   "Landscape Gardening" [1877]: *Johnson's New Universal Cyclopaedia*, 1878   350

   To the Board of Commissioners of the Department of Public Parks, January 2, 1878   358

   To Charles Henry Dalton, May 13, 1878   363

   To Robert Garrett, June 5, 1878   366

   "Notice to Watchmen for the Capitol Grounds," July 7, 1878   369

CHAPTER VII   JANUARY 1879–OCTOBER 1879   372

   Review of New York City Park Department Policies in 1878, January 8, 1879   373

   To Charles Sprague Sargent, January 27, 1879   387

   To Charles Sprague Sargent, January 29, 1879   388

   To Edward Clark, May 23, 1879   390

   To Édouard François André, June 6, 1879   393

   To Edward Clark, June 21, 1879   396

   To Henry Y. Attrill and Benjamin E. Smith, July 30, 1879   397

   To Henry Y. Attrill, September 23, 1879   417

   To James Terry Gardner, October 2, 1879   420

   To James Terry Gardner, October 3, 1879   422

   To Charles Eliot Norton, October 10, 1879   424

CHAPTER VIII   DECEMBER 1879–MAY 1880   427

   To Charles Henry Dalton, December 9, 1879   428

   To Tiffany & Company, December 9, 1879   431

   To Henry Whitney Bellows, December 22, 1879   433

CONTENTS

To Henry Whitney Bellows, December 24, 1879	434
"The Future of New York," *New-York Daily Tribune*, December 28, 1879	436
To Charles Eliot Norton, January 22, 1880	445
To Joseph Phineas Davis, January 24, 1880	447
To Charles Henry Dalton, January 24, 1880	450
To the Board of Commissioners of the Department of Parks of the City of Boston, January 26, 1880	451
To Barthold S. Schlesinger, February 9, 1880	464
To Charles Eliot Norton, February 15, 1880	471
"Notes by Mr. Olmsted." in *Special Report of New York State Survey on the Preservation of the Scenery of Niagara Falls for the Year 1879* [c. March 22, 1880]	474
"Improvement of the Back-Bay, Boston," *The American Architect and Building News*, April 3, 1880	481
To Charles Henry Dalton, May 5, 1880	484
To Charles Eliot Norton, May 7, 1880	488

Chapter IX May 1880–December 1880	491
To John Charles Phillips, May 11, 1880	492
To the Earl of Derby, June 11, 1880	497
To Thomas Wisedell, June 13, 1880	498
To William Oliver Buchanan, June 15, 1880	503
To John Charles Phillips, August 23, 1880	504
To Edward Clark, c. August–September 1880	507
To Sylvester Baxter, November 9, 1880	510
To Edward Clark, November 18, 1880	512
To Charles Henry Dalton, November 29, 1880	515
To the Commissioners of Parks, "Suggestions for the Improvement of Muddy River," December 1880	517

CONTENTS

CHAPTER X   FEBRUARY 1881–DECEMBER 1881   523

    To Horace William Shaler Cleveland, February 9, 1881   524

    To Paul Cornell, April 12, 1881   525

    To C. H. Dalton, "Mr. Olmsted's Report," May 17, 1881   528

    To Charles Eliot Norton, May 30, 1881   533

    To Barthold S. Schlesinger, June 17, 1881   535

    "Influence," c. July 1881   539

    To John Charles Phillips, September 27, 1881   549

    To Cornelius Rea Agnew, c. June–October 1881   555

    To Edward Clark, October 1, 1881   557

    To Charles Eliot Norton, October 19, 1881   561

    To Charles Eliot Norton, November 2, 1881   563

    To Charles Francis Adams, Jr., November 29, 1881   566

    To Charles Henry Dalton, December 29, 1881   567

    To John Sterling, December 30, 1881   572

CHAPTER XI   JANUARY 1882–MARCH 1882   574

    To Edward Henry Rollins, January 7, 1882   575

    To Edward Henry Rollins, c. January–February 1882   577

    "Central Park Circular," c. February 1882   583

    To George Kessler, March 5, 1882   588

    To John Charles Phillips, March 6, 1882   590

    To Charles Loring Brace, March 7, 1882   592

APPENDIX I   CHRONOLOGY OF FREDERICK LAW OLMSTED, 1874–1882   597

APPENDIX II   THE SPOILS OF THE PARK WITH A FEW LEAVES FROM THE DEEP-LADEN NOTE-BOOKS OF "A WHOLLY UNPRACTICAL MAN." (1882)   605

CONTENTS

Appendix III   PATRONAGE JOURNAL (1873–1877)   653

Appendix IV   LIST OF TEXTUAL ALTERATIONS   721

INDEX OF PLANT MATERIALS   735

GENERAL INDEX   739

ILLUSTRATIONS

FREDERICK LAW OLMSTED, C. 1878   Courtesy of the National Park Service, Frederick Law Olmsted National Historic Site, Brookline, Massachusetts   *Frontispiece*

VIEW OF U.S. CAPITOL WITH EARTH TERRACES, C. 1880   Courtesy of the Architect of the Capitol, Washington, D.C.   39

PLAN OF LOWER CENTRAL PARK, NEW YORK CITY, 1873   Courtesy of the Central Park Conservancy, New York, N.Y.   45

"PRELIMINARY STUDY FOR THE LAYING-OUT OF COURT OF UNITED STATES HOTEL AT SARATOGA SPRINGS, N.Y., DESIGNED BY FRED. LAW OLMSTED. J. WEIDENMANN, LANDSCAPE ARCHITECTS APRIL 1874" (Plan 602-1)   Courtesy of the National Park Service, Frederick Law Olmsted National Historic Site, Brookline, Mass.   56–57

"PLANTING MAP FOR CORTILE AT JEFFERSONVILLE DEPOT, IND. OF THE QUARTERMASTER'S DEPARTMENT U.S.A."   Fred. Law Olmsted, Landscape Architect, April 1874 Record Group 77, NARA   Courtesy of the National Archives and Records Administration, Washington, D.C.   60

[FREDERICK LAW OLMSTED], PLAN FOR U.S. CAPITOL GROUNDS, C. 1874 (Plan 2820-35)   Courtesy of the National Park Service, Frederick Law Olmsted National Historic Site, Brookline, Mass.   65

ILLUSTRATIONS

[FREDERICK LAW OLMSTED], "MOUNT ROYAL DESIGN MAP 1877" Courtesy of the National Park Service, Frederick Law Olmsted National Historic Site, Brookline, Mass. 88

"GENERAL PLAN FOR THE IMPROVEMENT OF THE U.S. CAPITOL GROUNDS" (1875) Fred. Law Olmsted, Landscape Architect Courtesy of the Architect of the Capitol, Washington, D.C. 95

PARAPET AND CURVED BLUESTONE SEAT ON EDGE OF PLAZA ON EAST GROUNDS OF U.S. CAPITOL Courtesy of the Architect of the Capitol, Washington, D.C. 97

BUFFALO PARK COMMISSION, "STUDY OF PLAN FOR IMPROVEMENT OF NIAGARA SQUARE," OCTOBER 1874 Fred. Law Olmsted, Landscape Architect Private Collection 100

PROPOSED CIVIL WAR MEMORIAL FOR NIAGARA SQUARE, BUFFALO, C. DECEMBER 1874 Henry Hobson Richardson, Architect Courtesy of Houghton Library, Harvard University, Cambridge, Mass. 102

VIEW OF WEST FRONT OF U.S. CAPITOL FROM SOUTHWEST SHOWING EXISTING CONDITION WITH EARTH TERRACES (1875) Rendering by Thomas Wisedell Courtesy of the Architect of the Capitol, Washington, D.C. 104

VIEW OF WEST FRONT OF U.S. CAPITOL FROM SOUTHWEST SHOWING TERRACES PROPOSED BY OLMSTED (1875) Rendering by Thomas Wisedell Courtesy of the Architect of the Capitol, Washington, D.C. 105

DEPARTMENT OF PUBLIC PARKS [NEW YORK CITY] "MAP OF THE RIVERSIDE DISTRICT WITH THE OUTLINE OF A PLAN OF A PARK EXTENDED OVER THE GROUND ORIGINALLY APPROPRIATED TO AN AVENUE AND DESIGNED TO COMBINE THE ADVANTAGES OF PARK AND AVENUE," JANUARY 18, 1875 Fred. Law Olmsted, Landscape Architect 110–11

"PROPOSED MODIFICATION OF PLAN HERETOFORE PRESENTED FOR A PART OF RIVERSIDE AVENUE INTRODUCING A RIDING WAY," MARCH 15, 1875 Fred. Law Olmsted, Landscape Architect Courtesy of the National Park Service, Frederick Law Olmsted National Site, Brookline, Mass. 169

[FREDERICK LAW OLMSTED], "PRELIMINARY STUDY FOR GROUNDS OF NEW CITY AND COUNTY HALL, BUFFALO, N.Y.," c. JANUARY 1876 (Plan

ILLUSTRATIONS

12106-Z1)   Courtesy of the National Park Service, Frederick Law Olmsted National Historic Site, Brookline, Mass.   *172–73*

"Map of Point Chautauqua Grounds . . . Laid Out by Prof. Fred. Law Olmsted" (1876)   Courtesy of Point Chatauga Historical Preservation Society   *180–81*

Façade of Doges' Palace, Venice   Courtesy of the Library of Congress, Prints and Photographs Division, Washington, D.C.   *185*

Model of Design by Thomas Fuller for New York State New Capitol, c. 1875   Courtesy of the Library of Congress, Prints and Photographs Division, Washington, D.C.   *189*

"New State Capitol at Albany. General Perspective View, Showing the Proposed Alterations"   From *American Architect and Building News*, March 11, 1876   *190*

Park Department, City of Boston, "Back Bay and Parker Hill Parks, Parker Hill & Jamaica Parkways," (1876)   Courtesy of the Francis Loeb Library, Harvard School of Design   *194*

Park Department, City of Boston, "Sketch Showing Arrangement for Park-way with Adjacent Streets and Building Lots, 1876"   From BCDP, City of Boston, *Second Report* (1876)   *196*

[Frederick Law Olmsted], Plan for upper Mount Royal without reservoir (Plan 609-36)   Courtesy of the National Park Service, Frederick Law Olmsted National Historic Site, Brookline, Mass.   *207*

[Frederick Law Olmsted], Plan for reservoir and promenade on Mount Royal (Plan 609-Z26)   Courtesy of the National Park Service, Frederick Law Olmsted National Historic Site, Brookline, Mass.   *209*

View of Tompkins Square, November 1870   Drawing no. 2663, Record Group   Department of Parks and Recreation   Courtesy of the New York City Municipal Archives   *214*

[Frederick Law Olmsted], "Late Additions to the Plan of Buffalo," c. 1876   Courtesy of the National Park Service, Frederick Law Olmsted National Historic Site, Brookline, Mass.   *232*

ILLUSTRATIONS

DEPARTMENT OF PUBLIC PARKS [NEW YORK CITY], "PLAN OF STREETS, ROADS AND AVENUES WITHIN THAT PART OF THE TWENTY-FOURTH WARD OF THE CITY OF NEW-YORK LYING WEST OF THE EASTERLY SIDE OF RIVERDALE AVENUE," FEBRUARY 21, 1877   J. James R. Croes, Civil and Topographical Engineer and Fred. Law Olmsted, Landscape Architect   Courtesy of the President of the Borough of the Bronx, New York City   261

"VIEW OF BALTIMORE CITY, MD. FROM THE NORTH"   E. Sachse & Co., c. 1862   Courtesy of the Library of Congress, Prints and Photographs Division, Washington, D.C.   268

[FREDERICK LAW OLMSTED], SKETCH FOR NORTH SQUARE (WINTER), WASHINGTON MONUMENT, BALTIMORE, MARYLAND, C. DECEMBER 1876   OAR/LC B2403   Courtesy of the Library of Congress, Manuscript Division, Washington, D.C.   270

[FREDERICK LAW OLMSTED], "EAST PARK," SKETCH FOR EAST SQUARE (SUMMER), WASHINGTON MONUMENT, BALTIMORE, MARYLAND, C. DECEMBER 1876   OAR/LC B2403   Courtesy of the Library of Congress, Manuscript Division, Washington, D.C.   271

[FREDERICK LAW OLMSTED], "WEST PARK," SKETCH FOR WEST SQUARE (AUTUMN), WASHINGTON MONUMENT, BALTIMORE, MARYLAND, C. DECEMBER 1876   OAR/LC B2403   Courtesy of the Library of Congress, Manuscript Division, Washington, D.C.   271

[FREDERICK LAW OLMSTED], SKETCH FOR SOUTH SQUARE (SPRING), WASHINGTON MONUMENT, BALTIMORE, MARYLAND, C. DECEMBER 1876   OAR/LC B2403   Courtesy of the Library of Congress, Manuscript Division, Washington, D.C.   272

[FREDERICK LAW OLMSTED], REVISED PLAN FOR NORTH SQUARE (WINTER), WASHINGTON MONUMENT, BALTIMORE, MARYLAND, C. MARCH 1877 (Plan 2403-3)   Courtesy of the National Park Service, Frederick Law Olmsted National Historic Site, Brookline, Mass.   274

[FREDERICK LAW OLMSTED], REVISED PLAN FOR SOUTH SQUARE (SPRING), WASHINGTON MONUMENT, BALTIMORE, MARYLAND, C. MARCH 1877 (Plan 2403-8)   Courtesy of the National Park Service, Frederick Law Olmsted National Historic Site, Brookline, Mass.   275

DEPARTMENT OF PUBLIC PARKS [NEW YORK CITY], "ROUTES FOR LOCAL STEAM TRANSIT IN THE TWENTY-THIRD AND TWENTY-FOURTH WARDS

ILLUSTRATIONS

of New-York City," March 20, 1877   Fred. Law Olmsted, Landscape Architect and J. J. R. Croes, Civil and Topographical Engineer   Courtesy of the President of the Borough of the Bronx, New York City   *309*

Department of Public Parks [New York City], "Plan of Streets, Roads and Avenues and Public Parks or Places in the Central District of the Twenty-third and Twenty-fourth Wards of the City of New York," March 28, 1878   [Frederick Law Olmsted, Landscape Architect], J. J. R. Croes, Civil and Topographical Engineer   Courtesy of the President of the Borough of the Bronx, New York City   *341*

Frederick Law Olmsted, "Map Showing Proposed Belt of Woods between Public Grounds West and South of the Capitol Grounds"   Courtesy of the Architect of the Capitol, Washington, D.C.   *391*

[Frederick Law Olmsted] "Plan for street communication through Reservation 17," Washington, D.C., June 20, 1879   (Plan 2820-40)   Courtesy of the National Park Service, Frederick Law Olmsted National Historic Site, Brookline, Mass.   *396*

[Frederick Law Olmsted] Plan II "Rockaway Point. Preliminary Plan," c. July 1879   (Plan 515-7)   Courtesy of the National Park Service, Frederick Law Olmsted National Historic Site, Brookline, Mass.   *408*

Frederick Law Olmsted, Plan III "Rockaway Point. Preliminary Plan, Enlarged Scale, of Districts A and B, Drawing No 1," July 29, 1879   Courtesy of the National Park Service, Frederick Law Olmsted National Historic Site, Brookline, Mass.   *413*

[Frederick Law Olmsted] Plan IV "Rockaway Point. Modified Preliminary Plan," c. July 1879   Courtesy of the National Park Service, Frederick Law Olmsted National Historic Site, Brookline, Mass.   *414*

Park Department, City of Boston, "Preliminary Plan for the Back Bay Park," February 13, 1879   Fred. Law Olmsted, Landscape Architect   (Plan 916-3)   Courtesy of the National Park Service, Frederick Law Olmsted National Historic Site, Brookline, Mass.   *429*

ILLUSTRATIONS

STREET PLAN FOR NEW YORK CITY, 1811   Courtesy of Eno Collection, Miriam and Ira D. Wallack Division of Art, Prints & Photographs, The New York Public Library Astor, Lenox and Tilden Foundations   *440*

PARK DEPARTMENT, CITY OF BOSTON, "REVISION OF NORTHERN PART OF PRELIMINARY PLAN FOR THE BACK BAY PARK" (DETAIL), MARCH 5, 1879   Fred. Law Olmsted, Landscape Architect (Plan 916-355)   Courtesy of the National Park Service, Frederick Law Olmsted National Historic Site, Brookline, Mass.   *448*

PARK DEPARTMENT, CITY OF BOSTON, "PROPOSED IMPROVEMENT OF BACK BAY" (1879)   J. P. Davis, City Engineer and F. L. Olmsted, Landscape Architect   Courtesy of the National Park Service, Frederick Law Olmsted National Historic Site, Brookline, Mass.   *452–53*

[FREDERICK LAW OLMSTED], "SKETCH NO. 1," BARTHOLD SCHLESINGER ESTATE, BROOKLINE, MASS.   (Plan 614-22)   Courtesy of the National Park Service, Frederick Law Olmsted National Historic Site, Brookline, Mass.   *465*

"SKETCH NO. 2," BARTHOLD SCHLESINGER ESTATE, BROOKLINE, MASSACHUSETTS, SEPTEMBER 2, 1879   Fred^k Law Olmsted L. A. (Plan 614-13)   Courtesy of the National Park Service, Frederick Law Olmsted National Historic Site, Brookline, Mass.   *468*

"IDEAL VIEW UP THE AMERICAN RAPIDS, AFTER THE VILLAGE SHORE AND BATH ISLAND ARE RESTORED."   After a drawing by Francis Lathrop, Plate 1, *Special Report of New York State Survey on the Preservation of the Scenery of Niagara Falls . . .* (Albany, 1880)   *476*

VIEW OF BACK BAY FENS FROM BOYLSTON STREET BRIDGE, 1896   Courtesy of Frances Loeb Library, Harvard Graduate School of Design, Cambridge, Mass.   *482*

PARK DEPARTMENT, CITY OF BOSTON, "MAP OF PROPOSED ARBORETUM, SHOWING ITS OUTLINES AND LOCAL CONNECTIONS, WITH A STUDY FOR PUBLIC DRIVE PASSING THROUGH IT," (1879)   Fred^k Law Olmsted, Landscape Architect (Plan 902-4, print 3)   Courtesy of the National Park Service, Frederick Law Olmsted National Historic Site, Brookline, Mass.   *486–87*

"PLAN OF THE PHILLIPS ESTATE, BEVERLY, MASSACHUSETTS"   From *Garden and Forest*, March 30, 1892   *493*

ILLUSTRATIONS

[FREDERICK LAW OLMSTED], "PRELIMINARY STUDY NO. 1," JOHN C. PHILLIPS ESTATE, BEVERLY, MASSACHUSETTS (Plan 12297-82) Courtesy of the National Park Service, Frederick Law Olmsted National Historic Site, Brookline, Mass. *494*

[FREDERICK LAW OLMSTED], "SKETCH NO. 2," JOHN C. PHILLIPS ESTATE, BEVERLY, MASSACHUSETTS (Plan 12297-13) Courtesy of the National Park Service, Frederick Law Olmsted National Historic Site, Brookline, Mass. *495*

[FREDERICK LAW OLMSTED], "PLAN OF HOME GROUNDS," JOHN C. PHILLIPS ESTATE, BEVERLY, MASSACHUSETTS (Plan 12297-78) Courtesy of the National Park Service, Frederick Law Olmsted National Historic Site, Brookline, Mass. *505*

PHOTOGRAPH OF GARDEN WITH PAVILION AND STONE ARCH, JOHN C. PHILLIPS ESTATE, BEVERLY, MASSACHUSETTS Courtesy of the National Park Service, Frederick Law Olmsted National Historic Site, Brookline, Mass. *506*

"SUGGESTION FOR THE IMPROVEMENT OF MUDDY RIVER AND FOR COMPLETING A CONTINUOUS PROMENADE FROM THE COMMON TO JAMAICA POND" (DECEMBER 1880) F. L. Olmsted, Landscape Architect Courtesy of the National Park Service, Frederick Law Olmsted National Historic Site, Brookline, Mass. *519*

OLMSTED, VAUX & CO., PLAN FOR SOUTH OPEN GROUND AND UPPER PLAISANCE SECTIONS (Washington Park) of Chicago South Park (1871) *526*

PARK DEPARTMENT, CITY OF BOSTON, "WEST ROXBURY PARK" From BCDP, City of Boston, *Second Report* (1876) *529*

[FREDERICK LAW OLMSTED] STUDY FOR REDUCTION OF SIZE OF WEST ROXBURY PARK, MAY 5, 1881 (Plan 918-649) Courtesy of the National Park Service, Frederick Law Olmsted National Historic Site, Brookline, Mass. *531*

VIEW OF SUMMER HOUSE ON U.S. CAPITOL GROUNDS, C. 1881 (Photograph 2820-2) Courtesy of the National Park Service, Frederick Law Olmsted National Historic Site, Brookline, Mass. *534*

VIEW OF SUMMER HOUSE ON U.S. CAPITOL GROUNDS, C. 1881 (Photograph 2820-3) Courtesy of the U.S. Commission of Fine Arts, Washington, D.C. *534*

ILLUSTRATIONS

View of south façade of Barthold Schlesinger house, Brookline, Massachusetts   Private Collection   537

[Frederick Law Olmsted], Sketch for path with octagonal terrace feature on south side of house, Barthold Schlesinger estate, Brookline, Massachusetts, Summer 1881 (Plan 614-Z3)   Courtesy of the National Park Service, Frederick Law Olmsted National Historic Site, Brookline, Mass.   538

View of John C. Phillips house, Beverly, Massachusetts   Courtesy of Boston Architectural Center, Boston, Mass.   551

View of principal terrace, John C. Phillips Estate, Beverly, Massachusetts   Courtesy of the George L. Batchelder III family   552

View of Montauk Association cottages, Montauk Point, Long Island   Courtesy of Carlton Kelsey Archive, Amagansett Historical Association, Amagansett, N.Y.   556

Park Department, City of Boston, "Proposed Park System from the Common to the West Roxbury Park including the Back Bay and Muddy River Improvements, Jamaica Pond and the Arnold Arboretum" (1882)   Courtesy of the National Park Service, Frederick Law Olmsted National Historic Site, Brookline, Mass.   570

View of U.S. Capitol with proposed terrace, from southwest (1882)   Courtesy of the Library of Congress, Manuscript Division, Washington, D.C.   578

Floor plan of basement of proposed terrace of U.S. Capitol (1882)   Courtesy of the Library of Congress, Manuscript Division, Washington, D.C.   580

Plan of "esplanade" of proposed terrace of U.S. Capitol with two details showing line of sight made possible by two-tiered form of terrace (1882)   Courtesy of the Library of Congress, Manuscript Division, Washington, D.C.   581

ACKNOWLEDGMENTS

This volume is dedicated to Charles Capen McLaughlin, the founding editor of the Frederick Law Olmsted Papers whose years of research laid the foundation for the editorial project. He served as Editor-in-Chief during the first decade of funding of the Papers and was chairman of the advisory board until his death in September 2005. Through a long career in teaching and editing he inspired many people with his knowledge of and concern for Olmsted's legacy.

The editors wish to give special thanks to the National Endowment for the Humanities and the National Historical Publications and Records Commission for their longtime support of the Olmsted Papers project and in particular the funds they provided for preparation of this volume. Editor Kenneth Hawkins began his work on the volume during his year as an NHPRC editing fellow. We also owe a special debt of gratitude to the National Trust for the Humanities for administering gifts from the Barkley Fund that provided important support for the volume. We thank the National Association for Olmsted Parks for maintaining the special fund that enables its members to contribute to our work. George A. Ranney, Jr., and Victoria Post Ranney have shown great generosity in their support of the project over the years and deserve special recognition and thanks.

We wish to recognize the help provided by the many members of the staff of American University, our sponsoring institution, who assisted in processing grant proposals and administering grants that facilitated preparation of this volume. Professor Roger Brown, chairman of the Department of History during much of the time of preparation of the volume, deserves special notice and appreciation. Several students at the university provided valuable assistance as researchers: they included Susan Hines, Julie Berebitsky, and Matt Clavin.

Former associate editor Jane Turner Censer made valuable suggestions concerning the volume's introduction, and David Schuyler provided a thorough and valued review of the annotation of the volume. Faye B. Harwell provided a close and helpful reading of the volume introduction.

Other assistance has come from good friends in the world of Olmsted scholarship. Arleyn A. Levee gave us the benefit of her knowledge of the career of John C. Olmsted and of Olmsted's work on the U.S. Capitol grounds. Francis R. Kowsky, the biographer of Calvert Vaux, answered numerous queries in his areas of expertise. Joy Kestenbaum provided significant information and located the plans by Olmsted and J. J. R. Croes for the street system of the Bronx.

Our work would not be possible without the assistance of the staff of the Frederick Law Olmsted National Historic Site, maintained by the National Park Service in Brookline, Massachusetts. Former site director Rolfe Diamant and current director Myra Harrison have helped in many ways, and assistant director Lee Farrow Cook has been an invaluable aide throughout. We have benefited greatly from the good will and knowledge of the collection of plans and photographs at Fairsted of archivists Jill Trebbe, Joyce Connelly, Michele Clark, and Michael Dosch. Allan Banks and Mark Swartz have assisted us through interpretation of the site. Lauren Meier of the Olmsted Center gave us valuable information concerning the grounds of the site, which she was in charge of restoring

The Library of Congress has also provided invaluable assistance. We owe a debt of gratitude to the Research Facilities of the library for providing us with a research carrel over many years, and to the staff of the Manuscript Division for the assistance they constantly provide during our research in the papers of Olmsted and his firm. We also have made frequent use of the resources of the Prints and Photographs Division and the Map Division. Barbara Wolanin of the Curator's Office, Architect of the Capitol, greatly assisted research on that key commission of Olmsted's. Others who have provided important aid are Mary Daniels of the Loeb Library of the Harvard Design School, Elizabeth Diefendorf of the New York Public Library, Kenneth Cobb and Evelyn Gonzalez of the Municipal Archives of New York City, Deborah Lelansky of the Cartographic and Architectural Branch, NARA, Terry Alan Bragg, archivist at McLean Hospital, Belmont, Massachusetts, and Kent Watson, FASLA. James Cerasoli and the Hon. Stanley Simon, president of the borough of the Bronx, provided valued assistance in our research on Olmsted's plans for that borough.

THE PAPERS OF
FREDERICK LAW OLMSTED

INTRODUCTION

On January 1, 1874, Frederick Law Olmsted and Calvert Vaux signed their last report to the Brooklyn Park Commissioners, a review of the past year's work on Prospect Park and the Brooklyn park system. This event marked the end of a partnership that had existed for all but two of the previous seventeen years. It would be another decade before Olmsted formed a new firm with another full partner. That partner would be his stepson and adopted son John C. Olmsted, who would begin his apprenticeship in Olmsted's office in the fall of 1875. In the years 1874 to 1882, Olmsted would turn to other experienced professionals for assistance. For the most part, he relied on the Swiss-born landscape gardener Jacob Weidenmann to assist him with small commissions at a distance from New York City and Boston. For architectural expertise he relied on the English-born architect Thomas Wisedell, who played a crucial role in the U.S. Capitol, the Washington Monument in Baltimore, Mount Royal in Montreal, and the Schuylkill Arsenal in Philadelphia. During this period, he collaborated with Henry Hobson Richardson and Leopold Eidlitz on the New Capitol of New York State. He also engaged Richardson to help him design the bridges of the Back Bay Fens in Boston, beginning a remarkable series of projects in the Boston area that would end only with Richardson's untimely death in 1886. For engineering assistance, Olmsted turned most frequently to George Radford and George Waring, Jr. His engineering mainstay in the New York area in these years was J. J. R. Croes, and Joseph P. Davis, the City Engineer of Boston, provided valuable guidance in planning the Back Bay Fens.

During the period of this volume, Olmsted was more directly responsible for the landscape design aspect of his commissions than was the case during any other portion of his career — either the years of his partnership with Calvert Vaux or the last decade of his practice when his partners included his pupils Henry Sargent Codman and Charles Eliot in addition to John C. Olmsted. Several commissions in the period 1874–1882 allowed Olmsted to use his imagination in contriving small, enclosed spaces with a special character. In them he used decorative brick and rustic stone, flowing water, and a profusion of plant materials often chosen for delicacy, scent, and shade-giving qualities. One of these was the summer house on the U.S. Capitol grounds; another was the sheltered grotto that he proposed for a corner of Tompkins Square in Manhattan; a third was the series of fountain-gardens he planned for the squares adjoining the Washington Monument in Baltimore; and a fourth was the sunken garden on the estate of John C. Phillips in Beverly, Massachusetts, with its massive stone arch and surrounding palisade of boulders. These designs demonstrated an attention to detail that he would seldom find opportunity to indulge as his commissions grew in number during the years of his residence in Boston after 1882.

At the same time, the period of the late 1870s brought Olmsted his most remarkable opportunities to work on a large scale. It was during those years that he carried out his most comprehensive regional plan, the street and rapid transit systems for the Bronx, an area six miles long by three miles wide. In Boston by 1882 he had drawn up the detailed conceptual design for a five-mile succession of parks from the Charles River to the projected West Roxbury Park — the core of the largest park system that he and his partners were to design. During these years, he also designed and directed the first phase of construction of his arguably most national project, the grounds and terraces of the U.S. Capitol in Washington, D.C. In the late 1870s, he also developed the remarkable concept for treatment of Mount Royal in Montreal as a public recreation ground, a commission that led to his publication in 1881 of the park report richest in landscape theory. In all, he drew up plans for over forty public and private spaces in these years. At the same time, he found himself embroiled in a larger number of intensely political commissions than at any other time in his career. The New York City parks, the New York State New Capitol, the U.S. Capitol, and Mount Royal in Montreal, were all demanding in this respect. Most intense was the constant pressure of patronage and politics that he encountered as an employee of the New York City Department of Public Parks. His final, abrupt dismissal from that arena, coming so soon after he began his most extensive series of projects for the city, led him to choose a new private and professional existence in the Boston region. Beginning in 1857 and continuing virtually uninterrupted for two decades, his chief professional concern had been the New York City parks. The memoranda that he recorded concerning the politics of its parks, presented in this volume, constitute his most detailed and impassioned testimony of their effect on him and on the city for which he labored for so many years.

INTRODUCTION

Olmsted and Vaux, 1872–1874

  The formal partnership of Olmsted, Vaux & Co. was dissolved in September 1872, but the two men continued through 1873 to collaborate on Central Park and Prospect Park, as well as in the planning of Riverside and Morningside parks in Manhattan.[1] Elsewhere, Olmsted soon began to advise on projects that he and Vaux had begun while partners. These included selection of a new site for Trinity College in Hartford, Connecticut, and informal advising on the Cornell campus, a role that had begun in 1867. Olmsted also continued to review work being done on the Buffalo park system that he and Vaux had planned in 1868–72, and he soon took on new commissions for that city—designing Niagara Square in 1874 and the grounds of Buffalo City Hall in 1875. New commissions in other places came quickly. In May 1873, U.S. Senator Justin Morrill requested Olmsted to plan the recently expanded grounds of the U.S. Capitol, and he began work on that project in early 1874. In the summer of 1874, Charles S. Sargent sought his assistance in a scheme to include the Arnold Arboretum of Harvard College in the projected Boston park system. By the fall of that year Olmsted was engaged to plan a park on Mount Royal in Montreal; in July 1875 he was appointed with Leopold Eidlitz and Henry Hobson Richardson to the advisory board for the New Capitol of New York State; in November, he was appointed with J. J. R. Croes to develop a plan of streets, parks, and rapid transit for the Bronx; and in the fall, the recently formed Boston park commission requested his help in planning the park system of that city.[2] Documents in this volume chronicle Olmsted's ongoing involvement in these varied projects.

  The last eight years of Olmsted's residence and practice in New York City, 1874–81 present a notable contrast with his role on Central Park during the previous decade. In 1865, he had returned from California to join Vaux as reinstated landscape architects of the park, despite the reluctance of Andrew H. Green, whose relations with Olmsted had become increasingly strained in the pre-war years.[3] Olmsted's efforts during the next few years focused on the design and construction of Prospect Park, and not on Central Park. He and Vaux developed the design concepts for Eastern and Ocean parkways in Brooklyn in these years, but they were given no role in planning the uptown boulevard and avenues that Green and his fellow commissioners were projecting for Manhattan at the same time. It was Green who wrote the reports of the New York parks commission on this subject.[4] Nor did the park board involve Olmsted and Vaux in planning for the newly annexed area of the Bronx, a process that began in 1872.

  During the brief hegemony of the Tweed Ring from May 1870 to September 1871, the new board dismissed Olmsted and Vaux and embarked on a program that would transform the park. They began to introduce such structures as the ostentatious "sheepfold" (later Tavern on the Green) on inappropriate sites, cleared out the dense plantings established by the designers, and transplanted trees and shrubs to smaller Manhattan parks. In early 1872 the reformers who ousted Tweed restored the partners as landscape architects to the Department of Public Parks, and Olmsted became general superintendent of the department as well. In May of that year he regained control of the Central Park keepers force after a hiatus of ten years. He also secured control of a small corps of gardeners in order to complete planting some parts of the park, his first such opportunity in an equally long time. But this promising situation lasted little over a year. A new city charter brought a new park board in June 1873. The board moved quickly to limit Olmsted's authority over the Central Park gardeners by creating an office of landscape gardening independent of him. By August the board had limited his authority further by forbidding the cutting of any trees on the park without specific approval. In September the board abandoned the new system for park keepers that Olmsted had instituted and relieved him of all duties of superintendence. Having sharply limited his authority on Central Park, the board set him instead to designing Riverside and Morningside parks, for each of which he prepared a report and preliminary plan before the end of 1873.[5]

The New York City Parks, 1874–1877

Such was Olmsted's situation in January 1874, at the beginning of the time period of this volume. Ironically, his final opportunity to direct work on Central Park came with the resurgence of Tammany Hall in the elections of 1874. The most important factor was the appointment to the park board of William R. Martin, a promoter of uptown development. The opportunities for park design and urban planning offered to Olmsted during the years of Martin's presence on the park board, from January 1875 to January 1878, were significant. The key turning point was March 19, 1875, the day that Olmsted regained control over the labor force of the Department of Public Parks. He immediately hired his valued horticultural assistants William Fischer and Oliver Bullard to thin neglected and overgrown plantings in Central Park. At this time, Olmsted also regained control of the keepers force. During 1875 the park board directed him to draw up new plans for Riverside Park and Avenue and selected him, with the engineer J. J. R. Croes, to plan streets, parks, and a rapid-transit system for the recently annexed twenty-third and twenty-fourth wards of the city, the Bronx. In succeeding years, the park board under Martin's presidency gave him the opportunity to redesign Tompkins Square on the East Side between 7th and 10th streets, and to begin planning East River Park (now Carl Schurz Park) between 84th and 86th streets.[6]

Olmsted's increased role in park affairs and his sponsorship by William R. Martin caused difficulties in his relations with an old colleague, Henry G. Stebbins, an early member of the park commission and its president from 1872 to May 1876. Stebbins was an ally of Andrew H. Green, whose animus toward Olmsted was of long standing. In the spring of 1876 the friction between Stebbins and Martin became increasingly heated. Green was seeking to consolidate his control of patronage of the Department of Public Parks by maneuvering to become mayor of the city and through his efforts in the state legislature to replace the park board with a single commissioner allied with him, thus countering the Tammany faction represented by Martin. Park employees remained in a constant state of excitement as the opposing groups saw their prospects rise and fall. By May 1876, Green's efforts had failed, and the addition of a new Tammany member to the park board brought William R. Martin the presidency. Green was quick to strike at Olmsted where he could. Olmsted was appointed a member of the State Survey Commission at the end of May and Green, as city comptroller, immediately withheld his salary, declaring that he had forfeited his position with the Department of Public Parks by accepting the state position. When the park board moved to reinstate Olmsted in July in anticipation of his impending resignation from the State Survey, Stebbins — as Green's principal representative on the board — proposed instead to abolish his position. Olmsted was forced to sue for his pay for the summer of 1876, finally receiving a favorable court decision in May 1877.[7]

Mayor Wickham removed Andrew H. Green as comptroller in November 1876, replacing him with the rising power in Tammany Hall, John Kelly. During the following year, Olmsted's principal task for the Department of Public Parks was developing plans for the twenty-third and twenty-fourth wards. This reflected a primary concern of park board president William R. Martin, but Martin's days in the Tammany Hall hierarchy were numbered, as were Olmsted's with the park board. An early sign of what was in store was the form letter Olmsted received in September from Kelly, as chairman of the Tammany Hall finance committee, directing him to contribute $112 to the Tammany war chest for the November elections. Olmsted presumably failed to respond, and the following month Kelly withheld his salary on the grounds that his full-time services were not needed by the park department during the winter months and that he had been absent on other employment every working day of November. This new crisis intensified for Olmsted the stress caused by physical debilitation brought on by the intense heat of the summer of 1877 and the return of an "old malarial complaint." His doctors insisted that he take a vacation from his work, and late in December the park board granted him a three-month leave of absence for a trip to Europe. As he prepared to depart, they moved to make his leave of absence permanent by abolishing the Bureau of Design and Superintendence and making him Consulting Landscape Architect without salary. While he was absent on his voyage a group of influential friends and supporters launched a protest against his dismissal but to no avail.[8] And so ended, in an abrupt and shocking way, Olmsted's official connection with the New York City parks he had worked so long and hard to plan and protect.

Olmsted returned from Europe little improved in health or attitude, and it was several months before his wife's regime of rest and horseback riding brought noticeable improvement.[9] He spent part of each of the next four years in the Boston region, beginning his design work on the park system there, but the fate of the New York parks still concerned him. Longtime supporters hoped to restore him to his old position there. Discussions in the fractious park board during the fall of 1881 brought proposals to secure the services of both himself and Calvert Vaux, but there was no agreement. Finally in November, to the surprise of most of those involved, the board appointed Calvert Vaux as Consulting Architect. Despite this change the board and its employees continued to carry out programs in Central Park that were the reverse of what Olmsted desired. Particularly troubling was the dedication of the new superintendent, appointed in August 1881, to "cleaning up" the park by clearing out the dense shrubbery and other undergrowth that Olmsted had carefully tended over the years, and by opening vistas into the park from surrounding residential areas. "How will it be," he mused, "when 'a free circulation of air and light' beneath every bush and brooding conifer has been secured; when the way of the lawn-mower has at all points been made plain, and the face of nature shall everywhere have become as natty as a new silk hat?"[10]

In response, and as his parting shot, Olmsted wrote and published a critique of the policies pursued by the park board since his dismissal. He titled his pamphlet *The Spoils of the Park, with a Few Leaves from the Deep-Laden Note-Books of "A Wholly Unpractical Man"* and published it himself in early 1882. Presented in this volume with explanatory annotation, it is a remarkable indictment of park policies and political patronage in New York City of the post-Tweed era. It was a companion piece to two other previously unpublished works that are included in this volume. One described the unfortunate effects of political forces on the final planning and construction of Riverside Park, a long article that Olmsted wrote in late 1879 after an independent commission of engineers revealed how irresponsible the officials in charge of construction of the park had been. He carried this project to the point of printing galley proofs and correcting them, but apparently abandoned the idea of publication.[11] The other statement was the article titled "Influence" that he wrote following the fatal wounding of President James Garfield in June 1881. He presented the manuscript to his old friend George W. Curtis, a leading civil service reformer and president of the Civil-Service Reform Association.

The other remarkable record that Olmsted made of the prevalence of patronage in the public life of his time was the informal journal on the subject that he kept during the years of this volume. The editors have given it the title "Patronage Journal" and have identified as fully as possible the persons and situations mentioned in it. The memoranda in the journal constitute a rare record of the inner workings of the political system of New York City. The journal also records Olmsted's attempts to reduce the wages of the park department employees who gained their employment through political influence, and to bring their pay more in line with that of private contractors during the hard times following the Panic of 1873. His description of the difficult conditions and slight compensation that workers in this period were willing to accept (the instance of the road builders on Mount Royal in Montreal is particularly appalling) are another aspect of this valuable record.

The New York State Capitol, 1874–1882

The arena of the city and state of New York was the crucial one for Olmsted in the period 1874–1877. At the same time that his work for the New York City Department of Public Parks greatly increased, he became involved in the many controversies surrounding construction of the New Capitol in Albany. Victory at the state level in the elections of 1874 brought Samuel Tilden to the capital as governor. His lieutenant governor was William Dorsheimer, a Liberal Republican who had abandoned his party in reaction against the policies of the Grant administration. Dorsheimer was a longtime associate of Olmsted's, having brought him to Buffalo to plan the park system there in 1868. He was also involved in development of the Buffalo Asylum for the Insane, designed by H. H. Richardson with grounds by Olmsted and Vaux, and he had been a member of the small group to whom Olmsted in 1869 had suggested creation of a public reservation at Niagara Falls. The change of state administration in 1874 gave rise to partisan controversy over the New Capitol. Dorsheimer expressed to Olmsted his misgivings about the architect Thomas Fuller's design of the New Capitol, which had been approved in 1867 during a Republican state administration. He proposed formation of an advisory board to pass on Fuller's design before further construction was authorized. Olmsted enlisted H. H. Richardson and they added the noted New York architect Leopold Eidlitz.[12] When they submitted their report in April 1876, this advisory board proposed that so far as possible the Capitol, already half completed, be finished according to a different plan and in a different style than previously—substituting Romanesque for Fuller's "Italian Renaissance." This proposed mixture of styles and the overriding of one architect's work in so politically charged an atmosphere drew immediate protest from the New York City chapter of the American Institute of Architects, chaired by Richard Morris Hunt. In the ensuing debate, Olmsted enlisted the support of his friend Charles Eliot Norton, professor of fine arts at Harvard College. Olmsted's group prevailed, Fuller was removed, and in September 1876 the three-man advisory board became the official architects of the New Capitol. They then formed the firm of Eidlitz, Richardson, & Co., with Olmsted as treasurer, to facilitate their work.

In the planning of the New Capitol, Olmsted's role was primarily to assist in defending the proposals of his colleagues and to write substantial parts of their reports. He also drew up a set of regulations for the Capitol's police force. Olmsted played a part in their artistic discussions as well—those "all-night debates" he later recalled that enlivened the advisory board's nocturnal steamboat trips between New York City and Albany. In those debates, Olmsted seems to have argued for simplicity of form and clear expression of the function of the building in its exterior.[13] The only elements of the building for which he seems to have made detailed designs were sidewalks on the north side of the Capitol and planting cases next to the windows in hallways. The latter were fabricated from plans that Thomas Wisedell drew up under Olmsted's supervision, based on suggestions of appropriate plant materials provided by Charles S. Sargent.[14]

The advisory board's victory of 1876 was not easy to sustain. A new series of attacks on the proposed changes in design of the New Capitol was launched by Thomas Fuller and his architectural and political supporters early in 1877. This led to halting of construction and a new round of legislative investigations during the spring. A key document relating to this controversy is the testimony that Olmsted presented in March to the joint committees of finance and ways and means. His efforts and those of his colleagues were unsuccessful: on March 23, a bare majority of the Senate Finance Committee recommended that the New Capitol be completed in the architectural style of Fuller's original design, and in May the legislature decreed that the exterior of the building should be completed "in the Italian renaissance style of architecture, adopted in the original design . . . ."[15] In consequence, Eidlitz and Richardson were required to devise a nominally "Renaissance" appearance for the rest of the New Capitol's upper stories. Their principal design projects in the interior, the Assembly and Senate chambers and related hallways and staircases, were not affected by the dictates of the legislature concerning the exterior of the building. Problems and controversies concerning the soundness of design and construction of these spaces, however, continued to arise. As late as the fall of 1882, Olmsted had to rush to Albany and work frantically drawing up a response to a critical review of Eidlitz's Assembly Chamber by a panel of architects that included George B. Post.[16] Through these years, he remained convinced that the root of the controversy was the desire for patronage and the power to award employment to political supporters.

The Campaign for the Niagara Reservation, 1879–1882

While he carried on his work on the New York state capitol, Olmsted became involved in another project related to the state — the campaign to create a scenic reservation at Niagara Falls. As early as 1869, Olmsted had discussed with his friends the possibility of removing the manufacturing and tourist buildings that marred the views of the American rapids at the Falls. It was nearly a decade later that a governor of the state, Lucius Robinson, embraced the issue. In January 1879, following a meeting with the Lord Dufferin, the governor-general of Canada, Robinson called on the New York state legislature to establish a public reservation there. The legislature then directed the New York State Survey Commission to establish appropriate boundaries. Olmsted and the director of the Survey, James T. Gardner, were already acquainted: Olmsted had hired him in 1865 to survey and map Yosemite Valley. The two men now joined forces to preserve an equally iconic site. The report of the State Survey of 1879, presented to the legislature in March 1880, included brief "Notes" by Olmsted on the special quality of scenery at Niagara. Gardner's accompanying report gave graphic descriptions, accompanied by numerous photographs, of the "disfigured banks" of the American rapids and other unattractive aspects of the area. The State Survey document also contained a petition in favor of a reservation signed by 270 luminaries from the United States and Europe, along with 400 unlisted signers, that Olmsted and Charles Eliot Norton had drawn up and circulated. A bill based on proposals contained in the report passed the state Assembly in May but failed to pass the Senate before the legislature adjourned. Norton then enlisted support in the British Parliament from the influential Earl of Derby, while Olmsted turned to organizing a new petition campaign. Any prospect of success during the following year was scotched by the hostility of the new governor, Alonzo Cornell. In the summer of 1881 Olmsted and Norton arranged to have a recent Harvard graduate, Henry Norman, write a series of articles for New York and Boston newspapers and by the end of the year were preparing to engage Jonathan B. Harrison, a New Hampshire clergyman, to write additional material. Their efforts bore fruit after Grover Cleveland became governor of New York in the fall of 1882. With his support, the legislature authorized creation of the Niagara Reservation the following year, and in 1885 followed that step by appropriating the funds needed to purchase the land. In 1887 Olmsted and his old partner Calvert Vaux drew up the plan and accompanying report for the needed construction. Their collaboration came as one more result of political antagonisms of previous years. Both William Dorsheimer and Andrew H. Green were members of the Niagara Reservation commission, and the former was determined that Olmsted should be engaged to draw up the plan of the reservation while the latter was equally determined that only his ally Calvert Vaux be chosen. The selection of both Olmsted and Vaux to prepare the plan was due to a grudging compromise on the part of both commissioners.[17]

The Boston Parks, 1870–1882

By the end of the time period of this volume, Olmsted had changed his place of residence from New York City to the Boston suburb of Brookline. As he observed to his old friend Charles Loring Brace, still in New York running the Children's Aid Society, "I enjoy this suburban country beyond expression." Recent friendships also drew Olmsted to the Boston region. By 1879 his old acquaintance Charles Eliot Norton had become his most important ally in the campaign for a Niagara reservation, and, most valued of all, his friendship and professional collaboration with Henry Hobson Richardson was rapidly growing in importance. In fact, Richardson proposed to design a shingle-style house for Olmsted on the architect's own property in Brookline.

It was while visiting Richardson in the winter of 1881–1882, so the story goes, that Olmsted observed the streets being cleared of snow on an early Sunday morning, directed by one of the selectmen, and concluded that a community with such attention to communal needs was the place best suited for him to live. In the summer of 1881 he moved to Brookline and two years later purchased the old farmhouse down the street from Richardson that he called "Fairsted."[18]

The professional attraction provided by Boston was the opportunity to plan a comprehensive park system for the city—something that only Buffalo had offered in previous years. Olmsted had been marginally involved in the debate about creating parks in Boston that took place in 1869. Some park advocates had urged him to testify on the subject and he delivered an address in Boston to the American Social Science Association entitled "Public Parks and the Enlargement of Towns." Further involvement came in 1874, when Charles S. Sargent, director of the nascent Arnold Arboretum of Harvard approached him for assistance in making the arboretum part of the projected park system. Olmsted had also been involved since 1872 in the search for a new location for the McLean Asylum of Massachusetts General Hospital.[19] In June 1875, Charles H. Dalton, for several years past a member of the committee charged with finding the new site, engaged Olmsted to review plans to be drawn up by the engineer Joseph Curtis for the property recently acquired at Waverly in Belmont. The following month, Dalton was appointed to the three-man park commission in Boston. By October he was soliciting Olmsted's advice on the location of parks and the decade-long association of the two men began in earnest. Olmsted visited the park commissioners in October 1875, combining park and asylum work. He reviewed their plans again in the spring of 1876, just before publication of their proposal for a park system. The principal effect of his comments at that time was widening of the proposed park at the Back Bay to provide a more impressive vista from Parker Hill over the marshes and Charles River. Several elements of the plan differed from the system of parks and parkways that Olmsted and his firm came to design over the next two decades, but the fundamental concept of a linear system extending from the Charles River and Boston Common to Jamaica Pond and a large park in West Roxbury, with a parkway extending on toward Boston Harbor, was established by the commissioners' plan of 1876.[20]

Up to this point, Olmsted had been merely an occasional and unofficial consultant, a fact at which he broadly hinted in his communications with the commissioners. This anomalous relationship caused difficulties in the next stage of building the park system. On March 1, 1878, while Olmsted was recuperating in Europe and unbeknownst to him, the Boston park commissioners announced a design competition for the Back Bay Park. Entries were due on May first and would be judged by the commissioners and their "consulting engineer," by which they meant Olmsted. One can imagine Olmsted's surprise when, a week after his return to this country, he received an urgent summons from Charles Dalton to come to Boston and help judge the competition. He quickly refused, citing the inappropriateness of such a role given his past and possible future relationship to the commissioners. He followed this with a systematic critique of the concept of design competitions. His response completely upset the plans of the commission. Henry Hobson Richardson convinced Dalton soon after that he must act quickly to secure Olmsted's counsel. Accordingly, the commissioners awarded their prize to Hermann Grundel, a florist whose plan was clearly inferior to those submitted by such respected landscape designers as Robert Morris Copeland, Ernest Bowditch, and Joseph Curtis. The *American Architect and Building News*, in its review of the competition, remarked that "We presume it would be too much to expect the commissioners to give the inquiring public a reason for their extraordinary choice, but we should be glad to know what were the merits which they discovered in Mr. Grundel's plan which in their judgment entitled it to the preference."[21] The answer seems to be that the commissioners believed that Grundel had no ambition to see his plan implemented, and no professional standing, leaving them free to enlist Olmsted as their designer. Their formal explanation was that none of the competition designs adequately addressed the engineering difficulties presented by drainage into the Back Bay of floodwaters from the Muddy River and Stony Brook. During the summer of 1878, Olmsted drew up his first concepts for the Back Bay Fens and by year's end the commissioners had formally engaged him to provide design and oversight of construction of the first section of their ambitious system.

Over the next four years, Olmsted developed his innovative plan for the Back Bay site. By installing a water gate at the Charles River he created a saltwater lagoon with only one foot of tidal rise and fall that would have an appearance similar to the salt marshes of the nearby Massachusetts coast. He dredged and mounded the soil of the bay to create a series of low-lying peninsulas with vegetation that would hinder the development of destructive surf when the basin was used to hold floodwater overflow from Stony Brook. Sanitary engineering considerations, he insisted, made it impossible to create on that site the usual labor-intensive and decorative urban park. The great challenge, he was to discover, was to develop plantings that would thrive in the difficult situation of those barely tidal Fens. Although in appearance it was a wild, natural marsh, Olmsted made sure to provide adequate access to and through the landscape he created there. He designed carriage drives along both sides of the Fens, connecting Commonwealth Avenue and Boylston Street with Huntington Avenue and Brookline Avenue, and added a separate half-mile-long bridle path on the east side. For pedestrians he provided a sidewalk along the carriage drive on the steep and narrow west bank, while on the east side he designed a sinuous path through the marsh. Several small beaches provided access to the water and a series of boat landings were planned for the water-trolley system he proposed to operate along the length of the lagoons. He worked through scores of sketches, considering many different treatments for the interior of the space. By the fall of 1878 he was ready to present several alternatives, all of which had more paths and other features in the interior than are found in the first published version of early 1879. Olmsted's report of January 26, 1880, in this volume is the document that accompanied his official presentation of this plan to the board. It was 1882 before the watercourse took its final form, running close to the eastern shore of the northern basin, and minor changes appear in the later published plan of 1887 and thereafter.[22]

As the documents in this volume indicate, Olmsted was determined that the bridges in the Fens not be designed by the city engineer, on whose professional skill he relied heavily in dealing with the issues of water control and sanitary engineering. He prevailed on the commissioners to let him engage H. H. Richardson for architectural design, and the two collaborated closely in providing concepts for the Boylston Street bridge in particular.

During these years, Olmsted was also engaged with Charles S. Sargent in securing a place in the Boston park system for the Arnold Arboretum. Sargent realized that he needed financial assistance from the city to achieve his ambitions for that institution. At first Olmsted was unsure that he could successfully combine an arboretum and a park, but he soon joined enthusiastically in the venture. Sargent gave him the task of deciding what land should be added to the existing holdings of Harvard College, and of planning the drives and walks. Olmsted also undertook to move the various parties—notably the city of Boston and the corporation of Harvard College—toward acceptance of the idea. "I always find the prospect bad when I arrive in Boston and good when I leave," he observed to Charles Eliot Norton at a crucial stage of negotiations. In 1878, authorization was secured from all quarters and the city of Boston purchased the Arnold Arboretum, along with the forty-five additional acres identified by Olmsted, and leased them back to Harvard for 999 years. For that investment, payment of the cost of constructing and maintaining drives and paths, and provision of police service, the city added the property to its park system and the university secured a truly exemplary arboretum. Olmsted began producing designs for the arboretum in the summer of 1878, beginning a collaboration between his firm and Sargent that lasted beyond Olmsted's retirement in 1895.[23]

During these years Olmsted was involved in development of other elements of the park system. In 1879 he designed the extension of Commonwealth Avenue across the northern end of the Back Bay Fens and connecting with Beacon Street. In the following year, he and Sargent drew up a proposal for replanting the trees along Commonwealth Avenue between the Public Garden and the Fens. In the spring of 1881, he reported to the park commissioners concerning the land most desirable to acquire for the principal park of the system, in West Roxbury. In a report of 1880, he proposed to connect the

Back Bay Fens to Jamaica Pond along the Muddy River and marshes and ponds above it, rather than constructing a parkway from a park on Parker Hill to Jamaica Pond as proposed in the commissioners' report of 1876. The river would be freshwater instead of brackish as heretofore, and would be separated from the saltwater Fens at Brookline Avenue by an underground conduit to the Charles River. The scenery along its banks, made accessible by carriage drives, walks, and a bridle path, would be that of a lowland stream, and the freshwater marsh above Tremont Street would become a pond for impoundment of flood waters. In this way the stream would keep its scenic character, saved from burial in a culvert and serving both recreational and sanitary needs of the area.[24]

Thus, by a series of campaigns, reports, and designs, Olmsted was able by early 1882 to submit the last report in this volume on the Boston park system, in which he offered a classic description of how the "Emerald Necklace," though decades from being named such, would offer a varied series of landscape experiences between the Charles River and what came to be Franklin Park.

Mount Royal, Montreal, 1874–1877

These extensive projects were only part of the public work that Olmsted carried out during the years covered by this volume. In 1874 he began to design a park on Mount Royal in Montreal, which offered him the challenge of creating a public recreation ground on a mountain site. The work engaged his attention during a period of three years. Over 100 letters that he wrote to the Montreal park commissioners and their staff for the period 1874–1877 have survived. They describe the difficulties that he encountered in attempting, from a distance, to guide the construction of the first park design that he created without Calvert Vaux's assistance. In the process, he became aware of the difficulties that developed when the group responsible for the park was not an independent commission, as had been the case in New York, Brooklyn, Buffalo, and Chicago, but rather a committee of a city's common council. The first major construction project on Mount Royal, the carriage drive up the mountain, was carried out with little reference to Olmsted's detailed plan. Later, the city chose to place a reservoir in the only area suited for truly parklike pastoral scenery. Further construction of a circuit drive atop the mountain closely followed his plans, but the charming "Crown of the Mountain" refectory and vista point designed for him by the architect Thomas Wisedell was not built, nor was the system of footpaths that he planned by which even visitors in wheelchairs could ascend to the summit. The difficulties Olmsted encountered in realizing his concept led him in 1881 to write and publish an explanation of his plan. That document, "Mount Royal. Montreal," stands as one of his richest and most impassioned statements on landscape design.[25]

INTRODUCTION

The U.S. Capitol Grounds, 1873–1882

    A professional commission of great importance that commanded Olmsted's attention through the whole period of the present volume was the design and construction of the newly expanded grounds of the U.S. Capitol in Washington, D.C., and the designing of terraces for that structure. The project began with a request in May 1873 from Senator Justin Morrill of Vermont, chairman of the Senate Committee on Public Buildings and Grounds, that Olmsted undertake the project. "I hope you may feel sufficient interest in this rather national project," Morrill urged, "not to see it botched."[26] It was indeed an undertaking of national significance. Olmsted saw the importance of creating grounds for the legislative halls of the Republic that assisted its efficient operation, and he wished to create a setting that heightened the grandeur and dignity of the building. Through subordination, visually and functionally, of the grounds to the Capitol he hoped as well to create a nationally influential example of good taste in landscape design—a demonstration that would counteract the current emphasis on decorative, horticultural display.

    Olmsted's first concern, as he expressed it to Justin Morrill in his first substantive letter of January 22, 1874, was to urge a coordinated treatment of the whole area between the Capitol and the Washington Monument and White House. In that entire area he found a confusion of spaces, each treated in a different way by different agencies and overseen by different congressional committees. Still aware of the issues of nationalism and states' rights that had so concerned him during the Civil War, he observed that "the capital of the Union manifests nothing so much as disunity." "What is wanting," he instructed Morrill, "is a federal bond." On March 27 he engaged to prepare a plan for the grounds of the Capitol, but attempted first to have a board of landscape architects consider his proposal "to bring all these grounds into subordination to a comprehensive scheme." His efforts, however, came to naught.[27]

    As for the setting of the Capitol itself, he observed that the earthen berms that provided terracing on the north, west, and south were insufficient for the enlarged building. On the east side, the eastern edge of the grounds must be lowered six feet to reach the level of newly constructed First Street East, and many trees in that area must be removed or transplanted. By June 1874 Olmsted had prepared a "skeleton plan" for the grounds. On the east side it simplified the approach to the Capitol by merging the fourteen streets reaching the grounds to half that number. By this time he had also worked out the shape of the two broad ovals of turf and trees in order to achieve an effect of spaciousness in the interior of the east grounds. He also arranged the plantings in a way that permitted views of the full façade of the Capitol from only the best vantage points. This plan did not provide for extending East Capitol Street directly into the grounds. It also contained the germ of the concept of an architectural terrace for the west front: but Olmsted at this time proposed simply to widen the earthen berm, introducing an architectural structure only in the form of two broad staircases with connecting walled terraces at their three landings. He and his architectural associate, Thomas Wisedell, made numerous alterations during the summer of 1874, and in September Wisedell drew up a large, colored version of their plan. It showed two-tiered architectural terraces on the north, south, and west sides of the building, and allowed for the full forty-foot extension of the West Front, as planned by the previous Architect of the Capitol, Thomas U. Walter. When U.S. Army Quartermaster General Montgomery Meigs, an opponent of the extension, queried Olmsted about that aspect of his plan, he replied that he had wished to intrude as little as possible on the purview of the architects. He added, however, that he had told Edward Clark, Justin Morrill, and others that among the various proposals being discussed for extending the east and west fronts, he "regarded that as the best by which they would be advanced the least."[28]

Most of the other features shown on Olmsted's plan of late 1874 were adopted and constructed. The most obvious difference is the plan's treatment of plantings on the west grounds along the walks of Maryland and Pennsylvania Avenue extended. The 1874 plan shows thick plantings of trees and shrubs that would have created an enclosure of dense shade in summer. Eventually, Olmsted lined these walks with formal rows of London Plane trees. The final treatment of the area between the staircases on the West Front also differed considerably from that shown on the plan of 1874, and the terraces never had the polychrome paving of red and blue that Olmsted proposed at that time. (Such pavement was, however, used on the sidewalks on the eastern edge of the Plaza on the east grounds.)

In explaining his plan in an article for the *New-York Daily Tribune* in November 1874, Olmsted wrote that his purpose was twofold: to "provide convenient approaches to and standing room about the Capitol" and to aid and heighten the effect of its "imposing dimensions and the beauty of its architecture." He emphasized the importance of subordinating the grounds to the structure, the landscape architecture to the architecture. Warning particularly against the introduction of distracting decorative features, he wrote:

> The same principle of subordination to the building will prevent the introduction in any part of the ground of local ornaments, whether in flowers, leaf-plants, or other objects imply curious or beautiful in themselves. Those matters only will be decorated which by their position and form carry out, repeat, and support the architectural design, nor will any decoration be such as to hold the eye of an observer when in a position to take a general view of the Capitol.[29]

This was the plan that Justin Morrill, Edward Clark, and others reviewed and approved on September 28, and that Olmsted presented to the Senate Committee on Public Buildings and Grounds in January 1875. The committee approved his plan on March 3, 1875. Construction moved forward steadily during the next four years, and much of the work on the grounds was completed in that period. But serious difficulties then developed. Thomas Wisedell had produced many architectural drawings, since it fell to him to provide all the detailed planning and rendering for the walls around and within the grounds, as well as the seats on the east grounds from which to view the façade, the two large fountains, and the numerous light posts. In the summer of 1879 he became ill, probably with the heart trouble that would cause his death five years later, and fell badly behind. For weeks he failed to respond to urgent requests for drawings, and even though he finally agreed to be more prompt, crucial construction was left unfinished when Congress convened in the fall of 1879.[30] The principal problem was the "summer house" that Olmsted planned in the northwest section of the grounds as a place of rest and refreshment. He used all of his ingenuity to create a unique and especially pleasing refuge—half-sunken into the hillside and surrounded by mounded earth heavily planted with shrubs. There was a fountain in the center, open to the sky, over which arched trees with delicate leaves. Several stone screens permitted foliage-scented and cooling breezes to pass through the structure, while at one end was a grotto-like enclosure with dripping water and moss. Olmsted even had the Tiffany firm contrive a carillon, run by the water of the fountain, that emitted a sound partly like music, partly like a purling stream. He adjusted every element to create the utmost effect of delicacy, and a cool, refreshing atmosphere. But by the time that Congress met in 1879, only the foundations were in place, standing raw and barren all through the winter. Several senators complained, and the general dissatisfaction was such that in the spring of 1880 Congress refused to authorize the first substantial appropriation for Olmsted's terraces. In an attempt to secure funding, Olmsted included a description of the terraces and their purpose in his annual report to Edward Clark in the fall of 1881. Then, in early 1882, he drew up an illustrated pamphlet explaining the terraces and distributed two hundred copies to members of Congress. However, the funds were finally authorized only beginning in 1884, the year that Olmsted lost responsibility for them. Wisedell had completed many of the plans needed by the end of 1882, but final plans were drawn up by August Schoenborn in the Office of the Architect of the Capitol.[31]

Hartford, Connecticut—Capitol and College, 1872–1877

In this period of patriotic construction of capitol buildings, Olmsted planned the grounds of a second state capitol, in his home town of Hartford, Connecticut. This was part of a twofold process, since the new capitol was sited on the edge of Bushnell Park on what was previously the campus of Washington—or Trinity—College. Unfortunately, no extensive description by Olmsted of his plans for the capitol has survived, although he did secure alterations to the section of the park near the building and worked diligently to provide convenient access between capitol and park. A fuller record has survived of his concept for the Trinity College campus. Part of this correspondence deals with the character that it was desirable to achieve for an American college campus, while other letters describe his plans for partial implementation of a quadrangle design by the English architect William Burges. Olmsted also wished to arrange several blocks for private residences surrounding the Trinity campus, a project that he was not able to carry out.[32]

Community Planning: The Bronx, 1875–1878

Olmsted's outstanding project in community design during this period was his planning of the street system of the Bronx with the engineer J. J. R. Croes. For years he had complained of the lack of an area in the New York region where a permanent residential quarter could survive — where a neighborhood could resist the constant transition from places of residence to places of commerce. He and Vaux had begun planning such an area for Washington Heights in 1860, but the commission they advised never submitted a formal proposal. The opportunity to plan the twenty-third and twenty-fourth wards in the mid-1870s was therefore doubly welcome to Olmsted. Much of the Bronx already had a gridiron street pattern. He proposed no major changes for these areas and concentrated on the hillside section between Riverdale Road and the Hudson River. There he planned a curvilinear street pattern that he hoped would lead to a stable "villa" neighborhood. At the same time, he was seeking to demonstrate the superiority to row houses of freestanding residences for city residents of means. In conjunction with this street plan, which was adopted in sections by the city between 1876 and 1878, Olmsted and Croes also devised a rapid-transit rail system that would serve the area on tracks at separate grades from the streets. It was a radical and comprehensive extension to a full city plan of the principle of separation of ways that he and Vaux had introduced in Central Park in the late 1850s. As for public parks in the newly annexed regions, one can see a number of small parks on the plans that Olmsted and Croes created, particularly along the line of the boulevard that eventually became the Henry Hudson Parkway. The reports describe a few other parks, but Olmsted's full conception on this subject is not known. The fullest explication of such a concept was written by William R. Martin — with what help from Olmsted it is impossible to estimate — in a report of 1875. In any case, the principal authors of the new plan for the Bronx — Olmsted, Croes, and Martin — all lost the power to realize their vision when they were dismissed from their positions with the Department of Public Parks in early 1878.[33]

Other Community Design, 1874–1879

New York State was also the venue during these years for other kinds of community designing, little of which came to fruition. In the mid-1870s Olmsted drew up a plan for a residential neighborhood, "Parkside," next to

Delaware Park in Buffalo. This was virtually his only commission for a residential community next to a park of his design. The plan went through several versions through the 1880s, as did other designs for subdivisions north of Delaware Park, but the final street pattern bore little relation to the elegant curves of Olmsted's first plans of the 1870s.

More ambitious was the detailed and imaginative proposal that Olmsted drew up in 1879 for a resort at Rockaway Point near New York City. There he combined an impressive analysis of the site itself with considerations of a resort that would combine a large hotel with many attractions for day visitors. His report for the project, which was not carried out, demonstrates the imagination that he could bring to bear on design issues when he was not constrained by the need to give primacy to issues of landscape experience. Another revealing design, which was carried out in large part, was that for Point Chautauqua on Lake Chautauqua in upstate New York in 1876. A summer colony for a religious group, the project gave Olmsted an opportunity to inveigh against the character of most sectarian summer communities and to analyze how best to secure a desirable result.[34]

Grounds of Private Residences, 1879–1882

The landscape design category that received least attention from Olmsted during the period of this volume — as in all other periods prior to at least 1890 — was the planning of the grounds of private residences. Olmsted felt that designing for residential communities — private or institutional — and the planning of public parks and recreation grounds was the most important work that he could do. And yet private residences involved a number of issues for which he felt considerable concern. Creation of freestanding residences was important because of the opportunity they offered to strengthen the family, the most important civilizing institution in American society, to develop taste, and to improve health through access to sunshine and fresh air. Realization of an urban alternative to that "relic of barbarism" the row house, a holdover from the ages when cities were constructed primarily for purposes of protection and defense, was a particularly important responsibility of nineteenth-century society.[35] The more a place of residence could strengthen the family, Olmsted believed, the stronger society would become. Creating the setting for the family residence, moreover, would enable householders to foster their own individuality by expressing their particular character. Such an approach would not consist of egotistical display or ornamental flower-gardening: rather it would, ideally, draw its character from the natural setting and serve as a training-ground for an aesthetic sensibility to subtle variation in tone, texture, and form of the plant materials used. Olmsted's apprentice Charles Eliot recorded such a response when Olmsted examined the site for the residence of G. Nixon Black on Manchester Harbor on the North Shore of Boston in 1883. Echoing his mentor's design standards, Eliot remarked that he saw "many ridiculously incongruous attempts at gardening" in the area. "Several proprietors have seen fit to 'smooth up' all their land that they possibly could, and here lawn mowers and hose are to be seen," he recorded, "—also ribbon beds of coleus and other foliage bedding plants—with circles of geraniums scarlet and other abominations." When the architect Robert S. Peabody asked Olmsted how he would demonstrate a more appropriate design approach, he replied, "I would not try to change the very pleasing natural character,—I would take this present character and work it up."[36]

Olmsted applied this concept to his designing of the grounds of two Massachusetts estates described in this volume. In both cases he was working without a partner, and his approach is of special interest. One estate was only half a mile from the farmhouse he would soon choose for his own residence. There, Barthold Schlesinger had recently purchased several properties as a setting for his mansion. Olmsted's correspondence with him published in this volume discusses issues of overall character, the siting of the house and approaches to it. In particular, Olmsted's letters provide his doctrine of terraces, of the importance of providing a zone of transition between the house and the grounds.[37] More extensive and important is the example of the estate of John C. Phillips on Wenham Lake in North Beverly that Olmsted began to plan in 1880. There he demonstrated how he wished to fit even a large country house designed by Peabody and Stearns into its setting. At the same time he showed his willingness to meet certain needs of the residents by bold reshaping of the land. He built a massive terrace in order to set the house closer to Wenham Lake. At the same time, he created on the terrace a large "open-air apartment" where the activities of the family could be moved out of doors. At the end of the lawn he placed a tea-house or "pavilion" with views of the lawn and house in one direction and overlooking a sunken flower garden in the other. In this fashion he carried out his concept of the varied spaces needed to meet the needs of the residents: "There should be a dry walk for damp weather, a sheltered walk for windy weather, and a sheltered sitting place for conversation, needle work, reading, teaching, and meditation." These features, the paved terrace next to the house, the enclosed lawn area, and the separate space for decorative gardening, represented Olmsted's key concepts for the grounds of private residences. For large country estates he had another purpose that he first implemented at John C. Phillips's estate, "Moraine Farm." This was the demonstration of advanced farming techniques and reforestation, which would reach its fullest and more resplendent realization at Biltmore Estate over a decade later.[38]

The Further Range of Commissions, 1874–1882

During these years Olmsted undertook numerous commissions not represented by documents published in this volume and for some of which the extent of correspondence, number of plans prepared, time period of work, and extent of execution of designs is not well understood. Working with Thomas Wisedell, for instance, he drew up plans for the Schuylkill Arsenal in Philadelphia at the invitation of Quartermaster General Montgomery Meigs, for whom he also planned the Jeffersonville Depot near Louisville. In Washington, D.C., while working on the U.S. Capitol grounds, he made suggestions to Senator William Windom for the grounds of his residence and to Senator Justin Morrill for the arrangement of Thomas Circle. He also drew up a plan for the campus of the Industrial Home School in the District. While planning the setting of the Washington Monument in Baltimore, he advised Reverdy Johnson, Jr., concerning use of the "Clifton" estate for the campus of Johns Hopkins University. In the Boston area he not only collaborated with H. H. Richardson on the bridges in the Back Bay Fens, but also prepared landscape plans for Richardson's Crane Library in Quincy and for the grounds of the house that Richardson designed in Cohasset for Olmsted's stepdaughter Charlotte and her husband, John Bryant. In Buffalo while engaged in the public projects documented in this volume Olmsted prepared a plan for Lafayette Square and, with George Radford, planned the Parkside subdivision adjoining Delaware Park. Elsewhere he planned a 385-lot subdivision, "Bellegrove," for John Watts Kearny in what became the city of Kearny in Hudson County, New Jersey, and designed a subdivision for the Aspinwall Hill Land Company in Brookline, Massachusetts. In addition to several private estates in Massachusetts and Connecticut, he planned two extensive estates on Long Island—those of Charles Anderson Dana on Dosoris Island at Oyster Bay and of Henry B. Heyde in Suffolk County. By early 1882, he was also engaged in planning a park on Belle Isle in Detroit.

Conclusion

The years 1874 to 1882, therefore, offered Olmsted a wide range of landscape design opportunities. He would find many new opportunities during the remaining dozen years of his professional practice, which he now began at the age of sixty, but a new domestic setting, a more benign political regime in the city of his principal park planning, and a growing number of employees and partners, meant that he would not be called upon to experience as intensely the principal difficulties he encountered in the years described in this volume. He would never again be the employee of a municipal bureaucracy, as he was during his years with the New York Department of Public Parks. Nor would he again be embroiled in political controversy to the extent that he was while a member of the advisory board for the New Capitol of New York State. As he reported to his friend Charles Loring Brace in the last document in this volume, "You can have no idea what a drag life had been to me for three years or more. . . . I am still delapidated—have a great noise in my head and a little exertion sets my heart bouncing but I sleep well and seem to myself to carry on my legs not quarter of the weight I did a year ago." His move from New York City to Boston, the satisfaction offered by the planning of the Boston park system, and the relief and renewed energy they brought him, meant that Olmsted was indeed entering on a new stage of his life.

Charles E. Beveridge

1. For the collaboration of Olmsted and Vaux after the formal dissolution of their partnership on October 18, 1872, see *Papers of FLO*, 6: 43–46, 651–58, and 664–71.
2. The commissions of Olmsted, Vaux & Co. that Olmsted continued to the end of that partnership made up a very small part of his landscape work over the next decade. The same was not true for Calvert Vaux. In 1872 he was fully involved with several important architectural commissions, most notably the Metropolitan Museum of Art and the American Museum of Natural History. His apparent winning of the competition for the major building at the Centennial Exposition of 1876 in Philadelphia ended in a bitterly disappointing loss of the commission, and major architectural work came to him infrequently thereafter. His work as a landscape architect was even more limited. Olmsted was the sole landscape architect of the New York Department of Public Parks from 1874 until his dismissal in January 1878, and Vaux returned to the park as Supervising Architect only in the fall of 1881. Vaux carried out few landscape commissions during the period of this volume — a small enclosed area for Trinity Church in Manhattan, the campus of Bryn Mawr College in Pennsylvania, and the extensive grounds of the suburban villas of Samuel Tilden in Yonkers and William B. Ogden at Fordham Heights, make up most of this list (See Olmsted & Vaux, Landscape Architects, "Report of the Landscape Architects," [January 1, 1874] [*Papers of FLO*, 6: 664–71]; see also Francis Kowsky, *Country, Park & City: The Architecture and Life of Calvert Vaux* [New York and Oxford, 1998], pp. 229–46, 248–51).
3. Calvert Vaux to FLO, May 30, 1865.
4. See *Papers of FLO*, SS1: 140–41; Andrew H. Green, "Document No. 3," in BCCP, *Minutes*, Jan. 11, 1866, pp. 1–75.
5. *Papers of FLO*, 6: 37–46; Olmsted & Vaux, "A Review of Recent Changes, and Changes which have been Projected, in the Plans of the Central Park" (*Papers of FLO*, SS1: 239–73).
6. As well as the expertise he offered, Olmsted was favored by Martin for personal reasons. His brother Howard Martin had been Olmsted's secretary in the early years of Central Park, and Olmsted had taken him first to Washington and then to California to assist him during the Civil War. After the war Olmsted had defended Howard Martin against attempts by Andrew H. Green to remove him from his post as chief clerk of the parks department; Laura Wood Roper, *FLO: A Biography of Frederick Law Olmsted* (Baltimore, Md., 1973), pp. 348–50. For the reports of Olmsted and Croes on the twenty-third and twenty-fourth wards, see their "Preliminary Report" and report on the area west off Riverdale Road in chapter 4, below, and the reports to William Runyon Martin of March 20, 1877 and Oct. 31, 1877, below. For Olmsted's proposal for Tompkins Park, see his report to William Runyon Martin of Aug. 9, 1876, below.
7. DPP *Minutes*, July 26, 1876; ibid., Aug. 4, 1876; *Forty Years*, 2: 108–9.
8. John Kelly and Tammany Hall Finance Committee, 1877, to FLO, Sept. 1877.
9. Mary Perkins Olmsted to Sophia Stevens Hitchcock Page, Nov. 24 [1881], William Page Papers, Archives of American Art, Washington, D.C.
10. See "Spoils of the Park," below, p.xxx.
11. See "Review of New York City Park Department Policies in 1878," Jan. 8, 1879, below.

12. FLO, "New York State Capitol Testimony," March 6, 1977, below. For the Buffalo Asylum, see *Papers of FLO*, 6: 452–54.
13. Mariana Griswold van Rensselaer, *Henry Hobson Richardson and His Works* (1888; rpt. ed., New York, 1969), p. 119; Cecil R. Roseberry, *Capitol Story* (Albany, N.Y., 1964), pp. 32–47; FLO, "To the Public," March 26, 1877, below.
14. Plan 608–08, c. June 3, 1878, and plan 608–10, NPS/FLONHS.
15. "Report of the Committee on Finance Relative to the Construction of the New Capitol Building," March 23, 1877, "Document no. 44," in New York (State), *Documents of the Senate of the State of New York, One Hundredth Session* (Albany, N.Y., 1877), pp. 1–3; New York (State), *Journal of the Assembly of the State of New York: At Their One Hundredth Session* (Albany, N.Y., 1877),1:602; "Veto of Supply Bill Items," *New York Times*, May 17, 1877, p. 2; "The New Capitol Appropriation," ibid., May 26, 1877, p. 8.
16. FLO to John C. Olmsted, Nov. 1, 1882; Leopold Eidlitz to FLO, Nov. 2, 1882; New York (State), Architects of the Capitol, *The New Capitol. An Examination of the Grounds on Which the Security of the Assembly Chamber is Held to be in Question.* ([Albany, N. Y.?], 1882).
17. Frederick Law Olmsted and Calvert Vaux, *General Plan for the Improvement of the Niagara Reservation* (1887) (*Papers of FLO*, SS1: 535–75). For documents in this volume relating to the Niagara campaign, see letters to James T. Gardner of Oct. 2 and 3, 1879; to Charles Eliot Norton of Oct. 10, 1879, Jan. 22, 1880, and May 30 and Nov. 2, 1881; to the Earl of Derby, June 11, 1880; to W. O. Buchanan, June 15, 1880; and "Notes by Mr. Olmsted," in *Special Report of New York State Survey on the Preservation of the Scenery of Niagara Falls . . . for the Year 1879*, below.
18. Cynthia Zaitzevsky, *Frederick Law Olmsted and the Boston Park System* (Cambridge, Mass., 1982), pp. 127–28; H. H. Richardson to FLO, Feb. 6, 1883; L. W. Roper, *FLO: A Biography*, p. 383.
19. Frederick Law Olmsted, "Public Parks and the Enlargement of Towns," *Journal of Social Science*, 3: 1–36 (*Papers of FLO*, SS1: 171–205). For the McLean Asylum, see FLO to Henry Bromfield Rogers, Dec. 13, 1872 (*Papers of FLO*, 6: 584–88).
20. FLO to Charles Henry Dalton, below; Charles Henry Dalton to FLO, April 11, 1876, B68: #900, OAR/LC; BCDP, City of Boston, *Second Report* (Boston, 1876).
21. H. H. Richardson to FLO, May 21, 1878, B68: #900, OAR/LC; *American Architect and Building News*, June 8, 1878, p. 202.
22. See Frederick Law Olmsted, "Paper on the Back Bay Problem and its Solution Read Before the Boston Society of Architects," April 2, 1886 (*Papers of FLO*, SS1: 437–59); see below, FLO to Charles Sprague Sargent, Jan. 27, 1879; ibid., Jan. 29, 1879; FLO to Charles Henry Dalton, Dec. 9, 1879; ibid., Jan. 24, 1880; FLO to BCDP, City of Boston, Jan. 26, 1880; FLO, "Improvement of the Back-Bay, Boston," April 3, 1880.
23. FLO to Charles Sprague Sargent, July 8, 1874; ibid., May 7, 1880; FLO to Charles Henry Dalton, May 5, 1880; C. Zaitzevsky, *Olmsted and the Boston Park System*, pp. 58–64.
24. For Olmsted's design work on Commonwealth Avenue, see FLO and Charles S. Sargent to Charles H. Dalton, Nov. 29, 1880, below; for his proposal to develop the valley of Muddy River as part of the Boston park system, see "Suggestions for the Improvement of the Muddy River," December 1880, below. For Olmsted's report on the landscape qualities and proposed boundaries for the West Roxbury Park, see "Mr. Olmsted's Report," May 17, 1881, below. See also his comprehensive 1886 report, "Notes on the Plan of Franklin Park and Related Matters" (*Papers of FLO*, SS1: 460–534).
25. See, below, FLO to John C. Olmsted, Oct. 7, 1877, reports of Olmsted to the Commissioners of Mount Royal Park, and letters to Horatio Admiral Nelson. For Olmsted's

final statement of 1881 on Mount Royal, see Frederick Law Olmsted, *Mount Royal. Montreal* (1881) (*Papers of FLO*, SS1: 350–418).
26. Justin Morrill to FLO, May 6, 1873.
27. See FLO to William Hammond Hall, March 28, 1874, below.
28. See FLO to Montgomery Meigs, Jan. 15, 1875, below.
29. FLO, "The National Capitol," Nov. 27, 1874, in *New-York Daily Tribune*, Dec. 5, 1874, below.
30. See FLO to Thomas Wisedell, June 13, 1880, below.
31. For the summer house on the Capitol grounds, see below, FLO to Tiffany & Company, Dec. 9, 1879, and FLO to Edward Clark, August–September 1880. For the U.S. Capitol terraces, see, below, FLO to Edward Clark, Oct. 1, 1881, FLO to Edward Henry Rollins, Jan. 7, 1882, and ibid., January–February 1882.
32. For Trinity College, see FLO to Abner Jackson, May 25, 1872, (*Papers of FLO*, 6: 561–66), and FLO to Thomas Pynchon, Feb. 25, 1875, below.
33. William R. Martin to Board of Commissioners of the Department of Public Parks, March 19, 1875 in "Document No. 65," DPP, *Minutes*, March 30, 1875, pp. 12–16. See, below, the reports by Olmsted and Croes of Nov. 15, 1876, Nov. 21, 1876, and (to William R. Martin) Oct. 31, 1877, on laying out streets in parts of the Bronx, and the report to Martin of March 20, 1877, on routes for local steam transit through the region.
34. For the Rockaway Point project, see FLO to Henry Y. Attrill and Benjamin E. Smith, July 30, 1879, and FLO to Henry Y. Attrill, Sept. 23, 1879. For Point Chautauqua, see FLO to Walter L. Sessions, Oct. 9, 1875, and FLO to J. H. Miller, Feb. 28, 1876, below.
35. For Olmsted's views on family residences, see "Report Upon a Projected Improvement of the Estate of the College of California, at Berkeley, near Oakland" (*Papers of FLO*, 5: 550–54). See also "The Future of New York," *New-York Daily Tribune*, Dec. 28, 1879, below.
36. Charles Eliot Diary, p. 71 (Sept. 3–7, 1883), Loeb Library, Graduate School of Design, Harvard University, Cambridge, Massachusetts.
37. See FLO to Barthold S. Schlesinger, Feb. 9, 1880, and ibid., June 17, 1881, below.
38. Charles E. Beveridge and Paul Rocheleau, *Frederick Law Olmsted: Designing the American Landscape* (New York, 1995), pp. 136–38. For Moraine Farm, see FLO to John Charles Phillips, Aug. 23, 1880, ibid., Sept. 27, 1881, and ibid., March 6, 1882.

EDITORIAL POLICY

The purpose of the Frederick Law Olmsted Papers project is to publish, in annotated form, the most significant of Olmsted's letters, unpublished writings, professional reports, and articles for newspapers and periodicals. The letterpress edition will consist of twelve volumes: nine volumes arranged chronologically, one volume containing major documents on park design and city planning, and two large-format volumes of plans and views of landscape designs.

Document Selection   Although the process is to some extent subjective, the editors require every document published to meet at least one of three criteria: that it provide insight into Olmsted's character, present valuable commentary on his times, or contain an important statement on landscape design.

Annotation   The editors believe that it is their responsibility to make clear the context within which Olmsted wrote the documents selected and to explain the significance of certain statements that readers not expert in the field might otherwise not adequately comprehend. They believe also that part of their function is to identify the persons, places, and events Olmsted mentions, and to explain his relation to them. The annotation in these volumes is fuller than it would be in a complete edition of Olmsted's papers, where the documents would more frequently annotate one another. To supply background information and provide continuity within each volume, the editors make use of volume introductions, biographical directories, and chapter headnotes, as well as chronologies, itineraries, genealogies, and other aids for the reader.

Treatment of Text   The intent of the editors is to provide a text as close to the original as possible without causing undue difficulty for the reader. In some instances we alter the original text in the interest of clarity: in such cases, we furnish guides to our alterations that permit recovery of the original text.

The complete existing text of each document is published. All of the words that Olmsted wrote and did not cross out are presented, with the exception of inadvertently repeated words. The treatment of illegible and missing words is as follows:

> {. . .} indicates illegible words or words missing because of mutilation of the manuscript.
> {*italic*} indicates the editor's reading of partially missing words.
> {roman} indicates a word supplied by the editors.

Where needed, these braces are supplemented by an explanatory endnote.

In the occasional instance where a passage does not make sense without substitution of a word or words for those in the original version, the editors make the needed substitution and supply the original wording in an endnote. When the word that Olmsted wrote appears not to be the one he meant to write and the correct word cannot be discerned, the editors suggest, in an endnote, an alternative word or phrase that seems closer to Olmsted's meaning. Where the document is not in Olmsted's hand and what appears to be incorrect wording may be due to the error of a transcriber or typesetter, one of these two approaches is used as well.

The published texts include words and phrases deleted by Olmsted only when they add material that does not appear at some other point in the document. If they are integral to the document, such deleted words are presented in the text in italics and in braces. If the deleted words are less directly relevant to the theme of the document, they are given in an endnote.

The principles of transcription stated here are applied by the editors to all kinds of documents, including drafts of articles and lectures that exist in "fair copy" as well as fragmentary drafts. When preparing a text from manuscript fragments that have no clear order, the editors construct a text, adding such indications as microfilm reel and frame numbers, extra spaces between lines of text, dividing lines, ellipses, and endnotes, to mark the transition from one segment of the original text to another. When a document exists in both printed and manuscript form, and Olmsted wrote the document for publication (as, for instance, with park reports), the most complete version is used as the basic text. If the other version or versions contain significant variations from that text, the differences are described and quoted in notes added at the appropriate places in the document. The first, unnumbered, endnote to the document explains the textual treatment in such cases.

For manuscripts that were published at a later date, the original version is used as the basic text. Differences between the two versions that appear to be printer's or transcriber's errors are noted in endnotes, as are changes apparently made by Olmsted for the published version; obvious typographical errors, such as incorrect, missing, or transposed letters, are silently corrected when a published version of a document is being used as the text.

At the end of this volume the editors provide a list of textual alterations, giving the original form of texts or quoted material where a change has not been indicated in endnotes or by braces in the text. The list indicates the original form of contractions that have been expanded. It gives each deleted or altered punctuation mark with the word preceding and the word following it and indicates added punctuation by giving the words preceding and following it. The list indicates the original form of misspelled words that have been corrected in the text, except as noted below.

Spelling Olmsted consistently misspelled words with double consonants (as "dissapoint" for "disappoint"). He frequently misspelled words with double vowels (consistently writing "lose" as "loose"), and he misspelled words with the diphthong "ie" (as "cheif" for "chief"). The editors silently correct these three kinds of Olmsted's misspellings. All other misspelled words are presented in the text as Olmsted wrote them. If the misspelling makes a word particularly difficult to interpret, however, it is corrected and its misspelled form is presented in the list of textual alterations. Terms such as "can not" and "no where" have been silently corrected to their modern-day forms "cannot" and "nowhere."

Paragraphing The editors follow Olmsted's indications of internal paragraphing. Where he indicated a paragraph by a long dash or a large space between sentences, we silently make a new paragraph. We do the same where he inserted a paragraph symbol or where a change in subject matter between two pages of manuscript indicates that he used the page change as a paragraph. Sections of conversations are silently rendered as paragraphs. Other paragraphing introduced by the editors is indicated in the list of textual alterations.

Contractions The editors present the original form of abbreviations and contractions. Superscripts are reproduced. Apostrophes are silently added if they are missing from the contraction "nt" (for "not"), from conjugations of the verb "to be," and from possessives. Particularly awkward or unclear contractions are expanded and the original form is indicated in the list of textual alterations.

Punctuation The editors do not regularize Olmsted's punctuation or make it consistently grammatical; but we do make changes in his punctuation when it would be difficult for the reader to work out the meaning of a passage in its original form. In long and convoluted sentences, or where the original text is likely to cause the reader to misread phrases, the editors alter punctuation. We occasionally delete punctuation where it unnecessarily complicates already difficult passages, and we add punctuation in order to clarify basic sentence structure. These changes are not indicated in the text itself by braces or other symbols, since that would introduce new distractions and complexity at the very place where they would be most troublesome. Instead, the changes are given in the list of textual alterations. We silently supply periods where the end of a line served for Olmsted as the end of a sentence.

Marginalia Material that Olmsted added in the margins is presented at the point where he indicated that it belongs. If such material has no clear place within the text, it is printed at the end of the document with an explanatory note. Notes or jottings on a document by other persons are not included in the text, but if informative are given in an endnote. Olmsted's infrequent footnotes are presented at the bottom of the page.

Place and Date of Documents Dates for documents are given as they appear in the original. The place of writing and date of a document is given as it appears in the original, but when the date appears at the end it is given in the upper right-hand corner of the published document. If that information is partial, incorrect, or missing, the probable date or time period is supplied in brackets, with an explanatory endnote if needed. Printed letterheads that are misleading are not reproduced but are noted in the first, unnumbered, endnote of the letter.

Arrangement of Documents Documents are presented in chronological order except for occasional pieces such as autobiographical fragments or reminiscences written at a later time than the period covered in the volume. Such pieces are presented with the documents from the period they describe.

Citation of Sources Full bibliographical information is provided in the first citation of a source in each chapter, except for sources that appear in a volume's list of "Short Titles Used in Citations." The latter are cited consistently by short title throughout the volume. A full listing of sources about an individual is given in the note accompanying the first mention of that person in the documents of a volume. In subsequent references, sources are given only for additional information supplied. Birth and death dates for persons mentioned in the text of the documents are given in the first note identifying them and, for selected persons, in the index.

No repository is cited if the document is from the Frederick Law Olmsted Papers, Manuscript Division, Library of Congress, Washington, D.C. For citation of manuscripts in other collections and repositories, documents with the same sender and recipient are cited in a series using "ibid." in place of the names of sender and recipient. The name and location of the collection is then given at the end of the series of citations so arranged.

SHORT TITLES USED IN CITATIONS

1. Correspondents' Names

BCCP	Board of Commissioners of the Central Park
BCPP	Board of Commissioners of Prospect Park
BCDP, City of Boston	City of Boston, Massachusetts, Board of Commissioners of the Department of Parks
BPC	Brooklyn Park Commission
DPP	Department of Public Parks (New York City)
FLO	Frederick Law Olmsted
FLO, Jr.	Frederick Law Olmsted, Jr.

2. Standard References

ANB	*American National Biography*
DAB	*Dictionary of American Biography*
DNB	*Dictionary of National Biography*
EB	*Encyclopaedia Britannica*
NCAB	*National Cyclopaedia of American Biography*
OED	*Oxford English Dictionary*

3. Books by Frederick Law Olmsted

    Walks and Talks *Walks and Talks of an American Farmer in England*, 2 vols. in 1 (New York, 1852).

SHORT TITLES USED IN CITATIONS

4. Other Published Works

Appleton's Cyc. Am. Biog.   *Appleton's Cyclopedia of American Biography*, ed. James G. Wilson and John Fiske (New York, 1887–89).

BCCP,—— *Annual Report* [18–]   New York City, Board of Commissioners of the Central Park, *Annual Report* (New York, 1858–70). Each annual report covers the calendar year preceding the year of publication.

BCCP,—— *Minutes*   New York City, Board of Commissioners of the Central Park, *Minutes of Proceedings of the Board of Commissioners of the Central Park* (New York, 1858–69).

BCDP, —— City of Boston, *Annual Report* [18–]   City of Boston, [Massachusetts], Board of Commissioners of the Department of Parks, Annual Report (Boston, 1875–).

BCPP,—— *Annual Report* [18–]   Board of Commissioners of Prospect Park, *Annual Report* (Brooklyn, 1866–68).

BPC, *Annual Reports, 1861–1873*   Brooklyn, Park Commissioners, *Annual Reports of the Brooklyn Park Commissioners, 1861–1873* (Brooklyn, 1873).

BPC, —— *Annual Report* [18–]   Brooklyn Park Commission, *Annual Report* (Brooklyn, 1869–1886).

DPP, —— *Annual Report* [18–]   New York (City), Department of Public Parks, *Annual Report* (New York, 1871–72). Each annual report covers the calender year preceding the year of publication.

DPP, *Minutes*   New York (City), Department of Public Parks, *Minutes* (New York, 1870–74).

FLO, A Biography   Laura Wood Roper, *FLO: A Biography of Frederick Law Olmsted* (Baltimore, Md., 1973).

Forty Years   Frederick Law Olmsted, Jr., and Theodora Kimball, eds., *Frederick Law Olmsted, Landscape Architect, 1822–1903 (Forty Years of Landscape Architecture)*, 2 vols. (New York, 1922–28).

Microfilm edition, FLO Papers/LC   Microfilm edition of the Frederick Law Olmsted Papers, Manuscript Division, Library of Congress, Washington, D.C.

Papers of FLO   *The Papers of Frederick Law Olmsted*, ed. Charles C. McLaughlin, Charles E. Beveridge, et al. (Baltimore, 1977–).

5. Unpublished Sources

OAR/LC   Olmsted Associates Records, Library of Congress, Washington, D.C. Citations give box or volume number, followed by (respectively) folder or page number (i.e., A21: 624 for volume A21, page 624, or B74: #1032 for Box B74, folder number 1032). The folder number is the

SHORT TITLES USED IN CITATIONS

same as the job number assigned a given project by the Olmsted firm — in this case project 1032 is Leland Stanford, Jr., University.

NPS/FLONHS   National Park Service, Frederick Law Olmsted National Historic Site, Brookline, Massachusetts.

NARA   National Archives and Records Administration.

PARKS, POLITICS, AND PATRONAGE
1874–1882

CHAPTER I

JANUARY 1874–AUGUST 1874

The principal topic of documents in this chapter is the early stages of Olmsted's planning of the expanded grounds of the U.S. Capitol grounds. The three letters to Senator Justin Morrill in this chapter mark the beginning of Olmsted's writing on the subject. In the letter of January 26, 1874, he reviews the condition of the center of Washington D.C., and demonstrates his longstanding concern with the relation of public open space to the overall city plan. The letter of June 9 describes his first preliminary plan for the Capitol grounds, while the letter of August 16 describes difficulties encountered in the process of construction. Other letters present a wide range of topics. "Country Living" reviews recent writings on landscape gardening by other practitioners, while the letter of March 23 to William Hammond Hall considers a current proposal for the campus of the College of California in Berkeley that Olmsted had planned in 1866. The letter to Salem Wales discusses the problem of placing statuary in large urban parks. The letter to Charles S. Sargent marks the beginning of Olmsted's involvement with the Arnold Arboretum in Boston. Other letters range from planning the grounds of a hotel in Saratoga, N.Y., to treatment of the Jeffersonville Depot near Louisville.

COUNTRY LIVING.*

[January 22, 1874]

These two books come together to the reviewer's table. The one from the East is a thick volume, designed to cultivate a love of nature, and to recommend simplicity of life. It is much better adapted to the first of these purposes than to the second, its method being to point out, as it does carefully and well, though sometimes in too much the manner of a catalogue, the leading points of beauty and interest in the natural objects of the old, neglected roads and paths and farmsteads of the less cultivated parts of Eastern Massachusetts, and to set in contemptuous contrast with these that which it is the chief purpose of the more modest little volume which meets it from the West to commend.

Mr. Flagg supposes that landscape gardeners and architects, in distinction from ordinary cultivators and builders, have it for their business to superadd artificial decoration to the beauties of nature. He regards them not only as the declared enemies of all natural simplicity, grace, and picturesqueness, but as the accepted ministers of the purse-proud, ostentatious, and vulgarly-conceited among men. His antipathy to them extends even to "popular writers on nature's aspects"—among whom he can never have thought of ranking himself—and those on landscape painting, who, "with all their *professed* admiration of nature, always place her in subordination to art." Mr. Cleveland, writing as a landscape architect, bases his work on the proposition that what is essentially important in his art lies back and absolutely independent "of mere decorations." The grouping of trees and shrubs, and the arrangement of fountains, flower-beds, rustic seats, and other such garden furniture, is but an incidental duty of his business, which is to adapt ground to the varied requirements of civilized society with artistic refinement of completeness. The gratification and cultivation of a love of nature he regards as but one among many such requirements.

The instructions of one author are directly contradicted by the other. Mr. Flagg says "the road that winds around the hill or the meadow is the one you must follow." "The old road is bordered with wild shrubbery, groups of trees of bold and irregular growth—there is no sameness." The new road, the landscape architect's road, is formal, unnatural, uninteresting, dreary. Mr. Cleveland says that in the old and common way of laying out roads "all the naturally beautiful or picturesque features have been destroyed or rendered

---

*"The Woods and By-Ways of New England. By Wilson Flagg, author of 'Studies in Field and Forest.' With [photographic] illustrations.' Boston: J. R. Osgood & Co.[1]

'Landscape Architecture as applied to the Wants of the West, with an Essay on Forest Planting on the Great Plains. By H. W. S. Cleveland, Landscape Architect.' Chicago: Jansen, McClurg & Co.[2]

hideous"; that the landscape architect asks, how can the road "be best adapted to the natural shape of the ground"? "How can any naturally attractive features, such as a river, a lake, or a mountain, near or distant, be made to minister to the beautiful or picturesque character of the place [neighborhood] by adapting the arrangement to the development of their most attractive aspects?"

Mr. Flagg loves the simplicity of the old, brown, slightly dilapidated house under the elms, its gambrelled roof studded with mosses, the greensward of its door-yard close cropped by the cows; he loves to follow the paths by which the cows stray from it through the adjoining huckleberry lots; he loves to pick his way from tussock to tussock along the edge of the lily ponds, and to point out the thousand charms offered on every side to the enjoyment of a lover of nature. It is in such neighborhoods, such houses, and such simplicity, might Mr. Cleveland say, that I have found women living more confined, dull, and dreary lives than in any barbarous country; caring less for simple, natural pleasures than any other women in the world; that I have found the chief objects of their admiration and ambition the furthest removed from nature and nature's grace; it has been in such homes that insanity, consumption, typhoid fever, and diphtheria have found more victims than in those even of the densest and dirtiest of cities.

Mr. Cleveland thinks that a civilized home is distinguished from a barbarous one by the convenience and economy with which those who live in it can command the conditions of health, and the gratification of healthful desires and tastes, and that, while there are beauties to be found by the side of a cow-path and on the boggy shores of a pond, it is also possible to have them where they can be enjoyed with more convenience, under conditions more favorable to health and more economical of civilized raiment. He assumes that to associate natural and artificial attractions successfully in a home, much more where many homes are found in a limited neighborhood, as in villages and towns, and to secure with them other conditions of health and happy life, requires much and varied study, a deep sympathy with and reverence for nature, a designing fancy, and a shrewd power in adapting means to ends. This he would say is what is required in a landscape architect. Unquestionably he is right. Mr. Flagg has been misled by quacks. The home of ignorance, conceit, and vulgarity is what he finds it not through excess, but through lack, of art.

The latter half of Mr. Cleveland's book is an urgent plea for forest planting, especially on the Great Plain and its borders, with a review of what little has been done, and some practical advice as to what should be undertaken. The publication is valuable, timely, and altogether of good omen for the West.

The text presented here is from the *Nation*, January 22, 1874, pages 64–65.

1. Thomas Wilson Flagg (1805–1884), naturalist and writer (*DAB*; *The Woods and Byways of New England* [Boston, 1872]).

2. Horace William Shaler Cleveland (1814–1900), landscape architect and writer (*DAB*; *Landscape Architecture, as Applied to the Wants of the West; with an Essay on Forest Planting on the Great Plains. By H. W. S. Cleveland* [Chicago, 1873]).

To Justin Smith Morrill[1]

209 W. 46th New York
January. 22^d 1874.

To the Honorable J. R. Morrill;
Chairman of Committee for Public Grounds
U.S. Senate.
Sir;
    Before anything more is done about the improvements of the public grounds in Washington concerning which you have asked my opinion,[2] the question, what shall be the motive of their improvement, should be conclusively settled.
    For convenience sake I will consider this question first with reference to the whole body of open ground from the Capitol to Lafayette Square,[3] and afterwards, more especially to that immediately about the Capitol.
    Within or on the borders of the larger ground stand the Capitol, the Executive Mansion and the several buildings occupied by the State, Judiciary, Treasury, and War and Navy Departments, the Agricultural Bureau and the Smithsonian Institution. To these the National Library and other buildings are expected to be added.[4]
    The larger part of the exterior of the existing buildings is of marble and granite elaborately wrought. Beyond the cost of all necessary accommodations for the business to be done in them, they represent an investment by the Nation of Millions of dollars, made solely with a view of producing certain impressions upon the mind of observers. Had this outlay been wisely and comprehensively directed to the purpose in view, no nation in the world would now possess as noble and fitting a capital as the United States. As it is, the effect produced is admitted to be a broken, confused and unsatisfactory one and is unhappily often alluded to as a standing reproach against the system of government which has been able to secure no better adaptation of means to such an end.
    That the result of so much architectural effort is so comparitively insignificant is largely due to the circumstance that the several government buildings are seldom seen under conditions favorable to the impression designed to be established; that this impression, so far as it might otherwise be

produced, is not sustained or supported by objects adjoining them and that long rows of other buildings have been intruded between the more important of them, the character of which is adapted only to bewilder and dissipate the desired effect.[5] In short the capital of the Union manifests nothing so much as disunity. This is not because of the distance between the government buildings simply: were this reduced one half, the intervening spaces remaining occupied as at present, the lack of any coordinating purpose would be felt none the less. What is wanting is a federal bond. Had the buildings been ranged about a single field of landscape all the other objects within which were not only objects of beauty but were consistent and harmonious one with another, a much more sustained and consequently more impressive effect would have been produced. Great breadth in this field of landscape and largeness of scale in all its features {provided it were consistently sustained} would not be felt in the least as a disadvantage.

It follows that if a space could now be introduced into the plan of the city by which the same result even in a modified degree could be gained, the capital would be more transformed and elevated in the scale of art than by any and all other means for the purpose that can be proposed.

It is my judgement that the canal district,[6] now mainly a dreary waste, with the adjoining public grounds, presents an opportunity for accomplishing this object, and this is my answer to the question, what should be the motive of any scheme for its improvement.

It would be requisite to the end in view that the motive should be absolutely controlling in all parts of the ground and the first obstacle to success would exist in the fact that certain portions of it have already been worked and are held and managed under divers committees and other authorities each with a different purpose.

General Babcock[7] showed me plans which had been prepared for other portions, the plan of each being substantially independant of that for every other, and he informed me that there was a project for improving yet other parts in the same way and for finally connecting each part with those adjoining it so that it would form a link in a chain of such grounds, extending from the Capitol to the Executive Mansion.

Under existing laws a project of this kind may be the best that can be adopted but with reference to the purpose of forming a ground which shall bring the various government buildings into a relation of landscape unity it can lead only to its antithesis.

Each building and other object of interest instead of appearing as one in the National assemblage will have its own little separate domain and seem more distinctly set apart from all the others even, than at present. And no matter how pretty each of these might be in itself by no aggregation of such prettiness can any great beauty or any fine impression of unity throughout all be produced.

I apprehend that the first step necessary to be taken toward a comprehensive improvement would be the most difficult one, that is, to place the control of all these grounds under one body so constituted that it would be likely to pursue a sustained policy year after year and not be led off by regard for special and temporary interests. The cost of carrying out such a plan as I suggest would probably be less — acre per acre — than of pursuing the project now entertained.

Before proceeding to the second question of the motive which should govern a plan for the improvement of the ground immediately about the Capitol, I will observe that too much importance seems to be generally given to the circumstance that the first Capitol building[8] was designed on the supposition that the city of Washington would be built on the East side of it and that it is therefore considered to be fronted to the East. A building may have two fronts and most noble buildings in fact are designed with two, of which not unfrequently that of the carriage or most used entrance is the less important architecturally and in the landscape. Such is the case with the palace of the Tuileries, of the Luxembourg and of Versailles, for example, as it is of the noblest halls of England.[9] It is much better for most purposes to which a large building is to be put that one side of it should be left entierly free from the disturbance of carriages and it is on that front that any beauty of architecture possessed by the building will commonly be seen to the highest advantage and on which any landscape beauty associated with it may be best enjoyed from within.

If the suggestion of a federal ground on the west should be carried out I should think the circumstance that the carriage front of the Capitol was on the East and that the question of the treatment of the ground on the West need not be complicated by the necessity of a grand approach road a fortunate one. I do not know the full history of the arrangement by which the West front surmounts an elevation looking out upon a space of ground gradually and symmetrically widening as the distance from it increases, extending to a broad river a mile away beyond which and toward the setting sun verdant heights terminate a prospect the natural elements of which are all broad, simple and tranquilizing, but if the most firmly established principles and the most satisfactory precedents in Landscape Architecture had been consulted the arrangement would not have been different. The cause of regret lies solely in the poor use that has been made of the opportunity thus originally secured.

The capitol building is a very large one and its design grand and imposing. The ground about it should be so managed as to sustain and minister to this design as much as possible. To this end its general features should be large in scale, simple in outline and in all respects as quietly dignified in character as the requirements of convenience will allow. Trees should be so placed that nature will gradually bring them into satisfactory landscape relation with the building.

Under present conditions advantages are nowhere found for fully en-

VIEW OF U.S. CAPITOL WITH EARTH TERRACES, C. 1880

joying the architectural design. There is no position on the East where the eye of the observer can hold it all in a fair perspective, none from which its base if seen at all must not be looked down upon. The sky lines of the trees about it do not compose satisfactorily with those of the architecture.

Looking from the West, owing to the disposition of the trees, there is no position from which a general view of it can be taken; none from which its real proportions are not apparently distorted. It is best seen as a whole from points on the Northwest or the Southwest but from these it appears crowding over the edge of the hill and to have no proper standing room.

The face of the hillside is broken by two formal terraces which are relatively thin and weak, by no means sustaining in forms and proportions the grandeur of the superimposed mass.[10]

These disadvantages of the Capitol are mainly due to the single fact that the base lines of the wings were not adapted to the ground they stand upon but were laid down with relation to those of the original much smaller central structure, and that the trees now growing about it were planted with no thought of the present building but only with regard to the old one. A considerable number of those on the East have also been introduced subsequently to the original planting and apparently without reference to the purposes then had in view. It is chiefly by these trees that the design of the architect is on that side obscured. On the West a few of the permanent trees were probably planted with consideration only for the effect they would have while young and small—others unquestionably with the expectation that they would be thinned out.[11]

Had this been done at the proper time the Capitol would be seen to much greater advantage than it now is and the general effect of the trees would be much more umbrageous as well as more harmonious with its architecture.

The proposed lowering of the surface to meet the new grade of the street which bounds the Capitol grounds on the East offers an opportunity for remedying the principal defects to which I have referred on that side.[12] It would not be a necessity of this lowering of the surface that the trees upon it should be destroyed but not more than half can, I think, be advantageously retained where they are. It is quite practicable by removing a part and introducing others to rehabilitate the ground in a short time with a larger body of foliage than is provided by the present trees and to have them grouped in much better relation with the enlarged building.

The defect of the West front is due, as I have said, to the fact that the new parts of the building are further advanced on the face of the hill side than they probably would have been had it been possible to design them with reference to it, and that the terraces by which this misfortune is designed to be relieved, being continuations of lines originally laid out with regard to a much smaller building, are inadequate to the purpose.

As the building cannot be moved back, the only remedy possible is to be found in bringing the face of the hill simply and boldly forward. This is especially needed on the flanks where the terraces are now run out with a constantly diminishing face. The material for this purpose could now be supplied at a moderate cost, by the proposed reduction of the surface on the East side but the work should not be undertaken until after the intended new lines on the West side have been most carefully studied in relation to the Architecture.

The text presented here is from an unsigned draft in a clerk's hand with numerous corrections and additions in Olmsted's hand. There is a copy in a clerk's hand signed by Olmsted and dated January 26, 1874, in Record Group 46, Records of the U.S. Senate, Committee on Public Buildings and Grounds, committee papers, SEN 43A–E17, NARA, Washington, D.C. A page is missing from this copy and it contains numerous errors of transcription. For these reasons, the editors have used the draft version for the text presented here.

1. Justin Smith Morrill (1810–1898), Republican senator from Vermont. Best known as the author of the Land-Grant College Act of 1862, he was also a leading member of the Senate Committee on Public Buildings and Grounds between 1870 and 1898. From this position he supported the planting of trees and lawns along Washington's streets undertaken by the Board of Public Work's "Parking Commission" in the 1870s. During this time, he introduced legislation that enlarged the eastern and western portion of the Capitol grounds to their present boundaries and appropriated funds to improve them from their long-standing condition, which he described as "little better than a common cattle-yard." For the nearly two decades it took to complete Olmsted's plan for the U.S. Capitol grounds, Morrill was his principal ally in Congress. His support was critical in funding construction of the terrace in the 1880s, and he conferred with Olmsted about revisions in the design of its central arcade after 1885 (*DAB*; A. J. Hal-

ford, *Official Congressional Directory of the Fifty-Fifth Congress*, [Washington, D.C., 1898], p. 114; James T. Gardner to FLO, Dec. 3, 1873; William Tindall, "The Origins of the Parking System of This City," *Records of the Columbia Historical Society* 4 [1901], pp. 78–81; [Glenn Brown], *Documentary History of the Construction and Development of the United States Capitol Building and Grounds* [Washington, D.C., 1904], pp. 1086–91, 1146; FLO to Edward Clark, Feb. 15, 1886, A1: 282, OAR/LC; Justin S. Morrill to FLO, Jan. 4, 1889, D4, OAR/LC).

2. Morrill first requested Olmsted's advice on the U.S. Capitol grounds in the spring of 1873. Although obligations to the New York City Department of Public Parks and an eye ailment prevented Olmsted from taking up the work that year, he advised that a topographical map of the grounds be prepared and promised to give further advice in the future (Justin S. Morrill to FLO, May 6, 1873; FLO to Justin S. Morrill, May 12, 1873; ibid., Nov. 26, 1873; ibid., Dec. 24, 1873; Justin S. Morrill to Henry G. Stebbins, May 10, 1873; Edward Clark to FLO, June 9, 1873; FLO to Edward Clark, June 11, 1873, Office of the Curator, Architect of the Capitol, U.S. Capitol, Washington, D.C.).

3. That is, the area extending west from the Capitol to the Washington Monument, known as the Mall, then north to Lafayette Square, which faces the White House from across Pennsylvania Avenue. Attempts to improve these grounds into a unified public promenade dated back to the original 1791 plan of the capital by French engineer Major Pierre Charles L'Enfant. In 1851, Andrew Jackson Downing, provided an alternative plan in the romantic style. Neither plan was completed on the ground, although significant work was done in accordance with both (Frederick Gutheim and Wilcomb E. Washburn, *The Federal City: Plans & Realities* [Washington, D.C., 1976], pp. 2–14, 78–85; David Schuyler, *The New Urban Landscape: The Redefinition of City Form in Nineteenth-Century America* [Baltimore, 1986], pp. 11–18, 67–76).

4. The "several buildings" included the U.S. Treasury Building, built between 1836 and 1869, just east of the White House; the State, War, and Navy Building (now the Old Executive Office Building), built between 1871 and 1888, just west of the White House; and the Justice Department, housed in a building across Pennsylvania Avenue from the Treasury. The Smithsonian Institution's "Castle," built between 1846 and 1855, is located on the south side of the Mall between Seventh and Twelfth streets west. Immediately to its west stood the Department of Agriculture Building, completed in 1868. A separate building for the Library of Congress, then housed in the Capitol, was first proposed in 1873 but Congress did not select its site across First Street east from the Capitol until 1886; it was completed in 1897 (The Junior League of Washington, *The City of Washington: An Illustrated History*, ed. Thomas Froncek [New York, 1977], pp. 182–83, 188–89, 257, 267, 299; National Park Service, Department of the Interior, *Historic American Buildings Survey: District of Columbia Catalog*, comp. Nancy B. Schwartz [Charlottesville, VA, 1974], pp. 136–37, 144–46).

5. Before the enlargement of the east Capitol grounds in 1872–73, an assortment of dilapidated boarding houses, saloons, and private residences stood near the Capitol to the northeast and southeast. "Under the very eaves of the Capitol," reported Major Nathaniel Michler, "the eye is forced to rest upon one of the most unfinished, unsettled, and offensive localities — and there are many of them — within the city limits." To the west of the Capitol, buildings crowded in on the present site of the Mall between Third and Sixth streets west. During the Civil War, railroad tracks were laid across the Mall at the latter street, and in 1874, with congressional approval, the Pennsylvania Railroad built a large station there, just south of the present Constitution Avenue. Finally, the area between the Mall and Pennsylvania Avenue, the present Federal Triangle, was a motley collection of slums, produce markets, and brothels known as "Swamppoodle." Each of these areas negated the unified appearance for Washington's public spaces and buildings envisioned in turn by L'Enfant, Downing, and Olm-

sted (Glenn Brown, *History of the United States Capitol*, 2 vols. [Washington, D.C., 1902], 2: 220; G. Brown, *Documentary History of the United States Capitol*, pp. 1090, 1120; U.S. War Department, *Annual Report* [Washington, D.C., 1868], 2: 893–94, 895–96; T. Froncek, *City of Washington*, pp. 186–87, 234, 242; F. Gutheim and W. E. Washburn, *Federal City*, pp. 22, 43).

6. The Washington Canal, included in L'Enfant's plan for the capital and built in the 1810s, ran from west to east along the northern edge of the Mall, on the present line of Constitution Avenue. It turned south and crossed the Mall near the foot of Capitol Hill and then ran southeast along the present line of Canal Street to the Anacostia River. It fell into disuse after the 1830s and became an open sewer (F. Gutheim and W. E. Washburn, *Federal City*, pp. 4, 8–9, 21, 114–15).

7. Orville E. Babcock (1835–1884), personal secretary to President Ulysses S. Grant and the officer in charge of public buildings and grounds for the U.S. Army Corp of Engineers, which gained authority over the maintenance and improvement of public spaces in the capital in 1867. Babcock served in this post between 1871 and 1875. He also sat, along with Olmsted, on a short-lived advisory panel to the Board of Public Works of the Territory of Washington, in early 1871. One of the panel's recommendations was the planting of lawn strips and trees along Washington's streets, a project carried out in following years by the "Parking Commission." Olmsted said later that Babcock's work on the Mall was that "of a gentleman who had previously shown no qualifications for the duty and who was prepared by no special education for it or, so far as publicly known, by any predilections or special disposition of taste" (*DAB*; F. Gutheim and W. E. Washburn, *Federal City*, pp. 23–24; Franklin T. Howe, "The Board of Public Works," *Records of the Columbia Historical Society* 3 [1900], pp. 261–63; [FLO], "Lecture to Architecture Students," 1892, manuscript draft).

8. That is, the building constructed in stages between 1793 and 1829 from plans by William Thornton, Benjamin H. Latrobe, and Charles Bulfinch. It consisted of a central section capped by a low dome, flanked by symmetrical wings on the north and south. The present dome and wings were designed by Thomas U. Walter, and constructed by Montgomery C. Meigs between 1851 and 1865. (N. Schwartz, *District of Columbia Catalog*, pp. 141–43; *Papers of FLO*, 4: 152).

9. The Tuileries Palace, built by Catherine de' Medici in the sixteenth century and burned by the Commune in 1871, was located between the Louvre and the Place de la Concorde in Paris. The royal palace of Versailles, commenced in the seventeenth century by Louis XIV, is located in the suburbs of Paris. Both palaces had fronts used for carriage approaches on one side, and more decorative fronts which overlooked gardens on the opposite side. Olmsted probably saw both during visits to Paris in 1856 and 1859. He visited numerous English country seats in 1850, 1856, and 1859 (*Papers of FLO*, 1: 394; ibid., 2: 484; ibid., 3: 232–39, 352; Pierre Lavedan, *French Architecture* [London, 1979], pp. 180, 185–90, 262–63; Jean-Claude Daufresne, *Louvre & Tuileries: Architectures de Papier* [Liege, 1987], pp. 121, 283).

10. Two narrow flagged terraces, built by Bulfinch in the 1820s, remained on the west front of the building. Following the completion of the new wings, earthen fill was used to extend them around the south and north sides of the building (G. Brown, *Documentary History of the United States Capitol*, pp. 1074–6, 1082).

11. During the 1820s, Senator John C. Calhoun of South Carolina obtained congressional funding to improve the west grounds of the Capitol, out of which several dozen fine maples were planted. Subsequently, James Maher, the public gardener appointed by President Andrew Jackson, planted silver poplars and silver maples around them. These were inferior trees which, when mature, crowded and damaged the better trees. In late 1851, A. J. Downing, already at work landscaping the Mall, was given authority over the improvement of other public spaces in Washington, including the Capitol

grounds. Downing tried to remove the offending trees, Olmsted later reported, but "in accordance with a custom still generally observed, was at once denounced for his presumption in doing so" (G. Brown, *Documentary History of the United States Capitol,* pp. 1146, 1155; [Frederick Law Olmsted], "Index to Trees About the Capitol, with Advice to Visitors Interested in Them," in *Annual Report of the Architect of the Capitol* [1882], appendix, p. 14; [Frederick Law Olmsted], "Lecture to Architecture Students," 1892, manuscript draft).

12. The "principal defects" were the trees that blocked the best views of the east front of the Capitol and the rise of the grounds in the direction of First Street east. The surface at the street was eight feet higher than the bottom steps of the east portico, putting the building at the foot of a long slope. Since the mid-1860s architect of the Capitol Edward Clark, along with Morrill and the committee on public buildings and grounds, campaigned for the grading down of the east grounds to give the building a more impressive position. Opponents in and out of Congress blocked the grading with the argument that it would involve the destruction of the mature trees on the ground. In the early 1870s, however, the city established the grade of First Street at the level recommended by Clark and Morrill. It was lowered with a cut which made a corresponding reduction of the east grounds necessary in order to recover the view of the Capitol building (G. Brown, *Documentary History of the United States Capitol,* pp. 1076, 1105–6; G. Brown, *History of the Capitol,* 2: 193–94; U.S. War Department, *Annual Report* [Washington, D.C., 1868], 2: 893; *Washington Evening Star,* Nov. 21, 1874, p. 5; "Work on the Capitol Grounds," undated c. Nov. 1874 newspaper clipping, scrapbook no. 1, Records Management Department, Architect of the Capitol, U.S. Capitol, Washington, D.C.; FLO to George E. Waring, Jr., July 19, 1874; F. L. Olmsted, "The National Capitol," Dec. 5, 1874, below).

To Salem H. Wales[1]

Department of Public Parks,
Office of Design and Superintendence,
New York, March 4, 1874.

To the Hon. S. H. Wales,
*President of the Board of Commissioners
of the Department of Public Parks:*
Sir:—

You ask us to report in answer to the following question:

Is it desirable that a statue, which with its pedestal would be thirty feet in height, should be placed in the centre of the oval plat of turf at the south end of the Mall of the Central Park?[2]

The position, outlines and color of every object in this part of the Park, as in every other, have been studied, first by reference to the main purpose of the Park, and afterwards with reference to special local purposes, consistent with and more or less contributive to that paramount purpose.

It may be assumed that the desirability of the introduction of any additional object at any point can best be determined by a similar process of study.

We shall consider the proposition, therefore, with reference, first, to the general design of the Park, and afterwards to the special design of the Mall, and other local conditions.

In providing for recreation from the effects of constant urban confinement of the people of a great city, it would but for one reason be better to have several comparatively small grounds rather than a single large one. This reason is that a sense of escape from the confinement of buildings and streets is in itself an important element of the desired recreation, and that the degree in which this is produced depends largely on the extent of open country which can be brought into view. The site of the Central Park was unfortunately selected with no regard for this desideratum, and happened to be divided in the middle by the reservoirs and further subdivided by rocky hillocks in such a way that in but few places was there any general rural view more extensive than might be found in a tract of land but one-tenth as large. It has consequently been a primary object in its design to get the better of this most conspicuous defect of the site, and to take the utmost advantage of such opportunities as were offered in the topography to make the visitor feel as if a considerable extent of country were open before him.

Such opportunities were therefore made key-points in the design of the park.

Of these key-points, the locality in question was considered to be of the first importance, for the following reasons:

The eminence at the southwest corner of the reservoir, called Vista Rock,[3] is the most distant natural object which can be seen from any point in the southern part of the park; and the Drive, south of the Mall, is the nearest point to the entrance from Fifth avenue at which it can be brought into view. A little to the right and left of the line of view towards it from this point, large rocky elevations[4] shorten the prospect by more than one-half. Further to the right and left, the prospect opens again much more broadly, but not to so great a distance. The strongest effect of distance can only be had, therefore, for a moment in passing this spot; and it was, in the estimation of the designers, worth so much that, to the enhancement of the possible impression it might make on the visitor, every element of the plan for long distances about it was subordinated. Not only, for instance, were the lines of the Mall, and the choice of trees upon it and its borders, controlled by this motive, but it influenced the courses of all roads and walks south of Seventy-second street; it led to the very costly excavation of large bodies of rock, and determined the selection of trees and color of foliage nearly half a mile away. The towered structure on Vista Rock[5] itself was placed where it is and designed, by its grey colors and the small proportions of its elevated parts, solely to further this purpose.

The middle line of the vista of the Mall is the line on which all these operations centre, and in looking along which everything tends most to favor

Plan of lower Central Park, New York City (1873)

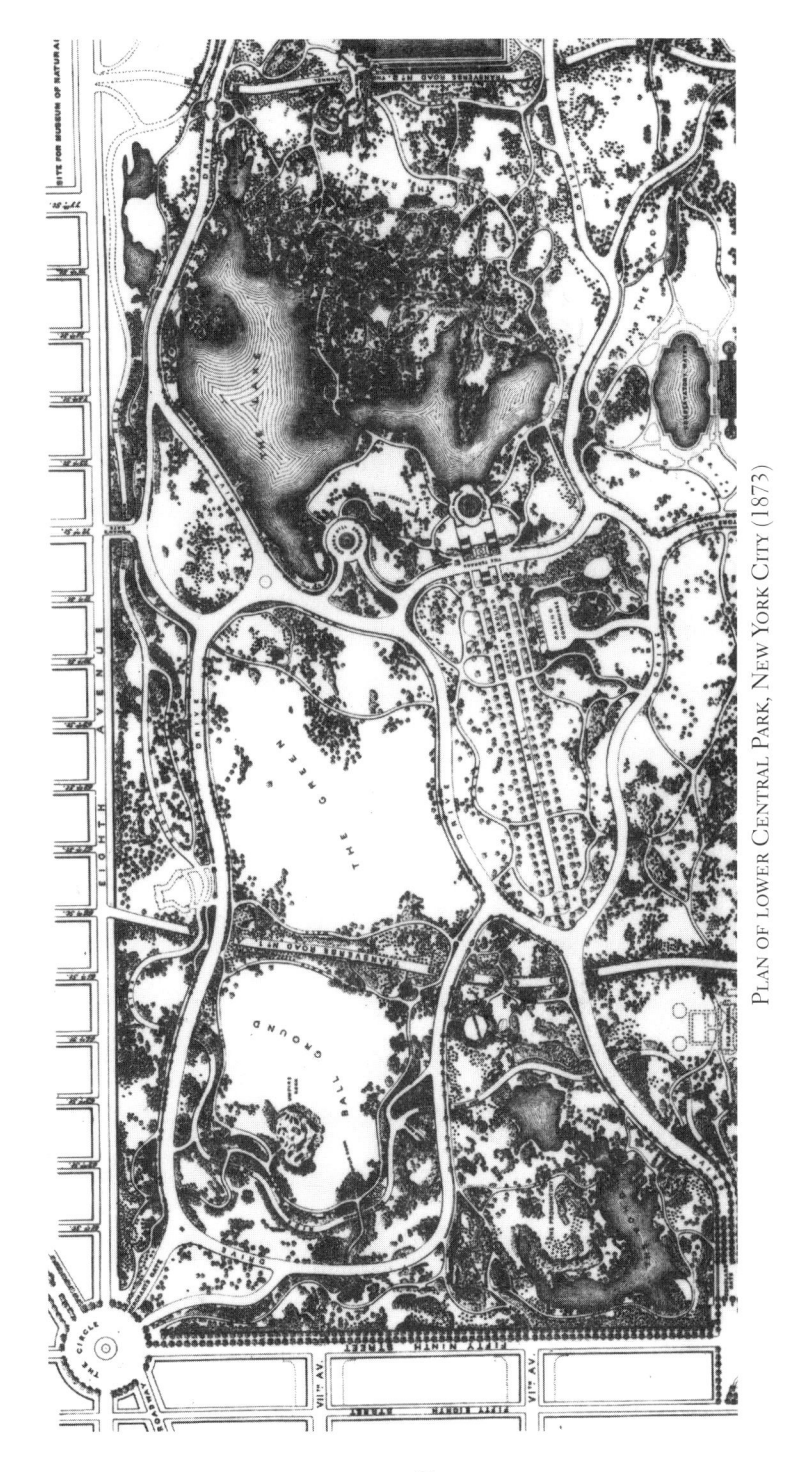

the desired impression. The space proposed for the base of the statue centres on this line of view, and if occupied as proposed, would interrupt it at a short distance from the most southerly point of observation.

It is obvious, then, that the adoption of the proposition would be a direct repudiation of the primary motive of the general design.

It may be said that the view would still be open on either side. It is true that it would, but aside from the fact of its being divided and narrowed by the introduction of the statue, if an object of the character proposed were so placed in the foreground the intended importance of the distant elements of the scene would certainly be lost.

So far also as the statue would be visible to those passing on the drive, their attention would be drawn by it to a lofty object near at hand and of course withheld from the distant scene below upon which it has heretofore been assumed that every means should be used to concentrate it.

With regard to the special purpose of the Mall, it is the only place in the park where large numbers of people are expected to congregate in summer, the walks elsewhere being designed for continuous motion, with seats and spaces of rest for small clusters of persons only.

Walks from all sides lead towards the Mall, the principal approaches being carried by arched passages under the carriage roads:[6] this element of the design of the park, therefore, stands, with reference to all others, as the hall of audience to the various other rooms, corridors and passages of a palace. Although the elms by which it is to be completely arched over and shaded are as yet not nearly half grown and but two of the many objects of art,[7] by which its dignity is expected to be supported and its perspective effect increased, are yet placed along its borders, it even now begins, in popular use, to assume its designed character. On a fine day in summer thousands of people who have been walking rapidly while in the various approaches to it, here move more slowly, often turning and returning, and the seats which are then placed at its side with accommodation for several hundred persons are often fully occupied.

The proposition is to place a colossal statue[8] in the middle of the south end of this grand hall of the park *with its back set square to the people.*

The impropriety of such an arrangement is plain.

But it is also to be remembered that a colossal statue in the proposed position would tend to establish a scale to which no other object in the vicinity has been or can be adapted. Relatively to it the adjoining walks and plats and the spaces between the trees would seem cramped and mean. It would have the effect of dwarfing and, so to speak, of casting in the shade the statue of Shakespeare and all others which are designed to be placed in the vicinity, of which there are four now provided.[9]

With reference to the value of what has already been acquired in the park, it is thus clearly not desirable that the proposition should be entertained.

We shall proceed to consider, whether, setting aside the fact that by far the greater number of visitors to the park would see only the back of the statue, the position proposed for it is one adapted to its favorable and dignified presentation.

On the elliptical plat of turf to be occupied there are four trees, and in the design of the park there are no more important trees upon it. They were the very first, or among the very first, planted on the park, and their trunks have already grown to be over one and a half feet in diameter. In a few years they will be three feet. The entire figure of the statue would be elevated above the point at which the branches spread out from these trunks.

If the base of the pedestal at the ground should be a square of about fifteen feet, as is probable, one of these trees would stand opposite each corner, at a distance from it of fifteen feet, and a quartering view of the statue from any greater distance would therefore be wholly obstructed.

Nearly at the same range, but a little more toward the front, stand two other trees of the same character; still further toward the front two more, all of which, as will be plainly seen by the annexed diagram,[10] would be between the statue and the carriage-way, and the most distant less than eighty feet from the base, and within equal distance, laterally, there are several others.

These trees have suffered from ice storms while young, and were, unfortunately, trimmed up under Mr. Sweeney's administration;[11] their heads have consequently not yet grown in fair proportion with their bodies, and are not well filled out, but it is only necessary for an observer walking around them today to imagine what they will be in June, five years hence, to be convinced that there is no point of view in which, during the summer, the proposed colossal statue would be even visible at the distance, and from the positions in which a colossal statue at the proposed elevation should be seen to the best advantage. If it were to be set up even two years hence, as it has been suggested that it might be, with a view to the centennial anniversary of Independence, and an audience were to gather as large as greeted the unveiling of the Shakespeare statue, not half of those assembled would be able to see the head of the figure.

If such a statue had been expected to stand in the proposed position, and the designers of the park had, at the outset, been instructed to arrange the foot approaches to the Mall, and to set the trees about the position in such a way that only the pedestal would be conspicuous, the result would be very much what it is.

Even were the dozen trees, which have been referred to, away, the position from which the statue would be seen to the best advantage is at the meeting of three carriage ways, and the busiest and most disturbed place in all the park, so much so, that it has long been the custom to station a keeper upon it to prevent people on foot from attempting to cross it, and to guard against collisions. Such a spot is certainly not one to be selected for the worthy contemplation of a great work of art.

The views which have thus been expressed as to the motives which should be controlling in respect to every object introduced at or near the point in question, are those adopted by the Park Commissioners before the first stroke toward the construction of the park was ordered. To show this, we quote from the explanation of the plan published by the Commissioners in 1858:[12]

> From this plateau a view is had of nearly all of the park up to the Reservoir, in a northerly direction, and in looking to the south and west we perceive that there are natural approaches from these directions, which suggest that we have arrived at a suitable point of concentration for all approaches which may be made from the lower part of the city to the interior of the park. Vista Rock, the most prominent point in the landscape of the lower park, here first comes distinctly into view, and, fortunately, in a direction diagonal to the boundary lines, from which it is desirable to withdraw attention in every possible way. We therefore *accept this line of view as affording an all-sufficient motive to our further procedure.*
>
> * * * *
>
> The idea of the park itself should always be uppermost in the mind of the beholder. Holding this general principle to be of considerable importance, we have preferred to place the avenue [or Mall] where it can be terminated appropriately at one end with a landscape attraction of considerable extent, and to *relieve the south entrance with only so much architectural treatment as may give the idea that due regard has been paid to the adornment of this principal promenade, without interfering with its real character.*

Mention should perhaps be made of the fact that a statue has once been offered to the Commissioners of the Park, with the expectation that they would place it on the spot now in question. The Commissioners declined to do so, and the offer was withdrawn.[13]

Respectfully,

FRED. LAW OLMSTED,
CALVERT VAUX,
Designers of the Central Park.

The text presented here is from "Document No. 57," in New York (City), Department of Public Parks, *Minutes*, March 4, 1874. A draft in Olmsted's hand survives in the Olmsted Papers. It was presented at the board of commissioners meeting of March 4, 1874. Less than a year before, a special committee consisting Calvert Vaux, Henry G. Stebbins and the landscape painter and former board member Frederic Edwin Church, had issued a report and rules on locating statues within the park. The rules, added to the bylaws in October 1873, stipulated that before statues were accepted they had to be approved for artistic merit by the heads of the Metropolitan Museum of Art, the National Academy of Design, and the American Institute of Architects. Statues commemorating men and events "of far reaching and permanent interest" were to be placed on each side of the main walk of the Mall, while symbolic or artistic statues could be placed throughout the park. In each case they were to

JANUARY 1874–AUGUST 1874

remain strictly subordinate to the landscape, on sites designated and approved by the board ("Document No. 46," in DPP, *Minutes*, July 17, 1873, pp. 9–10; DPP, *Minutes*, Oct. 1, 1873, p. 316; ibid., Jan. 12, 1874, p. 522; ibid., March 4, 1874, p. 590).

1. Salem H. Wales (1825–1902), journalist and businessman, was appointed to the Board of Commissioners of the Department of Public Parks in January 1873. He was elected president of the board in August of the same year (*Papers of FLO*, 6: 658).
2. At the previous meeting of the park board, February 25, 1874, Wales reported that Gordon W. Burnham had offered a colossal statue of Daniel Webster for Central Park, provided that it was placed at the south end of the Mall, the central feature of the lower park. The board designated Wales and Henry G. Stebbins as a committee to report on the advisability of the proposal and they apparently referred the question to Olmsted and Vaux. Although Vaux had assisted Olmsted the previous summer and autumn on plans for Riverside and Morningside parks, his primary work for the board was preparing plans for the Metropolitan Museum of Art on a commission basis. Since he no longer held a landscape position in the department, he and Olmsted signed this document (their last joint statement on Central Park) as designers of the park (DPP, *Minutes*, Feb. 25, 1874, pp. 585–86; ibid., March 13, 1874, p. 595; ibid., April 1, 1874, p. 614).
3. Vista Rock formed the southwest corner of the old Croton reservoir, now the site of the Great Lawn. It was the terminal point of the line of view northward along the axis of the Mall from the present intersection of the East and Center drives, the importance of which the authors described in the following passages.
4. These rock outcroppings flank the north end of the Mall on the west, northwest, and east.
5. The Belvedere, designed by Vaux with the assistance of Julius F. Munckwitz and begun in 1867, was nearly completed at the time of this report ("Belvedere: East Elevation," and "Belvedere Foundation Walls," Drawings 20 and 56, Department of Parks and Recreation Drawings Collection, New York City Municipal Archives; BCCP, *Eleventh Annual Report* [1868], p. 8; "Document No. 59," in DPP, *Minutes*, May 20, 1874, p. 4).
6. Instead of making pedestrians who approached the lower end of the Mall cross the carriage drive at grade, Olmsted and Vaux provided the Marble Arch and Willowdell Arch which allowed them to cross under the drive.
7. That is, the statues of William Shakespeare and Sir Walter Scott, placed near the south end of the Mall in 1872 (Issac Newton Phelps Stokes, *The Iconography of Manhattan Island, 1498–1909*, 6 vols. [New York, 1915–28], 5: 1949–50).
8. That is, a statue much larger than life size. The Webster statue was thirteen feet tall, and was to have a twenty-foot-high base (*New York World*, May 19, 1875, p. 5).
9. In addition to the statues of Shakespeare and Sir Walter Scott already in place, positions on the south end of the Mall had been designated for the statues of two other literary figures, Fitz Greene Halleck and Robert Burns (*New-York Times*, Jan. 22, 1869, p. 2; ibid., Oct. 3, 1880, p. 10; Elizabeth Barlow et al., *The Central Park Book* [New York, 1977], p. 41).
10. This diagram has not been found.
11. The Tammany-controlled park board headed by Peter B. Sweeny between May 1870 and November 1871 oversaw excessive pruning of many trees in Central Park (*Papers of FLO*, 6: 525–31).
12. Here Olmsted and Vaux quoted, with added italics, from their original description of the Greensward plan (*Papers of FLO*, 3: 125).
13. On April 1, 1874, the board of commissioners adopted the recommendation of the present document and instructed Olmsted to prepare plans "for a suitable terminal object" for the south end of the Mall, "in accordance with the original intention." Olm-

49

sted prepared preliminary drawings for a fountain that were adopted the next month, and Jacob Wrey Mould prepared working drawings later in the year, but the fountain was never built. The earlier offer of a statue for the south end of the Mall was not mentioned in the printed minutes, documents, and annual reports of either the Central Park commission or the Department of Public Parks. Following the adoption of the present report, Gordon Burnham pressed for another site for the Webster statue near the south end of the Mall. When the board again declined, he finally agreed to have it located subject to the established rules. Olmsted and Henry G. Stebbins chose the junction of the middle and west drives south of the Lake, where it was unveiled in the autumn of 1876. At the same time the board amended the bylaws to require that statues on the Mall be of heroic size, and that colossal statues be prohibited from the park (DPP, *Minutes*, April 1, 1874, p. 612; ibid., May 6, 1874, pp. 10–11; ibid., Nov. 24, 1874, pp. 363–64; ibid., March 3, 1875, pp. 553–54; ibid., July 29, 1874, p. 168; ibid., Aug. 10, 1874, pp. 183–84; ibid., Sept. 16, 1874, p. 259; ibid., Sept. 25, 1874, pp. 270–71; ibid., Oct. 18, 1876, pp. 358–60; *The City Record*, March 12, 1877, p. 369).

To William Hammond Hall[1]

209 West 46th Street,
New York.
March 23ᵈ 1874

Dear Mr. Hall;

I have just received yours of 12ᵗʰ inst. and as I am preparing to leave town for Washington you will please excuse an off hand and partial reply.[2]

I have your map and letter but not the printed report in regard to the Berkeley grounds before me. I have no maps or memoranda of the topography or of my old plan.[3]

There was an axial line in my plan extending from near the centre of the property toward the Golden Gate. There is a similar line in yours I think, but if so I doubt if the two lines correspond. Your line I judge is laid along the middle of a knoll or spur; mine through an adjoining valley. If so there is an obvious difference of motive between the two plans.[4]

You seem, however, to think that your plan may be imagined to involve an unjustifiable departure from the natural picturesque ideal in Landscape Gardening. My impression is that if I were to make a plan under your instructions, (I mean to meet present requirements), for this situation,[5] I should discard that ideal to a much greater degree than you have done. I think that you know my views in this respect. They are that the principles of English landscape gardening, which in this climate I am disposed to carry to a greater extreme than they have ever been carried in Europe, are out of place in the climate of California.[6] I should seek to cover the ground mainly with anything

JANUARY 1874–AUGUST 1874

by which I could secure a simply inoffensive low tone; not unnatural, never suggesting death or constant labor to keep alive. I should consequently have much less of open space than you have; should have much less respect for the present minor natural features — for wherever you put foliage in broad dense bodies you obliterate the old nature as effectively as if you had laid it over with bricks and mortar. I should then concentrate brightness, cheerfulness and elegance on a few plainly artificial elements, such as terraces, avenues and parterres, strictly formal and as unquestionably artificial as a necklace or a bracelet. You do less in this way than I should wish to do.

But you know that I should submit my views with great respect for the immeasureable advantage that you have gained in your much longer, closer, more special and practical study of the conditions in question in their bearing upon our common art.

Please present my compliments to President Gilman[7] and if he, or any other gentleman interested should have any doubt what my judgement would be in the point in question, I should be glad to have you show him this hasty letter — or, better, tell him from me that I could not be as bold as you in attempting English lawn effects in the climate of California, except in the smallest scale, as I might here plant a side garden of camelias, myrtles and fuschias,[8] but that I should wish to go much further than you propose to do in humble following of types which many centuries ago were enjoyed and accepted gratefully by artists in comparison with whom all now living are pygmies.

Faithfully Yours

Fred. Law Olmsted.

The text presented here is from a manuscript in Olmsted's hand in the William Hammond Hall Papers, Manuscript Division, The Bancroft Library, University of California, Berkeley, California.

1. William Hammond Hall (1846–1934), surveyor for the U.S. Army engineers in California after the Civil War, he designed Golden Gate Park in San Francisco and was its superintendent between 1871 and 1876. He was appointed California's first state engineer in 1879 and held the position for over a decade. Hall and Olmsted had corresponded since 1871, when Hall sought advice on landscape design and literature. In 1886, years after either had any official connection with Golden Gate Park, they contributed to a report on the management of its tree plantations (*Papers of FLO*, 5: 462–63; FLO to William Hammond Hall, Oct. 5, 1871 [*Papers of FLO*, 6: 468–69]; Raymond H. Clary, *The Making of Golden Gate Park The Early Years: 1865–1906* [San Francisco, 1980], pp. 7–8; *The Development of Golden Gate Park and Particularly the Management and Thinning of its Forest Trees* . . . [San Francisco, 1886], pp. 7–20).
2. Hall told Olmsted that he had submitted a plan and report to the regents of the University of California at Berkeley on landscaping the grounds of the institution. He had read, and quoted in his own report, Olmsted and Vaux's 1866 report on the same campus but had not examined the plan which accompanied it. The original of that plan had disappeared and the regents had since considered other designers and plans. Hall's plan,

which used terraces, had drawn criticism from faculty members and he wanted Olmsted's opinion of it (William Hammond Hall to FLO, March 12, 1874; *Papers of FLO*, 5: 401, 462–64, 546–73).
3. While living in California in 1865 Olmsted was commissioned to lay out the private College of California on a hillside site in Berkeley. He proposed to devote some thirty-five acres to the college campus proper and to create a suburban residential neighborhood on the rest of the one hundred acres, rather than creating the "park" that the trustees had envisioned as the setting for the college. In his report of 1866, Olmsted rejected the quadrangle arrangement of eastern colleges and instead carefully integrated neighborhood and campus in a plan that anticipated future growth in both and accepted climatic restraints on temperate zone plantings. While he proposed "a picturesque, rather than a formal and perfectly symmetrical arrangement" of the campus, its principal buildings were to be located on an artificial plateau, accented with an architectural terrace overlooking a formal *allée*. Despite renewed interest in the plan four years after the merger of the poorly funded college with the University of California in 1868, little or no work was ever done according to it (William Hammond Hall, "Report of an Engineer upon the Developments of the Grounds at Berkeley," in University of California, *Statements of the Regents of the University of California to the Joint Committee of the Legislature, March. 3, 1874* [San Francisco, CA., 1874], pp. 57–58; *Papers of FLO*, 5: 33–35, 398–400, 455–57, 546–73).
4. Olmsted is referring to the "formal avenue" in his plan, which led westward from the main college buildings and terrace toward the Golden Gate, just north of the present University Drive. He positioned the avenue between two spurs because they sheltered the trees and shrubs proposed to line it from the wind and the extra soil moisture there could support turf. Later plans, including Hall's, proposed axial lines on more elevated ground (*Papers of FLO*, 5: 398–400, 564–66; Paul Venable Turner, *Campus: An American Planning Tradition* [Cambridge, Mass., 1984], pp. 180–84).
5. That is, if Olmsted were to create a design adapted to the needs of the University of California, which had replaced the much smaller, private College of California. In describing this change, Hall testified that "the land was deeded to the State, upon condition that on it should be established a University, and that the entire site should be occupied for such purpose"(W. H. Hall, "Report of an Engineer," p. 58).
6. That is, because the open greensward, plantations and water suggestive of English landscape were inappropriate and prohibitively expensive in the semi-arid climate of California. Olmsted had argued against such attempts, and for a landscape style suited to the region, in his mid-1860s California landscape reports and in letters to Hall about Golden Gate Park beginning in late 1871 (Charles E. Beveridge, "The California Origins of Olmsted's Landscape Principles for the Semiarid American West," *Papers of FLO*, 5: 449–69; ibid., 6: 468–69).
7. Daniel Coit Gilman (1831–1908), educator and president of the university since 1872. In that year he invited Olmsted to re-examine the grounds at Berkeley and suggest improvements. Since the residential part of the plan had been abandoned and pressure to create an English-type park persisted, Olmsted declined the offer (*DAB*; *Papers of FLO*, 6: 48; FLO to Daniel Coit Gilman, Dec. 31, 1872, The Bancroft Library, Manuscripts Division, University of California, Berkeley, California).
8. That is, because camelia, myrtle, and fuschia are only semi-hardy and usually will not survive northeastern winters outdoors (Liberty Hyde Bailey et al., *Hortus Third* [New York, 1976], pp. 208–10, 489, 751).

To William Hammond Hall

> 209 West 46th Street,
> New York.
> March 28th 1874.

Mr. W. Hammond Hall:
My Dear Sir;

  I received your reply to my telegram of 26th inst. late the same evening. The occasion of my telegraphing you was this:

  There is in Washington a series of cultivated and of vacant grounds extending from those about the Capitol to about the White House; including the "public gardens," the "old armory square," the Smithsonian Grounds; the Agricultural bureau grounds; the (proposed) Washington Monument Grounds and a considerable area in process of reclamation from the Potomac flats.[1] They are managed in an absurd and wasteful way under advice and control of nearly a dozen independent Committees of Congress, assisted by nearly as many heads of bureaus and other officials, architects, surveyors and gardeners.

  I have twice been to Washington on invitation {of} Mr. Morrill of V^t, Chairman of the Senate Committee on Public Grounds, who wishes me to become their professional adviser and executive officer.[2] I have strongly urged that before anything more is done in regard to any particular ground an effort should be made to simplify and consolidate the present organizations and bring all these grounds into subordination to a comprehensive scheme and have requested that the question of policy involved in this proposition should be submitted to a representative board of American Landscape Architects; it being one which in my judgement concerns the credit of the profession and the honor and dignity of the country.[3]

  I yesterday accepted an engagement to prepare a plan for the grounds immediately about the Capitol but stated that I would prefer not to undertake any other duty until after the proposed board, if ordered, should make its report.

  I left Washington last night with the understanding that if there should seem to be a fair chance of carrying the proposition it was to be submitted to Congress.

  I named two gentlemen for it besides yourself and Mr Cleveland of Chicago[4] but Mr Morrill thought best to limit it to three.

  I undertook after receiving your telegram that the whole expense of the Commission should not exceed $1500.

  I shall promptly advise you if anything more comes of it.
  Respectfully Yours,

> Fred. Law Olmsted.

The text presented here is from a manuscript in Olmsted's hand in the William Hammond Hall Papers, Manuscript Division, The Bancroft Library, University of California at Berkeley, Berkeley, California.

1. Olmsted here listed, in order, the series of separate grounds and establishments which extended west from the Capitol along the length of the Mall. By the "public gardens," he meant the U.S. Botanic Garden, which adjoined the Capitol grounds on the west between First and Third streets. The garden featured greenhouse exotics brought to Washington in 1842 by members of the Wilkes exploring expedition. William D. Brackenridge, botanist of the Wilkes expedition and assistant to A. J. Downing on the Mall improvements and, after 1859, William R. Smith, who studied at Kew Gardens, planted native and exotic trees, shrubs, and flowers at the garden. (Olmsted's use of quotation marks to enclose his designation of the place, suggests that it reminded him of similar efforts at Boston's Public Garden.) The "old armory square" was the rectangular section of the Mall between Sixth and Seventh streets, on which Congress in 1855 erected a three-story brick building for the district militia. Following the Civil War, Nathaniel Michler and O. E. Babcock, officers of the army engineers in charge of the public grounds, drained, filled, and planted this square, and the reservations between it and the Botanic Garden. About 1874 the army engineers completed a carriage drive through these reclaimed areas, which connected with those of the Smithsonian grounds. Adjoining them to the west were the neoclassic style gardens of the U.S. Agricultural Bureau (later the U.S. Department of Agriculture), which erected a mansard-roofed building on the site in 1868. Beyond these was the unfinished shaft of the Washington Monument, which overlooked marshy grounds along the Potomac River and the Washington Canal. The process of draining and filling that extended the land west from the monument, and covered the canal, had just begun in the early 1870s, and took several decades to complete (Wilhelmus B. Bryan, *A History of the National Capital*, 2 vols. [New York, 1914–1916], 2: 325–27, 331; T. Froncek, *City of Washington*, pp. 267, 365; U.S. War Department, *Annual Report*, [1868], 2: 892–99; ibid., [1871], 2: 968; ibid., [1873], 2: 1152; ibid., [1875], 2: 803–4; F. L. Olmsted, "Index to Trees to Trees About the Capitol," pp. 10–11).
2. Although Olmsted had met with Morrill about the Capitol grounds as early as June 1873, it appears he did not visit Washington to inspect them until the middle of January 1874. At that time, Olmsted declined Morrill's suggestion that he supervise the project full-time in Washington. His counter offer to provide a general plan of the Capitol grounds for $1,500 plus expenses, made during his second visit to the Capitol in late March, was accepted by the committee on public grounds and buildings (James T. Gardner to FLO, Dec. 3, 1873; FLO to Justin S. Morrill, Jan. 26, 1874, above; FLO to Justin S. Morrill, March 26, 1874, and Justin S. Morrill and James H. Platt, Jr., to FLO, March 27, 1874, both in Records of the U.S. Senate, Record Group 46, SEN43A–E17, NARA, Washington, D.C.).
3. Morrill would undoubtedly have been the one to submit such a proposition to Congress, and during the spring and summer of 1874 he and Olmsted conferred with civic reformer Dorman B. Eaton on the improvement of public spaces throughout the capital. "In the end I hope you may have something to do with these also," Morrill wrote Olmsted in early September, "but at present we must wait" (FLO to Justin S. Morrill, Aug. 4, 1874, B134: #2820, OAR\LC; FLO to Dorman B. Eaton, Aug. 16, 1874; Justin S. Morrill to FLO, Sept. 7, 1874, B134: #2820, OAR\LC).
4. That is, H. W. S. Cleveland, then superintendent of the South Parks system in Chicago. In a memorandum written for the committee on public buildings and grounds, Olmsted stated that Calvert Vaux's presence on the proposed commission "would be a valuable addition, particularly so as he assisted Mr Downing in laying out Lafayette Sq. and

the Smithsonian Grounds and knows what his views were." The fourth person named by Olmsted was very likely Jacob Weidenmann (F. L. Olmsted, "Country Living," Jan. 22, 1874, above; [FLO], "Memorandum," [c. March 1874], Records of the U.S. Senate, Record Group 46, Committee on Public Buildings and Grounds, SEN43A–E17, NARA, Washington, D.C.).

To Seymour Ainsworth, Hiram Tompkins, and John L. Perry[1]

209 W. 46 NY,
April 21st [1874]

Messrs Ainsworth, Tompkins & Perry
Saratoga Springs;
Gentlemen;

In accordance with the intention expressed in my note of 17th inst. I have mailed you a traceing indicating the general features of a plan for your ground.[2]

If it fails to give as direct access as is desireable between any two points or is otherwise wanting in convenience, it is because I have not fully understood your plans & wishes in this respect, and it may be modified under more specific instructions.

After providing needed communications in all parts it is designed to offer considerable advantages for promenading and resting out of doors.

Lastly as much effect of space and distance and general air of luxury and refinemnt as the ground allows is aimed to be secured by a few simple central features.

Standing in what I understand to be the office and looking through the principal doorway you will observe that a vista would be commanded extending from end to end of the property; the foreground would be deeply shaded and inviting at all times of the day; in the middle distance would be a quiet sunny lawn, beyond it a fountain with rich shrubbery on each side, at a greater distance a pavilion would be distinguished and the view would terminate in a thicket of foliage.

Outside the door the first feature is a pergola the floor of which is designed to be on a level with that of the office. It is to be covered by a trellis and vines, and to serve as an outer sitting room overlooking the ground, shaded but airy.

Next, opening from the centre of the pergola is a gravelled area with four lines of trees and fixed seats. The trees would desirably be the weeping

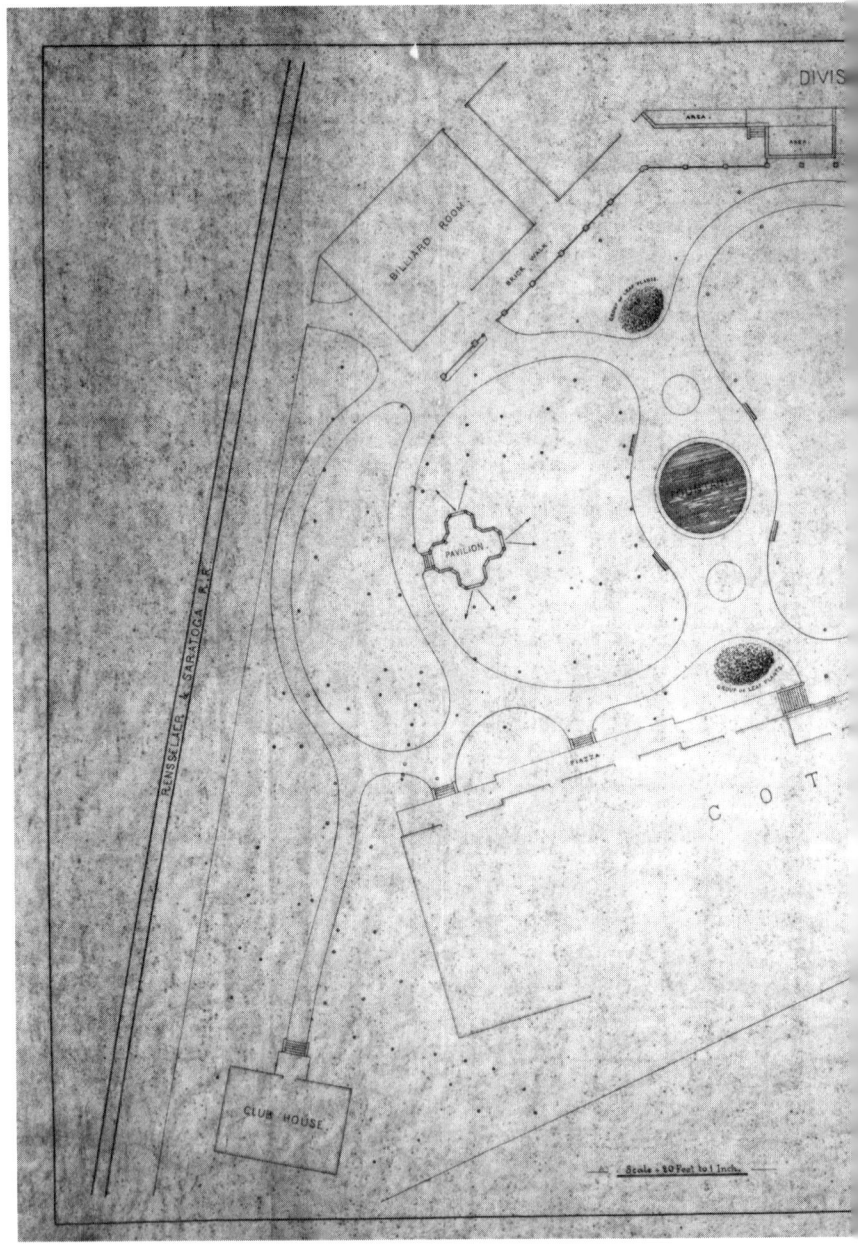

PLAN FOR THE GROUNDS OF UN

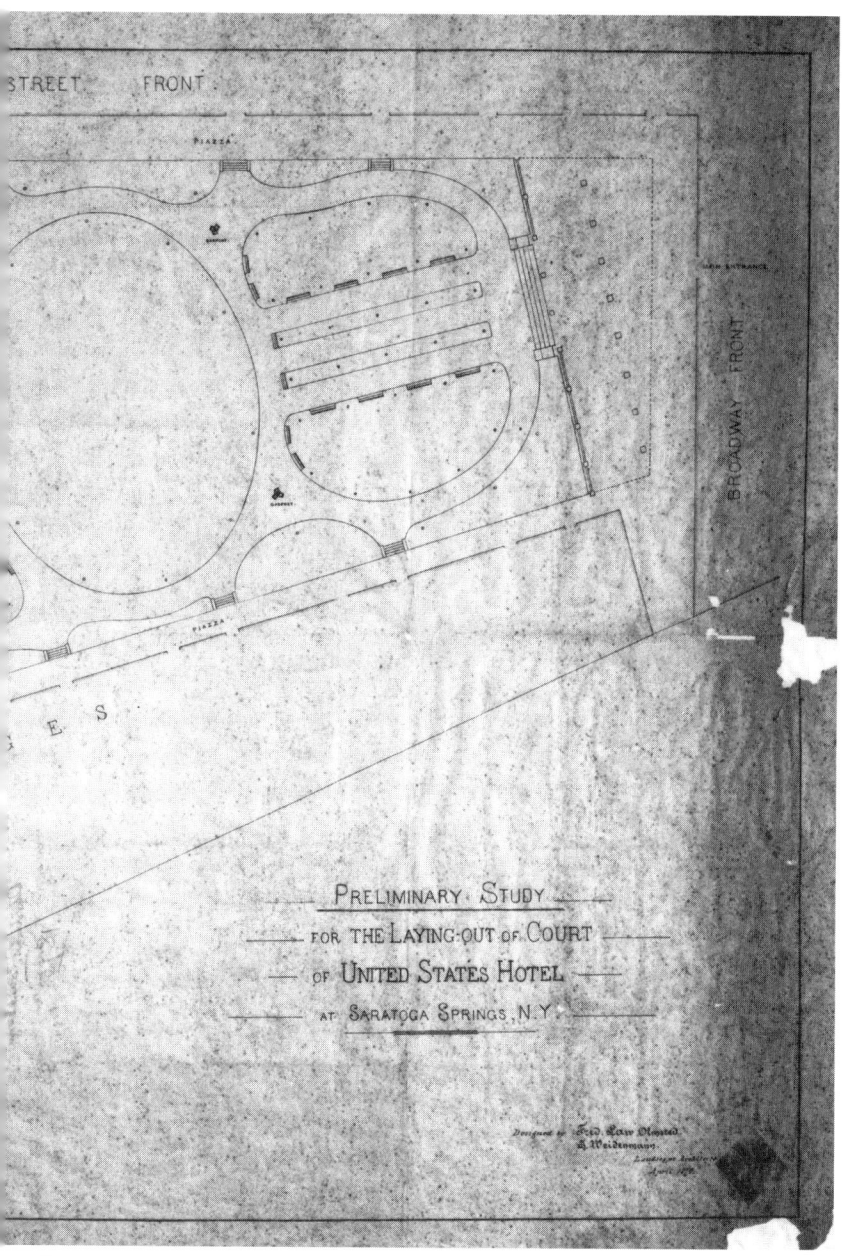

PRELIMINARY STUDY
FOR THE LAYING-OUT OF COURT
OF UNITED STATES HOTEL
AT SARATOGA SPRINGS, N.Y.

ash, to be trained to form a continuous canopy of verdure at a height of ten or twelve feet, as in old palace gardens. The space under them would be a shaded lounging place and a sort of ante room to the main court.

The next principal feature is a plot of turf 145x125 feet, designed with especial reference to croquet parties and children's dances.

The next compartmnt is a slope of turf to be planted on each side with banks of shrubbery, then comes a level area 5 feet higher than the croquet ground in the midst of which is a fountain.

Next a lawn terminated with a pavilion or summer house, beyond which a plot which is designed to be closely planted, with trees and under wood. A walk through this plantation gives a screened access to the Club House from the Billiard Room.

Fixed seats are designed to be placed around the fountain and croquet ground. Minor features will be observed that need no explanation.

The plan would require but slight changes in the present surface of the ground and could, except the fountain, under proper superintendence be carried out by ordinary laborers and carpenters. The pavilion may be simple and cheap or elaborate and costly at your discretion. For the fountain I think one can be found at the Architectl Iron Works imported from France that will do very well.[3] The pergola may be made entirely of pine joists and plank planed square and morticed together in the simplest way. To make it more elegant and to allow an effect to be produced the first season by annual vines, before the permanent vines could grow sufficiently to cover it, iron work as indicated in the enclosed sketch might {be} substituted with advantage for wooden posts.

Be so good as to return the study to me as soon as convenient with or without your instructions for maturing a plan.[4]

The text presented here is from a draft in Olmsted's hand.

1. Seymour Ainsworth (1819–1890), Hiram Tompkins (1824–1909), and John L. Perry (d. 1915), part owners and proprietors of the United States Hotel in Saratoga Springs, New York. Each had succeeded in separate business ventures and joined with other investors to rebuild the famous hotel, which had burned in the mid-1860s. Their ornate Second Empire building was nearing completion at the time of this letter (Francis J. Parker, comp., *Genealogy of the Ainsworth Families in America* [Boston, 1894], p. 83; *New-York Times*, April 14, 1915, p. 13; George Baker Anderson, comp., *A Descriptive and Biographical Record of Saratoga County New York* [Boston, 1899], pp. 506, 515–16, 519–20; Cornelius E. Durkee, comp., *Reminiscences of Saratoga* [Saratoga Springs, N.Y., 1929?], p. 59; James K. Kettlewell, *Saratoga Springs: An Architectural History, 1790–1990* [Saratoga Springs, N.Y., 1991], p. 56).
2. In early April 1874 Olmsted, in collaboration with Jacob Weidenmann, began work on a general plan for the open three-acre space enclosed by the hotel wings. Despite receiving word from the proprietors that they could not afford to implement improvements he had proposed in a letter of April 2 (now lost), Olmsted wrote them on April 17

that since work on the plan was nearly completed, he would send it for them to reconsider. If they still wished not to proceed, they could return the plan and pay only for the preliminary consultation (Seymour Ainsworth, Hiram Tompkins, and John L. Perry to FLO, April 13, 1874; FLO to Seymour Ainsworth, Hiram Tompkins, and John L. Perry, April 17, 1874).
3. The Architectural Iron Works, incorporated in 1856 by Daniel D. Badger, was one of the leading manufacturers of cast iron and wrought iron architectural products in the United States (Daniel D. Badger, *Badger's Illustrated Catalogue of Cast-Iron Architecture* [1865; rpt. ed., New York, 1981], introduction by Margot Gayle, v–xvii).
4. Although they considered his suggested improvements "very beautiful," the proprietors told Olmsted that other expenditures in finishing the hotel had to come first. They returned his plan and a check for $117. In 1875 Olmsted and Weidenmann furnished a plan for Congress Park, grounds adjacent to the Congress Hall hotel in Saratoga Springs, which was carried out, although not to Olmsted's satisfaction (Seymour Ainsworth, Hiram Tompkins, and John L. Perry to FLO, April 28, 1874; Jacob Weidenmann to FLO, April 20, 1875; FLO to C. C. Dawson, July 22, 1876; J. K. Kettlewell, *Saratoga Springs*, pp. 72–73).

To Montgomery Cunningham Meigs[1]

209 W. 46th St. New York; May 14th 1874.

Major Gen. M. C. Meigs; Q.M.G., U.S.A.
Sir;

    I herewith send you a design for completing the court and exterior ground of the Jeffersonville Dépôt of your Department.[2] Every condition required and every suggestion which I have recieved from you and from the officers of the Department is, I believe, complied with.

    The subdivision of the court is similar in motive to, and more convenient and symmetrical than that suggested by Col. Lee.[3]

    The trees within the court are all nut and fruit-trees and the shrubs are in part fruit-bearing.

    The trees are so arranged that when they are *full grown* the watchman in the tower will still have every door of the stores under observation.[4]

    In case of necessity, on the occurrence of war all the outer part of the court may be occupied for storage to the extent of three quarters of its entire area, without impediment from or injury to the important trees; (the smaller and rapidly growing fruit trees and shrubs only being removed), ample space for the movement of wagons being left between the larger and more valuable trees.

    The planting is so arranged that when the trees are well grown they will form a cone-shaped mass of verdure with the top of the tower at its apex;

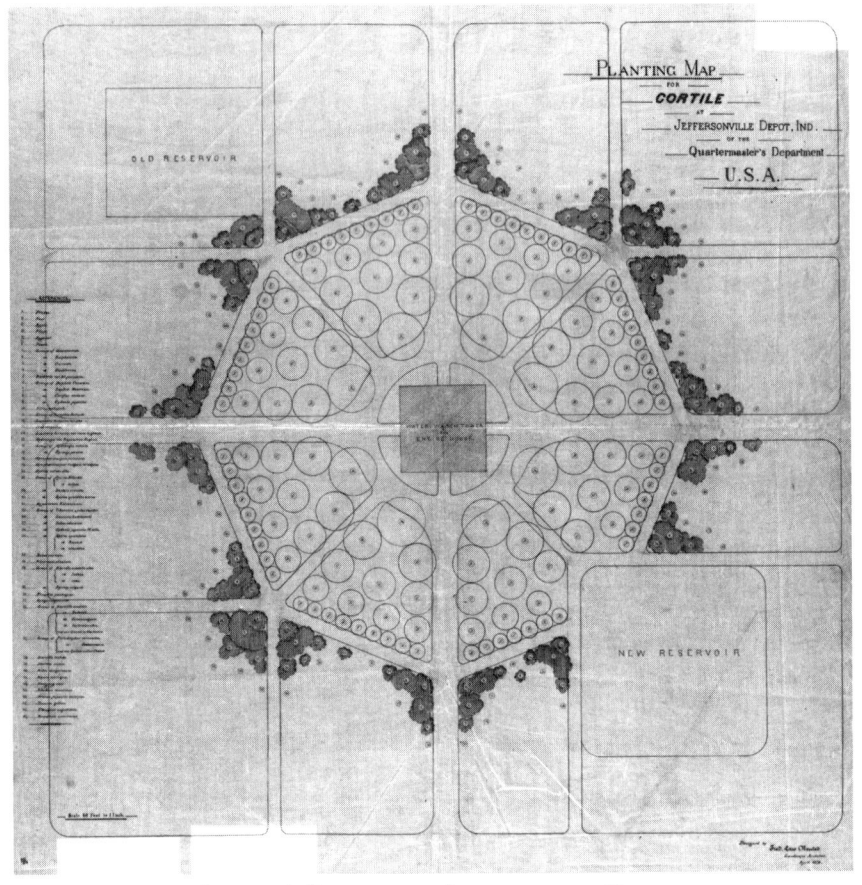

OLMSTED'S PLAN FOR THE JEFFERSONVILLE DEPOT
Circle nearest center is pecans; next circle is pears; third circle is plums;
outer row is, alternately, apricots and peaches.

the fruit bearing shrubs and the trunks and lower parts of the trees will be screened by the irregular fringe of decorative shrubs, leaving only the best of their foliage open to view.

An obvious adaptation of every elemnt of the plan to its special ends and the accommodation and consistancy of these special ends with the primary general ends of the Dépôt as a whole has been studied.

The satisfaction to be expected from the arrangement will depend entirely on the completeness with which the plan is executed — with a view to the health and perfection of growth of the trees and the consistent neatness of the whole establishment. This will, it is believed, be easily secured with such means as, after a few years of preparation, the officer in command will at all times be able to control.

To avoid an excessive shading of the building and to secure an effect of complete arrangement in the outer planting[5] it is proposed that the government property should be divided from the street only by a light rail or by posts and chains, and that the wall or stronger fence should be placed five feet within this outer line. By this arrangement the Dépôt may be bordered as proposed in the drawing, with a Mall of considerably more dignity than an ordinary sidewalk.

The trees of each double line should be of the same species and variety but each of the four double lines may be of a different species, as one of the Elm (American), one of the Lime (American), one of Maple, (sugar or scarlet) and one of Tulip. Or for either of the above English elm, Norway Maple or Sycamore Maple may be substituted if found more practicable.

In the detailed planting plan for the court *varieties* of the several kinds of fruit trees are not named as it will be easy for the officer in charge to obtain information of the results of local experience which would outweigh any advice that, without such special information, I could give. He will also be better able to judge than I of the most desirable proportions of early and late bearing kinds.[6]

I would repeat the advice offered in a previous communication to you that all trees designed to be planted should be first planted with a considerable excess of numbers in nursery on the ground; that the process of transplanting to their final position should be conducted with great care and deliberation and no tree set except under favorable circumstances, the work being continued, if necessary, through several planting seasons.

Particular caution may be necessary to prevent the trees from being planted at too great a depth. The swell of the roots (or "collar" of the tree) should be above the general surface.

The whole ground both where planted and where not planted should be trenched three spits deep[7] and heavily manured. It will be much better that this work should be done a season in advance of the planting so that the subsoil may be reconsolidated and the manure well incorporated.

That portion of the ground not to be planted should be treated in the same way, a soil rich at considerable depth from the surface being particularly desirable to avoid the bad effects of drouth. It should be brought to a fine surface tilth[8] and sown with two bushels of red-top and one of white clover seed to the acre. If Kentucky blue-grass is indigenous in the neighborhood it may be substituted for one half the quantity of red-top. Care should be taken to secure fresh seed. The ground should be rolled and as soon as the grass is generally two inches above ground, mowed. If very irregular in growth the first mowing may need to be by hand. Afterwards it should be mown with a lawn-mower once a fortnight or oftener except in periods of severe drouth, and frequently rolled until a firm close velvety sod is established.[9]

If to follow all the above advice would be too expensive, plowing with a subsoil plow, or trench plowing (plowing twice or thrice in the same furrow) or both may be substituted for hand trenching; the shrub and berry bushes may be dispensed with; the turf may then be kept by pasturing it closely with sheep instead of by frequent mowing and rolling.

If more display in decoration is desired, annual and perennial flowering plants may be set in the edge of the shrub plantations. The borders of the drives and walks may be planted with roses and other flowering shrubs grown as standards.[10] Either of these additions to the plan will however add much to the difficulty and cost of maintaining a high character of neatness and elegance which should be regarded as a matter of the first importance.

Respectfully;

Fred. Law Olmsted;
Landscape Architect.

P.S. The photographs[11] have been returned as requested to Quarter Master's Office. New York. The plans are sent by Express.[12]

The text presented here is from a document in a clerk's hand and signed by Olmsted, in Record Group 92, Records of the Quartermaster General's Office, Entry 225, Consolidated Correspondence File, "Jeffersonville Depot," box 472, NARA, Washington, D.C.

1. Montgomery Cunningham Meigs (1816–1892), engineer and quartermaster general of the U.S. Army. As quartermaster general of the Union army during the Civil War, Meigs helped Olmsted, then secretary of the U.S. Sanitary Commission, in a variety of ways. According to Olmsted, "the hospitality of no other single man was worth as much to our undertaking," and the two continued their professional relationship after the war. In 1866 Meigs urged Olmsted to apply for the position of commissioner of public buildings in Washington, D.C., and in 1870 obtained his advice on suitable landscaping for the national cemeteries. Meigs's thoughtful criticism of the proposed terrace of the U.S. Capitol in 1875 elicited Olmsted's first defense of it, and the same year he commissioned him to design the grounds of the Schuylkill Arsenal in Philadelphia (*Papers of FLO*, 4: 152, 178, 332; ibid., 6: 386–88; FLO to Montgomery C. Meigs, Jan. 15, 1875, and FLO to Montgomery C. Meigs, June 1, 1875, both below).
2. Meigs, in October 1873, asked Olmsted to prepare landscape plans for the interior courtyard and exterior grounds of the new supply depot of the Quartermaster General's Department in Jeffersonville, Indiana. The building, designed by Meigs, was the largest military depot and storehouse for clothing and camp and garrison equipment in the country. It surrounded a level eleven-and-one-half-acre courtyard from which supplies were unloaded and loaded, at the center of which stood a one-hundred-foot watchtower. The exterior grounds consisted of a thirty-foot-wide strip surrounding the building (Montgomery C. Meigs to FLO, Oct. 24, [1873] and *The United Presbyterian*, Dec. 11, 1874, in RG 92, Records of the Quartermaster General's Office, Entry 225, "Jeffersonville Depot," box 472, NARA, Washington, D.C.; J. D. Bingham to FLO, Oct. 28, 1873; U.S. War Department, *Annual Report*, 2 vols. [Washington, D.C., 1874], 1: 118).
3. Captain James Grafton Carleton Lee (1836–1916), assistant quartermaster of the Jeffersonville depot. Lee had submitted a list of trees and shrubs for the courtyard and

JANUARY 1874–AUGUST 1874

asked that they be planted before spring arrived. Meigs sent his proposals to Olmsted, who urged that nothing be planted in advance of the adoption of a general plan. He also gave detailed instructions on establishing a nursery on the property, which he condensed in the present report, below (*Who Was Who: 1897–1942* [Chicago, 1943], 1: 716; James G. C. Lee to Montgomery C. Meigs, Nov. 7, 1873; ibid., Jan. 26, 1874; FLO to Montgomery C. Meigs, Feb. 23, 1874, in RG 92, Records of the Quartermaster General's Office, Entry 225, "Jeffersonville Depot," box 472, NARA, Washington, D.C.).

4. In his initial instructions Meigs requested Olmsted to introduce fruit and nut trees be introduced in the courtyard, and not to plant trees of tall growth on its perimeter in order to retain the view of the warehouse doors from the watchtower (J. D. Bingham to FLO, Oct. 28, 1873; Montgomery C. Meigs to FLO, Feb. 16, 1874).
5. That is, the planting of the thirty-foot-wide strip surrounding the exterior of the building. The instructions in the next paragraph apparently apply to this area.
6. In November 1874 Captain Addison Barrett consulted several local nurserymen on the varieties of fruit and nut trees that would flourish in the courtyard and reported to the depot quartermaster. He suggested that English walnut, chestnut, and hickory trees be added to the pecans shown on the planting plan, the only nut-bearing trees Olmsted indicated. Plum and apricot trees did not grow well in the area, so he suggested that some of those on the plan be replaced with persimmon, papaw, peach, and pear trees. He also listed up to ten varieties of these and apple trees, gooseberries, raspberries, currants, and blackberries. Meigs reviewed Barrett's report and ordered that the better suited trees could be substituted but that Olmsted's plan should be followed "as closely as possible" (Addison Barrett to James A. Ekin, Nov. 16, 1874, and Montgomery C. Meigs to James A. Ekin, Dec. 15, 1874, both in RG 92, Records of the Quartermaster General, Entry 225, "Jeffersonville Depot," box 472, NARA, Washington, D.C.).
7. That is, the depth of earth penetrated by the length of three spades (*OED*).
8. Tilth refers to the physical condition of soil and its suitability for plant growth (ibid.).
9. Olmsted apparently intended that the outer plats of the courtyard, and between the trees and shrubs there and in the outer grounds, were to be planted as lawn. By the 1860s owners of large estates and park departments used lawnmowers drawn by horse, some of which cut swaths only three feet wide. Given the close quarters within the courtyard, however, it is possible Olmsted intended that they be mown with hand-pushed mowers, first mass-produced in the United States in the 1870s, and used at this time by the New York Department of Public Parks (Andrew Jackson Downing, *A Treatise on the Theory and Practice of Landscape Gardening, Adapted to North America*, with supplement by Henry Winthrop Sargent [New York, 1875], pp. 422–23; BCCP, *Tenth Annual Report* [1867], p. 16; Patricia M. Tice, *Gardening in America, 1830–1910* [Rochester, N.Y., 1984], pp. 64–65; DPP, *Minutes*, April 1, 1874, p. 610).
10. That is, grown standing on an erect stem of full height, not dwarfed or trained on a wall (*OED*).
11. Meigs had supplied Olmsted with three large photographs of the courtyard and building to help him envision the depot, which he did not visit while planning the grounds (J. D. Bingham to FLO, Oct. 28, 1873).
12. In July 1875 the depot quartermaster reported that the courtyard had been graded, its walks completed, and all trees and shrubs planted according to Olmsted's plan. The grounds outside the building were not yet improved (James A. Ekin, 1st endorsement [July 10, 1875], on Addison Barrett to James A. Ekin, July 9, 1875, in RG 92, Records of the Quartermaster General, Entry 225, "Jeffersonville Depot," box 473, NARA, Washington, D.C.; U.S. War Department, *Annual Report*, 4 vols. [Washington, D.C., 1875], 1: 262).

To Justin Smith Morrill and James Henry Platt, Jr.[1]

Washington, 9th June, 1874.

To the Hon. Justin S. Morrill and
Hon J. H. Platt, Chairmen
of the Committees of Congress on
Public Buildings and Grounds.
Gentlemen;

With a skeleton plan herewith exhibited the following explanatory statement is respectfully presented as a report of progress in the study of the design of the Capitol grounds.[2]

The chief object of the study is to determine the best means of sustaining and supporting the Capitol building consistently with convenience of approach to it.

The field of operations being small, relatively to the imposing dimensions of the building, the elements of the plan must be few, large and simple.

On the East side it is necessary that there should be an open carriage court extending the full length of the building about one hundred feet in width, essentially as at present.

Approaches to this court are desirable from the several streets, fourteen in number,[3] leading from all sides toward the Capitol. These fourteen approaches are designed to be reduced by converging junctions to seven, three to enter the court at each end and one opposite the main portico.

Those from the East are to be so laid out as to leave two unbroken plats of ground, elliptical in form, each five hundred feet in length and four hundred feet in breadth. These plats are designed to have a gently undulating, nearly flat, surface of turf broken and shaded only by a few groups of trees.

To enter the grounds in carriages from the approaching streets on the East, a reduction of six feet in the present surface is required at three points and the excavation must be continued over the greater part of the distance to the foot of the stairs of the porticos. The general surface of the ground must be so far conformed to that of the roads that the removal of the trees along the eastern border of the grounds is a necessity.

The ultimate character of the grounds east of the building would, under this arrangement, be park like; the surface nearly flat, the roads and walks laid out in long curves, and the trees large, umbrageous and standing in natural groups. The only artificial decoration proposed beyond the court will be in the form of three fountains at the junction of roads near the entrances and at the greatest distance from the building.[4]

The groups of trees would be so disposed that, when full grown, views of the building would be had from a distance in seven different directions, two of these being complete perspectives of the whole front.

JANUARY 1874–AUGUST 1874

"Skeleton Plan" for U.S. Capitol Grounds [c. 1874]
The plan shows the arrangement of paths on the West grounds as described in Olmsted's letter of June 9, 1874, but also shows his later extension of East Capitol Street in Capitol grounds.

The best of the trees now standing in the two groves nearest the Capitol building are not intended to be removed.[5]

On the west it is assumed that the breadth of the terrace which is now but thirty feet will be enlarged to fifty feet,[6] and that the present façade of the old capitol will eventually be replaced by a wall of marble corresponding in dimensions and architectural character to those of the wings.[7] Grand staircases are proposed leading from the terrace on each side of this central building to the natural surface of the ground below. In each of these staircases there would be three broad landings and the landings on each side would be connected by terraces, sustained by retaining walls of masonry, suitably decorated. The effect would be to greatly increase the apparent height and massiveness of that part of the building supporting the dome and to establish a relative proportion between these two parts of the structure which it is believed would be much more satisfactory than that now existing. The avenue extending from the foot of the present narrow stairs to the public garden, which consists chiefly of poor and short-lived trees, is proposed to be obliterated so that the whole support of the dome in the staircases, central terraces and the façade of the central building would be disclosed to view from a distance.[8]

The diagonal avenues leading from the foot of the old narrow stairs to Pennsylvania and Maryland Avenues are proposed to be retained.

A broad walk leading each way from the foot of the grand staircase on the level of the present surface is intended to extend north and south beyond the ends of the building where it would connect with walks leading from the several western entrances to the court on the East.

The only important structural features contemplated have thus been described.

All the spaces between the walks and roads are designed to have a gently sloping surface broken only by a few groups of large trees, but a nearly continuous grove would follow and shade the principal approaches and, with the exception already indicated, all of the borders of the ground.[9]

Respectfully,

Fred. Law Olmsted
Landscape Arch[t]

The text presented here is from a document in a clerk's hand and signed by Olmsted, in the Justin Smith Morrill Papers, Manuscript Division, Library of Congress, Washington, D.C.

1. James Henry Platt, Jr. (1837–1894) served in the Vermont volunteer infantry during the Civil War, settled in Virginia after the war, and was a Republican member of the State constitutional convention in 1867. He held a seat in the U.S. House of Representatives

from 1870 to 1875 and was chairman of the committee on public buildings and grounds (*BDAC*).
2. Since accepting the commission for the Capitol grounds in late March, Olmsted had worked on the plan several hours daily. In May he advised Morrill, who was preparing legislation to fund work during the fiscal year 1875, that from two to three hundred thousand dollars would be needed. The present report was composed by Olmsted during a two-day visit to Washington June 9 and 10. It differs in significant respects from the plan ultimately adopted and carried out on the ground. After he received this report, Morrill attached an amendment to the sundry civil bill, approved by the Senate June 23, 1874, appropriating $200,000 for the improvement of the Capitol grounds according to this plan (FLO to Justin S. Morrill, May 22, 1874, Morrill Papers, Library of Congress; ibid., June 11, 1874; FLO to Justin S. Morrill, June 4, 1874, B134: #2820, OAR/LC; G. Brown, *Documentary History of the United States Capitol*, pp. 1157–59).
3. That is, on the north, New Jersey Avenue, North Capitol Street, Delaware Avenue, and First Street east; on the east, B Street north (now Constitution Avenue), Maryland Avenue, A Street north, A Street south, Pennsylvania Avenue, and B Street south (now Independence Avenue); on the south, First Street east, New Jersey Avenue, South Capitol Street, and Delaware Avenue. Olmsted did not include East Capitol Street in this count because it did not enter the Capitol grounds at this time. In a revision of the plan presented to Morrill in mid-July 1874, he proposed to open it as a formal avenue leading directly to the east portico of the Capitol (FLO to Justin S. Morrill, July 16, 1874; FLO to Justin S. Morrill, July 20, 1874, Morrill Papers, Library of Congress).
4. Presumably, two of the fountains were to be located near the junction of entrance roads, beyond the north and south ends of the carriage court; the third fountain was to be at the junction of two curving roads opposite the east portico.
5. These two groves, located east of the Senate and House wings at the lower edge of the elliptical turf plats described above, were mostly remnants of plantings from the 1840s. A few of the trees, however, dated back to the turn of the century. While the poor condition of most trees in the east grounds necessitated their removal, considerable efforts were taken to save the more promising ones. In September, Olmsted arranged for the purchase from the Brooklyn park commission of a tree transplanting truck used at Prospect Park, and ordered another one custom-built from a carriage maker in Buffalo. He brought in his expert tree mover at Brooklyn, Oliver Crosby Bullard, to oversee this part of the work in Washington. One year later Olmsted reported to Edward Clark that 157 trees had "been transplanted by means of the tree-trucks, and re-arranged in appropriate groups, and at this date there are no indications of any of them having suffered from the change" (F. L. Olmsted, "Index to Trees About the Capitol," pp. 14–15; FLO, "The National Capitol," Dec. 5, 1874, below; FLO to Edward Clark, Sept. 18, 1874, in D2, OAR/LC; "Work on the Capitol Grounds," undated c. Nov. 1874 newspaper clipping, scrapbook no. 1, p. 8, Records Management Department, Architect of the Capitol, U.S. Capitol, Washington, D.C.; FLO to John A. Partridge, Aug. 4, 1875; FLO to Justin S. Morrill, Sept. 5. 1875, Morrill Papers, Library of Congress; "Report of Fred. Law Olmsted, Landscape-Architect," [Sept. 17, 1875], in *Annual Report of the Architect of the Capitol* [1875], p. 885).
6. That is, that the extension and widening of the earth embankments begun in the mid-1860s, and provisionally endorsed by Olmsted in early 1874, would continue (FLO to Justin S. Morrill, Jan. 26, 1874, above).
7. Olmsted here referred to the proposed extension of the west central portico and building, then under discussion (G. Brown, *History of the Capitol*, 2: 168–72).
8. This passage is Olmsted's first statement on the need to provide a visual base and support for the west front of the Capitol. The newly enlarged dome overwhelmed the older,

central part of the building it rested on, while the extended wings crowded to the edge of the earth embankments beneath them. Although the design problem remained constant, the plan Olmsted proposed here differed in important respects from the one he presented to Congress seven months later and which ultimately was adopted and built. Here the two grand staircases, with an architectural terrace limited to the space between them, were to descend from the earth and flagstone terraces which flanked each side of the central building. These earth and flagstone terraces were to be widened and extended across the remainder of the west front and around both north and south sides. Such an arrangement, however, did not satisfy Olmsted for long. While in Washington composing this report, he conferred with Edward Clark about the west front extension and requested sketches of it and photographs of the existing terraces and stairways. He spent a week on the Capitol grounds in July and, with the assistance of Thomas Wisedell, revised the proposal to include an architectural terrace extending from the each side of the central grand staircases on the west facade around both north and south sides of the Capitol (FLO to Justin S. Morrill, June 11, 1874, Morrill Papers, Library of Congress; Edward Clark to FLO, June 12, 1874, in D2, OAR/LC; ibid., June 15, 1874; FLO to Montgomery C. Meigs, Jan. 15, 1875, below).

9. For the continuous grove along the western approaches to the capitol, see the treatment of the borders of the paths on the lines of Maryland Avenue and Pennsylvania Avenue extended on the Capitol grounds plan of January 1875, page xxx below. This concept was later abandoned and rows of Plane trees were planted along these paths instead. The one section of the boundary to be left open was at the center of the west grounds; this opening of the grounds to view from the outside was made possible by removal of the old, straight avenue that ran westward from the foot of the central staircase below the west front of the Capitol.

To Charles Sprague Sargent[1]

July 8th, 1874.

My dear Sir:-

I have received yours of 5th inst. and thank you.

My charge of $200.00 was intended to be for a preliminary visit one object of which would be to enable me to judge of the scope and requirements of your scheme and the probable difficulties of a plan. I should not like to undertake to form a plan until I had seen the ground and discussed the general propositions with you. It might turn out that I differed with you radically about it or that I should advise a course and that you would adopt it which made it unnecessary for you to employ me on a plan. Indeed a park and an arboretum seem to me to be so far unlike in purpose that I do not feel sure that I could combine them satisfactorily. I certainly would not undertake to do so in this case without your cooperation and I think it would be better and more proper that the plan should be made by you with my aid rather than by me with yours.[2]

My usual charge for preliminary plans of parks is $15. to $20 per acre of ground covered.

Sincerely yours,
Fred. Law Olmsted.

C. S. Sargent, Esq.

The text presented here is from a draft in Olmsted's hand in B68: #900, OAR/LC.
1. Charles Sprague Sargent (1841–1927), professor of arboriculture at Harvard and at this time director of the Harvard Botanic Garden. Beginning in 1874 he and Olmsted developed plans for what became the Arnold Arboretum of Harvard, of which Sargent was the director for over fifty years (S. B. Sutton, *Charles Sprague Sargent and the Arnold Arboretum* [Cambridge, Mass., 1970], pp. 22–49; Cynthia Zaitzevsky, *Frederick Law Olmsted and the Boston Park System* [Cambridge, Mass., 1982], pp. 58–60).
2. At this point, Olmsted wrote and then deleted the following paragraph: "If you will come here and discuss the general question of your scheme with me & then give me your opinion of my plan for improving the Capitol, I shall be in debt to you."

To Justin Smith Morrill

209 W. 46th St. N York, 16th Aug. 1874.

Dear Mr Morrill;

I returned this morning from my third visit to Washington since you left.[1] Affairs at the Capitol ground have not moved rapidly or in other respects altogether satisfactorily. I have repeated to you on another sheet the few essential points of progress[2] and assume your interest in some minor occurrences which I shall here narrate.

On the first of my three visits, having found a man delivering manure on the lower or West Ground, I called the attention of Mr Clark to the mistake and advised what course should be followed to avoid a second handling of materials. Mr Clark, however, who left the next day for the Cape,[3] not thinking that much could be brought on in his absence and pressed with various duties, neglected to countermand his previous orders and consequently found when he came back, early in August, that some thousand loads of soil and manure so deposited that it will have to be lifted and carried up the hill to its proper place. I have given very explicit written directions to prevent the recurrence of such unnecessary labor.

I visited Washington again on the 4th inst. Mr Clark had opened and canvassed the bids for the preliminary grading, of which there were twenty or more, running from 14 to 35 cts. per cubic yard. I saw several of the lower bidders and their bondsmen but others were out of town and I returned to New York to meet an appointment, having an understanding with Mr Clark that he was if possible, to advance a plan in my absence by which the whole contract would have come into the hands of a strong and capable man by an arrangement between him and the lowest bidder. He found this, however, impracticable and concluded to let the lowest bidder go on at once with the work on his own resources. When he undertook to do so, however, he was, as it is reported, interrupted by a "mob," who threatened to prevent work being done unless a certain rate of wages should be paid — 50% higher than that current in the district on private works. The contractor at once showed the white feather and his hands scattered.[4] The next day, arriving early in the morning from New York and knowing nothing of all this, I walked over the ground and found about 25 second class field hands and as many boys and girls all lying on the ground near where work had been begun, a few smarter looking and rogueish men and two or three white policemen loafing about them. Pieces of paper were pinned on the trees bearing fairly well-written, ridiculous communistic war cries and an officer told me that a man whom he called an "International"[5] had been harranging the mob — which was when I saw it as peaceful, guileless and helpless a group of people in appearance as I ever saw. Fully one third of them were fast asleep. Afterwards I heard them singing hymns. The next day the contractor tried again in a very feeble way and the police easily prevented the slightest demonstration against his going on.

I finally concluded after much talk with the four lowest of the bidders to give them each a chance, the lowest having choice of ground, and so on. Of these four, two are honest men of small means, not regular contractors but probably each representing a cooperative association of poor cart-owners. Another has been a member of the District legislature[6] and does not promise well but his bondsman is strong and being a dealer in horsefeed &c. he probably has some interest in giving employment to his debtors. The fourth is a regular old contractor, probably a rogue but a close calculator, a driver, an owner of lots to be filled up and of many horses now eating their heads off in idleness. I mention these things because you will see that the work cannot be done at the prices with any direct profit and the probability of failure and of constant attempts at knavery made me very reluctant to deal with these men. However I explained the business very fully to them, assured them that the contract would be broken whenever they gave us difficulty and made the terms of the contract very stringent. Mr Clark thinks the bondsmen very good and they are bound to see the laborers paid punctually. I was the more inclined to make a trial of them because some of the larger bidders very plainly hinted that it would be much better that I should not. One fellow told me that he considered himself entitled to have the contract and at double the market rate as he had fully earned half of all he could get from it in lobbying your bill through last winter,[7] and a "syndicate" of six old public work contractors called on me in a body to warn me that the work could never be completed on better terms than they would offer—viz 35 cts and pay no man less than $1.50 for eight hours' work.

I had been expecting till last week to put an experienced park engineer in charge of the work at this time but when it came to the point of closing an engagement with my man his demands were so great that I was compelled to abandon my intention.[8] The man now appointed, Mr Partridge, was introduced to me some time ago by and is agreeable to Mr. Clark. He is of New England training, accustomed to hard work and to nice work, a methodical, deliberate prudent man, precise and exacting. He is a resident of Capitol Hill and President of the Washington branch of the National Assoc. of C. Engineers.[9] I had Mr. Radford (of whom I shall speak presently) on to help him in starting and shall send him a rod man, at low wages, who has had several years training in our parks. As soon as he has the work well in hand I shall have him come to New York, review our methods and see their results in the parks.

I employ Mr. Radford in the preparation of working drawings and specifications for grading, sewer, gas, water, basin, curb and gutter work. He is the best man I know for the purpose in the country.[10] I employ Mr Thomas Wisedell in a similar way for architectural work.[11] He was the architect under Mr Vaux of the work you chiefly noticed in the Brooklyn Park. Both work under my daily personal direction and review here and will receive their regular compensation for time employed. Mr Partridge is to be paid $150– per month, to give all desireable time to the work but not precluded from other business consistent with his duties. He intends to have nothing else of consequence.

I hope I have not overestimated your interest in these details.

I have had a correspondence with Mr Dorman B. Eaton, who makes a long series of good suggestions about improvements at Washington.[12] I advised him that you were much more strongly and intelligently engaged with the subject than anyone else. I find here now another note from him asking your address and whether you are likely to be in Narragansett Bay or at N York this summer? He is at Narragansett Pier.

I trust that you are getting abundant rest and refreshment and that Vermont air is doing much for Mrs Morrill.[13]

With much respect,
I am Sincerely Yours,

Fred. Law Olmsted.

The text presented here is from a manuscript in Olmsted's hand in the Justin Smith Morrill Papers, Manuscript Division, Library of Congress, Washington, D.C.

1. Morrill left Washington for his home in Strafford, Vermont, in the latter part of June and remained there through August. Olmsted's three visits to the capital took place on July 13–19, August 4–6, and August 14–15 (FLO to George E. Waring, Jr., July 19, 1874; FLO to Justin S. Morrill, July 20, 1874, Morrill Papers, Library of Congress; FLO, pay vouchers, Records Management Department, Architect of the Capitol, U.S. Capitol, Washington, D.C.).
2. In a letter written in Washington the previous day, Olmsted reported that he had hired the four lowest bidders for grading the east Capitol grounds, had marked a large number of trees for removal, and had appointed John A. Partridge engineer-in-charge of the work (FLO to Justin S. Morrill, Aug. 15, 1874, Morrill Papers, Library of Congress).
3. Edward Clark left Washington for Cape Cod, Massachusetts, on July 20 (FLO to Justin S. Morrill, July 20, 1874, Morrill Papers, Library of Congress).
4. When bids for the grading of the east Capitol grounds were opened on August 3, contractor Pat Sullivan entered the lowest at fourteen cents per cubic yard. When he reported to work with approximately 200 black laborers on August 13, none of them was willing to work for the $1 per day offered. Sullivan raised the pay to $1.25 and several men started to work, but retreated when others started throwing rocks at them and demonstrating. "These rowdies became so troublesome," reported Clark, "that the aid of the Capitol Police had to [be] called. After arresting a few of the ring-leaders and flourishing pistols at the others, the crowd was scattered" (*Washington Evening Star*, Aug. 13, 1874, p. 4; *The Capital*, Aug. 16, 1874, p. 8; Edward Clark to Justin S. Morrill, Aug. 22, 1874, Morrill Papers, Library of Congress).
5. A reference to the International Workingmen's Association, founded by Karl Marx and others in London in 1864. By the early 1870s the International had active membership in New York, Philadelphia, and Washington, and in 1872 its general council had moved from London to New York (Joseph G. Rayback, *A History of American Labor* [New York, 1966], pp. 149–51; Norman J. Ware, *The Labor Movement in the United States, 1860–1890* [New York, 1964], pp. 305–6).
6. That is, the popularly elected House of Delegates of the short-lived territorial government of Washington, which had been abolished by Congress only weeks before (Constance McLaughlin Green, *Washington Village and Capital, 1800–1878* [Princeton, N.J., 1962], pp. 332–61).
7. In early 1873 Morrill attached an amendment to the sundry civil appropriations bill providing $350,000 to grade and pave the streets and sidewalks around the Capitol and improve the Capitol grounds. Congress appropriated $125,000 on March 3, 1873 (G. Brown, *Documentary History of the United States Capitol*, pp. 1145–53).
8. In late July, Olmsted had offered the position to James C. Aldrich, a civil engineer for the Department of Public Parks in New York. Aldrich had prepared the topographical survey of the village of Riverside, Illinois, for Olmsted and Vaux in 1868. He later was superintending engineer of Riverside Avenue in Manhattan in 1876–78 (FLO to James B. Aldritch, July 22, 1874).
9. In a letter written the day before, Olmsted notified John A. Partridge of his appointment. He stipulated that the ground east of the Capitol was to be graded, underdrained, provided with permanent gas and water systems, dressed with a foot of topsoil, and prepared for lawn seeding by mid-November (FLO to John A. Partridge, Aug. 15, 1874).
10. George Kent Radford, English-born civil engineer who had worked for Olmsted and Vaux on various projects, including the Chicago South Park, Prospect Park in Brooklyn, and the Buffalo park system. During the 1870s, he assisted Olmsted on Mt. Royal in Montreal, the Parkside subdivision in Buffalo, and the grounds of the Schuylkill Arsenal in Philadelphia (*Papers of FLO*, 6: 651).
11. Thomas Wisedell (1846–1884), an English-born architect, whom Calvert Vaux had recruited to come to America in 1868. He was an assistant to the architectural firm of

JANUARY 1874–AUGUST 1874

Vaux, Withers & Company. His first important designs were for the Concert Grove buildings and stonework at Prospect Park, and the Martyr's Memorial at Fort Greene Park, in Brooklyn (*New-York Times*, Aug. 2, 1884, p. 4; *Papers of FLO*, 6: 672).
12. Dorman Bridgman Eaton (1823–1899), lawyer and civil-service reformer, conferred with Olmsted and Morrill in 1874 about providing permanent maintenance for the improvements then being carried out by the Parking Commission of the Board of Public Works (*DAB*; FLO to William Hammond Hall, March 28, 1874, above; FLO to Dorman B. Eaton, Aug. 16, 1874; Justin S. Morrill to FLO, Sept. 7, 1874, B134: #2820, OAR\LC; Dorman B. Eaton to FLO, Oct. 15, 1874).
13. Ruth Barrell Swan Morrill (1821–1898), (*New-York Times*, May 14, 1898, p. 4).

CHAPTER II

AUGUST 1874–JANUARY 1875

Reports in this chapter to Henry Stebbins and the commissioners of New York City Department of Public Parks spell out Olmsted's continuing concern for the policing, maintenance, and landscape management of Central Park. His report to Stebbins of January 15 describes his concept of a unified plan for Riverside Park and Riverside Avenue. The chapter also contains Olmsted's first description of his plan for a public recreation ground on Mount Royal in Montreal and his plan for Niagara Square in Buffalo with a proposed Civil War memorial arch by Henry Hobson Richardson. The article "The National Capitol" in the *New-York Daily Tribune* was Olmsted's first and fullest statement to the press concerning his plan of the U.S. Capitol grounds.

To Henry G. Stebbins[1]

DEPARTMENT OF PUBLIC PARKS,
OFFICE OF DESIGN AND SUPERINTENDENCE,
NEW YORK, August 27, 1874.

To the Hon. HENRY G. STEBBINS, *President of the Board*:
SIR—
As requested by you, I herewith submit estimates for ordinary maintenance expenses for parks and places for the year 1875. This estimate is based on a consideration of what has been accomplished by the Superintendent of

Parks,[2] the Director of the Menagerie,[3] and the Captain of Police,[4] with the means heretofore allowed them, and on the assumption that the rate of wages, the prices of materials to be purchased, and the degree of efficiency for their respective duties of the force employed will remain essentially unchanged.

For convenience of comparison I have tabulated the estimate for 1875, under various heads of accounts, together with (1) a statement of actual expenditures under the same heads for the year 1872; (2) the same for 1873; (3) estimates for 1874, as prepared in October last for the Board of Estimate and Apportionment; (4) estimates for 1874, as modified by the reduction made by the Board of Apportionment in June last,[5] this reduction being applied pro rata to the several items of the table; and (5) the expenditure for 1874, calculated on the assumption that the average rate will be maintained under each item during the last five months of the year that has obtained during the first seven months.

This comparative table, with the above explanation, renders argument in any other form for the estimates of 1875 unnecessary, except with reference to the increased expense proposed for the items of ice and police, and the two unusual items of special repairs of architectural structures and special improvement of plantations. Independently of these items and that of contingencies, the amount of the estimate for the Central Park is $43,000 less than that of last year, and $6,000 less than the amount actually expended in 1873.

You have requested me to fully state the occasion for the several items of proposed expenditure of a new or extraordinary character; to give testimony as to their necessity; and to state upon what grounds a postponement of them is to be deprecated.

I proceed to do so:

Ice.—The estimate for ice is much larger than the amount expended under the same head during the past winter, because the last winter was a remarkably open one, and there was scarcely any skating. The chances are that the next will be very severe, and the expenses of keeping the skating ponds and houses in good order unusually large. No permanent injury to the value of the park will occur if the public should be denied its customary use of the ice during the whole or part of the winter, but I need not say how much disappointment and discontent would be caused.

Police.—Having no official responsibility in respect to the Police,[6] my information is derived chiefly from the papers which you have referred to me, especially the reports from the Superintendent of Parks and the Captain of Police. I have also consulted the Landscape Gardener,[7] the Director of the Menagerie, and others who have responsibilities on the Central Park.

To justify the design of the park and the vast outlay which the city has made to carry out that design, a certain class of requirements must be met upon it for which no provision is made, unless through the expenditure designated "For Police." This class of requirements is not met by the Police, and the Captain of Police when called upon by you to account for the consequences, states that it is due to the insufficiency of his force in numbers. Assuming this to be the true and only reason, I have not the slightest doubt that the value of the city's property in the park not only now falls short of what it might economically be made by giving him a larger number of men, but that this value has diminished of late, and is diminishing to that degree; that for every dollar saved in Police wages, hundreds of dollars are wasted.

I shall but barely indicate the grounds of this opinion by a few illustrations.

An important object in the design of the park is to provide a place close at hand in which invalids, weakly and delicate persons, and children may obtain the relief from the confinement in the city which those of wealth and leisure gain by retiring to distant country-seats. For this purpose large districts of it have been designed to take the character of quiet seclusion, within which, as far as practicable, there should be a counterpart of the common scenes of fortunately disposed woodland glades; this not only in trees, and shrubs, and tender plants, but in the twittering of birds and such other rural charms as would help to the general result of simple, quiet, tranquilizing, and refreshing recreation. This purpose was at one time so far accomplished that under advice of physicians, not only invalids and convalescents, but numbers of school girls and children in delicate health were induced to spend much time in the park, and they did so without annoyance or any feeling of insecurity.[8] It is now becoming a much less prudent, agreeable, and beneficial custom for them to do so than it was a few years since, because of their liability to encounter rudeness, impertinence, dishonesty, and filth; and the special rural attractions referred to, instead of increasing, as they naturally should, if Nature were simply left undisturbed, are diminishing. I personally know of several cases in which heads of families have discontinued sending their children to the park, because of disagreeable and painful experiences to which they have been subjected while there. A physician, who ten years ago told me that he customarily sent a certain class of patients to the park every fine day in summer, and who regularly sent his own children to exercise in it, lately told me that he had been obliged to caution the same class of patients against going there, and to forbid his children their accustomed rambles. Numerous complaints of rudeness experienced, and disgusting things heard or witnessed in the park have been made by children to me personally, and parents have told me that while their children had formerly been eager to obtain leave to go to the park, they had lately found them reluctant to go there, and for the reasons I have indicated. Your Superintendent and other officers at the same time testify that it is evident that there are many persons who make a business of spoiling birds' nests and stealing plants from the park, and that in pursuing this business they break down and destroy trees, shrubs, and plants. A tree, six inches in diameter of trunk, standing in a prominent position, was the other day cut down with an axe by one of these rascals, in order to get from it a nest of young robins.

Your stock of swans and other water-fowl, and of wild birds, is now smaller than it was ten years ago. There is but one reason why it should not have greatly increased, and that is the stealing of eggs and young birds. This year you had, at one time, five nests containing twenty eggs, of swans, every one of them has been broken up and the eggs stolen; there have been a much larger number of eggs of the other fowl stolen, but in no instance have the thieves been detected.

Not a week has passed this summer that lead pipe, bronze ornaments, or other like property, has not been wrenched violently from its place and carried off the park, in consequence of which several structures have been rendered useless, and for some time closed to the public. The gardener states that it is evident that some of those who steal plants, know and select such as are readiest of sale and have the largest money value.

I refer to the obvious rapid increase of offences on the park, in themselves of comparatively small importance, as demonstrating the comparative security with which another class of offences are committed, which cause vastly greater injury to its value, as a place of wholesome resort, for the young, the pure, and the delicate.

Whenever it shall have become fully established that the park is the chosen resort of that part of the city's population which finds its chief pleasure there, as elsewhere, in the exercise of insolent, cruel, lewd, and dishonestly selfish propensities, the value of this costly recreation ground will have vanished. In other words, it will be seen that more than ten millions of dollars have been spent for an undesirable end.[9] That there is a strong and increasing tendency to that result, as things are, there is no room for doubt. If enlarging the number of the police force will effectually check it, there is as little room for doubt that it will be a measure of the strictest economy to make such increase.

Special Repairs and Improvement of Architectural Structures.—The estimate for this purpose is the result of a survey just completed by Mr. Munckwitz, your Superintending Architect,[10] and the object of it is to arrest the progress of numerous processes of injury, some recent and slight, but many first detected years ago, and which have been every year since increasing in magnitude. The longer, in each case, the required repairs are delayed, the greater will be the eventual cost to the city.

I propose to show how it happens that so large an accumulation of demands for repairs has occurred.

Previously to 1863 all expenditures on the Central Park were defrayed from the proceeds from the sale of City Bonds.[11] Since then it has been required that the proceeds of bonds should be applied solely to a particular class of expenditures; another class being met from taxation. The two classes of expenditure are designated, one as "Improvement and Government," the other as "Maintenance and Government." The terms are ambiguous, for a park is not wholly a human construction, but partly a growth, and the completion of so much of it as a human construction must to a certain degree wait upon and follow the process of growth. The continuous cost required on a park is not, on the other hand, strictly speaking, devoted solely to its maintenance, but largely to the stimulation, direction, and regulation of its growth, and in some degree to the modification of those elements which are not subject to natural growth in accommodation to the changes of those which are. A strict and true division between expenditures for "improvement and government" and for "maintenance and government" has never been practicable. For the purposes of their book-keeping, however, the Park Commissioners have always felt constrained by the law to assume that portions of the park, one after another, as the rougher preliminary work upon them has been completed, should be assumed to be completely improved, and to direct that all work thereafter expended on them should be reckoned as expended for their maintenance. It has, nevertheless, all the time been impossible to wholly ignore the obvious requirements of their continued improvement; and though there has been a great lack, and with a presumed motive of economy, a systematic withholding of intelligent direction for that purpose, the maintenance account has always been overloaded by charges for labor, which would not have been necessary were the park well grown and beyond the constant accidents and backslidings to which new garden work is subject.

It has happened, consequently, that the Commissioners have never been able to do what they themselves recognized and admitted it to be necessary to do, on these improved portions of the park in any one year since the attempt began to be made, without exceeding the limits of the allowance made to them for the purpose of maintenance. Repeated resolutions have been adopted that the utmost economy should be used, and every exertion made to prevent the recurrence of a failure in this respect, which they have felt to be a mortifying one, but always unsuccessfully. The average deficiency for eleven years past has been over $50,000 per annum: even omitting the extraordinary year of 1871,[12] when it was recklessly carried to $248,000, it has been above $30,000 per annum.

It cannot be surprising, under these circumstances, that a great many duties of maintenance, the neglect of which would not affect the satisfaction of the public for the time being in the parks, have been every year postponed. Such a course has been inevitable, and thus it has occurred that important constructions in stone, iron, and wood threaten to fall into a state of dilapidation, and some have already done so, because of processes of injury which might at one time have been arrested at almost trifling cost.

I shall not be misunderstood as finding fault with the law or with the Commissioners for taking the course they have under the law. It was, perhaps, impracticable to do better with the political conditions under which they have had to conduct their business; but it cannot be right that to avoid adding to the immediate requirements of taxation, or the bonded debt of the city, another form of liability should now be allowed to go on increasing at more than compound interest rates of enlargement, as this must, if no means are taken for stopping its insidious progress.

Special Improvement of Plantations.—There are certain places in the Central Park where there was originally a thick growth of sapling trees and bushes. In some cases, where it was desirable for landscape reasons, and also because of an intention to keep the surface of the ground in fine turf and to allow the public at times to range freely over it, the bushes were grubbed out and the trees so far thinned as to allow an expansion of the branches of those remaining. A part of those left were sprouts from the stumps and roots of old and decaying trees which had been felled, and for this and other reasons, not likely to be as healthy and vigorous as those which had sprung from seed. It was thought desirable to leave many such trees for a few years, lest too sudden and complete exposure of those designed to remain should be injurious to the latter.

The growth of the best trees, in these cases, has not been half as rapid as that of trees of the same species elsewhere on the park. This is due, in part, to the original thinness of the soil in which they were standing, and to the fact that the soil had been exhausted of the elements particularly required to sustain the trees, by their predecessors upon it, but it is also largely due to the excessive number of trees now growing upon it. The heads of the trees are interfering, and their satisfactory expansion is arrested.

I have repeatedly urged that a vigorous thinning out should be made among them,[13] and I now again advise this, and also that the ground, in some cases, be richly top-dressed, and other measures taken to advance the desired result.

Again, in parts of the park, when trees were planted, they were set much more thickly than they were intended to stand—permanently, partly for the sake of shelter, and partly for immediate effect.

Such excess of trees has been but partially removed; in many instances the trees designed to be permanent have been ruined by insufficient thinning, and in others greatly injured with reference to the results intended. The ultimate value of the park can never be as much as it might be had all desirable attention been given to this duty from year to year. It is unnecessary to recur to the conditions which have led to its neglect. The injury to the park, and the cost of such remedy as is practicable, increases with every year that its application is delayed, and to withhold it even for one year more would be the reverse of economical. I recommend an estimate for the specific object of thinning and improving old plantations to be adopted, as an item of the general estimate,[14] lest if a sum for the purpose should simply be added to the estimate "for plantations," it will be found to be required, and will be applied to meet other exigencies of the year having more apparent importance for the time being.

The estimate for the sea-wall at the Battery includes an amount of

$7,500 in addition to the estimate of last year, as the result of a more thorough examination of the premises.[15]

The estimate for the City Hall Park[16] pavement is the same as was made last year, nothing having been since expended there.

Respectfully,

FRED. LAW OLMSTED,
Landscape Architect.

The text presented here is from *The City Record*, September 11, 1874. It accompanied the estimates for 1875 expenses submitted by the Department of Public Parks to the Board of Estimate and Apportionment, the body which determined the annual budgets of municipal departments, raised taxes, and issued bonds. The board requested the park department's estimates in late July and the matter was assigned to its president, Henry G. Stebbins, the following month (*The City Record*, Sept. 11, 1874, pp. 1011–12; Issac Newton Phelps Stokes, *The Iconography of Manhattan Island, 1498–1909*, 6 vols. [New York, 1915–28], 5: 1954; DPP, *Minutes*, Aug. 28, 1874, p. 225).

1. Henry G. Stebbins (1811–1881), New York City banker and stock broker. Stebbins had served as a member of the Board of Commissioners of the Central Park, mostly as its president, from late 1859 until May 1870, when that body was replaced by the commissioners of the newly created Department of Public Parks. Following the collapse of the Tweed Ring in November 1871, Stebbins was reappointed to the park board. Except for a brief period in 1872 when Olmsted took his place, Stebbins served as president and treasurer until the summer of 1873, when Salem H. Wales was elected. Stebbins replaced Wales as president of the board on May 9, 1874, and served in that position for another two years (*Papers of FLO*, 6: 66–67; DPP, *Minutes*, July 31, 1873, p. 159; ibid., Aug. 29, 1873, p. 246; ibid., May 9, 1874, pp. 20–21; ibid., May 5, 1876, pp. 4–5).
2. Columbus Ryan had worked on Central Park before the Civil War and served as its superintendent until the Sweeny park board dismissed him in May 1870. In November 1871 he was reappointed to this position at Andrew H. Green's request. Several months later he also obtained a concession to operate a tavern at Mount St. Vincent in the northeast section of the park (*Papers of FLO*, 6: 524).
3. William A. Conklin (1837–1913) was connected with the Central Park menagerie since 1858 and was appointed its director by the Sweeny park board in 1870. He was retained by the Stebbins park board in May 1872 and served in that position for another twenty years. Reviewing the Central Park zoo in 1890, Olmsted stated that Conklin, "from the beginning, has been responsible for almost everything in the history of this affair that is not to be regretted" (*Appleton's Cyc. Am. Biog.*; DPP, *First Annual Report* [1871], p. 171; DPP, *Minutes*, May 8, 1872, p. 377; NCAB, 2: 256; FLO to Waldo Hutchins, March 18, 1890).
4. Henry Koster had been a keeper of Central Park since the early 1860s and was first appointed captain in 1867. A member of the Republican party, he was fired by the Democratic Sweeny park board in late 1870. Rehired after the fall of the Tweed Ring, he was reappointed captain in December 1872 (*Papers of FLO*, 6: 583; *New-York Times*, June 2, 1871, p. 5).
5. In the aftermath of the Panic of 1873 the City of New York reduced expenditures on public works. The Board of Estimate and Apportionment called for revised estimates

from the park board in May 1874 and fixed the reduced amounts the following month. During the same time, personnel reductions were made in the department's civil and topographical engineer's office and in the landscape architect's office, and Olmsted presented a report recommending the suspension of work on numerous construction projects (Seymour J. Mandelbaum, *Boss Tweed's New York* [New York, 1965], pp. 99–100, 111; DPP, *Minutes*, May 9, 1874, p. 13; ibid., May 20, 1874, pp. 32–42; ibid., June 3, 1874, p. 72; ibid., July 1, 1874, pp. 121–22; "Document No. 59," in DPP, *Minutes*, May 19, 1874, pp. 1–6).

6. The previous year Olmsted had reorganized the park keepers force in a plan that remained in effect only four months. The park board abandoned the plan and relieved Olmsted of superintending duties in late September 1873 (*Papers of FLO*, 6: 42–45).

7. Robert Demcker joined the Department of Public Park's Bureau of Landscape Gardening as a draftsman in March 1871, during the tenure of the Sweeny park board. The Stebbins park board retained him when it resumed its duties in late 1871 and made him head gardener several months later ("Document No. 30," in DPP, *Minutes*, Nov. 28, 1871, p. 11; *Papers of FLO*, 6: 523–31).

8. Olmsted, writing in 1865 for a San Francisco newspaper, drew attention to this use of Central Park, and did so again in an 1870 lecture before the American Social Science Association (Frederick Law Olmsted, "The Project of a Great Park for San Francisco," Aug. 4, 1865 [*Papers of FLO*, 5: 428]; Frederick Law Olmsted, "Public Parks and the Enlargement of Towns," Feb. 25, 1870 [*Papers of FLO*, SS1: 197]).

9. Expenditures for the construction and maintenance of Central Park through 1874 amounted to $13,064,535 ("Document No. 64," in DPP, *Minutes*, March 5, 1875, pp. 4–5).

10. Julius F. Munckwitz had assisted Calvert Vaux in the preparation of plans for structures on the park since at least 1867. He was appointed superintending architect in June of 1870 by the Sweeny park board and retained his position after the fall of the Tweed Ring. His report of August 28, 1874, detailed repairs needed on the park's bridges, arches, buildings, and the Terrace and was appended to the present text (Dennis Steadman Francis, *Architects in Practice in New York City, 1840–1900* [New York, 1980], p. 57; BCCP, *Minutes*, Nov. 1, 1867, p. 54; "Document No. 30," in DPP, *Minutes*, Nov. 28, 1871, p. 12; DPP, *Minutes*, Aug. 21, 1872, pp. 493–94; *City Record*, Sept. 11, 1874, p. 1012).

11. Olmsted is apparently referring to Chapter 85 of the laws of New York, passed in March 1860, that authorized the board of supervisors of the city and county of New York to collect taxes annually of up to $150,000 for the "maintenance and government" of Central Park. The mayor and aldermen were authorized to pay up to an equal sum for interest on "The Central Park Improvement Fund," which was to be secured by issuing bonds and was to be used "for the laying out, construction, government, improvement and regulation" of the park (New York [State], *Laws of the State of New York, Passed at the Eighty-Third Session of the Legislature* . . . [Albany, N.Y., 1860], chap. 85).

12. That is, the period when the Tweed Ring park board had control of the parks department.

13. In February 1872 Olmsted and Vaux reported to Henry G. Stebbins that the plantations had been in need of "extensive revision" before the arrival of the Sweeny park board two years earlier. At the same time Olmsted issued detailed instructions to landscape gardener Robert Demcker for the repair of the plantations, but this work was only partly done (Frederick Law Olmsted and Calvert Vaux, "A Review of Recent Changes, and Changes which have been Projected, in the Plans of the Central Park," Jan. and Feb. 1872 [*Papers of FLO*, SS1: 267]; *Papers of FLO*, 6: 525–31).

14. The appropriation for parks allotted to the department by the Board of Estimate and Apportionment in January 1875 was $150,000 less than requested and contained no

separate item for thinning and improving the old plantations. However, in February the park board abolished the Exotic and Propagating Department and the position of landscape gardener held by Demcker. The next month it authorized Olmsted to hire two of his most trusted gardeners from the early days of the park and from Prospect Park, William L. Fischer and Oliver Crosby Bullard, to thin the plantations. Within a few weeks Fischer was appointed to the new office of superintending gardener (DPP, *Minutes*, Jan. 6, 1875, pp. 429–30; ibid., Feb. 23, 1875, pp. 533–37; ibid., March 3, 1875, pp. 549–50; ibid., March 19, 1875, pp. 595–96; ibid., March 27, 1875, p. 604; ibid., June 11, 1875, p. 84; *City Record*, June 23, 1875, p. 977).
15. Department engineer John Bogart inspected the sea wall at Battery Park at the southern tip of Manhattan in June 1874 and was preparing a report on the necessary repairs (DPP, *Minutes*, June 25, 1874, p. 112; ibid., Sept. 2, 1874, pp. 235–36).
16. City Hall Park, thirteen acres bounded by Park Row, Broadway, and Chambers and Centre streets, was used for public events and outdoor meetings (DPP, *Statistical Report of the Landscape Architect, 31st December, 1873, Forming Part of Appendix L of the Third General Report of the Department* [New York, 1875], p. 344; *Papers of FLO*, 6: 536).

To Albert Gallatin Browne[1]

209 W 46 St
N.Y., 12 Nov 1874

Dear Mr. Browne;

If you will read the papers transmitted by the Department of Parks with its Estimates for 1875 to the Board of Apportionment, which includes one from me on the requirements of the parks,[2] you will find in it I think all you need. You will see so far as Central Park is concerned that the estimates were regulated by a consideration of what has been expended on the park the present and of late years and the results obtained.

In largely reducing this estimate the Board of Apportionment[3] says one of two things — either that this Department has paid an excessive price for what has been done heretofore or that too much has been done.

No doubt the Department does pay too much but it stands with all others in this respect & the Board of Apportionment does not I presume expect it to reduce wages, employ a better class of men, exact more from them or disregard the 8 hour law.[4]

I assume, therefore, that the Board of Apportionment means that the standard of keeping on the parks has been of late too high.

There are certain items of which the expense might be saved with no injury to the ultimate value of the park — as those of keeping the skating ground, providing music etc. But these on account of their popularity would be the last to be given up. The items on which expenditure will be saved are those by slighting which the developmnt of the park will be arrested and thwarted, by which the tendency to make it an unsafe, immoral and unpleasant place of recreation for young women & children will be increased.

I can't, while serving the Commissioners,[5] publicly criticise them or furnish you the means to do so, but my report gives you a sufficient clue to my views on the question whether the present standard in the keeping of the park is an economical one — Supposing that you will not want to use my opinion, but to save you the trouble of studying what I have written enough to guess what I think, I tell you that I think the park is going to the devil and have grave doubt whether the undertaking to provide a *rural* recreation ground upon such a site in the midst of a city like this was not a mistake, was not doomed to failure because of the general ignorance of the conditions of success and the impossibility of getting proper care taken of it.

See what I have said about the masonry, and consider how roadwork, turf, drains will suffer if too little cared for year after year or unless kept with a liberal conservation. Take the more subtle & indescribable elemnts such as bits of fern or ivy in just the right quantity & quality in a particular niche. Consider what vermin & insects do if they once get well the upper hand of a garden in a private place.

The Park can easily become a nuisance and curse to the city.

What is needed from year to year to prevent it is not to be hastily determined by men not constantly watching it and familiar with the conditions on which success or failure depends. There is no Board that should be distrusted less than the Park Board but you will find that the Board of Apportionment has made a larger proportioned reduction on the park board's estimates than on those of any other department.

I say nothing of the Westchester question which is not on my beat.[6]

As to the "mule," you are quite right in what you have said of his quarrel with Van Nort and its effects.[7] When you treat him or depend on him otherwise than as on a bucker you will not have to wait long to learn your error.

The text presented here is from a draft in Olmsted's hand.

1. Albert Gallatin Browne (1835–1891), managing editor of the *New York Evening Post*. Several days before this letter, Browne had visited the park department and talked with Olmsted and Henry G. Stebbins about the condition of Central Park and the inadequate appropriations for its maintenance (NCAB, 19: 316; *New York Evening Post*, Nov. 10, 1874, p. 3).
2. See FLO to Henry G. Stebbins, August 27, 1874, above.
3. On October 31, 1874, the Board of Estimate and Apportionment issued a provisional estimate, which was adopted in late December, some $150,000 less than the department

had requested for Central Park and the other parks and places under its control (FLO to Henry G. Stebbins, Aug. 27, 1874, n. 14, above; *City Record*, Nov. 2, 1874, p. 1279).
4. In 1870 the New York state legislature had established an eight-hour day for workers employed by New York City (*Papers of FLO*, 6: 628).
5. That is, the Board of Commissioners of the Department of Public Parks.
6. The Board of Estimate and Apportionment had reduced by half the amount requested by the department to continue surveying and laying out streets in the portions of Westchester County recently annexed to New York City. Although the Central Park commission had begun this work in 1869 and the Department of Public Parks continued it in the early 1870s, neither body assigned Olmsted to it until November 1875 (I. N. P. Stokes, *Iconography of Manhattan*, 5: 1954–55; *City Record*, Jan. 5, 1874, pp. 9–10; *New York Evening Post*, Nov. 11, 1874, p. 3; FLO, "Preliminary Report of the Landscape Architect and the Civil and Topographical Engineer, upon the Laying Out of the Twenty-Third and Twenty-Fourth Wards," Nov. 15, 1876, below).
7. The "mule" was probably Andrew H. Green, New York City comptroller, whose argument with commissioner of public works George M. Van Nort over the necessity of rapid city improvements filled the newspapers in the fall of 1874 (George Alexander Mazaraki, "The Public Career of Andrew Haswell Green," [Ph.D. diss., New York University, 1966], pp. 222–35).

To the Commissioners of Mount-Royal Park

209, WEST 46th STREET,
New York, 21*st November*, 1874.

To the Honorable, the Commissioners of Mount-Royal Park, Montreal.
Gentlemen,
    I have the honor to comply with your request, that I would repeat in writing the substance of certain observations verbally made to you last Monday, in regard to your property of Mount Royal.
    As a general rule, rugged and broken ground is the last that should be chosen for a public recreation ground in the immediate vicinity of a large city. It is unnecessary that I should show the objections to it; the simple fact that your property differs so greatly in its topographical characteristics from ground, which would be generally and properly described as "park-like," raises a sufficient presumption that it is unsuitable for a park.
    The question, whether it can, by any means, be economically adapted for the purposes for which you intend it, is, therefore, first in order, and, as it involves a consideration of the main features of a general design for dealing with it, it will be the chief object of my present communication to give you the conclusions of my judgment upon this question, and to indicate more or less distinctly the processes by which they have been reached.
    The chief elements of value of all recreation grounds for the use of

the general public of large towns are: 1st the change of air afforded; 2nd the power of their scenery to counteract conditions which tend to nervous depression or irritability; 3rd the ease and pleasure with which these advantages may be used.

Of the first two of these elements of value, Mount-Royal, in its present unimproved condition, offers a larger measure than any other place equally near so large a population of which I have knowledge, and by judicious means, as I shall indicate further on, its advantages of scenery may be heightened, its disadvantages lessened. The question, then, is, whether its possible value in these respects can be made available with due ease, comfort and economy? My doubts on this point were rapidly lessened after I got above the craggy face of the mountain toward the city, and found myself upon a surface but moderately broken and rugged, and essentially an undulating and wooded table-land, from nearly all points of which broad and delightful distant landscapes are commanded.

A survey of this district soon satisfied me that as far as roads, walks, seats and other conveniences of exercise, rest and refreshment are concerned, there is no extraordinary difficulty in providing within it all that is essential to your purpose, except as it may arise from the necessity of unusual precautions against the bolting of horses and the slipping of heedless persons over the steep declivities, and of establishing not merely security in this respect, but a tranquilizing sense of security in the minds of all classes of visitors.

Passing this point as one of detail, it is a more important and difficult branch of the question whether, these advantages being provided, the use of them can be had by the people generally of the city, with moderate ease, comfort and cheapness? The conditions necessary to be considered before giving an answer will, perhaps, be better recognized if the inquiry is made from the point of a physician considering the case of a poor patient, feeble, timid and nervous: or of a convalescent to whom change of air and scene would be highly beneficial, provided it could be had without too much fatigue, discomfort or exciting anxiety. First, then, the physician has to reflect whether what is likely to be gained through quiet, pleasurable recreation while moving or resting in the fresh air of the mountain, is likely to be neutralized or worse through the fatigue, worry and excitement that will be suffered in the journey to and from it: and, second, he has to consider whether his patient can afford the cost of the excursion? The conclusions which, in course of time, will be reached in thousands of such cases, will be favorable or unfavorable to the chances of recovery or of rapid or prolonged and tedious convalescence, of the patient, according to the arrangements which you will determine to make. Considering what is practicable, I find two possible routes for ascending the mountain without going to the rear of it: one on the north and north-west side; the other on the north-east and east. The first is more inviting near the base, but in the upper half of it tolerable grades and curves, for a road of desirable breadth, can only be obtained at great expense and, the ground being valuable for another purpose, I am disposed to think, at least for years to come, it will be better to have but a single main approach road, and that on the east side.[1]

Here, from the top of the mountain as far down, at least, as the McTavish monument,[2] there is no extraordinary difficulty in the way of preparing a road, two rods wide, by which a carriage may be driven up or down at a steady, moderate trot, moving smoothly and quietly, while beautiful distant views are opening to the south and west through frames of foliage that shut out any discordant nearer objects. A satisfactory connection might be made, though with more difficulty, between the mountain road at the monument and the nearest streets of the city now in use. But the grades of these streets are so much steeper than those of the roads above need to be, that, whether in ascending or descending, horses would be brought to a walk, and in passing through them at those periods of the day when the park would be the most attractive and its influence most beneficial, all the annoyances and dangers of a blocked street would often be experienced.

Those who have given little consideration to the subject will probably think that Montreal will hardly ever supply such a stream of travel to the mountain as I seem to imagine. I will remark, therefore, that no experience of Montreal under existing circumstances will much aid a judgment of what will result from a perfection of proper arrangements for pleasure driving, as a few facts will indicate. For instance, since the opening of the park drives in New York,[3] the number of persons keeping private carriages is estimated to have increased fully tenfold; the number and value of public carriages adapted to pleasure driving having also, in the same period, increased at a rate far beyond that of population and wealth. In Brooklyn the number of private carriages was thought to have doubled in two years after the opening of the park.[4] A similar, though less marked experience, has been had in Buffalo, Chicago, and other American towns.[5] The value of a pleasure carriage is, in fact, found to have been unknown as long as its use was limited to ordinary streets and roads.

Montreal is a prosperous city and rapidly enlarging its borders; the number of people able to keep carriages will in time be much greater than at present; the number able to employ public carriages will increase even more rapidly. The views commanded from the Mountain — surpassing in expanse, beauty and variety those of any of the common resorts of tourists on the continent — will, when they can be enjoyed with such ease and comfort as it will be practicable for you to secure, add largely to the number of visitors staying in the city who will supply another element in the throng to be accommodated.

A reasonable consideration of these conditions and probabilities will satisfy you that if the future travel to the mountain is to be all or mainly directed into any one of the existing streets by which the vicinity of the McTavish monument is approached from the lower ground, it would be wholly inadequate to carry it except, in a way which would be extremely tedious, provoking and often alarming.

Here, then, the physician would hesitate because here a hundred yards of movement would be liable to cause more fatigue and undesirable excitement to the patient than a mile beyond.

Here, then, also, the difficulty of cost would be largely augmented for, to ascend a grade like that of Peel, or worse, of McTavish Street, two horses would be required to move a load such as one would take with equal ease above, and the rate of wear and tear not only of horses, but of harness, carriage and roadway, would be fully doubled.[6]

Under such an arrangement the dividends to be obtained from the capital you shall invest in all your park arrangements, will be seriously less than they will be if you make such other approaches as I trust to be practicable. What ought to be hoped for in respect to the cost of a drive will be evident from what is accomplished elsewhere. For instance, the ordinary charge for carriage hire in the streets of New York is nearly double what it is in Montreal, but the Park Commissioners of New York have had no difficulty in causing a dozen or more carriages to be provided, comfortable low-hung covered vehicles suitable for weakly persons in which passengers are taken at a rate of fare of four cents a mile for a course of five miles, or of five cents a mile for a course of 2½ miles. In Brooklyn and Philadelphia, the Park Commissioners have done still better than this and the difficulty of doing better in your case lies less in the topography of the mountain than in the way your city has thus far been laid out and built up.

My present object is rather to show what should be the line of study to be pursued in planning your proposed improvements than to offer you even a suggestion of a plan for them but, to illustrate what I should hope to be practicable in respect to the approaches below the mountain, I will say that it might be something like this: To extend the road which I have suggested would be led spirally down the mountain-side from the southward with a regular moderate descent along the rear of Sir Hugh Allan's grounds[7] and afterwards by a more devious course across the steep and broken slopes to the northward, until, in the rear of the Hotel Dieu,[8] existing streets are reached running with an easy grade, in one direction, to the heart of the city, in the other, skirting its present advanced building line parallel to and on the side opposite the river front. It might then be further extended in the latter direction in the form of a broad boulevard or park-way exclusively for the use of pleasure carriages, crossing all streets running from the river.

This being done, from whatever part of the city north of Victoria Square,[9] carriages should be started to go to the mountain, they would enter the park drive north of the steep foot-slopes and, until this drive was reached and they were disengaged from all other street traffic, they would nowhere be concentrated or add materially to the ordinary number of vehicles in any street, while the average time required for entering upon a smooth quiet road with no liability to street obstructions would be less than half as much as it would, if the park drive was first to be south of the reservoir.[10] For the accommodation of those living to the south of Victoria Square, special branch

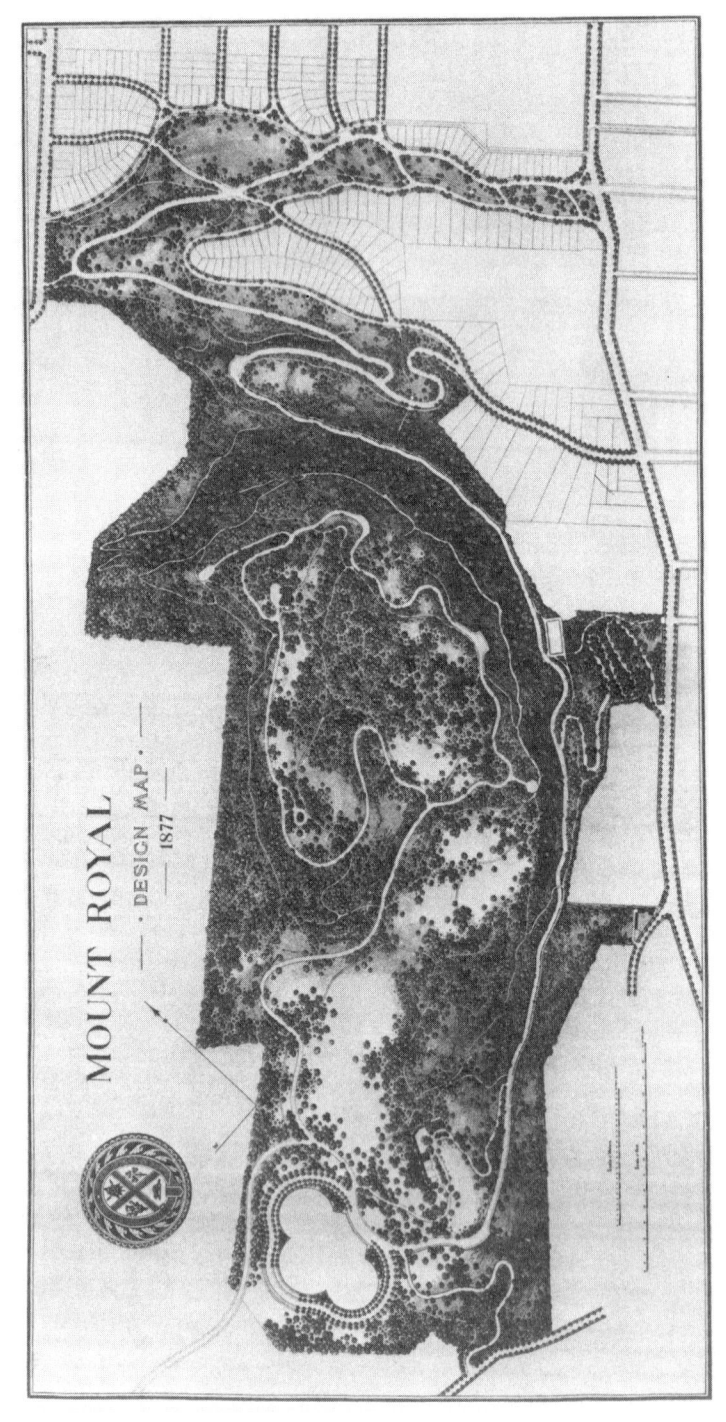

Olmsted's Plan of 1877 for Mount Royal

approaches to the same main approach would be required, one of which should be to the north of the Reservoir, another to the south of the McTavish monument. An additional sub-route of approach still further south is practicable through land not yet expensively improved, and two others from the Coté des Neiges road.[11] Foot approaches should closely follow the main carriage approach and its laterals, but it is desirable that there should also be one broad easy walk to the top of the mountain having attractions peculiar to itself, and several minor foot-paths scaling the crags more directly. Whenever street railways shall be laid to the foot of the mountain, an inclined lift or elevator will likewise be desirable to save feeble persons and young children the hard toil of its ascent.

Reverting to the matter of the general aspect of the scenery of the mountain, I would observe that the distant prospects in all directions, offer such controlling attractions that some of them, being commanded from nearly all parts of the ground, the immediate local landscape conditions are of much less consequence than they usually are in pleasure grounds, and that it is not undesirable that they should be subdued in character. Operations for their improvement should, therefore, not be ambitious, and should be intended, first, to relieve the surface of the mountain of the accidental and transient conditions through which it has at present an unnecessarily desolate and melancholy aspect; next, without destroying the essential picturesqueness of its natural features, to add a greater beauty of foliage; next, to hold attention in directions where the finest views will be seen to the best advantage and to furnish them with more harmonious and better composed foregrounds; next, to subordinate and, as far as may be practicable, obscure with suitable natural objects the constructions necessary to the convenient use of the ground (as these must in the end, be extensive and more or less too fine for harmony with its general character); and finally, to avoid in these and all respects an ordinary conventional gardening style of work, as finical, unseemly and out of character with the genius of the place.

I omit the observations made to you verbally in regard to the desirableness of a small park proper, in distinction from the larger mountain and forest district of your ground, because of the impossibility of doing justice to the subject without the advantage of demonstration on the site, or over a sufficient topographical map. I will merely observe that you have, in addition to the ground which I have thus far considered, a small area of a different character, and that it is fortunately situated to serve as a foil, through its natural amenity and the simple, quiet, secluded and pastoral character which can be given it, to the grandly local and rugged heights and declivities of the main body.[12]

Surveying the whole property with due regard for the considerations I have indicated; assuming that the treatment of the mountaintop shall be such as I have advised, and that some such arrangements as I have also suggested, shall be provided by which access to and ascent of the mountain shall be made as rapid, cheap, convenient and comfortable as is practicable, it will be seen that there is no reason to doubt that a public recreation ground can be formed within the limits of your property, which shall compare favorably as a means of health for the people who are to be invited to use it, with that of any other city of the world.

You are to be congratulated on the good judgment which has governed the selection of the parcels of land which you have had to purchase and in the good fortune which has allowed you to find so large an aggregate body of land on the immediate border of the city which could be acquired without change for costly improvements. Parts of some of the properties which you have obtained may, I think, be regarded as relatively unimportant for your purpose, and with a view to limit the cost of your undertaking, may be otherwise disposed of. There are yet also, on the boundaries of your ground, some small patches, of which, with a view to keeping under your control the best landscape effects, you should, if possible, obtain possession.[13] I cannot at present accurately define the bounds of these fragments but have no doubt that those which I think may be dispensed with, will exceed in market value those which I should recommend to be acquired.

I beg to express my obligations to Mr. MacQuisten, your city surveyor,[14] Mr. Smith, his deputy, and Mr. McGibbon your superintendent,[15] for their cheerful, zealous and valuable assistance in my examination of the ground.

I am, gentlemen,
your obedient servant,

FRED. LAW OLMSTED.

The text presented here is from the printed "Report of Fred. Law Olmsted on Mount Royal Park. 1874" in the Archives Municipales, Montreal, Canada. A draft of this report in Olmsted's hand is in the Olmsted Papers.

1. An approach road had already been planned for Mount Royal beginning at Peel Street before Olmsted agreed to lay out the park (see FLO to H. A. Nelson, Oct. 11, 1876, below).
2. The McTavish Monument is an obelisk marking the grave of Simon McTavish, who died in 1804. McTavish, a businessman, is credited with providing the foundation of Montreal's early commercial success (Charles W. Stokes, *Here and There in Montreal and the Island of Montreal* [Toronto, 1931], p. 49).
3. That is, the drives in Central Park.
4. That is, Prospect Park.
5. Olmsted and Calvert Vaux had prepared plans for the park system in Buffalo and for the South Park in Chicago (see *Papers of FLO*, SS1: 158–70, 206–35).
6. Peel and McTavish streets were located at the base of the mountain and paralleled each other. In arguing for an alternate approach road, Olmsted later wrote, "a pony, which would easily take a phæton with a lady and children to the top of the mountain,

if driven around by the way of Bleury Street, would be entirely unequal to taking the same load up such grades as those of Peel Street (1 in 7), or McTavish (1 in 9)" (Frederick Law Olmsted, *Mount Royal. Montreal*, 1881 [Papers of FLO, SS1: 402]).
7. Hugh Allan (1810–1882), a prominent Montreal businessman born in Scotland who was knighted in 1871. His estate "Ravenscrag" was located just east of the Crags (*Montreal from 1535 to 1914*, 3 vols. [Montreal, 1914], 3: 635–37; Edgar Andrew Collard, *Montreal: The Days that are No More* [Toronto, 1976], p. 264).
8. The Hotel-Dieu Hospital, originally built in 1644 near the St. Lawrence River, was moved in 1861 to a new location at the base of the mountain (Joseph Kearney Foran, *Jeanne Mance or "The Angel of the Colony"* . . . [Montreal, 1931], p. 57).
9. Victoria Square was in the old part of the city and slightly south of the line of Bleury Street, which Olmsted planned to make the entrance to the park (*Murray's Illustrated Guide and Pocket Business Directory to Montreal and Vicinity for 1892* [Montreal, 1892], p. 19; William D. Lighthall, *Sights and Shrines of Montreal* [Montreal, 1892], p. 33).
10. The McTavish Reservoir was located at the base of the mountain behind McGill College on McTavish Street.
11. Côte des Neiges Road began at Sherbrooke Street and ran close to the southern boundary of Mount Royal park.
12. Olmsted is referring to the flat, meadow land in the western section of the property of the estate of H. B. Smith, and which extended into the property of J. Tompkins adjoining it on the west. He drew up plans for an extensive meadow feature, which he intended to be the sole passage of pastoral scenery in the park, and which he proposed to encircle with a carriage drive. He wished to create a "truly park-like ground, broad, simple, quiet and of a rich sylvan and pastoral character, forming a harmonious, natural foreground to the view over the Western valley and all in striking contrast to the ruggedness of the mountain." The park commission did not acquire the Tompkins property and in July 1876 Olmsted acceded to the commission's instructions to plan for a reservoir in the section of the meadow area that was included in the park. Nonetheless, he retained his conception of the Glades section of the park as a pastoral interlude in the more rugged mountain scenery surrounding it and declared in his report of 1881 that "It can easily be made the finest spread of turf on the continent. But it will be best kept, when once well formed, with sheep and not with lawn-like smoothness" (FLO to H. A. Nelson, July 26, 1876, below; *Papers of FLO*, SS1: 386; "Contour Plan of Mount Royal Park, plan 609-30, NPS/FLONHS; plans 609-35, 609-36, and 609-48, NPS/FLONHS).
13. Olmsted tried without success to persuade the Mount Royal commissioners to purchase additional property along the park's southwestern boundary toward the Côte des Neiges Cemetery (FLO to W. J. Picton, Jan. 8, 1876, Archives Municipales de Montréal, Montreal, Quebec, Canada; ibid., March 18, 1876).
14. Patrick MacQuisten (1828–1877), city surveyor. Macquisten was born in Scotland and came to Montreal as a young man (Leona Bean McQuiston, comp., *The McQuiston, McCuiston and McQuesten Families, 1620–1937* [Louisville, Ky., 1937], p. 45; E. A. Collard, *Montreal*, p. 270).
15. William McGibbon, Mount Royal's first park superintendent, was appointed in 1874 and continued in that position for twenty-two years (*Gazette*, Montreal, Feb. 28, 1970, p. 1).

To Whitelaw Reid[1]

209 W 46th St. 26th Nov. 1874.

Dear Mr Reid;
    The length of this letter[2] requires an apology, first from me to you; then if you print it, from those you invite to read it.
    Consider, then, the importance the Capitol has as betokening and as tending to form and train the tastes of the nation, and the fact that the wisdom of destroying the old ground, was, before it was done, much questioned and excited a good deal of feeling. Besides these two considerations, I have had in mind this also, that few people seem even to imagine that designing grounds is a natural process of adapting means to ends — to a series of well considered and carefully ordinated ends — as much so as the planning of a ship or a factory or a newspaper, and that the same methods of design are not applicable to all kinds of grounds in all sorts of places. I have therefore given some slight suggestion of the true process toward the close of the letter.
    If it is too long have what you want taken out of it & made your own.
    I am just starting for Washington.[3]
    Yours Sincerely

Fred. Law Olmsted.

The text presented here is from a manuscript in Olmsted's hand in the Whitelaw Reid Papers, Manuscript Division, Library of Congress, Washington, D.C.

1. Whitelaw Reid (1837–1912), journalist and editor of the *New-York Daily Tribune*, supported Olmsted's work in the Department of Public Parks since the early 1870s. On November 17, 1874, the *New-York Times* published a detailed account of the Capitol grounds project by its Washington correspondent. Olmsted found the article misleading about important aspects of his plan and asked to write a response for the *Tribune*. The present letter to Reid accompanied the letter, printed below, which Olmsted returned for publication (*DAB*; *New-York Times*, Nov. 17, 1874, p. 3; FLO to Whitelaw Reid, June 25, 1872, Reid Papers, Library of Congress; ibid., Nov. 17, 1874; FLO, "The National Capitol," Dec. 5, 1874, below).
2. That is, the letter Olmsted enclosed on the Capitol grounds for publication printed below.
3. Olmsted visited Washington between November 26 and 29, 1874 (FLO, pay vouchers, Records Management Department, Architect of the Capitol, U.S. Capitol, Washington, D.C.; FLO to Edward Clark, Dec. 11, 1874, Office of the Curator, Architect of the Capitol, U.S. Capitol, Washington, D.C.).

New-York Daily Tribune, December 5, 1874

THE NATIONAL CAPITOL.

Mr. Fred. Law Olmsted on the
Improvements in Progress.

Characteristics of the Old Capitol Grounds — Details of
the Improvements — Due Allowance to be Made for
Architectural Effect — Progress of the Changes.

New York, Nov. 27, 1874.

To the Editor of the Tribune.
Sir:

    I cheerfully comply with your request[1] for the means of laying before your readers a more complete and detailed explanation than that supplied by the report of the Secretary of the Interior,[2] of the operations in progress on the ground east of the National Capitol. The need for it I presume to lie in the fact that, while much destruction is evident and a large force is at work, nothing is approaching completion, no improvement is found, and no intelligible plan can yet be recognized.

    The place was originally a flat table, slightly inclined toward the west, where a straight street, crossing it from north to south, formed the only approach for carriages to the Capitol from any direction.[3] East of this street there was a rectangular grass-plat bounded by straight walks; other trees appear to have been planted, at an early day, in imperfect rows alongside these walks, most of which died young. At various periods since then trees have been planted in and adjoining the first rows, some to take the place of those dying; some because of unwise haste to secure shade; some because they were of species newly arrived in the country and fashionable, and some with no intelligent purpose. A great number of rank upstarts were allowed to crowd and distort and starve the more permanent and valuable sort. The original thin soil had probably been worn out and washed away under colonial tobacco culture,[4] and left little but a sterile and exceedingly stiff brick clay, over which street-sweepings from the old dirt roads of Washington, with some Tiber mud,[5] have from time to time been laid. A careful forester's survey made this Summer indicated that the trees must have been generally taken from the woods, poorly lifted and poorly planted, and that their roots had rarely attempted to penetrate the clay but had sought food by running far and wide close to the surface. Three-fourths of them were in unsound condition, many far gone with decay, and the foliage of nearly all began to wilt after lacking rain but two weeks. With two exceptions the largest and best stood near the east boundary, their roots breaking out on a bank eight feet in hight formed by the recent grading down of First-st., which bank barred both approach and vision toward the Capitol. Shrubs and flower beds were dropped about here and there, many of the shrubs being of late sick or dead, and the flower beds overgrown by grass and weeds.

The Old Grounds Not in Harmony with the Capitol.

Looked at by itself, without reference to the Capitol; looked at in comparison with what is now to be seen in the early building stage of a designed improvement, or with any of the desert tracts which lie at short distances in all directions about it, it might be regarded as a beautiful place, and it tolerably served the purpose of a local playground for residents of the neighborhood.[6] Its devastation could not therefore be projected without some pathetic feeling, nor without giving occasion for honest, earnest, and rational remonstrance. The beauty of the trees and old associations connected with them have been feelingly described, and it has been urged that once removed they could not be replaced in fifty years.[7]

On the other hand, it was to be said that the Capitol could not be replaced at a cost of less that than $20,000,000, of which sum but a small part represents the body of conveniences provided for the transaction of the business of Congress, the remainder and larger part standing for the means of a suitably dignified, beautiful, and imposing effect in the vestment of these conveniences; that the ground, as it was, contributed not in the slightest degree to the conveniences for business of the Capitol, while, because of the inclination of the surface toward the building and the position of the trees, not half its due architectural effect could be enjoyed; that scarcely one of the larger trees had 50 or even 20 years' life in it; and the Capitol, being a permanent and monumental structure, the ground about it should be managed with reference not merely to present but to future effect.

The Old Park Swept Away.

This view has prevailed, and the old park has accordingly been swept away. Congress, at the close of its last session, having provided means for the purpose, the work began under contract on the 17th of August, since when there has been not yet quite time, with all the men who could be employed economically, to accomplish the grading, the amount of earth to be removed being about 150,000 cubic yards. Other operations seen in progress on ground where the grading is complete are the tillage and tempering of the newly exposed subsoil to the depth of two feet; the return to it of the old soil with additions to the depth of a foot; the taking up of the old sewer, drainage, water, and

"General Plan for the Improvement of the U.S. Capitol Grounds"
Drawn by Thomas Wisedell during the fall of 1874 and presented to Congress in early 1875.

gas pipes, and the laying of new and much better and more elaborate systems of each; the transplanting of some of the more thrifty of the old trees which have been preserved, to new places; and some laying of curb, gutters, gratings, and road and walk foundations, with a little pavement. These operations have seemed detached and purposeless because divided by those of grading, but the missing links are expected to be for the most part inserted before Winter stops work, when the plan will be more intelligible.[8]

Main Purpose of the Design.

The general design is very simple, and will be easily understood. It has two purposes: First, to provide convenient approaches to and standing room about the Capitol; second, to allow its imposing dimensions and the beauty of its architecture to have due effect, and so far as possible, to aid and highten that effect.

The idea of a park, flower-garden and play-ground is discarded, and the whole meager area of the little lot in which the Capitol is placed is to be treated as a court-yard and dependency of the building. A paved carriage-court is to extend all along its east front, giving access to each door. Walks and carriage-ways are to be formed between it and each of the fifteen streets leading from all sides toward the Capitol; the course of these approaches, with one exception,[9] will be curved, but each curve is to be governed by reference to a purpose of convenience. Where two purposes of convenience come in competition, that one is to be allowed the advantage by yielding to which greater breadth for turf surface will be gained; and by humoring this secondary purpose as much as possible, without an essential sacrifice of convenience on the whole, two elliptical spaces are to be obtained, measuring each from 400 to 600 feet across, in which a field of slightly undulating surface may be formed, unbroken, except by a few groups of trees.

Subordination of the Grounds to the Building.

As the trees to be planted grow, the larger part of the road and walk space will be shaded, but the object of happy compositions of the foliage with the Capitol, and of pleasant views from important points of the Capitol is not to be sacrificed to the object of making its court-yard, in all its parts and in all seasons, a perfectly comfortable lounging place or exercise ground.

The same principle of subordination to the building will prevent the introduction in any part of the ground of local ornaments, whether in flowers, leaf-plants, or other objects simply curious or beautiful in themselves. Those matters only will be decorated which by their position and form carry out, repeat, and support the architectural design, nor will any decoration be such as to hold the eye of an observer when in a position to take a general view of the Capitol.

VIEW OF U.S. CAPITOL SHOWING PARAPET AND CURVED BLUESTONE SEAT
ON EDGE OF PLAZA ON EAST GROUNDS

    The carriage-court will be bounded opposite the building by a walk or esplanade, laid with colored tile, and this will be separated from the broad turf spaces beyond it by a structure combining the purposes of a parapet or barrier, and a seat, so curved in plan, that unobstructed views of the Capitol may be obtained from it at various distances from 100 to 300 feet from the nearest point of its front, and at every practicable angle of vision. The parapet is to be formed of blue and red stone, and is to be also divided by piers, supporting bronze gas-posts. This work is under contract, and, if the weather is favorable, sections of it are expected to be complete before Congress meets.[10]

                FURTHER PLANS IN PROGRESS.

    The roads are designed to be of concrete, but only the base of gravel will be laid this year.
    Other details can hardly be explained without drawings, and what has been said will sufficiently indicate the general intention.
    No work has been done on the ground west of the Capitol, except in the deposit for storage of material taken from the east side. Designs for important improvements are, however, advanced, and are soon to be submitted to the Committee of Congress.[11] Your obedient servant,

                              FRED. LAW OLMSTED

The text presented here is from the *New-York Daily Tribune*, December 5, 1874, page 2.

1. Olmsted had told Reid in late October that he would write a piece on the Capitol grounds for his newspaper. He renewed the offer when the *New-York Times* article appeared on November 17 and returned the present letter just over a week later (Vincenzo Botta to FLO, Oct. 27, 1874; FLO to Whitelaw Reid, Nov. 17, [1874], Reid Papers, Library of Congress).
2. The annual report of the Architect of the Capitol, which in 1874 included a memoranda on the grounds by Olmsted, was printed as part of the annual report of the Secretary of the Interior (*Annual Report of the Architect of the Capitol* [1874], pp. 733–37).
3. This street was immediately adjacent to the east front of the Capitol, and connected with New Jersey Avenue on the south and Delaware Avenue on the north ("The Grounds of the Capitol," *Magazine of Horticulture* 8 [April 1842], pp. 127–28; [Glenn Brown], *Documentary History of the Construction and Development of the United States Capitol Building and Grounds* [Washington, D.C., 1904], pp. 1072–73; W. H. Morrison, *Morrison's Stranger's Guide for Washington City* [Washington, D.C., 1875], frontispiece map).
4. The land that eventually became the site of the Capitol was part of the properties granted by Lord Baltimore to his favorites in the mid-seventeenth century. Over the next century and a half large tobacco plantations owned by a few wealthy families and cultivated by slaves covered the area. When Olmsted visited Washington, D.C., in late 1852, tobacco was still the staple crop of outlying farms. These farms, he noted, were "cultivated most miserably on the same system as has long prevailed in the tobacco districts of the Middle States" (Wilhelmus B. Bryan, *A History of the National Capital*, 2 vols. [New York, 1914–1916],1: 49–56; Margaret Brent Downing, "The Earliest Proprietors of Capitol Hill," *Records of the Columbia Historical Society* 21 [1918]: 18–20; The Junior League of Washington, *The City of Washington: An Illustrated History*, ed. Thomas Froncek [New York, 1977], pp. 60–63; *Papers of FLO*, 2: 86).
5. That is, sewage muck taken from nearby Tiber Creek, which emptied into the Washington City canal just west of the Capitol.
6. Besides being a seasonal residence for members of Congress, Capitol Hill in the mid-1870s was home to government clerks, retailers serving Congress, and hundreds of skilled and unskilled workers employed at the U.S. Navy Yard at 8th and M streets. The east Capitol grounds served as the neighborhood park of these nearby residents. In the autumn of 1874 popular weekly band concerts and croquet games there had to be curtailed when tree removal and grading got underway (*Washington Daily Chronicle*, Sept. 3, 1874, p. 8; *The Sunday Herald*, Aug. 2, 1874, p. 4; Ruth Ann Overbeck, "Capitol Hill," in *Washington at Home: An Illustrated History of Neighborhoods in the Nation's Capital*, ed. Kathryn Schneider Smith [Washington, D.C., 1988], pp. 31–39).
7. For years the grading of the east Capitol grounds was opposed because it was thought the work would destroy the trees. When plans went forward in 1874, people expressed regret and proposed that certain of the trees be saved. In January, Senator Charles Sumner of Massachusetts extolled the beauty of a beech tree visible to the east of the Senate wing. "When it is clothed in all its foliage during the summer I know of nothing in the District of Columbia that is equal to it in beauty." Sumner died a few weeks after making these remarks and the tree, dubbed "the Sumner Beech," was spared. Another tree with important associations was a large elm located nearby, reportedly planted by George Washington. Although injured by neglect and poor pruning and recommended for removal by Justin S. Morrill, Edward Clark, and others, Olmsted requested the tree be saved. In 1882 he predicted that "it may yet outlive several generations of men." The tree survived until 1948 (G. Brown, *Documentary History of the United States Capitol*, pp. 1154–55; *Washington Evening Star*, Nov. 21, 1874, p. 5; *Washington Daily Chronicle*, Dec. 10, 1874, p. 7; Frederick H. Cobb to FLO, Nov.

4,1876; ibid., Nov. 18, 1876; ibid., Dec. 9, 1876; Oliver C. Bullard to FLO, Nov. 5, 1874, B134: #2820, OAR/LC; FLO to Edward Clark, [Nov. 6, 1874], draft of telegram, in D2, OAR/LC; [Frederick Law Olmsted,] "Index to Trees About the Capitol, with Advice to Visitors Interested in Them," in *Annual Report of the Architect of the Capitol* [1882], appendix, p. 14; *Washington Star*, May 13, 1948, p. B-1).
8. One week after writing this account, Olmsted reported to Reid that "the work has advanced so rapidly since that the design is much more obvious on the ground." A writer in the *Washington Daily Chronicle* noted that "the sidewalks of the broad avenue through the grounds to East Capitol street have been laid far enough to show how they will look, bordered by ornamental lamps" (FLO to Whitelaw Reid, Dec. 2 [1874], Reid Papers, Library of Congress; *Washington Daily Chronicle*, Dec. 10, 1874, p. 7).
9. The one exception to the curved drives was the formal avenue leading into the grounds from East Capitol Street. Olmsted introduced this change shortly after his preliminary report of June 9, 1874, which accounts also for the increase in his count of streets adjoining the grounds from fourteen to fifteen (FLO to Justin S. Morrill and James Henry Platt, Jr., June 9, 1874, n. 3, above).
10. In early October, Edward Clark signed a contract with the Bigelow Blue Stone Company of New York City for the stonework of the esplanade. The firm delivered stone to the Capitol grounds in late November but did not provide adequate markings with which to match the individual pieces before the second session of the forty-third Congress convened on December 7. Most of the esplanade was completed by the autumn of 1875 (article of agreement between Edward Clark and Bigelow Blue Stone Company, October 8, 1874, B134: #2820, OAR/LC; John A. Partridge to FLO, Nov. 26, 1874; *Annual Report of the Architect of the Capitol* [1875], p. 885).
11. Olmsted's preliminary report to the House and Senate committees on public buildings and grounds, submitted June 9, 1874, proposed an architectural terrace flanked by grand stairways on the central west front of the Capitol. He presented a revised proposal and drawings to the Senate Committee on Public Buildings and Grounds in early January 1875 (FLO to Justin S. Morrill and James Henry Platt, Jr., June 9, 1874, above; FLO to Montgomery C. Meigs, Jan. 15, 1875, below).

To the Buffalo Park Commission[1]

Buffalo, December 15, 1874.

To the Honorable the Park Commission of the City of Buffalo:
Gentlemen:
   I herewith present you a plan for the improvement of Niagara Square. In designing it, I have had in view the fact, that Niagara Square is the central feature of the plan of your city, and that broad streets approach and cross it from eight directions.[2] It is first of all a place of thoroughfare, and, in my judgment, nothing should be done which will seriously injure its character in this respect. For this reason I cannot approve the suggestion which has been urged upon me, and which I understand has been favorably entertained by many, of appropriating the greater part of its limited area to a public garden.

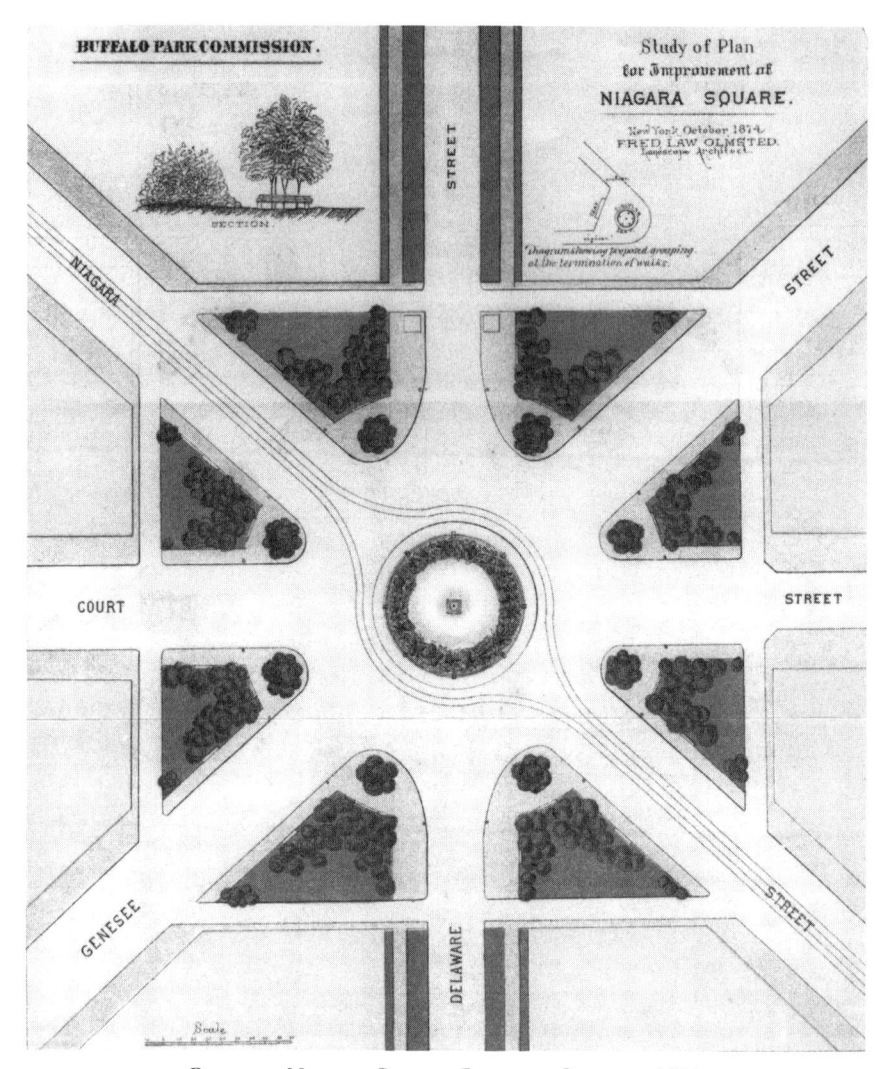

PLAN FOR NIAGARA SQUARE, BUFFALO, OCTOBER 1874

    Maintaining the present thoroughfares at their full breadth and on the same general plan as at present, eight triangles remain, the parts of which nearest the center of the Square are too narrow to be of any value. If they are reduced materially in depth the central space would be very large and need some effective decoration, neither breaking the view nor obliging travel to deviate abruptly or to an inconvenient distance from any of its present courses. For this purpose nothing would be better than a circular fountain basin at the center of the Square, provided convenience will allow it to be made large enough to appear suitable to a situation of so much importance, and in which it must be seen without support from adjoining objects.

This idea has been adopted in the plan: The fountain basin being made one hundred feet in diameter and designed to require as moderate a cost for construction as possible; its circumference being a low coping and rail; its center a body of spray without expensive masonry and a large part of the effect to be obtained by a belt near the circumference, of water plants; the design being similar to that of the new fountain in Union Square, New York, but larger in scale.[3] A wheel-way is then allowed around the fountain nowhere less than sixty feet in breadth.

The general plan of the remaining outer parts of the Square will be readily understood on examination of the drawing. The present trees of the Square so far as valuable are proposed to be utilized and others added so as to form effective groups which are to stand in turf plats. Seats are to be placed about and under the trees, the backs of which connected by railings will protect the turf and trees from injury.

My opinion has been asked as to several points under discussion in regard to a memorial of the late war.

There is a certain advantage to be gained by placing a memorial object in the midst of the city, rather than in its suburbs, which will fully justify the Commission in changing its original plan of assigning the Soldiers' Place to the proposed monument, if it is desired by those who have the matter in charge. A suggestion as to the form of the Memorial has been presented in a drawing of an arch.[4]

I think the design a very original and very noble one, and that it might be adopted with unusual confidence of an imposing and satisfactory result.

I should recommend that it be placed as indicated in the drawing on one side of the Square and so as to span one of the wheel-ways leading out of it. In this position it would be seen in its best aspect by all crossing the Square, and equally well from nearly all parts of it. Placed in the center, its principal front would be seen satisfactorily from only about a third part of the Square. There are several reasons why the position indicated on the north side of the Square, spanning Delaware street, is to be preferred to any other. The best light will then fall upon it; its inscriptions will therefore be more legible and its sculpture will have the best effect. The two spaces on which the largest number of visitors can stand on the Square, without disturbance by carriages, will be opposite to it, and at the best distance for viewing it comprehensively. The carriage-way is narrower than any other, and the arch could here be built at less cost. Its piers would stand, as shown, on ground at present intermediate between the wheel-way and the walks.

It is to be presumed that the private rights now held in the borders of Delaware street will at some time be extinguished, the trees and walks in them be arranged on an uniform system, and that it will in all respects be treated and used as a public promenade and approach road from the center of the city

H. H. Richardson's Proposed Civil War Memorial for Niagara Square, Buffalo, c. December 1874

to the Main Park, as was intended and expected when the park system was designed.[5] To such an approach and promenade the arch, placed as proposed, would form a fitting and noble entrance.

I recommend that, in case the Memorial Association should be willing to adopt a design of the character of that under consideration and to undertake its construction, the Commission offer to assign the site indicated on the plan (*aa*) and to lay suitable and sufficient foundations for it.

Respectfully,

Fred. Law Olmsted

The text presented here is from the *Fifth Annual Report of the Buffalo Park Commissioners. January 1875* (Buffalo, N.Y., 1875), pages 13–16.

1. The Buffalo Park Commission, created in 1869, was composed of sixteen leading citizens of the city who were responsible for the selection, location, and oversight of public spaces and approach roads in Buffalo (New York [State], *Laws of the State of New York, Passed at the Ninety-Second Session of the Legislature* . . . [Albany, N.Y., 1869], chap. 165).
2. Niagara Square was the center of Joseph Ellicott's 1804 plan for Buffalo. Located near Lake Erie, the square was bisected by four major thoroughfares: Delaware, Genesee, Court, and Niagara streets (Francis R. Kowsky, "Municipal Parks and City Planning: Frederick Law Olmsted's Buffalo Park and Parkway System," *Journal of the Society of Architectural Historians* 46 [March 1987]: 61–62).
3. A new fountain had been constructed during the past year in Union Square, Manhattan, according to changes proposed for the square by Olmsted and Vaux in 1872. The fountain and basin proposed by Olmsted for Niagara Square in Buffalo was sixty-five feet in diameter (Olmsted & Vaux, Landscape Architects to Henry G. Stebbins, March 13, 1872 [*Papers of FLO*, 6: 531–35]; Frederick Law Olmsted, "Memorandum of Proposed Works," June 21, 1873, Document No. 44, p. 15, in DPP, *Minutes*, June 23, 1873, p. 15).
4. Soldiers Place is a circle at the intersection of the three parkways—Bidwell, Chapin, and Lincoln—designed by Olmsted and Vaux for an approach to the western end of Delaware Park. The Ladies Union Monument Association of Buffalo, formed in 1874, had requested permission to erect a Civil War monument in Niagara Square and had engaged H. H. Richardson to create a design. In December 1874 Richardson forwarded drawings that Olmsted presented to the park commission on December 15, along with his plan for Niagara Square. The commission approved Olmsted's plan and the location of the memorial arch, but sufficient funds were not secured to make possible construction of the arch (James O'Gorman, *H. H. Richardson and His Office* [Cambridge, Mass., 1974], p. 188).
5. By the 1870s Delaware Street had become a primary residential street, and Olmsted and Calvert Vaux had incorporated it into their plan for the Buffalo park system as an approach road from the center of the city to Delaware Park (Francis R. Kowsky, "Delaware Avenue, Buffalo, New York," in *The Grand American Avenue: 1850–1920*, eds. Jan Cigliano and Sarah Bradford Landau [San Francisco, 1994], pp. 35–55).

To Montgomery Cunningham Meigs

New York, 15th January 1875.

Major General M. C. Meigs;
Dear Sir;

  I have received your favor of the 13th and thank you for your expression of interest in and kind consideration of the plan I have submitted to the Committees of Congress.[1]

  My duty has been with the grounds of the Capitol and I have avoided approaching the province of the architect further than was necessary to the presentation of the proposition of the terrace and stairways. As to the building

View of West Front of U.S. Capitol from southwest showing existing condition with earth terraces (1875)

View of West Front of U.S. Capitol from southwest showing terraces proposed by Olmsted (1875)

proper, I obtained drawings from Mr Clark representing a plan which I assumed to have been provisionally adopted and to this my plans have been strictly accommodated.[2] I stated to him as well as to Senator Morrill and to Senator Howe that, among the various propositions which (after forming my plans) I found under discussion in regard to the projection of the central porticos, I regarded that as the best by which they would be advanced the least, and that, as to the West portico, I thought that a reduction from the assumed projection of 40 feet beyond the line of the present wall would be better than any addition to it.[3]

In regard to your inquiry whether the wide terrace which I propose will not dwarf and conceal the Capitol, I must ask you to consider the question with the perspective drawing before you. To gain the advantage of the terrace without serious disadvantage in that respect has been the chief problem of my design. I think that with the aid of Mr Clark and of my architectural assistant, Mr Wisedell, I have fairly solved it.[4]

Before preparing the plan I experimented with a temporary staging and satisfied myself as to the line of elevation for the terrace at which the building would not suffer, assuming the terrace wall to be of marble and its parapet to be fully as open as that on the roof.

To place it low enough, an expedient was necessary that is not shown in the drawings exhibited though you may trace it on the plan of the grounds. It is that of dividing the terrace floor into two stages, the outer one being four feet below that against the walls of the Capitol. The top of the marble parapet is thus kept five feet below the lower course of marble of the building and it will be only on closely approaching it that any part of the building will be hidden.

I think that there is no point of view in which an observer can be expected to place himself (if my plan is adhered to) at which the Capitol will not appear more stately with the terrace than without.[5]

Very Truly Yours,

Fred Law Olmsted.

The text presented here is from a document in a clerk's hand with the closing and signature by Olmsted, in Record Group 92, Records of the Quartermaster General's Office, entry 294, General and Miscellaneous Letters Received, 1875, National Archives and Records Administration, Washington, D.C.

1. Olmsted visited Washington the second week of January 1875 to present his revised plan for the U.S. Capitol grounds to the Senate Committee on Public Buildings and Grounds. It included important changes introduced since the previous summer, and was illustrated by a general plan of the grounds and two perspectives of the Capitol from the southwest. One showed the building with the existing stairways and earthen embankments at its base; the second substituted grand double staircases ascending to an architectural terrace which extended around the west, north, and south fronts. Both

AUGUST 1874–JANUARY 1875

the plan and the perspectives included Thomas U. Walter's 1874 proposed extension of the west central portico of the building, intended to give added space to the Library of Congress.

    In the 1850s Montgomery Meigs had supervised the construction of the new wings and dome of the Capitol according to Thomas Walter's plans; he retained an interest in the building for the rest of his life. He had written Olmsted commending his design for the Capitol grounds and terrace but objecting to the extension of the building's central west portico that Olmsted's plan contained. He also expressed concern that the added width and height of the terrace would, "from all the western park, dwarf & conceal the Capitol" (FLO to Committees on Public Buildings and Grounds, Jan. 5, 1875, Office of the Curator, Architect of the Capitol, U.S. Capitol, Washington, D.C.; *Washington Evening Star*, Jan. 5, 1875, p. 1; ibid., Jan. 6, 1875, p. 1; *Washington Daily Chronicle*, Jan. 7, 1875, p. 8; Glenn Brown, *History of the United States Capitol*, 2 vols. [Washington, D.C., 1902], 2:166–69; Montgomery C. Meigs to FLO, Jan. 13, 1875, B134: #2820, OAR/LC; see also, Montgomery C. Meigs to Justin S. Morrill, Jan. 11, 1875, B134: #2820, OAR/LC; Charles C. McLaughlin, "The Capitol in Peril? The West Front Controversy from Walter to Stewart," *Records of the Columbia Historical Society*, 69–70 [1971]: 237–65).

2. In June 1874 Edward Clark had sent Olmsted a sketch of the west front of the building showing the extension of the portico, noting that this would require breaking up the old Bulfinch terrace (Edward Clark to FLO, June 12, 1874, in D2, OAR/LC).

3. Walter's proposal also contemplated an extension of the east central portico. During his Washington visit in early January and in correspondence the next week, Olmsted told Clark, Morrill, and Senator Timothy O. Howe, chairman of the joint committee on the Library of Congress, that a projection of the west central portico of forty feet or more "would be ruinous to the plan of a direct staircase approach to it from the ground below" (Thomas U. Walter to Timothy O. Howe, Oct. 30, 1874, Records of the U.S. Senate, Record Group 46, Committee on Public Buildings and Grounds, SEN43A–E17, NARA, Washington, D.C.; FLO to Justin S. Morrill, Jan. 12, 1875, Morrill Papers, Library of Congress; ibid., Jan. 14, 1875; Justin S. Morrill to FLO, Jan. 12, 1875, B134: #2820, OAR/LC; FLO to Edward Clark, [c. Jan. 15, 1875], B134: #2820, OAR/LC).

4. In mid-July 1874 Olmsted spent a week in Washington with Thomas Wisedell working on plans and drawings for the terrace. Wisedell finished several studies and perspectives by mid-August and completed a colored plan of the Capitol grounds in late September. Olmsted gained approval for his plan from Morrill, Clark, O. E. Babcock and others on September 28 (FLO to Justin S. Morrill, July 16, 1874; FLO to Thomas Wisedell, Aug. 12, 1874; ibid., Sept. 24, 1874; FLO and Thomas Wisedell, pay vouchers, Records Management Department, Architect of the Capitol; *Washington Daily Chronicle*, Sept. 29, 1874, p. 8).

5. The Senate Committee on Public Buildings and Grounds unanimously recommended Olmsted's plan for the terrace to Congress, which approved the entire plan of the grounds on March 3, 1875. The same day Morrill tried to attach an amendment to the sundry civil appropriation bill to provide $300,000 to fund construction of the terrace, but the amendment was defeated. Despite subsequent attempts by Morrill, money was not appropriated or work begun on the terrace until the early 1880s (G. Brown, *Documentary History of the United States Capitol*, pp. 1161, 1201–27; Justin S. Morrill to FLO, March 9, 1875, B134: #2820, OAR/LC).

To Henry G. Stebbins

Department of Public Parks,
Office of Design and Superintendence,
New York, 15th January, 1875.

To the Hon. Henry G. Stebbins,
President of the Board:
Sir,—

I have the honor to present a map of the Riverside territory belonging to the city, with the main outlines of a plan for its improvement.

What I have designated as the Riverside *territory* consists of two divisions: first, a strip uniformly 100 feet wide along its eastern side, named Riverside Avenue, and originally intended to be treated as other avenues of the city; second, a body of land of variable breadth named Riverside Park.[1]

Nearly all of the ground on both of these parts of the territory slopes with a rapid inclination to the west, so much so that the originally proposed avenue would require to be supported on the lower side by a strong retaining wall, generally not less than twenty feet in height.

The avenue (as laid out in 1868)[2] has a very crooked course, as is shown by the following line, representing a part of it equal in length to that part of Broadway south of Canal street.

Its variations of grade are also frequent, a change between ascent and descent occurring thirteen times, as represented by the following line (200 feet vertical; 4,000, horizontal, to one inch).

Many of the grades are severe, there being nine sharper than one in twenty, and on which trotting would be impracticable.

On each side of this avenue there is to be, at an average distance of less than two hundred yards, another avenue, straight in course, of better grades and equally wide.[3] These others would amply provide for through and heavy travel, and the breadth of 100 feet on Riverside Avenue, as originally designed, is therefore only required on the presumption that it will be used for the same purpose as the Park—that is to say, as a pleasure resort.

The advantage of the Riverside territory for this purpose lies in its command of views over the Hudson, which at several points are of great interest, and in its airiness.

This advantage is least, and will eventually be wholly lost, on its lower or westerly side, and is greatest, and will alone be of permanent value to the city, on its higher parts—that is to say: 1st, that part originally assigned to the avenue, and 2d, that part originally assigned to the park which, if the avenue should be built, would be close under its supporting wall (a, in the diagram).

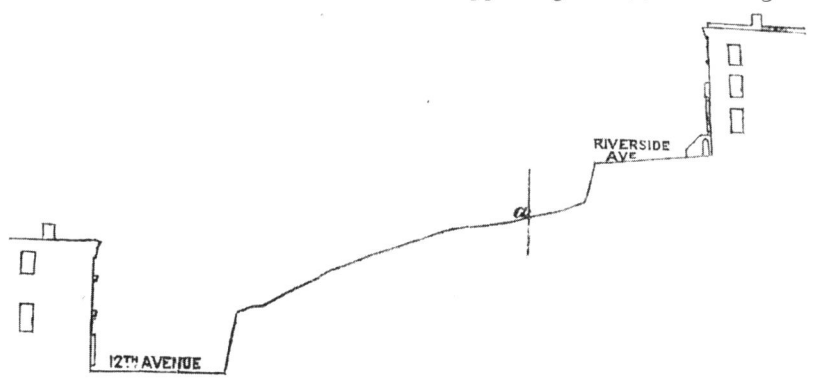

This part of the park, inclined as it would be to the west, with a wall of masonry on the east, would, when it might otherwise be most agreeable, be found insupportably hot, unless planted with large trees.

Trees upon it would, however, completely intercept the view over it from the avenue as originally planned.

This view being cut off, the avenue, with its steep grades and frequent undulations, would be the least attractive of all the avenues of the city for pleasure driving.

For this reason the Department was advised, in 1873,[4] that the imaginary line by which the site for the avenue was divided from the site for the park should be disregarded, and a plan prepared, with a view to utilize, in the greatest degree practicable, the advantages offered by the territory, as a whole, for the several purposes—first, of a means of access to the property on its east side; second, of a pleasure drive, commanding a fine view over the river, airy and shaded; third, of a foot promenade, commanding the same view, and also airy and shaded.

This proposition, after full consideration, received the unanimous approval of the Park Commissioners; it has since, also after cautious consideration, received that of all their successors; of the Commissioner of Public Works;[5] of all citizens interested, who have accepted the invitation of the Commissioners to examine the matter; of the Legislature of 1873, which passed a bill based upon it; and of the Senate Committee on Cities, of 1874, which recommended a bill intended to provide for it,[6] which failed to pass solely because of a question which arose under it as to the division of duties between the Departments of Parks and of Public Works.

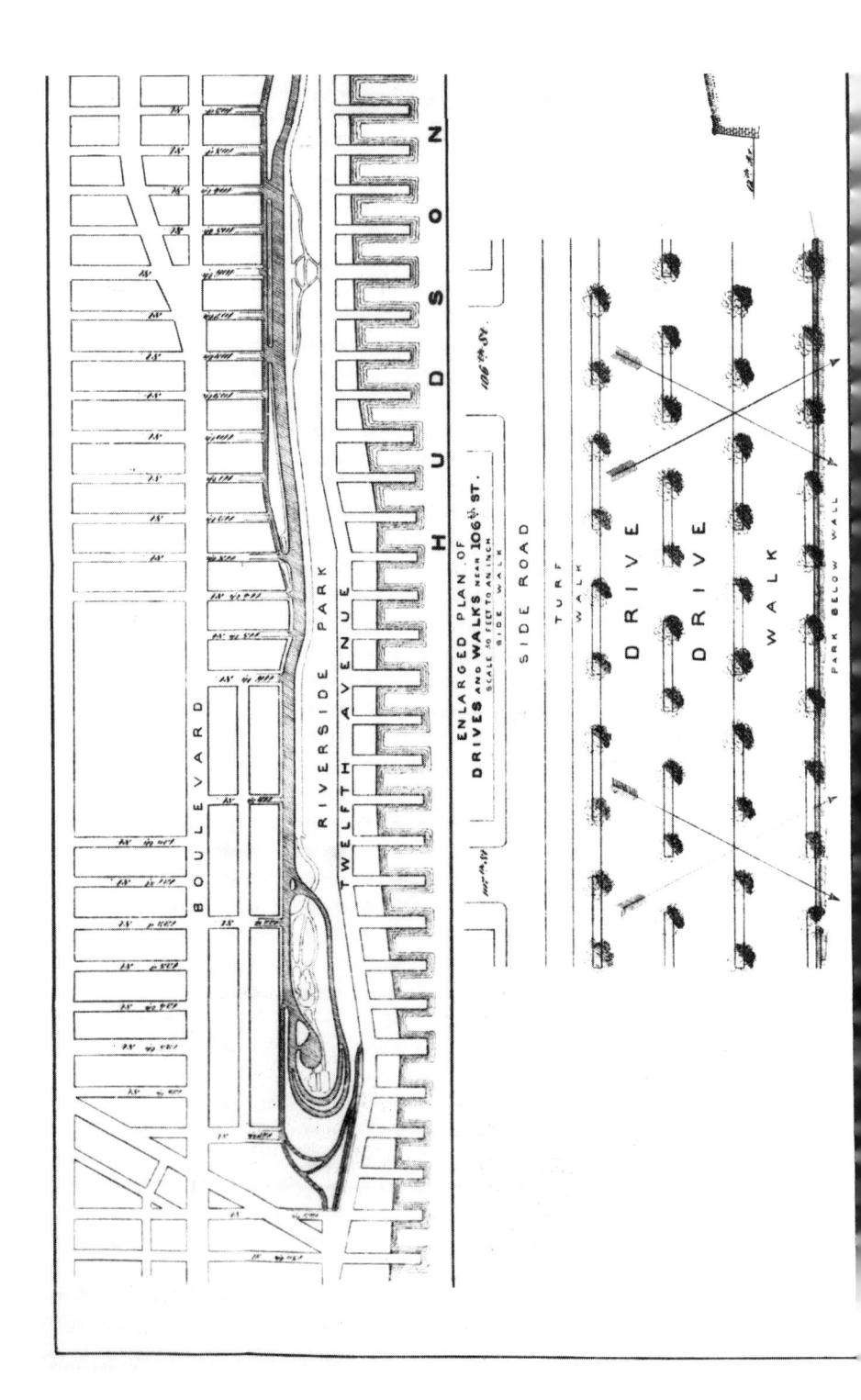

ENLARGED PLAN OF DRIVES AND WALKS NEAR 106th ST.
SCALE 40 FEET TO AN INCH

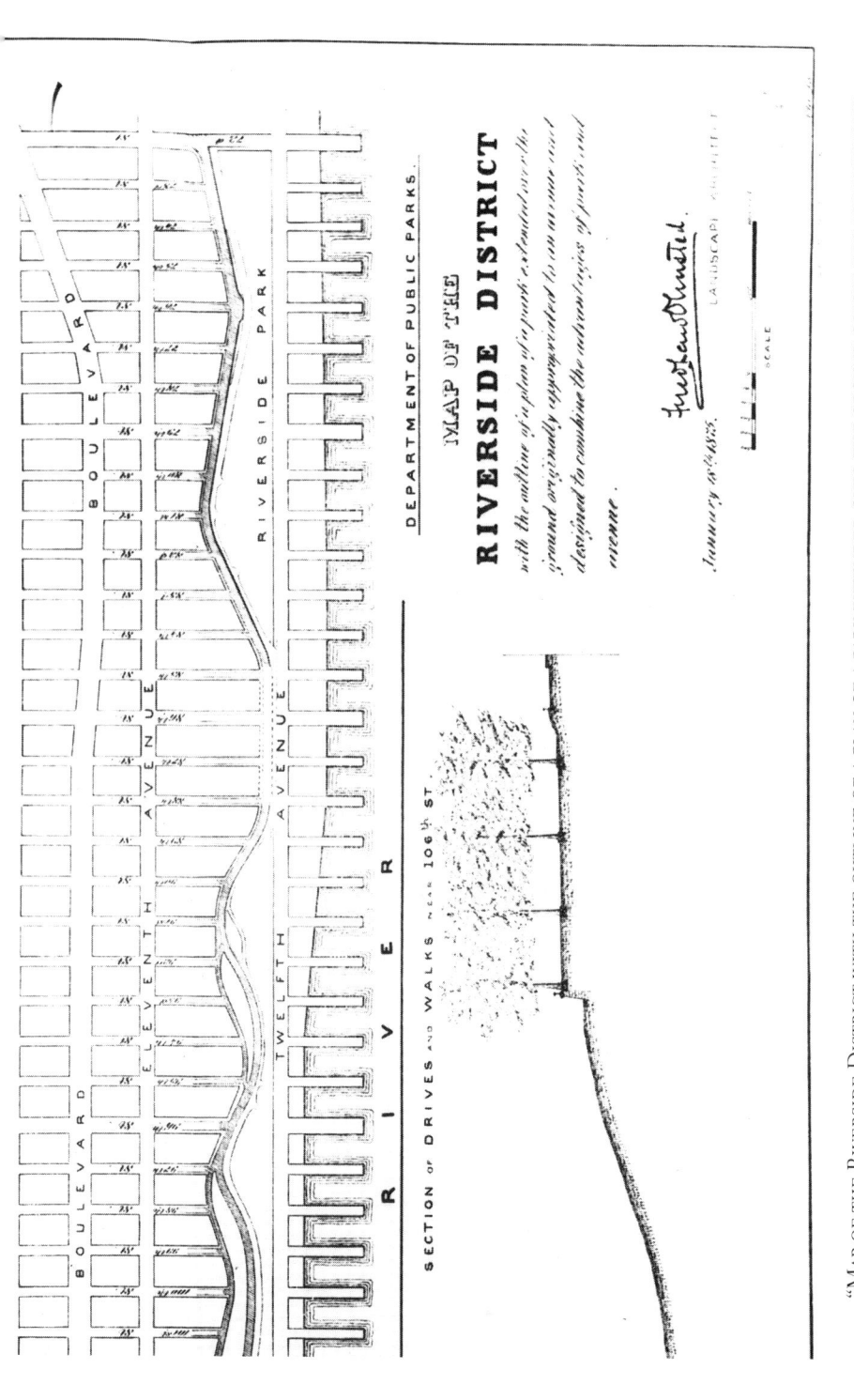

"Map of the Riverside District with the outline of a plan of a park extended over the ground originally appropriated to an avenue and designed to combine the advantages of park and avenue," January 18, 1875

The plan of which an outline is given in the accompanying map is prepared in accordance with the proposition which has been stated; that is to say, it is a plan for a combination of the avenue with the park. Comparing such a plan with one for a separate improvement of the two parts of the territory as originally intended, the general aim being as nearly as possible the same in both cases, the advantages which would be had under the combination plan, may be partly and moderately stated as follows:

1st. It would be less costly.

2d. The carriage way would, at all the more important points, command the view over the river, and would generally command better views; would be better shaded; would be breezier and cooler; would conveniently accommodate a much larger number of carriages, and would have much better grades. (See appended note, p. 9.)

3d. The accommodation for people on foot would be ampler; would have better views; would be better shaded; would have better grades, and would be more cheaply and efficiently policed.

In short the cost of the property under the new plan will be less than under the old, while its value to the city will be immeasurably greater.

There is a part of the Riverside territory to which the above observations do not apply, the park as originally arranged under the act of 1867,[7] not being continuous from the north to the south end, but the whole breadth from Eighty-fifth to Eighty-eighth streets being assigned to the avenue, the west line of which was made to coincide with the east line of Twelfth avenue, but with a difference of elevation of 65 feet.

A plan for dealing with this district has been prepared, under instructions from the Department of Public Works, by Mr. Leopold Eidlitz,[8] drawings of which, by favor of the designer, I am permitted herewith to present. It is proposed by this plan that instead of filling up with earth the great space over which the avenue would need to be constructed, it should be utilized as a building suitable for a market or other public purpose, the walls of which would thus have at this point the character of a terrace, commanding fine views of the river.[9]

It is not necessary that this plan should be carried out at present, but it has been thought best in designing the adjoining ground to keep it in view, and the dotted lines on the map imperfectly show how by means of it, the two parts of the general walk and drive system which has been described would be connected.

Respectfully,

FRED. LAW OLMSTED,
Landscape Architect.

AUGUST 1874–JANUARY 1875

NOTE AS TO GRADES.

On the Central Park it is found that the majority of horses are walked wherever the grade of the drives is steeper than 1 in 26. On the new Riverside plan, from Seventy-second to One hundred and twenty-seventh Streets (3 miles), there is no grade steeper than 1 in 28. More than an eighth part of that distance, on the old plan of the avenue, is on grades steeper than 1 in 20. On the descent from One hundred and twenty-seventh Street to Twelfth Avenue, the new plan offers a road with a grade of 1 in 20; the only road in the old is steeper than 1 in 10. By the following diagrams the differences of grade between the points indicated will be evident, the full line showing the old, the dotted line, and the new grades.

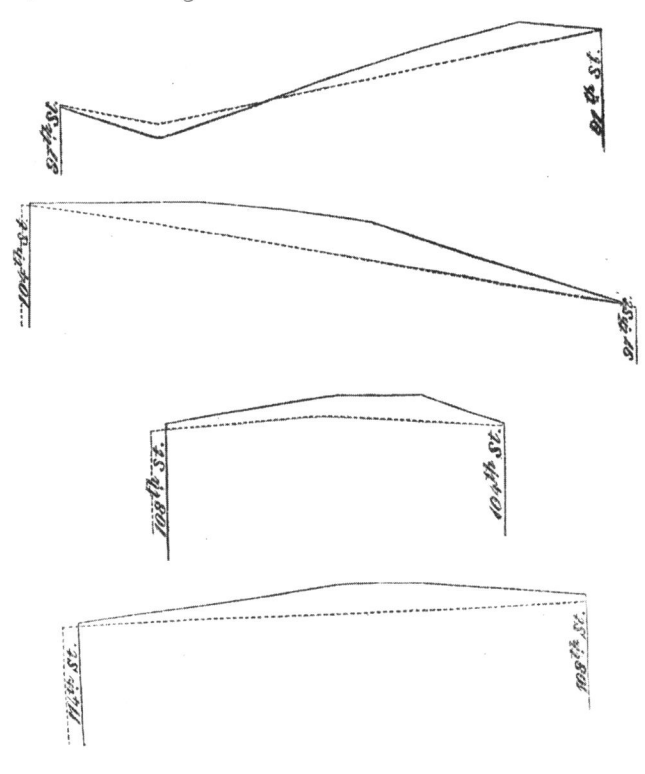

The text presented here is from "Document No. 60," in New York (City), Department of Public Parks, *Minutes*, January 20, 1875. Since Olmsted first urged the merger of Riverside Park and Riverside Avenue in March 1873, the park board had approved plans he prepared with the assistance of Calvert Vaux and engineer James C. Aldrich, and the state legislature had sanctioned the plan. Unfortunately, the legislation left unspecified whether the Department of Public Parks or the Department of Public Works would actually construct the avenue. The opportunities the project presented for patronage were vast and the fight to win control of the job produced several rival bills in early 1874 intended to throw it to one department or the other. No bill resolving the question was passed before the legislature adjourned and consequently the work was stalled for the rest of the year.

William H. Wickham, in his first message as new mayor on January 4, 1875, called for the prosecution of uptown improvements and in following weeks supported the construction of Riverside Park and Riverside Avenue by the park department according to Olmsted's plan. Two days after Wickham's message, the board of park commissioners, on the motion of William R. Martin, instructed Olmsted to report on the work done and still needed on Riverside Park, Riverside Avenue, and Morningside Park. Martin, a lawyer and real estate promoter, had just been appointed to the board by the mayor. He had urged the creation of a "riverside park" on the upper west side of Manhattan since the mid-1860s and communicated with Olmsted on the subject at that time. On January 9, as a member of the board's executive committee, he took under consideration Olmsted's preliminary report. At the board meeting of January 20 he presented the current text, along with a supplement by himself and commissioner Thomas E. Stewart. The board unanimously adopted it and sent a copy to the mayor so that he could obtain the Common Council's approval for construction. Despite Wickham's support, it was less than clear that the Common Council would give the work to the park department (since it did not dispense patronage jobs as liberally as did the Department of Public Works) or that the council even had the power to authorize the work. These unresolved questions, coupled with the adamant opposition of city comptroller Andrew H. Green on fiscal grounds, prevented all but minor work from being done on the project during 1875 (*Papers of FLO*, 6: 596–600; DPP, *Minutes*, Oct. 6, 1873, pp. 325–26; ibid., Feb. 17, 1874, pp. 567–70; ibid., Jan. 6, 1875, pp. 427–28, 438; ibid., Jan. 9, 1875, pp. 441–42; ibid., Jan. 20, 1875, pp. 463–64; FLO, Patronage Journal, Feb. 5–March 31, 1874, and July 21, 1875, below; FLO to Henry G. Stebbins, Jan. 9, 1875; "Report of the Executive Committee upon the construction of Riverside Park and Avenue," in "Document No. 60," DPP, *Minutes*, Jan. 20, 1875, supplement; S. J. Mandelbaum, *Boss Tweed's New York*, pp. 114–20; *New-York Times*, Jan. 3, 1875, p. 93; ibid., Feb. 12, 1875, p. 6; ibid., Oct. 14, 1875, p. 2; Andrew H. Green to the Honorable the Senate of the State of New York, April 28, 1875, "Document no. 85," in New York [State], *Documents of the Senate of the State of New York, Ninety-Eighth Session...* [Albany, N.Y., 1875], pp. 1–5; *City Record*, July 9, 1875, pp. 1073–75; ibid., Nov. 11, 1875, p. 1854).

1. Riverside Park is located west of Central Park between 72nd and 129th streets and overlooks the Hudson River. The area that Olmsted here designates as the Riverside territory is the present Riverside Drive and that part of Riverside Park east of the line of the present-day lower promenade. The lower promenade was built over the former line of the New York Central Railroad during the 1930s; the park to its west, and the Henry Hudson Parkway, were built on fill deposited there between the mid-1890s and the 1930s (Ann L. Buttenwieser, "Walls Upon the Water: Public Planning and the Development of the Manhattan Waterfront, 1870–1940," [Ph.D. diss., Columbia University, 1984], pp. 114–16, 190–201; Robert A. Caro, *The Power Broker: Robert Moses and the Fall of New York* [New York, 1974], pp. 525–66).
2. In April 1867 the New York state legislature gave the Central Park commissioners power to lay out the streets west of Central Park, north of 59th Street and south of 155th Street. Riverside Avenue and Riverside Park were shown on the commission map dated March 7, 1868. No documentary evidence suggests that either Olmsted or Vaux had any part in the 1868 plan, which Andrew H. Green, the dominant member of the commission, was pushing forward (New York [State], *Laws of the State of New York, Passed at the Ninetieth Session of the Legislature...* [Albany, N.Y., 1867], chap. 697; "Document No. 70," in DPP, *Minutes*, June 9, 1876, pp. 4–5).
3. That is, Eleventh Avenue and Twelfth Avenue.

4. A reference to Olmsted's March 29, 1873, "Report of the Landscape Architect on Riverside Park and Avenue" (*Papers of FLO*, 6: 596–600).
5. George M. Van Nort, a Republican who served as clerk to the Board of Commissioners of the Central Park between 1859 and 1870, when he was appointed comptroller to the Department of Public Parks by the Sweeny park board. Following the fall of the Tweed Ring, he was appointed commissioner of the Department of Public Works in late 1871. Although he concurred with the new design of Riverside Avenue in 1873, he fought in 1874 to have his department construct it (BCCP, *Minutes*, April 1859–May 1870; G. A. Mazaraki, "The Public Career of Andrew Haswell Green," p. 222; FLO to Salem H. Wales, Jan. 26, 1874; FLO, Patronage Journal, February–March, 1874, below).
6. The bill reported by the committee in late February 1874 retained the adopted design but gave the work of constructing the avenue to the Department of Public Works. The *New-York Times* and the mayor of New York, William F. Havemeyer, opposed the bill, and it did not pass the legislature (*New-York Times*, Feb. 25, 1874, p. 1; ibid., March 18, 1874, p. 8; ibid., March 19, 1874, p. 4; *City Record*, July 9, 1875, p. 1074).
7. See note 2 above.
8. Leopold Eidlitz (1823–1908), architect. Eidlitz designed churches and other buildings, including additions to the New York County or "Tweed" courthouse. His collaboration with H. H. Richardson and Olmsted on the upper stories of the New York State capitol in Albany began in July 1875 (*DAB*; see [FLO,] "Review of New York City Park Department Polices in 1878," n. 14, below; *New-York Times*, July 22, 1875, p.2).
9. In a letter to Henry G. Stebbins written two weeks after the present report, Olmsted reported that the Department of Public Works had approved Eidlitz's drawings for this structure. However, a "temporary wooden bridge" appeared in its place on a spring 1875 map of the park and avenue, and it was not mentioned in the specifications for the project published in 1876. By 1878 the department had bridged the ravine at this point with a wooden trestle (FLO to Henry G. Stebbins, Jan. 27, 1875; "Map of the Riverside Park & Avenue," document 2453, Department of Parks and Recreation Drawings Collection, New York City Municipal Archives; *Engineering News* 3 [Oct. 7, 1876]: 326–27; ibid., 3 [Oct. 14, 1876]: 334–35; ibid., 3 [Oct. 21, 1876]: 342–43; DPP, *Minutes*, May 1, 1878, pp. 1–2).

To Frederick William Poppey[1]

21st Jan. 1875

To Mr Poppey.
Dear Sir;
    I have recommended you for the position of Landscape Gardener to the Park Commission of San Francisco, am asked to ascertain your disposition in the matter.[2]
    The parks are large — each of several hundred acres — and lie between the city and the ocean, one of them reaching to the beach and being partly composed of drifting sands, the progress of which Mr Hall the Engineer in Superintendence is successfully arresting.[3] The site with the climate

renders a park, strictly so called, impossible (in my judgement). There is no turf — can be none except under artificial watering — and trees grow only in low thickets. But a very large range of low shrubs, vines and herbaceous plants grow, if properly cared for, with extreme luxurience. The summers are dry, cool and harsh; the winters very mild and agreeable, water seldom if ever freezing.

The general plan is established and roads built upon it.[4] What is now wanted is an assistant to Mr Hall of special knowledge for dealing with plantations & glades. The detailed design of these needs to be, in my judgment, wholly original — as adapted to make the best of circumstances which no man would ever intelligently choose as suitable for a pleasure ground.

I have been led to recommend you because of your experience in W. Texas — an arid country, — and because of your disposition to travel out of beaten tracks and find new methods for new conditions.[5] The pay would {be} $1500 per-annum in gold.

Supposing that you are otherwise favorably disposed, you should I think consider whether you can take up plans already formed by another man, and which you may feel to be imperfectly adapted to the official requirements of the situation and under his instructions, cordially aid in such developmnt of them as you find to be possible. One who cannot do this being, as I am instructed, to be carefully avoided.[6]

I may add that having no personal acquaintence with Mr Hall, I judge from his correspondence & reports that he is a gentleman of ability and estimable character, and that he is well read in the literature of Gardening and I know that he enjoys in a very high degree the confidence and respect not only of his commission but of some of the best citizens of California.[7]

The text presented here is from a draft in Olmsted's hand.

1. Frederick William Poppey, (b.c. 1832), landscape gardener. He was born in Prussia and studied at the Royal Educational College in Berlin. He travelled widely outside of Europe and, according to Olmsted, lived and practiced landscape gardening in San Antonio, Texas, for several years. He was living in San Antonio by 1860, and Olmsted may have met him during his visit to that area in 1854. In 1868, upon Olmsted's recommendation, he was hired as head gardener of the Hudson River State Hospital for the Insane, located north of Poughkeepsie, New York. Vaux, Withers & Company had designed the hospital building the previous year while Olmsted, Vaux & Company laid out the grounds. While working at the hospital in the late 1860s Poppey conferred with Olmsted on at least one other project nearby and apparently consulted in the planting of Prospect Park in Brooklyn (U.S., Census Office, 8th Census, *8th Census 1860. Texas* [Washington, D.C., 1860], Schedule 1, San Antonio, p. 429; "Testimony Taken Before the Assembly Special Committee Appointed to Investigate the Affairs of the Golden Gate Park, San Francisco," [San Francisco, 1876], pp. 130–32; FLO to William Hammond Hall, Feb. 24, 1874, William Hammond Hall Papers, The Bancroft Library, University of California at Berkeley, Berkeley, California; Frederick W. Poppey to FLO,

May 1, 1868; ibid., March 20, 1869; ibid., Oct. 28, 1869; ibid., July 3, 1877; Joseph M. Cleaveland to FLO, May 8, 1868; *Papers of FLO*, 6: 16–17).
2. Olmsted had been asked to recommend a man for this job in February 1874 by William Hammond Hall, who complained that "there is not a competent landscape gardener on this coast, that I can hear of." Olmsted suggested Poppey, who still worked at the Hudson River State Hospital, but a reduced California state appropriation for the park commission kept Hall from hiring him. When sufficient money arrived late the same year, Hall renewed his inquiry and again Olmsted recommended Poppey (William Hammond Hall to FLO, Feb. 13, 1874; ibid., March 12, 1874; ibid., Dec. 18, 1874; Joseph M. Cleaveland to FLO, Feb. 20, 1874).
3. The San Francisco park commission controlled three parks, two of which — Buena Vista and Mountain Lake — were less than fifty acres. Golden Gate Park covered over one thousand acres, its eastern third alone containing naturally stable soil and vegetation. Hall used structural barriers to reduce the sand that washed ashore on the western boundary of the property and planted a mixture of native beach grasses, barley, and lupine to secure the inland dunes for shrub and tree plantations (William Hammond Hall to FLO, Jan. 25, 1875, William Hammand Hall Papers, California Historical Society, San Francisco, Ca.; "Report of W. Ham. Hall," in *The Development of Golden Gate Park and Particularly the Management and Thinning of its Forest Tree Plantations...* [San Francisco, 1886], pp. 7–20; Raymond H. Clary, *The Making of Golden Gate Park The Early Years: 1865–1906* [San Francisco, 1984], pp. 14–19).
4. Hall's plan of the park was adopted by the park commissioners in December 1871 and construction of roads was started shortly afterward (William Hammond Hall to FLO, Jan. 15, 1872; FLO to William Hammond Hall, Feb. 20, 1872).
5. Poppey told Olmsted that he had worked with drifting sand in Potsdam, Nantucket, and Bermuda, while the dry California climate suggested the use of the "characteristic plants of Australia and the country watered by the Rio Grande" (Frederick W. Poppey to FLO, Jan. 22, 1875).
6. Poppey was hired as chief landscape gardener in February 1875 and moved to San Francisco with his wife and sons. Hall found him to be a good assistant, with a thorough knowledge of plants and "very correct in his taste and judgement of effect" (William Hammond Hall to FLO, Feb. 5, 1875; ibid., Jan. 8, 1876).
7. In 1876 state legislators refused to approve park construction bonds and conducted a hostile investigation of the park commission, causing Hall to resign in the spring. Poppey was dismissed the following year and returned to the east coast nearly destitute in 1879 (William Hammond Hall to FLO, Jan. 8, 1876; Frederick W. Poppey to FLO, July 3, 1877; ibid., Nov. 7, 1877; ibid., Feb. 23, 1879; R. H. Clary, *Golden Gate Park*, pp. 23, 26–27).

To the Board of Commissioners of the Department of Public Parks

[c. January-February 1875]

The Board has dismissed Captain Koster's charges against me as not entitled to consideration & on that point I have nothing more to say.[1] His letter has a significance, however, of another kind and before it is finally lost sight of I beg leave to call attention to it. I mean its significance as to his understanding of what is to be expected of *his* force.

The passages which throw some light on this subject have no direct bearing on the ostensible purpose of the letter and it requires a little reflection to see by what motive he was led to introduce them.

{*If Captain Koster had only wished to correct the alledged inaccuracies of the report half a dozen lines would have answered his purpose. There are epithets and allusions in his letter, however, which have no possible bearing upon such a purpose and I wish to inquire why they are introduced?*} Why, for instance, is the reference in my report to the design of the more rural parts of the park characterized as poetical, sentimental and faultfinding and why is a disappointment attending the realization of visionary ideas, spoken of?[2]

The writer of the report is the person supposed to have been disappointed; the visionary ideas in regard to which he has been disappointed are supposed to be identical with those uttered in this so called poetical passage about the design of the park, and a protest is thus directed not only against the alledged inaccuracies of the report but (in a prolonged undertone), against its assumption that a proper standard of duty for the police can be based on these visionary ideas. It would not require a *larger* force merely, Captain Koster means to suggest, to meet the requirements of such a standard but a force of a different character, different training, different discipline from that now employed.

To be sure that he did mean this, I have obtained a substantial acknowledgmnt under his own hand.[3]

Now I wish the Board to recall what was the cause of the disappointment to which Captain Koster refers and to look at it a little more below the surface than *he* is able to.

It is obvious that it can only have occurred through some act of the Board itself because the Board alone controls all questions of the design of the Park and if I have been disappointed in the setting aside of anything in which I have been deeply interested in respect to the design of the Park it has been through some action of the Board.

But the Board will look in vain for any such action on its part. What then, was in Captain Koster's mind when he wrote this letter? There can be no doubt as to the answer.

A year and a half ago a Committee of the Board recommended the abandonment of a temporary expedient for improving the discipline of the park-keepers which I, under its earlier instructions had just put in operation,[4] to the great indignation of those whose persistent evasion of their duty in respect to the protection of the timid, delicate & weak in their use of the more rural parts of the park, had made it necessary.

At the same moment, it was recommended that the force should no longer receive its instructions or make its reports through me. I earnestly labored with the Committee, as Captain Koster knew, to induce them to forego their determination in these respects, and, that I did so in vain, Captain Koster, also knew.

As affecting my personal interest, my ease and comfort, and even the dignity of my position, it could have been only a gratifying relief that was proposed to be given me; the duties from which I was to be retired, being in every respect, irksome, distasteful and burdensome. They took a great deal of time and energy which I could ill afford from occupations which were agreeable, honorable & profitable and they brought me large wages of senseless resentments.

Nevertheless Captain Koster is right in assuming that the action of the Board caused me deep disappointment. It would have been more than disappointment; it would have been a deep sense of injustice and of indignation, forbidding me to occupy the position in the service of the Board which I since have held,[5] but for one important circumstance. And that it may be realized what this circumstance is, (as for my argument is desirable), I must state the conviction that oppressed me as to the consequences which would result from the action by which my disappointment came. To show what that circumstance is I must explain the conviction I had as to the effect of the action of the Board to which I have referred. It was that the police would necessarily be confirmed in habits of leaving essentially uncared for those parts and elemnts of the Central Park which, to realize the intention of their design, require, more than any other, to be vigilantly watched, kept and protected. Because also I believe that they would be confirmed in habits of slighting, if not of regarding with contempt, those parts of their duty by which they should be distinguished from an ordinary street police. And I suffered peculiar pain in this prospect because it is in respect almost alone to the parts and elemnts of the design of the Central Park to which I refer, that it is, in my judgemnt, at all worthy of the fulsome praise it often gets, and because also, (as I may be allowed to add), it is in my share of the work by which these parts of it have been designed and partially and imperfectly developed that my best hope to be remembered kindly and gratefully must lie. I happen always to have had enough of that weak timber in my composition which Captain Koster calls poetry and sentiment to value this hope more than I have valued fortune or immediate applause.

In this respect, therefore, I suffered a disappointment. But it was not a disappointment of that personal character which would render me an unsuitable servant of the Board simply because I did not consider that I differed with the Board on any question of the design of the park, as I had, for example, with the Board of 1871,[6] but only on a question of practicability and method in pursuing that design. There was never a doubt expressed by a single Commissioner that such a result as I apprehended was greatly to be deplored, the only question was whether it would necessarily follow. The chairman of the Committee[7] will testify that I spared no pains to convince him that it would, and I will testify that he would never for a moment entertain the idea. When I asked him at last, how he supposed it could be guarded against he answered me emphatically, in these words: "By establishing a sufficiently high standard of duty in the force and maintaining it by the most relentless discipline." In this respect he added the Board would be found determined and inflexible.

This sentence if I am not greatly mistaken was the key to the whole policy of the Board then adopted. It was absolutely essential — literally so, it was the very essence of that policy — that a standard of duty should be set up adequate to sustain the design of the park in all particulars and that the force should be kept to it by a relentless discipline.

Captain Koster has been your agent for upholding that standard and for maintaining that discipline.

What then is the meaning of Captain Koster's coming now, a year and a half afterwards, to expostulate with the President on the publication of a few sentences setting forth the elements of the design in question and characterizing these sentences as sentimental, poetical and ill-natured?

It means simply this: that he knows that you know that he has never made the slightest effort to sustain the required standard of duty or to maintain discipline in the smallest degree with reference to it and that he feels it necessary to say something in excuse for himself.[8] It means a naive, half conscious, uneasy plea that the expectations ascribed to the writer of the report as if they were his alone, but which the writer justly and properly assumed to be those of his principal, the Board, were really unreasonable and based on visionary ideas.

With regard to which, I would only ask the Board to remember that, if everything now found on the park which was a visionary idea fifteen years ago should by any means be all at once swept out of existence there would remain absolutely nothing to show for the seven million dollars which in that time has been laid out upon it.[9]

The facts mentioned in the report[10] do indicate that much for which that outlay was made is in actual process of wasting away — and Captain Koster is perfectly right in intimating to the President, what *I* had not, even indirectly, ventured to do, however strong my conviction of it, that no mere enlargement of the Police in numbers can be expected to arrest that process. He is logically right also in claiming that what is being lost and wasted is simply the romance and poetry and fine art of the park — all, that is to say, that differentiate the scope of this Departmnt's duty essentially from that of the Departmnt of Works and the Departmnt of Police, and justify its distinct existence.

As soon as the views of the park and of the proper duties of its police upon which the police is now managed, come, through the gradual habituation of the public to them, to be generally accepted, either as desireable or as, from the political condition of the city, the limit of that which is practical, the whole business of the Departmnt will be gradually merged in that of water mains and pavements, sidewalks and sewers.

There are, as far as I can see, no sufficient grounds of argument against such a consolidation this very winter, except those which your Captain of Police deliberately and formally assures your President, are regarded with pity and contempt in the management of your police. I have for a long time believed this to be the case but you will find no intimation of such a belief in my report, no statements introduced in justification of it, and I should not have thought it proper to express it to you but for Captain Koster's volunteer testimony of the fact. With the class of men from which the police force has been largely recruited it could not perhaps have been confidently hoped to be otherwise, unless the force were placed under the constant and prolonged instruction either indirectly or better directly of someone of sufficient natural qualities of heart and mind, or of refinemnt through education, to respect, and revere, precisely that which Captain Koster gives you assurance that he wholly despises.[11]

The text presented here is from an undated draft in Olmsted's hand. The editors have dated it circa January–February 1875 because the park board's initial proposal to abandon Olmsted's plan for the Central Park keepers, which he notes as having occurred a year and a half earlier, took place in mid-July 1873. Because he uses the present tense to refer to Henry Koster as captain of the Central Park keepers, and the board suspended Koster on March 5, 1875, Olmsted undoubtedly wrote the text before that date (see notes 1 and 5, below).

1. In early September 1874 a letter by Olmsted critical of the management of Central Park and its police keeping in particular was quoted by the *New-York Daily Tribune* and published in full by the New York municipal journal *The City Record*. Henry Koster, captain of the Central Park keepers, responded to the criticism in letters to the park board president, Henry G. Stebbins. He charged that Olmsted misrepresented the facts in saying that no arrests had been made of people who vandalized bird nests in Central Park. The captain called the public airing of complaints by someone in the department "deplorable" and made it clear that he thought Olmsted's expectations of the police were unreasonable. Olmsted responded in at least two letters addressed to Stebbins in September and October. In mid-December Stebbins brought the attention of the board to the disagreement, and commissioners Thomas E. Stewart and David B. Williamson started a formal investigation. On March 5, 1875, the board, divided along party lines, came close to firing the captain but instead suspended him without pay. Commissioners Stewart and Williamson suspended their investigation a month later (FLO to Henry G. Stebbins, Aug. 27, 1874, above; *New-York Daily Tribune*, Sept. 7, 1874, p. 5; Henry Koster to Henry G. Stebbins, Sept. 9, 1874; ibid., Sept. 12, 1874; ibid., Sept. 22, 1874; FLO to Henry G. Stebbins, Sept. 19, 1874; DPP, *Minutes*, Dec. 19, 1874, p. 417; ibid., March 5, 1875, pp. 559–60; ibid., April 30, 1875, pp. 689–91).
2. Koster had found Olmsted's late-August report on Central Park to be "filled with sentiment and fault-finding" about the park's purpose and the failure of the police to promote it. "Disappointment," he concluded, "naturally follows when a realization of visionary ideas are expected in actual human affairs" (Henry Koster to Henry G. Stebbins, Sept. 12, 1874).
3. Koster confirmed Olmsted's characterization of their disagreement in a separate letter to Stebbins (FLO to Henry G. Stebbins, Sept. 19, 1874; Henry Koster to Henry G. Stebbins, Sept. 22, 1874).

4. In mid-July 1873 a committee of the new park board had proposed extensive revisions in the department bylaws. Among them was the recommendation that the management of the park keepers be made an independent office, removed from the management the old board had assigned to Olmsted several months earlier. Despite his protests, the full board adopted the revised bylaws in late August 1873 and specifically rescinded his organization of the park keepers one month later (*Papers of FLO*, 6: 42–45, 633–45, 659).
5. That is, the position of landscape architect.
6. In 1870 and 1871, contrary to the adopted design of Central Park, the Sweeny park board cleared the understory plantings that had been painstakingly introduced for picturesque effects and began construction of several inappropriate buildings (*Papers of FLO*, 6: 38–39, 392–95).
7. Philip Bissinger, chairman of both the committee on bylaws and the committee on reorganizing the park keepers (DPP, *Minutes*, July 18, 1873, p. 131; ibid., Sept. 25, 1873, pp. 296–97).
8. Koster was censured by the park board in late August 1874 for not enforcing proper discipline among the park keepers, several of whom had been found intoxicated while on duty. Olmsted described other long-standing discipline problems under Koster's command in his patronage journal (DPP, *Minutes*, Aug. 19 1874, pp. 214; ibid., Aug. 31, 1874, p. 233; FLO, Patronage Journal, March 25, 1875, below).
9. According to a department report of March 1875, the amount expended in the construction of Central Park since 1860 was $7,560,712 ("Document No. 64," in DPP, *Minutes*, March 5, 1875, p. 4).
10. That is, Olmsted's initial report to Stebbins (FLO to Henry G. Stebbins, Aug. 27, 1874, above).
11. Koster's suspension lasted until he was dismissed from the department in May 1876 (DPP, *Minutes*, May 31, 1876, p. 82).

CHAPTER III

FEBRUARY 1875–FEBRUARY 1876

During the period covered by this chapter, the advent of William R. Martin as a member of the New York City park board enabled Olmsted to regain control of landscape management and policing on Central Park. An area of special concern was the treatment of plantings and turf on Central Park, as shown in his communications to the park board, Henry Stebbins, and William Fischer. The letter to George Jones indicates the extent to which newspaper commentary on the park was tied to partisan, political concerns. In his letter to Stebbins of December 3, Olmsted discusses creation of a "promenade" section of Central Park, while on February 1, 1876, he proposes to conduct a scientific study of the growth and management of trees on the park. In another ongoing project, Olmsted instructs John Partridge on planting the U.S. Capitol grounds.

As for new projects, Olmsted's letter to Thomas Pynchon of February 25, 1875, discusses the desirable character of an academic campus in preparation for planning the new Trinity College site in Hartford, while his letter to Walter Sessions provides colorful commentary on summer communities created by religious organizations. The letter to J. H. Miller of February 28, 1876, accompanies his plan for such a village at Chautauqua Point in New York. In his letter to Dennis Bowen of January 1, 1876, Olmsted describes his plan for the City Hall in Buffalo. His letter to William Robinson explains his reluctance to design cemeteries, and his letter to Thomas Hill explores the issue of planting along the scenic section of a railroad in New Hampshire. His letter to H. A. Nelson considers desirable approaches to the park on Mount Royal in Montreal.

To the Board of Commissioners of the
Department of Public Parks, New York City

[March 1, 1875]

  The position which I hold being an irregular one, not provided for in the by laws or in any way by a distinct general order, its scope is to be inferred only by the class of duties which the Board habitually accepts of me.[1] If I may deduce from these a definition of the business of my office it is to advise the Board in regard to the design of grounds which have not yet been laid out, and the elaboration of such as have been; and more especially with respect to the Central Park to aid in the further true development of the original design and thus in the more complete realization of the objects which have been had in view in the larger part of the expenditure hitherto made upon it. I have no information to offer by which the Commissioners would be aided in just conclusions in regard to the future administration of either class of this business except the last.

  The design of the Central Park is well realized in respect to its drive and walk system and, but for a slight matter of detail, in respect to its rides. Nor need I at this time add anything to what I have recently reported in regard to its buildings, or in regard to the border parts of the park which have not been graded.[2] There remain two points in which the administration of the park is, in my judgmnt inadequate.

  First in regard to its plantations:

  The number of trees and shrubs which have been planted, with those allowed to remain of the indigenous growth on the Central Park is considerably more than half a million. They have stood (on the ground not occupied by roads, buildings, rocks, water and open meadows), on an average less than five feet apart. They were planted this closely for reasons perfectly familiar to every landscape gardener, with the intention that hardly one quarter of all should permanently remain. Once planted and growing, the designed effect was to be obtained by removal year by year of such as had exercised the influence desired of them upon the remainder and before they exercised, as in time, every one of them would do, an influence distructive of the design. The ultimate beauty of the park and the realization of the design of every important feature in it, even of the grading of the surface and the fertilization of the soil, would necessarily depend on the manner in which this work should be done, the proper trees left, the proper trees each year removed — neither too rapidly nor too slowly. This seems to me so self evident and is so well understood by all who have given any attention to the subject that I cannot without apology dwell upon it for a moment as if it could be questioned. I do so only because the course pursued by the Dept is certainly one directly at issue with the proposition. I may be allowed therefore to quote a few passages from a recognized authority, John Claudius Loudon's, (Encyclopedia of Gardening — p 962.)[3]

These precepts are laid down more particularly with reference to plantations of timber for commercial purposes, but the principles on which they are based apply with tenfold force to plantations for artistic ends.

It follows that the proper managment of the plantations of the C Park should be under the constant direction of a man who is not only throughly charged with the designs with reference to which they have been made and who has a sincere respect for them but who will steadily pursue through a course of years a long and complex series of artistic motives; who knows what the requisite measures for doing so successfully will be and who will proceed with such measures confidently and boldly.

I suppose that it is mainly because I have the first of these qualifications that I am employed by the Departmnt, yet two years ago a Committee of the Board proposed that another man should be appointed the Landscape Gardener of the Park and that he should proceed with his duties in absolute independence of my control or instruction.[4] This was a plain declaration that the Board preferred to have the original design of the park disregarded should the new Landscape Gardener be inclined to disregard it. On my intimation that the adoption of this recommendation would force me to leave the service of the Board altogether; the new Landscape Gardener was ordered to proceed under my direction in respect to landscape gardening but remained independent of me in respect to exotic & floral gardening.[5] And so, as far as the Bylaws of the Dept show, the matter now stands.[6] But suppose that I had accepted the responsibility of the managment of the plantations under this ambiguous arrangmnt, which I have never done, what opportunity had I for meeting it efficiently?

The Landscape Gardener who was to be my agent, has a force directly under his control for floral and exotic gardening — that is to say with reference to temporary & ephemeral decorations of the park but with reference to Landscape Gardening proper, the managmnt of the plantations, the realization of the permanently important purposes of the park, not one man. He directs no work except such as may be authorized and considered important by still another officer[7] who is not a Landscape Gardener and is profoundly ignorant of Landscape Gardening. To guard however against the possibility that either or all three of these officers[8] shall cause some work to be done, the reasons for doing which have not been fully understood and been reviewed & approved by the Commissioners it is ordered that not one of the many thousand trees {that stand} in excess on the park shall be removed without a special order of the Board — So far as I know an order for the cutting of a tree has never yet been given by the Board.[9]

If the Board were composed of the best experts in the world, with reference to this work, it could hardly adopt a course less likely to lead to efficiency; to having the proper work done at the proper time. But as a matter of fact so far from being a Board of experts, there has not in these 14 years been more than one of the 22 Commissioners of the Park who has professed to have even an elementary knowledge on the subject, and that one never so far as I know exercised the smallest degree of positive influence on the managmnt of the plantations. He simply acquiesced in a policy with regard to the park in this respect which he did not pursue in respect to his own private grounds.[10]

The consequence of the policy or want of policy which has been pursued is melancholy. Visitors who know how such plantations as those of the park should be managed cannot go through it without being deeply pained at the wastefulness of the neglect they see. Remonstrances on the subject, on the presumption that I am responsible, are frequently addressed to me. And although I have taken all reasonable precautions to clear myself of responsibility short of publicly protesting against the course which has been followed, I cannot but feel mortified both by the lack of proper confidence of the Commission in my professional discretion and executive ability with reference to a matter so comparatively small and by the result of that lack of confidence in the gradual stultification of the design of the Park.[11]

The other point on which I think the administration inadequate, is that of the park keepers.

I have never heard a Commissioner of the Park express dissent from the views which I have often and fully expressed as to what should be accomplished through the park keepers. When the measures which had been adopted by the Board at my suggestion for improving the efficiency of the police with reference to the practical realization of these views were abandoned,[12] the Chairman of the Committee who reported the resolution for that purpose {stated} that he thoroughly agreed with me as to the objects of the force and that the Commission did so without exception, that it was fully intended that those objects should be strenuously pursued and that the most relentless discipline would be applied to secure efficiency in their pursuit. Yet the Captain of the force[13] has within a few months shown that he regarded the most important and characteristic of these objects with contempt and, so far from wishing his subordinates to respect and induce the public to respect the design of the park as I understand it and as I suppose that the Board understands it, that he confidently and habitually treats it as a chimerical and romantic notion peculiar to a single soured and disappointed man and as a fit subject of ridicule in a deliberate and formal report to the President.[14]

I consider it a mistake of the Board to treat such an occurrence as unworthy of its notice. It affords the clearest evidence either that the Board has repudiated the original design of the park, which I do not believe, or that its

FEBRUARY 1875–FEBRUARY 1876

keepers force is not adapted to that design and is practically causing it to {be} set aside in favor of one radically different.

The force is tolerably efficient for the business to which it confines its attention but very inadequate to the purpose of giving the public the full value of what has been prepared for it in the park.

The text presented here is from a draft in Olmsted's hand, the last page of which he dated March 1, 1875, on the back and wrote the following notation: "verbal to D.P.P. on treatment of plantations Central Park — being asked to state what special defects in organization in my part of business." The printed minutes of the board report that he attended the meeting of March 3, 1875, and spoke about thinning the plantations of Central Park. However, his reference in the present tense to the independence of the landscape gardener, whose office had been abolished a week earlier, suggests that he wrote at least parts of the text before the date he assigned to it (DPP, Minutes, Feb. 23, 1875, pp. 533–34, 537; ibid., March 3, 1875, pp. 549–50).

1. By stating that his position was "irregular" and not provided for in the department bylaws or a standing order of the board, Olmsted did not mean his actual office of landscape architect and head of the Bureau of Design and Superintendence, which was named and defined in the bylaws. He apparently meant that the bylaws did not explicitly provide for the range of duties the commissioners had come to expect of him. In late August 1873, when new board members revised the bylaws, they narrowed the responsibilities he had held up to that time, vaguely defined those that remained, and reserved the power to enlarge or decrease them. Although they solicited reports from him on a variety of topics, on the whole their actions at that time and in subsequent months decreased his responsibilities and influence in the affairs of the department. Their revised bylaws made him responsible for issuing park maintenance orders, preparing landscape plans, and supervising the execution of both, but took other responsibilities from him and assigned them to three newly independent officers. Superintendent of Parks Columbus Ryan took over the allocation and supervision of laborers employed in park construction and maintenance. Landscape Gardener Robert Demcker, nominally under Olmsted's supervision in "the ornamentation and embellishment" of the parks, had complete control of the exotic and propagation department and was allowed to superintend any landscape plans that the board approved and assigned to him, including his own. Henry Koster took over the management and supervision of the park keepers. The commissioners removed a provision in the bylaws that required them to consult with Olmsted about actions that would change landscape plans already adopted, and by summer of 1874, occasionally made such changes without notifying him. In September 1873 they "relieved" Olmsted from supervising park maintenance, abandoned his plan of organization of the park keepers, and instructed him to work exclusively on the preparation of landscape plans for Riverside and Morningside parks "until further orders" (DPP, Minutes, Aug. 29, 1873, pp. 239–45; ibid., Sept. 25, 1873, pp. 296–97; FLO to Henry G. Stebbins, July 7, 1874; [FLO], "Main Divisions of Responsibility in the Park Organization," [1874], in Forty Years, 2: 328–29; Papers of FLO, 6: 44–45).
2. On January 29, 1875, Olmsted provided the board with estimates of costs for the repair of various architectural structures in the park and to complete grading work made necessary by the recent regrading of Eighth Avenue ("Document No. 63," in DPP, Minutes, January 29, 1875, pp. 2–7; DPP, Minutes, Jan. 29, 1875, p. 482).

3. John Claudius Loudon (1783–1844), Scottish landscape gardener and horticultural writer, whose *Encyclopedia of Gardening* was first published in 1822 and had many later editions. Olmsted apparently read passages in which Loudon quoted Edward Sang on the proper thinning of plantations, "a matter of first importance in their culture. However much attention be paid to the article of pruning, if the plantation be left too thick, it will be inevitably ruined." Loudon continued:

> With respect to the final distance to which trees standing in a mixed plantation should be thinned, it is hardly possible to prescribe fixed rules. . . . It may, however, be said in general, that if trees be allowed a distance of from twenty-five to thirty feet, according to their kinds and manner of growth, they will have room enough to become larger timber. . . . The operation of thinning and pruning, thickening or filling up, or renewing portions that cannot be profitably recovered, should thus go on year after year, as appearances may direct, on the general principles of tree culture.

(*DNB*; John Claudius Loudon, *An Encyclopedia of Gardening*, 2 vols., [London, 1826], 2: 1135–37).

4. In July 1873 newly appointed board members Salem H. Wales, Philip Bissinger, and David B. Williamson attempted to establish an independent office of landscape gardening headed by Robert Demcker (*Papers of FLO*, 6: 44–45; FLO to Henry G. Stebbins, July 30, 1873 [ibid., 6: 633–45]).

5. Despite Olmsted's opposition to the change and his intimation in late July 1873 that he would resign, the board revised the bylaws a month later to establish the office of landscape gardening for Demcker, and nominally placed him under Olmsted's direction (ibid.; see n. 1 above).

6. On February 23, 1875, less than a week before the date Olmsted assigned this document, the board had repealed the bylaw that provided for the office of landscape gardener and fired its head, Robert Demcker. Since Olmsted does not refer to this action in the document, it is probable that he wrote at least some parts of it before that date (DPP, *Minutes*, Feb. 23, 1875, pp. 533–34, 537).

7. The superintendent of parks, an office held until late January 1875 by Columbus Ryan, who resigned under pressure from board members Thomas E. Stewart and William R. Martin. Without a change in the bylaws, however, the person in the office could still undercut Olmsted by denying him the laborers needed to do landscape work properly. On March 19, 1875, the board adopted Martin's revision of the bylaws that restored to Olmsted the power to determine the allocation of laborers on the park and the nature of their instructions and superintendence (DPP, *Minutes*, April 7, 1874, p. 629; ibid., March 19, 1875, pp. 594–95; *The City Record*, Sept. 11, 1874, p. 1013; ibid., Feb. 5, 1875, p. 231).

8. That is, the landscape architect, the landscape gardener, and the superintendent of parks.

9. The board passed an order banning the cutting of all trees without its approval on August 20, 1873 (DPP, *Minutes*, Aug. 20, 1873, pp. 217–18).

10. A reference to the landscape painter Frederic E. Church, who served as a park commissioner from November 1871 to April 1873. During the same period he personally directed the landscaping of his Hudson River country estate, Olana, and had collaborated with Calvert Vaux on the design of the house (James Anthony Ryan, "Frederic Church's Olana: Architecture and Landscape as Art," in Franklin Kelly et al., *Frederic Edwin Church* [Washington, D.C., 1989], pp. 126–56).

11. On March 3, 1875, the board adopted Olmsted's recommendation that the plantations be thinned under expert supervision. In an 1889 report on the plantations of Central Park Olmsted referred to this report and noted that though it was not pub-

lished, "as a result of it a special force for thinning was allowed to be employed, and during an inclement season, when few visitors passed through the Park, within less than a month's time, more trees were felled than there had been altogether, probably, in ten years before" (DPP, *Minutes*, March 3, 1875, pp. 549–50; F. L. Olmsted and J. B. Harrison, *Observations on the Treatment of Public Plantations, More Especially Relating to the Use of the Axe* [Boston, 1889], p. 19; FLO to William L. Fischer, March 14, 1875, below).
12. In late September 1873 the board adopted the recommendation of a special committee chaired by Philip Bissinger to abandon Olmsted's plan for the park keepers force (DPP, *Minutes*, Sept. 25, 1873, pp. 296–97).
13. Henry Koster.
14. See FLO to DPP, c. January–February 1875, above.

To Thomas Pynchon[1]

[c. March 10, 1875]

To President Pynchon;
Dear Sir,
    I could perhaps as conveniently visit Hartford this week as at any time for several weeks to come but I should gain no advantage nor do I think that at this season you would do so by a visit to the ground.[2]
    It would be unsafe to adopt any conclusions as to the positions of the buildings without the topographical map and the only advice I could give you would be negative — advice against forming plans without all the necessary data which should be accurately weighed in their final and exact determination.[3]
    It is much to be desired that while securing opportunity for a large future extension the object & character of which cannot now be clearly forseen you should not involve yourself in the necessity of continuing for years with an outward aspect of raw make-shift, half dressed frontier life. Though so rarely done in this country it is by no means impossible to obtain in a few years order, completeness, maturity & finish of character throughout the whole of a large place (buildings & grounds) and yet hold the opportunity for large additions to its buildings.
    As you desire my personal interest in the matter, I shall take the liberty of telling you frankly where in my judgmnt you will find the principal difficulty in accomplishing this end and yet cutting your coat according to your cloth.
    Your trustees have had & will have I presume several ways of regarding what is to be aimed in your building enterprise — several problems in view, the perfectly satisfactory solution of each of which is not compatible with the perfectly satisfactory solution of all the others.

As for example 1st to provide an apparatus for an organized pursuit of learning by a chosen body of men, secluding themselves as a body for that purpose at least during certain hours of the day from the ordinary concerns of the community at large.

2. to rear a material monument of piety, learning and art.

3 The publication and public exaltation of a popular institution for the education of young men.

4. the gaining of something for the college endowment by the incidental commercial advantage which the building of the college will give to the market value of adjoining ground.[4]

As to the 1st, to honor and promote learning, the more set apart, shut in, retired and cloister like in character the site and the building the better. On the other hand, for publicity and display the more elevated the site, the larger the sky line of building, and the more open the situation the better.

The English colleges are designed with a strong predominance of the first motive.[5] They are not situated in parks but in the midst of cities and often entered from narrow public streets; their grounds are within and hidden from the public. The quadrangle is an expedient for securing by means of the inner court abundance of light and air consistently with a sense of retreat from the outer world. If they have additional grounds they also are arranged with a view to seclusion; not as a means for the display of the building. They are on the side opposite the public entrance. There is a consistent adherence in all this to the primary motive.

American college buildings have been generally placed and planned with an equally consistent regard for the other class of motives, to make the greatest public display possible. They are in this respect Greek and pagan as the English are Gothic and Christian.[6]

I do not mean that the quadrangular arrangement is by any means essential to convenience of collegiate life nor to the artistic manifestation of the pursuits of scholarship, nor do I mean that a range of buildings in a line cannot be made satisfactorily convenient and expressive of the purpose of a community of scholars but that there are advantages in the English arrangement for this purpose and disadvantages in the American, and we should not close our eyes to either.

That part of your ground which alone is considered with reference to the position of the buildings — is a very narrow plateau on an elevated ridge with a precipice of rock on one side and an inconveniently steep slope on the other. It is favorable to the American plan — a continous line of narrow buildings with a "campus" "yard", "lawn" or "park" in front of them, the plateau being wide enough, though barely so, for convenience, with such buildings so related one to another. It would not do to undertake to place a long series of buildings upon it in a straight line but a dozen buildgs of various character might be picturesquely ranged in adaptation to the topography very effectively along the summit of the ridge with a sufficient space of nearly level ground on each side of them for convenience & for an appearance both of convenience and of stability.

The same conditions are not at all well adapted to a quadrangular plan and you will find that in the end you will have made your choice between four alternatives, as follows:

1st   Abandonment of the quadrangle;
2d   abandonment of the site;
3d   a costly modification of the natural conditions of the site;
4   a compromise in which you will sacrifice something of the advantages of the quadrangle in order to save the ground & something of convenience in the surroundings of the buildings in order to save the quadrangle with the incidental result of a lack of happy relation, fitness and propriety between the buildings and the neighborhood and a difficulty laid over to your successors in regard to the placing & satisfactory correlating of additional buildings to those now definitely contemplated.[7]

As to your remark that someone will have to watch the progress of building with the eye of a lynx, let me recommend you to insist on the English plan of a clerk of the works, a professional watcher, constantly on the ground, looking to every detail as it is no part of the duty nor by any means in the power of the Architectural Superintendant to do. It will pay many times over and it will not pay but be a source of endless vexation, hard feeling, delay and embarrassment to undertake or allow a nonprofessional, occasional & desultory superintendence by yourself, your trustees or your building Committee.

The text presented here is from an undated draft in Olmsted's hand. The editors have dated it circa March 10, 1875, apparently a response to a letter from Pynchon of March 8 asking Olmsted to visit him at the site within two weeks. (see note 2 below).

1. Thomas Ruggles Pynchon (1823–1904), Episcopal clergyman and president of Trinity College between 1874 and 1883. Pynchon directed the relocation of the college from its original campus in the center of Hartford to its new property, selected with Olmsted's assistance in 1872, near the southwest outskirts of town (*DAB*; FLO to Abner Jackson, May 25, 1872 [*Papers of FLO*, 6: 561–66]).
2. In late February and early March 1875 Pynchon had asked Olmsted to visit Hartford and advise him how best to position the campus on the Rocky Hill site — approximately eighty acres that rapidly sloped upward to an elevated plateau, terminated on the west with a rock precipice, and commanded extensive views. In late 1873 Olmsted had noted in a report to the college trustees that the massive range of buildings and quadrangles in the plan they had adopted by the English architect William Burges would not fit on the plateau without modification or expensive embankments. Decreasing the width and increasing the length of the quadrangles would allow them to retain the plan, but Olmsted proposed instead that the college buildings, roadways, and facilities be arranged according to the existing topography. George Kent Radford, with whom he collaborated on the project, prepared a topographical map of the site and Olmsted drew up a preliminary plan that illustrated both options. In late 1874 the trustees decided not to un-

dertake construction of the complete Burges plan, but several months later opted to proceed with the construction of the west side of a smaller quadrangle based on Francis H. Kimball's revision. Pynchon then wrote Olmsted and reported that both the topographical map and plan that accompanied his 1873 report were missing but asked him to visit the site with the intention of fixing positions for the buildings (Abner Jackson to FLO, April 5, 1873; ibid., Oct. 6, 1873; FLO to Trustees of Trinity College, c. Oct. 1873; Thomas R. Pynchon to FLO, Feb. 25, 1875; ibid., March 2, 1875; ibid., March 4, 1875; ibid., March 8, 1875; FLO to Thomas R. Pynchon, Feb. 26, 1875; ibid., March 3, 1875).

3. Olmsted wrote and then deleted the following sentence: "If you will excuse so much frankness I will mention that from what I have heard I shd think there had been some confusion of motive in your councils heretofore & that there is need for some considerable sacrifice on one side or another and that there has been insufficient effort made to harmonize or reconcile them, the result being some confusion. These are the following ways of considering the thing to be done."

4. In his 1872 report evaluating available sites for the college, Olmsted recommended that if the Rocky Hill property were obtained about half of it should be laid out as a permanent suburban community adjacent to the campus. As he did with other campus plans he prepared in the 1860s and 1870s, Olmsted predicted that the market value of these lots would soon exceed the cost to the college of the entire property and that they would ensure a permanent domestic character for the surrounding district. Olmsted provided for residential building sites in his preliminary plan of late 1873 and conferred with college officials and Kimball on the question as they developed plans in the spring of 1875 (*Papers of FLO*, 6: 564–66; FLO to Trustees of Trinity College, c. Oct. 1873; FLO to Thomas R. Pynchon, May 27, 1875; Thomas R. Pynchon to FLO, June 1, 1875; ibid., June 16, 1875; Francis H. Kimball to FLO, June 11, 1875).

5. Olmsted, in his 1872 report, had cited Oxford University, Oxfordshire, and Winchester College, Hampshire, as examples of "slightly sequestered" colleges (*Papers of FLO*, 6: 563).

6. Many nineteenth-century American colleges located their campuses on prominent elevated sites, erected large imposing buildings, often in the Greek Revival style, or insisted on symmetrical quadrangles, while they neglected what Olmsted considered more desirable alternatives. He confronted such preferences when he advised officials at the College of California at Berkeley and the Massachusetts Agricultural College (1866), Cornell University (1867), and Amherst College (1870) (Paul Venable Turner, *Campus: An American Planning Tradition* [New York, 1987], pp. 89–93; *Papers of FLO*, 5: 546–70; ibid., 6: 9–16, 131–47, 193–98, 379, 562).

7. Despite Olmsted's recommendations here, officials at Trinity decided to proceed with the construction of the Burges quadrangle as revised by Kimball. In the remainder of 1875 and through 1876 Olmsted and Radford provided plans that fixed the position of buildings, roads, and walks, which included a bow-shaped terrace and esplanade on the rock ridge that formed the western boundary of the property. Although Pynchon admired this feature and it gained the approval of the building committee, it was never built. In the fall of 1878 the college opened the central buildings of the west side of the quadrangle but never fully completed the complex as designed (Thomas R. Pynchon to FLO, May 25, 1875; ibid., June 1, 1875; ibid., June 12, 1875; ibid., June 16, 1875; FLO to Thomas R. Pynchon, May 27, 1875; Francis H. Kimball to FLO, June 11, 1875; George Kent Radford to FLO, June 18, 1875, in B134: #2820, OAR/LC; *New-York Times*, July 28, 1875, p. 2; Trinity College to FLO, Oct. 1876, Trinity College Archives, Hartford Connecticut; P. V. Turner, *Campus*, pp. 217–21).

To William L. Fischer[1]

14th March 1875.

To Mr. Fischer;
My Dear Sir,

    I have been through the South Park[2] this morning and fear that you will not have nearly as much thinning out done as is needed before the Spring opens. Please call for all the men you can use and take every advantage of the opportunity that you can. There are many clusters of evergreens where the trees are destroying one another. Besides those to which I called your attention the other day please look especially to those East of the marble arch and the cluster on the knoll north of Bow bridge (north of the rustic seat). The deciduous wood still further north, (West of the Ramble), is also much too thick.

    The "pruning" has been stopped and will proceed only under your orders. Please order what you think particularly desireable but do not let this interfere at all with thinning out superfluous trees.[3] It is very desireable that suitable bushes *of good size* should be planted on the transverse road arches and wherever necessary to hide the transverse roads and subways and mask the bridges.[4] Please try to find a sufficient number of such bushes as you go about whereever they can be spared without serious loss; so that as soon as possible they can be moved. Consider this the first important business of the spring. I send you Robinson's Wild Garden, as I promised. I have marked various passages in the first 40 pages, which be so good as to observe attentively.[5] Robinson expresses the views I have always had for the Ramble, the winter drive district[6] and the more rocky and broken parts of the park. There can be no better place than the Ramble for the perfect realization of the Wild Garden, and I want to stock it in that way as fully and as rapidly as is possible. I shall be much obliged to you for any suggestions you can make for obtaining at the earliest day a large stock of hardy plants that will spread and cover the ground and take care of themselves, grow in shade and root out grass. Of such shrubs and vines, (as of Rubus, Lonicera, Clematis, Vinca and Hedera), as can be propogated this spring it is impossible to start enough. If an overstock were possible it would be soon absorbed on the Morningside and Riverside Parks.

The text presented here is from a draft in Olmsted's hand.

1. William L. Fischer (1819–1899) received his training as a gardener on private estates in his native Germany. He later went to England and worked in the gardens of the Royal Horticultural Society and, under Joseph Paxton, in the park and gardens at Chatsworth. By 1857 Fischer had immigrated to the United States and went to work on Central Park where he contributed to the preparation of planting plans and eventually superintended

the principal planting operations. He also operated a nursery in New York, from which he sold plants to the Central Park commission in the early 1860s. He remained on the park through the 1860s but apparently left when the Department of Public Parks replaced the commission in May 1870. On March 3, 1875, at Olmsted's recommendation, he was hired along with Oliver Crosby Bullard to supervise the thinning of the park's plantations. Five days after the present letter, he was appointed superintending gardener of the department. He kept this position until 1878, when he was dismissed with Olmsted and others, but regained his position in 1880. In 1884 Olmsted brought him to Boston to supervise the planting of Franklin Park (*Papers of FLO*, 3: 12; *American Gardening*, Dec. 2, 1899, p. 820; BCCP, *Minutes*, July 5, 1860, p. 65; ibid., Aug. 11, 1866, p. 27; DPP, *Minutes*, March 3, 1875, pp. 549–50; ibid., March 19, 1875, pp. 595–96; ibid., Aug. 14, 1880, p. 244; FLO to Henry G. Stebbins, Feb. 1, 1876, below; FLO to Smith E. Lane, March 4, 1882; ibid., March 31, 1882).
2. That is, the part of Central Park south of the Old Croton Reservoir at 79th Street, including the Ramble (FLO to Henry G. Stebbins, Dec. 3, 1875, below).
3. In March 1889 Olmsted inspected the park's plantations and commended the results of Fischer's work in 1875:

> The advantage gained where the thinning was most resolute is now conspicuous. It may be seen, for example, on the rising ground, between the two lobes of the North Meadow, the most park-like part of the Park; again on the north side of the eastern half of the road crossing the Park at Mount St. Vincent; on the borders of the drive mounting Bogardus Hill from the south; near the drive opposite Summit Rock; on Cherry Hill and at a few other points. A few complete clearances and replantings were made at this time. A group of hemlocks northwest of the Great Reservoir, for example, occupies ground in which a previous plantation had been ruined by the overgrowth of Norway spruce, the latter having been also ruined a little later, by their crowding of one another. It can be seen that these hemlocks have not been growing thriftily. This is because, in dread of a repetition of the first experience, they were planted too openly.

(F. L. Olmsted and J. B. Harrison, *Use of the Axe*, p. 19).
4. Olmsted here refers to the various architectural structures, largely masked by plantings, that provided for separation of vehicular, horse, and foot traffic inside the park. These included the sunken transverse roads that crossed the park at 65th Street and 79th Street, the heavy masonry arches that carried traffic over them, and the subways and bridges that carried horse and pedestrian paths under and over the drives and transverse roads.
5. William Robinson's *The Wild Garden*, first published in 1870, criticized the formal bedding-out of showy tender plants, a ubiquitous practice in domestic gardens and public parks at this time. Instead he called for informally arranged mixes of hardy native and exotic flowers, shrubs, and creepers set amidst the borders and wooded and rougher parts of gardens and parks. Not only did this approach give a more pleasing natural appearance but it reduced the yearly labor and expense of taking up and replacing beds of tender annuals. Both its aesthetic and economic advantages appealed to Olmsted, as he made clear in a report on the maintenance of Central Park at this time:

> During the last two years a considerable though quite inadequate stock of shrubs, creepers and hardy herbaceous plants has been obtained and partly planted out with a view to giving a wilder more natural and interesting character to certain parts of the park. The ultimate result of the intention of this work, if fully realized, would be a reduction of the maintenance expense of the park, the ground to be occupied having hitherto been mowed at frequent intervals at considerable expense,

whereas when once overgrown as designed it would require little or no attention from one year's end to another.

(William Robinson, *The Wild Garden* [London, 1870], pp. 1–39; FLO to William Robinson, c. March 20–30, 1875, below; [FLO], ["Report on Maintenance of Central Park"], [c. March 1875], p. 8. This is an untitled, undated report signed by Olmsted in the Olmsted Papers. See also, *Sunday Mercury*, April 25, 1875, p. 3).

6. That is, the area located west of the reservoirs between 72nd and 102nd streets, originally designed and planted with evergreens and shrubs to provide attractive landscape scenery when the park's deciduous plantings were bare (*Papers of FLO*, 6: 531).

To William Robinson[1]

[c. March 20–30, 1875]

Dear Mr. Robinson;

I send you herewith a photographic view in Spring Grove Cemetery which I think will answer your purpose.[2] Mr Strauch sends me with it a series of smaller views chiefly of monuments but among them there are two or three over the same lake, one of which you may perhaps find better adapted to your page. He also sends an account of Spring Grove Cemetery printed by the Association.[3] I have marked in the Table of Contents the parts which I think likely to be most useful to you and a few passages in each of these parts. Near the close there is a brief account of the more important rural cemeteries of the United States.

The course first adopted in forming our cemeteries, as at Mount Auburn and Greenwood[4] and till recently universally followed was to take a body of wooded land, open roads through it, divide the spaces between the roads in "lots", sell the lots and leave their owners to decorate them according to their fancy. It has been customary for the owners to mark their boundaries with walls, posts & chains, hedges or otherwise, and to plant trees, shrubs, vines and flowers within them, each owner according to his taste & knowledge or want thereof. Graves were made and monuments set up according to the taste and means of each lot owner, and much as in an English Church yard, except that a stronger inclination has here been manifest to extravagant outlay in this respect.

The result for a time, and particularly when compared with our older burial grounds, was very pleasing.

But I must say that it was never altogether satisfactory and the older and more crowded the ground, the more time operates upon the hedges and flower beds and posts and chains and Thujas and Spruces the further it is from being so.

I am giving you my strictly private opinion and for the purpose of a caution, which may be quite unnecessary, against the wholesale praise of the American Cemetery. And the more confidently because you seem to dislike the sticking of objects of architecture or sculpture upon a ground of a natural character or ground making pretensions that way, and to the breaking of its surface even with objects of gardening art. You dislike it, I detest it, and nothing has given me more pleasure in a long time than the article from the Saturday Review which you quoted lately which indicated that fashion was beginning to set against bedding art, which, as far as I can judge is ruin to the art of composing landscape effects.[5] (At the same time when you come here I expect to convince you that the arches in the Central Park were desireable and at any rate that not one of them was introduced as you were led to suppose for purpose of decoration.)[6] But as to the Cemeteries, you will see, how impossible, under the conditions I have described, any breadth or repose or simplicity of landscape character must be; how inevitable the opposite qualities in a high degree. And yet if art should do anything in a place of rest for our dead it should be to produce an impression of restfulness. How it is to be accomplished as a general rule near great towns where land has a high value, while we hold to our present habits, is more than I can yet tell. I do not think I could lay out a burial place without making conditions about the monuments such as I fear few but Quakers would be willing to accept.[7] But when I first saw Spring Grove Cemetery I found the problem more nearly solved by the taste and tact of Mr Strauch than I had ever expected to see it.[8] Parts of Spring Grove would be a very beautiful pleasure ground, with moderately broad, simple and quiet effects, if the monuments were not to be seen; and the custom of having but one monumnt to a family, and of reserving near the drives and especially at the forks of the drives good spaces of ground to be planted and treated by the association, at least secures a very grateful limit to the degree in which these effects shall be injured by monuments.

The offensive parts which in our older cemeteries mark the boundaries of lots, even before they are sold, were by Mr Strauch set so that their tops were out of sight below the surface of the ground, though so near it as to be easily found when necessary. Nearly the whole of the implanted space of the Cemetery, even under the groves is a smooth surface of turf.

The principles of the Spring Grove plan—sometimes carried out more thoroughly, sometimes less so than there—have been generally recognized in those of our cemeteries established of late years.

I do not {know} what you saw of our cemeteries and you will pardon me for writing as if I imagined you had seen nothing of them. For the substantial information of my package you are solely indebted to Mr. Strauch.

We are at New York just beginning our spring planting and in the colder exposures the frost is not yet out of the ground. In proper time I shall take care to meet your request for a view on the Central Park.

The text presented here is from a draft in Olmsted's hand. Olmsted wrote the letter around the first of April 1875: on March 20 he was still awaiting photographs from Adolph Strauch, which were promised "in a few days," and work on his article on Landscape Gardening for the *American Encyclopedia* may have delayed his writing of the letter. He may also have made use of a book and some pamphlets that a friend of Strauch's from Cincinnati delivered to him on April 8 (Adolph Strauch to FLO, March 17, 1875; FLO to Adolph Strauch, March 20, 1875; Jay Wilson to FLO, April 8, 1875).

1. William Robinson (1838–1935), English landscape gardener, writer, and editor of *The Garden*. Robinson and Olmsted met in 1870, became friends and shared information on landscape design over the years (*Papers of FLO*, 6: 552; ibid., SS1: 416; see also FLO to William L. Fisher, March 14, 1875, n. 5, above).
2. In February 1875 Robinson wrote to Olmsted requesting a fine illustration of landscape gardening in an American cemetery, suitable for engraving. Olmsted assumed the engraving would be used to illustrate an article in Robinson's journal *The Garden*, but instead it appeared in his book *God's Acre Beautiful; or, the Cemeteries of the Future*, published in 1880. Robinson specifically indicated an interest in Spring Grove Cemetery in Cincinnati, which he understood to be "very well arranged." Accordingly, Olmsted secured photographs and reports of the cemetery from its designer and superintendent, Adolph Strauch. Spring Grove had been consecrated in 1845, but in 1854 its directors hired Strauch to redesign the cemetery. He found the cemetery to be overly crowded with enclosures, multiple and gaudy monuments, excessive plantings, and crisscrossed with numerous avenues and pathways. In an effort to open up the grounds and provide for enhanced vistas, better light, and a more pastoral effect, he introduced what became known as the "lawn system" to Spring Grove Cemetery. With the full support of the cemetery's board of directors, Strauch was able to remove fences, hedges, and other enclosures and eliminate several drives. In addition, he urged lot owners to limit monuments to one monument for each family. By 1875 he noted that "the Lawn system is beginning to grow in favor with the people altho' they do make considerable opposition at first." Strauch's intent was to take control of the cemetery away from individual lot holders and place it in the hands of the cemetery staff. He wanted a more uniform appearance and one that was based on a coherent design (William Robinson to FLO, Feb. 21, 1875; FLO to Adolph Strauch, March 12, 1875; FLO to Adolph Strauch, March 20, 1875; see *Papers of FLO*, SS1: 614–15).
3. The Spring Grove Cemetery Association was created in 1844 with the purpose of selecting and purchasing a site for the cemetery. Strauch probably sent Olmsted a copy of *Spring Grove Cemetery: Its History and Improvements, with Observations on Ancient and Modern Places of Sepulture* [Cincinnati, Ohio, 1869], pp. 6–7.
4. Mount Auburn Cemetery in Cambridge, Massachusetts, the first "rural cemetery" in the United States, laid out in 1831. Green-Wood Cemetery in Brooklyn, New York, was incorporated in 1838 and opened for public interment four years later (David Charles Sloane, *The Last Great Necessity: Cemeteries in American History* [Baltimore, Md., 1991], p. 44; James Smillie, "Green-Wood Illustrated . . .," in *The Rural Cemeteries of America* [New York, 1847], p. 3; see n. 7 below).
5. Robinson had recently reprinted *The Garden* part of an article, "Queen Anne's Flowers" from the February 20, 1875, edition of *The Saturday Review*. By way of introduction to

the reprint, Robinson noted that "we are convinced that most gardeners would be pleased to reduce the 'bedding display,' as it is called; for it is the most expensive and troublesome mode of embellishing a garden; but it is for their employers to give the word" ("The 'Saturday Review' on Queen Anne's Flowers," *The Garden*, Feb. 27, 1875, pp. 170, 181–82).

6. In December 1871 Robinson wrote that in Central Park "one thing seemed a mistake — the making of many bridges over roads, with a view to separate equestrians from pedestrians; this is the most expensive and needless crotchet I have ever seen." Explaining his concern, he continued:

> In the Bois de Boulogne and in Hyde park we have a far greater number of equestrians, and no such thing is or will ever be necessary. When will the persons who arrange plans for such parks as these learn that park or garden is spoiled in proportion to the number of needless architectural works which it contains? This is particularly the case in a city. There should be no building in a public garden not absolutely necessary, and those that are indispensable should be inexpensive, and, as a rule, concealed by judicious planting.

(William Robinson, "Public Gardens. Parks and Public Gardens in America," *The Garden*, December 9, 1871, p. 45; see also, *Papers of FLO*, 6: 553).

7. A reference to the Society of Friends burial custom of having no marker of any kind on the grave (J. William Frost, *The Quaker Family in Colonial America: A Portrait of the Society of Friends* [New York, 1973], p. 43).

8. A reference to Strauch's insistence that only one monument per family be erected (Adolph Strauch, *Spring Grove Cemetery: Its History and Improvements, with Observations on Ancient and Modern Places of Sepulture* [Cincinnati, Ohio, 1869], pp. 70–71).

To Frederick Law Olmsted, Jr.[1]

209 W. 46 St.
New York.
13th May, 1875.

Dear Harry;

The cats keep coming into the yard, six of them every day, and Quiz drives them out. If I should send Quiz to you to drive the cows away from your rhubarb he would not be here to drive the cats out of the yard. If six cats should keep coming into the yard every day and not go out, in a week there would be 42 of them and in a month 180 and before you came back next November 1260. Then if there should be 1260 cats in the yard before next November half of them at least would have kittens and if half of them should have 6 kittens apiece, there would be more than 5000 cats and kittens in the yard. There would not be any place for Roseanna to spread the clothes unless she drove them all off the grass plot, and if she did they would have to crowd at the end of the yard nearest the house, and if they did that they would make a great pile as high as the top of my windows. A pile of 5000 cats and kittens, some of them black ones, in front of my window would make my office so dark I should not be able to write in it. Besides that those underneath, particularly the kittens, would be hurt by those standing on the top of them and I expect they would make such a great squalling all the time that I should not be able to sleep, and if I was not able to sleep, I should not be able to work, and if I did not work I should not have any money, and if I had not any money I could not send any to Plymouth to pay your fare back on the Fall River boat, and I could not pay my fare to go to Plymouth and so you and I would not ever see each other any more.[2] No, Sir. I can't spare Quiz and you will have to watch for the cows and drive them off yourself or you will raise no rhubarb.

Your affectionate father.

The text presented here is from a manuscript in Olmsted's hand.

1. Frederick Law Olmsted, Jr. (1870–1957), christened Henry Perkins Olmsted. He was later renamed for his father, the first instance of the name-change appearing in a letter from Olmsted to John Charles Olmsted in 1877 (Laura Wood Roper, *FLO: A Biography of Frederick Law Olmsted* [Baltimore, Md., 1973], p. 338; see FLO to JCO, Oct. 7, 1877, below).
2. Mary Perkins Olmsted had probably taken the younger children to visit Frederick Knapp and his family in Plymouth, Massachusetts (L. W. Roper, *FLO, A Biography*, p. 347).

To Henry G. Stebbins

18th May 1875—

To H. G. S. President

The attention of the Board has frequently been called to the manner in which the turf of the Central Park is abused and to the need of more effective measures for preserving it, especially to the necessity of employing a large number of men with the duty of cautioning visitors against breaking the rules for its proper keeping. Two years ago the Board adopted a plan under which a great improvement was gained, but from a necessity of reducing expenditure for maintenance it was soon discontinued[1] and during last summer the misuse of the turf continued and was, as I reported in September, greater than ever before.[2] It followed that during the dry weather fully a quarter of all the turf of the larger open spaces of the South Park[3] was trodden out and eradicated;

the soil having no protection was pulverized by those walking on it and blew away in dust. I earnestly beg that the Commissioners will now personally examine these grounds and observe the result.[4] The surface is very uneven owing to the depressions formed as above described and what should be, and once was, a smooth even fabric of fine close turf is a patch work consisting of three parts of poor and tufty grass with one of brown bare earth. The bare parts will probably now soon green over with weeds and annual grasses which will alternately wither and brown and spring up and become temporarily verdant according as the weather shall be hot and dry or cool and moist. These annuals having feebler roots and being in all respects less tough and fibrous than the proper turf grasses will wear out under foot more rapidly and the process above described will, if it is allowed to continue during the present summer, extend further. The result will be that although in the early summer the park will still appear green and promising, at that period when it {is} most resorted to by the mass of the people of the city and it is most important that its appearance should be cheerful and refreshing, it will lack the element most essential to its beauty and without which it can have but little rural charm.

 To repair this loss in the most direct, rapid and effective way the ground should be broken up, finely tilled and reseeded. A fine fresh turf might thus be had next year—but the small fund at the command of the Department must for the present prevent any such thorough operation; the next best thing is to level up the worse depressions by the addition of fine soil and to rake in the seed of good perennial grasses on all the bare and thinner parts.

 It would be of no avail to do this if the ordinary use of the turf shall be allowed this year as the tender young grass would be at once trodden to death.

 If such use is discontinued—if the public can be kept off and the turf be allowed a few months respite from wear—it may recover a tolerable condition. If such use cannot be discontinued it is certain to present a dreary and mortifying appearance and to bring discredit to the government of the city by midsummer of the centennial year.

 That the difficulty may be better understood I will repeat and state more fully in what way the turf is abused. First, however, it may be necessary to observe that the greater heat and drought of this climate is most unfavorable to the maintenance of good turf as compared with that of Great Britain and the north of Europe. During a certain period, usually in August, the grasses here lose their ordinary elasticity both in blade and root, their vitality is low and under pressure and friction may be completely exhausted. The dryness of the soil at this period is in the Central Park greater than elsewhere because of the fact that it has nearly everywhere a shallow made soil laid upon a solid flooring of rock. Almost anywhere for example on the Green and between the elm trees of the mall, when the ground is saturated with moisture a walking stick may be thrust down to the rock. When these grounds were prepared it was intended to provide a system of watering by the method in use in the Bois de Boulogne, but the plan which I laid before the Board for this purpose was rejected, partly to avoid the expense of the piping and partly because it was thought that at the season when alone it would be necessary the city could not spare the water for the purpose.[5] Even with watering, however, no such use as the public has here demanded and the Department allowed is made of the turf in the Bois de Boulogne.

The misuse of the turf which has resulted in its present condition as above described has been of three kinds: first, on the days when the public school boys are allowed to play on the Ball Ground & the Green hundreds of others, many of them beyond the school age have mingled with them.[6] Foreman Manning[7] says that often as many as 50 and sometimes as many as 200 full grown men have been on the Green at once, most of them rude fellows who by main force take possession of considerable parts of it, practically excluding the boys & depriving them of their legal rights. On every fair day the number of men and boys has commonly been much larger than should have been allowed.

2^d On days when it has not been legally permissable to walk on the turf it has been much trespassed upon. It is so now. While examining the turf of the Ball Ground this morning, there being but few visitors yet on the park, I saw in ten minutes 15 persons crossing parts of it illegally, without caution, protest or reprimand. Two of them were lying down in a conspicuous position during all of the time. I am informed that last Saturday a party of boys were for sometime playing ball there and I myself checked a party going on with bats, evidently with the intention of playing.

3^d Many walk across the turf, especially near the edges of the walks without reflection that they are doing it an injury or transgressing any rule. This chiefly occurs when the walks are crowded and knots and clusters of people stand so as to force others wishing to move rapidly to step off. As soon as the turf is thus trodden smooth at any point, especially if a distinct foot path is formed, every visitor seeing it reasonably assumes that when so many have been allowed to go before him he is free to follow. In a hot day, especially, the turf or the bare ground where the turf has been is more agreeable than any prepared walk can be, consequently once partially formed the wear upon these foot ways is very rapid.

Experience shows that greater standing, sitting and passing room is required at some points and I should recommend measures for this purpose if I did not know that the Departmnt was so stinted in its means that it would be useless. But such measures would help but little.

There are two ways in which the abuses which have been described may be guarded against. First, by fencing in the walks of the parks. To a certain extent this is done already and the foremen responsible for the condition of the turf, shrubs & plants, knowing that it is the only effectual means which they are at liberty to use are inclined to resort to it much more. It is a means which destroys the charm of the park as the pleasure ground of the people and which proclaims that it is impossible to secure a proper regard for regulations absolutely essential to its preservation except by physical force; a proposition which the earlier experience of the park demonstrated, in my judgment, to be fallacious and unjust.

The other means of guarding against these abuses is that of properly distributing a sufficient number of men who incidentally to other occupations shall have the duty of cautioning visitors against disobeying the laws, of interrupting and remonstrating with those engaged in doing so and in case of need of causing their arrest.

It is utterly futile to expect the park police as at present organized to accomplish the purpose.[8] The Board has sought in vain to obtain means for enlarging its number and has been compelled on the contrary to reduce it. It is insufficient for the proper regulation of the use of the roads alone.

Runaways and collisions owing chiefly to disregard of the rules are of almost daily occurrence, and by each one of them the lives of innocent and orderly visitors are put in peril. Five persons were thrown out or knocked down last week and one lady dangerously injured. A runaway horse has been able to pass at full speed for a distance of more than two miles through the park and out of one of its most frequented gates without arrest. As for the interior walks I have frequently been for hours upon them without seeing a single man bearing a sign of authority to caution or warn visitors or to help them on their proper ways. It is so evidently absurd to interfere with a single visitor in doing what hundreds of others may be doing, that the regulations for preserving the turf and tender plants are practically regarded by the keepers themselves as a dead letter.

I will add that it is also practically impossible for the foremen to repair damages as fast as they occur and to keep the park in as good order as has been usual, with the present force employed. Notwithstanding an unusual degree of activity and industry there is not a single class of all the work of the Departmnt that is not now behind hand or a single division of the park that is adequately manned. The roads are not sufficiently watered and their more rapid wear in consequence will cost more than the wages of the additional force required for watering them.

There is but one working gardener rated and paid as such for each 100 acres of the park and for the care on an average of more than 50.000 trees & shrubs to say nothing of the herbacious plants. The gardeners report from every division of the park the stealing of plants; the withdrawal of the gate keepers from two gates as a measure of necessary reduction of force is at once followed by an invasion of goats, some of them driven in by their owners to browse on the shrubs and girdle the young trees. They may easily damage the park in a single hour to an amount ten times their value to their owners and much more than the wages of the watchmen who would be required to guard against them.

I mention these facts that the Commissioners may be the better prepared for the inevitable consequences of the present policy of the city in reference to the park. It is absolutely necessary that the force should be still further reduced in order to keep the expenses of the Departmnt within the limit fixed by the Board of Apportionmnt or that this limit should be practically enlarged by a reduction of wages.[9]

With respect to the turf, I must advise the Board that the Ball Ground and the mall cannot be put in a condition to be used this summer as heretofore, without causing such injury to them as will destroy their value and as cannot be properly repaired except by breaking up and reforming them another year.

I believe that it would cause the least privation to the public and the least dissatisfaction to suspend ball playing & croquet playing and the usual Saturday and Sunday free range over all the turf of the South Park during the present year. The North Meadows might be prepared for the use of the school boys while the ball ground is recruiting.[10]

Respectfully.

The text presented here is from a draft in Olmsted's hand.

1. Olmsted is referring to his plan reorganizing the park keepers force, adopted by the park board in March 1873. Part of his printed instructions to the keepers emphasized the importance of healthy turf for the park experience. Because excessive foot traffic easily damaged the turf in Central Park, part of their duty was tactfully to enforce regulations that limited public access. The board rescinded its approval of Olmsted's plan in September 1873 (*Papers of FLO*, 6: 42–45; Frederick Law Olmsted, "Instructions to the Keepers of the Central Park," [Feb. 20, 1873], in *Forty Years* 2: 457–65).
2. The printed minutes and quarterly reports of the department for September 1874 do not mention any report by Olmsted on the condition of the turf at Central Park.
3. That is, the park south of the Old Croton Reservoir at 79th Street.
4. Olmsted presented the current text at the park board meeting of May 21, 1875. The commissioners agreed to meet him on the park the next day to examine the condition of the turf. Only William R. Martin and Joseph J. O'Donohue met with Olmsted, and it was not until June 9 that the full board formally responded to his recommendations (DPP, *Minutes*, May 21, 1875, p. 33; ibid., June 9, 1875, pp. 78–80; FLO, Patronage Journal, May 22, 1875, below).
5. In the autumn of 1859 Olmsted visited England and Europe to study the public parks and procured drawings of their irrigation systems. He made eight visits to the Bois de Boulogne in Paris, where engineers had built an extensive system of steam pumps, aqueducts, and reservoirs, to draw water from the Seine, pressurize it, and deliver it to the park via underground pipes and sprinklers. Based on his study of the system, Olmsted estimated that to irrigate Central Park below 86th Street between May and November each year would require over seventy-six million gallons of water (BCCP, *Minutes*, Sept. 27, 1859, pp. 146–47; Jean-Charles-Adolphe Alphand, *Les Promenades de Paris*. . . [1867–73; rpt. ed., Princeton, N.J., 1984], pp. 15–26; BCCP, *Third Annual Report* [1860], pp. 59–61; *Papers of FLO*, 3: 234–35, 349–51).
6. Since 1859 the Central Park commissioners had barred all but periodic access to select areas of turf. Beginning in 1866, they allowed school boys who had the permission of their principals to play on the turf areas of the south park from two to three days a week,

depending on the season and condition of the turf. Through the 1860s the commissioners denied applications by adult clubs to play baseball or croquet on these commons. Besides the considerable damage such active sport did to lawns, it clashed with the adopted purpose of the park to provide rural recreation for the entire public. By 1874, however, adults could play croquet on the East Green and the general public was allowed access to the Green and Ball Ground on music days, holidays, and weekends. Despite a serious drought that year, such use continued and enforcement of the general regulations about the turf was lax ("Regulations for the Use of the Central Park," [Nov. 3, 1860] [*Papers of FLO*, 3: 279]; BCCP, *Tenth Annual Report* [1867], pp. 35–40; *Forty Years*, 2: 406–14, 421–32; Clarence Cook, *A Description of the New York Central Park* [New York, 1869], pp. 113, 196–98; [FLO], [Report on Maintenance], pp. 6–7).
7. John W. Manning (b. 1833), a general foreman in the parks department (U.S., Census Office, 10th Census, *10th Census 1880. New York* [Washington, D.C., 1880], Schedule 1, Manhattan, p. 26).
8. Olmsted told the board shortly before writing the present report that the condition of the turf depended in some degree on the weather, but much more "upon the degree of industry, activity and judicious management exercised by the park keepers. Unless their duty is better done than it was last year, a larger expense for work to preserve the turf will not prevent it from becoming even more shabby than it is at present" ([FLO], [Report on Maintenance], pp. 7–8).
9. In January 1875 the New York City Board of Estimate and Apportionment had fixed the department's budget for park maintenance at $426,000, about $150,000 less than requested. Demands on this budget increased in late March when the department's construction budget was unexpectedly exhausted and all payrolls had to be paid out of the maintenance fund (DPP, *Minutes*, Jan. 5, 1875, pp. 429–30; FLO, Patronage Journal, March 25, 1875, below).
10. Instead of banning games and public access to the lawns of the south park as Olmsted suggested, the commissioners limited such use to the Ball Ground through the end of summer, when it was to be plowed under and replanted with grass. They also ordered a more thorough enforcement of the regulations controlling access to the lawn areas of the park. During this period the board took initial steps to install an irrigation system for the Ball Ground but no work was completed on it during Olmsted's tenure with the department (DPP, *Minutes*, May 14, 1875, pp. 28–29; ibid., June 9, 1875, pp. 79–80; ibid., June 29, 1875, p. 120; ibid., Sept. 6, 1875, p. 262; ibid., May 10, 1876, p. 25; *New-York Daily Tribune*, Dec. 31, 1877, p. 2).

To Montgomery Cunningham Meigs

[June 1, 1875]

M. Gnl. M. C. Meigs;
Q. M. General. U.S.A.
My Dear General;
    The improvments which I shall propose on the grounds at Schuylkill Arsenal are simple and the chief expenses required to carry them out will be

the renewal of the existing stone work (chiefly in curbs) which was never very good and is now delapidated with 70 years use.[1] Concrete paving also would be substituted with advantage for the present road surface, on the entrance way and in the Central Court, and flagging or concrete for plank on the rail way platform. The house originally designed as the residence of the officer in charge and now occupied by Captain Rogers[2] is a substantial building of the last century which yet lacks certain conveniences and appliances now commonly thought indispensable for a household living in a civilized town.[3]

Captain Hull's house is much smaller and is cramped, ill arranged, and approached in a most awkward and embarrassing way. It was originally intended as quarters for a mechanic and was but poorly planned for the purpose. Whatever the exigencies of military service may require on the frontier I cannot think it should be considered suitable for the family of an officer when stationed at Philadelph[a].

None of the inconveniences and deprivations which attach to a residence in these houses were pointed out to me by anyone at the depôt and the two officers more directly concerned were both slow to admit them and except as to the lack of any tolerable means of access to the smaller house indisposed to offer or entertain suggestions for their remedy. They obviously did not expect me to concern myself with them.

I am sure however that the defects to which I allude ought not be regarded as irremediable and permanent and as the simplest remedies for them would affect the question of approaches and other use of the adjoining ground I must consider it within my commission, unless you {are} otherwise distinctly instructed, to submit plans to you for some very modest improvments of the character indicated.[4]

The text presented here is from a draft in Olmsted's hand, which he dated on the back of the last page.

1. In 1798 Congress authorized the construction of an arsenal for the manufacture and keeping of armaments and military stores in Philadelphia. Two years later the secretary of war purchased eight acres of land along the Schuylkill River, on Gray's Ferry Road between Carpenter Street and Washington Avenue, and began erecting buildings for the Schuylkill Arsenal. Its main structures, completed in 1806, consisted of four brick warehouses grouped around a central court, a brick house for the commanding officer, a powder-magazine, and other structures. After the War of 1812 the army built a larger arsenal at nearby Frankford, and the Schuylkill Arsenal became the central depot for the quartermaster general's department. In May 1875 Meigs had invited Olmsted to examine its grounds and submit plans for their improvement, which he wanted finished "in a tasteful manner" before the Centennial Exhibition of 1876. Olmsted visited the arsenal, obtained a rough plat of its grounds and buildings, and sent Thomas Wisedell there to take measurements before making the present report (Joseph Jackson, *Encyclopedia of Philadelphia*, 4 vols. [Harrisburg, Pa., 1931], 1: 148–49; Montgomery C. Meigs to FLO, May 6, 1875, Record Group 92, Records of the Quartermaster General's Of-

fice, Entry 225, Consolidated Correspondence File, "Fred'k L. Olmstead," box 474, NARA, Washington, D.C.; John F. Rodgers to FLO, May 19, 1875; FLO to John F. Rodgers, May 23, 1875).
2. John F. Rodgers (1830–1899), U.S. Army military storekeeper and officer in charge of the Schuylkill Arsenal, was Olmsted's principal contact regarding improvements there (*The Washington Post*, August 26, 1899, p. 2; Records of the Adjutant General's Office, Letters Received by the Appointment, Commission, and Personal Branch, file 99 ACP 1873, NARA, Washington, D.C.).
3. Olmsted recommended that renovations to the house include enlarging the main hall and adding a coat and wash room, a water closet with outside ventilation, and a pantry with china closet, accessible from the kitchen and opening into the dining room. On the outside, he wanted to build a new front veranda and partially enclose the rear one (FLO to John F. Rodgers, June 18, 1875).
4. In June 1875 Colonel Rufus Ingalls, who acted as quartermaster general while Meigs was on assignment abroad, approved Olmsted's proposals and asked him to submit plans and estimates for renovating the buildings and grounds of the arsenal. In the latter half of 1875 Olmsted formulated the overall designs and, with the help of George Kent Radford, certified the work of colleagues on the project. Jacob Weidenmann drew up plans for drainage, walks and drives, and plantings, and superintended their construction. Thomas Wisedell provided studies and working plans for the architectural improvements, which included the two houses mentioned in this letter, the wall of the arsenal and its gate lodge. Olmsted observed that in the plans "it has been attempted to sustain the general style and character of the old buildings of the Arsenal but to extend it to a greater degree of interest of a quaint and picturesque type in such details as will admit of it." The project was completed by June 1876 (Montgomery C. Meigs to FLO, June 8, 1875; Rufus Ingalls to FLO, June 15, 1875; FLO, Schuylkill Arsenal bill, May 10, 1877; Jacob Weidenmann, Schuylkill Arsenal account, Aug. 4, 1876; Thomas Wisedell, Schuylkill Arsenal account, Aug. 30, 1876; FLO to Stewart Van Vliet, Sept. 25, 1875; U.S. War Department, *Annual Report*, 4 vols. [Washington, D.C., 1876], 1: 128, 169).

To John A. Partridge[1]

209 W. 46 ST.
NEW YORK.
9th Septr. 1875

J. A. Partridge Eq^r
Eng^r in Chg.
My Dear Sir;
   I have yours of yesterday.[2]
   If we are to have a very dry month, as you apprehend, would {it} not be useless to hasten to sow the seed? We gain nothing by having it in the ground, while, by a further process of harrowing, rolling, harrowing, picking and raking we shall gain much. I leave the determination to your discretion, only again, begging you to keep in mind that upon the refinement of the last

process before seeding depends the value of all the rest of our work. If seeding fails it can be done over again but when once seeded we are not likely to improve the lights and shades of the surface or give greater fineness and evenness of quality to the pap of our rootlets. I have always urged carelessness (cheapness of process and wholesale quality of superintendence) in the preparation of the ground up to this point because it is better and more economical to remedy all defects so occurring and to secure delicacy in one or two weeks of finishing work than to be always at it. Now, however, too much attention to detail — too much pains and refinemnt — cannot be taken.

There are two things to be secured, fine modelling, and fine tilth. As to the first it is so much a matter of constant local review of the work as it advances by the educated eye and artistic sense that I have nothing to say. The only danger is that with everything else you have the work will proceed too fast for you — will be run away with. I have only one thing to remind you of — what I wrote last spring & which was then forgotten. Take care that the spread of roots of each tree is fairly to be seen above ground and that the surface *slightly falls from,* never toward, each tree. If this rule is intelligently adhered to, (here a very slight, then a long and stronger slope according as space gives opportunity) the combination of curves that will (mechanically) result will be always pleasing. Thus the rule will save much consideration for this purpose. But be sure to fix in the mind of the graders that this rule is to be carried out never by heaping up about the trees, but always by combing out vallies between them, surplus soil to be carted away. I am sure there is still room for some improvement in this respect in the North plantation.

As to the tilth, you know that, except among close-planted trees, I would insist on having the greater part of the work done by the process the efficiency of which you have so thoroughly experienced: horses jumping with the harrow and frightened boys following them; the roller following as long as it crushes the lumps the harrow cannot be made to *knock* to powder. This is simply to save the necessity of spending as much time as would otherwise be necessary in the more costly process of pulverizing by the hand rake. Hand raking and perhaps here & there a little hand shovelling will be needed at last for the finish, but not much of it if men can be got to work briskly; it being quick action not strength that is required.

If you feel satisfied with the seeding of the South plantation let it stand. With a little patching here and there I think it likely that it will do, the weather having been so favorable since I examined it.

If you wish to seed before October, let me know as soon as you think that the surface will be satisfactory and I will, if I can, run on and inspect it. I am more anxious about it than anything else that remains to be done.

If you sow and, especially, if the seed barely or in part germinates before the occurrence of a drought you will have the worst condition to be anticipated. You must then be prepared to water finely and sedulously — an expensive operation which I hope will not happen to be necessary.

It would be desirable, with reference to a rapid early developmnt of roots, to sow with or upon the grass seeds, some fine quickly stimulating manure. You can judge by consultation with your seedsman or Mr Smith[3] what can best be bought, at this time in Washington, for the purpose & what would be a moderate top dressing.

One of the commercial mixtures of Peruvian Guano and Sup. Phosphate of lime[4]—if you can feel confidence against being cheated, would answer. For convenience of sowing and in order to secure adequate division & distribution it may be mixed with fine dry loam.

Excuse prolixity and repetition. This is a part of the business in which you have no *professional* knowledge or interest but in which my professional interest culminates.

Radford will tomorrow send you sketch for gas pipe. I should feel much better satisfied to have had it made with the benefit of a plan of the adjoining lighting on streets and the East grounds.

Yours Truly

Fred Law Olmsted.

The text presented here is from a manuscript in Olmsted's hand in the Office of the Curator, Architect of the Capitol, U.S. Capitol, Washington, D.C. During the spring and summer of 1875 John Partridge supervised work on the U.S. Capitol grounds according to Olmsted's plan and instructions. All of the east grounds (besides the roads, walks, and carriage court) were provided with subsoil drainage, a water supply, and covered with a fertile soil one foot deep. Although work was done on the west grounds, Olmsted instructed Partridge to give the east side more finish in order to make a good impression on congressmen when they convened in December. This policy, he told Partridge in June, was "the only *policy* I ever use and we must stand or fall by it. That is to say, we must leave our work in such shape that it will stand us in lieu of all lobbying" (*Annual Report of the Architect of the Capitol* [1875], p. 885; FLO to John A. Partridge, June 18, 1875).

1. John A. Partridge (1829–1898) (U.S., Census Office, 10th Census, *10th Census 1880. Washington, D.C.* [Washington, D.C., 1880], schedule 1, p. 46; Supreme Court of the District of Columbia, Register of Wills, Will of John A. Partridge [Washington, D.C., March 23, 1898], no. 8275).
2. Partridge was preparing to start plowing and harrowing the east grounds to sow rye grass, but feared the weather might be too dry for the seed to germinate properly (John A. Partridge to FLO, Sept. 7, 1875).
3. William R. Smith, head of the nearby U.S. Botanic Garden.
4. Bat guano from Peru, imported into the United States since the 1830s, was used to improve the structure and fertility of nitrogen-poor soils. Superphosphate was a fertilizing product manufactured by treating natural phosphates, such as limestone, shells, or bones, with sulfuric acid. By mid-October 1875, Partridge reported that the east grounds were green with rye and clover (Liberty Hyde Bailey, *Cyclopedia of American Agriculture*, 4 vols. [New York, 1907–09], 1: 455, 465–66; United States. Agricultural Research Service. Soil and Water Conservation Research Division, *Superphosphate: its History,*

Chemistry, and Manufacture [Washington, D.C., 1964], pp. 37–55; John A. Partridge to FLO, Oct. 11, 1875).

To WILLIAM HAMMOND HALL[1]

209 W. 46 ST.
NEW YORK.
13th Septr 1875.

Cemetery Plans

Wm Hammond Hall Eq^r
My Dear Sir;

I have just receivd yours of 4th inst.[2]

I must, in the first place, privately confess to you that I am so far from being satisfied with the prevalent fashions and customs in regard to the matter of your inquiry that I am less well informed than you might expect me to be. I have more than once advised applicants for my services in laying out burial places to go to someone with more experience and less out of tune in this respect than I consider myself to be. Mr Adolph Strauch of Cincinatti[3] and Mr J. Widenmann of New York[4] are the only respectable authorities whom I know on the subject.

For the above reason I am but poorly prepared to give you the information and advice you ask.

The more notable Cemetery Companies of which I have knowledge are as follows:

Greenwood and Wood Lawn, New York.
Mount Auburn —   Boston
Laurel Hill,   Phil^a
Cedar Hill,   Hartford;
Oakland,   Syracuse;
Forestlawn,   Buffalo;
Spring Grove,   Cincinatti;
Oak Wood —   Chicago;
Mount Royal (protst^t)
Cote des Neiges (Rom. C)   Quebec.[5]

Besides the above I have had occasion to visit cemeteries that seemed to be under good management and of the better class at Quebec, Springfield, Mass. Georgetown, D.C. and Louisville, Ky. but do not know their corporate designations.[6] There are many more which I have not visited.

The greater number of those grounds have been laid out, like Lone Mountain,[7] piece-meal or in desultory way, on no fixed principles of design. Every good thing in them stands by itself, gaining nothing from and adding nothing to the other elements of the scenery. Mr Strauch of Cincinatti has the honor of introducing what for this climate is, in this respect a great improvmnt, in what is known as the "lawn system."[8] It is not adapted to your climate but its main advantage of broad effects and the avoidance of petty and discordant details may perhaps be secured by other means. It allows, as a general rule, but one (family) monument for each burial lot, conceals the boundaries of lots, does away with posts and chains and iron work and gives the company the duty of setting and careing for all plants so that an appropriate general sylvan effect may be secured.

Some months since Mr Robinson of the Garden asked me to send him material for an article on American Cemeteries and I applied to Mr Strauch for assistance.[9] He was good enough to collect and send me a number of reports of Trustees of Cemeteries laid out more or less in accordance with his views, which together with every scrap of print I had on the subject I transmitted to London. But for this I might have been able to answer you more fully & satisfactory. A letter addressd by mail to the Trustees or the Secretary of either of the Companies I have named would, however, probably procure, in most cases, their last printed report and, in some, copies of the forms and blank used & of the by-laws.

I prepared a plan and report for a cemetery at Oakland while I was in California and both I think were printed.[10] So far as there was any originality in the design I do not think it was carried out nor could it be without some unusual pluck and capital. I don't think that I should be at all satisfied with it.

Respectfully Yours

Fred Law Olmsted

The text presented here is from a manuscript in Olmsted's hand in the William Hammond Hall Papers, Bancroft Library, University of California, Berkeley, California.

1. See FLO to William Hammond Hall, March 23, 1874, note 1, above.
2. In his letter of September 4, 1875, Hall wrote Olmsted that he was "about to organize a Rural Cemetery Association" in San Francisco and wanted any information Olmsted could provide about laying out cemeteries (William Hammond Hall to FLO, Sept. 4, 1875).
3. Adolph Strauch (see FLO to William Robinson, c. March 20–30, 1875, n. 3, above).
4. Jacob Weidenmann (1829–1893), landscape architect. Weidenmann designed Cedar Hill Cemetery in Hartford, Connecticut, in the early 1860s (David Schuyler, "Jacob Weidenmann," in *American Landscape Architecture: Designers and Places*, William Tishler, ed. [Washington, D.C., 1989], p. 44).
5. Laurel Hill Cemetery was established in 1836 in Philadelphia; Cedar Hill Cemetery was consecrated in 1863 in Hartford, Connecticut; Oakwood Cemetery was created in

1859 in Syracuse, New York; Forest Lawn Cemetery was laid out in 1853 in Buffalo, New York; Oak Woods Cemetery was established in 1853 in Chicago, Illinois; Mount Royal Cemetery for Protestants was acquired in 1852 and Côte des Neiges Cemetery for Catholics was established in 1853 in Montreal (for Mount Auburn, Green-Wood, and Spring Grove cemeteries see FLO to William Robinson, c. March 20–30, 1875, nn. 2 and 6, above; D.C. Sloane, *The Last Great Necessity*, pp. 56, 93; *Papers of FLO*, SS1: 169; John Irwin Cooper, *Montreal: A Brief History* [Montreal, 1969], p. 76).

6. The most highly reputed cemeteries in the places that Olmsted mentions were Mount Hermon Cemetery near the city of Quebec in Canada; Springfield (or Peabody) Cemetery in Springfield, Massachusetts; Oak Hill Cemetery in the Georgetown section of the District of Columbia; and Cave Hill Cemetery in Louisville, Kentucky (J. M. LeMoine, *Picturesque Quebec: A Sequel to Quebec Past and Present*, [Montreal, 1882], pp. 356–57; Alfred Minot Copeland, *A History of Hamden Country, Mass.*, 3 vols. [Boston, 1902], 2: 197–99; Wilhelmus B. Bryan, *A History of the National Capital*, 2 vols. [New York, 1914–1916], 2: 313–14; "Cave Hill Cemetery, Louisville, Ky.," *Park and Cemetery* 10 [Dec. 1896]: 380).
7. Lone Mountain Cemetery in San Francisco, California, established in 1854 (*Papers of FLO*, 5: 487).
8. See FLO to William Robinson, c. March 20–30, 1875, note 2, above.
9. See FLO to William Robinson, c. March 20–30, 1875, above.
10. In 1865 Olmsted prepared a report and plan for the Mountain View Cemetery Association in Oakland, California. The plan, however, was only partially carried out (Frederick Law Olmsted, *Preface to the Plan for Mountain View Cemetery, Oakland, California*, May 1865 [*Papers of FLO*, 5: 473–87]).

To Walter L. Sessions[1]

9th Octr 1875

The Hon W. L. Sessions;
Panama
Chautauqua Co.
Dear Sir,

I am sorry not to have seen you on my visit last Saturday to Mayville.[2] I could not fix the time for my going there until after meeting the Park Commissioners at Buffalo the night before and you doubtless received my telegram too late.

As I gave my professional opinion with reference to the land which I examined and on those points on which I was consulted to the Revd Mr Miller[3] and the other gentlemen interested whom I had the pleasure of seeing at Mayville I propose to write to you at this time personally and confidentially, having occasion to say some things which courtesy would hardly permit me to address to them on account of the connection which they have had with the Fair Point Camp, or so called "park" of Palestine.[4] It appeared to me that they regarded the proposed enterprise at Leets Point as one of similar character, hoping only for an improvement upon it. Also that, though in a certain qualified way, perhaps, but still positively, they regarded it — the Fair Point affair — with admiration.

I am far from doing so. Passing the arrangmnts for public worship which are, at least, thoroughly respectable, and the model of Palestine, which for a temporary exhibition designed to interest, instruct and please Sunday School children was a good notion though carried out in a slovenly and improvident way, not good for the education of anybody, there was nothing in the place, except the damaged natural features, that struck me at all agreeably while there was much that made me indignant.

When land is sold as it has been there, it is with a view to its occupation as a place of healthful summer recreation. Whoever has been led to buy land at Fair Point on that assumption has been swindled. The swindle is the more wicked that there is a pretence of organization by intelligent and educated men at its back, which is miserable quackery. Worse still, that there is a pretense of a religious motive, which is cant of the meanest and most despicable sort.

If you think I speak hastily, please consider that the main difference between a camp, village or city of a pagan and barbrous and of a Christian and enlightened people is that in the latter the results of experience and study are better applied to guard against the degrading and sickening influences which the lodging of great numbers of persons in close contiguity invariably tends to induce.

I have travelled nearly around the world and have fared with many tribes and nations but I have never before seen a place at which people had lodged in anything like the numbers they have at Fair Point — or as it has been deliberately intended by the managing of it that they should, for months together, in which the most firmly established laws of health and laws of morality for communities were so set at defiance as they appear to have been there.

Not doubting that there had been a certain degree of good motive in its origin and managment, I must think it in the last degree disgraceful to the intelligence of our country that 6000 people could have been found willing to live and expose their families to the danger of such arrangmnts. The wealth of the State of New York would not induce me to trust mine at Fair Point for a week.

It is a well known rule that the influence of such a manner of living affects men insidiously, silently and slowly, or that it shows itself at intervals in tempest-like bursts of pestilence. Hence it is not at all surprising that the danger has not made itself felt, but I would stake all the reputation I have earned on the prediction that if no radical change of arrangment is made at Fair Point and it shall continue to be resorted to as it has been or by half or quarter the number of people, it will, after a few years, become notorious as the place where hundreds have taken the seed of untimely death, and that it is not the worst to be feared from it.

It is needless to add that I will have nothing to do with the preparation of anything of a similar character.

But I have asked myself to what is the immediate popularity of such a place as Fair Point due? I suppose it is mainly and primarily to the opportunity which it is supposed to offer for a long summer relief from ordinary conditions of business and of household care; for gaining health by change of air, and for gratifying the gregarious, social and devotional inclinations of human nature at comparatively *small cost*. Except as to the devotional elemnt Fair Point has been expected to serve people of moderate means and simple tastes and habits in place of Saratoga, Long Branch or Newport.[5] In respect to the devotional element, as a prolonged and improved camp-meeting.

If this is the explanation of the crowds that remained for weeks at Fair Point last summer, the success of such miserable arrangements demonstrates the existence of a real public need of such urgency that in all probability the full and legitimate development of it has not yet begun to be witnessed. It is a case of demand undeveloped because of undeveloped supply. The demand jumps to meet the first weak pretence of supply.

I call it — the whole arrangement at Fair Point — a pretence because it will surely supply disease, not health, and as to the devotional element, the history of our race everywhere demonstrates that Godliness and cleanliness are in close contiguity and that there is such a thing as the material washing away of many sinful propensities as well as the typical washing away of sin. Fair Point will breed moral degredation as surely as a carcass will breed maggots.

An honest, well studied, substantial undertaking to satisfy this public want would be an honorable and beneficent enterprise, as well carried out it doubtless would be a perfectly sound commercial one.

Among the essential conditions of permanent and secure success in such an enterprise would be:

1st ample means and inoffensive methods of removing and disposing of wastes and filth of all kinds.

2d ample and convenient water supply.

3d Elements of attraction which would give promise by their character that the place would increase in beauty, comfort and popularity from year to year and not such as bear conspicuous seeds of dreary decay, shabbyness and delapidation, of disease, degredation and death.

What is wanted is, in fact, a summer city. No civilized family lives voluntarily in a city which lacks the two first provisions. No summer city will be long endurable without them. The elements which make places attractive as summer residences the world over, (aside from the social ones, which are not to be directly supplied like articles of merchandize) are trees, shrubs & flowers, with ample means of taking the air and enjoying prospects.

(Consider for a moment what nearly half the houses at Fair Point are in these respects. The windows of one look into those of another, the exhaled air and all the gaseous wastes of one drift directly into another, the slops of one soak under the sills of another. There is no foliage to be seen except overhead, where it serves to shut out the most important requirement for the preservation of health under such circumstances—the disinfecting and prophylactic influence of direct sunlight.)

The providing of the three conditions I have named must go far before those for public worship and social recreations. (If anything is an insult and abomination to the Lord, who has established the laws of health and of the preservation of decency and given us intelligence to understand them if we will, it must be public worship under such conditions as have been established at Fair Point). With them must come highways, not the false promises of highways of the map of Fair Point. To get these things there would be required not only the general Plan which I might furnish but a man of some degree of practical knowledge, experience and skill in such business to plan and determine the details and direct and superintend their execution.

Of course it is a problem how to realize these conditions in a manner consistent with the purpose of providing what is required at a sufficiently low price to the purchasers and tenants, a problem the proper solution of which requires ingenuity and special study.

I need not add that a much larger capital would also be required than has been used at Fair Point, but it would not be nearly as large as you might at first imagine if the plans were shrewdly designed in consideration of the fact that the arrangmnts were to be only for summer use & much ordinary provision against frost could be avoided.

In all probability the dividends on the necessary investmnt would not come so soon or be at once so large as they would on something more nearly imitating the Fair Point speculation, but in my judgmnt they would be surer to continue and be increasing for many years.

The Leets Point property, with strips along the shore running each way from it is well adapted to such an undertaking. There are many advantages as I explained to Mr Miller in confining operations mainly to the close vicinity of the shore. The cost of the works will be less, their value greater.

On the principle that it is better to sell 100 acres of land at a profit of $25 an acre than 25 acres at a profit of $50 an acre, I have little doubt that a more spacious and liberal character in the plan and the sale of land in larger measures than at Fair Point would be good policy.

I have said all that is necessary for my immediate purpose. For an undertaking such as I have indicated I would make a general plan, on my usual terms. I do not wish to do so and I would rather advise you to employ a man who would be able to give to the business more time and personal study and to aid more in the practical management of the work than I could.[6] Mr. H. W. S Cleveland of Chicago with whom I have heretofore cooperated with much satisfaction & who has done an extensive business at the first but is now I believe in want of occupation,[7] would, for example, be such a man — a most worthy, industrious and skilful Landscape Architect. You might possibly secure the service of Mr. F. J. Scott of Toledo,[8] who judging from his book must be fully as competent as I am — in some respects more so, but I fear he is not open to an engagment.

If you wish to make a demonstration next summer, which I would not advise, I would remind you that a camp of tents, skilfully displayed with suitable temporary decorations of bunting, annual vines, flowers, evergreens & various spectacular and theatrical devices on a green field is infinitely more attractive than one of shantees and that it would cost but little if anything more to make sanitary provisions of a temporary character for large number of people decent & complete than barely passable and indecent. Most of the requisite means for such a purpose could I presume be rented for the summer, transported to the ground and made ready for use on short orders.

Your obedient Servant

The text presented here is from a draft in Olmsted's hand.

1. Walter L. Sessions (1820–1896), was a lawyer and Republican politician from Chautauqua County in western New York. In the 1850s and 1860s he served in the New York state legislature and at the time of this letter had just concluded two terms in the U.S. House of Representatives. Active in the Baptist church, Sessions joined others of that denomination in late September 1875 in forming the Point Chautauqua Association with the purpose of creating a summer religious retreat on Chautauqua Lake. He was elected president of the association's board of directors and served on the committee that hired Olmsted to examine the 100-acre Leet's Point farm on the east shore of the lake. He examined the site on October 2, 1875, and upon his recommendation the committee purchased it early the next month (BDAC; Andrew White Young, *History of Chautauqua County, New York* [Buffalo, N.Y., 1875], pp. 664–65; *Chautauqua Assembly Daily Herald*, Aug. 8, 1877, p. 1).
2. Mayville, the county seat of Chautauqua County, is located on the north end of Chautauqua Lake.
3. J. H. Miller, Baptist minister from Mayville and secretary of the Point Chautauqua Association (A. W. Young, *Chautauqua County*, p. 665).
4. That is, the camp meeting and Sunday school association property operated by Methodists at Fair Point, on the western shore of the lake nearly opposite Leet's Point. It featured, as an aid to Sunday school instruction, an outdoor model of the Holy Land called Palestine Park. General educational topics came to characterize the meetings at Fair Point, which was renamed Chautauqua in 1877 and subsequently became the famed Chautauqua Institution (ibid., p. 664; B. Dolores Thompson, *Jamestown and Chautauqua County: An Illustrated History* [Jamestown, N.Y., 1984], pp. 61–62).
5. Saratoga, New York, was one of the most exclusive resorts in the United States, while the summer homes of the rich lined the seashore at Newport, Rhode Island. Long Branch, New Jersey, had developed as a seaside resort since the mid-1860s, and in 1866–67 Olmsted, Vaux & Company prepared plans for a subdivision of summer cottages there (*Papers of FLO*, 6: 104–10).

6. Olmsted did prepare a general plan for Point Chautauqua in the weeks following this letter, but became concerned when it appeared that Miller expected him to superintend its execution on the ground:

> Your undertaking is one with which I have a profound sympathy and if you could place everything in my hands and it was possible for me to take up the affair in that spirit I should be delighted with the opportunity. There is nothing I have ever done that I would like better than to be able to carry out my own ideas of what such a place should be. But this is impossible.

Olmsted could not spare the time from his other engagements to superintend this plan himself and stressed that it would be a failure unless it was "followed by a great deal of study and close superintendence on the ground by some man experienced in works combining problems of Engineering, Architecture, and Gardening" (FLO to J. H. Miller, Dec. 13, 1875; ibid., Jan. 5, 1876; FLO to J. H. Miller, Feb. 28, 1876, below).

7. Cleveland had been in charge of implementing the Olmsted, Vaux & Company's 1871 designs for the South Park commission in Chicago but since the economic depression of 1873 that work had been interrupted several times. In May 1875 he wrote Olmsted in search of steadier employment. In December 1875 Olmsted followed up his recommendation here by proposing to Miller that Cleveland join him in preparing the Point Chautauqua plan and that Cleveland's firm then superintend it. Nothing came of the proposal (FLO, "Country Living," Jan. 22, 1874, above; Horace William Shaler Cleveland to FLO, May 26, 1875; ibid., June 8, 1875; FLO to J. H. Miller, Dec. 13, 1875).

8. Frank Jesup Scott (1828–1919), landscape gardener and author of *The Art of Beautifying Suburban Home Grounds* (1870), which Olmsted reviewed for the *Nation* in 1871. Trained under A. J. Downing, through whom he met and became friends with Calvert Vaux, Scott had an architecture practice in Toledo, Ohio (*Papers of FLO*, 6: 472–77).

To Horatio Admiral Nelson[1]

11th Oct 1875

To Hon H. A. Nelson
Copy
My Dear Sir

I have just received your favor of the 9th. My plan for the mountain approach roads went from here on the 7th and should have been in your hands when your letter was written.[2] I hope that it has since been received and found satisfactory. Be so good as to advise me.

I would be glad to have your attention particularly given to the suggestion of an approach from the corner of the Reservoir.[3] It is important to keep in mind that your object is a *pleasure* drive and that, provided the route is interesting, a few minutes more or less to be spent upon it is a matter of small consequence — in some respects even an advantage, {for} which excessive crookedness and steepness are very objectionable. Your pleasure is not to be all concentrated on the top of the mountain and the base treated as a disagreeable necessity to be got through with in the shortest possible way at any cost. Looking at it all as a part of your park—the ascent of Peel Street or the upper part of McTavish can never be made a pleasure drive—it will be postively painful. On the other hand, with moderate improvements in the lower part of McTavish Street you may be able to drive from Sherbrooke by the way I suggest to the top of the mountain at a trot, with pleasanter scenery and easier turns. It is true that with a strong horse and harness you could make the distance about 5 minutes shorter by Peel Street, but to do so you would make a toil of pleasure.

Perhaps from the point of view to which you have been obliged to accustom yourselves in Montreal my objections to such a comparatively short piece of steep road may not seem very weighty, but you will remember that study of refinement in such matters is the main part of my business.

Looking either to comfort in ascending the mountain or to the most refined art in landscape effect I should advise no approach from Peel Street. If the commission think it necessary I am willing to do all I can to make the best of it, but I fear that at its best it will be an ugly job. The whole impression of a drive in the park—up the mountain—will be a more consistently impressive one, if the reservoir route is taken and no other is opened to the South of it.

Your obedt. Servant

The text presented here is from a draft in Olmsted's hand.

1. Horatio Admiral Nelson, chairman of the Mount Royal park commission (see FLO to the Commissioners of Mount Royal Park, Nov. 23, 1874, n. 1, above).
2. On October 7, 1875, Olmsted provided the park commission with a map and report for laying out the road up the mountain to the Glades section. He intended to have the primary entrance be on Bleury Street (now avenue du Parc on the northern side of the park), although he wished to visit the place again before making a final plan for the drive through what was to be the côte-placide section of the park. Nelson, however, preferred an approach from Peel Street and responded to Olmsted's plan on October 9 by urging him to concentrate his efforts on that approach (which Olmsted had only indicated tentatively with dotted lines in his plan of October 7). Nelson had earlier informed Olmsted that

    I should like it if you lay out the Peel Street connection so that work may be commenced on it at once, this or McTavish Street will be the short way on to the Mountain and will be much more used than the round about way via Bleury Street, as the larger number of the Driving Teams are owned in the Western part of the City, & the great attraction will be the top of the Mountain, it is getting to be a great place of resort already.

   (FLO to H. A. Nelson, Oct. 7, 1875; H. A. Nelson to FLO, Sept. 13, 1875; ibid., Oct. 9, 1875; FLO to Patrick Macquisten, Oct. 7, 1875).
3. Olmsted describes here the alternative approach that he proposed, and which he included, along with the switch-back approach from Peel Street, in his plan of 1877. This

second approach was to run up McTavish Street to the reservoir and then pass on its northern side, following the line to the park of present-day avenue Docteur-Penfield. The park commission did not adopt this part of Olmsted's plan and that section of the park was eventually occupied by the Royal Victoria Hospital (FLO to Patrick MacQuisten, Oct. 7, 1875).

To Thomas Hill[1]

209 W. 46 ST.
NEW YORK.
3rd November, 1875.

My Dear Doctor Hill;
    I have just received your favor of the 30th ulto.
    I believe that the word exotic is something more than a synonym of foreign or strange — it carries a sense of unnatural, out of harmony with local natural conditions. If so, you take for granted the sole point to which the argument of my last letter was directed. If the attention of more than one in ten or fifty thousand, and that one other than a botanist, is to be supposed divertible in the slightest degree from the landscape as a whole by the plants I have named and stand for more than by those you stand for, my advocacy of them falls to the ground. Does the occurrence of the little red or yellow clover or the buttercups in the pastures of Walpole or the barberry on the hills of Andover distract attention from the loveliness of the Connecticut or the Merrimac vallies?[2]
    I go with you and beyond you on the line of your argument, for I have no doubt at all about the misfortune of the profile, and stand ready to contribute to blow its nose off with gunpowder without waiting for an earthquake.[3] That is precisely what landscape gardening should do I think, make improvements by design which nature might by chance make through the action of earthquakes, storms, frosts, birds and insects.
    (I have this in print, and will send it to you if I can get a copy of my paper.)[4]
    I fully endorse every word you say, except that I am not disposed to regard the trumpet creeper as necessarily a permanent exotic in the White Hills, and should not wait to be sure that it had found its way there by chance already before using it as a very valuable means of preventing the railroad from doing the scenery an injury.[5]
    Very truly and respectfully,

Fred. Law Olmsted.

FEBRUARY 1875–FEBRUARY 1876

The text presented here is from a document in a clerk's hand and signed by Olmsted.

1. Thomas Hill (1818–1891), Unitarian minister and president of Harvard College from 1862 to 1868. Hill vacationed in the White Mountains of New Hampshire, sketching landscapes. Olmsted probably met Hill through their mutual friend, Frederick Knapp. In 1869 Olmsted, Knapp, and Hill invested in a cranberry farm in Sutton, Massachusetts, and were still partners at the time of this letter. By 1875 Hill was living in Portland, Maine, where he was minister of the Unitarian church. The railroad through Crawford Notch in the White Mountains with whose effect on the landscape Olmsted and Hill were concerned at this time was probably the Portland & Ogdensburg Railroad, which was being constructed through the notch in 1875 (*DAB*; William G. Land, *Thomas Hill: Twentieth President of Harvard* [Cambridge, Mass., 1933], p. 237; *Papers of FLO,* 6: 340; Robert M. Edgar, "North of Franconia" White Mountains Railroad, 1848–1873 [New York, 1953], p. 22).
2. Apparently, Olmsted's letter to Hill has not survived. In his response to Olmsted concerning "exotics," Hill wrote on October 30:

> The rough edges of the new R.R. divert the attention disagreeably from the grand panorama. I find fault with them for being disagreeable & wish to improve them; so do you. But I also object to their diverting my attention at all; and I wish so to improve them as to make them pass unnoticed by those who go to the Notch, as thousands will go during the next decade, to see the grand mountain masses on the Easterly side of the defile;—and on the West. I think that if we put exotics there, it will distract the attention, & lead to a silent questioning & discussing the principles of your letter, & I would avoid that in the passage of the Notch. About the Crawford House, even about the section men's houses in the Notch, I have no objection to exotics, as beautiful and showy as you please. But in the presumed wilderness where you are expecting to enjoy the sight of the Mts themselves, I do not want the attention diverted by any other object however beautiful. Wild plants will please without diverting the attention. But exotics will have, in a mild degree the distracting effect of those confounded finger boards pointing to "Profile" "Old Maid" "Elephant's Head," "Guardian of the Notch" "White Horse," and other ridiculous resemblances in the outline of the rocks, which draw the attention of the tourist from the Majesty and beauty and loveliness of the natural scenery to fix it on the quips & quirks & fancies of foolish fellow men

(Thomas Hill to FLO, Oct. 30, 1875).
3. The Profile or "Old Man of the Mountain" located on Profile Mountain in Franconia Notch was a rock formation resembling a man's profile (Samuel C. Eastman, *The White Mountain Guide Book,* 11th ed. [Concord, Mass., 1873], pp. 127–28).
4. An example of Olmsted's designing of a landscape that would appear to have been formed by natural processes, see his description of the proposed lagoons in the Chicago South Park in 1871 (*Papers of FLO,* SSI: 213).
5. In January 1876, Hill reported to Olmsted that three thousand seeds of the native grape had been sown along the railroad in Crawford Notch, and two thousand plants of Virginia Creeper (*Parthenocissus quinquefolia*) were about to be planted. "I think Mr Ramsays 2000 rooted Ampelopsis will *tell* in a very few years," he wrote, "& you may congratulate yourself that your single word, crystallized action so speedily." Hill added that he had seen trumpet creeper growing without protection in Portland and would plant some in the Notch (as Olmsted had proposed). Olmsted later apparently contributed funds for planting along the railroad (Thomas Hill to FLO, Jan. 24, 1876; ibid., Feb. 5 [1876]).

To George Jones[1]

209 W. 46th St. 19th Nov. 1875.

My Dear Mr Jones:
Though your personal acquaintance with me, (which began just 23 years ago with my appointment as a "Times Commissioner")[2] has been but slight you probably know that as a public servant I have been in the habit of minding my own business and strictly avoided the service of any political party, clique, faction or individual speculator in legislation. If you would assure the present editor of the Times[3] of this and of your confidence in my sincerity, he would not, I hope, think it impertinent that I should wish him advised that the recent attacks of the Times on the Department of Parks[4] are based in some important respects on a misapprehension as to the facts.

For example, the few defects which are obvious in the drainage and sewerage of the Central Park originated and should have been repaired years ago. The present Commissioners are not only not responsible for them, but as the Times has assured, but may claim credit for being the first to see about their remedy. This they did some months ago.[5]

Again, the water of the lake ran low this summer as it always has done whenever the Department of Works has found it necessary to cut off the supply from the reservoirs.[6] When at the lowest, the forms of vegetation usually seen in stagnant waters made their appearance. They did so at the same moment in the Croton water and, unless you were more fortunate than most citizens you must have seen traces of them even in ice water which had passed through ordinary filters. I have drawn them within three weeks from pipes in my own chamber. They disappeared from the park waters but little if any later than from those of the reservoirs.

But if the condition of the park lakes in this respect is reprehensible, as it certainly is objectionable, the present Commissioners are again entitled to credit at the expense of their predecessors, for they have taken all practicable measures to remedy this evil—measures such as have been neglected under their predecessors.

As to the actual sanitary condition of the park, the general health of the men and women employed upon it should afford the best evidence. As to this, I have, at the request of President Stebbins, made particular enquiries and I am confident, not only that there has been no special suffering this year from malaria but that since operations began 18 years ago, there has been no year in which there has been so little illness. Notwithstanding the statement of the boatman quoted by the Times I must even say that I much doubt if there has this year been a single case of fever and ague originating within the year on the Central Park.[7] I doubt even more whether there is an acre of ground elsewhere in New York or its suburbs in which a man is as little likely to be poisoned by malaria of local origins as he would be at any point within the improved parts of the Central Park. I say that while clearly recognizing some conditions of possible danger still existing, a remedy for which I have long desired.

At the lowest stage of water in the lake I may mention that I repeatedly took my own children out upon it in the evening with no bad consequences.

As to the turf question, all I need to say for my present purposes is that the public has had a longer use of it during the last summer than was ever had under the old Commissioners of the Central Park whose administration has so often been held up as a model by the Times.

Frankness, however, may require me to add something upon a question which it is almost useless to attempt to deal with as one of definite facts, since those most important to a full understanding cannot in this case as in the others be easily established by the inquiry of any intelligent reporter. As a matter, then, in which weight of opinion should be considered I will remind you that I have given the best and largest part of my life to a study of the various elements — sanitary, horticultural, political and social — of this question, visiting and examining and watching closely the management of every notable public park of Europe and America for the purpose. Also that in connection with Mr Vaux I laid out and superintended the formation of both New York and the Brooklyn Parks and have been the professional adviser of both Commissions.

As such I urged the Brooklyn Commission to try the experiment, an experiment which, so far as I know, was at that time essentially untried in this climate, of allowing the public unrestricted use of a certain piece of turf (about five times larger than any piece in the Central Park) which had been specially designed and prepared with reference to this purpose from the outset.[8] Four years ago, also, the Commissioners of the Central Park were induced by Mr Vaux and I to allow the public a much larger use of the turf than had been before thought prudent, (Comptroller Green earnestly protesting against the policy).[9]

I mention my special responsibility in the matter in order that it may be seen that with a certain foundation of knowledge and study I have had a strong bias of personal disposition and that my pride and selfish interests have been all engaged on the side advocated by the Times. I regret nevertheless to say that the manifest results of each experiment are in my judgement not simply unfavorable but absolutely disastrous to the hope that the turf of the Central Park can ever be made use of by the public more unrestrictedly than it has been. I know that this opinion strikes almost all who have not given special study to the matter as preposterous but whenever those who shall be in trust of the Park shall have been led to yield to the popular opinion I shall be glad to have my conviction remembered that not many years will pass before the results will be recognized as a grave public calamity and the unseemly and offensive expedients will be vainly advocated for recovering the ground which has been lost.

Although I have said that this can hardly be made a question of facts, still with a certain amount of labor I am disposed to think it practicable to put the facts, by observation of which my conviction has been fixed, in such connected, exact and statistical form that no intelligent man who would take the trouble to candidly and thoroughly weigh them could avoid adopting the same conclusion.

I trust that you will recognize the motive of this letter which is written without the knowledge of any Commissioner and is, of course, strictly personal and private.

Yours respectfully,

Fred Law Olmsted.

Immediately after the receipt of this the attacks ceased.[10]

F.L.O.

The text presented here is from a letterpress copy in Olmsted's hand.
1. George Jones (1811–1891), publisher of the *New-York Times*: he co-founded the newspaper in 1851. The paper printed numerous exposés which led to the fall of the Tweed Ring in 1871, and it continued to criticize Tammany Hall (*DAB*; *New-York Times*, Feb. 8, 1875, p. 5).
2. That is, when Henry Raymond, co-founder of the newspaper, commissioned Olmsted in 1852 to write a series of letters describing his travels through the slave states of the South (*Papers of FLO*, 2: 9).
3. Louis J. Jennings edited the newspaper between 1869 and 1876 (Frank Luther Mott, *American Journalism* [New York, 1941], p. 383).
4. Since Democratic mayor William H. Wickham appointed William R. Martin and Joseph J. O'Donohue commissioners in January and May 1875; the *Times* had repeatedly accused the park board of being a tool of Tammany Hall. In November the paper printed an editorial claiming that "malaria in the most aggravated forms" emanated from the lakes and ponds of the park. It also criticized as overzealous the enforcement of rules about keeping off the grass. Between these "vexatious restrictions" and the "malaria," it seemed that "the Central Park Commissioners do their best to drive the public out of their own property" (*New-York Times*, May 25, 1875, p. 6; ibid., Aug. 25, 1875, p. 4; ibid., Nov. 15, 1875, p. 4; see FLO, Patronage Journal, Nov. 19, 1875, below).
5. In August 1875 the park superintendent, Julius Munckwitz, reported that algae and muck had collected in the lakes and ponds throughout the park. Over the next several months Munckwitz supervised about two hundred laborers in removing the material and in repairs to the general drainage system of the park. About the same time it was found that small amounts of sewage from the water closets near the Kinderberg, Dairy, and Ball Ground house emptied into the Pond. Olmsted reported that such arrangements were not part of the original design of the park, and he could find no record

of when or by whom this work had been authorized. In October engineer John Bogart began a special examination of the park's drainage system, which comprised over ninety-five miles of buried pipe and tile. His investigations lasted into the early months of 1876 (DPP, *Minutes*, Aug. 18, 1875, pp. 206–7; ibid., Sept. 29, 1875, pp. 303–4; Feb. 5, 1876, p. 603; ibid., March 18, 1876, p. 676; FLO to Henry G. Stebbins, Nov. 16, 1875).

6. Although the main reservoirs of the municipal water system (the "Croton water works") were located within the park, the supply was controlled by the Department of Public Works. During the dry summer of 1875 that department ordered the water supply for park use sharply curtailed. Even then shortages persisted throughout New York City (DPP, *Minutes*, Aug. 4, 1875, p. 170; "Document no. 79," in New York [State], *Documents of the Senate of the State of New York, Ninety-Ninth Session . . .* [Albany, N.Y., 1876], pp. 25–31).

7. The *New-York Times* editorialist stated that "one of the boatmen assured us, a few weeks ago, that all his companions had been down with chills and fever — caught on the lake." Olmsted interviewed the supervisors of those whose employment kept them constantly on the park, including the surgeon of the police force, and found no cases of "malarial illness" traceable to their work. On their way to and from work, however, most employees passed over the sunken, poorly drained ground bordering the park where "malarial influences unquestionably prevail" (*New-York Times*, Nov. 15, 1875, p. 4; FLO to Henry G. Stebbins, Nov. 16, 1875).

8. Olmsted is referring to the Green, or Long Meadow, of Prospect Park in Brooklyn. In 1866 he and Vaux recommended that at most times it should be open to persons on foot as a common. They believed that thoroughly underdrained ground, planted with good grasses, supplemented by efficient supervision of visitors by dedicated park keepers, could prevent damage to the turf (BPC, *Annual Reports, 1861–1873*, p. 106; *Papers of FLO*, 6: 356–57, 668).

9. Surviving records do not indicate any such recommendation by Olmsted and Vaux c. 1871. It is unlikely that Olmsted and Vaux would have proposed in 1871, following the period of the Tweed Ring, to "allow the public a much larger use of the turf than had been before thought prudent," in Central Park, and the printed minutes and reports of the board do not record any such proposal at that time. Olmsted probably meant to write "Fourteen years ago," since in November 1860, with Vaux's help, he had formulated regulations for Central Park that permitted walking on the grass in certain areas. This was the first major expansion of public access to the lawn areas of the park. As he then wrote Andrew H. Green, comptroller of the park, "I do not at all like to have published a positive interdict upon all grassed ground, with no promise of a let up. Judging from my own feelings as well as my observation of the public, nothing would be more unpopular" ("Regulations for the Use of the Central Park," [Nov. 3, 1860] [*Papers of FLO*, 3: 279]; *DAB*).

10. Olmsted later added this sentence in pencil to his copy of the letter.

To Henry G. Stebbins

DEPARTMENT OF PUBLIC PARKS,
OFFICE OF DESIGN AND SUPERINTENDENCE.
NEW YORK, 3d December, 1875.

To the Hon. HENRY G. STEBBINS,
President of the Board:
Sir,
  The want has long been recognized of a place in the Central Park arranged suitably for a promenade, side by side, of drivers, riders and walkers under conditions favorable to a certain degree of social enjoyment. It has also been recognized that it would be a grave error to provide an arrangement for this purpose, which, while likely to establish a custom and stimulate an irresistible public demand, should fall far short of satisfying it. It has been considered especially that any considerable sacrifice of the results of the expenditure already made on the park in order to gain such an imperfect arrangement, would be unpardonable. Whether any of the existing constructions of the park can be so far improved and supplemented as to supply what is needed, and, if not, how much it would be necessary to sacrifice in order to introduce entirely new constructions for the purpose, was therefore to be determined upon a careful forecast of the detail of conditions which would be favorable or otherwise to the enjoyment of those engaging in the promenade. There are three constant elements of such enjoyment to be considered, one being that of the spectacle; the second, that arising from recognition of friends and observation of special objects, as faces, dresses, horses and equipages; and the third, that of such personal conversation as is possible for those moving side by side in a crowd.
  Every person present becomes a part of the spectacle, and may contribute to each of the other two elements. The position and movements of each person is consequently a matter of interest to every other present. It is desirable, therefore, that during the hours of the promenade, the ground used for the purpose should be well filled. It is desirable that there should be a continuous movement of all engaged, and that the attention of none should be unnecessarily held to other matters in such a way as to interfere with the enjoyments which are special to the promenade. The more the movement of each person is regulated with reference to the enjoyment of all by fixed conditions, and the less by the constant effort of his individual judgment; the more the vision of each over the promenade before him is unobstructed, and the more complete and extended his command of the spectacle, the greater will be the enjoyment of all.
  Whenever obstructions, however slight, occur, tending to suddenly arrest movement at particular points, or to hinder or to make unnecessarily indirect the movements of individuals, and especially of carriages and riding

horses, the consequence will be at one place crowding, apprehension of collisions, and more or less demand on the attention of each person near by to the circumstance, and at another breaks and gaps in the spectacle and the irregularities of movement to which these would invite. The turning of carriages on the promenade, their entrance upon it, and their withdrawal, create more or less unavoidable disturbance; therefore, there should be no frequent opportunity or temptation for these movements; at the same time the space prepared for the promenade should not be so long that its necessarily restrained movement would become very tedious before those entering upon it could, if they desired, escape, and move more at will.

The following specifications of requirement are readily deducible from the above considerations:

1. A devious course is to be avoided; the more nearly straight the promenade the better.

2. A steeper grade than one in forty and much variation of grade is to be avoided. A "hogsback" is particularly objectionable. The more nearly level the promenade the better.

3. No other thoroughfare should cross or intersect the line of the promenade.

4. There should be no necessity for driving freighting vehicles over it late in the day.

5. Its direction should not be such as would bring the sun in the eyes of those resorting to it late in the day.

6. All parts of it should be as much as possible shaded late in the day.

7. At each end it should be practicable for visitors to do either of three things with the least possible confusion and disturbance, and with reasonable ease and convenience, viz.: To turn around and continue on the promenade; to make an excursion in the park beyond the promenade and out of its crowd; or, lastly, to quickly leave the park on the shortest course home.

8. The promenade should be fully half a mile in length and will desirably be somewhat longer.

9. The total space to be occupied by the drive, ride and walks cannot well be less than 150 feet in breadth.*

According to the degree in which these desiderata can all be combined in any arrangement it will be likely to prove permanently satisfactory, while in so far as one or more of them shall be secured at the sacrifice of others the public demand designed to be met will be greatly increased but not adequately fulfilled.

In 1872, after the return of the present President of the Department from Europe,[1] the subject was, at his request, more thoroughly canvassed than

---

*This allows 60 feet for the driving-way, 40 feet for the riding-way, 40 feet for two walks and 10 feet for two rows of shade trees.

ever before. After demonstrating objections to two suggested plans, which were recognized to be conclusive against them, I was then asked to select the least objectionable route to be found in the South Park and prepare a definite plan for laying it out. In doing so I was assisted by Mr. Vaux, and the plan which resulted has been seen by all the Commissioners of the Department.[2] It has never been formally presented to the Board, however, because of its acknowledged numerous defects and the injury, which would unquestionably result from undertaking to carry it out, to the park as it now stands.

The conclusion of the study then given the subject may, therefore, be stated as follows:

That no plan at all adequate to the requirements of the city in a promenade can be carried out on the South Park, except at a cost in direct outlay and in the waste of results of outlay already made, for which its value would be no sufficient compensation.

Bearing in mind and giving but their just weight to each of the desiderata that have been enumerated, and considering a few broad general facts of the topography of the park, the conditions which enforce this conclusion are easily recognized.

The South Park is one mile in length from north to south and half a mile in width, and is divisible topographically into three tolerably distinct elevated ranges and two intermediate valleys, all trending across the line of the greater distance. Each range of high ground is a continuous ledge of rock, with a coating of earth, for the most part artificially laid on, not exceeding two feet in average depth. The difference of elevation between these ranges and the valleys which divide them is from thirty to ninety feet. It is only by circuitous courses or by heavy rock cuttings and embankments that roads of tolerable grade can be carried from north to south, and only by crossing these existing roads and numerous walks, lawns and plantations, that a moderately direct road of even a third of a mile in length could be made from east to west. In either case the reduction of a space of ground 150 feet in width and the necessary length, so nearly to a plane surface as would be necessary to the purpose, could only be accomplished by the destruction of the most valuable landscape features of the ground.

Difficulties similar in character to those which have been indicated are found in all of the North as well as the South Park, and also in the strip of ground through which the communication with it from between the two is carried on the west. The only space where they do not obtain in the property under the control of the Department is that of the straight, narrow belt of land on the east side of the great reservoir. The drive which passes along this belt has already been selected by the public as more nearly than any other meeting the requirement of the promenade, and this in spite of the fact that there is neither a walk nor a bridle road alongside of it.

It is not only more traveled by carriages than any other on the park, but late in the day they are often driven back and forth upon it as on a proper promenade. The reasons for its use in this manner are: 1st, that it is straight; 2d, that it is level; 3d, that late in the day it is shaded; 4th, that it does not look toward the setting sun.

Observing that speed of movement was more checked by the conflux of carriages here than elsewhere in the park, the Commissioners of 1871[3] thought to make an improvement simply by widening the wheelway, giving no consideration to any other public requirement of the locality, and accomplishing the little that was attempted with such narrow study of the circumstances that the relation of the widened drive to adjoining objects was left incomplete, unsymmetrical and offensive to the eye. To adapt the arrangement to the purpose for which the public is obviously inclined to use the locality, the straight reach of drive needs to be still further widened and, if possible, lengthened, and a broad walk and riding-way to be formed adjoining it. To gain the necessary space for this purpose without encroaching on the reservoir it would be necessary to appropriate a part of the sidewalk on the west side of Fifth Avenue, to remove and reconstruct the present retaining wall, and to give increased height as well as breadth to the embankment on which the drive is now carried. I present a preliminary study of a plan in which these, with several minor improvements, are proposed.[4] If this plan were carried out every one of the desiderata of a promenade would be realized in full degree almost precisely as they have been stated.

Certain objections to the proposition are obvious: First, that of its cost; second, that of the distance of the locality from the present centre of residence of the city;[5] third, that the length of the promenade (being barely half a mile) is rather less than is desirable. The fact that it is now more resorted to for carriage exercise than any other part of the park, shows that the second objection already has no very important weight; with the advance northward of population it will annually have less. The fact, again, that whenever the improvement of Riverside Avenue is made, the city will be possessed of another promenade nearly a mile in length, and better in all important respects than any other in the world, lessens considerably the weight of the third objection.[6]

That the promenade would adjoin Fifth Avenue may be considered an advantage, as an alternate route is thus provided for those who may wish to pass rapidly north from the South Park when the promenade is crowded and the less occasion is left for the intrusion upon it of an undesirable class of vehicles. The entrance at the south end from the avenue would meet a local demand which has been the subject of repeated memorials to the Department.

I submit this study to the consideration of the Board as indicating the least objectionable way of providing for a public demand which is likely to increase, and any less complete arrangement for meeting which would probably prove temporary, and therefore more costly, and in all respects objectionable.

The work could now be all put under contract at $250,000.[7]
Respectfully,

Fred. Law Olmsted,
Landscape Architect.

The text presented here is from "Document No. 67," in New York (City), Department of Public Parks, *Minutes,* December 3, 1875.

1. Henry G. Stebbins traveled to Europe between May and October 1872 (*Papers of FLO,* 6: 41).
2. The three plans Olmsted discusses here were not mentioned in the printed minutes of the park board in late 1872 or early 1873. During this period, however, Olmsted and Calvert Vaux prepared plans for an extensive promenade in nearby Riverside Park (FLO to Henry G. Stebbins, Jan. 15, 1875, above).
3. That is, the park board dominated by Tammany Democrats Peter B. Sweeny, Henry Hilton, and Thomas C. Fields.
4. This plan has not survived.
5. Earlier in the year Olmsted estimated that the center of New York City's population was within 600 yards of Tompkins Square on the lower east side, some three miles south of the proposed promenade (Henry G. Stebbins to William H. Wickham, Jan. 27, 1875, Mayor's Papers, box 1263, New York City Municipal Archives).
6. Following approval of his January 1875 plan for Riverside Park and Avenue, Olmsted revised it in March by introducing a bridle path to the promenade section of the park. Although the park board approved his modification immediately, the department was not authorized to begin construction of the avenue until June 1876 (FLO to Henry G. Stebbins, March 16, 1875; DPP, *Minutes,* March 17, 1875, p. 571; FLO to Édouard André, Nov. 3, 1876, below).
7. Beyond ordering that the present text be printed, the board took no further action on Olmsted's recommendations.

To Dennis Bowen[1]

Dennis Bowen Esqr Buffalo

1st Jany. 1876.

My Dear Sir;
I shall send you by Express a preliminary study of a plan for the City Hall[2] grounds which I will thank to examine and return to me with comments. I see two particulars in which work already done would perhaps have to be undone in carrying out this plan but they are not of weight against the advantages to be gained.[3] There may be necessities to be accommodated,

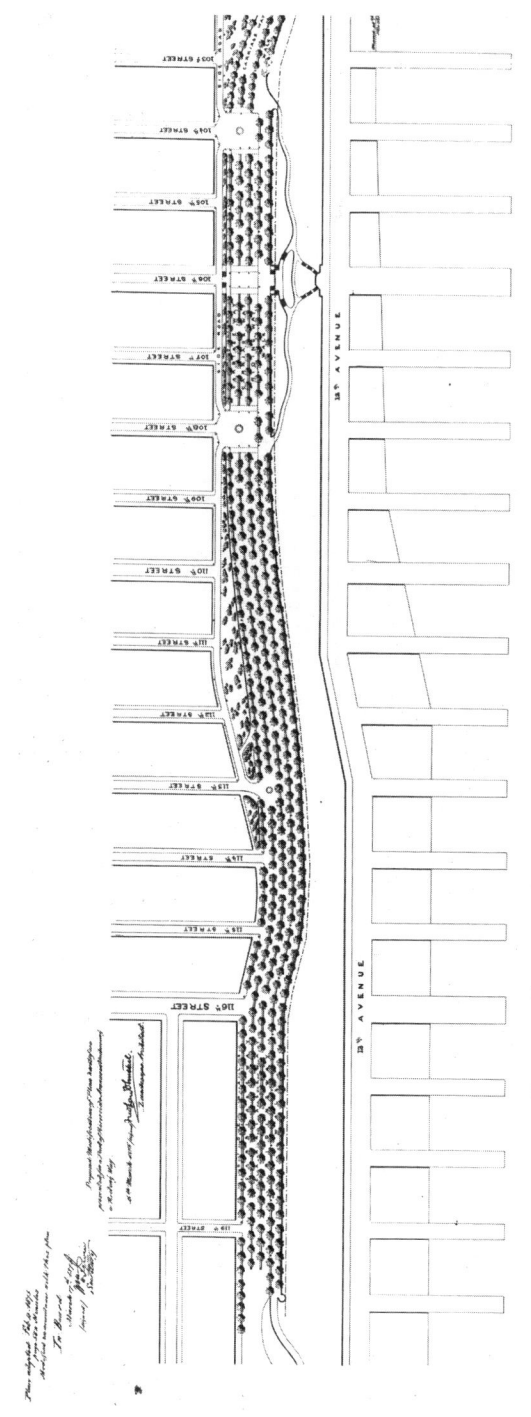

Plan for Riverside Avenue with Addition of Riding Way, March 15, 1875

however, which the drawings have not exhibited to me and which you have not indicated. If so I should like to make any necessary modification of the arrangments proposed before submitting the plan to your Board. So far as I am well advised of the construction and purposes of the building the plan has been very carefully studied.

I have had four principal considerations in mind.

1st that under ordinary circumstances the more important business of the City Hall is of a quiet, orderly, bureau character, with reference to which a certain degree of seclusion of the building from the streets and of elegance in the grounds would be convenient, fitting and in accordance with what is customarily attempted, but

2d that the building is nevertheless one for public business and should appear open and free to the public; that business is liable to be done in it having great popular interest and on certain occasions the grounds and even the streets near it will need to serve the purpose of outer lobbies. Public guests may at times be received at the building and reviews and receptions if not meetings held before it. More liberal and spacious arrangmnts of standing and passage room should for this reason be provided all about the building than if it were designed for private residence or trade or even for ward or district public business.

The City Hall in the old world is nearly always placed in the midst of an open public place, usually a noisy market place. In our own country small parks are more commonly formed around or at least in front of such buildings. These at first are neatly finished and their appearance satisfactory but I do not know a case where in a populous town they have long remained so — in which, that is to say, the edgings of the walks have not been soon obliterated, and the trees, shrubs and turf sadly abused or the ruling expression of which has not in a few years become one of inefficient governmnt, seediness and delapidation. I do not think you will need to look far to find illustrations of what I mean.

If you want to avoid a similar destruction of your work you must see to it that wherever there is likely at any time to be much public pressure, no kind of decoration is attempted that will not bear rough usage or which, after the tramping over or about it of a turbulent crowd, cannot be made as good as new with water and a scrubbing brush.

3d a very important item in the cost of the construction of your City Hall is for means of securing an elegant and imposing exterior effect. You want some degree of seclusion and sylvan beauty about your building but you do not want this architectural effect to be lost in a grove of trees. On the contrary any foliage should be so disposed as not merely to reveal but to fix attention upon the more important architectural elements from those points of view and at the distance at which they will be seen to the best advantage.

4th It is not desirable that the building should seem to have been thrust abruptly through a flat bed of turf. The grounds should be so arranged as to obviously be one in design with it and to support it. This is particularly necessary because the building is so tall and straight and independent of other buildings. It not only needs a verdant drapery to set it off but solid outworks that will have the effect of a pedastal in connecting it with the ground.

    You will see that each of these four considerations conflicts more or less with the others and that you will recognize that they cannot be expected to be reconciled except by means more substantial and expensive than we find in every day use nor without a very nice and accurate adjustmnt of the different provisions to be employed. I expect to furnish you with elaborate working plans and specifications and it will be important that they be strictly adhered to. Hence I shall be anxious to have the preliminary plans cautiously scrutinized before their adoption.

    The studies are on a small scale and only indicate the larger features of the design but you will see by a little comparison of the different sketches what sort of detail is intended and, as I think, to detect the motive of everything proposed. You will observe the distinction between trees and shrubs & will see that the few fine lawn trees and all the shrubs and turf proposed are to be guarded from injury by means which are designed in strict harmony with and as auxiliary to the architectural effect of the building. At the same time the more striking parts of the building are exhibited to the best advantage and all the arrangments, even to the street, will have, as I hope, a broad, spacious and hospitable effect {*such as in my judgment should distinguish the locality of a building for business of importance to the whole community of a city.*}

    I have thought it necessary that provision should be made for removing prisoners by or receiving them from a carriage and also for receiving needed materials for repairs & other purposes in freedom from a crowd. I have therefore arranged a small closed court in which a waggon can stand and turn and in which materials may be piled, mats & carpets cleaned etc. without being seen from the street or obstructing the public passages.

    There will be no occasion for anyone to enter the purely ornamental grnds except in careing for them and they may with little labor be kept as nicely as the daintiest private garden.

    I do not know that the architect has intended that the building shall be so terraced about as to hide the basement but if not I have no doubt that on reflection he will see that it will gain much by such an arrangement as I propose. At least to me it would appear more firmly placed, its position more commanding and its proportions more agreeable to the eye {*rising from an unbroken base*}.[4]

ALLEY.

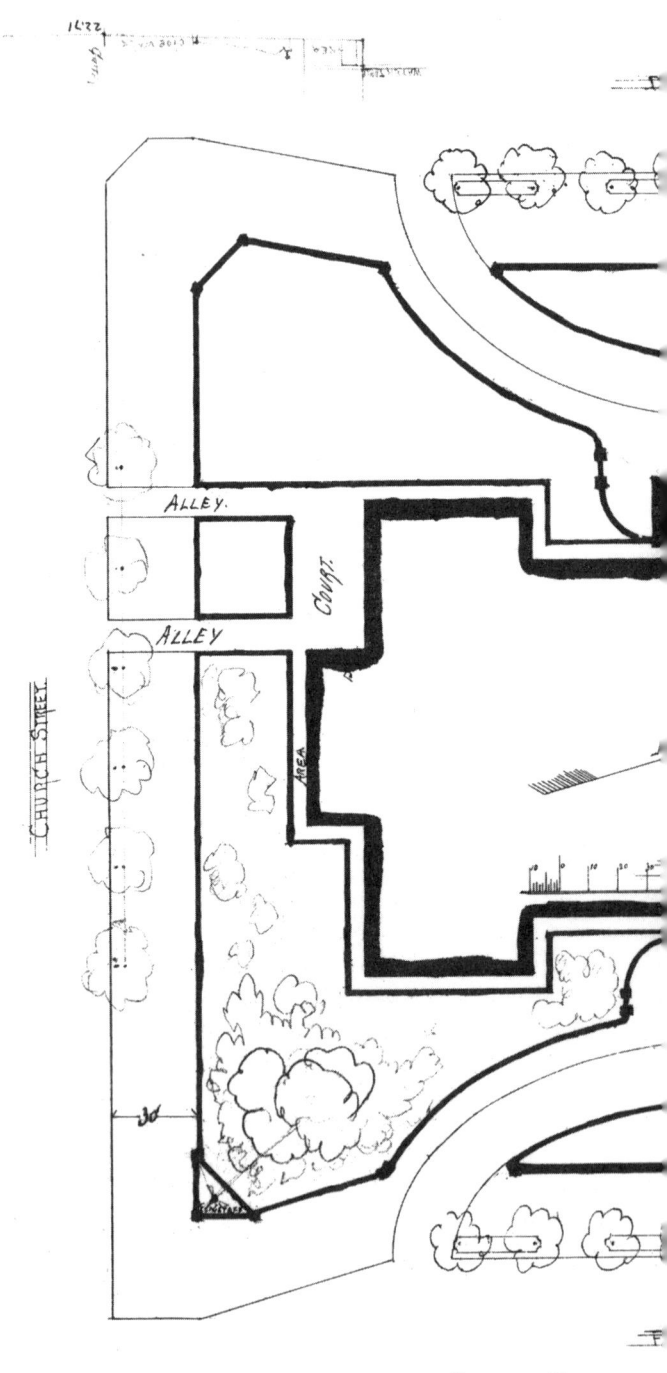

ALLEY

CHURCH STREET

COURT.

AREA

PLAN FOR GROUNDS O

FEBRUARY 1875–FEBRUARY 1876

PRELIMINARY STUDY FOR
GROUNDS
OF
NEW CITY AND COUNTY HALL
BUFFALO, N.Y.

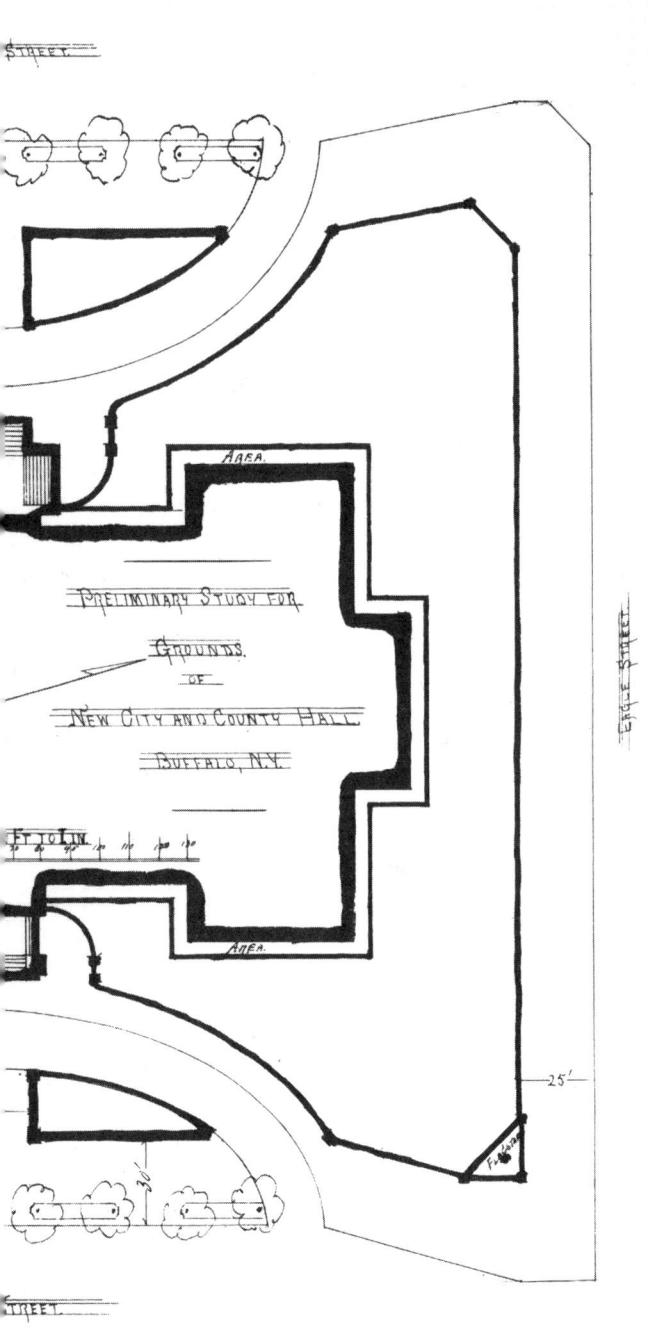

County Hall, Buffalo

The text presented here is from a draft in Olmsted's hand.

1. Dennis Bowen (1820–1877), a prominent Buffalo lawyer, was one of the organizers of the city's park movement and in 1869 served on the first park commission as chairman of the committee on grounds, a position he held until his death. In November 1875, as a member of the commission on the new city and county hall, he asked Olmsted to provide a plan for the grounds of the building. Olmsted began work on preliminary studies for a plan in early December (H. Perry Smith, ed., *History of the City of Buffalo and Erie County*, 2 vols. [Syracuse, N.Y., 1884], 2: 480–81, 489, 493–96; Dennis Bowen to FLO, Nov. 27, 1875, B65: #700, OAR/LC; FLO to Dennis Bowen, Dec. 11, 1875).
2. That is, the City and County Hall, located at Franklin and Church streets, presently known as Old County Hall. Designed by Rochester architect Andrew Jackson Warner in High Victorian Gothic style, the building was constructed between 1871 and 1876. Warner also had been superintending architect of H. H. Richardson's Buffalo State Asylum for the Insane since 1871, a project for which Olmsted and Vaux had designed the grounds (Reyner Banham et al., *Buffalo Architecture: A Guide* [Cambridge, Mass., 1981], pp. 64–65; *Papers of FLO*, 6: 454–55).
3. Olmsted is probably referring to stone walks recently installed around the building, which Bowen had noted were not to be disturbed, and to a paved space on one side of the Delaware Street entrance that clashed with "the otherwise perfectly symmetrical arrangement of the place." Having noted these features on the plans furnished him to start the design, Olmsted had asked Bowen to suspend any further work on grading, flagging, steps, lamps, etc., "until all the outside arrangements have been studied as parts of one" (FLO to Dennis Bowen, Dec. 11, 1875).
4. Bowen's committee quickly approved Olmsted's preliminary studies, for in April 1876 he sent a revised working plan and detail plans, complete with specifications and instructions for carrying them out. He estimated the cost of the stonework, including foundations, to be $14,000 and the cost of lamps, posts, and railings to be less than $3,000. Thomas Wisedell drafted the plans and made at least one inspection visit to Buffalo on Olmsted's behalf. William McMillan superintended the grading and planting of the grounds without detailed instructions, as Olmsted trusted him to use his own discretion "within the conditions presented by the drawings." Andrew Jackson Warner superintended the architectural portion of the work, which was nearly ready for the erection of lamps and flagstaffs by October 1876. Olmsted requested a payment of $800 from the commission in late December 1877 (FLO to Dennis Bowen, April 14, 1876; ibid., Oct. 19, 1876; FLO to William McMillan, Dec. 29, 1877, B65: #700, OAR/LC; Thomas Wisedell to MPO, Jan. 19, 1878, B65: #700, OAR/LC).

To HENRY G. STEBBINS

1st Feby 1876

To the Prest—

I wish to submit a proposition to the Board and that its bearings may be better understood to briefly introduce it.

An important branch in the organization of almost every civilized government of the world but our own is that relative to the conservation of Woods and Forests. That this subject will soon be one of great national concern to ourselves cannot be doubted. Our sources of supply for all productions of the forest are rapidly shrinking, while the demand for them on the whole is prodigiously increasing.

The cultivation of trees for decorative purposes alone is already an important business and with the growth of the country in wealth and refinement of taste will be much more so. At present a very consider-[1]

* * * * * *

{dis}eases to which they are otherwise subject and even brought from an uninhabitable condition to support a large and prosperous population.

What are the special properties by which trees act in these cases; in what degrees different trees possess these properties and under what conditions of soil, climate and culture they may be developed and made available are questions which open fields for scientific investigation of great promise and the exploitation of which is barely begun.

The chief discouragement to the scientific study of trees and the chief obstacle to their intelligent managmnt is the slowness with which individual experience is acquired. An entire life history of most of the plants we cultivate is witnessed every succeeding summer, while the natural life of our more valuable trees is extended much beyond that of mankind. Hence the value of public provisions for continuous observations upon trees and of the careful preparation and safe transmission of public records and statistics of the effects of disease, accidents, temperature, culture and other conditions upon the growth & value of trees.

From these general considerations I ask the Board to turn its attention to the opportunity offered in this respect by the Central Park.

Although so young and although it has some striking deficiencies there is no other collection on the continent of equal age containing examples of so many species and varieties.

Specemins of the greater number of them have been growing where they now are fifteen years or more[2] and a record of the more important conditions to which many of them have been subject from the seed to their present stage of growth, the manner of their planting, their subsequent treatmnt, the meteorological conditions by which they have been influenced, their health and rate of growth, is still possible, all having been planted under my superintendence and the more immediate supervision of Mr Fischer your present Superintending Gardener.[3]

If the considerations which have been referred to, or the experience of all other civilized peoples should have weight with the Department, it will be regarded as a matter of some national interest that such a record should be made and hereafter presented and continued. The Central Park would then form a Museum of Arboriculture arranged and catalogued suitably for profitable study. Its value for this purpose would however be greatly increased by an adjunct collection of various matters illustrating the growth, management and uses of trees, with suitable books of reference.

I have, with the assistance of Mr Fischer, taken some preliminary measures toward this end, a small collection of tree sections and other material, having been made, and data collected for such a record as has been indicated.

I had last year prepared a report on the subject with a suggestion that the Board should authorize a simple and inexpensive arrangement for the furtherance of such a project as I have indicated, but the action of the Board of Apportionment and the resulting embarrassmnt which has come upon the Department in regard to all its business has led me to defer presenting it.[4]

As the Centennial Commission of Philadelphia has recently undertaken a somewhat similar collection[5] to that proposed I have also thought it might be best to avoid any apparent competition with it in this respect.

I have nevertheless thought it desirable to bring the subject to the attention of the Board and to ask, if it should be thought fit, that some action may be taken whereby Mr Fischer & I may be justified in quietly soliciting gifts, collecting information and speaking and writing with reference to the object as are sanctioned by the Department and officially committed to us.

Such an inchoate and purely provisional arrangmnt may prove of trifling value and may lead to nothing better but there is also a possibility that what the Department would gain and hold under it would form the necessary inducemnt to the foundation at a later period of an institution of no little importance.

To give a more definite idea of the character and value as a popular educational entertainmnt of what might be hoped soon to result, I append a form which I had prepared with a view to a public invitation for voluntary aid in the matter.

Respy.

F.L.O.
L.A.

The Board of Commissioners of the Department of Public Parks of the City of New York, contemplate forming as an adjunct of the plantations of the Central Park, a collection of matters of interest relatively to Forestry, Aboriculture, and Landscape Gardening.

The collection is designed to be of a practical character with reference to the following purposes:

1st The propogation, culture, managmnt, transportation and manufactures of and from trees and shrubs with reference to

(a) Commodities in the form of timber, fuel, paper, cordage, dyes, gums, perfumes, drugs, clothing, food, drink, and otherwise, or (b) to their use while living for sanitary and decorative purposes, as for road side planting, for screens and for landscape gardening.

A collection of illustrations is desireable for each species and distinct variety of tree and shrub, and especially of each growing in the United States, as follows:

1st   a section across the trunk of not less than 6 nor more than 10 inches in thickness. This will be ordinarily best obtained by sawing with a two hundred cross cut pit saw. Care should be taken to preserve the bark.

2d   A billet plank[6] or board 18 inches in length, showing the grain of the wood from the heart to the bark: if valuable for cabinet work, an additional billet showing the same polished.

3d   A slab or strip of the bark. This will desireably be 1½ foot in length by 1 foot in breadth.

4th   Specemins of the fruit, nuts or seeds, and seed vessels.

5th   Specemins of the foliage;

6th   Specemins of the flower;

7th   Specemins of various forms of the commercial products;

8th   A portrait of the living tree photographed, drawn or painted.

9th   Pictorial illustrations of its landscape character singly or in groups or masses.

10th   Pictorial illustrations of various conditions and processes of treatment of the tree and its products.

11   Illustrations of its physiology and especially its diseases and their effects, and of remedies for these and their effects.

12   Illustrations of insects and vermin affecting the tree while living, of their effects and of modes of preserving it against them and of counteracting their attacks.

13th   Illustrations of insects and other agencies of destruction to its timber or other commerical products and of modes of preventing and counteracting the same.

Illustrations of shrubs of a similar character, are also desired. Where the trunk of trees or shrubs is less than six inches in diameter the sections may be 18 inches long and split sections will serve in place of billets.

Contributions to the Collection are especially desired in any of the above forms.

Those coming under the 1st 2d 3d 5th 9th 10th 11th & 12th sections will be much increased in value if accompanied by exact memoranda of facts & observations of all special conditions by which the growth, constitution and landscape character of the tree may have been affected, such as, the soil, subsoil, climate, exposure, and situation with reference to moisture and prevailing winds of the locality in which the tree has grown. If the tree is known to have been artificially planted, transplanted, grown from suckers, cuttings, or been irrigated, lopped, pruned or grafted it is important that the fact should be stated.

Those proposing to make contributions are requested when practicable to communicate with the undersigned before doing so, in order that an excessive duplication of specemins may be avoided.

Resolved that incidentally to the main object of the Central Park the opportunities which it affords for instruction in the science and art of tree culture and landscape gardening are valuable to the public and it is desireable that nothing which will increase their usefulness should be lost through inattention.

Resolved that the Board approves the proposition of the Landscape Architect for increasing the value of the park in this respect and that he is authorized with the assistance of the Superintending Gardener to prepare such records of the plantations of the park as may be practicable, to provide for the continuance and preservation and for such collection and arrangmnt of materials and means of information on the subject of forestry, arboriculture and landscape gardening as may be found desireable and practicable without special expense to the Department.[7]

The text presented here is from a manuscript in Olmsted's hand.

1. At this point one or more pages are missing from the manuscript. At the point where the text resumes, Olmsted was apparently discussing the beneficial effect that introduction of trees had had on unforested or deforested areas.
2. The first trees were planted on Central Park in October 1858 (DPP, *Statistical Report of the Landscape Architect, 31st December, 1873, Forming Part of Appendix L of the Third General Report of the Department* [New York, 1875], p. 7).
3. William L. Fischer.
4. In 1875 the New York City Board of Estimate and Apportionment substantially reduced the park department's budget, forcing it to lay off employees and curtail some work (FLO to Henry G. Stebbins, May 18, 1875, n. 9, above).
5. The horticultural department of the United States Centennial Exhibition in Philadelphia took up over forty acres of the exhibition grounds at Fairmount Park. Part of this area was devoted to an arboretum with hundreds of ornamental trees and shrubs, which were donated to the Fairmount Park commission after the exhibition closed (U.S. Centennial Commission, *Official Catalogue* [Philadelphia, 1876], n.p.; The National Museum of History and Technology. Smithsonian Institution, *1876: A Centennial Exhibition*, ed. Robert C. Post [Washington, D.C., 1976], p. 71).
6. Originally, a piece of wood cut to a size suitable for fuel (*OED*).
7. The park board received and tabled Olmsted's report and proposed resolutions on February 5, 1876, and took no further action on them (DPP, *Minutes*, Feb. 5, 1876, pp. 602–3).

To J. H. Miller

28th Feby 1876.

The Rev. J. H. Miller.
Secy. Point Chautaqua Assc[n]
Dear Sir;

I send you by today's Express the plan for laying out Chautauqua Point prepared in accordance with instructions.[1]

The number of building lots not including those for the meeting house and hotel is 466, of which 21 are about 1/4 of an acre and 445 1/8 of an acre in area, measuring in each case to the middle of the road way. A general study of design for the improvment of the public grounds by planting and otherwise is incorporated with the plan for roads and lots.[2] The landing is shown as I should recommend it to be extended from the plan of that now understood to be under construction, so as to accommodate two boats at once lying broadside to the length of the wharf and with a block and pavilion at the outer end, with the object heretofore explained.[3]

The roads are so laid out that no grade will be required, or should be permitted, under the most unfavorable circumstances steeper than 1 in 20.

It is indispensable to a good result under this plan that the company should plant the roads and campground.

It is also indispensable that the company should organize and provide some systematic and adequate method for the removal of waste and for the supply and removal of water.

I have ascertained that a system of water works on the Holly plan, supplying water to each lot on this plan, to a height at low pressure of 130 feet above the lake, and a total quantity of 320,000 gallons per diem, will cost not exceeding $15.000, the interest on which with running expenses would amount to an annual tax on each lot of a little over $6—.[4]

I recommend a correspondence with the Holly Company and send a pamphlet giving more particular information.

If your association wishes to consider the question of an Earth Closet System, I recommend consultation with Col. George E. Waring, Sanitary Engineer, Newport, R.I.[5]

I enclose my account and am
Respectfully Yours,

The text presented here is from a draft in Olmsted's hand.

1. In October 1875 Olmsted began preparing a general plan for Point Chautauqua, New York, despite reservations he had about securing expert superintendence to carry it out on the ground. His instructions were to lay out roads and lots on the property for its

PLAN FO

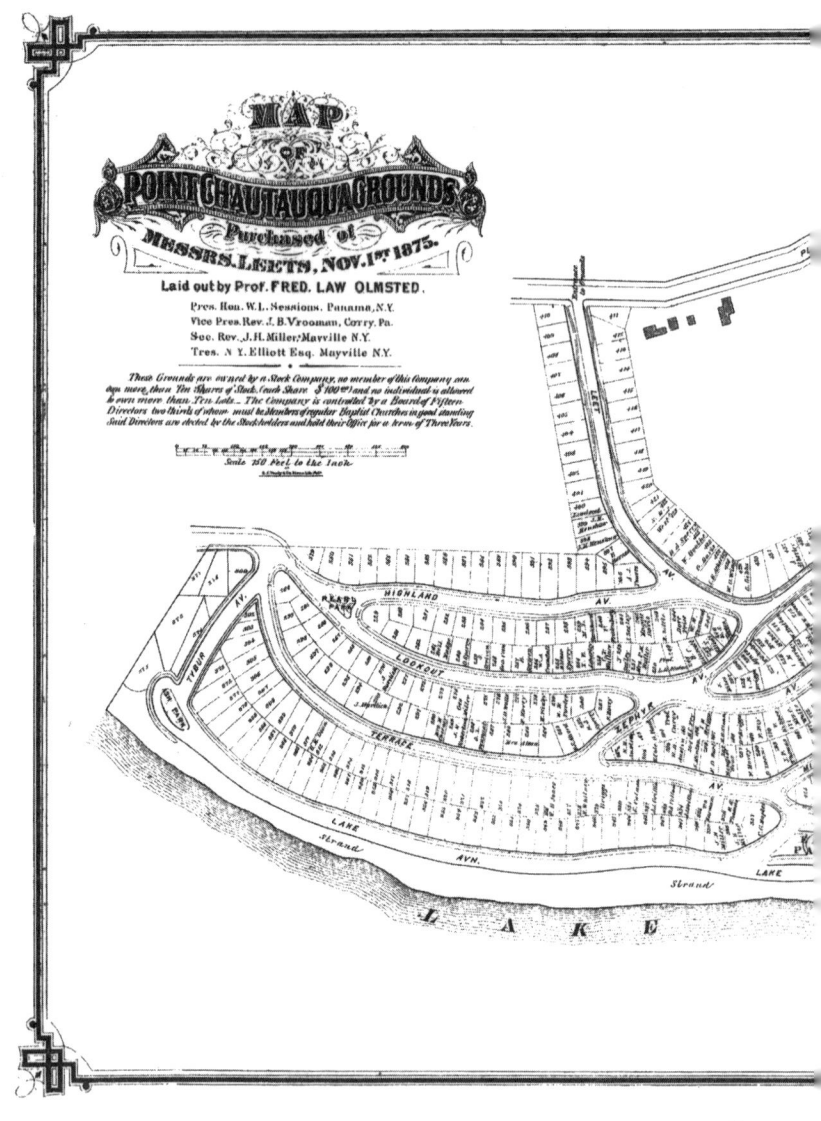

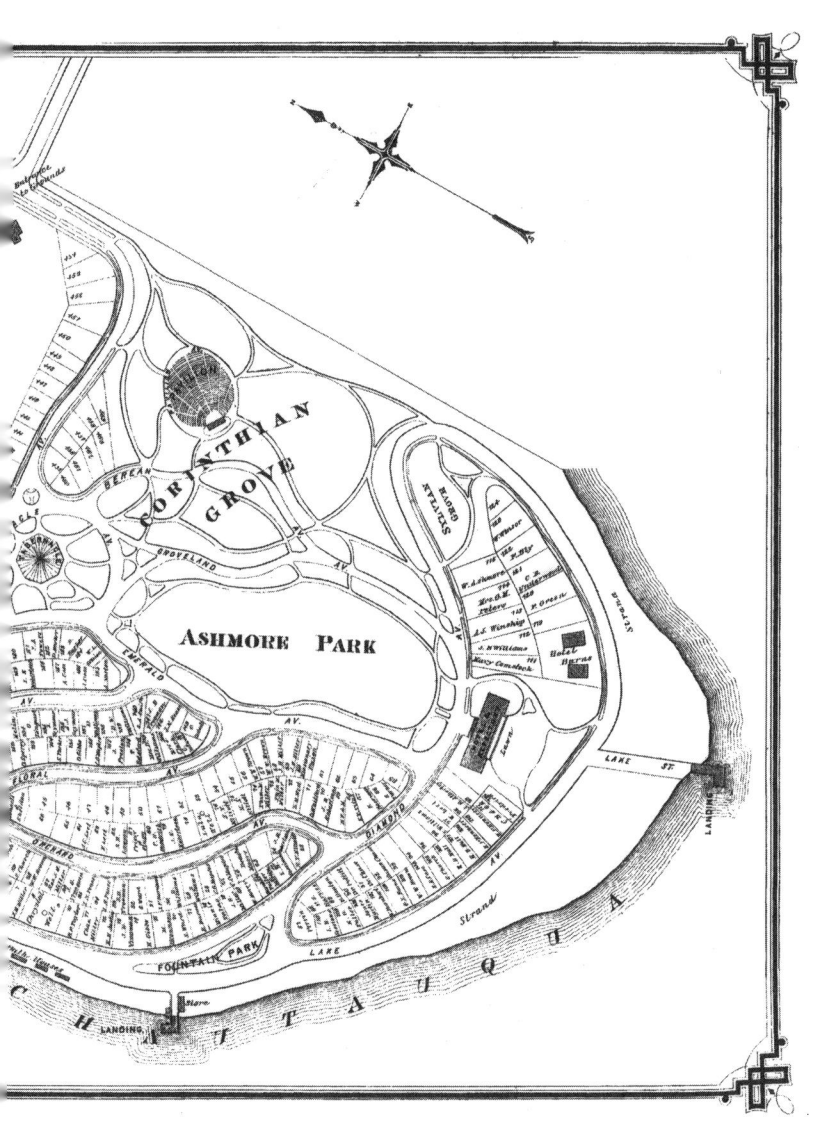

AUQUA (1876)

occupation as a "summer village," with a landing place on the lake, a meeting place in the woods and a site for a meeting house. J. H. Miller asked him to provide at least three hundred residential lots one-eighth of an acre in size, for those who purchased individual shares in the association, and larger lots for holders of multiple shares. Olmsted prepared the plan with the assistance of Jacob Weidenmann. Although the original does not survive, the Point Chautauqua Association officers had it copied for filing with the county clerk and prepared a lithographed copy for publicity purposes. A pencil draft of the plan that includes Olmsted's place name designations and some planting information is in the Olmsted Papers (FLO to Walter L. Sessions, Oct. 9, 1875, above; J. H. Miller to FLO, Dec. 10, 1875; FLO to J. H. Miller, Dec. 19, 1875; Jacob Weidenmann, "Acct with Fred Law Olmsted," c. Aug. 4, 1876; "Plan for laying out the Summer Village of Chautauqua Point," map 94, Chautauqua County Clerk's office, Mayville, New York).

2. Olmsted's plan showed plantings and walks along the roadways and in the public areas, the southern portion of which he designated the campground. The association's lithographed copy left out these details and named the campground Ashmore Park and the area to its northeast the Corinthian Grove.

3. In early January 1876 Miller reported that the association intended to begin constructing a small wharf at once and asked Olmsted to comment on a plan of it. He replied that they should make it larger and that "a prettily designed shelter on the outer block, such as would be suitable for a small railway station, would be not only a convenience but make the wharf an agreeable resort when no boats were coming to it and give a pleasanter first impression to people arriving than they would obtain from a wharf which was nothing more than an ordinary convenience or bare necessity" (J. H. Miller to FLO, Jan. 11, 1876; FLO to J. H. Miller, Jan. 18, 1876).

4. The Holly Manufacturing Company of Lockport, New York, pioneered the use of steam pumps to carry water directly into mains without the use of a reservoir. The water pressure in the system could be varied at will, allowing it to be delivered at moderate pressure for domestic use and high pressure for fire fighting. Olmsted intended that the water be pumped directly from the lake but the association decided to draw water from springs on the property (J. J. R. Croes, *Statistical Table of American Water Works* [New York, 1887], n.p.; FLO to Holly Manufacturing Company, Jan. 8, 1876; *Westfield Republican*, June 7, 1876, p. 3).

5. George E. Waring, Jr. (1833–1898), sanitary engineer, began working for the Central Park commission in 1857 and designed and installed the park's elaborate drainage system. He advocated the use of earth closets instead of water closets and published a treatise on the subject in 1870. Olmsted supported experimentation with the earth closet and several of them were installed at Prospect Park and at Riverside, Illinois. Although the devices proved a failure, Waring was the leading sanitary engineer in the country and collaborated with Olmsted on various projects later in their careers (*Papers of FLO*, 6: 554–55).

CHAPTER IV

APRIL 1876–DECEMBER 1876

This chapter marks the early stages of three remarkable projects in Olmsted's career—the New York State Capitol, the Boston Park system, and creation of a city plan for the Bronx. Letters to William Dorsheimer and Charles Eliot Norton describe the aftermath of the protest of the New York chapter of the American Institute of Architects to the proposal of the advisory board of Olmsted, Leopold Eidlitz, and H. H. Richardson to complete the state capitol in a different architectural style than that adopted for the first stories of the edifice. The letter to Charles Dalton of April 8, 1876, shows the influence that Olmsted exerted on the 1876 proposal by the Boston park commissioners for an extensive park system in their city. The reports of November 1876 by Olmsted and the engineer to J. J. R. Croes spell out the general principles of their plan for the Bronx and explain their design for the first section, between Riverdale Road and the Hudson River.

Other documents present Olmsted's design proposals for public parks in several cities during this period. The report to William Martin of August 1876 describes in detail Olmsted's proposal for a new design for Tompkins Square in Manhattan, while his letter to Thomas Lanahan contains his imaginative proposal for the treatment of four small squares adjoining the Washington Monument in Baltimore. Three letters to H. A. Nelson describe issues relating to major design elements of the work on Mount Royal, and the letters to William Macmillan and Dennis Bowen chronicle ongoing construction of the Buffalo parks. The letter on Landscape Gardening to *The Garden* provides a clear statement on Olmsted's views concerning the use of monumental and architectural objects in parks.

On more personal topics, the letter to his son contains a curious, cautionary tale, while his comments to Charles Eliot Norton of December 27, 1876, reveal the intensity of his response to the presidential election of that year.

To WILLIAM EDWARD DORSHEIMER[1]

[April 2, 1876]

The Hon. William Dorsheimer
Dear Sir;
    I returned from Boston this morning and have only since seen the remonstrance against the plans of our Board[2] signed by Mr Bloor for the N.Y. Chapter of the Institute of Architects.[3] Eidlitz and Richardson are here and I find from them that the statement that it represents the unanimous opinion of the Chapter was certainly unwarranted. But if it did it would none the less be a shamefully unsound document. We anticipated charges of the same general character, considered whether we should be at all weak with reference to them and satisfied ourselves that we should not, but we did not think that they would be presented in such a form nor that they would have a backing so apparently respectable.
    From the first distinct charge it must be inferred, either (a) that a Romanesque superstructure would be "absolutely inharmonious" with a Roman base, or that (b) the simpler forms of Italian Renaissance are incongruous with those of its Roman parent, or (c) that the lower parts of Fuller's design[4] are not of the simpler forms of Renaissance, neither of which positions could be seriously sustained.
    But if such a misassociation is for the sake of argument assumed, it would, again be inferred from the whole drift of the paper that the association of Romanesque and Gothic forms with Renaissance was held in horror by good architects. There are numerous instances in which distinguished Renaissance architects have practiced in defiance of this opinion: notably Sir Christopher Wren, who repeatedly did so and who even introduced Renaissance features in the most prominent positions in Westminster Abbey.[5] There are hundreds of notable instances in which others have deliberately done the same. You may recall examples in the Ducal palace, the Duomo of Milan, the Certosa of Pavia, and various other well known edifices.[6] As to the statement about the introduction of brilliant color—you perfectly know its falsity & its futility.
    The statement that it has always been considered indispensible to

FAÇADE OF DOGES' PALACE, VENICE, WITH GIANT'S STAIRCASE, SHOWING UPPER WINDOWS NOT ON AXIS WITH THOSE OF LOWER STORIES

persue the axial lines of windows — has no pertinance except as it is assumed that ours is a purely Renaissance design. There are many buildings which are largely Renaissance in style, & are among the most interesting & important buildings in which renaissance appears in which this condition is disregarded — I have an example before me in a photograph of the Giants stairs of the Doge's palace.[7]

In Cambridge I saw Prof[r] Norton,[8] who said "I was so much pleased with your report[9] that I immediately read a large part of it to my class" [in the History of Art][10]

As to the propriety of the imposition of a Romanesque superstructure upon a Roman though somewhat Renaissance base he said he had no doubt.

If we are to do anything publicly about the matter we should prefer to do so in answer to official inquiries from you.

The text presented here is from a draft in Olmsted's hand.
1. William Edward Dorsheimer (1832–1888), lawyer and politician in Buffalo, New York. Dorsheimer and Olmsted had been friends since the late 1860s when Olmsted and Calvert Vaux had designed the Buffalo park system. It was Dorsheimer, in his capacity as lieutenant governor of New York and head of the New Capitol Commission created in 1875 after the old commission was abolished, who transferred the designing of the New York state capitol to Olmsted, Leopold Eidlitz, and Henry Hobson Richardson in 1876 (*Papers of FLO*, SS1: 168).
2. A reference to the advisory board to the New York State New Capitol Commission composed of Olmsted, Leopold Eidlitz, and Henry Hobson Richardson.
3. Olmsted is referring to an appeal to the state senate of New York from the New York Chapter of the American Institute of Architects, dated March 29, 1876, and signed for the chapter's president, the architect Richard Morris Hunt, and for himself, by its secretary, Alfred J. Bloor (c. 1828–1917). This "remonstrance" appeared in several New York City newspapers. It contained a strong attack on the advisory board's proposed changes to the state capitol. It read in part:

> The chapter finds that the projected work is designed in direct antagonism to the received rules of art. It finds that Italian renaissance under-stories are surmounted by other absolutely inharmonious romanesque stories; that no successful attempt has been made to avoid the abrupt transition from one style to the other; that the axes of windows have been totally disregarded; a feature the preservation of which is indispensable to renaissance work of importance; that the whole is surmounted by roof towers and a dome of discordant character, renaissance in form, gothic in treatment; that it is proposed to introduce brilliant color in the facades and roofs, which is not only utterly out of keeping with the work already done, but which will be destructive of the repose and dignity of a structure of this class and material; and that the new work is extravagantly rich and expensive in parts, while in others it is meagre to baldness.

Alfred J. Bloor was well known to Olmsted. He had assisted Olmsted and Calvert Vaux in 1859–61 in their work on Central Park and other landscape designs, and then spent more than two years as Olmsted's assistant with the U.S. Sanitary Commission. After the Civil War he worked with the two men on architectural projects until the end of 1867 (*DAB*, s.v. "Bloor, Alfred Janson;" *Papers of FLO*, 4: 90–4; "Remonstrance of the New York Chapter of the American Institute of Architects, against the Proposed Changes in the Plans for the Building of the New Capitol," March 29, 1876, "Document no. 65," in New York [State], *Documents of the Senate of the State of New York, Ninety-Ninth Session* . . . [Albany, N.Y., 1876]).
4. Thomas Fuller (1822–1898), architect. Born and educated in England, Fuller immigrated to Canada in 1857. In 1858 he joined the partnership of Robert C. Messer and Chilion Jones, both civil engineers. Messer left the firm the next year but Fuller and Jones remained partners until 1863. During his partnership with Jones, Fuller received his greatest success. The two won the design competition for the Parliament Building in Ottawa in 1859, and the building was completed in 1866.

It was with Jones that Fuller entered the first design competition for the new New York state capitol in 1863. Although they won the competition no action was taken to build the structure at that time. Four years later a new competition was held and Fuller, now working with the Albany firm of Nichols and Brown, submitted a new design. His design was selected and with minor alterations served as the plan for building the new capitol until 1875 when work was halted due to charges of graft and inefficiency (*Dictionary of Canadian Biography*, 12: 343–46).

5. Christopher Wren (1632–1723), English architect who was in charge of restoration work on Westminster Abbey from 1698 until his death (*DNB*).
6. Probably the ducal palace of Urbino, built for Duke Federigo Montefeltro. Construction of the residence began in the 1460s and was completed in 1482. Most of the features were designed in a Florentine style; however, the arcaded courtyard was Renaissance. The Duomo of Milan, one of the largest churches in Europe was begun 1386 in the Gothic style; however, by the time it was completed in the nineteenth century many Renaissance-style windows had been added to it. Construction of the Certosa di Pavia, began in 1396 in the Gothic style. The monastery building was not completed until 1465, and many of its features including its galleries, pinnacles, and cloisters were designed in the Renaissance style (*EB*).
7. The Remonstrance of the New York Chapter of the AIA had asserted concerning the plans of the advisory board "that the axes of windows have been totally disregarded; a feature the preservation of which is indispensable to renaissance work of importance." This was presumably a reference to the fact that, due to the large number of windows on the third story of the design for the New Capitol proposed by the advisory board, those windows were not in most cases placed directly above the windows of the lower stories. The façade of the Doges' Palace in Venice with the Scala dei Giganti, to which Olmsted refers, had a two-story arcade with windows on axis designed during restoration of the structure c. 1484 by the architect Antonio Rizzo; the two upper stories, with a very different arrangement of windows, were designed by Pietro Lombardo beginning fifteen years later (Karl Baedeker, *Italy from the Alps to Naples* [Leipzig, 1909], pp. 76–77; Ludwig H. Heydenreich and Wolfgang Lotz, *Architecture in Italy, 1400 to 1600* [London, 1974], pp. 92–93; "Remonstrance of Certain Citizens of the State of New York, against the Changes which have been, and are being made, on the New Capitol Building," December 1876, "Document no. 28," in New York [State], *Documents of the Assembly of the State of New York, One Hundredth Session*...[Albany, N. Y., 1877], p. 1).
8. Charles Eliot Norton (1827–1908), professor of fine arts at Harvard College (*Papers of FLO*, 4: 285).
9. A reference to the report of March 2, 1876, of the advisory board to the New Capitol Commission, of which Olmsted wrote a substantial portion. It provided an extensive critique of the design of the capitol by applying the time-honored standards for architectural style and monumentality provided by the Parthenon of Classical Athens, which Norton greatly admired. The report identified two qualities of the Parthenon that were of special importance. One was that "there is nothing to be found in it–not so much as a tool mark–that does not manifest a refined building purpose, followed simply, conscientiously and with consummate executive skill, and because, also, there is not one such purpose to be detected, that has not been kept in harmony with every other, and in strictest subjection to the general purpose of all." The report also asserted that all elements of a structure should contribute to "consistency, congruity and unity of meaning" of the whole. The report was printed as New York Senate Document No. 49 and was also published separately (*Report of the Advisory Board [Frederick Law Olmsted, Leopold Eidlitz and Henry H. Richardson], Relative to the Plans of the New Capitol* [Albany, N.Y., 1877], pp. 11, 13–4; Kermit Vanderbilt, *Charles Eliot Norton: Apostle of Culture in a Democracy* [Cambridge, Mass., 1959], pp. 126–29).
10. Olmsted's brackets.

To Charles Eliot Norton

209 W. 46 ST.
NEW YORK.
2nd. April, 1876,

My Dear Norton;
    While I was talking with you, the dam burst here and out leapt the muddy torrent of the Institute of Architects' remonstrance against our proposition to modify the design of the State Capitol.[1] You will I think regard the matter as one of considerable importance, knowing how generally this cant about style is made to apologize for and sustain lazy and contemptible architecture. It was at once made the occasion and ground for a proposition presented by the Finance Committee of the State Senate (the Chairman of which was chairman of the Commission which ordered the building on Fuller's design)[2] to make further appropriations for the building only on the condition that the attempt to modify that design should be abandoned. Fuller's design is expected to be published in this week's American Architect, and the editor, Longfellow, will probably take sides.[3]
    You will observe that the remonstrance of the Chapter has been hastily prepared. I am told that but few members were consulted and that it is by no means true that it expresses their unanimous opinions. I think that we shall try in some form to get up a counter professional demonstration. I know of no architect of any standing who does not condemn Fuller's design.
    You will observe that the chapter itself indicates that it might do so, but it is to be considered that it has allowed it to stand nearly nine years without a word of remonstrance and first speaks when an attempt to improve is made.
    I send you copies of our drawings. The Capitol is built to the top of the third story—the last but one below the roof.
    Now I should be very glad to be advised whether the lower stories are, in your judgment, so far modified from the Roman, and so distinctly Renaissance, that the change of an abrupt transition from Renaissance to Romanesque is well grounded; whether the suggestion for surface decoration of the granite is properly described as an "introduction of brilliant color" and which would be "destructive of dignity and repose,"[4] and, generally, how far I can feel confidence that thorough study of the matter will satisfy competent men that the Chapter has seriously blundered?
    I ask this for my private advice, but if you will allow me, I may be glad to show it also to Dorsheimer and his Commission,[5] who, I believe, will resign rather than carry out Fuller's design if this should be required by the legislature.
    Faithfully Yours,

Fred Law Olmsted.

APRIL 1876–DECEMBER 1876

Model of Thomas Fuller's 1867 design for New Capitol of York State

The text presented here is from a manuscript in John C. Olmsted's hand in the Charles Eliot Norton Papers, Houghton Library, Harvard University, Cambridge, Massachusetts. Olmsted explained the circumstance of the writing of the letter in another letter to Norton that he also dated April 2, 1876:

>I had John write my letter to you of yesterday in duplicate, that it might have the better chance of going by last night's train. This effort means simply that I feel that within a few days I must make up my mind as to some policy to be pursued in the matter of the Capitol in which I find my position a particularly unpleasant one, the whole architectural profession being just now under a strong lead to condemn and hold up to public scorn views which I have gone out of my way to advocate. I have taken my course with sufficient consideration, deliberately, cautiously and substantially I have not a doubt that I am right. I feel on my own account and on that of my associates very defiant but I also feel that I am to fight in a field in which I am an intruder and that I may find it necessary to take my position at any moment. Dorsheimer's commission meets tomorrow & will have some compromise proposition to consider &, I hope, to refuse. Wednesday the matter comes before the Senate in some form & on Thursday is to be debated. Under these circumstances I should greatly value any word of caution or of encouragment from you.

189

DESIGN BY ADVISORY BOARD OF OLMSTED, RICHARDSON, AND EIDLITZ
FOR NEW CAPITOL (1876)

1. See FLO to William E. Dorsheimer, April 2, 1876, note 3, above.
2. On March 31, 1876, the Senate Finance Committee had proposed the appropriation of one million dollars for the New Capitol, with the provision that construction must be completed to the roofline according to Fuller's design. The chairman of the committee, Hamilton Harris, had been chairman of the New Capitol Commission when it selected Fuller's design in 1867. He resigned from that commission in 1875 and was elected to the state senate (*American Architect and Building News*, April 15, 1876, p. 121; *New-York Times*, April 1, 1876, p. 10; *Who Was Who: 1897–1942* [Chicago, 1966], 1: 524).
3. On April 15, 1876, the *American Architect and Building News* published a perspective view and floor plans of Fuller's design for the capitol. The editor, William Pitt Preble Longfellow (1836–1913), made no editorial comment on either Fuller's plan or that of Olmsted, Eidlitz and Richardson (*American Architect and Building News*, April 15, 1876, pp. 124–25; *DAB*).
4. Olmsted is quoting from the New York Chapter of the American Institute of Architects' "Remonstrance" dated March 29, 1876 (see FLO to William Dorsheimer, April 2, 1876, n. 3, above).
5. A reference to the New Capitol Commission (see FLO to William Dorsheimer, April 2, 1876, n. 2, above).

To Horatio Admiral Nelson

4th April 1876.

The Hon. H. A. Nelson.
President —
Dear Sir;
 There would be many and serious disadvantages attending the erection of a temporary refectory on the mountain adapted to serve your purpose for five (5) years, as you have proposed and, on considering the matter more carefully I have thought it better to submit to you another proposition.[1] I have for this purpose had prepared a study for a plan for a house to be built at the crown of the mountain, in accordance with a suggestion before made to you, which I herewith send.[2] The whole plan would provide tables and seats for nearly 300 visitors at a time but is adapted for the serving only of light refreshments & for summer use, it being assumed that you will have another house in a lower and more sheltered position for a dinner business & for winter. The plan will, upon a little study, sufficiently explain itself. I need only remark that what is named "the bar" is the place for the manager and for the sale of hand articles — cakes, cigars, & soda water &c. The room marked "parcels &c" is a place of deposit for baskets, cloaks &c. for visitors; the space marked "Ombra" is an open gallery or veranda similar to but broader than that showed on the opposite of the house in the perspective sketch A.
 The house is designed to be built of wood in a common and inexpensive way, its effect depending on the form & general style adopted, which is not essentially different from that of the best old French farm houses of the Dominion. It is to be covered chiefly with shingles, except the canopy of the tower which is designed to appear at a distance like a crown and to be overlaid with tin — or if you can afford it with gilded copper. The architect has not quite met my intention in the tower but you will recognize the general idea.[3]
 I mean the tower to be high enough to be seen from and to command a view over the nearer part of the city and I have arranged a large open belvidere over the main body of the house at a height at which it is expected that more distant views will be obtained over and through the tops of the trees. It is intended that this place shall also be used for the refectory business.
 I propose that you shall immediately build so much of this structure as is shown on Sheet C. and shall for this summer place a tent where, in the full plan, the room lettered "Refectory" stands. This will give you in good form all the special conveniences needed & accommodations for the lodging &c of the manager and servants.
 Considering the greater economy of the arrangment in the long run, I do not think that the cost of adopting this plan will be so much beyond what you have intended to lay out upon a temporary house that you will feel that you cannot afford it.

Not knowing your laws, I suggest that it may be practicable for you to make an arrangment by which the whole of the structure might be built at once at the expense of a lessee on a long lease with proper conditions & security.

Please return the studies and inform whether my proposition can be entertained.

Yours respectfully,

The text presented here is from a draft in Olmsted's hand.
1. On February 21, 1876, Commissioner Nelson wrote Olmsted requesting his opinion on building a "refreshment stand" in the Upperfell section of the mountain. It was to be located near the top of the stairs ascending from the reservoir above the Peel Street entrance, close to the present-day Grand Chalet. In March Nelson again asked Olmsted about the possibility of building a temporary restaurant or café "in the most central position, on the top of the Mountain" (H. A. Nelson to FLO, Feb. 21, 1876; ibid., March 9, 1876; ibid., March 21, 1876).
2. The plans for this refectory have not survived, but its footprint appears in the northeast part of the Upperfell on Olmsted's "Mount Royal Design Map 1877."
3. Thomas Wisedell was the architect that Olmsted engaged to provide plans for the refectory. The refectory that Olmsted proposed here would have cost $8,000 to build, but the City Council refused to approve the needed appropriation and the building was never constructed (see FLO to Justin Smith Morrill, Aug. 16, 1874, n. 11, above; *Papers of FLO*, SS1: 417, n. 56).

To Charles Henry Dalton

8th April 1876.

Dear Mr Dalton;[1]

I have not written sooner and shall make no formal report to the Commission upon your scheme because I have not found myself ready to give you any definite advice upon the few points on which I am not fully satisfied with your scheme and on which I have not already sufficiently expressed my views.

I do not feel that I have mastered the conditions which should be controlling or that I can help you much until you have a better map of the proposed (main) park property

I have not taken hold of the matter as I should had you chosen to place upon me a definite professional responsibility and, going about, as I have under your lead, in a desultory way, taking up the various matters to which you have invited my attention from the point of view to which they had been previously carried in your minds, without having approached them by the same road, the lack of what has thus been excluded from my consideration by which I am compelled to look mainly at the positive & not the comparative value of what you have selected, is embarrassing.

I will however, briefly review the matters which you have more particularly asked me to consider.

The proposition of the Charles River Embankmnt[2] I regard with unqualified satisfaction. I would advise no more and no less than you propose.

The outline of the ground between the Embankmt and the main land, below the Parker Hill Reservoir, as sketched when I left on your map shows the minimum of what should be taken with a view to a park. The area would be desirably enlarged especially at the broadest part.[3] If necessary from considerations of cost to contract it, it would be better to change the motive and substitute for the park a broad park way.

If any of the ground marked to be taken on the last sketch on your map, between Francis Street and Fisher Avenue must be dispensed with I should advise the reduction to be made at the West end at the nearest point to Tremont Street. If by throwing out land at this point you could enlarge the gap at Bumpstead lane I should advise you to do it.[4]

The Jamaica pond[5] plot is unquestionably very desirable. The chance that such a pond in the midst of a dense neighborhood will become pestilential and the certainty that if defended and used as you propose, it will be a great sanitary advantage is conclusive.

As to your main park, the locality seems to possess more advantages for the purpose than any other I have seen near Boston and some of these are of great positive value, while the negative advantages—mainly in the fact that so large a space can be found so near the center of population, so little occupied & expensively improved, are remarkable.[6] The topography has defects and presents difficulties which to overcome without excessive cost will require much consideration and in the attempt to select and aggrandize the more valuable opportunities of the site I apprehend that some adjustment of its boundaries both by contraction and expansion will be found necessary This is the only ground you propose to take on which it is practicable to form a park properly so called and the advantages of a park can be obtained upon it much sooner and the value of it will be much greater acre for acre if you take as much land as you propose than if you try to get on with a smaller amount. There are some circumstances about it (so far as I now see necessary circumstances) which are not satisfactory but in the whole the possibility of obtaining a tract of land so near a large city equally well adapted to be formed into a park, and so free from costly improvements is a rare piece of good fortune and if advantage should not be taken of it in all probability the city would hereafter be compelled to go further and fare worse with much greater expenditure. The Elm Hill and adjoining properties[7] might I believe be in some way turned to

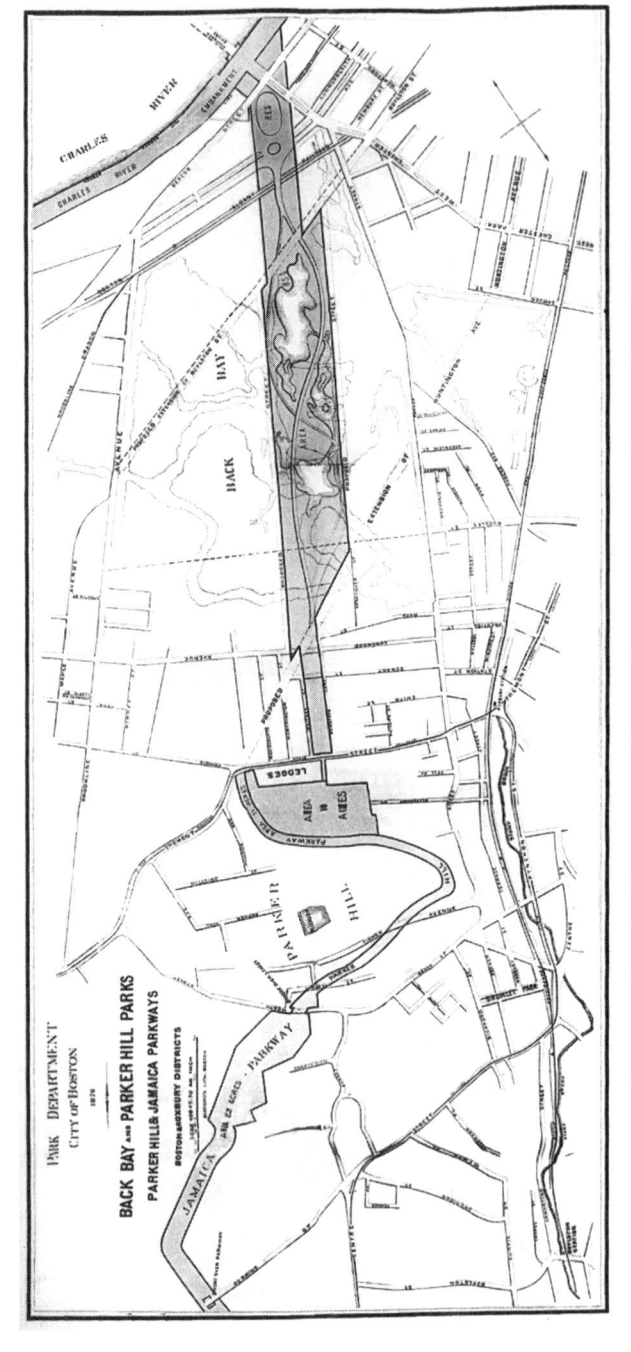

Plan for Back Bay Park, park on Parker Hill and parkway to Jamaica Pond (1876)

good account for the improvement of your scheme in this particular but you cannot make an approach through them that will not assume the character of your most important approach and establish the grand entrance to your park and for this purpose I can shape out nothing in my mind as yet that does not lack artistic completeness.[8]

I have little doubt that something better than I now see can be done but it will probably require an adjustmnt of boundaries.

On the whole if you were compelled to reduce your scheme at all materially, I should prefer to leave out the Elm Hill property to any other–especially would I do so rather than reduce the size of the park or run any great risk of being compelled to reduce it or of failing in your immediate purpose.

On the other hand if any enlargmt of the scope or costliness of your scheme were now admissable I should advise greater liberality in the new park ways and bolder and more sweeping improvemnts of existing streets leading toward the park, than you seem to contemplate.

The most defective part of your scheme certainly is that of the approaches to the park. It must be reached from all distant points by very indirect routes, such as in any other of our cities but Boston would be regarded as intolerable. Those from the denser parts of the city, which are the least open to this objection, though more or less agreeable at present, will after a few years, be (comparatively speaking and with reference to the purpose) mean streets, cramped inconvenient and awkward.

I am much afraid that your plan of a Park-way without side roads will not prove satisfactory. A back yard is an indispensable part of a house and I can see no way of arranging a domestic establishmnt with your plan for the streets, that will not defy many prejudices and have great economical disadvantges.[9]

You have a precedent for it, I know, in the arrangmt of the villas about Regent's Park[10] but even if the plan is there regarded as satisfactory the difference between the social conditions and customs of London and Boston render the experience of little value. In the approaches to the Bois de Boulogne a different and I think a much more available theory was adopted and certainly works well.[11]

I must, therefore, suggest, with all deference to your judgmnt, that it would be better not to be bound to this feature. It is at least open to objections that may bring prejudice against your whole project.

You will see from all I have said that in whatever degree you are disposed to be influenced by my advice I should still be chiefly anxious that it tended to keep the boundaries of the various plots as far from an exact determination as possible, leaving them to be adjusted after the general theory of a plan for laying out the ground had been sufficiently developed to allow it to be done more intelligently & judiciously than I should imagine would be possible at present.

A private citizen under ordinary circumstances must take land as he can find it, that is as it may have been platted off by others without reference

Sketch of Parkway proposed by Boston Park Commissioners (1876)

APRIL 1876–DECEMBER 1876

to his particular wants. In laying out grounds so obtained, one must, of course, generally make the best of what thus happens to be available. It should be possible and it would be much better in your case to let your land be chosen more definitely with reference to your ideal after this had been in some degree defined by a plan accommodated to the topography of the neighborhood

Very truly yours

F L. O.

The text is taken from a draft in Olmsted's hand. The Boston park commission was appointed in July 1875 and began a series of public meetings in September, after which it was available daily for several months for the presentation of plans and proposals. On October 26, Olmsted examined a number of the sites being considered at that point. In November the secretary of the park board, Charles H. Dalton, sent him a map of the properties being considered, expressing the hope that Olmsted could return for a week once the park sites had been selected. He did make a two-day visit to the commissioners on March 31 and April 1, 1876. Arriving back in New York on the morning of April 2, he was greeted by news of the American Institute of Architects' "Remonstrance" against the advisory board's proposals for completing the New York State capitol. The ensuing furor may account for the tardiness of Olmsted's reply to the Boston park commissioners, which he sent only two weeks before they issued their report of April 24. The principal change the commission appears to have made in response to his critique was to widen the southern end of the Back Bay Park, making it eight hundred feet wide for most of its length. This made it possible to secure the vista from the Parker Hill Park over the Fens toward the Charles River that Olmsted wished to secure. Another likely result of this letter was the omission in the commissioners' report of any mention of "Elm Hill and adjoining properties." (Cynthia Zaitzevsky, *Frederick Law Olmsted and the Boston Park System* [Cambridge, Mass., 1982], pp. 43–44; BCDP, City of Boston, manuscript Minutes, October 14, 1875, ff.; Charles H. Dalton to FLO, Oct. 18, 1875; ibid., Nov. 3, 1875; ibid., Nov. 15, 1875; FLO to Charles H. Dalton, April 14, 1876).

1. Charles Henry Dalton (1826–1908), Boston businessman and a member of the Boston park commission from its founding in 1875 until 1885, and president of that body during most of that time. Dalton played an important part in creating the congenial setting for Olmsted's work with the Boston parks. Their political allegiances were similar as well. Dalton was representative for the Commonwealth of Massachusetts in Washington during the Civil War, overseeing supplies sent by the state to the Union Army. After the war he was active in the Loyal Publication Society, which Olmsted helped to found. The first recorded contact between the two men came in May of 1873 when Dalton, as a member of the committee of the Massachusetts General Hospital charged with finding a new site for the McLean Asylum, wrote Olmsted asking him to examine a newly proposed site. In this, Olmsted was continuing a role that he had begun when he examined proposed sites for the asylum in late 1872. In fact, Olmsted's first visits to Boston to consider sites for parks were combined with ongoing consultation concerning the asylum (Roger Bigelow Merriman, "Memoir of Charles Henry Dalton," in Massachusetts Historical Society, *Proceedings* 42 [April 1909]: 287–312; Charles H. Dalton to FLO, May 3, 1873; ibid., Oct. 18, 1875; *Papers of FLO*, 6: 584–88).
2. The proposed embankment was to extend along the south bank of the Charles River from Leverett Street (near the present site of the Charles River Dam and Museum of

Science) for three miles to the Cottage Farm Bridge (now Boston University Bridge). As designed by Olmsted and his firm in 1887 and 1892, the embankment extended only the half mile from Leverett Street to the bridge at Cambridge Street (BCDP, City of Boston, *Second Report* [Boston, 1876], pp. 15–16; C. Zaitzevsky, *Olmsted and the Boston Park System*, pp. 96–97).

3. The widest section of the proposed Back Bay park, as presented in the park commission's *Second Report* of April 1876, was a straight-sided parallelogram between Boylston Street and Huntington Avenue eight hundred feet wide and containing a curving drive, a narrower drive or bridle path, and four connected lagoons.

4. Olmsted is suggesting a reduction of the sixteen-acre area of parkland proposed by the commissioners on the northeast slope of Parker Hill above an area of ledges along Tremont Street. The gap that he refers to was the very narrow section of parkland — only sixty feet wide — southwest of Tremont Street between Whitney Street and Bumpstead Lane (now St. Alphonsus Street) extended. This narrow strip was to provide passage to the base of the ledges on Parker Hill (not included in the park acreage) with steps leading to Parker Hill Park above (BCDP, City of Boston, *Second Report*, p. 20).

5. The commissioners proposed to take for park purposes the seventy-acre pond and fifty-two surrounding acres, approximately the area and configuration of the park for which Olmsted and his firm created plans c. 1892 (BCDP, City of Boston, *Second Report*, pp. 28–30; C. Zaitzevsky, *Olmsted and the Boston Park System*, pp. 86–88)

6. The proposed site for the large park in the system was 485 acres in the West Roxbury section of Boston, three miles from Boston Common. It was approximately the same area as the 512 acres that Olmsted planned as Franklin Park beginning c. 1884. The principal expansion of the site that occurred by that time was extension of the park boundary to Morton Street along the full length of the southwest side of the park.

7. The Elm Hill neighborhood is located on the opposite side of the park's northeast boundary along Seaver Street, west of Blue Hill Avenue. It could have provided an entrance experience for the park for visitors approaching directly from the city along Warren and Hampden streets.

In the original version of the end of this sentence, Olmsted wrote "and for this purpose I can shape out nothing in my mind as yet that is not rather weak and incomplete and pretentious."

8. At the end of this sentence, Olmsted originally included the following phrase: "and without a decided urban nor decidedly suburban aspect."

9. The section of the commissioners' report on parkways was so general that it did not describe the aspects of their plan to which Olmsted objected; but the illustration of a parkway published in the commissioners' report appears to lack the streets on the outer sides of the parkway, providing access to houses by front-yard entrances, that Olmsted desired. (On one side in the illustration the pedestrian promenade runs along the front yards of residences; on the other side there is a forty-foot-wide street "for traffic," but it does not appear to provide access to the houses) In their report, however, the commissioners said that the parkways might be "approached by ordinary parallel streets in the rear or front," the front-yard access presumably meeting Olmsted's criteria.

Their plan showed a series of parkways, some two hundred feet wide and others one hundred feet, that would provide a connected, six-and-one-half-mile circuit from Charlesbank through Back Bay and Parker Hill parks, Jamaica Park, the main park in West Roxbury, and on to Neponset Avenue in Dorchester. They also called for a parkway, running for the most part through the village of Brookline, that would connect Charlesbank with a proposed 391-acre suburban park at Chestnut Hill Reservoir in Brighton (BCDP, City of Boston, *Second Report*, pp. 11–12, 18, 27–28, 31–33; "Sketch Showing Arrangement for Park-way with Adjacent Streets and Building Lots," ibid., opposite p. 12 [see p. 196]).

10. The residential terraces surrounding Regent's Park in London, planned by John Nash in 1812, are serviced by streets at their rear, which also serve as their principal entrance-point (John Summerson, *Georgian London* [1945, rpt. ed., Cambridge, Mass., 1978], pp. 179–84).
11. A reference to the Avenue de l'Imperatrice in Paris, that extended from the Place de l'Etoile to the Bois de Boulogne. It had a wide central promenade area for carriages, equestrians, and pedestrians, flanked by broad planted strips outside of which were side roads for access to the villas that lined it (Jean-Charles-Adolphe Alphand, *Les Promenades de Paris.* . . [1867–73; rpt. ed., Princeton, N.J., 1984]).

To Charles Eliot Norton

209 W. 46 ST.
NEW YORK.
22^d April 1876.

My Dear Norton;

  I received yours of 18th tonight, on my return from Washington and Eidlitz & Richardson being here was glad to read it to them as it is persuasive toward my policy. But I am sorry to say that I cannot hope the measure you urge can be adopted.[1] Perhaps I can't explain just why not. I think, however, it is because of the strong bent of mind which in their long consideration of the subject the architects have acquired. I judge by a sort of echo of their sentiments in my own mind. It is more than that with Eidlitz who says simply "I cannot"—(work in Renaissance). Richardson, on the other hand, would, had he taken up the problem alone at the outset, almost certainly have kept to Renaissance, yet he equally seems unable to return to it now.[2]

  I think we agree in the mind that we should not (& will not) allow these attacks, which are coming with increased rapidity and force,[3] to deter us from doing precisely that which we best can to bring about the most satisfactory result to the public and for this purpose we agree that less difference of style in the two parts of the building is very desirable. The tendency is to reach the result, however, not so much by abandoning what we will call Romanesque in the upper part as, if possible, by some slight changes in the lower part, making its Renaissance character less pronounced. I confess to a little doubt whether the two styles do not spring from such different roots that the sap of one cannot flow into the other—whether in the Romanesque part we must not see the skin of what is beneath and in Renaissance a raiment worn over the real creature, so much that the amalgamation will be monstrous, but this doubt goes for little in my faith in Richardson's instinct & Eidlitz clear head. Judging by his works, Eidlitz is safer to come out right than any other architect we have.

Eidlitz admits that there is a jar between the lower & the upper parts of the design and that there probably will be when we have done all we can to sooth it, but, he says, if a good Renaissance architect had undertaken to complete the building from the same point and to do so in Renaissance and as smoothly as he could, a great difference between the character of his part and of Fuller's would have been inevitable. There will be a jar between good architecture and bad even if they are in the same style.

Do you feel quite sure yourself, that in such a case, the more audacious way is not the safer way?

I have no doubt that the enmity toward us will increase as you suggest and I would do anything in reason to conciliate our enemies but I am afraid that nothing we can do now will have any effect. The prejudice against us is likely to be stimulated by the removal of Fuller, which if he should fail to resign I do not think that we now can prevent.[4] His course has been insubordinate and almost insulting to the Commission & it is plain that he is not a fit person to superintend the execution of plans which he regards as outrageously bad. Nothing has of late been said to us on the subject and all that we have so far said has been with the hope that he might be retained.

You will not suppose that I write with the expectation of being answered but I would like to keep you informed in the matter and I am very much obliged to you for taking the trouble to write as you have.

You will be pleased to know that La Farge is quite as strongly on our side as you are.[5]

Faithfully Yours,

Fred Law Olmsted

The text presented here is from a manuscript in Olmsted's hand in the Charles Eliot Norton Papers, Houghton Library, Harvard University, Cambridge, Massachusetts.

1. In his letter of April 18, Norton was uneasy about the proposal to place upper stories in the Romanesque style above the existing Renaissance stories. "It would be safer, and in my judgment probably productive of a better artistic result," he counseled, "to keep to the style in which the building has thus far been constructed, so far as the outside is concerned." In a further expression of his concerns, he wrote:

    Now, although there is no principle of art violated by the superposition of a story with Byzantine forms, on one of Renaissance design, it seems to me that a principle of good judgement, and possibly of good taste, is contravened. A change in technical style in a building should be justified either by some utilitarian advantage, or by some historic change of national temper. Otherwise the change indicates a mere difference of individual taste, and is likely to displease the greater number even of the few men competent to form a judgement on an architectural design, as appearing the result of a purely arbitrary choice. In this case the question is not the abstract one of whether Romanesque or Renaissance is the better style, but whether a mingling of the two is better than the Renaissance alone.

This doctrine was presumably the part of the letter that Olmsted welcomed as "persuasive toward my policy" (CEN to FLO, April 18, 1876).
2. However, a year later Richardson admitted confidentially to Olmsted that "I hope Dorsheimer will be firm but I do believe entre-nous that the building can be well finished in Francois 1er or Louis XIV which come under the head of Renaissance" (H. H. Richardson to FLO, March 10, 1877).
3. A reference to the attacks from several New York architects.
4. The New York State New Capitol Commission dismissed Fuller on July 1, 1876 (Cecil R. Roseberry, *Capitol Story* [Albany, N.Y., 1964], p. 33).
5. John La Farge (1835–1910), American artist and writer and friend of Olmsted's (*DAB*).

To Horatio Admiral Nelson

6th June 1876.

To Mr. Nelson
Sir,

In several interviews with your commission week before last, I pointed out to you some of the serious mistakes which had been made in the laying out and construction of the road up the mountain.[1]

Justice to the purposes which led you to employ me require however that I should more distinctly take the occasion which this experience offers to urge you to establish certain conditions which a much more extended experience that I have elsewhere had convinces me are not only necessary to make my services of any real value to you but indispensable to an economical managment of your work.

I therefore ask your special consideration of certain facts, as follows:

1st That in what has thus far been done the drawings and the written advice given in and accompanying my report to your Board and the extended written and verbal instructions given your Engineer have been practically lost sight of and all the study which I had given to them wasted.

2^{d} That so far as any comprehensive plan has been had in the work done, it is one of a radically different character from that which I supplied you, the great majority of the objects I had studied to effect being carefully avoided & the results which I studied to avoid being in many instances pursued as if desirable.

3rd   The superintendent of the work[2] who was not under the orders of the Engineer[3] and who varied at pleasure from his advice did not during the progress of the work ever see my report to you, nor had he been informed in any manner of the most essential instructions which I had prepared for the work.

4th   The engineer occasionally employd, (apparently only to indicate the general course of the road & give levels), never read my detailed instructions, never saw the detailed drawings & denied all responsibility for the plan which was followed, many of the simply engineering errors of which he was nevertheless aware of but had no power to prevent.

5th   Neither the Superintendent nor the Engineer nor again your secretary[4] was able to refer when required to my drawings or written instructions, or to copies of them nor upon search were they to be found distinctly in the custody of any one of them; two papers among them being particularly called for could not be found and I am informed that it is necessary that I should reproduce them.

6th   You have principally as the result of the undefined responsibilities and insubordination which these facts exemplify, a road such as, (the lowest & the highest point being given & the maximum grade being fixed) any boy who had been a year with a surveying party might have laid out & any intelligent farmer might have constructed, in which a great deal of costly material has been unnecessarily used and which nevertheless will require you to obtain from other sources a much larger amount of this same material than if any well considered plan had been followed would have been necessary.

Whatever *beauty* you enjoy in going over it exists simply in spite of the work that has been done, not in the least because of it—and opportunity of making such an attractive way up the mountain as I had designed, has been lost forever.

The injury which I must inevitably suffer from being supposed to be the designer of a work of which any tyro in my profession would be ashamed, and for which it is wholly out of your power to make me a compensation, could never have occurred had the work been under the Superintendence, as you had led me to understand that it would be, of a man, however little qualified by previous training for it, who would be influenced in the least degree by a sense of professional responsibility in the matter.

I put the case thus plainly before you, with no desire to reproach the Commission for a course which I know was followed with the best of motives, but as my justification for not only recommending on grounds of public interest but for earnestly requesting as a matter of simple justice to myself that you adopt some fundamental rules in the form of By Laws or otherwise so that they may not be too readily set aside, for guarding against similar waste in the future.

To this end I submit the following suggestions:

1st   That no construction shall be ordered or authorized until after the Landscape Architect has had opportunity to report on it and his plans or recommendations have been distinctly adopted or distinctly rejected by the Commission.

2^d That an Engineer shall be appointed, to whom the adopted general plans and approved instructions of the Landscape Architect shall be given and who shall have such control over the work that he may secure conformity to the plans in its progress.

3^d That all orders of the Commission relating to construction work shall be issued to and through the Engineer [orders relating to police & maintenance work going *directly* to the Superintendent].

4th That copies of all orders of the Commission relating to construction shall be furnished to the Landscape Architect.

5th That as to matters of detail not defined by the general plans as adopted by the Commission the Engineer shall consult with and proceed under the instructions of the Landscape Architect.

6th That as to deviations of detail from the general plans adopted by the Commission, which may be found by the Engineer to be desireable on account of conditions of topography not shown on the topographical map, he shall submit suggestions to the Landscape Architect. If approved by him the work shall proceed in accordance with such modifications except when they are of such a character that the cost of the work would be materially affected by them, in which case they shall first be submitted to and acted on by the Commission.

I am confident that the adoption of and rigid adherance to such a routine as would thus be prescribed, whatever its immediate inconvenience, would in the end lead to results much more satisfactory to the Commission than can be otherwise attained and that the course of proceeding thus suggested is essential to secure due value to the service which I am engaged to render.

The text presented here is from a draft in Olmsted's hand.

1. Anxious to provide employment during a severe depression, the Montreal park commission constructed a road up the mountain in the midst of the bitterly cold winter of 1875–76. The work began in November and was completed in February, carrying the road as far as the edge of the Glades section. Finding geological conditions different from those anticipated by Olmsted, the engineers in charge altered his plans at will. In particular, this resulted in wide areas of grading on either side of the road, instead of the walls and terraces by which he had intended to avoid alteration of the natural terrain. Warned by his engineering associate George Radford, he urged that the commissioners allow him to visit the site and devise a new plan where necessary, but the work was com-

pleted without his involvement. Commenting on this construction in his report of 1881, he observed:

> ... had it been desirable to display barrenness on its borders, and to make the fact apparent that the road was a rude and hasty construction, made with no regard to those considerations for local and foreground scenery which I sought to explain in the early part of this discourse, the same amount of labor could hardly have been better applied to the object.

(*Papers of FLO*, SS1: 33, 405–06; FLO to H. A. Nelson, Dec. 25, 1875; FLO to H. A. Nelson, Jan. 6, 1876, Archives Municipales de Montréal, Montreal, Quebec, Canada).
2. W. J. Picton.
3. Probably William McGibbon.
4. P. O'Meara.

To Charles Eliot Norton

209 W. 46 ST.
NEW YORK.
7th June 1876.

My Dear Norton;

We have submitted revised designs of the State Capitol, the roofs elevated, towers reduced and porches given a Romanesque character.[1] I think the roof a great improvement but it is greatly injured by large Renaissance dormars which are pets of Richardson's and the whole has I fear a patch work character.[2] I trust it will be lessened as we go on.

It was adopted without delay by the Capitol Commissioners but in the Land Board there was much debate,[3] the Anti Tilden Democrats[4] repeating the phrases as well as they could recollect them of the Memorial of the Institute of Architects and Fuller repeating his remonstrance and quoting Hunt and Upjohn.[5] A comprehensive resolution of approval failed. A resolution of approval "to the roof line," (so as to allow work to proceed this summer) was then offered and after further weak debate adopted by one majority (in a Board of Seven). The change was with Comptroller Robinson[6] who thought the roof "looked like a hencoop" but was willing to let us go as far as we could below the roof before the next legislature could take it in hand.

I have received no reply to my letter to Hunt[7] and am told that the matter will be brought before the general convention of the Institute in November. Fuller will, I presume, be dismissed if he does not now resign.[8]

Considerable improvements have been made in the interior.

The business is in various ways very embarrassing to me. I think that I am in a false position as the head of a Board charged with the duty of architectural superintendence but Eidlitz and Richardson both insist that they will resign if I do.

    Faithfully Yours

                          Fred Law Olmsted

The text presented here is from a manuscript in Olmsted's hand in the Charles Eliot Norton Papers, Houghton Library, Harvard University, Cambridge, Massachusetts.

1. Olmsted, Eidlitz, and Richardson submitted revised plans for the capitol before a joint meeting of the New Capitol Commission and the commissioners of the Land Office. The revisions were minor, but the advisory board hoped to quiet the protests against their original design (*American Architect and Building News*, June 17, 1876, p. 193).
2. Richardson's dormers were designed in François I French Renaissance style, while Fuller's design had been in Italian Renaissance (C. R. Roseberry, *Capitol Story*, p. 41; Henry-Russell Hitchcock, *The Architecture of H. H. Richardson and His Times* [Cambridge, Mass., 1970], p. 169).
3. The Land Office board was composed of seven commissioners: Lieutenant Governor William Dorsheimer, Secretary of State John Bigelow, Comptroller Lucius Robinson, Treasurer Charles N. Ross, Attorney General Charles Fairchild, State Engineer and Surveyor John D. Van Buren, and Speaker of the Assembly James W. Husted. In this particular meeting to which Olmsted here is referring, the comptroller, Lucius Robinson, refused to approve the new design of the upper part of the building. Lieutenant Governor William Dorsheimer then modified the bill so that construction only had to be approved "to the roof-line." The resolution was then passed (John Bigelow, *Manual for the Use of the Legislature of the State of New York*, [New York, 1876], pp. 228–33; *American Architect and Building News*, June 17, 1876, p. 193).
4. Anti-Tilden Democrats were "opposed both to the Tilden Presidential programme and to the policy enunciated in the platform." At first Tilden Democrats tried to identify this element as those involved in the Canal Ring (*New-York Times*, Feb. 20, 1876, p. 2).
5. A reference to the memorial of the New York Chapter of the American Institute of Architects of March 29, 1876, criticizing the design for the capitol of Olmsted, Eidlitz and Richardson as published in the *American Architect and Building News* of March 11, Thomas Fuller's response to William Dorsheimer of March 20, 1876 concerning that design, and testimony critical of the design by the eminent architects Richard Morris Hunt and Richard Michell Upjohn that Fuller included in his response ("Remonstrance of the New York Chapter of the American Institute of Architects, Against the Proposed Changes in the Plans for the Building of the New Capitol," March 29, 1876, "Document no. 65," in New York [State], *Documents of the Senate of the State of New York, Ninety-ninth Session* . . . [Albany, N. Y., 1876]).
6. Lucius Robinson (1810–1891), a Democrat, was elected New York state comptroller in 1875. A year later he was elected governor of New York (Robert Sobel and John Raimo, *Biographical Directory of the Governors of the United States, 1789–1978* [Westport, Conn., 1978], p. 1088).
7. On April 4, Olmsted wrote a letter to Richard Morris Hunt, protesting the action of the New York chapter of the American Institute of Architects in addressing a remonstrance to the legislature without according Olmsted and his colleagues on the advisory board an opportunity to respond. Olmsted allowed that the precipitousness of the action of the chapter might have been due to belief by its members that Olmsted and his associates

on the board had intentions, or were employing means "which, in the interest of the profession and, of justice, it was important should be resisted instantly and by the most direct means." If anything had been spoken or written in meetings of the chapter to foster such a view, he asked to be informed of it. "Further," he wrote, "if anything in my action professionally considered, or in that of any member of the Board over which I have the honor to preside has appeared to be in question before the Chapter, or to be thought to fall short in the slightest from the highest standard of professional decorum and polity, or to be unjust or ungenerous to any professional brother, or if anything has been uttered to which if I had been present I should have been expected by you from regard to my good name or that of my associates to reply, I ask to be fully and promptly and as soon as possible advised of it" (FLO to R. M. Hunt, April 4, 1876)
8. Fuller was dismissed as resident architect on July 1 (see FLO to CEN, April 22, 1876, n. 4, above; C. R. Roseberry, *Capitol Story*, p. 22).

TO HORATIO ADMIRAL NELSON

209 W 46 ST.
NEW YORK.
26th. July. 1876.

H. A. Nelson, Esq[r],
Chairman, M[t] Royal Park Commission.
Dear Sir;
    Having been advised by you that the project of a reservoir had been fully adopted, to be situated on the meadow of the Smith property, originally intended to be included in your park,[1] I prepared a study of an outline to the same such as I thought would best suit its necessarily close relations with the park, while fully meeting the requirements of the Water Works.[2] This study I requested Mr. Picton[3] to submit, as a basis of discussion to Mr. Lesage.[4] Mr. Lesage, last week, wrote me expressing his satisfaction with my suggestion and stating that he had recommended its adoption and that it had been definitely adopted by the Water Works Committee. As it lies wholly within the property now held by your Commission, and as in determining its form I had in view a highly important feature of the Park, I shall expect, in due time to submit the whole project to your Board.
    Its adoption will involve a change in the general theory of design for laying out all the upper part of the mountain. The element, which I have hitherto considered a very important one, of a piece of truly park-like ground, broad, simple, quiet and of a rich sylvan and pastoral character, forming a harmonious, natural foreground to the view over the Western valley and all in striking contrast to the ruggedness of the mountain proper, must be

Plan by Olmsted for upper Mount Royal without reservoir, c. April 1876 abandoned. This is much to be regretted, but as it has been determined upon, I shall turn the new conditions to the best account that I can, and in the arrangements which I shall propose you will find I trust much approach to compensation for what has been lost.

Either by opening a broad road from the Reservoir to the Cote des Nieges road East of the Cemetery or by some other expedient yet to be devised, it will be necessary that the City guard strenuously against the erection of any building by which the view might be cut {off} or disturbed, which in that direction is so very lovely and distinct in character from all others to be enjoyed from the mountain.

I have proposed an outline to the reservoir adapted to admit of the construction about it of a grand promenade half a mile in length which will include driving, riding and walking ways, nearly level in grade. Accommodations of this class can thus be provided much better and at less expense than on the upper part of the mountain and, situated here, they will have several advantages, each of no little value.

First, as a place of social gathering, the locality will be a mile nearer the City than that previously proposed to be similarly used.

Second, it will be a safer place for the congregation of large numbers of carriages and horsemen.

Third, it will be available for its intended use with comfort earlier in the spring and later in the autumn, being sheltered from northerly winds.

{Fourth}, horses having had a mile less of up-{hill work} to do will reach it in fresher condition, {and} visitors will find it a pleasant relief to {turn} out upon its level course on their way to the "Crown of the Mountain."[5]

Fifth, the material excavated from the reservoir, and not required in the construction of the promenade around it, will materially help to mend the defects of the road from Bleury Street up the mountain.[6]

Sixth, having provided a much more satisfactory course for horsemen than was previously practicable, there will be no need of constructing one in the upper part of the mountain, which will leave the latter a much safer place for the rambles of women and children.

Seventh, the addition at this point of a broad, level promenade drive, will justify a reduction of width, and the use of steeper grades and more frequent and rapid changes of course in the drive of the upper part of the mountain, the natural features of which will thus be less subject to injury, while the road will be more harmonious {and in}character with the scenery.

I shall as soon as practicable submit a plan presenting the whole project in definite form which I have little doubt will receive your approval. Inasmuch, however, as the introduction of the grand promenade will make little essential difference in the course of the circuit drive of the upper part of the mountain, which has already been surveyed in and which you have informally approved, I have given Mr Picton instructions for such modifications as will be desirable in the preparation of the working plan upon which, when

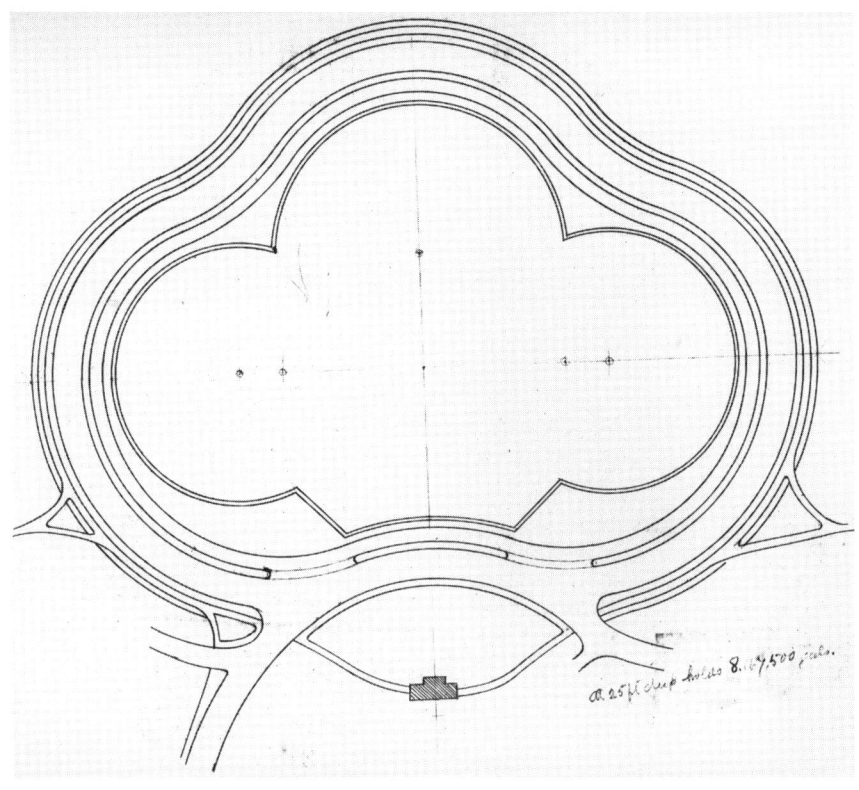

PLAN BY OLMSTED FOR RESERVOIR AND PROMENADE IN GLADES SECTION
OF MOUNT ROYAL, C. JULY 1876

approved, your Board can, if thought best, order construction to proceed this summer.

   Respectfully,

               Fred Law Olmsted.

The text presented here is from a manuscript in Olmsted's hand in the Archives Municipales de Montréal, Montreal, Quebec, Canada. The words in brackets are supplied by the editors where a preceding, folded and stapled page covers some of the text.

1. The Estate of H. B. Smith, of which the farmhouse is still standing in the park, made up much of the western part of the park. Olmsted expected that much of the flat meadow land at the western end of the property would be acquired for parkland, as well as a section of the meadow that lay in the property of J. Tompkins that abutted the Smith property on the north. With this expectation, he drew up plans for the extensive meadow feature that he refers to in this letter, encircling it with a carriage drive. He intended the meadow to be the sole passage of pastoral scenery in the park. In his report of 1881 he

wrote that "It can easily be made the finest spread of turf on the continent. But it will be best kept, when once well formed, with sheep and not with lawn-like smoothness." The park commission did not acquire the Tompkins property and, as this letter indicates, Olmsted then acceded to instructions of the commission to plan for a reservoir in the meadow. The commission at first stipulated an area of twenty acres for the reservoir, but when Olmsted objected, agreed instead to five acres. In his plan, Olmsted made the reservoir a central feature of the park by designing promenades around it for carriages, equestrians and pedestrians. Olmsted included this formal feature in his plan of 1877 but it was never constructed. The present-day lac au Castors, designed by the landscape architect Frederick Todd in 1936–37, is on the approximate site of Olmsted's proposed reservoir (Plan 609–36, NPS/FLONHS; plan 609–30, "Contour Plan of Mount Royal Park," NPS/FLONHS; plan 609–Z26, NPS/FLONHS; *Papers of FLO*, SS1, p. 386; FLO to H. A. Nelson, April 11, 1876; Louis LeSage to H. A. Nelson, April 15, 1876).
2. That is, the Montreal waterworks commission.
3. W. J. Picton, the city engineer.
4. Louis Lesage (1827–1889), the engineer in charge of the Montreal waterworks (American Society of Civil Engineers, A *Biographical Dictionary of American Civil Engineers* [New York, 1972], p. 150).
5. The "Crown of the Mountain" was the highest point on Mount Royal, where Olmsted proposed to site a refectory and belvedere (FLO to H. A. Nelson, April 11, 1876; Louis LeSage to H. A. Nelson, April 15, 1876; *Papers of FLO*, SS1: 418, n. 63).
6. Olmsted planned to make Bleury Street (now Avenue du parc), the principal access route to the park from the city.

To William Runyon Martin[1]

Department of Public Parks;
Office of Design and Superintendence.
New York. 9th August, 1876.

To the Hon. Wm. R. Martin,
President of the Board:
Sir,

You inform me that some of the present Park Commissioners, not having been members of the Board when the plans for the improvement of Tompkins Square were first discussed,[2] feel imperfectly informed as to the reasons for the works which have been started there; and you ask that, when I report, under the instructions of the Board of the 31st of May as to the northwest arbor, I will reply also to the question: What is the need of such expensive operations as have been undertaken, and why would not something more of the ordinary kind be better adapted to the locality, more readily appreciated, and more nearly conform to public demands and expectations?[3]

There is an idea abroad, to which, I presume, the last branch of this inquiry is to be referred, which seems not to be based on any examination of your drawings or other authentic information, but chiefly on surmises as to the possible purposes of what is called a "hole in the ground," found in the Square. Such an excavation being unusual as a preliminary to a gardening work, it is conjectured that something is to be attempted of an extraordinary, sumptuous and extravagant character, which will be much out of place in this locality. I refer to it only that I may at once say, that in looking at the plans, now on the table of the Board, it will, to avoid prejudice, be well to bear in mind that the ordinary attractions of a Park[4] are so far prohibited by the necessity of occupying the larger part of the Square with the Parade Ground and its accompaniments, that the Department cannot acquit itself of its duty to the people of the locality without getting out of the ordinary rut. There is one small and not very expensive group of details of the design, which cannot be quite clearly described or shown in the drawings, and with regard to which, if they appear fanciful or over-refined, something must be trusted to the common sense, taste and practical knowledge of his business, of the designer.

I shall, however, describe this, as well as all other features of the plans, as fully as I can in the present report, and that their leading motives, at least, may be clearly understood, shall explain the circumstances under which they originated.

Partly with this object and partly to show how far the Department would be from meeting its responsibility as the trustee of the permanent interests of the city, if it allowed itself to look no further than to the active public demand of the day, in matters of this class, I shall give a slight introductory narrative of the experiences which the city has already had in dealing with this piece of its landed property.

The site of Tompkins Square before any improvements were made upon it was low rolling ground, into which extended shallow water from the East River. It was for this reason, first laid out as a public market place, with the intention of making a canal through the lowest ground, of sufficient breadth and depth to furnish material for bringing all other low ground to a satisfactory elevation, and to allow produce to be floated directly to the heart of what was then expected to be the great centre of trade of the city.[5]

In the progress of years this idea was lost sight of, and at length a speculation in the land about the Square occurred, with the belief that it might be brought into successful competition with that about Washington Square[6] as the fashionable residence quarter of the city. Some houses built in furtherance of this scheme are still to be seen in the vicinity.

With the same object in view the low ground was, about 1836, filled in, all the natural inequalities obliterated, and what was then the "regular thing" for a park in all respects done with it. It was enclosed, that is to say, with a high fence, against which, on the inner side, a border of shrubbery was planted; straight walks were made through it, and rows of trees planted.

Rules to preserve the turf and trees from misuse were of course posted about, as a part of the due furniture of such a ground, but the idea then prevailed that the people who were the true owners of the property could not justly be interfered with in making such a use of it as they thought proper; and if some superserviceable public servant ever construed literally the orders formally and gravely given him, and which he was sworn to enforce, by making an arrest on account of a disregard of those rules, public opinion called him a Jack-in-office, and even magistrates were more ready to reprove his officiousness than to punish the offender.

It naturally followed that the life was soon stamped out of the perennial grasses of the turf, and that annual grasses and weeds took their place; bare streaks and patches followed, and at last the whole surface took on the dreary character of a neglected waste.

The trees and shrubs also were slowly mutilated, starved and murdered by accident, by wanton injuries, and through the desire to find employment upon them for men incompetent to fight the battle of life without the aid from the city treasury which they thus obtained grounds for claiming.

When its condition became intolerable, and it could no longer be regarded from the point of view of a pleasure ground, a third appropriation was made of the property. This time it was seen to be just the place for a parade ground.[7] (Washington Square had in the meantime been a parade ground, and while so, had moved ahead and become a centre of fashion.)

The trees in Washington Square had been found in the way of its use as a parade ground; when, accordingly, Tompkins Square was to be improved for the purpose, so much of its original plantation as remained alive, the trees being then about thirty years old, was mainly cut away, a few trees only being left along the outside. The Parade Ground proper was to be a clean, smooth, green field.

After three years, it was found that turf could not stand the necessary wear, and it was concluded that the best exercise ground for soldiers would be a simple flat table with a hard uniform surface, black as night, and free from all suggestions of ease and lassitude. The high fence was accordingly removed and the remains of the effeminate turf overlaid with pitch and sand. When the latter operation had been extended over about half the surface of the Square, however, the conviction obtained that it manifested too much of a brutal martinet spirit for citizen soldiers. A border ground of trees and shrubs was therefore planted, an orchestral pavilion and two dainty sentry boxes were built, the half of the interior not yet plastered with pitch was graveled and a sort of rim introduced to the parade, formed of a composition of which coal tar was the principal ingredient. Finally the whole was again enclosed with a very handsome new Gothic stone and iron fence.*[8]

---

*It is perhaps worth remembering that while this improvement was making on Tompkins Square, Washington Square was being improved by the opposite process, namely, the removal of its fence.

Except in the matter of the fence and the little wooden buildings, the work done on Tompkins square was all of that plain, easily understood character, which, by virtue of its simplicity, is commonly assumed to be economical. Before long, however, the black composition upon the parade proved not only to be a plain, straightforward piece of work, but cheap, fraudulent and nasty, creating a nuisance more intolerable than the dust and mud it had been expected to abate. The border planting was too thin, too hastily done, in insufficient and unsuitable soil, and no adequate precautions were taken to protect it. The costly fence was for this purpose worthless, because it covered but one side of the border; the other was left to the guardianship of the keepers, for whose comfortable rest the pretty little sentry boxes had been provided. The border was half a mile in length, and when a few hundred boys gathered in the Square, as they did not unfrequently in the evening, the keepers were powerless to prevent them from trooping over it.

Feeling before long as if in some way advantage had been taken of their ignorance, the residents about Tompkins square now adopted the idea, as those in Washington square had previously, that the Parade Ground itself was an unjust imposition upon them, and began to demand that it should be moved, and the Square laid out solely with a view to use as a pleasure ground again.*

Between 1872 and 1875, the Department of Public Parks was frequently urged, in the newspapers, by formal addresses, and by much verbal representation of the demands of the people, to set about a sweeping and comprehensive improvement of the Square. It was alleged that the quarter of the city in which it was situated was further removed from parks than any other; that the property holders were taxed for parks by which their property had not at all been benefited, and that the people of this vicinity, on account of the close manner in which it had been built up and the number of its crowded tenements, stood in greater need of a park than any other, and this claim was sustained by reference to the statistics of mortality, especially of nursing infants during the summer.[10]

One of the addresses to the Board, to which I above refer, was in the form of a petition from the mothers of the vicinity, pleading for their little children.[11]

It was admitted that the Parade Ground served the boys tolerably as a

---

*Being asked to suggest a locality for the Parade Ground, one of the gentlemen interested indicated the Green of the Central Park, a tract of land, as he said, now entirely useless, there being no buildings, no walks and no shade upon it. To the objection that a mere green place in the city was rather pleasing to many people, and that the crowd attending a parade would not only destroy the turf but even the trees about it, he rejoined that this could be prevented by proper rules, and an efficient police to enforce them. These views would probably be popular for a year or two, and they have in effect been sustained by many.[9] If adopted, they would nevertheless in a few years lead to the waste of property for which the city has paid some millions of dollars.

View of Tompkins Square, New York City (1870)

place for athletic sports, but it was asserted that with reference to women, children of tender years, invalids, convalescents, and all those to whom a park should be most attractive, it was simply repulsive and dangerous.

In 1873 the Park Commissioners ordered the replanting of the strip of shrubbery near the fence, which was done with much more care to secure proper conditions of growth than before, but the result was not regarded with satisfaction by the people, and with reference to the usefulness of the Square as a place of recreation, it had in fact no particular value.

The following year the demand for more radical measures accordingly became stronger. The Mayor, the Common Council and the Legislature were appealed to on the subject. In the Legislature a bill was introduced providing for the abolition of the Parade Ground, and the formation of a park upon its site. It was defeated or withdrawn late in the session upon representations that the Department of Public Parks had the question of the improvement of the Square under consideration.[12] As the Department, however, afterwards took no action, a bill with the same object was introduced early in the session of the succeeding year, and the Department was advised that its passage was imminent. The Department adopted the position that a ground in the lower part of the city which could be used for military exercises and various other purposes for which Tompkins Square was suitable, was a necessity; that no other place could be found for it; that it would be imprudent to abandon it; and, admitting that there was reason for the demands which had led the Legislature to consider the question, the Department argued that it would be possible to provide some valuable means of recreation upon the ground without appropriating all of it to the purpose. A copy of a letter to the Mayor is appended in which this position is more fully set forth. The Mayor promptly acted on its suggestions; and upon the strength of his statements, and those of the Commissioners, that such changes were to be made in the Square as would meet the essential needs of the people living near it, the bill was no further pressed.[13]

In accordance with the understanding thus reached, the Legislature was then asked to provide the Department with the sum of $60,000 for work to be done on the Square during the year 1875, and it did so.[14]

Thus was determined the sixth project for making this piece of property useful to the city, each having a purpose in view of a distinct character.

I recapitulate them as follows:

I.—A grand central market-place;
II.—An enclosed green grove for a promenade and airing ground;
III.—A meadow for parades;
IV.—An unenclosed, paved place-of-arms;
V.—An enclosed pleasure-ground parade;
VI.—A place-of-arms, with detached arrangements for the refreshing rest of women, little children, convalescents and others specially needing

relief from the generally surrounding conditions of foul air, heated pavements, &c.

The Department now had to meet the following problem:

To find room in Tompkins Square, without materially impairing its value for the exercise of arms, for such provisions as would supply a grateful and healthful relief to the class more particularly proposed to be benefited.

The first proposition, devised to this end, was declared by Major-General Shaler[15] to be entirely inadmissable. He stated that, to answer any valuable purpose of the National Guards, a square of ground was required of which each side should be as long as the existing Parade Ground. A second proposition was afterwards contrived of quite a different character, to which at length the General's somewhat reluctant consent was obtained. This proposed a field of square form which, within the area strictly under the Department's control, was of less than the requisite dimensions. It was shown, however, that by taking down the useless fence at its angles, a military line might upon occasion be extended to the length which had been stipulated, and that by making a special provision for spectators elsewhere, the area for military occupation would be practically scarcely less than it had been before. The new square for parades was so placed that outside of it there remained four small triangular spaces. One of these, as a necessity resulting from the requirements of the military, was appropriated to the use of spectators of parades, refreshments, storage and latrines, a second to the orchestral pavilion already built and other requirements of promenade concerts.[16]

There remained, then, but two small places, each somewhat less in area than the oval of the Bowling Green,[17] within which any special provisions for the recreation, in the Square, of women and children of tender years were to be confined.

There are two conditions under which the discomforts and dangers to invalids and weakly people of a visit to a garden are liable to outweigh the pleasure and benefits received. One of these is that of chill, windy weather in the spring and autumn, the other that of midsummer heat, when it is difficult to escape from the sun. The parade ground being essentially treeless and bleak, and its main object of military exercises requiring that it should remain so, it was thought best to provide separately, within the two triangles, for these very different conditions. In that at the southeast corner accordingly, the surface of the ground was designed to have a dell-like form, the lower parts to be several feet below the adjoining plain of the parade, a broad walk was to be carried through it with a loop, and ordinary park seats were to be placed facing the centre, where the adjoining streets and parade ground would be out of sight. The central part was to be a small lawn, with a few groups of shrubs and spring flowers; the outer parts to be planted more densely, so as to form a screen from the wind and secure an aspect of semi-seclusion. No part of the enclosure was intended to be hooded over by trees to the complete exclusion of sunshine.

No construction was designed to be introduced except the seats; and the plan was as simple and as inexpensive to execute as any that could be proposed with an intelligent purpose to accomplish what had been undertaken.

The little triangle in the northwest corner was left to be planned and in it all that was yet unfulfilled of the duty of the Commissioners to the people of the locality, was to be provided for.

Should it be treated in a similar simple way with the southeast corner just described, Tompkins Square would offer not a single additional object of that class, which to many constitutes the only entirely tangible and sure source of attraction in parks, such as fountains, monuments, statues, pavilions, rockworks, cascades &c.

During the extreme heat of summer, when the bare ground of the parade would be not only forbidding in aspect, but glowing with fervent heat, and when it would be most important that mothers especially should be drawn away from the turmoil, bustle and glare of the streets, as well as from the foulness of crowded houses, there would, in the middle of the day, be no place to which they could resort; there would be nothing to be seen to gratify even the simplest tastes without discomfort, and even danger, and the Square would be hardly of more use than it had been before the Department was charged with its improvement.

In devising how the deficiencies thus indicated could best be economically met within the narrow limits of the northwest triangle, the difficulty and cost of maintaining any arrangements in tolerable order in this locality was a matter of at least equal interest with that of the immediate expense to be incurred for construction.*

It was required, then, in the northwest triangle, to provide shaded seats and something pleasant to the eye to be enjoyed from them, and to accomplish this by means as much as possible beyond the reach of wanton or accidental ill-usage.

The arbor, which is to be the principal provision for this purpose, is approached from each side by a walk sixteen feet wide, which descends towards it between rocky and steeply inclined banks. By this means not only is the bare, heated parade ground to be the sooner and more completely lost

---

*An illustration of one class of obstacles to improvements really adapted to permanently accomplish the objects in view, is to be found in the fact that of the trees formerly planted in the Square nearly all had had their limbs broken down and their trunks hacked and sometimes completely girdled by knives or bayonets inserted between the bars of the iron cages vainly placed for their protection; another in the fact that a border of herbacious plants having been placed close adjoining a walk in the nearest of the small City Parks,[18] all of them to the number of over a thousand were very soon pulled up by their roots; another in the fact that in the same ground the turf edgings have been trodden into dust and mud, the seats hacked and whittled, birds' nests stoned and broken up, and that it is impossible to preserve tolerable neatness because of the ease with which trespasses and depredations may be committed unobserved.

sight of, and a shady glen-like seclusion, under partially overhanging shrubbery, made possible, but a barrier against straggling where straggling might otherwise do serious injury is to be gained.

These walks are to lead from each side, by two transepts, to an aisle, floored with concrete, one hundred feet long by twenty wide, with over two hundred lineal feet of fixed seat room at its sides. The space is to be walled in on three sides to a height of six feet, and is to be covered by a trellis, which is to be overgrown by the foliage of vines trained upon it from the beds on the outside of the wall, and inaccessible to the public. The object of shade by foliage for so large a space can thus be obtained with certainty in two years, while, by planting nursery trees, it could not in ten.

The whole structure, with the exception of the hard wood slats of the seats, is to be iron and concrete, and the vines with which it is to be veiled are to be nowhere within arms' length of a man on the floor.

The danger of both malicious and careless injury of the essential conditions of beauty and comfort within the arbor, if not thus entirely removed, are at least studiously reduced to a minimum.

Every advantage is also secured for cheaply keeping the place clean, and there is nothing to be put out of order.

Except in the foliage overhead there is, however, no beauty, and, as before suggested, something seems desirable to be added which will be gratifying not only to good taste but to the popular liking for objects of spectacular or scenic interest. For this purpose there is to be placed at the end of the arbor furthest from its entrance, a grotto, separated from its floor by a pool of water, guarded by a railing. The grotto is to be formed with walls and three successive recesses, the visible openings of which diminish in size as they recede from the spectator in the arbor. The walls are to be laid with natural rock, covered with mosses and fernlets, and the whole is to be kept damp and rendered slightly misty and mysterious by small fountains of fine spray in the recesses. The banks of the pool in front are to be faced with rocks, and to be overgrown with ferns, ivy and small water-edge plants. The trellis of the arbor is to be extended over the pool and the light from above obscured, in such degree as may be found desirable, by vine foliage.

All these arrangements are to be inaccessible to the public and are studied with a view to cheapness of maintenance as well as protection against pilfering and wanton abuse.

Both the grotto and the arbor are planned, by a graduated reduction in size of all the parts and otherwise, with a view to produce a slight ocular deception, increasing the apparent distance and depth of the misty recess in which the vista is to terminate.

The water of the pool is to be lighted through a hidden opening below the surface, and is to be clear and stocked with gold fish.

The slight fall of water from the grotto to the pool, the dropping of water and spray within the grotto, and the escape of the overflow, are expected to furnish the musical effect of a small tinkling and murmuring mountain rivulet.[19]

The amount of water needed will, nevertheless, be less than is required for the fountains in other small city parks.

Attractive places for free birds, with water, feeding-ground, and nesting-boxes, inaccessible to the public, are provided adjoining the arbor.

The effect of the grotto will depend on the skill and care with which the details of the work are handled; but the materials proposed to be used being all simple, and their arrangment and association natural, somewhat gross mismanagement will be required to produce either a ridiculous or a wholly commonplace result.

The ground below the floor of the arbor is to be thoroughly drained, and its surface concreted; the trellis is to be carried on double and asphalted walls, and harmful dampness is not to be apprehended.

The whole triangle within which the grotto is to be situated is enclosed by a strong high fence, and is designed to be closed at night when shade is unnecessary and the beauty of the plants cannot be enjoyed.

The Board sometime since directed the excavation and foundation work for the arbor to be done,[20] and some progress has been made upon it; the drainage and fencing is almost complete. It is estimated by the Superintending Architect[21] that the completion of the arbor and grotto above the foundation-work, will cost about $10,000. The facing of the grotto and the planting could not be sufficiently described in specifications to be let to the lowest bidder, but should be done by men of special aptitude for such work, under the immediate direction of the designer.

None of what may be regarded as the more fanciful details of the arrangement described are of an expensive character, and probably nine-tenth of the expenditures required will be for ordinary materials, in ordinary mercantile forms, to be contracted for in the open market under active competition.

With regard to the expenditures which have been made upon the Square as a whole, and those which will be required, I beg to say that it was never represented to the Board, nor, so far as my knowledge, recollection or belief goes, was it ever represented to the Mayor who favored the appropriation, nor to the Legislature which authorized it, that a sufficient scheme of improvements could be carried out for $60,000.

I recommended that the sum of $50,000 should be used for the first year's operations, and stated that, with this expenditure, all parts of the work might be expected to be so far advanced as to give the public use of them, except the tribune for spectators, which could wait a further appropriation.

Of the sum of $60,000 which was to have been expended last year, $25,000 remains. This is probably short of what will be needed to accomplish the results expected from ten to fifteen per cent. The reason the work so far done has cost more than was anticipated is not to be given in a word. At least five causes or classes of causes have plainly contributed to it:

1. Parts of the work have been done by the day, which it was presumed would be contracted, at rates based on lower wages for labor.

2. Foremen and men have been employed who were newly recruited and organized, and these have been more or less demoralized by doubts whether they were legally employed; whether they would be paid, and whether their employment would continue.[22]

3. The work has lacked a continuous, responsible engineering supervision, the organization for the purpose having been broken up in order to reduce salary expenses.[23]

4. The force of laborers employed has been very variable, and has been more than once suspended at an unfavorable moment.[24]

5. The work has been unexpectedly impeded and its management embarrassed by quicksands and floods, the effect of which has been aggravated by the suspensions and irregularities above noted.

FRED. LAW OLMSTED,
Landscape Architect,
D.P.P.

The text presented here is from "Document No. 71," in New York (City), Department of Public Parks, *Minutes*, August 16, 1876. It was presented to the park board and its proposal approved on that date (DPP, *Minutes*, Aug. 16, 1876, pp. 248–49).

1. William Runyon Martin (1825–1897), lawyer and real-estate speculator. Appointed to the park board by Democratic mayor William H. Wickham in January 1875, Martin took over its presidency from Henry G. Stebbins in May 1876 when another appointment gave Democrats a majority on the board. Long an advocate of uptown improvements in streets, municipal services, and parks, Martin, in 1865, was the first to call for the creation of Riverside Park, about which he consulted with Olmsted two years later (William R. Martin Historical Collection, New York University Archives, New York City; *New-York Times*, May 9, 1876, p. 6; *Papers of FLO*, 6: 599; DPP, *Minutes*, May 5, 1876, pp. 3–5).
2. Tompkins Square, laid out and named in 1833, is located between Avenues A and B and East 7th and 10th streets. In June 1875 the park board instructed Olmsted to prepare plans to allow its use both as a military parade ground and as a recreation ground for residents of the neighborhoods surrounding it. His plan addressing these needs, which he reviews in the present text, was first adopted in late September 1875. The only member of the park board not then in office was William C. Wetmore, whose term began in May 1876 (Isaac Newton Phelps Stokes, *The Iconography of Manhattan*

Island, 1498–1909, 6 vols. [New York, 1915–28], 5: 1719; DPP, *Minutes*, June 29, 1875, p. 121; ibid., Sept. 29, 1875, p. 296).
3. In October 1875 preparatory excavations were started for a sunken arbor in the northwest corner of the square. After receiving complaints about its sanitary condition the following spring, the board ordered Olmsted to submit a report on the arbor's proposed treatment and its expense (*The City Record*, Nov. 11, 1875, p. 1854; DPP, *Minutes*, March 3, 1876, pp. 655–56; ibid., April 19, 1876, pp. 748–49; ibid., May 31, 1876, pp. 75–76).
4. In 1875 Olmsted touched on the main attractions of a park which he defined as "a space of ground used for public or private recreation, differing from a garden in its spaciousness and the broad, simple, and natural character of its scenery, and from a 'wood' in the more scattered arrangement of its trees and greater expanse of its glades and consequently of its landscapes." Such broad landscape features and effects were not possible in the ten acres of Tompkins Square (Frederick Law Olmsted, "Park," [1875] [*Papers of FLO*, SS1: 308]).
5. The Public Market or Grand Market Place was laid out on the Commissioners Plan of 1811 and extended across the site of Tompkins Square from the East River to First Avenue. The state legislature abolished the market in 1829 ("Tompkins Square," in *Twenty-Third Annual Report of the American Scenic and Historic Preservation Society* [Albany, N.Y., 1918], p. 173).
6. Washington Square is located at the south end of Fifth Avenue, between Waverly Place, West 4th Street, MacDougal Street, and University Place. Used as a potter's field since the late eighteenth century, it was laid out and dedicated as a parade ground in the mid-1820s. In following decades it became the center of a fashionable neighborhood ("Washington Square," in ibid., pp. 166–72).
7. In April 1866 the state legislature dedicated Tompkins Square as a parade ground for the First Division, New York State National Guard (*Papers of FLO*, 6: 632, n. 3).
8. The work Olmsted describes here took place between 1868 and 1871. In 1868 the legislature appropriated $60,000 to pave the square under the direction of then street commissioner William M. "Boss" Tweed. His department of public parks, created in May 1870, carried out the remainder of the "improvements" ("Tompkins Square," in *Twenty-Third Annual Report of the American Scenic and Historic Preservation Society*, p. 174; DPP, *First Annual Report* [1871], pp. 45–46, 241–43).
9. In early 1873 the park board reaffirmed its policy that no part of Central Park was suitable for use as a military parade ground and took steps to acquire a site Olmsted had designated near Fort George at the north end of Manhattan. When the proceedings to acquire it stalled in 1874, a member of the state legislature introduced a bill to compel the board to set aside a temporary parade ground in Central Park, but it did not pass ("Document No. 40," in DPP, *Minutes*, Oct. 16, 1872, pp. 2–4; Salem H. Wales to William F. Havemeyer, Dec. 30, 1873, Mayor's Papers, box 1237, New York City Municipal Archives; *New-York Times*, April 23, 1874, p. 4).
10. The tenements surrounding Tompkins Square, along with those near the Battery and Five Points, were the most crowded and unhealthful in the city (*New-York Times*, April 23, 1874, p. 4; *Sunday Mercury*, July 26, 1874, p. 6; *New-York Daily Tribune*, June 1, 1875, p. 2).
11. In August 1873 the park board received petitions from "Mothers of the 11th and 17th wards," the wards surrounding the square (DPP, *Minutes*, Aug. 6, 1873, p. 169).
12. On January 26, 1874, "An act to provide for the improvement of Tompkins square, in the city of New York," was introduced in the state assembly, passed in April, and was sent to the state senate. The two bodies disagreed whether the work should wait until a new parade ground was established, and by the time a joint committee worked out a compromise version in late April, the legislature adjourned without taking action

(New York [State], *Journal of the Assembly of the State of New York: At Their Ninety-Seventh Session* [Albany, N.Y., 1874], 1: 132, 872; ibid., 2: 1647, 1771; ibid, 1: 702, 792, 837, 904, 1108–9).
13. The second bill to improve Tompkins Square was introduced in January 1875 and quickly gained the approval of the assembly. Olmsted summarized here a letter to the mayor he drafted in late January for Henry G. Stebbins to sign. The senate rejected the bill in early February (New York [State], *Journal of the Assembly of the State of New York: At Their Ninety-Eighth Session* [Albany, N.Y., 1875], 1: 81, 131–32, 143–44; *New-York Times*, Jan. 29, 1875, p. 1; ibid., Feb. 4, 1875, p. 1; FLO to Mayor, Jan. 27, 1875; Henry G. Stebbins to William H. Wickham, Jan. 27, 1875, Mayor's Papers, box 1265, New York City Municipal Archives).
14. This amount was part of the general appropriation of $575,000 granted to the department in late May 1875, obtained through the lobbying efforts of commissioners Martin and O'Donohue (FLO, Patronage Journal, May 23, 1875, below; *New York World*, March 25, 1875, p. 8; New York [State], *Laws of the State of New York, Passed at the Ninety-Eighth Session of the Legislature* [Albany, N.Y., 1875], chap. 608; [William R. Martin], "Report on the Subject of Tompkins Square," in DPP, *Minutes*, June 9, 1876, pp. 92–93; William R. Martin to William H. Wickham, June 10, 1876, Mayor's Papers, box 1263, New York City Municipal Archives).
15. Alexander Shaler (1827–1911), joined the Seventh Regiment of the New York State National Guard in 1848 and, after serving in the Civil War, commanded the regiment from 1867 to 1886. In 1872 Shaler had consulted with Olmsted on the location of an alternative parade ground in northern Manhattan (*NCAB*, 4: 458; *New-York Times*, Dec. 28, 1911, p. 9; see n. 9 above).
16. Olmsted is referring to the orchestral pavilion designed in May 1870 by Jacob Wrey Mould and built that year by the Sweeny park board, which stood in the northeast corner of the square. This corner, in Olmsted's 1875 plan, was to be laid out "in broad formal walks" with the pavilion at its center. The southwest corner was to have a terraced mound designed "in the form of a raised tribune from which 5000 persons at once can command a complete view of the parade ground." This feature was reminiscent of the "grand terrace or tribune" for spectators and dignitaries that Olmsted had planned between a playing field and parade ground in his proposal of 1866 for a system of public pleasure grounds in San Francisco (DPP, *Minutes*, May 31, 1870, pp. 72, 74; DPP, *First Annual Report* [1871], p. 242; "Tompkins Square," in DPP, *Minutes*, June 9, 1876, p. 92; FLO to Henry G. Stebbins, Sept. 23, 1875; ibid., Oct. 2, 1876; *New-York Daily Tribune*, March 3, 1877, p. 5; *Papers of FLO*, 5: 532–34).
17. The Bowling Green, located at the foot of Broadway, dated to the early eighteenth century and was New York's first park. In the mid-1870s it covered just over one-half acre (Charles Lockwood, *Manhattan Moves Uptown: An Illustrated History* [Boston, 1976], pp. 33–34; DPP, *Statistical Report of the Landscape Architect, 31st December, 1873, Forming Part of Appendix L of the Third General Report of the Department* [New York, 1875], p. 40).
18. Stuyvesant Park, a square of just four acres, which flanked Second Avenue between 15th and 17th streets (ibid.).
19. The grotto that Olmsted describes here is strikingly similar to a feature in the summer house that Olmsted created on the U.S. Capitol grounds, with working drawings by Thomas Wisedell, beginning c. 1877 (see FLO to Edward Clark, c. June 1879–June 1880 and FLO to Frederick H. Cobb, May 30, 1881, below).
20. The board ordered this work in April 1876 (DPP, *Minutes*, April 19, 1876, pp. 748–49).
21. Julius F. Munckwitz.
22. In the months following the approval of Olmsted's plan for the square in September 1875 a conflict arose between park department president William R. Martin and city

comptroller Andrew H. Green. Green felt that under the provisions of the city charter the work must be done by contract rather than by the day. Martin, backed by a favorable opinion of the New York City corporation counsel, favored paying laborers by the day and pressed the board to hire more men to prosecute the work. Commissioners Stebbins and David B. Williamson agreed with Green and opposed Martin's actions. Some work was accomplished by December, until Green delayed and then withheld the laborers' payroll, effectively stopping the work in January 1876 (*City Record*, Nov. 11, 1875, p. 1854; "Tompkins Square," in DPP, *Minutes*, June 9, 1876, pp. 92–93; William R. Martin to William H. Wickham, July 26, 1876 [ibid., pp. 186–88]).

23. In March 1875, due to a shortage of funds, members of the department's engineering force were placed on half pay or suspended. This situation continued throughout the year and the Board of Estimate and Apportionment, headed by Green, did not help matters by reducing the department's 1876 budget below previous amounts. In January 1876 the board suspended the pay of superintending engineer John Bogart (DPP, *Minutes*, March 24, 1875, p. 600; ibid., Jan. 13, 1876, pp. 516–17; ibid., Jan. 18, 1876, pp. 543–52; ibid., Jan. 31, 1876, p. 566; FLO, Patronage Journal, March 25, 1875, and July 8, 1875, below).

24. After several stoppages in the autumn of 1875, work was entirely suspended on Tompkins Square in January 1876 ("Tompkins Square," in DPP, *Minutes*, June 9, 1876, pp. 92–93).

Mr. Olmsted on Landscape Gardening.

[August 12, 1876]

To the Editor of "The Garden."—[1]

I am gratified to have the good opinion which led you to think me the author of an article in the "Gardeners' Monthly," quoted in *The Garden* of July 1, and which you pleasantly make the occasion for showing how you and I, from our different points of view, may observe a subject of common interest.[2] You rightly assume that I have been placed by circumstances in a position to regard the relation between the professions of landscape gardening and architecture with more than usual interest. I must confess, however, that as far as this relation has a bearing on the question of professional education, I yet stand a little too much in a waiting and enquiring attitude to write upon it with satisfaction. Still if you care to know my view of the subject, you are entitled to have an authentic report of it, and so far as I can give you this, I will do so with pleasure. It has long been a practice to introduce temples, pagodas, pavilions, "ruins," bridges, arches, obelisks, and other monuments, in works of landscape gardening, not alone where they were required by considerations of health and convenience, but with a view to give interest, character, and finish to the scenes in which they appear. In the war on this practice which you are leading, I claim to be with you. With, perhaps, a single justifiable exception, no architectural object has ever yet been introduced in any work of landscape gardening with my consent which was not first devised with a view to some other purpose than of display or effect in the landscape.[3] But what are the grounds of objection to the practice? To find and substantiate them, I think it is necessary to see, more clearly than most intelligent men seem ready to do, in what the essence of landscape gardening consists. Loudon, after making an extended study of the manner in which the term is used by a series of authors, says (§ 7181, Ency. of Gard.) of a simple example: — "All the parts unite in forming a whole which the eye can comprehend at once and examine without distraction. Were this principle not prevalent, the groups of trees, the lake, and the building would only please when considered separately, and the result would be as poor a production as a machine, the wheels of which are accurately finished and nicely polished, but which do not act in concert so as to effect the intended movement."[4]

The objection, then, to monumental and architectural objects in works of landscape gardening is this, that, as a rule, they are not adapted to contribute to any concerted effect, but are likely to demand attention to themselves in particular, distracting the mind from the contemplation of the landscape as such, and disturbing its suggestions to the imagination. But the object of producing an effect on the imagination being to make the life of man more agreeable, war on architectural objects may be carried too far whenever the objects which it removes are likely to add more to the satisfaction of life than they deducted from it by their injury to the landscape. Where the number or extent of artificial objects thus called for is large as compared with the ground to be operated upon, landscape gardening, properly speaking, is out of place; gardening material should then be made to support, strengthen, and aggrandise architectural design. But there are intermediate cases where the landscape gardener, as such, will neither retire from the field nor refuse to yield anything of landscape effect to convenience. If, in laying out a ground which is to be used by a hundred thousand people of all classes, we seek to have no more numerous or more substantial artificial structures than we should if it were to be used only by a quiet, private family and its guests, we shall overreach ourselves. It is better that the ultimate special requirements of the situation should be foreseen from the outset, that provisions for them should be ample, that the necessary structures, however inconspicuously they may be placed, should be substantial, and their real character not only undisguised but artistically manifested, and that, finally, they should become as far as possible (preserving the above conditions) modest, harmonious, and consistent elements of a general landscape design, in which no more ambitious landscape motives are to be admitted than will allow them to be so assimilated. In such cases it is obvious that the architect would work with reference to the same general idea as the gardener, and should take pride and pleasure in subordinating his art to it. It follows that no architect is perfectly fit for the duty who cannot enter heartily into the spirit of a general design embodying landscape considerations; considerations, for example, of the modelling of ground-surface and of the disposition of foliage, as to density and colour and shade and sky-line. It is to be said that architects are often shamefully ignorant in this respect, and I have no doubt that they are sometimes somewhat conceited and presumptuous in their ignorance. But we do not, as a rule, find that men trained as shoemakers have a propensity to chequer their hats with leather, nor men trained as hatters to slash their boots with felt; and I do not believe that it is a necessary result of properly educating an architect that he should be irresistibly disposed to patch a lawn with bricks and mortar. Whenever such a mania manifests itself, we may be sure it signifies too crude, not too refined a professional training.

But our present business is rather with the question of the education of landscape gardeners than of architects. Let me ask then, if it be a just cause of reproach to an architect that he cannot comprehend, and therefore cannot avoid overdoing his proper part in a landscape design, whether it is not equally true that the landscape gardener, who cannot upon occasion work hand-in-hand with the architect cheerfully, loyally, and with fore-reaching sympathy, is unqualified for his duty? Practical occasion for this close alliance of the two professions is not uncommon; indeed, in the greater number of cases where either is called in, there is to be a building or group of buildings, the site, aspect, elevation and outline of which cannot be properly determined without an understanding as to how the adjoining grounds are to be managed; as to where an approach is to be laid, as to where trees are to close the view and lawns open it, as to where the surface is to be gentle and quiet, and as to where it is to be abrupt, broken, and picturesque. On the other hand, it is equally impossible to properly design the walks and drives, the slopes, lawns and foliage, without regard to the position, the height, the breadth, the openings, the sky-lines, and even the decorative details of the buildings. There is then, properly, no distinctive field of general design for each profession; there is only a distinctive field of operations under the general design, the landscape gardener being responsible in the outlying parts of that of which the special field of the architect is the centre. The house comes first, because shelter is the first necessity, and it is only with increasing wealth and refinement that the garden part grows out of it. In the familiar aphorism of Lord Bacon, the art of pleasure-gardening is thus regarded as a higher development of the art of architecture;[5] and, in fact, if we look to the origin of the word we shall find that an art worker in soils and living plants is as accurately an architect as one who is confined to brick and mortar. But you suggest that if the landscape gardener interests himself in architecture and other fine arts, it will be likely to overmuch distract his mind from another class of interests which, if not essentially, are yet closely connected with landscape gardening, such, for example, as those of tropical botany and exotic horticulture. The range of study which is called for in these is already so greatly extended that simply to call by name the various plants that are to be found under glass in England, a man must have gone through an amount of special mental discipline which would have been appalling to a gardener of fifty years ago. And yet this range is rapidly enlarging, and no one can guess where it will end. If, then, a young man, in addition to the study necessary to the practice of landscape gardening pure and simple, is to make himself master of tropical botany and exotic horticulture, and a perfect adept in all other branches of botany, I question if there will not come in time another danger to the art of more gravity than that which I am disposed to apprehend exists in its disalliance with architecture.

To recognise what I mean, please ask yourself what is the one sure product which any professional education in landscape gardening must be adapted to cultivate? It surely is that of a special sensibility to the characteristic charms of broad, simple, quiet landscape compositions, united with a power of analysing these charms, and of conceiving how they may be reproduced through other compositions adapted to different topographical circumstances and different requirements of convenience; and this united again with a power of organising and directing means through which, after many years, these conceptions may be realised. In order to acquire such a wide range of information and of skill as will before long evidently be required of a gardener professing to be equipped at all points, a man of ordinary abilities must begin young, and must for some years be thoroughly absorbed in his work. This cannot occur without a strong tendency to establish a propensity to regard trees and plants from mental points of view in which the special qualities of each are to be of interest only as they favourably affect broad harmonies of landscape. It appears to me that the likeness of the materials and processes of botanical and exotic gardening to those of landscape gardening, instead of being an advantage in this respect, really establishes an insidious danger greater than that which you apprehend from an interest in an art dealing with such different materials and processes as that of architecture. It is a matter of history that the revolution in which landscape gardening originated[6] was practically led more than by any other man by one (his monument should be in Westminster Abbey) who was educated as a coach painter, grew from that to be an historical painter, from that again wandered as a student of the fine arts in general into Italy, and finally on his return started in business as an architect before making his first imperfect essay in landscape gardening.[7] How we should now rank his more mature work, and that of his contemporaries, few of whom were gardeners bred from youth, is an interesting question, for the profitable study of which there may yet be opportunity in England. How we should rank it as an arboretum, how we should rank it with regard to brilliancy of colouring, how as a living museum of botany, how as an exhibition of the fashionable plants of the day, there can be no doubt; but I mean what should we think of it as a work of art? what would be its influence on the imagination? We know that in its day it compelled the unbounded admiration of the most cultivated people, not only of England but of all Europe, and we may presume that if it lacked the incident and varied interest of modern work, it was not without some impressive poetical qualities. We may be sure, I think, that the profession of landscape gardening has not since been gaining as steadily in power to affect the imagination as it has gained in working material and in science. It is possible that it has lost something; and if so, I should judge from descriptions, and from a few old engravings, that it was in the qualities of breadth, consistency of expression, subordination of all materials used to a general ideal simplicity, tranquility, and repose. I do not want to give undue importance to this suggestion, but it is obvious that defects with reference to these qualities are precisely what should be expected to result from an overlong absorption of mind in questions of classification and nomenclature, from an excess of interest in conservatory, winter garden, terrace garden, and bedding-out effects, and from the resulting necessity of a forced retreat from the border grounds of allied arts and professions.

My *alter ego*, if you please, of the "Gardeners' Monthly" apparently regards the title of landscape architect as one in which an assumption of superiority is affected toward those who beforetime have been called landscape gardeners. I do not see the assumption, but to remove the suspicion, however it arises, in at least one case, I will mention that the word architect, as applied to the manager of a public work, of which landscape gardening should be the chief element, was here in America adopted directly from the French, and was first fastened upon the occupant of such an office, who was not an architect in the English usage of the term, in disregard of his repeated remonstrances.[8] As it is not wholly without an etymological propriety, as it has a certain special value in addressing a public which, in my humble judgment, is too much rather than too little inclined to regard landscape considerations as one thing and architectural considerations as quite another, and as it has now been fairly accepted as an intelligible term on this side of the water, I will submit to whatever reproach must follow on the other in subscribing myself, in all goodwill,

FREDERICK LAW OLMSTED, Landscape Architect.
New York.

The text presented here is from *The Garden*, August 12, 1876, pages 149–50.

1. William Robinson was editor of *The Garden* (see FLO to William Robinson, c. March 20–30, 1875, above).
2. B. S. Olmstead, a landscape gardener from Rye, New York, published an article entitled "Who Shall Lay out our Ornamental Grounds?" in the June 1876 edition of the *The Gardener's Monthly and Horticulturist*. William Robinson mistakenly attributed the article to Frederick Law Olmsted and quoted a large part of it in the July 1, 1876, edition of *The Garden* (B. S. Olmstead, "Who Shall Lay out our Ornamental Grounds?" *The Gardener's Monthly and Horticulturist* 18 [June 1876], pp. 164–66; William Robinson, "Landscape Gardeners of the Future," *The Garden*, July 1, 1876, pp. 1–3).

3. Possibly Olmsted is alluding to the Martyrs' Monument in Fort Greene (Washington) Park designed by Olmsted and Calvert Vaux and completed in 1873 (*Papers of FLO*, 6: 207, n. 7; *Frederick Law Olmsted's New York*, text by Elizabeth Barlow and illustrative portfolio by William Alex [New York, 1972], pp. 146–47).
4. Olmsted is quoting from John Claudius Loudon's *An Encyclopædia of Gardening*, book iv, part iii, section 7181 (*DNB*; John C. Loudon, *An Encyclopædia of Gardening*..., 4th ed. [London, 1826], p. 1000).
5. Francis Bacon (1561–1626), lord chancellor of England and writer. Olmsted is paraphrasing a section of Bacon's essay "Of Gardens." Bacon writes

> God Almighty first planted a garden; and, indeed, it is the purest of human pleasures; it is the greatest refreshment to the spirits of man; without which buildings and palaces are but gross handyworks; and a man shall ever see, that, when ages grow to civility and elegancy, men come to build stately, sooner than to garden finely; as if gardening were the greater perfection.

(*DNB*; Francis Bacon, *Bacon's Essays and Wisdom of the Ancients* [Boston, 1884], pp. 249–50).
6. A reference to the changing style in landscape gardening beginning in the early eighteenth century from a more formal garden design to the "picturesque" with serpentine waterways, meandering paths, and more naturalistic plantings. William Kent is credited with starting this revolution (Edward Hyams, *Capability Brown and Humphry Repton* [London, 1971], pp. 4–5).
7. William Kent (1684–1748), English painter, architect, and landscape gardener was first apprenticed to a coach-painter when he was fourteen years old. At nineteen he traveled to London and attempted historical and portrait painting. Local patrons financed his way to Italy where he studied art under the master Cavalier Luti. While in Italy, he attracted the attention of the third Earl of Burlington, Richard Boyle (1695–1753), who became his lifelong friend and patron. Kent returned to England with Burlington and eventually turned his talents to architecture and later to landscape gardening. Horace Walpole credits Kent with being the "father of modern gardening, the inventor of an art that realizes painting and improves nature." Kent's "first imperfect essay in landscape gardening" may be a reference to his work for the Earl of Burlington at Chiswick House in London (*DNB*; Michael Wilson, *William Kent: Architect, Designer, Painter, Gardener, 1685–1748* [London, 1984], pp. 191–92).
8. In his article in *The Gardener's Monthly and Horticulturist*, B. S. Olmstead had observed that many gardeners and engineers seemed to be ashamed of the title landscape gardener. "They had themselves printed and called landscape architects, landscape engineers, rural architects, artists in grounds, etc., etc.; anything but landscape gardeners."
The distinction in the meaning of the term "architect" to which Olmsted is apparently referring here is between the British definition of architect as meaning a builder, with emphasis on craftsmanship, and the French inclusion of the element of art—"Celui qui exerce l'art de l'Architecture, l'art de bâtir."
The first application of the term to a public work of which landscape gardening was a chief element was the choice of "architect-in-chief" as Olmsted's title when he assumed responsibility for directing the construction of Central Park in 1858. Olmsted seems to be saying that this title was taken from the French title "architecte en chef." This title was given to managers of public works in Paris—as, for instance, "architecte en chef des Promenades de Paris." Olmsted objected to the title at the time, and was never fully satisfied with the term "landscape architect" (B.S. Olmstead, "Ornamental Grounds," p. 165; *OED*, s.v. "Architect;" *Le Dictionnaire de l'Academie Française* [5th edition, 1798], s.v. "Architecte;" FLO to Calvert Vaux, Nov. 26, 1863 [*Papers of FLO*, 5: 147]).

To William McMillan[1]

10th Sept [1876]

Mr W^m McMillan;
Superintendent, Buffalo Park.
Dear Sir;
 I have just received yours of the 7th inst. and am chagrined and disappointed beyond expression by its news.
 You will remember that in reply to repeated warnings and injunctions I have been constantly assured that you would see to it that sufficient funds were retained to employ this fall as large a force as could be desirable in the planting and finishing operations which have been so long postponed and the postponement of which has been to me such a grievance. There can possibly have been no work done within the year in which the necessary amount of money could be spent as desirably or anywhere near as desirably. The amount required is not large and I hope you will strongly protest for yourself and for me against its being used on Fillmore Avenue or anywhere else or in any other way which to prevent the work in question from being done. And if the money cannot be otherwise obtained I hope that you will find something that can be sold to raise it. All the buildings and furniture that we have been spending money for are simply a disgrace to us if money is wanting to provide what they are intended to serve in the park itself.
 If there is no other way I shall try to have a statemnt made to the public and a popular subscription asked to repair the blunder.
 As to the clearing out of the trees on the "line of sight" and the adjustmnt of the trees and shrubs along the North shore of the lake, employ all necessary men the moment the season admits of its being done and have it done without fail promptly and well.[2] What cannot be otherwise paid for I will pay. I would not for twice all it can cost let it be neglected another year. If there is any obstacle to your doing this let me know at once.
 As to the cold frame, all you positively require at once that you have not ready at hand is a sash or two of glass. Can't you borrow this? If not why not board up one of the windows of the boathouse[3] and take it from that? You might restore it in May. I suppose that oiled cotton supported on lath might tolerably answer your purpose.
 Of course we have now to go through a period of extravagant cutting {and} paring. Its your business and mine to guard by every ingenious contrivance we can bring into play against penny-wise pound-foolish waste of the property under our care until sound economy can again be steadily sustained. You are in a first rate position to run under short sail for a time and let the public overtake you except for your planting. Strain every nerve to accomplish what you have so often promised to do in this before next winter. You can manage to do nearly all without purchasing. Willow and poplar trees cost you

nothing. The great point is to get every man and boy at work that you possibly can; to anticipate the usual planting season and let nothing draw you off from the first moment you dare begin, until the ground freezes. André[4] told me that in Paris they had done a great deal of successful planting with the leaves on the trees. It is only necessary that the transference should be rapid; that the roots should not at all dry.

Can you not reduce wages? Can you not employ two boys in place of one man? Can you not let your watchman's duty be neglected and apply the wages saved to trees? Can you not screw some work out of your licensees? Can you not abandon all maintenance work? It will be only a temporary inconvenience if the roads & walks suffer ever so much. Don't spend a cent on watering except it is to save the life of trees which ten years hence will be more valuable than those which the saving would enable you to plant. Leaves evaporate so little from this time out that I should take the risk in almost every case, no matter how great the drought. If you can put the whole of your 12 men from this time out strictly at the work & let everything else go, and if the season is prolonged you can get everything done that was proposed except the screen, the gathering of seeds &c. and some part of the shrubbery and vines for which last you can at least start cuttings. Can you not exchange trees for shrubs? Is there no nursery man who will contribute what you specially need on a statement of your necessities? Please write me often and fully and I will help you in any way possible.

The text presented here is from a draft in Olmsted's hand. Apparently, McMillan's October 7, 1876, letter has not survived.

1. William McMillan (1830–1899), landscape architect and superintendent of the Buffalo parks from 1871 until 1898. Despite the impatience demonstrated in this letter and the September 11 letter presented below, Olmsted valued McMillan's work on the Buffalo parks, and in 1893 he noted that McMillan had performed his duties more efficiently and intelligently than any other superintendent he had encountered (*Papers of FLO*, SS1: 596, n. 24).
2. A reference to the lake, or Gala Water, in Delaware Park.
3. The boathouse, a wooden structure designed by Calvert Vaux, was constructed in 1874. It was located on the southern shore of the Gala Water (Francis R. Kowsky, "Municipal Parks and City Planning: Frederick Law Olmsted's Buffalo park and Parkway System," *Journal of the Society of Architectural Historians* 46 [March 1987]: 54–55).
4. Édouard André (see letter of Olmsted to André, Nov. 3, 1876, below).

April 1876–December 1876

To Dennis Bowen[1]

[September 10, 1876]

Before every spring and fall planting season I have gone over the ground anew, urged McMillan[2] to have everything in readiness early and begged the Commission to take care that no work should be required which would not leave him individually free to give himself for two months exclusively to the personal direction of the men to be employed in making good the result of the original haste and lack of detailed oversight. At my request, a deputy superintendent[3] was employed expressly to secure this end—and you personally and other Commissioners have repeatedly assured me that you would see to it that he should not be allowed to occupy himself with anything else while this repairing remained to be done. Nevertheless I have at the close of every planting season, fall & spring, had a letter from Mr McMillan telling me that some unexpected circumstances, orders and requiremts of the Commission had again obliged to postpone this most important work, and every time I have come to Buffalo it has made me sick to see the offensive objects growing constantly more offensive.

Last autumn enough was done to show how easily the Park might be vastly improved by good managemnt in this respect but the greater part of the work promised was still left undone. In the Spring scarcely anything was accomplished toward the desired result. This summer I have again had Mr McMillan's repeated promise and assurance that all the work of the Summer should be arranged expressly with a view to devoting as large a force as could be managed in the fall to paying off the old scores. Yet such was my anxiety because of previous disappointments that it was the principle object on my mind in my last visit to Buffalo to go over the ground again and impress upon him a sense of the importance of what was to be accomplished and satisfy myself that nothing would again be allowed to interfere with it.

I returned as well assured as I could be, yet again was so anxious that last week I wrote him recapitulating the points in which I most dreaded neglect and urging him to take care that no possible means were lacking for starting the work at the earliest moment and putting its accomplishment beyond peradventure.

I receive now in return a letter telling me that all the funds now in the hands of the Commission must be expended on Fillmore Avenue.[4] If this is the case I cannot but think it a perfectly scandalous piece of bad management nor can I help feeling a personal disgrace in it. It is not possible that having been so long in your employment I can be held free from responsibility for the persistent and systematic misuse of the large amount of preparatory work which is distorted and hidden by the hasty and imperfect premature attempt at a show of finish.

Of course I do not want to fight with the inevitable or cry over milk

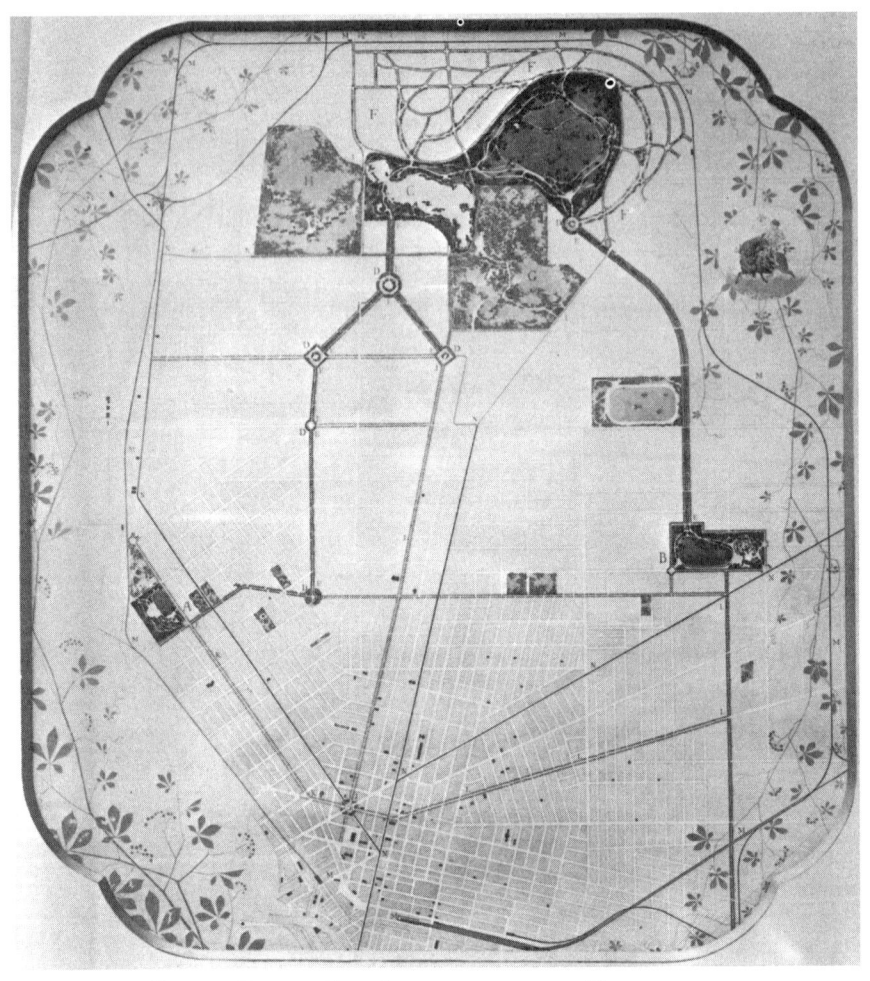

PLAN OF BUFFALO PARK SYSTEM DRAWN UP BY OLMSTED FOR
CENTENNIAL EXHIBITION IN PHILADELPHIA (1876)

that is entirely and hopelessly spilt but I must write to beg of you that, as a matter of justice to me as well as to the enterprise which owes so much to your wise prudence that everything now possible shall be put at McMillan's disposal for this long neglected duty and that he shall be positively forbidden to concern himself with anything else while the weather permits him to be engaged with it.

    I write to you individually because I long ago pointed out the facts on the ground to you & you know all I say to be true, and also because you know better than I what can be & what needs to be said to the Commission on the subject.

    Is there not something that can be sold by which a fund can be realized, and if not could not those whose interests compel the Commission to proceed with Fillmore Avenue this Fall be induced by a frank statement of the facts to allow this vastly larger interest of the City to be dealt with more justly.

  I don't think it necessary to enter into an argument to satisfy you that it is the more important interest of the City for which I plead. As I have often said to McMillan the value of all the work which has been done on the Park — the dividend which the City is to obtain for all that it has invested — depends entirely on the refined management of its plantations. You might just as well go to all the expense of purchasing a vein of gold bearing rock, of opening a mine upon it, getting out the quartz and crushing it and then be careless in the amalgamating process, letting half your gold go down the stream, as to make a park and let the work on the plantations be rushed, wholesaled and slighted.

  I hope it will be remembered that I long ago said this not only to McMillan but in effect before your Board.

The text presented here is from a draft in Olmsted's hand.

1. Dennis Bowen (see FLO to Dennis Bowen, January 1, 1876, n. 1, above).
2. Parks superintendent William McMillan.
3. The assistant superintendent was George Troup, hired by the commission in October 1874 ("General Superintendent's Report," in City of Buffalo. Park Commission, *Fifth Annual Report of the Buffalo Park Commissioners. January, 1875* [Buffalo, N.Y., 1875], p. 36).
4. Fillmore Avenue extended two miles south from the Parade, providing a connection to the park and parkway system from the western part of the city. During 1876 the commissioners carried out the extensive filling and other construction needed to make the avenue passable. As a result, they stated in their annual report of the following year, "all the boulevards of the park scheme are now practically opened to travel on the sub-grade or bed of the permanent roadway" (City of Buffalo. Park Commission, *Seventh Annual Report of the Buffalo Park Commissioners. January, 1877* [Buffalo, N.Y. 1877], p. 7)

To William McMillan

                Sep^t 11th 1876

Dear Mr McMillan;

  Yours of 9th just received. Don't show my memorandum letter — of 6th. I have written Mr Bowen.[1]

  You don't tell me that you have moved the pines. You promised to do so *immediately* when I was with you and to write me of your progress from week to week.

Now you must not allow anything else to stand in the least in the way of the planting and shore work.

Take the risk and bear the blame of something else's going wrong. You can do your professional duty and, if necessary, offend the public and the Commission, who never can & never will know the need of it.

It is no disgrace to the Commissioners that they do not understand our business and mismanage it, it is a disgrace to us if we neglect or allow ourselves to be driven from it year after year and nobody has a right to compel us to disgrace ourselves. A Superintendent is a man exercising discretion for others. Take the largest discretion and let the results justify you.

Have the leeward shore of the lake[2] put in the best shape possible early this fall, if you neglect wholly everything else. You can steal material from other parts of the park less prominent in landscape, less marred by hasty work and less difficult to make satisfactory.

Remember it was that bit of all your work which needed to be done before all others with the greatest amount of personal care and steady refinement and artifice and it is the last to be properly taken hold of.

You can take out a third of the shrubs along the drive from the Parkway to the bridge[3] and with good management the park will be no worse three years hence for the thinning & setting back. Almost everywhere the shrubs are too near the edge of the drive; the large ones should be removed & smaller ones, or creepers and broader margins of turf substituted.

If you lack low shrubs you can raise them and replant in another year or two but at any rate crowd the leeward bank of the lake and by every means that can be contrived force out a low thicket which the wind cannot prevent from becoming strong, overhanging, picturesque & varied in form, with light and playful spray and which shall give a fine, soft, natural, mysterious and poetic quality to this most prominent feature of all the park in place of the bare, lumpy, bald shorn, machine shaped character which is now fixed upon it.

The text presented here is from a draft in Olmsted's hand.

1. See FLO to Dennis Bowen, Sept. 10, 1876, above.
2. Olmsted appears to be concerned particularly with the western part of the southern shore of the Lake, between the boathouse and the promontory called "Spirehead," with the Spire House structure. This section of the shore was especially visible, and early photographs show it less densely planted than other parts of the lakeshore.
3. That is, remove a third of the shrubs along the carriage drive in the western part of the park between Lincoln Parkway and the bridge over the Lake.

April 1876–December 1876

To Horatio Admiral Nelson

28th Septr 1876

To Mr Nelson.
Dear Sir,
    I have read with regret yours of yesterday just received. Referring to my advice of 25th you state that with your present imperfect arrangements travel to the mountain is greatly increasing.[1] It would cost little to double the convenient carrying capacity of the present road at the place in question and make it during the summer a quieter and in every way more agreeable road than one of stone can be. It is only for the early spring and after showers that an earth road is not much better for pleasure driving than a McAdamized road.[2]
    That with your present awkward arrangmnts the travel is larger than you have expected is a slight indication of the value which may be developed for the city by proper improvemnts of the mountain and a sound reason for carefully avoiding false steps.
    The road plans I have furnished you, both for the bit of road particularly referred to and all of the remainder, have been designed with the reservoir in view as one element of the work of which they were another and I can only recommend construction to proceed on any part of the road hand in hand with that of the reservoir.
    I observed in my last that slight differences might be found desirable in the plan of the reservoir which should modify the plan of road with regard to which you questioned me.[3] It is now obvious from what you say that after a year or two, with returning prosperity, an increase of population, rapid progress in building, new members of the Common Council, new Committees and possibly a new water works engineer, the whole project of the reservoir is liable to be reconsidered; that a larger one may be required or a different situation preferred.[4] In that case the entire plan of roads which I have given you beyond the road already made will have been badly designed and, if carried out, will be regarded as a costly and vexatious mistake. As to the stretch of road which you are more particularly anxious to undertake it would in that case be a barbarism, for which, speaking as a friend, I should be very sorry to have you in the long future of the mountain held responsible.
    I fear that the necessity of making the project temporarily popular is constantly urging a policy on the Commission which if its results could be fully recognized would be anything but popular.
    Allow me to point out to you why this work should stand on a different footing from other city works in this respect and be managed through quite different methods of administration.
    The best results of sewer, pavement, lighting and water supply improvments are demonstrated the moment the expenditure required for them

has been made. Their profit is simple, direct and may in a great degree be so measured and stated in advance as to be readily comprehended. Each step in the progress of construction has a comparatively direct and intelligible bearing on the promised result. Hence with rare exceptions the practice of managing them through Common Council Committees is as safe, conservative, economical and efficient as any that has yet been tried.

Park improvments are of a wholly different class. They do not look to the immediate relief of tangible, serious and generally felt public inconveniences. Public opinion cannot, therefore, act in the same manner upon those having them in charge as in the case of other works for the public benifit. There may or may not be some immediately valuable results of the work as it advances, appreciable by the general public, but whether there are or not, such results are the last and least that should be considered in laying them out. They can by no possibility ever furnish a sound justification for the required expenditure and if the disposition of ignorant and inconsiderate critics to look upon them in that light is in the least encouraged or the right of any man to judge them in this manner admitted, the administration will ncccsarily be condemned and come to grief.

With sound managmnt after a year or two the real purport and value of the improvemnts will begin to develop and will thereafter increase at a rapidly advancing rate of augmentation for a period of at least fifty years. Money cautiously spent for such a result is likely to be well spent. Money spent for the immediate gratification of the public is almost sure to be extravagantly spent.

Consequently when works of this kind have been managed by Committees dependent from season to season for their funds upon the satisfaction which is immediately felt by the public with what they appear to superficial observers to be doing, they have in every instance within my knowledge after a few years proved mortifying disappointments. On the other hand every one which is generally recognized as a great success, and in which there is general pride and satisfaction has been managed by a proper Commission specially constituted for the purpose in a large degree independent of the Common Council and employing funds, raised expressly with a view to carry out the whole of a particular scheme, usually by a loan specially negociated for the purpose and secured by pledge of the property to be improved.[5]

Of course, I do not mean to suggest that this is the only way in which such a work can be judiciously managed, but I will not conceal my opinion that it is most unfortunate that any attempt should be made to improve such a noble property as the mountain at all while so many elements of uncertainty exist as to the conditions by which its character must be affected & with a policy toward it on the part of the Common Council so unfixed and uncertain from year to year.

APRIL 1876–DECEMBER 1876

The text presented here is from a draft in Olmsted's hand.

1. On September 25, Olmsted had again recommended a delay in constructing a permanent road in the area of the proposed Reservoir that would connect the road built up to the Glades in the winter of 1875–76 and the new road that he had planned around the Upperfell. Two days later Nelson wrote him that it was vital to move ahead with the plans for the road since six hundred carriages a day were driving up the mountain and were inconvenienced by the narrowness of the drive in the Glades section (FLO to H. A. Nelson, Sept. 25, 1876; H.A. Nelson to FLO, Sept. 27, 1876; see also n. 4 below).
2. The McAdam system of road construction, which Olmsted also refers to as a "stone" road, consisted of layers of broken stones of which the top two inches were one inch in size. The "earth" road that he preferred for a carriage drive in a park had much finer surface material, which was compressed by heavy rolling machines (Ivan Sparkes, *Stagecoaches & Carriages, An Illustrated History of Coaches and Coaching* [New York, 1975], p. 116; *DNB*, s.v. "McAdam, John Loudon").
3. Regarding the existing temporary road between the section already McAdamized and the carriage drive on the upper mountain, Olmsted had written, "I advise your Board to make some slight and inexpensive improvements so that carriages may meet and pass upon it, and, for the present, to be content with it" (FLO to H. A. Nelson, Sept. 25, 1876, Archives Municipales de Montréal, Montreal, Quebec, Canada).
4. In his letter of September 27, Nelson noted that

> . . . in refering to what you say about the Reservoir, I beg to say, that the Council have decided to adopt your plan for it, and to allow you to make your plan accordingly, but it may be years before the reservoir is made, therefore it would not do to delay the Park plan for the Building of it, but I think the drives could be made, and the site of the reservoir turned into a Flower Garden in the meantime, or excavate part of it, in order to get the material to make slopes of the road &c and any defacing of the place covered by a Ceder Hedge, until the reservoir was required. . . .

5. The Montreal Park commission was not a separate entity but rather a committee of the City Council. The park commissioners were also members of the Board of Aldermen, subject to politics, public opinion, and reelection. The frustration that Olmsted felt in dealing with the Montreal Park commission poured forth in his *Mount Royal. Montreal*, published in 1881 (*Papers of FLO*, SS1: 414, n. 33).

To Frederick Law Olmsted, Jr.

209 W. 46th St. N. York.
1st Oct. 1876.

Dear Henry,[1]

Once there was {an} old colony engine[2] whose name was SUCCOTASH. He was very proud of his name and had it put on his side in brass letters. He lived in a Round house when he was at home and he had a man by the name of John Grinner who fed him and washed him and put him to bed and woke him up. He was pretty old for an engine but engines hardly ever live to be as old as a man and John Grinner was a good deal older and old Succotash looked up to him and respected him and when John Grinner took him out he was very careful to mind every little hint he gave him. He would go slow and carefully or go fast; he would stop short and would back, he would whistle or exhaust or move along quietly just as John Grinner said.

There was a young rat who lived in the turntable. He was not bigger than a good sized mouse but he had got his second teeth and he thought he felt his wisdom teeth coming and had a good opinion of himself. His name was Tzaskoe, a family name that came from Norway. Tzaskoe used to come in the night when Succotash had cooled down and lick his axles. There was a taste of oil there which he liked. But old Succotash felt it to be a delicate attention in the little fellow and he did not care what the motive was. So he encouraged Tzaskoe's visits and after a time there came to be a great friendship between the two.

Old Succotash did not care for anything to eat himself but kindling wood and coal. "Only give me coal enough and a few slivers of wood, and all the cold water I want", he used to say to John Grinner, "and I would not give a puff for all the lobsters and molasses candy and such like kickshaws there are in all Boston."

But John Grinner's wife, when he went out, always used to put him up a snack of hard boiled eggs and cheese and after he had fed Succotash the fourth time he would eat it.

Succotash found out that Tzaskoe was very very fond of toasted cheese. So he used to save up the crumbs that John Grinner dropped and warm them and then in the evening he would invite Tzaskoe up on his cab and it pleased him very much to see how quickly he would leap up and how nimbly he would nibble the crumbs. After a time he was sorry to find that there were no more delicate attentions from Tzaskoe. But he continued to love Tzaskoe more and more.

As for Tzaskoe he was very proud to be made so much of by a great old engine and when he met the wharf fellows used to boast that old Succotash would do anything for him. After a time he used to take even higher airs and talk about "that old engine" and pretend that Succotash could not get along without him and that he could turn him on the end of his tail. He got so much in the habit of talking in this way that at length he began to think so.

Old Succotash's regular work was to draw a train to Boston and back every day. After he got back he had nothing more to do but John Grinner would wash him and rub him bright and put him to bed in the round house.

But one day there was a young engine who lived in the same round house who did not do as he was told and first thing he knew he was off the track and tumbled up against a wood pile near Silver lake and threw the man who took care of him into an apple tree and tore his clothes and broke the glass and bent the reflector of his own headlight.

The man got down and tied a handkerchief over the place and sent out his red flags and ran all the way to Kingston where he sent word to John Grinner by telegraph to come up with old Succotash and pull Nipyac upon the track again. Nipyac was the name of the foolish engine.

Tzaskoe had just jumped up on the cab to get his toasted cheese when John Grinner opened the round house door and told Succotash what had happened, and Tzaskoe did not like it at all. So he whispered to Succotash, "Dont go!"

"Why! What do you mean, my little Tzasky?" said Succotash, "Of course, I must go."

"No you must not", said the ratlet, "you will be very disobliging if you budge an inch."

"Why", said Succotash, "you surprise me; think of that poor Nipyac with a banged eye and off the track, and all the people that are waiting for me and the three train nearly due and the track all crowded up."

"You think a great deal of that silly Nipyac and you don't think anything of me", said Tzaskoe.

"Oh!" said Succotash, "how can you say so, I think everything of you my dear little Tzaskie but this you see is a question of duty."

"If you are a friend of mine, it's your duty to think of me", said Tzaskoe, "you are not a friend of mine, you are a false hearted, unfeeling brazen faced old coal eater, that's what you are."

When he heard these hard names Succotash choked and blubbered a little, he felt so badly, but he soon recovered himself and said very seriously and quietly "You forget how much we both owe to John Grinner: he feeds me and waters me every day; he is even now getting ready to give me an extra meal, and he gives me the cheese which I toast for you, you surely would not have me refuse to mind him would you."

"John Grinner, John Grinner; I'm tired of hearing of John Grinner", said the pert little nincumpoop of a rat; "When John Grinner asks you to go out after your day's work is done and you are engaged in social duties, he is not a reasonable being."

"How strangely you talk," said Succotash, "John Grinner is a great deal older than I and it is not for me to say that he is not reasonable."

"I don't care about John Grinner" said Tzaskoe, "I say you shan't go."

"Shan't?" asked the engine.

"No, you shan't, I shall not allow you", said Tzaskoe, and he jumped down and ran along to the rail in front of Succotash. "Now then, we will see if you prefer duty to me", said Tzasko, and he really thought that Succotash loved him so much and was so soft hearted that he would never think of running over him. But Succotash said, "My dear Tzasko-Tzasko; John Grinner takes care of me, and gives me coal and water and watches over me and tells me what to do, and keeps me out of accidents and without him I should not be able to do anything. If he makes mistakes it is his fault not mine, but if I don't do what he tells me to it is my fault and I should be a mean, ungrateful smokey old humbug if I stopped a second when he said go; so I pray and beg of you to get right off the track."

But the conceited little fool of a ratlet said, "I don't want to hear any of your talk, I tell you to stand still; that's all I have to say."

Bye and bye, John Grinner, who had not heard this conversation, but had been feeding and kindling and watering Succotash and wondering how it was he was so unusually leaky, came round to the front and lighted the head lamp, and Tzaskoe ran away.

Then Succotash brightened up and said "Oh! it was a joke of my dear little Tzasky: what an old fool I have been to think that he was so wicked", but no, the moment John Grinner got up on the cab again, back came Tzaskoe, looking crosser than ever, and took his position on the right hand rail just in front of the cow catcher.

"My dearest pet", said Succotash, "John Grinner is just ready to touch the throttle valve and when he does, I must move. This is dangerous joking. Do — please move a little further off."

"I am not in the habit of joking with my friends", said Tzaskoe, and turned his back.

John Grinner struck the bell and Succotash gasped and whistled and shrieked but Tzaskoe affected to be very much interested with the end of his tail and not to notice anything that was said.

The next minute John Grinner said go!

"It's all over now", said Succotash, bursting into tears as he began going.

Tzaskoe instantly felt the rail tremble under him. Up to that moment he had not believed that his big friend would really do his duty but now he was in such an agony of terror that he could not attempt to jump even if there had been time. He crouched down and the cow catcher passed over him but so close that it almost crushed him and forced him down on one side so that before the wheel came up he had all but rolled off.

A scalding hot tear fell from poor Succotash right on the top of his head and the wheel was just in time to take his interesting tail off, right smash up to its roots.

Succotash went on about his business, Tzaskoe fainted.

When he came to he had a terrible head ache and a terrible back ache and was in a high fever. He tried to make his way down to the wharf, so he could cool his head and get a sea-weed poultice for the end of his back but he had the greatest difficulty in keeping his balance and steering the way he wanted to go. First thing he knew he ran almost into the mouth of {a} horrid old terrier. The terrier looked right at him as if he were a curiosity. Tzasko could not think why he did not eat him till he came to the wharf and looked down at his image in the water and did not know himself. Just then he heard some of the wharf ratlets talking, and one of them asked "What sort of an animal is that? It has not any tail and it has not any ears, but it is not a toad because its hairy except a bald spot on its head." The fact is the tear that Succotash let fall had just scalded his ears and all the hair on the top of his head off.

Tzaskoe when he heard what the other ratlet said knew that the terrier had not suspected that he was of a rat family, and he was so mortified that he dropped himself off into the water wishing that he might be drowned. But his head was too light and he had not strength to hold it under long enough.

So after bobbing up and down till he was frightfully sea sick he was washed ashore. He was very cold and very sick and very, very sore and he said. "What can I do! what can I do! I am too miserable to live and I can't die, I wonder if my old daddy would know me."

Early the next morning after Succotash had returned bringing back the wounded Nipyac and Nipyac had been plastered and bandaged up and they had both been washed and put to bed and the round house door closed, a most respectable grave gray old gentleman walked up into the roundhouse through the floor and approaching old Succotash said,

"Sir, will you kindly condescend to let me detain you from your well earned repose for a few brief moments that of your greatness I may ask a favor?"

"Willingly" replied Succotash, "but be brief."

The grey old Norwegian then stated that he was the unfortunate father of the wretched Tzaskoe. He described the disgusting figure in which Tzaskoe had returned to his home and how he begged to be relieved of his misery. A cat had been decoyed toward him but she only touched him with one claw and turned up her nose. The town had been searched and fortunately a sufficient dose of genuine rats bane found, "but before what is left of my miserable child destroys itself", said the venerable rat, "he desires me to thank you for your generosity, to acknowledge his own meanness and folly and to ask your forgiveness."

"Stuff and nonsense", said old Suc. "Bring my dear little Tzasky to my cab at once. I was an ass to cry and scald his dear little head. As for his tail — that I could not help, he carried the joke too far, that's all, but I will get John Grinning to make him a new tail and in a week we'll have him out as bright as ever."

"Pardon me, noble sir"! replied the stern parent, "my son owes a duty to his family. Your bright example Sir, has at last awakened him to a sense of it. With tail gone, ears gone, scalp gone, he has gained what is more than all — the spirit of a rat. In five minutes he will die. And I — and I —

(emotion choked his utterance)

In the presence of this grief Succotash recovered his equanimity. After a pause he said, "and you Sir, you were about to say?"

"I sir, have a favor to ask of you."

"Of me? too happy I am sure", said Succotash.

"It is that his poor mother and myself may have passage with you tomorrow to the port of Boston without the bother of tickets."

"What in the world are you going to do in Boston"?

"There we shall easily put ourselves on board some shipping by which we can betake ourselves to the land of our fathers. After what has occurred we cannot of course remain on this continent."
"Of course not—I see. Don't give yourself the slightest uneasiness. I'll make it all right with Grinner, If I don't I'll burst my head off. But now go and put little Tzasko out of his misery. My love to him."
"Good night."
"Good night."

The text presented here is a manuscript in Olmsted's hand.
1. Frederick Law Olmsted, Jr., who at this time was still called Henry Perkins Olmsted (see FLO to FLO, Jr., May 13, 1875, n. 1, above; *Olmsted Genealogy*, p. 109).
2. The Old Colony Railroad that ran between Boston and Plymouth, where Olmsted's wife, Mary Perkins Olmsted, and their son and daughter were staying (Mary Perkins Olmsted to John C. Olmsted, Sept. 28 [1876]).

I.

Preliminary Report of the Landscape Architect and the Civil and Topographical Engineer, upon the Laying Out of the Twenty-Third and Twenty-Fourth Wards.

CITY OF NEW YORK,
DEPARTMENT OF PUBLIC PARKS.
15th November, 1876.

The Hon. WILLIAM R. MARTIN,
President of the Board:
SIR:
   The undersigned have the honor to present a report introductory to a series of plans for laying out the new wards of the city. The first of these plans can, if desired, be laid before the Board at its next meeting; a second and third are in preparation, and the whole series is in progress of study.[1]

The great advance northward in the building of New York, since 1807, has been strictly according to the street plan which a commission of its citizens then laid down for it.[2] The objections at first hotly urged against this plan (chiefly by property holders whose lands it would divide inconveniently, whose lawns and gardens it would destroy and whose houses it would leave in awkward positions), have long since been generally forgotten, and so far as streets have been opened and houses built upon them, the system has apparently met all popular requirements. Habits and customs accommodated to it have become fixed upon the people of the city. Property divisions have been generally adjusted to it, and innumerable transfers and pledges of real estate have been made under it with a degree of ease and simplicity probably without parallel. All the enormous changes in the modes of commerce, of means of communication, and of the styles of domestic life which the century has seen, have made but one slight local variation from it necessary.[3]

These facts, taken by themselves, may seem to leave little room for doubt that the system was admirably contrived for its purpose, and that, as far as can be reasonably expected of any product of human skill, it remains perfect.

There are probably but few men in the community who, in the course of a busy life, have given any slight attention, and but slight attention, to the subject, who are not in the habit of taking this view of it, and in whom, consequently, a pre-judgment is not in some degree deeply rooted in favor of the system. That it should be extended, whenever practicable, over that part of the city not yet laid out, and where this is forbidden by extraordinary difficulties of topography, that no greater variation should be made from it than is necessary to bring the cost of preparing streets within reasonable limits of expense, seems, to all such persons, a matter of course.

All the work of the undersigned will, nevertheless, have been done under the influence of a quite different conviction and its results can only be fairly judged, after a candid and patient balancing of the advantages to be gained, and the advantages to be lost by the adoption of a variety of proposed arrangements always differing, and often differing widely from those with which commissioners and the community are familiar under the regular system.

They, therefore, wish to submit, in advance of any plans, a few general considerations adapted, as they think, to give a different impression of the merits of the system from that which appears to be ordinarily accepted, and by which the Commission has hitherto, to some extent, almost necessarily been influenced.

New York, when the system in question was adopted, though vaguely anticipating something of the greatness that has since been thrust upon her, viewed all questions of her own civic equipment, very nearly from the position which a small, poor, remote provincial village would now be expected to take.

The city had no gas, water or sewer system. The privies of the best houses were placed, for good reasons, as far away from them as possible, in a back yard, over a loose-bottomed cesspool. If the house stood in a closely built block, the contents of the cesspool, when necessary to be removed, were taken to the street in buckets carried through the house; the garbage of the house was often thrown, with its sweepings and soiled water into the street before the front door, to be there devoured by swine, droves of which were allowed to run at large for the purpose.

Under these circumstances, it was not to be expected that, if the utmost human wisdom had been used in the preparation of the plan, means would be aptly devised for all such ends as a commission charged with a similar duty at the present day must necessarily have before it.

So far as the plan of New York remains to be formed, it would be inexcusable that it should not be the plan of a Metropolis; adapted to serve, and serve well, every legitimate interest of the wide world; not of ordinary commerce only, but of humanity, religion, art, science and scholarship.

If a house to be used for many different purposes must have many rooms and passages of various dimensions and variously lighted and furnished, not less must such a metropolis be specially adapted at different points to different ends.

This it may chance to be if laid out by the old cow-path method, or more surely if laid out in greater or less part with carefully directed intention to the purpose, such as is now being used for instance in London, Paris, Vienna, Florence, and Rome.[4]

There seems to be good authority for the story that the system of 1807 was hit upon by the chance occurrence of a mason's sieve near the map of the ground to be laid out. It was taken up and placed upon the map, and the question being asked "what do you want better than that?" no one was able to answer. This may not be the whole story of the plan, but the result is the same as if it were. That is to say, some two thousand blocks were provided, each theoretically 200 feet wide, no more, no less; and ever since, if a building site is wanted, whether with a view to a church or a blast furnace, an opera house or a toy shop, there is, of intention, no better a place in one of these blocks than in another.

If a proposed cathedral, military depot, great manufacturing enterprise, house of religious seclusion or seat of learning needs a space of ground more than sixty-six yards in extent from north to south, the system forbids that it shall be built in New York.

On the other hand it equally forbids a museum, library, theatre, exchange, post office or hotel, unless of great breadth, to be lighted or to open upon streets from opposite sides.

There are numerous structures, both public and private, in London and Paris, and most other large towns of Europe, which could not be built in New York, for want of a site of suitable extent and proportions.

APRIL 1876–DECEMBER 1876

The Trustees of Columbia College sought for years to obtain the privilege of consolidating two of the uniform blocks of the system, into which their own property had been divided, in order to erect sufficient buildings for their purpose, in one unbroken group, but it was denied them.[5]

There is no place under the system in New York where a stately building can be looked up to from base to turret, none where it can even be seen full in the face and all at once taken in by the eye; none where it can be viewed in advantageous perspective. The few tolerable sites for noble buildings north of Grace Church[6] and within the built part of the city remain, because Broadway, laid out curvilinearly, in free adaptation to natural circumstances, had already become too important a thoroughfare to be obliterated for the system.

Such distinctive advantage of position as Rome gives St. Peter's, Paris the Madeleine, London St. Paul's,[7] New York, under her system, gives to nothing.

But, if New York is poor in opportunities of this class, there is another of even greater importance in which she is notoriously still poorer. Decent, wholesome, tidy dwellings for people who are struggling to maintain an honorable independence are more to be desired in a city than great churches, convents or colleges. They are sadly wanting in New York, and why? It is commonly said because the situation of the city, cramped between two rivers, makes land too valuable to be occupied by small houses. This is properly a reason why land, at least in the lower part of the island, should be economized, and buildings arranged compactly. The rigid uniformity of the system of 1807 requires that no building lot shall be more than 100 feet in depth, none less. The clerk or mechanic and his young family, wishing to live modestly in a house by themselves, without servants, is provided for in this respect no otherwise than the wealthy merchant, who, with a large family and numerous servants, wishes to display works of art, to form a large library, and to enjoy the company of many guests.

In New York, lots of 100 feet in depth cannot be afforded for small, cheap houses. The ground-rent would be in too large proportion to that of the betterments. In no prosperous old city are families of moderate means found living, except temporarily in the outskirts, in separate houses on undivided blocks measuring 200 feet from thoroughfare to thoroughfare. It is hardly to be hoped that they ever will be in New York under the plan of 1807.*

The inflexibility of the New York plan, and the nature of the disadvantages which grow out of it, may be better recognized upon an examination

---

*Various attempts have been made on a small scale to get the better of this difficulty, the most successful being the introduction of an alley by which a tier of 100 feet lots is divided into two of 42 feet each, one tier facing upon the back of the other. A philanthropic scheme is now under discussion for cutting up a whole block into short lots for poor men's houses by 16-feet alleys.[8]

245

of certain peculiarities with which Commissioners must be familiar as distinguishing the city.

These are to be found, for instance, in the position usually occupied by the kitchen and menial offices of even the better class of houses; in the manner in which supplies are conveyed to them, and dust, ashes, rubbish and garbage removed. This class of peculiarities grows out of the absence from the New York system of the alley, or court, by which in all other great towns large private dwelling houses are usually made accessible in the rear.*

It is true, that in other cities, as they become dense and land valuable, the alleys and courts come to be much used as streets, that is to say, small houses and shops, as well as stables are built facing upon them, and the dwellings only of people of considerable wealth are carried through to them from the streets proper. But this practice does not do away with the general custom of a yard accessible from the alley by an independent passage, and of placing the kitchen and offices of all large houses in a semi-detached building. Out of this custom come the greater ease and economy with which streets are elsewhere kept in decent order, and the bad reputation which New York has always had in this respect; and again, the fact that New York houses of the better class, much more than those of other cities, are apt to be pervaded with kitchen odors.

Another peculiarity of New York, is to be found in the much less breadth and greater depth of most of the modern dwellings of the better sort. There are many houses not much wider than the hovels of other cities, which yet have sixty or seventy feet of depth, and fifty to sixty feet of height, with sculptured stone fronts and elaborately wrought doors. This incongruity results from the circumstance that a yard at the back of the house, when no longer needed for a privy and where there is no alley to communicate with it, has little value; consequently, to economize ground-rent, two house lots of the size originally contemplated are divided into three or four, and houses stretched out upon them so as to occupy as much of the space as the Board of Health,[10] guarding against manifest peril of public pestilence, will allow.

The same cubic space is now obtained in a lot of 1,700 square feet, or

---

*THE SANITARIAN, for January, 1877, received as this is printing, contains the following professional notes on Boston, by Doctor E. H. Janes: "The streets of Boston present quite a contrast with those of New York in point of cleanliness." "Their system of alleys, by which access is obtained to the rear yards, renders it unnecessary to disfigure the sidewalks, or defile the gutters and pavements with every variety of house refuse and filth. At the appointed time the cartman rings the bell at the rear gate, receives from the housemaid the garbage, deposits it in a water-tight cart. * * * * The garbage is taken to the country and used for feeding swine. The ashes are collected in a similar way, and, being entirely separate from garbage, or any putrescent matter, can be used for filling low ground." * * * "I wish some such system could be adopted with us, as I am confident it would reduce the rate of mortality among our tenement house population."[9]

even 1,300, as formerly on one of 2,500, and the depth between the front and rear windows of houses of corresponding area has been nearly doubled.[11]

That this change has been forced also by the street system, and is not a matter of fashion, nor the result of a caprice in popular tastes, is evident from the fact that no corresponding method has obtained in other cities, new or old, nor however situated; none, for example, in London, Liverpool, Philadelphia, Baltimore, Buffalo, Chicago, or San Francisco.

The practice is one that defies the architect to produce habitable rooms of pleasing or dignified proportions, but this is the least of its evils, for in the middle parts of all these deep, narrow cubes, there must be a large amount of ill-ventilated space, which can only be imperfectly lighted through distant skylights, or by an unwholesome combustion of gas. This space being consequently the least valuable for other purposes, is generally assigned to water-closets, for which the position is in other respects the worst that could be adopted.

Still other, and perhaps even graver, misfortunes to the city might be named which could have been avoided by a different arrangement of its streets. The main object of this report will, however, have been secured, if the conviction has been shown to be justified that an attempt to make all parts of a great city equally convenient for all uses, is far from being prescribed by any soundly economical policy.

"Equally convenient," in this case, implies equally inconvenient. "As far as practicable," means within reasonable limits of expense. But there are no reasonable limits of expense for such an undertaking. Even on a flat alluvial site, like that of Chicago, it is essentially wasteful and extravagant. In proportion as a site is rugged and rocky it is only more decidedly so; not simply because in this case it involves greater unnecessary cost, but because variety of surface offers variety of opportunity, and such an undertaking often deliberately throws away forever what might otherwise be distinctive properties of great value.

The important question in dealing with a site of greatly varied topography is, whether, and in what manner, advantage can be so taken of the different topographical conditions it offers, that all classes of legitimate enterprises can be favored, each in due proportion to the interest which all citizens have in its economical and successful prosecution.

It would be easy, of course, to attempt too much in this respect, but the range of practicability is more limited than at first thought may be supposed. The value of a particular situation for a certain purpose may be determined as far as the depth which is left available for building is concerned, by the distance apart of two adjoining streets, and as far as aspect, accessibility to the public, and the cost of transportation to and fro, are concerned, by their courses and grades; but as to the breadth of ground that shall be available for any particular purpose, as to the manner in which it shall be graded and otherwise dealt with; whether it shall be cut down or filled up, terraced, or used in a more natural form — these are questions which the street system must necessarily leave to be settled by private judgment under the stimulus of competition.

Hence, while it is held that the capability of the ground should be studied for purposes more or less distinctly to be classed apart, and that, as topographical conditions vary, it should be laid out with reference to one class or another, an extended, exact, and dogmatic classification for this purpose is not to be apprehended.

A judicious laying out of the annexed territory requires a certain effort of forecast as to what the city is to be in the future. In this respect, there is a great danger in attempting too much as in attempting too little. Before New York can have doubled its present population, new motive powers and means of transit, new methods of building, new professions and trades, and new departures in sanitary science, if not in political science, are likely to have appeared. If half its present territory should then be built up and occupied as closely as its seven more populous wards now are, the other half would need to lodge but one-seventh of its total population. Assuming that in this other half there should be but a moderate degree of urban density along the river side and near the railway stations, there would still remain several square miles of land which could only be occupied by scattered buildings. It is, then, premature, to say the least, to attempt to overcome any topographical difficulty that may be presented to a perfectly compact and urban occupation of every acre of the ground to be laid out.

Respectfully,

FRED. LAW OLMSTED,
Landscape Architect.
J. JAMES R. CROES,[12]
Civil and Topographical Engineer.

The text presented here is from "Document No. 72, Part I," in New York (City), Department of Public Parks, Minutes, December 20, 1876. In January 1874, with the annexation to New York City of the Westchester County towns of Morrisania, West Farms, and Kingsbridge, creating the city's Twenty-third and Twenty-fourth wards, the Department of Public Parks accelerated its surveying and planning of street, water, and sewage systems for these areas. Olmsted assumed direction of the project from department engineers in November 1875 and collaborated with civil engineer J. J. R. Croes in devising entirely new plans. The present text, their first report on the subject, was presented to the board on November 22,

APRIL 1876–DECEMBER 1876

1876, and laid over until December 20. It originally appeared as part one of "Document No. 72." Their second report, on the Riverdale district, was part two of the same document and is presented below separately (I. N. P. Stokes, *Iconography of Manhattan*, 5: 1954–55; *City Record*, Jan. 5, 1874, pp. 9–10; DPP, *Minutes*, Nov. 5, 1875, pp. 369–70; ibid., Nov. 22, 1876, p. 417; ibid., Dec. 20, 1876, pp. 479–80; "Document No. 73," in DPP, *Minutes*, Dec. 20, 1876, pp. 2–27).

1. The first plan completed by Olmsted and Croes was for Riverdale, the elevated district which overlooks the Hudson River north of Spuyten Duyvil and south of the city boundary with Yonkers. On December 20, 1876, they presented it and a report on the district to the board. Their second plan, presented without a report on February 28, 1877, was for the district immediately to the east, between Riverdale Avenue and Broadway. Three weeks later they presented a report and plan on local steam transit routes for the entire Twenty-third and Twenty-fourth wards. The board approved the first two plans within five weeks, following community review and some minor revision by the designers. The board adopted the plan for local steam transit in January 1878. Olmsted and Croes were also at work on plans for the districts east of the Harlem River from Jerome Park to Morrisania, and the Hunt's Point District to the southeast (FLO and J. J. R. Croes to William R. Martin, Nov. 21, 1876, below; J. J. R. Croes and FLO to William R. Martin, March 20, 1877, below; FLO and J. J. R. Croes to William R. Martin, Oct. 31, 1877, below; *Transactions of the American Society of Civil Engineers* 48 [June 1907]: 524–31; *Civil Engineering* 8 [October 1938]: 702–3; *City Record*, July 24, 1874, p. 798; DPP, *Minutes*, Nov. 12, 1875, pp. 384–85; S. S. Haight, "Surveying, Laying Out and Monumenting the New Wards of New York," *Engineering News*, March 5, 1881, p. 96).
2. In 1807 the New York state legislature created a commission to lay out the permanent street system of the city. Their plan, a gridiron of rectangular blocks, was adopted in 1811. It provided avenues 100 feet wide running north and south and streets only 60 feet wide running east and west (with fifteen wider streets to facilitate crosstown traffic). All the blocks were 200 feet deep and from 420 to 920 feet long. The plan covered Manhattan Island from approximately 14th Street to 155th Street (BCCP, *Tenth Annual Report* [1867], pp. 118–25; "Document No. 73," in DPP, *Minutes*, Dec. 20, 1876, p. 11; David Schuyler, *The New Urban Landscape: The Redefinition of City Form in Nineteenth-Century America* [Baltimore, 1986], pp. 17–20).
3. A probable reference to the 1867 action of the Central Park commissioners in altering the lines of adopted streets and creating new ones near Morningside Park to circumvent the cliffs and steep terrain of the area (BCCP, *Eleventh Annual Report* [1868], pp. 148–51; *Papers of FLO*, 6: 658–59).
4. Of the cities mentioned by Olmsted, Paris and Vienna had the most extensive programs of urban planning and renovation. Between 1852 and 1870 overlapping agencies in Paris headed by Baron Georges Eugène Haussmann revised the city plan, cleared away narrow streets and tenements, introduced spacious boulevards, and built several large parks and numerous neighborhood squares. Haussmann was dismissed in 1869 but work continued according to his plans well into the 1870s. In the late 1850s Emperor Franz Joseph ordered the transformation of the old defensive glacis and wall surrounding Vienna into the Ringstrasse, a grand boulevard lined with cultural, educational, and government buildings and affluent residential districts. Work on the project lasted into the 1890s. In London, municipal authority was diffused among dozens of local parishes, but beginning in 1855 the Metropolitan Board of Works was empowered to undertake large public works projects. Over the following decades it built a city-wide sewage system, cleared congested slums, and opened new streets for improved traffic circulation. Florence, the national capital of Italy between 1864 and

1871, implemented several expansion and development plans by the architect Guiseppe Poggi. Two years later, when Rome was named the capital, a plan was approved for the clearance and redevelopment of its central areas (Donald J. Olsen, *The City as a Work of Art: London, Paris, Vienna* [New Haven, Conn., 1986], pp. 12–13, 24, 44–59, 69–81; Donatella Calabi, "Italy," in *Planning and Urban Growth in Southern Europe*, ed. Martin Wynn [London, 1984], pp. 42–43).

5. In the spring of 1857 Columbia College had moved from its downtown location near City Hall to a two-block-square property bounded by Fourth Avenue, Fifth Avenue, and 49th and 50th streets. The trustees approved construction of a building by Richard Upjohn almost three hundred feet long, but the project required closing Madison Avenue to consolidate the two blocks, and they abandoned it by the early 1870s (*A History of Columbia University 1754–1904* [New York, 1904], pp. 129–30, 160).

6. Grace Church is located at Broadway and 10th Street.

7. These great churches were located on elevated sites which allowed them to be viewed from a distance, or had special avenues or plazas which served as ceremonial approaches to them.

8. Olmsted's first example probably refers to tenements built since 1867, when the state required that alleys from ten to twenty-five feet wide separate tenements built behind those fronting on a standard one-hundred-foot-deep lot. His second example refers to the proposal by New York architect Edward T. Potter, first made in late 1866, for model tenement houses in which north-south alleys would introduce open space for light, ventilation, and the removal of trash and refuse. Potter refined his plans in late 1876 and described them in a private circular and before the American Social Science Association, with which Olmsted had been affiliated for ten years. Olmsted again drew attention to Potter's scheme in an 1879 newspaper article on the future of New York (*New-York Daily Tribune*, Dec. 3, 1866, p. 2; Sarah Bradford Landau, *Edward T. and William A. Potter, American Victorian Architects* [New York, 1979], pp. 393–96; I. N. P. Stokes, *Iconography of Manhattan*, 5: 1928; FLO, "The Future of New York," Dec. 28, 1879, below).

9. Dr. Janes's letter appeared in *The Sanitarian* 5 (Jan. 1877): 11–12.

10. The Metropolitan Board of Health, created in 1866, made sanitary inspections of tenements and enforced the space provisions of the 1867 tenement law (Seymour J. Mandelbaum, *Boss Tweed's New York* [New York, 1965], pp. 65–66).

11. Olmsted is describing a trend that accelerated after the Civil War, in which older house lots of twenty-five feet frontage, designed for one or two-story dwellings, were divided to accommodate narrower buildings. These newer buildings had additional stories and were extended farther back on the lot over ground formerly occupied by privies and outbuildings, increasing the amount of cubic space of the structures on a given plot of ground.

12. John James Robertson Croes (1834–1906), had been a civil engineer in the New York City area for fifteen years. In 1860 he joined the New York City's Croton Aqueduct Department and, under General George S. Greene, worked on the construction of the large receiving reservoir in Central Park. During the Civil War, he assisted in the completion of the waterworks for Washington, D.C., after which he returned to work under Greene in the Croton Aqueduct Department on the design and construction of Boyd's Corner dam. In 1871 he joined the Department of Public Parks as a division engineer under William H. Grant, and worked on the surveys of New York City north of 155th Street and parts of Westchester County. In June 1874 Greene replaced Grant as chief engineer of the department's civil and topographical office and Croes took charge of the surveys and plans for the north end of Manhattan. His appointment as chief engineer of the office in November 1875 probably came at Olmsted's recommendation, as it followed by only a week the landscape architect's assignment to for-

APRIL 1876–DECEMBER 1876

mulate new plans for the annexed district. His promotion, recalled another engineer in the department, "gave encouragement in well doing to all members of the force, as it was felt to be in the nature of reform, a promotion consequent upon approved service." Croes held this position until March 1878 and he resigned from the department in 1879. Over the next two decades he consulted on numerous private and public civil engineering projects and held several executive positions, including president with the American Society of Civil Engineers (*Transactions of the American Society of Civil Engineers* 48 [June 1907]: 524–31; *Civil Engineering* 8 [October 1938]: 702–3; S. S. Haight, "Surveying, Laying Out and Monumenting the New Wards of New York," *Engineering News*, March 5, 1881, p. 96).

II.

Report of the Landscape Architect and the Civil and Topographical Engineer, Accompanying a Plan for Laying Out that Part of the Twenty-Fourth Ward Lying West of the Riverdale Road.

CITY OF NEW YORK,
DEPARTMENT OF PUBLIC PARKS,
21st November, 1876.

The Hon. WILLIAM R. MARTIN,
President of the Board:
SIR:
 The undersigned have now the honor to submit, as the first of a series, a plan for a primary road system for that part of the new wards lying west of the Riverdale Road.[1]

 The Commission has had the problem of laying out this district under debate since 1872. It has heretofore at various times called four engineers into its counsels upon it, and has considered five separate plans covering the ground wholly or in part.[2] Much difference of opinion and something of partizanship with regard to these plans has appeared, and conflicting private interests concerned in the issues developed have been urged with warmth.
 These, with other circumstances, the force of which the Commission will recognize, made it desirable that the purely professional and official char-

251

acter of the duty given the undersigned should be strictly guarded, and that for the time being, they should keep out of view any private ends to be affected.

For this reason, and also because it would be impracticable to give a fair hearing to everyone concerned, they have, since they took the matter in hand,[3] declined conversation upon it, have denied all requests for an examination of their study plans, and have neither expressed opinions nor accepted advice upon the subject.

They are now, consequently, under obligations to explain more fully than might otherwise be thought necessary, the grounds upon which the judgments have been formed which are embodied in the plan herewith presented.

In a previous report[4] the objections have been indicated which prevail with them against one of the ruling motives upon which New York, so far as built during the present century, has been laid out and upon which most American cities are now building; the motive, that is to say, of securing in all quarters as nearly as practicable without excessive expense, an equality of advantages for all purposes.

They proceed, on the contrary, with the conviction that the principle of a division of labor may, with advantage, be measurably applied to the plan of a city; one part of it being laid out with a view to the development of one class of utilities, another to a different class, according as natural circumstances favor.

Under the first method, the great variety of topographical conditions found in the site of New York is regarded as a misfortune to be overcome, under the latter, as an advantage to be made available.

Having in view all the territory to be occupied before laying out any part of it, according to the preferred method, the topography of that part is to be questioned as for what class of private undertakings it is comparatively unsuitable, and as for what it is comparatively suitable.

I.

THE DISTRICT TO BE LAID OUT.

The district lies within and forms the larger part of the great promontory, the shank of which is crossed by the line dividing Yonkers from New York, and which terminates three miles to the southward in the abrupt headland of Spuyten Duyvil. Its ridge line seldom drops much below an elevation of 200 feet, and its highest point, which is also the highest in the city, is 282 feet above tide.

Its surface is much broken by ledges, and there are numerous steep declivities on its hillsides which can rarely be directly ascended without encountering a grade of from 15 to 25 in a hundred. Its ruggedness has prevented its being occupied for agricultural purposes, except very sparsely, and it is largely wooded and wild.

The only noticeable improvements have been made in connection with a number of private villas, and with a large convent and seminary, the grounds of which were also first prepared for a private pleasure ground.[5]

That the district is not more generally occupied in this manner, is due first, to the uncertainty which exists as to how it is to be laid out and generally built over; second, to the fact that it is affected by malaria, of a mild type, however, and resulting entirely from superficial conditions easily to be removed; third, to its lack of suitable roads. The local scenery is everywhere pleasing, except as it is marred artificially. Generally, it is highly picturesque, with aspects of grandeur, and from nearly all parts, broad, distant prospects are commanded of an extended, interesting, and even very impressive character.

II.
The Unsuitability of the District for the More Common Purposes of the City.

To what needs of the city is such ground as has been described, well adapted?

The authors of the five plans for laying it out, of which transcripts upon a uniform scale are herewith exhibited, all knew well, from much experience, the convenience of the ordinary city division of real estate, and each plan represents an amount of patient and ingenious study in fitting streets of rectilinear or nearly rectilinear courses, to the highly curvilinear contours of the topography, that can be fully appreciated only by those who have had some experience in similar tasks.

Under neither of these plans could any considerable part of the ground to which it applies be subdivided into building sites of the usual form and dimensions of city real estate, or be built upon advantageously in compact ranges. This may be considered as conclusive testimony that the attempt to lay it out with such a purpose in view, would be impracticable.

The ascent of the slopes will be nowhere easy, and two horses, on an average, will be required within it to accomplish the work, which, in most other parts of the city, could be done by one.

There will be no thoroughfares adapted either to heavy teaming or to rapid driving, and in none of the plans heretofore prepared, is a single short-cut proposed across the district.

On these grounds, it may be concluded that factories, (at least of heavy goods,) shops, warehouses, or stores for general trade, except possibly to a limited extent at the foot of the slopes, can be brought here only by some forced and costly process. The city holds much better ground for them in large quantity elsewhere.

The nearest part of the district is ten miles away from the present centre of population,[6] and within that distance, there is but little other ground in which the call for houses of low rent for families of small means, could not be more economically met. The cost of preparing each site for such a house, and rendering it accessible, would be excessive, and the average space which would be appropriated for each, would be much larger than would be elsewhere required.

III.
THE QUESTION OF A PERMANENT SUBURBAN QUARTER.

There remains to be considered the question of its further general and permanent occupation by that class of citizens to whom the confinement, noise, and purely artificial conditions of the compact city are oppressive, and who are able to indulge in the luxury of a villa or suburban cottage residence.

What are the chances of its being occupied in this manner advantageously?

IV.
THE POSSIBILITY OF A PERMANENT SUBURBAN QUARTER.

Of course, although manufactories and commercial buildings on a large scale are not to be apprehended, a perfectly uninterrupted succession of private villas and cottages is not to be hoped for. Here and there a shop or a range of shops will be necessary, but being adapted only for local custom, they are not likely to be lofty or excessively obtrusive. Now and again buildings for other purposes would probably occur; a school with its play grounds, a church set in a proper churchyard; a higher institution of learning with its green quadrangle, academic grove or campus; a public hall, library or museum; a convent with its courts and gardens; a suburban inn or boarding-house with its terrace, commanding grand prospects over the Hudson. All who have lived abroad know how buildings of these classes and many others may come into a villa suburb (their sites being chosen so as to gain an advantage from appropriate natural circumstances), in such a manner as not to disturb but to give point and emphasis to its proper aspect.

The nearest approach to urban building likely to be frequent, if once the general character proposed is obtained for the district, would be what the English call a terrace, a range of dwellings set back from the public street and reached by a loop-road, the crescent-shaped intermediate space being either a quiet slope of turf, a parterre of flowers, a play ground for children, or, if the topography favors, a picturesque rocky declivity treated perhaps as a fernery or Alpine garden. There will be, whatever the plan of roads, a great number of situations well adapted to such an arrangement, and which could be made suitable for no other except at much greater cost.[7]

Old neighborhoods, more or less of the character indicated, are to be found near almost every great city of Europe, and there are towns like Bath, Leamington, and Brighton, and scores on the continent, noteable parts of which have had something of it for generations past, and hold it still.[8]

But in none of these cases, except perhaps that of one of the suburban quarters of Edinburgh, were the natural conditions nearly as unfavorable for the more common manner of town building, and at the same time as favorable for a permanent, highly picturesque neighborhood, combining the conveniences of the town with the charms and healthfulness of the country.[9]

It is not to be doubted that the promontory may, throughout its whole extent, be so laid out and occupied as to have an interest and attractiveness far excelling in its kind that of any other locality in America; nor that, if this result can be secured, it will hold great numbers of wealthy people within the city who would otherwise go away from it to find homes to suit them, and will draw many to it from without the city. Its effect will, in this respect, be similar to that which has been experienced from the Central Park, but with this difference, that the gain to the city will be in conditions the cost of which will have been mainly defrayed by the voluntary and self-directed contributions of the private owners of the land, not from the public treasury.[10]

It may be questioned whether, even in a locality as yet so remote from dense building and so rugged in its topography, the demand for land for various other purposes will not, in time, crowd out all rural and picturesque elements, and whether, for this reason, it would be prudent to lay it out with exclusive reference to suburban uses? All that can be said in reply, is that thus far in the history of other great cities there is nothing to sustain such a doubt.

After a certain degree of density has been attained, the proportion of people who are disposed and able to live under suburban conditions, relatively to those who may be content or obliged to live under rigidly urban conditions, becomes larger the larger the town, but there is yet no city in the world so large that it has not luxurious suburban quarters much nearer to its centre than is the promontory, even to the outer part of New York as now densely built. London has fairly grown around and stretched beyond some clusters of fine old suburban residences without seriously disturbing them. There are private gardens in which the town is almost lost sight of at not many minutes walk from Hyde Park.[11] Within a range from the heart of Old London of less than one-third the distance of Riverdale from the City Hall,[12] there are hundreds of acres of gardens and villa and cottage grounds; and, with a city adding much more annually to her population than New York, costly villas are every year built, and villa neighborhoods are steadily enlarged without becoming less distinctly suburban in character.

Districts of villas exist and others are forming also but a little way from dense parts of Paris. Under Haussmann, roads were laid out expressly for villas closely adjoining the grand route between the Champs Elysées and the Bois de Boulogne, every site upon which is now occupied by a semi-rural residence.[13] Other and extensive districts of the same class have been laid out since with confident reference to permanence as an integral element of the attractions of the city.

V.

THE ADVANTAGES OFFERED BY THE PROPOSITION TO THE CITY.

It is reasonable to infer that New York will have such quarters. It remains a question whether they shall be formed by a co-operation of public and private work, or by private enterprise in making the best of unsuitable public arrangements. The importance of the question will be recognized if it is considered what a difference there would now be in the attractiveness, and consequently in the wealth of the city, if twenty-five years ago, when it was quite practicable, Fifth avenue from Madison Square[14] to the Central Park, had been laid out fifty feet wider than it is, with slightly better grades, a pad for riding horses, broad sidewalks and an avenue of trees.

It will cost much less to lay out and prepare the promontory admirably as a permanent suburb than to prepare it tolerably for any other use.

A given sum expended upon it for the purpose will have important results much sooner than if expended for any other.

All other purposes which the city needs to have in view can be provided for at much less cost and much more conveniently in other parts of its present territory.

Treated as a suburb, the district is likely to make larger contributions to the city treasury, and to begin to contribute to it in important amount sooner than if treated in any other way.

What is meant by treating the district as a suburb is, that the development of a distinctly suburban and picturesque character should everywhere be kept frankly in view as a source of wealth, and that the roads should be adapted to a population living less densely, and with which pleasure driving and walking are to be, relatively to heavy teaming, more important than in the streets of the compact city.

If the policy which has been indicated does not, upon reflection, fully commend itself to the Commission, the plan now submitted is not entitled to further examination. It is professedly adapted to no other.

If, however, the soundness of the policy is accepted, the manner in which the district should be laid out, in order to its success, remains to be considered.

VI.
The Question of Laying Out a Specially Picturesque and Convenient Suburb.

The custom of laying out roads in the outskirts of cities only upon right lines, under any circumstances which leave it possible to do so, is so strongly fixed in our country that the Commission cannot entertain the idea of abandoning it before carefully weighing what is to be gained and lost by doing so. It should remember, however, that the custom is largely due to the disposition of land owners, to act on the imagination, by showing lots which, as represented on paper, differ in no respect from the most valuable in the city, and thus to feed the pernicious propensity which prevails among the ignorant for gambling on small means under the name of speculation in real estate.

Again, it is to be remembered that it is not customary to think of the laying out of any part of a city as a matter in the smallest degree of esthetic design; but, if the policy of carrying on a series of constructions in a manner sympathetic with picturesque landscape effects has any claims to adoption by the Commission, it necessarily involves a serious application, in however humble a way, of the laws and the spirit of art.

The more tangible and weighty advantage to be urged in favor of keeping as nearly as practicable to straight lines of road, is one commonly expressed under one of the following specifications:

1st. That of the comparative ease and simplicity of the business of laying out the roads.

2d. That of the comparative rapidity and convenience with which surveyors' measurements and calculations are made when dealing with straight lines.

3d. That of the greater convenience of a straight front when land is to be divided or described with a view to sale or mortgage.

It is not questioned that these advantages should be waived in the case of very difficult topography, such as must often occur on the promontory. (It will be observed that each of the six plans[15] before the Commission proposes a considerable extent of curved line). It apparently follows that whether the straight street should yield to the winding road at any point, when it is otherwise desirable, is, at the worst, a question of employing surveyors competent to deal with curved lines. No plan has been proposed to the Commission for laying out the promontory, under which a local surveyor to whom curved lines were a serious matter, could honestly earn his living. The whole amount of the class of expenses in question, under the most difficult circumstances, would be relatively inconsiderable, and if any essential, permanent advantage to the community is at stake, regard for them should not be allowed to obstruct the very best arrangement that can be devised.

The third specification above refers to the facility which straightness in a street gives for laying off properties in lots the dimensions of which may be expressed in two numbers, and to the convenience of the custom, to which this advantage is essential, of dividing property for sale in a series of parallelograms of uniform length of frontage, as in the case of city lots. As to this custom, it is to be remembered that if it should be generally adhered to on the promontory it would not affect the desired result favorably, but otherwise, for this reason.

In broken and rolling ground, and especially in rocky ground, sites for houses can be well chosen only with an intelligent consideration of local circumstances. If a hundred lots are to be laid off, each one hundred feet wide, and with the dividing lines all at right angles with the street line, in many parts of the promontory the dividing lines will so occur, that on not half the lots will an entirely satisfactory site for a building be found, and, on several, building will be impracticable until after much labor has been given to transform the natural surface. Let the same property, on the other hand, be laid out with a judicious adjustment of lines to the local conditions, and an equal number of lots may be made of it, each offering an admirable and conveniently approached site. Of course, however, they will vary in size.

As to the general attractiveness of the region, and as to the total or average value of all its real estate, there are certain well established principles by which men of taste throughout the civilized world, when living among rural or even rus-urban conditions are almost invariably guided when laying out the private carriage approaches to their houses.* The motives growing out of well established experience which enforce this practice, apply equally in the case of a common approach to two houses as to one, and if to two, equally to twenty or to two hundred. Though the propriety may be questioned of advancing toward a house indirectly when it is situated on a plain, there is no question that in a hilly country the principles referred to always lead to the use in roads of winding courses in greater or less degree of correspondence with the natural surface.

VII.
The Economical Advantages of the Proposition.

The comparative economy of straight and winding roads is partly a question of what is desirable under given circumstances as to grades. The

---

*Exceptions occur when the approach is short, crosses flat ground, and can be seen from end to end in one symmetrical composition with the house; conditions to which there will be none corresponding in the roads of the promontory.

shortest line between two points is not always that which can be passed over at the least cost of time or in wear and tear.

A carriage load that requires two horses and a given strength of harness to be drawn over a road with grades by which one foot in elevation is overcome in ten feet of distance, as in the case of some of the present roads of the promontory, can be as easily and safely drawn by one horse and with a harness one-half lighter on a road in which twenty-four feet is allowed for overcoming the same elevation. If a man in haste at a given point wishes to drive a horse of ordinary quality with a light wagon to another point 180 feet higher on a hillside, he can do so in shorter time upon a curved road 800 yards in length than upon a straight road of 600 yards.

If the hillsides of the promontory are to be occupied chiefly by families in comfortable circumstances it is evident that for the great majority of occasions a road carried between two points, one at a greater elevation than another, upon a curve regulated by the curve of the hillside along which it will be passing, though longer horizontally, will be passed over in shorter time, and with less wear and tear, than a straight road between the same points. The straight road might, because it was the shortest, cost less for construction. The probabilities are, that ploughing straight through whatever was in the way, it would cost more. But, whether so or not, in running along an alternately swelling and retreating surface, the more unswerving the course the more it would be necessary in grading the road to cut through the protuberances and to fill across the depressions.

From this consideration it follows, that unless a level can be kept, which in this district it rarely can for any distance, access will be had from a road laid on natural lines to adjoining building sites with much less violence and at less cost, on an average, than it can from a straight road, and, again, that the amount of walling, sloping, turfing or other operations necessary to a tidy road-side, or the attractive presentation of the adjoining properties, will be less with the winding than the straight road.

VIII.
THE IMMEDIATE CONVENIENCE OF THE PROPOSITION.

One advantage to be gained by adopting winding and picturesque roads, as far as conveniently practicable, rather than straight and formal streets, remains to be suggested.

Formal streets, especially when far extended on a straight line at an even grade, their every line of curb, sidewalk and lamp-posts, being truly set, and when bounded by continuous walls of stately houses, have an imposing effect, and satisfy good taste. But in streets which, by alternate cuttings and embankments, are carried, here through woods, there across open fields, here are flanked by the ragged face of blasted ledges or raw banks of earth, there by a varied prospect, even when fine houses are occasionally built fronting upon them, straightness gives no dignity and expresses little but incongruity and imperfection.

To make such a street tolerable to the eye it needs from the beginning as perfect lines and as perfect surfaces in its curbs, gutters and lamp-posts, pavement and flagging, as the densely occupied street of the city. If a cheap temporary wheel-way is made in it, or temporary sidewalks, any deviation from a straight line, or even any short flexions of grade in them are unsatisfactory. If trees are set between the walks and the wheel-way they seem out of place, and add to a general expression of untidiness, incompleteness, disorder and shiftlessness, unless they are evenly spaced in continuous lines parallel with all the other features. The slightest disarrangement of such a road, scattered patches of grass and weeds, a sucker growth of trees and bushes on the bordering banks, even the general heaving outward and inward of the fences that form its outlines, all claim attention as defects and shortcomings from what is attempted.

Nothing of this is true of roads laid out with a natural motive. The wheel-way may have a somewhat variable width, as economy shall require; its grade may dip and rise within a hundred yards; the courses of the walks may vary a little from that of the wheel-way, may rise a little in a cutting or fall a little on an embankment, may rise on one side and fall on the other; wild plants may spring up, here and there, in random tufts, or, again, the roadsides be all filled out (as some in the district now are), with a thick growth of low brambles, ferns, asters, gentians, golden-rods; roadside trees may be irregularly spaced and of various sizes and species, great opposite small, ash over against maple, elm bending to oak; fine old trees may be left standing, and, to save them, the wheel-way carried a little to the right or left, or slightly raised or lowered. It may be desirable, simply for convenience sake, to go to the expense of avoiding such conditions, but, as a matter of taste, they are far from blemishes; they add to other charms of picturesqueness, and they are a concession to nature, tending to an effect not of incongruity and incompleteness, but of consistent and happy landscape composition.

Hence, roads on natural lines, which may be so far worked, at moderate cost, as to meet the ordinary requirements of convenience of a considerable community, will much sooner and more uninterruptedly give results of a presentable, comely and attractive character. In this manner, indeed, the most agreeable roads in the world have been made.

IX.
GENERAL REQUIREMENTS.

Adopting the general conclusion which has thus been sustained, there is still much room for difference of judgment as to the location of roads, their breadth and grades.

The existing divisions of land, the positions of houses, of fences, of

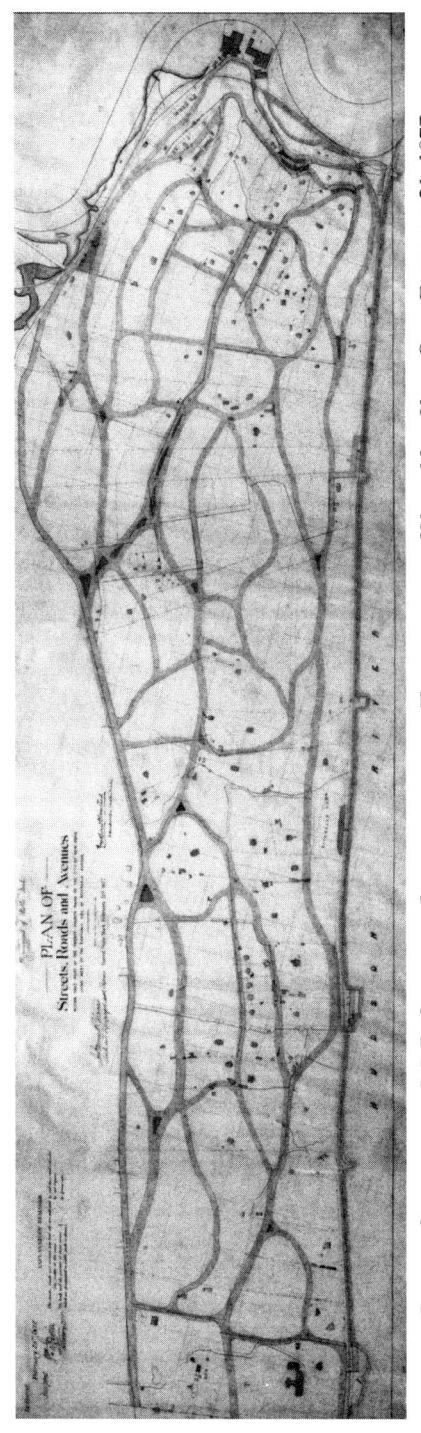

Plan by Olmsted and J. J. R. Croes for Riverdale area of Twenty-fourth Ward, New York City, February 21, 1877

roads, have been determined without regard to such an occupation of the district as is now to be prepared for. Individual interests, based on existing arrangements, must necessarily be, in greater or less degree, at issue with those general and lasting interests of the public of which the Commission is the guardian. There must be limits within which the latter are so far paramount that not the least compromise between the two is admissible. To keep on the safe side of those limits, it has appeared to the undersigned best to perfect a conclusion, in the first place, as to what roads are necessary as routes, or links in routes, of extended, general and unquestionably desirable, in distinction from local and limited, communication. This they have done in the plan now presented, except that they have adopted the judgment of the Board, as heretofore indicated, on three points not materially affecting the general design.[16]

X.
By-Roads.

If the Commission should substantially adopt the system, and afterwards think proper to consult the judgment and wishes of each land-owner as to cross roads or by-roads, it can do so with confidence, that no conclusions to which it may then be led can be seriously detrimental to the general interests. Any one of the divisions left by the plan might even be subdivided, for example, by rectilinear roads without destroying the consistency and harmony or lessening the convenience, of the main system. If, on the other hand, such minor roads within any division should, in order not to mar a series of natural building sites, be made very indirect and circuitous, the worst result would be a slight inconvenience to a few residents within the division and those calling upon them, which, to these, would be compensated by the greater beauty and local convenience of the buildings. The public in general, keeping to the primary roads, would suffer no inconvenience.

It is believed, too, that the proprietors will be much better able to form a sound judgment as to the requirements of their own interests in the minor roads if they are allowed to become familiar with the proposed general system, and with the theory which it represents of the interest of the district as a whole.

XI.
Requirements of Detail. Planting Arrangements.

It should be recognized that to carry out a natural or informal system judiciously, so that a good share of its possible advantages may be surely realized, much study of detail is required. Both for economy and beauty local circumstances must be diligently consulted, and the treatment of the road adapted to them. Variety in this respect should be sought, not avoided. Every turn should bring something of fresh interest into view within the road as well as beyond it.

In this detail very well-considered provisions should be made for road-side planting. Ordinarily in the suburbs of rapidly growing American towns, trees are planted most injudiciously and wastefully, ill-chosen as to species for the locality, ill-placed, ill-planted, and with no suitable provision for a continuous, healthy growth. Science is yearly placing a higher estimate on the sanitary value of street trees. Paris now maintains a great nursery with a view to the systematic supply of all the city with this means of dissipating malaria and infection. London is just entering upon a similar duty. The matter of supplying New York streets with trees has been much debated by her sanitarians.[17] The difficulty lies in the fact, that the street arrangements of the city being all designed with no reference to the purpose, the introduction of trees, with the conditions necessary to success, would be very costly and inconvenient. In laying out a new system, especially for a quarter designed to offer a beautiful and healthful relief to the more general conditions of city life, this requirement should be thoroughly well attended to.

The tracing submitted represents the outline of a general plan, the adoption of which is recommended subject to such slight adjustments, immaterial to the essential design, as may be found desirable.[18]

A drawing is also exhibited which will serve to indicate more fully the purposes in view.[19]

Respectfully,

FRED. LAW OLMSTED,
Landscape Architect.
J. JAMES R. CROES,
Civil and Topographical Engineer.

The text presented here is from "Document No. 72, Part II," in New York (City), Department of Public Parks, *Minutes*, December 20, 1876.

1. That is, the elevated district which overlooks the Hudson River north of Spuyten Duyvil and south of the city boundary with Yonkers.
2. Since 1869 the Board of Commissioners of the Central Park and, after May 1870, the Department of Public Parks, had charge of preliminary surveys of districts subsequently annexed to New York City from Westchester County. With the topographical surveys completed, plans for the street system were commenced in 1872. The board contracted with Thomas C. Cornell in February of that year to prepare a plan for streets in the southwest parts of the town of Kingsbridge, later known as Riverdale. He did not complete the plan and William H. Grant, superintending engineer of Central Park during its construction and department civil and topographical engineer between September 1871 and June 1874, took over the task with the assistance of consulting

civil engineer John J. Serrell. On January 29, 1873, the board approved a plan signed by Grant but shortly thereafter it ordered the plan revised with the advice of property owners in the area, one of whom even submitted his own plan. Grant presented a second plan in October 1873 which was revised again, submitted to Serrell and approved by the board in late December. When Grant became chief engineer of the bureau of construction for the new wards in June 1874, his successor as civil and topographical engineer, General George S. Greene, undertook new plans for the Riverdale district. The board considered Greene's new plan for the area on November 12, 1874, but in January 1875 allowed Grant to reconcile it with his own earlier plan of December 1873. Grant's hybrid plan was not taken up by the board until late April 1875 and was not approved. By then William R. Martin had convinced the board to consider yet another approach to laying out the area, which resulted in the plans and reports of Olmsted and Croes (*City Record*, Jan. 5, 1874, pp. 9–10; *Papers of FLO*, 3: 253; "Document No. 30," in DPP, *Minutes*, Nov. 28, 1871, pp. 11, 38–42; "Document No. 45," June 25, 1873, pp. 5–6, 24–31; "Document No. 74," in DPP, *Minutes*, Feb. 28, 1877, pp. 2–26; DPP, *Minutes*, Jan. 29, 1873, pp. 651–52; ibid., Feb. 5, 1873, p. 663; ibid., Oct. 16, 1873, pp. 350–51; ibid., Dec. 15, 1873, p. 450; ibid., Dec. 23, 1873, p. 465; ibid., May 10, 1874, pp. 42–43; ibid., June 3, 1874, pp. 71–72; ibid., Nov. 12, 1874, p. 344; ibid., Jan. 12, 1875, p. 446; ibid., April 21, 1875, p. 665).

3. That is, since November 1875.
4. FLO and J. J. R. Croes to William R. Martin, November 15, 1876, above.
5. Since the late eighteenth century, the Riverdale district had proved an attractive area for country estates. In 1847 actor Edwin Forrest purchased fifty-five acres in the far northwest corner of the district and built a Gothic castle there which was completed in 1852. In 1857 his estate was purchased by the Sisters of Charity, a benevolent organization of Vincentian Sisters whose original convent and seminary, Mount St. Vincent, had recently been incorporated into Central Park. They built a large administration building and opened the new Academy of Mount Saint Vincent in 1859, presently known as the College of Mount Saint Vincent-On-Hudson (J. Thomas Scharf, *History of Westchester County, New York*, 2 vols. [Philadelphia, 1886], 1: 759–60; Donald M. Reynolds, *Fonthill Castle: Paradigm of Hudson-River Gothic* [Riverdale, N.Y., 1976], pp. 12–23; *Papers of FLO*, 3: 231).
6. That is, from the lower East Side neighborhoods near Tompkins Square (FLO to Henry G. Stebbins, Dec. 3, 1875, n. 5, above).
7. Along with limiting through streets between a suburban district and its town to ensure seclusion, Olmsted in 1860 had recommended English crescents to one of the commissioners charged with laying out streets in the Fort Washington district, immediately south of Riverdale. He and Calvert Vaux served as landscape architects to the commission, which produced no report before its duties were taken over in 1865 by the Board of Commissioners of the Central Park (FLO to Henry H. Elliot, Aug. 27, 1860 [*Papers of FLO*, 3: 263–67]; BCCP, *Tenth Annual Report* [1867], p. 125).
8. Bath developed as England's premier health resort by the early eighteenth century and, besides its famous Royal Crescent, featured dozens of residential crescents and terraces built starting in the 1760s on the steep hills behind the town. Brighton was also a popular resort at this time, and by the 1840s its terraces, squares, and crescents stretched along the shore for four miles. Leamington, noted for its saline springs and baths, was not popular as a resort until the nineteenth century. Olmsted visited Bath on his trip to England in 1850, and Brighton and Leamington (where his friend Alfred T. Field lived) in 1856 (Mark Girouard, *Cities and People: A Social and Architectural History* [New Haven, Conn., 1985], pp. 196–98; Laura Wood Roper, *FLO: A Biography of Frederick Law Olmsted* [Baltimore, Md., 1973], pp. 67–76, 113–19, 146–48; *EB*; *Papers of FLO*, 2: 385, 484; ibid., 6: 432).

APRIL 1876–DECEMBER 1876

9. Olmsted is referring to the New Town at Edinburgh, Scotland, first laid out in 1767 by James Craig on an elevated district north of town. Nineteenth-century landlords added dozens of crescents, terraces, and circles with views of the city on one side and the Firth of Forth on the other. Olmsted visited Edinburgh in 1850 and 1856 (M. Girouard, *Cities and People*, pp. 231–32; L. W. Roper, *FLO, A Biography*, p. 75; *Papers of FLO*, 2: 381).
10. As early as 1865 Olmsted had drawn attention to how Central Park kept wealthy residents from moving away from New York City and attracted new residents. William R. Martin presented similar arguments in March 1875 when he convinced the park board to consider new plans for the annexed district. He noted that in the previous decade the population increase of suburban counties adjacent to New York City outstripped that of the city itself. An attractive, well-planned suburban quarter inside New York would keep some of those in search of desirable living quarters from moving away and would substantially increase the city's tax base. Here Olmsted adds that private expenditures on improving houses and grounds in the area would benefit the city (through increased value of real estate and tax income) without public expense (Frederick Law Olmsted, "The Project of a Great Park for San Francisco," Aug. 4, 1865 [*Papers of FLO*, 5: 427–28]; "Document No. 64," in DPP, *Minutes*, March 5, 1875, pp. 28–30; "Document No. 65," in ibid., March 30, 1875, pp. 4–5, 24–25).
11. The neighborhoods to the south and east of Hyde Park, one of the parks in London's West End, were laid out as suburbs beginning in the 1820s. Some of them, such as Mayfair, Belgravia, and others, remained intact to the late-nineteenth century. In addition to his visits of 1850 and 1856, Olmsted spent several weeks in late 1859 studying London's parks (Donald J. Olsen, *The Growth of Victorian London* [New York, 1976], pp. 162–64; *Papers of FLO*, 3: 234–35).
12. That is, about four miles.
13. Olmsted is referring to the Avenue de l'Impératice, now the Avenue Foch. Completed under the direction of Prefect of the Seine Georges Eugène Haussmann in 1856, the avenue was bordered by hundred-foot-wide strips planted with lawn and trees, which were adjoined by roads serving residential villas. The width of the combined elements was 460 feet (*Papers of FLO*, 6: 411, 425–26; David H. Pinkney, *Napoleon III and the Rebuilding of Paris* [Princeton, 1958], pp. 98–99).
14. Madison Square, opened by the Common Council in 1847, is located at the intersection of Broadway, Fifth Avenue, and 23rd Street (C. Lockwood, *Manhattan Moves Uptown*, p. 210).
15. That is, the five plans considered by the commission since 1872, plus the one by Olmsted and Croes submitted with the present report (see n. 2 above).
16. To help preserve the district's residential character, Olmsted and Croes provided no thoroughfares for heavy teaming or fast driving, nor any short-cuts across the district, as they noted near the beginning of the report (see p. 253, above).
17. As early as 1861 Olmsted had called attention to the extensive use of street trees along the boulevards opened up in Paris by Haussmann and Jean-Charles-Adolphe Alphand. A member of the American Public Health Association since its 1872 founding, Olmsted discussed before that organization and elsewhere the theory that trees, by removing excess ground water and arresting airborne malaria with their foliage, were important features of a healthful urban environment. In 1875 he reported that Paris had 117 miles of shaded boulevards, New York only 8 miles (F. L. Olmsted, "Park" [*Papers of FLO*, 3: 348–49]; Stephen Smith, "Historical Sketch of the American Public Health Association," in American Public Health Association, *Public Health Reports and Papers* 5 [1879], pp. xiv–xv, 252; FLO to Edward Clark, May 23, 1879, n. 2, below; FLO to Manton Marble, Dec. 16, 1873, in *The Druggist* 11 [1873]: 185; DPP, *Statistical Report of the Landscape Architect, 31st December, 1873*, p. 42).

18. In February 1877 the department publicly exhibited the Riverdale plan, which was prepared with the assistance of landscape architect Jacob Weidenmann, for the review of residents in the district. A delegation of residents approved it in late February 1877. Over the dissenting vote of Henry G. Stebbins, the board approved the plan on February 28, 1877 (DPP, *Minutes*, Dec. 15, 1876, pp. 476–77; ibid., Feb. 21, 1877, pp. 625–26; ibid., Feb. 28, 1877, pp. 645–47).
19. The editors have not located any such drawing.

To Thomas M. Lanahan[1]

New York, December 23rd 1876.

T. M. Lanahan, Esq.,
Chairman of the Commissioners of the Washington
Monument Grounds; Baltimore.
Dear Sir:—
 I received the revised map of your grounds through Commissioner Garrett[2] on the 15th inst. and have since given some study to the question of their plan. I have an idea of a design upon which, before I undertake drawings, I should like your judgment and to introduce it I shall indicate the course of reflection through which it has come to me.
 The areas to be laid out have been hitherto simply reserves of space by which the monument was kept open to view. That they might be neat and seemly they have been graded each to a plane surface, coated with turf and enclosed by an iron fence. Nothing could be better adapted to its purpose than this simple and consistent treatment.
 The design of the monument to which the grounds are thus made auxiliary belongs to the last rather than to the present century and of the period which it thus represents the country has no better architectural memorial. There is not and there never will be another monument to Washington more accordant with his own tastes.[3] Faulty in conception, according to the best art judgment of our day, it is undeniably stately and impressive. No other American city holds an heirloom of equal value nor one which is as sure to command the veneration of posterity.
 While the grounds in their present condition are consistent with the monument and, as a part of its apparel, meet every requirement of good taste, they are small in area, narrow and not well adapted in form to be used as public pleasure grounds.
 I confess that in view of all these considerations I have shrunk from the duty of advising any considerable departure from their present design and

that I doubt if any can be made by which something of their value as with reference to the monument will not be lost. But considering their central position in the city, the large densely built and populous area in which they are situated and the lack of public squares in Baltimore;[4] considering also that they cannot long be left open as they are without becoming desolate places, the demand for a change of arrangement seems justified.

The considerations I have indicated nevertheless make it necessary that in attempting any material change, something shall be had in view of more than ordinary consequence; something which shall be of permanent and substantial value, thoroughly creditable to the city and likely to outlast, with the monument itself, many changes of fashion.

If laid out in what may be described as a common, modest, inexpensive way, such as would be suitable if they were designed for the use of a respectable family, or even a score or two of respectable families, the result would not prove satisfactory even temporarily. In the first place gardens of that character, in the midst of a public place and in direct association with dignified public structures, would seem puerile, paltry and fussy and, in the second place, they would be actually cramped and inconvenient; they would consequently be ill used and a shabby and forlorn aspect would become inevitable.

If, on the other hand, a broad simple arrangement should be attempted consisting of a spacious alley extending from end to end of each plot, bordered by symmetrical strips of turf and set in the midst of a formal avenue of trees, the grounds would assume a more intimate and important relation to the monument than they have at present, namely that of exterior halls or grand approaches.

This is the idea presented in the report which you sent me of a committee of the Common Council, in which the removal of the slight iron fences and the separation of the whole arrangement from the wheel ways of the adjoining streets by a low wall is justly recognized as a necessary condition of its success.[5]

It is practicable to carry out this proposition in such a manner as to produce a good and dignified result, but to obtain a sufficient impression of unity of design between the monument and its approaches it would be necessary that the walls and their copings, the edgings of the walks and such steps, ramps, piers and terminals as there might be found occasion for should be large in scale and of an effective, massive and enduring character, commensurate with that of the monument.

Although this theory of design has had your provisional approval I am not quite satisfied to set to work upon it for the reason, among others, that I am sure that the result relatively to the public enjoyment of it would seem to have been too costly. There would be, for instance, nearly 3000 linear feet of the low enclosing wall alone to be built of which a large share of the expense would be under ground.

Washington Memorial and adjoining squares, Baltimore, c. 1862

The appearance of the four approaches would be very much the same and in each case would be monotonous, formal and stern rather than cheerful or entertaining.

To relieve this aspect fountains might be introduced, as has been suggested,[6] but they also would have to be kept in general accord with the ruling motive of dignity and grandeur which would involve simplicity and sobriety.

There would also be an infelicity in advancing by four similar alleys toward an object of which the crowning feature would face toward but one. The approach to the front should be broader, but would in fact be narrower than those toward the sides of the statue.[7]

I would not say that all those objections cannot be overcome so far as to produce a result in which they will not be seriously felt, but if some theory of design could be hit upon which would practically lend itself more readily either to gaiety or to some pleasing poetic association further removed from the hard, common-place prose of the streets it would be preferable.

What is desirable in this respect is a general theme of which, to borrow a term from music, each of the four plots should present a distinct movement, each movement admitting a contrast in detail with all the others.

It would cost more, I judge, considerably, to carry out the idea to which, as I said, these reflections have brought me, than that which you have had in mind, but the result would I am confident be much more than proportionally valuable.

What I would like to do is this:

The monument is at a distance of nearly a hundred feet from the nearest part of the grounds to be laid out and is divided from them by public streets. If the trees, now obviously misplaced, and the fences, at the ends of the grounds nearest the monument were removed, (as they would be in carrying out the idea of the straight alleys), the imagination would bridge the intervening space and connect the grounds with the monument. If, on the other hand, in the place of the present straight fence there should be a distinct architectural line of masonry, then, in looking toward the monument from within the grounds, it would seem to stand, as in fact it does, upon a broad, level, central plateau or terrace. The grounds would then appear much more distinctly detached and would be more readily regarded apart from the monument and their treatment might be much more complex in its interior detail without incongruity and without serious injury to the effect of the monument.

As the proposed walls would not be seen together it would not be necessary to have regard for symmetry of arrangement in determining their position. I would, then, place that on the east side at such a distance from the monument that the principal doors of the Peabody Institute and the church opposite would give fairly upon the terrace and that on the south side at a still greater distance.[8] As the natural surface of the ground falls away on both these sides, the base of the walls would be several feet below the base of the monument; I would build them up to an equal height with it and make the inter-

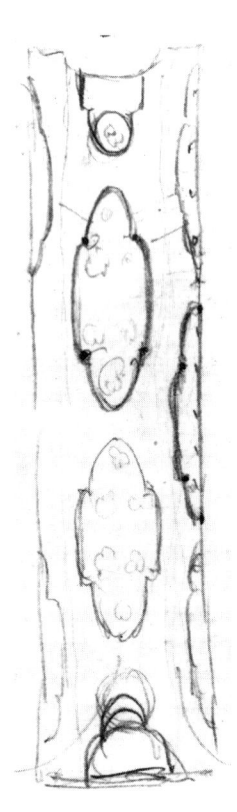

OLMSTED'S SKETCH FOR NORTH SQUARE (WINTER) ADJOINING WASHINGTON
MONUMENT IN BALTIMORE, C. DECEMBER 1876

mediate spaces level by embankment. The walls would then need to be surmounted by a pierced parapet or balustrade.

On the garden side of each of the structures thus crudely indicated I would have a wall fountain and the walls about its issue should be formed with a view to sculptural decoration in relief. The design in each case should be significant of one of the four seasons. Then, through each of the gardens below I would have a recurrence, in some more or less distinct form, of the special motive of the fountain at its head. I do not mean emblematically but in such manner that according as it should be spring, summer, autumn or winter, the visitor should find in one or the other specially grateful and appropriate conditions.[9] For example, I would have one fountain framed in Cyclopean masonry,[10] to be run over by ivy and let the garden below it be adapted to and take its character largely from evergreen shrubbery. The frame of another should simulate a cool grotto and the garden below it be provided with shaded walks; a third should indicate harvest bounty, and the garden below it rural

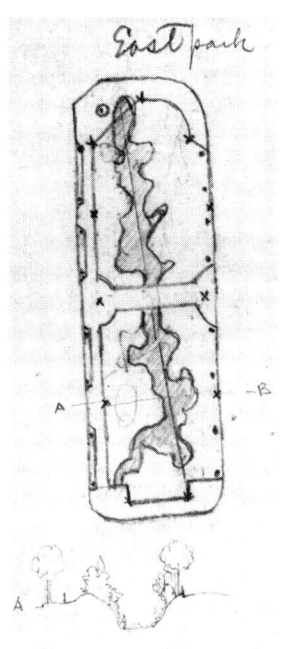

Olmsted's sketch for East square (Summer) adjoining Washington Monument in Baltimore, c. December 1876

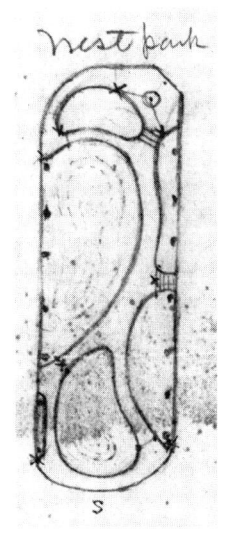

Olmsted's sketch for West square (Autumn) adjoining Washington Monument in Baltimore, c. December 1876

OLMSTED'S SKETCH FOR SOUTH SQUARE (SPRING) ADJOINING WASHINGTON
MONUMENT IN BALTIMORE, C. DECEMBER 1876

quietness with the bright hues of the foliage and flowers of the ripening year.[11] In the fourth fountain, placed lower than the others on the south side, the waters from all the rest should unite and burst out again and again, and in coverts sheltered from the winds and open to the sun there should be the earliest bloom and verdure of the year.

Such a general theme could, if there were breadth enough, be best worked out by a plan which a little below the fountains would run into the natural style, but I doubt that this could be well done in spaces so narrow and I should probably rather aim to secure something of the quaint character of the old fashioned flower garden, always maintaining, however, largeness of scale and convenience of passage and looking more to turf and shrubs for decoration than to florist's materials.

It would be a month's work at least to fully digest this suggestion and define it in drawings so that a trustworthy estimate of the cost of realizing it

could be made. I hardly think it would be worthwhile to undertake it however with a less sum in view as likely to be required, than $50,000.[12]
Respectfully

Fred Law Olmsted.
Landscape Architect

The text presented here is from a document in a clerk's hand with the closing and signature by Olmsted.

1. Thomas M. Lanahan, a prominent Baltimore attorney, in 1875 had served on a commission that asked the mayor and city council of Baltimore to appropriate $40,000 to renovate the four squares surrounding the Washington Monument at Charles and Monument streets. The council took no action until October 1876, when it approved $12,000 for the project and asked the mayor to appoint a new three-member commission to oversee it. The mayor approved the scheme and appointed Lanahan chairman of the commission. By late October 1876 Lanahan had asked Olmsted to advise the commission, and in early November sent him a plat of the ground and the first commission's report (*The Biographical Cyclopedia of Representative Men of Maryland and District of Columbia* [Baltimore, 1879], pp. 35–36; "The Report of the Commission for the Improvement of the Squares at Mount Vernon and Washington Place," [c. June 24, 1875]; Thomas M. Lanahan to FLO, Oct. 25, 1876, in B124: #2401, OAR/LC; ibid., Nov. 2, 1876; *Journal of Proceedings of the Second Branch City Council of Baltimore, at the Sessions of 1875–76* [Baltimore, 1876], pp. 430–32).
2. Robert Garrett (1847–1896), banker and railroad executive, served on the commission appointed in October 1876. As son of the president of the Baltimore and Ohio Railroad, John W. Garrett, he was at this time head of one its subsidiary lines, the Valley Railroad of Virginia, and helped in its merger with the larger line and in the development of associated telegraph networks. Before Olmsted composed this preliminary report, the two Garretts invited him to dinner, where their offer to pay for fountains and sculpture on the squares persuaded him to include these features in his plan. (Lanahan had told him that the commission had abandoned the idea of including fountains because it could not afford them.) Although the multiple fountains described in the report were not built, the Garretts did pay for a fountain and a bronze statue placed on the squares (*NCAB*, 18:4; FLO to Robert Garrett, Dec. 23, 1876; Thomas M. Lanahan to FLO, Nov. 2, 1876, in B124: #2401, OAR/LC; J. Thomas Scharf, *History of Baltimore City and County* [Philadelphia, 1881], p. 280).
3. The monument, designed by Robert Mills and completed in 1829, consists of a 160-foot high Doric marble column topped by a heroic statue of George Washington (J. T. Scharf, *Baltimore City*, p. 266).
4. At the time of this report Baltimore had at least ten public squares within its limits, but those surrounding the Washington Monument were the only ones in its central district (F. Klemm, *Map of the City of Baltimore* [Baltimore, 1875]; J. T. Scharf, *Baltimore City*, pp. 279–81).
5. Olmsted is referring to the design proposed in the June 1875 "Report of the Commission for the Improvement of the Squares at Mount Vernon and Washington Place," signed by Lanahan and four others (see n. 1 above).
6. The commissioners who reported in 1875 proposed that "handsome fountains" be erected on the outside ends of each of the four squares surrounding the monument.

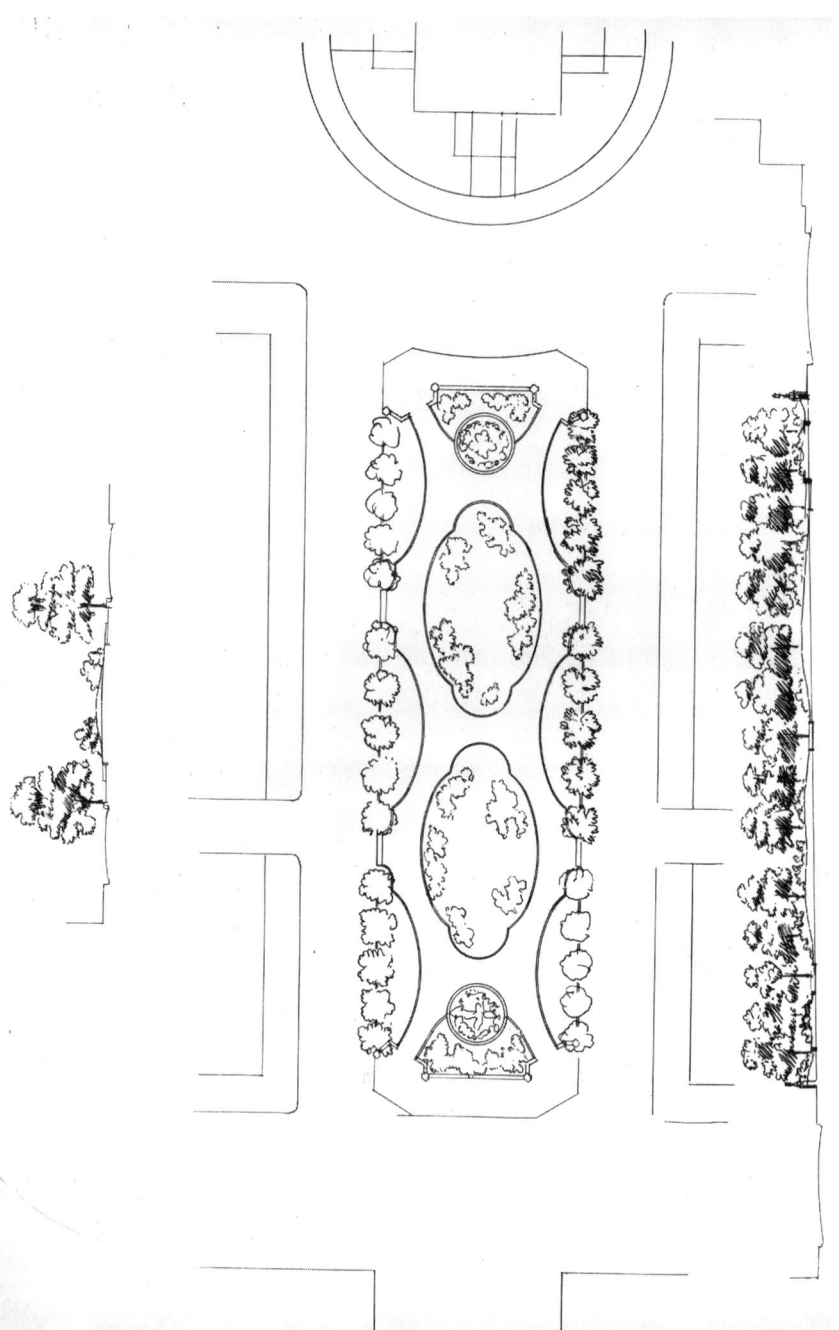

Olmsted's revised plan for North Square (Winter) adjoining Washington Monument, Baltimore, c. March 1877

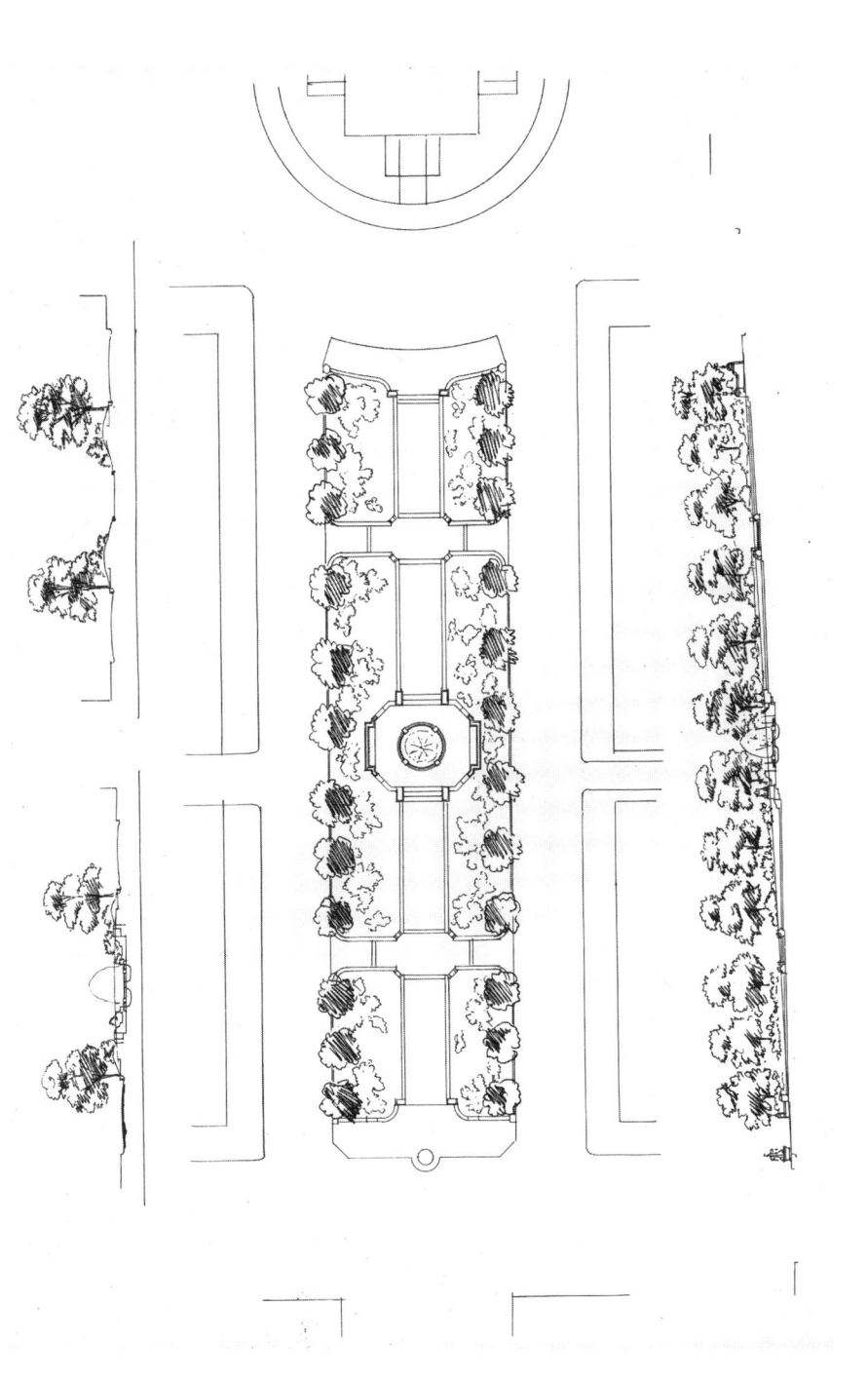

Olmsted's revised plan for South square (Spring) adjoining Washington Monument, Baltimore, c. March 1877

7. The statue of Washington atop the monument faces toward the south square, which is the narrowest.
8. That is, the east and south walls were to be removed further from the monument than those on the north and west. The Peabody Institute, a free library, music academy, and art gallery founded in 1857 by the American philanthropist George Peabody (1795–1869), was located on the southeast corner of Charles and Monument streets. The Mount Vernon Methodist Episcopal church stood on the northeast corner of the intersection (*DAB*; J. T. Scharf, *Baltimore City*, p. 266).
9. In his August 1876 plan for Tompkins Square in New York City, Olmsted had introduced a sunken dell and a combination arbor/grotto with the intention, similar to his proposal here, that each would offer particular advantages according to the season (FLO to William R. Martin, Aug. 9, 1876, above).
10. An ancient style of masonry in which the stones are of large size and irregular shape (*OED*).
11. Olmsted further described the intended effect of the autumnal garden in a letter to Robert Garrett dated the same day as the report published here. The treatment of the space was to be

> rich and suggestive — embodying the ideas of harvesting the ripe fruits of labor and of plenty, bounty, liberality and copious outflow. Much could be done in this way by sculpture in low relief and subdued in detail, at comparatively moderate expense. There would be occasion for short flights of stairs in order to pass on the right & left between the terrace & the garden and whole affair could be worked up into a striking architectural composition.

Olmsted wrote this passage to explain how the garden would provide a foreground for a statue of George Peabody that Robert Garrett and his father proposed to donate and to place opposite the Peabody Institute. The garden, Olmsted observed, "would be complete without the statue but would acquire a new and I think a happy significance with it" (FLO to Robert Garrett, Dec. 23, 1876).

12. In January 1877 Commissioners Lanahan and Garrett expressed admiration for Olmsted's proposed treatment of the squares but since it would cost too much they asked him to prepare simpler plans for only the two squares north and south of the monument. During the following three months, assisted by Thomas Wisedell, he supplied them with sketches and finished drawings that embodied something of the "broad simple arrangement" he admired in the report of the 1875 commission. In both squares there were walks paved with colored cement of black, red, and yellow (the colors of the Maryland state flag) and laid in patterns, a version of the "patriotic polychromy" of the sidewalks in patterned blue and red cement that Olmsted had already installed on the U.S. Capitol grounds. A marble fountain stood in the center of the main walk, which was flanked by slight earth berms that were to be planted with shrubs and trees. The central axis of the north square had two oval panels, which were to be planted with ivy and low-growing shrubs, flanked by eight half-oval panels around its perimeter. The stonework at both squares used cut North River blue stone for edgings and steps, and brown sandstone and light stone for dwarf walls and entrance piers. Olmsted recommended that the commissioners hire his former colleague on Prospect Park, the engineer John Bogart, to superintend construction of the squares, which they did in April 1877. Construction began immediately and was largely completed by the end of the year. In 1878 conflicts arose about the finishing of the paving, lamps, and planting of the squares, about which Olmsted wrote commissioner Robert Garrett (Thomas M. Lanahan to FLO, Jan. 26, 1877; ibid., Jan. 31, 1877; Robert Garrett to FLO, Feb. 1, 1877; ibid., March 29, 1877; ibid., Aug. 29, 1877; contract between John Bogart and commissioners for the improvement of the north and south parks, Washington Place, Baltimore, May 19, 1877, in B124: #2401, OAR/LC; FLO to Thomas M.

Lanahan, Jan. 29, 1877; ibid., March 9, 1877; *American Architect and Building News*, April 27, 1878, p. 148; "The Report of the Commissioners of Mount Vernon Squares," c. Nov. 20, 1877, City Archives and Records Management Office, Baltimore, Maryland; FLO to Robert Garrett, June 5, 1878, below).

To Charles Eliot Norton

209 W. 46 ST.
New York.
27th Dec. 1876

My Dear Norton,

    I am very glad that you imagine that I agree with you in politics for since the Nation stampeded I have felt lonely.[1] Before any guess could be made as to the votes of at least three states, the World and every other Democratic paper that I saw began systematically to sound the public mind and prepare the way for a *pronunciamento*.[2] There was no excuse for it whatever except that Chandler and the republican newspapers did not all at once accept a solid South for Tilden as a foregone conclusion.[3] I had never any fear that anything substantial would come of it for I know Tilden and I know what Copperhead bluster means but I remembered the draft riots, and my family being not one block away from a considerable cluster of Irish tenement houses I felt a little savage about it.[4] Finding that the republicans proper did not scare very badly that game has been abandoned and one can look at the matter quietly. The only difference is that it obliges me, at least, to look at it more strictly from the point of view of a republican than I might otherwise. I can't help feeling, that is to say, that there was before "McDowell advanced on Manassas"[5] a pretty deep difference of opinion as to the true basis of statesmanship between Mr. Chas O'Connor[6] and myself and that there is today the same difference between Mr Tilden and myself—a difference which has justified the killing of great many thousand men and the waste of a vast amount of honest industry. I do not welcome as President a man with whom I have that difference. I prefer a man who has less ability, who is less of a reformer, even one who can regard as friends and give public trusts to men less respectable than John Morrisey, Jimmy O'Brien and Andy Green.[7] Standing in this position even ten years after the men of Mr Tilden's ways of thinking had their arms taken away from them I simply do not think that it has been so fully proved that Mr Tilden has become our President elect by the honest legal vote of the nation that it is my duty to abandon hope of the contrary. And on this point I don't propose to be thrown off my balance by an impatient apprehension of injustice to those with whom I differ any more than I propose to be bullied into acquiescence in their plans. Ever since the day of the election as I understand, Mr Tilden has had Mr O'Connor and 50,000 young men, (candidates for 2^d class clerkships), engaged in the compilation of his case.[8] When he has completed it and the Nation has reduced it to a comprehensible statement of proven facts then I shall be ready to consider it fairly I hope and to accept a reasonable conclusion. But so long as there is reasonable room for doubt I mean that the theory of the nation which I have hitherto upheld shall have the benefit of it and if anybody wants to fight about it I shall refer them to my man of business whose name for the present is U. S. Grant.

The situation is critical but I don't on the whole think it a bad one. The republicans are doing a good deal of thinking without being any less republicans. The democrats are learning that their antebellum tactics don't have precisely the effect on their opponents that they formerly did, and that there are other men in the country whom neither firearms nor commercial depression can frighten out of their senses besides the Fire eaters.[9] I don't believe that the republicans are weakening any more than I believe they are Mexicanizing.[10] If Tilden is elected he will be President and if he is President he will be opposed by a much stronger, better disciplined, more serious and earnest party than he would have been had there been no doubt of his election and no demonstration of the continued dangerous character of his own party.

I have not seen Sturgis[11] for a year past but I believe that he knows that we of the Advisory Board (now the firm of Eidlitz, Richardson & C° Architects to the Capitol)[12] have stood by his friend Eaton[13] and between him and his pursuers all the time, formally and informally, publicly and privately. I should not have any fear that a hair of his head would be touched if Uncle Sammy[14] were not so very past finding out and if he had not taken such a mysterious interest in the matter.

The design of the Capitol has since last winter grown more Romanesque but also, I hope, a little more quiet and coherent.

There will be much historical incongruity in it and some that I would gladly have escaped. But we must take men as we find them and Eidlitz would not if he could have it otherwise. If he had been a man who could and would we might have more weak and meaningless and pottering work and it is a comfort that we are likely to escape that.

I have just returned from Albany. Fuller has given notice that he intends to appeal to the legislature and I suppose that he will have his old backing.[15] I don't know what we have to expect, but, though Dorsheimer has both branches of the legislature against him, his colleagues unhappy and the governor not personally friendly he seems resolute & confident.[16]

While writing, the Nation of today has been laid on my table and I have glanced at the work to see if there is any change. None.[17] I wonder if the World and the Sun and the Express and the Albany Argus, all of which I have chanced to see within a few days, & the World daily, are never seen in the Nation office. I am demented if Zach Chandler and the Times and the very hottest of the republican mercenaries have at any time shown more rabid partisanship, impudence, arrogance and "Mexican" spirit than Mr Hewitt[18] and the coolest and most cultured of the Democratic press that I see.

Ah! well, I'm afraid we none of us have advanced so very far from the simplicity of savage life. We are all alike crazy when our blood is up. & it seems to get up without our knowing it.

I sent my boy[19] on last week to see Richardson's church before the scaffolds were taken down. I want very much to see it myself—perhaps I shall. I should like to know if you like it.

Kindest regards for the New Year for your mother, your sister & yourself from

Yours affectly.

Fred Law Olmsted.

The text presented here is from a manuscript in Olmsted's hand in the Charles Eliot Norton Papers, Houghton Library, Harvard University, Cambridge, Massachusetts.

1. Olmsted is referring to statements by E. L. Godkin in the *Nation* of November 30, 1876. Godkin declared that if the electoral votes of the Reconstruction governments of Florida, South Carolina, and Louisiana were cast for Hayes, the country would be faced with the disastrous situation of a disputed election. The way to avoid this, he proposed, was for a single Republican elector to vote for a third candidate, thus creating a situation where the House of Representatives would select the next president. This, predictably, would be Samuel Tilden: but such an outcome would be preferable to a disputed election, which had never before occurred in the history of the republic. Olmsted was appalled that Godkin would abandon the sure Republican victory that would come by accepting the highly questionable results in the three southern states. Godkin also appealed to Hayes not to accept the votes of the obviously corrupt Louisiana Returning Board, whose vote was widely anticipated to provide the margin of victory in the electoral college for the Republican candidate ("A Disputed Election or a Failure to Elect," *Nation*, no. 596 [Nov. 30, 1876], pp. 319, 322).
2. That is, the *New York World* and other Democratic newspapers began to prepare the public for a declaration by the Democratic party that it would resist any decision that gave the election to Rutherford P. Hayes.
3. Zachariah Chandler (1813–1879), a longtime Republican senator from Michigan, who was appointed secretary of the interior in the Grant administration in 1875 and served as chairman of the Republican party during the 1876 presidential campaign. He acted vigorously to rally support for Hayes when numerous newspapers indicated an expectation immediately following the election that Tilden would be elected (*DAB*).
4. The term Copperhead was applied during the Civil War to northern opponents of the use of military force against the southern Confederacy. The New York Draft riots, begun in opposition to the first use of military conscription to secure soldiers for the Union army, occurred for five days in mid-July of 1863. The mobs focused their attacks on Blacks and leading Republicans, resulting in much destruction of property and the

death of over one hundred persons. During those days Olmsted was in the area of Gettysburg directing U.S. Sanitary Commission relief operations following the battle, but declared to his wife that "I do so want to be in the thick of it in New York. I never had such a passion for fight before." Olmsted meant in the statement in this letter that his residence in 1876 of 209 W. 46th Street in Manhattan was near a cluster of tenement houses: in July of 1863 his family's residence was still in Washington, D.C., and his wife and children were in the Connecticut hill town of Litchfield (FLO to MCO, July 15, 1863; ibid., July 20, 1863; ibid., July 27, 1863).
5. That is, when General Irvin McDowell (1818–1885) commanded the Army of the Potomac in the first battle of the Civil War, near Manassas Junction, Virginia (*DAB*).
6. Charles O'Conor (1804–1884), a leading New York lawyer and Democratic politician, noted for his steadfast attachment to states rights and legal inferiority of Blacks. He opposed military coercion of the seceded southern states and when Jefferson Davis was indicted for treason after the Civil War, O'Conor helped to pay his bail bond and provided him with free legal counsel (*NCAB*, 3: 387; *New-York Times*, May 14, 1884, p. 5).
7. Here Olmsted links together his old antagonist on Central Park, Andrew H. Green, a close associate of Tilden and a partner in his law firm, and reputed as a gentleman-reformer, with Democratic politicians with less respectable reputations. One was John Morrissey (1831–1878), a prize-fighter who served two terms in the U.S. House of Representatives and at this time was a New York state senator. The other was James O'Brien (1841–1907), a colorful anti-Tammany leader and speculator. In early November, 1876, the *Nation* had made special mention of the role of the three men Olmsted names in the creation of a unified and victorious Democratic party in the presidential election in New York (*DAB*; *Herringshaw's Encyclopedia of American Biography of the Nineteenth Century* (Chicago, 1907), s.v. "O'Brien, James;" *New-York Times*, March 6, 1907, p. 9; "The Week," *Nation*, no. 593 [Nov. 9, 1876], p. 277).
8. During the two months following the presidential election of 1876, Samuel Tilden oversaw a group of men in the preparation of a long document providing precedents concerning the counting of electoral votes that he hoped would convince Congress to facilitate his selection in the contested presidential election. In early January 1877 he published this compendium under the title of *The Presidential Counts: A Complete Official Record of the Proceedings of Congress at the Counting of the Electoral Votes in All the Elections of President and Vice-President of the United States; Together with All Congressional Debates Incident thereto, or to Proposed Legislation upon That Subject. With an Analytical Introduction* (Keith Ian Polakoff, *The Politics of Inertia: The Election of 1876 and the End of Reconstruction* [Baton Rouge, La., 1973], pp. 234–35).
9. The fire eaters were southerners during the antebellum period who argued for the protection of southern rights and called for secession from the United States.
10. That is, to become like Mexico, especially in respect to frequent revolutions. On December 21, 1876, the *Nation* published an article entitled, "What is 'Mexicanization'?" It noted that the prevailing definition was "the use of armed force to decide political contests or legal disputes, or to set aside the result of elections, or settle conflicting claims to power or authority" (*OED*; *Nation*, Dec. 21, 1876, p. 365).
11. The architect, critic, and art historian Russell Sturgis (1836–1909), who was collaborating with Charles Eliot Norton in the preparation of the *Catalog of . . . Ancient and Modern Engravings, Woodcuts and Illustrated Books, Parts of the Collections of C. E. Norton and R. Sturgis*, published in 1879 (*DAB*).
12. On September 12, 1876, the members of the advisory board officially replaced Thomas Fuller as Architects of the New Capitol. They then formed a company, Eidlitz, Richardson & Company, with Olmsted as treasurer, to carry on the Albany work (C. R. Roseberry, *Capitol Story*, p. 33; Paul A. Chadbourne, *Public Service of the*

APRIL 1876–DECEMBER 1876

State of New York During the Administration of Alonzo B. Cornell, Governor, 3 vols., [Boston, 1882], 2: 70).
13. James W. Eaton (1817–1891), an Albany, New York, building contractor appointed superintendent of construction on the New York Capitol project in 1874 (*New-York Times*, June 14, 1891, p. 2; C. R. Roseberry, *Capitol Story*, p. 31; for the architects' defense of Eaton, see, for instance, "The New Capital Investigation," *New-York Times*, March 9, 1877, p. 2).
14. That is, New York governor Samuel Tilden.
15. A reference to the appeal of architect Thomas Fuller to regain approval of his plan for the state capitol in Albany that led to the hearing by a joint committee of the legislature to which Olmsted presented his address of March 1877 (above).
16. The lieutenant governor of New York, William Dorsheimer, who had been responsible for engaging Olmsted, Richardson, and Eidlitz as an advisory board concerning the design of the New Capitol. At this time Dorsheimer had lost some of his political power, making the advisory board more vulnerable to attack. He had expected to be chosen by the Democratic party as candidate for governor in 1876, but was passed over in favor of Lucius Robinson (Geoffrey Blodgett, "Lieutenant Governor William Dorsheimer and the Politics of Architectural Reform," in Temporary State Commission on the Restoration of the Capitol, *Proceedings of the New York State Capitol Symposium* [Albany, 1981], p. 56).
17. On December 28, 1876, the *Nation* noted that

> Mr. "Zach" Chandler still insists that Hayes has been surely elected, and that the Vice-President will surely declare him elected, and that nobody else has anything to say about it, and that he will be inaugurated peaceably or forcibly as the Democrats please, and that there is no room in the matter for any compromise or for any respectable difference of opinion about it, and so on; and the *New-York Times* supports him in this view with a wonderful tick-tock accuracy and regularity

(*Nation*, Dec. 28, 1876, p. 375).
18. Abram Hewitt (1822–1903), a New York iron manufacturer and Democratic politician who was chairman of the Democratic National Committee during the presidential campaign of 1876 (*DAB*).
19. Olmsted had sent 24-year-old John C. Olmsted or 19-year-old Owen Olmsted to see Trinity Church in Boston, which was consecrated on February 9, 1877.

CHAPTER V

JANUARY 1877–OCTOBER 1877

This was a time of intensifying political pressures in New York, both at the state and local levels. In early 1877 came a second round of opposition in the state legislature to the plans for the New Capitol of Olmsted, Eidlitz and Richardson, leading to investigations by legislative committees. Olmsted's address to one of these on March 6, 1877, was his most extensive review of the ongoing controversy and defense of himself and his colleague architects. "To the Public" is a draft for a counterappeal to the architectural profession that apparently was not carried out. The issue became a moot point when the state legislature in May 1877 directed that the New Capitol be completed "in the Italian renaissance style of architecture, adopted in the original design," and not in the Romanesque style proposed by the advisory board.

Olmsted continued to be involved in the management of Central Park, as indicated by his letter to William Martin on the adverse effects of crowds attending the dedication of the statue of the writer Fitz-Greene Halleck. At the same time, Olmsted and J. J. R. Croes continued their planning for the Bronx: the report to Martin of March 20, 1877, spells out their innovative proposal for a rapid transit system for the area that would secure both speed and safety by complete grade separation of the system's tracks from city streets. Letters to H. A. Nelson deal primarily with proposals to place inappropriate structures on Mount Royal, while the letter to John C. Olmsted describes Olmsted's poorly attended speech in Montreal in October. To his wife, Mary Perkins Olmsted, he reports on events in New York during the railroad strikes of 1877 during a summer whose intense heat brought on a crisis in his own health.

January 1877–October 1877

Memorandum on New York Capitol Patronage

1877

Early this year an elaborately organized attack on the administration of the State Capitol & expressly upon the revised plan & the architects or Advisory Board suddenly appeared in the legislature and public prints. I was called to Albany & attended several sessions of the Joint Committees of Finance & Ways & Means at which the matter was discussed very violently, with great exaggeration & misstatement.[1] While there I was told by half a dozen men of high & low standing and of both parties that the sole object of the attack was to get patronage. The Chairman of the Capitol Commission[2] said, "There is not a single member of the legislature who is not dissatisfied with us, not even one of our own party — not because of our plans, that is only a pretext; not because of our administration, for that has been unprecedentedly economical and efficient & everybody knows it, but simply because not one thinks we have given him as much patronage as he ought to have had." Again he said, "I could settle all this opposition in a moment, if I would simply consent to give up the patronage."

We (E. R. & Co)[3] were asked at the outset to see two members whose favorable influence it was thought desirable to gain. We were, if good opportunity offered, to remove any false impressions they might have adopted. I called on one, a man of wealth and good education who went to the legislature purely from patriotism, a man of the highest character. Within two minutes after I entered his room he introduced the subject of the Capitol by remarking that he had been to the Capitol to see if he could not get a few men put on the work. (The work was wholly stopped by order of the legislature; nevertheless applications were incessant from members who had voted for the stoppage). Eidlitz went to see the other, a young man of good and rapidly rising reputation.

"Well," said I, "how have you succeeded with him?"

"Oh, he has a man who must be taken care of before he can take any favorable interest in the matter and I had to promise he should be." Next day he said "Well I have taken care of ——'s man and now I find him quite open to argument."

"How did you take care of him?"

"I told him to go to a stonecutter in New York and gave him $5 to pay his passage & then I wrote to the stone cutter that he must try him and if he could not earn his wages for a week I would pay them. If he is a good man he'll keep him. If he is not he's had his chance & can't complain."

Of another member of the legislature of uncommonly good standing I asked the President of the D.P.P.[4] "Is he a friend of yours?"

"That depends on how much patronage I have."

The text presented here is a record that Olmsted made of the role played by considerations of patronage in the controversy over the design of the New York State capitol that took place in early 1877.

1. These meetings of the joint committees took place during the first two weeks of February 1877 (see FLO to Charles Eliot Norton, Feb. 15, 1877, below).
2. William Dorsheimer.
3. That is, the firm of Eidlitz, Richardson &Co., created to facilitate work on the new capitol in Albany after the advisory board consisting of Olmsted and those two architects became the official architects of the new capitol in September 1876.
4. William R. Martin.

TO CHARLES ELIOT NORTON

209 W. 46th St. NYork.
15th Feby 1877.

My Dear Norton;

Miss Theodora[1] arrived this evening to our pleasure, after a rather more than usually fatiguing journey from Boston, (the train being nearly an hour behind time), but apparently unfatigued & in good spirits.

I am very warmly engaged in the fight upon the Capitol just now, having been most of the time during the last two weeks in Albany. The question of tearing down what we have done and returning to the old plan is before a Joint Committee and we have been for several hours daily attending its sessions but have not yet had a chance to say one word for ourselves.[2] Fuller is present with a sharp and brassy lawyer who opened with a very violent and extravagant attack upon us, accusing us of falsehood & knavery; Two or three members of the Committee also took active part against us. The Commissioners[3] replied and so effectively in the end that it became ludicrous & the Committee retreated into Executive Session. It was then agreed, as we are told, to send for Renwick and Hunt, and a country architect who has built a block of stores for one of the members of the Committee & who, as this member said, assured him that our work was barbarous.[4]

Every charge will be abandoned except that of passing from Roman to Romanesque in the exterior and that of "making a dungeon" of the Assembly Chamber. As there is something new in this I will tell you of it. The Assembly Chamber is a hall nearly 150 feet long, 100 wide & 50 high, with two tiers of windows on each of its longer sides—very light. Fuller narrows it at the bottom, shuts out half the light by partitions, hangs a cast iron ceiling over it and covers its walls with Parian marble—viz. a form of "hard finish" with that name, and large plaster "decorations." In our plan the walls are of three tints of sand stone, (ashlar of the lightest Ohio quarry) with polished red

JANUARY 1877–OCTOBER 1877

granite columns supporting a grand vaulted ceiling. It is admitted to be a much more conveniently arranged room for its purposes as far as floor and galleries are concerned. But one questions if such a ceiling can be made safe?— Think of sitting right under a great piece of stone without a strap or bolt to hold it up! Then it would be so gloomy with stone walls all around. Moreover, we are told, that some of the Committee think that the sand stone would absorb the air that had been breathed in the room and retain so much of the poisonous exhalations from the lungs of the Assembly that it would soon become dangerous to sit near the walls. Finally Mr Renwick has already told the Chairman of the House Committee that a vaulted ceiling would render the room wholly useless for its purposes on account of its echoes. It would be impossible to speak intelligibly in it.

This chairman of the House Committee,[5] when it was first stated against us that we intended to make a ceiling of stone, interrupted the speaker, with an exclamation of incredulity and when again and again assured that it was so, threw up his hands with a great groan, then sank back, closed his eyes and said "That is enough for me!" Actually, the possibility of such a construction seems to be doubted.

The Committee is strongly against us but so far we have gained in the debate and in the canvass. Apparently the majority of the Democrats are disposed to sustain the Commissioners who are now all state officers of their own party.[6] The reform republicans, the soberer country members, are also at least disposed to give us a hearing, being jealous of the men who are leading against us who are notoriously corrupt & who are after the patronage. How it will be when the authority of the profession is brought against us and the rural member has been sufficiently educated in the cant of schools and styles I don't know. We are now chiefly anxious that when Hunt & Renwick are examined, we may be present and allowed to question them.[7]

I am glad to hear that you like Richardson's church.

Yours Sincerely

Fred Law Olmsted.

The text presented here is from a manuscript in Olmsted's hand in the Charles Eliot Norton Papers, Houghton Library, Harvard University, Cambridge, Massachusetts.

1. Norton's sister-in-law Maria Theodora Sedgwick (1851–1916) (Hubert M. Sedgwick, *A Sedgwick Genealogy, Descendants of Deacon Benjamin Sedgwick*, [New Haven, Conn., 1961], p. 213; *Boston Herald*, April 8, 1916, p. 12).
2. In response to the remonstrance against the change of architectural style of the New Capitol introduced by the advisory board, a joint committee consisting of the Senate Finance Committee and the Assembly Ways and Means Committee held a series of hearings on the matter in early 1877. The chairman of the committee was Senator Hamilton Harris, who had been chairman of the original New Capitol Commission

that approved Fuller's plan and appointed him resident architect in 1867. The remonstrance to which the committee was responding had petitioned the legislature "to cause the work now executed, varying from the original design, to be removed and reconstructed in accordance with the original plan." Two days before Olmsted wrote the letter presented here, Dorsheimer and Fuller had appeared before the committee and presented conflicting views of the cost of carrying out the plans of Fuller and of the advisory board (C. R. Roseberry, *Capitol Story*, p. 22; Geoffrey Blodgett, "Lieutenant Governor William Dorsheimer and the Politics of Architectural Reform," in Temporary State Commission on the Restoration of the Capitol, *Proceedings of the New York State Capitol Symposium* [Albany, 1981], pp. 56–57; "Remonstrance of Certain Citizens of the State of New York, against the Changes which have been, and are being made, on the New Capitol Building," December 1876, "Document no. 28," in New York [State], *Documents of the Assembly of the State of New York, One Hundredth Session*...[Albany, N. Y., 1877], pp. 1–2; *New-York Times*, Feb. 14, 1877, p. 5).
3. That is, members of the New Capitol Commission.
4. The noted architects James Renwick, Jr., and Richard Morris Hunt and an unidentified "country architect."
5. The Chairman of the House Committee on Ways and Means was James W. Husted (1833–1892) (*New-York Times*, Feb. 16, 1877, p. 4; ibid., Sept. 26, 1892, p. 1)
6. The Commissioners of the New Capitol at this time were William Dorsheimer, Charles S. Fairchild, and George W. Schuyler (Paul A. Chadbourne, *Public Service of the State of New York During the Administration of Alonzo B. Cornell, Governor*, 3 vols., [Boston, 1882], 2:73; G. Blodgett, "Politics of Architectural Reform," p. 53).
7. The group of architects who finally testified before the joint committee on February 28, 1877, consisted of George B. Post, Richard Morris Hunt, Napoleon Le Brun, Henry Dudley, and Detlef Lienau, all fellows of the American Institute of Architects practicing in New York City. They asserted in a letter, published in New York City newspapers on the day that the testimony of the advisory board was reported, that the board's change of style of the Capitol was an admission that they were incompetent to complete the building in its original Renaissance style, and that they should, accordingly, resign. The architects further asserted that the advisory board's design, if executed, "would be totally wanting in unity, and consequently an architectural failure." Olmsted and his colleagues were not allowed to question the testimony of these architects, as they had wished (Dennis Steadman Francis, *Architects in Practice in New York City 1840–1900* [New York, 1980]; "The Battle of Styles," *New-York Times*, Mar. 7, 1877, p. 2).

To Whitelaw Reid

Private

2^d March 1877.

My Dear Mr Reid.

Let me call your attention to the fact that a bill has been favorably reported in the legislature for *occasionally* occupying a part of the Central park as a parade ground.[1]

Bills for this purpose have often been introduced but have been strongly resisted and I believe that never before has one appeared equally likely to pass.²

If it is desirable to maintain a rural character in the park and to prevent its degenerating from a sylvan retreat into a place for boisterous fun and rough sports—a sort of Metropolitan Common or Fair Ground, the most energetic protest should be made against this bill.

The ordinary rules for the protection of the characteristic elements of the park must be practically suspended when the troops enter. Inter arma silent leges³ would apply with peculiar significance. For you know very well that the characteristic spirit and tone of manners of a crowd attending any great muster of militia is always one peculiarly antagonistic to that which has hitherto been in a large degree preserved in the park.

To a certain extent the scenes of the park have hitherto impressed the rough element of the city as with something of sacredness and to this fact the park owes all that has hitherto made it peculiarly enjoyable (among parks) to the more refined and delicate of the community. All of its domestic character.

I do not believe that for a single occasion measures could be taken which would be effectual against actual damage to the park of a most serious character (from the point of view of a lover of nature), but even if with special exertions this might be accomplished, nothing is more probable than that such precautions would be soon neglected and the park at times become subject to the humor of a multitude as uncontrollable and as dangerous to all that is peculiarly valuable in it as a street mob is found to be when it has broken into a private house.⁴

The text presented here is from a draft in Olmsted's hand.

1. On the morning that Olmsted wrote this letter the state assembly passed a bill making the Green of Central Park available to the First Division of the State National Guard for parades and reviews between May 1 and July 1 of each year. The bill then was forwarded to the state senate for final approval (*New-York Times*, Feb. 13, 1877, p. 5; New York [State], *Journal of the Assembly of the State of New York: At Their One Hundredth Session* [Albany, N.Y., 1877], pp. 239–40, 371).
2. In 1864 officers of the First Division of the State National Guard had attempted without success to have part of Central Park set aside for a parade ground. Although Tompkins Square in lower Manhattan was dedicated to this purpose in 1866, its shortcomings led to renewed pressure to allocate space in the park. In 1869 Governor John T. Hoffman took preliminary steps to have the legislature authorize this but yielded to Andrew H. Green's arguments in favor of a site just north of the park. A site farther north, recommended by Olmsted and General Alexander Shaler, was approved by the legislature in 1871 but proceedings to acquire the property stalled. In 1874 a bill setting aside a parade ground in Central Park failed to pass the legislature (BCCP, *Thirteenth Annual Report* [1870], pp. 153–71; FLO to William R. Martin, Aug. 9, 1876, nn. 7 and 9, above).
3. An allusion to Cicero's phrase, "*silent leges inter arma*," meaning "laws remain inactive in the midst of arms" (F. M. Payne, *New Explanatory Pronouncing Dictionary of Latin Quotations* [New York, 1899], p. 65).

4. Shortly after Reid received this letter, the *New-York Daily Tribune* characterized the bill as an "invasion of Central Park. . . . The only way to preserve it now from gradual encroachment and sure deterioration is to stamp the life out of schemes like this the instant they show their heads." The senate committee on the affairs of cities rejected the bill on March 7. Olmsted's concern regarding the results of military parades in the park was confirmed less than eight weeks later when a crowd following one into the park to attend a statue unveiling caused extensive damage to trees and plants (*New-York Daily Tribune*, March 7, 1877, p. 4; ibid., March 8, 1877, p. 5; New York [State], *Journal of the Senate of the State of New York: At Their One Hundredth Session* [Albany, N.Y., 1877], pp. 239, 251; FLO to William R. Martin, May 17, 1877, below).

New York State Capitol Testimony

[March 6, 1877]

Mr Chairman.[1]

Shortly before I last left Albany I chanced to remark to my associates[2] that if I were a member of your Committee I did not believe that with every desire to be fair and candid and thorough I should have been able to keep my mind free from impressions and sentiments more or less prejudicial to a just conclusion. I added that if I were to have an opportunity to speak with you I should be disposed before taking up the technical question with which you are laboring to ask you to try to understand a little better than it is likely that you do for what we are accountable in this business, and how we have come to be accountable for it. More importance seems to have been attached to this remark than I desired or intended and it has thus turned out that something like an engagment has been made with you in my behalf. Distrusting my readiness to say what I had vaguely in mind as desireable to be said by way of introduction to more essential matters I have attempted, necessarily very hastily in the short time at my disposal, to give it consistency in the paper from which I read.

We who today are first permitted to address you[3] have had as you know for nearly two years past a definite professional duty as the advisers of the State in regard to a building in the construction of which it is engaged. We have been regularly retained and are in the pay of the State for this service.[4]

The occasion for the special inquiry which your Committee has been instructed to make arises from the fact that a number of our professional bretheren not so retained and without invitation from the state have taken it upon themselves to advise that our counsel to it should be rejected. They have also procured and caused to be laid before you a series of papers from numerous other gentlemen which altogether are adapted to convey the idea, are in part at least designed to convey the idea, and without other information must irresistably give you the idea, that we have committed a grave professional offence — an offence — if I should not rather say a crime, which has profoundly shocked the sensibilities of the whole body of architects of the country; that the profession has risen to repudiate us and to warn the state, our employer, that as architects we are unworthy of its respect or confidence.

The state is told for example, (I quote from documents of which two editions have been officially published and which have been industriously disseminated) that the advice we have given it is *ridiculed* by *all competent* critics,[5] that its errors are *unpardonable*; that it is in direct antagonism to all received rules of Art, that its adoption would for ages vitiate the public taste, that it would result in a monstrosity, in a horrid nightmare,[6] in an absurdity so glaring as to require no criticism, and so on.

If it were possible for you to receive these representations literally as the unprejudiced opinions of the architects of the country, you must have been inclined to doubt if the debasement of politics could reach a lower depth than that marked by the state's employment for such a duty of charlatans so base and so brazen as those before you.

But you well know that no such deduction is possible to be entertained by any well informed man.

Look at it.

My friend Mr Richardson here is no stripling and yet had you questioned the gentlemen who have been before you on the subject they would not have been able to name one other man who in the same period of practice has obtained a more generally recognized, more assured or more brilliant professional success. Only last week, some of these very gentlemen, fresh from giving their evidence before you here in Albany, came to greet him with warm congratulations upon the last illustration of this success,[7] and I believe that there is an unusual concurrence of opinion that his success is fair, legitimate & well deserved.

Mr Eidlitz again could point you to more than 30 churches and other edifices of public importance which he has built in our land and it may be doubted if any other active architect can show as many which have been found equally acceptable to men of acknowleged taste. Mr Eidlitz is old enough to have had an honored name among the architects of the state before a majority of those who now caution the State against him had drawn their first shop fronts.

Your Committee very well knows, Sir, that my associates are the peers of the best architects of the country. There are none better-grounded in the principles of Art, none better able to guide the state by those principles, none better schooled or better equipped for the duties the state has asked them to assume. Two years ago not one of these gentlemen now trooping to the attack upon them would have failed had you made the inquiry to confirm this estimate of them.

Suppose if you please Sir, that these men, my associates, are men of very bad private character, low lived, dissolute, malicious and thoroughly dishonest. Still they must be recognized as artists—unquestionably they have an established standing as artists, and that implies a great deal. It implies for a selfish and base man that his selfishness and his baseness are applied to means of indulging his artistic propensity. It does not mean and it is wholly inconsistent with the idea that he is utterly indifferent to the requirements of art, to the conditions of beauty and that whenever it serves to put money in his pocket he snaps his finger at these requirements. As for the third member of our partnership I may be allowed to say for him that if he has a reputation for lightly accepting public trusts or of acquitting himself of them ignorantly, recklessly or faithlessly, it is one of quite recent growth.

Take us at any measure you please, are we men, Sir, who are likely either ignorantly or carelessly or with deliberate sinfulness to have committed an offence against our art which *in itself* would give reasonable occasion for such an outcry as you have heard from these gentlemen.

If you can imagine for an instant that I have been the marplot of this business, ask whether such men as my associates are likely to have been drawn into a grave professional crime by a man who deems himself unworthy to uphold alone the title of Architect.

Before the opinion was given which has been made the occasion of so much reproach to us, we had been eight months engaged in the investigation and discussion of the matters dealt with. We had had more than fifty meetings for debateing it. Our opinion was finally expressed in a methodical way and with argumnt and illustration as carefully as possible freed from all technical obscurity. How was it on the other side?

The gentlemen who took it upon themselves to come between us and our employer, ostensibly formed the judgmnts which have been given you mainly upon a newspaper publication of two drawings taken from among those furnished the Commission.[8] These drawings had not been presented by us as complete; they had not been presented by us as designs which we should unqualifiedly recommend to be adopted. Their publication was not made at our request or at our instigation. Not one of the gentlemen had seen the drawings or fully knew the advice which we had given the Commission. Nevertheless their action was plainly concerted and systematic. It seems to have been to some extent prearranged and prepared for. With such pretext upon such appearance of an occasion as the publication of these drawings afforded, their protests began at once to pour in upon the legislature from different parts of the country far and near.

Were you previously aware that the architects of the country had their eyes fixed on the Capitol of New York, that they watched it with such eager interest? Do you know of another case in which architects have hurried up from all parts of the country to protest against an act of vandalism? There are hundreds of stately buildings in the World, in which one style in architecture has been placed over another. Did it ever occur before that there was a general uprising of architects to arrest the progress of such an atrocity?

You know perfectly well Sir, that the whole story has not been told — that however sincere these gentlemen were in what they said they had been moved to say it by some other consideration, some other purpose, than that which is plainly expressed in their memorial & their letters.

It must be plain to you Sir, if you look it all over, that this demonstration is a demonstration not as these gentlemen imagined it to be simply of architectural orthodoxy but of architectural partisanship.

But what was the impulse from which this partisanship proceeded; what {was} its motive, bent and aim?

Had it grown out of a cooperative devotion to purity of style? I question Sir if there are any architects who are more given to mixing styles than some of the gentlemen who have been most zealous in this matter.

It has been suggested that they are chiefly men who are accustomed to work in the renaissance style and that they have felt that the proposition to depart from the customs of the renaissance in the treatmnt of the Capitol was equivalent to a condemnation of that style for any and all purposes and consequently a condemnation of themselves and their work, a condemnation which they were bound to resist and resent.

Illogical and inconsequent, this explanation cannot account to you for all the feeling that has been manifested.

I ask you then to look with me a little further.

First, you will please to observe that except in our official reports and in answer to pertinent and respectful inquiries, we of the Advisory Board have been perfectly silent as to how we came to be in the affair, on what terms; with what understanding; with what views and intentions; how we have managed our business, what has been one man's part & what anothers. Of all that you are ignorant; the public is ignorant, and these architects are and have been all the time utterly in the dark.

Now Sir, you know that in affairs where large public interests are inextricably mixed with diverse private interests, (and when their direction in whole or in essential parts is likely to affect for better or worse personal fortunes and personal reputation) you know how it is that doubts and suspicions spring up like weeds and how it is also that from these doubts and suspicions, conjectures, surmises, suppositions and guesses develop, and yet again you know how surely many of these creeping branches break out into positive rumors and reports and presently there is a crop of what pass current for authentic facts. And you know how it is that no self respecting man unfavorably affected by these poor fruits of an unhealthy imagination is ever inclined to lay aside his proper work and set about killing them. And you know how little use it would be if he were. For after all, the roots of suspicion and doubt and distrust are below the surface and if you cut off one sprout from them a dozen may presently rise in its place. A man has nothing to do as a general rule but live them down. And yet you know that these miserable weeds are sometimes factors in personal and in political history of no trifling importance. Every member of the Committee probably knows that there are men whose minds are in some degree poisoned against himself through the gradually accumulating effect of observations such as are contained in a single obscure line of the local items of a newspaper, which by itself it would be absurd to contradict or in any way take any notice of.

And every member knows that there is no place in the world, where a soil is found so rich, deep, warm and fructifying to these often utterly ridiculous but nonetheless very noxious plants as that in which this Capitol stands. Few men have suffered more in this way and we are in some respects prepared to testify that few men have suffered more unjustly in this respect than some here present and not I regret to say of our side.

Let the members of your Committee take all the circumstances into consideration and ask themselves whether it is likely that we of the Advisory Board have suffered not at all — in like manner, and whether it is not possible — that a more or less ill defined distrust of us, *otherwise than as artists* has arisen here and has been propagated and extended its growth so at last to strike its roots into the mind of some of our professional bretheren?

Let us suppose that a possibility appears rising to them that a custom is to be disregarded in an instance which will be prominent and notorious; which custom is so necessary to be observed for the interests of the profession that it has with them more than the sacredness of a law — the custom I mean which requires that the designer of a building shall, whenever his design is used, be allowed to earn the fees of supervising its construction.

Starting with a clue of this kind, and remembering that architects have much the same human nature with men of other callings, look, if it please you, for a moment at certain facts which are well known to you and see if you can trace no connection between them and the sudden outburst witnessed last year of professional interest in this building.

Mr. Thomas Fuller comes here, a worthy gentleman from Canada and engages in a competition for the position of architect of the new Capitol. He is not at once successful but as the final result of a series of arrangments, compromises, combinations and of partnerships with rivals, such as the questionable custom of professional competitions often compels architects to resort to as the necessary condition of success, he at length works his way to the place.[9] He holds it for a series of years. In the language of the profession the Capitol has become his building, his right to it is unquestioned. But at length the Capitol comes under the management of men of whom he knows little except that they are chosen of the party which has thrown out those who have hitherto kept him where he is and who have given him their confidence. One day the head of this new Commission suddenly walks into Mr Fuller's office bringing three strangers who he states have been employed by the Commission to assist it in an examination of his building and of his plans with a view to some contemplated changes and improvements.

Suppose this to occur to a man, who however thoroughly a gentleman, disposed to credit others as far as possible with good and honorable motives, had been living for ten years in the noisome atmosphere of suspicion, rumor, gossip, slander and detraction which so often hangs about this Capitol, suppose an English gentleman whose first and only experience of republican life had been in this atmosphere and who had for ten years been schooling himself to carry on his work under such tortures as it supplies to any man of refinemnt. How, I ask you, would he be likely to regard these intruders and what would he be likely to imagine as to the motives and ultimate objects of their appointment?

It is not fair to speak in this way of Mr Fuller and leave it unsaid for a single moment that in the very difficult position in which he was placed toward us he bore himself with entire dignity and courtesy and that in this particular he gained and he holds our hearty respect. We have a difference with him and we necessarily stand here his opponents but our difference is purely a difference of judgemnt. Placing ourselves however in his position, with his slight knowledge of us and with such knowledge and impressions as he was likely to have obtained of the Chairman of the new Commission and of the manner in which Americans carry on their public business, can we suppose that he took a wholly favorable view of our position; of our motives, purposes and intentions?

What were his friends and allies here and elsewhere likely to imagine? from such rumors of the occurrence as would naturally come to them.

Is there a man here, not of ourselves who is at this moment completely free from a suspicion that we were intending, and expecting to open a way to get into such a position as that we now hold; to supercede Mr Fuller as the Architects of the building, and that there was an understanding to that effect; some sort of a plot to bring it about between us and the new Capitol Commission?

Are there not men here now who think that they see how the thing managed, how the pipes were laid and the whole business glossed over with the intention — they would have it the vain intention — to avoid raising the indignation of the public? Are there not men here who have talked and written of the new Capitol ring as if something notorious.

Is it to be imagined that the idea occurred to no one until quite lately that Mr Fuller was liable to be made the victim of a dirty political intrigue. Or that from no one to whom it may have occurred was it possible that that mysterious phenomenon called an authentic rumor should emanate and spread? That no man to whom such a rumor should come would be capable of feeling shame as an American that this English gentleman coming here at the expense of the State should be so threatened? Is it impossible that the good judgmnt of more than one such indignant person might be carried away and run him into rash and extravagant courses before he had severely questioned just how much basis of fact such a rumor might have? Do you see no provocation to partisanship in these circumstances? Would it not be rather creditable than otherwise to Mr Fuller's friends here in Albany and elsewhere that they had some feeling in the matter and that they sought to propogate that feeling?

We know Sir that they did use means adapted to that end.

I spoke just now of Mr Fuller's allies — You know that he was at that time at the head of a Society of Architects here in Albany and that that Society was in affiliation and in correspondence with other societies of architects in New York and other cities. Possibly you may not know that every man among those who came so promptly forward to protest to the legislature against the change of styles was a member of one of those societies.

I say Sir that we know that means were used adapted to the end of firing the hearts of these our professional bretheren; that there was a certain amount if you please of waving of the bloody shirt. We know, for example, that our professional bretheren were informed that on a given date we were all here in Albany lobbying with the legislature, that articles published at the time in the newspapers were attributed to us and that false statemnts in them discreditable to Mr Fuller, phrases in them unkind and ungenerous to Mr Fuller were quoted and passed around as proceeding from us. We know that a circular letter was sent out asking the cooperation of Architects' in other cities in the rescueing movemnt and we know that while this appeal struck some as highly improper, undecorous and unprofessional, the hearts of others were fired by it to the utterance of such professional advice as you have heard. All this we know Sir, not through any search we have made for such knowledge but through the voluntary statemnts of certain cooler heads of the profession who have thought it better that we should be advised of it.

It was all well intentioned Sir, all prompted by chivalric feeling, all creditable to the hearts of all concerned.

But whether it was throughly just and sound and based on a true knowledge of the facts & whether the indignation expressed was wholly representative of a settled well considered professional judgmnt upon the matter of styles, that we do not know. Whether on the whole it is a good, prudent, and always trustworthy method to introduce for guarding against abuses of the Civil service of the state and whether as such it is desirable to be encouraged, it is for you and not for us to consider.

Upon the point of prudence and safety, perhaps it may be best to mention that every one of the rumors about ourselves to which I have referred and doubtless many others, were purely offsprings of the imagination.

We had not, for instance, written or caused to be written a single word for the newspapers. The publication more particularly referred to had been made without our knowledge or consent & was very disagreeable to us. We had never spoken to a member of the legislature on the subject of the Capitol except when he had introduced it and desired information upon it; there was not a word of truth in any reports of our doings by which we were made to appear as taking our steps in this matter beyond the strict line of the requiremnts of our official and what we believed to be our professional obligations.

Whether we were right in our view of our professional obligations and in accepting the official obligations that we did, is another matter. That you might, if you should come to do so, better judge us in this respect I should like, if I could count on your interest, to give a full and detailed narrative of our connection with this business and to make known to you all that we know; but as that is out of the question I will say that if there remains a lurking suspicion with anyone that there is anything in it which we would wish to keep out of the light, I shall take as a favor if he will now or at any other time question me about it.

But I propose to tell you if you will permit me here & now how our connection with it began. To reveal the very inception of the plot in all desirable detail.

In June 1875, I was travelling Eastward on the Central RRoad and found Mr Dorsheimer, the Lt Governor on the train. He asked me to sit with him and began almost at once to speak of the Capitol. He told me of the action of the legislature making the new commission; of his position upon it; and of his great regret that he was upon it. He said that there was great public dissatisfaction with the building and that after as careful an examination of it as he had been able to make it appeared to him that there were abundant grounds for it. He expressed a strong repugnance to the association of his name with such a work but said that the law was such that he could not now escape the responsibility. He did not know much of Mr Fuller, he believed that the parliament houses at Ottawa were respectable buildings and if Mr Fuller had really designed them of which he appeared to harbor a doubt he ought to be able to do better work than he had done in the state capitol, as far as that was concerned it seemed to him to be thoroughly bad and he greatly distrusted his ability. He then undertook to explain to me what he regarded as the more prominent faults of the building and to discuss with me the possibility of getting the better of some of them. This conversation — or rather this discourse for I took little part in it — lasted for several hours and it certainly impressed me strongly with the conviction that Mr Dorsheimer's mind was much burdened and perplexed with the matter. At length, when we had nearly reached Albany he observed that the Commission was expected to have ready for the next session of the legislature plans for the completion of the building which should have received the unqualified approval in all respects of the Commission & that this approval was to be binding so that thereafter no alteration could be made without the written consent approval of all the Commissioners. Mr Dorsheimer went on to say that the plans to be made by Mr Fuller would be very numerous, that they could not be completed much before the opening of the session, that they were then to be passed under review by the Commission, that neither he nor either of his associates had the technical knowledge, experience or training, nor would they have the time to give the plans when Mr Fuller should have them ready such critical examination as they ought to receive, that only an expert could adequately judge them and that of course they could not ask Mr Fuller's assistance in criticising his own plans. Moreover, he added, he felt sure from what he had seen of Mr Fuller's work that there would at least be parts of them which they could not fully approve — and if not, he asked, how would it be possible to comply with the requirments of the legislature to report complete plans fully approved? He did not see but that they were at Mr Fuller's mercy. Did not see but that the state would be compelled next year to build exactly as Mr Fuller should propose, or not build at all.

Finally he said that the only way to meet the difficulties of the case that had occurred to him was to get the aid of a Board of experts, and he asked if I did not think that would be a practicable and proper thing to do?

I answered that I believed that the custom had been established in England and that the Institute of Architects had I thought recommended its adoption here, that when laymen were required to pass upon architectural plans of special importance, as in the case of the compilation drawing for the Courts of Law in London[10] that they should take counsel with an architect. It would be a sort of duty, that of passing judgment on the work of another, that no respectable architect would court, I added, but I supposed that it would be a perfectly proper one and one which if called upon by the state no architect would be justified in refusing.

"Well", said he, "if we conclude to adopt that course I shall call upon you."

"But I am not an architect."

"You are a member of an architectural firm are you not?" he asked.

"I have been",[11] I replied, "but nonetheless I never have offered my services to the public as an architect."

"Its no matter", he said; "what we need is a complete Board of Experts, and you are an expert in the administration and managemnt of public works which include architectural works" and there the matter ended for the time.

This conversation occurred nearly two years ago, and it is not to be supposed that I now recall it literally or in its exact sequence — but I do so as nearly as I can & I am sure that substantially what I have said then passed between us. I did not regard the part personal to myself as necessarily serious.

Some little time after this Mr Dorsheimer asked Mr Richardson and me to meet him in Albany, and I learned that Mr Richardson had had a conversation very similar to mine with him. Mr Richardson and I talked of the matter and we agreed in taking much the same view of it that I have just now expressed.

I ought to mention perhaps that Mr Dorsheimer had had some previous experience in dealing with both Mr Richardson and myself in a professional capacity. This had come to him as a Commissioner of public works on which we were employed.[12]

After some debate with the Lieut' Governor, being urged by him first as a personal favor to himself and secondly as a matter of duty to the State, we consented to serve as he wished. We were then consulted as {to} an additional member or members of the proposed board. Seven architects and two engineers, were named. The Lieut Governor observed that no engineer was likely to be needed and after thoroughly canvassing the architects, referring in the case of most to such of their works as he had seen, selected Mr Eidlitz distinctly on the ground of his large experience and the general satisfaction he had himself experienced with many of his important works, and on no other.

He finally said that he would propose that we should receive a round sum of $1500 each for the service—he understood that it would be inadequate but he did not think the Commission would consent to making it larger.

To this we made no reply but met with him before the Board where the arrangment was confirmed.

I wrote to Mr Eidlitz and he joined us. Immediately upon his coming into the room where we were, he said, "So far as I understand what would be expected, the duty of this proposed board would be one of the most disagreeable that an architect could be called upon to perform, and, of course, $1500 would be no compensation for it but I considered when I received your note that you were not a man to blunder into such a business or who would propose to me that I should join you in it unless you thought that by doing so we might be in the way of rendering the state some service."

Much in these words if not literally, and in this spirit we all of us accepted the duty of our office and in this spirit we pursued it. It may better show you this if I say that there is not one of us who has not at different times, when certain stages of our task have been passed asked of his associates if they would not consent to his retirement. I have myself been most particularly anxious to withdraw, and have been prevailed on to remain only by the declaration of both my comrads that if I refused they would themselves immediately resign. Of course this was before the attacks made upon us, or after they ceased and when we had no idea that they would be renewed.

There are two things more, Sir, of which I wish, if you please, to speak—because they seem to have been misunderstood. First, as to our attitude toward Mr Fuller.

To explain this it may be necessary that I should say that there is a custom which seems fixed in this country, a custom to which our people are tenaciously attached, but which every competent architect believes to be a bad one; at least a very questionable one. I mean the custom of obtaining plans and selecting the architects for public buildings by a certain method of public competition. The method adopted in the case of this Capitol building was not one, as architects believe, which was calculated to obtain for the state such plans as it should have had or all such architectural service as it needed. The custom is based as we think on a wrong idea of the proper duties of the architect and of the most desirable relations between an architect and his client. No man who has ever been for his private ends in proper relations with a good architect can need to be informed what these are. The architect should not stand in the position of a mere scrivener, clerk or amanuensis to his client, but in the confidential position of his lawyer or physician. He should not merely follow, in many important respects he should lead. He should not be instructed only, in many important respects he should instruct.

The usual process I say is based on a mistaken view of the responsibilities of the architect and a most exceedingly mistaken under estimate of what may properly and what should be asked of him. And this mistaken view having been adopted at the outset is thereafter almost unavoidably maintained, and the architect selected in this manner never comes into his proper position, never feels his proper responsibilities, is never able to fully give his client that benefit which he should have of his knowledge, training, experience and art. I wish that this could be realized but there seems to be a difficulty about {it} where an architect is concerned.

A man needing medical treatment would do a very foolish thing, as anyone can see, if he should undertake to describe his own symptoms and advertise that he would receive prescriptions for them and choose that man for a physician whose prescription he liked best. A man would make grave mistakes who in like manner selected his lawyers, and in like manner had his contracts drawn.

When a building plan is the result of such a process as public opinion is supposed to require to be followed generally with our public buildings, architects are not surprised to find crudities in it, evidences of inexperience and imperfect study in many respects.

We explained this to the Commission; we explained more than once or twice, we explained many times that Mr Fuller was not necessarily responsible for many things which under the constant searching inquiries of the Commission we were obliged to speak ill of in the building, and here I may testify that no man on trial for his life before a French justice was ever more shrewdly and persistently examined & cross examined and obliged to show himself from every point of view than we have been in the Commission's process of examining this building through our eyes and our minds.

But the Committee should distinctly understand that we were never asked, certainly we never undertook, to pass judgment on the Architect of the Capitol, or to pass judgment on the Commission which had been superceded. We were asked to give expert opinions upon the building as we found it, on the plans as we found them, and on the best available means of bettering them and of bettering it. After a time — it was no part of our original undertaking,—we were asked to prepare plans in accordance with the advice we had given.

The only advice we have ever given the Commissioners or any of them with respect to Mr Fuller was that they should not hold him accountable for all the faults of the building and that they should not think of dismissing him.

On one occasion I remember that in answer to some observations of ours the Lieut Governor said, "If you can satisfy us that Mr Fuller is not responsible for these faults — if you can satisfy us that he is throughly competent for the work — understand that we have no prejudice against him, on the contrary we would like nothing better than to strengthen him and sustain him and give him a chance to show the very best that he can do."

I don't mean to be understood as intimating that at the time Mr Fuller was dismissed, after all that had then occurred it was not right and necessary that he should be dismissed. But that was not a part of our business and there was never an effort to make it so. Until after Mr Fuller's dismissal we had no knowledge of any intention to dismiss him.

I am not conscious of ever having said a word of Mr Fuller that was not a word of respect. I am not aware that I or that the present architects of the Capitol have at any time to any person or any body of persons said one word against his work, that we {were} not required to say in reply to questions addressed to us. If as he supposes, we did so in our published report[13] it escaped us unintentionally and its significance was not recognized. That report was a report on the building not on its architect.

I know that it is difficult to think of them apart but that was what we were required to do, and that was what we did do.

We trace and in our minds we constantly have traced all the faults of the building — its excessive costliness more particularly, back to method under which most of its important characteristics seem to us to have probably been determined — that is to say by a body of gentlemen, having many differences of opinion needing to be reconciled as best they could and dealing with a subject with which no one of them had adequate experience, yet under the influence of a bad but strongly fixed custom denying to themselves the only method which the most highly educated and cultivated men in any part of the world have ever found to result satisfactorily.

Finally I wish to say a few words as to the matter of what is called the change of styles — we did not fall into that accidentally. We all of us recognized it as a somewhat grave matter and we did consider at great length; with much study; with prolonged debate in many sessions and with sketches and drawings both by Mr Richardson and Mr Eidlitz, whether it was practicable to accomplish what we were instructed to aim at, as well by any means which would not be open to that form of criticism and we were satisfied that it would not.

When I read the Memorial of the architects — gentlemen whom I greatly respect, gentlemen who had conferred upon me an honorary distinction[14] which I greatly valued and for which I felt very grateful to them, gentlemen whom I regarded as personal friends. I confess that when I read their apparently unqualified, indignant, instant and unanimous condemnation of a judgment to which my associates had been brought so deliberately and with so much care, I confess that I felt extreme surprise and great concern. And though I saw that it was hasty, inconsiderate {and} that it contained unconsciously & unintentionally, of course, errors of fact and allusions and insinuations for which there did not exist the slightest shadow of justification — I felt a momentary doubt whether we had not been in some way deceived in supposing that we had found a means of increasing the dignity, repose and harmony of aspect of the building — whether what we had imagined to be harmony might *not* be, as these gentlemen asserted "absolute want of harmony." Turning it over in my mind I said to myself — "Why! it is not necessary that a man should be a practicing architect to determine such a question." I called, then, on a distinguished painter and asked how it struck him — I called on a distinguished sculptor and asked him. The question was answered with a smile.[15] Then I bethought me that there was one gentleman in the country who was peculiarly fitted to set me right if I was wrong in the matter. A gentleman who had made this very question of the historical sequence of styles — of schools, their origins and motive a special study and thus with advantages for the purpose such as no architect in the country has enjoyed — a devotee of art and a scholar withal of high culture. A man who has spent years in the close investigation of the more interesting architectural monumnts of Europe and whose business it has been to deduce general principles of art from what he found in them. A man who from his official position and the special studies which have qualified him for that position was likely to be peculiarly sensitive on the very point in question. Unquestionably, I suppose, the highest authority we have upon the subject. I mean the gentleman who occupies at Harvard University the chair of Art History.[16]

I sent Prof.ʳ Norton copies of the printed plans and of the protest of the architects, and asked him to kindly advise me whether it struck him that their point was well taken. I will if you please sir read a part of his reply — you shall have the whole if you desire. It was not written for publication but he has kindly given me permission to read it to you.

> The protest of the New York Chapter American Institute of Architects against the designs of your Advisory Board for the completion of the State Capitol Building — does not pay any attention to the most important features of your designs, namely the general treatment of the walls so as to secure breadth of mass, and simplicity and dignity of aspect; and, secondly, the essential change in the character of the roof, a change which coincides in effect with your treatment of the walls, and is, apparently, further recommended by great constructive advantages. It is hardly credible that the Chapter does not recognize the excellence of your design in these respects under the given conditions by which it was primarily determined. The work

had advanced so far before you were called upon for advice that your designs are to be looked upon as simply the best modifications you can suggest in a structure radically vicious; and in this view they seem to me in all essential points excellent. I certainly do not find in them any "direct antagonism to the received rules of art." They are antagonistic, it may be, to certain canons of building laid down by some architects of the Renaissance, canons deduced *not* from principles of art but from what were assumed to be classical models.

  The objection of the New York Chapter to the surmounting of Italian Renaissance under-stories by "absolutely inharmonious Romanesque stories," might have force if it were not a very open matter of question whether your upper stories are "absolutely inharmonious" with the lower. They seem to me to accord sufficiently in general character—not in simply technical style—with the part of the original building on which they are to rest.[17]

  Prof[r] Norton a few days after writing this letter authorized me to make any use of his opinion that I wished.[18] We have received expressions of convictions similar to those which it expresses from other gentlemen whose opinions upon the question are entitled, certainly, to as much respect as those which have been given to the legislature. We did not think it necessary and we questioned if it were decorous for us while holding our present position to engage in a public controversy on the subject or to seek to fortify the advice which as the appointed advisors of the state in the matter we have already given by bringing in volunteers to our assistance.

  A quotation from the letter, however, I have thought that you would excuse, because not only of the exceptional position held by its author as a special scholar in the history of architectural art which you have been told that we have outraged but because it justifies me in assuring you that this question is one upon which it is not necessary that a man should be an architect in order to form some opinion for himself. The question as Mr Norton points out really is are the upper stories essentially inharmonious with the lower in general character or are they not?

  I have as great deference as any man for the trained judgment of professional architects and I have always yielded to it in all proper occasions but it is a fact that upon this question trained judgments differ, and it is a fact that upon this question it is quite competent for a layman—for any member of the Committee—to form an opinion for himself and not be dependent on the possibility of rightly determining on which side the weight of professional judgment really lies. It cannot be done lightly. It cannot be done while you sit here in the Committee room, but it is not a mystery of the dark ages which can only be unlocked by one of the priesthood of art. I pray the Committee to use its own eyes and its own judgmnt.

  We much regret Sir that we had no warning and no reason to suppose that the question of the plans as last year adopted under the direction of the legislature was to be thus reviewed. Not knowing this we had prepared no perspective drawings—no show drawings—the Protesting architects cautioned the legislature against allowing its judgments to be beguiled by deceptive pictures. Go to the plan room Sir, and judge for yourself whether if such a caution was needed against whom it was needed. The only perspective of ours which you will find there—a pen and ink drawing, not glazed—was a drawing prepared to aid our judgmnt on a particular question upon which we were in some doubt. One of the Commissioners saw it in an office and asked us to have it filled out and framed. It is an accident that we have even so much, but while without an effort of the imagination such as few men without special training can use, you may not see the whole building before you as a picture— you will find the elevations and working drawings quite sufficient for an intelligent determination of the question which you have more particularly asked to decide.

The text presented here is from a draft in Olmsted's hand, read before the joint committees of finance and ways and means of New York State Legislature on March 6, 1877, as part of the testimony of the advisory board on the Capitol, which also included a presentation by Leopold Eidlitz and, presumably, one by H. H. Richardson (*New-York Times*, March 7, 1877, pp. 1–2).

1. Senator Hamilton Harris (1820–1900), Chairman of the Senate Finance Committee (*New-York Times*, Dec.16, 1900, p. 5).
2. That is, H. H. Richardson and Leopold Eidlitz.
3. That is, we who are finally permitted for the first time to address you officially after being present at your hearings during much of your month-long investigation.
4. In a letter of explanation of 1880 to lieutenant governor George G. Hoskins, Olmsted stated that "We are retained by the State (not as individual architects but) as a firm known as Eidlitz, Richardson & Co., and are paid for our services the sum of $20,000, $10,000 of which we receive to compensate us for all cash disbursements heretofore paid by the state." This arrangement occurred following the dismissal of Fuller as of July 1, 1876, after which the three members of the advisory board became jointly "Architects of the Capitol." (FLO to Hoskins, c. July 19, 1880; Cecil R. Roseberry, *Capitol Story* [Albany, N.Y., 1964], p. 33).
5. Olmsted is referring to remonstrances by architects against the advisory board's proposed changes in the state capitol that were published as documents of the state Senate for the 1876 session. One, dated March 30, 1876, was "Remonstrance of Thos. Fuller, Architect, Against the Proposed Changes in the Plans for the Building of the New Capitol," in which Fuller supplemented his own letter with a quotation from a letter by Richard M. Upjohn and a letter signed by the architects Richard Morris Hunt, Henry Dudley, and Detlef Lienau. Soon after, Fuller submitted several additional letters and quotations from still others in opposition to the advisory board's proposals. Also published as a Senate document was the "Remonstrance of the New York Chapter of the American Institute of Architects, Against the Proposed Changes in the Plans for the Building of the Capitol," signed by Richard Morris Hunt and A. J. Bloor. This phrase "ridiculed by all competent critics" appears in "Remonstrance of Certain Citizens of the State of New York, Against the Changes Which Have Been, and Are Being Made, on the New Capitol Building," dated December 1876 with 52 signatories ("Document nos. 64, 65, and 67," in New York [State], *Documents of the Senate of the State of New York, Ninety-Ninth Session*. . . [Albany, N.Y., 1876]; "Document no. 28,"

in New York [State], *Documents of the Senate of the State of New York, One Hundredth Session*. . .[Albany, N. Y., 1877]).
6. In a letter to the *New-York Times* published on March 2, 1877, Richard T. Auchmuty, a fellow of the American Institute of Architects, asserted that the proposal to have two stories of a building in one style and two in another "is a violation of all acknowledged rules of art." The assertion that the advisory board's design "would vitiate instead of educating the taste of the people" appears in a letter to the *New-York Times* of March 6, 1877, from the architects George B. Post, Richard Morris Hunt, Napoleon Le Brun, Henry Dudley, and Detlef Lienau; The term "monstrosity" occurs in a letter by J. C. Cochrane, a Chicago architect, of March 27, 1876; the term "horrid night-mare" appears in a letter by Frank W. Vogdes, architect of the Kentucky state capitol, of March 24, 1876, both presented by Fuller in his second remonstrance (D. S. Francis, *Architects in New York City, 1840–1900*, s.v. Auchmuty, Richard Tylden; "The Battle of the Styles," *New-York Times*, March 2, 1877, p. 4; "The Battle of the Styles," *New-York Times*, March 7, 1877, p. 2; "Document no. 66," in New York [State], *Documents of the Senate of the State of New York, Ninety-Ninth Session*. . . [Albany, N.Y., 1876]).
7. A reference to the dedication of Richardson's Trinity Church in Boston.
8. A reference to the publication of drawings of the Capitol in the March 11, 1876, issue of *American Architect and Building News*.
9. English-born architect Thomas Fuller had won the design competition for the Centre Block of the Parliament buildings in Ottawa in 1860. In 1863 he submitted a design for the New York State capitol. When the Capitol Commission was formed in 1865, he joined with Augustus Laver to submit a new design, and in 1867 a new design that Fuller drew up with the Boston architect Arthur D. Gilman was officially adopted (Shirley E. Woods, Jr., *Ottawa: The Capital of Canada* [Toronto and New York, 1980], pp. 124–25; C. Roseberry, *Capitol Story*, pp. 21–22).
10. A reference to the design competition for the new courts of justice in London of 1865–66, which was presided over by a royal commission consisting of representatives of the legal profession. (David B. Brownlee, *The Law Courts: The Architecture of George Edmund Street* [Cambridge, Mass., 1984], pp. 77–78).
11. Olmsted had been a partner in the architectural firm of Vaux, Withers, & Co. from c. 1865 to c. 1872.
12. William Dorsheimer had been a leader in the formation of a park system in Buffalo and was a member of the original park board, serving on that body until 1872. He had also been involved in 1874 in the selection of Richardson to design a proposed Civil War Memorial in Niagara Square, which Olmsted was redesigning. Dorsheimer was also influential in the selection in the early 1870s of Richardson to design the Buffalo State Hospital, for which Olmsted planned the grounds. Olmsted does not mention that, in addition, Richardson had designed a house for Dorsheimer in Buffalo in 1868–71, and prepared plans for him for a house in Albany in 1874–75 after he was elected lieutenant governor (Jeffrey Karl Ochsner, *H. H. Richardson: Complete Architectural Works* [Cambridge, Mass., 1982], pp. 54–55, 78–79, 144–47).
13. "Report of the Advisory Board (Frederick Law Olmsted, Leopold Eidlitz and Henry H. Richardson), Relative to the Plans of the New Capitol," "Document no. 49," in *Documents of the Senate of the State of New York, One Hundredth Session*. . .[Albany, N. Y., 1877]).
14. Olmsted had been made an honorary member of the American Institute of Architects in 1867 (*Papers of FLO*, 6: 677).
15. The painter that Olmsted consulted was probably his friend John La Farge, who at this time was creating the interior decoration of H. H. Richardson's Trinity Church in Boston. The sculptor was very likely J. Q. A. Ward, whom Olmsted and Vaux had advised in 1868 on the design of the Seventh Regiment Memorial in Central Park. Ward

secured a commission to do historical bas-reliefs in the New York State capitol and accompanied Olmsted, Richardson, and Eidlitz on one of their overnight steamboat trips to Albany from New York City (Henry Adams, et al., *John La Farge* [Pittsburgh and Washington, D.C., 1987], p. 242; John La Farge to FLO [c. November 1878]; FLO to Charles Eliot Norton, Jan. 22, 1880, below; Sara Cedar Miller, *Central Park, An American Masterpiece* [New York, 2003], pp. 202–03; Cecil R. Roseberry, *Capitol Story*, pp. 41, 55; Montgomery Schuyler, *American Architecture and Other Writings*, 2 vols., eds., William Jordy and Ralph Coe [Cambridge, Mass., 1961], 1: 177).

16. A reference to Charles Eliot Norton.
17. Olmsted is quoting from a letter to him from Charles Eliot Norton of April 4, 1876. The only substantive statement that Olmsted deleted occurs in the ellipsis represented by the long dash in the first sentence, within which Norton asserted that the New York Chapter's protest "is not only a foul blow but a weak one." Olmsted also added the emphasis of italics to the word "not" in the last sentence of the first paragraph that he quoted (Charles Eliot Norton to FLO, April 4, 1876, Charles Eliot Norton Papers, Houghton Library, Harvard University, Cambridge, Massachusetts).
18. Norton had written Olmsted "I have just written to you a letter that may be shown to anybody, or used in any way you see fit" (Norton to FLO, April 4, 1876, Charles Eliot Norton Papers, Houghton Library, Harvard University, Cambridge, Mass.).

To William McMillan

McMillan

16th March 1877.

My Dear Sir,
I have just recvd yours of 14th and look for your next with anxiety. Whatever occurs I hope that you will regard the present aspect of affairs as temporary. Public opinion and even Aldermanic opinion will turn again. At any rate parks must be taken care of and one element of competency in taking care of them lies in adjusting the method of managment as far as indispensably necessary to existing conditions of municipal government. The report of Mr Evarts' Commission after two years study of the subject records the conviction that there is no use in attempting to overcome the chief source of bad government of cities while the conditions of service of the general government remain what they have been.[1] In what is now occurring at Washington let us hope that we see a glimmer of better days dawning.[2]

The names on your map now strike me with one or two exceptions as studiously common place and cheap. If you set about fixing names on the park don't you think there should be found some slight flavor of quaintness among them and that it is possible to have this without running into mawkishness? I think that I should prefer, unless the process can be carried further and better, to continue to omit names from the map—at least to omit all the matter of course descriptive names, such as the South bay, the North bay, the East bay. I don't like the "Look Out" because the place is not sufficiently entitled (rather than any other) to the distinction—besides it is a cheap appropriation. I think that I would not note the landings and if I did so I would not say (superfluously) *boat* landing. The French *entrance* is very bad when we have the better English *gate*. If the Commission have an objection to gate it is probably based on a misapprehension. It means a passage not the instrument for barring a passage. The city gate is the entrance and outlet of the city not the port cullis which stops entrance and outgoing. I would now substitute Bosky-banks for Coppice banks—(coppice means wood never allowed to grow large) "North Meadow gate" strikes me now as cumbrously long. I should prefer—though it is cheap—North gate. Northmead gate, Southmead gate would perhaps do better. I would certainly not say "Park-way Gate"—better Beechbank gate or Lincoln gate—or Main gate or City gate. By all means Sedgwood gate not South meadow.

I think that I will give any of the Douglass farm trees that remain worth moving to Central Park. Please send me an authorization to take them which can be used by Mr Fischer or any one sent from the park.[3]

The text presented here is from a draft in Olmsted's hand.

1. William Maxwell Evarts (1818–1901), lawyer and statesman. On the heels of widespread corruption and fraud, first with the Tweed Ring in 1872 and then the Canal Ring in 1874, the governor of New York in May of the following year appointed a commission to "devise a plan for the government of cities in the State of New York." The commission was made up of well-known lawyers and professional men, and Evarts was elected its president. In March 1877 the commission released its report. The commission made several recommendations for the improvement of city government such as increasing home rule, strengthening the power of mayors, creating popularly elected boards of aldermen, creating boards of finance, and limiting indebtedness. The state legislature, however, failed to act on any of the recommendations (*DAB*; Chester L. Barrows, *William M. Evarts: Lawyer, Diplomat, Statesman* [Chapel Hill, N.C., 1941], pp. 194–95; "Document no. 68," in New York [State], *Documents of the Assembly of the State of New York* [Albany, N.Y., 1877], pp. 17–20, 30).
2. A reference to President Rutherford B. Hayes's pledge for civil service reform in his inaugural address on March 5, 1877. On March 10, 1877, at his first cabinet meeting, Hayes asked William Evarts and Carl Schurz to draft rules for civil service appointments (Charles R. Williams, *The Life of Rutherford Birchard Hayes*, 2 vols. [New York, 1971], 2: 8–9; Arthur Bishop, ed., *Rutherford B. Hayes, 1822–1893* [Dobbs Ferry, N.Y., 1969], pp. 14–15).
3. William L. Fischer.

To WILLIAM RUNYON MARTIN

CITY OF NEW YORK,
DEPARTMENT OF PUBLIC PARKS,
20th March, 1877.

The Hon. WILLIAM R. MARTIN,
President of the Board:
SIR—
In compliance with your request,[1] the undersigned have the honor herewith to present a map, showing proposed routes for local steam transit through the Twenty-third and Twenty-fourth Wards, and connections of the same with lines, or proposed lines extending to the south end of the city.

I.

The speed which is maintained on our railways in passing through rural districts is generally checked the moment a dense population is reached, and within our large towns the chief advantage of this great improvement upon older methods of traveling is in a great degree lost. Where, as is the case with New York, the distance between the business centre and the residence centre is great, the deprivation is a serious one, and the demand that it should be obviated has long been pressing.

The reason for the diminution of speed on entering a town lies in the fact that the long-established plan of laying out towns is not adapted to the conditions essential to rapid movement, having been devised before the necessity for it was felt, and indeed before the means of accomplishing it had been invented. Now that its accomplishment has been proved to be mechanically practicable and its necessity is recognized, it would be unpardonable, in devising plans for laying out a large territory for the accommodation of a more or less dense population, not to provide for it in advance.

II.

In the existing condition of the mechanical appliances for travel at high speed it can only be accomplished by the use of heavy trains of vehicles moving on rigid lines with light gradients. For safety such lines must be so located that pedestrians and vehicles adapted to use on ordinary roads can by no possibility encounter the trains. The routes selected must, therefore, at all points of contact with common roads, be either above or below their grades. Any plan which involves adherence throughout the entire route to an invariable type of construction, whether elevated or depressed, is inconsistent with economy in any region like new wards, the topography of which is very uneven.

The conditions to be fulfilled are best found in a road running either along a hillside, in a narrow valley, or on a narrow ridge, in such a manner that intersecting streets may be carried either over or under it, as local convenience may dictate, with moderate expense.

III.

It has hitherto been customary in laying out routes for railways to disregard the requirements of ordinary travel and the existing and future division of property. It has, on the other hand, been usual, in dividing property by common streets, to pay no attention to the possible introduction of railway transit.

As a result of these customs, difficulty is now encountered on New York Island in arranging rapid transit routes, and in the suburban wards in obtaining safe and convenient roads adjoining and crossing existing railroads. Inasmuch as steam roads admit of less flexibility of line and grade than common roads, the determination of their location should in a plan aiming to combine the two systems satisfactorily, precede the establishment of the complete subdivision of the property, but the practicability of a proper subdivision must always be kept in view. The construction of a system devised to combine the two undoubtedly involves more expense for each, considered by itself, than if the combination could be avoided, but not so great expense or injury as the adjusting of one to the cheapest location of the other.

IV.

The experience of the last twenty-five years has demonstrated that the chief obstacle to the accomplishment of speedy communication between distant points in New York City, is the difficulty of obtaining the right of way for steam roads.

There are three methods possible for acquiring the land needed:

1st. It may be purchased by the corporation which is to furnish the means of transportation.

2d. The right of way over a highway already devoted to the public uses may be granted to such corporation.

3d. A new route to be used exclusively for the purpose may be provided at the public expense.

Where the transporting corporation purchases the land, the whole burden falls on the travelers, who are forced to pay in fares the interest on the purchase money, as well as on the cost of construction.

Capitalists object to this method, from a conviction that it will oblige the imposition of so high a rate of fare as to repel, rather than invite travel; or if low fares are established by legislation, that the result will be a loss to the management.

Where a street is taken which has been already acquired by the public for ordinary traffic and for access to the property fronting on it, the burden falls partly on the travelers, who pay the interest on the cost of construction, receiving an equivalent however for their money, and partly on the owners of such property as is injured, who receive no equivalent.

This method is objected to by owners of property, on the ground that it imposes the cost of the right of way on them, not indeed directly as an actual pecuniary disbursement, but indirectly, through the depreciation of the value of their property, and the diminution of their business resulting from the presence in the street of an obstruction to ordinary traffic.

Where a new route is furnished by the public, part of the burden is borne by the travelers, as in the other cases, and the rest by the property which is benefited by the facilities for travel, which includes alike the business centres and the remote residence districts.

By this method, the injury to property is reduced to a minimum, and the burden is distributed equitably among the persons who are benefited.

V.

In accordance with the considerations thus presented, the plan now submitted contemplates the laying out of a system of roads on such routes and with such grades that their use can be restricted to steam travel, that they will afford moderately direct communication between the desired points, will be easily accessible from all points which they do not directly touch, will nowhere cross ordinary high ways at the same level, and will not as a rule interfere with satisfactory divisions of property.

In the arrangement of the routes the following principles have been kept in view.

(1.) The crossings of the Harlem River must be as few as possible.

(This is alike desirable whether such crossings are by bridge or by tunnel; if by the former it is important that navigation should be as unobstructed as practicable, if by the latter the expense of many crossings would be too great.)

(2.) All crossings of the river must be at such points that connection can be easily had with lines on New York Island.

(3.) Lines must be so laid out that trains passing from the city through one district may return by a loop or circuit through another.

(This not only gives to the residents of each of the districts the advantage of communication between the two, but also gives them, with the same number of trains, more frequent opportunities to reach the business centre than they would have with single lines.)

(4.) While every opportunity must be afforded to existing lines of trunk freight and passenger railroads to co-operate in the local passenger

Plan for local steam transit routes Twenty-third and Twenty-fourth wards, New-York City, March 20, 1877

traffic, routes and river crossings must be provided which will be independent of their control.

VI.

With reference to the crossing of the Harlem River, the following considerations are presented:

There are but two existing railroad crossings of the river. The New York Central & Hudson River Railroad enters on New York island by a bridge at Spuyten Duyvil, and the extension of the same road by the Spuyten Duyvil & Port Morris branch crosses at Fourth Avenue by the bridge of the Harlem Railroad, which is also used by the New Haven Railroad.

The Rapid Transit Commissioners,[2] in 1875, authorized a crossing of the river at First Avenue, to connect with the Portchester branch of the New Haven Railroad, and another near the High Bridge, to connect with the partially constructed New York & Boston Railroad.

Both of these lines are so situated as to render it very unlikely that any crossing will be constructed upon them for many years to come, if at all.

As regards the first, a bridge would cause too great obstruction to navigation at a point which is now the centre of a considerable water traffic, and a tunnel is not likely to be built upon it as long as it is possible, within a mile, to construct, at one-tenth of the cost, a bridge which will not very seriously interfere with the interests of commerce.

As regards a crossing near the High Bridge, the authorized approach on the Manhattan shore passes for more than a mile along the base of a precipitous hill, which can never have a sufficient population to support a local road, and from the crossing, when made, extensions of the road can be made with advantage in only one direction.

A bridge from One hundred and forty-fifth Street, on the south side of the river, connecting with the loop line authorized by the Rapid Transit Commission, along the exterior street, and crossing to One hundred and forty-ninth Street, on the north side, will be open to neither of these objections. It will afford all the facilities for crossing which will be needed, for several years at least, and will be at such distance from any other bridge that little inconvenience will occur to navigation, even after the projected improvement of the Harlem River is made.[3]

VII.

In determining the arrangements which should be provided for steam transit after crossing the river, existing railroads must be taken into consideration.

Along the Hudson River the New York Central & Hudson River Railroad affords facilities for travel; along the Harlem River runs the Spuyten

JANUARY 1877–OCTOBER 1877

Duyvil & Port Morris Railroad; in the Mill Brook Valley the Harlem River Railroad furnishes accommodation; and further to the eastward the Portchester Branch Railroad has an opportunity for building up a large local travel as far north as West Farms Village.

Of these the Spuyten Duyvil & Port Morris branch, in connection with the Hudson River Railroad, is the only one which at all supplies the desideratum of a circuit or loop line. It is defective, in that its termini lie on opposite sides of the city, and too far north.[4]

The other lines mentioned must always remain pre-eminently routes of through travel, and as such their managers cannot be expected to give the attention to local convenience which the interests of the city will demand.

Being, nevertheless, too important to be overlooked in any comprehensive scheme, they may be considered available as links of a system as yet incomplete, and opportunity must be given them for combining with other lines.

The three main divisions of the territory which are as yet wholly unprovided with facilities for access to old New York, are the valley lying east of the Spuyten Duyvil Promontory and extending to Yonkers, the Jerome Avenue Valley, and the Southern Boulevard District.

During most of the year, the pleasure and comfort of water travel over the route by steamboat from Harlem to the eastern lower portion of the city will always attract a large passenger traffic. It is essential, therefore, that provision should be made for the delivery of passengers from local railroads at the point now occupied by the terminus of the Portchester road, situated at the head of unobstructed navigation.

VIII.

The plans submitted herewith exhibit the following main features:

(*a.*) A central crossing of the Harlem River between Fifth and Sixth avenues at a point about equidistant from the two authorized routes on New York Island, running parallel to its axis.

(*b.*) A main circuit line up the Jerome Avenue Valley to Jerome Park, thence crossing to the Harlem Railroad, by the route of the Jerome Park Branch Railroad, and following a route generally parallel to that of the Southern Boulevard to the Boston Road, thence down the Bound Brook Valley to the Westchester Road, thence to the Port Morris branch, at St. Mary's Park, and thence, crossing North New York, between One hundred and forty-fourth and One hundred and forty-fifth Streets, over the Harlem Railroad, and through Buena Ridge to the bridge at One hundred and forty-ninth Street.

(*c.*) A loop line, connecting with the main circuit and with the Port Morris Branch Railroad at St. Mary's Park and passing through the Notch at One hundred and forty-first Street, and southerly between St. Ann's and

Brook Avenues, to a connection with the Portchester Depot, and thence, along the river, to the crossing at One hundred and forty-ninth Street.

(d.) A loop line, connecting with the main circuit at Mount Eden, and following the Valley of the Ice Pond Brook, passing under the Harlem Railroad at One hundred and fifty-fourth Street, and thence, between Morris and College Avenues, to line (c), near the Portchester Depot.

(e.) A line, connecting the main circuit and the Portchester Railroad, near Fox's Corners.

(f.) A loop line *via* the Port Morris Branch Railroad.

(g.) A line from Kingsbridge to Ludlow's Dock and Yonkers, by way of the Broadway Valley.

(h.) A route from High Bridge to Yonkers, up the valley of Tibbett's Brook, being an amendment of the route of the partly-built New York, Boston & Montreal Railroad.

All of the above described routes are so located as to be intermediate between streets intended for ordinary travel, and all such streets will cross them, either over or under the grade.

The maximum gradient will be 80 feet to a mile, and the minimum radius of curvature 521 feet. These extremes are closely approached but in a few instances.

Respectfully,

J. JAMES R. CROES,
Civil and Topographical Engineer.
FREDERICK LAW OLMSTED,
Landscape Architect.

The text presented here is from "Document No. 75," in New York (City), Department of Public Parks, *Minutes*, March 21, 1877.

1. No specific request for this report and map was recorded in the board's printed minutes or quarterly reports. However, William R. Martin considered rapid transit access to the new wards integral to their overall planning and development. In March 1875 he reported to the board that elevated rail lines would be too expensive to build in the area. To avoid at-grade crossings, therefore, "a depressed or viaduct road" should be built where the lines crossed thoroughfares. "This feature of the plan," he concluded, "should receive the first consideration." Upon receiving the report and map, the board resolved that they be printed and the subject laid over. It approved the plan for local steam routes on January 16, 1878 ("Document No. 65," in DPP, *Minutes*, March 30, 1875, p. 14; DPP, *Minutes*, March 21, 1877, p. 693; ibid., Jan. 16, 1878, p. 522).
2. In June 1875 the New York state legislature authorized the organization of county rapid transit commissions and granted them power to determine the routes of rapid transit lines, passenger rates, and, if necessary, to organize companies to build them. By early September 1875 New York City's commission presented a report to the Board of Alder-

men, which adopted it, fixing the location of routes on Manhattan and crossings over the Harlem River to the north (Isaac Newton Phelps Stokes, *The Iconography of Manhattan Island, 1498–1909*, 6 vols. [New York, 1915–28], 5: 1958–59; *New-York Times*, Sept. 7, 1875, p. 2).
3. The present 149th Street bridge, completed in 1905, occupies the site recommended here by Olmsted. In April 1876 the New York state legislature had given permission to the United States to improve the channel of the Harlem River and Spuyten Duyvil from the Hudson River to the East River. The work was carried out by the U.S. Army Corps of Engineers (Stephen Jenkins, *The Story of the Bronx* [New York, 1912], p. 206; I. N. P. Stokes, *Iconography of Manhattan Island*, 5: 1964).
4. The Spuyten Duyvil and Port Morris branch railroad was the only existing line that crossed the area from west to east. Its western terminus was at Spuyten Duyvil station on the Hudson River and its eastern terminus was at Port Morris on the East River. Olmsted and Croes proposed three additional west-east lines south of it in Morrisania.

To Horatio Admiral Nelson

Mr Nelson.

26th March 1877

Dear Sir,
  I have recevd yours of 21st. The objection to the Small Pox Hospital lies in the effect it will have on the imaginations of the people. Of course the park is the last place in all of the unoccupied suburbs of the city where it can stand appropriately and there is no position in the park where it can go without being an offence to good taste.[1]
  The special objection to the position you suggest is that a small pox hospital there would render valueless good house lots, now city property but which may otherwise be expected in a few years to be brought favorably into the market with the advantages of frontage on the park, of a street railroad passing close by, of good roads, and a near market, church, post office &c (at St Jean Baptiste).[2] Also that it would be even at present much nearer to this village than it is proper to place such a hospital. St Jean Baptiste, whenever the park begins to exist as a park, will be sure to gain rapidly in population and prosperity and will spread over the park lands. There is no ground in the rear of the Hotel Dieu[3] in which the necessary buildings could stand so that there would be a space of more than a hundred feet between them and a public road, as roads are proposed and will soon need to be laid out. I have no doubt that it will in the end cost the city a great deal more if the hospital is placed

here than in the location I have advised. The latter is much the more isolated site really and apparently.[4]

The objection you present does not appear to me weighty for this reason. The site you propose would be closely passed in going to the other which I have suggested, therefore until after passing that point, whichever is taken, the same route would ordinarily and might by regulation always be followed. The occasion for moving patients is not frequent. They should be moved in close vehicles in no way specially noticable and they would rarely be observed or known to be bound for the hospital until after leaving the public road. The actual danger is nothing. The only important question is that of the remoteness of the hospital itself and in this respect the site I advise has obviously very greatly the advantage.

I think that it would prove a great injury to your property to place the hospital anywhere between Bleury Street or the Frothingham property and St. Jean Baptiste.

As to your inquiry about planting, a little reflection will show you that if trees could be made to grow in rows at regular intervals on each side of the present wheel way of your half built road up the mountain they would simply call attention to and make more marked the present prominent, rude, artificial character of the cuttings and embankments between which it is carried. These have been made with such misunderstanding of the purpose with which the road was laid out that I believe that it would be true economy to tear the whole work up and build it over again.[5] But if it is out of the question as I suppose it is just now, there is little to be done to improve the road until you begin the excavation for the Reservoir. Every spade full that comes from that should be used with the greatest possible care and judgement to hide and make less conspicuous the unnatural character of the embankment on which the road rests. When this has been done, but not before, it will be desirable to plant trees & bushes near it, not by any means in rows and at regular intervals but naturally, in groups and clusters and thickets, with frequent glades and openings where under favorable circumstances distant views can be best commanded.

What you chiefly need at present is to be getting the proper assortment of trees and shrubs for the purpose growing in proper permanent nurseries, particularly the Siberian trees & others which I recommended you to get as seedlings from Scotland.

Planting such as you did last year without system or design is a waste of money.

The text presented here is from a draft in Olmsted's hand.

1. On March 15, 1877, Nelson wrote to Olmsted about a new location for the small pox hospital. Nelson suggested that the hospital be "placed directly back of the Hotel Dieu

Mall, and nearly over to St Urbane Street. . . ." Olmsted replied that if it was necessary to build such a hospital on park grounds, it should certainly be placed "at the greatest practicable distance from any of its roads or walks and from any dwelling house or public street or ground likely to be so occupied." On March 21, Nelson reiterated his suggestion for placing the hospital behind the Hotel Dieu, stating that that location would be more accessible by existing thoroughfares (H. A. Nelson to FLO, March 15, 1877; ibid., March 21, 1877; FLO to H. A. Nelson, March 19, 1877).
2. The village of St. Jean Baptiste was north of Mount Royal Park and the proposed extension of Bleury Street, and northwest of the Hotel Dieu.
3. See FLO to Mount Royal Park Commissioners, Nov. 23, 1874, note 8, above.
4. Olmsted advised that the small pox hospital be located on the park grounds but 600 feet from the nearest road on what was the Benjamin Hall property. Nelson's suggestion for the location of the hospital would have placed it just east of Olmsted's main approach road, Bleury Street, and made it very conspicuous as one entered the park. Olmsted's suggested placement, however, moved the hospital to the west of the approach road and inside the park, in essence hiding it from view (FLO to H. A. Nelson, March 19, 1877).
5. At this point Olmsted included the following text but then crossed it out, "If this could be done I would gladly contribute a thousand dollars to bring this about, myself, so mortifying it is to me."

To the Public

Mch 26. 1877

To the Public.

A controversy has lately grown out of the changes of plan which have been adopted for the new capitol of this state in the heat, haste and confusion of which we apprehend that there is danger that a too prevalent impression may with some be confirmed and strengthened. For this reason rather than because we wish to appear as partisans of either of the plans in dispute we think that while the public mind is more than usually awake to the matter, a word of caution may be timely.

The impression referred to is of this nature.

That the essence of architecture lies in overlaying the substantial structure of a building with what are termed architectural forms applied in certain combinations suggested by personal fancy, these having no necessary relation to the uses, purposes, or materials of the building but selected and used with this single qualification, that they have been taken from the store house of history and all belong to a given period of time, or if belonging to two or more periods that they have heretofore been joined together by someone who has himself by the lapse of time become historical.

This impression is a false and a pernicious one. Architecture is the Art of building, not merely of ornamenting nor in any way of veiling or covering up of a building. It is a living art; an art which deals always directly with its special problems as they arise, seeking first of all to use its materials in the best mechanical way for the particular purpose in hand; looking to the past not for forms but for the cause of forms, and avoiding all useless construction, uncalled for ornament and especially all imitation in one situation or in one material of forms appropriate to another situation and another material.

It is only in this way that architectural monuments have ever been produced, the merits of which are recognized at all times, by men of all degrees of culture, under all changes of fashion. The unity of style which distinguishes such structures is never due simply to the reproduction or imitation of forms first designed in adaptation to conditions of an earlier age or to the needs and customs of a different people and which are for the time in which they are built without meaning or life, but to the direct rational and logical process by which they have been built.

But let us give the question a practical form, a form in which if it does not come before us today it may tomorrow.

Supposing a great and costly building to have been already partly erected which under the rule we have laid down is not a work of true architecture, its plain rude exterior walls having been superficially overlaid with copies of parts of old buildings all possibly in one style but which as to that which is within have no meaning. Suppose that it cannot be taken down, one question is whether it is the duty of an architect always to carry it on as it has been begun?

We answer unhesitatingly that it is not. It is the duty of the architect as soon as possible to deal with it rationally and frankly for what it is; to make outside as far as it is in his power expressive of that which is within, to give it outwardly as well as inwardly a life and a character of its own. Then also if he is allowed it is his duty to touch carefully what has already been done, bringing it as far as may be into an essential harmony with that which is built upon it. {*It is his duty to adjust that which is bad to that which is good, not that which is unformed to that which is bad.*}

Not all of us have had an opportunity of examining the capitol at Albany and it is not our duty to pronounce whether it is or is not a case in point.

We simply would not, on any account, have it supposed that if it had been so, if its exterior had at any stage in its progress been found by an architect called in consultation by the state, to be inappropriate, insignificant, meaningless with reference to its purpose, its interior arrangment and its construction, that there is any rule or established understanding in our profession that would require him to pursue purity of style at the expense of purity or truth or dignity of expression, still less at the expense of integrity of material or soundness of construction.[1]

JANUARY 1877–OCTOBER 1877

The text presented here is from a draft in Olmsted's hand. It was apparently intended to be a public statement signed by architects that would counteract the numerous "remonstrances" that architects had issued in opposition to the advisory board's proposals concerning the state capitol. It was to be issued in April 1876 in the "counter professional demonstration" that he had contemplated in response to the protest by the American Institute of Architects in April 1876 (see FLO to Charles Eliot Norton, April 2, 1876, above).

1. The view expressed in this sentence is reminiscent of Olmsted's later statement that Eidlitz and Richardson proposed to complete the capitol in a Romanesque style "chiefly for the reason that they were of the opinion that it would give a better opportunity for a true expression exteriorly of the internal structure, arrangements and special services of the building. (This was certainly the reason I gave my adherence to the proposition)" (FLO to Marianna Griswold Van Rensselaer, Dec. 21, 1887).

To the Mount Royal Park Commission

28 April 1877

To the Mount Royal Park Commisn.
Gentlemen.
 I have recevd an inquiry through your Secretary asking my judgmnt upon an application for permission to erect a commemorative monument upon the mountain. The character of the monument and the object of commemoration not being stated I can only briefly indicate a few general rules which I think should govern the city in determining questions of this class.
 The chance of getting a monumnt that will not in any position which would be selected for it be in some way out of place is a small one. A monumnt that would appear appropriate and dignified in a public place of moderate extent framed in by buildings will appear meanly and discordantly in the midst of natural scenery of large scale. And the essential object of monuments is much better served if they are placed in the midst of the people in their daily lives, rather than in positions where they will be chiefly looked upon as holiday sights and seen incidentally to a very different form of amusement.
 Regarded as ornaments it must be always remembered that the mountain is a mountain and all finished artificial ornaments upon it will be more or less incongruous. Every artificial object upon it should be placed there only and obviously only to serve in some practical way the main purpose of the enjoyment of natural scenery, and the less conspicuous it is the better.
 All funereal monumnts and all with which would stir sad associations, all monumnts tending to kindle or keep alive differences of creed, of

race, of politics or which would be provocative of antagonism of any kind should be excluded.

Finally no monuments should be admitted which are not works of art of a high and dignified type, such as very rarely offer.

Whatever the character of the monumnt now offered and the occasion of it, I would strongly urge you not to accept it until you have adopted a general plan to which every detail can be systematically subordinated.

I am aware that what I have said would exclude all monuments and I must admit the possibility of public interests which would overrule this position. I can only say therefore that on general principles monumnts should be admitted if at all with extreme caution and careful circumspection.

My draft of the plan has been for some weeks complete and I have two draughtsmen engaged upon the final drawing. The hand work of this is very tedious, much more so than that of any other plan I have ever undertaken. Judging from the rate of progress thus far the drawing cannot be completed within a month from this time.

The text presented here is from a draft in Olmsted's hand.

To WILLIAM RUNYON MARTIN

NEW YORK, 16th May, 1877.

The Hon. WILLIAM R. MARTIN,
President of the Department of Public Parks.
SIR:—
On the 9th inst. the Board was informed that the statue of Halleck was intended to be unveiled on the 15th, and that plans had been formed for the occasion for the carrying out of which its sanction and aid were needed.[1]

It was ascertained that the committee having the matter in charge had already made an engagement with the President of the United States, and numerous distinguished persons, to take part in the proceedings, and also to associate with them a military display under the form of an act of courtesy to the President. A thousand invitations had been printed and mainly sent out, each promising a secured seat for two persons; sixty special guests of the committee were also to be provided for upon the platform or in reserved seats adjoining it.

These arrangements had been so far advanced that, on the whole, it seemed best to take the risks of carrying them through than to attempt to have them changed.[2]

Preparations were made on the ground as follows:—A square in front of the statue, large enough to contain seats for the required number was enclosed by a line of posts connected by a strong rope and by a line of iron framed settees, set back outwards, below the rope. An entrance was left at the middle of the Mall, on the south side, and another at the platform. The approach to the rear of the platform from the drive, and the space to be occupied by the military, was enclosed by a rope carried by posts and trees, and, where pressure was likely to be greatest, by a well-braced fence of scantling.[3] The total line of enclosure was 1,600 feet.

The force available for preserving order consisted of a captain and fifty men of the 7th Regiment, and the lieutenant of the park keepers, three sergeants and sixty-nine uniformed privates. The force, coming on the ground a little before two, at once, and without difficulty, cleared the enclosure of about 3,000 persons who had previously occupied it, and was then distributed along the lines above defined and the drives leading to them.

The two nearest carriage entrances to the Park from Fifth Avenue[4] were closed except to footmen, and no one was allowed to pass on the drives except those bearing passes from the committee. After the crowd, pressing towards the platform, had become so large and dense that a lane could no longer be kept open without constant exercise of force, visitors with passes were sent along the drive and through the military lines and were able to the last to come to the seats with comfort. Ushers had been provided in addition to the keepers, but, as visitors would not be guided by them, or remain where placed unless in seats near the platform, the attempt to regulate the seating was abandoned.

Just before the military procession reached the ground an inspection was made of the entire line of enclosure and of the approaches to it for several hundred yards each way. At every point on a frontage of more than 3,000 feet there was a pressing crowd, and it appeared everywhere to be deep and compact. Every rock and other elevation from which it could be at all overlooked was seen to be packed with people, and between these and the standing mass pressing toward the ropes there were moving swarms. From the southern and eastern entrances to the park, streams of visitors choked and overflowed all the walks and poured through the borders and shrubberies. From the enclosure of the seats near the platform southward to the end of the Mall there was a mass so dense that one of the park keepers who undertook to carry a prisoner through it, states that for a distance of fully 250 feet no one could move in it except by pressing others back. Many women begged to be assisted in getting out. A great many people, mostly women and children, when they came near enough to see the standing crowd, turned aside or back and made their way through the vines, shrubs and evergreens, seeking either a place where they could sit in the shade or where the passing crowd could be overlooked. It had been announced that the military would pass out of the park escorting the President along the approach from the Scholar's Gate, and for more than an hour all the ground adjoining this road and every point on each side from which it could be observed was occupied. Boys climbed into the trees, and girls, to pass away the time, made garlands of flowers and leaves, which they picked as if in the wild woods.

At the same time the Concert Ground, the Pergola, the Casino, the Terrace,[5] and all the open spaces nearly a quarter of a mile away to the northward are stated by those in charge of them to have been crowded, chiefly by people who had abandoned the attempt to get a standing place within sight of the platform.

The gatekeepers report that at times the people came in like a mob, in such numbers that the attempt to count or estimate them was abandoned. The general report is that never before had half so many been seen passing in. The influx continued till the end of the ceremonies, when the current was suddenly reversed.

Apprehending that on the approach of the military there would be a general movement toward the point at which it was to enter between the two wings of the fixed crowd, the military guard and keepers' force on the drive near by that point was strengthened, that near the platform being correspondingly reduced.

With the entrance of the procession upon the park came an additional press of people who had been previously attracted to the review by the President in Seventy-fourth Street.[6]

The belief that when the President, rising upon the platform to remove the veil from the statue, would stand so high as to be seen even in the rear of the standing crowd, led the greater number of those who had been roving on the outside of it, as the bands were heard approaching, to move from all sides toward the statue, which, draped in flags, was a conspicuous object. This movement adding to the previously great pressure, became almost unendurable to those nearest the ropes. Some women were drawn out fainting, and a line, chiefly of children, was allowed to be formed sitting under and outside the ropes.

The request of the committee that 2,000 seats should be reserved for guests bearing their invitations, and 30 immediately in front of the platform for those with special cards had been strictly complied with, but of the first not more than a third and of the last but a sixth had presented themselves. Between the main body of spectators and the platform there was consequently an empty space when the President arrived, large enough to contain several thousand persons standing. This, it is needless to say, was an exasperating sight to those on all sides who were under the torture of the crowd constantly struggling to get nearer.

As the President passed from his carriage toward the platform, a distance of 400 feet, there was some struggle by those a little back of the front line to place themselves nearer, and to lift themselves, so as to get sight of him. A few were thrown over the ropes, and in the flurry others followed, and ran after the Presidential party toward the platform, but there was no general break.

As the President appeared on the platform there was a general movement toward it, with loud and continuous cheering and clamor, in the midst of which several of the iron frames of the settees gave way, and a number of persons leapt or were pitched into the but half-filled enclosure. The reserved seats were instantly occupied, and there was for a few moments considerable crowding and confusion within the enclosure, but no violent rush, and fortunately not the least panic. The band played the opening piece of music, the assembly became quiet, and the exercises went on in regular order.

At their close the President and his party returned without difficulty to their carriages, and the military column formed and moved out of the park, followed closely by the greater part of those present.

To these minutes we shall add some general observations.

The day was fair, the temperature warm for the season, but not oppressive, and the park in the richest possible condition of foliage and bloom. The so-called "Carnival" procession in the forenoon had been extensively advertised, and had brought in a great many people from the country who had made it a part of the plan of their holiday to visit the park. A considerable proportion of the men present had their wives and children with them, and throughout all of the crowd there were many women. The proportion of decided roughs was nowhere large, and that of quiet, civil and well-disposed people nowhere small. The spirit of the crowd as a body was patient, good-natured and accommodating. With a very few individual exceptions, there was not only a willingness but an evident good-will and effort to meet the requirements of the authorities, and to maintain such a degree of order and decorum as was appropriate under the circumstances. We did not hear a harsh word, nor witness any violence. We did not see a drunken man, and not a personal injury to anyone has been reported.

In view of all these facts it is gravely significant, and we trust that the lesson will not be overlooked, that as with respect to all the special regulations which are necessary for the development of the park as a place of rural recreation, *the crowd was essentially a mob, lawless and uncontrollable.* Had the whole police force of the city been on the ground, it could have done little toward protecting the property which it is the essence of the department's special trust to preserve. Judging from all experience, it would have made no attempt to do so. The keepers of the park, who are supposed to be trained especially for this duty, looked upon the most flagrant offences against the ordinances of the department in thousands of instances under an impression apparently that they were for the time being suspended.

An hour after the military had left the ground we saw keepers repeatedly pass by a group, mainly of children, who in their play were trampling upon and about a piece of rockwork, the crevices of which were filled with delicate plants in bloom and the edges fringed with ferns and mosses. The life of these was stamped out, and in places the ground was left beaten hard, and without a tinge of green remaining.[7]

We saw women and girls breaking off branches of lilacs loaded with bloom, and others carrying aloft bundles of similar branches, passing out of the park by way of the police station, perfectly oblivious of the fact that it subjected them to arrest and punishment. We asked two men openly breaking the law, if they knew that they were doing so; both answered smilingly that the law just then was not of much account.

Long after the President and the military had disappeared, people, especially children, continued to rove off the walks, quietly breaking down and trampling over shrubs and vines, and seemed surprised when remonstrated with.

The turf in the park was in the best condition for hard wear, growing rapidly, and the ground neither moist nor dry. The trees and shrubs were also sappy and pliant, and bent to force as they would not at any other season. The crowd centered at the point where it could least do harm, the surface of the ground being level, covered for a large space with turf and gravel, and bearing no shrubs or low branched trees.

For all these reasons the damage done was comparatively slight, and every pains being taken to repair it as rapidly as possible, under favorable conditions of weather, it is now hardly to be noticed. The turf was soaked with water, and except where the crowd was densest, warm moist weather following, will generally recover. There are hundreds of spots from one to two, or three, feet across, however, where it has been tramped out completely, and the soil ground to dust. These will not, probably, again green over again this year unless it be with coarse annual grasses and weeds.

Forty of the settees were smashed, the iron frames of six being broken. The statues between that of Halleck and the south end of the Mall were loaded with men and boys when the President passed, but suffered no harm. Had there been any delicately cut stone work in the vicinity like that at the Terrace it would have been ruined. No limbs, but hundreds of small branchlets, were broken from the trees.

The city has expended, within the area of the park, nearly ten millions of dollars,[8] and, if it is closely considered for what purpose, in the last analysis it will be found to be to produce certain influences on the imagination of those who visit it, influences which are received and which act, for the most part, unconsciously to those who benefit by them. These influences come exclusively from the natural objects of the park as they fall in passing them into relations and sequences adapted to the end in view. The value of the park is greater or less according to the success with which arrangements for this purpose have been made. If the value of the natural elements is lessened, the value of the artificial, as the roads, bridges and arches, lessens correspondingly. With the increase in beauty and influence on the imagination of the one increases the value of the city's property—the amount of the city's income—in the other. A very much higher degree of beauty and of poetic influence would be possible but for the necessity of taking so much space for that which in itself is not only prosaic but often dreary and incongruous, that is to say the necessary standing and moving room for the visitors.

The area thus appropriated in the park is considerably more than a hundred acres, and much study has been given to the object of distributing it in fair proportion to the requirements of the public in different parts, and of keeping it as inconspicuous as practicable. Its extent can nowhere be enlarged, nor can the public be allowed to occupy unprepared ground without destruction and waste of what has been laid out for the main object in the natural elements.

Whenever, therefore, the park is used for any other than its primary purpose, and especially for spectacles entirely foreign to it, like that of a military display, which tend to concentrate visitors, the regulations designed with reference to that purpose are necessarily, in a greater or less degree, out of place, and are overruled; its custodians, as well as its visitors, become accustomed to regard them without respect, customs suitable to paved streets or commons override them, and the result, directly and indirectly, is incalculably wasteful of the public property.[9]

Respectfully,

FREDERICK LAW OLMSTED,
Landscape Architect.
JULIUS MUNCKWITZ,
Superintendent D.P.P.

The text presented here is from New York (City), Department of Public Parks, *Minutes*, May 16, 1877.

1. On May 9, 1877, William R. Martin informed the park board that he had received letters from William Cullen Bryant and James Grant Wilson, members of the committee presenting the city with a statue of the late American poet Fitz-Greene Halleck for placement in the park, in which they outlined arrangements they had already made for the unveiling ceremony at the south end of the Mall (DPP, *Minutes*, May 9, 1877, pp. 22–23).
2. Although military parades had always been forbidden in Central Park, the Halleck committee requested permission to allow the Seventh Regiment of the New York State

National Guard to accompany newly elected President Rutherford B. Hayes to the ceremony. Despite its reservations about allowing a military parade to enter the park and the large crowd sure to come see the president, the board concluded that refusing permission might be misinterpreted as a slight to Hayes on his first visit to New York, just two months after the outcome of his disputed election over Democratic rival Samuel J. Tilden (ibid., May 16, 1877, p. 42).
3. That is, a fence of small, upright timbers (OED).
4. The two nearest carriage entrances were the Scholar's Gate, at Fifth Avenue and 59th Street, and the Inventor's Gate at 72d Street.
5. Olmsted is referring to locations and structures around the north end of the Mall.
6. Before the ceremony President Hayes reviewed the Seventh Regiment on 74th Street, which then marched with him into the park by the Inventor's Gate (New-York Times, May 16, 1877, p. 8; New-York Daily Tribune, May 17, 1877, p. 5).
7. Park superintendent Julius F. Munckwitz, who signed the present report with Olmsted, told a reporter that the damaged rockwork and plantings, some of the oldest and most delicate in the park, were along the East Drive. "It has taken fully eight or ten years to get these plants to the condition they were in when this terrible horde came tramping like an army of Bashi-Bazouks carrying wreck and ruin. The rockwork is simply a wreck, and will have to {be} commenced over again" (from an undated newspaper clipping in the Olmsted Papers).
8. Olmsted's figure was for construction expenses; adding maintenance costs brought the total to over thirteen million dollars (FLO to Henry G. Stebbins, Aug. 27, 1874, n. 9, above).
9. The board resolved strictly to enforce its prohibition against military parades in the park after receiving this report (DPP, Minutes, May 23, 1877, p. 66).

THE CENTRAL PARK.

NEW YORK, May 19, 1877.

TO THE EDITOR OF THE AMERICAN ARCHITECT.[1]
Sir,—
I have hesitated to recur to the matter of my former brief note,[2] but submit that the credit of the profession your journal represents is enough concerned to justify the publication of a fuller statement of the facts which prove to be in question. The case is this: The Institute of Architects had published an interesting paper prepared by its Secretary for a national and international occasion,[3] and which was likely to be preserved abroad and at home as an abstract of the history of architecture in America. Its compiler, living in New York, had given special consideration to the work of his contemporaries of that city, which he registered by decades. Half the space of the sixth decade he thought proper to appropriate to the Central Park, in the account of which I

was credited with all that is respectable of the general design, and Mr. C. Vaux as holding a consulting and somewhat questionable position with reference to the architecture only.

Regarding this account as defective from inadvertence, I could not do less than supply the brief correction which you published on the 14th ult. It appears, however, from the note which it has drawn out, that there was no inadvertence, and that it is still believed that in all particulars of special interest to architecture the record is authentic and complete.[4]

In my judgment, if the design of the park has any special interest to architects at all, it lies in a few circumstances which have been thus wholly lost sight of, and which, to relieve them for the moment as much as possible from any personal bearing, I will narrate as follows:—

Years ago a young English architect, returning from a professional tour on the Continent, contributed drawings to an exhibition in London, the subjects of which and their treatment led to his being sought out by Mr. A. J. Downing, at whose invitation he soon afterward came to and established himself as an architect in America.[5] He here became not only the intimate friend but the professional partner of Mr. Downing, a man who more than any other in my knowledge possessed the attributes of genius both in the art of landscape-gardening, and in that of conveying to others an understanding of the conditions of success in that art. It was through the exertions of Mr. Downing that the project of a park in New York first became popular; and when five years after his lamented death a plan for the Central Park was wanted, there was no man to whom it came more naturally, properly, and in due sequence of a strictly professional career, to undertake to provide it, than to the architect who had been his chosen disciple, and enjoyed the privilege of aiding him in his latest and best work.

In due time with the co-operation of an associate whom he had selected, invited, and with some difficulty persuaded to join him, a study was produced, which being submitted in competition was adjudged the best of thirty-three which had been offered in conformity with the rules prescribed, all but two or three of the remainder being the work exclusively of men untrained in architecture.[6] The design was adopted, and though many details have been introduced in an outlay since made of over eight millions of dollars, it has been substantially adhered to. After nearly twenty years of growth following labor, and labor waiting on growth, the intended landscape effects are beginning to be disclosed. They are found worthy of praise in an architectural record; but all the circumstances above indicated, by which they are more directly related to the interests of architecture as a professional pursuit, are forgotten.

There is a popular impression about architects, on account of which, if there were no other reasons, it is proper they should be recalled. I mean the impression that the special training of an architect, and his habit of dealing almost exclusively with rigid materials, disqualifies him for co-operating intimately, cordially, and successfully, in works of landscape design.

For the same reason, testifying now as the associate of Mr. Vaux in the design of the Central Park, I personally owe it to his profession to say that in his discussion even of such matters as the shaping of embankments, the disposition of rocks, the outlining {of} shores and of plantations, and in determining the exact adjustment to natural conditions of roads and walks, with the purpose of bringing means of convenience relatively large into tolerable subordination to means of developing picturesqueness through objects necessarily restricted in breadth and in detail, methods of study acquired in the training of the architect proved not only no obstacle to satisfactory results, but manifestly a great furtherance.

You will see by the accompanying copy of the London *Garden* that I have before now been led by the conviction thus expressed, in addressing those who stand for the other side of the question, to urge that architects should always be associated in the general design of important landscape undertakings;[7] and in the public works in which I have been engaged since my partnership with Mr. Vaux expired, I have secured such co-operation.[8]

And I may properly add that a gentleman who has had a wider range of practice, and been connected with more important works in landscape than any other in Europe,[9] has, since this publication in the *Garden*, privately advised me that his own experience has led him to place a similar estimate in this respect on the value of architectural training as an auxiliary element in landscape design.

There is a second question as to which I will, if you please, at another time state facts which have equally been forgotten with those mentioned in this letter.[10] What I have now said must make it sufficiently clear that in an architectural minute as to the design of the Central Park, if but one man's name is to be mentioned, it is courtesy overmuch to make it that of your obedient servant.

FREDERICK LAW OLMSTED

The text presented here is from the *American Architect and Building News*, June 2, 1877, page 175. Olmsted wrote it in response to an article published there on March 24, 1877, by Alfred J. Bloor, national secretary of the American Institute of Architects. In reviewing American architectural history, Bloor claimed that Olmsted alone had made the landscape design of Central Park. Vaux's role he considered only consultative, limited to the preliminary design of its architectural structures, the important details of which were "designed and elaborated by a small staff of architects and draughtsmen." In 1867 Bloor had quit an assistant position in the architectural firm of Vaux, Withers & Company and held a grudge against Vaux well into the 1880s (*American Architect and Building News*, March 24, 1877, supplement; *Papers of FLO*, 4: 90–93; FLO to William Dorsheimer, April 2, 1876, above).

JANUARY 1877–OCTOBER 1877

1. William Pitt Preble Longfellow, assistant architect of the U.S. Treasury Department in the early 1870s. He edited the *American Architect and Building News* between 1875 and 1880 (*DAB*).
2. Olmsted, in a letter published in the issue of April 14, 1877, stated that no one, himself included, had more claim to the landscape design of Central Park than Calvert Vaux. That is, as the two men had agreed in public statements and in a lengthy debate over the question after Olmsted moved to California in late 1863, their contributions to the design were equal and indivisible. He also wanted the record set straight on Vaux's other contributions: "As to its distinctively architectural works, during twelve years he made the original studies for them; and his superintendence of their details was personal, direct, and controlling" (*American Architect and Building News*, April 14, 1877, p. 120; FLO, "Park," [1861] [*Papers of FLO*, 3: 355]; FLO to Calvert Vaux, Nov. 26, 1863 [*Papers of FLO*, 5: 144–53]; FLO and Calvert Vaux to Henry G. Stebbins, March 4, 1874, above).
3. The article by Alfred J. Bloor was originally presented in October 1876 to the tenth annual convention of the American Institute of Architects.
4. Bloor responded that giving Vaux credit for the original studies of the park's architectural works and superintendence of their details denied due credit to others on the architectural staff, presumably himself included. He had left the firm of Vaux, Withers & Company in 1867 with a strong sense of having been ill-used and with an animus against Vaux that seems to have persisted undiminished for years thereafter (*American Architect and Building News*, April 28, 1877, p. 135; *Papers of FLO*, 6: 92).
5. Here Olmsted describes the circumstances by which Vaux met A. J. Downing in England in 1850 and moved to New York that fall to be Downing's architectural assistant. By the end of the year he became partner in the firm of "Downing and Vaux." They secured a commission to improve the public grounds of Washington, D.C., and were well along in that and other projects when Downing died in a steamboat accident in 1852 (George B. Tatum and Elisabeth Blair MacDougall, eds., *Prophet with Honor: The Career of Andrew Jackson Downing, 1815–1852* [Washington, D.C., 1989], pp. 37–38, 291–311; *Papers of FLO*, 3: 63–68).
6. Olmsted and Vaux's Greensward plan won the design competition for Central Park on April 28, 1858 (*Papers of FLO*, 3: 453).
7. See "Landscape Gardening," Olmsted's letter to William Robinson, editor of *The Garden* above, pp. 223–27).
8. Since Olmsted's partnership with Vaux ceased in October 1872 he had collaborated with several other architects on public projects. Among these were Thomas Wisedell and Architect of the Capitol Edward Clark who, starting in 1874 helped him with the design of the grounds and terrace of the U.S. Capitol. Leopold Eidlitz contributed a design for an architectural terrace for Olmsted's 1875 design of Riverside Park in New York City, and in 1876 joined Olmsted and H. H. Richardson on the advisory board to the New York State New Capitol Commission. Richardson, who in the early 1870s collaborated with Olmsted and Vaux on the state insane asylum at Buffalo, joined Olmsted in 1874 on a design for Niagara Square in the same city. Olmsted also worked during these years with the architects of the New York City Department of Public Parks, Jacob Wrey Mould and Julius F. Munckwitz.
9. Probably French landscape architect Édouard André, who toured the United States in the autumn of 1876, and for whom Olmsted had written letters of introduction and hosted a farewell dinner in New York (FLO to Édouard André, Nov. 3, 1876, above).
10. Olmsted did not write further letters to the journal about the design of Central Park, but the question of Vaux's contribution to the design reappeared in public in early 1878 while Olmsted was in Europe (FLO to Henry W. Bellows, Dec. 24, 1879, below).

To Horatio Admiral Nelson

Private
Mr Nelson.

24th July 1877

Dear Sir;
In reply to yours of 20th I am sorry to say that I should not at all like such an arrangment as you propose.[1] I cannot write in a popular way upon my subject and I have no gift for public speaking. I could not make myself heard by such an audience as might assemble on the mountain, nor if I could should I be likely to long hold its attention.

But I might write a semi scientific treatise on Public Parks with special reference to the conditions presented by the city of Montreal and by the topography of Mount Royal and I could read such a paper intelligibly to a considerable audience under favorable circumstances. I have done something of this kind in other cities with good results.

I should prefer to address particularly the class of men indicated in the opening of my last letter to you,[2] and those conservative citizens who while well disposed to philanthropic and educational interests look with some jealousy upon the park as an extravagent play thing by which the city is liable to be drawn into excessive expenditures.

The success of the park scheme in Buffalo was largely influenced by getting a small hall full of such people together with the Common Council by special invitations, opportunity being given at the end of my lecture for questions and debate.[3]

This might not be a convenient or proper way of proceeding in your case & I only mention it to show you how my judgment points.

But I know I could do nothing out of doors & that there is no place on the mountain in which my plans could be suitably shown and explained.

The text presented here is from a draft in Olmsted's hand.
1. Nelson proposed that Olmsted lecture to a gathering on the mountain to which the general public would be invited. He also suggested that Olmsted make reference to the rules of the park including "no Funeral Badges No destruction of Trees, Shrubs or Plants, not desirable to set aside Plots of land for the use of Societies or for Games &c, Or the allowing the Erection of Monuments, &c &c" (H. A. Nelson to FLO, July 20, 1877).
2. In his letter of July 14, Olmsted proposed inviting the members of the City Council and those "citizens who care most for the larger and more permanent interests of the city" (FLO to H. A. Nelson, July 14, 1877).

3. On August 25, 1868, Olmsted had addressed a public meeting, chaired by former president Millard Fillmore, to offer his suggestions for park development in Buffalo, New York (David Schuyler, "Cityscape and Parkscape," in *The Best Planned City: The Olmsted Legacy in Buffalo*, ed. by Francis R. Kowsky [Buffalo, N.Y., 1992], p. 10).

To Mary Perkins Olmsted

24th July [1877]—night.

Dear Mary.

The city is essentially under martial law, the whole of its military force having been since yesterday afternoon waiting orders at the armories, ready to march with ammunition and rations. But that is all. You see the uniformed men at the windows in passing and a small crowd of boys and tramps looking at them and nothing else, the streets being a little quieter than usual and no excitement apparent.

Dr Elliott called last night and had evidently been among people who were a little panicked. He thought the boys safer at Harrisburg than here and apparently came to induce me to telegraph Owen to stay there but agreed that Phoenixville would be better still, and I advised Owen accordingly.[1]

I see that our neighbors are a little excited tonight and think we may have mobs tomorrow.[2] Mr Carey is spending the night at the 7th Regt Armory, serving as a substitute, being himself an ex-member.

I have no fear, the precautions taken being I think adequate. However, after Dr Elliott left last night I doubled the sentries and directed the armorer to load the individual mountain howitzers.

He, (John) went off early this morning to Brooklyn & staid late, returning less tired than usual, though he says he walked all over the park.

We have heard nothing from Owen since yesterday morning. There was a little row at Harrisburg late last night very promptly and neatly put down by the citizens.[3] In fact Harrisburg has behaved better than any other town.

The sultry weather continues.
Affectionately—

The text presented here is from a manuscript in Olmsted's hand. This and the following letters to Mary Perkins Olmsted in this chapter describe Olmsted's experiences while stranded in New York City during the railroad strikes of the summer of 1877.

1. It is possible that the physician referred to here was Dr. Ellsworth Eliot (c. 1827–1912), who lived and practiced in Manhattan and was a native of Guilford, Connecticut,

where Olmsted had lived in 1847–48. His thirteen-year-old son, Ellsworth Eliot, Jr., may have been the friend "Elliot" who was staying with Olmsted's son Owen at a lodging house in Harrisburg, Pennsylvania. Owen was engaged in a college project on the use of turbines in the iron and steel industry and had planned to visit an iron works in Phoenixville, near Philadelphia, owned by the father of a former schoolmate (Wilimena Emerson,. . .*Genealogy of the Descendants of John Eliot, "Apostle to the Indians," 1598–1905* [New Haven, Conn., 1905], pp. 167–68, 194; *New-York Times*, Dec. 11, 1912, p. 13; NCAB, 34: 477–78; Owen Olmsted to John C. Olmsted, July 9, 1877).

2. The neighbors that Olmsted refers to here were presumably residents of the "considerable cluster of Irish tenement houses" less than a block away from his residence at 209 West Forty-Sixth Street (See FLO to Charles Eliot Norton, Dec. 27, 1876, above).

3. The situation at Harrisburg was still ominous, with one thousand soldiers prepared to defend the state arsenal there against a reported crowd of three thousand strikers. During the 23rd several groups of soldiers had been captured and disarmed by the strikers, who then acceded to an appeal by the city's mayor that they give up the arms upon the assurance that the arms would not be used against them. Later in the day the mayor halted a break-in at a gun shop by direct personal appeal to the strikers. Thereafter the sheriff gathered a posse of five hundred citizens, supplemented by firemen, that prevented the burning of a newspaper office, and citizens formed a Vigilance Committee to guard various buildings. The *New-York Times* reported that "a reign of terror exists, but a show of firmness may have the effect of subduing the mob" ("Serious Outbreak in Harrisburg," *New-York Times*, July 24, 1877, p. 1).

To Mary Perkins Olmsted

25th July [1877] night

All as yesterday. Three regiments have gone off quietly.[1] There are fewer people to be seen and there is less noise and bustle in the streets — transportation business having mainly ceased. The soldiers with their legs hanging out of the armory windows look very hot and weary. They keep sentinels patrolling the sidewalks in front and we hear the drums for morning and evening parade. Mike says that the people up his way generally sat up all of last night fearing riots. But except with the newsboys I know of no other signs of excitement. Now that their boss is gone the newsboys cry aloud late at night without restraint or temperance.

Meats have gone up 2 to 4 cts a pound and if the embargo[2] is not broken in two days the supply of the city will be exhausted. We are fattening Curry in a little pen and baiting cats and doves in the yard. When these are exhausted we shall have the rats and spare the canaries to the last. How little we thought that Providence was providing for us when we complained of the rats forming a colony in our house! Last evening I found a bug on my couch. (Rats can support life on bugs).

 Richardson is here. Mary Barret is not.
 We have not heard from Owen.
 John is very well.
 You know that although I speak and read French fluently I do not always catch what French people are saying when they talk rapidly or excitedly. You have observed my difficulty? There is a clerk at the office who has the same. And today I saw a painful thing in his efforts to converse with a very tall, very excited Frenchman who had a longer hesitation and a more explosive termination to hesitation in his speech than any English speaking man I have known.[3] I found myself wholly unable to assist him. It was as unintelligible to me as a language which I did not speak.
 Affectionately

The text presented here is from a manuscript in Olmsted's hand.

1. A reference to National Guard regiments that were dispatched from New York City to other cities in the state — Hornellsville, Albany, and Buffalo (*New-York Times*, July 25, 1877, p. 1).
2. The *New-York Times* reported on July 25 that due to cessation of railroad traffic caused by the strikes only eight railroad cars of beef cattle had arrived in New York City since July 20th, and that nine hundred carloads were stranded at Pittsburgh and Buffalo (*New-York Times*, July 25, 1877, p. 3).
3. Olmsted's sketch of the Frenchman's "explosive termination" consists primarily of a semi-circle of words (illegible and only partially formed), each followed by an exclamation point.

To Mary Perkins Olmsted   [August 18, 1877]

                           10th Aug.

 So we have jumped to the end of another week.
 I recvd last yours of 14th.
 John is well again. I had Dr Campbell come in twice to see him. We liked the D^r very well. He is a pleasant friendly old scotch Presbyterian I

judge—with rather a twinkle in his eye, with the ways of an easy doctor gentleman. He was sufficiently thorough in his inquiries, approved the treatmnt in progress and added only a little pepsin and acid—and at his second visit said "you are all right—drop the velpean & keep on with the pepsin and boiled milk for a few days."

I was so well I could not smuggle anything for myself.

I counted as much as I could on John's apathetic habit, but after I got your approval of his transatlantic vacation I could not keep down my own excitemnt in sympathy with him. I took a day to lead him toward it and after circulating nearer and nearer, I had him lying in the prostrated back Richardson's chair, while I hid behind my pigeon holes and writing. As if I was not thinking much about it, I observed that I had been thinking that perhaps it might do to take a trip across the Atlantic for his vacation & have a glimpse of things in Paris & London. He made no reply. Knowing that at his age such a suggestion might naturally have thrown me into a fit I peeped over my barricade and saw him looking rather cross and down hearted, reading Repton.[1]

After a minute or two—I asked—"What would you think of it?" No reply. "John! What would you think of it?"

"I should hardly think it was worthwhile."

And nothing more was said for twenty four hours. Then I told him that it *was* worthwhile and he was to go under orders as a matter of business—"All right," and since then he has been deliberating upon it and begun reading up. He suggested that the best he could do would be to read two or three French novels just to get up his conversational French. But I put him in a course of Robinson and Alphand.[2]

I don't know why you suggest the London line for passage. Why not the Havre—to get up "conversational French?" (Please answer)

I don't think he would have time for the Fields.[3]

When are you coming home? We are doing very well.

Dr Campbell said he did not think there would be much left of John's dyspepsia if he went to Paris & back this fall.

The Doherty's are having a new back put in to their house.[4] They say the rain drove in everywhere. The fault lay with the West neighbor, who refused to correct it & they will declare independence.

Is Molly[5] rowing steadily?—

Affectly

The text presented here is from a manuscript in Olmsted's hand.

1. English landscape gardener Humphry Repton (1752–1818), author of several influential works on landscape design (OCG).
2. William Robinson, English gardener and prolific writer, including the book *Parks and Gardens of Paris* (1869), and Jean-Charles-Adolphe Alphand (1817–1891), French en-

gineer, landscape architect, and administrator and author of *Les Promenades de Paris* (1869–73) (OCG).
3. Olmsted's friend Alfred T. Field (1814–1884) and his family, who lived in Leamington in Warwickshire (*Papers of FLO*, 1: 342, n. 11).
4. Probably Olmsted's next-door neighbors Charles W. Doherty and family who lived at 211 West 46th Street (*Trow's New York City Directory. For the Year Ending May 1, 1877* [New York, 1877], p. 343).
5. Marion, Olmsted and Mary Perkins Olmsted's fifteen-year-old daughter (*Olmsted Genealogy*, p. 108).

To John Charles Olmsted

209 W. 46 ST.
NEW YORK.
7th Oct[r] 1877.

Dear John,

I have just reached home from Canada and the East, and read your letters from ship board and Chester (latest 23[d]). They are in all respects admirable and give us great pleasure. They show that you were well prepared to profit by the journey; better than I had supposed, & I am now sure that it will be of great profit to you in every way. Your notes are just what I want; full & nothing redundant. I look with great interest for what are to follow. I read them all aloud to the family at breakfast this morning.

My lectures were a farcical failure as far as reaching the people is concerned.[1] The Commissioners thought apparently of nothing but how they could get out the business without incurring expense for which they had no funds. They took the hall at 3 p.m. because it could be had at half price; sent invitations only to the city officials, Common Council &c.; bid no advertizing but only requested editors to inform the public. The hall was a large & fine one with seating for 1200.[2] When mother[3] & I went into it at the hour fixed, the floor had just been washed & it was dark, damp & cold. There were present 3 commissioners, Mrs Nelson & another lady; Ansley, the Engineer[4] and four men whom I did not know; no other member of the city gov[t] nor did the mayor or commissioner of Health or any others come at all. In the course of half an hour the audience increased to 30 or 40. There were 5 reporters. I read my first paper. Of the reports, one had five lines saying that I thought the mountain an unfortunate site, another about the same with — different & equally absurd misstatement.[5] Another had reserved a column for it & filled it up with very injudicious & misprinted selections from my MS.[6] The next day

I had a little better & a much more intelligent audience, including Principal Dawson of McGill College[7] &c. & was thanked & complimented, but not one of the papers referred to the lecture or the plan. But it is to go to the City Hall & the lectures are to be printed.[8]

A few days before I went to Montreal I spent several hours with D[r] Gray[9] and Sir Joseph Hooker (Supdt. Kew Gardens) (he has lately been knighted & is now President of the Royal Society)[10] on the Central Park. After Montreal I went to Boston & had two days there (partly with Sir Joseph) and Professor Sergeant in the suburbs & at the Botanic Garden.[11] I had a long talk with Sargent & others pretty determined to lay out the new arboretum for Harvard (130 acres).[12] The result is that I think under advice that you had better take still another week (adding 2 to the original plan) & if you think necessary one more (adding 3) chiefly to study botanical gardens & arboretums more thoroughly and to visit Waterers.[13]

Prof[r] Sargent especially urges this (Waterer & if practicable some other great nurseries). Prof[r] Norton also wished me to urge you to spend a day or two on the British Museum & the National Gallery which he apparently thinks more important than South Kensington.[14] What you had better do you are now much better able to judge than I. But we are likely to have something to do with Botanic & Gardens & Arboretums & I should be in possession of all that is good & know how to avoid what is bad. You may possibly think best to go to Queenstown by Dublin & visit the Glasnevin Horticultural garden[15] which is one of the best — & the Zoological garden in Phoenix park.[16] But I think you can learn more by close attention to Kew. Sir Joseph sailed yesterday & if you go there call on him. He will welcome you & give you every aid. And I would out of regard to Prof[r] Sargent, see Waterer's specemin trees & shrubs. Mr. Field[17] may go with you to a great nursery at Worcester.[18] He will probably take you to Birmingham Botanic Gard[n].[19] I think it is little more than a public pleasure ground. Derby Arboretum[20] it is not worth your while to go out of your way to see, as I remember it. I forget the name but have had something from it for Brooklyn. — Oh! one thing more, Sargent wants you to visit Dropmore; the earliest of the large collections of new conifers.[21] It is near Windsor, & as you will then be near by also, says you should see Birnham beeches.[22]

It has been suggested to me that the Zoological Society[23] might send me out with Bickman[24] to study the subject of Z. & Bot. gardens. If so it would probably be in November. There is no prospect of additional business. The Boston parks projects are nearly dead.[25] I offered to lay out (the walks &c) for the Arboretum at a low price, thinking the connection a very desirable one for you.

The only thing I regret in your change of plan as to Warwick is that the leaves will be off the trees by the time you return from the continent & you will lose the park beauty of Stoneleigh, Charlcote & others there.[26]

Prof[r] Sargent is particularly anxious to hear what you find about André[27] with whom he has had an experience in many respects identical with mine. He is remarried. I hope you will not have failed to see him.

Someone from Paris expresses the highest opinion of St. Gauden's recent work.[28]

Mother comes back from the mountains in better health than she has had for years it appears to me. All the rest are well, except that I am worn out & the doctor says in great need of a prolonged rest.[29] I shall try to take things easier for a while.

Wisedell has been very delinquent — overstaied his vacation a week, left everything in the lurch, & has done nothing so far as appears since his return.[30] I shall probably go to Washington tomorrow. Mary Barnett leaves the house tomorrow & Mary Smith has given warning. Mother proposes to try a China man. Chatty is back at her kindergarten & Molly at Miss Errington's (till Mrs Field.)[31] We think in certain contingencies of sending Rick there. (Henry, Frederick, 'Erick', Rick).[32] Miss Errington, Molly, who is at home today (Sunday) reports to be in better health this fall.

We have all been terribly shocked by the forgeries of Gilman,[33] who though you have seen perhaps nothing of him, was with his wife a close friend of your mother's, of Godkin's & of mine. The newspapers will have told you all I know. He was the last man of whom such a crime could have been thought possible & we have all been in deep grief & sympathy for his wife, whom I knew well as a child in Hartford.[34]

I send this through Mr Field, your program having been so changed that I do not know how else to catch you.

Your affectionate father.

F.L.O.

The text presented here is from a manuscript in Olmsted's hand. At this time, John C. Olmsted had begun a trip to Britain and the Continent that lasted until April 1878. He landed at Liverpool and soon visited Chester in Cheshire, one of the first towns that Olmsted visited during his first trip to Europe. Olmsted joined him in January, and together they traveled in England, France, and Italy (*Walks and Talks*, 1: 111–32; [FLO] European Travel Journal, Olmsted Papers; Laura Wood Roper, *FLO: A Biography of Frederick Law Olmsted* [Baltimore, Md., 1973], pp. 361–62).

1. A reference to the two lectures on Mount Royal Park that Olmsted presented on September 28 and 29, 1877 (Frederick Law Olmsted, *Mount Royal. Montreal* [1881] [*Papers of FLO*, SS1: 32, 355]).
2. The Mechanic's Institute, located on St. James Street, included a hall large enough to seat 800 people. It was the primary hall used for meetings in Montreal at this time (William Henry Atherton, *Montreal, 1535–1914*, 2 vols. [Montreal, 1914], 2: 353).
3. Mary Perkins Olmsted.

4. Unidentified.
5. It is unclear which newspaper stated that Olmsted thought Mount Royal was an unfortunate site, but the other newspaper may have been the *Montreal Herald and Daily Commercial Gazette*. On September 29, 1877, the newspaper in a statement entitled "Public Parks, Their Use and Abuse" noted that "Mr. F. Law Olmsted delivered his first lecture on the above subject yesterday afternoon in the Mechanics' Hall treating on the motives for which public parks were made in large cities, the principal one being to supply a breathing place and recreation ground for the masses" (*Montreal Herald and Daily Commercial Gazette*, Sept. 29, 1877, p. 4).
6. Probably a reference to the article on page 2 of the Montreal *Gazette* of September 29, 1877.
7. The naturalist and educator Sir John William Dawson (1820–1899). Dawson became principal of McGill University (W. Stewart Wallace, *The MacMillan Dictionary of Canadian Biography*, 3d ed. [London, 1963], pp.176–77).
8. Olmsted did not submit his lectures to the commission for printing at this time. In October 1878 the commission requested that he forward the manuscripts, reserving the right to publish them at some future date. Olmsted did not comply with the commission's request, and in 1881 published a report on Mount Royal himself with the title *Mount Royal. Montreal*. It is unclear how closely the published report followed the lectures, because Olmsted's manuscripts have not survived (see Frederick Law Olmsted, *Mount Royal. Montreal* [1881] [*Papers of FLO*, SS1: 350–418]).
9. Asa Gray (1810–1888), botanist and professor of natural history at Harvard from 1842 until his death. (*DAB*; see also *Papers of FLO*, 1: 70, 369 and 3: 78).
10. Sir Joseph Dalton Hooker (1817–1911), director of the Royal Botanic Gardens at Kew, near London, from 1865 until 1885 and president of the Royal Society of London for Improving Natural Knowledge, the oldest scientific society in Great Britain (*EB*)
11. A reference to Charles Sprague Sargent who at this time was director of the Harvard Botanic Garden.
12. That is, the Arnold Arboretum.
13. Anthony Waterer, Sr. (1822–1896), owner of Knap Hill Nursery in Bagshot, Surrey, from whom Olmsted often ordered rhododendrons for his design commissions (David G. Leach, *Rhododendrons of the World, and How to Grow Them* [New York, 1961], pp. 17, 504).
14. The museum at South Kensington, near Hyde Park in London, precursor of the Victoria and Albert Museum, was founded in 1851 to house industrial exhibits from the Great Exhibition of 1851 and to promote "industrial education." It contained exhibits of ornamental and applied art (John Physick, *The Victoria and Albert Museum: The History of Its Building* [Oxford, 1982], pp. 19–20; Karl Baedeker, *London and its Environs* [Leipsic, 1892], pp. 281–82).
15. The Royal Botanic Gardens at Glasnevin were created by an act of the Irish Parliament in 1790 (David Moore, *Guide to the Royal Botanic Gardens, Glasnevin* [London, 1885], p. 2).
16. Phoenix Park in Dublin, which Olmsted had visited in 1850 and 1859. The zoological garden in the park was laid out in the early 1830s (Patrick A. Reilly, *Wild Plants of the Phoenix Park* [Dublin, 1993], p. 99; *Papers of FLO*, 3: 101; FLO, "Park," [1861] [ibid., 3: 360, n. 4]).
17. Alfred T. Field.
18. The extensive nursery of Richard Smith & Co. at St. John's, a suburb of Worcester (Michael Fardon, ed., (reprint, *Worcester the Faithful City* [1897], Worcester, U. K., 1997], pp. 35–39).
19. The sixteen-acre Birmingham Botanical Garden was laid out by John Claudius Loudon in 1831. Olmsted had visited the site in 1859 (Melanie Louise Simo, *Loudon*

JANUARY 1877–OCTOBER 1877

and the Landscape: From Country Seat to Metropolis, 1783–1843 [New Haven, Conn., 1988], p. 178; FLO to the Board of Commissioners of the Central Park, Dec. 28, 1859 [*Papers of FLO*, 3: 234]).

20. The eleven-acre arboretum, located just south of Derby, was laid out by John C. Loudon in 1839–40. Olmsted had visited the Derby arboretum the day prior to his visit to the Birmingham Botanical Garden (M. L. Simo, *Loudon and the Landscape*, p. 191; FLO to the Board of Commissioners of the Central Park, Dec. 28, 1859 [*Papers of FLO*, 3: 234]).
21. The Dropmore estate located near Burnham and Slough just west of London. The collection of conifers that Olmsted mentions was planted by Lord Grenville between 1792 and 1830 (Edric Holmes, *London's Countryside* [London, 1928], p. 55).
22. The 444-acre tract of woodland known as the Burnham Beeches was located north of Burnham in Buckinghamshire.
23. American Zoological and Botanical Garden Company in New York City (See L. W. Roper, *FLO, A Biography*, pp. 366, 523, n. 11).
24. Albert Smith Bickmore (1839–1914), educator. Bickmore was one of the founders of New York city's Museum of Natural History and served as its superintendent from 1869 until 1884 (*DAB*).
25. In the early summer of 1876 the Boston park commissioners had proposed a park system and requested the city to appropriate some five million dollars to purchase the land, but as debates in the city council continued, the commissioners in early 1877 closed their offices and discharged their clerk. The city council finally appropriated $450,000 for the purchase of at least one hundred acres of land for a park in the Back Bay, but few people believed the funds would be sufficient, and there was widespread expectation that the endeavor would fail, ending the whole effort to create a park system (C. Zaitzevsky, *Olmsted and the Boston Park System*, pp. 44–45).
26. That is, the grounds of Stoneleigh Abbey and Charlecote estate, both in Warwickshire. The grounds of Stoneleigh Abbey were designed by Humphry Repton in 1809. Charlecote was laid out by Lancelot "Capability" Brown in the 1750s and 1760s. Olmsted had visited these sites in 1859 (Edward Malins, "Humphrey Repton at Stoneleigh Abbey, Warwickshire," *Garden History* 5 [Spring 1977]: 21–29; Dorothy Stroud, *Capability Brown* [London, 1975], pp. 56–57; FLO to Sir William Hooker, [c. Nov. 29, 1859] [*Papers of FLO*, 3: 232–33]).
27. Edouard André.
28. Augustus Saint-Gaudens (1848–1907), American sculptor. Saint-Gaudens's recent work, to which Olmsted here refers, was probably the relief panels for St. Thomas Church in New York City. Saint-Gaudens prepared the reliefs in a studio in Paris and sent the finished panels to the United States on September 20, 1877 (*DAB*; Homer Saint-Gaudens, ed., *The Reminiscences of Augustus Saint-Gaudens*, 2 vols. [New York, 1913], 1: 190–99).
29. See L. W. Roper, *FLO, A Biography*, p. 358–59.
30. Since early September, F. H. Cobb had been anxiously waiting for Thomas Wisedell to send plans for the walk, coping and ramps of the U.S. Capitol's West Front approaches along the line of Pennsylvania Avenue (FLO to Clark, Sept. 6, 1877; Cobb to FLO, Sept. 26, 1877, in D2, OAR/LC; ibid., Oct. 4, 1877).
31. "Chatty" was Olmsted's niece and stepdaughter Charlotte Olmsted (1855–1908), and Molly was his sixteen-year-old daughter Marion. Harriet Errington (1812–1896) had been the Olmsted family's governess during their stay in California in 1863–65, and ran a school on Staten Island. Mrs. Field was her sister, Charlotte Errington Field, wife of Alfred T. Field and a neighbor of Olmsted's on Staten Island in the 1850s.
32. Frederick Law Olmsted, Jr., had originally been christened Henry Perkins Olmsted, but his name was changed when he was seven years old.

33. William Charles Gilman (b. 1833), a New York insurance broker convicted of forgery in 1877 (*New-York Times*, Oct. 3, 1877, p. 1; ibid., Oct. 4, 1877, p. 5; ibid., Oct. 13, 1877, p. 8).
34. Katherine Beecher Perkins Gilman (1836–1879), daughter of the Hartford lawyer Thomas Clap Perkins and Mary Foote Beecher Perkins, sister of Harriet Beecher Stowe. Olmsted knew the family from childhood and had a long courtship with Katherine's sister Emily that resulted in their being briefly engaged to be married (Charles Brush Perkins, *Ancestors of Charles Brush Perkins and Maurice Perkins* [Baltimore, Md., 1976], p. 265 ; *New-York Times*, Dec. 4, 1879, p. 1; ibid., Dec. 5, 1879, p. 3; *Papers of FLO*, 1: 89–91).

CHAPTER VI

OCTOBER 1877–JULY 1878

During this period Olmsted was removed from his position as landscape architect with the New York parks department, losing all official connection with Central Park and the other city parks and leaving the final stages of the street planning for the Bronx in the hands of J. J. R. Croes. His health deteriorated during the period and was little improved by a four-month trip to Europe.
    The report to William R. Martin of October 31, 1877, presents the plan of Olmsted and Croes for the Central District of the Bronx, the section between Jerome Avenue and Third Avenue. Olmsted's report to the New York park commissioners of January 2, 1878, just days before his departure for Europe and subsequent dismissal, treats the question of where in Central Park it would be acceptable to place a menagerie. It demonstrates Olmsted's willingness to examine proposals for which he had little sympathy, rather than dismissing them out of hand. The letter to Charles Dalton of May 13, 1878, with its severe critique of design competitions, played an important role in convincing the Boston park commissioners to engage him to design the Back Bay Fens section of their park system, rather than using the result of their current competition. The article that Olmsted wrote for *Johnson's Cyclopedia* makes clear the difference between landscape gardening and "parterre and specimen" types of gardening; in it he demonstrates how the principles of landscape gardening could be applied to domestic grounds with limited space.

To William Runyon Martin

CITY OF NEW YORK,
DEPARTMENT OF PUBLIC PARKS.
31st October, 1877.

The Hon. WILLIAM R. MARTIN,
President Department of Public Parks:
SIR:
The plan presented herewith covers the district between Jerome avenue, and Third avenue with its continuation Berrian avenue, from One hundred and sixty-first street to Woodlawn Cemetery.[1]

It was originally laid before the Board on the 20th of June,[2] and under its orders has since been open to the inspection of the property owners, large numbers of whom have examined it with much interest.

So far as can be judged, it meets with the approval of the great majority of those whom it directly affects. There are instances in which complaints are made that individual properties are injuriously affected, but this is unavoidable in laying out roads which will meet public requirements in a district so large as this, and in which there are more than fifteen hundred different owners of property.

In entering upon this district, we pass from the region of villa residences into one well adapted to a different occupancy. In applying here the principles which were laid down in our first report as guiding the formation of plans for the new wards, it is evident that a different mode of treatment from that used in the districts, the plans for which have already been approved by the Board, must be adopted.[3] The full development of this mode has been obstructed by the existence of many previous partial efforts at improvement. A large number of farms have been independently sub-divided from time to time, within the last thirty years, each in such manner as to give the greatest practicable number of rectangular "city lots," and rarely has any attention been paid in arranging the streets, to the manner in which the adjoining property was laid out; to economy of construction, or to convenient connections and extensions.

It will be readily seen that in treating such territory it has been a difficult task to avoid injury to property and interference with vested rights, and at the same time to preserve a general harmony and consistency of plan while providing for continuous longitudinal and transverse lines of travel on easy grades.

The district comprises about twenty-five hundred acres, and is divided by certain marked characteristics due to both natural and artificial conditions, into four distinct sections, which will be separately considered.

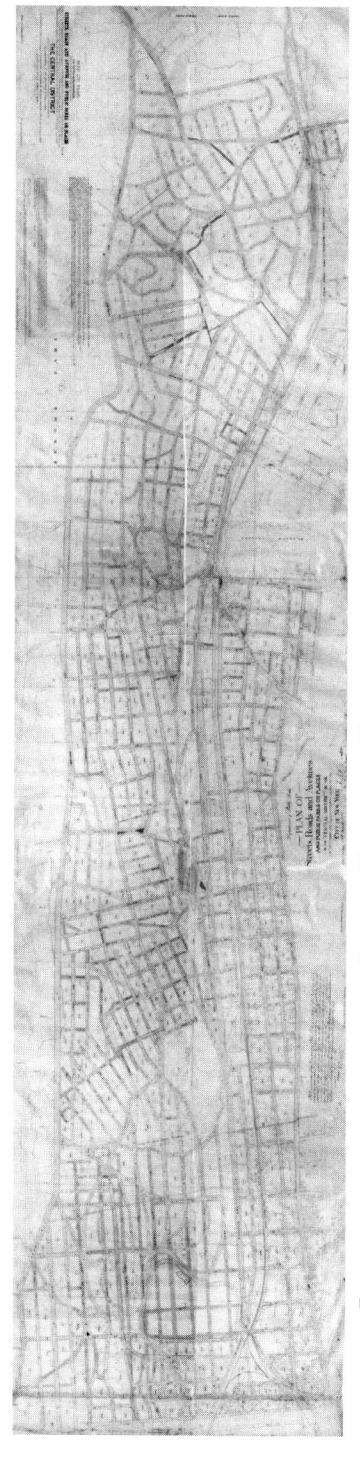

Plans for streets and parks for Central District of Twenty-third and Twenty-fourth Wards, New York City, June 20, 1977, as revised and submitted March 28, 1878

I.

THE VALLEY OF MILL BROOK, FROM ONE HUNDRED AND
SIXTY-FIRST STREET TO FORDHAM STATION.

This section, included between Third avenue and Webster avenue, is and must always remain, preëminently a business district.

It is traversed from end to end by the Harlem Railroad, which now furnishes communication with the Grand Central Depot[4] twenty-six times each way daily, the trip occupying from twenty to thirty minutes. The result of these facilities for intercourse with the city is shown in the fact that the narrow strip on the east side of the railroad which has been laid out in streets by the owners of the property, contains 765 houses, most of which are occupied.

The corresponding strip on the west side of the railroad is hardly settled at all.

This is due principally to the fact that through it runs the Mill Brook which is liable to freshets which overflow the low ground on each side.

For a distance of nearly two miles southwardly from Fordham Station, five avenues traverse the section. Four of these are continued southwardly to One hundred and sixty-first street.

The two exterior avenues, Third and Webster, the lines and grades of which were established by the Board in 1876, are, respectively, 80 and 100 feet wide.

Of those intermediate, Madison and Washington avenues are each 50 feet in width.[5] Both are extensively built upon. The houses are in most instances set back from the street line, and the sidewalks lined with trees which have attained considerable size.

By the plan, these avenues will be widened five feet on each side, but the additional width thus obtained will not increase the roadway, which is now of the proper width for a sixty-foot street.[6]

The effect of the widening will only be for the present to prevent encroachments by stoops and areas on the present sidewalks, which are now not wider than is needed for pedestrians.

The New York Ordinances, which by the Annexation Act are made applicable to the Twenty-third and Twenty-fourth Wards, prescribe a definite width of sidewalk for each width of street, and no new curb can now be set on either of these avenues at the distance from the house line at which the present curb stands; a conformity with the ordinances would therefore, unless the avenue is widened as proposed, bring the fine trees which line the streets into such a position as to render their removal necessary for convenience of travel.[7]

Few existing buildings are required to be set back in order to accomplish the proposed widening.

The fifth avenue in the section was laid out by the original owners of the property immediately along the line of the Harlem Railroad.[8]

It is difficult at this day, in the light of the experience gained on the Fourth and Eleventh avenues in New York City,[9] to understand the motives which influenced such an arrangement.

As a highway such a road is unsafe and uncomfortable, and will be used neither for business nor for pleasure when other routes can be found, nor does it make the land fronting upon it desirable for residence purposes.

In a suburban district the disadvantages of the arrangement are not felt to so great an extent as where population has become more dense, and, consequently, travel on both the railroad and the street more frequent. But even in this section its effects can plainly be seen by a comparison of both the number and the character of the buildings erected on the Railroad avenue, with those of buildings on streets of no greater natural advantages, but situated away from the railroad.

Thus on the Eastern Railroad avenue, from One hundred and sixty-fifth street to Fordham, with a frontage of 12,011 feet, lots amounting to a frontage of 7,554 feet are unoccupied, while immediately in the rear of these the properties fronting on Washington avenue which are unoccupied have an aggregate frontage of only 3,800 feet.

But when such a street becomes more thickly occupied, one of two results must follow:

Either considerations of safety will compel a reduction of speed in the steam travel, (as in Eleventh avenue, from Thirtieth to Sixtieth streets, where thirty heavily laden trains pass daily, creeping along at less than nine miles an hour, and even then causing frequent accidents,) or else the magnitude of the nuisance will compel the expenditure of an enormous sum to put the road out of sight, and where it cannot be entered upon or crossed by the public.

The first remedy is not to be thought of at this day.

As regards the second, it must be borne in mind that if the public compel the expenditure by a corporation of a large sum, the corporation will by some means or other take care that the public bears its full share of it. It may do so either by procuring the payment by the public at large of at least a portion of the cost of improvement, or by forcing the payment of excessive fares for travel, or by furnishing meagre and shabby accommodations: or by all three methods combined.

Another serious objection to a railroad street is that it is only one-sided, and that therefore the expense of its construction and maintenance is twice as great to the abutting owners as that of a street which is improved on both sides.

These considerations lead to the conclusion that it is better to make at the outset such provisions for rapid transit that enormous additional expense will not be called for in a few years; and from this conclusion springs naturally the decision that the street along the Harlem Railroad ought to be discontinued, and a street substituted for it which is out of sight of passing trains, and both sides of which will be available for occupation.

In the particular case now under consideration the possibility of encountering legal obstacles has induced a reconsideration of the plan first suggested to the Board,[10] which was to close the Railroad avenue, and substitute for it a street 100 feet from the railroad and 200 feet from Washington avenue.

Several years after the Harlem Railroad Company had acquired title to the land which they now occupy, the owners of the adjoining lands on the east divided at different times their properties into lots and streets, laying out a street fifty feet in width adjoining the railroad land.

The tracts so divided were five in number. The most northwardly, the Thomas Bassford farm, was sold in parcels by W. C. Wetmore, as executor. The deeds executed by him conveyed to the grantees in express terms the fee to the centre of the street on which the several plats abutted.

The second tract was sold in parcels by Ida E. Bassford, the guardian of the infant heirs of Abraham Bassford. The deeds conveyed the property to the line of the street only.

The third tract, known as Upper Morrisania, was sold in lots by Gouverneur Morris,[11] the lots being bounded by the streets laid down on a map referred to in them.

The fourth tract, or Central Morrisania, was sold under somewhat different provisions.

On January 10th, 1851, Charles, John and Alexander Bathgate executed an agreement with Nicholas McGraw to sell to him, or to such persons as he might designate, all the land included within certain lots designated by numbers on the map, together with the land contained within the streets and avenues designated and described on said map.

On December 1st, 1855, Nicholas McGraw executed a certificate, which was duly recorded, acknowledging that the Bathgate Brothers had fulfilled their part of the above agreement, by conveyances dated May 1st, 1851.

The fifth tract, called the Village of Morrisania, was sold under still other provisions.

It appears from the records that —

(1.) Gouverneur Morris agreed, on June 20th, 1848, to sell to J. L. Mott, N. McGraw and C. W. Houghton, the whole tract.

(2.) He failed to fulfil this agreement, but had the land laid out in streets and lots, and conveyed away the lots (September, 1848) by deeds, the descriptions in which bound the property by the streets and avenues.

(3.) To satisfy Mott *et al.*, he agreed, on November 8th, 1848, for the consideration of $100, to convey to the town of Morrisania, by warrantee deed, all the lots designated on the map as Parks, Schools and Public Squares, and to quit-claim all his title to the streets on the map, to whomsoever might be authorized to receive the deeds, for the benefit of the inhabitants of the village of Morrisania.

(4.) He afterwards executed these deeds.

In examining the tenure of the land under these various conditions of sale, it appears probable that the whole of Railroad avenue, as laid out, would, if closed, revert to the abutting owners on the east side in the fourth and fifth tracts.

In the first tract, it might be questioned whether the westerly half of the avenue would not revert to the original owners.

In the second and third tracts, the question might arise as to whether, in the absence of any stipulation, the abutting owners on the east had any rights further than to the centre of the avenue, and if not, whether the railroad company had any rights as abutting owners.

The necessity for a solution of these questions may be avoided, as proposed by the plan,[12] by retaining the westerly half of Railroad avenue as a public alley, 25 feet wide, for access to the rear of existing lots and for certain advantages for drainage which would thus be secured.

The street or avenue for travel, and for giving a frontage to existing lots, is laid out 120 feet from this alley, and is made 60 feet wide. This gives the property fronting on Washington avenue another front, and leaves the block between the two avenues 140 feet in depth.

Although this arrangement may operate hardly upon a few of the present owners, it is believed that it will be found much more advantageous on the whole than the present block of 300 feet in depth, with one front on the railroad.

All crossings of the railroad are by bridges over the track. The injury to existing improvements will be slight.

II.
West of Webster Avenue and South of the Morrisania Town Line.

This section is almost entirely unimproved, and is owned in large tracts.

It was laid out by the Commission of 1868,[13] in rectangular blocks, without regard to its topography. The cost of construction of the streets, on the lines then proposed, would exceed the value of the land, and the grades of the cross streets would prohibit the movement of heavy loads.

In preparing the present plan, the attainment of light grades, with slight cuttings and fillings, at moderate cost, has been aimed at, rather than adherence to straight lines or directness between distant points. Wherever practicable, ranges of straight and parallel streets have been introduced for the subdivision of property, but very long and straight avenues, either longitudinal or transverse, have not been sought where their introduction would involve heavy expense. As a matter of economy and of convenience, the straight road is often the dearer, although it may be shorter. On a street of 80 feet in width, to be paved and sewered, and furnished with gas and water, every foot of cutting which can be saved in construction will admit of an increase of over 5 per cent. in length of street without increase of cost, and with increase of ease of travel. This estimate does not take into account the saving in the cost of preparing the abutting lots for occupation.

The only objection to curved streets which has been made by any person out of more than four hundred who have examined the plans, has been that under the usual method of selling city property, the sale of rectangular lots is more easily managed. This view of the matter neglects all consideration of the cost of improvements.

The original owner is expected to make all the profit, and the unfortunate purchaser is left to be taxed and assessed until his means are exhausted, and his property taken from him under a foreclosure suit.

The object of the study bestowed upon the plans now submitted, has been to avoid this result, and to produce a system of roads adapted to the progressive improvement of property at the minimum of cost, with a certainty that when the operations are completed the gradients will be easy, and communication as direct as possible.

The topography of the section makes it impossible to procure without steep ascents and heavy cutting and filling, perfectly straight lines from the railroad to Jerome Avenue, and where such lines have been previously planned, they have been abandoned.

On the summit of the ridge a space of about twenty acres has been designated as a park.[14]

III.
FROM THE MORRISANIA TOWN LINE TO THE JEROME PARK BRANCH RAILROAD ROUTE,[15] WEST OF WEBSTER AVENUE.

In the division of this section into independent villages, the proprietors provided no continuous lines of road from North to South, and the few transverse roads from Jerome Avenue to the Harlem Railroad were laid out without regard to directness or ease of travel.

This, in itself, is not remarkable, but it is a little surprising to find that within a short distance of each of the steep old roads leading from the bluff to the valley, and at the intersection of which with the railroad, important stations have been established, routes heretofore neglected exist, by which access can be had from these stations to the elevated land, on easy grades and at slight cost of construction.

On such routes the plan establishes main thoroughfares with no gradient exceeding five feet in 100.

For longitudinal travel, good routes are generally attained by following existing streets and introducing connections. In the plots which lie intermediate to the main routes thus established, the existing divisions of property are in most cases retained. Two small plots are reserved for public greens near Fordham and Tremont Stations, and at the southerly extremity of the district, a particularly desirable tract of about twenty-five acres, which has never been subdivided, is reserved as a park.[16]

IV.
North of the Line of the Proposed Jerome Park Branch Railroad.

In this section the land is still owned in large tracts and is now mainly used for farming purposes.

The ground is high; in some parts nearly level, in others broken and undulating. The views are entirely inland, overlooking the Bronx and Mill Brook Valleys.

The treatment of this section is governed almost entirely by topographical considerations. There is considerable variety in the subdivision, parts being rectangularly laid out, and other parts being divided so as to admit of a more rural character of roads.

On its southern limit, a natural water course of considerable importance gives opportunity for the continuation of the Parkway and chain of small parks which, with those already adopted, will connect the Hudson and Bronx Rivers.[17]

As a summary, the plan submitted provides for business sections in the valleys of Mill Brook and Cromwell's Creek; for a section for residences on the elevated ground along the centre of the district, for a section for suburban homes at the northern limit, for avenues of easy grade, opening into small parks at suitable distances, traversing the whole length and breadth of the district, and for routes for present and prospective steam travel, so placed that they will not interfere with other roads.

Respectfully,

FRED. LAW OLMSTED,
Landscape Architect.
J. J. R. CROES,
Civil and Topographical Engineer.

The text presented here is from "Document No. 76," in New York (City), Department of Public Parks, *Minutes*, November 7, 1877.

1. The area discussed in this report presently includes, from south to north, the Bronx neighborhoods of Morrisania, Tremont, Fordham, Bedford Park, and Norwood. At the time of this report it was called the Central District of the Twenty-third and Twenty-fourth wards. Woodlawn Cemetery, a 400-acre rural cemetery at the north end of the district, opened in 1865 (James Lee Wells et al., *The Bronx and Its People: A History 1609–1927*, 2 vols. [New York, 1927], 2: 706).
2. The first plan prepared by Olmsted and J. J. R. Croes for the Central District of the Bronx was presented on June 20, 1877, to the parks board, which ordered that it be made available for public inspection for the remainder of the summer. This plan apparently has not survived. On October 31, 1877, the date of the report presented here, the board convened and received comments from over one hundred property owners from the district. Many of them object to the closing of the avenue adjacent to the line of the New York & Harlem Railroad, as proposed by Olmsted and Croes. On November 7, 1877, the designers presented a revised plan, also not extant, with the report published here. In March 1878 the board instructed Croes to make revisions that it approved the following month. As Croes reported to Olmsted, this revised plan (see page 341) eliminated the two parks and one small public green proposed by the designers in the present report. It retained the existing railroad avenue along the New York & Harlem Railroad, but did not otherwise alter the street system proposed here (DPP, *Minutes*, June 20, 1877, p. 123; ibid., Oct. 31, 1877, pp. 368–70; ibid., Nov. 7, 1877, p. 381; ibid., March 23, 1878, pp. 687–88; ibid., April 17, 1878, pp. 741–42; J. J. R. Croes to FLO, March 24, 1878).
3. In their preliminary report for the planning of the Twenty-third and Twenty-fourth wards, Olmsted and Croes stressed that different parts of New York required various treatments suited to the peculiar topographical, economic, and social characteristics of each area. Here they reiterated that the kind of curvilinear street plans already adopted for Riverdale, Mosholu, and Kingsbridge, and the area east of the Harlem River to Jerome Avenue, would apply only in part to the Central District, notably in its southwestern and northern sections. Much of the area was already platted in unconnected sections with a gridiron street pattern. Olmsted and Croes proposed to add curvilinear streets that would provide easy grades and more direct communication between these areas (see page 346, above).
4. The Grand Central Station, located at 42nd Street and Fourth Avenue and completed in 1871, was the terminus for the New York & Harlem, the New York Central and Hudson River, and the New York, New Haven and Hartford railroads (Isaac Newton Phelps Stokes, *The Iconography of Manhattan Island, 1498–1909*, 6 vols. [New York, 1915–28], 5: 1946).
5. That is, the officially adopted width of these streets, including sidewalks, was fifty feet. Since the roadway in use was thirty feet wide, only ten feet remained on each side for sidewalks. Part of this space was taken up by trees, pushing the walkways onto private property.
6. The additional width obtained would allow the sidewalks to be extended to their proper width while retaining the street trees. The roadway would remain thirty feet wide.
7. The New York municipal ordinances prescribed sidewalks of thirteen feet on each side for a street fifty feet wide, leaving a road width of twenty-four feet. Building a new curb to these specifications, thirteen feet from the private property line, would narrow the road and place the street trees in the middle of the sidewalk. Increasing the official width of the street to sixty feet retained the existing width of the roadway, the curb line, and the street trees and added five feet to each sidewalk (New York [City], *Ordinances*

of the Mayor, Aldermen and Commonalty of the City of New York [New York, 1866], chap. 15).
8. In 1877 this avenue (later renamed Park Avenue) was called Railroad Avenue.
9. In Manhattan the New York & Harlem Railroad ran along Fourth Avenue, and the New York Central and Hudson River Railroad ran along Eleventh Avenue (J. L. Wells, *Bronx and Its People*, 2: 762–67).
10. That is, the plan dated June 20, 1877.
11. Gouverneur Morris, (1813–1888), railroad entrepreneur. He was the son of Gouverneur Morris (1752–1816) the noted Federalist statesman and owner of the estate of Morrisania (*New-York Times*, Aug. 21, 1888, p. 2).
12. That is, the plan which originally accompanied the report presented here.
13. In 1868 the state legislature appointed commissioners to lay out and construct streets in the Westchester County town of Morrisania. The following year it granted broader powers to the Board of Commissioners of the Central Park for the towns of West Farms and Kingsbridge, immediately to the north, and ordered that the board coordinate its plans with those of the Morrisania commission. In the early 1870s the Department of Public Parks continued planning the street system in the two northerly towns. Its authority was not extended to include the town of Morrisania until the entire area was annexed in 1874, and the plan completed by the earlier commission was retained until Olmsted and Croes began their work in late 1875 (*The City Record*, Jan. 5, 1874, p. 10; BCCP, *Fourteenth Annual Report* [1871], pp. 41–42; "Document No. 45," in DPP, *Minutes*, June 25, 1873, p. 12; "Document No. 62," in ibid., Jan. 20, 1875, p. 2).
14. The site of this proposed park, which is not shown on the plan adopted in 1878, was probably on the present site of Grand Concourse in the vicinity of 167th and 170th streets.
15. In their report on local steam transit routes in the new wards, Olmsted and Croes had proposed a loop railroad running as far north as the northern end of Jerome Park near present-day East 205th Street (FLO and J. J. R. Croes to William R. Martin, March 21, 1877, above).
16. The plan approved by the board in April 1878 shows a public green only near the Tremont station, in a position that corresponds with the present Echo Park. The proposed public green near the Fordham station was presumably the park "on the Hill at Fordham" that the park board removed from the plan, according to the report of J. J. R. Croes to Olmsted in 1878. The "particularly desirable tract" at the southern end of the district was formerly the country estate of Martin Zboroski. When they adopted the plan for this section, according to Croes, the park board ordered that designation of this area as a park be removed – "that is, simply not colored green: the surrounding streets not to be changed." The city acquired the site soon after and dedicated it as Claremont Park c. 1884. Beginning in 1927, the Olmsted firm drew up plans for the park (J. J. R. Croes to FLO, March 24, 1878; Stephen Jenkins, *The Story of the Bronx* [New York, 1912], pp.291, 319; John Mullaly, *The New Parks Beyond the Harlem . . .* [New York, 1887], pp. 98–101; See Claremont Park correspondence, in B39: #527, OAR/LC).
17. Although Olmsted and Croes did not discuss small parks or parkways in the Twenty-third and Twenty-fourth wards until the present report, such spaces were indicated on the plans they prepared that had been adopted by the board in the first half of 1877. William R. Martin, in a report that accompanied the designers' preliminary report, detailed a scheme for distributing small parks throughout the area and connecting them with parkways "of sufficient width for the adjacent country to be planted out, so as to preserve the appearance of a park to the persons who walk or drive along them." Olmsted and Croes followed this scheme in the present report and on the earlier plans.

Beginning at the northern end of the Central District, the designers' proposed parkway followed the Mill Brook northwest to its headwaters beyond Jerome Avenue, presently the route of the Mosholu Parkway. Following a curvilinear route, the parkway, varying in width from 80 to 130 feet, turned west and skirted the south shore of Van Cortlandt Lake (now part of Van Cortlandt Park). It crossed Broadway at the line of the present Manhattan College Parkway. The proposed parkway turned south almost immediately and followed Tibbet's Brook, the line of the present Tibbet Avenue, to Spuyten Duyvil. The present Manhattan College Parkway follows the curvilinear line of a chain of small parks proposed by the designers, which turned south and merged into another parkway, called the Spuyten Duyvil Parkway, now occupied by the Henry Hudson Parkway between West 239th and West 227th streets ("Document No. 73," in DPP, *Minutes*, Dec. 20, 1876, pp. 14–17).

Landscape Gardening.

FROM
JOHNSON'S NEW UNIVERSAL CYCLOPAEDIA

[1877]

Landscape gardening is a branch of horticulture, the highest results of which may be attained by processes of a comparatively simple character — simpler, for instance, than those of kitchen or of floral gardening. Failure of success in it being oftener due to a halting purpose than to lack of science, of means, or of skill, this article will be chiefly given to establishing the definition and limitation of the general end proper to the art; some indications being incidentally presented of the manner in which, under the requirement of different individual tastes and different local conditions, it may be judiciously pursued.

There are two other branches of horticulture, which in ordinary practice are often so much confounded with that of landscape gardening that the reader may find it convenient to have them set apart from it at the outset. One of them is the cultivation of plants with special regard to an interest in their distinctive individual qualities. The other is the cultivation of plants (trees, shrubs, perennials, and annuals) with a view to the production of effects on the principles commonly studied in the arrangement of precious stones, enamel, and gold in an elaborate piece of jewelry, or of flowers when sorted by colors and arranged for the decoration of a head-dress, a dinner-table, or a terrace. Whether, in any undertaking, one of these two leading motives or that of landscape gardening be adopted, it may be presumed that the result will satisfy that motive in proportion as it shall be followed to the end with singleness of purpose. We now turn, therefore, from the two which have been defined to consider what, in distinction from them, the leading motive of landscape gardening may be.

Derivatively, the word "landscape" is thought to apply only to such a scene as enables the observer to comprehend the shape of the earth's surface far before him, or, as we say in common idiom, "to get the lie of the land," the land's shape. Consistently with this view, it will be found, on comparing a variety of scenes, that those which would be most unhesitatingly classed as landscapes are distinguished by a certain degree of breadth and distance of view. Looking at the face of a thick wood near at hand or of a precipitous rock, we do not use the term. Pursuing the comparison farther, it will be found that in each of those scenes to which the word more aptly applies there is a more marked subordination of various details to a characteristic effect of the scene as a whole. As Lowell says, "A real landscape never presents itself to us as a disjointed succession of isolated particulars; we take it in with one sweep of the eyes — its light, its shadow, its melting gradations of distance."[1] But there are many situations in which plant-beauty is desired where the area to be operated upon is so limited, or so shaped and circumstanced, that the depth and breadth of a landscape scene must be considered impracticable of attainment. In America gardening is required for the decoration of places of this class many thousand times for one in which such restraining conditions are not encountered; and the question may be asked whether they must all be excluded from the field of landscape gardening, and if not, what, in these cases, can be the significance of the prefix "landscape"? As a general rule, probably, so many purposes require to be served, and so many diverse conditions to be reconciled, that the only rule of art that can be consistently applied is that of architecture, which would prescribe that every plant, as well as every moulding, shall bear its part in the "adornment of a service." To this end, parterre and specimen gardening are more available than landscape gardening. But it may happen that where, with due regard to considerations of health and convenience, there would be scant space for more than two or three middle-sized trees to grow, there will yet be room for a great deal of careful study, and, with careful study, of success in producing effects the value of which has nothing in common with either of the objects of horticulture thus far defined.

As an example, suppose a common village dooryard, in which are found, as too often there may be, a dozen trees of different sorts planted twenty years before, and that, by good chance, among them there is one, standing a little way from the centre, of that royal variety of European linden called *Alba pendula*. Trampled under by its coarser and greedier fellows, and half starved, youth and a good constitution may yet have left it in such condition that, all the rest being rooted out, sunlight given it on all sides, shortened in, balanced, cleaned, watered, drained, stimulated, fed, guarded from insidious enemies, its twigs will grow long, delicate, and pliant; its branches low and trailing, its bark become like a soft, finely-grained leather, its upper leaf-surface like silk, and its lower leaf-surface of such texture and tint that, with the faintest sunlight and the softest summer breeze, a constant wavering sheen, as of a damask hanging, will be flowing over the whole body of its foliage. While it regains its birthright in this respect it will also acquire, with fullness of form and moderate play of contour, a stateliness of carriage unusual in a tree of its age and stature. If landscape gardening is for the time to take its order from this princess of the fields, and all within the little court made becoming with her state, the original level surface of the ground need be but slightly modified, yet it may perceptibly fall away from near her, dipping in a long and very gentle wave to rise again with a varying double curve on all sides.[2] There cannot, then, be too much pains taken to spread over it a velvet carpet of perfect turf, uniform in color and quality. Looking upon this from the house, it should seem to be margined on all sides by a rich, thick bank, generally low in front and rising as it recedes, of shrubs and flowering plants; the preparation for which may have required for years a clean-lined border, curve playing into curve, all the way round. A very few plants of delicate and refined character may stand out in advance, but such interruptions of the quiet of the turf must be made very cautiously. Of furniture or artificial ornaments there must be none, or next to none, for even bodily comfort may willingly defer a little to the dainty genius of the place. They may well walk, for instance, a few steps farther who would take a lounging seat, put up their feet, and knock the ashes from their pipes. Yet a single Chinese garden-stool of a softly mottled turquoise-blue will have a good effect if set where a flickering light will fall upon it on the shady side of the tree. The rear rank of shrubs will need to stand so far back that there will be no room to cultivate a suitable hedge against the street. The fence will then best be a wall of cut stone, with decorated gate-piers; or with a base of stone it may be of deftly-wrought iron touched with gilt. By no means a casting with clumsy and overdone effort at feeble ornament — much better a wooden construction of less cost, in which there is a reflection, with variety, of the style of the house if that is of wood also, or if it is not, then something like a banister-rail of turned work, but with no obviously weak parts. The gateway being formed in a symmetrical recess of the fence nearly opposite the tree, the house-door being on the side, the approach to it will bend, with a moderate double curve, in such a way as to seem to give place to the tree, and at the same time allow the greatest expanse of unbroken lawn-surface. Near the gateway, and again near the corner farthest from it, there may be a small tree or a cluster of small trees or large shrubs, forming low, broad heads (dogwood grown in tree-form, sassafras kept low, or, to save time, the neat white mulberry), the tops of which, playing into that of the loftier linden on the right, will in time give to those sitting at the bay-window of the living-room a flowing sky-line, depressed and apparently receding along the middle. If there is a tall building over the way with signs, or which otherwise offends, and the sidewalk space outside admits, we will plant upon it two trees only, adjusting them, as to both kind and position, so that they will almost repeat the depressed line of the nearer foliage, at no greater distance than is necessary to obscure the building. Quite hidden it need not be, lest, also, there should be some of the sky lost, banishment from the lower fields of the sky being a punishment that we should strive not to need. But let us hope that at the worst we have but our neighbor's stable opposite, and that the tops of more distant trees may be seen over it; we shall then still be glad to have the chance of bringing up two trees, set somewhat farther apart than before, on the roadside, as their effect will be to make an enlarged consistency of character, to close in and gather together all that makes up the home-scene, and to aid the turf in relieving it of a tendency to pettiness and excitement which lies in and under the shrubbery.

Let a different theme be sung on the same ground. Suppose that it is an aged beech that we have found, badly used in its middle age as the linden in its youth — storm-bent, lop-limbed, and one-sided, its veteran trunk furrowed, scarred, patched, scaly, and spreading far out to its knotted roots, that heave all the ground about like taut-set cables. If we had wanted a fine-dressy place, this interesting object would have been cut away though it were the last tree within a mile. Accepting it, nothing would be more common, and nothing less like landscape gardening, than to attempt to make a smooth and even surface under it. Let it be acknowledged that fitness and propriety require that there should be some place before the house of repose for the eye, and that nowhere in the little property, to all parts of which we may wish at times to lead our friends in fine attire, can we risk danger of a dusty or a muddy surface. Starting from the corner nearest the tree, and running broader and deeper after it has passed it and before the house, there shall be a swale (a gentle water-way) of cleanly turf (best kept so by the cropping of a tethered cosset and a little play now and then of a grasshook, but if this is unhandy we will admit the hand lawn-mower). Now, to carry this fine turf right up over the exposed roots of the beech would be the height of landscape gardening indelicacy; to let it come near, but cut a clean circle out about the tree, would be a landscape gardening barbarism. What is required is a very nice management, under which the turf in rising from the lower and presumably more humid ground shall become gradually thinner and looser, and at length darned with moss, and finally patched with plants that on the linden's lawn would be a sin — tufts of clover and locks and mats of loosestrife, liverwort, and dogtooth-violets; even plantain and sorrel may timidly appear. The surface of the ground will continue rising, but with a broken swell towards the tree, and, in deference to its bent form, hold rising for a space on the other side; but nowhere will its superior roots be fully covered.

Suppose that we are to come to this house, as it is likely we may, three times out of four from the side opposite to where the beech stands; our path then shall strike in, well over on that opposite side and diagonally to the line of the road; there will be a little branch from it leading towards and lost near the tree (the children's path), while the main stem bends short away toward a broad bowery porch facing the road at the corner nearest the gate. The path must needs be smooth for ease of foot and welcomeness, but if its edges chance to be trodden out a little, we will not be in haste to fully repair them. Slanting and sagging off from a ringbolt in the porch there is to be a hammock slung, its farther lanyard caught with two half-hitches on an old stub well up on the trunk of the beech. A strong, brown, seafaring hammock. There shall be a seat, too, under the tree of stout stuff, deep, high-backed, armed, and, whether of rustic-work or plank, fitted by jointing (not held together by nails, bolts, or screws). It may even be rough-hewn, and the more checked, weatherworn, and gray it becomes, without dilapidation or discomfort to the sitter, the better; here you may draw your matches and clean out your pipe, and welcome. We will have nothing in front to prevent a hedge, but must that mean a poor pretence of a wall in leafage? Perhaps it must have that character for a few years till it has become thick and strong enough at bottom, and always it may be a moderately trim affair on the roadside, otherwise we should be trespassers on our neighbors' rights. But its bushes shall not be all of one sort, and in good time they shall be bushes in earnest, leaping up with loose and feathery tops, six, eight, and sometimes ten feet high. And they shall leap out also towards us. Yet from the house half their height shall be lost behind an under and out-growth of brake and bindweed, dog-rose and golden-rod, asters, gentians, buttercups, poppies, and irises. Here and there a spray of low brambles shall be thrown out before all, and the dead gray canes of last year shall not be every one removed. There will be coves and capes and islands of chickweed, catnip, cinquefoil, wild strawberry, hepatica, forget-me-not, and lilies-of-the-valley, and, still farther out, shoals under the turf, where crocuses and daffodils are waiting to gladden the children and welcome the bluebird in the spring. But near the gate the hedge shall be a little overrun and the gateposts overhung and lost in sweet clematis; nay, as the gate must be set-in a little, because the path enters sidewise, there shall be a strong bit of lattice over it, and from the other side a honeysuckle shall reinforce the clematis; and if it whirls off also into the thorn tree that is to grow beyond, the thorn tree will be none the worse to be held to a lowly attitude, bowing stiffly towards the beech. Inside the gate, by the pathside, and again down by the porch, there may be cockscombs, marygolds, pinks, and pansies. But nothing of plants tied to the stake, or of plants the names of which, before they can command due interest, must be set before us on enameled cards, as properly in a botanic garden or museum. Above all, no priggish little spruces and arborvitæs, whether native or from Satsuma;[3] if the neighbors harbor them, any common woodside or fence-row bushes of the vicinity may be set near the edge of the property to put them out of sight; nannyberry, hazel, shadbush, dogwood, even elder, or if an evergreen (conifer) will befit the place, a stout, short, shock-headed mountain-pine, with two or three low savins and a prostrate juniper at their feet. Finally, let the roadside be managed as before. Then, if the gate be left open not much will be lost by it; not all the world will so much as look in, and some who do will afterwards choose to keep the other side of the way, as it is better they should. Yet from the porch, the window beyond, or the old seat under the tree there will be nothing under view that is raw or rude or vulgar; on the contrary, there will be a scene of much refinement as well as of much beauty, and those who live in the house, especially if they have a way of getting their work or their books out under the beech, will find, as the sun goes round and the clouds drift over, that taking it altogether there is a quality more lovable in it than is to be found in all the glasshouses, all the ribbon borders, all the crown jewels of the world.

The same will be equally true of the result of the very different kind of gardening design first supposed. We come thus to the question, What is the distinctive quality of this beauty? In each case there has been an ideal in view, and in each element introduced a consistent pursuit of that ideal, but it is not in this fact of consistency that we find the beauty. We term it landscape beauty, although there is none of the expanse which is the first distinguishing quality of a landscape. This brings us to the consideration that from the point of view of art or of the science of the imagination we may ask for something more in a landscape than breadth, depth, composition, and consistency. A traveller, suddenly turning his eyes upon a landscape that is new to him, and which cannot be directly associated with any former experience, may find himself touched as if by a deep sympathy, so that in an instant his eyes moisten. After long and intimate acquaintance with such a landscape it will often be found to have a persistent influence which may be called its charm — a charm possibly of such power as to appreciably affect the development of the character and shape the course of life. Landscapes of particular type associate naturally and agreeably with certain events. Their fitness in this respect is due to the fact that, through some subtle action on the imagination, they affect the same or kindred sensibilities. If in these dooryards there is something to which every element contributes, comparable in this respect to a poetic or a musical theme, as well, in the one case, of elegance and neatness, carried perhaps to the point of quaint primness, as in the other of homely comfort and good-nature, carried close to the point of careless habits, then the design and process by which it has been attained may lay some slight claim to be considered as a work of art, and the highest art-significance of the term landscape may properly be used to distinguish its character in this respect.

In the possibility, not of making a perfect copy of any charming natural landscape, or of any parts or elements of it, but of leading to the production, where it does not exist, under required conditions and restrictions, of some degree of the poetic beauty of all natural landscapes, we shall thus find not only the special function and the justification of the term landscape gardening, but also the first object of study for the landscape gardener, and the standard by which alone his work is to be fairly judged.

There are those who will question the propriety of regarding the production of the poetic beauty of natural landscape as the end of landscape gardening, on the ground that the very term "natural beauty" means beauty not of man's design, and that the best result of all man's labor will be but a poor counterfeit, in which it is vain to look for the poetry of nature. Much has been written to this effect; with what truth to the nature of man it will be well cautiously to consider.

It is to be remembered, however, with reference to landscape effect, that nature acts both happily and unhappily. A man may take measures to secure the happy action and to guard against the unhappy action in this respect with no more effrontery than with respect to the production of food or protection from lightning, storm, frost, or malaria. He need not take the chance that a certain thick growth of saplings will be so thinned by the operation of what are called natural causes that a few of them may yet have a chance to become vigorous, long-lived, umbrageous trees. Knowing how much more valuable a very few of these will be in the situation, with the adjoining turf holding green under their canopy, than the thousands that for long years may otherwise occupy it, struggling with one another and barring out the light which is the life of all beneath them he may make sure of what is best with axe and billhook. The ultimate result is not less natural or beautiful when he has done so than it would have been if at the same time the same trees had been eaten out by worms or taken away, as trees sometimes are, by an epidemic disease.

On the other hand, there are several considerations, neglect of which is apt to cause too much to be asked of landscape gardening, and sometimes perhaps too much to be professed and attempted. The common comparison of the work of a landscape gardener with that of a landscape painter, for example, easily becomes a very unjust one. The artist in landscape gardening can never have, like the landscape painter, a clean canvas to work upon. Always there will be conditions of local topography, soil, and climate by which his operations must be limited. He cannot whenever it suits him introduce the ocean or a snow-capped mountain into his background. He cannot illuminate his picture with constant sunshine nor soften it by a perpetual Indian summer. Commonly, he is allowed only to modify the elements of scenery, or perhaps to bring about unity and distinctness of expression and suggestion in a locality where elements of beautiful landscape already abound, but are partly obscured or seen in awkward, confusing, and contradicting associations. This is especially likely to be the case in undulating and partially wooded localities, such as in America are oftenest chosen for rural homes. Again, the artist in landscape gardening cannot determine precisely the form and color of the details of his work, because each species of plant will grow up with features which cannot be exactly foreknown in its seed or sapling condition. Thus, he can see his designed and imaginary landscape only as one may see an existing and tangible landscape with half-closed eyes, its finer details not being wholly lost, yet nowhere perfectly definable. Still, again, it is to be remembered that works in landscape gardening have, as a general rule, to be seen from many points of view. The trees which form the background, still oftener those which form the middle distance, of one view must be in the foreground of another.

Thus, the working out of one motive must be limited by the necessities of the working out of others on the same ground, and to a greater or less degree of the same materials. Finally, the conditions of health and convenience in connection with a dwelling are incompatible with various forms of captivating landscape beauty. A house may be placed in a lovely situation, therefore, and the end of long and costly labors of improvement about it prove comparatively dull, formal, and uninteresting. What is lost is a part of the price of health and convenience of dwelling. The landscape gardener may have made the best of the case under the conditions prescribed to him.

It has been said that landscapes of a particular type associate naturally and agreeably with certain events. It is to be added that the merit of landscape gardening consists largely in the degree in which their designer has been inspired by a spirit congenial to elements of locality and occasion which are not, strictly speaking, gardening elements. The grounds for an ordinary modest home, for instance, may desirably be designed to give the house, gardens, and offices an aspect of retirement and seclusion, as if these had nestled cozily down together among the trees in escape from the outside world. The grounds of a great public building—a monument of architecture—will, on the other hand, be desirably as large in scale, as open, simple, and broad in spaces of turf and masses of foliage, as convenience of approach will allow, and every tree arranged in subordination to, and support of, the building. The grounds of a church and of an inn, of a cottage and of an arsenal, of a burying-place and of a place of amusement, will thus differ, in each case correspondingly to their primary purpose. Realizing this, it will be recognized that the choice of the site, of the elevation, aspect, entrances, and outlooks of a building for no purpose can be judiciously determined except in connection with a study of the leading features of a plan, of its approaches, and grounds. Also, that in the design of roads, walks, lakes, and bridges, of the method of dealing with various natural circumstances, as standing wood, rocks, and water; in a determination of what is possible and desirable in respect to drainage, water-supply, distant prospects to be opened or shut out, the avoidance of malaria and other evils,—all these and many other duties are necessarily intimately associated with those of gardening (or the cultivation of plants) with a view to landscape effects.

FREDERICK LAW OLMSTED

The text presented here is from volume 2 of *Johnson's New Universal Cyclopaedia: A Scientific and Popular Treasury of Useful Knowledge* (New York, 1878), pages 1627–30. While preparing this article, Olmsted forewarned the editor of the *Cyclopaedia*, Frederick A. P. Barnard, that he would be offering his own idiosyncratic concept of the subject. Barnard replied, "I am rather gratified to know that your views are peculiar to yourself. I prefer to have "Landscape Gardening" as you understand it, rather than any repetition of what others have said" (F. A. P. Barnard to FLO, June 21, 1875).

1. This quotation with slight changes comes from James Russell Lowell's essay "Spenser" written in 1875 (James Russell Lowell, "Spenser," *The North American Review* 120 [April 1875]: 339).
2. Here Olmsted is describing the "ogee" curve that he frequently used in grading the land. It is a continuous S-shaped double curve, convex above and concave below.
3. Satsuma, a province on the Japanese island of Kyushu.

To the Board of Commissioners of the Department of Public Parks

NEW YORK 2d January, 1878.

To the Board of Commissioners of the Department of Public Parks:
Gentlemen,—

The present menagerie of the Department has become what it is by successive desultory steps taken with no view to permanence or completeness in any respect.[1] It is so placed as to be a serious injury to the Central Park; it is ill arranged, ill equipped, not adapted to economical maintenance. Under these circumstances, though closely, prudently and skillfully managed, it adds a weight to the annual appropriations for the Park which tends unjustly to the public discredit of its administration.

The existing objections to it will be more obvious as its slight wooden buildings fall more and more into disrepair. The cracks and openings caused by the shrinkage, decay and warping of timber in them are now so many and so large that after another year, should an extraordinarily severe winter occur, it will be hardly practicable to keep the tropical animals alive, unless considerable and expensive rebuilding is undertaken. The Board can, therefore, not long hold to a waiting policy with respect to it, but will be compelled to adopt some radical measure.

Still more unsuitable and economically indefensible, except as makeshifts, have been all the arrangements hitherto employed by the Department for purposes such as are met by the well-known Floral and Exotic Public Gardens of Europe.[2]

The Park Commissioners of different periods, always expecting that some permanent and well-arranged plan would soon be carried out, have tentatively entertained two radically different classes of projects, one having in view the management of the proposed gardens by the city direct, the other the management of them by an association especially formed for the purpose.

With reference to the first class, four different localities have been successively appropriated; plans adopted suitable to them, and twice operations have been begun in carrying out these plans.³ Each of these appropriations has at last been reconsidered, and all of the plans abandoned. With reference to the second class, numerous organizations have been undertaken, and two have been so far matured as to obtain special acts of legislation,⁴ but no one has been able to secure such concessions, assistance, and privileges as its promoters thought necessary to success, and all are now defunct.

During the last three years I have been asked to report upon five projects,⁵ some of one of these classes, some of the other, on neither of which has the Commission as yet taken definite action. As the subject is likely to be further agitated during my intended absence,⁶ I propose at this point briefly and without extended argument, to state certain general conclusions which, in my judgement, may be wisely adopted.

1st. New York demands advantages corresponding to those found in the acclimatization, zoological, botanic, and horticultural gardens of other metropolitan cities.

2d. The best way to secure such advantages would be one in general accordance with the policy which has been heretofore adopted, and which is already, to a certain extent, in succesful operation in the American Museum of Natural History and the Metropolitan Museum of Art.⁷

3d. This policy would lead to a contract between the city and a society, for the purpose, under which the city would give the society the use of land and aid in obtaining buildings and collections, while the society would give the public the use of the same at certain times, gratuitously, and at others in payment of moderate admission fees, and would undertake the current expenses of the enterprise.

4th. Botanic or exotic gardens need to have many of the same plants and the same appliances as zoological gardens. A zoological garden, as generally managed, is, to some extent, a botanic garden, and each of the propositions for a zoological garden, now before the Department contemplates a combination of botanic and zoological interests.⁸

In view of the difficulty which has been experienced in raising the necessary capital to start either a zoological or a botanic garden on an adequate basis, and in view of the objections to inclosing any more of the area of the Central Park than is necessary for the purpose, it is not wise to contemplate, at present, two or more distinct gardens — one for zoology, others for different branches of botany or floriculture — each to be aided by the city.

5th. No garden of the kind proposed could be established on the Central Park without taking away from the public advantages for which a high price has been paid. Nowhere in the middle parts of the park, nor on its southern borders, could such a garden be placed without great waste and disastrous results. Not even on its more northern borders could any body of land be taken for the purpose which would not be found cramped, and, in some respects, inconvenient — requiring large outlays to make it satisfactory.

6th. On the other hand, no garden of the class contemplated

would be likely, for a long time to come, to make adequate returns through admission fees, if situated much further north than the Central Park.

7th.   Under all these conditions, the Department would be justified in providing, whenever it shall be found practicable by the method proposed, for the more immediately useful, attractive, and popular departments of a combined zoological and botanic garden upon the Central Park, taking land for these purposes in which the buildings could be so arranged as not to break up the broader landscape scenes, and recovering for the Park the land now occupied by the menagerie.

8th.   But it is desirable that, in addition to this, that the Department should designate some considerable tract of suburban land as a public ground to be specially reserved for an arboretum and horticultural garden, and, perhaps, other scientific uses in the future. Suitable land for such a purpose may be found in that portion of the new wards, the plans of which remain to be determined.[9]

9th.   Having in view a Zoological and Botanic garden to be situated in the Central Park, which would compare favorably with the best in the world in respect to popular entertainment and instructiveness, though lacking space for scientific completeness, a site should be sought within which a considerable extent of surface would be found (1) an exposure to the south, (2) protection from northeast, north and northwest winds, (3) perfect drainage, (4) ample flowing water supply, (5) direct association with a considerable pond or broad body of water, which would lie within the same enclosure.

10th.   The only ground in other respects available where these advantages are offered in the Central Park lies on the west side of the Park, south of the great hill, from Ninety-sixth to one hundred and fifth Streets. A garden might be found to which this locality would be central, containing from twenty to thirty acres, in which the necessary buildings and fences of a zoological and exotic garden would be inconspicuous, if not wholly invisible, from any part of the park proper. No other equal space of ground upon the park could be taken for the purpose of a zoological and botanic garden with less sacrifice of advantages for the proper general purposes of the park.

In conclusion, I beg to urge that if the Commission is of opinion that it is necessary to appropriate some portion of the Central Park to a zoological garden, and any association can be found, having public interests in view, like the existing organizations managing the Natural History and Art Museum, and not looking to pecuniary profits, which is able and disposed to assume due responsibilities in the matter, it is very desirable that negotiations with a view to the lease for the purpose of the ground I have indicated, should be entered upon at an early day.[10]

Respectfully,

(Signed) FRED. LAW OLMSTED,
Landscape Architect.

OCTOBER 1877–JULY 1878

The text presented here is from New York (City), Department of Public Parks, *Minutes*, January 9, 1878, pages 503–6.

1. At this time the menagerie consisted of approximately 700 animals, kept mostly in cages and wooden buildings adjacent to the arsenal in the southeast corner of the park. The Central Park commission had not originally contemplated a zoological garden within the park and the Greensward plan did not include one. In the early 1860s public interest led the commissioners to investigate the question at length without settling on a plan. They did begin to accept gifts of animals and, after keeping some inside the Arsenal itself, erected what were intended to be temporary pens and sheds around it. In 1866–67, Olmsted and Vaux had prepared a plan for a zoological collection in Manhattan Square, between 77th and 81st streets and Eighth and Ninth avenues. Andrew H. Green was reluctant to have the plan submitted to the full park board, and when that finally occurred in December 1867 the plan was referred to a committee. In 1871 the state legislature chose the site for the American Museum of Natural History (DPP, *Report of the Director of the Central Park Menagerie* [New York, 1878], p. 7; *Papers of FLO*, 3: 218, 236; *Forty Years*, 2: 83–84; *Papers of FLO*, 6: 184–89).).
2. That is, the planting of ornate beds of showy exotic annuals in the park, which Olmsted considered detrimental to broader, more essential landscape effects. Such plantings were done by gardeners hired by the Tweed Ring park board and the practice was continued between 1873 and 1875, despite Olmsted's protests, by Robert Demcker in the exotic and propagating department (DPP, *Minutes*, Oct. 10, 1871, pp. 222–24; FLO to [DPP], March 1, 1875, above).
3. In addition to the "temporary" menagerie near the arsenal, the board had designated sites and approved plans to move the collection to Manhattan Square, adjacent to Central Park on the west (1867), the north meadows of Central Park (1870–71), and, at Olmsted's recommendation, to distribute it among several sites, including areas in Central, Riverside, and Morningside parks (1873–74). The Manhattan Square location saw only preliminary drainage work until it became the site of the Museum of Natural History. Actual construction of a building got underway on the north meadow in Central Park and of a deer park on Riverside Park. Both, however, were soon halted (*Papers of FLO*, 6: 184–88, 392–95, 651–60; "Document No. 51," in DPP, *Minutes*, Oct. 11, 1873, pp. 2–5; DPP, *Minutes*, Sept. 25, 1873, p. 300; ibid., March 5, 1874, p. 605; ibid., May 13, 1874, p. 26; FLO to Henry G. Stebbins, May 15, 1874; New York [City], Department of Public Parks, *Third General Report of the Board of Commissioners of the Department of Public Parks . . . from May 1st, 1872, to December 31st, 1873* [New York, 1875], pp. 9–10).
4. In 1860 the New York state legislature incorporated the American Zoological and Botanical Society and instructed the Central Park commissioners to allot sixty acres in the park for the society to establish a combined zoo and botanical garden. Olmsted and Central Park commissioner Robert J. Dillon were among the New Yorkers named in the act of incorporation. The park commission did not allot ground for the society's project but continued to investigate the question. The second group Olmsted had in mind may have been the Botanical Garden of the City of New York, incorporated by the legislature in April 1877 (New York [State], *Laws of the State of New York, Passed at the Eighty-Third Session of the Legislature* . . . [Albany, N.Y., 1860], chap. 256; *Forty Years*, 2: 84; "Document No. 79," in DPP, *Minutes*, April 24, 1878, pp. 7, 11).
5. In January 1875 the park board asked Olmsted to report on a proposal to remove the department's deer herd from the park near 81st Street and Fifth Avenue, where construction of the Metropolitan Museum of Art had just started. Later that spring he reported adversely on a proposal to relocate the entire menagerie to the vicinity of the Tweed Ring's sheepfold building, conspicuously ill-sited west of the Green. Shortly afterward the board referred to him the request of a committee from several New York

colleges to establish a botanical garden on the park. In late 1875 and early 1876 Olmsted drew up a general plan to relocate all the menagerie buildings around the arsenal to its west side. In addition to these four projects, it is probable that Olmsted prepared this document in response to recent proposals for combined zoological and botanical gardens in the park (DPP, *Minutes*, Jan. 30, 1875, p. 488; ibid., March 6, 1875, p. 566; ibid., April 30, 1875, p. 683; ibid., Nov. 17, 1875, pp. 388–89; ibid., April 8, 1876, pp. 738–39; FLO to Henry G. Stebbins, March 2, 1875; *New York Herald*, Jan. 15, 1878, p. 5; see n. 8 below).

6. That is, Olmsted's trip to Europe in 1878, for which he had requested and received a three-month leave of absence from the board (DPP, *Minutes*, Dec. 26, 1877, pp. 458–59).

7. The American Museum of Natural History was being built adjacent to the park on Manhattan Square. It was opened in 1877. Work on the first building of the Metropolitan Museum of Art, located in the park at Fifth Avenue between 80th and 84th streets, was started in late 1872 and completed in 1880 (I. N. P. Stokes, *Iconography of Manhattan*, 5: 1950, 1956, 1967, 1973).

8. Several proposals for zoological and botanical gardens were before the board at this time. In early 1877 it had received several communications from a gentleman who inquired if part of the park could be leased "to proper parties" in which to establish a zoological garden. In July 1877 the American Zoological and Botanical Company requested that the board appropriate space in one of the city parks for a combined garden. Shortly after the present report became public, this group requested that the site Olmsted recommended in this report, on the upper west side of Central Park between 96th and 105th streets, be set aside for their use. Finally, trustees of the Botanic Garden of the City of New York, mostly property owners along Manhattan Square, began discussions with the board in August 1877 to acquire the northern part of the square for a botanic garden (DPP, *Minutes*, Jan. 10, 1877, p. 526; ibid., June 20, 1877, p. 124; ibid., July 11, 1877, p. 146; ibid., Aug. 22, 1877, p. 244; ibid., Feb. 27, 1878, pp. 621–22; "Document No. 79," in ibid., April 24, 1878, pp. 7, 11; *New York Herald*, Jan. 15, 1878, p. 5; *New-York Daily Tribune*, Dec. 31, 1877, p. 2).

9. The only part of the Twenty-third and Twenty-fourth wards of which the board had not seen plans by Olmsted or Croes was that section along the banks of the Harlem River, east of Third Avenue and north of the Boston Road. In the mid-1880s the city dedicated a large part of this section as the Bronx Park, now the location of the Bronx Zoo and the New York Botanical Garden.

10. On March 6, 1878, the park board rejected the proposal of the American Zoological and Botanical Garden Company because it proposed to charge admission to the zoo and pay dividends to those who invested in its stock. In 1890, in his last official document on Central Park, Olmsted reviewed the entire zoo question and advised the park board against relocating the menagerie to the north meadow (DPP, *Minutes*, March 6, 1878, p. 650; FLO to Waldo Hutchins, March 18, 1890, in *Forty Years*, 2: 511–17).

OCTOBER 1877–JULY 1878

To CHARLES HENRY DALTON

13th. May, 1878.

Chas. H. Dalton, Esq.,
Chairman, Boston Park Commission,
My Dear Sir;
  I am sorry that you are disappointed at my conclusion not to aid you in deciding the result of your competition for plans for the Back Bay Park.[1] The confidence you have heretofore given me may perhaps require that I should explain why I have thus failed to meet your expectations.

  For whatever reasons and with whatever expectations you determined upon the competition, the public to which you are responsible supposes that by means of it you will be likely to intelligently determine who among the competitors is best able and best entitled to be appointed to lay it out and direct its development.

  In this I believe the public to be most egregiously misled. I will try to indicate briefly how and why.

  Although no building can appear to the eye of an observer under ordinary circumstances as it is represented in the "elevations" of an architect, yet, assisted by the personal explanations of the designer, it is possible for a man with much study and sufficient exercise of the imagination to form from them, together with ground plans and sections a sufficient idea of a building to be constructed from them to understand somewhere near in what degree it will answer his purposes and satisfy his taste.

  Thus in dealing with the profession of architects it is supposed to be practicable to determine the best among several for a particular purpose as no one thinks of attempting to do in choosing a lawyer or a physician. Hence architectural "competitions" have become common.

  Yet the difficulties of forming a just judgment among architectural plans when got up for this purpose are so great that every respectable architect the world over looks with extreme distrust upon such competitions, even as best conducted, and held under professional advice. Many refuse under all circumstances to engage in them and there are I suppose none of any considerable experience who are not satisfied that a better building is likely to be obtained where an architect of even inferior ability, if fairly qualified, is employed from the outset in direct consultation with his clients than where they are to obtain one as the result of a competition. There are reasons for this not generally understood which I need not attempt to give. It is sufficient for my present purpose to say that my own experience with architects and architectural undertakings strongly confirms such a view. I have closely watched many competitions. I do not know one of the usual kind, (corresponding at all with that you have invited) which has not had unpleasant and reprehensible results. Now it is not enough to say that the difficulties to which I have referred in the case of architectural competitions are greatly increased when the choice of a plan for dealing with *grounds* is in question. The plans and sections of designs for this purpose are extremely deceptive to all but the most practised eyes, *while no such aid to the imagination as is afforded by the elevations* of an architect is possible. Even perspective views from particular points are delusive. It is simply impossible, in the nature of the case, to foresee from such drawings as you have called for what would follow from the adoption as the basis of your work, of the plan which you will select as the best. The most important ultimate results would depend on measures and courses which the successful competitor might be able to direct or advise from time to time subsequently, but which could not be assumed from his drawings to be intended, like those of a good building from the drawings of an architect.

If you do not conclude to employ the author of the premium plan to superintend its development, you will select someone else who cannot possibly do justice to it; who, starting from it, will probably develop at great economical disadvantage a plan widely differing from that which has been in the mind of its author and with reference to which alone any merit it has should be determined.

If you do employ the author of the premium plan, you must do so either because of a knowledge of him which has been obtained otherwise than from his drawings or you must take a large and probably an unjustifiable risk, the consciousness of which will prevent your giving him that degree of authority and discretion which is essential to his efficiency and success.

For reasons thus suggested, while your selected plan may possibly have such conspicuous advantages in respect to general arrangement, and its author such unquestionable practical ability that the course to be subsequently followed will be in the main a plain one, the chances are I fear against you.

Another class of probable results you may well feel able to meet as they rise, but they may nevertheless turn out to be not unimportant.

You are dependent on a public which is not only exceedingly ignorant in respect to the concerns with which you are to deal but which is always ready to act on superficial views of them with great and dangerous energy.

From whatever misjudgment and trouble the competition saves you, you cannot fix upon the premium plan without causing a great deal of toil, study and anxiety to result in what will be felt by those whom you have induced to give it to you as a snub to cherished ambitions if not as a rankling injustice. You are thus likely to have established many prejudiced centres for the propagation against you of more or less bitter criticism, misunderstanding and misrepresentation.

There have been many difficulties attending the administration of the New York Parks which I am able to trace to causes having their root in the jealousies, disappointments and animosities bred in a competition in which Mr. Vaux and I were successful 20 years ago.[2]

No aid I could give in the selection of a plan to receive your premium would materially lessen either class of objections to the competition, which I have indicated. Advising your choice I should place myself in a leaky boat with you. Keeping out of it I retain a professional position in which it is possible I may yet be of service to you.

I need not add that I declined your invitation with great reluctance or repeat my regret that you were disappointed by my decision.

I am faithfully Yours,

(signed) Fred^k Law Olmsted

The text presented here is from a document in a clerk's hand and signed by Olmsted.

1. On March 1, 1878, the Boston park commissioners voted to hold a competition and award a $500 prize for the best plan for laying out Back Bay Park. On May 6 Dalton wrote to Olmsted asking him to come to Boston on "Thursday next" (i.e., May 9 or perhaps 16) to assist the commissioners in judging the competition, for which submissions had been due on May 1. Olmsted wrote to Dalton two days later declining the offer and stating that "the relation in which I have hitherto stood to your general scheme and that in which you may wish me to stand hereafter require in my judgment that I should abstain from giving advice as to the comparative merits of the plans submitted to you." The commissioners awarded the prize to Hermann Grundel, a florist, but decided not to construct the park following his plan. They explained that none of the plans submitted provided adequate solutions to the problems posed by the tidal flow of the Charles River and by the surface drainage of the Stony Brook watershed. The commissioners stated that they had not sufficiently understood those problems, and that they "found the perplexities to grow more formidable as progress is made in the study of the premises." But Henry Hobson Richardson reported that at a meeting in mid-May, presumably immediately after Charles Dalton received the letter published above, Dalton told him that the two letters that Olmsted had written the park commissioners in May, following his return from Europe in late April, had entirely upset their plans. In his letter of May 8 he had refused to take part in judging the competition for the Back Bay park while in the other, printed here, he had offered a strong critique of design competitions in general. These letters and Richardson's observation that it would be unfortunate for Boston to lose Olmsted's services resulted in Dalton's declaring "that they must have you and would have you." This event took place nearly three weeks before the Commissioners awarded the competition prize to Grundel. By October they had worked out an agreement with Olmsted and in December they formally engaged him to develop a viable plan for the Back Bay site (BCDP, City of Boston, manuscript Minutes, March 1, 1878, p. 84; ibid., Dec. 10, 1878, pp. 115–17, Boston Department of Parks and Recreation Archives, Boston, Massachusetts; Charles H. Dalton to FLO, May 6, 1878; FLO to Charles H. Dalton, May 8, 1878; Cynthia Zaitzevsky, *Frederick Law Olmsted and the Boston Park System* [Cambridge, Mass., 1982], p. 54; City of Boston, *Reports of Proceedings of the City Council of Boston, for the Municipal Year 1879* [Boston, 1879], pp. 61–62; FLO to Charles Dalton, May 8, 1878; H.H. Richardson to FLO, May 21, 1878; Charles Dalton to FLO, Oct. 21, 1878)
2. Olmsted is referring to the Central Park competition in 1858 in which his and Calvert Vaux's Greensward plan was the winning design.

To Robert Garrett

To Mr Garrett.

5th June 1878.

Dear Mr Garrett;
I was very sorry not to see you when I was last in Baltimore.[1] In the brief interview that I had with Mr Lanahan I promised that I would write to you in regard to one matter which gave me concern and for which he said that you were responsible but I don't like to take that one and leave others unnoticed, all of which have I fear a common root and one which does not exist in your mind alone.

While I write to you therefore what I say will have a general application and I will thank you to communicate the substance of it, if you please, to your fellow Commissioners.

When your Board first did me the honor to seek my advice[2] I was told that you intended to give me so large a degree of trust that whatever fault should be found with the work that should afterwards be done you could say "that is entirely the fault of Mr Olmsted." You believed that I knew my business and you proposed within due financial and legal limits to trust me implicitly and take the risk of the results.

Now my experience had been such in other city works of a like character that I perfectly well knew that before any plan which I should recommend to you in the premises, could be well carried out, there would be a long interval in which you would have to bear up against much misconception and false and impatient judgmnt rashly & clamorously expressed. I knew that with those from whom the clamor would arise the fact that I had accomplished results popularly satisfactory elsewhere and that I had had in view a result only to be obtained by a process of developmnt extending through a period of some years would have not the slightest weight. I knew consequently that you were likely long before a popular success should crown your work to find it a weary and thankless task.

Accordingly, as you will, I doubt not, remember, I then, (that is to say, in our first interview) advised you to consider well whether it would not be wiser to forego the intention of reconstructing the parks upon an entirely new plan. I distinctly expressed the opinion that with a much smaller expenditure than would be necessary for that purpose you might get most satisfactory results by simply revising and improving them in general accordance with the original plan.[3]

You decided not to adopt this suggestion, and I proceeded to prepare such plans as I thought would be found permanantly satisfactory under the peculiar circumstances of the situation.

When I finally submitted the plan for the South Park[4] you will remember that I distinctly informed you that it involved the sacrifice of all the trees good and bad on its borders, and that if you adopted it you must be prepared for a great outcry from those who would not understand the necessity for this proceeding nor realize for years afterwards what adequate gain was to be obtained for the loss.

Nor have I at any time since given you the slightest room for supposing that a result satisfactory to the public, or one by which any part of your outlay would be obviously justified, could be expected until after the designed elements of permanent foliage had been slowly developed by adequate skilful labor.[5]

For this reason I have the more urged that everything possible should be done to secure and preserve neatness, firmness, accuracy in these elements of the park not to be covered and enriched by foliage and the substantial, well designed qualities and fitness for their purposes of which could be in a great measure appreciated at once by every passerby.

I begged last winter just before I sailed for Europe, that your new gardener might be made, by every practicable exertion, to feel that no neglect on his part in this particular could be passed over for a single day without its being observed and reproved by the Commissioners individually and by others interested in establishing a high standard of excellence in the keeping of the parks.

I begged also that you would take every care that he should not be influenced in the slightest by the popular demand for immediate results other than these, such as it would be perfectly easy to secure at trifling expenditure (for example by tricking out the parks with bedding or foliage or subtropical plants), because it would be sure to divert him from the only course of managmnt by which it would be possible for you to present within reasonable time any sound justification of the outlay you had made in construction.

Accustomed as I am to disappointmnts in these respects, even to see my best work entirely wrecked by impatience of the slow processes through which alone it has any worth, I confess that I felt very much grieved when I came to Baltimore this spring to observe how completely you had abandoned all thought of pursuing such a policy.

There are everywhere people who are savagely impatient of well studied and prolonged processes of serving any purpose, even for their own good, and who have a ravenous appetite for smart superficial criticism of matters of which they are themselves profoundly ignorant. How much it is necessary to concede in your case to the weight and drag which directly and indirectly such people have in all city politics it is for you to judge, but you must be aware that for such parks as you are likely to have if you neglect such necessary managmnt of them as I have from the outset assumed would be practicable I cannot justly be held in any way responsible.

Mr Lanahan is greatly disturbed about the lamps which you received while I was absent in Europe.[6] I believe he has been led to greatly overestimate their defects and I fear has been induced to adopt unnecessarily expensive means of remedying them. But if I am mistaken it is a comparatively small matter, for the lamps are of little essential importance in the main design. Other lamps, at least, of considerably different character might be substituted for them without vitiating it. It will not be so if you substitute a bed of rank grass & weeds for a close mantle of ivy, in the very centre of one of the parks or if you neglect the essential conditions of healthy growth in the largest and most important element of the other, or if you take no trouble to make the simplest repairs in connection with the stone work the necessity of which I have so particularly enjoined in advance.[7]

If you need, which I hardly suppose, to have what I refer to more particularly pointed out, Mr Wisedell will be able to show it to you and to advise what can now best be done.

The main point at this moment is to have the old trees removed, it being wholly impossible for the designed bodies of foliage to be formed under their shade.

The text presented here is from a draft in Olmsted's hand.

1. Olmsted probably visited Baltimore in May 1878, during a trip he made to Washington in the middle of the month. He examined the work done on the squares north and south of the Washington Monument in Baltimore, plans of which he had provided in 1877 to the commission on which Garrett served, and wrote the present letter to protest its poor management (FLO, pay voucher, and "Daily Log," p. 30, Records Management Department, Architect of the Capitol, U.S. Capitol, Washington, D.C.; FLO to Thomas M. Lanahan, Dec. 23, 1876, above).
2. In October 1876 Thomas M. Lanahan, commission chairman, asked Olmsted to visit and give advice on the squares on all four sides of the monument. Olmsted conferred with Robert Garrett about the project in December 1876, prepared study plans for all four squares shortly thereafter, and submitted general plans for the north and south squares to the commissioners in February 1877 (FLO to Thomas M. Lanahan, Dec. 23, 1876, above).
3. Olmsted is referring to the arrangement of the squares when he first examined them, as level grass plats surrounded by an iron fence, which kept the monument open to view. "Nothing could be better adapted to its purpose than this simple and consistent treatment," he declared (ibid.; FLO to Thomas M. Lanahan, Jan. 29, 1877).
4. That is, the square immediately south of the monument.
5. Olmsted told the commissioners that since cutting down only the sick trees lining the squares would leave but a few healthy ones standing, it was better to cut them all down and "begin anew with foliage fully adapted to the design." Both Garrett and Lanahan agreed with him, and the removal of thirty trees was made part of the contract for the reconstruction of the squares. Nonetheless, many of the trees remained at the time of this letter (FLO to Thomas M. Lanahan, March 14, 1877; Robert Garrett to FLO, March 29, 1877; Thomas M. Lanahan to FLO, July 18, 1877; contract between John Bogart and commissioners for the improvement of the north and south parks, Washington Place, Baltimore, May 19, 1877, all in B124: #2401, OAR/LC).

OCTOBER 1877–JULY 1878

6. Square and oval brass lamps, designed by Thomas Wisedell specifically for use on the squares, had been manufactured by W. Staehlen, Jr., of New York. Some problems arose in installing them on the stone lamp piers and the bevelled glass in them developed cracks after use. Wisedell felt that the glass was installed too tightly to allow for expansion in heat and cold, and Olmsted assured Lanahan that the problem could be remedied "by slight and inexpensive adjustments such as have almost always to be made in objects of this class when first executed from drawings of entirely original design" ([FLO], North and South Parks, Washington Place, Baltimore, statement of payments and liabilities, Dec. 1877, and Thomas Wisedell to FLO, June 18, 1878, in B124: #2401, OAR/LC; FLO to Thomas M. Lanahan, June 5, 1878).
7. Olmsted's warnings about the stonework were apparently given in interviews with the commissioners and possibly had to do with faulty maintenance. This and the other problems he mentions, such as the removal of ivy in the oval panels in the north square and the retention of existing trees on the square although they shaded important plantings too much, persisted after he wrote this letter. In mid-June 1878 Wisedell reported that the gardener on the square constantly neglected the plantings established that spring by Oliver Crosby Bullard according to Olmsted's design. When Wisedell mentioned this to Lanahan, the commissioner replied "that next season they thought of placing some 'pretty Japanese Vases one in each plot, and fill them with flowers.'" Olmsted did not confer in person with the commissioners before leaving to spend that summer in Cambridge, Massachusetts, and as late as December 1879 was requesting that they pay him and Wisedell the full amount of money owed them for the design and work. In June 1883, according to his student Charles Eliot, Olmsted had yet to be paid (Thomas Wisedell to MPO, April 9, 1878, in B124: #2401, OAR/LC; Thomas Wisedell to FLO, June 18, 1878, in B124: #2401, OAR/LC; FLO to Robert Garrett, Dec. 26, 1879; Charles Eliot diary, June 17, 1883, pp. 29–30, Loeb Library, Graduate School of Design, Harvard University, Cambridge, Massachusetts.).

Notice to Watchmen for the Capitol Grounds.[1]

[July 7, 1878][2]

The greatest practicable order and neatness is to be maintained in the Capitol Grounds & their turf, plants & other fittings and decorations are to be preservd from all unnecessary wear & ill usage.

To this end it is chiefly required that practices which if generally indulged in would be inconvenient, disorderly and inconsistent with the beauty and fitness of the grounds should be *prevented* and that no one should at any time do what all cannot do at any time without obvious misuse and damage of the premises.

Watchmen are employed to guard against such practices and are expected to do so chiefly by the influence they may exert in preventing all persons wherever they may be upon the grounds from being careless or indifferent to the requiremnts which common sense upon due reflection would enforce.

It is of much less importance for this purpose that actual warnings or remonstrances should be addressed to visitors than that they should be made to feel that all misuse of the grounds is watchfully guarded against and that they are liable at any moment to be observed and interrupted in any improper conduct.

The ground is so large relatively to the number of watchmen that the duty thus required of them can only be performed by rapid and frequent movements of each man between the different parts of his beat and by his preserving such an attitude and manner as will show that he is really on the watch and not himself careless & indifferent to the object.

For these reasons watchmen are forbidden when on duty to sit, lounge, stand idly, to smoke, read newspapers or engage in conversation not necessary to their duty.

Men who find themselves unable to maintain activity of movement and a vigilant wide awake attitude and to attend exclusively to the business for which they are employed for the required periods of duty must be considered physically disqualified for the position of watchmen.

Watchmen are required to maintain good temper, to avoid threatening language & all unnecessary irritation of words or manner and to do their duty with the least possible disturbance and with as much civility, quietness and good nature as practicable but in the case of aggravated offences or determined and persistent perversity to arrest the offenders promptly & firmly, using any force necessary for the purpose. When necessary they will call to their assistance other watchmen or any men in the government service on the grounds.[3]

The text presented here is from a draft in Olmsted's hand.

1. Olmsted had been dissatisfied with the policing of the U.S. Capitol grounds for several years. Police jobs were awarded as political favors and little attention was paid to the performance of duties. His complaints in 1876 to Edward Clark, who served as chairman of the Capitol police commission, and to Justin S. Morrill led that year to an act of Congress intended to improve protection of the grounds.

   Matters did not improve over the next year, according to the new engineer-in-charge of the grounds, Frederick H. Cobb. He complained that hundreds of shrubs and plants had been stolen, trees vandalized, and cattle let into the grounds due to "the total lack of police" after dark. Olmsted renewed pressure on Clark for "proper police & police regulations." Clark told the chairman of the Senate committee on public buildings and grounds that "idlers are continually lounging around the most attractive parts of the park, rendering it unpleasant and unsafe for ladies and children." On June 20, 1878, Congress appropriated money for the salaries of six watchmen for the Capitol grounds. They were placed under Clark's direction and were to be employed day and night. When Olmsted visited Washington in early July, Cobb shared his doubts about their willingness to perform their duties, which likely prompted Olmsted to write the present text detailing what was expected of them. His insistence that they move rapidly over their beats and conduct themselves politely recalls instructions he issued to the watchmen of Central Park in 1859 and 1873 (FLO, "Patronage Journal," Nov. 1, 1875, below; Committee on House Administration, *A Statutory History of the United States Capitol Police Force* [Washington, D.C., 1985], pp. 13–17; *Annual Report of the Architect of the Capitol* [1877], p. 903; Edward Clark to H. L. Dawes, June 15, 1878, Records Management Department, Architect of the Capitol, U.S. Capitol, Washington, D.C.; FLO, "Rules and Conditions of Service of the Central Park Keepers," [March 12, 1859] [*Papers of FLO*, 3: 219–21]; FLO, "Report of the Landscape Architect on the Recent Changes in the Keepers' Service," [July 8, 1873] [ibid., 6: 610–30]).

2. The date is written on the back of the text and coincides with the visit Olmsted made to the Capitol grounds and consulted with Cobb on their policing.
3. The destruction and theft of plants remained a problem on the Capitol grounds despite the presence of the watchmen. "I commend the police to your fatherly guidance," an exasperated Olmsted wrote Cobb in 1881. "I agree with Capt. Brown that some of them would best be guided off the ground" (FLO to Edward Clark, Nov. 18, 1880, below; FLO to F. H. Cobb, April 11, 1881, Office of the Curator, Architect of the Capitol, U.S. Capitol, Washington, D.C.).

CHAPTER VII

JANUARY 1879–OCTOBER 1879

This chapter is in part retrospective, beginning with Olmsted's detailed but never-published account of chicanery and official malfeasance in the construction of Riverside Park. This article, written in early 1879, is a precursor and companion piece to *The Spoils of the Park* that Olmsted published three years later. The story ends with the dismissal, in the months following Olmsted's own, of his associates and supporters engaged in the Riverside Park work. Concerning other issues, the letter to Edward Clark presents his proposal for planting an area south of the U.S. Capitol grounds for protection against malaria. The letter to Charles S. Sargent deals with the difficult problem of selecting viable plant materials for the Back Bay Fens. The extensive reports to Henry Attrill and his associate spell out Olmsted's imaginative program for creating a hotel and resort at Rockaway Point near Brooklyn. Of equal interest with the imagination shown is his analysis of the sanitary and ecological conditions of the site. Letters to James Terry Gardner and Charles Eliot Norton represent early stages of planning for the Niagara reservation and the campaign to secure it.

JANUARY 1879–OCTOBER 1879

Review of New York City Park Department Polices in 1878

West Forty-sixth Street, 8th January, 1879.

If any apology should be needed for what I am now to write it would be found in a large pile of newspaper-cuttings, preserved for me by a friend, which testify to no little public interest in my removal a year ago from the position which I had for a long time held in the Department of Public Parks of this city; in the great kindness which these evince toward me personally (if there was anything else it has been omitted from the collection); and in the earnest remonstrance against the action of the Park Commissioners which a large and most respectable body of citizens did me the honor to make.[1]

My private life for many years has been one of so much seclusion that few of those who, as I have since learned, took an active interest in the matter are personally known to me, and this fact, while it increases my obligation to them compels me to think of it much less as an obligation to individuals than to the public.

The general interest taken in my removal was obviously in some degree due to the circumstances under which it occurred, and as these may now have a new significance I shall beg briefly to recall them. The principal works of the Department had been suspended for the winter, and leave of absence had been given me for three months upon a physician's certificate of the immediate and imperative necessity of my release from duty.[2] I was to use the opportunity thus occurring to review the principal works of my profession in Europe, and it was with a knowledge of my motives and intentions that, on the day which had been first appointed for my departure, my removal was resolved upon. No intimation that such action was contemplated had been given me. I was notified of it only as I was going on board the steamer and the final act of removal occurred after I had landed in Liverpool.[3]

The object was said to be to save the amount of my salary; but as my salary was to be stopped during the period of my sick-leave, the motive did not account for the abruptness and apparently unpremeditated character of the action. It might be suspected that, in taking leave, I had given the Commissioners some ground for sudden offence with me which they had taken this method to resent; but they had provided against such an idea by passing a complimentary and grateful resolution, and by a promise that if, after my return, they should find that they had anything to do in my line, they would take pleasure in giving me an occasional day's work.[4]

It was not a matter for a coroner's jury, and such interest as had been taken in it soon blew over. For more than five months afterwards I avoided looking at a New York newspaper, and when I returned[5] I could no longer with propriety say some things which it might have been becoming in me to do had I been at home while the public concern with it continued.

A recent occurrence having revived interest in the doings of the Commission, occasion seems offered me for three duties:

First, to give my thanks, as I heartily do, to the remonstrants against my removal; second, to express my regret that an exaggerated view should have been taken by some of the writers for the press of the responsibilities with which I had for some time previously been entrusted, and credit given me for services to the city which belonged wholly or in part to others;[6] and, lastly, to point out that the circumstance of my removal was in itself of less public interest than that of the adoption of a general policy in the business of the Department of which it was but the first step — a fact which has not, I think, obtained that degree of consideration which it would have received had it been frankly stated at the time.

I shall not explain or characterize this policy, but briefly give a few examples by which it may be better understood.

The duty of laying out that part of the city lying north of the Harlem River had been given, some years before my removal, to Mr. J. J. R. Croes, C.E., and myself jointly. I may be permitted to say that it was a duty which, for several reasons, I had strenuously endeavored to avoid, and which I took up only when not to do so would have compelled me, according to my notions of official propriety, to resign other duties very dear to me.[7] To get adequate command of the conditions of so large, complex, and in many respects original a problem had been necessarily a work of time, and would have been much more so but for the familiarity with them which Mr. Croes had already gained. This, however, had been accomplished, and when my removal occurred the whole of our common design had been studied, its leading lines laid down, its principles and motives determined; about two-thirds of it had been elaborated, half of it laid before the Commissioners, discussed with them, and remitted to the property-holders; their protests, requests, and comments given the most careful consideration; the plans laboriously revised, again submitted for discussion, and finally accepted and adopted. Perhaps a quarter of the whole had been surveyed in, filed, and fixed.[8] So much as had been gained toward what remained of the work by prolonged study, by experience, by debate, by increasing familiarity with and confidence in the general principles adopted, and by practice in their application; whatever had been gained by intimate knowledge of the ground and of all records, precedents, laws, usages, and prejudices to be consulted, rested, after my removal, with Mr. Croes. His removal, however, as a measure of economy, soon succeeded mine.[9]

Another followed, doubtless with the same motive — that of the Superintending Gardener of the Department, Mr. W. L. Fischer.[10] Mr. Fischer had been first employed in the Central Park in 1857, and two-thirds of the trees and shrubs planted upon it had been set by his hands. He is the only man now living, except myself, who has a close, intimate, intelligent, and sympathetic understanding of the design of the Park plantations, and who fully knows what is necessary to their due development. A man of admirable qualities, he loved the trees of the Park as his children, and his heart was wholly in his work.

The cases of Mr. Aldrich, the engineer whom I left in charge of the Riverside Avenue (and the only man in the Department to whom I had fully explained the aims and motives of its design), and of the several surveyors, draughtsmen, and inspectors under him, also removed in pursuance of the general policy of the Department,[11] have gained some attention of late, because of the publication of a report upon the subsequent progress of that undertaking,[12] but I must doubt if the full significance of this report has been appreciated. It cannot be unless the circumstances which led to the enquiry and under which it was prepared, are well considered. Briefly stated they are these:

A few months after the removal of Mr. Aldrich the comptroller of the city was advised, by a resident and owner of land fronting upon the Avenue, that the work of the contractors upon it was plainly not proceeding in accordance with the terms of the city's agreement with them, and that on this ground assessments for it could be successfully resisted—a serious charge for many reasons. The comptroller thereupon suspended payments to the contractors and notified the Park Department. The Commissioners replied by sending him a copy of a report from their engineer, denying the statement, and by presenting certificates calling for further payments to the contractors. At the same time being urged to make a more thorough enquiry into the matter, they refused to do so. In the end, however, they were compelled to assent to a proposition for this purpose.[13]

Payments to the contractors requiring the concurrence of both the mayor and the comptroller, each of these officers, to guard his responsibility against further imposition, if imposition there had been, independently selected an engineer to examine the work, and the two thus chosen were joined by a third, who was specially appointed for the occasion by the Department of Parks.[14]

The report lately published gives conclusions reached unanimously by the three examiners thus enlisted.[15] It is silent not only upon any points left in doubt in the mind of either one of them, but also as to much of the construction which, in the short time allowed for their scrutiny and with the means at their disposal, they could not uncover. They did not ask for the observations of others, made while the covered work had been in progress. The language of the report is technical and guarded, and the restraint of gentlemen meeting a thankless duty, reflecting upon more than one of their own profession, and addressing employers neither one of whom could be held wholly free from responsibility for anything wrong in the affair, is strictly observed.

I repeat that it is only when the unusual circumstances under which the report was made and the restricted range of the enquiry is kept well in mind that even the professional reader of it is likely to recognize how often the conclusion is reiterated that since Mr. Aldrich's removal the contractors have been allowed to draw large sums from the city treasury for work which has not been done but which they had engaged to do and which it was the particular function of the Department to insist that they should do.

I must go further and say that no engineer even, without some previous knowledge of the ground and of the plan and motives of the work, which are quite distinct from those of ordinary engineering constructions, will be able to infer from the report how great a wrong to the people of New York is told in its cramped recitals.

I have not personally examined the work since my return, and I am not expressing my opinion or giving my evidence about it. I simply want at this point to fix it in the reader's mind that down to the moment of Mr. Aldrich's removal there is no evidence that the city had been defrauded, while such evidence as I have indicated has been given to the public that since his removal, the contractors have been allowed to do much as they pleased, and that they have been pleased to do what it would have been much better for the city that they had not done.

Another proof thus occurs of a delusion which, though often exposed, even in such startling instances as those of the successive disasters of the Forty-second Street tunnel,[16] appears yet to have a strong hold. It is commonly supposed, that is to say, and the city's charter is shaped to the assumption, that by giving public work, under open competition, upon recorded specifications, checked by high officers of the city, an assurance is obtained against waste, misappropriation, and extravagance. The theory fails in practice in ways innumerable.

That it should work well requires not only that there should be trained, skilled, painstaking, honest, and honorable setting-out, inspection, and accounting by subordinates, but resolute integrity and absolute independence on the part of the directing and auditing officers. Our frequent and sudden changes both of subordinate and superior public servants; the insecurity of any official's tenure; his dependence on the caprices of others, on tastes, whims, personal, party, and faction interests which are constantly changing, and on judgments formed hastily, rashly, on imperfect information, and from which any form of review or appeal is a deceptive formality, sufficiently account for the dangerously speculative way in which contracts are often taken. It should not be surprising, when the character of the temptation which the public thus offers is considered, that contractors should be found who carry the principle of *caveat emptor* so far as to be constantly experimenting on the honor and keenness of those who stand for the interest of the public. In the affairs with which I have been connected I do not now recall a single important instance in which the penalties provided for delays in a contract have been finally enforced. When a contractor finds that he is at all exactingly dealt with, the temptation to speculate on changes of superintendence, and take his chance to rush upon new-comers, hoodwink, embarrass, and outrun them, if nothing worse, is obviously great. Give him time enough, and there are many other chances before him. The general result is unfortunately but too well known.

Yet the public is slow to draw the inference that only by sustained method, system, training, and discipline, and by so establishing men's positions and making clear their responsibilities that they may be in some measure independent of back-door influence, can essential improvement occur. New York is not now, so far as I can see, essentially more secure in this respect than when Mr. Tweed's great operations began.[17]

The change required is not, as it seems to me — for I would speak with no assurance on such a matter — simply one in respect to methods of appointment and removal and of conditions of holding office, but also one in respect to the classifying and fixing of official responsibilities. In the fifteen years in which I have served the city I do not think that there has been any period of six months in which my official status has not been distinctly modified; in which a material change has not occurred in my official relations with my superiors, colleagues, and subordinates, sufficient in most cases to much disturb if not wholly upset the routine, form, method, and the whole system of checks of my business. This in a department with which the legislature and the Common Council has perhaps less interfered than with any other. That the evil of shifting and uncertain official responsibilities exists under the able single-minded administration of the Department of Public Works was clearly shown by the statements given to the public after the Forty Second Street disasters last summer. Two recent trials in the Police Department have made it ludicrously apparent there.[18] And I have heard gentlemen connected with another branch of our municipal service deplore constant conditions in it obviously growing from the same root, or more directly from the jealousies, apprehensions and intrigues which branch from it.

The design of the Riverside work had engaged my best study during a period of four years, and to bring the cost of realizing it down to a point at which its simplest desiderata could be saved without laying the Department open to the charge of extravagance, the plans for it had been again and again revised with the aid of an engineer of more varied experience in such works than any other I know.[19]

The design had been adopted under the administration of Colonel Stebbins, and, in its earliest form, with the assistance of Mr. Richard M. Blatchford, Mr. Robert C. Dillon, and Mr. F. C. Church, the artist. It had been reviewed and confirmed under the presidency successively of Col. Stebbins, Mr. Wales, and Mr. Martin, and I had twice taken drawings of it to Albany and obtained the approval of legislative committees.[20]

The carrying out of so much of the general design as applies to what is known as the Avenue — an unfortunate misnomer — was to form the largest piece of contract-work of its class ever let by the city; its letting, consequently, attracted much attention. Among the bidders were some of the most respectable contractors in the country, and they had been aided in their calculations by some of the best engineers for the purpose.

The bid at which, under the provision of the charter to which I have referred,[21] the Department was compelled to let the work was lower by more than two hundred thousand dollars than the average of the bids, and there were large portions of the work, chiefly those which would come late in its progress, which no well-informed man supposed could be executed at the prices determined, without heavy loss to the contractor.[22]

If I should have any readers to whom it is supposable that, in long pondering over such duties as I have had the priviledge to be called upon by the city of New York to undertake there may possibly enter some degree of the labor and spirit, love and pride in which great works of the imagination grow, they will, perhaps, understand how the fact last mentioned became at once to me, and has ever since remained, a matter of deep concern.

The possibility that what I had pictured to myself as the ultimate results of the Riverside work would ever be realized, the possibility that its construction would not prove to me a great humiliation, rested wholly on the chance that the superintendence should be such that, while aiding and encouraging the contractors to meet their obligations in good faith, it should persistently resist all attempts to escape them.

The appointment of Mr. Aldrich as the certifying engineer of the work[23] was not made at my solicitation, but was most satisfactory to me, for I not only had had knowledge through other engineers of his successful dealings with contractors on other works, and of his shrewdness, manliness, and fidelity, but some personal experience of his accuracy and conscientiousness.

I knew nothing to the discredit of the contractors, but it was too much in the natural way of things, under all the circumstances, for me to be much surprised when, soon after the work opened, I began to hear that the appointment of Mr. Aldrich was a good deal talked of as a strange one; that it was asked whose man he was; that it was doubted if he was an engineer; that it was confidently asserted that he could have had nothing to do before with public works; that he did not seem to understand the specifications; that he was not accurate in measuring up work; and that he was a thoroughly unpractical sort of man. And after this I was less surprised to learn that he had persistently refused to give the contractors certificates for work which they were quite sure that they had done, and that he had even insisted that some of the work for which they had asked certificates should be taken down, because, as he said, it did not come up to the specifications.

Nor yet was I surprised when frequently-recurring appeals were made from his decisions to the Park Commissioners; nor yet, again, when counsel and advocates (not all free of the bar)[24] were brought in to reinforce these appeals.

On one of these hearings, having said that the contractors must be expected to govern themselves by the requirements of the contract as defined in the specifications, one of them, standing before the Commissioners, laughed at the suggestion, and declared that no contractor who attempted to work up to his specifications could get his living, and that no one with any practical knowledge of public works would think of expecting him to do so.

I shall not recite all the long and sickening history, but move on at once to the point of time when, according to the terms of the contract, the work should have been completed.[25] I believe that at this period not one-third of the necessary outlay to complete it in accordance with the terms of the contract had been made, and its slow, halting, irregular progress could be rationally accounted for only on the surmise that a change of superintendence was expected. This was Mr Aldrich's opinion. When I was about leaving last winter, not yet knowing of my own intended discharge, he said: "You will not find me here when you return. How it will be managed I can't guess, but I shall have to go."

How it was managed, by whom it was managed, or that there was any management required I do not know, but some time before my return it had so happened that Mr. Aldrich and his corps, now thoroughly organized, instructed, and trained, familiar with the ground and their several duties upon it, and working to an admirable system, had been got away.

It may be an unworthy suspicion which suggests some connection between the circumstances before stated and this event, and that it was, like the other removals of last winter, "a measure of economy"; but it is to be observed that the city saved not one dollar in salaries or wages by the operation, and, since the report of the examining engineers, it is unnecessary to say to whose interests the economy was applicable.

This chapter of my story having been written, it is time again to take up a thread which I dropped with the cases of Mr. Croes and Mr. Fischer.

Mr. Croes had several times during the appealing period been taken from his proper duties north of the Harlem River to resurvey and reinspect the Riverside work, with a view to advising the Board how far the complaints made by the contractors against Mr. Aldrich could be justified, the result being in every case a disappointment to the contractors.[26]

Mr. Fischer's duty on the Riverside work had been of the slightest, but he had been over it with me in conference about the plantations, and under my instructions had marked some of the old trees to be felled, and others on the Park beyond the limits of the Avenue, in order that the engineer might see that particular care was taken to prevent them from being injured by the contractors. These are the trees the grubbing out of which is shown by the report of the examining engineers to have followed quickly upon that of Mr. Fischer.

Though there are no more like instances of economy to be referred to, I shall have occasion before I close to pick up the thread once again by which the interests of the contractors are associated with the general economical policy of the Commissioners.

I could not consider the report of the examining engineers without pointing to the demonstration which it offers, that the fancied security against extravagance of the provisions of the city charter in respect to contracts is but a stimulant to the worst kind of waste, so long as present methods in the appointment and removal of the professional servants of the city are sustained.

If any ask what I would have, I answer that, after a silence, demanded by official propriety, of twenty years,[27] I am speaking of certain evils of which, as a servant of the city, I have had experience. It has not been my business to look for a remedy for them, and upon that question I have nothing to say. The great body of those whose business it has been plainly believe that under our form of government no permanent remedy is practicable and that the conceded evils of our present methods should be accepted as a part of the price that we pay for the advantages we gain by it. But if so, should not the consequences be more frankly accepted and the state be spared the yearly agitation for changes of the charter of the city and other temporizing, superficial and futile expedients, of which with whatever good purpose they may be urged by some the preponderating motive and the more conspicuous result nearly always is the gratification of personal or political spite or friendship?

But there is another lesson for the people of New York even less likely, I fear, to be attentively considered than that which I have been aiming to emphasize, and it may be believed that I shall indicate it with reluctance, and only because of the obligation which the action of so many good citizens last winter places upon me.

Perhaps I should admit, however, that I am unwilling that the public should wholly overlook a matter of some moment to my craft.

I will not claim that my craft has as yet a perfectly firm and well-defined place among the callings by which the mark and measure of every people's civilization is so largely determined; but that there is a field of public as well as of private work which engineers as such cannot be expected to fully occupy, and in which thorough devotion of life is to be desired, I feel sure that no intelligent man will be disposed to question; and possibly the very conditions which make such a vocation as yet a comparatively inconspicuous one among the professions should rather commend a great city to be cautious of treating it with contempt than be regarded as a justification for its doing so.

The opportunity of permanently endowing itself at small cost with a noble work—a work not simply of engineering or of architecture or of gardening; a work which would be in more than one respect without a parallel—which is owned by New York in the site of Riverside Park and Avenue, though it is as yet so little appreciated by its citizens, is really an important item of their corporate property. The difference between well-studied and ill-studied dealings with it, that is to say, may easily be in the future a matter of several millions of dollars.

The question how far the dealings of the Department of Parks with this property during the last summer were, in respect to design, well-studied or ill-studied, refined or brutal, did not come before the examining engineers. It is touched in their report only incidentally to the proper purpose of it; but, incidentally, facts are stated which unquestionably show a reckless disregard of the interests of the city. And this is a matter responsibility for which can in no degree be shifted from the Commissioners to their engineer. It was not the business of an engineer to be able to properly determine a class of questions such as their engineer was allowed, consulting with no one, to determine finally — such as, after giving my life to them, I have never thought of determining without reporting to, and obtaining the approval of, my official superiors.

The waste which the contractors were permitted, and even aided, to make, through the destruction of opportunity and the accumulation of obstacles and conditions of costliness to valuable results previously intended — waste against which due guardianship had been provided for in the contract — is a matter much more to be regretted, and which will yet be much more regretted, than that which the examining engineers more distinctly report.

If the changes of design — but they cannot be designated by so mild a term — if the botchings of the design of the Avenue and the Park which are indicated in the report of the examining engineers — I have not examined the work, and I speak only of testimony which I find published — if these botchings and mutilations were also a measure of economy, need I point out again that it is not the taxpayers of New York who are to benefit by it?

If the circumstances which I have stated suggest, as they seem to me to do, that a good-natured disposition toward the contractors rather than toward the general body of taxpayers of the city may by some indirect process, hardly understood, perhaps, by the Commissioners themselves, have been combined with some peculiar theories of economy in the removal of Mr. Croes, Mr. Fischer, Mr. Aldrich and his company, I must mention a circumstance having a possible bearing on my own case.

Something more than a month before I was so suddenly shot out of the Department, with resolutions expressive of gratitude, respect, and confidence toward me, and with an intention to take me in again, but in another form, when I should be thought to be needed, some persons had confidently supposed that my removal might be accomplished in a manner which would have occasioned no public curiosity as to its motives, and which certainly would have been attended by no kindly resolutions or promises.

I was to have been discharged on the ground of delinquency and unfaithfulness to my duties. The specifications of a charge of this character were such as could have been honestly framed only by information from one who had made it a part of his daily business to furtively inform himself of my every movement beyond the doors of my house.

I would not, if I could well avoid it, provoke a comparison between this incident of my life and the celebrated case of Mr. Eugene Wrayburn,[28] but frankness compels me here to say that I had, in fact, observed, and had stated for the amusement of my friends, that I certainly was being mysteriously "worked up," and that I had allowed myself a slight indulgence in those peculiar "pleasures of the chase" to which that unfortunate gentleman was addicted. I should still, perhaps, refrain from mentioning so ridiculous a thing, if I did not possess evidence of another piece of meanness even more contemptible, tracing very distinctly from the same direction.

I was informed that the charge against me had been made in writing by several hands. I did not see this writing. I did not ask who the writers were. I was not told. It looked to me as if the whole device had been the work of a very clumsy workman, or that its object had been expected to be accomplished quietly, without examination of witnesses, at least without cross-examination. I was not called to make any formal answer to the charge by the Commissioners. I did not think that I was called to do so by self-respect. The story is worth the telling because it shows how a certain class of the community may suppose that it is practicable to deal with public servants who stand in their way, and because it exemplifies again the demoralizing influence of the present methods of appointment and discharge of public servants, especially professional public servants, in whom a certain degree of personal dignity is of decided economic value.

Will it be believed that, upon evidence of such a character as I have indicated, my name was actually struck from the pay-rolls of the Department, that my salary was stopped, that the accusation was given in its full absurdity to the public press, and that my casting out in disgrace was publicly announced? All this actually occurred.[29]

Someone even took the trouble to send me, from the office of publication apparently, a weekly newspaper in which I was set out in prominent capitals as The Great Leech who had for twenty years been gorging himself on the life-blood of the taxpayers of New York.[30] This pleasing bit of condensed biography was followed up by a column of details not to be found in the "American Encyclopædia," and which must have required a good deal of research, in which the various plants were described by which I had outwitted, one after another, all the old political leaders of both parties in the city and State, from my participation with the Red-handed Vaux in stealing the plan of the Central Park down to my leadership of the Gravel Ring and the snooping of the Capitol with my pals, the Artful Archer and Dickson the Deft.[31] That my gory taking-off should have been accomplished after all by a shepherd banker and a shepherd broker,[32] with little stones from the brook of financial purity, was almost too good to be true, and pointed plainly to the class of men from which, if the city is ever to know a genuine reform, it would have to look for its mayor.

The full folly of the effort to accomplish the end in view of this movement, with whomsoever it originated, was only too soon arrested by a plain recital, by the then President of the Department,[33] of facts within his knowledge, and by reference to the Commissioners' minutes; and I must not neglect to say that, while giving long, frequent, and patient hearings to the Riverside contractors, and showing much anxiety that the work should go on, and that they should not be annoyed by mere red-tape exactions or in any way unnecessarily hampered, he in the end always acknowledged that Mr. Aldrich had been substantially right, and backed him in insisting upon what was due the city.

As to the other Commissioners I trust that in suggesting a possible relation of cause and effect between the condition of the Riverside work and the dissatisfaction of the contractors in 1877; the discharge of the several professional servants of the city whom I have named, and the condition of the same work as reported by the examining engineers less than a year afterwards, I shall not be thought in the least to imply that my late official superiors are not all honorable men.

To explain the dubious position in which they seem to have been placed I would, without wishing the analogy to be very closely drawn, recur to a common experience which teaches us that when a man who has expended his vigor in toiling up the ladder of pecuniary self-satisfaction takes a fancy to divert his well-earned leisure in agricultural pursuits, or in any others, for which he has no natural aptitude or acquired proficiency, and toward a sound understanding in which all his established tastes and habits sternly interpose, it would nearly always be as well for the public that his virgin essays should be made at his own rather than at their expense.

It is a matter of ordinary observation that amateurs of this class fall into habits of excessive credulity and over-ready good fellowship on the one hand and of morbid distrustfulness on the other. By taking advantage of their weakness in the first respect, cow doctors, tree-peddlers, dealers in patent fertilizers and other practical men, make them very useful in their respective branches of business. Their distrustfulness applies more particularly to men to whom the matters of their amusement have long been the subject of deep and absorbing interest and who are disposed to apply to them a degree of method which would be suitable to affairs of business. If I should add that anything looking like professional pride in such matters, or, worse still, anything looking like a delicate conscience such as would be shown by pottering and worrying over what they regard as trivial and pedantic details, is extremely offensive to them, I should do so only to report more distinctly, that no analogy of this kind should be thought to apply more closely than would be consistent with all due respect to the Commissioners. But that there are those among

them who have suffered under an infirmity more or less of the nature thus suggested, I have had reason, in personal experience, to imagine, and I doubt if any explanation of their dealings with the Riverside work can be made which will more redound to their credit.
Respectfully,

FREDERICK LAW OLMSTED.

The text presented here is from a galley proof with revisions in Olmsted's hand. Olmsted apparently wrote this document between December 26, 1878 and January 8 the following month, and had it set in type soon after. It is not clear why he did not proceed and publish it.

1. Numerous public complaints followed the Department of Public Park's actions in January 1878 to abolish the Bureau of Design and Superintendence which Olmsted, as landscape architect, had headed since late 1872. Newspaper editors castigated the decision and published letters against it, including one by E. L. Godkin that sparked a separate debate over who originally designed the park and one signed by over 160 New Yorkers, among them Albert Bierstadt, Clarence King, and Whitelaw Reid. Olmsted's friend and office clerk, Howard A. Martin, saved newspaper articles about his ouster (DPP, *Minutes*, Jan. 5, 1878, pp. 489–90; ibid., Jan. 23, 1878, pp. 545, 553, 556–57; *New-York Daily Tribune*, Jan. 11, 1878, p. 2; *New York World*, Jan. 22, 1878, p. 5; Howard A. Martin to FLO, Jan. 11, 1878; ibid., Jan. 15, 1878; ibid., Jan. 25, 1878).
2. Dr. J. L. Campbell certified that Olmsted's poor health required that he stop work for two or three months (DPP, *Minutes*, Dec. 26, 1877, pp. 458–59; see above).
3. On Saturday, January 5, 1878, the day Olmsted had originally intended to sail, the board resolved to abolish his office. He postponed his departure until the following Tuesday, January 8, when he embarked on the *Montana*. On January 23, 1878, the board formally abolished his office by revising the department bylaws (DPP, *Minutes*, Jan. 5, 1878, pp. 489–90; ibid., Jan. 23, 1878, p. 553; *New York Herald*, Jan. 10, 1878, p. 5).
4. Olmsted's annual salary in 1877 was $4,500. When the board removed him from the position of landscape architect, it appointed him consulting landscape architect, noting that "his services to be paid for at such rate as this Department shall determine from time to time as they are availed of" (DPP, *Minutes*, Jan. 24, 1877, p. 565; ibid., Jan. 23, 1878, pp. 556–57; see Frederick Law Olmsted, *The Spoils of the Park with a Few Leaves from the Deep-Laden Note-Books of "A Wholly Unpractical Man"* [Feb. 1882], p. 648, n. 61, below).
5. Olmsted returned to New York from Europe in late April 1878 (FLO to Edward Clark, April 16, 1878, Office of the Curator, Architect of the Capitol, U.S. Capitol, Washington, D.C.).
6. E. L. Godkin and others had issued public remonstrances that gave Olmsted sole credit for the design of Central Park, and Calvert Vaux replied with an angry letter to the editor of the *New-York Daily Tribune*. Godkin responded but Olmsted's stepson Owen stopped the exchange with a letter in the same paper stating that no one had authority to claim for his father more than equal share with Vaux for the design of the park. Olmsted, in an attempt to stave off a similar fight in late 1879, recalled the exchange to Henry Whitney Bellows (see FLO to Henry W. Bellows, Dec. 24, 1879, below).

JANUARY 1879–OCTOBER 1879

7. Olmsted and Croes were instructed to design the street, rapid transit, and park systems of the Twenty-third and Twenty-fourth wards in November 1875. The duties to which Olmsted refers were presumably those relating to Central Park, where his organization of the gardeners force had been reinstituted in September 1875.
8. See FLO and J. J. R. Croes to William R. Martin, Nov. 15, 1876, note 1, above, and FLO and J. J. R. Croes to William R. Martin, Oct. 31, 1877, notes 2 and 3, above.
9. The board dismissed Croes on March 27, 1878 (*The City Record*, May 16, 1878, p. 781).
10. The board dismissed William L. Fischer on February 20, 1878 (ibid., p. 782).
11. The board dismissed Aldrich on March 13, 1878, and eight others working on the Riverside project one week later (ibid.).
12. Olmsted is referring to the report by an independent commission of engineers that criticized the construction of Riverside Avenue. Their report, dated December 26, 1878, was published in several New York newspapers and in the *Engineering News* ("Document No. 85," in DPP, *Minutes*, Jan. 15, 1879, pp. 5–14; *New York World*, Dec. 28, 1878, p. 1; *New York Herald*, Dec. 28, 1878, pp. 4, 9; *New-York Times*, Dec. 28, 1878, p. 8; *Engineering News*, Jan. 4, 1879, pp. 4–5; see n. 15 below).
13. On October 4, 1878, architect Leopold Eidlitz, who resided at Riverside Avenue and 87th Street, informed comptroller John Kelly of numerous defects in the construction of the avenue. Because the defects violated the agreement between the city and the contractor, he noted, property owners would be able to contest assessments upon them for the cost of the work. Within two weeks, the park commissioners returned to the comptroller a report by the project's superintending engineer, Thomas Franklin, denying Eidlitz's charges. At the same time they voted down a motion introduced by their fellow commissioner, Smith E. Lane, to begin an investigation by Eidlitz, the full board, department engineers, and the comptroller. They then presented certificates to the city's finance department for payments to the contractor, over the objections of their treasurer, Smith Lane. He had personally inspected the work and declared that Franklin's approval of it was incorrect. By late November the full board assented to an investigation of the project by independent engineers (*Trow's New York City Directory... for the Year Ending May 1, 1878* [New York, 1878], p. 40; DPP, *Minutes*, Oct. 9, 1878, pp. 295–98; ibid., Oct. 16, 1878, pp. 311–12; ibid., Oct. 30, 1878, p. 338; ibid., Nov. 20, 1878, pp. 377–78; *New-York Times*, Oct. 10, 1878, p. 8; *New-York Daily Tribune*, Oct. 10, 1878, p. 8).
14. Democratic mayor Smith Ely, Jr., appointed William E. Worthen and comptroller Kelly appointed Charles H. Haswell to the commission of engineers. The park board first asked Montgomery A. Kellogg, engineer-in-chief of the department under the Tweed Ring. When he declined the appointment the board chose John Bogart, who had worked with Olmsted and Vaux in the department and elsewhere (DPP, *Minutes*, Dec. 4, 1878, pp. 390–91; *Papers of FLO*, 6: 162, 560).
15. Among their findings, the engineers reported that the superintending engineer, on his own and without notifying the park board, changed the lines, grades, and widths of the avenue, walks, and park surfaces from Olmsted's design. He also changed the design of the retaining wall upon which much of the avenue and walks were to be supported and allowed plain earth to be used as backfill instead of rock. Portions of the avenue and walks had already subsided as a result. Flagging was laid in soft earth without using gravel or sand as a foundation. Topsoil removed earlier and stored for use in the future was used for fill. Finally, hundreds of old trees that Olmsted and Fischer had marked to be saved were cut down ("Document No. 85," in DPP, *Minutes*, Jan. 15, 1879, passim).
16. On June 29, 1878, a section of a tunnel being constructed between First and Second avenues and 42d Street collapsed killing two men. The Department of Public Works

had designed the tunnel and was responsible for inspecting its construction. Under the provisions of the city charter, a private contractor, as the lowest bidder, was constructing the tunnel. Blame fell on the city inspector, who was fired, although independent engineers found that the design of the tunnel, supplied by the commissioner of public works, was faulty. Work continued using the same design and a second section of the tunnel collapsed on October 20, 1878, whereupon the commissioner fired his chief engineer (*New-York Times*, July 12, 1878, p. 8; ibid., Oct. 25, 1878, p. 8; *American Architect and Building News*, July 20, 1878, p. 18; ibid., Nov. 2, 1878, p. 145).

17. That is, the period of the notorious Tweed Ring control of the government of New York City, from May 1870 to November 1871.

18. In November 1878 the board of police commissioners tried two police captains charged with selecting polling places where liquor was sold during a recent election. Their defense, eventually accepted by the board, was that the practice by which election officials instructed police captains to choose polling places was an informal one, unaffected by any regulation of the police department; thus they had broken no rules of the department (*New-York Times*, Dec. 18, 1878, p. 2; ibid., Dec. 28, 1878, p. 3; ibid., Jan. 22, 1879, p. 2).

19. James C. Aldrich, an engineer who in 1868 had prepared the topographical survey for Olmsted and Vaux's plan of Riverside, Illinois. In October 1873, on Olmsted's recommendation, Aldrich was named "Assistant Landscape Engineer" on Riverside and Morningside parks (*Papers of FLO*, 6: 271; DPP, *Minutes*, Oct. 6, 1873, pp. 325–26).

20. Olmsted and Vaux began the preliminary design of Riverside Park in the late summer and autumn of 1872, various times during which Blatchford, Dillon, and Church sat on the park board. The board first approved the design in early 1873, when Henry G. Stebbins was its president, and approved revised plans in 1874 under Salem H. Wales and in 1876 under William R. Martin. Olmsted twice presented drawings of the design to legislative committees in early 1874 during political fights over the project (*Papers of FLO*, 6: 596–600; FLO to Henry G. Stebbins, Jan. 15, 1875, above; FLO, Patronage Journal, Feb. 18 and c. March 19, 1874, below).

21. That is, article 16, paragraph 91 of the New York City charter of 1873, which required the city to accept the lowest bid entered for public projects (New York [State], *Laws of the State of New York, Passed at the Ninety-Sixth Session of the Legislature* [Albany, N.Y., 1873], chap. 335).

22. The department accepted the bid of $516,161.25 offered by Nicholas H. Decker and George W. Quintard (DPP, *Minutes*, Oct. 4, 1876, p. 330; ibid., Oct. 9, 1876, p. 343).

23. The board appointed James C. Aldrich as superintending engineer of the Riverside Avenue project on November 22, 1876 (ibid., Nov. 22, 1876, pp. 422–23).

24. That is, some of them had stood at the bar as defendants in law suits.

25. The contract specified that work on the avenue be completed by October 31, 1877 (ibid., Dec. 15, 1877, p. 442).

26. The printed minutes of the board do not indicate when Croes examined the Riverside work. His inspections probably took place between mid-1877, when the contractors complained that Aldrich was too demanding, and March 1878, when Aldrich was dismissed and replaced by Thomas Franklin (ibid., July 18, 1877, p. 171; ibid., Aug. 1, 1877, pp. 192–93; ibid., Oct. 24, 1877, pp. 358–59; ibid., Feb. 13, 1878, pp. 595–96; James C. Aldrich to FLO, May 22, 1877, B38: #505, OAR/LC).

27. That is, the period of approximately twenty years that Olmsted had been identified with the public parks of New York.

28. A young lawyer in the novel *Our Mutual Friend* (1865) by Charles Dickens. In his search for his lost love Lizzie Hexam, Wrayburn finds that he is being followed by her other suitor, the schoolmaster Bradley Headstone, and delights in throwing him off

JANUARY 1879–OCTOBER 1879

the trail (Gilbert Ashville Pierce, *The Dickens Dictionary* [Boston, 1880], pp. 467–69, 490).
29. On December 12, 1877, New York City comptroller John Kelly informed the park board that he was withholding Olmsted's salary, because he understood that the parks were mainly finished and no longer required a landscape architect and that Olmsted's absences from his duties in New York to work in other cities were "frequent and prolonged" (DPP, *Minutes*, Dec. 12, 1877, pp. 433–34).
30. The editors have not located a newspaper article describing Olmsted as a "Great Leech" and giving the biographical information suggested here, but two articles from this period in the Tammany newspaper the *Sunday Mercury* are examples of similar attacks in the press. The first, on December 9, 1877, with the title "Cornering a City Leech," announced that comptroller John Kelly had refused to authorize Olmsted's salary for November because he had so little to do during the winter months. The article asserted that only one member of the Board, William R. Martin, was aware of what had taken place. On December 12 the park board received a communication from comptroller Kelly stating that he had withheld Olmsted's salary as Landscape Architect "for the reasons that he has been informed Mr. Olmsted renders little or no services in that capacity; that his duties outside of the City of New York render his absence necessary and frequent, that he had been absent from his duties for twenty-six days during the month of October, and that the parks are in the state of completion that the services of an architect can be dispensed with." William R. Martin, apparently forewarned, offered a reply to the comptroller's charges. A later biographical article in the *Mercury*, anticipating by three days Olmsted's formal dismissal as Landscape Architect, claimed to show by evidence from the park board's minutes that Olmsted was not the person whose plan for Central Park had won the design competition of 1858 ("Cornering a City Leech," *Sunday Mercury*, Dec. 9, 1877, p. 1; "Light on a Muddled Subject," ibid., Jan. 20, 1878, p. 5; DPP, *Minutes*, Dec. 12, 1877, pp. 433–34).
31. This is apparently a reference to Olmsted's two associates on the capitol advisory board, giving them names suggestive of criminals: the "artful archer," with its veiled allusion to the artful dodger, a character in the novel *Oliver Twist* by Charles Dickens, is the name that he gives to Leopold Eidlitz, who was both artful and a designer of arches (since he declared he must work in the Romanesque style with its distinctive arch-form); Olmsted's term for Richardson, "Dickson," is simply the diminutive form of his name.
32. That is, park board president Samuel Conover, president of the Produce Bank, and commissioner James F. Wenman, president of the Cotton Exchange (*New-York Daily Tribune*, Jan. 11, 1878, p. 2; *New York Telegram*, June 14, 1879, p. 2).
33. William R. Martin answered Kelly's charges against Olmsted on December 12, 1877 (DPP, *Minutes*, Dec. 12, 1877, p. 434).

To Charles Sprague Sargent

27th Jan. 1879.

There are two broad divisions of beauty of vegetation in tidal lands. (1)that of what I know as salt meadows, the beauty of which is in the complete occupation of nearly level surfaces by a short fine grass — in lawn like breadth and repose. This is our salt hay grass. I don't know its botanical name — (2) that of taller, graceful waving reeds, rushes and sedges, in which interest may lie much in the variety and contrast of forms and tints

I suppose that the grass of the first class grows only where the ground is nearly of the elevation of ordinary high water — its roots being but occasionally covered. That is to say where I want the broad quiet effect, I had better arrange level surfaces (of rich, salt marsh mud?) which will usually be barely covered by the tide, (for half an hour) once in twelve hours. Of the taller and coarser vegetation I suppose that I may have two classes, one to grow on ground which would not often be reached by the tide but would be moistured by infiltration at the depth of three to six inches every twelve hours, the other on ground most of the time covered by salt water, that is to say near my low water mark (which will be but a foot below high water).

Please tell me if I am wrong and tell me the botanical names of a few plants which I could be most sure of success with — or which would be most likely under operations of nature to predominate, in the three situations, (1) slightly above ordinary high water; (2) slightly below ordinary high water, and (3) near and below ordinary low water.

If I make a bank at an angle of 45° and sod it between high & low water with the ordinary sedge of salt marshes (of salt creek banks) the tide rising and falling over the whole face, will it be likely to live and hold. (This apart from the question of washing away & gullying?)

The text presented here is from a draft in Olmsted's hand. In this letter Olmsted describes the issues relating to vegetation with which he had to deal in planning the Back Bay Fens. For his further explanation after receiving Sargent's reply, see FLO to Sargent, Jan. 29, 1879, below.

To CHARLES SPRAGUE SARGENT

N.Y. 29th Jan. 1879.

My Dear Mr Sargent;
I have recevd yours of yesterday and thank you for its prompt reply to my inquiries.[1] I did not fully present my general idea, and in doing so partially, with reference to particular points, have a little misled you.

I am now thinking of a basin as extended (above grade 9) as practicable; the shores to vary much in character, sometimes sandy and beach like, sometimes abrupt, sometimes and as much as can be afforded rocky; the bank above also variable, in degree of steepness, and to be, as a rule, overgrown thickly, in a picturesque, natural, completely informal even negligent manner, so that after a few years such slight damages as would occur (with the precautions I have in view) would at worst be inconspicuous. In my inquiry with respect to strictly tidal ground plants I had little reference to the foot of this bank, or to any islands which would bear trees or shrubs.

But I wish to avoid large areas of open water, and also, in order to spread the occasional floods over as much surface as possible and so avoid vertical rise of water to have large flats bearing vegetation which would tend to prevent the formation of waves.

I have large quantities of mud to be dredged and disposed of. I can form flats by making enclosures of solid earth and filling them with mud.

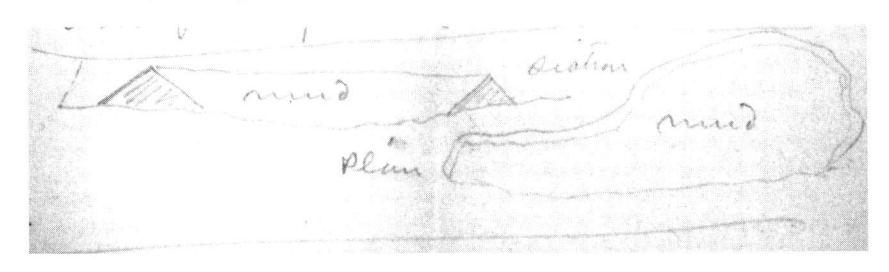

I shall have also large areas of mud and sedge bank already formed, the present surface of which, being several feet above the proposed high water level, must be pared down so that flood water may pass over it.

On these flats I can have a thin layer of any soil I choose and I can allow their surface to vary from a few inches above ordinary high water level to a few inches below ordinary low water level. Thus, as far as practicable, with a rise & fall of but one foot of tide, I can imitate the conditions in which any of the tidal ground plants best flourish. What I chiefly want is to be sure that I can perfectly cover these flats with marshy plants in considerable variety. There are a number of such plants which I know, and which I think could be used by planting sods of them, but upon all these I find myself in doubt as to the most suitable elevation having regard to a tide of one foot. I suppose that the "black grass"[2] wants to be a little above *ordinary* high water. What I know as sedge (probably different species) grows both above and below this—in sand and in crevices of rocks. Whether it is soil or period of submergence that determines the position I don't know.

There are many plants with which I have a general familiarity, as making pretty effects on the edges of tidal brackish water, which I fear might not grow where the water is as salt as it will be in the Backbay.

But in general I infer from your letter that without raising the surface of the flats more than a few inches above ordinary high water level I can have a large variety, including in the uppermost possibly certain Solidagos, asters and bullrushes and lower the two or three plants which chiefly cover the marshes between Cambridge and Brighton.

The text presented here is from a draft in Olmsted's hand.
1. On January 27, 1879, Olmsted wrote to Sargent asking him for information regarding plants that would do well at Back Bay (FLO to Charles S. Sargent, Jan. 27, 1879).
2. Black grass (*Juncus gerardi*) is not a grass but rather a member of the rush family and grows in salt marshes above the high-water line (Lauren Brown, *Grasses: An Identification Guide* [New York, 1979], p. 114; Cynthia Zaitzevsky, *Frederick Law Olmsted and the Boston Park System* [Cambridge, Mass., 1982], p. 187).

To Edward Clark[1]

New York, *May* 23, 1879.

Edward Clark, Esq.,
Architect of the Capitol, Washington, D.C.:
My Dear Sir:
Scientific students of the subject are divided between two theories of the nature of malarial poison, and differ as to the manner in which trees act upon it,[2] but the following propositions satisfy either theory, and their soundness is, I believe, unquestioned.

1st. If malarial poison originates in a particular locality, and there is a free movement of air between the locality and a hill a mile away from it in the direction in which the prevailing winds of summer move, the poison is likely to be more felt upon the upper part of that hill than in the intermediate valley.

2d. But if there is a belt of trees crossing the direct line between the two localities the entire higher ground to leeward is often found to be wholly, and nearly always partially and in an important degree, protected from the action of the poison.

If, therefore, there was a body of trees along the base of Capitol Hill, the ground beneath them being well drained and not in itself adapted to the production of malaria, it would in all probability be an efficient means of protection to the Capitol from malarial poison originating on the banks of the Potomac and in the low grounds between the river and the hill.

Your suggestion that a plantation for this purpose could be formed upon the government property along the line of the old canal[3] seems to me an excellent one.

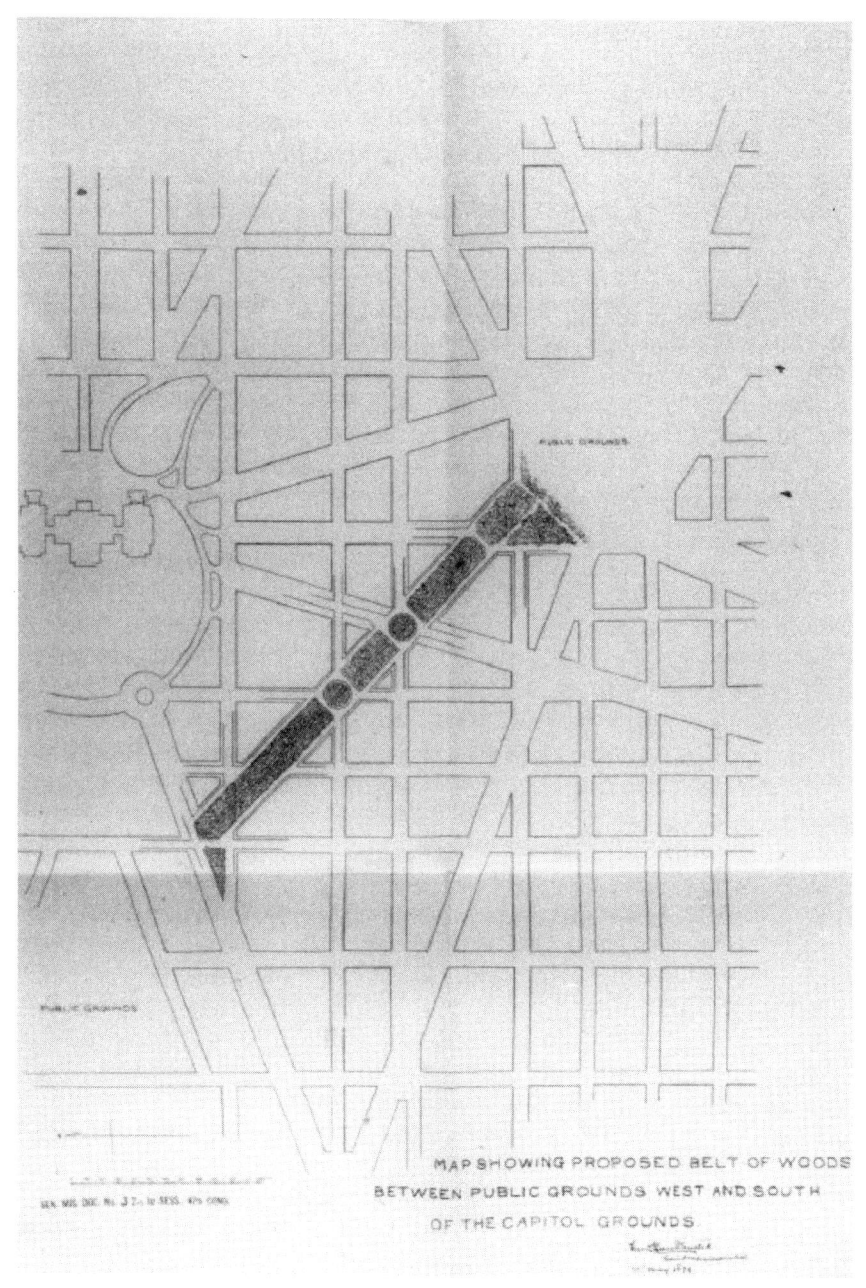

PLAN FOR TREE PLANTING ALONG LINE OF OLD CANAL BETWEEN
INDEPENDENCE AVENUE AND RESERVATION 17

I have attempted to give it a more definite form in the accompanying map, by which it will be seen that while maintaining with unimportant exceptions the existing and intended lines of public communication, a continuous belt 160 feet wide could be planted so as to connect the existing plantations of the Botanic Garden with another to be formed upon reservation 17.[4] I have proposed a walk 20 feet wide through the middle of the belt, as the branches of the trees standing at its sides would soon meet overhead and form an unbroken body of foliage. I think it desirable to avoid so large a gap as would be needed for a central drive and walks.

The desired result would of course be much sooner and more effectively obtained if the plantation could be extended over the space between the proposed belt and the Capitol grounds, and this would give a much needed opportunity for enlarging the collections of the National Botanic Garden, and add greatly to the dignity of the Capitol itself.[5]

But the suggestion could be carried out as indicated on the map without the purchase of any land, at very moderate outlay for soil, trees, and planting, and with confidence in results of value to Congress and to the public.[6]

Respectfully,

FRED'K LAW OLMSTEAD,
Landscape Architect.

The text presented here is from United States Senate, 47th Congress, 1st session, miscellaneous document 32, page 2.

1. Edward Clark (1822–1902), architect, worked in the Philadelphia office of Thomas U. Walter and came to Washington with him in 1851 to work on the extension of the U.S. Capitol. Appointed Architect of the Capitol in 1865 after Walter's resignation, Clark held the position until his death. Throughout the duration of the Capitol grounds project he was Olmsted's closest associate and ally in Washington, and he frequently obtained his advice and services on related projects. Since at least 1876 Clark had worked to improve the ventilation of the House chamber of the Capitol and obtained the design for its ventilation shaft from Olmsted and Thomas Wisedell. It was under construction by the time of this letter, but many people, including Olmsted, suspected that the air it drew from outside the building carried malaria and other poisons from nearby areas. Most of the stagnant Washington Canal along the Mall had been filled by this time, but the section south of the Capitol, and the sanitary condition of the city on the whole, remained dismal. Swamps and marshes along the Potomac and Anacostia rivers surrounded the city on three sides; the outlets for the city's raw sewage emptied directly into these wetlands. The combination of rank vegetation, sewage, and high summer temperatures created, according to one newspaper, "a pestilence breeding nuisance of unbearable offensiveness." Clark apparently asked Olmsted's advice on how tree plantations could help purify the air reaching the Capitol (Glenn Brown, *History of the United States Capitol*, 2 vols. [Washington, D.C., 1902], 2: 193–94; *Annual Report of the Architect of the*

JANUARY 1879–OCTOBER 1879

Capitol [1876], p. 755; ibid., [1877], pp. 900–5; Washington Evening Star, Jan. 29, 1879, p. 2).
2. The Staten Island Improvement Commission of 1870–71, on which Olmsted served with physician and sanitarian Elisha Harris, had discussed the latest theories of malaria and the effect of trees upon it. While scientists agreed that it originated in swamps or poorly drained ground as an invisible, poisonous gas or vapor, one group held that it was produced by the microscopic spores of certain water plants, another that decaying vegetable matter released it. Planting trees near such areas helped abate the problem. Opinion differed on the question of whether their roots removed the excess ground water that hosted malaria, or, instead, their foliage physically arrested malarial spores or neutralized them with "oxygen and volatile aromatic material" (Papers of FLO, 6: 34–36; Frederick Law Olmsted, Elisha Harris, J. M. Trowbridge, and H. H. Richardson, Report to the Staten Island Improvement Commission of a Preliminary Scheme of Improvement [New York, 1871], pp. 30–35).
3. A reference to the section of the old Washington Canal, now Canal Street, that ran between the U.S. Botanic Garden on the Mall and the parcel of U.S. government land (Reservation 17) at the intersection of New Jersey and Virginia avenues.
4. Olmsted sent Clark a plan the following month for planting and carrying streets through Reservation 17 (FLO to Edward Clark, June 21, 1879, below).
5. The area that Olmsted here proposes to use for tree-planting is south of the Capitol, bounded by Independence Avenue, Canal Street, and either South Capitol Street or New Jersey Avenue. Part of the area is now occupied by the Rayburn House Office Building.
6. In his annual report for 1879, Edward Clark recommended that Olmsted's plans be adopted by Congress as "the most important step that can be taken to procure purer air" for the Capitol. Appropriations were made in February 1880 to fill, drain, and put "in good sanitary condition" the old canal south of the Capitol, but nothing was provided to plant or open communication through it or Reservation 17 according to Olmsted's plans (Frederick H. Cobb to FLO, May 22, 1879, in D2, OAR/LC; ibid., May 27, 1879; FLO to Edward Clark, June 21, 1879, Office of the Curator, Architect of the Capitol, U.S. Capitol, Washington, D.C.; Annual Report of the Architect of the Capitol [1879], p. 322; Statutes at Large of the United States of America [Washington, D.C., 1881], 21: 300).

To ÉDOUARD FRANÇOIS ANDRÉ

209 W. 46th St
New York, 6th June 1879

My Dear Mr André

I have just recvd, on returning to New York, your kind note of 21st ult°. The package of books was delayed for some time in the Custom House and on getting it I did not at once make my acknowledgts because I thought I should receive a letter from you with directions for the disposal of the volumes not inscribed to me. I surmised your intention, however, and after waiting a fortnight

393

sent one to Prof[r] Sargent,[1] the other (with the botanical work) to D[r] Thurber.[2] (Prof[r] Sargent is now in the mountains of Carolina on a botanical tour with D[r] Gray & others.[3] I have just called on Dr Thurber but failed to find him).

Of course with my exceedingly limited knowledge of French I read your book with difficulty, imperfectly & slowly but I am going through with it in course as best I can, asking assistance when necessary and getting a written translation of many of the more important pages. Having been travelling much of the time I am as yet only at the ninth chapter.

Before I last left home I took the liberty to send the book to our largest publishers (the Harpers)[4] telling them that it was by far the most complete and satisfactory book on the subject yet issued in any language and was likely to long remain the standard authority; that a translation of it would be of great value to our country and the demand for it would be permanent. I also said that with your consent I should be proud to appear as the editor of a translation if they thought such an endorsemnt desirable. They now return it saying that in the present depression of the book trade they are not willing to undertake so large a work. When I see Thurber I shall urge him to advise his publishers to undertake it and if they decline shall try others. A few years ago I should have had no difficulty in accomplishing my purpose but have little hope of success just now. I shall try, however, and you will please write if you object to my doing so and if you would be willing to allow me if successful to edit the translation, with an introduction and notes.

Of course I should not make this proposition and request if I did not most sincerely respect & admire your work nor if I did not think that it met a great public want & met it in a spirit with which I heartily sympathize. My interest centres in Chapters 5, 6 & 7[5] and I am greatly pleased to find how thoroughly I agree with you upon the main principles of criticism with respect to art in Gardening. I am particularly glad that you have taken ground so strongly against the common abuses of decorative gardening.

If you are likely to publish a new edition at any time (revising the letterpress at all) there are one or two errors as to American affairs which I could point out to you—unimportant to your purpose but worth correcting if occasion offers.

It may interest you to know that though what you regard as the Italian and English use of the word picturesque is not wholly obsolete here in America, it is much less common than that which you say is French. I have never from childhood used the word otherwise than as you do.[6]

Downing (Landscape Gardening Chap II) objects to Price's definition (it is rather Lauder's than Price's) and speaks of the picturesque as "an idea of beauty or power strongly and irregularly expressed."[7] This is not in itself a satisfactory statement but it shows how far he was from accepting the Italian or old English idea and if you read all that he says on the subject you will see that he means by picturesque much the same that you do. So would most Americans.

JANUARY 1879–OCTOBER 1879

I should be glad to know more of your Mediterranean work.[8] I am doing but little professionally, my most important active work being the Capitol Grounds at Washington. I am in the employmnt of the City of Boston and have made plans which are accepted for what they call the Back Bay Park. The Arnold Arboretum waits certain treaties in progress for a rectification of boundaries which I have recommended.

The subject which most interests me is a movement which I am actively urging for the purchase by the State of New York and the province of Ontario in Canada of territory adjoining Niagara Falls including Goat Is^d with a view to the removal of the buildings upon it & the restoration of natural conditions. I enclose a statement privately circulated about it.[9]

My son joins with me in hearty congratulations to you & also in begging to be kindly remembered to Mad. André.

The text presented here is from a draft in Olmsted's hand.

1. Charles Sprague Sargent.
2. George Thurber (1821–1890), botanist and horticulturist. Thurber edited the *American Agriculturist* from 1863 to 1885 (*DAB*).
3. Asa Gray, Charles Sprague Sargent, William M. Canby of Wilmington, Delaware, and John H. Redfield, curator of the herbarium of the Botanical Department of the Philadelphia Academy of Natural Sciences traveled to the North Carolina mountains on a botanical expedition between May and July 1879 (Jane Loring Gray, ed., *Letters of Asa Gray*, 2 vols. [1893; rpt. ed., New York, 1973], 2: 686–87, 692–93).
4. That is, Harper & Brothers publishing firm.
5. These chapters were titled, respectively, "Du Sentiment de la Nature," "Principes Generaux de la Composition des Jardins," and "Division et Classification des Jardins" (Édouard André, *L'Art des Jardins: Traité General, de la Composition des Parcs et Jardins* [Paris, 1879]).
6. André declared that in Italian and English usage the term "picturesque" meant having the quality of being a proper subject for a painting. The French definition said of a picturesque object that "il faut qu'il donne une impression soudaine, étrange, en meme temps qu'agréable" (that is, immediate, strange, and at the same time agreeable). In addition, André described certain qualities that are found in picturesque objects, but not in beautiful ones: rudeness, irregularity, showing the effect of disease, or richly ornamented (ibid., pp. 114, 115).
7. Olmsted is quoting from Andrew Jackson Downing, *A Treatise on the Theory and Practice of Landscape Gardening, Adapted to North America* . . . (New York, 1875), p. 54, and referring to commentary by Sir Thomas Dick Lauder in his 1842 edition of *Sir Uvedale Price* on the Picturesque. . . .
8. André carried out several commissions in Monaco and Rome, including designing gardens in the English style for the Villa Borghese (*OCG*).
9. The circular to which Olmsted refers was presumably a precursor of the one presented in Olmsted's letter to James T. Gardner of October 2, 1879, below.

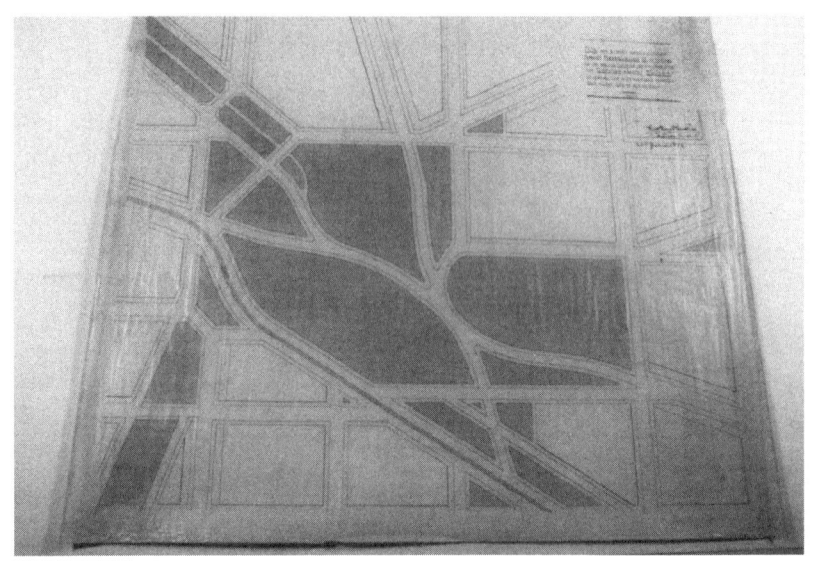

"Plan for street communication through Reservation 17, with a view to its being planted as a screen for the Capitol against Malaria"
In connection with proposed planted belt along line of old Canal, June 20, 1879.

To Edward Clark

New York, 21ˢᵗ June, 1879.

Edward Clark, Esq.,
Architect U.S. Capitol;
My Dear Sir;
 I send a plan for carrying street communication through Reservation Seventeen,[1] with a view to planting the ground, the object being to get as large bodies of planting as practicable without too much interrupting passage. It would cost little to plant the ground. There is no probability that Congress will want to make another small park for recreation for the vicinity of Capitol Hill for a long time to come. To leave the openings suggested for streets and plant all the rest of the ground with young stock would be a comparatively inexpensive operation. It would have considerable sanitary value, and if at any time it should be thought to give a park treatment to any part of the ground all desirable openings could be readily cleared.
 I think of coming to Washington again the last of next week.[2] If you are not likely to be at home, please let me know.
 Very Truly Yours

Fredᵏ Law Olmsted.

JANUARY 1879–OCTOBER 1879

The text presented here is from a document in a clerk's hand and signed by Olmsted, in the Office of the Curator, Architect of the Capitol, United States Capitol, Washington, D.C.

1. That is, the twenty-three-acre parcel of U.S. government land located one-half mile south of the Capitol at the intersection of New Jersey and Virginia avenues. One of the original seventeen reservations of land set aside for federal uses in the L'Enfant plan of Washington, it was the only one remaining in public ownership without a building on some part of it (U.S. War Department, *Annual Report* [1885], 2: 2351; DeBonneville Randolph Keim, *Keim's Illustrated Handbook. Washington and Its Environs* [Washington, D.C., 1876], pp. 21–23; Wilhelmus B. Bryan, *A History of the National Capital*, 2 vols. [New York, 1914–16], 2: 330–31).
2. Olmsted visited Washington from June 26 to June 30, 1879 (FLO, pay voucher, Records Management Department, Architect of the Capitol, U.S. Capitol, Washington, D.C.).

To HENRY Y. ATTRILL AND BENJAMIN E. SMITH[1]

Report

209 West Forty Sixth Street,
New York, 30th July. 1879.

H. Y. Attrill, Esq.,
B. E. Smith, Esq.,
Gentlemen;

On the 8th. instant I received your instructions to examine Rockaway Point; consider the opportunities it offers for making a place of summer resort, more particularly as compared with those of Coney Island, and to suggest how they might be most profitably turned to account.[2]

I have since spent nearly three weeks on the Point and have sought information from all local sources. The topographical survey in progress is not so far advanced that I can make much use of its results and my estimates of distances and quantities must be subject to correction, but they will be found, I believe, sufficiently accurate for your present purpose.

This being a report for your private information, I shall speak first of circumstances unfavorable to your object which you are liable to have underestimated.

First the stench of decayed fish is perceptible on the Point whenever the wind sets toward it from Barren Island[3] which it frequently does at night. It might be prejudicial to a hotel even at the East end. Coney Island lying to the Westward of Barren Island suffers less from this source because Easterly winds are less frequent in summer and, being more violent, when they occur the odor is apt to be dissipated before reaching the hotels.

Next as to Flies and muskitoes. These are always to be found in countless numbers among the bushes. I am assured that in passing through the thickets even in January, clouds of muskitoes are stirred up. They swarm to the sea-side in summer whenever there is not a fresh breeze. They have been annoying at the Surf House[4] nearly every night. The residents are cautious in speaking of them but it is admitted that they have, at times, been an intolerable pest.

Flies also swarm on the Point and at times during my visit it has been difficult to take a meal because of them, they so covered the food and filled the air.

I think it practicable to so far abate both these nuisances that they will be of no serious prejudice to your object.

Flies are now bred in vast numbers in the privies and the slops, offal and waste thrown out at the back doors of the taverns, as well as in the dead fish &c on the strand.

Mosquitos are generated in stagnant water and find their proper sustenance while in the larvae state only in decaying matters at the bottom of pools or puddles. They mature and harbor, after taking the insect form, in bushes and herbage where they can escape from wind. Much of the eastern part of the Point presents exactly the conditions most favorable to their propagation, in moist hollows in which shallow pools form with every shower, surrounded on all sides by dense thickets, with sand hills to make a lee for every wind.

I am not likely to undervalue the beauty of the natural low growth of the Point and it goes against my professional grain, as I know it will disappoint your expectations, that I should advise you that it had better be sacrificed. But in doing so I only express my reluctant judgment of the risk which it involves of bringing a dangerous reputation upon your property. You had better burn every living thing, level every sand-hill and give the breeze a clear sweep rather than build a great establishment and have your guests even once driven away by these pests, and the newspapers tell the story as newspapers would.

By clearing off the bushes, draining the low ground and providing for the prompt removal of decaying matters, there is every reason to suppose that you may avoid the danger. Thorough measures, and perhaps rather costly measures, for drainage, sewerage and the washing away of all manner of filth, which are needed for this, are, as I shall presently show, for other reasons of the first importance.

Lastly, I must point out that though you have a certain extent of better building ground than was originally found at Coney Island, the advantages of the Point in this respect may not be quite as extensive as you have supposed, for the reason that the sand-hills are so disposed and so conspicuous that in any view at the East End a deceptive idea is obtained of the general elevation of the land.

North of the line of dunes which protects it in storms from the wash of the surf and, from a line half a mile from the East end to the extreme west, very little of the property is a foot above ordinary high-water and probably nine tenths of it is occasionally flooded. The relative standing of different parts as affected by this consideration may be seen in Diagram No 1. In this the part lettered A, shows an area (lying just back of the sea-beach) which consists of an undulating ridge of sand often 20 feet in height. Here a plateau might be formed of local material at a distance of from one to two hundred feet from ordinary high-water-mark on the beach, having a length of three quarters of a mile, a depth of a hundred and fifty feet and an elevation of ten feet above high-water of Spring tides.

This narrow district along the beach is the best building-ground upon the property. I will compare it later with the ground correspondingly situated on Coney Island.

Further to the South west, the same ridge continues with much less average elevation. Still, at several points upon it, there are sites suitable for large hotels. The block on the diagram, lettered B indicates the district now referred to.

The space lettered C. represents an average elevation of at least three feet above that of any considerable part of the property lying West of it, and is, in all respects, the best site for shops & residences, and nearly all buildings not desirable to be more closely connected with the beach. To prevent an inconsiderate occupation of any part of it which would stand in the way of good final arrangements, lines of streets and lots of various depths, suitable to different objects, should be laid down at once, to which all constructions and all sales and leases of land may conform.

In the remainder of the property there are numerous hillocks but no considerable space which is more than a few inches above ordinary high-water. Most of it is marshy, but I have not found any to be miry. By dyking on the Bay side and closing a few gaps in the sand-hills through which water above the general level of the sea is urged in great storms, and by some drainage through tide-gates, aided, if necessary, by wind-mill pumps, a large part of this area, (say 450 acres) may be reclaimed. It will then be available for many purposes, but hardly desirable for large hotels or residences. The westernmost part is liable to be swept by the sea and no building would for the present be safe upon it in a severe storm with spring tides and ice afloat in the bay, unless set upon strong piles well above the present surface. The extreme point is gaining, however, and there is good reason to expect that it will continue to gain both in extent and elevation.[5] Not improbably within two years the capabilities and value of this last district will be decidedly greater than at present.

Dyking the bay side of the Point might be expected to accelerate the extension and elevation of the extreme point by strengthening the westerly current after a storm and increasing and carrying further out the eddy in the edge of which sand is deposited.

Before passing from the subject of the elevation of the property, I will observe that communities occupying such low ground, and especially temporary and shifting communities, are particularly open to contageous and endemic diseases. As an outbreak of one of these would be liable to be magnified by rumor, raise a panic, empty the hotels and create a permanent prejudice against the place, no unnecessary risk of it should be taken. This danger, as well as that from flies and mosquitos, is to be mainly provided against by abundant water supply and efficient sewerage and plumbing. The need of these to the highest success of your proposed enterprise will appear from another consideration.

The people of New York and its suburbs are peculiarly cursed by conditions which tend to establish malarial troubles and are hard upon children, hundreds dying in consequence of them every year as soon as extreme summer heat occurs. There is no place as near and easily & cheaply accessible from New York as Rockaway Point which is also as far removed from conditions of the same class, or in which, barring the liabilities which I have pointed out, conditions exist as favorable for recovery and the working off of malarial and diarrhetic trouble. It is at least five times as far removed from local malarial conditions as any part of Coney Island; ten times as far as parts of it, and is separated from them, as Coney Island is not, by a body of water[6] so large that it will be recognized by Sanitarians as a perfect barrier to their influence. There is no other locality equally secure in this respect within twice the distance. Whenever this fact is well understood by physicians it will much recommend the Point as a place of summer resort and no risk should be taken, in order to save outlay in sewerage arrangements or otherwise, of sacrificing this advantage.

To avoid fouling the Bay water for bathing, the nearest point at which sewage should be discharged is a mile west from your eastern boundary. As the sewers must be carried below the level of high-water, an efficient and economical arrangement will require expert planning and the matter should have early and careful study.

The sewage of the Brighton and Manhattan Beach Hotels[7] is discharged into Sheepshead Bay at a distance of about 3000 feet by twelve inch pipes. Complaint is made of the arrangement and a larger sewer to convey it further, with steam-pump to secure a better discharge is projected. Both houses are supplied through pipes with water pumped upon the main land. The first large hotel upon the Island was supplied at first from local wells, but whenever much drawn upon the water became brackish. A special Company to bring a much more abundant supply of water to the Island is reported to be forming.[8]

I have now stated all the difficulties and drawbacks, for your purpose, of the property which I can suppose are not already patent to you. I will proceed to show some of its advantages more especially as compared with Coney Island.

The beach in both cases varies so much with different conditions of wind that in some particulars it is difficult to generalize accurately about it, but the same winds produce like results in each case, and I shall speak of what appears common with ordinary tides and the usual summer breezes.

At Rockaway Point for a mile and a half the beach has a more regular slope. The breakers ordinarily reach it more unbroken and with equal force of wind are a little larger. There is usually a larger proportion of powdered shell in the composition of the surface stratum; it is consequently firmer in grain and it is less apt to be pebbly. The water being further from the outflows of the Hudson, Raritan and other streams and the sewers of New York, Brooklyn & the New Jersey towns, must be supposed to be purer sea-water.[9] This part of the beach is not only a better bathing beach than any part of Coney Island but better than the beach to the eastward which gave Rockaway its old reputation[10] and which I find is generally preferred, by those who have had experience of both, to the Coney Island beach. I have watched it & tested it in all states of tide and I do not think that it has a fault from which it is possible that a sea beach shall be always free. I do not know that there is anywhere a better bathing beach.

Beyond a point a mile and a half to the westward of your east line the beach has a longer slope but for another mile and a half is still an excellent bathing beach, quite as good as that of the favorite bathing resorts further east, or those of Coney Island. I find no more evidence of "undertow" than at Coney Island.

The statement above that the breakers are larger than at Coney Island may suggest that they are likely to do more damage along shore as well as make bathing more dangerous. This is not the case in any appreciable degree for this reason. At a distance of about a hundred and fifty yards from the shore and parallel with it is a bar upon which, with the ordinary afternoon sea-breeze, the waves pass undisturbed, but if the wind freshens and the waves run higher and deeper they are checked or broken upon it and consequently come to the shore with abated force. I have three times seen this illustrated during my visit and Captain Donn of the Coast Survey[11] tells me that the bar has been long established and is to be considered a permanent circumstance. Winter storms sometimes work gaps through it but these are quickly repaired and it is never broken during the bathing season.

On the opposite side of the Point and at a distance of 450 yards from the Ocean, your property fronts again upon the lagoons of Jamaica Bay. Vessels drawing twelve feet of water can run in at the lowest ebb of the tide from the open sea, find a land-locked harbor and come to a wharf at a hundred yards from the shore. Small-craft can come to the natural banks. The lagoons offer twenty square miles of quiet water surface which can be used without danger of sea-sickness and which is otherwise well adapted to and much frequented by sailing and rowing parties. They are also celebrated for their fishing and shooting advantages. I have seen their value in all these respects fully demonstrated during my visit.

At the nearest point of the lagoons to the best bathing place upon the ocean there is a smooth, soft, clean, gently-sloping, sandy beach admirably adapted for still-water bathing for delicate persons and all who find the surf unpleasant. Further to the westward there are other such beaches on your property.

At Coney Island not only are all these advantages growing out of the lagoons wanting, but the ground immediately back of the principal hotels and upon which some of their dependencies stand is a marsh intersected by narrow creeks and washed by the tide, disagreeable if not even repellant. There is nothing which invites to yachting or boating, nor, off the beach, to walking, driving or riding. Embankments are now being formed adjoining to and back of the hotels upon the marsh with sand drawn from the beach and loam from the main land, and it is reported that in one case a large operation of this character is intended, with a design for pleasure grounds, in which ponds for amusement with boats will be a feature; showing that the need is felt of the class of advantages which you so abundantly possess.

This large body of water in your rear in place of the narrow marsh gives you also the advantage of cooler nights when the wind is northerly. A gentleman who has spent much time at Coney Island tells me that during periods of northerly wind he has often found it as warm there as at New-York. I have heard the same said of Long Branch.[12] With northerly winds I have found an agreeable coolness in the air at Rockaway.

One other advantage of your property I find in the beach to the eastward of it. At low-water the drive along this beach, after passing the group of inns, for a distance of five miles is surely one of the finest of the kind in the world. It is better than that from the Cliff House at the Golden Gate and equal to that of the celebrated Lynn Beach.[13] A finer riding course cannot be imagined.

It is to be noted, however, that nowhere along this beach are the same advantages to be found for a summer hotel as those you possess; the land in the rear being less elevated and the space between extreme low and extreme high water two or three times as broad — an advantage for driving, a disadvantage for bathing.

For the reasons I have thus sufficiently indicated and having due regard to the accessibility which is promised,[14] it is my opinion that Rockaway Point might be made not simply, more attractive to the public than Coney Island but quite the most complete and popular sea-side resort, *adapted to very large numbers*, in the world.

It should not be forgotten that forty years ago "The Beach at Rockaway" was the most fashionable sea-shore resort in America,[15] drawing visitors from all parts of the country, and that only three years ago, with poorer accommodations, it had more visitors than Coney Island; 50,000 coming to it in one day. Considering the present furor for Coney Island and its numerous superior approaches the fact that Rockaway even now draws 20,000 a day is significant as to its undeveloped capabilities.

In discussing how a property of these capabilities should be dealt with in order to secure the largest profit, the chief difficulty I find lies in an apprehension that such measures as a prudent estimate of immediate results may call for, may restrict and embarrass such a development of its value as will be justified when its merits shall have been established in the estimation of the public.

There is, in my judgment, sound reason for believing that a much larger number of visitors may yet be drawn to a suitable resort upon the sea shore than has yet been known at Coney Island.

The fame which in two years three or four independent undertakings more boldly and liberally designed than any of the class before them brought to Coney Island has drawn many thousands to the sea-shore who never before left home for recreation; thousands besides who had hitherto gone for their summer recreation elsewhere than to the sea-shore; and thousands more who had before been accustomed to go to other resorts on the sea-shore. Yet there is no reason to suppose that this success has been obtained at any serious and permanent cost to other like enterprises. It seems rather to have stimulated the business at various points. A substantial hotel of brick 800 feet in length has just been opened at Cape May.[16] Newport, Narrangansett Pier[17] and other resorts to the Eastward are reported to have more visitors than ever before. The Telegram of today reports that the number of visitors at Long Branch, both of lodgers at the hotels and of "excursionists" coming for a day, has never been as large as it is now.[18]

The growth of the business does not come exclusively, though it does largely, from the great cities. It is evident that the field is opening very widely. Of the visitors to Rockaway during my stay there parties of a few hundred each have come from Connecticut; from Central New York; from distant parts of New Jersey and from Eastern and Western Pennsylvania. I have talked with those engaged in getting up such parties and am assured on intelligent grounds that these hundreds are not unlikely soon to be thousands.

Again, I have observed a statement, and it seems to me true, that more than three quarters of all the visitors to Brighton Beach have thus far come from Brooklyn and that much more than double as many people came to the Island as a whole from Brooklyn in proportion to population as from New York. It must be inferred that with better provisions, better knowledge of them, better facilities of transport and better times there may be a vastly greater number of people drawn out from New York to the sea-shore than there yet has been.

That the enlargement of the business shall be attracted chiefly to Rockaway Point the main requirement is that those coming there shall carry away a more decided and pleasurable impression of its adaptation to public wants than they can obtain elsewhere.

By observing how and in what degree different points at Coney Island are occupied, something is to be learned of the manner in which visitors are acted upon in this way.

Within certain defineable limits it is evident that substantially all take their pleasure alike. All, for instance, enjoy the outlook upon the sea; the great expanse. All enjoy the dash and sparkle of the breakers close at hand. All enjoy to feel the full force of the sea-breeze and nearly all enjoy to take their pleasure in these things while walking slowly up and down the beach, or if the sun is hot, the verandas of the hotels. Beyond these the inclinations of visitors are diversified and they rapidly divide off, according to their tastes and dispositions, as affected by age, sex, education and means.

Out of 50,000 visitors on a fine day at least 49000 will have stood or strolled before the end of it on the beach or the verandas; nearly that number on both. But I do not suppose from what I have seen that more than 10,000 of these will have taken a "square meal" at the hotels or more that 1000 have paid for a room. I doubt if 20,000 will generally have paid for anything at all at the hotels. Rarely 10,000 pay for baths. Then come a variety of special provision for the public entertainment of which each draws a few. The Aquarium, the Prospect Tower, the Race Course, the Balloon, The Shooting Galleries, Billiard Rooms and so on down to the Mud Pie establishment, Aunt Sally[19] and the Scups.[20] Not one in a hundred of all who attend the concerts or walk on the verandas may be seen at any of these, yet few fail to see and be pleased with some one of them and each contributes to a general gay, grand, popular holiday effect and thus to make people of all tastes and of all classes go away satisfied, disposed to come again and to stimulate their neighbors to come.

Hence in forming the general scheme of a resort of this class it would be a wild mistake to measure the value of an object by the money it is likely to directly bring in, or even by the degree in which is to be voluntarily used by visitors. It may be, as I have said, that at Coney Island, much less than half the visitors on a particular day contribute anything to the revenue of the hotels. But to a man who does not enter the hotels, who even does not use their free verandas, they are by no means an unimportant element in his experience and will influence very much the story he will tell of the place. That is to say these great, gay complex structures, if they do not feed his belly do feed his eyes. They please his fancy. He feels them, with all the rest, to be admirable and they help perhaps as much as everything else to the common exclamation. "It's a Great Place!"

And, in the long run, the revenue of the hotels is dependent on the common fame of the place and will, in some degree, rise or fall according to the satisfaction taken in it even by men who directly contribute nothing to it.

Looked at in this light it will be evident that the capital invested in the hotels might have been much more profitably used had it been under one control and had the prospective value of the common fame of the place been appreciated.

For example, with reference to general popular admiration of the place, nothing perhaps is more talked of, or counts for more, than the single circumstance of the length of the verandas. "Such a glorious piazza"! You hear people exclaim again and again. Yet the longest hardly exceeds four hundred yards. If all the verandas on the island had been set end to end it would have made one more than a mile in length.

Let it be supposed that the four principal buildings for public entertainmnt on the island[21] instead of being set a quarter of a mile apart and one obscured from the other by petty structures, had been skilfully grouped together with a view to producing a single strong impression of the same kind which has been more or less judiciously aimed at in the composition of each. Suppose that the several bathing establishments connected with them had been in like manner consolidated and brought into range and harmony of effect with the mass and that the small buildings for various purposes which huddle about them had been added and then suppose that a single spacious arcade had been carried along the entire front of the whole. Let this have been done by an architect alive to the opportunity and it is certain that at no greater cost and at no sacrifice of convenience a result might have been obtained which in its effect in pleasing the fancy and producing a strong impression of spaciousness, liberality and adequacy to the public needs, would have been a much more marked success than has in fact been realized on Coney Island.

Hence, as you are situated, with a frontage of four miles on the Ocean beach and another frontage of four miles upon the Lagoons; with every important advantage which Coney Island possesses and many of great value which she lacks and, with the opportunity of a far broader and more comprehensive organization of all the elements of your improvements with reference to general effect, it would be a mistake to look closely upon Coney Island as a model or to take the numbers which it has drawn as the measure of those for which you should make provision.

Successful as the arrangmnts of Coney Island have been it is apparent that they were not contrived either as a whole, or (except in a few later constructions) in particular parts, with direct regard to the character and extent of the business which has actually been drawn to them. From fifty to a hundred thousand people, largely in families, in which the little children have to be taken care of without the aid of hired nurses, often come to the island in a day. At the same time there may not be upon it more than one thousand such visitors as usually fill a first-class hotel. Yet it is apparent that the plans of the central, most conspicuous, most famous and most costly constructions upon the island have been conceived in the first instance wholly from the point of view of the ordinary hotel-keeper. Both at Manhattan Beach and at Brighton

Beach there is a building known as the Pavilion specially prepared for vistors who do not want a room and do not want regular meals. But they are comparatively plain and inconspicuous structures; are set on one side, are evident after-thoughts; and the hotels have as distinctly the aspect of hotels simply, as if they had been designed for Saratoga or Niagara.[22] The great outlay for music, for turf and for flowers is all for the hotels. The ground about the Pavilions is shabby and neglected.

Now the class of people for whose use the Pavilions are more especially intended do not as individuals spend much money; they are not at all the sort of people whom first-class hotel keepers like to fill up with because of their frugality and the small number of "extras" they call for. But of the class of men who are well able, and who are growing rapidly to be more disposed than they have hitherto been, to come with their "wives, their cousins, their sisters and their aunts" and more especially their little children for an occasional holiday to the sea shore, there are in New York and its various suburbs and in all the country penetrated by the rail ways and steam boat routes centering at New York, not hundreds merely to one of those for whom first class hotels are more particularly designed, but absolutely thousands.

I have not any doubt that your best policy is to provide directly, frankly, ostensibly and with manifest pride, as the foremost matter of your enterprise, for the accommodation and gratification of immense numbers of this class—the great industrious, moderately-thriving, decent, self-respecting class, the children of which mainly fill the Common Schools.

Even with the very unsuitable provisions which now exist, the business of the inns at Rockaway Point has at once a large increase when the Public Schools of New York close and their profitable season ends abruptly when the schools open again.[23]

I do not mean that ample and wholly suitable provisions even surpassing that made at Coney Island, should not also be made for the more free-spending and luxurious class but that the larger profit on the whole would be found in placing the hotel for these where it would not seem intended to be the focus of attraction; even by giving it a slightly retired and reserved if not exclusive character.

Hardly anyone even at a pleasure resort does not prefer to command occasional quiet and an opportunity to draw himself well away from a multitude. Hardly anyone, on the other hand, does not like, in his own good time, to join a great festive throng. It is better, then, not to complicate the problem of the festive arrangmnts with the problem of the hotel. It is only necessary that there should be convenient communication between the two.

It is to be remembered that large numbers and apparent expectation and preparation for large numbers go far to secure large numbers, as is so well established in respect to theatres and all public shows and exhibitions. The gregarious instinct of human beings is as evident as that of crows or buffaloes. And that immense numbers are drawn to a play or a concert or a preacher does not stand in the way of rich, exclusive, refined people's being drawn with the rest. Unless there is some special element of rowdyism or coarseness in the crowd, of which there is always less danger in the case of a very large than of a moderate sized assembly, the gregarious disposition manifests itself in the rich quite as much as in the poor and this equally whether it is the Black Crook[24] or a sermon that is the centre of attraction.

This idea, thoroughly-well carried out, of remanding the hotel element of a watering place to its proper subordinate position and magnifying and glorifying the Pavilion element would have this incidental advantage, that the new place would not seem to be quite so much Coney Island over again as there is danger that it otherwise must be. It should be remembered how much Coney Island owes to the immense gratuitous advertising which it has received from the newspapers. There is nothing newspapers are more averse to than repeating an old story. Every element of originality that you can secure, whether it be novel in its purpose or simply novel through the advance made in carrying out in a large and grand way purposes previously realized more cautiously and contractedly, will compel the Press to help you, will compel people to talk about you. Nothing can be more fatal than failure in this respect.

A realization of the topographical conditions which the diagram (No 2) before you is intended to broadly exhibit will leave no doubt as to where you should aim to fix the centre of attraction and provide most amply for the public accommodation. The division marked by the letter A is your most elevated and firmest ground and that which will be first closely approached by rail from New York. There is no area on the sea-coast from New York to beyond Far Rockaway and none on the New Jersey coast for a much greater distance from New York than Long Branch which is quite as well adapted for a building or a range of buildings close upon the strand and from which an equally simple sweeping ocean overlook may be secured.

Make the most that is practicable of these three elements — the great breadth of the ocean view, the surf tumbling in at your feet and the expression of amplitude and liberality in your provision for general public entertainment, and you will not only stand in advance of any other place of summer resort but all competition must be permanently at disadvantage.

And I advise you to bring all your main structures into one line, partly for the reason which I have already suggested and partly to avoid the flanking out of the view of the sea as the view from the hotels is flanked out by the bath houses, rail way-stations and other structures at Manhattan Beach.

Finally I advise you to place the front of this range as near to the Strand as shall be found consistent with perfect security and convenience. That is to say, as your guests come to enjoy the sea-shore, I advise you to place your principal accommodations for them as closely as practicable to the sea-shore.

This would give you another distinction. It is not a customary arrangment and it is not partly because it is not generally practicable. From the

II

ROCKAWAY POINT.
PRELIMINARY PLAN.

Showing on what parts the several principal requirements of a large summer resort can best be met.

A. Space for Hotels, Bath Houses, Sanitarium, Concert Gardens, Theatres and Dancing Halls, and the shops and establishments to be naturally associated therewith.

B. Site which may be temporarily occupied by shows, menageries, merry-go-rounds and other means of amusement and trade available for additional building, in the future.

C. For Baymouth reservation.

D. Site for Summer Cottages.

E. Camp Ground.
F. Railway Station.
G. Stores, shops and showers.
H. Gardens and Play Ground.
I. Town plot; to be laid out in streets and blocks and held permanently for all special purposes to which, or front on the beach or not particularized by associable.
J. Exhibition Ground and Race Course.
K. Rifle and Artillery Range.
L. Steamboat Landing.
M. Landing for yachts, boats, etc., and Boatman's Quarters.

N. Still-water Bathing, Swimming School, &c.
O. Military Camp and Parade Ground.
P. Shoemaking Grounds.
Q. Quarters where whole may be Fish Pond, Fish House, Aquarium, Menagerie, Boarding Establishment for Nurses, Water Fowl, and Poultry; also Aviary and amusements for Children.

SCALE - 1 MILE.

SCALE - FEET.

ROCKAWAY POINT, PLAN II, "PRELIMINARY PLAN," C. JULY 1879

veranda and the lower windows of the Manhattan Beach House the beach cannot be seen and all the glory of the surf breaking upon it is lost. It is the same at Cables[25] and at the principal hotels at Long Branch. To visitors who come to stay but a few hours at most upon the sea-shore of a hot day the deprivation seems almost a cruelty.

Is it compensated by the customary front flower-garden? I question the art which under such circumstances places such an object as a flower-garden where to be enjoyed it must be in competition with and through distraction from such another object as the Ocean. I question if it does not involve an unnecessary incongruity with sea-coast scenery which it would be better under any circumstances to avoid.

If a garden is desireable in connection with a sea-coast house, to occupy all the ground between the house and the beach with it is to place it where as an object of interest from the windows it is least needed, where it must be formed and maintained at the greatest cost and where perfection of plant-growth is, at whatever cost, least likely to be secured.

In Sketch No. 2 you will see more distinctly the position which I have thus recommended to be held for your principal architectural demonstration. (The dark space on the right marked A) Within the limits indicated a range of buildings can be stretched out nearly three quarters of a mile in length. According to the depth and height adopted for them, their entire capacity might be less than that of the two principal hotels with their dependencies on Coney Island, or it might be greater.

For convenience of reference in what is to follow I will call this proposed range of buildings facing the Strand, the Terrace, and will now proceed to point out the best positions for other provisions of a large Summer resort which cannot, or for various reasons should not, be incorporated with it.

Referring again to sketch No. II., the terminal railway station of the roads from New York will be observed (F) fixed upon a direct prolongation of the present tracks and to avoid bringing unnecessary noise near the Terrace at a distance from the latter of 200 yards. A narrow-gauge road leads each way from it, the southern branch showing two way-stations in the rear of the Terrace. The Steamboat Wharf (L) is at the point where boats of 10 feet draft can come nearest to the shore, and a straight, broad street leads directly from it, passing the main railway station, to the Terrace. The ground immediately to the West (I) is proposed to be reserved for a village plot for all shops and residences for which close association with the beach is not important.

The northern line of narrow gauge railway is to follow down the northern shore of the Point upon an embankment which will form a dyke. Of the land thus to be reclaimed, the highest and firmest is on the ocean side of the Point half a mile to a mile west of the Terrace. Here (J) provision is made for an enclosed Exhibition Ground with a mile race track; buildings for spectators and a level sward for cricket, base and foot ball; arrangements for acrobatic performances, school & club festivals, fireworks, &c., the whole as much as practicable open to the sea breeze and accessible by special trains direct from New York and Brooklyn.

Still further West an area of nearly 200 acres (O) is proposed to be adapted to military maneuvres on a larger scale than is practicable on any Parade Ground in the country. I assume that, with the advantages that could be offered, brigades would be likely to be drawn from New York & Brooklyn,[26] and Regiments from a greater distance, to camp upon the Point, forming an attraction for other visitors. They could be landed from boats or the railway upon the ground. This being for maneuvres in line and column, the region further West, (P) consisting largely of low, broken sand-hills with slight growth of vegetation, will be suitable for skirmish practice. A range for rifle and light artillery target practice being desirable, not only for military but for general use, the best position for it is shown just west of the Steamboat Landing at K. The extreme length of this range would be 1200 yards, which is equal to the longest in the country.

An intermediate area, marked Q, is proposed to be enclosed for a variety of objects by which the attractions of the Point would be increased. I have in mind for this some of the more popular features of European Zoological Gardens. In several of these there is, for example a model dairy in which cows are exhibited in a luxurious stable and milk from them, as well as other dairy products, as cream-cheese, ice creams and custards made on the spot, are sold to visitors. Another establishment would be for the breeding of large numbers of swans, geese and ducks, the greater number to be sent out during the day to give greater interest to the Lagoon water. A large poultry yard and dove-cote would be another. An elephant and a few camels to make tours, carrying children, would be desirable. A pond in which children could sail small boats. A fish pond and a house for fish dinners would be placed near the railway station and the boat-landing on the shore. At this house there should be large glass tanks from which guests could select the fish to be served to them. A grotto of artificial stone leading into a subterranean aquarium, in which day light would come to the visitor only through tanks in which the fish would be seen, after the style of that last year in the Paris Exposition.[27] Each of these features, as I intend it, would be a novelty and would be particularly pleasing to the large class of people who would come to the Point with their children. They would probably be directly profitable in admission fees, sales and charges, but their chief profit would be indirect in swelling the general tide of popular interest in the locality.

I may here barely touch upon several matters of detail in most of which every place of summer resort in America is deficient as compared with many like places of repute in Europe. For example, at one where I spent a week or two, years ago,[28] there were hundreds of wheel-chairs held to let, and they were more used by visitors than public carriages. The streets of the town were adapted to them, there being slopes instead of curbs at the crossings. I think from experience at the Philadelphia Exhibition,[29] that they would be much liked here and that there would be no difficulty in managing so that one could travel in them without a jar from the steamboat landing to and along the whole length of the Terrace if not further. Other desirable equipments would be pony phaetons for the beach with broad tired wheels, and riding ponies and donkeys to let.

The beach and surf should be thoroughly illuminated for a distance of a mile. This could be accomplished by the use of low-grade electric lights set at frequent intervals along the veranda of the Terrace, with clear glass toward the sea and opaque glass toward the buildings.

Fire works, except what are called fixed or exhibition pieces, appear to the best advantage when seen at a greater distance than is usual in exhibition grounds and best of all when fired over water. A nightly display of colored fires, bombs and rockets from a hulk moored so far off-shore that they would be well seen from the ends as well as the centre of the Terrace would be very attractive.

A mere squirt of water such as commonly passes for a fountain at our hotels is a poor thing and especially so if it comes from coarse and pretentious iron-work. But as an abundant supply of water and a powerful pumping engine will be needed for reasons I have given and also to guard against fires it would add but little to the cost for hydraulic works to provide some simple fountains, both wall and jet, which would be an element of great splendor. Of course they should be on the land side not the sea side of the buildings.

On the strand, however, gay awnings thrown out from the veranda of the Terrace at frequent intervals with comfortable seats under them will not be out of place and elsewhere numerous public seats with awnings fixed to them will be desirable. A provision of row-boats much more gaily painted and furnished than is usual would give an element of life to the lagoon side. There are several additions which could be made to the ordinary bathing arrangements which would be gratefully regarded by the public but these are details for the future.

The district along the shore West of the Terrace I advise to be given with suitable preparation to shows, hucksteries and means of amusement such as can be accommodated with slight temporary buildings, or none at all, so that the ground will remain available whenever required for adding to the length of the Terrace or for another detatched hotel and bath-house. I mean such things as Punch and Judy and other puppet shows, circuses and minstrels, conjurers, performing birds, tents and enclosures for walking, leaping, & wrestling matches, quoits, Scotch games and travelling exhibitions of curiosities, scups, swings, flying horses & so on. I would take care that they were so arranged and displayed with bright colored awnings and bunting and in such positions with reference to the beach, that without being obtrusive or offensive they would add to the general festive character of the scene.

Still further West beyond Mr. Degraw's villa site,[30] I suggest a range of small cottages or cabins and beyond these again, where the ground near the beach is too low for slight houses to stand safely during the winter, a provision of tents to be let with all requirements for camping. I believe that, well organized, under a superintendent and a police officer who would have their headquarters at a store at which supplies would be sold to the Campers, such an arrangement would find many patrons, single, by clubs and in families, and that the whole affair would not only pay fairly in rent of tents, &c., but add another object of interest to the Point.

I have thus sufficiently for the present set forth the germ of a general plan and what seems to me to be the best disposition for various purposes of the different parts of the property.

Drawing No. III. shows to a larger scale and with more suggestion of detail the proposed position of the Terrace group, the Stations, Landings, Still-water Baths, the Village Plot, the Hotel Garden and Play Grounds. The walk from the Terrace to the Station and Steamboat Wharf is designed to be shaded by a trellis and vine foliage.

A Concert Garden is suggested, in connection with the Terrace, in which a large audience would occupy the ground where in the afternoon it would be shaded. Great amphitheatrical galleries are suggested to be carried around this space in which, suitably divided, open to the breeze from the North and South & with a view over the ocean, the principal business corresponding to that of the Pavilions and restaurants of Coney Island would be done. A continuous arcade along the entire front of the Terrace is indicated. At points where the different sections of the Terrace could be desirably separated, the supports of the arcade might be of iron and the roof and floor moveable, with a view of guarding against sweeping fires in winter.

Sketch No. IV., shows the general design with some modifications and more elaborately than No. II.

All the drawings are to be regarded simply as elementary suggestions of matters of general design to serve as a basis for a more mature discussion of your scheme.

It would be inexpedient to proceed further except in consultation with an architect to whom you would entrust the design of the buildings.

I am, Gentlemen,
Your obedient Servant

Fred[k] Law Olmsted
Landscape Architect.

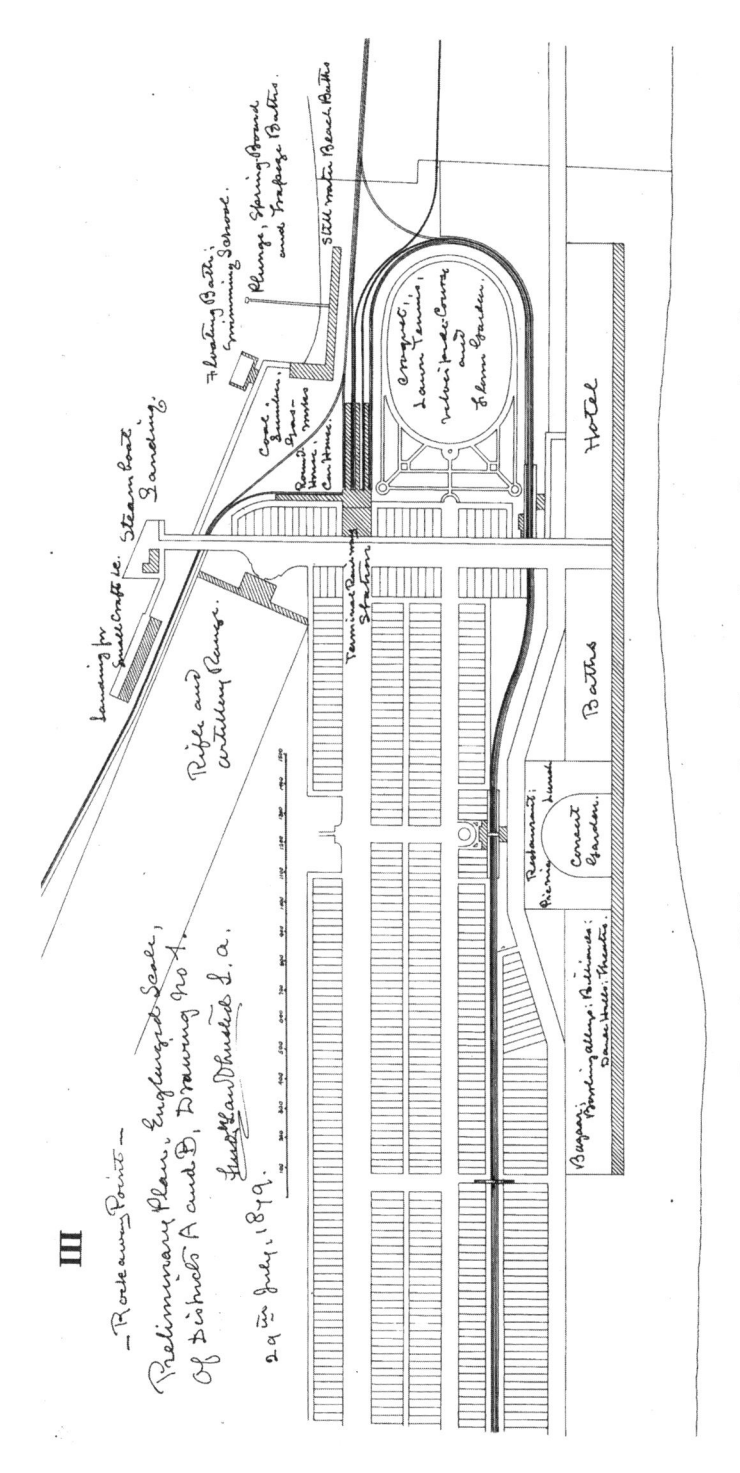

Rockaway Point, Plan III, "Preliminary Plan, Enlarged Scale, of Districts A and B, Drawing No 1," July 29, 1879

ROCKAWAY POINT.
MODIFIED PRELIMINARY PLAN.

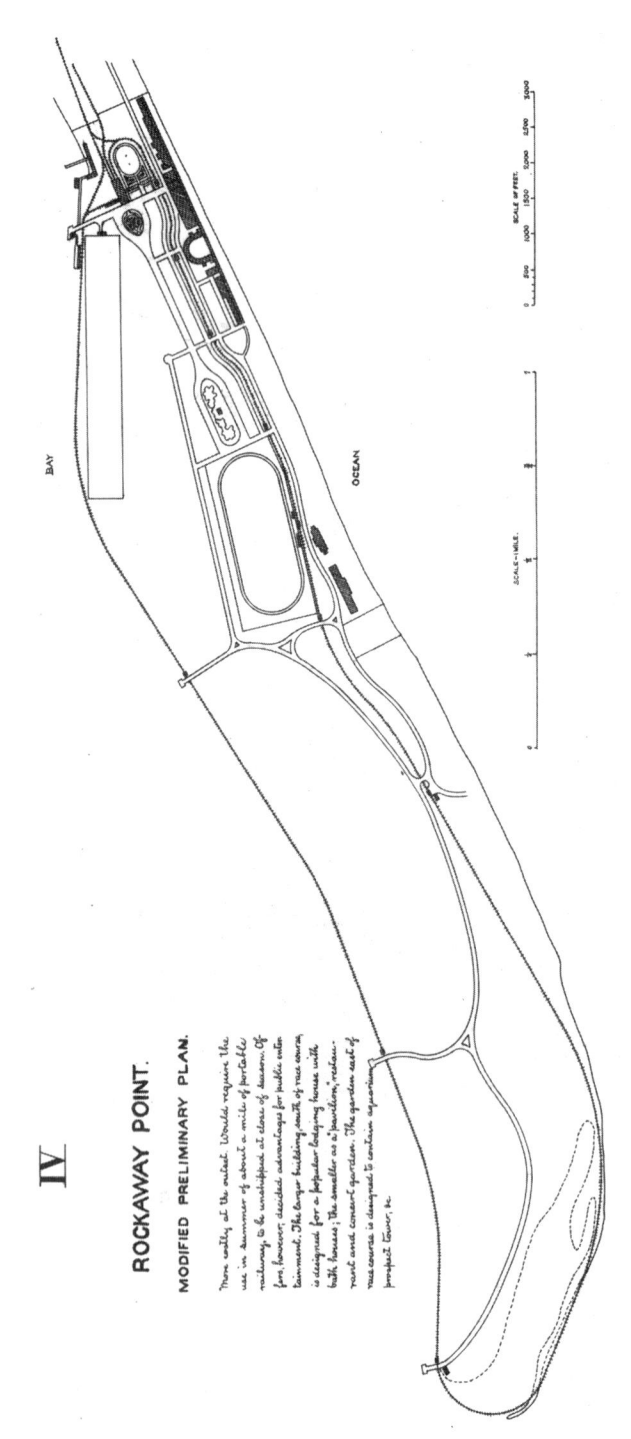

Rockaway Point, Plan IV, "Modified Preliminary Plan," c. July 1879

JANUARY 1879–OCTOBER 1879

The text presented here is a draft in a clerk's hand and signed by Olmsted and with extensive corrections and revisions in his hand. He first titled it *Report upon Rockaway Point* but then crossed out the last three words.

1. Henry Y. Attrill, Baltimore businessman and president of the Rockaway Beach Park Association, and Benjamin E. Smith, president of the Cleveland, Columbus and Indiana Central Railroad.
2. Attrill and Smith led a group of investors who raised more than one million dollars to create a summer resort at Rockaway Beach, Long Island, twelve miles southeast of New York City. Throughout the summer of 1879 they purchased approximately 700 acres of the sandy peninsula that extends west from Far Rockaway and separates Jamaica Bay to the north from the Atlantic Ocean on the south. In early July of that year, Olmsted agreed to examine the property, which he calls here Rockaway Point, and to provide advice in regard to its general layout, positions of buildings, railway line and depot, docks, a hotel, "and other features to be devised" (*New-York Daily Tribune*, Aug. 2, 1879, p. 1; Alfred H. Bellot, *History of the Rockaways from the Year 1685 to 1917* [Far Rockaway, N.Y., 1918], pp. 24–26, 104–5; FLO, "Memorandum," July 8, 1879; FLO to Henry Y. Attrill, July 8, 1879; FLO to Henry Y. Attrill, Sept. 23, 1879, below).
3. Barren Island, located just northwest of the western tip of the Rockaway peninsula. Together they formed the inlet to Jamaica Bay (Porter R. Blakemore, *Historic Structures Report: Floyd Bennett Field, Gateway National Recreation Area*, 2 vols. [Denver, Colo., 1981], 1: 9).
4. Hillyer's Surf House, one of the first hotels erected at Rockaway Beach in the mid-1870s (A. H. Bellot, *History of the Rockaways*, p. 104).
5. That is, the tide constantly deposited large amounts of sand on the western point of the peninsula and increased its length. At the beginning of the nineteenth century the west point was located near the present intersection of Rockaway Beach Boulevard and 120th Street. By the time of Olmsted's visit and report it had moved nearly two miles further west, near the present site of Jacob Riis Park. Presently, the west point of the peninsula is due south of Coney Island, another three miles having been added since 1879 (ibid., p. 22; *Report of the Superintendent of the U.S. Coast and Geodetic Survey Showing the Progress of the Work During the Fiscal Year Ending with June, 1879* [Washington, D.C., 1881], pp. 22–23).
6. Jamaica Bay.
7. The Manhattan Beach Hotel, built in 1877, and the Brighton Beach Hotel, built in 1878, were two of Coney Island's largest and fanciest hotels. Each had long verandahs facing the ocean and extensive landscaped grounds (John F. Kasson, *Amusing the Million: Coney Island at the turn of the Century* [New York, 1978], pp. 31–32).
8. In 1880 Benjamin F. Stephens built a waterworks for a private company to supply Coney Island. Fifteen wells were sunk on Long Island and the water was pumped by steam engines to a large standpipe tank near the beach hotels (J. James R. Croes, "The History and Statistics of American Water-Works," *Engineering News Record*, March 3, 1883, pp. 100–1).
9. A newspaper report on the Rockaway Beach venture noted that the sewage that passed out through the Narrows from these cities often made the surf at Coney Island "very unpleasant" (*New-York Daily Tribune*, Aug. 2, 1879, p. 1).
10. The "beach to the eastward" was that between present-day Seaside and Far Rockaway, the latter renowned as a summer resort since the 1830s (see n. 15 below).
11. John W. Donn of the United States Coast and Geodetic Survey performed triangulation surveys of Jamaica Bay and the southern shore of Long Island between 1877 and 1880 (*U.S. Coast and Geodetic Survey, 1879* [Washington, D.C., 1881], pp. 22–23; ibid., 1880 [Washington, D.C., 1882], pp. 16–17; John W. Donn to FLO, Aug. 1,

1879, B39: #515, OAR/LC; Gustavus A. Weber, *The Coast and Geodetic Survey: Its History, Activities, and Organization* [New York, 1923], pp. 1–9).

12. Long Branch, New Jersey, an ocean-front resort town since at least the mid-1860s. In 1866–67 Olmsted and Vaux advised Howard Potter and prepared a plan for his proposed colony of summer cottages that featured a public recreation area overlooking the beach (*Papers of FLO*, 6: 104–10).
13. The beach drive to San Francisco's Cliff House, overlooking the Pacific Ocean just north of Golden Gate Park, and the Long Beach stretching southward from the town of Lynn on Massachusetts Bay, were both famous carriage drives at this time (Louis M. Babcock, ed., *Our American Resorts* [Washington, D.C., 1883], p. 148; *Sutro Baths, Cliff House, Sutro Heights*, illus. by I. West Taber [San Francisco, 1895], p. 6).
14. A branch of the Long Island Railway already reached Rockaway by way of Springfield, but a more direct line that crossed Jamaica Bay directly to the beach, called the New York, Woodhaven and Rockaway Railroad, was being built by a separate group of investors. Travellers on this line were promised only a forty minute ride to Rockaway from 42d Street in New York, considerably quicker than the steamboats already in service from the city and other points. It opened service in 1881 (*New-York Daily Tribune*, July 17, 1879, p. 8; ibid., Aug. 2, 1879, p. 1; ibid., March 22, 1880, p. 2; ibid., June 6, 1881, p. 8).
15. Olmsted is referring to beaches east of the Attrill and Smith property, primarily that of Far Rockaway. In 1833 an association of wealthy New York families purchased a tract of land at Far Rockaway, built a fancy hotel, the Marine Pavilion, and opened a special turnpike to make it accessible from the city. The Marine Pavilion established the location as an exclusive summer resort and attracted national attention until it burned in 1864, by which time numerous other hotels had opened on the beaches to the west (A. H. Bellot, *History of the Rockaways*, pp. 83–86; Ralph Henry Gabriel, *The Evolution of Long Island: A Story of Land and Sea* [New Haven, Conn., 1921], pp. 173–74).
16. In late 1878 a fire destroyed the commercial district of Cape May, New Jersey, including several of its large hotels. Among these was Congress Hall, which was rebuilt in brick the following spring (George E. Thomas and Carl Doebley, *Cape May, Queen of the Seaside Resorts: Its History and Architecture* [Philadelphia, 1976], pp. 31–32, 62, 120).
17. Newport and Narragansett Pier, located on opposite sides of Narragansett Bay, Rhode Island, were among the most exclusive summer resorts in nineteenth-century America (*A Guide to Narragansett Bay* [Providence, R.I., 1878], passim).
18. Hotel owners at Long Branch reported the arrival of more guests for both limited and extended visits than for the past six or seven years (*New-York Evening Telegram*, July 30, 1879, p. 2).
19. The Aunt Sally was a game in which a figure of a woman with a pipe in its mouth was set up and the player threw sticks at it to break the pipe (*OED*).
20. Scups are a kind of swing (ibid.).
21. Olmsted is referring to the Manhattan Beach Hotel, the Brighton Beach Hotel, the Ocean Hotel, and, possibly, the Oriental Hotel (Townsend Percy, ed., *Percy's Pocket Dictionary of Coney Island* [New York, 1880], 18–19, 52–53, 59–61).
22. Saratoga Springs and Niagara Falls, two of New York's most popular resort and scenic attractions.
23. During the 1870s, New York City public schools closed in mid-June and opened in early September.
24. "The Black Crook," by Charles M. Barras, was a popular melodramatic musical. It opened in New York in 1866 and was the most successful Broadway play up to its time (Gerald Bordman, *The Oxford Companion to American Theatre* [New York, 1984], pp. 81–82).

25. Olmsted is referring to Cable's Hotel, opened in 1875 by English restaurateur Thomas Cable at Brighton Beach on Coney Island (Edo McCullough, *Good Old Coney Island* [New York, 1957], pp. 41–42).
26. In 1868 Olmsted, Vaux & Company had presented to the Brooklyn park commission a report and plans for a parade ground adjacent to Prospect Park. From about the same time, state national guard regiments in New York City had agitated for a larger parade ground than the one assigned to them at Tompkins Square in lower Manhattan. In the mid-1870s Olmsted, as landscape architect for the park department, had argued against using any part of Central Park for the purpose, proposed a new site in upper Manhattan and, when that failed, prepared plans to renovate Tompkins Square to accommodate both military and recreational uses (FLO to William R. Martin, Aug. 9, 1876, and FLO to Whitelaw Reid, March 2, 1877, both above; *Papers of FLO*, 6: 309–10).
27. Olmsted visited the Exposition Universelle in Paris during his trip to Europe in early 1878.
28. Olmsted may be referring here to one of the resorts at Bath, Brighton, or Leamington, which he visited during a business trip to England in 1856 (FLO to William R. Martin, Nov. 21, 1876, n. 8, above).
29. That is, the Centennial Exposition held in Philadelphia in 1876.
30. In 1879 Aaron A. DeGrauw, Jr., whose father had property interests on the Rockaway peninsula since at least 1866, purchased a plot of land that was surrounded by Attrill and Smith's property. Olmsted indicated its position on map two of his preliminary plan with the letter "C" (A. H. Bellot, *History of the Rockaways*, pp. 23–26).

To Henry Y. Attrill

209 W 46th St. New York.
Sep 23rd 1879.

H. Y. Attrell Esq.
My dear Sir.

You are drifting into a corner in the Rockaway business from which you cannot get out.

The chief advantage you possess on the Coney Island enterprises is that of holding so long a space of ground as you do free from all local rivalry upon which you can organize your business comprehensively. So that each part will complement any other part & all insure to your benefit and not that of others. If my general scheme for this purpose is not a good one you should put it aside and get another. What you should not do is to proceed upon no general plan to which each particular division of the work as you take it up can be adjusted. To settle upon particular things first & then work up to generals is to lose the chief element of value in the situation. This is just what you are doing. Mr Smith told me on Sunday that you had sent for me that I might finally settle some things with him. The first was the front line of the hotel—and the elevation of the plateau upon which it was to stand. Of course this cannot be done even approximately—without some understanding as to the plan of the hotel, its sewerage system, connection with the railway station and landing; position & character of the bath house &c. It thus appeared that Mr Smith had made up his mind upon all these points or was ready to do so on the moment. He did not care even to discuss them.[1]

    His notions about them were naturally such as had come to him from what he had seen at Coney Island; very different from those which I had suggested in my report to you, which he had not appearently given the least attention to, and in no way based upon the special local circumstances and apportion. This for something radically better of the locality. After an hour's argument which I insisted upon as to one of the points upon which his mind had been made up, I succeeded in making him realize the objections to it. These objections having reference to effects quarter of a mile away—which had not before occurred to him—and which I should not now have got him to recognize if Mr Brown his engineer, had not come to my assistance.

    But yesterday Mr Smith told me that half a dozen architects and landscape architects were at work making plans in accordance more or less with his notions about these matters. That he had advised with some of them—*given them instructions.*

    You may say that you are not bound to accept any of them—which is true. But—you will presently be in haste to get to work. Some one of these plans will suit you more nearly than another,—will have a generally attractive effect & be approximately satisfactory. It will compare favorably with the plan of the Manhattan Beach house. If you consult me about it I shall probably say this—shall say that it is an admirable plan for the purpose which the architect (under Mr Smith's advise) has had in view. It would fit the Coney Island conditions perfectly but not having been designed with reference to the general plan which I have recommended you to adopt is not suitable to it. I may add that if you will give me time to indoctrinate an architect, not already committed to a theory, with the results of my month's study of the special problem, I shall be sure of getting a plan for a hotel which will be more profitable to you.

    Are you likely to share my confidence, or to proceed without losing any more time, upon your preconceived ideas—derived chiefly from Coney Island?

    You remember that when I first took up the matter I advised you to appoint an architect at once, with whom I could work from the start. I am sorry that I did not go further; make it a condition of taking it up.[2]

    Had Mr Smith told me then what he told me yesterday was to be considered as settled and {no} longer open to discussion, I should have made you a very different general plan, and given you different advice in many subjects. Now simply to put myself right I ask and advise you to let me employ an architect at your charge to make a sketch plan of buildings adapted — to the theory of arrangement of my general plan. I will have the work done as cheaply as I can and will charge you nothing for further personal services in the matter.

I wish to be fully clear of responsibilities for what will otherwise occur.

I have an appointment at Niagara Falls which will probably keep me out of town nearly all of next week. Telegraph me to go ahead and will confer with an architect and about the work before I go.[3]

I put this to you personally because you have told me that your interests were not identical with Mr Smith's and have invited confidence.[4]

Yours Truly,

sgd. Fred[k] Law Olmsted.

The text presented here is from a draft written and signed in a clerk's hand.

1. Olmsted agreed to visit the property with Henry Attrill and Benjamin Smith to discuss the project on Sunday, September 21. Attrill was unable to attend the meeting, and Smith not only failed to understand Olmsted's proposals, he wanted to start construction without a general plan ("Rockaway Beach," memorandum of conference with Attrill dated Aug. 30, [1879], B39: #515, OAR/LC; Henry Y. Attrill to FLO, Sept. 27, 1879, B39: #515, OAR/LC).
2. Olmsted proposed this arrangement in early July 1879 without effect (FLO to Henry Y. Attrill, July 8, 1879).
3. There is no evidence that Attrill authorized Olmsted to confer with an architect, as he requests in this letter, and it is possible that Olmsted sent him the letter that he drafted on the same day in which he formally withdrew from the project and disclaimed all responsibility for design and construction of the hotel. Attrill went ahead with his own plans for the site, constructing what was claimed to be the largest hotel in the world, which measured 1200 feet in length and 250 feet in length with over 100,000 square feet of piazzas. This structure was similar in length but much wider than the one proposed by Olmsted in July 1879, and had only one-third of the beach frontage that the series of structures in Olmsted's plan would have created.

    Attrill's venture did not fare well. It is claimed that only one wing of the hotel was ever opened, and only for the month of August 1881. By that time the company had been in receivership for a year, and the receiver, James W. Husted, forced Attrill to sell the property at auction in May 1882. The successful bidders were the trustees of Attrill's own company. Meantime, Attrill developed a new scheme free of the receivership that tied up his first venture at Rockaway. In the autumn of 1881, he and a new partner, Frederick A. Phipps, informed Olmsted of their plan to provide railroad access from South Ferry in Brooklyn to a new hotel and cottages that they would build at the northern end of Rockaway Point. Attrill understood that Olmsted was willing to assist him, and the newspaper article that announced his new venture, which appeared on the same day as the news of the auctioning of his original hotel, stated that "Supervising Architect Olmsted, of Central Park, in this City, is now drawing the plans for the projected sea-side city." No correspondence between Attrill and Olmsted later than November 1881 has survived, however (A. H. Bellot, *History of the Rockaways*, p. 105; "Rockaway's Big Hotel," and "Another Sea-Side Project," *New-York Times*, May 2, 1882,

p. 3; *New-York Times*, Aug. 4, 1880, p. 8; Henry Y. Attrill to FLO, Oct. 26, 1881; ibid., Nov. 1, 1881; ibid., Nov. 10, 1881).

4. Attrill, in his response to the present letter, said that had Smith "been possessed of ordinary reason, the Hotel and upper grounds would have been half finished by this time" (Henry Y. Attrill to FLO, Sept. 27, 1879, B39: #515, OAR/LC).

To James Terry Gardner

209 W. 46 ST.
NEW YORK.
2ᵈ Oct. 1879.

My Dear Gardner;[1]

Please consider whether it would not be well to print the enclosed (with such revision as you may choose) on a half sheet of thin note paper, to be sent to all whose aid in getting signatures &c may be desirable, and as a courtesy to all who have aided. It would follow English usage in like matters only that in England it would be signed by a lot of honorable promoters. I think no signature is necessary. It should only be used enclosed in a written note which of course would be signed.

Yours

F. L. O.

Confidential.

The project of relieving and preserving the scenery of Niagara Falls from certain offensive conditions has taken the form of a proposition (1) that the islands and a strip of land along the shores of the river from the head of the Rapids to the bridge quarter of a mile below the cataract shall be purchased by the State of New York on one side and either by the Province of Ontario or the Dominion of Canada as may be determined, on the other; (2) that the present dams, piers, sluice-ways, retaining walls, mills and shops near the river shall be removed and buildings at a greater distance obscured by planting; (3) that natural conditions shall as far as possible be everywhere restored and preserved, only such artificial constructions being permitted as are essential to convenient communication and observation of the scenery, and these to be as modest and inconspicuous as possible; (4) that only a single small fee shall be required for admission to the reservations the proceeds to be used to defray the necessary expenses of maintenance, and that visitors shall as far as possible be relieved of all other of the present numerous interruptions to their enjoyment of the scenery in the form of tolls, fees, huckstering and solicitations for employment.

The proposition as thus defined has been favorably considered by the Commission appointed by the State of New York to examine the matter and by the Council of the Province of Ontario.[2] It will be officially recommended to the Legislature of New York.

It is expected to be resisted as a measure involving a large outlay to be defrayed by the taxation of people who will generally receive from it no special benefit and it is hoped will be carried by an appeal to their pride and public spirit.

Letters or memorials sustaining the project have been received from several United States senators; the Secretary of State, the heads of numerous institutions of learning; from Emerson, Longfellow, Whittier, Holmes, and other eminent Americans, and from Carlyle, Ruskin, Sir James Stephen, Lord Houghton[3] and others in England. Aid in the developmnt and expression of favorable public opinion, through the Press & otherwise, is invited from all to whom the matter is of interest. Decisive debate of the question may be looked for early next year.

The text presented here is from the James T. Gardner Papers, New York State Library, Albany, N.Y. The note to Gardner is in Olmsted's hand. The memo marked "Confidential" is in a clerk's hand with corrections by Olmsted, except for the last two sentences, which are in Olmsted's hand.

1. James Terry Gardner (or Gardiner) (1842–1912), who at this time was director of the New York State Survey. Responding to an appeal by Governor Lucius Robinson in January 1879, the state legislature had instructed the commissioners of the State Survey in May to report on measures it would be expedient for the State to adopt for carrying out the governor's proposal for collaboration with the government of Canada in protecting visitors to Niagara Falls from "improper annoyance." The commissioners then instructed Gardner to join with Olmsted in preparing a report on the condition of the Falls area and to consider what action the State should take regarding it. Olmsted knew Gardner from his time in California, where Gardner was working on the California Geological Survey. In the fall of 1864 Olmsted hired him and Clarence King to survey the boundaries of the newly created Federal grant of Yosemite Valley. In 1879 Gardner was assisting Olmsted in gathering signatures for the petition calling for a public reservation at Niagara Falls that Olmsted had drawn up, and Olmsted was planning to have him "direct & control the agitation" on the American side (*DAB*; Thomas V. Welch, "How Niagara Was Made Free: The Passage of the Niagara Reservation Act in 1885," in Buffalo Historical Society *Publications* 5 [1902], p. 325; *Papers of FLO*, 5: 513, n. 12; FLO to J. T. Gardner, Oct. 1, 1879, James T. Gardner Papers, New York State Library, Albany, N. Y.).

2. A reference to the meeting at Niagara Falls of four members of the New York State Survey and the premier and members of the Council of Ontario that Olmsted describes in his letter of October 10, 1879 (below). Gardner proposed that Olmsted end the "Confidential" text at this point. "I think we should not state in print in advance of our report what that report will be, nor assume that there will be opposition," he counseled, "and

above all it seems to me improper for us to appear to be working up public opinion to favor a definite proposition not yet submitted to the legislature" (J. T. Garner to FLO, Oct. 2, 1879).
3. Sir James Fitzjames Stephen (1829–1894) and Richard Monckton Milnes (1809–1885), first Baron Houghton (*DNB*).

To James Terry Gardner

209 W. 46 ST.
NEW YORK.
3ᵈ Oct. 1879.

Dear Gardner;
    Yours of yesterday recvd.
    With regard to buildings the usual course is to take them under condemnation and afterwards sell at auction with the condition that they shall be removed before a date fixed. We should take care that what can be got in this way is available for improvemnts—as a discretionary fund to be used to eke out anything else that is short in construction, maintenance, or incidental expense accounts. I inquired about the Tugby building[1] & was told that it was a balloon frame & could not be moved, but I think it can, by inserting a sill & strengthening the frame work. You might get Eaton's[2] opinion.
    I have slept out a clear conviction upon a point as to which I must at times have appeared temporarily muddled. It is important to us to get as much as we can of the back part of Prospect Park[3] and to form a distinct, capacious, well arranged ante-room to the American reserved ground. It is not desirable that this should be held as a picnic ground or a park or common by the village or by private owners. It will play a most important part in the scheme of managmnt and the larger the area that can be secured for it the better.
    I wish now, before defining the boundary lines, that I could have a close topographical map of the American shore as far back as we can think of taking land & go at once to work upon a plan of laying it out—not an official work but precautionary—with a view to determining safely just what will prove to be important and the relative importance of every foot.
    I am making up my mind that the military project must be fought[4] at the outset & very warily, & that we must stand or fall upon cardinal principles which will exclude the idea & every other idea but that of the simplest enjoyment of natural scenery. People must not come to the reservation for any other purpose & must be even required to submit to some inconvenience and restraint (such as is not required in public "parks") for the sake of oppor-

JANUARY 1879–OCTOBER 1879

tunity for contemplativeness. It is a big problem. I feel as I get nearer to it and the liklihood of its becoming real increases that if not the most difficult problem in landscape architecture to do justice to, it is the most serious — the furthest above shop work, that — the world has yet had. All practicable room to work in should be secured.

Although we must look to separate administrations; the *International* idea must be kept prominent. We can resist the militia best by making it so and pointing to the impropriety of *showing our arms*, under the circumstances. I suppose that we can arrange that an admission on either side passes the admittee free on the other.
Yours.

F.L.O.

I send you Holley book[5] by mail tonight as you may like to look it over en route. You should review the geological chapters.

The text presented here is from the James T. Gardner Papers, New York State Library, Albany, N.Y.
1. Tugby's Bazaar, a three-story structure at the mainland end of the bridge to Goat Island, that offered "a full and complete collection of curiosities, articles representative of Indian life and manners, toys, bijouterie, fancy goods, and all similar products" (Ralph Greenhill and Thomas D. Mahoney, *Niagara* [Toronto, 1969], plate W, p. 126).
2. James W. Eaton, the superintendent of construction of the New York state capitol. Gardner planned to have Eaton go to Niagara Falls the following week to estimate the cost of removing buildings from the proposed reservation site (James T. Gardner to FLO, Oct. 2, 1879).
3. Prospect Park, an amusement park, was on the mainland adjacent to the American Falls. In Olmsted and Vaux's plan of 1887, the boundary of the reservation in this area was set some 850 feet back from the falls, and in the "Upper Grove" in the Prospect Park area the designers placed administration buildings and a large reception building where visitors could prepare for their visit to the reservation.
4. Goat Island was an area of special concern for Olmsted, since it was the one part of the proposed reservation area that had not been despoiled by industrial and commercial structures. The Porter family had owned the island since 1816 and had preserved the vegetation and scenery of the place while making it available to tourists. It was anticipated at this time that the Porters would soon be forced to sell the island because of an impending suit by some of their heirs for division of the property. One of the proposals being urged at this time was to use Goat Island for military encampment. Olmsted tried without success to dissuade one of the principal proponents of this "military parade," William Findlay Rogers (1820–1899), a brigadier general in the New York State Militia. Rogers had been mayor of Buffalo when Olmsted submitted his original proposal for a park system for the city in 1868, and was a strong supporter of the plan from

the outset. He was a member of the board of park commissioners from its creation in 1869 until 1887, serving most of those years as secretary and treasurer. He was also active in the establishment of the Buffalo State Asylum, designed by H. H. Richardson, for which Olmsted planned the grounds in the early 1870s (James T. Gardner to FLO, Oct. 3, 1879; FLO to James T. Gardner, Oct. 2, 1879, James T. Gardner Papers, New York State Library, Albany, N. Y.; Peter A. Porter, *Goat Island* [Niagara Falls, N.Y., 1900], pp. 33–34; *New-York Times*, April 1, 1880, p. 2; Melvin G. Holli and Peter d'A Jones, eds., *Biographical Dictionary of American Mayors, 1820–1980: Big City Mayors* [Westport, Conn., 1981], pp. 309–10; *The Men of New York* . . ., 2 vols. [Buffalo, 1898], 2: 28–30).
5. A reference to George W. Holley, *Niagara: Its History and Geology, Incidents and Poetry, with Illustrations* (New York, 1872), Chapters 6 through 8 deal with geology—one on the origin of the falls, one on the recession and retrocession of the falls, and one on their future recession.

To CHARLES ELIOT NORTON

209 W. 46 ST.
NEW YORK
10th Oct 1879.

My Dear Norton;
I want briefly to report progress to you about Niagara. We have had a meeting at the Falls of four of the N. York Commissioners and the Premier & Members of the Council of Ontario.[1] The general outlines of a scheme which I presented was fully approved by all.[2] The Ontario party was unwilling to make it a govermnt measure, fearing that it would be resented as an extravagance by the farmers & might force them out of office. They rather thought they would try to have it made a Dominion matter feeling sure of the favor of the Governor General[3] but fearing strong opposition from the lower provinces, who would claim that it was no affair of theirs. There was more confidence & more boldness on our side—perhaps because no one had anything to lose by it if confidence was misplaced. On both sides it was felt to be a question how far the pride of the people could be touched. Geddes,[4] a good representative of the better farming class, said, "New York farmers will not want to appear before the world as *mean* in a matter of this kind" and Mowatt,[5] the Ontario chief, said: "If your people move strongly ours will be ashamed to hold back." They all thought that the publication of our memorial with weighty names would have much effect.
Someone in the Provinces has gone abroad, promising to get *many* English signatures and I am afraid that it has been circulated as a popular thing in Canada. To a certain extent it has got out of my hands.

What I now propose is to get as many signatures of the really notable men of the time of all countries as I well can — and publish the Memorial, say in December, with the names and (generally) the leading distinctions of those attached. To bind the originals and give them as valuable autographs to the Governor, but to recall one of the volumes and if the measure is successful, let it be kept at the Managing Office at Niagara as a matter of historical interest. (Not simply because of its historical interest, but because it would help to keep alive and enforce the idea ever after that the proper protection of the Falls was a matter of dignity & world-wide interest.)

As a wider range must be given the memorial than I had at first designed, would you be disposed to solicit a few more signatures? It is for you to judge whose — Any men whose names are to live or which ought to live. There is Darwin,[6] at any rate, who should not be omitted, & I should like you to consider the artists, as well as the Scientific men of the time.

You will see that I have two thoughts about it now. One to touch the pride of our people at the moment — The other to give a weight to the undertaking for the future. And as the range of selection is to be enlarged there are more men whom I would not like to have omitted and I can't trust to the judgment in selection of the unknown canvassers. I mean to retain the power, within certain limits of dropping off — or at least of determining prominence in the publication, if not the final disposition of the signatures.

Would you think it intrusive too much to ask Carlyle[7] for his original signature, in this new view of the matter?

I hope to be in Cambridge for a day or two in about a fortnight.

Very Cordially Yours

Fred[k] Law Olmsted.

P.S. I will send what number you may be willing to use of the blank memorials.

The text presented here is from a manuscript in Olmsted's hand in the Charles Eliot Norton Papers, Houghton Library, Harvard University, Cambridge, Massachusetts

1. That is, a meeting of three commissioners of the New York State Survey with Sir Oliver Mowat, premier of Ontario and members of the Council of Ontario, the upper house of the provincial legislature.
2. Presumably the proposals contained in the "Confidential" note that Olmsted attached to his letter to James T. Gardner of October 2, 1879 (above).
3. John Douglas Sutherland Campbell, the Marquis of Lorne (1845–1914) who succeeded Lord Dufferin in 1878 and served as governor general until 1883 (*DNB*).

4. George Geddes (1809–1883), a commissioner of the New York State Survey, with whom Olmsted had spent six months studying farming in the summer of 1846 (*Papers of FLO*, 1: 77–79, 393–94).
5. Sir Oliver Mowat (1820–1903), prime minister and attorney general of Ontario from 1872 until 1896 (W. Stewart Wallace, *The Macmillan Dictionary of Canadian Biography*, 3rd ed. [London, 1963], p. 535).
6. Norton was a likely choice for securing Charles Darwin's signatures, since Darwin's son William was married to Norton's sister-in-law Sara Sedgwick (Peter Brent, *Charles Darwin: "A Man of Enlarged Curiosity"* [London, 1981], p. 264).
7. Norton was a logical choice for securing the signature of Thomas Carlyle: they had become good friends during the winter of 1872–73 that Norton spent in London, and Carlyle had agreed for Norton to be the literary executor of his correspondence with Ralph Waldo Emerson (Kermit Vanderbilt, *Charles Eliot Norton: Apostle of Culture in a Democracy* [Cambridge, Mass., 1959], pp. 113, 167).

CHAPTER VIII

DECEMBER 1879–MAY 1880

This was a very active time for Olmsted, both in planning the Boston park system and developing the campaign for the Niagara reservation. Letters to Charles Dalton, Joseph P. Davis, and the Boston park commissioners describe the approach that he devised for dealing with the complex conditions of the Back Bay Fens, while his letters to Dalton and Charles Eliot Norton of May 5 describe the arrangement he was working to realize between Boston and Harvard College concerning the Arnold Arboretum. His "Notes" in the report of the New York State Survey for 1879 offer his first description of the "distinctive charms of Niagara scenery," and his letter to Charles Eliot Norton of January 22 indicates the status of the petition campaign for Niagara that they were organizing. His letter to Barthold Schlesinger of Brookline, Massachusetts, demonstrates his analysis of the site for a residence and his process of developing a design appropriate to it. The letter to Tiffany & Co. describes the water-driven carillon that he installed in the summer house on the U.S. Capitol grounds as the final touch for creating an atmosphere of variety, intricacy and "delicacy" in that distinctive space. Working on a different scale, that of the city region, he presents in his letter to the *New-York Daily Tribune* on "The Future of New-York" his critique of the gridiron street system of New York and his views on the row house as a form of urban residence.

To Charles Henry Dalton

Mr Dalton;

9th Dec. 1879.

My Dear Sir;
    Yours of 1st inst has only just now come to me having been first mailed unstamped.
    I must confess that I would greatly prefer to drop the word Park[1] and am disposed to stick to Back Bay. What you are to have is hardly more a park than it is a theatre or a market and to designate your salt marsh and water a park implies a feeling that the real thing is not as pleasant and favorable to the value of real estate as you could wish it to be. It is a puff and a wholly unnecessary puff, for the real thing will be better in the place, than any park could be. Then as to the park like margin the word park will be a constant invitation to unjust criticism and to demands for what may properly be demanded in a park but cannot be in a promenade with a sylvan border of the character designed.
    As to Back Bay all that is to be said is that it is of the class of proper names which though prosaic at first or if regarded analytically are most permanently satisfactory such as Cornhill, Pallmall, High Gate, Brick Yards — (Tuileries), Long Branch, New Port, Cam Bridge, Dobb's Ferry.[2] (They tried changing the name of Dobb's Ferry & for several years the P.O. there was Greenburg, but the public would not adopt it). Back Bay is not very euphonious nor a quite pleasant alliteration, but it is appropriate, sensible and of historical value.

    Of the names you suggest I prefer that of Water Park. But I would much rather reverse the order and call the interior the Park Water — and give special names to different parts of the outside Park. I do not object as a prefix or descriptive term before another as in Park Way.
    On the whole I advise you to call the basin part of the affair,
    The Everglade.
    Though we hardly know this term except as applied to the Florida glades, it is a descriptive and not a proper name meaning (see Webster) "a tract of land covered with water and grass", that is to say exactly applicable to the locality.
    However, if you think the association unpleasant, which I do not, then say
        The Salt Glades

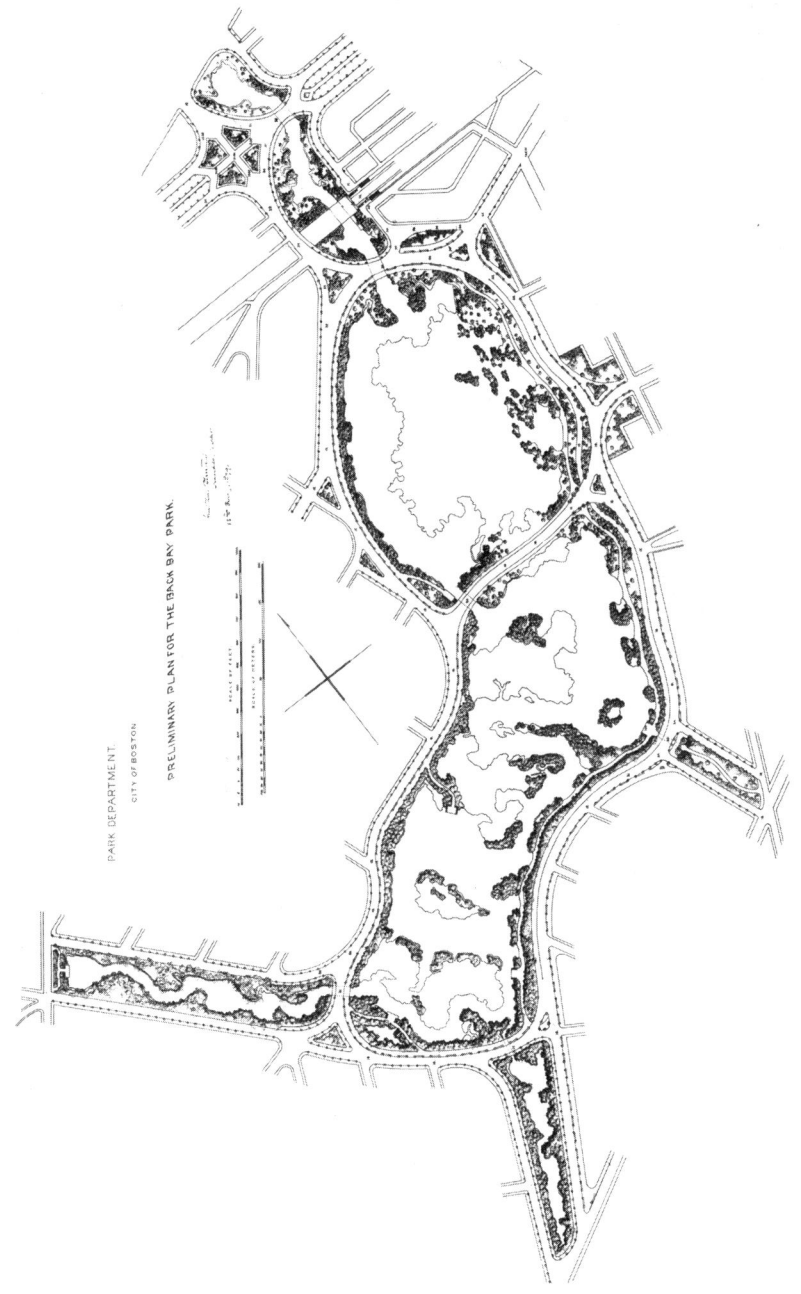

"Preliminary Plan for the Back Bay Park," February 13, 1879

The Sedgeglade
The Sea Glades,
or
The Glade Water.

Then give different stretches of the banks and roads about it such names as the following.
Everglade Parkway,
(or Gladewater Parkway,)
Hawthorne Place,
Allston Road,
Aggasis Terrace,
May Flower Walk.
Boylston Bridgeway
Charles Gate
Sedgefare
Westland Cross
Westbay Terrace
Northbay Terrace.
Eastover Place.
Longview
Saltcroft.
Fair Leat
Bankshaw
Blooming Bank.
Lowell Road
Whittier Place
May Flower Road
Alden Terrace.

The text presented here is from a draft in Olmsted's hand.

1. Olmsted further explained his opposition to calling the area he designed in Boston's Back Bay a "park" in a letter he wrote to a friend in 1895:

    Its too bad that people so generally call the place the Back Bay *Park*; it being no more park-like than it is orchard-like or corn-field-like. This was the reason that before the first stroke of work was done upon it, we had its name officially changed to that of the Fens. . . . (I have an English dictionary of 1706, in which the signification of Fens is "Marsh or Boggy Ground"). The name Fens should preserve the fact that there are at *this* time hundreds of acres of land and water to which this term is perfectly appropriate, being descriptive of a natural condition which in the public pleasure ground that we have made has been attempted to be, to a small extent, preserved, partly as a matter of historical interest.

(FLO to W. Bowen Murphy, Aug. 3, 1895).
2. Dobbs Ferry named for William Dobbs who started a ferry on the Hudson River at Willow Point in 1730. The community took that name until 1873 when it incorporated and assumed the name of Greenburgh, New York, after the town where the ferry was located. In 1882 residents persuaded the state legislature to change the name of the town back to Dobbs Ferry (William J. Blanck, ed., *Life of a River Village: Dobbs Ferry* [Dobbs Ferry, N.Y., 1974], pp. 4–5, 33).

To Tiffany & Company[1]

9 Dec. 79.

Messr Tiffany & C°
Gentlemen,

I should like to place under the floor of a Summer House[2] now building on the Capitol Grounds at Washington a small carillon[3] of sufficient power to be heard only some 20 or 30 yards away. It should be set to play a few simple airs, should be strong and enduring; not liable to get out of order or be injured by rust or frost. I would arrange to have it worked by water power at intervals, having the discharge of a drinking fountain to dispose of.

Will you please inform me if you have anything likely to answer my purpose? If not, do you think that it could probably be found ready made in Europe? If not could you have it made to order? I should not require it for three months to come, and could wait if necessary nine months. I shall be glad to have advice as to probable cost &c.

16th Dec. 1879.

Tiffany & Co. Mr Gray,

One other desideratum occurs to me which it may be as well to have in view in devising the chimes for Capitol Grounds. Suppose the barrel is adapted to a single "change"[4] upon 8 or 9 notes, to be repeated say seven times and followed by silence for an equal period of time. It would be desirable that it should be hardly distinguishable at first, and only heard in full force the fourth time, rising gradually and then dying out or lost in the tinkle of the waters. The simplest way to accomplish this that occurs to me would be to place the chimes in a box, with close fitting lids top and bottom. At first they would be closed, then the lower lid gradually drawn out thru the upper. The operation afterwards reversed. This to be done by the clock-work if clock work is used.

The text presented here is from a draft in Olmsted's hand.
1. The New York firm of jeweler and silversmith Charles Louis Tiffany, which in 1878 won the Grand Prix at the Exposition Universelle in Paris for its work. Three years earlier Olmsted had relayed to Edward Clark an offer by Tiffany to gild the statue of Freedom atop the Capitol dome (John Loring, *Tiffany's 150 Years* [Garden City, N.Y., 1987], pp. 10–12; FLO to Edward Clark, Sept. 6, 1875, Office of the Curator, Architect of the Capitol, U.S. Capitol, Washington, D.C.).
2. The summer house is a picturesque hexagonal brick structure set into the hillside northwest of the Senate wing of the U.S. Capitol. Its origin dates to 1877 when Capitol grounds engineer Frederick H. Cobb, architect Thomas Wisedell, and Olmsted planned to conceal the opening of a ventilating shaft for the House chamber in a structure variously termed a shelter, temple, or summer house. It was to have a fountain and would, according to Cobb, "afford a cool and pleasant resting place on the way to the building." By late 1879 a tower of rock-faced ashlar dressed with granite, designed by Olmsted and Wisedell, had been chosen instead and was under construction. However, demand had persisted for a shady resting place and drinking fountain for those walking up Capitol Hill from Pennsylvania Avenue, the most traveled portion of the grounds. With Thomas Wisedell's assistance, Olmsted designed a summer house incorporating all but the ventilating features of its predecessor, and construction began in October 1879 (FLO to Edward Clark, June 8, 1877, Office of the Curator, Architect of the Capitol, U.S. Capitol, Washington, D.C.; Frederick H. Cobb to FLO, June 11, 1877, and Frederick H. Cobb to Thomas Wisedell, Jan. 24, 1878, both in Records Management Department, Architect of the Capitol, U.S. Capitol, Washington, D.C.; Frederick H. Cobb to FLO, Oct. 3, 1879, in D2, OAR/LC; *Annual Report of the Architect of the Capitol* [1879], p. 324; ibid., [1880], pp. 439–40).
3. In March 1881 Tiffany & Company was paid $200 for a carillon that was installed under the floor of the completed summer house by late May. It was powered by the runoff water of the fountain, but despite almost constant attention by Cobb, it worked only sporadically (FLO to Tiffany & Company, May 27, 1881, Records Management Department, Architect of the Capitol, U.S. Capitol, Washington, D.C.; FLO to Frederick H. Cobb, June 27, 1881, Office of the Curator, Architect of the Capitol, U.S. Capitol, Washington, D.C.; E. Hennessey to FLO, March 23, 1881, in D3, OAR/LC; Frederick H. Cobb to FLO, July 27, 1881, in D3, OAR/LC; ibid., Dec. 18, 1881).
4. That is, the order in which the bells of the carillon were struck by pegs of its revolving barrel. In Olmsted's example, the sequence in which eight or nine bells were struck would produce the notes of a single "change" (*OED*; *The Harvard Dictionary of Music* [Cambridge, Mass., 1986], p. 147; FLO to Frederick H. Cobb, May 30, 1881, below; FLO to Frederick H. Cobb, May 30, 1881, below).

DECEMBER 1879–MAY 1880

To Henry Whitney Bellows[1]

209 W. 46 ST.
NEW YORK.
22^d Dec. 1879.

My dear friend;

As I was getting my children's books tonight I recevd a surprising Christmas present myself. A package of proofs was put in my hand with the remark that I might find something of interest in them.

I have been looking through them with no little emotion — partly for the honor you are heaping on me — partly because of a haunted feeling. What! You don't mean to say that I wrote that! The Ghost of Christmas past.

Really, Doctor, you know they are not wholly authentic, those letters to which you sign my name. I know at least that a very kind editorial hand has been upon them.

I am more than grateful that you can have had it in your heart to so deal by me. And I don't repine that the fact of my life falls so very far short of what you have wished to think it.

I can only wish you in return a Merry Christmas & many of them, being always

most affectionately yours

Fred^k Law Olmsted.

As a matter of proofreading: F.L.O was not the *originator* of the Central Park. That word belongs to Downing[2] if to any man. And the *design* is equally Vaux's. If the page (10) is cast & not printed could you not at least substitute *executive*? It is not quite the thing but it would fill the space of *originator*.[3]

The text presented here is from a manuscript in Olmsted's hand in the Henry Whitney Bellows Papers, Massachusetts Historical Society, Boston, Mass.

1. Henry Whitney Bellows (1814–1882) was president of the U.S. Sanitary Commission during the time that Olmsted was its general secretary, and played a crucial role in selecting Olmsted to serve in that position. Bellows had been very distressed when Olmsted left the commission and went to California in 1863 as general manager of the Mariposa Estate. They apparently had little contact in the years following the Civil War, but when Bellows published a memoir in 1879 on the founding of the Union League Club of New York in early 1863, for which Olmsted had offered valuable advice, he included a most complimentary discussion of Olmsted's role. He testified that Olmsted was the

first person to whom Oliver Wolcott Gibbs turned for advice; "Those who know the capacity, the thoughtfulness, the statesman-like qualities of Mr. F. L. Olmsted, will not wonder that Dr. Gibbs found him readiest and ripest for the plans he had in view, and the best able to suggest the method by which it was to be carried out. The United States Sanitary Commission have always been proud to acknowledge the great part which Mr. Olmsted, the first Secretary of the Commission, had in giving practical body and form to the enterprise. It is doubtful if anybody else could have carried the ideas of its founders out into such a commanding and successful achievement as it finally was." Bellows praised Olmsted's work in the creation of Central Park, concluding that "Mr. Olmsted has, perhaps, rendered greater public services with less reward and less appreciation from those who have most profited by them, than any citizen of New York" and quoted nearly the entire text of two letters he wrote on the issue to Oliver Wolcott Gibbs, excising two short phrases and disguising the names of some of the men referred to (Henry W. Bellows, *Historical Sketch of the Union League Club of New York: Its Origin, Organization, and Work 1863–1879* [New York, 1879], pp. 10–18; *Papers of FLO* 4: 83–90, 466–70, 477–78).
2. Andrew Jackson Downing whose editorial "The New-York Park" in his periodical *The Horticulturist* of August 1851 has generally been viewed as the effective beginning of the movement for creation of a major urban park in New York City (*Papers of FLO*, 1: 74–77).
3. Bellows apparently did not have time to alter his reference on page 10 to Olmsted as "the originator of our Central Park," but he instead devoted most of his errata page to the question, asserting that Calvert Vaux deserved equal credit with Olmsted for the design of the park, that Downing was said to deserve credit for the idea of the park, and that Olmsted's friends, including Bellows himself, had claimed more credit for Olmsted than was his due.

To HENRY WHITNEY BELLOWS

209 W. 46th St.
24th Dec. 1879.

My Dear Doctor;
I thank you with all my heart for all you say.

You appear not yet to have noticed that arms-bearing is printed *alms-bearing*. It was the alms, not the bearing, that I objected to. It is of little consequence. The other matter is more so. You will see why if I recall an occurrence which can hardly have wholly escaped your notice when, two years ago, I was dismissed from the Departmnt of Parks, being then absent in Europe on sick leave, Godkin, in a letter to the Tribune, referred to me in some such way as you have done, perhaps as "the Creator of the Central Park." Thereupon Vaux published in all the papers a sharp, excited, bitter and sarcastic protest, in much such terms as he might have used if *I* had claimed to have made the park all by myself. Thereupon the Times, being then engaged in "booming" Andrew H. Green, took the opportunity of intimating in a leading article that in point of fact my part in the making of the Park had been a very insignificant one and that I was a humbug. The truth was that so far from making such claims I had taken particular pains to publish Vaux's rights in the matter and to give him quite all the credit he could ask. Godkin replied courteously denying that he had meant to represent me as the exclusive designer and my son published a few lines to set me right.[1] Vaux then called on my wife[2] to say that he was sorry; acknowledged that I had done him full justice but thought that some of my friends habitually neglected to do so and confessed that he was morbidly sensitive about it, feeling that he had never had nearly the credit due him for his work on the Park, which is unquestionably true. Much truer of him than of me. I am sure that if the word "originator" stands it will painfully stir him up nor can any note to be added salve it over.

    I hope that you will ask if my suggestion is not feasible — that is, if the page is cast, to cut out the work *originator* and substitute *executive*. Of course I should prefer some other phrase as "one of the joint designers", or "a leading spirit", or a more direct recognition of Vaux if that were practicable — Vaux's son[3] is Putnam's proof reader, and I must not be known in the matter. I am sure you will excuse my anxiety about it.

    Faithfully & Gratefully,

Olmsted.

The text presented here is from a manuscript in Olmsted's hand in the Henry Whitney Bellows Papers, Massachusetts Historical Society, Boston, Mass.

1. In a letter to the *New-York Daily Tribune* of January 11, 1878, Edwin L. Godkin, Olmsted's friend and the editor of the *Nation*, discussed at length Olmsted's accomplishments and standing as a landscape architect, and respect accorded the art of landscape design in Europe. He made no mention of Calvert Vaux's role in the design of Central Park, but said of Olmsted "that he who designed the Park, and has for twenty years, nearly, watched over its execution, holds a leading position among the professors of this art; that his position is fully conceded to him in Europe, and that his work in this city and Brooklyn is acknowledged everywhere to be second to nothing of the kind anywhere. The credit due to him is heightened by the fact that no other American has worked in the same field with equal success." In a letter to the *New-York Daily Tribune* of January 25, 1878, Godkin further discussed the attitude of the park commissioners who had removed Olmsted, observing that they had no intention of seeking his advice thereafter and stating that he had been the "main obstacle" to changes that would transform Central Park into "the politician's ideal of a public garden — a mixture of a popular cemetery, camp — meeting ground, fair ground and race course." The emphasis on Olmsted's primary role in the parks by those protesting his dismissal was increased by a petition by 158 leading citizens of New York, submitted to the park commissioners on January 22, which called him the "main designer" of both Central Park and Prospect

Park. On February 19, Vaux published a short note in the *Tribune*. Despite the fact that Olmsted had been out of the country since before the affair began, Vaux began by saying that he had waited sufficiently long "to allow of Mr. Olmsted's disavowal of the designs for the Central and Brooklyn Parks, of which I am the author in every respect, equally with Mr. Olmsted." Now, he complained, E. L. Godkin, as Olmsted's representative had had "the repulsively bad faith to step forward publicly and administer our joint estate; To F. L. Olmsted, everything; to C. Vaux, the cut direct." Two days later, several New York newspapers carried a brief statement from Owen Olmsted, speaking in his father's behalf, (and written by his mother, Mary Perkins Olmsted) stating "that no one has, or can have, the smallest authority for claiming for Mr. Olmsted either more or less than an equal share with Mr. C. Vaux in the designs of the Central and Brooklyn Parks." In the *Tribune*, Owen's letter was preceded by a short note by Godkin that included the assertion that "I need hardly say that the acknowledgement it contains would have been cheerfully made at any time during the past month, if Mr. Vaux had requested it." ("Mr. Olmsted's Dismissal," *New-York Daily Tribune*, Jan. 11, 1878, p. 2; "Mr. Olmsted's Removal," *New-York Daily Tribune*, Jan. 25, 1878, p. 5; "Local Miscellany. Asking for Mr. Olmsted's Retention," *New-York Daily Tribune*, Jan. 22, 1878, p. 8; "The Central Park Plan. Mr. Calvert Vaux's Part in It," *New-York Daily Tribune*, Feb. 19, 1878, p. 5; "The Central Park Plan," *New-York Daily Tribune*, Feb. 21, 1878, p. 6).

2. Mary Perkins Olmsted reported that E. L. Godkin had "written two pretty plain spoken notes to Vaux, to the last of which he answers humbly and says the devil must have prompted him . . ." Indeed, she continued, Clarence Cook and Thomas Wisedell said that Vaux was "almost out of his head with worry that he has no business" (Mary Perkins Olmsted to John C. Olmsted, Feb. 24, 1878).

3. C. Bowyer Vaux (1855–1928) (C. Bowyer Vaux to FLO, June 17, 1881).

New-York Daily Tribune, December 28, 1879

The Future of New-York.

Views of Frederick Law Olmsted.
Organizing the Business of a Continent — New-York's
Commercial Advantages — Defects in its Streets and
Houses — the Vicious System of Blocks — What a City Must
Have to Take Rank as a True Metropolis.

Considerable changes are occurring in the courses of trade, and some branches of business which have hitherto contributed to the prosperity of New-York are passing from it. The question what is likely to be the result on the whole is one of the deepest interest to New-Yorkers. The following observations upon this question were mainly drawn out in a recent casual conversation by a Tribune representative with Frederick Law Olmsted. The commercial advantages of New-York are touched upon. Its recent progress toward the rank of a true metropolis is referred to, and some of the evils and obstacles in the way of that progress are pointed out. The bad results of the unfortunate plan of the streets and the crowding together of houses in blocks are dwelt upon, and the tendency in large cities to concentration for business purposes and dispersion for domestic purposes is considered.

Aids and Checks to Progress.

If a wise despot had undertaken to organize the business of this continent, he would have begun by selecting for his headquarters a point where advantages for direct dealing with all parts of it were combined with advantages for direct dealing with all parts of Europe. He would then have established a series of great and small trading posts, determining their positions by regard, first, to the local resources of various parts of the country, and secondly, to facilities of transportation. Each of these would be an agency of exchange for a district, but, the several districts not being strictly defined, there would, as trade developed and individual enterprise came more and more into play, be much competition between different agencies, and by greater economy of management one would often draw away trade from and prosper to the disadvantage of, another. But except in a limited and superficial way, abnormal to the system, the interests of the central and of the local agencies would be identical, and the relation between them not one of rivalry but of coöperative and reciprocal service. The business of the general agency would be proportionate to the business of the country; its local profits to the profits of trade generally. Whatever it gained would as a rule be a gain to every community on the continent.

The general agency would, unless special obstacles interposed, soon come to be the best place for comparing, testing, appraising and interchanging information and ideas on all concerns common to the New World and the Old. It would therefore take the foremost place in affairs of fashion and luxury. It would be the headquarters of dramatic and musical enterprises. It would be a centre of interest in matters of science and art. It would be the readiest point for making collections and for comparing and testing values for a great variety of affairs not usually classed as commercial. All this would cause people to resort to it, either as occasional visitors, or with a view to residence, more than to any other place on the continent. It would thus become the best market for high ability in crafts of refinement. It would be the best "shopping place." As the resources of the continent were more and more fully exploited, it would thus tend to become a metropolis. Special advantages of climate, topography or of personal leadership and particular enterprise might give a local agency a leadership in some particular field; but the tendency, as a matter of continental economy, to concentrate leadership in general, even social leadership, at the trade centre, could be permanently overcome only by local conditions which would make life in it decidedly less secure, healthy, peaceful, cleanly and economical than elsewhere. Considerable natural disadvantages in this respect, even, might be gradually overcome.

The Great Peter of Russia and his successors, in fact, proceeded much in this way which has been supposed. The position which he selected for a general centre of exchange for Eastern Europe and Western Asia was in many respects unpromising; the harbor shallow and nearly half the year closed by ice, the land marshy and malarious, natural scenery tame and sad, and the climate most inclement. Nevertheless St. Petersburg has been made not only the centre of commercial exchanges, but the chief seat of learning, science and art, and of all intellectual and social activities, for a vast population of more varied and antagonistic races, creeds, tastes and customs than that of America.

Commercial Position of New-York.

New-York has long been the general centre of commercial exchanges for the continent. There is not the least likelihood that any other city will supercede it. Even if any other had somewhat superior local advantages for the purpose, it is not desirable in the general interests of commerce at this stage that a change should be made. The cost of the rearrangement would be too great. Such transfer of particular branches of business to other growing towns, as now occurs, is simply a modification of commercial organization by which the mutual business of New-York and the country at large is to be done with more profit on the whole to both. St. Louis, Cincinnati and Chicago are in rivalry with one another but never except in a temporary and superficial way, with New-York. Boston, Philadelphia and Baltimore are more plainly in competition with New-York; yet in the main they likewise so far coöperate with her that New-York gains more than she loses by every advance that is made by either of them.

But New-York is yet hardly ready to assume the full duty and take the full profits of a metropolis. In some respects Boston leads New-York, Philadelphia in others; in still others Cincinnati at least aims to do so. And in many respects New-York is not as yet nearly as well equipped as many cities of Europe of less than half her population and commercial prosperity. Treasures of art and the results of popular familiarity with treasures of art must be gained slowly, and New-York can in a long time only partially overcome its inevitable disadvantages in this respect. Yet, as to the higher results of human labor, in general attractiveness to cultivated minds and as a place of luxury, New-York has probably been gaining of late, even during the hard times, more rapidly than any other city in the world. She has gained, for instance, the Natural History Museum, the Art Museum, the Lenox Library, the Cathedral, the railways to and the great plant for healthful recreation at Coney Island.[1] She is decidedly richer and more attractive in libraries, churches, clubs and hotels. The display of her shops is very greatly finer than it was a few years ago. Shops more attractive in general effect are now hardly to be found in any older city. Great advances have been made also by half a dozen of her business concerns which are all large employers of the finer artisans and artificers: wood carvers, workers in metal, enamels, glass and precious stones, decorative painters. Better workmanship can now be had here in almost anything than was available five years ago. Take pottery, wood-engraving, upholstery, gas-fixtures, furniture, for example; in all these we could now make a better show than we did in the Centennial Exhibition.[2] Without doubt that exhibition did much for New-York; possibly more than for Philadelphia. It is, at least, certain that New-York has since had better workmen, better designers, better tools and a more highly educated market; and all these things have distinctly advanced her metropolitan position.

Unfortunate Plan of the City.

Next to the direct results of a slipshod, temporizing government of amateurs, the great disadvantage under which New-York labors is one growing out of the senseless manner in which its streets have been laid out.[3] No city is more unfortunately planned with reference to metropolitan attractiveness. True, it may be said that large parts of many old world cities have not been planned at all, but their accidental defects are compensated by their accidental advantages. The tenement-house, which is the product of uniform 200-feet-wide blocks,[4] is beginning to be recognized as the primary cause of whatever is peculiarly disgraceful in New-York City politics, through the demoralization which it works in the more incapable class of working-people. It is a calamity more to be deplored than the yellow fever at New-Orleans,[5] because more impregnable; more than the fogs of London, the cold of St. Petersburg, or the malaria of Rome, because more constant in its tyranny.

On the other hand, the first-class brown-stone, high-stoop, fashionable modern dwelling house is really a confession that it is impossible to build a convenient and tasteful residence in New-York, adapted to the ordinary civilized requirements of a single family, except at a cost which even rich men find generally prohibitory.

Dr. Bellows[6] once described the typical New-York private house as "a slice of house fifteen feet wide, slid into a block, with seven long flights of stairs between the place where the cook works and sleeps;" and really, the family is now fortunate which gets twenty feet and which has more than two

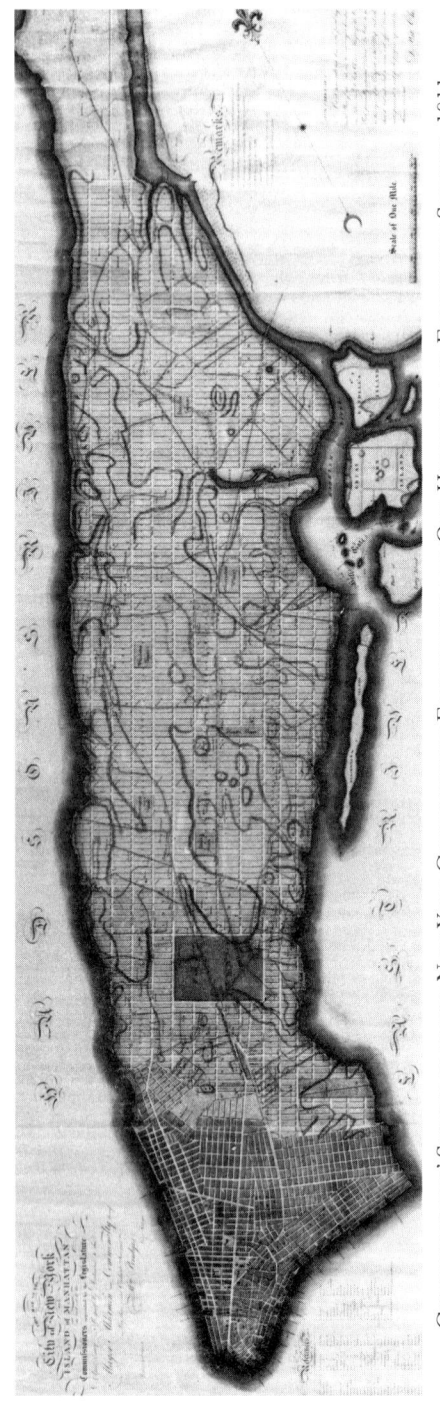

Commissioners' Street plan for New York City between Fourteenth and One Hundred and Fifty-fifth Streets, 1811

rooms out of three of tolerable proportions with windows looking into the open air.

There are actually houses of less than fifteen feet wide, to which men, who anywhere else in the world would be in comfortable circumstances, are obliged to condemn their families. A gentleman of rare attainments and in every way a most valuable addition to any community, whose private professional library and collections must have cost him $10,000, has been obliged to compress his family into a five-floored stack, the party walls of which are but twelve feet apart.

In none of those older towns in which domestic convenience has been systematically sacrificed to considerations of military expediency is a man of like value condemned to such a preposterous form of habitation. Its plan is more nearly that of a light house built upon a wave-lashed rock, than of a civilized family home.[7] New-York has need of great attractions to draw people into quarters of this kind from such houses as they could better afford in any other American city.

The Same Defects Up-Town.

But what is worst in the lookout for New-York is that the elevated roads and the up-town movement lead as yet to nothing better; for even at Yorkville, Harlem and Manhattanville,[8] five or six miles away from the centre of population, there are new houses of the ridiculous jammed-up pattern, as dark and noisome in their middle parts and as inconvenient throughout as if they were parts of a besieged fortress.

Nay, there is a prospect of even worse to come, for on the slopes south of Manhattanville there are new streets, some of them paved and flagged, which, out of respect to the popular prejudice in favor of continuing the regular system, are laid out on just the worst course possible, so that in passing through them you must mount an inclination of one in six, eight or ten. What this means may be guessed by thinking of the steeper grades in the lower part of the city. That of Fifth-ave, north of Thirty-fourth-st., for instance, is one in twenty-five, and it brings every omnibus and most hackney coaches from a trot to a walk. Every ton of coal dragged up such a street, every load of garbage gathered and taken from it, is to cost three or four times as much in horse-power as it would in the lower part of the town, and yet in the lower part of the town we cannot afford to prevent great mounds of garbage from lying before our doors for weeks at a time. Its daily removal is found to be too costly.

Small families who do not wish to entertain many friends may find some relief in the better of the new apartment houses. But still, what these offer, as compared with what is offered in other cities, is of most extravagant cost. They are no places for children, and to any really good arrangement of apartments the 200-foot block still bars the way. Apartment houses in the old countries, of corresponding luxury in other respects, have much more spacious courts. The court, instead of being regarded as a backyard and every inch given to it and every dollar laid out upon it begrudged, often gives the noblest and usually the pleasantest fronts to the house. What are advertised as apartment houses for people in New-York of more moderate means, such as must be looked to by teachers, artists, artisans, writers, and nearly all the rank and file of the superior life of a metropolis, are as yet only a more decent sort of tenement-house, nearly half their rooms being without direct light and ventilation. The same classes that are compelled to live in them in New-York would regard them as intolerable in Philadelphia, or in London, Paris or Vienna.

Many attempts have been made to subdivide the block so that comfortable small houses which would come in competition with the tenement-houses might be built. The result in the best cases is that family privacy and general decency in fact and appearance are attained at an outlay which in any other large city would be thought preposterous. A better arrangement than any which has been tried is probably that proposed by Mr. Potter,[9] which consists essentially in subdividing the block by a series of lanes running from street to street; but capitalists as yet draw back from it.

ORIGIN OF THE EVIL.

How did the city come to be saddled with this misfortune? Probably by a process of degeneration. In the old city of Amsterdam, after which it was first named, many houses are still to be found which approach in proportions the fashionable New-York house. But from the beginning these had one great advantage. At their back, running lengthwise through the middle of the block, there was a canal. Into this the closet and kitchen drains had direct discharge. Dust, ashes and garbage could be shot down to the lower floor and then passed directly into boats and floated off to farms in the suburbs. At the base of the house, on the street, there was a narrow brick terrace, and outside the front door a little open-air sitting-room, and everything on that side was kept as neat as a pin. The streets of old Amsterdam were, indeed, as much celebrated in the seventeenth century for their cleanliness as those of New-Amsterdam have since ever been for their filthiness.

New-York is in short a Dutch town with its canals and cleanliness omitted and its streets straightened and magnified. Long after the present street plan was adopted it was the custom of its citizens to throw their slops and garbage out of the front door, and droves of hogs got their living in the gutters. Out of this state of things New-York streets have been slowly improved to their present condition and New-York houses have come to be more inconvenient, uncomfortable and unhealthy, for the money and labor spent upon them, than those of any other American city.

But when we speculate upon the future of New-York as a metropolis we must not think of it as confined by arbitrary political boundaries. As a metropolis, Newark, Newport and Bridgeport, as well as Brooklyn, Yonkers and Jersey City, are essential parts of it. For all scholarly and scientific purposes Yale College with its thousand students is already annexed to New-York, and is possibly today a more actively important element of its intellectual life than either or all of the four colleges which stand within its political limits.

In fact, the railway, the telegraph and the telephone make a few miles more or less of so little consequence that a large part of the ideas of a city, which have been transmitted to us from the period when cities were walled about and necessarily compact and crowded, must be put away.

Concentration and Dispersion.

There is now a marked tendency in most large and thriving towns in two opposite directions — one to concentration for business and social purposes, the other to dispersion for domestic purposes. The first leads toward more compact and higher building in business quarters, the other toward broader, lower and more open building in residence quarters. The old-fashioned "country houses" of city people are growing more and more out of vogue, but residences in a greater or less degree combining urban and rural advantages, neither solitary on the one hand nor a mere slice of a block on the other, wherever they can be had in healthy and pleasing localities, with quick and frequent transit to business, social, artistic, literary and scholarly centres, are gaining favor. They are springing up in hundreds of charming neighborhoods about London and Paris; Boston and our Western cities are largely formed of them. They are as yet less used by New-Yorkers than by the people of any other large town. The reason is simply that hitherto there have been no thoroughly healthy suburban neighborhoods sufficiently accessible about New-York. In time such neighborhoods will be formed. Whenever they are, the metropolitan advantages of New-York and the profits of its local trade must be greatly increased by constantly increasing accessions to its population of men who have accumulated means elsewhere, and who wish to engage in other than purely money-making occupations. Such men, living under favorable circumstances and with capital and energies economically directed to matters of general interest, are the most valuable constituents of a city; and it is by their numbers, wealth and influence, more than anything else, that a city takes the rank in the world of a metropolis.

The text presented here is from "The Future of New-York," *New-York Daily Tribune*, December 28, 1879.

1. The City had recently gained the American Museum of Natural History, designed by Calvert Vaux and begun in 1872; the Metropolitan Museum of Art, designed by Vaux with construction beginning in 1874 and formally opened in March 1880; the library of

art objects and books collected by James Lenox, designed by Richard Morris Hunt, with the first displays opened to the public in early 1877; and St. Patrick's Cathedral, designed by James Renwick and dedicated in May 1879. At this time there were at least six railroads that provided access from parts of Brooklyn to the growing number of bathing establishments at Coney Island. They supplemented Ocean Parkway, designed by Olmsted and Vaux and completed in 1876, that connected Prospect Park with Coney Island (Francis R. Kowsky, *Country, Park, & City: The Architecture and Life of Calvert Vaux* [New York, 1998], pp. 225–27, 231–37, 274–80; Harry Miller Lydenberg, *History of the New York Library, Astor, Lenox and Tilden Foundations* [New York, 1923], 99–107; Federal Writers' Project of the Works Progress Administration, *The WPA guide to New York City* . . . [New York, 1982], p. 34; Edo McCullough, *Good Old Coney Island* [New York, 1956], pp. 42–43; J. Disturnell, comp, *Summer Resorts and Watering Places* . . . [New York, (1877)], p. 53).
2. A reference to the Centennial Exposition held in Philadelphia in 1876.
3. A reference to the street system for Manhattan between First and 155th streets established by a special commission in 1811. Most of the blocks created by the plan were rectangles 800 feet long and 200 feet deep. In Olmsted's view, this arrangement made it impossible to take advantage of the opportunities for variety offered by the natural terrain of the island, made it difficult to site important buildings properly, produced unnecessarily steep grades for streets, and laid the basis for construction of many tenement houses lacking adequate ventilation and exposure to the sun (David Schuyler, *The New Urban Landscape: The Redefinition of City Form in Nineteenth-Century America* [Baltimore, 1986], pp. 17–20).
4. The depth of New York City blocks led to the proliferation of housing for the city's poor that consisted of multi-story "tenement" houses over seventy feet deep on narrow lots. These were built on a standard city lot that was one hundred feet deep and twenty-five feet wide. This created narrow buildings with minimal space between them.
5. New Orleans had suffered numerous yellow fever epidemics; the most recent, and one of the most severe, had occurred in 1878 (Jo Ann Carrigan, *The Saffron Scourge: A History of Yellow Fever in Louisiana, 1796–1905* [Lafayette, La., 1994], pp. 112–29).
6. A reference to Olmsted's friend and colleague in the U.S. Sanitary Commission, the Unitarian minister Henry W. Bellows, pastor of All Souls Church at Union Square.
7. Olmsted here uses a simile that he had previously applied to another "relic of barbarism," the isolated plantation of the slaveholding South–whose owners he described as being in "a condition approaching in comfort that of the keeper of a light-ship on an outer-bar" (*Back Country*, p. 398).
8. The old village of Manhattanville was on the west side of Manhattan above 125th Street.
9. The architect Edward T. Potter (1831–1904). In 1866 he proposed a plan for constructing two residential buildings instead of one on a standard Manhattan lot, and after his retirement in 1877 further developed this approach. In 1878 he published a series of articles in the *American Architect and Building News* in which he offered an analysis of the problem similar to the one Olmsted presents here and a number of solutions. His principal concept for both tenement and apartment houses was to have air passages between the buildings, secure ventilation and light for all rooms, and achieve cross-ventilation by eliminating interior hallways and providing access instead by exterior stairs and landings (Adolf K. Placzek, ed., *Macmillan Encyclopedia of Architects*, 4 vols. [New York, 1982], 3: 465–66; Sarah Bradford Landau, *Edward T. and William A. Potter, American Victorian Architects* [New York, 1979], 390–97; Edward T. Potter, "Urban Housing in New York," *American Architect and Building News*, March 16, 1878, pp. 90–92; ibid., "Urban Housing," ibid., April 20, 1878, pp. 137–38; ibid., May. 18, 1878, pp. 171–73; ibid., May 24, 1879, pp. 163–64; May 31, 1879, pp. 173–74; ibid., Sept. 27, 1879, pp. 98–99).

december 1879–may 1880

To Charles Eliot Norton

Capitol Grounds.
Washig[n] 22[d] Jan 1880.

My Dear Norton;
 I have been occupied with some pottering work in which I have had to keep my eyes constantly on the workman and to do something with my own hands.[1] By night I have been so dogged tired that I could hardly sit up. So I have been putting off writing you.
 Stout,[2] of the Commission, offered to reprint the Memorial & he & others promised aid in canvassing. But very strangely no one has done anything & except from you I have had no assistance. Gardner, the Director of the Survey, has been preparing an elaborate report, with maps and cuts & photolithograph. A part of these were burned in the Boston fire. Since that I have heard nothing from him & only know that his proceeding is delayed. I have been expecting a summons to Albany about it for a fortnight but if it came should not at present be able to go. I have been hoping that the debate in the legislature would be so long postponed that I could take the business up again, canvass myself for signatures and get it in good shape. I want also to get time to write a report to be printed with Gardner's report. In another week I hope to be more free.
 What I have written will sufficiently show you the state of the case.[3] I feel humiliated by my own inefficiency but I had reason to expect assistance which has failed me and I have been swamped with other & more imperative duties.
 I still hope that the Memorial may be a factor of some importance in the affair. If so it will be mainly because of what you have done. I shall be glad to get the results of what you have done not already rendered but I cannot ask or advise you to be any further trouble. Only now please send me your own signature, & if convenient get Parkman's.[4] I need not say that I appreciate & regret the concern which your friend in Paris has had.[5]
 An incident today calls my attention to a matter which ought to way heavily on you. A question asked by two school girls led me to the knowledge that our common schools are provided with two works on Art & that by means of them Art is a regular branch of instruction. These girls had been through one & had had the wit to observe, soon after taking up the other, that the Art of one was not the Art of the other. One is Kane's Elements,[6] edited as a class book for the American market, the other is by "Mr Long" of Boston.[7] I only mean that for good or evil it is a matter of importance. It strikes me that an elementary primer of art for common life would be very different from Kane's Elements & that if Mr Long has made one which is in the least respectable, he deserves much more general public credit than he has received.[8] I do hope that it is possible to give to common country folk even some idea of what art

is—enough for a starting point of such self education as may be possible toward a softer & finer life. Letting the leaves of Mr Long's book slip through my fingers I get the impression that it is Picture Gallery Art that it mainly means. La Farge.[9] came here with me. In the car I thought he had been some time asleep. He explained to me that he was greatly enjoying the landscape & colour in the low lying rain clouds, the beauty of which he then made me see—And I don't suppose that in all the state of Delaware there were two others to whom it was apparent. This is a part of my idea of the true line of common School Art Education.

I write under a shed in the rain, while my men are off for dinner. Yours affctly

Fred[k] Law Olmsted.

The text presented here is from a manuscript in Olmsted's hand in the Charles Eliot Norton Papers, Houghton Library, Harvard University, Cambridge, Massachusetts.

1. At this time, Olmsted was supervising construction of the summer house on the U.S. Capitol grounds.
2. Francis A. Stout (1833–1892), a New Yorker of prominent family and a vice president of the American Geographical Society, who had been a leading figure in the campaign to create a New York State Survey (*New-York Times*, July 21, 1892, p. 3; John Meredith Read, *Francis Aquila Stout* [New York, 1894], pp. 24, 46–51).
3. See "Notes by Mr. Olmsted" in *Special Report of the New York State Survey on the Preservation of the Scenery of Niagara Falls . . . for the Year 1879* below.
4. Norton's longtime friend the famous historian Francis Parkman (1823–1893) (*DAB*; Kermit Vanderbilt, *Charles Eliot Norton: Apostle of Culture in a Democracy* [Cambridge, Mass., 1959], p. 32).
5. The noted philologist and professor of English at Harvard, Francis J. Child (1825–1896). In December, Child, in Paris, had responded to Norton's request that he gather signatures by giving a lukewarm agreement and recounting the great difficulty that he would experience in the process. Norton also volunteered to enlist his friend the French lexicographer and philosopher Maximilien Paul Émile Littré in securing the signatures of fellow members of the *Academie française* (*DAB*; C. E. Norton to FLO, Jan. 13, 1880; F. J. Child to C. E. Norton, December 1879).
6. A reference to *Elements of Chemistry, Including the Most Recent Discoveries and Applications of the Science to Medicine and Pharmacy, and to the Arts* by the Irish scientist and professor of chemistry and natural philosophy Sir Robert John Kane (1809–1890). First published in Dublin in 1841, it went through several American editions beginning in 1842 with the additional subtitle "An American ed. with Additions and Corrections, and Arranged for the Use of the Universities, Colleges, Academies and Medical Schools of the United States." The American editor was the English-born chemist and historian of science John William Draper (*DNB*; *DAB*).
7. Probably Samuel P. Long, *Art: Its Laws, and the Reasons for Them, Collected, Considered and Arranged for General and Educational Purposes* (New York, 1871).
8. Norton replied: "Your suggestions about an Introduction to the Fine Arts set me thinking. There is no book that can be recommended for the purpose. If I could I should like to write one that you would approve" (C. E. Norton to FLO, Jan. 26, 1880, Charles

DECEMBER 1879–MAY 1880

Eliot Norton Papers, Houghton Library, Harvard University, Cambridge, Massachusetts).
9. The American artist John La Farge (1835–1910), who had recently completed a series of murals for H. H. Richardson's Trinity Church in Boston (*DAB*; Henry Adams, et. al., *John La Farge* [New York, 1987], pp. 241–42).

To Joseph Phineas Davis[1]

Mr Davis.

24th Jan. 1880.

My Dear Sir,

I reply to yours of yesterday.

I don't understand what is now wanted in the way of estimates other than parts of what you prepared last year or why you should revise those then made except as required by the rise in price of iron &c.

I am much disinclined to abandon any of the propositions which you place in question;

As to the bridge over the railroad, of course grace and symmetry and especially continuous unity of motive must be regarded as primary objective points {equally with safety and convenience of transit.}[2] A broken curve in the curb of the drive, that is to say, would be displeasing. And if the parapet of the bridge is not set parallel with the curb, or at worst if it is not a chord of its curve & this symmetrical, (showing unity of design with it) the awkwardness would be a constant offence to a nice eye.

On the whole I would prefer a girder construction below the floor at the expense of a slight increase of grade in the approaches from Commonwealth Avenue. The law would oblige the underside of the girder to be 18 feet above the rails, I believe. The distance to be spanned is, say, 85 feet, but of this less than half is occupied by the rails and their bed. I asked some railroad man, probably Mr. Rockwell,[3] whether something might not be gained in piers or brackets upon the 20 feet or more of spare space on each side {of} the tracks? He thought it could by consent of the Company. I would go to any trouble, even that of getting a special permissive act, to gain all that is thus possible and then adopt the lowest girder construction consistent with safety. This construction I would take as a platform to build the superstructure of the bridge upon, maintaining all curves both vertical and horizontal in the top work exactly as if working on an earth bed.

The less people passing {over} this bridge are aware that they are off

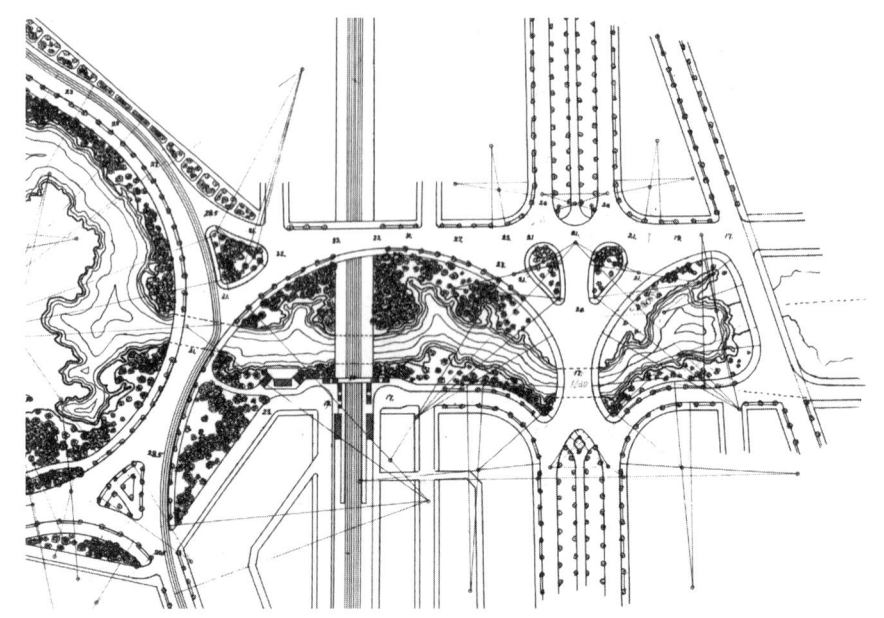

SECTION OF PLAN SHOWING NORTHERN SECTION OF BACK BAY FENS (BOYLSTON STREET BRIDGE TO COMMONWEALTH AVENUE), MARCH 5, 1879

the ground the better. (It is not so with the others.) The walks and parapets might overhang the girders.

  The Boylston bridge will be the most conspicuous object in all the scheme. It will be forced on the attention above and below and on each side. It will dominate everything & be seen from Charles River to Parker Hill. People will rest & lounge upon it & look at it more closely than anything else on the Bay. A natty, formal elegant structure would put all rural elements of the Bay out of countenance. It would be a discord. The bridge must, if possible, have a rustic quality and be picturesque *in material* as well as in outlines & shadows. It does not seem to me that I should want to conceal the spiral lines of the arch. What I would greatly prefer is a long elliptical arch[4] of rough stone and I do not think I should want to conceal the spiral lines as you suggest. The more the real structure is evident the better. I would like an arch of Roxbury pudding-stone;[5] or an arch of boulders, or of rough field stone, with voussoirs &c of cut stone or brick; or an arch wholly of cheap rough brick. I would much prefer wood to iron. I would not at all object to a timber bridge of almost the simplest and cheapest possible construction. I would with such a bridge prefer greater distance between the abutments than the printed plan calls for and two or four timber piers on iron piles, making three or six spans. If such a bridge could be made to last with moderate repairs fifteen or twenty years would it not be fairly economical? After that the question of a stone arch could come up again. I should certainly like a wooden bridge in this situation much better than the most beautiful iron bridge. Let us have iron everywhere else if economy requires but on Boylston Street, though I would always prefer a brick arch or arches at the same cost.

As to the Commonwealth Avenue bridge, I would say the same as of the railroad bridge. Let us have, that is to say, girder construction, if you please, but a superstructure maintaining curves as on the printed plan (and more accurately on diagram enclosed).[6] Have *three* spans if required but a single central pier is to be avoided if practicable. Two are much to be preferred. Head room below is of no importance but I should think that two piers, and a simple beam construction would appear best.

You will find enclosed a diagram showing plans & positions of bridges and radii of curves.

Before making up my mind more definitely about designs of bridges, especially Boylston Street Bridge, I should want to take counsel with an architect. If you think it desirable to further settle conclusions before making your report let me know & I will come on but I want, if I can, to be here now till Friday.

The text presented here is from a draft in Olmsted's hand. The letter discusses the bridges at the northern end of the Back Bay Fens: the bridge carrying Boylston Street over the Fens, and the bridge over the Boston & Albany Railroad tracks between the Boylston Street bridge and Commonwealth Avenue.

1. Joseph Phineas Davis (1837–1917), a civil engineer, had worked with Olmsted and Calvert Vaux on the construction of Prospect Park in Brooklyn in the 1866–67. He became city engineer of Boston in 1871, a position he held until 1880 (NCAB, 25: 51).
2. Olmsted crossed out the phrase in braces. In an earlier version, the first part of which is missing, he apparently observed that the use of girders for the understructure of the bridge would be acceptable. ". . . we are not bound to please the eye with grace or symmetry from that point of view," he continued, "but grace and symmetry and especially unity of motive are *primary objective points* in the drive and walks above—" His draft then continues with the sentence beginning "A broken curve in the curb of the drive."
3. Alfred Perkins Rockwell (1834–1923), a mining engineer and from 1876 to 1879 the president of the Eastern Railroad Company, which ran between Boston and Salem (NCAB, 21: 466).
4. Here Olmsted wrote, and then crossed out, "like that of the Trinity bridge at Florence," a reference to the Ponte Santa Trinita, noted for the beauty of the curves of its arches (Elvira Grifi, *Saunterings in Florence* [Florence, Italy, 1899], p. 373).
5. H. H. Richardson's first sketches for the bridge, in line with Olmsted's wishes, show it faced with boulders. The commissioners could not be convinced to adopt this scheme and the bridge was instead faced with square-cut pieces of granite (Cynthia Zaitzevsky, *Frederick Law Olmsted and the Boston Park System* [Cambridge, Mass., 1982], pp. 164–66).
6. The diagrams referred to by Olmsted in this letter have not survived, or cannot be identified.

To Charles Henry Dalton

Mr Dalton

24th Jan 1880.

Dear Mr. Dalton;
    I enclose copy of a letter which I send in reply to one from Mr Davis.[1] I want you to have it in mind that the points he questions me upon are critical. Davis looking from the Engineer's point of view don't realize that they are so and if you don't guard them well his influence will all be against you, not intentionally or consciously but from the habitual drift of the Engineering mind. I don't suppose that it is necessary at this moment to take a new step but with the professional itching for the tried, prudent and *common-place* he will be constantly inclined to find opportunities for backing away from the more refined purposes of your undertaking. The time may not have come for employing an architect — I should think, that is to say, that it was unnecessary for the purpose of a preliminary estimate to do so, but I judge he does not contemplate having any upon the bridges in the future. To an Engineer bridges are engineering works. It would be better therefore that you let him see on proper occasion that you expect the City Architect to finally make the plans for iron bridges in consultation with him (Davis) & with me.
    But as to the Boylston Street bridge, when you have read the enclosed, I wish that you would consider whether you could not let me have Richardson's assistance?[2] Either with stone, or brick or timber, this bridge can be made very effective, and it is the first thing you have to do as a Commission in which a striking success, giving artistic people confidence in your ability to lead the city, is practicable.
    I hope the Arboretum map[3] answers your purpose & the scheme is growing in favor.

The text presented here is from a draft in Olmsted's hand.

1. See FLO to Joseph P. Davis, January 24, 1880, above.
2. Olmsted and Henry Hobson Richardson did collaborate on the design of the Boylston Street Bridge, with Olmsted assuming a major role. He later asserted that the "single, sweeping arch" of the bridge had been planned by his firm in 1879, with the height and span being designated, and that "Richardson's first drawing, made in 1882, for that bridge, closely follows memorandum drawings prepared by the landscape designers of the Fens, in which drawings, the outline of the arch; its full plan, elevations and cross sections; the batter of the wall; in short, every important feature except the tourelles and the shape of the coping of the parapet, — had been prescribed as fundamental *landscape requirements of a bridge in that locality*" (FLO, "A few Annotations, for Private Use Only, Upon 'Architectural Fitness,' Humbly Submitted to the Consideration of His

Omniscient Editorial Majesty, by His Prostrate Servant, F. L. O." [c. August 27, 1891], in Cynthia Zaitzevsky, "The Olmsted Firm and the Structures of the Boston Park System," *Journal of the Society of Architectural Historians* 32 [May 1973]: 170–71).
3. See BCDP, City of Boston, "Map of Proposed Arboretum, Showing its outlines and local connections, with a study for public drive passing through it" (1879), p. 486–87.

To the Board of Commissioners of the Department of Parks of the City of Boston

[January 26, 1880]

The Board of Commissioners of the Department of Parks of the City of Boston:—
Gentlemen,—
 I have had the honor to prepare the accompanying plan in coöperation with the City Engineer,[1] under instructions embodying the main results of prolonged debates of your Board; and the present report is written to meet your request for an explanation of it suitable to be offered through the City Council to the public.
 It should be understood that though classed as a parkwork, the amount to be expended under this plan to facilitate recreation is comparatively small. Its main ends are drainage, wholesome air, and convenience of communication between different quarters of the city, in a locality offering some unusual obstacles to these objects. The provisions for them are simply to be so supplemented that appliances for rest and exercise in the open air may be also secured to the public by a very moderate additional outlay.
 I will briefly describe the conditions to be dealt with.

 Back Bay is the common estuary of Muddy River and Stony Brook. When the tide is in, it is a broad pool; when the tide is out, a narrow creek between broad, deep, and fetid mud-banks, in parts of which soundings have been made to a depth of thirty feet without reaching firm bottom. Offensive exudations arise from the mud when exposed by a falling tide to the summer's sun, which are perceptible at a great distance.
 Private enterprise is filling up and building over the adjoining marsh, and, notwithstanding the embarrassment caused by the bay, the city on three sides is rapidly moving toward it; the fourth is its mouth, and as yet impracticable of private improvement.

"Proposed Improveme[nt]"

DECEMBER 1879–MAY 1880

BAY," C. DECEMBER 1879

A serious check and disturbance to what would otherwise be the natural growth of the city is thus established, which must sooner or later be got the better of.

Remembering that no considerable extension of the city in compact blocks beyond the Public Garden was nearly as likely to occur when that improvement was projected,[2] as a like extension now is beyond and about the Back Bay, it has been generally recognized that whatever is to be done should be fitting to what is thus to be anticipated.

Accordingly it was generally expected, when the city bought the property and gave it in your charge, that the two streams of Stony Brook and Muddy River would be diverted from the bay, the mud-banks filled over, and the site transformed into a public park; and you for some time proceeded with this course in view.[3] It was found, however, to have serious difficulties. Legal authority to turn Stony Brook from its outlet was wanting, and necessary legislation for the purpose was likely to be obstructed by opposing private interests. Under the recently adopted plans for the drainage of the upper valley of Stony Brook, this stream would at times bring down a much larger body of water than at present.[4] To carry it harmless from the upland region south of Back Bay to Charles River would require a very large sewer-like conduit, which would have to be built for a long distance over deep marshy ground upon piles; its cost would be excessive, and it could not probably be undertaken without drawing the city into prolonged litigation. The difficulties and hazards thus arising would be liable to defer the completion of the work indefinitely, and such delay would work serious injustice.

As, in abandoning the idea of a public park and adopting that here to be presented, it may appear that you are following a less liberal policy in dealing with this part of the city, it may be well to add that the property had been purchased for the corporation in various parcels under a provision that none should be taken for which the previous owners refused to receive a certain rate of compensation, and the principles which would otherwise have determined its outline as a site for a park had been necessarily disregarded. Its form was, consequently, unfortunate for the purpose.[5] The difficulties thus presented, in addition to those growing out of the topography, were further complicated by the necessity of reference in laying it out to several more or less independent street systems which had been established at no great distance from its border, and for accommodating lines of transit between them.

More than a score of plans for laying out the property as a park, representing in several cases prolonged, arduous, and painstaking study by highly capable men, came under the consideration of your Board, and it was your conclusion, reached unexpectedly and reluctantly, after due deliberation, that none of them promised a park of sufficient value to the city at large to justify its cost, taking into account the continuous cost which its satisfactory maintenance would involve.[6]

Your Board was thus brought to inquire whether a form of improvement, of a less ambitious character than that implied in designating the ground a park, might not, on the whole, better serve the interests of all concerned.

Taking up this question, and regarding first the nuisance and inconvenience, relief from which was the more pressing necessity, it was obvious that a good deal might be gained, while retaining the bay as an estuary, by simply banking out upon the mud flats and so reducing its breadth. By a dam at its mouth the water in it could be prevented from falling below the level of ordinary high water in Charles River and the new banks would be firm slopes, which might be shaped and planted in a natural and more or less picturesque way.

To this proposition the objection was apparent, that as, in extraordinary tides, the water is liable to rise from four to eight feet above its usual high-water level, the sloping face of an earth embankment would, at more or less distant intervals, be in part submerged and in part washed by breaking {waves} and spray, and that whenever this occurred any vegetation upon it would be liable to be drowned out, or killed by salt.

A deposit daily, between high and low water, was also to be apprehended of the filthy slime which is usually found where the organic matter of fresh-water streams is first thrown into salt water.

It was your judgment that these objections were conclusive against the proposition.

It was suggested that they might be lessened by substituting a vertical wall for the slopes. But as such a wall, needing to be built on piles, would be very costly, and at best but comparatively inoffensive, you decided against it, holding out for something which would be positively, permanently, and constantly wholesome and agreeable.[7]

It finally became evident that no plan would be satisfactory which failed to provide the following *desiderata*: —

1. The floods of Stony Brook to be carried off through the bay.
2. The exposure of muddy banks by falling water to be adequately guarded against.
3. A continuous embankment to be formed on the boundary of the city property, reducing and defining the outlines of the bay.
4. Streets to be made on the embankment.
5. At least two public streets, besides Commonwealth Avenue and Beacon Street, to be carried through the property, crossing the bay.
6. No important public thoroughfares already laid out approaching the bay to be interrupted, seriously diverted, or made less commodious.

7. A public promenade to be laid out which would include a commodious and well-appointed pleasure drive and walk, and a pad, or stretch of soft riding-way, for speeding saddlehorses without danger of collisions.

8. This promenade to be on that side of the city property nearest to Huntington and West Chester Park Avenues, and readily entered from them, and also to be agreeably connected with the existing public promenade of Commonwealth Avenue, the contemplated Charles River Embankment, and the proposed parkway leading to Parker Hill and Jamaica Pond.[8]

9. All of the city property, which is not to be occupied by artificial constructions under the above requirements, to be so treated as to present an agreeable aspect, appropriate to a first-class residence neighborhood.

10. This aspect to be obtained without resort to costly methods of decoration, such as architectural terraces, pavilions, fountains and parterres.

11. Arrangements which would call for large future outlays, for repair and maintenance, or for guarding against accidents, to be avoided.

The plan now shown is designed to meet these requirements, as follows:—

Muddy River is to be diverted as originally proposed.[9] (There are no legal difficulties about it, and the operation will not be very costly).

A covered conduit is to be formed within and near the south-eastern boundary of the property, by which the waters of Stony Brook, when at an ordinary stage and when the tide is not above ordinary high-water level in Charles River, will be discharged. When the tide rises above the outlet of this conduit it is to be self-closing.

A basin is to be formed into which the waters of Stony Brook will flow whenever the mouth of the conduit is closed, and in which they will be held until the tide falls again below the outlet of the conduit.

Within this basin there is to be a body of water nearly thirty acres in extent, with outlines, as shown in the drawing resembling those of a salt-creek with coves. This will be tide-water but with no more ebb and flow than is necessary to avoid stagnation, the efflux and reflux being regulated by a self-acting water-gate[10] the position of which is shown on the extreme right of the drawing. Its surface elevation, under ordinary circumstances, is to correspond with that of Charles River at mean high-water.

There will also be within the basin a body of level land of nearly equal extent with the water, having an elevation a few inches higher.

When freshets occur in Stony Brook coincidentally with easterly winds and spring tides, which would temporarily prevent an outflow into Charles River, the water of the brook is to be turned into the basin, and the creek, rising, will overflow this level ground. Usually such an occurrence would be anticipated and, by drawing down the water of the creek at the preceding ebb of the tide, a rise of more than a foot above the ordinary level avoided. Having, when at this height, a surface of fifty-two acres to spread over, a rise of more than four feet, by reason of floods of Stony Brook, will not be likely to occur under the most unfavorable circumstances. Even should special precautions be neglected, it will not probably happen more than once in ten years, nor will the water ever be liable to stand more than two feet above the ordinary level longer than two hours at a time. As the lighter fresh water will not at once mingle perfectly with the salt, when the body of water is more than two feet above its ordinary level, there will be an upper stratum of but moderately brackish water.

This ground designed to be occasionally overflowed is to be formed of marsh mud, with a superficial coating of sand or light gravelly loam, through which salt sedges and grasses may grow. Besides the more common vegetation of salt-marshes, there is a considerable variety of perennials to which an occasional wash of brackish water does no harm. There is also a range of shrubs, including beach-plums, berberries, candleberries, cydonias, tamarisks and the sea-buckthorn.

Such shrubs and plants are to be grown along the foot of the slope on the margin of the basin, and on the small points and islets by which, as will be observed on the drawing, the level ground is here and there broken.

The wind having nowhere a long sweep upon the water, and the rushy vegetation acting to check its movement, there will be no swell of importance, and no spray will be thrown beyond these marginal plantations, and immediately above them any desirable trees and shrubs may be safely grown.

Just what can be accomplished on the level ground may be regarded as doubtful, but it is believed that, at the worst, it may in a few years be mantled with sedges, rushes, and salt-grasses, with slashes of such golden-rods and asters as are now found in profusion on the tidal banks of the Charles and the salt-marshes at the head of the bay.

The plan, so far as the chief difficulty to be dealt with is concerned, has thus been sufficiently explained. The vital question about this element of it is, whether the conditions to result would be unfavorable to the health of adjoining parts of the city? Upon this question you have called in consultation Dr. Folsom, of the State Board of Health,[11] who has confirmed the opinion that so far as the proposed body of salt water, and the salt vegetation within the basin, would have any influence upon the air of the neighborhood, that influence would be purifying and salutary, and that the occasional floods of fresh water, being rapidly drained off, would be harmless. The conditions would be more rather than less favorable to the health of the neighborhood than those of an ordinary park.

As to the secondary question, of the fit aspect of the result, it may be confidently anticipated that, under judicious detailed treatment, the several broader constituents which have been named—the waving fenny verdure, meandering water, the blooming islets, and the border of trees and underwood following the varied slope of the rim of the basin, like the hanging woods of a winding river-bank—would dispose themselves in compositions of a pleasing character.

The effect would be novel, certainly, in labored urban grounds,[12] and there may be a momentary question of its dignity and appropriateness; but this question will, I think, be satisfactorily answered when it is reflected that it represents no affectation or caprice of taste, but is a direct development of the original conditions of the locality in adaptation to the needs of a dense community. So regarded, it will be found to be, in the artistic sense of the word, natural, and possibly to suggest a modest poetic sentiment more grateful to town-weary minds than an elaborate and elegant garden-like work would have yielded.

It is doubtless true that to many the predominant associations of a sea-coast marsh are dreary; but this is probably due in the main to circumstances which would not be found on the Back Bay when improved as proposed and built about. They belong, that is to say, to marsh scenes in which there is a great extent of low, damp and bleak ground, with creeks and sloughs barring passage across it. The tints, lights and shadows and movement of salt-marsh vegetation when seen in close connection with upland scenery, are nearly always pleasing, and sometimes charming.

(The right bank of Muddy River, on the reach below Longwood bridge, illustrates the character of the slopes and plantations which I should think well to have in view in forming the margin of the basin, and the brackish swamp nearer Brookline[13] will give a suggestion of what may be hoped for on the ground to be subject to flooding. This swamp is a neglected and ill-used waste, but it has at times remarkable beauties.)

I think that it may be justly added that public taste has been lately drifting toward a better appreciation of quaintness and subdued picturesqueness in scenery, and that this circumstance is favorable to the ultimate popularity of what is likely to grow out of the plan.

It may still be questioned whether the bay would not be too much wanting in attractions of popular interest for a public property so near the heart of a city. A larger part of the value of public grounds of the smaller class lies in the pleasure which children find in them, and in that education of the observing powers which cannot be obtained in the nursery or the school-room.

One element of value in this respect may be used more largely and brought to a higher degree of perfection in the Back Bay, as proposed to be revised, than it has been or can be with advantage in any public park in the world; I mean that of birds, and especially of water-fowl. The rushy glades and bushy islands will supply well-guarded seclusions in which they can breed; the extent of quiet water and of shores, and the character of the vegetation upon them, will allow large numbers and a great variety to be taken all necessary care of with little trouble or expense. While well protected, there will be convenient opportunities for observing them closely and for visitors to feed them.

The collection of water-birds should not be confined, as it usually has been in parks, to a few sorts of swans, ducks, and geese, but include as many varieties of these as practicable, and also pelicans, cormorants, cranes, and other waders, and fishers.

The bay would be too warm for deep-sea fishes, but it could doubtless be made to swarm with other sorts of interesting salt-water life.[14]

The necessary narrowness of the water at certain points and its crookedness would prevent the bay from being used by the public in row-boats or sail-boats without too great liability to collisions and disorders. The plan has, therefore, been studied with reference to a regular service of small pleasure packets, moved by compressed-air engines, or, if that should not prove practicable, by steam, and specially adapted to the circumstances. This would avoid the evils sure to result from the movements of irresponsible boatmen out of view of the police, and such injury as would occur to the shores and water-fowl from the careless or unskilful use of oars. It would admit of the enjoyment of boating by children or timid persons with a sense of security and a degree of convenience not otherwise practicable, and the service might be expected to be popular and a source of income. The entire length of shore is to be about four miles, and the boating tour of the bay about three miles, making an excursion of half an hour. But a direct line of small omnibus-boats could be run between the Back Bay station of the Albany Railroad at Commonwealth Avenue and the most distant landing (which is four hundred yards from Chapel station, Longwood), on a course of a mile and a quarter, in ten or twelve minutes.[15]

The requirement of the promenade is met as shown on the lower part of the drawing.[16] It includes a walk twenty-five to forty feet wide, a drive forty feet, and a riding pad twenty-five feet. These are carried side by side for a distance of three-quarters of a mile, and are subject to crossing in that space but once, one transverse wheelway being indispensible under the fifth requirement. A sub-crossing is provided by which visitors can obtain access from Westland Avenue to the walk on the water side, without interrupting the movement of carriages and horsemen. There is a stretch of riding-way, without crossing, nearly half a mile (2,300 feet) in length.

The grade of the promenade is nearly level, and its course at all points is slightly curving. The requirements of access from West Chester Parkway and Huntington Avenue are fully met.[17]

To connect the promenade with Commonwealth Avenue, it is necessary to pass over the Albany Railroad at an elevation fifteen feet higher than that of the avenue. One route for carriages will be as convenient as two; and a central route is to be avoided because, at the required elevation of the bridge, it would destroy breadth, unity, and openness of view through the opening. By going as far as possible to the north-west the easiest turn is obtained for carriages coming from the east.

Boylston Street is carried through the property with a curve which, for a short distance, combines it conveniently and economically with the approach from Commonwealth Avenue to the Promenade. Its grade must be lifted to carry it over the bridge; but the steepest inclination is but one foot in fifty, which is satisfactory with respect to the proposed horse-railroad.[18]

The requirements as to roads for crossing the bay is fully met, and with a little study of the drawing, attention being given to figures of grade, the motives governing the entire arrangement of roads and walks will be obvious. It needs only to be stated that the depth of mud and water on the proposed shore opposite the promenade is greater than elsewhere. (Solid bottom is not found within forty feet of the street grade.) Neither a broader roadway nor a shorewalk could, consequently, be introduced, except at considerable additional cost for embankment. It is believed also that the comparative quietude here proposed by the plan, with the bank of wood unbroken from the street to the shore, will, on the whole, be more satisfactory.

The enclosure and buildings shown on the Westland crossroad[19] are for administration purposes. They include storage, cart and tool sheds, repair shops, and winter quarters for water-fowl. Their walls are to be of brick, as low as practicable, and roofs of tile, and they are to be mainly overgrown with creepers.

The plan calls for no other buildings, except the necessary small gate and landing-houses, and for no construction simply for ornamental purposes. The landing-houses are designed to serve as shelters in case of sudden showers, and are so placed as to be readily accessible from all parts of the public ways. The landings will have the effect of terraces and balconies in connection with them. Except at a few points, where beaches are designed,[20] and others which will be made rocky, the shore at the water's edge is intended to have a long, sedgy slope, and the necessity of pitching or curbing to be avoided. It would be generally overhung by foliage, and its character entirely natural.

The Boylston-Street bridge will necessarilly be nearly as high as that crossing the railroad, and twenty-three feet above the water. This elevation will give it a commanding view over the fens on one side, over Charles River on the other, and its arch will be the frame of a quiet, distant, rural scene from the bridge on Commonwealth Avenue, which, to make the most of this opportunity, should have no greater height than is necessary. The Boylston-Street bridge will be the most conspicuous object on the bay and its architecture should be studiously appropriate to the circumstances.

There being no turf to be kept under the scythe, except narrow strips on the margins of the roads, no flower-beds or exotic planting, the waters ordinarily self-regulating, the public ways subject to little wash, and no secluded paths, the police, repair, and maintenance of the grounds will be simple and inexpensive.

Since the action, a few days since, of the City Council, extending Commonwealth Avenue upon a line diverging from its original course,[21] you have asked me to consider the feasibility of adopting a new plan in that part of this important public promenade remaining to be laid out.

The principal reasons for proposing a change I understand to be that a continuous production of the same formal plan would be tiresome; that the central walk is, during much of the year, useless; the public, in winter, crowding to the north sidewalk for the sake of its sunshine and the lee of the houses, in the heat of summer to the south sidewalk because more densely shaded.

The disadvantage of doing away with the central feature and substituting, as some have proposed, a single wheelway for the two of the present arrangement, with a broad turf border on each side, is that the turf must be cut into petty plats, in order to give access by walks to the houses facing the avenue; and that the distance between the curb and house door (85 feet) would be excessive. Any plan to accomplish the purposes in view satisfactorily must, in my judgment, be much more radically different from the old one.

I suggest that a broad public drive be so laid out as to leave room for a walk of but moderate width on the north side, access to houses on the south side being provided for by a narrow wheelway; a broad walk to follow the main drive, and a narrow walk the side drive, both on the south side. A space equivalent to that of the two green strips of the present arrangement would remain between the main and the side drive to be turfed and planted, and there would be a row of trees between the broad walk and the adjoining drive. The main drive and walk would then be shaded in summer; there would be a winter promenade in the lee of the houses on the north side, unshaded; and the houses on both sides would be within convenient distance of a carriage-way.

As shown on the drawing, the suggestion offers the further advantage of terminating the vistas of the straight avenue with borders of foliage, of easing the turns from West Chester Parkway into the avenue, and of providing a graceful transition from the formality of the straight avenue to the more picturesque and natural conditions of the Back Bay.

Respectfully submitted,

FREDERICK LAW OLMSTED,
Landscape Architect Advisory.

The text presented here is from BCDP, City of Boston, *Fifth Annual Report, for the Year 1880* (City Doc. No. 15) [Boston, 1881], pages 6–16.

1. The city engineer was Joseph P. Davis.
2. In 1837 a group of amateur horticulturists proposed to use the partially filled site adjoining Boston Common on the west for a public botanic garden. In 1856 the city acquired clear legal title to the site, beginning a process that led to laying out the grounds as a public garden in 1859–60 (C. Zaitzevsky, *Olmsted and the Boston Park System*, pp. 15, 33–34).
3. The commissioners' plan of 1876 contemplated a "Back Bay Park" with lagoons and carriage drives, and in 1878 they had held a design competition for a park on the land that they had acquired for that purpose (BCDP, City of Boston, *Second Report* (City Doc. No. 42) [Boston, 1876], pp. 19–22).
4. Stony Brook had a drainage area of some twelve square miles, primarily in West Roxbury and Dorchester (CharlesW. Folsom, "The Surface-Drainage of the Metropolitan District," Massachusetts. State Board of Health, *Seventh Annual Report*, [Jan. 1876], p. 511).
5. The authorization by the City Council on July 23, 1877, of expenditure of $450,000 for land for the Back Bay park stipulated that the park commissioners must purchase at least one hundred acres within a described area, and that the purchase price should not exceed ten cents per square foot (BCDP, City of Boston, *Sixth Report* (City Doc. No. 104) [Boston, 1877], p. 1).
6. A reference to the design competition held by the park commissioners in 1878. The official reason they gave for not using any of the competition entries, however, was not that their cost of maintenance would be prohibitive but rather that none adequately addressed the problems of handling floodwaters from Muddy River and Stony Brook. (see above, p. 365, n.1)
7. For a further description of Olmsted's development of his plan, see FLO, "Paper on the {Back Bay} Problem and its Solution Read Before the Boston Society of Architects," *Papers of FLO*, SS1: 442–48.
8. West Chester Park Avenue is now called Massachusetts Avenue. For the parkway to Parker Hill and Jamaica Pond, which the park commissioners had included in their plan of 1876, see City of Boston, Park Department, "Back Bay and Parker Hill Parks, Parker Hill & Jamaica Parkways" (BCDP, City of Boston, *Second Report* (City Doc. No. 42) [Boston, 1876]).
9. Perhaps a reference to chapter 267 of the year 1872, in which the state legislature empowered Brookline and Boston "to divert the waters of Muddy River so as to make them flow in a more direct line to the Charles River." In early 1878 the park commissioners made it clear that they would insist that Muddy River be diverted to the Charles River by a conduit west of Brookline Avenue (City of Boston, *Reports of Proceedings of the City Council of Boston, for the Municipal Year 1878* [Boston, 1879], pp. 95).

10. For the self-acting gate mechanisms for controlling water flow into the Back Bay Fens, see Edward Willard Howe, "The Back Bay Park, Boston," in *Proceedings of the Boston Society of Civil Engineers*, [Boston, 1881], pp. 130–32.
11. The physician Charles Follen Folsom, a specialist in hygiene and mental diseases, at this time the secretary of the Massachusetts state board of health (NCAB, 19: 375).
12. By this phrase, Olmsted presumably means in public recreation grounds that, like the Boston Public Garden, required expensive and labor-intensive maintenance for their decorative floral displays.
13. That is, the section of the Muddy River between Longwood Avenue and Tremont Street.
14. Olmsted hoped to amass in the Back Bay Fens a collection of "small whales, porpoises, dolphins, narwhals or other cetaceous mammals, flying fish, bonita, sturgeons, or other fish that would make some display under the circumstances." In 1871 Olmsted and Vaux had proposed to design islands in the lagoons of the Chicago South Park so as to provide safe breeding places for a variety of birds, and he was to make a similar proposal for the South Park of Buffalo (not constructed) that he proposed in 1888 (FLO to A. E. Verrill, Feb. 8, 1879; see *Papers of FLO*, SS1: 227, 585–86).
15. Olmsted's plan for the Back Bay Fens of 1879 shows six boat landings, the one most distant from Commonwealth Avenue being at the "water gate" at Brookline Avenue. Both stations referred to were on the line of the Boston and Albany Railroad.
16. That is, the separate promenade routes for pedestrians, equestrians, and carriages that ran along the eastern edge of the Fens from Boylston Street to Ruggles Street.
17. The Common Council's authorization of July 1877 stipulated that the land acquired should include approaches to the park from Beacon Street west of Chester Park, the extension of Boylston street west from Chester Park, and from Huntington Avenue extended (BCDP, City of Boston, *Sixth Report* (City Doc. No. 104) [Boston, 1877], p. 1).
18. The plan shows the tracks of the proposed horse-car railway running along Boylston Street.
19. That is, the drive crossing the Fens from Westland Street that came to be called Agassiz Road.
20. Olmsted planned four beach areas on the eastern side of the Fens—one between the Boston and Albany Railroad bridge and Boylston Street bridge, and three between Agassiz Road and the Huntington Entrance near the Stony Brook water gate. The beaches had direct access from paths and provided a gradually shelving surface that extended a sufficient distance into the water to make them safe for wading.
21. On December 26, 1879, after a considerable period of debate and input from interested citizens, the Boston Common Council authorized the borrowing of funds to extend Commonwealth Avenue from Chester Park Way to Beacon Street in accordance with plans approved by the Street Commissioners in 1878 that called for Commonwealth Avenue to angle in a northerly direction in order to intersect with Beacon Street instead of extending in a straight line as earlier intended (City of Boston, *Reports of Proceedings of the City Council of Boston, for the Municipal Year 1879* [Boston, 1880], p. 731).

To Barthold S. Schlesinger[1]

Mr Schlesinger.

9th Feby 1880.

Dear Mr Schlesinger:
I have recvd yours of 7th & the plans.[2]
Be so good as to remember that when you first did me the honor to ask my counsel you said that you did not want me to make a plan for your grounds but only to advise you upon the question of house site and a possible division of the property. This I have done and I doubt whether, as I am only occasionally in Boston, it would be worth your while to employ me to make plans and give you advice as to details in a situation of such difficulty. In truth I do not feel much inclined to be the responsible planner of your grounds partly because I think that whoever plans them ought to direct the work more closely than I probably should be able to, and partly because I do not feel that you and Mrs Schlesinger[3] would be quite satisfied with what I should be moved to aim at.

It is true that I have already gone beyond your first commission and made several sketch plans but I did this only because I could not otherwise fully state my views of the question of site. Further than was necessary for this purpose my planning did not go. I had to say: "Here is a site which I can recommend, provided you are willing to accept such and such an arrangment of approaches &c. as this or even such as this other." Thus I put before you several alternatives. If I failed to make my opinion plain to you it was because you seemed to be ready to accept the conditions which, as to one of these sites, I had in view. Your present letter, however, leads me to think that you do not accept the conditions as they lie in my mind; in which case I must take care that you do not accept the site as upon my recommendation. What I should have said before had I not thought you agreed with me, I must say now, namely that the Amory property does not contain a site suitable for such a house as you contemplate unless you are willing to put up with some conditions which many people would regard as eccentric, queer and unsuitable to be associated with so fine a house as you mean to have but which I should hope would carry their own justification and therefore simply secure an individuality of character appropriate to the house. This being, however, a matter in a certain degree of personal tastes and habits, it is one which you should decide with your eyes open.[4]

The question is of the general ideal to be had in view.
This Amory site has a certain poetic character as it stands, more or less obscure and more or less mangled by the buildings, roads, fences, planted trees, &c. What you are to do will either result in pretty well destroying it and

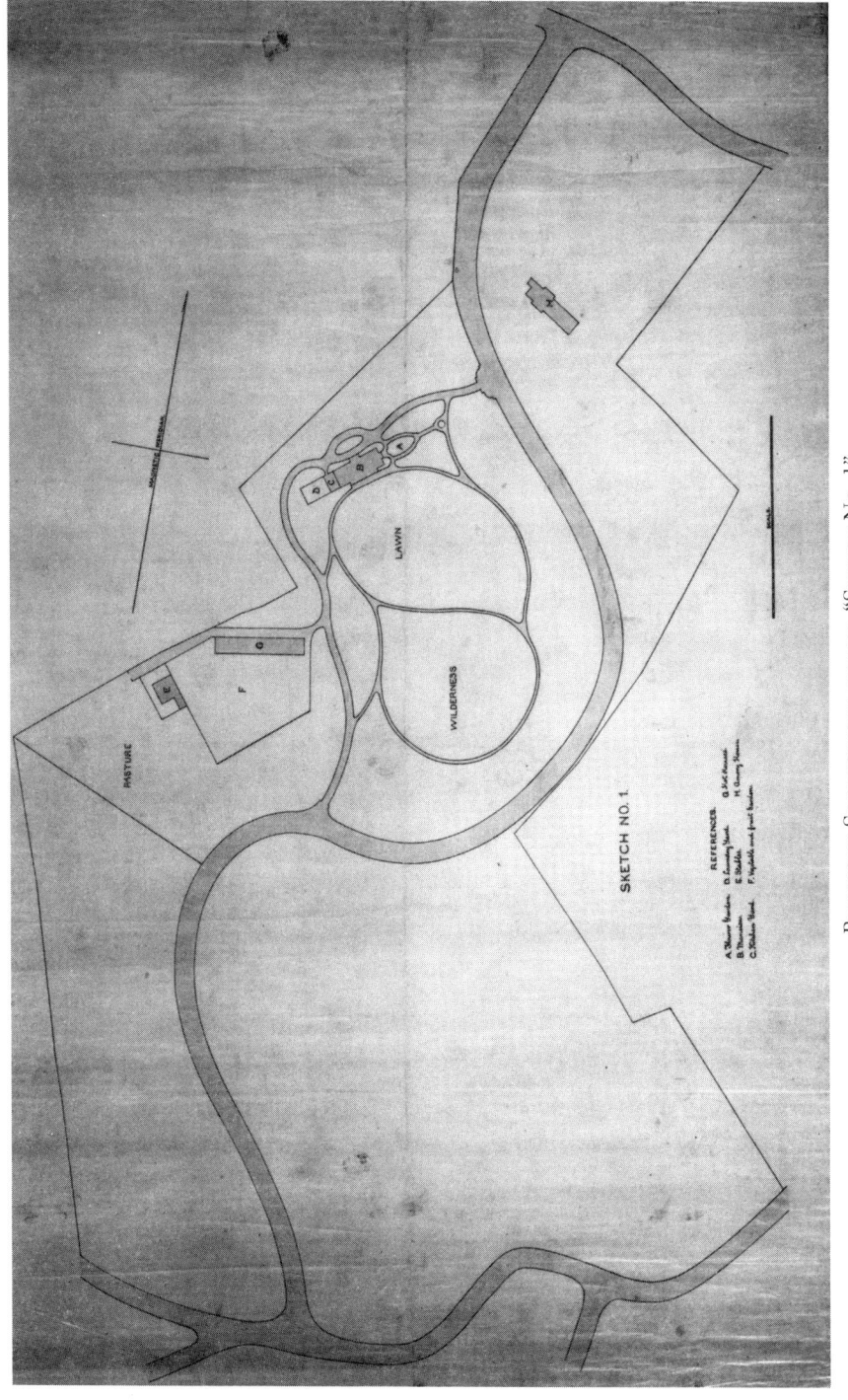

Barthold Schlesinger estate, "Sketch No. 1"

substituting another character, or in unveiling and developing it in a much higher degree.[5]

I have not a spark of the sentimentalism which would prevent me from adopting the first course if I thought I could get on the whole a more satisfactory result—satisfactory as to convenience, health and beauty. But I have very maturely considered the question and I do not think so.

The question with me, therefore, as to your suggestions of varying from my plan, is what way do they tend? To a better recovery and development of the old poem of the place or to putting it away and composing a new one?[6]

Of course you see certain small difficulties in the way of what you would like. You may understand better what I mean—it is not easy to explain—if you suppose these difficulties to be all just a little greater.

Imagine the highway a little more on a hill side and a little more crooked, the descent from it into the place a little steeper, the valley a little deeper, the hill of the house a little higher, its slope a little sharper, the distance between the boundaries a little less, the space available for a house and lawn a little more contracted and the neighbors a little nearer. Give a few minutes practical study to the question where you would enter, under these circumstances; where you would carry your road and at what grades; where you would place your kitchen, your stable and all your dependencies; how you would grade about your house and what general landscape quality you would aim at. Do this and you will find I suspect, that you would come to my conclusion, either to abandon your building altogether upon this site or else to abandon making the place one of such a character as you are now inclined to. If so, this shows that it is only necessary that the objections that I feel to what you propose should be a little more obvious to be conclusive to you also. And this again proves that what you are trying to do if not quite bad is hardly good. Now the dishing and garnishing (if you take so very poor a view of the outside part of your proposed home) of such a house ought to be more than hardly good. It should be perfectly excellent *of its kind*.

You may recall houses built in situations of like but greater difficulties, more cramped and rocky and crooked, as on little seacoast promontories about which you have found a peculiar charm.[7] Why? Largely because all the arrangments in such a case were compelled to be what they are by the difficulties of the topography. What would elsewhere be a defect becomes under such circumstances, a merit, and each adds to the general quaint fitness of the artificial to the natural.

Now, although your ground only approaches in character to such a situation it is too much like it to be dealt with on a different principle.[8] Adopt that principle and an admirable result is possible. Undertake to smooth down and bridge over the difficulties, as for instance by a more direct descent into the valley,[9] by forcing a back road, by long indirect communications between your kitchen and your stables and by aiming at a dress ground or "front yard" character between the rear of your house and the highway and you could hardly fail to emphasize all the natural disadvantages of the situation. Everything would have a certain awkwardness. At best, as it seems to me, you would attain only to a respectable common place character.

If I state it too strongly it is to make the difference between what I should be *inclined* to and what you, I think, are *inclined* to more obvious.[10]

I will even confess that I almost think Mrs Schlesinger's old quarrel with the green-house an unfortunate one.[11] I feel that the green house was put where it is for a good reason in the natural circumstances. This reason remains; it is obvious and it not only qualifies and compensates for the blemish but to my mind makes it a beauty — at least a picturesqueness which if it were gone I should miss.[12]

Again, if I found the place with a square entrance like Mr Sargent's[13] near the middle of its front I would, if needed at great expense, abolish it & get a corner entrance with a long easy sweep toward the house as suggested in my drawing,[14] and if I were willing to spend more on the improvemnt of this entrance & approach I would apply it to making the occasion for an entrance so far different from what is commonly looked for, *more decided*, by banks, retaining-walls and the planting of rocks and large trees in that part of the ground where a more common sort of entrance might possibly be otherwise forced in. I would make it appear that no more had been done than was necessary to obtain access in the easiest way from the public road across an interposing valley to a fine situation upon a neighboring height. There should not be a suspicion of effort about it for anything but convenience. If there were well grown Norway Spruces on this part of the ground I would fell them because in such a place they would be fussy and destroy the unsophisticated character at which I should be aiming.

If the kitchen end of the house must be to the Eastward, (which, if there is a chance of your getting some of the White property, I think more than ever a mistake), I should prefer to let the stable be seen (barely seen) between the house and the main road, primarily because it would be the most convenient situation but partly also because it would help to make sure that the place would not be judged by ordinary standards—that it would appear to be a law to itself.[15] Also because it would a little suggest that the house was not built because of what was between it & the highway, {and that the ground passed through was not a "front yard"}[16] but that the key of the whole arrangment was to be looked for on the other side of it — its domestic, not its public side.

Thus I would find in each of the difficulties of the situation not a difficulty but an advantage.

I have not meant to give definite advice upon any one of the points of your inquiry. Perhaps (except as to the Spruces) I should, upon more full consideration upon the ground see reasons for agreeing with you. I think not however, and at any rate all I have said is pertinent as to the question of the general scope of improvemnt to be attempted. If you should adopt my views you will be certain to hear much good natured remonstrance, be told that you are

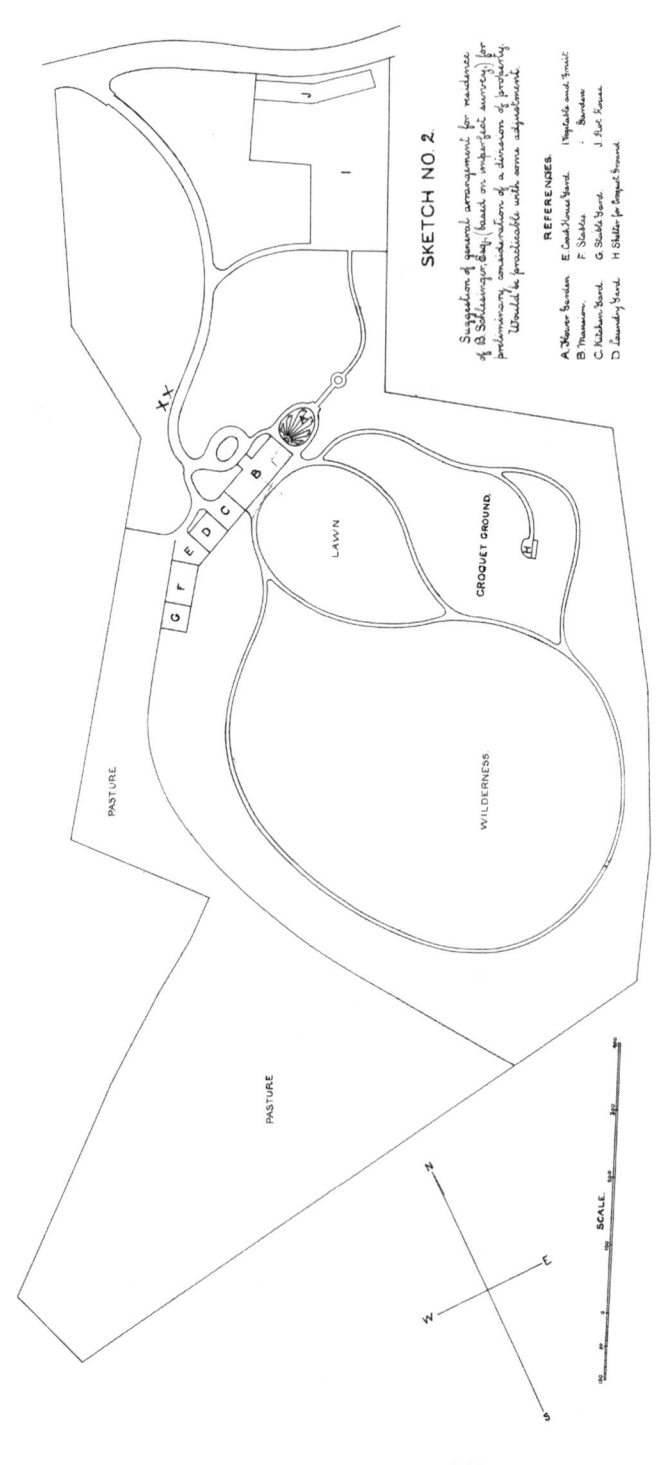

BARTHOLD SCHLESINGER ESTATE, "SKETCH NO. 2," SEPTEMBER 2, 1879

DECEMBER 1879–MAY 1880

transgressing receivd rules of landscape gardening and oftimes be tempted to insipid compromises. Nor can I honestly say that I think that you would save a great deal in outlay. To do well what is unusual is always costly and if you try to overleap common standards you must expect to use spur and whip more than on the beaten track. In aiming at less than would commonly be thought appropriate to so fine a house you must be sure of success in what you undertake at whatever cost.[17]

I am sure that you and Mrs Schlesinger, to whom I beg to be most respectfully remembered, however little you may like what I have said, will not fail to appreciate the friendly object of this long letter and will believe me
Always faithfully Yours

The text presented here is a fragmentary draft in Olmsted's hand that appears, by editorial indications of paragraphing and capitalization, to be the version he had ready for a copyist to transcribe into fair copy. It is located on reel 17, frames 503–26 in the microfilm edition of the Frederick Law Olmsted Papers in the Manuscript Division of the Library of Congress. The editors have used all the text that Olmsted wrote and did not then delete. We have used endnotes to describe and present deleted passages that he did not incorporate at another place in the text. Most of these significant deleted sections occur at transition points where Olmsted revised the text by changing his wording or the direction of his argument in order to soften the tone of his opposition to his clients' preferences. These deletions were not included in the version of the text prepared by Frederick Law Olmsted, Jr., and Theodora Kimball in the 1920s that is in the Olmsted Papers collection. That version contains no material not found in the existing manuscript, which indicates that no pages of the manuscript have been lost in the intervening years. The present editors, after considering a number of possible arrangements of the text, have followed the order of the text as arranged by Olmsted and Kimball.

1. Barthold S. Schlesinger (1828–1900), a wealthy Boston businessman and real estate investor, asked Olmsted in August 1879 to advise him on the siting of a new house and the division of fifty acres he had just purchased from the Amory and Ellis families in Brookline, Massachusetts. Olmsted visited the property that month and found that its variable topography and contracted limits made it difficult to create broad landscape compositions. In addition, he felt that the house that the architect George E. Harney had already designed for Schlesinger was too large and ornate for the property. In early September 1879 Olmsted presented plans for two alternative arrangements. Of these he preferred the plan that placed the house on the former Amory property atop the only long, southward-facing slope available, with a curving approach road on the opposite side of the house. Olmsted apparently assumed that Schlesinger accepted his proposed arrangement until he received the letter to which he responds in the text presented here. (*Boston Evening Transcript*, July 14, 1900, p. 4; Barthold S. Schlesinger to FLO, Aug. 13, 1879, B63: #614, OAR/LC; FLO to Barthold S. Schlesinger, Sept. 2, 1879; John Nolen, "Frederick Law Olmsted and His Work, III: The Schlesinger Place, Brookline, Mass.," *House and Garden* 9 [1906]: 217–22).

2. Schlesinger's letter of February 7 has not survived. In it he apparently inquired whether Olmsted would provide a landscape design for his estate and superintend its execution. Olmsted's response indicates that Schlesinger contemplated departing from the general plan that Olmsted had provided him in September 1879, particularly

in reference to the drives through the property and its overall landscape character. The plans to which Olmsted refers that he had received from Schlesinger may have been topographical or drainage plans prepared by George E. Waring, Jr., or plans for the house itself by architect George E. Harney (Barthold S. Schlesinger to FLO, Aug. 13, 1879, B63, #614, OAR/LC; George E. Harney to FLO, Sept. 13, 1879; ibid., Oct. 2, 1879).
3. Mary McBurney Schlesinger (1836–1924), in later years a noted suffragette, took an active role with her husband in deciding how their property was to be arranged (*Boston Evening Transcript*, Oct. 20, 1924, p. 20).
4. At this point Olmsted wrote, revised, and then deleted the following sentence: "I have only to repeat that if you don't take my view of these conditions, I really think you ought not to build on such a site but sell the property and seek a site better suited to your tastes elsewhere."
5. Olmsted here wrote, and then deleted, "So far as I studied a plan it was a plan to accomplish the latter purpose."
6. In a deleted section of the draft of this letter, Olmsted considered the possibility that the Schlesingers would decide that they valued what they would lose by Olmsted's plan more than they valued what they would gain. "Then, I repeat," he countered, "it seems to me that you make a mistake in building at all upon such a site because what you value is not to be had upon it *except in a moderate way at immoderate cost.*"
7. Schlesinger had a summer place at Nahant, a small resort town located on a promontory jutting into Massachusetts Bay north of Boston (Louis M. Babcock, ed., *Our American Resorts* [Washington, D.C., 1883], p. 104; FLO to Barthold S. Schlesinger, June 17, 1881, below).
8. At this point Olmsted wrote and then deleted the following passage:

    All your aim is to tame it, and make it go in common harness. You can't do it with any tolerable success. You will destroy its qualities & picturesqueness and not obtain the well dressed drawing room quality you seek.

9. Olmsted's first version of this clause, which he deleted, indicates something of Schlesinger's intent regarding the entrance drive: "as for instance by making a square entrance and direct descent into the valley...."
10. At this point Olmsted wrote and then deleted the following passage: "You can say you prefer the commoner path as the path of safety. And I admit that I should have some anxiety for the result if you took my advice against your own convictions." The abrupt transition between this and the following paragraph, which begins at the top of a new sheet, indicates the possibility of missing material at this point.
11. Here Olmsted first wrote "Mrs Schlesinger's child-" and then crossed out the last word, indicating that he had begun to write "child-like quarrel," but then softened the statement.
12. Concerning the greenhouse and perhaps other outbuildings, Olmsted wrote and then deleted the following passage: "They were put there for a good reason existing in the natural circumstances. If they were to burn down I would rebuild them just there and possibly of much the same character as at present."
13. Olmsted is probably referring to Holm Lea, the country estate of Charles Sprague Sargent, located in Brookline near the Schlesinger property
14. See Sketch no. 2.
15. The proposed location of the Schlesinger house was close to the east side of the property and to land owned by F. A. White. Olmsted's preliminary sketches had placed the kitchen, kitchen yard, and stables on the west side of the house. Ultimately, Schlesinger had them placed on the east side (Plan 614–22 ["Sketch No. 1"] and plan 614–13 ["Sketch No. 2," Sept. 2, 1879], NPS/FLONHS.

16. Olmsted deleted the words in braces.
17. In May 1880 Olmsted agreed to plan the grounds of the Schlesinger estate and with John Charles Olmsted's assistance worked on the project through 1881. In the months following the present letter, he debated with Schlesinger on the location of the main approach road to the house, an element he considered to be "the most important and most permanent of controllable features." He prevailed in the final choice of location, but in 1881 found Schlesinger opposed to his proposal to use an architectural terrace to ease the transition between the house and the grounds (FLO to Barthold S. Schlesinger, May 8, 1880; ibid., Aug. 12, 1880; ibid., Dec. 12, 1880; John Charles Olmsted to Mary Schlesinger, July 8, 1904, B63: #614, OAR/LC; FLO to Barthold S. Schlesinger, June 17, 1881, below).

To Charles Eliot Norton

209 W. 46th St. NYork
15th Feby 1880.

My Dear Norton;

Since I last wrote I have placed copies of the Niagara Memorial at three Club Houses and have a man taking signatures at Buffalo and Montreal. I shall have them all in a few days. Next week I shall want to print & present it. But in what order? Its as puzzling as an English dinner. I state the puzzle not expecting you to help me but shall be very glad if you do. It seems to me that the Englishmen, as guests should come first, but if so, must not we put Carlyle & Ruskin first? Is it expedient to give the demagogues & ranters such an opportunity as this would offer — quoting the ugly sayings of these men about us?[1]

Then, on our side, I am inclined to put Church, the artist, first, because he was the first, as far as I know, to advance the proposition & I believed he brought it before Lord Dufferin.[2] But then — Emerson & Longfellow to come after? And the Vice President, Supreme Court, Senators, Bishops, where are they? I expect even the Cardinal![3]

Can I resolve it by the Alphabet? If so shall I jump as the alphabet requires from Oxford to Buffalo, Buffalo to Caribou & Caribou to Washington?

Finally, shall I attempt to give each or any man his proper tail? Shall I write "*Lord* Houghton." (He signs "Houghton-Tipton (?) Hall."[4] "B. Jowett", adds "*Master of Baliol & Reg. Profr of Greek at the University of Oxford.*" But few do so. If I do anything of the kind, I shall need to have you go over the list. Gov. Seymour & others of the Comsn[5] are afraid. They must not be made responsible for anything which can be thought extravagant or opposed to Democratic instincts. Dorsheimer made a draught which he thought they would come to and has allowed me to add a good deal to it. As thus amended it is a good starting point & I have two signatures to lead off with. Probably Seymour will want to cut out a part.[6]

I have not much confidence of success because nobody at Albany is interested but it would be shameful not to do all we well can. I wonder if your Nation came to you all cock-abill.[7] Ours did & it seemed to me that it must have gone through an edition. I have not dared to ask Godkin. He is still stranded with boils and I fear regards all of us who are not as frivolous creatures.

I felt that I was rather weak in being drawn into St. Botolph.[8] (I am pining for the lives of the Saints) but I saw it might in a pinch serve to define my ecclesiastical position and as my business lies now more in Boston than N.York, I might soon prefer to drop the Century. I was finally comforted when I saw your name.

Yours affectly

Fred^k Law Olmsted.

The text presented here is from a manuscript in Olmsted's hand in the Charles Eliot Norton Papers, Houghton Library, Harvard University, Cambridge, Massachusetts.

1. Both Thomas Carlyle and John Ruskin had published statements critical of American society. In his *Latter-Day Pamphlets*, Carlyle had asserted that Americans had as yet accomplished nothing great or noble of their own. Their one notable achievement was that "They have begotten, with a rapidity beyond recorded example, Eighteen Millions of the greatest *bores* ever seen in this world before: — that, hitherto, is their feat in History!" In his "Essays on Political Economy," John Ruskin provided a litany of the qualities of American life: "Lust of wealth, and trust in it; vulgar faith in magnitude and multitude, instead of nobleness; . . . total ignorance of the finer and higher arts, and of all that they teach and bestow . . ." (Thomas Carlyle, *Latter-Day Pamphlets* [Boston, 1855], p. 27; John Ruskin, "Essays on Political Economy," *Fraser's Magazine for Town and Country* [1863] 67: 447).
2. The landscape painter Frederic Church, who Olmsted understood to have suggested creation of a public reservation at Niagara sometime in the 1860s, and who c. 1878 proposed creation of an international reservation there to Frederick Temple Blackwood, the Earl of Dufferin, Governor General of Canada. In the Niagara Memorial as finally issued in the spring of 1880, Church's name is simply listed with those of other private citizens of the United States and Canada (*New York World*, April 1, 1880, p. 4; FLO to Thomas Welch, Feb. 16, 1889; C. Dow, *State Reservation at Niagara*, p. 12).
3. R. Waldo Emerson and Henry W. Longfellow were the first private United States citizens to be listed in the Memorial. Olmsted did secure the signature of John, Cardinal McCloskey, Archbishop of New York and those of eight bishops. Their names were scattered through the list (DAB).
4. Richard Monckton Milnes, First Baron Houghton (1809–1885), poet and man of letters, was the first British signer in the published list, appearing simply as "Houghton." He was the owner of Fryston Hall, near Leeds in Yorkshire. The eminent classicist

DECEMBER 1879–MAY 1880

Benjamin Jowett (1817–1893), master of Balliol College and Regius Professor of Greek at Oxford, was listed as "B. Jowett, University of Oxford." (James Pope-Hennessy, *Monckton Milnes: The Flight of Youth 1851–1885* [1951; rpt. ed., New York, 1955], pp. 108–11).

5. Horatio Seymour (1810–1886), governor of New York State in 1852–54 and 1862–64, and president of the State Survey (DAB).
6. The text of the printed "Memorial Addressed to the Governor of New York, and the Governor-General of Canada" was as follows:

> To Alonzo B. Cornell, Governor of the State of New York:
>
> The undersigned, citizens of several states and countries, address you by reason of the suggestion lately made by Lord Dufferin, that the State of New York, and the Dominion of Canada should secure and hold, for the world's good, the lands adjacent to the Falls of Niagara.
>
> The Falls of Niagara are peculiarly exposed to disastrous injury. The heights of snow, the precipitous crags of great mountains, however they may be disfigured by man, can rarely be applied to uses which would destroy their sublimity. But should the islands and declivities of the Niagara River be stripped of their natural woods, and occupied for manufacturing and business purposes; should even the position, size, and form of the constructions which the accommodations of visitors will call for, continue to be regulated solely by the pecuniary interests of numerous individual land-owners, the loss to the world will be great and irreparable. The danger may be measured by what has already occurred. The river's banks are denuded by the noble forest by which they were originally covered, are degraded by incongruous and unworthy structures, made, for advertising purposes, willfully conspicuous and obtrusive, and the visitor's attention is diverted from scenes to the influence of which he would gladly surrender himself, by demands for tolls and fees, and the offer of services most of which he would prefer to avoid.
>
> Objects of great natural beauty and grandeur are among the most valuable gifts which Providence has bestowed upon our race. The contemplation of them elevates and informs the human understanding. They are instruments of education. They conduce to the order of society. They address sentiments which are universal. They draw together men of all races, and thus contribute to the union and the peace of nations.
>
> The suggestion, therefore, that an object of this class so unparalleled as the Falls of Niagara should be placed under the joint guardianship of the two governments whose chief magistrates we have the honor to address, is a proper concern of the civilized world, and we respectfully ask that it may, by appropriate methods, be commended to the wise consideration of the Legislature of New York.
>
> A similar memorial has been addressed to the Governor-General of Canada.

(Charles Eliot Norton and Niagara Falls collection, Manuscript Division, Library of Congress, Washington, D.C.).

7. A nautical term meaning awry or not properly arranged (*OED*).
8. The St. Botolph Club, founded in Boston in 1879 on the model of the Century Club in New York City, to which Olmsted already belonged. Many of Boston's intellectual elite, including Charles Eliot Norton, were members of the club from its founding (Joseph Henry Curtis, *The St. Botolph Club: Its Birth and Early Club History* [Boston, Mass., 1880], pp. 1–8).

Special Report of New York State Survey on the Preservation of the Scenery of Niagara Falls, and Fourth Annual Report on the Triangulation of the State. For the Year 1879.

James T. Gardner, Director.

Notes by Mr. Olmsted.

[c. March 22, 1880]

The few notes which I propose to append to Mr. Gardener's report will be directed to a single point.

There are those, and I fear that most of the people of Niagara are among them, to whom it appears that the waterfall has so supreme an interest to the public that what happens to the adjoining scenery is of trifling consequence. Were all the trees cut away, quarries opened in the ledges, the banks packed with hotels and factories, and every chance-open space occupied by a circus tent, the Falls would still, these think, draw the world to them. Whatever has been done to the injury of the scenery has been done, say they, with the motive of profit, and the profit realized is the public's verdict of acquittal.

It must be considered, therefore, that the public has not had the case fairly before it. The great body of visitors to Niagara come as strangers. Their movements are necessarily controlled by the arrangements made for them. They take what is offered, and pay what is required with little exercise of choice. The fact that they accept the arrangements is no evidence of their approval.

The real question is, how, in the long run, is the general experience of visitors affected by measures and courses which are determined with no regard to the influence of the scenery?

I have myself been an occasional visitor at Niagara for forty-five years.[1] My attention was first called to the rapidly approaching ruin of its characteristic scenery by Mr. F. E. Church, about ten years ago.[2] Shortly afterwards, several gentlemen, frequenters of the Falls, met at my request, to consider this danger, one of them being a member of the Commission now reporting on the subject.[3] I have thus had both occasion and opportunity for observing the changed courses into which the public has been gradually led and of studying these courses and their results.

When the arrangements by which visitors were conducted were yet simple; when there were few carriages, and these little used; when a visit to the Falls was a series of expeditions, and in each expedition hours were occupied in wandering slowly among the trees, going from place to place, with many intervals of rest, there was not only a much greater degree of enjoyment, there was a different kind of enjoyment from any now generally obtained. People, then, were loth to leave the place; many lingered on from day to day after they had prepared to go, revisiting ground they had gone over before, turning and returning; and when they went away it was with grateful hearts and grateful words.

The change from this to what is described in the second section of the Commissioners' report[4] has been gradual and, while something must be attributed to modern ease of travel, a greater influx of visitors and to habits of quicker movement and greater restlessness; much must also be referred to the fact that visitors are so much more constrained to be guided and instructed, to be led and stopped, to be "put through," and so little left to natural and healthy individual intuitions.

The aim to make money by the showman's methods; the idea that Niagara is a spectacular and sensational exhibition, of which rope-walking, diving, brass bands, fireworks and various "side-shows" are appropriate accompaniments, is so presented to the visitor that he is forced to yield to it, and see and feel little else than that prescribed to him.

But all the time there are some who, because of better information and opportunities, and as the result of previous training, get the better of this difficulty, and to these the old charm remains. Take, as an illustration, the experience of the writer of the following passage. It is that of a man who has traveled extensively for the express purpose of observing scenery and comparing the value, as determined by the influence on the imagination, of different types of scenery. It is recorded in a little book which treats more especially of the scenery of the Alps and of what are designated "nature's gardens" among them.*

But says the author:

"The noblest of nature's gardens that I have yet seen is that of the surroundings and neighborhood of the Falls of Niagara. Grand as are the colossal falls, the rapids and the course of the river for a considerable distance above and below possess more interest and beauty.

"As the river courses far below the falls, confined between vast walls of rock—the clear water of a peculiar light-greenish hue, and white here and there with circlets of yet unsoothed foam—the effect is startlingly beautiful, quite apart from the falls. The high cliffs are crested with woods; the ruins of the great rock walls forming wide, irregular banks between them and the water, are also beautifully clothed with wood to the river's edge, often so far below that you sometimes look

*Alpine Flowers, by William Robinson, F.L.S. London: John Murray, 1875.

"Ideal View Up the American Rapids, after the Village Shore and Bath Island are Restored"

from the upper brink down on the top of tall pines that seem diminished in size. The wild vines scramble among the trees; many shrubs and flowers seam the high rocks; in moist spots, here and there a sharp eye may detect many flowered tufts of the beautiful fringed Gentian, strange to European eyes; and beyond all, and at the upper end of the wood-embowered deep river bed, a portion of the crowning glory of the scene — the falls — a vast cliff of illuminated foam, with a zone towards its upper edge as of green molten glass. Above the falls the scene is quite different. A wide and peaceful river carrying the surplus waters of an inland sea, till it gradually finds itself in the coils of the rapids, and is soon lashed into such a turmoil as we might expect if a dozen unpolluted Shannons or Seines were running a race together. A river no more, but a sea unreined. By walking about a mile above the falls on the Canadian shore this effect is finely seen, the breadth of the river helping to carry out the illusion. As the great waste of waters descends from its dark grey and smooth bed and falls whitening into foam, it seems as if tide after tide were gale-heaped one on another on a sea strand. The islands just above the falls enable one to stand in the midst of these rapids, where they rush by lashed into passionate haste; now boiling over some hidden swellings in the rocky bed, or dashing over greater but yet hidden obstructions with such force that the crest of the uplifted mass is dashed about as freely as a white charger's mane; now darkly falling into a cavity several yards below the level of the surrounding water, and, when unobstructed, surging by in countless eddies to the mist-crested falls below; and so rapidly that the driftwood dashes on swift as swallow on the wing. Undisturbed in their peaceful shadiness, garlanded with wild vine and wild flowers, the islands stand in the midst of all this fierce commotion of waters — below, the vast ever-mining falls; above, a complication of torrents that seem fitted to wear away iron shores; yet there they stand, safe as if the spirit of beauty had in mercy exempted them from decay. Several islets are so small that it is really remarkable how they support vegetation; one, looking no bigger than a washing-tub, not only holds its own in the very thick of the torrents just above the falls, but actually bears a small forest, including one stricken and half cast-down pine. Most fortunate is it that these beautifully verdant islands and islets occur just above the falls, adding immeasurably to the effect of the scene."[5]

I have spoken of the *distinctive* charms of Niagara scenery. If it were possible to have the same conditions detached from the falls (which it is not, as I shall show), Niagara would still be a place of singular fascination; possibly to some, upon whom the falls have a terrifying effect, even more so than it is now.

Saying nothing of the infinitely varied beauties of water and spray, and of water-worn rock, I will, for a purpose, mention a few elements which contribute to this distinctive charm.

The eminent English botanist, Sir Joseph Hooker, has said that he found upon Goat Island a greater variety of vegetation within a given space than anywhere in Europe, or east of the Sierras, in America; and the first of American botanists, Dr. Asa Gray, has repeated the statement.[6] I have followed the Apalachian chain almost from end to end, and traveled on horseback, "in search of the picturesque," over four thousand miles of the most promising parts of the continent[7] without finding elsewhere the same quality of forest beauty which was once abundant about the falls, and which is still to be observed in those parts of Goat Island where the original growth of trees and shrubs has not been disturbed, and where, from caving banks, trees are not now exposed to excessive dryness at the root.

Nor have I found anywhere else such tender effects of foliage as were once to be seen in the drapery hanging down the wall of rock on the American shore below the fall, and rolling up the slope below it, or with that still to be seen in a favorable season and under favorable lights, on the Canadian steeps and crags between the falls and the ferry.[8]

All these distinctive qualities,—the great variety of the indigenous perennials and annuals, the rare beauty of the old woods, and the exceeding loveliness of the rock foliage,—I believe to be a direct effect of the falls, and as much a part of its majesty as the mist-cloud and the rainbow.

They are all, as it appears to me, to be explained by the circumstance that at two periods of the year when the northern American forest elsewhere is liable to suffer actual constitutional depressions, that of Niagara is insured against like ills, and thus retains youthful luxuriance to an unusual age.

First, the masses of ice, which, every winter are piled to a great height below the falls, and the great rushing body of ice-cold water coming from the northern lakes in the spring, prevent at Niagara the hardship under which trees elsewhere often suffer through sudden checks to premature growth; and, second, when droughts elsewhere occur, as they do, every few years, of such severity that trees in full foliage droop and dwindle, and even sometimes cast their leaves, the atmosphere at Niagara is more or less moistened by the constantly evaporating spray of the falls, and in certain situations frequently bathed by drifting clouds of mist.

Something of the beauty of the hanging foliage below the falls is also probably due to the fact, that the effect of the frozen spray upon it is equivalent to the horticultural process of "shortening in;"[9] compelling a denser and closer growth than is, under other circumstances, natural.

Reference is made at page 9, of the Commissioners' report to a marvelous effect in scenery above the Falls.[10] It is that to which the following account by the Duke of Argyle applies:[11]

> The river Niagara, above the falls, runs in a channel very broad, and very little depressed below the general level of the country. But there is a steep declivity in the bed of the stream for a considerable distance above the precipice, and this constitutes what are called the rapids. The consequence is that when we stand at any point near the edge of the Falls, and look up the course of the stream, the foaming waters of the rapids constitute the sky line. No indication of land is visible — nothing to express the fact that we are looking at a river. The crests of the breakers, the leaping and the rushing of the waters, are still seen against the clouds, as they are seen in the ocean, when the ship from which we look is in the trough of the sea. It is impossible

to resist the effect on the imagination. It is as if the fountains of the great deep were being broken up, and that a new deluge were coming on the world. The impression is rather increased than diminished, by the perspective of the low wooded banks on either shore, running down to a vanishing point and seeming to be lost in the advancing waters. An apparently shoreless sea tumbling toward one is a very grand and a very awful sight. Forgetting, then, what one knows, and giving oneself to what one only sees, I do not know that there is anything in nature more majestic than the *view of the rapids*[12] above the falls of Niagara.

FREDERICK LAW OLMSTED.

These "notes" were published in the New York State Survey's report for 1879 following the report of the commissioners of the State Survey, and a report by the Director of the Survey, James T. Gardner. Gardner's report gave an extensive description, with accompanying photographs, of the "disfigured" condition of the banks of the American Rapids due to the presence of numerous commercial and industrial structures.

1. Olmsted first visited Niagara in 1828 at the age of six (*Papers of FLO*, 1: 391).
2. Olmsted later declared that "This is not an accurately true statement." In a letter in 1889 to Thomas V. Welch, a leader in the campaign for a Niagara reservation who became superintendent of the reservation after it was established, Olmsted went on to say:

    Mr Vaux had said that before the meeting at Cataract House in 1869, he had heard Mr Church talk at the Century Club of the injury which was occurring to the scenery. I do not think that I had ever heard a word from Mr Church, or from any other source of what he had said on the subject. But as I was a member of the Century, (though not a frequenter of the Club House), and might have done so, I thought it right to assume that I had . . . .I do not in the least doubt that Mr Church had talked on the subject. I think it likely that he had before 1869 suggested that the State and Dominion Government should take action in the premises but if he had it was wholly unknown to me, to Mr Dorsheimer or, I believe, to any of the gentlemen meeting at Cataract House in 1869.

    (Calvert Vaux, "A Natural Park at Niagara," *New-York Daily Tribune*, Oct. 5, 1878, p. 4; FLO to Thomas V. Welch, Feb. 16, 1889).
3. On August 7, 1869, Olmsted was at Niagara Falls with H. H. Richardson and William Dorsheimer, who was a member of the New York State Survey Commission. While rambling on Goat Island Olmsted broached the idea of creating a scenic reservation at Niagara, and that evening they gathered in Dorsheimer's rooms at the Cataract House to discuss the matter further. Present at that meeting were several other men from Buffalo with whom Olmsted had been associated while planning the Buffalo park system and designing the grounds of Richardson's Buffalo State Asylum (FLO to C. K. Remington, May 28, 1888; FLO to Thomas V. Welch, May 28, 1888, as quoted in Charles M. Dow, *The State Reservation at Niagara: A History* [Albany, N.Y., 1914], pp. 10–11).
4. In the second section of their report, the State Survey commissioners observed that "though it receives a great number of transient visitors, it is believed that at no other notable pleasure resort or Europe or America is the stay for travelers so short. It may be added that, if the public press for years past is to be credited, from none do so many vis-

itors depart in ill-humor" (New York (State), *Special Report of New York State Survey on the Preservation of the Scenery at Niagara Falls . . . for the Year 1879* [Albany, N.Y., 1880], p. 8; "Document no. 86," in New York [State], *Documents of the Assembly of the Senate of the State of New York, One Hundred and Third Session...* [Albany, N.Y, 1880]).

5. Olmsted's quotation here is a fairly close rendition of the passage on pages 24–26 of William Robinson's *Alpine Flowers for English Gardens*, published in London in 1875. Olmsted omitted two short sections that he presumably viewed as digressions from the theme he wished to emphasize. At the end of the first sentence, and as part of it, Robinson had written: "and very suggestive it is to those interested in forming artificial or improving natural cascades and the like." Before the last sentence quoted by Olmsted, Robinson had written, "It looks a home for Gulliver in Brobdingnagian scenery."

6. Sir Joseph Dalton Hooker, (1817–1911) and Asa Gray (1810–1888), professor of Botany at Harvard, visited Niagara together in September 1877. On Goat Island they identified thirty kinds of trees and twenty different shrubs. In a paper that he delivered to the Royal Institution of Great Britain the following year, Hooker chose Goat Island as one example of the richness of flora in what he called the "Great Eastern Forest region" of the United States, which reaches from the Atlantic to beyond the Mississippi. The other example he chose from this region was a patch of native forest on the Missouri River near St. Louis, where he and Gray counted forty trees and some twenty shrubs. "I know of no temperate region of the globe," he wrote, "in which any approach to this aggregation of different trees and shrubs could be seen in such limited areas, and perhaps no tropical one could afford a parallel" (*DNB*; *ANB*: Joseph D. Hooker, "The Distribution of the North American Flora," in Royal Institution of Great Britain, *Notices of the Proceedings at the Meetings of the Members . . . 1875–1878* 8 [1879]: 572–73; see P. M. Eckel, "Botanical Evaluation of the Goat Island Complex, Niagara Falls, New York" [Buffalo, N.Y., 1990]).

7. A reference to Olmsted's journey on horseback from the vicinity of Tuscaloosa, Alabama to Lynchburg, Virginia, in the summer of 1854, as recounted in his *Journey in the Backcountry*, combined with numerous trips in states further north, ranging at least as far as the White Mountains of New Hampshire. He presumably includes his horseback trips in the region of the Mariposa Estate and the Sierra Nevada during his two years, 1863–65, in California (see *Papers of FLO*, 2: 481–82; ibid., 5: 768–69).

8. The ferry ran from the Canadian side of the gorge to the base of the American Falls (Theodora Vinal, *Niagara Portage: From Past to Present* [Buffalo, N. Y., 1949], p. 92).

9. "Shortening-in" or "heading-in" is the shortening of limbs of trees, usually in the process of transplanting (Liberty Hyde Bailey, *The Standard Cyclopedia of Horticulture* 3 vols., [New York and London, 1925], 1: 354).

10. On page 9 of their report, the State Survey commissioners stated that although the expanse of smooth water above Goat Island and the turbulent river in the narrow gorge below the falls are significant elements of the whole landscape experience of the place, the "distinctive interest of Niagara, as compared with that of other attractive scenery, is remarkably circumscribed and concentrated" –that is, in the area of the rapids on either side of Goat Island.

11. George Douglas Campbell (1823–1900), eighth Duke of Argyll, visited the Niagara region during the summer of 1879 and published an account of his visit in *Fraser's Magazine* after his return in the Fall. It was reprinted in the January 1880 issue of *Littell's Living Age*. The passage quoted here immediately followed the Duke's description of the falls, and he prefaced his description of the rapids by saying "I am inclined to think, however, that the most impressive of all the scenes at Niagara is one of which comparatively little is said." His description of the rapids is one of the most eloquent evocations

of the scenery there that Olmsted especially valued, but it served other purposes as well. Olmsted was concerned about the lack of serious consideration of the reservation proposal in Canada, where the Duke's son and heir, John Douglas Sutherland Campbell, Marquis of Lorne, was governor general. As he indicated to Sara Sedgwick Darwin when forwarding his proposal of June 11, 1880 to the Earl of Derby (below) that there be discussion of the reservation issue in the House of Lords, "Anything tending to show that the leading men of England really care for it & think it worthy of their earnest attention will help to overcome this provincial indifference." The Duke's rhapsodic description of the rapids at Niagara was a valuable demonstration of such appreciation of the scenery of Niagara (*DNB*; Duke of Argyll, [George Douglas Campbell], "First Impressions of the New World," in *Littell's Living Age*, Jan. 3, 1880, p. 38; Canada. Centennial Commission, *The Founders and the Guardians: Fathers of Confederation, Governors General, Prime Ministers; a Collection of Biographical Sketches and Portraits* [Ottawa, 1968], p. 84).

12. Olmsted's italics.

IMPROVEMENT OF THE BACK-BAY, BOSTON.

[April 3, 1880]

To the Editor of the American Architect:[1]
Dear Sir,—

My attention is called to an objection offered in your issue of 20th inst.,[2] to the plan for the improvement of the Back Bay now before the Boston City Council, and which, if the writer's assumptions were accepted, might stir up a strong property interest against it, and defeat the pending appropriation. As I had not thought it necessary to anticipate this objection in my report on the subject, quoted by the writer, you will kindly allow me to explain my neglect to do so.

The objection is that there must be a constant rapid deposit of filthy silt in the proposed Back-Bay basin, from the water supplied to it out of Charles River; that this silt will foul the shores, and fill up the channel from which it must be removed at frequent intervals by a very costly process and with great offence to all living in the vicinity. The objection is unsound for the following reasons:

In summer all the supply required from the Charles may be let in within an hour before and after high-water, and may be all drawn from within three feet of the surface. At and near the turn of flood, the river is without perceptible current, and the water within three feet or more of the surface carries no silting matter. I have observed it frequently, when, so far as the eye could detect, it was perfectly clear.

When, under extraordinary circumstances, the water is unusually turbid, it will be unnecessary to let it into the basin. The gates may be always

VIEW OF BACK BAY FENS, C. 1896

closed against in-flow during stormy weather if it is thought desirable. In winter they may be closed for a month at a time without harm.

But it is urged that as population increases on its banks, the river will be increasingly dirty. Both the present city engineer and his predecessor in office, and the city superintendent of sewers, are of a different opinion.[3] The completion of works now in progress is expected to relieve the river of Boston sewage; and, looking further ahead and beyond Boston, it is likely that other expedients will in time be adopted for maintaining it in tolerable cleanliness. In no probable event is it to be anticipated that the annual deposit of silt within the basin from tidal water will be more than a mere film, or that it will be offensive.

To obtain satisfactory results upon the Back Bay without excessive expense, is a complicated problem. I acknowledge especially a certain degree of uncertainty as to what may be accomplished under the novel conditions proposed for the low ground, and I should be grateful for advice upon this point from any of your sea-coast readers, who may have had experience of approximately similar conditions. The descriptive terms of our language applicable to land subject to occasional overflow from the sea are unfortunately limited, and for want of better I spoke of that proposed to be formed in the Back-Bay as marshy and fenny. Your contributor's second objection[4] to the commissioners' plan is based, however, upon a more restricted use of these terms than I had supposed to be necessary. There are many sea-coast nooks of Massachusetts Bay with wooded banks into which the tide occasionally rises, and which are commonly spoken of by country people as marshy, very different in character and appealing in a very different way to the imagination from the marsh which he assumes that I have had in view.

As to his somewhat authoritative assumption of the "unloveliness" of all possible marsh detail under the circumstances, you will pardon me for repeating the familiar words of the poet:—

> "Dear marshes! Vain to him the gift of sight,
> Who cannot in their various incomes share."[5]

Respectfully yours,

FREDERICK LAW OLMSTED.

The text presented here is from *The American Architect and Building News*, April 3, 1880, page 145.

1. The editor of *The American Architect and Building News* was William Pitt Preble Longfellow. Longfellow became the first editor of the journal when it was created in 1876, and he resigned from the position a month after this article was published (NCAB, 23: 239).
2. The article to which Olmsted refers was highly critical of his plan for the Back Bay Fens ("The Back Bay Park in Boston," *American Architect and Building News*, March 20, 1880, pp. 117–18).
3. Joseph P. Davis and his predecessor, Nathaniel Henry Crafts (b. 1828), who was City Engineer of Boston from 1864 to 1871. The Superintendent of Sewers was William Hammatt Bradley (b. 1835), who held that position from 1863 to 1883 (James Monroe Crafts, comp., *The Crafts Family* [Northampton, Mass., 1893], p. 422; Frederick Law Olmsted, "Paper on the Back Bay Problem and its Solution Read Before the Boston Society of Architects," [April 2, 1886] [*Papers of FLO*, SS1: 456, n. 21]).
4. The objection was that:

> Mr. Olmsted has made the mistake — which would not surprise one in a beginner, but which is astonishing in a veteran landscapist — of undertaking to create in a small space, hemmed in narrowly by city streets, a great natural feature. In such a space, out of grass and water we may make a garden, a lawn, a stream, or a pond, and be reasonably certain that nature will not mock at our modest efforts. But a marsh is a feature of the natural landscape which needs, as much as any other, unlimited size. What is it that makes a marsh interesting but the play of light in broad masses, the broad reflections of sky and cloud in the water, the low light, the opposing rise of horizon lines, the opposing colors of horizon hills, seen afar against the sky, the far-reaching and repeated alternations of land and water? These are charms which make us forget or overlook the unloveliness of detail. Well, in Mr. Olmsted's marsh or "fens," as he sometimes prefers calling them, these effects, if they are to be had at all, must be got within a breadth varying from four hundred to nine hundred feet, and confined between close blocks of city houses, which may, perhaps, by great

good luck be veiled in a generation or two by the thin foliage of city trees. It does not seem possible (even supposing the attempt at clothing the marsh with some sort of coarse growth, such as Mr. Olmsted permits himself to expect, should be successful) that the result should not be lamentably prosaic if not worse. That it should prove to be, in the words of the report, "positively, permanently, constantly agreeable" is beyond belief. ("The Back Bay Park in Boston," p. 118.)

5. Olmsted is quoting from James Russell Lowell's poem "An Indian-Summer Reverie" (Majorie R. Kaufman, *The Poetical Works of James Russell Lowell* [Boston, 1978], p. 70).

To Charles Henry Dalton

May 5—1880.

C. H. Dalton Esqr
President Park Dept. Boston;
My Dear Sir,

    Enclosed is a statement of the terms recommended to be adopted for an arrangment between the city and Harvard College as to the Arboretum. As explanatory of the proposition I submit the following observations.

    Regarding the Arboretum as a public pleasure ground, there would under the proposed arrangment be a space of 125 acres to be planted and maintained partly in the form of natural woods, (the trees standing for the most part closely or in groups and completely shading the ground), and partly, as an open grove, (much as the majority of trees stand at present on the Common). Besides this planted space there would be about 11 acres of ground kept mainly clear of trees in order to give the public the benefit of distant views from the heights, and an additional open space of five acres of turf at all suitable times available as a play ground for children.[1]

    There would be a total space of 145 acres of ground to be used by the public, precisely as well regulated and much frequented public parks are commonly used, no restrictions or regulations being necessary that are not in force on the Central Park, or the Park of Monceau (St James's Park).[2]

    The Arboretum is to be open daily to the public from sunrise to sunset, except that if it shall at any time hereafter be found desirable to avoid the disturbance of necessary operations on the ground or of instructions to students it may be closed upon due public notice until 10 in the morning.

    There will be ten acres of ground (not included in the 150 acres above described) which the college is to be permitted to occupy with special collections of plants, nursery and propagating gardens and by such buildings for administration and instruction as may be required, the use of which reserved ground will be subject to regulation by the college.

This being the scheme to carry it out, the city is to provide less than a fourth of the land to make and maintain a public drive and walk leading through it, to protect the property and preserve order and decorum in its use and to supply water necessary to keep down dust and water the plants.

The college is to supply three fourths of the land required, to establish and maintain the plantations and keep the entire grounds in good order, without expense to the city.

Briefly the city has the opportunity of acquiring a public ground of a distinct, interesting and valuable character promising to be the best of its kind in the world, which will cost it neither for construction nor for maintenance more than a quarter as much as it would without the cooperation of the college.

The college gains the opportunity of making its arboretum more complete and more generally useful to the public than would otherwise be practicable. I know of nothing else it has to gain and in my efforts to bring about the result proposed, I have nothing else in view.

Accompanying letter to Dalton 5 May '80.

I recommend the following as terms of an arrangement between the City of Boston and Harvard College for establishing and maintaining the proposed arboretum.

1. The land proposed to be used for the Arboretum to be provided as contemplated in the act of the legislature.[3]

2. The college to hold the right to appropriate certain areas, not exceeding altogether ten acres in extent for administrative and special purposes bearing upon the object of the Arboretum as a scientific institution, including sites for museums, lecture rooms and nurseries.

3 The college to establish and maintain the plantations of the Arboretum, including a collection of trees and shrubs suitably classified and labelled adapted to the advancement of the science of Botany and arboriculture and the instruction of the public.

4 The city to provide the land proposed to be added to the Arboretum (as shown in the map attached to the Fifth Annual Report of the Park Commissioners);[4] to make and maintain a road and walk on or near the line proposed for a road in said map; to take all measures necessary to the protection of the property and to preserve order and decorum in the use of it by the public and to supply the water required for keeping down dust and watering plants.

1879
PARK DEPARTMENT.—CITY OF BOSTON.

MAP OF PROPOSED

ARBORETUM,

SHOWING ITS OUTLINES AND LOCAL
CONNECTIONS, WITH A STUDY FOR
PUBLIC DRIVE PASSING THROUGH IT.

SCALE

FRED! LAW OLMSTED,
LANDSCAPE ARCHITECT.

PLAN OF PROP
Showing five-acre play area next to Centre Street and adjacent to Adams Ne

ld Arboretum, 1879
m, and open area on hilltop with carriage concourse southeast of play area.

	5 The Arboretum to be open to the public from sun rise to sunset, daily, but the college to hold the right, if it shall hereafter be found necessary for efficient and economical administration or to secure the best use of the ground for purposes of science and instruction, to its exclusive use until ten o'clock in the morning.
	6 Whenever the Arboretum is open, the public to have free access to all its parts (except the reservations proposed in ¶ 7.)[5] with only such limitations, commonly adopted on well-kept public grounds which are largely used, as may be found necessary to prevent injury to the trees and plants.

The text presented here is from a draft in Olmsted's hand.
1. The eleven acres kept open for distant views were in the vicinity of the concourse on Bussey Hill, and the five-acre area of turf for children's play can be seen next to Centre Street adjoining the Adams Nervine Asylum grounds on Olmsted's plan for the Arboretum dated 1879 on page 486.
2. The Parc Monceau is in Paris, while St. James's Park is one of the Royal Parks in London.
3. Chapter 144 of the Acts and Resolves of the General Court of Massachusetts of 1880, which became law on March 29, 1880, authorizing the Boston park commissioners to acquire the land of the Arnold Arboretum from Harvard College, to purchase adjoining tracts, and to lease all of that land not needed for park-ways and public recreation grounds to the college for use as an arboretum.
4. See map on pages 486–87, and map of November 1880 (plan 902-7), which more clearly shows the land the Olmsted had selected for the City of Boston to purchase to fill out the boundaries of the Arboretum and to provide for a parkway along its eastern side.
5. Olmsted meant to identify paragraph 2 at this point, not the nonexistent paragraph 7.

To Charles Eliot Norton

209 W. 46th St. N.Y.
7th May. 1880.

My Dear Norton;
	You are always so quick and thorough in helping me in any matter that I bring to your attention that I am learning reserve. Otherwise I should[n't] have been a week in Boston without saying a word to you about the arboretum, which project is at a crisis.[1] I don't think there is anything for you to do about it but I guess that you will like to know about it.
	The college has 118 acres appropriated to the arboretum. Not more

than half of it is really well adapted to a classified collection. The rest will do for illustrations of forestry &c. The city is now authorized upon my proposition to condemn 37 acres in two parcels, one at each end of the college tract.[2] On the 155 acres, much the best arboretum in the world can be formed. The scheme is that the city shall lease the condemned land to the college on a nominal rent for a thousand years and that the college shall establish and maintain the arboretum; that the city shall in good time lay out a road & walk (2¼ miles) through it & that the public shall be admitted to it under no regulations or restrictions other than such as are usual in well-kept public grounds. The college is to reserve the right to keep the gates closed when it shall think desirable until 10 o'ck in the morning. The college is also to hold exclusively within the enclosure 10 acres of land to be used for special collections, museums, lecture rooms and administrative duties. The city is to provide police and water without charge.

This is the whole of the scheme as I would have it. I am sure that it is a capital bargain for both parties. If it fails it will be because of some reserve, caution or lack of push at the college end and of indifference and jealousy, growing from ignorance at the city end.

I am perfectly confident that if any man fully understanding the case were to make it his business to talk it over and explain it to the Common Councilmen, it could be carried. I always find the prospect bad when I arrive in Boston and good when I leave. The difficulties are all difficulties of ignorance or of the imagination.

The arrangment would cost the college nothing and the result would be immeasurably more creditable to it. The city would get a very valuable, novel and interesting pleasure ground at about one quarter what it would otherwise have to pay for it.

The sole difficulty is that nobody (feeling free to act) is really alive to the opportunity. I have been shaking Dalton and Sargent and have tried to stir up Mr Pulsifer[3] of the Herald upon whom I called for the purpose. I hope something will come of it next week but not confidently.

Yours affctly

Fred[k] Law Olmsted.

The text presented here is from a manuscript in Olmsted's hand in the Charles Eliot Norton Papers, Houghton Library, Harvard University, Cambridge, Massachusetts.

1. The "crisis" was created by the decision of the Boston Board of Alderman on May 3, 1880, after years of consideration of the question, to authorize the park commissioners, as soon as possible, to report to them what terms could be made with Harvard College regarding inclusion of the Arnold Arboretum in the Boston park system. This action followed close upon the passage by the state legislature on March 29 of a bill authorizing

the City of Boston to purchase the Arnold Arboretum and adjoining property for that purpose. It was therefore important to galvanize support for the proposition quickly.
2. A reference to the land that Olmsted proposed to have the City of Boston purchase in order to fill out the boundaries of the arboretum.
3. Royal Macintosh Pulsifer (1843–1888), owner and publisher of the *Boston Herald* from 1869 until his death (*Proceedings of the Bostonian Society at the Annual Meeting, January 8, 1889* [Boston, 1889], p. 15; *Boston Herald*, Oct. 21, 1888, p. 4).

CHAPTER IX

MAY 1880–DECEMBER 1880

The principal focus of the documents in this chapter relates to the Boston park system. The document addressed to Charles Dalton consists of a report by Olmsted and Charles S. Sargent on replanting Commonwealth Avenue between the Back Bay Fens and the Public Garden, while the report to the park commissioners presents Olmsted's first proposal to transform the valley of the Muddy River between the Fens and Jamaica Pond. A further letter to Sylvester Baxter encourages the development of a metropolitan system of scenic reservations.

Two letters to John C. Phillips describe the stages of Olmsted's planning of that important commission, "Moraine Farm" in Beverly, Massachusetts, which became the most fully realized of Olmsted's early plans for a country estate. The letters relating to the U.S. Capitol grounds touch on a number of issues: the letter to Thomas Wisedell shows Olmsted engaged in reasoning with a professional colleague about difficulties in their relationship; one letter to Edward Clark describes Olmsted's imaginative concept for the summer house on the grounds and the other records difficulties of policing the area.

To John Charles Phillips[1]

11th May 1880

To Mr Phillips.
My Dear Sir,
I send you two suggestions for treatment of your house site on Wenham Lake. As the charm of the situation lies wholly in the look down upon and over the lake, whatever increases the down-looking and overlooking effect adds to its value. This is the first consideration; the second is that as you do not mean the house to have the character of a villa but rather of a forest lodge for the summer, the more you avoid the common-places of a villa or a suburban cottage and the more bold, rustic and weather-proof consistently with substantial comeliness and comfort you make the immediate outworks of the house, the better.

For these two reasons I advise the house be set high, pushed as near the lake as it conveniently can be & that it shall be supported by a terrace boldly projected, following natural lines, "country-made" and highly picturesque in its outlines and material.

I should aim to obtain on this terrace wall something of the character and beauty of very old masonry. It should remind one of a ruin without being an imitation of one. The material to be mainly field-stones, laid with a large but variable batter and with many crannies.

The figures on the drawing on the West side of the wall show the elevation above the lake of proposed surface of garden; those on the East side the present elevation of ground upon which the wall would stand. The difference will be the height of the terrace wall except that two feet must be added for a parapet.

Supposing the entrance hall of the house to be carried through 20 feet from the South end, as suggested by Mr Stearns[2] and that it should serve as a billiard room &c., I have supposed that the end toward the lake would have a large window, which could be thrown wide open. The space A in study no 1 would in that case be a level flagged floor serving as an out of door extension of the hall, ending in a balcony overhanging the face of the terrace and at a point where there is a natural depression of the hill slope below. The whole might be covered with an awning.

The surface of the terrace is designed as the figures will show to slope gently away on both sides of the balcony, so that at the end of the lawn a man's head would be below the level of the eye of one sitting at the balcony. This will allow the garden to be sufficiently furnished with rich forground shrubbery without shutting off the view.[3]

At the South end of the garden a pavilion is to be placed partly overhanging the terrace wall. This is designed to be not a mere shelter but a useful

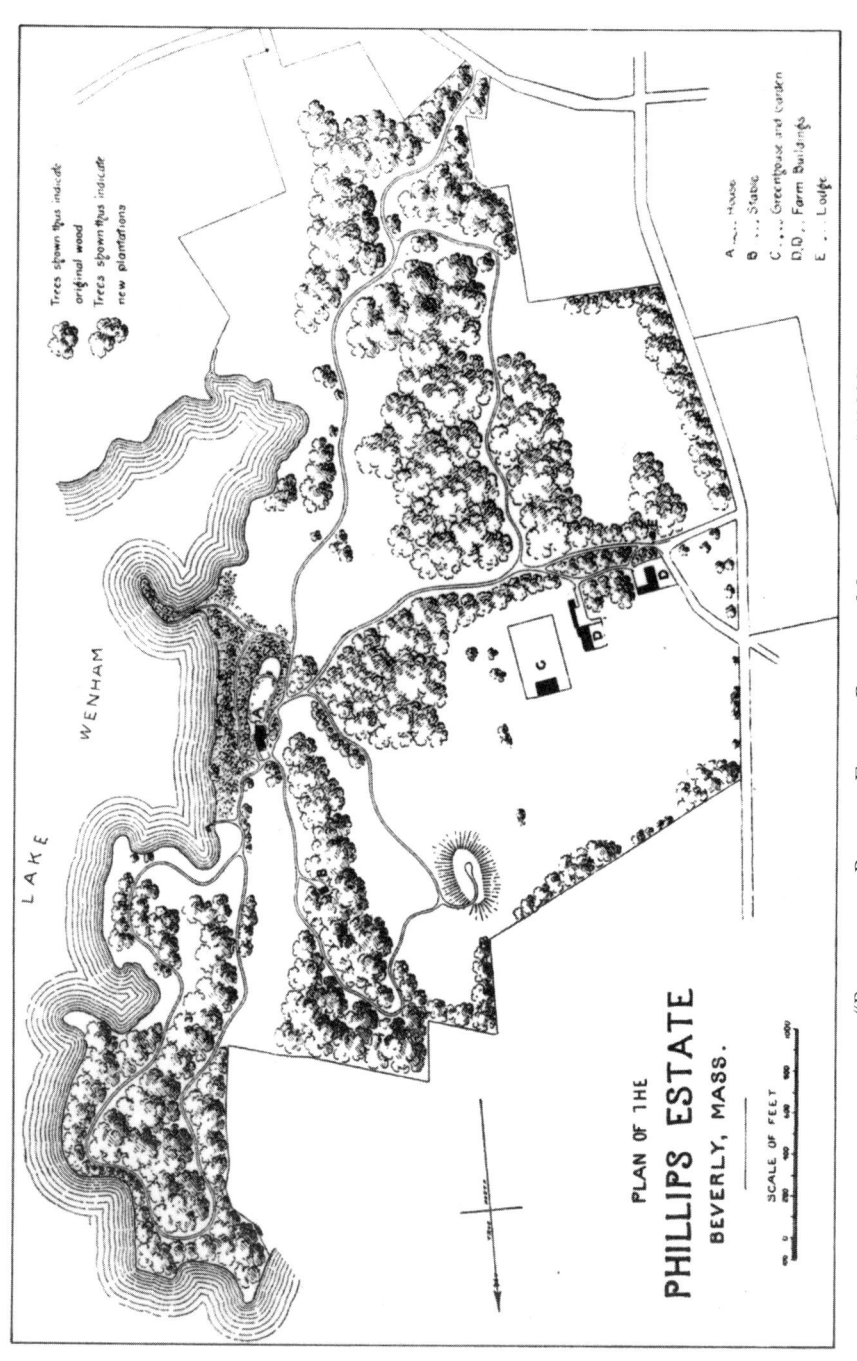

"Plan of the Phillips Estate, Beverly, Massachusetts" (1892)

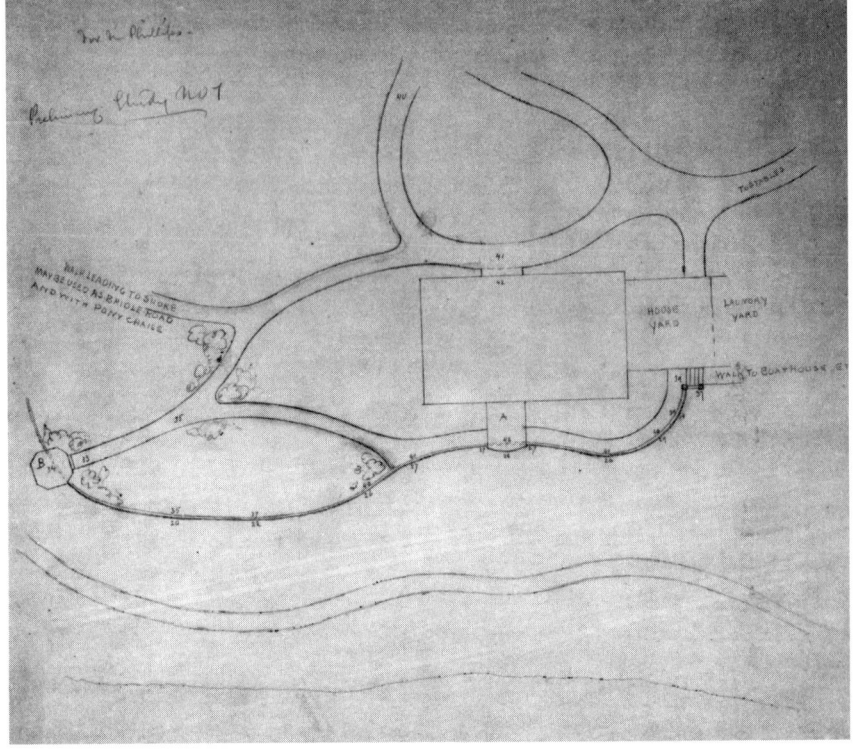

JOHN C. PHILLIPS ESTATE, "PRELIMINARY STUDY NO. 1"

room, large enough for a coffee, reading or ladies'-work room, with windows, and shutters.

The plot between the walk leading to it from the central balcony and the parapet of the terrace is to be of finely kept turf with a few shrubs as indicated but vines and creepers are to be planted all along the base of the parapet & grow over it.

The ground below the terrace wall is to be a "wild garden;" with ferns and perennials seen among groups of low trees which like the sumachs and dogwoods, and pinus Mugho might appear to advantage when looked down upon.[4]

In study no 2 a modification of the same plan is shown, by which at some additional cost, considerable would be gained.

The pavilion stands over the lake and is approached by an easy stairway carried in a wall thrown out from the terrace. This wall is to be pierced by an archway and from the pavilion stairs lead on down to a road carried under it. The stair-case and the garden-wall of the terrace is to be covered with a trel-

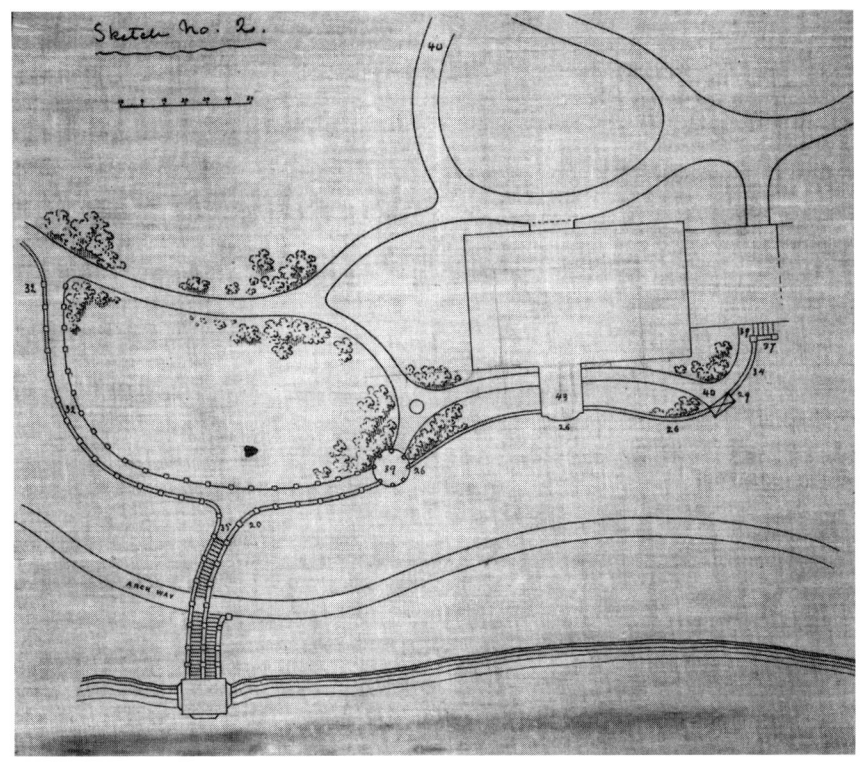

JOHN C. PHILLIPS ESTATE, "SKETCH NO. 2"

lis the posts of which only are shown. These posts may be roughly quarried granite columns (such as farmers often use for fence posts) forming a pergola in the old Italian rustic style.

Built as I have suggested of field stones well clothed with lichens, and shaded by vines, this entire arrangement would be extremely interesting even quaint, but not affected because it grows naturally out of the situation.

The pergola would give you an agreeable shady promenade, long before it would be possible to obtain much shade by trees, and its top may be kept so low as to interfere much less than trees would do with the Southerly views from the house. On a line South from the balcony the top of the trellis loaded with vines would be six feet below the line of the eye of a man standing on the floor of the balcony. You will observe that the natural slope of the hill favors this arrangment.

The house is outlined in accordance with the largest dimensions each way which were named when we were on the ground. I do not expect the form or dimensions to be adhered to but the outline of terrace is well fitted to the ground, and it is desirable that the house be designed to correspond with it as nearly as shall be found practicable. This could be done just as well if the suggestion of Mr Stearns of a diagonal kitchen wing should be adopted. Of course all the walks &c can be readily adjusted to a narrower or shorter house.[5]

The text presented here is from a draft in Olmsted's hand.

1. John Charles Phillips (1838–1885), a nephew of abolitionist Wendell Phillips, prospered as a commission merchant in New York and Boston during the 1860s and 1870s. His success in business allowed him to engage in philanthropy and to pursue horticulture and farming as hobbies. In 1877 he contributed money toward the establishment of the Arnold Arboretum, and the following year accompanied its director, his friend Charles Sprague Sargent, on a botanical expedition in Nevada and California. Shortly after this trip, Phillips inherited from his father a large farm on Wenham Lake north of Boston. Olmsted, accompanied by Sargent, conducted a preliminary examination of the property for which he submitted an invoice in January 1880 for $100. In early 1880 he agreed to provide Phillips with advice and plans on the location of a new house, roads, walks, and planting of the property, and visited it with him in late April.

    A remarkable element of the plan that Olmsted developed was the massive terrace, fifteen feet high on its outer edge, that provided the foundation for the house and the lawn area adjacent to it on the south. On the lake side of the house he designed a terrace paved with tiles that is one hundred and forty feet long with a curving outer edge and a width that varies from twenty-one to thirty-five feet (*Boston Evening Transcript*, March 2, 1885, p. 4; ibid., Nov. 7, 1878, p. 4; NCAB, 47: 138; S.B. Sutton, *Charles Sprague Sargent and the Arnold Arboretum* [Cambridge, Mass., 1970], pp. 54–56; FLO to John C. Phillips, Jan. 20, 1879 [probably 1880]; John C. Phillips to FLO, Feb. 11, 1880; ibid., Feb 29, 1880; ibid., March 15, 1880; ibid., April 25, 1880; measured plan of terrace by George Batchelder, July 30, 1998, private collection).

2. John Goddard Stearns, Jr., (1843–1917), architect, engineer, and senior partner in the Boston firm of Peabody and Stearns. He apparently was present during Olmsted's April 1880 visit to the Phillips property. Born and schooled in Brookline, Massachusetts, he graduated from Harvard's Lawrence Scientific School in 1863 and apprenticed in the firm of Ware and Van Brunt until 1870. In the latter year he formed a partnership with Robert Swain Peabody and began a diverse practice in domestic, public, and church architecture that lasted until 1917. In 1878–79 the partners designed a house for Phillips on Commonwealth Avenue in Boston. Their consultation with Olmsted about the Phillips property in Beverly during 1880–81 was the first of several collaborations during the 1880s (Henry F. Withey and Elsie Rathburn Withey, *Biographical Dictionary of American Architects [Deceased]* [Los Angeles, Ca., 1956], p. 568; Adolf K. Placzek, ed., *Macmillan Encyclopedia of Architects*, 4 vols. [New York, 1982], 3: 380–82; FLO to John C. Phillips, Jan. 20, 1879; John C. Phillips to FLO, April 25, 1880; Peabody and Stearns to FLO, July 21, 1880; ibid., April 4, 1881; FLO to Peabody and Stearns, April 15, 1881).

3. Plan no. 68 shows the highest point of the terrace at datum 43 and the floor of the pavilion at 33 or 35 (plan 12297–68, NPS/FLONHS).

4. Olmsted is calling for the treatment advocated by William Robinson in *The Wild Garden* (1870)—that is, informally arranged combinations of native and exotic flowers, shrubs, and creepers, ideal for borders and rough sections of landscaped properties (see FLO to William L. Fischer, March 14, 1875, n. 5, above).

5. Six weeks after the date of this letter Phillips told Olmsted he had not yet decided upon the final ground plan of the house and requested that he visit the property. Olmsted did so in late July. In late August he provided revised plans of the terrace wall and grounds immediately around the house. He abandoned the lakeside pavilion and terrace-edge pergola proposed here and substituted, at the end of the lawn south of the house, a pavilion set above a massive stone arch and overlooking a flower garden. That autumn John H. Watson, who in late 1879 had constructed the stone grotto of the summer house on the U.S. Capitol grounds, commenced the stonework of the terrace wall and the pavilion foundation and arch. Construction of the Phillips house began in the spring of 1881 (John C. Phillips to FLO, June 21, 1880; ibid., July 16, 1880; ibid., Oct. 7, 1880; ibid., Oct. 21, 1880; ibid., Dec. 27, 1880; Peabody and Stearns to FLO, July 21, 1880; ibid., April 4, 1881; FLO to John C. Phillips, Aug. 23, 1880; FLO to Peabody and Stearns, April 15, 1881; A. J. Merritt to FLO, Dec. 12, 1879, D3, OAR/LC).

To the Earl of Derby

The Right Honorable the Earl of Derby.[1]
Draught

209 West 46th Street;
New York, 11th June, 1880.

My Lord;
    Mr Darwin having kindly sent me a copy of your Lordship's note to him of last November, expressing interest in the movement to restore the natural scenery of Niagara Falls, I sometime since sent you a copy of the report of the New York Commission on the subject.[2]
    I am sorry to say that though advocated by a great number of the more eminent men of letters and other esteemed citizens both of Canada and of the United States and received with considerable official favor, the legislative bodies of the Dominion, of the Province of Ontario and of the State of New York have all adjourned without taking favorable action upon the project. A cautious policy with reference to the present Presidential canvass had to do with the failure in New York. In Canada I am advised that the chief obstacle lay in the difficulty of gaining a serious interest among members of Parliament in a subject so far without the field of their ordinary political discussions.
    The agitation will be revived in the autumn and I beg to say that an inquiry upon the subject in the House of Lords as kindly proposed in your lordship's note to Mr Darwin, would, as an indication of the interest of the subject to the world beyond Canada and the United States, have a valuable

influence and be gratefully regarded by those who have here led the movement,[3] writing in whose behalf,
    I have the honour to be
    Your Lordship's,
    very obedient servant

                          Frederick Law Olmsted.

The text presented here is from a manuscript in Olmsted's hand.
1. Edward Henry Stanley, fifteenth Earl of Derby (1826–1893) (*DNB*).
2. Charles Darwin had apparently approached the Earl of Derby about signing Olmsted's petition concerning Niagara Falls. The Earl replied that he did not sign such petitions, but that he was "entirely and cordially sympathetic in the object of the memorial," and would be glad to forward the endeavor as far as he could. He suggested that he might ask a question concerning the status of the reservation issue during the next session of the House of Lords (Earl of Derby to Charles Darwin, Nov. 13, 1879).
3. Derby replied to Darwin on June 27 that he could raise a question in the House of Lords only if there had been communications on the issue from the Americans and Canadians. On July 7 he reported to Darwin that he had made inquiries both at the Foreign Office and the Colonial Office and neither of them had heard anything from America on the Niagara question. Under those circumstances it was useless for him to raise the issue in Parliament. "We on this side of the water can help when the project is started," he reiterated, "but the first steps must be taken between Canada and the U.S." Derby wrote a similar explanation to Olmsted that apparently has not survived (Earl of Derby to Charles Darwin, July 7 [1880]; FLO to CEN, July 20, 1880, Charles Eliot Norton Papers, Houghton Library, Harvard University, Cambridge, Massachusetts).

To Thomas Wisedell

                              13th. June 1880.

My Dear Wisedell.
    Having had no more uncomfortable thing to ride me in these restless nights since John's interview with you the other day, I have had to think over his report of what then occurred and what must have been back of it.[1]
    John may not have been able to tell me just what provocation he offered you, but I had given him no message to you and I think that I can judge what he was likely *not* to say well enough to be safe in assuming that you could have been driven to repeat to him the bitter protest against my courses with

you which you have before addressed more than once to me, by the consideration that I had made no sufficient reply to it, and that it had had no apparent effect upon me.

That I have not appeared to give it more consideration is because I did not at the time I heard it think that the circumstances were favorable to candor of debate with either of us and because on afterwards deliberately reviewing your words I was led to conclude that they were temporary expressions of feeling inconsistent with your more abiding sentiment. I have not neglected to consider them.

We are both of us invalids, both suffer from a similar form of nervous irritability, extremely provocative of impatience, and if your malady is the hardest, I am much the older man, more hardened in my habits and less tractable.

Therefore as to mere expressions of impatience and petulance we have within us much to boast of, and between ourselves I don't think we need attempt to cast up accounts. If you do and find a balance against me, it can only be a case for forgiveness as to the little over and I ask your forgiveness.

Let us turn from these superficial matters of nerve and temper to those of continuous and deliberate conduct of life.

Taken thus by itself apart from all mere irritations of manner the charge which you make against me, I understand to be chiefly in this: That for some time past I have fallen into ways of dealing with you which imply rights on my part and obligations on yours which are wholly unwarranted, and which proper professional self-respect and regard for your professional position compels you to resist and warmly protest against as you do.

If you think that I have changed my bearing toward you intentionally, I can only deny it. If you cannot take my denial, that is the end of the matter. I cannot engage in discussions with you as to my veracity or sincerity.

If you think that I have fallen into a different habit from that of my earlier dealings with you unconsciously, I can only say that having given the question mature consideration I am satisfied that you are mistaken and that further reiteration of your conviction is not likely to change my opinion.

There is only one way in which I can account for such a conviction having taken root in your mind and I shall suggest it with no thought of insisting upon it, much less of reproaching you with it, if you think it wrong.

I put myself in your place and reflect that since the early Charles Street days there have been greater changes with you than with me.[2]

You now have children. You are living in your own house in the country; You have your own office; you have a partner and you have undertaken and carried through important works on your own account; works which should bring you fame — and which do so, though less than you deserve.[3]

Putting myself in your place, I don't think that an arrangment which I should have been satisfied to make before such changes would latterly have been perfectly congenial to me. There can be no reproach then, in asking you to consider whether you do not feel that something more is due to you now than in the Charles Street days and whether it is not this feeling which is at the bottom of your conviction that I have grown unjust and am trying to deal with you in a way derogatory to your professional rights?

Is this not quite as likely as that I, a much older man as I have said & more hardened in my habits should have changed in the manner you suppose?

If you recognize that this may be possible or may even partly account for the hard feeling which you feel compelled to express toward me I beg you to reflect that in the organization of the Washington work I stand in a very different position from that of a private client, the head of a private office, or the head of a public office. I have to do with it under an ambiguous, ill-defined, wholly irregular form of obligation[4] to accomplish certain ends as best I may under certain conditions and with the use of certain means which are extremely unsatisfactory to me and which I think most injudicious, embarrassing and wasteful. But I have accepted the duty subject to its contingencies. I have not thought it necessary to throw it up as the difficulties have been developed, and until I do so with due notice I am in honor bound to use all my energies, and all the energies I can by any means tackle in, to accomplish the best results thus left possible.

I perfectly understand that it remains in a great degree dependent on other men what these results shall be — men whom I have not selected, whose duties I have not determined and whose tastes, personal interests, prejudices and misinformation may be very unfavorable to my purposes. I know that they are not efficiently under my command. But through these men by such persuasion and education as my constitution of mind is adapted to use, and theirs to receive I must operate, or not at all. The conditions in this respect are not worse than I have had to meet more than once before. I have therefore been prepared to take a good deal for granted which you say that I do not know.

Perhaps I should not be in more favorable humor for what I need to do if I knew it better — at any rate I do not want to know it better for it ought not to affect my course if it were ten times worse.

Provided nothing waits which it is my duty to supply and that I do all the best possible to anticipate, guard against and piece out the short comings of others, then if the work after all fails here and there to be promptly, regularly, systematically and economically done and the results to be satisfactory I need not blame myself.

But as to your part in this work the case is wholly different. If anything for which I depend on you fails to work in perfectly; if the business is in any way disconcerted through your being behind hand or not in perfect rapport with me, I am as much responsible for it as for anything to be done solely by my own head and hands.

That is to say you are the only man whose work is done theoretically in my office.[5] If what I depend on you for is not opportunely and fittingly done

MAY 1880–DECEMBER 1880

it reflects not at all on the Committees of Congress, Mr Clark, Mr Cobb, Captain Brown or Mr Cogan,[6] nor publicly upon you. The blame all comes upon me and upon me alone. The arrangment is not the best or the justest possible but it was originally made, as far as the making of it lay at all with me, to suit you and I believe it was the very best and justest that could then have been obtained. The alternative would probably have been to have the architectural work done in Mr Clark's Office.

As far as I can judge it is still the best that is practicable provided your present business arrangments allow you to second me in it as fully and promptly as ever and that you still accept it with the hearty good will which you once assured me that you did.[7]

If such is not the case I cannot think that the fault is mine, and it can do no possible good for you, in dealing with me to assume that it is. It can only give me and provoke me to give you useless pain, and that result I hope that you are as desirous to avoid as I am.

I would close with some expressions of good will but if you have thought my conduct toward you evinced ill-will such professions could only make matters worse. For unquestionably

I am what I have been

The text presented here is from a draft in Olmsted's hand.

1. Thomas Wisedell had worked on the U.S. Capitol grounds project under Olmsted's direction since the summer of 1874. He designed the piers, lampposts, and fountains of the east carriage court, the curb and stonework at street and walk entrances, and assisted in the design and prepared drawings for the ventilating tower, summer house, and the proposed terrace. In the summer of 1879 Wisedell fell ill and was late in providing working drawings for the summer house. He broke several promises to deliver them and left letters calling for them unanswered. As a result, work on the structure did not begin until late in the working season that autumn and its unfinished condition attracted unfavorable criticism from Congress in the early spring of 1880. Several days before the present letter was written senators denounced the summer house and denied funding for the proposed terrace.

    Olmsted had sent his stepson John to determine the cause of Wisedell's delay once before and another such visit prompted an exchange which led to the present letter (Thomas Wisedell, pay vouchers, 1874–80, Records Management Department, Architect of the Capitol, U.S. Capitol, Washington, D.C.; FLO to Justin S. Morrill, Aug. 16, 1874, n. 11, above; FLO to Montgomery C. Meigs, Jan. 15, 1875, n. 4, above; FLO to Tiffany and Company, Dec. 9, 1879, n. 2, above; FLO to Frederick H. Cobb, Aug. 30, 1879, Office of the Curator, Architect of the Capitol, U.S. Capitol, Washington, D.C; FLO to Frederick H. Cobb, May 30, 1881).

2. Between 1874 and 1876 Wisedell resided at 29 Charles Street in New York City. Thus, during "the Charles Street days" (and since 1868, when he began working for Vaux, Withers & Company,) Wisedell had served as an architectural assistant (FLO to Justin S. Morrill, Aug. 16, 1874, n. 11, above; FLO to Thomas Wisedell, Aug. 12, 1874; *Trow's New York City Directory for the Year Ending May 1, 1876* [New York, 1876], p. 1416).

501

3. Wisedell, his wife, and their three children lived in rural Yonkers. In 1879 he formed a partnership with architect Francis H. Kimball, and opened an office on Broadway in New York City. His designs of several well-known New York theaters won recognition for Wisedell in the architecture profession (FLO to Frederick H. Cobb, June 7, 1879, Office of the Curator, Architect of the Capitol, U.S. Capitol, Washington, D.C; Thomas Wisedell to FLO, Sept. 10, 1879; *Trow's New York City Directory for the Year Ending May 1, 1881* [New York, 1881], p. 1630; *New-York Times*, Aug. 2, 1884, p. 4).

4. Although Congress in 1874 and 1875 adopted Olmsted's plan for the Capitol grounds and named him to superintend it, the exact terms of his employment were not specified. Justin S. Morrill, Edward Clark, and Olmsted verbally agreed that he would be paid $2,000 annually to direct the work from New York and visit Washington as needed as well as occasionally employing professional assistants. Olmsted was never officially appointed landscape architect of the Capitol and continued from year to year at the behest of the committees on public buildings and grounds. Clark drew his salary from the annual appropriation for the Capitol grounds (++[Glenn Brown], *Documentary History of the Construction and Development of the United States Capitol Building and Grounds* [Washington, D.C., 1904], pp. 1159, 1201, 1219; FLO to Edward Clark, Aug. 4, 1876, Office of the Curator, Architect of the Capitol, U.S. Capitol, Washington, D.C.; Edward Clark to FLO, Aug. 7, 1876, Records Management Department, Architect of the Capitol, U.S. Capitol, Washington, D.C.; FLO to Carl Schurz, Aug. 18, 1877, in Records of the U.S. House of Representatives, Record Group 233, 45A–F28.1, NARA, Washington, D.C.).

5. In the early part of the Capitol grounds project, Olmsted had brought in, besides Wisedell, engineer George Kent Radford and tree expert Oliver Crosby Bullard as assistants. By 1880 their contributions had diminished while Wisedell's were becoming more prominent.

6. That is, respectively, the Senate and House committees on public buildings and grounds, the Architect of the Capitol, the engineer-in-charge of the Capitol grounds, the superintendent of laborers, and the head gardener (Frederick H. Cobb to J. B. Stubbs, May 10, 1881, Records Management Department, Architect of the Capitol, U.S. Capitol, Washington, D.C.; Frederick H. Cobb to Edward Clark, Aug. 18, 1881, Records Management Department, Architect of the Capitol, U.S. Capitol, Washington, D.C.).

7. Wisedell apparently gave assurances of his willingness to continue on the terms Olmsted demanded. He supplied reports and drawings for the summer house through the rest of 1880. Soon he again fell seriously behind on drawings for the terrace, and in 1881 and 1882 he neglected or ignored correspondence (Thomas Wisedell to FLO, July 21, 1880, B134: #2820, OAR/LC; FLO to Frederick H. Cobb, July 15, 1881, Office of the Curator, Architect of the Capitol, U.S. Capitol, Washington, D.C; ibid., Sept. 9, 1881; FLO to Francis H. Kimball and Thomas Wisedell, Sept. 11, 1881; FLO to MPO, Aug. 7, 1882; FLO to Edward Clark, Aug. 10, 1882, Office of the Curator, Architect of the Capitol, U.S. Capitol, Washington, D.C.).

To William Oliver Buchanan

To W. O. Buchanan, E^{sq1} 15th June, 1880

My Dear Sir;
 I am much obliged for yours of the 12th.
 I do not understand the course of things at Albany. Mr Brush[2] assured me that he would personally superintend the work; would see to the drawing of the Bill, &c. I infer that he did not. I also understood that the member from Niagara[3] would make it his business and again Mr Gardner assured me that he would do so.[4] I have seen none of these gentlemen & heard from none, nor from any one else interested in Albany, since February. I have supposed that they made up their minds at a certain time that the Bill could not be carried thro' the Senate, and abandoned effort.
 I had not seen the Bill when it was presented. I strongly advised that my name should not be in it — simply because I thought some other name would give it more strength. But as the service required was not of a professional character and was not to be paid for, I don't understand the objection you say has been felt to it.[5] Still I should like it to be known to those interested that I did not wish to be a commissioner.
 I think what you propose as to petitions very desirable and beg that you will do what you say.[6]
 I should advise a very short and simple form. Perhaps this would answer:
 "The undersigned, referring to the Memorial on the subject of Niagara Falls, formerly addressed to the Governor of New York and embodied in the report of the Commission of the State Survey of 1880, beg to express their concurrence in the views of the many eminent signers of that Memorial and earnestly pray your Honorable Body to adopt such measures as in your wise discretion may be thought most expedient for accomplishing the essential ends therin set forth."
 I rather think that after the Presidential canvass is over, it will be best to send blank forms of petition to different quarters of the state and get as many signatures as practicable.
 I send copies of the Memorial as you request.
 I should be glad if you would let Mr. Whitney of the Cataract House[7] know what I have written you.

The text presented here is from a draft in Olmsted's hand.

1. William Oliver Buchanan (1820–1904), a civil engineer and entrepreneur who was attempting to establish a private corporation that would build a park and hotels at Niagara, as well as a toll road or railway along the Canadian edge of the gorge. He corre-

sponded with Olmsted about affairs at Niagara from 1879 to 1883 (A. W. Patrick Buchanan, *The Buchanan Book: The Life of Alexander Buchanan, Q.C., of Montreal* . . . [Montreal, 1911], p. 246; Pierre Berton, *Niagara: A History of the Falls* [Niagara Falls, 1992], pp. 193–95).
2. Presumably Alexander Brush (1824–1892), Republican mayor of Buffalo in 1880–81, and previously mayor of the city for two terms in the early 1870s (Merton M. Wilner, *Niagara Frontier: A Narrative and Documentary History*, 4 vols. [Chicago, 1931], 1: 465; Michael Rizzo, comp., "Alexander Brush," in *Through the Mayor's Eyes: The Only Complete History of the Mayor's of Buffalo, New York* [buffalonian.com, 2001]).
3. A reference to James Low, the state assemblyman from Niagara Falls, and James T. Gardner.
4. The bill to authorize purchase of land for a public reservation at Niagara Falls was introduced in the state legislature on April 1, 1880, by Assemblyman James Low of Niagara Falls. It named Olmsted as one of the five men to be made commissioners with the responsibility of choosing the land to be purchased for the reservation (serving without compensation). The bill passed the Assembly on May 6, and the Senate finance committee, to which the bill was referred, recommended it for consideration by the full Senate: but no vote to approve it occurred before the Senate adjourned on June 3 (New York [State], *Journal of the Assembly of the State of New York* . . . [Albany, N.Y., 1880], pp. 694, 1296; New York [State], *Journal of the Senate of the State of New York* . . . [Albany, N.Y., 1880], pp. 760, 1170; *New-York Times*, "Discussions at Albany," April 2, 1880, p. 1).
5. In his letter to Olmsted of June 12, Buchanan had written: ". . . you will excuse me for saying what I hear, that your name being among the Commissioners, coupled with your professional interest is spoken of as unfortunate." Indeed, during 1880 Rowland F. Hill of Niagara Falls published several statements asserting that the Niagara reservation was a scheme devised by Olmsted and a small group of hotel owners for their profit (*Letter of Rowland F. Hill Relative to the International Park or State Reservation at Niagara Falls* [Albany, N. Y., 1880]; *Niagara Falls Gazette*, Nov. 3, 1880).
6. Buchanan had written that he planned to place a petition at each of the Niagara Falls hotels for guests to sign. He asked Olmsted to send him some copies of the text of the 1879 Memorial to use in books for signatures that he would make up (W. O. Buchanan to FLO, June 12, 1880).
7. Solon Miron Napoleon Whitney (1815–1883), a proprietor of the Cataract House on the bank of the American Rapids in Niagara Falls, N. Y. (Frederick Clifton Pierce, *Whitney. The Descendants of John Whitney* . . . [Chicago, 1895], p. 417).

To John Charles Phillips

Brookline Mass.
23rd Aug. 1880.

J. C. Phillips, Esq.
My Dear Sir;
    I send you enclosed, drawings, by which you can set about the work of subgrading your home grounds and building the terrace wall.[1] In this plan

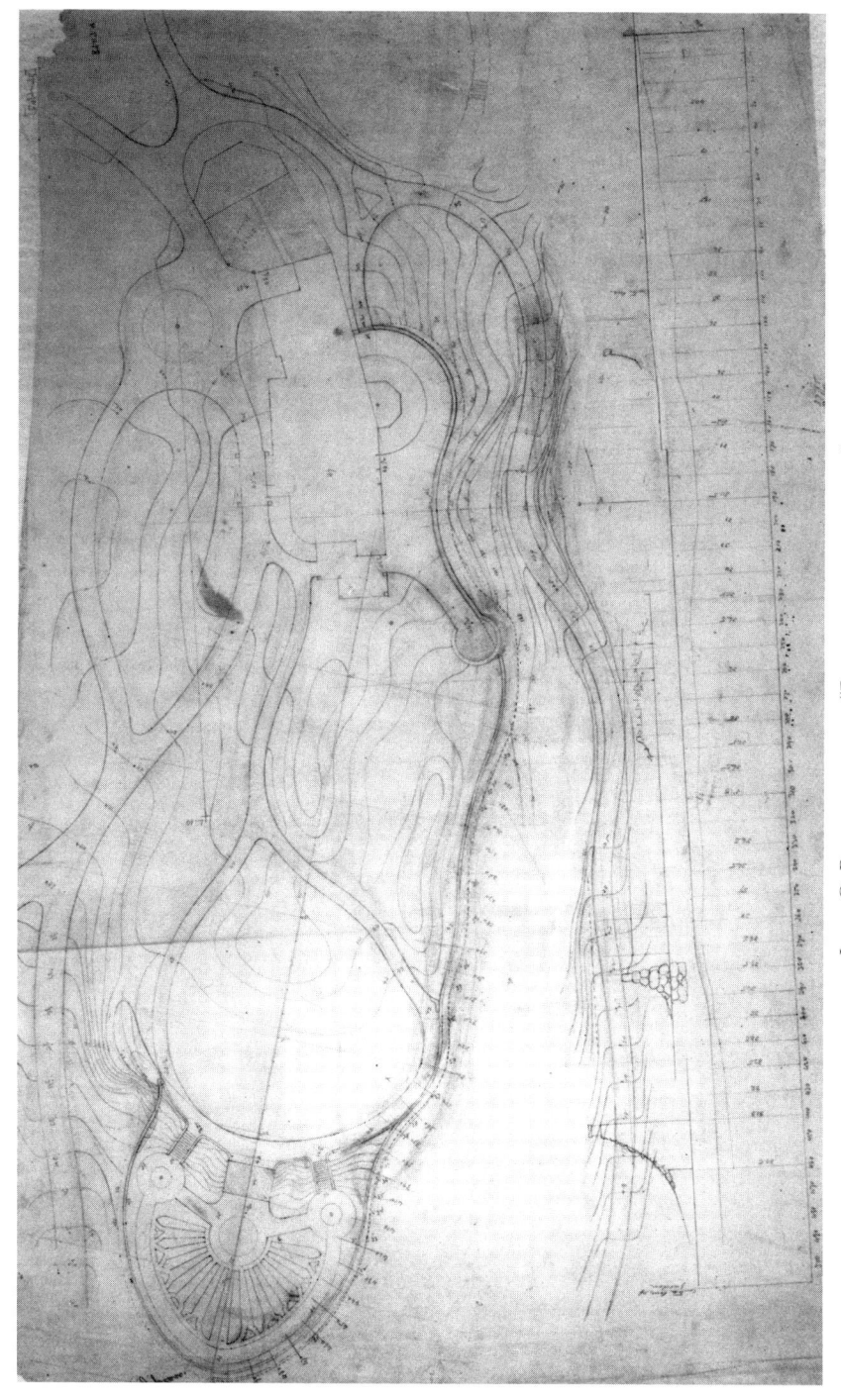

John C. Phillips estate, "Plan of home grounds"

JOHN C. PHILLIPS ESTATE, GARDEN AREA WITH PAVILION AND STONE ARCH

the height of the wall is less than has been contemplated in our conversations. I think the result will be on the whole equally satisfactory and the cost less. The only important modification or addition to the plan grows out of Mrs. Phillip's[2] wish for "an old fashioned flower-garden."[3]

An old fashioned flower-garden is largely made up of a class of perennials which at times have a sprawling habit and close under the windows of a house are apt to appear disorderly and a little out of place. I have therefore planned a garden of the old fashioned kind at the south end of the lawn so situated that it will be looked down upon from the pavillion. The outline of this garden fits the ground nicely. The larger part of it is intended to be in turf with beds defined by box edgings. The surface is to decline gently from the outside to the central circle, like a palm leaf fan pressed down by the handle. If you think it too extensive as thus laid out the beds can be reduced and the proportion of turf increased or the periphery contracted. Mr. Haskell[4] will be able to lay the work out from these drawings. If he should be in doubt at any point, let me know and my son[5] or I will come up.

The text presented here is from a draft in Olmsted's hand.

1. Presumably the undated plans no. 33 and no. 78, which give elevations for the terrace wall on the eastern side of the house, and for the contours of the land near the house. Plan 78, entitled "Plan of home grounds/ copy of working plan," shows a design for the garden south of the pavilion that fits the description in this letter. A nearly identical design for the garden appears on plan no. 17, which bears the date August 12 and 13, 1880. (Both sets of numbers assigned by the Olmsted firm to plans for this project, most of which are undated, appear to have been added at a later time and do not seem to reflect knowledge of the order in which the plans were prepared). (Plans 12297–17, 12297–33, and 12297–78, NPS/FLONHS).
2. Anna Tucker Phillips (c.1847–1925) (*Boston Globe*, April 25, 1925, p. 3).
3. The old-fashioned garden became popular in the aftermath of the Centennial Exhibition held in Philadelphia in 1876. Part of a broader cultural interest in the Colonial era, the gardens contained hollyhocks, poppies, foxgloves, and other perennials that, as Charles S. Sargent wrote, "enlivened the borders of long ago." These flowers were generally displayed in beds lined with boxwood or in formally arranged sections of gardens (Charles S. Sargent, "Old-Fashioned Gardens," *Garden and Forest* 8 (July 17, 1895): 281–82; see May Brawley Hill, *Grandmother's Garden: The Old-Fashioned American Garden, 1865–1915* [New York, 1995]).
4. The surveyor J. H. Haskell of Beverly, Massachusetts (J. H. Haskell to FLO, Aug. 6, 1880)
5. John Charles Olmsted, who helped prepare plans for this commission and may well have worked out the design of the flower garden.

To Edward Clark

[c. August–September 1880]

Edward Clark Esq.
Architect of the Capitol.
Dear Sir;

I write the following at your request.[1]

The use of the ordinary park seats, either moveable or fixed, is to be {avoided} on the Capitol Grounds both as a matter of taste and propriety and because of the disorder and misuse to which they would lead.

The inconvenience of having no place for resting in them would however be too great and if this were attempted some unsuitable expedient would probably in the end be adopted, as such expedients have been heretofore.

The summer house in question is designed principally to provide for persons passing through the Southwest quarter of the grounds,[2] a cool and shady place in which a few minutes rest can be taken without interruption to the walks or breaking the leading lines of view. Secondly to provide a drinking fountain about which a number of persons may stand without obstruction to the walks, and lastly, incidental to the above purposes, to secure conditions favorable to certain types of beauty in vegetation.

It is designed in materials and forms to be enduring and to offer the least temptation or opportunity to careless or wanton injury, or for indecent or unseemly practices.

Standing well out of the walks, the seats which it contains are open to view from them and a watchman in passing by will be able to see all within. The seats are divided so they can be used only as seats, not as lounges. The entrances are furnished with lock-gates to be closed at night.

The walls are thick and double for coolness. It is so built into the hillside that to one coming down the slope it does not obstruct the western prospect.

When over grown with ivy it will be indistinguishable in any general view across the grounds, being merged in the adjoining verdure. By placing the floor on a level with the walk on the down-hill side ample head room is obtained under the roofs with the least possible exterior exposure of walls

The walls back of the seats on the two lower sides above the level of the ground are of perforated stone to allow a circulation of air. For the same reason the central portion is open to the sky. On the uphill side a deep alcove of rock work is provided, looked into from the house through an oval stone frame through which a rivulet is carried (being the waste water from the old fountain at the west entrance to the Capitol.) The alcove is shaded and the rock-work is designed to be mainly covered with the more delicate ivies.

It is also provided with numerous crannies opening into deposits of wood earth back of the walls for ferns and several flowering mountain plants. The arrangement is such that they will be inaccessible to pilferers and once established, may be expected to thrive with little gardening care. Moderate soil-moisture during extreme droughts is secured by several, slowly percolating tanks back of the walls. The aim is to produce in the hottest and driest season an effect of coolness, moisture, shade and airiness in association with deep, rich and luxurient verdure. No exotics are to be used.

The parting of the rivulet in the rock-work and the outflow of the simple drinking fountain to stand in the centre of the house will contribute to the effect. The water of the drinking fountain passes into filtering tanks to give moisture to the ivy on the South and West sides and thence falls six feet into water under the floor grating. The roof is designed to be mantled with ivy both within and without. There are openings in the brick work for the ivy to creep through. The roof tile and parts of the brick-work are roughened to give it a better hold.[3]

It will take about three years for the plants to grow to a point at which the esthetic motives of the design will begin to be realized.

MAY 1880–DECEMBER 1880

The text presented here is from a document in a clerk's hand with corrections by Olmsted. A shorter version appeared in the *Annual Report of the Architect of the Capitol* (Washington, D.C., 1880), page 440, and was used to supply a word missing from the text. The editors have dated it circa August–September 1880 because in early August Frederick H. Cobb requested that Olmsted write a statement about the summer house for the annual report. On October 1, 1880, Edward Clark signed the report in which the short version appeared (Frederick H. Cobb to FLO, Aug. 5, 1880, D3, OAR/LC).

1. Although it was Cobb who requested this memorandum, it is likely that Olmsted and Clark had discussed the need for one to clear up confusion about the summer house. Olmsted had hoped to finish enough of the structure during the autumn of 1879 to avoid any misunderstandings when Congress convened in December. Unfortunately Thomas Wisedell did not deliver his drawings when needed and only the foundation and rockwork were completed by the time winter arrived. In April 1880, Eli Saulsbury, a Democratic member of the Senate committee on public buildings and grounds, complained that the summer house would become a nuisance and that it had not been authorized in the original plan of the grounds. He threatened to introduce a Congressional resolution to have it removed at once. He relented when Justin S. Morrill, Edward Clark, and finally Olmsted himself, explained its purpose and convinced him that it would not appear to full advantage until the plantings around it matured in several years.

    The summer house stirred opposition of a more serious nature just weeks later. On the Senate floor in early June, Morrill moved to add $90,000 to the Capitol grounds budget to start construction of Olmsted's proposed terrace. Senator James Beck, a Democratic member of the appropriations committee who had favored eliminating all funding for the Capitol grounds several years before, rose in opposition. He undercut support for the terrace by ridiculing the two fountains Olmsted had introduced in the east carriage court ("Dutch spittoons") and the unfinished summer house: "I heard that it was a house for some man's monkey." Other senators then questioned Olmsted's authority to introduce the summer house without specific authorization from Congress. Henry M. Teller, who shortly afterward became secretary of the interior, set the tone by declaring "I think if he is going to build any more summer rests or roosts, the matter had better be submitted to Congress." The senators then voted down the appropriation for the terrace.

    From the start of construction Olmsted had feared that the summer house would be misunderstood and invite ridicule. His intent, he reminded Cobb in June 1880, had been to complete it during the previous year's congressional recess.

    > Now as we failed to accomplish this and have got into a scrape let us try to make the best of it. I have certain purposes to be accomplished. They are good and sensible purposes and if the work is allowed to stand three years the necessary outlay for them will be justified. In the meantime it will be under a constant ill-natured investigation.

    (FLO to Frederick H. Cobb, Sept. 4, 1878, in Office of the Curator, Architect of the Capitol, U.S. Capitol, Washington, D.C.; ibid., Sept. 8, 1879; FLO to Edward Clark, April 17, 1880, in Office of the Curator, Architect of the Capitol, U.S. Capitol, Washington, D.C.; Justin S. Morrill to Edward Clark, April 15, 1880, B134: #2820, OAR/LC; Edward Clark to FLO, April 24 1880, D2, OAR/LC; ibid., May 5, 1880; A. J. Merritt to FLO, April 16, 1880; ibid., April 19, 1880; FLO to Frederick H. Cobb, June 13, 1880, D3, OAR/LC; G. Brown, *Documentary History of the United States Capitol*, pp. 1207–9).

2. The summer house under construction when Olmsted wrote the present text is located in the northwest quarter of the Capitol grounds. However, as late as the summer of 1881 a second summer house, not constructed, was planned for the southwest grounds (FLO to Frederick H. Cobb, Dec. 18, 1879, Office of the Curator, Architect of the Capitol,

U.S. Capitol, Washington, D.C.; ibid., June 27, 1881; Frederick H. Cobb to FLO, July 27, 1881, D3, OAR/LC; Frederick H. Cobb to Edward Clark, Aug. 12, 1881, B134: #2820, OAR/LC).

3. Olmsted specified that Dahurican and Irish ivies and evergreen honeysuckle be planted to cover the walls of the summer house; large cavities over the arches of the structure were to be planted with yuccas, prickly pear cactus, and sempervivums. Delicate ivies, mosses, and ferns flourished in the moist enclosure of the rockwork. The ground near the rockwork was planted with yuccas and evergreen honeysuckle; the remaining ground around the structure was to be covered with ivy, periwinkle, and mouse-wort. The trees close by, although hardy, were to present "a somewhat quaint or exotic aspect." They included the Willow oak, Cedrella, Oleaster, two kinds of Aralias, and the Golden Catalpa (FLO, "Planting Memoranda Spring 1880," Records Management Department, Architect of the Capitol, U.S. Capitol, Washington, D.C.; William Cogan to FLO, May 31, 1880, D3, OAR/LC; ibid., Nov. 21, 1880; FLO to CEN, May 30, 1881, below; [Frederick Law Olmsted], "Index to Trees About the Capitol, with Advice to Visitors Interested in Them," in *Annual Report of the Architect of the Capitol* [1882], appendix, p. 921).

To Sylvester Baxter

Brookline 9th Nov. 1880.

Sylvester Baxter Esq[rl]
My Dear Sir,

I have recev[d] your note asking advice about the Middlesex Fells project.[2] The scheme when I visited the ground was yet so indefinite and my observations were so cursory that I do not know upon what points advice is needed which I am qualified to give.

You use the word park however with reference to the project and I have heard something said of the fitness of certain localities for particular purposes which indicated a disposition to associate, with the main purpose, various side shows such as are generally thought of in connection with a park scheme — some of which would lead on to structures and to a garden like treatment of parts of the property.

This will perhaps justify me in stating what I think to be the most important lesson of my professional study. Since this began thirty years ago, I have not only been in supervision of several large parks and numerous smaller grounds but have a number of times personally reviewed the principal public grounds of Europe & closely followed their history. In all I have found the difficulty of pursuing any one leading purpose through a series of years in a consistent and single minded way the chief source of inefficient managmnt, extravagance & waste.

This difficulty lies mainly in an unrecognized conflict between interest in the main & interest in minor motives of the works in question. Hence I say that I have learned nothing of more importance than the wisdom of rigidly limiting the objects to be pursued on each piece of ground and of developing in the highest degree whatever may be the distinguishing characteristics of each particular property.

I may add that lovers of nature without special experience seldom realize how much more difficult it is to obtain and preserve in much frequented public grounds what is asked for under the name of simple natural aspects of scenery than to secure the most elaborate and finished gardening effects.

The natural drift of men in prosecuting improvements of ground is almost irresistably to the undue multiplication of features & incidents and to formality and fussiness. The capacity and disposition to apply art to the concealmnt of art though much talked of & professed is exceedingly rare.

Therefore it should be kept in mind that when as in this case the impulse of an undertaking comes from an appreciation of the beauty & use of absolutely wild sylvan scenery it is most desirable to avoid complicating the purpose of preserving & developing such scenery & making it available to the public with any other of the more generally recognized purposes of public parks and gardens.

If the scheme succeeds as soon as the work is well under way it will be found that all the means that can be obtained for it will be inadequate to do all that is desirable in respect to its initial purpose in a thoroughly excellent manner.

There will be a question whether the results of the general policy which it is my aim to suggest would be of sufficiently varied popular interest to obtain public support. I recognize that there is a misled & misleading public opinion in this respect which at the outset may have to be somewhat boldly met but I am confident that after a short time, the pride and pleasure which the public interested would have in a ground perfectly unique in character, that character being consistently sustained in all its borders with artistic completeness & finish would be much greater than it would be in any ground of more complex & sophisticated character.

The topography of Middlesex Fells is most unsuitable for a park. To give it a park character and adapt it to ordinary park managemnt and use would be an absurdly costly operation.

What is adviseable & what can be done cheaply, profitably and with a wise and noble beneficence, is to take it as it stands, develop to the utmost its natural characteristics, and make it a true retreat not only from town but from suburban conditions.

The few structures and blots of cultivation which already mar its natural character should be removed; operations for its public use either inconsiderately crude or out of keeping through unnecessary nicety should be avoided; the intrusion upon its prospects of all objects and scenes incongruous with its natural characteristics should be as much as possible guarded against; every inducement should be offered visitors to ramble and wander about and the least possible temptation should be put in their way to come together in clusters, crowds and throngs; most of all everything of a show, museum or toy shop order, everything smart or splendid, everything spectacular, sensational, bustling and fussy should be kept as far away as possible.

    I trust that this advice is not needed but if you think it will tend to strengthen sound convictions and intentions it is heartily at your service.

The text presented here is from a draft in Olmsted's hand.

1. Sylvester Baxter (1850–1927), newspaper reporter and publicist, a leading figure in the creation of the Boston metropolitan park system. Baxter had published an article in the *Boston Herald* in November 1879 urging preservation as a public reserve of the four thousand-acre area of rocky terrain, woods and ponds north of Boston to which he gave the name Middlesex Fells. Various citizens of the regions supported him in his campaign, and Olmsted had visited the area with one of the proponents, the naturalist and author Thomas Wilson Flagg (1805–1884), a short time before. Olmsted had reviewed Flagg's book *The Woods and By-Ways of New England* in the *Nation* in early 1874 (See FLO, "Country Living," above: DAB; *Who Was Who: 1897–1942* [Chicago, 1943], 1: 71; Cynthia Zaitzevsky, *Frederick Law Olmsted and the Boston Park System* [Cambridge, Mass., 1982], pp. 122–23).
2. In letter to Olmsted of November 5, 1880, Baxter reported that a group was working to "secure the Middlesex Fells as a public domain." He solicited Olmsted's advice as to "how it could best be treated simply, effectively, and with little expense." "I suppose the idea of an elaborate park would frighten the towns out of the idea," he observed, "although the plan will improve them wonderfully." He immediately thanked Olmsted for the letter presented here, apologizing for his use of the word "park" in describing his concept for the Fells (Sylvester Baxter to FLO, Nov. 5, 1880; ibid., Nov. 10, 1880).

To Edward Clark

Private.

Brookline 18th Nov[r] 1880.

Dear Mr Clark:

    I know something of the difficulties and don't want to complain or say that matters *can* be better ordered. Especially I don't want to cross Mr Cobb but as he has I believe twice officially reported that the police of the capitol grounds is satisfactory,[1] I think that I ought to tell you how very unsatisfactory it is to me. When I last went on the ground with Cogan[2] I noticed that some plants which I had seen before had disappeared; asking him about them he said they had been stolen, and immediately pointed out several plants that had apparently been pulled up by the roots & left on the ground within a few hours. He said that this was of daily occurrence and that at least 3000 plants had been pulled up and most of them taken away since last spring. Afterwards he begged that I would not have the temporary rail about the rockwork of the summer house taken down and urged that additional barriers should be made. I then spoke to the watchman of the beat explaining to him that it was of first importance to prevent boys from leaving the walk while the summer house was still a novelty and to guard against bad habits being started. I told him that on Sundays especially, he must give special attention to this, if necessary giving his entire time to it, everything else being of comparatively small consequence. He promised me to do so and to repeat what I had said to his relief. I also begged Mr Cobb to give the matter his special attention and reinforce my instructions to the watchman.

I asked Cogan to report to me if there should be any disorder and to-day I have a note from him saying:

"*I am very sorry to be obliged to report further injuries to plants &c.— at the summer house on Sunday a hundred people were on the roof and rockwork during the day and made beaten paths all about.*"

He had twice previously reported (as I instructed him to) that ivy had been jerked violently from the walls, broken and pulled up. He has also reported that boys continue to play at night among the choice evergreens (as I have seen them) and have lately done serious injury to them.[3]

I have written to Mr Cobb—had written him before getting this last report from Cogan.[4] I know that he can't be expected to give much personal attention to these matters and especially on Sunday. And I don't suppose that anything can be done to secure greater police efficiency. Still I think I ought to submit the matter to you and I suggest for one thing that from this time to winter at least it would be better to reduce the day force if necessary to have one or two active men on at night, and that the day watchmen should be instructed not to patrol the roads, there being less need for them on the roads than anywhere else. I also suggest the employmnt of a detective. Is it not wrong that where plants are disappearing by the thousand, year after year, arrests should hardly ever be made or the petty rascals punished?

The whole difficulty—apart, of course, from the all pervading political difficulty—lies in the fact that with the single exception of Cogan, who counts for little, the professional training and habits of all in authority on the grounds, from Mr Cobb to the watchmen themselves, make it hard for them to regard what is wasted in the manner I have indicated as of any serious consequence. To me it is the soul of the affair, without which the engineering and architectural work and even much of the coarse planting is but what the foundations & rough brickwalls of the Capitol are to the carvings of the marble.

I hate to add a feather's weight to the load you have to carry but having written yesterday to Cobb suggesting that he should speak to you about a night watch, I thought that I had better frankly let you know how different his point of view may be from mine. I really don't mean to complain or ask what may be impracticable.[5]

Very Truly Yours

Fred^k Law Olmsted.

The text presented here is from a manuscript in Olmsted's hand in the Office of the Curator, Architect of the Capitol, U.S. Capitol, Washington, D.C.

1. Vandalism against plants, trees, and fixtures on the U.S. Capitol grounds had concerned Olmsted since 1875. However, Frederick H. Cobb, engineer-in-charge of the Capitol grounds, had reported in his annual reports of 1879 and 1880 that the policing of the grounds was good and had "prevented depredations in a large degree" (FLO, "Notice to Watchmen," [July 7, 1878], above; *Annual Report of the Architect of the Capitol* [1879], p. 324; ibid., [1881], p. 440).
2. Olmsted visited Washington from October 26 to 30. William Cogan, the head gardener, had been employed on the Capitol grounds since at least 1875. He had been recruited for the job by Oliver Crosby Bullard, whose chief assistant he was at Prospect Park in Brooklyn (FLO, pay vouchers, Records Management Department, Architect of the Capitol, U.S. Capitol, Washington, D.C.; FLO to John A. Partridge, Aug. 4, 1875; John A. Partridge to FLO, Oct. 7, 1875).
3. Cogan had reported vandalism of the plantings around the summer house and among the evergreens at the Pennsylvania Avenue entrance in August and again in November. Here Olmsted quotes from a letter Cogan had written two days before the present letter (FLO to Frederick H. Cobb, Aug. 2, 1880, Office of the Curator, Architect of the Capitol, U.S. Capitol, Washington, D.C.; Frederick H. Cobb to FLO, Aug. 5, 1880, and William Cogan to FLO, Nov. 14, 1880, D3, OAR/LC; ibid., Nov. 16, 1880).
4. In the letter to which he refers, Olmsted had asked that a night watchman be put on duty near the summer house. Cobb complied but reported that Cogan had exaggerated the amount of damage done to plantings (FLO to Frederick H. Cobb, Nov. 17, 1880, Office of the Curator, Architect of the Capitol, U.S. Capitol, Washington, D.C.; Frederick H. Cobb to FLO, Nov. 19, 1880, D3, OAR/LC).
5. Arrangements for a night watchman appear to have been temporary. Cogan soon reported that Clark had only instructed the watchmen to pay more attention to the interior of the grounds than to the roads and had authorized him to put one of his gardeners on full-time duty at the summer house. Olmsted renewed his complaints about the policing of the Capitol grounds the following spring (William Cogan to FLO, Nov. 21, 1880, D3, OAR/LC; ibid., Nov. 29, 1880; FLO to Frederick H. Cobb, April 11, 1881, Office of the Curator, Architect of the Capitol, U.S. Capitol, Washington, D.C.).

may 1880–december 1880

To Charles Henry Dalton

Arnold Arboretum, Harvard University,
DIRECTOR'S OFFICE,
BROOKLINE, MASS., November 29, 1880.

CHARLES H. DALTON, Esq., Boston.
My Dear Sir,—

In compliance with your request, we have examined Commonwealth Avenue with the view of recommending a scheme for re-planting the central greens.[1]

It is a well established rule in urban planting that only trees of one variety can be used in the same continuous street. If this rule is disregarded, and trees differing widely in habit, rate of growth, and in the period of putting on or losing their leaves, are planted side by side, incongruous and disagreeable effects will result; and such disagreeable effects will increase rather than diminish as the trees approach maturity and assume the widely different characters peculiar to different species. The advantage of using one instead of several varieties of trees in the same street or avenue will be readily seen by comparing the Beacon Street Mall below Joy Street, or the Charles Street Mall,[2] with the plantation in the older portions of Commonwealth Avenue.

In order to obtain in Commonwealth Avenue the uniformity which seems to us so essential to the future beauty and dignity of the finest street in the city, we recommend that it be entirely re-planted from Arlington Street to West Chester Park;[3] and that, instead of the double row of trees now used, a single row be planted on each side of the central walk, ten feet from the line of the street.

We recommend that European elms, of one variety and of a standard size, should be used for this purpose. This selection is based on the fact that the European elm has been thoroughly tested in Boston and its immediate vicinity during a period extending over more than a hundred years,—a period long enough to show its entire adaptability to our climate; and because the largest and finest trees which have ever been planted in Boston have belonged to this species, which in this climate seems better fitted than any native tree of a similar class to withstand the droughts, heat and dust, to which all city trees are necessarily subjected.

We recommend a single rather than the double row of trees now used, and that the trees should stand at least forty feet apart in the rows, in order that in the future they may attain a development worthy of the wide and stately thoroughfare which is to join the Common and Public Garden with the new system of city and suburban parks.[4]

If Commonwealth Avenue is re-planted in accordance with these suggestions, it will not be necessary to remove at once the trees now growing in the older portions of the street, or at least many of them. The new plantation can be made by inserting the new trees between existing ones; and these can be gradually removed as they encroach on the young plantation.

We find that the total length of the eight grass plots between Arlington Street and West Chester Park is 4100 feet, and that to plant it in the manner proposed will require 180 trees, namely: —

24 trees between Arlington and Berkeley Streets.
22 " " Berkeley and Clarendon "
24 " " Clarendon and Dartmouth "
24 " " Dartmouth and Exeter "
26 " " Exeter and Fairfield "
22 " " Fairfield and Gloucester "
16 " " Gloucester and Hereford "
22 " " Hereford and Chester Park.

Total, 180

Suitable trees for this purpose can be imported from England at a cost which, including freight, duties, etc., should not exceed $1.00 each.

It is needless to remind you that the soil of Commonwealth Avenue plots (a few inches of loam overlaying loose, porous gravel) is entirely unsuited to grow large and long-lived trees. In order to produce a lasting and satisfactory result, it will be wise to make a considerable outlay in preparing the ground for the new plantations. We recommend that pits at least ten feet square and four feet deep should be made for each tree, and that the soil excavated should be entirely replaced by the best virgin loam procurable. Even larger pits are desirable; for, the existing soil being unfit to support plant-life for any length of time, the size and age to which any trees planted there will be able to attain must depend on the amount of artificially prepared nourishment which can be supplied to them.

If Commonwealth Avenue is to be re-planted next spring, it is desirable, should the weather permit, to have the ground prepared this winter, that the new loam in the pits may have time to become properly settled and compacted before the trees are planted. The order for the trees, too, should be sent to England at once, as it may take some time to pick up there a sufficient number of suitable size and shape. Even if it should be found impracticable to plant next spring, it might be desirable to send for the trees now and grow them on the Austin Farm until needed for Commonwealth Avenue, and in this way gain the advantage of their larger size.

Yours very truly,

CHARLES S. SARGENT.
FREDERICK LAW OLMSTED.

The text presented here is from a typescript in the Library of Gray Herbarium, Harvard University, Cambridge, Massachusetts.
1. In this letter Sargent and Olmsted proposed a new planting plan for the trees along Commonwealth Avenue between the Public Garden and Back Bay Fens.
2. Olmsted refers here to two allées of trees in Boston Common: one along its western edge at Charles Street, facing the Public Garden, and the other in its eastern section connecting Joy Street with West Street or Winter Street (M. F. Sweetser, *New Map of Boston* [Boston, 1880]).
3. That is, Olmsted and Sargent proposed to replant the trees along the full distance of the straight section of Commonwealth Avenue between the Public Garden and what is now Massachusetts Avenue — after which the Avenue was planned to angle northward in order to intersect with Beacon Street at Brookline Avenue.
4. Commonwealth Avenue intersected at the Back Bay Fens just beyond Massachusetts Avenue with the linear park system that Olmsted was planning that extended from there to Franklin Park and, eventually, beyond to Marine Park.

Suggestions for the Improvement of Muddy River

BOSTON, December 1880.

To the Commissioners of Parks:—
GENTLEMEN,—

In a plan which I had the honor, in conjunction with the City Engineer, to submit to you a year ago,[1] the drainage difficulties of Back Bay were proposed to be met by forming a part of it into a basin in which water would, under ordinary circumstances, be maintained at a nearly uniform level, but in which, when an unusually high tide would for a few hours prevent outflow, a larger amount could be harmlessly stored. Public roads were to be laid out around and across this basin, and its banks to be planted, and otherwise treated picturesquely.

The plan was adopted, and with the concurrence of the City Council work is now advancing under it. In presenting it last January to the Council, you pointed out that while its scope was limited to that part of the Back Bay which had some years before been placed in your charge with a view to a public park, the evils which it was designed to meet would still remain to be dealt with in that arm of the bay known as Muddy River.

The question has since been raised whether the best plan for this purpose might not be found in extending a corresponding arm of the Back Bay basin to the head of tide-water in Muddy River, and the present report is designed to present this suggestion (as far as practicable in advance of surveys and mature study) in a form to invite preliminary discussion.

The tidal part of Muddy River above the basin now under construction has the usual character of a salt creek winding through a valley, the marshy surface of which, lying from fifteen to twenty feet below the general level of the adjoining uplands, is partially submerged at extreme high-water. The tide ordinarily flows to a point about a mile above the basin.[2] Streets have been laid out upon the uplands upon no continuous system; those of each side independently, and regardless of what may be eventually required in the low lands; the leading motive being to make small bodies of land immediately available, at little cost, for suburban residences. The city is rapidly advancing in compact blocks towards the region, and public convenience will, before many years, require a more comprehensive treatment of it.

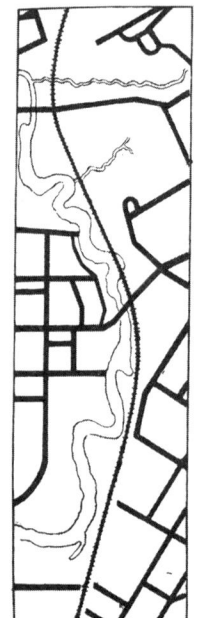

It usually happens when a town is building up on both sides of a small water-course and valley that the sanitary and other disadvantages of the low ground prevent it from being much occupied, except in a way damaging to the value of the adjoining properties. In process of time the stream and valley and the uses to which they are put, come to be regarded as a nuisance; and radical measures, such as the construction of a great underground channel, and the filling up of the valley, are urged as the only adequate remedy. The cost of these, and the local disturbance they make, excite opposition to them; their complete beneficial operation is long delayed, and the character of the district becomes so strongly fixed before this period is reached that it can only be partially changed. Though necessary, therefore, to public health and convenience of general transit through the district, the result in the increased tax-bearing capacity of the locality is no compensation for the required outlay.

As an alternative to such a possible course the policy now suggested for Muddy River would look to the preservation of the present channel with certain modifications and improvements adapted to make it permanently attractive and wholesome, and an element of constantly increasing advantage to the neighborhood. Except where the valley is now narrowest, it would be reduced in width by artificial banks, so that the river with its shores would everywhere have a general character, resembling that which it now has near Longwood bridge, only that its water would be kept at a nearly uniform level, and guarded from defilement by intercepting sewers and otherwise. The Brookline margin would be the broadened base of the present railroad embankment,[3] bearing a woody thicket. The opposite or Boston bank would have an elevation above the water of ten feet where wholly artificial, rising where the natural bank is used to twenty feet. Upon this would be laid out a public way ninety feet wide in continuation of that now forming upon the Back Bay basin; divided like that into foot,

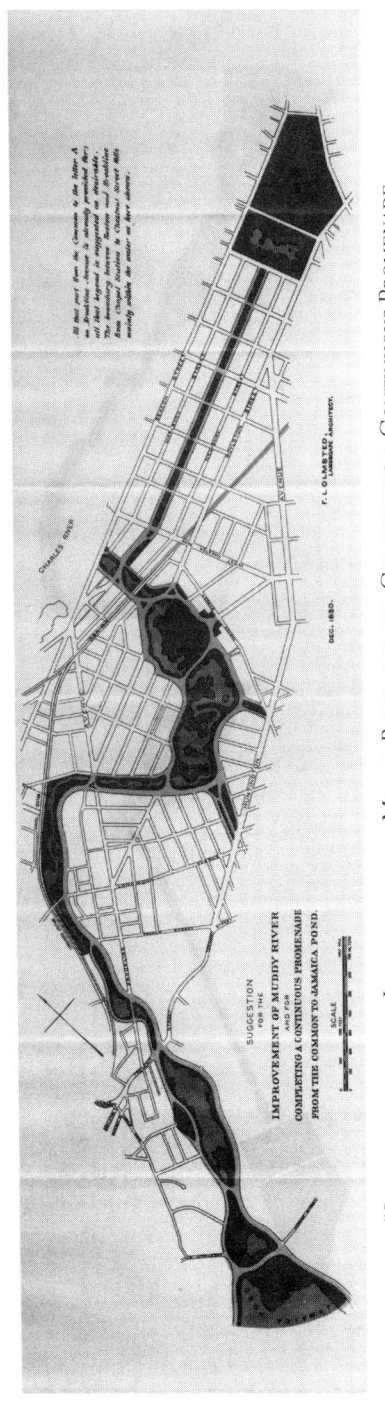

"Suggestion for the Improvement of Muddy River and for Completing a Continuous Promenade from the Common to Jamaica Pond," December 1880

carriage, and saddle courses, and designed to serve as a public promenade along the river bank, as well as a trunk line giving an element of continuity to the street system of the neighborhood.

It is proposed that this parkway should be continued along the small water-course above and through the valley to Jamaica Pond, which would add another mile to its length. There are three smaller ponds near the head of the valley, which would thus be skirted, and below them a large marsh, which, though formerly reached by the tide, is now a fresh-water swamp,[4] and cannot long remain in its present condition without great peril to the health and life of the increasing population of the adjoining parts, both of Boston and Brookline. Physicians practising in the neighborhood believe it to have been already the source of serious epidemics.

The supply of water to it from local springs is supposed to be large enough to maintain a pond to be formed by a dam at the lower end, by which it would be changed from a foul and noisome to a pleasing and healthful circumstance. The property is of little value speculatively, and of none otherwise, and the improvement thus projected would be neither difficult nor costly. If the fresh-water supply should finally be thought insufficient for the purpose, it would be possible to extend the salt-water basin to cover the ground.[5] The swamp-soil excavated would be of value for covering the slopes below, and the operation would not be costly.

Adopting either expedient, the result would be a chain of pleasant waters, including the four closely adjoining ponds above the swamp, extending from the "mill-dam" on Beacon Street[6] to the far end of Jamaica Pond, all of natural and in some degree picturesque outline, with banks wooded and easily to be furnished with verdure and foliage throughout. Except at one point where there are about a dozen cheaply-built wooden dwellings and shops,[7] the whole would be formed on land of little value, occupied by no buildings, and for no productive purposes, and all of it now in a condition hazardous to public health.

Such a chain of waters, even if connected and having a sweeping current, always becomes objectionable in a town, when streets are so laid out that its immediate borders are private property, or have private properties backing upon them. In such case it is found necessary to give it the character of a canal, to wall its banks with masonry, and, if the water supply greatly fluctuates, to take other measures to prevent its becoming a nuisance. At the best it is an eyesore. But if uniformly filled, its banks made comely, and kept neatly, in the usual manner of public parks, and if no private property is allowed to abut upon them, any natural water-course will be attractive and wholesome.

On the other hand, private property looking upon the parkway would at small cost be well drained; there would be nothing objectionable in its rear but in general a pleasant neighborhood, already formed, and, as it would lie midway between an attractive urban and an attractive suburban residence district, agreeably connected, there would be no doubt as to its ultimate character, or that it would be rapidly taken up for dwellings of a superior class. This prospect would have an immediate favorable influence on adjoining properties, and the entire operation would be attended by an advance of market and taxable values securing the city a rapid return for its outlay.

The indirect course of the parkway, following the river bank, would prevent its being much used for purposes of heavy transportation. It would thus, without offensive exclusiveness or special police regulation, be left free to be used as a pleasure route.

The Brookline Branch Railroad and the drive of the parkway, where they come nearest together, would be 200 feet apart, and there would be a double screen of foliage between them.

Taken in connection with the mall upon Commonwealth Avenue, the Public Garden and the Common, the parkway would complete a pleasure-route from the heart of the city a distance of six miles into its suburbs. These older pleasure-grounds, while continuing to serve equally well all their present purposes, would, by becoming part of an extended system, acquire increased importance and value. They would have a larger use, be more effective as appliances for public health, and every dollar expended for their maintenance would return a larger dividend.

The scheme offers hardly less advantage to Brookline than to Boston, and a plan of equitable coöperation in carrying it out is probably feasible.

If the interests of the city required that the region affected should be largely occupied for manufacturing and commercial purposes, and that for this reason it should be provided with frequent, continuous, and direct lines of communication upon easy grades, the proposition would be more open to objection. But such provisions would be very costly, and if the tendency at present manifest on every side to make the district a residence quarter, with only such provisions for trade as local convenience may call for, is not desirable to be checked, then the suggestion would seem to offer a much-needed sanitary improvement at moderate cost, and with a promise of large incidental profits.

Respectfully,

FREDERICK LAW OLMSTED.

The text presented here is from BCDP, City of Boston, *Sixth Annual Report, for the Year 1881* (City Doc. No. 12) [Boston, 1881], pages 13–17.

1. See FLO to BCDP, City of Boston, January 26, 1880, above
2. The Muddy River was tidal approximately as far as the Huntington Avenue crossing (Route 9).
3. The embankment for the Brookline branch of the Boston & Albany Railroad, located near the river on its western side.
4. The site of present-day Leverett Pond.

5. This extension of salt water from the Back Bay Fens would have required dredging the swamp and running the Muddy River through a conduit to the Charles River from a point above the pond being created.
6. The Mill Dam along the line of Beacon Street was constructed across the Back Bay in 1818–22 to provide a source of water power for industries (Nancy S. Seasholes, *Gaining Ground: A History of Land Making in Boston* [Cambridge, Mass., 2003], pp. 155–60).
7. The buildings were in the area of Downer Street, which lay east of Brookline Avenue between Aspinwall and Tremont (now Boylston) streets.

CHAPTER X

FEBRUARY 1881–DECEMBER 1881

During the time period of this chapter, Olmsted rented his house in Manhattan and moved his family permanently to Brookline, Massachusetts. Two reports of these months deal with new aspects of the developing Boston park system. The report of May 17 examines the proposed site in West Roxbury for the principal park of the system, and the report of December 29 contains Olmsted's first description of the linear system of parks and parkways running from Charlesbank and Boston Common to the West Roxbury park. In addition, the letter to Charles Francis Adams, Jr., encourages the movement in suburban Quincy to reserve the area of Merry Mount for park purposes. The letter to John Sterling marks the beginning of Olmsted's planning in Detroit of the park on Belle Isle.

In the letter to Edward Clark, Olmsted provides his fullest explanation of the process by which he planned the West Front terrace and other terraces of the U.S. Capitol. On a similar theme, his letter to Barthold Schlesinger sets forth his doctrine of terraces as applied to private residences. The letter to Charles Eliot Norton of October 19 is an impassioned statement of his continuing efforts to discover and publicize a comprehensive and coherent definition of landscape design. Other letters to Norton chart the development of the Niagara reservation campaign. The letter to Cornelius Agnew explores issues of private and public space in a community, as applied to a summer colony being designed at Montauk by the firm of McKim, Meade and White.

The assassination of President James Garfield in the summer of 1881 moved Olmsted to write the article "Influence," containing a concise and forceful review of his experience with the politics of patronage during his years on Central Park. This he submitted to his friend George W. Curtis, president of the Civil Service Reform Association, for use in a new campaign.

To Horace William Shaler Cleveland

209 W. 46th St. N. York.
9th Feby 1881.

My Dear Mr Cleveland;
    Thank you very much for your kind note of 4th just received. My life is a slow but steady and wearing fight with the common ignorance and presumption which denies that our profession is an art and will not allow it the position of a trade.[1] There is not a public work with which I have {been} connected & have left which is not being despoiled by men who have neither knowledge or interest in its purposes much less of the processes by which they are to be served. It all makes me sick and keeps me sick — though I have been rather better in health of late through a systematic cultivation of patience. I have often asked myself whether I could not do something to influence people in Providence[2] to trust to you and sustain you. Is there anyone there you would like me to send a copy of the pamphlet to? I am nearly out but could spare one or two.
    I heard of your great loss[3] last summer through your sister — not however until long after it occurred. Otherwise I should have written to express the strong sympathy I felt. I was then, however, expecting soon to see you.
    Sincerely Yours,

Fredk Law Olmsted

The text presented here is from a manuscript in Olmsted's hand.
1. Cleveland had written Olmsted thanking him for a copy of the article "A Consideration of the Justifying Value of a Public Park," a lecture that Olmsted had delivered to the American Social Science Association in September, 1880, and that was published, with many errors, in the December 1880 issue of the Association's *Journal of Social Science*. Olmsted published a corrected version as a separate pamphlet in early 1881. Cleveland expressed his pleasure in the appearance of the pamphlet and declared "I have read it twice through with appreciative interest & profit" (Cleveland to FLO, Feb. 4, 1881; see *Papers of FLO*, SS1: 31–32, 331–49).
2. Cleveland had drawn up a plan for Roger Williams Park in Providence, Rhode Island, in 1878.

3. Cleveland's eldest son, Henry, a mechanical engineer, had died at Barranquilla, Colombia, in June 1880, at the age of thirty-four. He left a widow and three children dependent on Cleveland's financial assistance. Cleveland's sister-in-law Sarah Paine Perkins Cleveland (1818–1893), the widow of his brother Henry Russell Cleveland (c.1809–1843) had informed Olmsted of the tragedy in August 1880. The member of a rich and influential Boston family, she sought at various times to promote Cleveland's career. She was a close and valued friend of George W. Curtis and Charles Eliot Norton, both of whom wrote to Olmsted on Cleveland's behalf, at her behest, after he lost his job in early 1868—an effort that apparently led to his being employed for a few months on Prospect Park in Brooklyn. In her letter of August 1880, Sarah Perkins again urged Olmsted to help her brother-in-law, specifically mentioning that he hoped soon to have more work in Providence (Edmund Janes Cleveland and Horace Gillette Cleveland, comps., *The Genealogy of the Cleveland and Cleaveland Families*, 3 vols. [Hartford, Conn., 1899], 2: 1072–76; H. W. S. Cleveland, "Ancestry and descendants of H. W. S. Cleveland, in line from Moses Cleveland of Woburn, Mass., 1635," manuscript in Rare Book Room, Library of Congress, Washington, D.C.; George W. Curtis to FLO, March 30, 1868; Charles Eliot Norton to FLO, April 10, 1868; Sarah P. Cleveland to FLO, Aug. 20, 1880).

To Paul Cornell

N. York 12th April, 1881

My Dear Sir;

When I saw you in Chicago last fall you asked me if I could explain the intention of some rather incoherent lines and dots in the very rough lithographic representation of our plan for the South Park. I was not at the moment able to do so but {*as it just now comes back to me*}[1] I will now try to give you an understanding of it.

Imagine a plane of an acre or more with a finely gravelled surface except for a series of circles six feet in diameter arranged thus: The space between centres of circles to be 16 ft. These circles are to be pits 3 ft. deep filled with fine soil. Ample provision to be made for agricultural drainage and for surface drainage by gratings and pipes. Suppose four posts to have been set in each circle: posts to be a foot in diameter and 10 or 12 ft in height above ground. Connect the posts with strong floor joists in this way. Upon these joists make a floor of lattice-work in the usual manner of pergolas (Examples in Skizzen Buch)[2] uniformly covering the entire space. Plant vines in the pits between the posts. Train them straight up the inside of the posts, taking care they do not cross, and from the head of each post train out each vine fan-fashion. If the soil is sufficiently

Olmsted, Vaux & Co., Plan for South Open Ground and Upper Plaisance sections of Chicago South Park (1871) Pergola overlooking South Open Green is shown on concourse near 56th Street entrance.

rich I judge from my experience that in two years you could have the entire space under a leafy canopy of Virginia creeper. There is no objection to using a variety if you prefer, being governed in choice by experience in your climate. Common wild grape vine will be appropriate. Trumpet creepers and Wistarias, possibly. But Virginia Creeper would be surest to give satisfaction, quickly under all circumstances.

Between the pits, upon the ground, you can place tables and chairs for the serving of refreshments. Thus: (the cross showing the table), or the tables can be omitted on intermediate lines, AA. The entire space may be so used if there should be found occasion.

The distances I have given may be considered minimum distances to allow passage between the tables and the posts — and may be enlarged at discretion.

The whole affair is to form a shaded promenade concert ground. On one side would be the concourse, on the other the house in the lower story of which would be the offices but mainly large covered spaces for shelter in case of sudden rains. The upper floor would be a covered esplanade, commanding a view over the top of the pergola, the relative heights being such that the nearest parts of the meadow would be in full view from all parts of the esplanade and a complete view had of parades, matches &c. upon it.

Vines from the pergola should creep up the posts supporting the overhanging roof of the house and the whole affair kept as quiet and unobtrusive in the landscape as possible consistently with its main purpose of shade and shelter for a great multitude.

It should be purely a summer affair, and very distinctly a Café and not a hotel or restaurant. I would ask for nothing more than is absolutely necessary to fulfil the requirements — trusting the vines to cover and decorate everything except the roof of the house.

Very Truly Yours

Fred^k Law Olmsted.

The text presented here is from a manuscript in Olmsted's hand.

1. Olmsted wrote and then lined out the words in braces. The recipient was probably either Chicago South Park commissioner Paul Cornell or, possibly, W. M. Berry, the park superintendent. Cornell was the one commissioner with whom Olmsted carried on a correspondence, exchanging letters from 1869 to 1880. However, the technical detail of Olmsted's explanation of the Pavilion that he and Calvert Vaux had proposed for the concourse at the southern end of the Southopen Green of the inland park (now Washington Park) suggests that he was writing a person who was in a position to supervise its construction. Both Cornell and Berry presumably accompanied Olmsted on a visit to the park in late September 1880. Writing to Olmsted the previous week, Cornell said

that he and Berry and commissioner Martin J. Russell would accompany him on his tour (Paul Cornell to FLO, Sept. 18, 1880).
2. *Architektonisches Skizzen-buch* (architectural sketch-book), a bimonthly journal published in Berlin.

MR. OLMSTED'S REPORT.

17th May, 1881.

C. H. DALTON, Esq., *Chairman of the Park Commission:*—
SIR,—

In reply to your inquiry of 24th inst., I beg to observe that the all-important feature of the site proposed for a park at West Roxbury[1] is a gentle valley, nearly a mile in length and of an average breadth, between the steeper slopes of the bordering hills of less than a quarter of a mile. Relieved of a few buildings, roads, causeways, and fences; given an unbroken surface of turf, and secluded by woods on the hillsides, their edges breaking into bays, capes, and detached groups, a perfect example would be had of a type of scenery which is generally thought more soothing in its influence than any other. A man might wander for hundreds of miles through the country without coming upon one as complete and free from incongruity. No site has been proposed for a park near Boston which is to be compared with it in this respect.

Natural tranquility, without bareness or deadness, is the quality more to be valued in a public recreation-ground. There is simply the difficulty connected with it of reconciling the necessary apparatus of public use with the requirements of consistency and harmony of expression,—of making them, that is to say, sufficiently modest and unobtrusive. Assuming that this difficulty can be met with fair success, the opportunity is an exceedingly valuable one, and it would be improvident for the city, with its present prospect of increased population and future prosperity, to neglect to secure it.

The quiet, pastoral dale, the natural beauty of which is now broken and obscured by roads, buildings, orchards and crops, with so much of the adjoining elevations as would be necessary to control it, occupies less than three-quarters of the tract first recommended by your commission to be taken for a park. The remaining part of the original area is mainly of two descriptions, a part being outlying dale-land detached in landscape, more or less, from the main valley; the other part rough upland, mostly shaded by rather stunted woods, but with many grand rocks, and adapted to yield at moderate expense to a picturesque development.[2]

The value of the smoother outland lies in the fact, first, that if it were not available, the main valley would be likely to be used for various special methods and appliances of popular recreation, which, as before suggested,

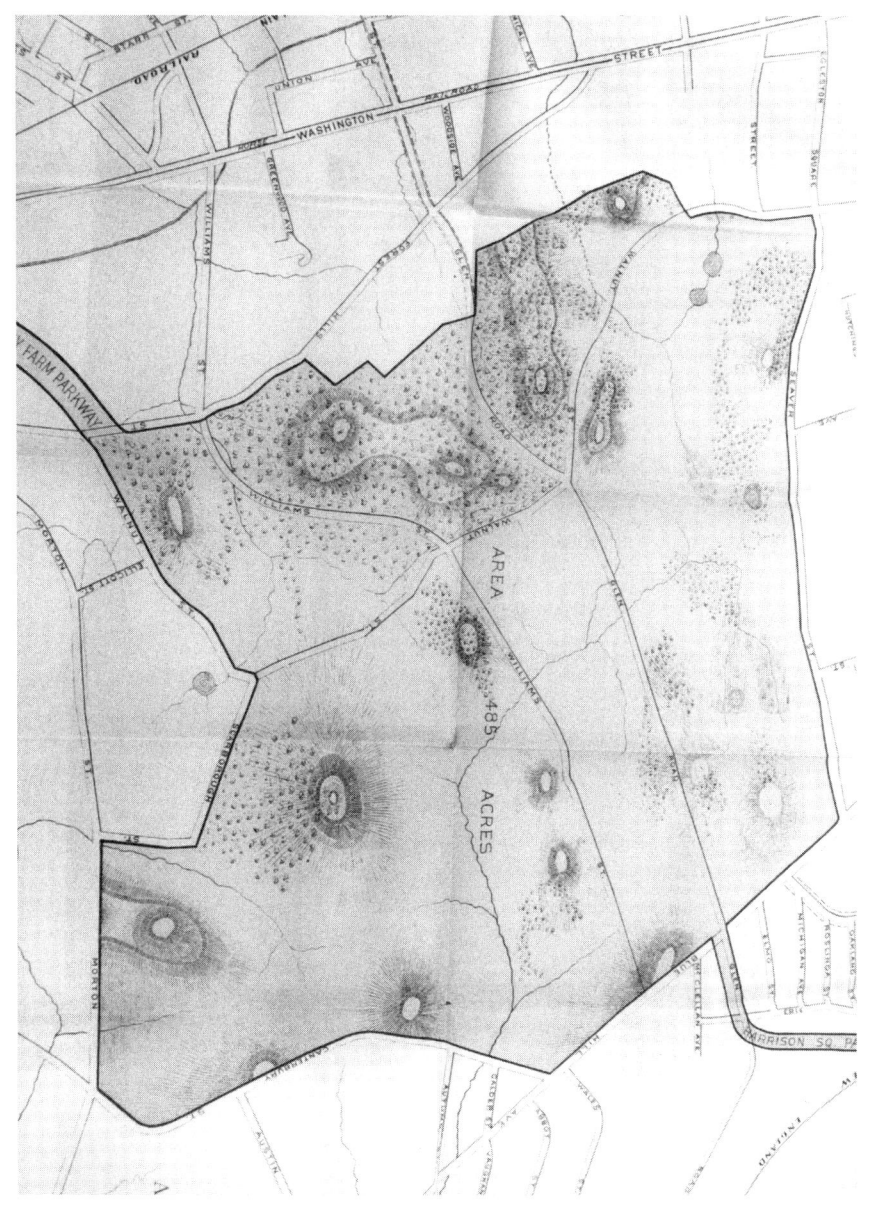

Area proposed for West Roxbury Park by Boston Park Commissioners (1876)

would be an injury to its scenery; second, in the readier and greater seclusion which plantations upon it would give the main valley; third, in the more varied rural attractions which might be offered in the park by skilful use of it; and, fourth, in the greater length of roads which it would allow to be made without cutting into the central sweep of greensward.

The special value of the outlying rough and wooded land consists in its immediate availability as a shaded, rambling, and picnic ground; in the distinct interest of its picturesque elements, and in the heightened effect which would be obtained by contrast of character in passing between it and the dale scenery.

The question now raised is whether any notable part of the outlying land of either class can be dispensed with without a serious diminution of the value of the site as a whole for public use? It is mainly a question of what use the public will, in the future, need to make of it, and this again is mainly a question of what is elsewhere to be provided.

If this were to be the only considerable provision of the city for out-of-door recreation, the whole would be inadequate to the purpose, and for this reason:—

In time the numbers resorting to it, on days its unrestricted use would be most valuable, would be so large that the provisions for them first made, in roads, shade, houses of refreshment, and arrangements for special forms of recreation, would be found too limited; and to obtain an enlargement of them the quiet of the valley would be invaded, and little by little the only special charm which had led the locality to be selected as a park would be destroyed. Therefore this question cannot be prudently considered without reference to others which your commission has heretofore brought to the attention of the City Council, and to one more particularly.

Within a mile of this West Roxbury site the city has been offered 120 acres of land, for a public recreation ground, with the condition that it shall add about 40 to it, and allow parts of it to be occupied by certain plantations, to be paid for out of a fund of which Harvard College has been made the trustee in perpetuity.[3]

Portions of this ground are much better adapted to be used as a rambling and picnic ground than any at West Roxbury. It is already furnished with much finer trees, and it has the advantage for this purpose of more open, higher, and more breezy elevations, commanding extensive and beautiful distant views.

If the city shall accept the gift of this land, make a road through it, and connect this road with the roads of the West Roxbury park, the two grounds would be used a good deal in connection. They would also be used by many alternately, one holiday being given to one, the following to the other, and the provisions for the public of one would complement and fill out those of the other.

A smaller extent and less cost of roads, walks, buildings, and planta-

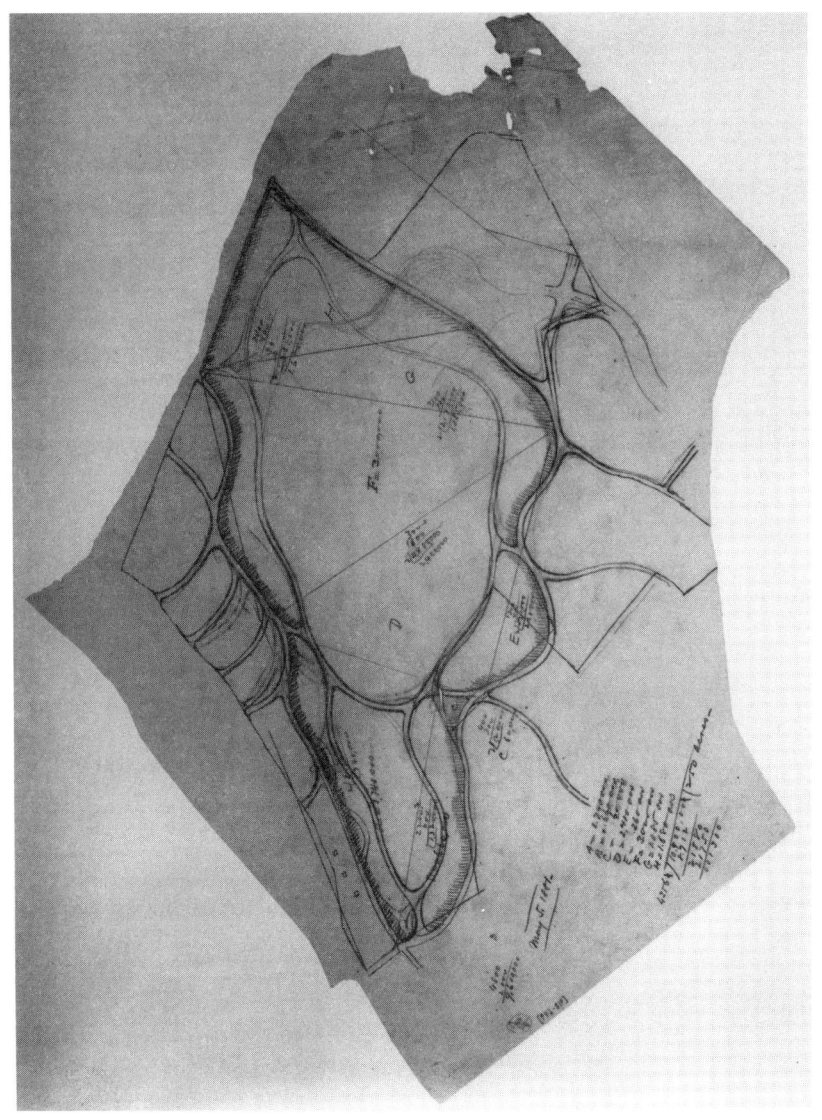

OLMSTED'S STUDY FOR REDUCTION OF SIZE OF WEST ROXBURY PARK
The proposed new boundary is indicated by the shaded area along the boundary drive.

tions for shade would therefore be required on the ground now more particularly under consideration, and a distinct character of scenery, distinct horticultural attractions, and contrasting points of interest in other respects being provided on the Bussey site, it would be much easier to maintain the distinctive beauty of the West Roxbury park free from the embarrassments and incongruities with which it would otherwise be threatened. It follows that a much smaller body, of what I have termed the outlying land, would be necessary to secure the essential purpose which justifies its selection.

I have, at your request, gone carefully over the ground, and have considered the assessed valuations of the different properties as published in your former report, and am satisfied that if the course above suggested is adopted, portions of the outlying lands, originally proposed by your Board to be taken, may be set off, aggregating over 150 acres, the value of which would probably be more than a third that of the entire area,[4] leaving a park of great value because of its unity of character and the strong distinctive and desirably distinctive quality which it may, with very moderate works of improvement, be made to possess.

If I may be allowed, in closing, to express a judgment, based on a careful study of the experience of many other cities, I should say that there is no part, division, or quarter of Boston, which would not gain greatly by the city's acquisition of such a park. I may go further. So far as I know, there is no body of land within the limits of the city in which a considerable expanse of tranquil, "park-like," natural scenery could be obtained nearly as economically; and, if not, an outlay sufficient to make it available would be a better investment in the long run, in my judgment, even for the most distant and least benefited part of the city, than {if} an equal sum would be laid out within that quarter, with a view to a park of more detailed and spectacular interest.

It is wonderful that so large a body of naturally attractive land, so near a densely built city, should be so free from costly "improvements." After a much more careful examination of it than I have heretofore made, my opinion of the good fortune of your commission in finding such a piece of ground, and its good judgment in selecting it as the site of the principal park in common of the citizens of Boston, is greatly strengthened.

Respectfully,

FREDK. LAW OLMSTED,
Landscape Architect, Advisory.

The text presented here is from "Report on the Committee on Public Parks," City of Boston, *Documents... for the Year 1881* (City Doc. No. 93) [Boston, 1882], pages 3–5.

1. The site for a park in the park commission's proposal of 1876, located for the most part within the present bounds of Franklin Park.
2. Presumably a reference to the areas of Ellicottdale, and the Wilderness in Franklin Park. Ellicottdale served both as an expanse of pastoral scenery and as a place for lawn tennis played with temporary nets.
3. A reference to the Arnold Arboretum.
4. As shown in the study on page 531, Olmsted proposed to retain the areas that became the Playstead, Schoolmaster Hill, Nazingdale, and Abbotswood in Franklin Park, and to

exclude most of what became the Greeting, Long Crouch Woods, the Wilderness, Ellicottdale, Scarboro Hill, and Scarboro Pond.

To Charles Eliot Norton

209 W. 46th St.
30th May, 1881.

My Dear Norton;

The Governor's contemptuous opposition[1] has left no hope that anything will be done through the State for the protection of Niagara and I am thinking whether it may be practicable to obtain a refusal of the properties more important to be secured for the purpose and accomplish the result by a popular subscription to a joint stock company. I am going a fishing tomorrow and {if} I get any encouragmnt may probably in a day or two afterwds try to get some men together and raise a little money for preliminary expenses.

You may remember that when I last talked of it with you, you thought you could find a man who for a compensation would make a business of writing up the matter for the newspapers. Can you do so now? If you think it likely that you can, please give me some idea of what would probably be required to secure him.[2]

Of course it is a forlorn hope but I don't think it would be right not to do something more out of respect for those whose aid on {it} {I} have asked and obtained.

I enclose photographs of a structure[3] for which I was much ridiculed in the Senate last year and which is still an object of the writings of the Washington newspapers. The best things of it are not photographable. The tile are from my model. They have a rough surface with marks of hand-modelling and are a dark variable red with glints of gray. It is to be completely clothed with ivy. There are cavaties over the arches of the size of bathing tubs in which yuccas, prickly pears and sempervivums are to grow. The central object is a drinking fountain.

I call the whole thing a summer-house but the d.f.s will have it "the subterranean grotto"!

Yours affctly

Fred[k] Law Olmsted.

VIEW OF SUMMER HOUSE ON U.S. CAPITOL GROUNDS, C. 1881, SHOWING PLANTINGS AND CENTRAL FOUNTAIN

VIEW OF SUMMER HOUSE ON U.S. CAPITOL GROUNDS, C. 1881

FEBRUARY 1881–DECEMBER 1881

The text presented here is from the Charles Eliot Norton and Niagara Falls collection, Manuscript Division, Library of Congress, Washington, D.C.

1. Cornell's contemptuous comment apparently occurred at a meeting with William Dorsheimer close to the time Olmsted wrote this letter. The Niagara bill had passed the Assembly and had a good prospect of passing the Senate. Concern then arouse that Cornell would veto the bill, and Dorsheimer met with him on the matter. Cornell declared that he did not consider preservation of the scenery at the falls to be of any consequence. When Dorsheimer countered that the banks of the rapids were lined with manufacturing structures, Cornell remarked, "I don't see that it will make any difference — the water will run over the falls all the same" ("Cornell and the Niagara Park," *The Washington Post*, Sept. 14, 1882, p. 2).
2. In July, Norton and Olmsted arranged to engage Henry Norman (1858–1939), a recent Harvard graduate, to write a series of articles for newspapers on the situation at Niagara Falls and the need for creation of a public scenic reservation there. He published several articles before returning in December 1881 to his native England. Thereafter he enjoyed a distinguished career as a journalist, serving as London correspondent for the *New-York Times*. He was a member of Parliament for twenty-three years and held several important governmental offices (FLO to Charles Eliot Norton, Aug. 25, 1881, Charles Eliot Norton and Niagara Falls collection, Manuscript Division, Library of Congress, Washington, D.C.; *New-York Times*, June 5, 1939, p. 21).
3. Olmsted is referring to the summer house on the U.S. Capitol grounds.

To Barthold S. Schlesinger

Porch & Terrace

Brookline 17th June 1881.

My dear Sir,
  Before we meet next Friday, I want you to please think over the objections which lie against what is proposed in the drawing given me by Mr Harney at your request. Mr Harney and Mr Colburn each tell me that they have pointed out what seem to them conclusive objections.[1] As they relate to matters of local detail I will not repeat them but submit simply the difficulty which I find in reconciling the proposition in this case with what I know to be your wish in respect to the general expression of the place.
  You must well know that if you scantily furnish a large and stately room with cheap little cottage tables and chairs, you don't make it cottage like by doing so, on the contrary the height of its walls appears to be increased; its spaces to be in every way enlarged. Its stateliness becomes oppressive. The effect of a narrow walk carried stiffly up to the central door of a large house — between flat beds of turf would be the same.
  That a house should bear an expression of private social and domes-

tic life rather than institutional you need to see something which indicates that its occupants go in and out as they please not with the directness that belongs to places of business or under strict rules and orders. You want to feel that they often turn about between outside and inside occupations and can step out for a moment without change of house attire. You need a place outside the door obviously suited to be so used & to be conveniently occupied at times by a group of people and this place needs to be furnished and embellished in a way that neither belongs to a lawn or garden nor to the inside of the house. Your porch at Nahant last year told the story exactly.[2] Something of this kind is as essential to the ideal of a rural home for a family as a roof or chimneys. It may take the form of a terrace, veranda, portico or porch or simply of a farm house "stoop" with its tubs of oleanders &c. The lack of it makes either a wretched habitation as in the Irish cabin or an official building, barrack, office, jail, hospital or monestery. To make a square place some distance in front of the door does not help the matter. Take away the platform on which you had such a charming effect by the informal grouping of flowers, vines and vases of lovely hues with inviting chairs about a central passage to the door and substitute something with a motive like this drawing of Mr Harney's and your cottage would very well front on the esplanade of a military station; the bit of square pavement being supplied with a flag staff in the centre and a field piece on each side of it —

What is more commonly done with well considered houses similarly situated is probably the most convenient and the least open to sound objection. Your house has a long front planted on sloping ground, the surface of which at one end being a rocky knoll, at the other a gentle swell. Under such circumstances experience for centuries has found it best to form a level shelf, sustained by a wall or embankment which gives the house a stable base and supplies a convenient out step. Elsewhere in the world this is almost universally done; here we have fallen into the way of getting over the difficulty by shaded verandas, which are simply cheap and shabby terraces in most cases: darkening the rooms looking upon them; their wooden decks or columns always rotting away and needing yearly repair & paint. I think that you are right to abandon this expedient but I can't but feel that something terrace like is essential to a domestic aspect of the building & I feel very certain that if you adopt the plan now proposed you will soon be compelled by its inconvenience to adopt some make shift modification.

You object that a portal or door would prevent greenery about the door. On the contrary it would be the proper and convenient place for tub and pot plants, it would increase it. If the objection is to the color you can have a concrete of any color you please. I have laid hundreds of yards of it at less cost than flagging and in all colors.[3] You can have mats made or you can cover all that you do not want to tread upon with trays of moss. If you want to grow vines at any point against the wall you can have openings to deep beds of soil below for the purpose. I have done this and the vines flourish perfectly. If the objec-

VIEW OF SOUTH FAÇADE OF BARTHOLD SCHLESINGER HOUSE, SHOWING
WHERE OLMSTED PROPOSED TO CONSTRUCT A TERRACE

tion to the terrace is that it would add to the stateliness of the house I must think that, on the contrary it would, by its strong unbroken horizontal line bring it down as a dado does a wall.[4] Nothing relieves a house from an unquiet and fussy appearance like a strong base. Your house is not unquiet or fussy but the effect of a terrace would be to give it greater repose and simplicity of aspect, and the gain in actual convenience and comfort would be very great.

I write because I want to be away for a week and shall not see you till we meet next Friday to reach a final decision.[5] I can't make the drawings I promised simply because I can't devise anything satisfactory without a portal.

Respectfully yours

Fred[k] Law Olmsted

The text presented here is from a document in a clerk's hand. Olmsted added the notation *"Porch & Terrace"* at the top of the first page.

1. George Edward Harney (1840–1924), architect, began his career in the late 1850s writing articles for the *Horticulturist* and renovating country estates on the Hudson River. In 1873 he moved to New York City and had a flourishing practice well into the twentieth

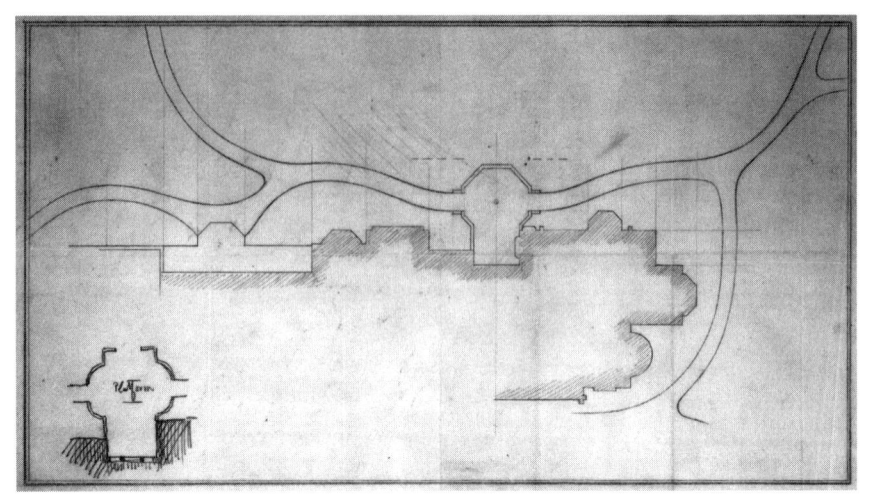

SKETCH FOR PATH WITH OCTAGONAL TERRACE FEATURE ON SOUTH SIDE OF HOUSE,
BARTHOLD SCHLESINGER HOUSE, JULY 29, 1881

century. Besides numerous commercial buildings he designed in New York, Harney designed a house at Trenton, New Jersey, for Washington A. Roebling, the chief engineer of the Brooklyn Bridge. He worked on the design for Barthold Schlesinger's house in Brookline, Massachusetts, from its August 1879 inception and consulted frequently with Olmsted on that project through letters and joint visits to the property. In October 1880, as construction on the house neared completion, he reported that Schlesinger had objected to an architectural terrace that Olmsted had planned for its south front. The sketch by Harney to which Olmsted refers presumably presented a concept of Schlesinger's for treating the grounds next to the south side of the house that the architect did not approve. Olmsted's comments suggest that the plan showed a square paved area before the front door, connecting by narrow walks with the house entrance and the grounds. Mr. Colburn, possibly an assistant to Harney, had worked on the project since at least November 1880 (*NCAB*, 1: 371; Dennis Steadman Francis, *Architects in Practice: New York City, 1840–1900* [New York, 1980], p. 37; George E. Harney to FLO, Sept. 13, 1879, B63: #614, OAR/LC; ibid., April 17, 1880; ibid., Oct. 1880; FLO to George E. Harney, Nov. 6, 1880; ibid., June 30, 1881; Barthold S. Schlesinger to FLO, April 5, 1881).

2. In August 1880 Olmsted had visited Schlesinger at the coastal resort town of Nahant, Massachusetts (Barthold S. Schlesinger to FLO, Aug. 11, 1880, B63: #614, OAR/LC).
3. Olmsted had used colored concrete laid in patterns on the walks of the east grounds of the U.S. Capitol and at Washington Square in Baltimore.
4. A dado is the lower part of an interior wall, if treated differently from the remainder of the wall, as in wainscoting (*OED*).
5. Dated sketches show that in June and July 1881 Olmsted experimented with a variety of treatments for the Schlesinger terrace. He began with designs that showed a low, straight terrace along most of the south front and finished with a design for an octagonal platform connected to the house at the main door with slighting curving walks running east and west along the front of the building. On August 2 he sent Harney a copy of the latter design and told him that Schlesinger had accepted the concept of an octagonal plat-

form, and had suggested that it measure eleven feet on a side. Ultimately, however, Schlesinger built neither the octagonal platform nor the extended terrace but settled for a narrow walk next to the house (FLO to George E. Harney, June 30, 1881; ibid., Aug. 2, 1881, B63: #614, OAR/LC; Barthold S. Schlesinger to FLO, n.d.; John Nolen, "Frederick Law Olmsted and His Work, III: The Schlesinger Place, Brookline, Mass.," *House and Garden* 9 [1906], pp. 217–22; Plan 614–16, July 29, 1881, NPS/FLONHS).

INFLUENCE.

[c. July 1881]

Both influence and advice are words now used in a sense so different from that formerly common that without discrimination they will lead in the pending national discussion to much darkening of counsel. "A man of influence" once meant what might be supposed from Webster's definition — "moral power; power of truth operating on the mind; rational faculties or will." A few illustrations will indicate the present more technical sense of the term.

A tramp of the Guiteau stamp but more seedy and sottish[1] touched my elbow as I was about entering a government building and whispered: "Don't you want my influence, General?" While in a public office I heard a girl say, "I can't do anything about it today. My influence is out of town," (presumably with reference to obtaining some favor or escaping some penalty), and a young man asking the return of some papers: "I'm a gone sucker without my influence." In a single newspaper I have seen four advertisements of influence "wanted", the influencer being promised a share of what could be got from the public till or in consequence of the desired trade. I was present when a poor sickly haggard old man offered himself as a recruit for the public service. "You can see my influence" he said, showing a varied assortmnt of what he thus designated, that of most recent date being a paper signed by several members of Congress begging that some place might be found for him, a part of the wages for which should be held back until a sum had accumulated sufficient to send him to the distant part of the country from which older influences had drawn him.

Wrecks of influence like this are so common in Washington I was told that the Police have a wholesale arrangment with certain railroads for removing them at reduced rates of fare.

Another shade of meaning I have seen illustrated in a note addressed to the head of an office, to this effect. "J.B stands for my influence with you. He tells me some charge is to be made against him — If so please overlook it and oblige Yours &c. ———"

Also, I once heard a subordinate when asked to explain a gross neglect of duty, reply, "You want an explanation do you? Well, [laughing] there it is": handing a writing: "If there is anything against C.D. Please let him off and charge to account of Yours Respy."

Influence when used in the sense of these examples is often accented in the penultimate — inflúence, and it would be convenient to accept this variation.

A civil service system of which it is a cardinal point that places in it shall be obtained & held less by merit than through influence, can be maintained only because no satisfactory alternative offers. But one proposition has been made, the adoption of which would do more than beat the devil of influence about the bush; it is that prominently brought forward by Mr Pendleton's bill.[2] There is a strong, sincere and thoroughly respectable repugnance in many minds to this alternative. It rests mainly on connections of the class commonly designated as of common sense, and partly on clear scientific ground.

The scientific ground is that upon which much modern statesmanship is based, that the most efficient bar against bad service lies in competition and that the advantage which the present system secures through the danger that bad service will tend to the defeat of the party dispensing patronage would be thrown away by the change proposed.

What seems to many the common sense objection to the proposed change is probably in part simply a habit of mind established in adaptation to customs indirectly growing out of the present system.

It is for example largely due to the present system that the line has been in so great a degree obliterated which originally divided the class of public servants who are responsible for the choice of measures by which laws and policies are to be carried out and those whose official business lies in the pursuit more or less by set methods and under rules and discipline of measures determined independently of them. And the mental confusion due to this custom is aggravated by another, that of so overloading heads of administration with patronage business that they are compelled to neglect or throw upon their subordinates their own proper duties.

Two notions on the subject have thus far been more distinctly lodged in the public mind. First that the time and strength of the President and chief officers of the federal government are absorbed in dealings with influence to a degree that cannot but be cruel to them and detrimental to all other public business, second that the evil has its origin and the remedy must be looked for with the people.

Something would be gained if it could be realized first that what the President suffers is simply a more conspicuous example of an evil extending to nearly all public business; second that instead of the common figure of a stream of which Washington is supposed to be the mouth, and private sentimnt the sources, it would be more apt to regard the seat of government as the heart of a system between which and its extremities there is a ceaseless flux & reflux of influence.

How the system operates in this respect in many Custom-Houses, Post Offices and Indian Agencies is notorious. A few illustrations which I propose to offer from points still more remote from the federal centre may aid a better understanding of its difficulties.

The experience upon which I shall draw for these has been obtained in professional engagmnts in township affairs. Engagmnts in every case coming unsolicited, through votes from both national parties, in boards composed of men generally of enviable repute, in easy circumstances, serving the public without pecuniary compensation, with pride in their duty; not selected by the caucus process or elected by popular suffrage.

By a board of this class, in the city of New York I was unexpectedly called in 1857 to find work for and employ a thousand men upon the site for the Central Park in advance of the adoption of a plan for laying it out. The order led to the accumulation of a store of road-metal which it was assumed would be valuable under any plan.[3] The morning after it passed, and before it reached me officially, I was told by an appalled domestic that twenty men were outside my street door each with a letter which he wished to deliver to me with his own hands and that four of them had forced their way into the house. To reach my office that morning I had to penetrate a body of men estimated by some of the newspapers to be five thousand strong. They were mostly laborers but a number of members of the legislature and aldermen were among them. As I worked my way through the crowd, no one recognizing me, I saw & heard a man then a candidate for reelection as a local magistrate addressing it from a wagon. He urged that those before him had a right to live; he assumed that they could live only through wages to be paid by the city; and to obtain these he advised that they should demand employment of me. If I should be backward in yielding it — here he held up a rope & pointed to a tree, and the crowd cheered. Men pushed letters at me wherever I went, stuffed them into my pockets, set their wives to waylay me, tossed letters through windows to me. I fully believe that some thought that if they could hit me with a letter I should be magically made their benefactor. Several applicants were at my door whenever I came home & when I went out in the morning. Their influences joined me as I walked in the streets and sat with me in rail-cars.

The President of the Board of Aldermen — the vice-mayor[4] — apologized for introducing himself while I was at breakfast on Sunday morning by a {. . .}[5] harrowing narrative of the pressure for patronage which he suffered. He obtained my promise to give personal attention to a certain number of men whom he would select as the most worthy & efficient out of a large number for whom the pressure was most irresistible. One of these, when they came, I was told by the police had lately served a term in the state prison. He was assigned to a stone-breaking gang; looked morosely at the work for a moment and then turned his back. Another assigned to a gang opening a ditch at the time he came upon it, was given a shovel by the foreman and told to fall in with those in the trench. Whereupon he threw the shovel down with a great oath, turned his back and was seen no more. I asked the smiling foreman who reported this to me what it meant. "Why, it means", said he, "that Johnny will find that he can't pay his debts with any such jobs as you give these fellows." Of fourteen men employed under this official's influence not one remained on our rolls at the end of three weeks. Some had resigned, some been dismissed for intoxication, indolence or insolence.

So constant and rapid was the process of elimination thus illustrated that during a period of two years in which I was in uninterrupted superintendence of this work[6] more than ten thousand recruits were enlisted for it, the force at work never reaching 4000 and being hardly more than 2000 on an average. For the 10,000 successful in securing an opportunity to serve on it there were probably more than ten times that number of letters or other forms of influence receivd from office-holders or candidates for office.

A general design having been adopted, it became the policy of the Board to advance the work as rapidly as possible in order to have its leading features so stamped on the ground as to distance the constant projects of politicians for getting possession of it through specious charges against the purposes and taste which it embodied.

To keep a large, shifting and mainly raw force under efficient organization and discipline; work it with reasonable economy; cut out and superintend its work, secure adequate checks against fraud and negligence and be at all times prepared to supply conclusive proof against the innumerable charges against the managmnt brought by the discharged and disaffected and which after having {been} dealt with by the Board directly in charge, led to five successive Investigating Committees of superior legislative bodies,[7] each believed by the Board to have its origin in jealousies of appointing influence, and all this with an executive staff not one man of which had ever before been engaged in an undertaking having the same objects, conducted on the same principles and with the same forms and methods, would have well taken all the time and strength I could give it had I been wholly guarded from influence. With my best possible efforts I should have failed disastrously in my distinctive professional duties had it not been for a strong set of public favor and for the enthusiasm which the nature of the business seemed to inspire in my associates who generally worked twelve to fourteen hours a day. There were nine engineers who habitually took their work home with them & often did more at night than by day. More than once some of them remained in the office all of two successive days & nights of full sixty hours in harness. Three of the most devoted were disabled by over-work one after the other, each showing incipient or fully developed brain-fever.[8] In all this time, the larger part of my day-light was claimed by business growing out of the demands for patronage of men in such public positions that, as I was assiduously instructed, custom & policy required that they should be respectfully dealt with & if possible conciliated. I several times officially reported this fact to my superiors and measures were taken to relieve me as far as was thought practicable in respect to certain details, but as long as I remained in charge of the work the wear and tear from this cause greatly exceeded that from all others. More than 90 percent of my correspondence and of the time occupied in conference about matters of my office, other than with my subordinates, was taken up with it. That I had any other and more important duties seemed to be generally forgotten, not by my direct but my indirect superiors. My real work, that of forecasting scenery to be formed, to contrive means of securing its gradual development under difficult conditions and of making it available to great bodies of people, was of deep interest to me. I had none in life that compared with it, and every minute to be saved for deliberate and absorbed study of it was deeply precious. Under these circumstances, one day when hardest pressed, a note came marked "important" asking me to call at a certain hour upon a party leader. "The biggest boss over all." To do so took me from my office three hours and the heart out of my day. I rearranged my appointmnts and as soon as possible stood at a guarded door[9] while others passed in and out—a senator, the highest local federal officers, a Commissioner of Police. When at last my turn came I was received with a charmingly benignant manner and the business occupied less than a minute. "A man will call with my card. Do me the favor to see that he obtains some employment that will satisfy him."

"I shall hope to do so."

"Good bye."

"Good bye Sir."

The efficient manager had sent for me simply to repeat face to face what he had previously written and after all the object of his solicitude never delivered his card. He had probably set his heart upon a consulship and knew that I could have no office to fill with which he would put up.

Of course it was not recruiting alone that gave occasion for these demands upon my time. We sometimes used fifty barrels of gunpowder a day in blasting rock, for a long time more than half that and besides thousands of laborers & hundreds of horses we had within limited space great numbers of visitors—men, women & children, to guard from danger. For this among many reasons a degree of discipline was needed and was maintained, seldom attempted in public works. Many of those calling upon me were seeking the restoration of officers or men, dismissed after fair trial for disregarding the rules or for other forms of negligence or insubordination. The "pressure" on this account was very trying, and I must add that a painful part of it though not the most venomous began with men not themselves "in politics," not a little with some for whom I had a sincere regard and to whom I felt under private friendly obligations. Unsuccessful in direct appeals to me, these often sought also to bring political influence to bear in favor of their wrong-headed charities. Among them who did so I recall one zealous clergyman who urging the reappointment of a backslider as an encouragement to a renewed effort for a better life, made me responsible for the culprit's soul. The appointing officer of another work told me that he had been obliged to restore a man of infamous character, grossly insubordinate and always damaging through the relentless insistence and pressure of one of the foremost leaders of benevolent and religious movements in all the country, a doctor of laws.

The harrassments to which I was subject by day forced me to leave matters for absorbing study chiefly for the night. I was often out with my associate in the design[10] or others going over the ground until after midnight and engaged upon maps and plans or writing instructions until after day-break.

The time at length came late in the season when the doctor said— "an entire change for a few days at once, or I will not be responsible for the consequences." He obtained for me a week's leave of absence and sent me off, but letters and telegrams followed and before the week was up I was advised from headquarters to hasten my return. I did so to reach the work in a delirious condition, disabled for duty for several months and with injuries {from} which I have never recovered.[11]

In 1872 the government of New York passed through a change which left its affairs in a more confused and provisional state than revolutions in France have left those of Paris.[12] The status, rights and duties of its several offices were in many respects doubtful and all their business proceeded under consequent difficulties aggravated by injunctions of Court & other legal proceedings. This was especially the case with the department of parks upon which devolved a variety of extraneous business. Its managing board contained two of the recognized heads of the revolution and one of the Tweed faction who remained very active & singularly vigilant, bold and resolute in obstructing its business until late in the year when he also fled abroad.[13] Extensive operations had been begun under the overthrown Ring and some of them, ill-judged, tasteless & extravagant, were in that condition that it was a hard question whether what had been accomplished should be taken as a basis for further proceedings or demolished.[14] Upon the decisions to be made large private interests were at stake. In nearly all the works of the departmnt, and in nearly all parts of each work, revisions of design and policy were called for. To increase the difficulties thus arising, the Chief Engineer, the chief gardener, the Secretary, the bookkeeper and a large number of the subordinate officers upon the works had resigned or been removed. The office of Treasurer was combined with that of President and the President was given extraordinary powers as to purchases, appointments and removals. But the President was also a member ex officio of an extraordinary Board recently appointed to audit the accounts against the City run up by the Ring,[15] many of them just claims but many fraudulent & more exhorbitant, yet pressed by skilful lawyers, so that the duty required deliberate study of bodies of conflicting testimony. This and other important duties outside those of the departmnt proper so took the time and mind of its chief that as far as possible he had, in the lack of others whom he was disposed to trust, laid upon me a great variety of his discretionary duties & depended much upon my study & reports. Suddenly he was obliged by private business to be absent for some weeks from the country. He thought it best and it was thought best by the leaders of the reform movement & by the Mayor that his responsibilities should be added to those proper to my professional office. I reluctantly yielded to their and his request to take them. A plan for the purpose was devised and carried out. I took my seat at once in three boards over one of which I presided.[16] At the first meeting of this body four questions were referred to me to investigate with a request that I would report on them at the following meeting and I found fourteen similar requests with which my predecessor had been unable to comply & which he had left over to me. As I came out from this meeting there were lawyers and others waiting to press affairs upon my attention, nearly all with letters of introduction from men in high official station. One man presented a claim which he declared & which was afterwards conceded to be just, long over due, the prompt payment of which he assured me would save him from bankruptcy. There were papers on my desk addressed to me in all four of my functions, among them an order of Court requiring immediate attention.

I have mentioned these things as an indication of the work other than that of recruiting that at this period needed my time and strength. As to recruiting, in the pressure of multifarious duties upon my predecessor he had allowed our works to be overstocked and the payrolls were much larger than our appropriations justified. He had advised me of this and that in consequence a reduction of force was imperative. In addition therefore, to a notice to that effect which he had posted at the outer door, I at once advertized that under no consideration would any new appointments be made. Nevertheless a crowd of applicants bearing letters from officials so blocked the sidewalk, that a police officer was needed to keep a passage open, and during all business hours members of the Reform Committee, of the legislature and of the city councils were waiting to press claims for patronage upon me. A clerk experienced in the duty was instructed to receive them; to explain the situation to each and to request that I might be excused from receiving them. Many upon this withdrew but many declined to do so. When Sunday came I took a few notes. I find one to the effect that I had not during the week, had five minutes in my office uninterrupted by a card sent or by some gentleman who had been unwilling to take my written notice or my clerk's verbal assurance that I could make no appointmnts and who either held such a position in politics or brought such letters that the clerk did not feel justified in refusing to present his request to see me.

All this occurred in the midst of a storm of reform declamation. My visitors mostly classed themselves as reformers and often brought me letters urging their claims as such from the recognized reform leaders. (Nevertheless, singular as it may seem, some actually made themselves of consequence because of their friendship with Mr Tweed and the confidence that had been given them under the broken Ring. (as to be shown later))

Mainly all my time in office hours when not attending Board or Committee meetings was given to patiently satisfying such callers that my written declaration was sincerely made. I studied to do this considerately and conciliatingly but before the end of the second week one of those upon whose advice I had taken the office sent for me to say that complaint came to him of my inaccessibility and he feared that the cause of reform might suffer if this continued.

I reminded him that, needing no recruits, every hour that I gave to the business of recruiting was wasted for any of my essential duties but he advised me to realize that I could have no duty so essential as that of maintaining good relations with those who made the laws and determined appropriations. That I could commit no more serious offence than to deny to them the right and opportunity of conferring and advising with me and he suggested that if their views in this respect did not seem sound to me it was hardly becoming in me to set up my private political theories against those clearly established in the customs of the country & accepted by the people.

I had occasion to confer with the head of another departmnt of the city governmnt. While my card went in I waited with eight men whom I had previously seen at my office with influence, and when I was admitted found others with the Chief. I was passed on into a small inner room while he was putting them off. When they had left he came to me; apologized for having kept me waiting, reclined on a sofa and said he was well nigh worn out.

"Can you be as much rundown by these men as I am?" I asked.

"Oh! More so, I'm sure."

"That is impossible, but do tell me, when are you able to give attention to the more essential business of your office"?

"I don't often get a moment for it during office hours. I come early and stay till after seven."

"What about your meals?"

"I have them sent in from the Astor House."

"Is there no way of avoiding this waste of your time & strength."

"No it is the established order of things."

I met a statesman of national renown with whom I had had the honor of a friendly acquaintance and as he kindly invited me to take counsel with him I told him of my situation and said, "Here I am paid ten thousand dollars a year, furnished with a luxurious office & given clerks to aid me in a public duty and it is demanded that on an average a full working day of my time shall be given every twenty four hours to assuring people who wish to share in the patronage of my office that there is no patronage to share and so softening the assurance to them that they shall not go away with a disposition from which the interests of the city might suffer. Must I yield to such a preposterous demand?"

He answered in effect, by asking, "Do you think it would be judicious for you all alone to rebel against a system universally accepted, national in its scope and as clearly representative of the genius of the people as any institution we have?"

Of a score of public men of considerable rank and hundreds of subordinate standing having weight in party managmnt, of whose private convictions I have had a somewhat confidential knowledge there are none whom I believe would give a different answer. I thoroughly believe also that it would be generally honest and that in many — perhaps in most cases — it would express a conviction adopted reluctantly and held with a sadness not without a tinge of remorse.

I have often sought to understand the grounds of this abandonment of faith in the republic of our fathers, and think that a good deal of them would appear in a frank argument somewhat as follows:

More distinctly than England has become a Nation of Shop-keepers, our people have become filled by the spirit not so much of mere shop-keeping as of trading adventure, bolder & less closely considerate and rule-bound than shop-keeping spirit. Except in a few tiny garden patches of genuine Poetry, Art, Science & Scholarship, nothing holds out against this spirit. For example, tricks of trade, advertising methods of trade, trade language and forms not only pass as natural and proper in the managmnt of church & church charitable and even church propogandist and devotional efforts, but a scrupulous avoidance of them would be commonly felt to argue lack of practical ability if not of earnestness & religious zeal. Much more so would their avoidance in politics show a man to stand apart from the people. Nay if bishops and ministers, elders and deacons, evangelists and colporteurs are required to yield a little of their dignity and straight-lacedness to the spirit of trade & speculation; is it to be supposed that politicians can afford to be nice & fine in their ways with offices, votes, patronage, influence? All this is a weight to be deplored but for the present it handicaps all statesmanship if not all law and gospel and those who cannot carry it must be distanced.

The text presented here is from an undated draft in Olmsted's hand. He apparently wrote it in the summer of 1881, following the shooting of President James Garfield on July 2 by Charles J. Guiteau, a mentally unstable supporter of Garfield who was angry at not receiving a patronage appointment for his imagined role in the recent presidential campaign. Garfield died of his gunshot wound on September 19. Olmsted evidently wrote this article for the use of his friend George W. Curtis who, as president of the Civil-Service Reform Association, was launching a renewed campaign following the attempted assassination. No proposal to Curtis by Olmsted has survived, but in a letter of July 17, Curtis wrote him saying "Your idea is capital and I will see what can be done. We are just issuing a circular to every considerable newspaper in the country, enclosing a postal card for reply addressed to our Secretary, engaging to furnish all material that they may desire for the discussion — if they wish to discuss." The editors have found no evidence that Olmsted provided Curtis with a finished article or that anything of the sort by him was published or circulated (George W. Curtis to FLO, July 17, 1881).

1. Olmsted first wrote, and then deleted, the following introductory phrase to this sentence: "As I was entering a public building in Washington a tramp who from the description of him might have been the unfortunate Guiteau only that he was a little more seedy and decidedly sottish. . . ." Guiteau "wore his hair brushed up in front, which gave him a startled look," and was reported on one occasion to have called on a U.S. Senator in winter "bareheaded, with a pair of sandals on, without stockings on his feet" (*DAB*; *Washington Post*, July 3, 1881, p. 1; *New-York Daily Tribune*, Nov. 25, 1881, p. 1).
2. The bill of Ohio senator George Hunt Pendleton, introduced in the U.S. Senate in February 1881. It authorized creation of a civil service commission that would carry out competitive examinations, wherever practical, of candidates for employment by Federal offices in Washington and the larger custom houses and post offices (*DAB*; Adelbert B. Sageser, *The First Two Decades of the Pendleton Act: A Study of Civil Service Reform* [Lincoln, Nebraska, 1935], pp. 40–42).
3. As Olmsted made clear in the original version of this sentence, preparation of the road metal called for hiring laborers to break up stone by hand. He wrote: "The order resulted in the preparation of a great store of road-metal obtained by reducing thousands of 'nigger-head' (diorite) boulders."
4. John Clancy (1830–1864), a Democratic politician closely associated with Tammany Hall (New York (City). Board of Aldermen, *Proceedings of the Board of Aldermen of the City of New York* 67 [New York, 1858], n.p.; *New-York Times*, July 2, 1864, p. 8).
5. At this point a word inserted by Olmsted is missing due to a torn corner of the page.
6. Olmsted is probably referring to the period from September 1857, when he became Superintendent of Central Park, to September 1859, when he took a ten-week trip to Europe.
7. See, for instance, *Papers of FLO*, 3: 287–88 and 322.
8. See, for instance, Olmsted's anecdote concerning the engineer John H. Pieper, *Papers of FLO*, 3: 302.
9. At this point Olmsted originally wrote "at a door of the Astor House."
10. That is, Calvert Vaux.
11. Olmsted had gone to Saratoga Springs for a rest, but Andrew H. Green summoned him back to the park before the end of his week's leave (*Papers of FLO*, 3: 230).
12. A reference to the overthrow of the Tweed Ring in New York City and the creation of revolutionary communes in Paris and other French cities in 1871.
13. Leaders in the defeat of the Tweed Ring who became commissioners of the new Department of Public Parks were Andrew H. Green and Henry G. Stebbins. The member of the Tweed faction was Thomas C. Fields.
14. See the review by Olmsted and Calvert Vaux of the activities of the Tweed park board in *Papers of FLO*, SS1: 255–73.
15. Henry G. Stebbins, who became president and treasurer of the parks board in November 1871, was a member of the Board of Audit created to review financial claims against the city following the overthrow of the Tweed Ring. This board held its first meeting on February 1, 1872 (DPP, *Second Annual Report* [1872], pp. iii, iv; "The Board of Audit," *New-York Times*, Feb. 2, 1872, p. 8).
16. During the time from May 29 to October 23, 1872, when he replaced Henry G. Stebbins as president and treasurer of the Board of Commissioners of the Department of Public Parks, Olmsted presided over that board and was a member of the Board of Audit and the Board of Apportionment of New York City (*New-York Times*, June 10, 1872, p. 4).

To John Charles Phillips

To Mr. J. C. Phillips;

Bkline, 27th Sep. 1881.

My Dear Sir;

I am sorry to have missed you in my flying visit today.[1] I don't know that I have anything new to say but I would have been glad of a chance to further urge just at this point some ideas that I have before presented.

I found the place impressing me less pleasantly than usual and that I felt uncertain & worried about it. As the house was not in itself disappointing I finally concluded that the trouble lay in the suggestion of a quality of smugness in its surroundings given by the new dressing of the hillside on the West front.[2] This slope was simply tame and uninteresting before. Now with its smooth, soft, even green surface & its few stuck up nursery trees (as evidently artificial as your chimneys), disposed park-fashion, it is as foreign to the locality as a prairie. With good luck, (in whirlwinds and borers) these trees will after a long time come to something agreeable but for years they can only serve to emphasize the effect manifest in the surface — anything that would grow & take shape of itself having apparently been discarded from the design, rooted out or green-washed over, through preference for an artificial quality.[3]

I tell you my impression & what chiefly produced it because it confirms to my mind that which I had when you first asked my advice & I can't give it too strongly. The difficulty to be always contended with is the ease of a costly commonplace result — a result which though neither fowl, flesh nor good red-herring shall leave no man room to say that he is not satisfied. You may spend ten times what you are willing to and in forty years have either a tolerable poor park-like place, or a farm with less farm beauty than hundreds of other farms to be bought ready made. But the house you have now put upon it is suited neither to a park nor to a farm. It will be incongruous with the ideal of either — still more with an agglomeration of both. It is a proper summer lodge, so placed in the midst and near the edge of a forest as to command an opposite forest over a sheet of water, with an oasis of ladies' ground strongly but rudely & in forest fashion built in to the wild hillside with it.

Now what I mean by forest is not full grown trees; it is an aspect of nature such as is found where neither crops nor prepared pasturage occupy the ground. If it were practicable every word of my advice would stand just as well if instead of forest, I said down, or heath or moor. I have been in a most attractive place found in the edge of a treeless space half overgrown with patches of broom, the contrast of which with the fine lawn, trees & shrubbery of the enclosed ground was very effective.

To induce the necessary forest character with all its possibilities of pure forest beauty, and to secure desirable convenience so that it will appear to have been found & not made, (without showing your hand, as it were) is the point of the game. I think it is in the cards to do it completely, but if it is not, I am sure that the next best thing is to come as near to it as you can — and at least to let the intention of any effort that must be betrayed be so evidently the helping of nature to escape from the farmer & the landscape gardener, that the imagination of what is finally to come shall be consistent & satisfactory. If the gardener shows himself outside the walls,[4] "off with his head." I am sure that it is only by following this rule unflinchingly that you will ever reach a result worthy of your effort.

I could not but think how little satisfactory any ordinary result of gardening — of high gardening — would be as a fore-ground or background for your house, compared with precisely what you have in the pine hillside opposite — And the larger and more unvexed the mass of it, the greater would be the dignity of the place. I much doubt today whether about the cheapest thing you *could* do would not be the best — this being to sow seeds of pine & larch and let such indigenous growth of birches, hickories, sumachs and bushes grow up with them as would; trusting to the axe a few years hence for selection & grouping & to top dressings for more thrift than could otherwise be expected. I am moved to say this the more from having lately visited the plantations of Mr Forbes at Naushon[5] & Mr Fay at Woods Hole;[6] so sowed — (but not so thinned out or fed.) Your situation is much better than theirs for the purpose but I would rather have done what Mr Fay (working blindly & ignorantly until taught by experience,) has done than what Mr Hunnewell[7] has. Mr Fay has made an immense landscape improvemnt self sustaining & self perpetuating. His planting yields him annually more than it costs at least, while Mr Hunnewell's wants several thousands a year spent on it to hold it from becoming very seedy if not from going to destruction.

I seriously advise this course. It puts you at once in the way of getting what you most want; In a single year it will begin to establish the true character of the place and shut off the comparison of it with cockney villa grounds, sure otherwise for some time to come to be consciously or unconsciously made to its disadvantage by everyone. Except your 40 acres of dairy ground, I would this month carry tree-seeding over the whole place — Then if you want to plant nursery stock in a regular way on well tilled ground at any point next year or next after, the cost of the seeding will not have been so much that it need prevent you. Meantime, on all ground whereon you don't interrupt nature, she will be giving you something at least more satisfactory for your August landscape than potatoes, beets, rye or hay stubble, more agreeable even than pasture unless it is pretty bad pasture.

I thought that the house promised exceedingly well — the skylines & the proportions and grouping of the roofs very pleasing and the stone more

View of John C. Phillips house, designed by Peabody and Stearns showing roofline and wooden terraces on south side

VIEW OF TERRACE ("TILED TERRACE"), JOHN C. PHILLIPS HOUSE

charming in color & texture(?) than any new stone work I ever saw before. I was glad to hear from Watson[8] that you intended to build the yard walls of the same. That will I think much help the whole house especially if near it you carry them up pretty well. I hope that you may be able to retain the inside dimensions of the yards. The first one is more of a court than a yard & should be open for visitors to drive under the shed if they like.

 I like your wood-work terrace less now that I see more clearly how it is to appear in connection with the solid stone wall than I did when I first did not like it. I am sure that the raft now framing on the west front[9] is wrong and I must advise you strenuously to take it away. But as I don't think that you will, I enclose tracing of the best arrangmnt that I have been able to make for bringing it into connection with the approach & the lawn. I don't think it is very good but I can't think of anything better. I intend the lawn to be graded flush with the floor of the terrace all along the South face of the house. It must drop off a little at first to make a water way, as I explained to Watson.

 The plans I saw & the work done look as if it was still proposed to put some sort of screen or break between the covered wooden and the open tile terrace at A (on the sketch enclosed). You had something of this sort in view before the open terrace was planned but in designing the open terrace, I assumed that the intention would be abandoned.[10] If it is not to be, my work is wrong but I can't see the use or propriety of any obstruction at that point & think its retention if it is retained must be an oversight. If not, the line of the terrace walk needs revision. All the time I am sure that it would be better to have gravel all the way round than to divide between tile & boards, if the question is of expense — the wood lying in the position most favorable to decay will always contradict the effect of the stone walls, and the wood floor subject to the same use and the same destructive agencies on one side of the dotted line A as on the other will seem a piece of make shift patch-work. I see no argumnt for a wood floor on the South side that does not apply to the East. The conditions differ only in that a part of one is to have a wooden awning & a part of the other an awning of canvas.

It struck me that your road was likely to be unpleasantly conspicuous & to appear meaninglessly meandering for some time to come — There is really a reason for every curve and as the borders become woody it will be all right. But perhaps in finishing you may reduce the breadth a little. Where water will not run off from the sides, a broad shallow turf gutter is much better than a narrow deep one & I hope no paving will be needed at any point. The border of the road should never be abrupt, the ground should invariably rise or fall from it with a long curving slope, so that the road may not be an evident or very pronounced construction.[11]

so —

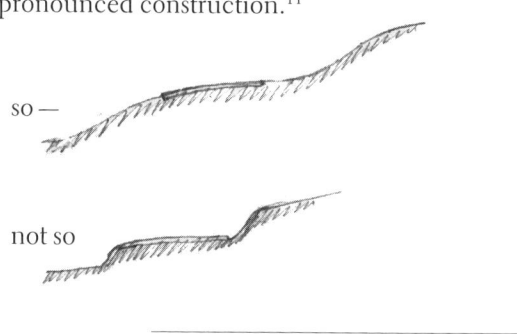

not so

Could you not be planting some prostrate junipers & Pinus mugho along the bottom of {the} terrace-wall now? It looks so badly as it is & the regular deciduous planting season is so short & hurried. Next summer this wall should fully realize its design.

The text presented here is from a draft in Olmsted's hand.

1. Olmsted had visited the estate of John C. Phillips in Beverly, Massachusetts. Since early 1880 he had actively advised Phillips on the location of a new house there designed by Peabody and Stearns, and provided plans for its terrace, walks, roads, and garden. Several days before the date of this letter Phillips had asked Olmsted to visit and

give advice on grading in front of the house and how best to make use of the remaining weeks before winter weather prevented outside work (FLO to John C. Phillips, May 11, 1880, above; John C. Phillips to FLO, Sept. 23, 1881).

2. Olmsted first wrote "that the trouble lay in the greater smugness which you had brought into association with the house by putting a crop into the hillside on the West front."
3. Olmsted first wrote "they can only serve to emphasize the present effect — which is just as unseemly as it can be, because all natural character in the premises — anything that would grow & take shape of itself has so plainly been rooted out or green-washed over, through preference for an artificial quality."
4. Olmsted first wrote "outside the fortress." This suggests that while he wished to relegate flower-gardening to the garden that he sited below the pavilion, he was willing to have some gardening effect on the filled land that contained the house, tiled terrace, lawn and pavilion. Further from the house the landscape should not appear to be the result of art. He may, however, have been referring only to the garden, which had a fortress-like appearance, encircled as it was by a wall of boulders, with the terrace side consisting of the same palisade-like upright stones that lined the eastern edge of the lawn.
5. John Murray Forbes (1813–1898), prominent Boston businessman and railroad builder. He had known Olmsted since at least 1861, when he worked for the Boston branch of the U.S. Sanitary Commission and raised large amounts of money for the organization. According to Olmsted, Forbes had established forest plantations in the 1830s on his estate on Naushon Island in Buzzards Bay, Massachusetts, and had obtained advice on them from A. J. Downing (*Papers of FLO*, 4: 240–41; *DAB*).
6. Joseph Story Fay (1812–1892) in 1850 purchased an estate overlooking Buzzards Bay at Woods Hole, Massachusetts, and established a tree nursery there in the late 1850s. In the 1880s Olmsted purchased trees from him for planting in the Boston Fens (Mary Lou Smith, ed., *Woods Hole Reflections* [Woods Hole, Mass., 1983], pp. 254–55; "Our First Summer Resident," *Falmouth Enterprise*, May 17, 1863, Section F; FLO to Joseph Story Fay, Dec. 3, 1884, A1: 103, OAR/LC; ibid., July 28, 1887, A1: 918, OAR/LC; ibid., April 10, 1889, A3: 462, OAR/LC; Joseph Story Fay to FLO, April 13 and 14, 1889).
7. Horatio Hollis Hunnewell, whose country estate outside Boston Olmsted had visited in 1877 and 1878. It included, besides a pinetum and an English garden, an ornately planted and expensively maintained replica of an Italian Renaissance garden (FLO to George O. Shattuck, Dec. 31, 1877).
8. John H. Watson, the stone mason who constructed the terrace wall and the pavilion foundation and arch at the Phillips estate.
9. Olmsted is apparently referring here to an open, wooden "piazza" that appears in several plans on the west side of the house between the covered, wooden porches along its southern end and the porte-cochère at the main entrance in the middle of the west side (see, for instance, plan no. 14 by Peabody and Stearns (1881) (Plan 12297–14, NPS/FLONHS).
10. Olmsted first wrote, "This portion of the plan had been designed essentially before the tile terrace was planned, and in designing the tile terrace, I assumed that it would be abandoned." (He used the phrases "tile terrace" and "open terrace" interchangeably, referring to what became the open, tile-floored terrace along the east side of the house). As shown in several plans, and as finally constructed, the south end of the house had a wooden porch with a roof over it and a partially open octagonal structure that stood between that porch and the open, tile-surfaced terrace on the east. The sketch to which Olmsted refers has apparently not survived.
11. Olmsted here illustrates the "ogee" curve that he used so frequently in grading next to paths and drives.

FEBRUARY 1881–DECEMBER 1881

To Cornelius Rea Agnew[1]

[c. June–October 1881]

My Dear Doctor,

As to the fitness of what you are going to do at Montauk it has to be considered from two opposite points of view — one being that of the great natural landscape as seen from the proposed cottages; the other that of the aspect of each cottage and of the settlement as a whole in respect to suitability and attractiveness in itself.

Much the most powerful impression of the scenery is to be had from the higher ground. Every cottage placed on the lower ground would not only be an injury to it but the cottage seen under these circumstances would appear lonely, bleak, incongruous and unsuitable.

By placing the cottages as I have proposed along the hillsides, you avoid the first objection wholly, and through the appearance of companionship and mutual support gain a great advantage in respect to the second.

All this I pointed out to you and I also argued the value of fences and outdoor furniture in manifesting the fact of family and domestic independence in the constituents of the community. What I did not explain sufficiently is that all my advice (as to the general design) had in view also the esthetic advantage which is always gained in placing a richly intricate body of detail upon a field of great breadth and simplicity. To secure this you need the two elements of unity (to be served in this case by an obvious close association and connection of the different houses) and of intricacy (to be served by variety in the patterns of houses and the outdoor furniture which will more or less occupy the spaces between and before them.)

But there is something to be gained also by the same means with respect to the landscape from the cottages. Without forming any essential obstruction to the view seaward, appropriate objects in front of them will serve the purpose which leads painters to desire to bring emphatic fore-ground features into pictures; that is to say to soften the middle distance and give increased effect of aerial perspective to the back ground.

I shall hope to see a certain continuity apparent between each house and the road, so that the design of the house may seem to be supported and carried out in the arrangment of approaches, hand rails, fences, shrubbery, trellises &c. Each private ground being thus furnished there will, in general effect, be a connection between it and the next on each side, and the unity of the community more fully expressed.

When you come to choice of lots to be built upon, it will be well to have compactness of settlemnt a little in view, avoiding unnecessary vacant lots, and it will help the desired effect if the Association will undertake at once to form a continuous fence along the entire street line.

This may be in part a hedge, in part a low trellis, to be overgrown with

VIEW OF MONTAUK ASSOCIATION COTTAGES, DESIGNED BY MCKIM, MEAD, AND WHITE, MONTAUK POINT

vines, and in part a stone wall to be dressed with rock-plants and creepers. The last is the best and I would adopt it at least for the front of all lots not to be immediately built upon, allowing those who are building their choice.

The advantage of the wall is that, made of the neighboring field stone, you are sure at once of a thoroughly respectable & satisfactory result, modest and appropriate to the circumstances, while with hedges and vines the effect desired will be delayed and the result not perfectly certain.

I write this however not to urge any special measure so much as to commend certain principles to {be} had constantly in view.

The text presented here is from a draft in Olmsted's hand.

1. Cornelius Rea Agnew (1830–1888), a New York physician, had been a member of the executive committee of the U.S. Sanitary Commission when Olmsted was general secretary of the organization in 1861–63. Although their relations were not especially cordial at that time, they maintained a casual friendship after the Civil War, dining together occasionally and exchanging some professional services. Agnew treated Olmsted for problems with his eyes and Olmsted, on at least one occasion, provided advice on landscape design issues. This instance was the subject of the letter presented here, in which Olmsted advised on the arrangement of a group of cottages at Montauk Point being planned by Agnew and six acquaintances calling themselves the Montauk Association. They engaged the architectural firm of McKim, Mead & White to design the cottages, along with a common stable and laundry and a common Association Hall with recreational facilities. The group decided to differ from Olmsted's proposals sufficiently that they offered not to assign him professional responsibility for what they constructed. Agnew reported that "We have not adopted your idea of the small lots, nor have we

agreed to reserve the entire rolling plateau in front of the line of hill sites" (*A Monograph of the Works of McKim Mead & White 1879–1915* [1915, rpt. ed , New York, 1977], p. 24; C. R. Agnew to FLO, Oct. 13, 1881).

To Edward Clark

October 1, 1881.

Sir:

When the new wings of the Capitol had been built, much of its due value was evidently lost because of the incongruous objects by which it was surrounded and the unfavorable circumstances under which it had to be observed. Congress then ordered the demolition of the nearest adjacent buildings and a design to be prepared for a suitable laying out of an enlarged Capitol ground.[1]

At this time the earth thrown out from the foundations having been heaped up within geometric outlines and grassed over, had begun to be known as the terrace. In the climate of Washington a semblance of turf laid on a steep formal bank is often for long periods as devoid of verdure or of any quality of beauty or architectural dignity as a dust-heap. Under the most favorable circumstances it must appear but a shabby make-shift for a terrace suited to the situation and adapted, as such a terrace would be, to support and augment the grand effect of so august a structure as the Capitol. The term thus rather suggests what is left lacking than what is supplied by the earthwork in question.

At once impressed with this consideration, when I had the honor to be asked to prepare a plan for laying out the ground my first step was to ask your assent, as Architect of the Capitol, to the introduction of a feature at the base of the building designed to remedy this defect. Your assent having been promptly and cordially given, and the general character of the structure for the purpose provisionally agreed upon, the entire plan of the grounds was afterwards worked out with constant reference to it.[2]

Before presenting the plan to the joint committee of Congress having oversight of the work, scaffolds were set up to indicate the dimensions of the proposed terrace and to aid judgment of its effect on the building. The committee, after taking counsel with you, called in, also, with reference to the particular question of the terrace, your venerable predecessor, Mr. Walters, and the then Architect of the Treasury, Mr. Potter, both of whom warmly supported the proposition.[3]

After prolonged consideration the entire plan was approved and favorably reported by the committee without a dissenting voice and subsequently adopted by Congress.[4]

Photographic copies of the plan and the perspective sketch of the terrace have since been widely distributed. In the several years that they have been under review but one criticism is known to have been drawn out. It assumes that the terrace would injuriously intercept views of the lower part of the Capitol building as it now stands. If the assumption were sound it should have condemned the entire plan of the grounds, since mainly carried into execution. To understand its unsoundness it needs to be considered that the full proportions and beauty of a great building like the Capitol can only be comprehended from a distance at which its various parts will fall into a satisfactory perspective. Accordingly, in planning the grounds, after determining as before stated upon the general character of the terrace, the next step was, again in consultation with you as the Architect, to fix upon twelve points of view from which the Capitol would be seen to advantage in as many different aspects.[5] The route and grade of the various roads and walks leading in from the several points of entrance determined by the abutting streets; the shaping of the surface elsewhere and the disposition of the trees and shrubbery upon it, as well as the planning of the terrace in more detail, was then determined in studious adjustment to these points of view, care being taken, of course, that no part of the building should be undesirably obscured from any one of them.

To accomplish the object the terrace was so designed that its upper line would, at critical points, be a few inches below the height of the present earthworks, and these, from any point at which a pleasing full view of the Capitol can be had, will be found to barely obscure the granite base stones upon which the marble walls of the Capitol rest. An examination of the premises can thus easily be made by anyone interested which will show the alleged objection to be groundless.

Considering that the motive which has mainly controlled the outlay of more than ten millions of dollars on the Capitol is that of investing the Halls of Congress and the Supreme Court[6] with suitable dignity and beauty, it will be found that the sum required for adding the proposed terrace will, as the entire structure now stands, accomplish more to that end than an equal amount has done anywhere heretofore expended on it.[7]

For example, the terrace being supplied:

First. The western front of the building will appear as standing on a much firmer base, and thus gain greatly in the supreme qualities of stability, endurance, and repose.

Second. The marble mass, being larger in all its dimensions as well as more firmly planted, will no longer be overpowered and as it were put out of countenance by its crowning feature, the dome.

Third. The opportunity of the higher relative elevation, the more genial exposure, and the far-spreading, varied, and charming landscape of the Potomac front, now lost to most who visit the Capitol, will be turned to profitable account, and the more so because of the freedom of the west side from the disturbance of carriages, and the immediate presence of a foreground harmonious in forms and color with the distant Virginia horizon.

Fourth. The larger part of the city, the Executive Mansion and the other government buildings will no longer appear to tail off to the rear of the Capitol, but what has been considered its rear will be recognized as its more dignified and stately front.

Fifth. Yet another gain is to be accomplished by the terrace, the value of which is not perhaps as readily to be appreciated in advance as those above enumerated, but which is assured by much experience. It is the augmentation of architectural effect in a structure of classic style, where there stands interposed between it and the adjacent ground a considerable feature, partaking of its leading characteristics and extending its material, yet carrying up toward it some outgrowths as it were of natural decoration.[8] So seldom has anything been done with us to secure this advantage, and it seems so little a matter of familiar knowledge, that it is available that I will add to my assertion of it, in a note at the end of this report, the evidence of two out of many masters of art who might be quoted for that purpose.

Of the advantages of the terrace as planned otherwise than with a view to architectural effect, I will briefly refer to two only:

First. The increased convenience which it will offer to all visiting the Capitol, coming from the west on foot.

Second. The provision which it will afford of spacious, dry, fire-proof, and otherwise secure and suitable exterior vaults for the storing, handling, and using of coal and all other supplies needed for the business of the Capitol, but which cannot be brought within its walls proper, without also bringing dirt, noise, and confusion too near its halls and offices.

Respectfully,

FRED'K LAW OLMSTED.
Landscape Architect.

Edward Clark, Esq.,
Architect of the Capitol.

NOTE.

Sir Walter Scott (in the introduction to Quentin Durward) observed: "In by far the greater number of sites the intervention of architectural decoration seems necessary to relieve the naked tameness of a large house planted by itself in the midst of a lawn, which looks as much unconnected with all around as if it had walked out of town upon an airing." And again: "I am content to subscribe to the best qualified judge of our time [he refers to

Uvedale Price], who thinks the neighborhood of a stately mansion requires some more ornate embellishments than can be derived from meager accompanyments of grass and gravel."[9]

Robert Kerr, professor of architecture in King's College, lays it down as established, that "for a building of classic design on a grand scale, a considerable amount of Italian landscape gardening ought to be introduced in order to carry out the principle of stately severity which is enthroned in the building as the center of the composition.

"The essential character [of good work in this respect] is always the same — that of a symmetric composition in which the architecturesque principle governs the primary features. * * * In other words, the primary features will be terraces, flights of steps, basins, fountains, sculptures, &c."[10]

The text presented here is from the *Annual Report of the Architect of the Capitol* [1881], pages 832–33.

1. The new wings of the U.S. Capitol were completed in 1865. Congress enlarged the east Capitol grounds by condemning and demolishing two blocks of buildings east of the new Senate and House wings in 1872–73, and in January 1874 ordered that a landscape plan be prepared of the enlarged grounds ([Glenn Brown], *Documentary History of the Construction and Development of the United States Capitol Building and Grounds* [Washington, D.C., 1904], pp. 1073–1155; FLO to Justin S. Morrill, Jan. 26, 1874, above).
2. Olmsted received the commission for the U.S. Capitol grounds in March 1874. His earliest consultations with Edward Clark, and the formulation of the terrace proposal, took place during the spring and summer of that year.
3. Olmsted's temporary scaffolds, used to indicate the lines of the proposed terrace, were probably set up in July 1874. He presented his general plan incorporating the terrace, and perspective sketches of the building with and without it, to the committee on public buildings and grounds of the Senate and House on January 5, 1875. There is no official record that Thomas U. Walter or William A. Potter testified before the Senate or House committees on public buildings and grounds at this time. Later that month, however, Morrill wrote Olmsted that both architects were scheduled to speak before the Library Committee in regard to Walter's proposed extension of the Capitol's west front. Although Walter knew about Olmsted's terrace proposal at this time, no evidence survives to corroborate Olmsted's claim that he supported it. In early 1877 Walter told the editor of the *American Architect and Building News* that the "elaborate design for terracing the western front . . . would greatly injure the appearance of the building." Nonetheless, in 1885 Olmsted quoted Walter as saying that the terrace "would be the making of the building" (FLO to Montgomery C. Meigs, Jan. 15, 1875, above; Adolf K. Placzek, ed., *Macmillan Encylcopedia of Architects*, 4 vols. [New York, 1982], 3: 467–68; Thomas U. Walter to Justin S. Morrill, Jan. 20, 1875, Morrill Papers; Justin S. Morrill to FLO, Jan. 22, 1875, B134: #2820, OAR/LC; Thomas U. Walter to W. P. P. Longfellow, Feb. 10, 1877, Archives of American Art, Smithsonian Institution, Washington, D.C.; FLO to Mr. Perry, March 20, 1885).
4. On March 3, 1875, Morrill reported to the Senate that the committee on public buildings and grounds unanimously endorsed the terrace proposal. Congress approved the

entire plan of the grounds the same day but refused to appropriate money to build the terrace (FLO to Montgomery C. Meigs, Jan. 15, 1875, above).
5. The "twelve points of view" of the Capitol were probably decided during Olmsted's July 1874 visit to Washington. They can be discerned on the general plan of the grounds first completed that month.
6. The U.S. Supreme Court met in the old Senate chamber of the Capitol between 1860 and 1935 (The Junior League of Washington, *The City of Washington: An Illustrated History*, ed. Thomas Froncek [New York, 1977], p. 254).
7. Olmsted's first estimate for the cost of the terrace and lower staircases, submitted to the committee on public buildings and grounds January 5, 1875, came to $315,519. An estimate prepared by engineer Frederick H. Cobb in January 1882 amounted to $657,402 (FLO to Committees on Public Buildings and Grounds, Jan. 5, 1875; FLO to Frederick H. Cobb, Nov. 10, 1881, Office of the Curator, Architect of the Capitol, U.S. Capitol, Washington, D.C.; "Estimate for new Terrace," Jan. 11, 1882, B134: #2820, OAR/LC).
8. That is, the use of vegetation on the terrace, which Olmsted proposed to accomplish by placing plant-filled vases on the stairways and balustrades of the terrace, and by a line of small trees, shrubs and ground cover extending around the north, west and south sides in planting "cases" along the edge of the terrace's upper level.
9. Sir Walter Scott (1771–1832), Scottish novelist and poet, published the novel *Quentin Durward* in 1823. Scott's narrator made these remarks, which Olmsted renders with fair accuracy, in the preface to the novel. He cites Uvedale Price's *Essays on the Picturesque*, and makes particular reference to the section of the "Essay on Decorations Near the House" in which he gives a sorrowful description of his own destruction of an "old-fashioned garden" on his familial estate.
10. A quotation from Robert Kerr (1823–1904), *The Gentleman's House*, 2d ed. (London, 1865), pp. 324–25, 334–35.

To Charles Eliot Norton

Brookline, 19th Oct[r] 1881.

My Dear Norton;

Though I know that you will respect the strong feeling which has impelled me to print this booklet, I send it to you with some reluctance and shamefacedness,[1] because I know that it deals with a subject on which I am not qualified to write. I am constantly impelled to write upon it because of the deploreable neglect of it by so many who could so easily be better qualified and the horrible barbarous waste which goes on because of this neglect. I see now a new folly arising here about Boston which cannot fail to be demoralizing and I can hardly refrain from lifting up my voice about it, but I none the less feel how great a risk I should run in doing so of blundering in argument, however right I know that I am in practice. I am always working away at it just to the last point of my strength — many printed reports, two encyclopedia articles and no end of private urgings & remonstrances. I have written twenty letters about it in the last week besides a long horticultural magazine article and what I have been doing about Niagara & my regular business in Boston & Washington — An unusual batch rather because I am stirred up by what I have heard of the destruction going on in Central Park, complacently called improvement. I have no reason to suppose that half a dozen men have yet read anything I have written, and as far as argument goes it all tells for nothing. A doubt of my own sanity in keeping on at it often comes upon me but I can't help it. Now & then I do meet a man who says: "I know what you think and I think—" with me or otherwise as may happen but always with the assumption that I have original and peculiar ideas and am not what I only want to be, the expounder, vindicator and applyer of views which are — not views at all but well established science.

But how can I feel any confidence in myself in this duty, when I find myself so much alone and all I say and think on my topic treated by the best of men — as this book illustrates? I can't & while I work like a horse at it, I take every step shrinkingly & look back upon it when taken half repentantly, as an act of effrontry.

This is all preface to saying that I do wish you would look over page 22 to page 32[2] so much of this little thing — not little to me — and tell me surgically if I have been going out of my depth — off solid bottom or if I have been preaching essentially false doctrine? But if I have been, also I want to ask you, if you can advise me nothing to read, going beyond what you know I must have read, whereby I can better ground myself?

Where shall I find the definition of Art which I want to correct me — a definition which will include landscape modification and accentuation? Is it absurdly incomplete to say as I do that the prime object of a work of art is to affect the emotions? Of course I don't ask you to answer this but can you tell where I will find the instruction I want, without learning a new language or building another story to my education? Of course I can't begin at 60 a University Course but it does seem that I should find solider ground than I feel that I do in the books. You see I want to distinguish the motive & purpose of what I have to call gardening from that of the florist & confectioner, on the one side, & from that of the engineer & brick layer on the other. I think it ought to be done better than it has been and that the public indifference to it — no, not the public indifference but the indifference of the proper leaders of the public in matters of Art — ought to be exploded.

We are again under the tension of a great domestic anxiety. A telegram saying that our boy Owen is "very low."[3] He is two days journey from a telegraph office. We have telegraphed for a doctor to be sent & our John started by the first train to go to him—will have reached Chicago tomorrow, but without an hour's rest it will take him a week to get to him & we cannot look for another message under ten days.

 Yours affecty

Fred^k Law Olmsted.

The text presented here is from a manuscript in Olmsted's hand in the Charles Eliot Norton Papers, Houghton Library, Harvard University, Cambridge, Massachusetts.

1. Olmsted was sending Norton a copy of the pamphlet *Mount Royal. Montreal*, which he had just published.
2. Pages 22 to 32 of *Mount Royal. Montreal* constituted section 6 through 10, in which Olmsted discussed his plan for Mount Royal as a work of art and explored the special qualities that make up the "charm" of natural scenery (see *Papers of FLO*, SS1: 366–72).
3. At this time, Olmsted's stepson Owen Frederick Olmsted (1857–1881), the son of John Hull Olmsted and Mary Perkins Olmsted, was operating his own cattle ranch on the Powder River in Montana. He had spent two years learning the business on a ranch in Wyoming of Olmsted's friend the geologist Clarence King. In 1880 King had secured funds for Owen to form the Rocky Mountain Cattle Company and buy a herd of fifteen hundred. At the time of this letter Owen was fatally ill with tuberculosis, the disease from which his father had died at the age of thirty-four (Laura Wood Roper, *FLO: A Biography of Frederick Law Olmsted* [Baltimore, Md., 1973], pp. 388–89).

To Charles Eliot Norton

Brookline, 2^d Nov. 1881.

My Dear Norton;

 Your proposition and Mr. Harrison's[1] letter please me very much but I don't think that we are free to make any arrangmnt requiring funds. Mr Potter[2] approved and favored all our suggestions but said very distinctly that until he had passed round the hat and tested his friends he could not be responsible for any further expenses. His expectation was that we should supply him with a list of persons properly to be brought together to discuss the matter, and sometime after he shall have moved into town (about 15th Nov), he would invite them to a meeting at his house. A general plan of campaign then would be discussed. He would also see whether he could obtain money by subscription for further preliminary agitation. He wanted the paper[3] which Mr Norman is printing for both purposes, expecting to put {it} in the hands of friends as he should meet them in the street.

I think Mr Harrison's letter will please and encourage him and I shall take leave to send it to him.

Meantime if you are disposed to have Mr Harrison go to Niagara at once[4]—that is that he should see it before winter—I will advance half of what is necessary. Of course "the season" is already past and the nuisances of Niagara mainly withdrawn.

I hope Mr Harrison would be able to canvass New York a little in person. I don't think he would be a bad sort of man to {tackle} Governor Cornell if there should be occasion.

Would it not be well to ask Mr Norman to prepare a part of his letters for publication,[5] as you proposed, in a pamphlet?

Can you look forward to going to N. York to attend the meeting at Potter's & can you induce some other Massachusetts and Harvard gentlemen to come with you? What day would suit you best about the middle of the month?

We yesterday had our first word by mail from John after he had found Owen.[6] He was at a "hotel" at Spearfish creek & looked better than John had imagined that he would. He was to write again after seeing the doctor. Several telegrams since indicate that Owen is mortally ill, and we are prepared to hear of his death at any moment. Yet there are expressions which imply that John does not realize immediate danger. We shall probably have a letter tomorrow giving us a better understanding of the facts. As yet the history is dark to us. Mrs Olmsted is very deeply stricken. Our hopes have always centered on him. He had what all our other children conspicuously lack.[7]

Affectly Yours

Fred[k] Law Olmsted

The text presented here is from the Charles Eliot Norton and Niagara Falls collection, Manuscript Division, Library of Congress, Washington, D.C.

1. At this time Charles Eliot Norton was proposing that a protegé of his, Jonathan Baxter Harrison (1835–1907), be hired to write articles on Niagara as part of the next campaign to create a reservation there. At this time Harrison, a Unitarian minister at Franklin Falls, New Hampshire, was completing a series of articles in the *New-York Daily Tribune* and *Atlantic Monthly* based on a tour he had recently made of the South. In preparation for that tour, that Norton played a crucial role in arranging, he secured advice from Olmsted concerning the approach he should take in his search for information. Norton proposed that he go to Niagara at once to study the conditions at the same salary he received as a minister, with additional payment of ten dollars a column for published articles. Harrison was concerned about finding a replacement acceptable to his congre-

gation, but expressed great interest in the undertaking. "I visited Niagara a dozen years ago," he wrote Norton, & ever since have been deeply, sadly, interested the subject of the preservation of the scenery there. I should rejoice to be able to do anything to aid a movement so important and so vitally related to the civilization of the world" (*Boston Globe*, June 18, 1907, p. 7; Timothy Crimmins, "Frederick Law Olmsted and Jonathan Baxter Harrison: Two Generations of Social Critics of the American South," in Dana F. White and Victor A. Kramer, *Olmsted South: Old South Critic/New South Planner* [Westport, Conn., 1979], pp. 137–43; FLO to Charles Eliot Norton, Sept. 19, 1878, Charles Eliot Norton Papers, Houghton Library, Harvard University, Cambridge, Massachusetts; J. B. Harrison to C. E. Norton, Nov. 1, 1881; C. E. Norton to FLO, Nov. 2, 1881).

2. Howard Potter (1826–1897) New York banker and active in the formation of voluntary organizations, including the U.S. Sanitary Commission and numerous New York philanthropic and cultural institutions. Potter was an important financial contributor to the Niagara reservation campaign (Margherita Arlina Hamm, *Famous Families of New York* . . . [New York, 1902], p. 56; *Papers of FLO*, 6: 110; FLO to CEN, May 25, 1880, Charles Eliot Norton Papers, Houghton Library, Harvard University, Cambridge, Massachusetts).

3. Probably a reference to a three-page flier that Norman was preparing, labeled "Confidential" and dated November 1, 1881, that described the situation at Niagara Falls and the need for action to protect the scenery there (Charles Eliot Norton and Niagara Falls collection, Manuscript Division, Library of Congress, Washington, D.C.).

4. The hiring of Harrison to write on Niagara was postponed until the summer of 1882, during which he published eight letters in New York and Boston newspapers (Howard Potter to FLO, June 16, 1882; see J. B. Harrison, *The Condition of Niagara Falls, and the Measures Needed to Preserve Them*. . . [New York, 1882]).

5. That is, preparation of a compilation of Norman's newspaper letters on Niagara, which Norman completed before leaving for Europe in December 1881–a 39-page pamphlet published as *The Preservation of Niagara Falls. Letters To the Boston Daily Advertiser, The New York Evening Post, Herald, and Tribune, in August and September, 1881.*

6. Olmsted's stepson Owen had progressed only as far as the railroad at Spearfish in far western South Dakota, some one hundred miles east of his ranch on the Little Powder River in Montana. His brother John C. Olmsted met him there and brought him East by train. Olmsted and his wife met the young men at Buffalo on November 20, but Owen was already unconscious and died the following day (L. W. Roper, *FLO, A Biography*, p. 389).

7. From early childhood, Owen had displayed a freedom of spirit, energy, and enthusiasm that were conspicuously absent in his siblings. Olmsted's first surviving description of Owen, at Bear Valley in California at the age of six, is characteristic: "Owen is a perfect cub—the climate seems only to make him more clumsy, imperterbable, ravenous and prone to fall anywhere but on his feet than ever." A photograph taken at that time bears out the description. As a schoolboy, Owen wired the house and neighborhood with telephone lines and later, while attending the Columbia School of Mines, thoroughly immersed himself in a summer project on steam turbines. In 1880, after two years of experience on the Wyoming ranch of Olmsted's friend Clarence King, Owen set up his own ranch and enthusiastically launched into the demanding work of running it (*Papers of FLO*, 5: 235–36; L. W. Roper, *FLO, A Biography*, 347, 388–89).

To Charles Francis Adams, Jr.[1]

NEW YORK, 29th November, 1881.

Charles Francis Adams, Jr., ESQ.
Dear Sir,—
   It would need little to adapt the ground you have shown me to immediate public use as a park; and while thus readily available, it is susceptible of great improvement. For this purpose neither costly constructions nor elaborate methods of culture are wanted, so much as the pursuit of simple courses of husbandry, tending to the improvement of the soil and the development of the better elements of the natural growth. Thrifty management in this respect would result in more luxuriant and sustained verdure, and in harmonious, refined, and effective bodies of foliage.
   A park of such sylvan beauty as would thus be gradually gained, mainly as an outgrowth under judicious selection and treatment of natural conditions, and interestingly distinctive of the locality,—situated on the margin of a picturesque bay, with outlooks upon the ocean,—would be one of rare interest, and the citizens of Quincy are to be congratulated on the opportunity of acquiring it as cheaply as seems to be practicable.
   Yours truly,

FREDERICK LAW OLMSTED,
Landscape Architect.

   The text presented here is from "Appendix. 1. Letter of F. L. Olmsted" in *Report of the Merry-Mount Park Association. February, 1882* (Cambridge, 1882).

1. Charles Francis Adams (1835–1915), railroad expert, civic leader and historian. At this time Adams was overseeing construction of the Thomas Crane Public Library in Quincy, Massachusetts, designed by H. H. Richardson and with grounds planned by Olmsted. Adams was also involved in the association founded in Quincy to create a "Water Park and Beach Drive" at Merry-Mount, the fabled hill overlooking Quincy Bay. In June 1881 Adams had urged Olmsted to visit him and give his opinion of the site. In the simplicity of treatment that Olmsted proposes here, he is suggesting an approach to reservation of scenic sites in cities that he was to express more strongly in his article "A Healthy Change in the Tone of the Human Heart," in the *Century* magazine of October 1886 (*DAB*; Jeffrey Karl Ochsner, *H. H. Richardson: Complete Architectural Works* [Cambridge, 1882], pp. 226–27; Charles Francis Adams to FLO, June 8, 1881).

FEBRUARY 1881–DECEMBER 1881

To CHARLES HENRY DALTON

BOSTON, December 29, 1881.

CHARLES H. DALTON, Esq., *Chairman of the Park Commission:—*
SIR,—
  The Park system for Boston, advised by your Commission, though of smaller area than that of many other cities, differs from all others in the scope of its landscape design; and this is, in part, due to topographical opportunities possessed by Boston, which, for the purpose in view, are probably unrivalled.
  On the other hand, as my counsel has heretofore been asked by several other cities, when engaged with municipal problems of the same general class as that of which your proposed system is offered as a solution, it will not, I trust, be thought beyond my duty if I point to a circumstance which appears to me to be operating as yet not a little to the disadvantage of Boston.
  It is that the Boston of to-day is largely made up of what were formerly a number of distinct local communities, each habituated to regard its public affairs from an independent point of view, and sometimes in a spirit of competition and jealousy toward the others. The larger part of Boston, territorially considered, has till lately been so divided.[1] Possibly, also, the marked topographical divisions of the old city induced separate local interests in an unusual degree.
  There is now a habit of looking upon the proposed parks of the city, each apart and independently of its relations to others of the system, as if it were to be of little value except to the people of the districts adjoining it. And this is so much evinced by intelligent and generally well-informed citizens that it must be supposed to be an inheritance from those older conditions. It presents a difficulty which should be contended with; for, unquestionably, if it is maintained and allowed influence in legislation, it will be likely to nullify half the value to the city of the properties now proposed to be acquired for parks.
  For example, a site has been selected at West Roxbury for a large park, because of the topographical advantages for a particular class of park purposes which nature has there provided. It is not uncommon to hear it referred to as if it were to be a special property of the West Roxbury community, and its chief value lie in what that community would gain from it. If this were just, the project would not be worthy of a moment's consideration. Moreover, if it were to be adopted and carried out in this limited spirit at the cost of the city, the people of the locality would not gain those advantages from it that a wiser policy would have in view for them.
  A site for a park to stand by itself and be little used except by those living near it should be a very different one from that for a park designed for more general use, and especially for a park which is to stand as one of a series. In the latter case the fitness of a site will largely be found in its adaptation to supply some form of park refreshment that others of the series are ill-

adapted to supply or are naturally excluded from supplying. The qualities of a park which the West Roxbury site offers in generous measure at very moderate cost, could not, for example, be gained in a tenth part of that measure at ten times the cost on the proposed park-site near Chestnut Hill,—"Brighton Park,"[2]—or on any other which the city has had under consideration. But the converse is equally true; the Brighton site offers features of great interest, ready made, which could not be as well provided in the West Roxbury tract by an outlay in millions. Moreover, the attempt to introduce the more valuable qualities to be thus found at Brighton in the midst of those to be found at Roxbury, would be destructive of the latter, and any expense incurred for the purpose in behalf of the city would be much worse than wasted. In one word, the aim of design under the policy of the city which your Commission has been so long trying to establish, can only wisely be to develop qualities in each locality which will give it a more distinctive and grateful interest because of the development of quite other distinctive qualities elsewhere.

The accompanying map shows a series of sites which are now under consideration by the city government, and which your Commission has been authorized to purchase—if it shall be found possible to do so within fixed limits of price—together with the connections which are contemplated between them and by which they would, should the scheme be carried out, be tied to existing city properties.

It will be obvious at a glance, to anyone having a superficial knowledge of the several localities named upon the map, that, if due advantage is taken of the distinctive capabilities of each and due respect paid to the distinctive limitations of each, the results to all concerned, of whatever part of the city resident, will be incomparably more interesting and valuable than they can possibly be under a policy such as seems to be commonly entertained of regarding each proposed park and parklet as an independent affair, deriving no interest from its relation to others, land imparting nothing of value to the interest of others.

Regarding the natural opportunities and limitations of the several localities to be named below, it will be found that each will, through a judicious method of improvement, be adapted to induce a distinct impression; and that, in each, the space to be applied to this impression is sufficient for the purpose, yet none too large to accomplish it with a determined avoidance of peep-show and theatrically scenic effects. While, except at West Roxbury, which is the one ground in the entire series to be with strict propriety called a park, the spaces to be taken are nowhere to be broad, the impressions which under judicious designing will be had in view are such as may be obtained within the limited scopes proposed.

The following is a memorandum which may suggest to anyone looking at the map one or two of the more distinctive landscape qualities of the several locations mentioned, the note being in each case of the briefest, and intended only to give a slight lead to the imagination:—

february 1881–december 1881

Memorandum.

The Common, Public Garden, and Commonwealth Ave.—Turf, trees, water, and other natural objects unnaturally arranged, but not in the main unpleasingly in consideration of the stately rows of buildings and other architectural and artificial objects with which they must stand associated, and the necessary thoroughfares passing among them.
Charles River Embankment.—Broad bay and river views with a rus-urban background seen from a stately promenade.
Back Bay.—Scenery of a winding, brackish creek, within wooded banks; gaining interest from the meandering course of the water; numerous points and coves softened in their outlines by thickets and with much delicate variety in tone and color through varied, and, in landscape art, novel, forms of perennial and herbaceous growths, the picturesque elements emphasized by a few necessary structures strong but unobtrusive.
Muddy River.—The natural sequence upon slightly higher ground to the last in following up a fresh-water course bordered by passages of rushy meadow and varied slopes from the adjoining upland; trees in groups, diversified by thickets and open glades.
Upper Valley of Muddy River.—A chain of picturesque fresh-water ponds, alternating with attractive natural groves and meads, the uppermost of these ponds being—
Jamaica Pond, a natural sheet of water, with quiet, graceful shores, rear banks of varied elevation and contour, for the most part shaded by a fine natural forest-growth to be brought out overhangingly, darkening the water's edge and favoring great beauty in reflections and flickering half-lights. At conspicuous points numerous well-grown pines, happily massed, and picturesquely disposed.
The Arboretum.—(Independently of its imposed features.) Rocky hill-sides, partly wooded with numerous great trees, and a hanging-wood of hemlocks of great beauty. Eminences commanding great distant prospects, in one direction seaward over the city, in the other across a charming country-side to blue distant hills.
West Roxbury Park.—Complete escape from the town. Open country. Pastoral scenery. A lovely dale gently winding between low wooded slopes, giving a broad expanse of unbroken turf, lost in the distance under scattered trees.

  To the above, as constituent features of the sylvan system of Boston, as had in view by your Commission, are to be added two pieces of ground not shown in the present map; one commanding a close view of the lower harbor, and a distant outlook over the ocean; the other having grandeur of rocks with extraordinary beauty of form and tinting, and such interest of forest wildness as might be looked for in the midst of unpeopled mountains.[3]

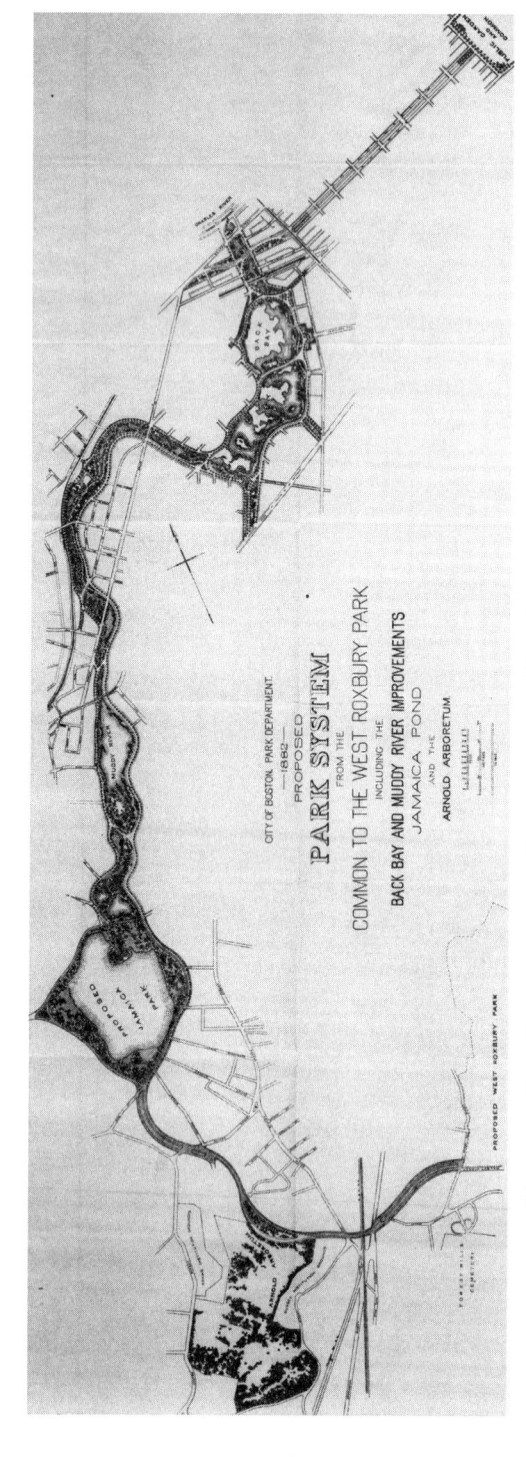

"Proposed Park System from the Common to the West Roxbury Park including the Back Bay and Muddy River Improvements, Jamaica Pond and the Arnold Arboretum" (1882)

FEBRUARY 1881–DECEMBER 1881

The above hint as to what may be ultimately hoped to result from the improvements in progress on the Back Bay, looks in a direction so diverse from that formerly entertained, and which seems still to be adhered to by many, that it will be right again to briefly characterize that undertaking, at present more prominently before the public than any other of the series.

The leading and only justifying purpose of the Back Bay Improvement, under the present design, is the abatement of a complicated nuisance, threatening soon to be a deadly peril to the whole city as a propagating and breeding-ground of pestilential epidemics. A second purpose is the reconciliation of convenient means of general public communication through the adjoining districts of the city with the means taken to accomplish the first purpose. A third purpose is the dressing and embellishment of the banks, basins, bridges, and causeways, requisite under the first and second, suitably to the relation in which they will stand to the adjoining streets, and the improvements which it is the interest of the city that private enterprise should be encouraged to make upon them. A fourth purpose is to thriftily turn to account whatever shall be found requisite under the first, second, and third, as a distinctive incident, element, and feature in a general scheme of sylvan improvement for the city, looking to the development of local variety harmonizing in one comprehensive design. It may be observed that the continued application of the term *park* to an undertaking of the character thus indicated tends to perpetuate an unfortunate delusion, and to invite unjust expectations and criticisms.

A like fourfold purpose has controlled the selection of ground and the plan, as shown on the map, of the projected Muddy River Improvement. In general design, these two sections of the park system are one, the only division between the two being a concealed bar,[4] which, in the Muddy River section, will permit fresh-water vegetation to be used along the water sides.

Respectfully submitted,

FREDERICK LAW OLMSTED,
Landscape Architect Advisory.

The text presented here is from BCDP, City of Boston, *Seventh Annual Report, for the Year 1881* (City Doc. No. 16) [Boston, 1882], pages 24–28.

1. Between 1868 and 1874, Boston annexed the towns of Roxbury, Dorchester, Charlestown, West Roxbury, and Brighton, adding over 16,000 acres to the pre-existing 3,300, an area five times as large as the previous city of Boston.
2. The 160 acres of forest and rugged, rocky terrain adjoining Chestnut Hill Reservoir in Brighton that the park commission in 1876 proposed to use for park purposes.
3. That is, "Brighton Park" and a proposed park at the City Point Battery on Boston harbor

at the eastern end of the South Boston peninsula. This was the eventual site of Olmsted's "Pleasure Bay," or Marine Park.
4. A dam and water gate at Brookline Avenue, separating the salt water of the Back Bay Fens from the fresh water in the proposed Muddy River section of the park system.

To John Sterling

Copy

Brookline, Mass.
30th December, 1881.

Mr Jno Stirling, Sec'y.
Belle Isle Park Commission;
Dear Sir:
    I have your favor of 27th, suggesting that a third part of the proposed park for Detroit might be laid out independently of a general plan and asking if I will prepare a plan for such a part at the rate per acre of my usual charge for the general planning of a park.
    There are doubtless reasons for the suggestion of which I am ignorant but I should hope that the end in view might be reached through some less objectionable expedient. I cannot but think it of the first importance that all parts of a park work should be in subordination to a comprehensive design, each part being made helpful to and being helped by every other part. In devising a plan therefore every part should, in my judgemnt, be subject to revision until every other part is provisionally determined. It would be better to plan the wing or corner of a dwelling house without knowing what the main part is to be than to take a like course with a great park. I would therefore submit to the Commissioners that it will be better to give me an opportunity of examining the entire property and of conferring with them before requiring an answer to the question.
    And upon this proposition I beg to observe also that before a park can be fully planned it is inevitable that ideas will be advanced which are more or less in conflict with one another. The making of a plan should be to some extent a gradual process of weighing the comparative importance of these ideas, throwing out those which would make the plan too complicated and incoherent and of adjusting and fitting together such as can be harmoniously used. It should not therefore be the straight-forward work of an expert representing his own ideas without consideration for others and most certainly not if the expert is a stranger to the people in whose behalf the work is to be undertaken

and unfamiliar with the circumstances under which it is to be done. Hence I advise as the first step a free conference between the Commissioners and myself if they entertain the idea of employing me, such as there would be as a matter of course between a client & his intended counsel in an important case at law.

I do not wish to be engaged in the matter nor can I suppose the Commissioners wish to be unless it is considered one of importance; and as a work of art, demanding in its design the best and most mature study that can be given it, nor unless it is likely to be prosecuted with a view to the best results attainable with the means at command.

Very Respectfully,

Fred[k] Law Olmsted.

The text presented here is from a manuscript in Olmsted's hand. This letter is a characteristic refusal by Olmsted to plan a portion of park before adopting a comprehensive general design for it. Sterling's letter may have come as a result of a recommendation made in November 1881 by Salem Wales to James Macmillan of Detroit, at that time a member of the commission responsible for the planning of a public park on Belle Isle, that Olmsted should be engaged to design the park (Salem Wales to FLO, Jan. 21, 1882).

CHAPTER XI

JANUARY 1882–MARCH 1882

This chapter marks the completion and publication of *The Spoils of the Park*, Olmsted's parting shot concerning Central Park and his final effort to win support for its proper administration. The "Central Park Circular" that he wrote at this time to enlist testimony from qualified experts was never circulated. The final letter in the chapter, to his old friend Charles Loring Brace, reviews the effect of *The Spoils of the Park* and expresses his pleasure at living and working in the new setting of the Boston suburbs.

Other documents in the chapter describe important ongoing design work. The letter to John C. Phillips explains the importance of forest planting on his country estate and stresses the need to avoid "the ease of a costly commonplace result." The report to Edward H. Rollins accompanies and explains a sketch-view of the U.S. Capitol with the proposed terraces as Olmsted strove to secure funding for their construction.

JANUARY 1882–MARCH 1882

To Edward Henry Rollins[1]

Washington, *January* 7, 1882.

To the Hon. E. H. Rollins,
Chairman Senate Committee on Public Buildings and Grounds:
Sir:
  I respectfully ask your consideration for the fact that the air of the Capitol is always, during the larger part of the year, charged with poisonous miasma.[2]
  If the fact is questioned I will submit reasons for asserting it. For the present I assume it, and also that no session of Congress can be carried into the spring, or held during the summer or fall, without a distinct impairment, because of this miasmatic poison, of the health, vigor, and ability for their duty of its members, while, in the usual interval between the sessions of Congress, the efficiency of all who are employed in the business of the Capitol is lessened by it.[3]
  The source of the poison is the low ground lying from half a mile to a mile south of the Capitol. Rising from this locality it is floated northward by the summer winds to the Capitol.
  The evil may in time be cut off at its origin by embankments and drainage, but adequate operations for the purpose will be costly, and are likely to be prolonged. While in progress their immediate effect will be an aggravation of the evil.
  The movement of the poison may, however, be arrested by means, which will not be costly, of planting the strip of land now held by the United States along the base of the Capitol Hill on the south.[4] The situation and the scope of the planting required are indicated on the subjoined map.
  Should there be doubt with your committee of the value of the purpose of the expedient thus proposed, it is respectfully suggested that it might be removed by inquiring of the National Board of Health.[5]
  The proposition originated in a question addressed to me in 1879 by Mr. Edward Clark, the Architect of the Capitol, my reply to which, attached to the map below, more fully defines the very simple scheme.[6] I will add here that the trees required to carry it out could probably be obtained without cost from the overstock now in the nurseries of the Commissioners of the District of Columbia;[7] that the proposition is in all respects a frugal one, and that it would have very desirable incidental advantages, which, should your committee be pleased to entertain the question, I would ask the honor to be allowed to explain from the windows of the committee room.[8]
  Very respectfully, your obedient servant,

FRED'K LAW OLMSTEAD,
Landscape Architect of the Capitol Grounds.

The text presented here is from United States Senate, 47th Congress, 1st session, miscellaneous document number 32, pages 1–2. Olmsted presented the text and plans to a joint meeting of the Senate and House committees on public buildings and grounds at the Capitol on January 11, 1882 (*Congressional Record*, 47th Cong., 1st sess., 1881–82, 8: 346).

1. Edward Henry Rollins (1824–1889), businessman and politician. Prominent in the New Hampshire Republican party before the Civil War, Rollins sat in the U.S. House of Representatives between 1861 and 1867. After serving as secretary and treasurer of the Union Pacific Railroad during the 1870s, Rollins was elected to the U.S. Senate and served between 1877 and 1883. He was a member of the Committee on the District of Columbia and chaired the Senate Committee on Public Buildings and Grounds between 1881 and 1883 (*BDAC*; *Index to the Congressional Record*, 46th Cong., 1st sess., 1879, pp. 362–363).
2. The atmosphere surrounding the Capitol was suspected of carrying malarial vapors from the canal district and marshes along the Potomac River to the south (FLO to Edward Clark, May 23, 1879, above).
3. The health of those at the U.S. Capitol was an issue of national interest. In 1879 Julian Hartridge, a member of Congress, died in Washington, and the miasmic atmosphere of the city was widely blamed for his death and the illnesses of other members. Sanitary conditions worsened during the summers, when Congress recessed, and added to the city's morbid reputation. Olmsted personally knew people whose work at the Capitol building made them vulnerable. John A. Partridge, engineer in charge of the Capitol grounds, his successor, Frederick H. Cobb, and head gardener William Cogan all suffered periodically from "chills & fever" (*Washington Evening Star*, Jan. 29, 1879, p. 2; ibid., Aug. 4, 1879, p. 1; Alexander Y. P. Garnett, "Observations on the Potomac Marshes at Washington, D.C.," in American Public Health Association, *Public Health Papers and Reports* 7 [1881], pp. 186–88ff; John A. Partridge to FLO, Sept. 3, 1874; William Cogan to FLO, Dec. 8, 1878, D2, OAR/LC; E. Hennessey to FLO, Jan. 28, 1879, D2, OAR/LC).
4. Olmsted had first proposed planting a belt of trees along the old canal bed for this purpose in May 1879. In 1880 drainage and filling work was done, but no trees were planted (FLO to Edward Clark, May 23, 1879, above).
5. In early 1879 Congress created the National Board of Health composed of prominent physicians, scientists, and sanitary engineers. It was charged with regulating quarantines against yellow fever and giving advice to state and municipal governments on public health questions (Jon A. Peterson, "The Impact of Sanitary Reform upon American Urban Planning, 1840–1890," *Journal of Social History* 13 [1979], pp. 83–103; U.S. National Board of Health, *Annual Report* [Washington, D.C., 1879], p. 1).
6. Olmsted appended his May 23, 1879, letter to Clark, printed above.
7. That is, the nurseries on the grounds of the Washington Asylum at Georgia Avenue and 19th Street southeast which supplied trees for the street planting operations of the Parking Commission of the District of Columbia (William Tindall, "The Origin of the Parking System of this City," *Records of the Columbia Historical Society* 4 [1901], p. 84; DeBonneville Randolph Keim, *Washington and Mount Vernon* [Washington, D.C., 1893], p. 54).
8. The House Committee on Public Buildings and Grounds met in a first floor room on the southeast corner of the House wing of the Capitol, which overlooked the area being discussed. Rollins also sat on the Committee on the District of Columbia, which reported a bill during the same session appropriating money to continue draining and filling work on the canal tract and Reservation 17. Congress appropriated $20,000 for the work in August 1882, and it was carried out by the U.S. Army Corp of Engineers in charge of public spaces in the District. It does not appear, however, that Olmsted's plans were followed in the improvement of either the canal tract or Reservation 17. The latter

place was renamed Garfield Park in 1883 (*Congressional Directory* [Washington, D.C., 1882], pp. 102–3; *Congressional Record*, 47th Cong., 1st sess., 1881–82, 8: 631, 986, 2305–7; U.S. War Department, *Annual Report* [Washington, D.C., 1883], 2: 2099, 2107; ibid. [Washington, D.C., 1885], 2: 2344, 2351).

To Edward Henry Rollins

[c. January–February 1882]

THE HON. E. H. ROLLINS,
Chairman of the Joint Committee of Congress on Public Buildings and Grounds.
Sir:
    Illustrations are here presented for the more convenient consideration by your Committee of the plan of an architectural terrace, designed to supersede the present earth-work covering the unfinished base of the Capitol.[1]
    The perspective on this page {see page 578} is taken from the point which would be occupied by a man coming up the hill in a carriage, where the first unobstructed view of the building would be had.[2] It is at this point that the obscuration of the main walls by the new construction would be greatest. A few yards farther to the eastward there would be none. As this effect of the terrace is the only objection raised to the plan, poles with cross-bars at top have been set in the ground south of the building, showing the height and position of its upper line; and in passing to or from the Capitol on the House side, the Committee may readily see what the objection amounts to. The granite base-course of the present marble walls of the Capitol will be found in looking from the road within the grounds to appear a little *above* the cross-bars. What remains to be seen of this granite above the line, will in the end be obscured by the foliage to be introduced upon the terrace, and the effect of the arrangement will be to re-establish a granite base on the natural surface of the ground, all the visible structure above being of marble. A better understanding of the facts may be had from the small section on the right of the third page.
    The above plan {see page 580} shows the enlargement of the basement room of the Capitol to be gained through the construction of the terrace. The additional space is 1,400 feet long by 60 feet wide, divided into rooms opening from a central corridor. Ten of these correspond in form and dimensions with the best of the present upper committee rooms, each having two or three windows looking upon the existing courts in the same manner as those of the architect's office in the present basement. These court-yards are to be made attractive winter gardens.[3] (The rooms in question are marked A on the

View of U.S. Capitol with proposed terrace, by Olmsted

plan, which differs from that lately submitted to the committee, in accordance with suggestions made by some of the members.[4] A small perspective at the top of the next page shows the character of the rooms. The walls are 14 feet high to the spring of the arch). The other rooms shown are expected to be used (1) for the storage of coal and other materials now within the walls of the Capitol; (2) for the keeping, with convenient arrangements of access and reference, of the archives and documents, now stored in bulk and inaccessible in rooms within the walls of the Capitol, and every year rapidly accumulating; (3) for the temporary deposit of current documents of Congress, sorting, folding, packing and other working purposes; (4) for extraordinary committee and clerks' rooms when needed. These rooms will be fire-proof, dry, and may be gas-lighted and steam-heated at pleasure. They will have day-light and be ventilated through the construction to be shown on the next page, and will also be furnished with deck-lights. Of the class of rooms thus described there are 78, but any number of them may be thrown into one by archways in the walls; disconnected, they vary from 20 to 44 feet in length and from 16 to 24 feet in breadth. Most of them will resemble the present basement committee rooms. The plan of this floor provides for a sub-way, by which coal, ashes, and all goods not desirable to be passed through the upper entrances, may be conveyed underground to or from a postern in the government work-yard on South B street. It also provides for an enlargement of the present boiler-rooms.

The above plan {see page 581} shows the esplanade or deck of the terrace. It is to be in two parts, the division running midway between the outer walls of the present building and the outer walls of the proposed new work. The inner one of these two parts is to be level with the foot of the several short flights of steps opening from the porticos, the outer one four feet lower.[5] The two levels are to be connected by flights of steps opposite those from the porticos. (The arrangement will be most readily understood from the small section on the right.) In line with these lower flights, and following the division between the two levels, there is to be a channel eight feet wide and four feet deep, the bottom of it on the lower level, the top a little higher than the upper. (See section on the right.) This is to be filled with soil and planted and decorated in the Italian manner of gardening, consistently with the architectural style of the Capitol.[6] Sufficient openings are to be made through the outer wall of this terrace garden for lighting and ventilating the corridor below. By thus setting the outer part of the terrace at a lower level than the inner part, its parapet will not harmfully obstruct views from or toward the building, while it is believed that the architectural effect to result will be in all other respects fitting and satisfactory.

The Committee is asked to consider:

That it is more than twenty years since the problem of a suitable treatment of the northern, western and southern bases of the Capitol was first forced upon Congress; that the present plan has been prepared under special orders of Congress as a solution of it; that it is five years since it was presented

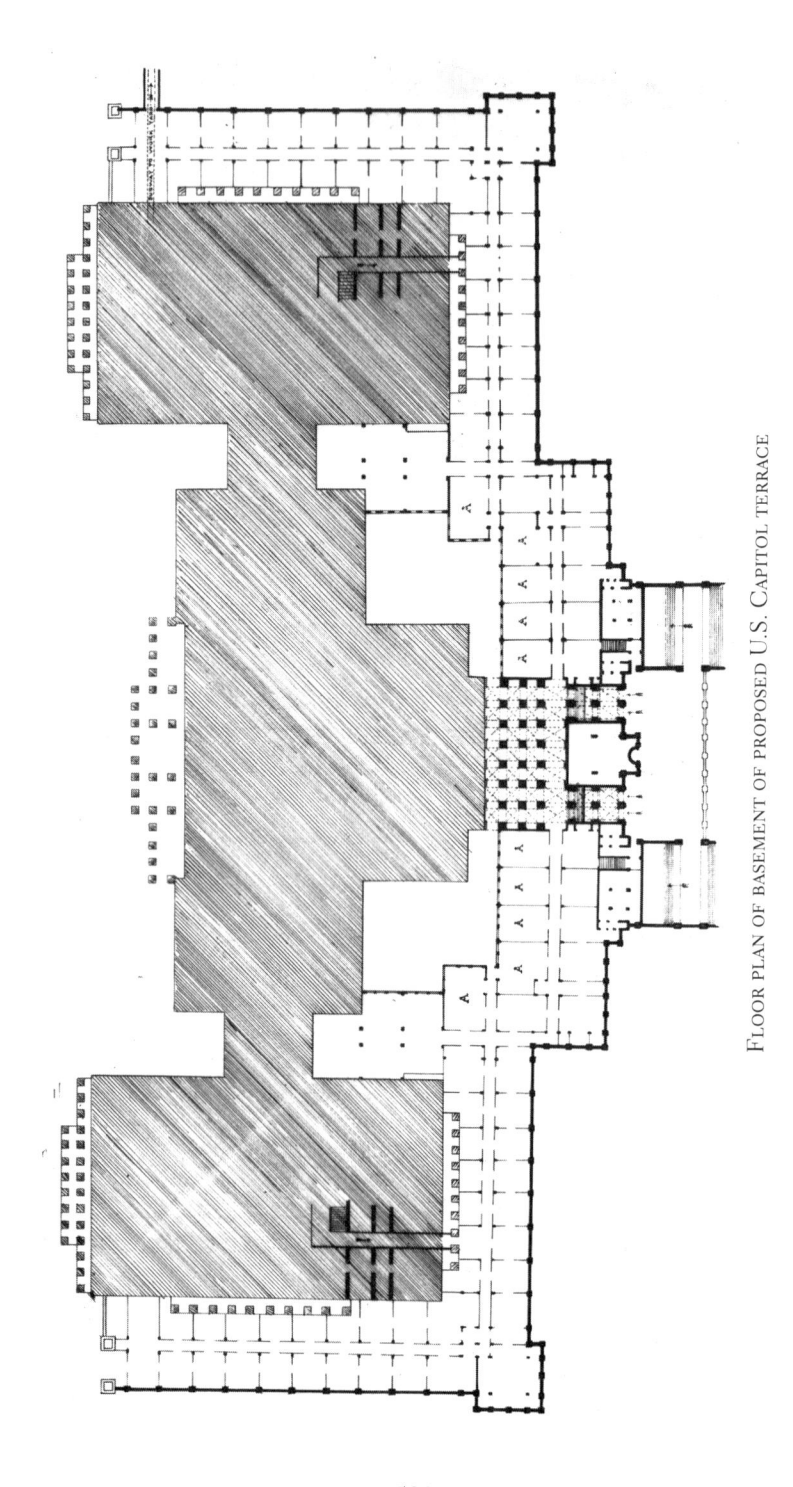

Floor plan of basement of proposed U.S. Capitol terrace

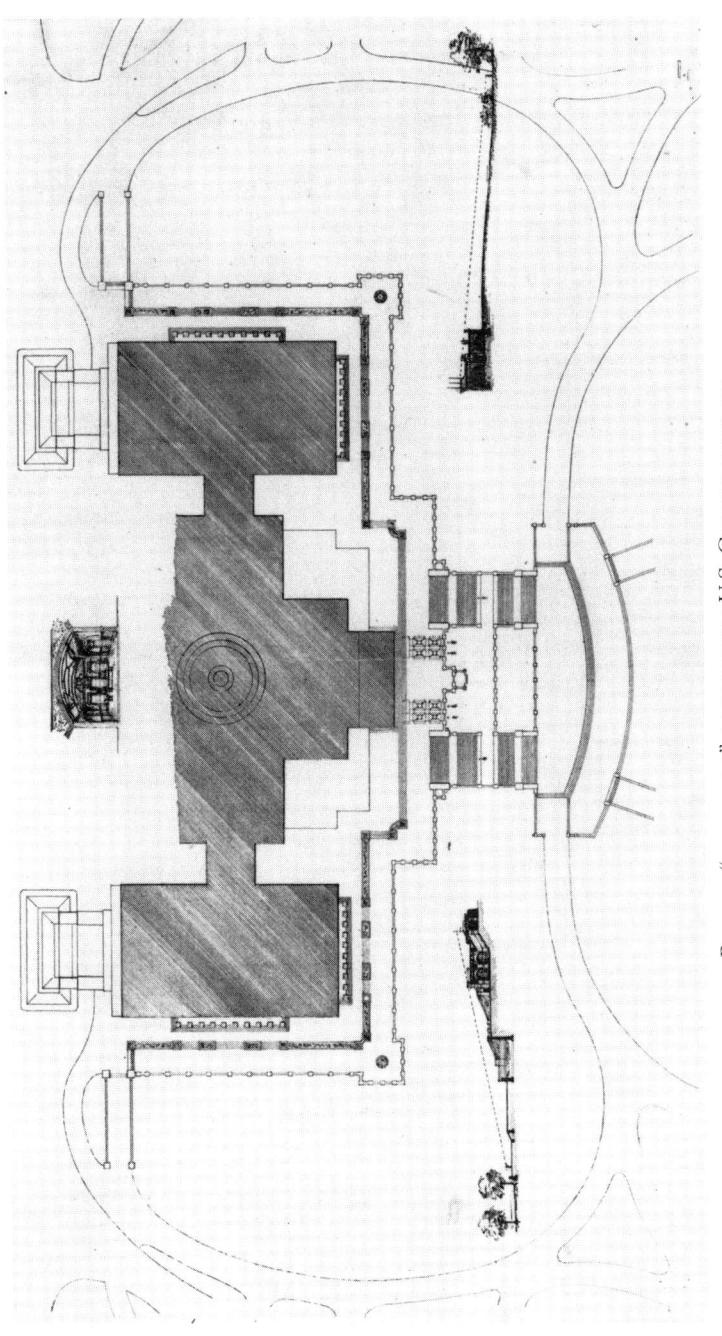

Plan of "esplanade" of proposed U.S. Capitol terrace
Two details show the line of sight made possible by two-tiered form of terrace.

and adopted by Congress as a satisfactory solution;[7] that while other plans have from time to time been devised for occupying the ground, none of them have met with favor, none have contemplated as small an outlay; none would involve as little destruction of work already done, and none have been designed with a single eye to support, sustain and augment the primary architectural motive of the Capitol; finally, that the merit neither of what has been obtained in the Capitol, nor upon its grounds, can be realized until the gap between the two is harmoniously closed, as it is designed to be by the proposed construction.

And in view of these considerations the question whether it is sound economy to further delay entering upon the work is respectfully submitted.[8]

FREDERICK LAW OLMSTED, Landscape Architect.

The text presented here is from a printed circular in the Olmsted Papers.

1. On January 11, 1882, Olmsted appeared before a joint meeting of the Senate and House committees on public buildings and grounds and showed drawings and elevations of his proposed terrace for the U.S. Capitol. Within weeks he prepared the present undated text to explain the project further and generate congressional support for it. He sent the "terrace circular" to Edward Clark in mid-February 1882 and asked that it be shown to Justin S. Morrill. Frederick H. Cobb reported that both men had read and approved it and that copies had been distributed to committee members. Some two hundred printed copies were distributed to Congress in early April 1882 (Minutes of House Committee on Public Buildings and Grounds, Jan. 11, 1882, p. 8, in Records of the U.S. House of Representatives, Record Group 233, 47A–F24.7, NARA, Washington, D.C.; *Washington Evening Star*, Jan. 12, 1882, p. 1; FLO to G. G. Vest, Jan. 12, 1882; FLO to Edward H. Rollins, Dec. 30, 1882; FLO to Edward Clark, Feb. 17, 1882, in Office of the Curator, Architect of the Capitol, U.S. Capitol, Washington, D.C.; ibid., April 8, 1882; FLO to Frederick H. Cobb, March 7, 1882, in Office of the Curator, Architect of the Capitol, U.S. Capitol, Washington, D.C.; Frederick H. Cobb to FLO, Feb. 22, 1882, D3, OAR/LC ; ibid., March 23, 1882).
2. This view was drawn in October 1881 by Thomas Wisedell and was probably a copy of the large colored drawing which he prepared when Olmsted first presented the terrace proposal to the Senate Committee on Public Buildings and Grounds in January 1875. Wisedell also drew the plans referred to below (FLO to Montgomery C. Meigs, Jan. 15, 1875, above; Thomas Wisedell, pay vouchers, Oct. 20, 1881, Records Management Department, Architect of the Capitol, U.S. Capitol, Washington, D.C.; ibid., April 20, 1882).
3. Olmsted was not proposing to cover these courtyards with glass to make a traditional winter garden but rather to take advantage of their sheltered position and plant evergreen shrubs and ivies that would provide color through the dreary winter months. In his 1866 proposal for San Francisco's pleasure grounds, Olmsted had designated as a "Winter Garden" a sheltered (but not covered) promenade to be planted with laurel, myrtle, rhododendrons, Chinese magnolias, and ivy. The U.S. Capitol courtyards were not planted until after the completion of the west terrace in 1889. At that time Olmsted ordered that "a large plat of good turf" be planted in each area instead of the winter gardens because of congressional plans to extend the western front of the building (*Papers*

of *FLO*, 5: 541; FLO to William Cogan, Aug. 2, 1889, A5: 94, OAR/LC; William Cogan to FLO, Oct. 1, 1889, D4, OAR/LC; ibid., Oct. 25, 1889).
4. Thomas Wisedell and Frederick H. Cobb had drawn up detailed plans for the terrace between October and December 1881. Olmsted presented them in his appearance before the committee in early January and, at the request of members at that meeting, revised them to include committee rooms (Thomas Wisedell to FLO, Nov. 26, 1881; Frederick H. Cobb to FLO, Nov. 14, 1881, D3, OAR/LC; ibid., Nov. 23, 1881; ibid., Dec. 15, 1881; Thomas Wisedell to Edward Clark, April 26, 1882, and Thomas Wisedell and Frederick H. Cobb, pay vouchers, Records Management Department, Architect of the Capitol, U.S. Capitol, Washington, D.C.; FLO to Edward H. Rollins, Dec. 30, 1882).
5. Unlike the 1874–75 general plan of the Capitol grounds, which showed the lower deck of the terrace covered with mosaic pavement, this plan omitted such a treatment.
6. In the mid-1880s, Olmsted attempted to introduce formal plantings, including low-growing trees, on the terrace, expressive of Italian gardening and complementing the classic architecture of the Capitol. He relented, however, when Justin S. Morrill, Edward Clark, and others conveyed their own and public disapproval (Justin S. Morrill to FLO, Nov. 28, 1883, B134: #2820, OAR/LC; FLO to Justin S. Morrill, Nov. 30, 1883, Morrill Papers, Library of Congress; William Cogan to FLO, April 24, 1886, D3, OAR/LC; Justin S. Morrill to Edward Clark, April 21, 1887, Office of the Curator, Architect of the Capitol, U.S. Capitol, Washington, D.C.).
7. In fact, seven years had passed since Olmsted's terrace proposal was first approved by Congress (FLO to Montgomery C. Meigs, Jan. 15, 1875, above).
8. Despite opposition from Democrats on the Appropriations Committee, Congress in August 1882 provided money to begin work on the north approach to the terrace ([Glenn Brown], *Documentary History of the Construction and Development of the United States Capitol Building and Grounds* [Washington, D.C., 1904], pp. 1211–17; FLO to Edward H. Rollins, Dec. 30, 1882).

Central Park Circular

[c. February 1882]

[33: 521] This circular will be addressed to a number of men who may be presumed to have had their minds for considerable periods directed to questions of a corresponding character to those which occur in public parks.[1] It is designed to submit to their consideration without concert, a few simple propositions applicable to the managmnt of a park under the circumstances of the Central Park. The object is to ascertain whether those who have given the subject studious attention free from political biases, agree in holding such propositions to have been established and to be so far authoritative and binding that disregard of them implies culpable ignorance, negligence or perversity.

The circumstances in question to be first more particularly considered are these: [33:524] The Central Park occupies a body of land two miles square (exclusive of parts given to other than park purposes)[2] in what is expected to be the heart of a great commercial city, interrupting its two central avenues and fifty streets which would otherwise cross from one of its navigable waters to another.[3]

[33: 529–32] The circumstances to be particularly considered are that the ground is to be enclosed by high buildings from some of which no part of it will be more than quarter of a mile distant; its surface is diversified but no part of it of higher elevation than the tops of such of those buildings as have been already erected. It is everywhere underlaid with granite rock of which the usual surface form is that of long undulations.

In five sixths of the field the earth, soil and boulders overlying this rock are not naturally on an average more than three feet in depth while at frequent intervals there are outcrops of the ledge and considerable spaces where it is insufficient to sustain large trees or maintain a tolerable turf. By excavating near the base of conspicuous rocks and exposing portions of rock surface originally thinly covered, material has been obtained for increasing the original depth of earth in selected localities, the aim being to obtain the greatest practicable breadths of greensward in the interior parts of the park.

To avoid frequent interruptions of the distinctive use of the park by ordinary street traffic it is crossed in the 2½ miles of its length by four subways, and where those would otherwise be conspicuous the ground is tunnelled.[4] Elsewhere they are everywhere walled to a height of at least 8 ft., the pavement being generally 10 ft below the natural surface. This brings within the park two miles of masonry which has to be considered in addition to the structures which are to surround it and those by which its two principal parts are divided.

The soundness of certain ends which have been had in view in laying it out and of certain principles which have been regarded in pursuing these ends has been often very vehemently denied, never by any landscape gardener, but by men whose influence and authority has nevertheless been sufficient to induce great departures from the courses which would otherwise be pursued. At the present time there is a complete reversal in important particulars of those courses and a profession of counter purposes and principles.[5] It is desired to obtain the judgmnt of those to whom this circular will be addressed upon the questions thus at issue, and it is proposed after returns from it shall have been received to embody the general sentimnt in a paper which will again be submitted for consideration with a view to a public declaration on the subject.

[33: 523] It is hoped that questions growing directly from actual practice may be presented with this object in view, the answers to which will show that a certain footing has been firmly established for Landscape Gardening among the arts of Design and that it is only ignorance which assumes to conduct a public undertaking involving outlays and affecting the value of property to amounts of many millions of dollars in denial of such laws as may thus be recognized as fixed for that art.

[33: 541] The Central Park is a work of more than local and immediate importance. The direct outlay of public money already made upon it amounts to upwards of $15,000,000, important parts of it being yet unimproved, encumbered and unused. The expense in which it must indirectly involve the city will be much larger than that of this direct outlay. Great public treasures in addition to those classed with the park are accumulating within and adjoining it.[6] Not only will these circumstances give it extraordinary celebrity but from its situation in the heart of the principal city of the continent it will be brought more under general observation than any other work of its class.

[33: 526–28] The managment of the Central Park, directly and through the discussions growing out of it must largely influence customs, fashions, manners, opinions and tastes throughout the country.[7] The differences of opinion which now appear upon the subject are so radical they touch the value of property of such enormous value and they are sustained with so much assurance as to leave open to question among all to whom the subject has not been one of special study, whether there are any fixed principles applicable to the treatmnt of pleasure-grounds public or private, or by which the administration of trusts with regard to them needs to be regulated. Doubt on the subject is doubt of the value of all study that has been given to the art of Landscape Gardening by a large number of eminently wise and worthy men and of the utility of the profession of landscape gardening. It is thought that something may be done to lessen this doubt if an expression of conviction can be obtained from the gentlemen to whom this circular will be addressed upon a few simple points, even though a wide field for difference of opinion and diversity of policy shall be left open, and that these points can be best presented in answers to questions having reference to the particular circumstances of the Central Park.

[33: 533–39] Thirty millions of dollars have already been invested in parks by a few of our leading cities and the outlay upon them is continuous. Their actual value depends on their managment from year to year—Their managment is generally controlled by boards the composition of which is subject to change from year to year. No previous knowledge or consideration of anything distinctive in the business of parks is required in the members of these boards.[8] There is a custom of using the term landscape gardening as if there were a recognized art, with fixed laws, in some degree applicable to a part of the business, but some regard this as cant to cover quackery and to few has the term any meaning so far fixed and clear that its use serves otherwise than to darken counsel. It is substantially denied that there are any principles or canons covered by the term that any man of ordinary intelligence may not be presumed to be familiar with or which he may not honorably assume himself qualified to apply under any circumstances, even in cases where the value of millions of trust property is at stake.

If there is ground for this denial it lies in the fact that within the proper field of landscape gardening and under such laws and precepts as constitute the frame work of the art, there is room for such differences of opinion and of practice that to superficial observers there is nothing settled.

This circular will be sent to a number of persons who are known to have given the subject more thorough study than is common and who if not of professional standing may justly be regarded as experts within the limits of landscape gardening which will be brought under consideration. The object will be to demonstrate that, within these, under given circumstances there is a perfectly well established understanding among all men having any authority in landscape gardening, as to what is right and wrong, true and false, reputable and disreputable.

[33: 522] The first proposition is that by no other treatmnt of such a property consistent with its designation as a park can it be given as much value to the people of a great city, as that which will make available to them upon it the enjoymnt of beauty in natural scenery, or in scenery designed to affect the imagination and sensibilities of men by a semblance to natural scenery such as may be accomplished through the art of landscape gardening as its objects, principles and processes have been defined by Gilpin, Repton, Price, Loudon, Downing and other standard authors on the subject.[9]

The text presented here is an unpaginated, fragmentary draft in Olmsted's hand. It is repetitive and discursive, and appears to consist of drafts of the same document. The reel and frame numbers of the Frederick Law Olmsted Papers microfilm on which the text fragments can be found are given in brackets throughout the text published here. Using all the sheets that Olmsted did not cross out except two, the editors have constructed a text that best provides a coherent progression of the related themes of the manuscript. We have also drawn upon our understanding of the circumstances under which Olmsted wrote it. The first theme concerns the way that the principles and techniques of landscape architecture had been used in the peculiar topography and urban surroundings of Central Park to create extended passages of pastoral scenery, and how a recent, misguided maintenance program on the park constituted a repudiation of those principles and techniques. The second theme concerns the fact that since Central Park was the country's first and most prominent park, its management served, for better or worse, as an example for the rest of the country. The third theme is the need for codification of the basic principles of park management and adherence to them by the officials sworn to administer such properties as public trusts. This manuscript appears to consist only of the introductory section of the intended circular. It lists only the first of what Olmsted apparently intended to be a series of propositions concerning principles of park design on which a selected group of experts were to comment.

The editors have dated the text circa February 1882 because the specific mismanagement of the park that prompted Olmsted to write it began in the fall of 1881 and because his pamphlet *The Spoils of the Park* of February 1882 mentioned the possibility of issuing a circular about the problem to experts in landscape gardening. Olmsted appears never to have issued such a circular. A differently arranged, partial version of the text presented here was published by Frederick Law Olmsted, Jr., and Theodora Kimball as a footnote in *Forty Years of Landscape Architecture* (*Forty Years*, 2: 145; Frederick Law Olmsted, *The Spoils of the Park with a Few Leaves from the Deep-Laden Note-Books of "A Wholly Unpractical Man"* [Feb. 1882], p. 632, below).

1. In *The Spoils of the Park*, Olmsted named twelve men that he considered qualified to review changes in the management of Central Park (F. L. Olmsted, *Spoils of the Park*, p. 632, below).
2. In referring to sections of the park devoted to non-park purposes, Olmsted presumably had in mind the old and new Croton reservoirs in its center and the area occupied by the Metropolitan Museum of Art.
3. The park discontinues Sixth and Seventh avenues between 59th and 110th streets and blocks cross town streets for those fifty blocks.
4. That is, the four transverse roads crossing the park at 65th, 79th, 85th, and 97th streets were constructed below grade and bordered with plantings to insulate park visitors from the sight and sound of their traffic. The transverse roads were tunneled under the ground at most points where park's circuit drive crossed them, and the 79th Street transverse road ran through a long tunnel just south of Vista Rock, from which it would otherwise have been particularly conspicuous.
5. In the summer of 1881 the park board appointed Aneurin Jones, a Welsh carpenter, as superintendent of Central Park. That fall he began an indiscriminate program of cutting down trees and shrubs throughout the park with the avowed aim of opening vistas from the streets around it. He also removed plantings carefully established to mask its bridges, arches, and architectural structures. Although his actions constituted a repudiation of the adopted design of the park, and were changes that had to be approved by the park board, the commissioners did nothing to stop him. Olmsted privately described his work as "a rash ignorant and absurd attempt to destroy the main object hitherto in view in all that has been done on the park" (*New-York Daily Tribune*, Oct. 3, 1881, p. 4; ibid., Oct. 17, 1881, p. 5; FLO to William L. Fischer, Oct. 19, 1881; William L. Fischer to FLO, Nov. 7, 1881; Roy Rosenzweig and Elizabeth Blackmar, *The Park and the People: A History of Central Park* [Ithaca, N.Y., 1992], p. 288; see *The Spoils of the Park*, above).
6. A reference to the Metropolitan Museum of Art and the American Museum of Natural History.
7. At the end of the previous paragraph, Olmsted wrote and then deleted a sentence that is best placed at this point: "Whatever its merits or demerits therefore it cannot fail to be of great influence in the education of the republic. If managed in successive periods with a view to differing and irreconcilable ends, or upon opposing principles, the result must be calamitous & nationally humiliating."
8. In a passage which he deleted, Olmsted elaborated on the absence of professional park management in municipal affairs:

> In all of these divisions of public business some forms of authority are recognized by which the ends to be had in view and the means and methods of pursuing them are prescribed and limited within certain ranges of discretion. But in parks it is held that no corresponding restraints exist. Every successive administration may be a law to itself, free to adopt purposes the reverse of those which have been previously entertained & to use such means & methods as shall suggest themselves to men to which the business is new.
>
> Of this class of works the Central Park is the oldest and the most renowned in the country. It has cost and is annually costing more than any other

(see reel 33, frame 525, Microfilm edition, FLO Papers/LC).

9. William Gilpin, Humphry Repton, Uvedale Price, and John Claudius Loudon were British writers on landscape and agriculture whose works Olmsted had read early in life and whose ideas influenced his practice of landscape architecture throughout his career. A. J. Downing, the preeminent American landscape gardener of the 1840s and 1850s, particularly influenced Olmsted's ideas about the civilizing influences of domestic and landscape architecture (*Papers of FLO*, 1: 74–77, 117, 120–21; ibid., 3: 40–41; ibid., 6: 468–70).

To George Kessler[1]

Bkline 5th March 1882.

Mr Geo. Kessler,
My Dear Sir;

I have only today, after returning from the West, been able to look over your drawings. My object in asking you to send them was simply to know for what work I could if opportunity offered suggest your employmnt, not to criticise or advise. But as you invite me, I will observe that it strikes me that your study & practice so far as indicated has been too much limited to small pleasure-ground work in which consistent broad effects of natural landscape are out of the question. The only illustration of what I regard as the higher field of landscape gardening is that to which you refer of the work of Puckler Muskau, which I wish much that I had seen.[2] I don't mean to speak disrespectfully of pleasure ground & flower garden work such as is nearly always called for near a house and which alone gives much general employmt to gardeners but only to urge you to be ambitious to be master in higher fields, as to which you can learn little in the Central Park or in any of the situations open or likely to be open to you. Take any of these therefore as means of living and make yourself as perfect as possible in all that pertains to them & all that you can learn in them, but by reading & reflection and such excursions as you can afford for *enjoyment* of natural scenery educate yourself above them. For this purpose a day's walk along the valley of any stream or among the foot hills of any mountain range would be worth more to you than a year in the park. I do not mean to advise you to neglect study of improved scenery. There are various places on the Hudson, Hyde Park laid out by Dr Hosack;[3] for example, in which magnificent nature gains by foregrounds of art. You will find most referred to in Downing's Landscape Gardening. But bear always in mind that landscape gardening has natural scenery and the art to conceal art as its highest aim and that where we have one man qualified for work of this higher kind there are thousands in competition for the lower fields.

Aim to free yourself from German associations, not because they are not excellent but because you have been too much confined in your education to them and they are likely to cramp your capabilities and limit your influence and opportunities. Remember that in America the German demand for landscape gardening is likely to be but a small part of all that is to come and you don't want to be tied to it, or, give the impression that you are. Your writing shows that your English is much affected by German idioms & your English vocabulary not as copious as desirable. Hold yourself one of the universal republic of art, free to receive light, free to work, on all sides.

Seek in the public libraries and read, study deliberately, the older English works on landscape gardening. Repton, Loudon, Gilpin, above all Price (on the Picturesque).[4] All are faulty & to be read discriminatingly but all are in earnest and of high ideals, and in your present stage will be of invaluable service in keeping them before you.

A railway company in Missouri may want a man to take charge of a public picnic or excursion ground. The President is to be in New York soon and having your address may ask you to call on him. He is himself a landscape gardener of great ability.[5] I mention it only that if he should send for you, you may {be} prompt and prepared to present yourself to advantage.

The text presented here is from a draft in Olmsted's hand.

1. The landscape architect George Edward Kessler (1862–1923). Born in Germany, Kessler immigrated to the United States with his parents three years later. In 1878 he returned to Germany, where he spent two years studying botany, forestry, and landscape design at the Belvedere park in Weimar and working on the extensions of parks in that area. He also studied at several other gardens and institutions. Kessler returned to the United States in October 1881 and met John C. Olmsted soon afterward, while working at a nursery in New York City. He then wrote Olmsted seeking employment, and was asked to send his credentials and examples of his work. In doing so, Kessler requested Olmsted's advice on whether to accept one of two current offers of employment—one as a gardener on Central Park, which Salem Wales had offered to provide, and the other as a florist at Woodlawn Cemetery in the Bronx. Through Olmsted's good offices, referred to in this letter, Kessler was instead employed by Hollis H. Hunnewell to operate the pleasure park of one of his railroads in Kansas. From this beginning, Kessler developed an extensive practice of subdivision and park system design, particularly in Kansas City and the Midwest (Charles A. Birnbaum and Robin Karson, eds., *Pioneers of American Landscape Design* [New York, 2000], pp. 212–15; NCAB, 20: 296–97; Kessler to FLO, Jan. 22, 1882; ibid., Feb 15, 1882).
2. Hermann Ludwig Heinrich von Pückler-Muskau (1785–1871), German prince and landscape gardener, who created an extensive park in the English picturesque style on his estate at Muskau in Silesia and designed similar landscapes for several other German estates. He was strongly influenced by the writings of Humphry Repton and himself wrote a significant theoretical work, *Hints on Landscape Gardening*. In the sinuous flow of his paths and drives, and in the forming of spaces and massing of vegetation, his work was closer in spirit to that of Olmsted than most of the French and English landscape gardening that Olmsted experienced in his travels (OCG; Elizabeth Barlow Rogers, *Landscape Design: A Cultural and Architectural History* [New York, 2001],

pp. 259–60; Samuel Parsons, ed., *Hints on Landscape Gardening by Prince von Puckler-Muskau* [Boston, 1917]).
3. Dr. David Hosack (1769–1835), physician and teacher, who developed great landscape beauty on his 700-acre estate at Hyde Park on the Hudson River. Downing asserted that at one time it was the finest country seat in America (*DAB*; Andrew Jackson Downing, *A Treatise on the Theory and Practice of Landscape Gardening*, 9th ed. [New York, 1875], pp. 29–30).
4. A reference to the British landscape writers whom Olmsted read assiduously—Sir Humphry Repton, John Claudius Loudon, William Gilpin, and Uvedale Price.
5. Horatio Hollis Hunnewell (1810–1902), Boston banker, railroad financier and horticulturist. Hunnewell had developed forty acres of widely admired ornamental grounds on his estate "Wellesley" near Boston. Through Olmsted's intercession, Hunnewell engaged Kessler to lay out a pleasure resort being developed by the Kansas City, Fort Scott and Gulf Railroad near Kansas City, Missouri (Laura Wood Roper, *FLO: A Biography of Frederick Law Olmsted* [Baltimore, Md., 1973], pp. 394–95; A. J. Downing, *Treatise on Landscape Gardening*, pp. 442–45).

To John Charles Phillips

Bkline, 6th March 1882.

Jno C. Phillips Esq
My Dear Sir,
Yours of 17th ulto was duly recvd & I should have replied to it sooner but that I have had to be away from home.[1]

If I had to consult solely my own judgmnt, (taste, sense of fitness and practicable ideals) I should have no landscape gardening, no composition, grouping or display of foliage effects on your moraine place at all. I should have dense forest right up to & about the house, with only such breaks and openings as would come of themselves in seeking convenience and comfort in roads, walks, house-garden, lawn, yards, and the walls, hedges, thickets, stairways & out-structures. As a matter of comfort and propriety I would seclude the lawn &c from the road, the thicket for this purpose serving as a windbreak from the chilly N.W. wind; I would guard against trees growing up where they would keep the morning sun from the house, lawn & terrace, and I would decorate the artificial features of the house wall & lawn with bushes & vines. As the trees grew up, I would thin them out, with a little more care to develop beauty of individuals, groups & masses to be seen from the house than in ordinary commercial forestry but with equal care to avoid suggesting a lawn or park or any effort & study for the purpose. I would use no sythe, broom or rake on this side and if this left the ground forlorn, would scatter about low bushes, vines and creepers enough to screen it.

I would dispense with all views to the westward from the house except into or, for the front, over, the wood, and would have a stranger arrive and enter the house without a suspicion of the broad & extended views in its East & South outlooks; the unexpectedness of these and the strong contrast of character in all detail & scenery of the domestic and confidential lawn & terrace with that of the carriage, public, woodland, stable & kitchen sides of the house being its most striking distinction from the common run of villas & country seats.

As I could never get you to quite fully accept or even Sargent[2] to approve of this idea I suppose I must consider it extreme to the point of offensive eccentricity. Then the question is, how much dilution of common-place is necessary? Suppose the wood as it exists about your stable extended over the house site, there being several hundred trees from five to fifty years old to the acre. What would you cut out? Having in view the expanse from N.E. to S.W. from the terrace & lawn, what openings on the other side would you feel bound to make? I send a skeleton map with suggestions in pencil for groups of park-like treatment, leaving from 100 to 150 feet in which sufficient light would fall on the ground to allow a fair close turf to be maintained. If this would be so far satisfactory (all beyond to the West & N. West being close-planted forest), I will if you wish send a detailed planting map. (I should use chiefly elms & bass wood with a view to rapid lofty growth grouping with the house, in views of it from the E., North & South).[3]

Between the lawn & the approach road AAA I should aim at an impervious thicket of small trees, as horn beam, hop-horn, dogwood, white birch, laburnums, Kohlreuteria, sassafras, mountain ash, moose wood &c. faced with bushy shrubs, and on the lawn side I would bring this thicket to a regular formal hedge of hornbeam, or if you prefer something more delicate or elegant, of privet, buckthorn or Cydonia Japonica. If, however, you want more of proper shrubbery than the few groups required for furnishing the lawn or than could be consistently introduced in the wild garden below the terrace, then I would make the garden face of this thicket (AAA) the shrubbery.

The points to be guarded are (1) that the house shall seem in approaching it from Beverly to be standing in the midst or on the edge of a wild forest, (2) that nothing shall be seen of the Eastern outlook or of the lawn or finished ground from the approach (3) that the lawn, terrace & the part of the house opening upon them shall appear all one affair, refined, domestic and sharply seperated, secluded and distinct in quality from everything else in the vicinity. So that in going or looking from it, you will seem to be everywhere going or looking into an outer world.

I write & send you the map that you may return the latter with a more definite statement of what you feel to be desirable, when I will fill it out sufficiently for working purposes.[4]

The text presented here is from a draft in Olmsted's hand.

1. On February 17, John C. Phillips had asked Olmsted for "more definite instruction" for planting the open ground immediately around his house on Wenham Lake in Beverly, Massachusetts. He acknowledged Olmsted's intention for plantings and a walk below the terrace on the east side of the house and his desire for "forest effect" on the west. That left, as Phillips observed, "more or less space" next to the lawn for planting his "shrubs &c."
    Olmsted had been delayed in replying to Phillips due to a trip to Detroit to begin planning a park on Belle Isle and to Syracuse to advise W. T. Hamilton on siting his house, designed by Peabody and Stearns (John C. Phillips to FLO, Feb. 17, 1882; Frederick L. Ames to FLO, Feb. 16, 1882; Robert Swain Peabody to FLO, Feb. 28, 1882; FLO to John Sterling, March 3, 1882, above).
2. Charles Sprague Sargent, who had accompanied Olmsted on an early visit to the site.
3. This map apparently has not survived.
4. Phillips did not respond specifically to Olmsted's suggestions here nor request a more detailed planting map. He replied:

    > I perfectly understand your desire to strive after a forest effect about the house, and believe in it too, but how best to do, that is the question that I cannot answer to my satisfaction. I suppose time will solve it perhaps, and be my best assistant

    (John C. Phillips to FLO, March 10, 1882).

To Charles Loring Brace[1]

Brookline, 7th March 1882.

Dear Charley;
    I am glad to get your note of yesterday from Hartford, & glad that you can ease up & recruit when there is occasion. That promises a comfortable & useful old age. You can have no idea what a drag life had been to me for three years or more. I did not appreciate it myself until I began last summer to get better. The turning point appears to have been our abandonment of New York. I am still delapidated—have a great noise in my head and a little exertion sets my heart bouncing but I sleep well and seem to myself to carry on my legs not quarter of the weight I did a year ago. I have done much hard & steady work. The pamphlet[2] of which you speak was mostly written after midnight & did not prevent me from getting regularly five or six hours refreshing sleep. I enjoy this suburban country beyond expression and in fact, the older I grow find my capacity for enjoyment increasing. We have had great trials & agitations in the last year but their result on the whole has been withal tranquilizing. I am to turn sixty with two grandsons.[3]
    I am receiving many letters from strangers asking copies of the Spoils of the Park but yours is the second letter commenting upon it and I think it sin-

gular that the Press takes so little notice of it. I have seen but three references to it in New York & these all turning it to some partisan account — not looking to the rescue of the park, which, of course, is a disappointment to me. But no doubt the fact is it hits hard on all sides & disturbs all manner of plans. Few men of influence in New York are not interested directly or by regard for friends in some scheme which would cross good managment of the park for its proper ends. I fear that its ruin is inevitable & it is very depressing to me. But my mind is pretty well made up to it, and this probably is my last blow. Of course, you understand that but for wounding the feelings of well-intentioned men, I could have given more effective and disgusting illustrations, and also that entente between Vaux, Parsons, Green & Tilden, regard for the memory of Col. Stebbins,[4] & consideration of the responsibility of several men of good standing for some of the more atrocious bargains obliged me to steer as delicately as possible. I consider it as bread thrown on the waters.

The one man in New York who has given me encouragmnt & solace of late is your friend Potter.[5] He has been bold, generous, sympathetic & liberal — all with reference to Niagara but the spirit of it has refreshed me in everything.

You will see Field I suppose — poor fellow. His life now must be very lonely. Even his old companion elms swept away. Give my love to him. And Rosa, whom I suppose you will find mistress of Hanwell.[6] I wish that Field could make us a visit. I am sure he would enjoy Boston suburbs.

With love to Letitia[7]

Affctly yours

Fred[k] Law Olmsted.

The text presented here is from a manuscript in Olmsted's hand.

1. Charles Loring Brace (1826–1890), Olmsted's childhood friend and longtime director of the Children's Aid Society in New York City.
2. A reference to *The Spoils of the Park*.
3. Olmsted's grandson's were the sons of John Bryant and Charlotte Olmsted Bryant, his stepdaughter and the daughter of his wife, Mary Perkins Olmsted, and his brother, John Hull Olmsted. They were John Bryant (b. 1880) and Owen Bryant (b. 1882) (*Olmsted Genealogy*, p. 155).
4. The "entente" to which Olmsted seems to be referring was related to the effort of Calvert Vaux in 1880–81 to regain the position of landscape architect to the parks department that he had given up to Olmsted in 1872, his appointment in October 1881 as superintending architect, and his insistence that Samuel Parsons, Jr., be made superintending gardener. Andrew H. Green was a longstanding patron of Vaux's, having been instrumental in securing him various architectural commissions, including work on two houses of Samuel Tilden's, Green's law partner. In 1880 Green had returned to the park board after several years absence while comptroller of the city — a position he lost to "Honest John" Kelly in December 1876. In the unruly meetings of the park board

during the fall of 1881, Green consistently supported Vaux's candidacy and opposed all attempts to return Olmsted to a management position on Central Park. Olmsted's friends and colleagues William Fischer and Jacob Weidenmann were both strongly opposed to Vaux's attempt to install Parsons. Fischer was distressed because Vaux was proposing to have Parsons replace him as superintending gardener. ". . . to give a young man, who understands according to Weidenmann's testimony nothing at all about Landscape Gardening the position as superintendent of planting, is more than I can endure," he wrote Olmsted, "and if the Commissioners should concede to these conditions of Vaux, my self esteem shall require my resignation." Fischer had been in charge of the landscape gardening work during the years of construction of the park — 1858 to 1875 — and was angry at being disrespected by Vaux. Jacob Weidenmann was also distressed, dismissing Parsons as not possessing "the slightest gift for the art" of landscape gardening. In addition, he said that Parsons and his father, who maintained a nursery in Flushing, N.Y., had for years been seeking to do away with the Central Park nursery in order to supply the park department themselves. With Green's support the father had written a long review of the "unpractical" management that characterized the planting of Central Park from the beginning, and the present attempt was simply one more chapter in the plan of the two Parsons men to gain control of that department. Olmsted must have had all of this testimony from his friends in mind when he asserted the existence of an entente between Tilden, Green, Vaux and Parsons (William A. Fischer to FLO, Dec. 28, 1881; Jacob Weidenmann to FLO, Jan 13, 1882; *New-York Daily Tribune*, Dec. 25, 1881, p. 6).

5. Howard Potter
6. Olmsted's English friend and former neighbor on Staten Island Alfred Field (1814–1884), whose wife, Charlotte Errington Field, had died in 1880. His daughter, Rosa, was married in March 1882 to Dr. Henry Rayner, a specialist in nervous diseases who presided over The Asylum at Hanwell, Middlesex (*Papers of FLO*, 1: 342; L. W. Roper, *FLO, A Biography*, p. 439).
7. Brace's wife, Letitia Neill Brace (1822?–1916), whom Olmsted and Brace had met at her parents' home in Belfast, Ireland, during their walking trip of 1850 (*Papers of FLO*, 1: 69, 368).

APPENDIXES
INDEXES

I

CHRONOLOGY OF FREDERICK LAW OLMSTED
1874–1882

1874

January	Olmsted inspects U.S. Capitol Grounds
February 17	Committee on Legislation of New York City Department of Public Parks organized to lobby against legislation to authorize the Department of Public Works to construct Riverside Avenue.
March	Olmsted offers to make general plan of the U.S. Capitol grounds for $1,500 plus expenses: accepted by the committee on public grounds and buildings
April	Olmsted provides plan and report for grounds of U.S. Hotel in Saratoga Springs, N.Y.
May 9	Henry Stebbins elected president of New York City Board of Commissioners of Department of Public Parks
May 14	Olmsted's report to Montgomery Meigs on Jeffersonville Depot, Indiana
June 9	Olmsted submits "Skeleton Plan" for U.S. Capitol grounds
July 8	Olmsted agrees to assist Charles S. Sargent in making the Arnold Arboretum part of the Boston park system
September 28	Olmsted's plan for U.S. Capitol approved by Justin Morrill, Edward Clark, and O. E. Babcock
November	William H. Wickham of Tammany Hall elected mayor of New York City; Samuel Tilden elected governor of New York State, William Dorsheimer elected lieutenant governor
November 21	Olmsted submits report on park for Mount Royal, Montreal
December 5	Olmsted's article "The National Capitol" published in *New York Daily Tribune*

APPENDIX I

December 15	Olmsted submits plan for the improvement of Niagara Square, Buffalo
1875	
	Olmsted and engineer George Kent Radford draw up plans for Parkside subdivision next to Delaware Park, Buffalo
January 5	William R. Martin appointed to New York City park board
January 15	Olmsted presents report on Riverside Avenue and Park to New York City park board
January 20	New York City park board adopts Olmsted's Riverside Park and Avenue plan
March 3	Congress approves Olmsted plans for U.S. Capitol grounds and terraces
March 5	Henry Koster suspended as captain of Central Park Keepers
c. March 16	Olmsted revises plan of Riverside Park and Avenue, adding bridle path to promenade section
March 19	Olmsted regains control over Central Park labor force
May	Report to New York legislature by Senate Finance Committee criticizing cost and construction of New Capitol
June 1	Olmsted submits report and plans for Schuylkill Arsenal, Philadelphia
June	New Capitol Commission created by New York state legislature, with William Dorsheimer as chairman
July 15	Appointment of the New Capitol advisory board of Olmsted, Richardson and Eidlitz
September 6	New York City park board reinstates Olmsted's plan of organization for gardeners on Central Park
Fall	John C. Olmsted begins work as draftsman and apprentice
October 7	Olmsted submits plan for Mount Royal approach roads
October 26	Olmsted examines sites being considered for Boston parks
November	Olmsted corresponds with Thomas Hill on landscaping of railroad through Crawford Notch in the White Mountains
November 5	Olmsted and engineer J. J. R. Croes are authorized to plan street and rapid transit systems for 23rd and 24th wards of New York City (the Bronx)
Winter 1875–76	Construction of road up Mount Royal
1876	
January 1	Olmsted submits plans and report for Buffalo City Hall
February 28	Olmsted submits plan for laying out summer community at Chautauqua Point on Lake Chautauqua, New York
March–April	Bill to create one-commissioner New York City park board before NY legislature: fails of passage

CHRONOLOGY OF FREDERICK LAW OLMSTED, 1874–1882

March 2	Report of the advisory board to the New York State New Capitol Commission
March 11	Plans of advisory board for the New Capitol published in *American Architect and Building News*
March 23	$70,000 error in accounts of New York Department of Public Parks discovered — construction staff laid off
March 29	Remonstrance of New York Chapter of AIA against plans of advisory board for the New Capitol
March 31–April 2	Olmsted makes a two-day inspection of proposed Boston park sites
April 8	Olmsted submits report on proposed sites for Boston parks
May 6	William R. Martin elected president of New York City park board
May 31	New York State Survey Commission meets with Olmsted as member
June	Plans for the New Capitol by advisory board approved
June 14	City Comptroller Andrew H. Green withholds Olmsted's salary as landscape architect of the Department of Public Parks because of his appointment to State Survey Commission
July 1	Thomas Fuller dismissed as Resident Architect of New Capitol
July	Olmsted plans reservoir and formal promenade in Glades section of Mount Royal
August 4	Olmsted is reinstated as landscape architect to Department of Public Parks
August 9	Olmsted submits report on improvements for Tompkins Square New York City
August 10	Olmsted resigns from State Survey Commission
September 1	Olmsted, Eidlitz and Richardson officially replace Fuller as architects of the New Capitol
September 12	Firm of Eidlitz, Richardson & Co., with Olmsted as treasurer, is formed to facilitate work on the New Capitol
November 4	Presidential Election: uncertainty of outcome lasts until March 1877; in New York State, Lucius Robinson elected governor, William Dorsheimer lieutenant governor
November 15	First report by Olmsted and J. J. R. Croes to New York City park board on 23rd and 24th wards (the Bronx)
November 21	Report and plan by Olmsted and Croes for 24th Ward west of Riverdale Road
November 22	New York City park board appoints James C. Aldrich superintending engineer of Riverside Avenue project
December 7	John Kelly replaces Andrew H. Green as Controller of New York City
December 23	Olmsted submits report on grounds of Washington Monument, Baltimore

APPENDIX I

1877

January–March	With Thomas Wisedell, Olmsted prepares revised plans for squares north and south of Washington Monument, Baltimore
January	New remonstrance against plans for New Capitol of Eidlitz, Richardson & Co. submitted to state legislature by numerous citizens; joint committee of legislature begins hearings
February 28	Submittal by Olmsted and Croes of plan for section of 23rd and 24th wards between Riverdale Road and Broadway
February 28	Group of architects testify before the joint committee against plans for New Capitol of Eidlitz, Richardson and Co.: they include George B. Post, Richard Morris Hunt, Napoleon Le Brun, Henry Dudley, and Detlef Lienau
March 6	Olmsted presents his testimony on plans for the New Capitol to joint committee of New York State legislature
March 20	Olmsted and Croes submit report and plan for steam transit routes for 23rd and 24th Wards
March 26	Olmsted prepares counter-remonstrance concerning the New Capitol
April 11	Olmsted and Croes submit report for district of 23rd and 24th wards west of Jerome Avenue
April 25	New York legislature directs that the New Capitol is to be completed in the original "Italian Renaissance" style employed by Thomas Fuller
May 15	Unveiling of Fitz-Greene Halleck monument in Central Park
June 20	Olmsted and Croes submit plans for Central and Hunt's Point districts of 23rd and 24th wards
July	Railroad strikes isolate New York City for several days
September 28–29	Olmsted presents two lectures in Montreal on his plan for Mount Royal
c. October	Olmsted suffers break-down in his health
October 31	Olmsted and Croes submit report for Central District of the 23rd and 24th wards
December 12	New York City controller John Kelly withholds Olmsted's salary
December 26	New York park board grants Olmsted three-month leave of absence for reasons of health

1878

January 5	New York park board resolves to discontinue Bureau of Design and Superintendence, abolishes its offices, and appoints Olmsted Consulting Landscape Architect
January 8	Olmsted sails to England: travels for three months in England, Holland, Belgium, Germany, Italy, and France
January 16	William R. Martin removed from New York City park board, James F. Wenman replaces him as president of the board

CHRONOLOGY OF FREDERICK LAW OLMSTED, 1874–1882

January 22	A petition by 166 taxpayers and citizens of New York City is submitted to the park board protesting Olmsted's dismissal
January 23	New York park board receives letter from Olmsted, read by Howard A. Martin, requesting that action on his dismissal be postponed until his return from Europe. The board removes him as Landscape Architect of the Department of Public Parks and confirms his appointment as Consulting Landscape Architect without salary
March 1	Boston park commissioners vote to hold a design competition for Back Bay park
March	James C. Aldrich and J. J. R. Croes dismissed by New York park board
April 29	Olmsted returns from England
May 6	Charles Dalton requests that Olmsted come to Boston to review competition submittals for Back Bay park
May 13	Olmsted refuses to participate in judging Back Bay park plans
June 3	Hermann Grundel awarded prize for Back Bay park design competition
Summer	Olmsted and family living at E. L. Godkin's in Cambridge, Mass.
June 28	Olmsted makes presentation to Connecticut State Capitol Board, goes on to draw up plans for grounds of the new Capitol
October 24	Olmsted submits first preliminary plans for Back Bay Fens to Boston park commissioners
December 10	Olmsted enters into formal contract with Boston park commission to provide preliminary plan and construction drawings for Back Bay park
December	Olmsted draws up plan for subdivision near Newark, N.J., for John Watts Kearny
December 26	Report by independent commission of engineers criticizes the construction of Riverside Avenue
1879	
c. January	Olmsted visits property of John C. Phillips in Beverly, Mass.
January 8	Olmsted completes writing and sets galley proofs of his review of policies of New York Department of Public Parks since his dismissal in January 1878
January 9	Governor Lucius Robinson calls for creation of a commission to confer with Ontario authorities concerning creation of public reservation at Niagara Falls
May 19	New York State legislature instructs State Survey Commission to report on measures to adopt for creation of Niagara reservation: commission directs Olmsted and James T. Gardner to prepare a plan
May 28	Olmsted and Gardner visit Niagara Falls
Summer	Olmsted and family living at Allens' on Dudley Street, Brookline

APPENDIX I

Summer	Thomas Wisedell becomes ill and is late in providing working drawings for summer house on U.S. Capitol grounds
Summer	Olmsted prepares plans for Arnold Arboretum
July	Olmsted spends three weeks examining site for resort and hotel at Rockaway Point on Long Island
September	Olmsted presents plans for grounds of Barthold Schlesinger estate in Brookline, Mass.
September 27	Olmsted presents proposal for Niagara Reservation to Ontario and New York State commissioners

1880

c. January	Olmsted engages H. H. Richardson to assist in designing Boylston Street bridge and other bridges in Back Bay Fens, Boston
March 29	General Court of Massachusetts authorizes Boston park commissioners to acquire the land of the Arnold Arboretum from Harvard College
March 30	Publication of Special Report of New York State Survey on the preservation of scenery of Niagara Falls; includes petition signed by 268 leading citizens of U.S., Canada, and England collected by Olmsted and Charles Eliot Norton
April 1	Bill to authorize purchase of land for a public reservation at Niagara Falls is introduced in the state legislature
May 1	Olmsted sends John C. Phillips plans for his estate on Wenham Lake, Beverly, Mass.
May 3	Boston Board of Aldermen authorizes park commissioners to work out terms with Harvard College for incorporating Arnold Arboretum into Boston park system
June	U.S. Senate refuses to provide appropriation for construction of Capitol terraces
Summer	Olmsted and family living at Allens' on Dudley St., Brookline
September 10	Olmsted delivers lecture, "The Justifying Value of a Public Park," to American Social Science Association meeting at Saratoga, N.Y.
c.September 25	Olmsted visits Chicago, reviews condition of South Park
November	Plan by Olmsted showing land to be acquired by city of Boston adjacent to Arnold Arboretum
November 29	Olmsted and Charles S. Sargent submit report on planting for Commonwealth Avenue in Boston
December	Olmsted submits proposal for treatment of Muddy River as part of Boston park system

1881

May 17	Olmsted submits report on site for park in West Roxbury, Mass.
May 30	Final efforts in New York state legislature to pass bill creating Niagara Reservation: not successful

CHRONOLOGY OF FREDERICK LAW OLMSTED, 1874–1882

July	Olmsted and Charles Eliot Norton engage Henry Norman to write for newspapers on proposed Niagara Reservation
June–October	Olmsted begins planning grounds for cottages of Montauk Association
July 2	President James Garfield shot
July	Olmsted writes "Influence" for use by George W. Curtis in civil service reform campaign
August 15	New York City park board appoints Aneurin Jones, a Welsh carpenter, as Superintendent of Parks
Summer–Fall	Olmsted and family living at Mrs. Perrin's, Walnut St. Brookline; leases New York house at 209 W. 46th Street and spends winter in Brookline — permanent move from New York
August–September	Publication of Henry Norman's newspaper articles on Niagara Falls
October	Olmsted publishes *Mount Royal. Montreal*
November	Olmsted writes Charles Francis Adams, Jr., supporting creation of Merry-Mount Park, Quincy, Mass.; works with Adams and H. H. Richardson on Thomas Crane Memorial Library in Quincy, Massachusetts
November 21	Death of stepson Owen Frederick Olmsted
November 19	New York park board votes to appoint Calvert Vaux as Superintending Architect
December	Olmsted suffers injury, is incapacitated for short time
December	Olmsted draws up plans and report for Industrial Home School in Washington, D.C.
December 27	City Council of Boston authorizes purchase of Arnold Arboretum and leasing of it back to Harvard University
1882	
January 2	Proposal for plantings along Canal Street SW to counteract poisonous miasma at U.S. Capitol
January 11	Olmsted appears before joint meeting of the Senate and House committees on public buildings and grounds and shows drawings and elevations of his proposed terrace for the U.S. Capitol
February 13 & 15	Bills are introduced in the New York State legislature to replace the park board of New York City with a single Superintendent of Parks, who would be appointed by the mayor with no provision for confirmation by the Board of Aldermen
February 17	Olmsted submits proofs of printed circular on proposed U.S. Capitol terrace to Edward Clark
c. February 25	Olmsted publishes *Spoils of the Park*

II

THE SPOILS OF THE PARK.

WITH A FEW LEAVES FROM THE DEEP-LADEN NOTE-BOOKS OF "A WHOLLY UNPRACTICAL MAN."

They that have done this deed are practical;
What private griefs they have I know not
That made them do it; they are wise and practical,
And will with reasons answer you.[1]

BY FREDERICK LAW OLMSTED

One of the Designers of the Park;
Several Years its Superintendent; and
Sometime President and Treasurer of the Department.[2]

February, 1882.

The demand for a change in the management of the parks has taken a more distinct form, even since I left the last of this pamphlet in the printers' hands.[3] If I had been seeking office, it would have been a most foolish thing to write it: yet it may be best to refer to the fact that the frequent appearance of my name, either as a candidate or otherwise, in the debates of the Park Board, has in every case been against my repeatedly expressed wishes; that, whenever privately consulted, I have advised the immediate employment of men who could give the assurances of *efficiency with reference to the proper ends* of park management, which are only to be found in professional standing and in arrangements for this purpose, which left my own employment out of the question.[4] I was more immediately moved to write by the opinion of a shrewd observer that Mr. Vaux's employment was the last thing that a *majority* of the Board had ever intended, and by seeing Mr. Wales blamed for "wrangling."[5] I had in view, at starting, only to point out good-naturedly that Mr. Wales's view of his Board's course was not that of a too contentious, so much as that of a too lenient man.[6] Having taken up the case from this point of view, I found a more thorough treatment of it necessary. Though it is the first time I have written critically of the business of the Department, except officially and with official sanction, it must be well known to my friends that the views expressed are of very old standing. In their more important points they are not even original with me, and are as far as possible from having been developed for the occasion. Though often urged to write on the subject, I have done so now without conference with anyone, and, except in closing, without reference to any plans of legislation.

F.L.O.

Detroit, Mich., Feb. 23, 1882.

I.

"This disorganized body has been masquerading before the public, a headless trunk, without policy, without order, without well-defined purpose."[7]

The words of my text were of late given to the World by one of the members of the body they depict, sometime, withal, its president, worthy Master Salem Wales,—a man-of-peace, across whose shapely bows my yet more peaceful shallop could never hold her course but with the falling topsail of deferential salutation. Occasion cometh now in this wise:—

Having been kept much from home, seeing the Board and its works only through the eyes of the Press, and thus taking, if a less perspicuous, yet a more distant and therefore more comprehensive, view of its proceedings than Mr. Wales can have done, I fancy that I recognize a general drift in them of which he seems unconscious. I am the more moved to show the difference between his perspective point and mine, because I have observed, that, whereas till lately the meetings of the Board have been regarded by the Press as a sort of brawling farce, and as such, for amusement's sake, liberally reported, now for some little time back, through a growing weariness of them as it is made to appear, an entire performance often gets no other notice than a single contemptuous paragraph. Thus I see a gaining tendency to look upon the Commissioners as an incapable and harmless set of witlings, with whose doings no sensible man can be expected to much concern himself. Such an impression is clearly unjust to Mr. Wales himself, else why should he be able to do so little with them as he tells us that he is? Yet the brief characterization of

THE SPOILS OF THE PARK (1882)

the Board which I have quoted, and with which much else that he has written tallies, tends to confirm the impression that it is pursuing a heedless, aimless, and essentially a harmless course.

Comparing his accounts with those of the newspapers, and judging both in the light of my experience in affairs of the Department, I am strongly drawn to think that there is more of tragedy than of farce in what is going on; and were the integrity, frankness, and manly straight-forwardness of all his colleagues at all less assured than it is, I should be disposed to think, that so far from being without policy, order, or purpose, the Board's proceedings had been all along nicely directed by the most wary gauging of the city's patience and credulity, and with a most craftily-formed and long-ripening purpose,—a purpose, I should add, that would seem to me in direct conflict with that which the Commissioners are sworn to pursue.

Without ambition to appear as an advocate of such a view, I think it may subserve the city's interests, if, rather as a witness than an advocate, I state how it is that I can be at all tempted toward conclusions so different from those of the better-informed Mr. Wales. In the end, having on my way there shown my right to do so, I expect to testify as an expert witness. For the sake of compactness I shall confine my purpose to a review of some aspects of the Board's business with Central Park. As introductory to this, I wish to bring a few considerations to mind, upon which so much will hang of what is to follow, that I beg those in haste to get to the point, that they will not, because of the apparent self-evident character of my persuasions, leap them over. Their lack of self-evidence to many minds has cost the city millions of dollars.

1. After an investment of some fifteen millions in the Park, now in the twenty-fourth year of its growth, what is the proper business of the Commissioners with it? It is my experience that the answer given by men, in their conduct toward and in their comments upon the business as actually conducted, varies greatly with special points of view: that, for example, of a man who visits the Park on foot only, differing from that of one who sees it habitually from a carriage; and this again from the view of riders; and this yet again from that taken by those who would, but cannot, see it from "the silent steed."[8] There are various real-estate points of view. There is a view from behind a trotter; there is the view of an employment broker; and there is the remote view of statesmen, to whom the paltry interest of the mere local community of New York, in its vacant lots called "parks," is of consequence only as it may at a pinch be turned efficiently to account in affairs of great national and international concern.

Some more or less distorted reflections of these and of a hundred other special views may often be detected in the newspaper reports of the Commissioners' familiar discords. Putting them all aside as inadequate, and regarding the business as a trusteeship, my experience further is, that, asking what is the essence of the trust, not many business-men are to be found in Wall Street, nor yet in Water,[9] who have ready upon it a business-like opinion.

APPENDIX II

It is simpler to determine what it is not; and, by knocking off a few answers that may be suggested, we may converge toward a satisfactory conclusion.

For example: the Commissioners have elected, if I have reckoned aright, five several principal architects, one after another, to their business-staff; not one and four coadjutors, but five masters, each to a separate duty, dismissing none to make room for another. It is true that two are not appointed directly for building-duties (one being chief-of-staff, and another chief executive officer), and also that the last election was made with conditions that rendered its acceptance impossible;[10] but as it was intended to supersede none of the previous building-strength at the Commissioners' command, sufficient, as it already was, for taking in hand all at once four great cathedrals, it strengthens the occasion for asking, At this stage, is building the distinctive and essential business of the commission? And no man can, upon reflection, fail to see that it is not.

The very "reason for being" of the Park is the importance to the city's prosperity of offering to its population, as it enlarges and becomes more cramped for room, opportunity of pleasurable and soothing relief from building, without going too far from its future centre. What else than this purpose justifies the reservation from commercial enterprise of more than a hundred blocks of good building-land right in the line of the greatest demand? Building can be brought within the business of the Park proper only as it will aid escape from buildings. Where building for other purposes begins, there the Park ends. The reservoirs and the museum are not a part of the Park proper: they are deductions from it. The sub-ways[11] are not deductions, because their effect, on the whole, is to enlarge, not lessen, the opportunities of escape from buildings. Were they placed above the general surface, and made intentionally conspicuous; had they been built—as for a time it was difficult to convince people, even intelligent critics, that they were not—as decorative objects, it would have been in contravention, not in furtherance, of the essential business of the Park. Of late years they have, in the summer, almost disappeared from general view; and, by their action in facilitating passage clear of the drives and rides, {their} much less apparent construction serves the general public purpose of the Park. If through ignorance and mismanagement their present seclusion is destroyed (as the Commissioners have promised that it shall be, as far as their means go), it must tend not to further, but to obstruct, the proper course of the Commissioners' business. It must be concluded, then, that the Commissioners' trust is essentially the reverse of that which the affluence of architectural force at its headquarters might be thought to imply.

If the essence of the Commissioners' business is not to be found in building, neither is it in engineering, nor in inn-keeping, nor in the decorative art of gardening, nor in a display of nurserymen's samples, nor in forestry. All these callings may have their place; but it is at best a subordinate and incidental or auxiliary place, as calendar-printing in insurance business, as astronomy and pastry-cooking in steamship business.

THE SPOILS OF THE PARK (1882)

2. A man may be strong for any other business commonly pursued in the city, yet unfamiliar with and inapt to acquire a sound understanding of the ends, to grasp the principles and to seize the critical points of management in the business of the Park.

3. By changes made for the purpose in the laws every few years, and by the rotation of new men into office as often as practicable, the composition of the Commission is never long the same.[12] Its members, receiving no pay for the study they give the park business, abandon no other to take it up, and rarely make any change in their habits on account of it. Most of them deal with it, as reports of their proceedings exemplify, more in the habit of mind with which prosperous gentlemen take up their diversions, as of whist or euchre, yachting, or trotting horses, than in that with which they earn their living.

It is as unbusiness-like for the city to assume them masters of the business, in an executive or an expert sense, or to allow them to assume themselves so, as for the stock owners of a great railway to allow a constantly changing board of directors to take upon themselves the duties of its Chief Engineer.

4. The view which has been thus suggested of what the Commissioners' trust is not, and of what the business-like method of dealing with it for a board constituted as theirs is cannot be, is set forth more at length and more forcibly in a communication addressed to their predecessors in office four years ago, to which are attached such names as MORGAN, BROWN, BELMONT, STEWART, WARD, CISCO, COOPER, HAVEMEYER, POTTER, PHELPS, DODGE, MORTON, JAY, JESSUP, SISTARE, HAMILTON, SCHUYLER, LIVINGSTON, ROOSEVELT, SHERMAN, MARSHALL, GRISWOLD, JOHNSTONE, BABCOCK, GUYON, ROBBINS, LAIDLAW, WALLACH, JAFFRAY, COLGATE, THURBER, CLAFLIN, HARPER, APPLETON, CARTER, SCRIBNER, PUTNAM, WESTERMANN, HOLT, CRAVEN, and of leading merchants, artists, physicians, and barristers, each master in his own business, ranging with these on the roll of the city's worthies to the number of more than ninescore.[13]

If Mr. Wales's name is not among them, it is probably from motives of delicacy, in view of his former connection with the Commission which the paper in question calls to account; but if otherwise, as Mr. Wales has of late been a commissioner of a public hospital[14] as well as a commissioner of parks, he might ask himself whether, if his colleagues of the hospital trust had undertaken to manage it without aid of doctors, or with that only of doctors of divinity, he would have thought it implied but a weakness of purpose? Is it not such weakness that fills our prisons?

II.

FOR years there was an office of the Board which at different times had different sorts of duty given it, and was designated by different titles, as the fancies of succeeding commissioners varied. It was once officially described as "the Chief Executive office by or through which all orders for the work should be executed and all employees supervised and governed;" at another and the latest period it could give no one an order—could govern nothing, only advise. But through all, one duty it held constantly, and that was to keep the Park under professional landscape-gardening supervision, with a view to the furtherance of consistency of purpose in the business of the Commissioners with it; to which end the occupant of the office had a seat with the Board, and was free to take part in its debates, though without a vote. When slighted as to this responsibility, the occupant offered his resignation, and the office was temporarily suspended.[15]

In 1859, when it was working upon Central Park near upon four thousand men, and the records of the time say with extraordinary efficiency, the Board numbered eleven members. On the ground that it was too large for efficient *executive* management, it was gradually reduced. In January, 1879, when it was working less than two hundred men, and the records say inefficiently, it numbered four members. In this month, unexpectedly to those interested in the Park otherwise than as a field of statesmanship, an element in the real-estate business, or some other specialty, the Commissioners concluded to extinguish such little (advisory) life as had till then been suffered to remain in the office.[16] Since the day they did so, there has been no office under the Commission looking to landscape considerations; and the only man in its employment competent to advise or direct in matters of landscape-gardening has been degraded to an almost menial position, and this by methods and with manners implying a perfectly definite purpose to prevent him from exercising professional discretion, and to bring his art into contempt.[17]

Reference is here more particularly made to occurrences imperfectly brought to public attention by reporters of the press two years ago or more; but Commissioner Wales has lately shown, to his honor expostulatingly, that the same policy is still pursued by the same methods, and with the same manners; the unfortunate representative of landscape art having been changed,[18] and the tools of the ignoble work being new, and expressly adapted to it.

No plea will here be made that Landscape-Gardening is an art having due place side by side with the fair sisters, Poetry, Architecture, Music, Acting, Painting, and Sculpture. For nearly two centuries our greatest and our most popular teachers — as Sir Walter Scott, for example — have given it that rank;[19] and I know not one man of accepted authority who has made bold to differ with them. Who are they that do so now? Is there an artist in any field who is with them? Is there a friend of art whose friendship is not the cloak of a hopeless snob? I am assured not one. Standing, then, for the youngest and modestest of the serene sisterhood, I know that not only every artist under every name of art, but every gentleman and every gentlewoman of New York, stands with me in challenging the Board to reconcile its course in casting out the profession of landscape art from the Park with faithfulness to its most sacred trust.

Where shall one be found more sacred?—a trust for all who, from our time onward, from generation to generation, are to be debarred, except as they shall find it in the Park, from what one of old aptly styled "the greatest refreshment of man;" from what our own Lowell calls "the wine and the oil for the smarts of the mind;" what our Emerson says "yet soothes and sympathizes in all our toils and weariness;" and again our Longfellow,—

> "If thou art worn and hard beset
> With sorrows that thou wouldst forget;
> If thou wouldst read a lesson that will keep
> Thy heart from fainting, and thy soul from sleep,
> Go"—[20]

Where shall the poor man go when the Park has become what persistence in such management will make it?

III.

For a few days after the determination of the Commissioners to leave the office of landscape out of their business was publicly reported, there was much interest to know their motives; and, in the absence of a satisfactory explanation, disapproval of their course was generally expressed. I had been holding the position in question, with the title, under the last shift, of Landscape Architect Advisory; and a friend had the kindness to make for me a collection of more than seventy cuttings from the journals of the time, bearing on the matter, which are now before me.[21] Looking them over, I find, that, however differing in terms, they bear uniform testimony on a few points, which at this distance I would wish to have recalled: as, first, that to that time the people of New York had, notwithstanding some grumblings, on the whole, been proud of the Park, and especially proud of its landscape promise; second, that the business-view set forth in the previous chapter in regard to the landscape office had been generally accepted; third, that there was a general, though not generally a very definite, perception of danger involved in its abolition.

So strong was the feeling for the moment, that a Park Defence Association was organized, and at least one older organization joined with it in urging the common conviction upon the Commissioners.[22] It may be thought strange that it should have led to no debate or remark in the Board; but is it stranger than that, against constant outcry for fifty years, New York streets should have continued till now to be the dirtiest to be found in all the large towns of Christendom?

One of the Commissioners is reported to have said, in the midst of the stir, "It will soon blow over." He appears to have been right; but, if I mistake not, a little silent breeze is even now perceptible, and if, after the revelations of the last four years, it once more gets up, it may not prove so easy to ride it gayly out.

May I refer to one thing more that appears all through these leaves?— such kind feeling toward me personally, as I have no words to acknowledge, but to which I can hardly avoid the poor response of drifting, as I write, into more personal narration than might otherwise befit my purpose.

IV.

I HAVE shown what the highest authorities in the commercial business of the city hold to be the essence of the Commissioners' business with the Park, and what is essential to their success in it. But it must be known that a strong party has always stood opposed to this view, and from the start has been incessantly laboring, and never without some measure of success, to compel a disregard for it. The counter view is commonly termed by those urging it the *practical* view; and, if this seems strange, it must be considered that a given course is called practical or otherwise, according to the object had in view at the moment by the speaker. To relieve the charity of friends of the support of a half-blind and half-witted man by employing him at the public expense as an inspector of cement may not be practical with reference to the permanent firmness of a wall, while it is perfectly so with reference to the triumph of sound doctrine at an election.[23] It will be important, in what follows, to keep in mind this relativeness of meaning in the word.

First and last, there have been some pretty dark rams in the Park Commission; but on the whole it has been the worthiest and best intentioned body having any important responsibility under the city administration in our time, and it has, till lately, had rightly more of public respect and confidence than any other, its distinction in this respect being not always pleasing to some other constituents of the government. Yet with all the advantage their high standing might seem to give them, the Commissioners have rarely been able, when agreed among themselves, to move at all straight-forwardly upon the course, which, left to themselves, they would have marked out. Commissioner Wales has more than once, of late, referred to what he calls the "embarrassments" of the department, and has been careful to state, that, so far from these being new, he had in former years, when the public confidence in the Commissioners was much greater than at present, matched his strength with them till the breaking-point was reached, when he was compelled to resign, and go abroad to recruit his vigor in preparation for the renewed struggle in which he is now engaged.[24]

He will excuse me for thinking that he has left the nature of these embarrassments in some obscurity, and for wishing to throw a little light upon it. I am going further on to mention circumstances connected with the dissociation of landscape-gardening from the business of the Park, which, if I had been in New York when the Commissioners' action for the purpose was taken,[25] and had been disposed to make them public, would have added to the distrust and apprehension so generally expressed. They will even now cause surprise, even tax the credulity of many; and partly to lay a foundation for them, partly to give a clew to their significance, partly to reveal what

THE SPOILS OF THE PARK (1882)

Mr. Wales probably means by the embarrassments of the Board, I will, in this chapter, relate a few incidents of my earlier experience. My object being to throw light on methods and manners, for which we, citizens of New York, are every man responsible, and not to assail parties or persons, I shall aim to avoid names and dates.

My first narration will be of a commonplace character, and be given only to supply a starting-point.

1. The mayor once wanted to nominate me for the office of Street Commissioner.[26] After some persuasion, perfectly aware that I was taking part in a play, though the mayor solemnly assured me otherwise, I assented, with the distinct understanding, that, if the office came to me, it should be free from political obligations; that I should be allowed to choose my own assistants, and, keeping within the law, my own method of administration. "Which," said the mayor, "is just what I want. It is because I felt sure that you would insist on that, that I sent for you." I smiled. The mayor preserved his gravity, and I took my leave. Within half an hour I received a call from a gentleman whom I had held in much esteem, to whom I had had reason to be grateful; who had once been a member of Congress,—a man of wealth and social position, but at the time holding no public office, and not conspicuous in politics. He congratulated me warmly, hoping that at last New York would be able to enjoy the luxury of clean streets. Conversation turned upon the character of the Board of Aldermen. The gentleman thought there need be no difficulty in getting their confirmation, but suggested that it might be better for me to let him give a few confidential assurances to some who did not know me as well as he did, as to my more important appointments. He soon afterwards left, regretting plaintively to have found me so "unpractical" in my ideas. It was his opinion that half a loaf of reform was better than no bread. It was mine, that a man could not rightly undertake to clean the streets of New York with his hands tied confidentially.*

Soon another, also not holding an office, but president of a ward club, and as such having a certain familiarity with practical politics, called to advise me that —— wanted an understanding that I would give him fifteen per cent of my patronage. Not having it, he feared that —— would throw his weight against me. I need not go on. When one of the mayor's friends in the city-hall understood that I seriously meant to be my own master, or defeated, he exclaimed, "Why, the man must be a fool!"

2. At one time, in a temporary emergency, I had the honor to be called to the quarter-deck, having been appointed a commissioner, and elected by the board of the period to be its president.[27] In the few months that I held the position, I had some wonderful experiences, of which, for the present purpose, I will relate, because of their bearing on what follows, but five.

---

*The word "unpractical" is not found in common dictionaries, but is so useful in our mandarin dialect, that I shall make bold for this occasion to adopt it.

613

That unpractical men may realize the wonder of them, it must be remembered that I was riding on the very crest of the glorious reform wave.

(1) A "delegation" from a great political organization[28] called on me by appointment. After introductions and handshakings, a circle was formed, and a gentleman stepped before me, and said, "We know how much pressed you must be, Mr. President, and we don't want to be obtrusive, sir, nor exacting; but at your convenience our association would like to have you determine what share of your patronage we can expect, and make suitable arrangements for our using it. We will take the liberty to suggest, sir, that there could be no more convenient way than that you should send us our due quota of tickets, if you please, sir, in this form, *leaving us to fill in the name.*" Here a pack of printed tickets was produced, from which I took one at random. It was a blank appointment, and bore the signature of Mr. Tweed. "That," continued the spokesman, "was the way we arranged it last year, and we don't think there can be anything better."

(2) Four gentlemen called by appointment on "important business." Three were official servants of the city: the fourth stated that he came from and was authorized to represent a statesman of national importance. Their business was to present a request, or rather a demand, so nearly naked that it would have been decenter if there had been no pretence of clothing it, for the removal of some of the minor officers of the Park, in order to make places for new men, whose names they were ready to give me. They said nothing to recommend their candidates, except that they were reformers. The fact that the men whose removal they called for had been long enough employed to understand their duties, and to have proved their faithfulness and unpracticalness, was a sufficient reason that they should go. They had had their "suck." After a little conversation, which I made as pleasant as I could, I said smiling, "But excuse me, gentlemen, if I ask if you consider this to be reform?" There was no responsive smile (rather the contrary), and the representative of statesmanship said sharply, "What's the use of being a reformer, if it isn't?" And seriously, to these efficient public servants, this was the high-water mark of reform.

(3) Calling at this period upon another department head, and finding his lobby packed as mine was, when, after half an hour's waiting, I was admitted to a private interview,—of which the head took advantage to eat a cold lunch that had been waiting for him,—I said, "Is it possible that you are as hard beset by these gentlemen as I am?"—"Oh! more so, I think."—"Then, when do you get time for the proper business of your office?"—"Only before and after office-hours, when they think I am gone."

(4) Among those calling on me was one official of the city, who came regularly once a week, and, having been admitted, remained sometimes two hours, saying plainly that he did not mean to go until I had given him at least one appointment. At length I remonstrated with him somewhat severely. "Well, Mr. President," he replied, "you must excuse me. You know this is

my business now, and I must attend to it. If I didn't, where should I be? But I'll let you off for to-day, and go round to ——'s office, and see what I can do with him."

(5) Twice it occurred to me, after passing through a large public office with many deputies and clerks, that the Chief remarked to me, "Among them all, there is but one man who is here by my own free choice, or in whose faithfulness I have confidence."

3. It has occurred five times in succession that I have been at the headquarters of the Department of Parks on the first visit of a new commissioner, and when, after a few passages of introductory courtesy, he has, as his first official movement in the business of the parks, asked to be furnished with a list showing the places at its disposal, the value of each, and the vacancies at the time existing. I believe that each of these gentlemen had been certified to the reporters to be entirely free from political obligations, and to owe his appointment solely to his eminent qualifications for the particular post of a park commissioner; but it will not be surprising, that, in view of my experience, I doubted the accuracy of the certificate.

4. A commissioner once said in my presence, "I don't get any salary for being here; it would be a pretty business if I couldn't oblige a friend now and then:" this being his reason for urging a most unfit appointment.

5. Writing of unfit appointments, nothing could be more ludicrous, if the anxiety they gave me had left room for a humorous view of them, than many most strenuously urged. A young man was pressed for my nomination as a topographical draughtsman. I asked to see some of his work, and, after explanations, was answered, "I don't know that he ever made any maps or drawings on paper." — "How could you think he was qualified as a draughtsman?" To which the reluctant reply was this: "The fact is, he was a little wild a few years ago, and ran away to sea on a whaler, and when he came back he brought a whale's tooth, on which he had made a picture of his ship as natural as life. Now I think that a boy who could do that, you could do most anything with in the drawing way." The very man who said this, and, incredible as it will be thought, said it seriously, was nominated by the mayor for a park commissioner. Can the reader say, that, if the favorite remedy for the moment, and that advocated by Mr. Wales, for all the evils of the present park mismanagement,[29] shall be adopted, this same good business-man may not next year be chosen to exemplify the efficiency of a single-headed administration?

6. I once expressed to a gentleman surprise at the accuracy of certain information of which I found him possessed. "Oh! that's nothing," he said. "There is not a workingman living in my district, or who comes into it, or goes out of it, that I have not got him down on my books, with the name and ages of his wife and all his children, what house they are in, what rooms they occupy, what his work is, who employs him, who is to look after his vote, and so on. I have it all tabulated, and posted up. I have to make a business of it,

you know. If a man means to succeed in politics, he must. It is not a business you can play with."

7. Another illustration of practical business-methods was given by a president of the Department as follows:—

"I want you to know," he said, after opening the door, looking out, closing and locking it, "of some things going on here. Yesterday a man applied for a certain position, bringing a letter dated at Albany the day before, in which the writer stated that he understood that the late holder of the position had been discharged. I told the applicant that he was mistaken; but he insisted that he was not, and I could hardly get rid of him. Here is a report coming this morning from the Park, making charges against the man in question, and advising his discharge. Information of a prospective opportunity of an appointment had gone to Albany and back, before it came to me here. You see how closely they watch us. But here is another example of it. I signed to-day an appointment which I had not determined to make five minutes before. I sent the appointee directly up to the Park, starting myself, at the same moment, for the city-hall. When I reached there, reference was made to the appointment by the first man who spoke to me, showing that not a moment had been lost in reporting it. But who made the report, and how, so quickly? I confess I hardly dare inquire. But there is something yet more inscrutable. I suspected the lock of my private drawer to have been tampered with. Last night I placed a bit of paper where it would be dislodged if the drawer was opened, and another in my memorandum-book of vacancies, applications and intended appointments. This morning I found both displaced."

8. There was an intrigue to remove a valuable officer by destroying his character, in order to make an opening for the advancement of a subordinate strongly backed with "influence." I asked and obtained a committee of the Board to try the case. The subordinate made oath to a statement which was proved to be false; and for the perjury he was dismissed. Shortly afterwards he met me on the Park, offered me his hand, and, with much flourish, thanked me for having brought about his removal, as it had compelled his friends to make proper exertions, and he now held a position much more to his taste than any on the Park could have been.

9. At a dignified public ceremony on the Park, I saw, while listening to the oration of the day, a roughly-dressed man approach the point where the Commissioners were arrayed, all in proper black, and facing a great crowd. As the man neared their position from the rear, he reached out a walking-stick, and punched one of them. The commissioner turned; and the man threw his head back, as if to say, "Come here, I want a word with you." The commissioner fell out, and there was a whispered conversation. "Now, what does that mean?" I asked. "Don't you know? Why, that is one of our new foremen; and he and the commissioner are both members of the same district committee. He is laying in with him to make a place for some fellow whose help they need in the primaries."

THE SPOILS OF THE PARK (1882)

10. I suspended a man because of evidence of gross disobedience of a standing rule. He told a very improbable story; and I gave him a fortnight to produce corroborative evidence of it. Instead of doing so, he set a number of his "friends" after me. His special patron was a man in office, and proprietor of a weekly newspaper.[30] A copy of it was sent me, with a marked article containing absurd and scurrilous abuse of me, and of the Commission for employing me. As this official had shortly before called at my house, and been profuse in compliments and professions of regard, I went to see him. Referring to the article, I said, "It would have given you but the slightest trouble to ascertain that you had been imposed upon in the statements to which you have given currency." He smiled, and asked, "Would you like to see an article I intend to publish to-morrow?" handing a galley-proof to me. I read it, and said, "I have marked and numbered with my pencil seven statements in this article, which, I give you my word, can be ascertained, by anyone coming to the Park, to be quite untrue." The next day a copy of the paper was sent me containing the article without the change of a word. The suspended man at last confessed, hoping to be pardoned, but was dismissed. The paper continued to be sent me every week for perhaps a year, and I was told that every number had some attack on the Park. At another period another paper pursued a similar course. One day the editor, finding the president of the Department on a railway-train going to Albany, gayly saluted him in terms of friendship. "I am surprised, sir," said the president, "that, after what you have been saying of our Board in your paper, you can offer me your hand."—"Oh!" replied the editor, "but that was business."

11. During all my park work it was a common thing to receive newspapers, addressed by unknown hands, containing matter designed to injure me; sometimes, also, anonymous threats and filthy caricatures. The object I take to have been to impress me with the insecurity of my position, and the folly of the unpractical view of its duties.

12. A foreman of laborers, discharged from the Park against strong political influence, was, at the next election, a candidate for the Legislature.[31]

13. At one time, shortly after the police of the Park had a second time been put under my superintendence, I undertook an improvement of it.[32] Asking the officer in charge to account for his own failure to secure the conviction and removal of some whom he described as "regular dead-beats," who had "never performed one honest tour of duty since they were taken on," he answered, "Why, damn 'em, they are every man laying wires to go to the Legislature, and they carry too many guns for me."

14. As my first step, I wrote an order to the surgeon, directing a medical survey of the force. The surgeon called on me, and said, "I am under your orders, sir, and if you insist I shall act on them to the letter; but perhaps you do not realize, as I do, what the consequences will be to me."—"What will they be?"—"Only that I shall have to eat my bread without butter for a while."—"I understand; but I must do my duty, and you must do yours." He

did, reporting a quarter part of the entire force physically incapacitated for any active duty, and indicating that it had been used as an asylum for aggravated cases of hernia, varicose veins, rheumatism, partial blindness, and other infirmities compelling sedentary occupations. The surgeon was supported by the highest authorities of his profession, and had established on the Park an excellent character, professionally and otherwise. He had gained the affection and confidence of the force, but, in obeying orders without consulting its friends, had proved himself an unpractical man, and, as he had anticipated, was soon afterwards dismissed by order of the Board.[33]

15. I asked an officer before me on a grave charge what he had to say. With a laugh, and a wink to his comrades, he answered, "You want to know what I have to say? Well, that's what I have to say," handing me a crumpled note which read, "If there is anything against officer ——, please remember that he is my man, and charge it to account of Yours Truly, —— ——." He was dismissed.

16. I set a watch upon the night-watch; and five men, receiving three dollars a night for patrol-duty on beats of which two were a mile and a half apart, were found together in the middle of their watch in a necessary building, which they had entered with false keys. They had made a fire, taken off their boots, and, using their rolled-up coats for pillows, were fast asleep; and this had doubtless been long their habit. With the sanction of the Board I changed the system, much reducing its cost, and employed mechanical detectors on the principle of those used for the night-watch of great mills. They were broken from their fastenings, and carried away. I devised a stronger and simpler apparatus. In several instances, within a week it was broken, as if by sledges, great force being necessary.[34]

17. The eldest of the watchmen had been originally employed for several years in the Park as a land-surveyor. He had received a good education, and, after his discharge as a surveyor, had suffered grievous domestic afflictions, and been left very poor. He was a religious man, had been active in church charities; and it was in part upon a letter from his pastor setting forth his trustworthiness that I had obtained his appointment as watchman. He had refused to join the others in their conspiracy, and was looked upon as a spy — wrongly, for he had given me no information. He was waylaid at night, murderously struck down, and left for dead. It was several weeks before he was able to leave his bed, and when he did so he was scarred for life.

18. Several other measures were adopted, all with the knowledge and sanction of the Board, and believed at the time, by the excellent gentlemen composing it, to be perfectly business-like.[35] But they were all very unpractical in the view taken by many of the force and their friends, who consequently united in measures designed to convince the Commissioners of their mistake, and for self-protection against my cruelty. A fund was raised, and a "literary gentleman" regularly employed to write me down. At this time I received confidential warnings indirectly from high quarters outside the Com-

mission, that I would not be allowed to succeed in what I was attempting, and had better drop it. I did not drop it, but worked on with all my might; and presently the literary gentleman got also to his work, first in some of the Sunday papers. At length, by one of those accidents that seem liable to occur in any great newspaper establishment, he managed to get a powerful article prominently displayed in a leading daily,[36] in which, after referring to the reputation of the force with the public, gained by its alleged uniform activity, efficiency, civility; its high state of discipline and *esprit du corps*, it was represented, that, through some unaccountable freak of the Board, it had recently been placed under the orders of a silly, heartless, upstart, sophomorical theorist, through whose boyish experiments it was being driven into complete and rebellious demoralization. One of the Commissioners told me that he was asked a day or two afterwards, "Who is this young chap that you have put in charge of the police? How could you have been stuck with such an unpractical fellow?" Now it happened that I was one of the few men then in America who had made it a business to be well informed on the subject of police organization and management. I had made some examination of the French system; had when in London known Sir Richard Mayne, the organizer of the Metropolitan force, upon the model of which our New York Metropolitan force is formed; had been favored by him with a long personal discourse on the principles of its management, and been given the best opportunities for seeing them in operation, both in the park service and in all other departments. I had made a similar study of the Irish constabulary.[37] I had originally organized, instructed, and disciplined, and under infinite difficulties secured the reputation of this same Central Park force. Finally, by a singular coincidence, I had nearly twenty years before, when my defamer was himself a school-boy, been an occasional editorial writer for the journal which he thus turned upon my work, and had contributed to it much of the matter, which, collected in a volume, had been later twice reprinted in London, and in translations in Paris and Leipsic.[38]

I was asked by the president of the Department to make a public reply, and was allowed by the editor to do so in the same columns.[39] I must gratefully add that the editor afterwards made all reparation in his power consistently with the ordinary rules of newspaper business. Nevertheless, the article served its purpose, was largely circulated among practical men, and I had reason to believe that even some of my friends thought there must be something in its ridiculous falsifications. The end was, that I was relieved of responsibility for the police of the Park.[40] My duty was mainly assumed by a committee a majority of whom were new to the business; and the only two men who, besides the surgeon, had been conspicuously resolute in carrying out my orders, and sincere and faithful in efforts to enforce them, were dismissed — neither honorably nor dishonorably discharged, but simply notified that their services were no longer required.[41] I am sure that the commissioners whose votes frustrated my efforts had been thoroughly convinced by the advice of friends that they were acting for the best interests of the city; that my intentions were good but impractical; and that in everything they were doing God's service. The president to the last sustained me. Because he did so, and asked it as a personal favor and act of friendship, I consented, after having resigned my office, to resume service under the Commission upon a modified arrangement, vindicating my professional standing and securing me against another similar experience.[42]

19. Within two years the rules which the Board had been persuaded to adopt to prevent unsuitable men from being recruited, and to secure advancement by proved merit, had become a dead-letter;[43] and the force was left to drift into the condition in which one of the Commissioners lately stated in a Board meeting that he had found it, and which led to a beautifully drawn resolution that hereafter no man who could not read and write should be taken for it.[44] How soon to become in its turn a dead-letter, who can say? Some time after my defeat, a gentleman told me that he had walked, in a fine day, through the interior of the Park from end to end without seeing an officer. There was no lack of them on the fashionable drives; but in the most secluded and sylvan districts prostitutes were seeking their prey without hindrance, and it was no place for a decent poor woman to bring her children. I myself, since I left the Park, have seen an officer within a hundred yards of a carriage when it stopped, and when the coachman bent down an overhanging lilac-bush loaded with bloom, from which the occupants broke large branches, afterwards driving off without interruption or reproof. The officer, doubtless, thought it an unpractical thing to have lilac-bushes in the Park, as the present Commissioners think anything like sylvan seclusion unsanitary.[45]

At another time I met seven small boys coming from the Park, all carrying baskets. They were showing one another the contents of these as I came upon them; and I found that they were each filled with beautiful rock-moss, which they were going to sell for the decoration of hanging-baskets. The Park has always been very deficient in this lovely accompaniment of rocks, and it is difficult to secure it. I asked the boys if the police allowed them to strip it off. "No," said one: "we waits till their heads is turned." "No," said another: "they don't care; they just minds the carriages, they does." Nor are these incidents by any means the most alarming that I might report.

Do the owners of houses building near the Park fancy that its vicinity will be a more agreeable place of residence because of this practical style of management? I have seen a newspaper report that already last summer great numbers of tramps and gypsies regularly lodged in the Park. When the police was under unpractical direction, I have repeatedly walked through its entire length after midnight, finding every officer in his place, and not one straggling visitor. Hyde Park is closed at nightfall, as are all other city parks in Europe; but one surface road is kept open across Hyde Park, and the superintendent of the Metropolitan Police told me that a man's chances of being garroted or robbed were, because of the facilities for concealment to be found in the Park, greater in passing at night along this road than anywhere else in London.

If these incidents give little idea of the number, weight, and constancy of the embarrassments with which the Park Board has to struggle, they may have made plainer the nature of them, and the soil on which they grow.

But I must add a few more, that may, in some degree, remove misapprehensions as to the responsibility for various matters which are occasionally referred to in the interest of practical park management, as if they were the result of the ignorance or perversity of which the Commissioners intended to rid the Park in abolishing the landscape office.

For several years before that event, the management of the parks had, as before stated, not been under my direction. I had only to advise about it.[46] But even before this, there was, for some time, a standing order in force, forbidding me to have a single tree felled without a specific order, to be obtained by a majority vote of the Board.[47] Before this order was passed, men seen cutting trees under my directions have been interrupted and indignantly rebuked by individual commissioners, and even by the "friends" of commissioners, having no more right to do so than they would for like action on a man-of-war. I have had men beg me, from fear of dismissal, to excuse them from cutting trees, and, to relieve them, have taken the axe from them, and felled the trees myself. I have been denounced to commissioners by their friends as "a Vandal" and a "public robber," because nurse-trees were cut from the plantations of the Park under my directions. It may have been noticed, that, notwithstanding much talk of the necessity of thinning plantations, Mr. Wales, in a triumphant way, announced lately that not a single live tree had been cut this winter. Why not? Nothing had been cut but bushes, the removal of which, one by one, would pass with little notice from the vigilant friends of the Commissioners. Who is there, with any authority on the Park, competent to judge what trees should and what should not be cut, with a view to the purpose for which the Park has been formed?

Rocky passages of the Park, which had been furnished under my direction with a natural growth of characteristic rocky hill-side perennials, have been more than once "cleaned up," and so thoroughly that the leaf-mould, with which the crevices of the ledge had been carefully filled for the sustenance of the plants, was swept out with house-brooms in the interest of that good taste which delights in a house painted white with green blinds, whitewashed cherry-trees, plaster statuettes on stumps; and patty-cakes of bedding-plants set between rocks scraped of their dirty old lichens and mosses,—and all in the heart of an Appalachian glen. Whereupon Mr. Robinson, in that invaluable addition to the literature of landscape art, Alpine Flowers, writes (I quote from a copy kindly sent me by my good friend the author, 2d London edition, p. 8),—[48]

"In the Central Park of New York are scores of noble and picturesque breaks of rock, which have not been adorned with a single Alpine plant or rock-bush." He might have said, from which not only all such adornments, but even all the natural growth of rock-bushes, vines, perennials, and mosses, has again and again been cleaned away as exhibiting a low, depraved, and unpractical taste. The work is going on, I am assured, at this moment; and when it is finished, and August comes round again, and all the yellow turf and the dead, half-covered outcrops of smooth-faced, gray and brown ledge are fully exposed to view, God help the poor man who can find no better place of escape from the town!

20. The landscape office had been twice dispensed with for a time before its last abolition in 1879.[49] During one of these intervals a much boasted improvement in the plan of the Park had been put through with the energy and efficiency characteristic of a bull earning his passage through a China shop. Later, something was found defective in the drainage of the adjoining region. After a tedious and costly exploration, it was ascertained that a large main drain had been cut through at a critical point, and that the tile had been so broken and deranged as to make a complete dam, after which the excavation had been filled up, and built over. This led me to look at the drainage-maps, several sheets of which proved to have been lost. I begged to have a survey made for their renewal; and a man was employed for it who had been previously engaged in the work. While he was still occupied with the duty, what passes for economy in practical park management came and dismissed him.[50] I doubt if complete drainage-maps will be found in the Department to-day. I will undertake to satisfy a fair jury of respectable sanitarians, that, if there is reason to believe that a single case of malarial disease has originated in the Park in twenty years, it has been due to conditions which have been established or maintained against the advice of the landscape office. The reverse has been asserted or implied in scores of publications, for which no commissioner, as such, has ever been responsible.

21. The more "practical" Commissioners have often given me advice received by them from friends having no official responsibility for the parks, and which betrayed exceptional ignorance, even for city-bred men, on matters which had been my life-study; which ran also directly counter to the practice of every respectable member of my profession; the folly of which I have often seen exposed in our agricultural journals, and the agricultural columns of our newspapers, but which they regarded, and expected me to regard, as of controlling weight. Some such advice I have, since I left the Park, seen carried out in practice.

22. The president once notified me that a friend of his was to come before the Board as spokesman for a "delegation" of citizens, to advocate the introduction of a running-course on the Park.[51] He would ask me to explain some of the objections to the project, but hoped that I would do so in a way as little likely to provoke the gentleman as possible, as he had great weight in politics, and it would be in his power to much embarrass the Department. I

followed these instructions as I best could; but it was impossible for me not to refer to the landscape considerations. At the first mention of the word the gentleman exclaimed, and by no means "aside," "Oh, damn the landscape!" then, rising, he addressed the president to this effect: "We came here, sir, as practical men, to discuss with your Board a simple, practical, common-sense question. We don't know anything about your landscape, and we don't know what landscape has to do with the matter before us."

23. It will have been asked by many, as they have been reading, Why did you not appeal to public opinion? Why did not the Commissioners, who were superior to the courses through which your professional judgment was overruled, if they could not otherwise overcome these embarrassments, lay them frankly before us, and see what we could do? Might not a corresponding question be asked in regard to what everybody knows is going on at this moment, and has been for years going on, of the highest officer of the nation?

If the reference seems presumptuous in one respect, let me show that it hardly can be so in another; I mean in respect to the absorption of time and energy of public servants, through the pressure of "practical advice." As superintendent of the Park, I once received in six days more than seven thousand letters of advice as to appointments, nearly all from men in office, and the greater part in legislative offices upon which the Commissioners have been much dependent for the means of accomplishing anything they might wish to do,—either written by them directly, or by Commissioners at their request. I have heard a candidate for a magisterial office in the city addressing from my doorsteps a crowd of such advice-bearers, telling them that I was bound to give them employment, and suggesting plainly, that, if I was slow about it, a rope round my neck might serve to lessen my reluctance to take good counsel. I have had a dozen men force their way into my house before I had risen from bed on a Sunday morning, and some break into my drawing-room in their eagerness to deliver letters of advice. I have seen a president of the Park Board surrounded by a mob of similar bearers of advice, in Union Square, carried hither and thither by them, perfectly helpless; have seen policemen make their way in to him with clubs, drag him out, force him into a passing carriage, and lash the horses to a gallop, to secure his temporary relief from "embarrassments," the nature of which I trust that I have now sufficiently illustrated.[52]

I do not remember ever to have seen the office of the Board without a poster, reading, "No laborers wanted;" and I do not believe that there has in twenty years been a time when nine-tenths of the intellectual force and nervous energy of the Board has not been given to recruiting duty.

V.

During all of the summer before the Commissioners agreed to "damn landscape," I was aware that the practical view was getting the upper hand of them.[53] It would take too much space to tell how I became conscious of it. There were symptoms such as this: that, while observing great ceremony of politeness with me, there were three of them whom I was never able to get to meet me on the Park (nor on any park). In the case of two, I was careful not to let a month go by without separately asking the favor of an appointment for the purpose, and in reply was always assured of a desire and intention to make it soon. Twice an appointment was actually made; and each time the commissioner failed to keep it, afterwards courteously apologizing.[54] Thus and otherwise, there was no doubt left in my mind, that, with respect to my part of the business of the parks, these amiable gentlemen cared only how not to do it. If there had been, occurrences which have followed the abolition of my office would have removed it.

But it was not simply from observation of mere symptoms that I knew that the embarrassments affecting them were of an unusual character. I myself received from without the Board several warnings, both direct and indirect. By indirect, I mean threats made in such a manner as to leave me in no doubt that it was intended to guard against a public accountability for them. By direct, I mean not only friendly, confidential hints, but such as were given me, for example, in my own house, by a man who brought a line of introduction from a high public officer. After he had called three times (on each occasion while I was at dinner), I informed the introducer that his bearing had been such, that, if he called again, I should ask the protection of the police. I knew that my movements were being furtively dogged, and I presumed that they were so with a view to obtaining pretexts upon which to urge my removal.

Let it be understood what this meant to me,—the frustration of purposes to which I had for years given all my heart, to which I had devoted my life; the degradation of works in which my pride was centred; the breaking of promises to the future which had been to me as churchly vows. However I was able to carry myself by day, it will not be thought surprising that I should have had sleepless nights, or that at last I could not keep myself from over-wearing irritation and worry. The resulting depression, acting with an extraordinary prostration from the great heat of the summer, and the recurrence of an old malarial trouble, brought me, late in the season, to a condition comparable to that often produced by a sun-stroke, perhaps of the same nature. It has taken me four years to recover the strength which I then lost within a week. In view of this loss, I was advised by three well-known physicians to seek at once a change of air, scene, and mental occupation. I knew that any prolonged absence from New York would give an opportunity to the plotters against my work that might be fatal to it; and while I hesitated an incident occurred which made my retirement for a time impossible. A newspaper was sent to my house with a marked passage stating that disgraceful charges were pending against me. The president of the Department knew nothing of them at the time; but within two days he informed me that the report was authentic.[55]

The charter, so called, of the city, provides, that, when anyone in its service stands accused of official misdoings, there shall be a form of trial open to him before his dismissal.[56] I determined to take no notice of the charges until I had the opportunity, thus supposed to be secured to me, of looking my accusers in the face. But it never came. On the strength of the charges,—deliberate and circumstantial lies, invented, as I imagine, by spies to cover their ill success from their employers,—my name had been struck from the payroll.[57] A month afterwards I found it restored; and the installment of salary, which had been due when the charges were made, and payment of which had been stopped on account of them, was silently sent me. Thus, though no words of retraction or explanation, of vindication or apology, followed, I was left to infer that the attempt to cast me out as a culprit had been abandoned.

Of many incidents emphasizing the character of this occurrence, I will make room for but one. I have shown that the charges were given to the press before they were officially known to the Board or to me. I have to add that this which I now make more than four years afterwards is the first public mention, to my knowledge, of their falsity or abandonment.

It is not to be supposed that I was gaining ground upon my nervous disorder during this month. At its end winter was setting in, and the principal work on the parks had stopped for the season. As soon as I was released from arrest, so to speak, I presented the medical certificate I had been holding back, showing my need of temporary relief from duty; and upon it leave of absence, with suspension of salary, was given me till spring. It was while this act was fresh and operating, and I was yet on the sea, that my office was abolished.[58]

The general mistrust of the press, that the determination to do away with it had had other motives than those officially recorded, led to some "interviewing" of the Commissioners, under the torture of which one of them admitted that I had been suspected of having had "a pretty fat thing" in supplying the parks with trees.[59] It happens that I had been anxious to obtain a few comparatively rare and costly trees for the Park. But I knew that the Commissioners were averse to authorizing purchases which might be taken as illustrations of extravagance. Moreover, the Park was in great need of another elephant; it actually did not possess a single rhinoceros; the gilding on the weathercocks was much tarnished; and the bronze nymph at Mount St. Vincent was almost as black as before she had, by the order of an older commissioner, been cleaned up, and painted white.[60] Therefore I had, with the aid of friends, procured the trees I specially wanted without expense to the city. The value of the gift was, I believe, less than two hundred dollars; but that any such thing could be done from interest in the scenery of the Park had not probably occurred to the sufferer, and a confused recollection of something inexplicable about it led him, when squeezed, as I little doubt, to blunder upon the expression caught by the reporter. Still, in view of my absence from the country, to have been betrayed into such an innuendo is not characteristic of a lofty soul; and this may explain why it was also said that the Commissioners had had enough of "high tone."

But not too much importance should be given to these hasty expressions. I do not doubt that the Commissioners were quite sincere in stating that they abrogated the landscape office because they found it "of no practical use." That they really had the completest confidence in my integrity, esteem for my professional ability, and held me to have deserved well of my fellow-citizens in all official duty, they were forward to testify by placing a series of resolutions to that effect on their minutes, and also by giving me an appointment that the public has been often advised, through the published proceedings of the present Board, remains uncancelled; that, namely, of Consulting Landscape-Architect (without salary).[61] Considering the form of this appointment,* it is significant, that, while I have been holding it, the Board has permitted designs prepared under its orders in my office, long discussed, laid before the public, and, after most mature deliberation, adopted by unanimous vote, to be, in some cases, strangely mutilated by men not of my profession, and of no public standing in any profession; in others, to be superseded by wholly new and radically different designs.[62] The main object of the changes in these cases had been before most carefully considered with the aid of comparative drawings, models, and other demonstrations, and the Board satisfied that objections of a conclusive character applied to them. In the reconsideration, partly or wholly by new commissioners, no thought of these objections appears to have been had. I have been allowed no opportunity to point them out, or to defend, in any manner, the work for which I had been made publicly responsible; and they are now to be established by slow, provoking, and expensive public experience. Why was I appointed? and how is it that I still hold the office of Consulting Landscape-Architect to the Board? In the four years since it was made, there has been no communication between the Board and me.

In Victor Hugo's story, the practical M. Nortier says,—

"*In politics we do not kill a man: we only remove an embarrassment; that is all.*"[63]

VI.

WHEN Mr. Vaux and I first put our heads together in study of the design for the Central Park, we agreed to treat nothing as of essential consequence, except with reference to results which might be looked for, at nearest, forty years ahead. And with an outlook at least that far along, all our work and

---

*"Whereas Mr. Frederick Law Olmsted, long identified with the Central Park and its improvements, and enjoying the confidence of the community and the respect of this Department since its organization, should be placed in a position where this Department can avail itself of his large experience and intimate knowledge of the designs and objects of the work on the different parks," etc.

THE SPOILS OF THE PARK (1882)

our advice has since been given. In this has consisted a large part of its unpracticality.

If a park be got up mainly with the use of money borrowed in long loans; if the ground upon which it is formed be mortgaged as security for the ultimate payment of the loans; if the conduct of the business be placed in the hands of men who accept the trust without salary, as a consolation for the loss of a paid commissionership in a business of a very different character, or a place on a party committee, or a nomination for alderman, and who are far too knowing to accept advice except from practical men and of an instantly practical character:—if the business of these men be conducted with a view, first, to aid the cause of honest government at the next election; second, to suit the convenience of political contractors with notes coming due next month; and, lastly, to secure immediate satisfaction from one election to another of the public, it would not be surprising if even this *immediate* public satisfaction was not all they could wish.

It would be going further than is necessary to my purpose, to say that just this has occurred; but it may be well to ask if facts do not suggest methods of business which correspond nearly with what might be expected if it had. Let us see.

The Park Board, stimulated by the stings of the press and the public, and by the formal remonstrances of the leading business men of the city, has now had full four years in which to prove how well its business can be managed under the practical view, by practical men, and free from the embarrassment of professional advice and professional superintendence; and with what result?

Unless every newspaper that I have been in the way of seeing has been bearing false witness, and everything that comes to me verbally is deceptive, no branch of the city government has ever failed so completely and humiliatingly to earn public respect and confidence. As supplying the only available pleasure-roads, the Park is yet, perhaps, with an increasing driving and riding population, increasingly resorted to in the fashionable driving and riding season; that is to say, by that part of the population who least need to have opportunities of rural recreation brought nearer to them. But spite of all that should have been gained after twenty years, by four years' growing together of trees planted with the design of securing broad, quiet, massing effects, the Park is reported to have been steadily losing attraction, and, relatively to the entire population of the city, to be made less use of, and less valuable use of, than before.[64]

Notwithstanding the obvious fact that the motive of the management has been favorable to what may be termed the uniformly smug and smart suburban door-yard style, in distinction from a more varied treatment admitting here and there of at least a subdued picturesqueness, the verdict appears to be, that the Park has even taken on a slovenly and neglected aspect. This is not by any means the worst of the story; but, for the present, stopping here, if an explanation is needed, may it not be given in the one word "IGNORANCE"?— not ignorance of practical politics; of the stock, cotton, or iron markets; of Greek, physics, or botany; of horticulture, floriculture, or garden decoration, but ignorance—complete, blind ignorance—of the principles, even of the motives and objects, of an art to which many men of great wisdom and venerated character have thought it right to give as long and arduous study as is often given to any other form of art, or to any learned profession,—an art to which it is no more reasonable to suppose that a man can turn at middle life, and in a few months be prepared to assume the responsibility of a great public work, than that he can, in like manner, qualify himself to take command of an army, to serve as corporation counsel, superintending physician of Bellevue Hospital; as a sculptor, chemist, or lapidary.

VII.

WHAT has just been declared impossible many have been led to believe to be just what Mr. Vaux and I attempted, and with the result of leading the city, by our unfitness for the duties we accepted, into disasters such as the present commissioners have been seeking to mitigate. I have little doubt that many commissioners before the present, have, one after another, given a certain degree, at least, of credence, to statements made with this object, and I know that not a few estimable citizens must have done so. It is a matter of some moment to the city; it is of considerable interest to my profession; and I believe it to be due to the cause not alone of my art, but of all art, that the true state of the case should be known. The delusion so common and so melancholy, that because a boy has, or thinks he has, a natural gift for sketching, or modelling, or mimicry, he may hope to mount to distinction as a painter, sculptor, or actor, without far greater labor than is required for learning a trade, has its full counterpart in respect to landscape-gardening. I cannot say with what pity I have seen young men advertising themselves as landscape-engineers, etc., on the strength of having chanced to be employed as assistant surveyors for a few months in the ruder preparatory processes of park-making. Nay, I have seen even greater effrontery than that.

Mr. Vaux had, years before he took up the work of the Park, been the chosen co-operator of the greatest master in America of landscape-gardening, and had been associated with him in the most important and best public work that had been done in the country.[65] He was personally familiar with the most useful of European parks through having shared from childhood in their popular use. He had made, in company with other artists, long sketching-tours on foot, both in the old country and in the new; had more than ordinary amateur skill in landscape-painting, and had had thorough professional training in architecture.

I myself began my study of the art of parks in childhood. I had read, before I was fifteen, the great works upon the art,—works greater than any of the last half-century,—and had been under the instruction of older and more observant students of scenery, under the most favorable circumstances for a sound education.[66] And there had been no year of the twenty that followed before I entered the service of the Park Board, that I had not pursued the study with ardor, affection, and industry.

I had twice travelled in Europe with that object in view; had more than a hundred times visited the parks of London and Paris, and once or oftener those of Dublin, Liverpool, Brussels, The Hague, Berlin, Vienna, Florence, Rome, and other old cities. I had travelled five thousand miles on foot or in the saddle, and more than that by other private or public conveyance, in study of the natural scenery of this continent.[67] I had been three years the pupil of a topographical engineer, and had studied in what were then the best schools, and under the best masters in the country, of agricultural science and practice.[68] I had planted with my own hands five thousand trees, and, on my own farm and in my own groves, had practised for ten years every essential horticultural operation of a park. I had made the management of labor in rural works a special study, and had written upon it acceptably to the public. I had been for several years the honorary secretary of two organizations, and a member of four, formed for the discussion of rural themes and the advancement of rural arts. I had by invitation written for the leading journal of landscape-gardening, and had been in correspondence with and honored by the friendship of leading men in its science on both sides of the Atlantic.[69]

And essentially what I have thus said of myself had been known to the Commissioners, if not otherwise, then through those who introduced me to them, among whom were Mr. Irving, Mr. Bryant, Professor Gray, Mr. Greely, Mr. Raymond, Mr. Godwin, General Hamilton, Peter Cooper, Russell Sturgis, Charles H. Marshall, Edmund Blunt, Cornelius Grinnell, and David Dudley Field.[70]

It is notoriously too easy to get the use of names, one following another: therefore I add, that most of these well-known men had been either my hosts or my guests; all had met me socially, and testified of my training not without some personal knowledge.

Since then, the work of Mr. Vaux and myself speaks for itself; and judgment upon it has been given, not by New York alone, which in natural landscape art, at least, might easily for a time be misled, but by the highest authority living.[71] On what more worthy works rests the authority of those who tell the people of New York that we were quacks and knaves, and that our designs require such recasting of competent park-makers as it is now with all possible energy receiving?

If I seem tending to their level in thus speaking for myself, let it be considered that I have yet something more to say, and that I wish it to have all the weight that my rightful good name should entitle it to; let it be considered, also, that I have twenty times seen the assertion in print, made by some of the practical hounds, to whom this is my first reply in twenty years, that Mr. Vaux and I were brought upon the Park unknown, ignorant, incompetent pretenders, to serve a knavish scheme of base politicians; and that I happen to know that inquiries have been lately making in the vain hope to find ground of support for reiteration of the stupid fabrication.

And yet, in what has been spread abroad of this sort, there is just that yarn of truth that is usually to be found in the work of practised falsifiers. It is true that I had not set up to be a landscape-gardener before I came upon the Park. I had not thought myself one, and had been surprised and delighted when I was asked if I would accept even a journeyman's position in the intended work.[72] Why? Simply because I held the art in such reverence, that, to that time, it had never occurred to me that I might rightly take upon myself the responsibilities of a principal in its public practice. My study of it had been wholly a study of love, without a thought of its bringing me pecuniary reward or repute: in many matters of detail, therefore, it was defective (it is still very defective); and it is perfectly true, for this reason, if no other, that the task which was ultimately given me in the Central Park would have been an impossible one, had I not been so fortunate as to enjoy, for a time, the ardent and most loyal aid of men better qualified in some important respects than myself.[73] But I am more inclined to question now than I was when I accepted my first unsought and most unexpected appointment,[74] whether, if I had been more elaborately fitted than I happened to be, I should have been more strenuously or more intelligently bent on serving, with all such skill as I could command, the highest ends of the art, or better fitted to escape beguilements from them through the pedantries or the meretricious puerilities which hang on all its skirts. Let me illustrate my meaning.

During the last twenty years Europe has been swept by a mania for sacrificing natural scenery to coarse manufactures of brilliant and gaudy decoration under the name of specimen gardening; bedding, carpet, embroidery, and ribbon gardening, or other terms suitable to the house-furnishing and millinery trades. It was a far madder contagion than the tulip-mania, or the morus-multicaulis fever of our youth.[75]

It ran into all park management, the only limit often being that fixed by annual appropriations. Long ago, for example, it seized Hyde Park, and put completely out of countenance the single charm of broad homely sylvan and pastoral simplicity which the fogs and smoke of London, and its weary miles of iron hurdles, had left to it. Why? I asked the old superintendent. "Well, you know the fashion must have its run, and it just tickles the nursery-maids." I take some credit for my schooling, then, that so far as Central Park has been under my guardianship, it has been perfectly quarantined; not a dollar having been spent, nor a rood of good turf spoiled, for garishness, under my superintendence, nor at any time, except against my protest.

THE SPOILS OF THE PARK (1882)

Thirty years ago, before the Park was dreamed of, as a farmer, and with no more idea that I should ever be a professional landscape-designer than that I should command a fleet, I had printed these thoroughly unpractical words:—

"What artist so noble as he, who, with far-reaching conception of beauty and designing-power, sketches the outlines, writes the colors, and directs the shadows, of a picture so great that Nature shall be employed upon it for generations, before the work he has arranged for her shall realize his intentions!"[76]

VIII.

In the last chapter I observed that a loss of popular favor through slovenliness and neglect was not the worst misfortune that had befallen the Park. If it had been, I should have been still constrained to hold my peace. Neglect for considerable periods may do no serious permanent harm. Hence, while in the service of the Commission, I yielded much in that way to the practical policy. Neglect, if it continues not too long, may even have its advantages. The landscape-architect André, formerly in charge of the suburban plantations of Paris, was walking with me through the Buttes-Chaumont Park, of which he was the designer, when I said of a certain passage of it, "That, to my mind, is the best piece of artificial planting, of its age, I have ever seen." He smiled, and said, "Shall I confess that it is the result of neglect? I had planted this place most elaborately, with a view to some striking immediate effects which I had conceived, and others, to be ultimately obtained by thinnings. I had just worked out my plan, when the war came;[77] and for two years I did not again see the ground. It was occupied as a camp; horses were pastured in it; it was cut up by artillery; fires were made in it. As a park, it was everywhere subjected to the most complete neglect. When, at length, I came back to it, expecting to begin my work over again at all points, Nature had had one summer in which, as well as she could, to repair damages; and I declare to you, that, on arriving at just this point, I threw up my hands with delight, for, spite of some yet unhealed wounds, I saw at once that in general aspect there was a better work than I had been able to imagine. That which was weak and unsuitable in my planting had, by natural selection, disappeared; and in the struggle for existence nearly all that remained had taken a wild character, such as in an art we may aim at, but can hardly hope to attain." (But see how the true artist at once bowed himself before his tutor, and recognized and seized the opportunity.)

Hence, were ignorant neglect and feeble-minded slovenliness the worst qualities of the Board's management, I should yet have had nothing to say. The reason I must now speak is, that the Park is at last, avowedly, boastfully, and with much brag of energy, managed in distinct contemptuous repudiation of the leading motives with which it was laid out. This means, not as

Mr. Wales says, with no well-defined purpose, but with a purpose defined with perfect distinctness to undo, as far as practicable, what at least six million dollars of the city's debt have been heretofore spent to do. And of these six, two millions may be safely reckoned to be represented in structural works, which are to be found under the present policy simply obstructive to what is designed; so obstructive, that the results of this policy can at best be but botchwork.[78] Hereafter it will always be open to say of these results, I mean, that they would have been vastly better but for the obstructions which the original purpose had placed in the way of those responsible for them.*

The end will be that the park to be substituted for the original Central Park, without change of name, will be one better adapted to practical management; in which, for example, every operation can be directed and performed by men who have been unable to earn living wages in sewer and pavement work, in railroad and house-building work; who have broken down from incompetency in the hat-making and in the painting and glazing lines; and the services of whose sons and grandsons in carrying torch-lights, and stocking the primaries, must in some way be suitably acknowledged. The whole story is not told in this explanation; but, if it is considered how a constant gravitation in a general direction finally operates through many thousand channels of influence, it will be found to tell a good part of it.

I will later testify that the pretended landscape-gardening cloak under which this proclivity is disguised is a poor, tawdry piece of motley; but for the present let it be supposed that it is what it is claimed to be,—a much better-considered, wiser, and completer design than the old one; that it represents a higher culture and a nobler art, and as such is entitled to all possible respect. Then, I want to ask, was this respect paid to it, and did it mark a high sense of the Commissioners' responsibilities, and was it studiously deferential to the intelligence of the people of New York, that it should have been adopted, and work energetically begun upon it in the manner that it has been? With, so far as can be judged from the newspaper reports, absolutely no debate in the Board upon it, even apparently upon informal orders or verbal permits of Commissioners acting individually; with no public discussion, no opportunity for asking explanations, none for hearing remonstrances; without the publication of a single drawing, map, or plan, to aid an understanding of the great

---

*It is to be hoped that this will be denied. I should be glad to submit the grounds of the assertion to a jury of experts; to any number, for example, of the following gentlemen, to whom the principles of landscape-gardening must have been a serious study: Adolph Strauch, Cincinnati; Henry Winthrop Sargent of Woodenethe; H. W. S. Cleveland, Chicago; H. H. Hunnewell of Wellesley; W. Hammond Hall, Sacramento, Cal.; William McMillan, Buffalo; Col. F. L. Lee, Albany; Professor Robinson, Harvard Arboretum; E. W. Bowditch, Boston; John Sturgis, Brookline, Mass.; F. J. Scott, Toledo; Professor C. E. Norton, Harvard College. There are others whom I should include, as Mr. Weidenmann, but that I happen to be informed of their views. Several of these named are personally unknown to me, and with none have I had any conversation on the subject.[79]

undertaking? (I will soon show more fully the contrasting methods in which the first Park Commissioners proceeded, but may mention here, that, in the first four years in which their design was developing, they issued over thirty maps and drawings, several thousand of which were distributed gratuitously, and that in some cases electrotype copies of them were supplied for newspaper publication.)

How many of those who read this paper will not, for the first time, know from it that an entirely new motive of design has been lately adopted, and vigorous work in pursuing it entered upon?

It is due to the enterprise of a single newspaper reporter, moved, it would appear, rather by a sense of the ludicrous than the grave aspect of the matter, that the completest exposition of the new policy has come before the public at all.[80] Were it a question of the refurnishing and decorating of their board-room, the Commissioners could not have observed less formality, given less evidence of deliberation, forecast, and study, or used fewer of the commonest business precautions against foolhardy blundering, than they have in all this proceeding.

IX.

The points of identity between such of the purposes and motives of the present attempt to reform the Park as have been drawn out by the reporters, and those of that which was made at the cost of a million or more in 1871,[81] are so many and so marked, that what is deficient in our information may be fairly taken to be supplied from what is of record as to what was then in view. The difference is only in the present lack of boldness, and a disposition to generalize rather than come to definite particulars. With this additional light upon it, the character of the scheme can be made comprehensible; and it is plain, that, if there had been knowledge and skill enough at the Commissioners' command, it would have been asserted for it that a new school of landscape-gardening had arisen, adapted especially to urban parks; that it had for them great advantages; and Mr. Robinson[82] might have been quoted, and the experience of thousands of New York visitors to Paris cited, in confirmation of this statement. It would have had the value, too, for purposes of deception, of being true; and it is apparent that a dull sense of this truth has been mixed with another dull sense of the ideal of cockney villa-gardens in determining what should be said to reconcile the public to the destruction of the original Central Park. Let us see what the new school, thus clumsily serving as a decoy, really is.

It is in fact that of which M. Barillet-Deschamps is by repute the father, and M. André the most judicious and successful practitioner. It had its origin in the revision of the small interior public grounds of Paris, undertaken by Napoleon the Third; became very popular, largely because of the striking and spectacular effects rapidly obtained by profuse use of certain novel, exotic, and sickly forms of vegetation; and was allowed to have a certain degree of influence, always unfortunate, in the detailed management of much more important works.[83] Meaning no disrespect to it, holding it in admiration in its proper place, I should say that it bears a relation to natural landscape-gardening, like that which the Swiss peasants of Mrs. Leo Hunter's costume lawn-party bear to the healthy cow-girls of Alpine pastures.[84] As a fashion, it has had its run in Europe; and of those who have taken and carried it on as a fashion, and the results they have obtained, it is M. André himself who gives his opinion thus: "They did not see that this new art was in great part conventional." Then, after describing the misapplication of it upon works of larger scale, and in connection with genuine rural conditions, he continues, "Under the false pretext that lawns, trees, waters, and flowers are always pleasant, they have substituted for the old geometrical garden a still more artificial style. The former, at least, avowed its aim to show the hand of man, and master nature. The latter borrows the elements of nature, and, under pretence of imitating it, makes it play a ridiculous — I was going to say an effeminate — part." "It is not this — we say it emphatically — it is not this that constitutes landscape art. If art seeks means of action in nature, it is in order to turn them to account in a simple and noble way." (*L'Art des Jardins*, chap. V.)[85]

The best that can be claimed for the new design of the Central Park is, that it is in part an attempt to reclothe its rocky frame with second-hand garments of the fashion thus truthfully characterized by the master to whose ability the fashion itself is a tribute of ignorant reverence.

Further, I will not attempt to characterize it, certainly not to criticise it; but I will ask any who have been induced to suppose there is a real landscape purpose in it to reflect in what respect such conception as they have been led to form of it differs in its ideals of landscape from such as might be appropriately adopted on a site like that of Union Square,[86] and then to ask themselves whether the ends and motives suitable to the area and topography of the one city property are probably at all such as should be had in view in business with the other; whether, with no intrinsically different purpose, it is justifiable — pardonable — to close from all ordinary use, from all commercial occupation, for all the future of the city, a hundred and fifty ordinary blocks, with the avenues and streets between them, in one continuous body, and that at the point where it will cause the most inconvenience, — the very centre of the city that is to be? Could a theory of the use and value of the Park be propounded better adapted to open it continually to schemes of subdivision, intrigues of "real-estate sharps," and to all manner of official corruption?

Can Commissioner Wales be right in basing his opposition to it on the ground that this means only indecision of purpose? Is not what he calls "no definite purpose" as distinctly a default of trust as a purposeless leaving-open the vaults and the outer doors of a bank? What is "no definite purpose" under such circumstances? What would be thought of a jury that would acquit the cashier or night-porter responsible for it?

I will further ask those who may suppose that the plan of the Park needs such general revision as is now promised, in the interest of what is called "utility," if they suppose that the only utility which can be held to excuse the attempt to form a park of such dimensions, on such ground, in such a situation, has heretofore been wholly disregarded in its design?

Yet another question for these gentlemen to put to themselves. If a direct cut is to be offered between every two points where a manifest utility is to be served by permitting it, fifteen millions more may easily be spent to accomplish the result, and in the end the Park will have been obliterated. A dozen projects have already been urged for opening additional roads through the Park, and more than that for entrances and walks through parts of it. There is not one of them, which, if the process of cutting up the Park could stop with it, would not, for the time being, tell to the advantage of somebody's real estate. But how will it be in the end, if the bars are once taken down?

Are there any who suppose that those are sincere who seek to create an impression that considerations of public utility and convenience in this respect had no weight in the old design of the Park? If so, I would ask them simply to recall the fact that that design had for its starting-point the necessity of provisions for carrying the ordinary traffic of the city across it in such a manner as not to interfere with its recreative use; that it was the only one of more than thirty plans submitted by different persons and associations in which this necessity had been so much as thought of; and that the chief opposition to the accepted design rested on the assertion that such provision was unnecessary, and, in the manner proposed to be used, absurdly impracticable. It has now been in use twenty years precisely as proposed; and not one of the objections said to have been made to it by "eminent engineers" has been heard of in all that time.[87]

Are those who used this forecast likely to have been otherwise indifferent to motives of utility?

A very different objection to this arrangement will soon appear, if the aims lately announced in behalf of the Park Board are sustained, and if the work now said to be in energetic progress shall be long pursued. By a most careful disposition of plantations and underwood the sub-roads[88] have been so obscured (as have with equal care most of the more finished architectural structures originally so disconcertingly conspicuous), that they make no impression upon those passing through it. I have known visitors to make the tour of the Park several times without being aware of their existence. How will it be when "a free circulation of air and light" beneath every bush and brooding conifer has been secured; when the way of the lawn-mower has at all points been made plain, and the face of nature shall everywhere have become as natty as a new silk hat?

X.

But one poor apology can be contrived for the course the Commissioners have been following. That apology they have not as yet put forward,—those responsible for recent barbarities have not yet begun to think of apologizing,—but attempts to supply a base for it have been often seen; and some of the younger generation may have been led to suppose them to have substance. They are of precisely the same character, and they have the same origin, and the same motives and purposes, with those I have already cleared up in respect to Mr. Vaux and myself; and to assist the truth, a slight repetition of what I believe to be the facts may be necessary.

In 1857, twenty-five years ago, eleven citizens of New York were asked to take upon themselves, as a Board of Commissioners for the purpose, the extraordinary and gravely difficult duty of preparing for the transformation of a broken, rocky, sterile, and intractable body of land, more than a mile square in extent, into a public ground, to stand in the heart of a great commercial city. The project was without precedent, and remains without parallel. There were political motives in the determination of the arrangement, and governing the choice of the Commissioners selected. Among them, most prominent, was the desire of the leaders of the Republican party to reconcile the Democratic party, largely in majority in the city, to a relinquishment of the spoils of office in the proposed work. For this purpose they provided that no one of the Commissioners should, under any pretext, be entitled to pecuniary compensation for his services. They selected for Commissioners several men unknown in politics, but of high standing in liberal, benevolent, and unpartisan patriotic movements; others, who, if known in politics, were unknown as office-seekers, or, as the term is commonly used, as politicians. In a Board of eleven the Republicans were supposed to have a majority of one; but the first President elected was a Democrat;[89] and seldom if ever (I remember not one case) from the first, in any important matter, did a division occur on party lines. When, near the first city election after the organization, an attempt was made to obtain a party advantage on the work, under orders given by one of the Commissioners, I as superintendent at once arrested it, suspended the foreman, who had acted upon the order, and was sustained in doing so by the vote of every other Republican in the Board.

It was obvious that such a ground as has been described, of very broken topography; rocky, sterile and intractable, in the situation contemplated; to be enclosed by a compact busy city, would, under any possible treatment, entail many and great public inconveniences, and that it could only be kept in suitable order at constant great expense. Whatever its treatment, it was to be anticipated that the land would in time come to have enormous value for purposes other than those to be at first had in view, and that crafty attempts would be made to obtain advantages from it for various selfish ends. It was plain that varied and competing purposes and interests, tastes and dispositions, would be concerned in its management; and that there would always be those, who, however it might be managed, would believe that it should have been very differently treated, and that certain elements of value should have been more amply or less lavishly provided.

From considerations such as these, it followed that the foremost, paramount, and sternest duty of the Commissioners was to be cautious in determining the ends and motives with reference to which the ground should be laid out and treated; to act only upon the most thorough study, and under the most carefully digested advice attainable.

That this duty was recognized, accepted, and deliberately and laboriously met, is a matter of plain, circumstantial, and irrefutable record. This record will also show that different theories of what the circumstances would call for, different opinions, ideals, tastes, and dispositions, were given patient consideration; that views widely different from those finally adopted were ably and warmly represented in the Commission itself; and that the problem had prolonged, earnest, and elaborate discussion.[90]

It is to be added, in view of the very different way in which the undertaking to reverse, as far as practicable, the results of this deliberation, has come to the knowledge of the public, that no body of men charged with a like public trust has ever taken more pains to invite and give opportunity for general public discussion of what it was debating, and review of what it determined; and that discussion and review were prolonged and earnest. There were great differences of opinion; but, in the judgment of those responsible, public opinion steadily moved to a more and more intelligent acceptance of the conclusions adopted in the earlier management, as wisely foresighted.

The Commissioners entered upon their duty under a cloud of jealousy and distrust, and every device of what in city politics passes for statesmanship was employed to keep them there. There were desperate men using desperate means for the purpose; there were misled honest and worthy men who labored to the same end. Nevertheless, as public discussion proceeded, the Commission steadily advanced into the sunshine of public confidence, gained the good will of the more respectable of all parties; and from that day to this no man or party has appealed fairly to public opinion against their conclusions with any degree of success.

There have been strong alliances and combinations to do so. A most energetic attempt was made, as I have before said, in 1871; but it met with decided popular reprobation, and those responsible for it retreated in very bad order, two of them going abroad to escape criminal prosecution.[91]

Essentially, the work now being energetically pushed in the Central Park is a revival of that then defeated: it has the same avowed objects; it has the same obscured ends; it is supported by the same sophistries; it calls for a like popular rebuke.

XI.

Is the honest and business-like management of the city's park business to be always "embarrassed," as it has hitherto always been, and must a dead stop and reversion of its true course be come to every ten years, in the future as in the past? If not, how is it to be avoided?

His Honor the mayor has given the more important part of the answer in his message to the aldermen on the occasion of the assassination of President Garfield.[92]

Beyond that, possibly the time may come when the management of the parks may be overlooked, and their business audited by a body of men, among whom there shall be representatives of those to whom the wholesome charm of simple natural scenery has been, as with most of the members of the National Academy of Design,[93] for example, a matter of business-like study, and to whom the permanent reconciliation of a certain practicable degree of such charm, with the necessary conveniences of rest and movement of a vast multitude of people of all classes of the population of a great city, would not be felt a contemptible matter, even in comparison with the immediate practical requirements, from day to day, of republican government.

I cannot see, though it is so apparent to some true friends of the Park, what is to be gained of permanent value by saying to any one man, "Go work your sweet will there, till we find that we have had enough of you;" taking no security, making no official provision for watching, against that man's personal hobbies and freaks, ambitions and weaknesses. The concentration of executive functions in one man's hands is of too obvious advantage to ever need debate; but beyond and above this, in my judgment, it would be far better to return to something like the original arrangement, in which all questions of general administration, or of sub-legislation for the Park, and especially all determinations affecting its general design, ends, and aims, should be subject to review, discussion, and at least to veto, by an unpaid board of citizens, so large, and of such established reputation because of interest otherwise evinced in affairs allied to those of the proper business of the Park, that there could be some rational confidence that they would exercise conservative control. The labor of such a board need not be great,—a quarterly meeting would probably be sufficient for the auditing of accounts, the passing upon projects, and a review of operations upon previously prepared official reports. An annual report to the mayor would present the entire business satisfactorily to the public.

THE SPOILS OF THE PARK (1882)

Postscript.

This pamphlet had been so far written, and in part printed, before I knew that a practical proposition had been prepared—the first of the present session, and introduced in the form of a bill before the Legislature had organized—to amend the city charter in such a way as to provide for the abolition of the Park Board, and the substitution for it of a Superintendent, responsible directly to the mayor.[94] Assuming, as I must, from the favor with which it is instantly received by friends of the Park, that there are no private, or party, or local interests moving the proposition; that there is no understanding as to who the superintendent is to be, whom he is to appoint, and what work he is to prosecute,—I can only recur to what I was just saying. If the man shall be qualified by the special study and training required for his duty, and shall have given proofs of it, and shall take up his duty with an earnest and serious purpose, he cannot but desire the moral weight which would be gained by such an arrangement as I have above been suggesting.

Considerations against the plan as I have seen it set forth are these:—

The results to which good management of the Park will be directed are not to be brought about quickly, by strokes, but gradually, by courses extending through several years. Good courses, consequently, require time for their vindication. A man cannot reasonably hope to be allowed to steadily pursue any courses looking solely to good results in the Park. He will be constantly pressed with advice from men who are neither competent nor disposed to give sound advice with reference to results of such limited scope,—men who will be not at all accountable for his failure to reach vindicating results; men who will never be known to the public to have had anything to do with the matter; men who, nevertheless, will make a business, if he fails to be ruled by their advice, of obstructing his way upon any desirable course, and who, by one shameful means or another, will so accumulate embarrassments for him, that he will be fortunate if he succeeds in escaping a mortifying and apparently disgraceful failure.

Again: with whatever confidence we may look to the present mayor's intentions and shrewdness, it is not to be forgotten that no arrangement for the guardianship of the park property could be more tempting to a sly, smooth, and double-faced schemer, than that proposed; and that such an one, unscrupulous in making bargains for the purpose, ready to resort to falsehood and all manner of vile intrigues, would have unlimited advantages in contending with an honest man.

To come to a point, no well-matured scheme for the government of Central Park will fail to recognize that it is an essentially different form of city property,—on the one hand, from ordinary urban squares and places; on

APPENDIX II

the other, from the great suburban parks of other cities,—nor will it fail to embody features nearly equivalent to the following:—

First, A definition of the trust, giving some fixed idea of what may and what may not be legally aimed at in its management.

Second, Provision for a board of directors with the ordinary duties of a commercial board of directors, in which board there will be, by some ex-officio appointment, representatives of the art of landscape-painting, of standing previously fixed by their fellow-artists.

Third, Provision for an executive office, with the executive duties of which the directors will be restrained from interfering.

Fourth, Provision for a professional adviser, qualified by study and practice in the art of landscape-gardening, with such prescribed duties and rights as will make him responsible for an intelligent and consistent pursuit of the main landscape-design of the Park; this office to be combined, or not, as may be found best by the directors, with the executive office.

Fifth, All such provision as legislators will think practicable for restraining, with reference to the park-service, that form of tyranny known as advice or influence, and that form of bribery known as patronage.

Olmsted wrote this document during the late fall and early winter of 1881–82, as a result of his growing dismay at the destruction of the landscape in Central Park that was being carried out by the new superintendent, Aneurin Jones. The concept of himself as an "unpractical man" was particularly galling to Olmsted in relation to Central Park, and seems to have had its origin in his first encounter with his superiors in the park administration. In September 1857, at the end of his first meeting with the park's engineer and chief officer, Egbert Viele, when Olmsted was seeking appointment as superintendent of the park, he was dismayed by Viele's dismissive comment that "he would rather have a practical man." Olmsted's account of those first days with the park's commissioners and staff describes how universally they viewed him as "unpractical." This description became part of a longer memoir that he entitled "Passages in the Life of an Unpractical Man" (*Papers of FLO*, 1: 98–113; ibid., 3: 79–84.)

1. This quotation is taken from Marc Antony's funeral oration for Julius Caesar in William Shakespeare's *Julius Caesar*, Act 3, scene 2: Olmsted substituted the word "practical" for Shakespeare's "honorable."
2. Olmsted had been superintendent (and beginning in 1858 architect-in-chief as well) from September 1857 to May 1863. From May to September 1872 he had taken the place of Henry Stebbins as president and treasurer of the board, while Stebbins was absent from the city on a trip to Europe. This was the only period during which Olmsted was a member of the board of commissioners of the New York Department of Parks.
3. Olmsted's statement here is probably based on information he had received in a letter of February 21 from William R. Martin, a former park commissioner and supporter. Martin informed him that a plan was being developed to create a two-member park board for New York City. One seat would go to the Republicans and one to the Tammany Hall Democrats, while supporters of the anti-Tammany faction led by Andrew H. Green would be excluded. The result, so Martin claimed, would be to give

Olmsted control of the superintendence of the parks (William R. Martin to FLO, Feb. 21, 1882).

4. Presumably Olmsted means that any arrangement for superintendence of the New York City parks would require the kind of close and constant attendance that he had provided, whenever permitted, during the past quarter-century. A year later he expressed to Calvert Vaux his reluctance to assume such responsibilities again, saying "For my part, for my personal health and welfare it is everything not to be living in New York which would be hell to me" (FLO to Calvert Vaux, Jan. 6, 1883, Calvert Vaux Papers, The New York Public Library, Humanities and Social Sciences Library, Office of Special Collections, Astor, Lenox and Tilden Foundations, New York City).

5. In the debates in the park commission during the fall of 1881, commissioners Smith Lane and Salem Wales had proposed to give Olmsted a role in directing landscape architecture in the parks department, either by himself or jointly with Calvert Vaux. Commissioners McLean and Olliffe, representing Andrew H. Green's faction of the Democratic Party consistently voted against any new engagement with Olmsted and instead proposed appointing Calvert Vaux or Samuel Parsons, Jr. On November 19, 1881, after more than a month of controversy during which the commission's meetings were frequently referred to in the press as reminiscent of a "bear garden," three of the four commissioners voted to appoint Calvert Vaux as Superintending Architect and to demote Julius Munckwitz from that position to that of Architect (*New-York Times*, Oct. 20, 1881, p. 7; *New-York Daily Tribune*, Oct. 20, 1881, p. 1; *New-York Daily Tribune*, Oct. 27, 1881, pp. 4 and 8; *New York World*, Nov. 11, 1881, p. 5; *New-York Times*, Nov. 20, 1881, p. 13; DPP, *Minutes*, Oct. 19, 1947, pp. 297–300; ibid., Oct. 26, pp. 318–19; ibid., Nov. 19, 1881, p. 389).

6. A reference to the statement by park commissioner Salem H. Wales that Olmsted quoted at the beginning of the body of his text (below).

7. Olmsted here quotes from the characterization of the park board by commissioner Salem H. Wales in a letter to the *New York World* of December 18, 1881. He went on to say that "The public is disgusted with this grotesque exhibition and they cannot be blamed for its disgust." Salem Howe Wales (1825–1902) a prominent civic leader and managing editor of the *Scientific American* for over twenty years. He was active in the Union League Club and the Century club and was a founder and official of the Metropolitan Museum of Art. Wales was appointed to the parks commission in January 1873 and served as its president from August 1873 until his resignation in June 1874. He was appointed to the commission again in December 1880 and resigned in 1885, during which time he made numerous attempts to arrange for Olmsted's return to management of the New York City parks (*New-York Times*, Dec. 3, 1902, p. 9; NCAB, 3: 310; DPP, *Minutes*, Dec. 15, 1880, p. 397; FLO, Patronage Journal, May 9, 1874, above).

8. The "silent steed" was the bicycle, which was excluded from New York City parks at this time (DPP, *Minutes*, July 7, 1880, pp. 143–44).

9. Water Street, an area of commercial establishments, abuts Wall Street and runs from Battery Park to the Brooklyn Bridge.

10. On September 22, 1880, the commissioners of the Department of Public Parks had appointed the architect Jacob Wrey Mould as "Architect of Morningside Park." Following its formation with three new members in December 1880 and January 1881, the board that was in place at the time that Olmsted wrote *Spoils of the Park* made five additions to its architectural and general management staff. These were: the appointment on July 26, 1881, of J. C. Cady as superintending architect for construction of the American Museum of Natural History; the appointment on August 15, 1881, of Aneurin Jones as Superintendent of Parks; the appointment on September 7, 1881, of J. C. Cady to superintend the construction of the approaches to Central Park at

APPENDIX II

Eighth Avenue and 77th and 81st streets; the appointment on November 19, 1881, of Calvert Vaux as Superintending Architect of the Department of Public Parks; the appointment on the same day of then Superintending Architect Julius Munckwitz as Architect of the department. The "last election" to which Olmsted refers was the appointment of Vaux, who insisted as a condition of his acceptance that Samuel Parsons, Jr., his partner in the firm of Vaux & Company, be appointed Superintending Gardener in place of William Fischer. At the time Olmsted completed writing this pamphlet, the board had not yet agreed to such an arrangement: as late as February 1, 1882, an evenly divided board had failed to approve that proposal (DPP *Minutes*; Charles A. Birnbaum, "Parsons, Samuel, Jr.," in Charles A. Birnbaum and Robin Karson, eds., *Pioneers of American Landscape Design* [New York, 2000], pp. 287–91; "The Park Board Still Trifling," *New-York Daily Tribune*, Dec. 25, 1881, p. 6; Calvert Vaux to FLO, Nov. 20, 1881; Calvert Vaux to FLO, Dec. 9, 1881).

11. That is, stone arches designed to carry pedestrian and bridle paths under carriage drives in Central Park. Olmsted and Vaux masked these arches with plantings so as to merge them into the landscape. Since his appointment in the summer of 1881, superintendent Aneurin Jones had undertaken to trim back these plants in order to make the arches more visible (*New-York Daily Tribune*, Oct. 17, 1881, p. 5; William L. Fischer to FLO, Nov. 5, 1881).

12. The Board of Commissioners of the Central Park was organized in 1857 with eleven members. The so-called Tweed Charter for the city in 1870 replaced this commission with a five-member Board of Commissioners of the Department of Public Parks. In 1874 the state legislature reduced the number of commissioners to four. Under each arrangement the terms of the commissioners were staggered so that the board's membership changed frequently (New York [State], *Laws of the State of New York, Passed at the Eightieth Session of the Legislature* [Albany, N.Y., 1857], chap. 771; ibid., [1870], chap. 137; ibid., [1873], chap. 335; ibid., [1874], chap. 300).

13. A reference to a letter submitted to the park board by 166 prominent New York citizens protesting Olmsted's dismissal in January 1878. It urged the commissioners to allow his close professional stewardship of the original Central Park design to continue. It cited the frequently changing membership of the board of commissioners as a reason for securing that continuity of management of the park. The letter also cited the economic benefits arising from the ability of the park to attract tax-paying residents to the city: anything that undermined those benefits would surely cost the city more than the $4,500 ostensibly saved by eliminating Olmsted's salary. The board filed this communication without comment (DPP, *Minutes*, Jan.23, 1878, pp. 544–46; *New York World*, Jan. 22, 1878, p. 5).

14. Wales was one of the founders of the New York Homeopathic Hospital and Medical College in 1860 and served on its board of trustees for many years (*New-York Times*, Dec. 3, 1902, p. 2; William Harvey King, *History of Homeopathy and Its Institutions in America*, 4 vols. [New York, 1905], 2: 288).

15. Olmsted here refers to the offices he had held on the park and the diminution of their power over time. As architect-in-chief between May 1858 and May 1863, his office controlled all work done on the park and the labor allocated to it, as stated in his quotation from the *Minutes* of the park board upon his appointment. When Olmsted and Vaux returned to Central Park in July 1865, they were appointed "landscape architects to the Board, upon such terms and conditions as the Executive Committee, or a majority of said committee, may deem expedient." After the removal of the Tweed Ring Board in November 1871, Olmsted and Vaux were appointed "Landscape Architects Advisory to the Board," with the stipulation that "no structure be placed on the Central Park until after they have first seen a plan of the same, and reported thereon to this Board." In January 1872 the board created the position of "Landscape Architects

and General Superintendents," who were to "plan and supervise the improvements that may from time to time be undertaken by the Department . . . ." In November 1872 the board created the Bureau of Design and Superintendence "through which all orders for the service of the Department of Parks and Places, not relating to payments and financial accounts, shall be given, and their execution supervised and controlled." The Landscape Architect of the department was to be the head of the bureau. Olmsted held the position of Landscape Architect from November 1872 until his dismissal on January 23, 1878. In the summer of 1873, as the board implemented plans to revise its bylaws to remove duties of superintendence, policing, and even landscape matters from his office, Olmsted tendered his resignation. For several weeks in August and September the office of superintendence and design was effectively suspended, after which he consented to resume the position with duties considerably reduced and mostly limited to providing designs upon orders of the board (BCCP, *Minutes*, May 17, 1858, p. 31; ibid., July 19, 1865, p. 39; DPP, *Minutes*, Nov. 23, 1871, p. 235; ibid., Jan. 30, 1872, p. 289; ibid., Nov. 6, 1872, p. 565; ibid., Jan. 5, 1878, p. 490; *Papers of FLO*, 3: 27; ibid., 6: 44–46, 633–41; FLO to DPP Board, [March 1, 1875], above).

16. A reference to the park board's abolition of the Bureau of Design and Superintendence, which took place on January 23, 1878, and not in 1879 as stated in the published text (DPP, *Minutes*, Jan. 23, 1878, pp. 556–57).

17. On the day that it abolished the Bureau of Design and Superintendence, the park board invested the position of Superintendent of Parks with authority to oversee all gardening work in the parks. In consequence, foreman of gardeners William Fischer had little authority for managing the plantings in the park, and in any case he was fired on February 20, 1878. He returned to the parks department in 1880 as superintending gardener. With the advent of Superintendent Aneurin Jones in the summer of 1881, however, Fischer acquired an unsympathetic superior, although remaining the department's "representative of landscape art." Calvert Vaux's desire to have Samuel Parsons, Jr., take Fischer's position in the department was presumably another aspect of the "degrading" of his position to which Olmsted refers in this passage (DPP, *Minutes*, Jan. 23, 1878, p. 553).

18. Olmsted is referring principally to articles critical of the management of Central Park that appeared in the *New-York Times* in the fall of 1879. On August 27, the *Times* published a letter by Calvert Vaux entitled "A Plea for the Artistic Unity of Central Park," which was quickly followed by an article by Samuel Parsons, Jr., that criticized the loss of trees in some areas of the park and the lack of pruning and thinning of vegetation in others. The *Times* then published an article stating Vaux's approval of the article by Parsons and calling for constant agitation of the issue in the public press. A few days later the *Times* published an interview with August Hepp, the superintending gardener at that time. Hepp denied responsibility for several recent instances of mismanagement in Central Park, which included the cutting down of the central row of elm trees at the entrance at Fifth Avenue and 59th Street, neglect of trees along the 59th Street sidewalk, and removal of turf from an "expensively made lawn." Hepp asserted that Superintendent John F. Dawson controlled the management of the park and that his own recommendations went unheeded. He said that "There was neither head nor tail to the management. It was all mismanagement." At the time that Olmsted wrote *The Spoils of the Park* the "unfortunate representative of landscape art" on the park was Superintending Gardener William Fischer, who had replaced Hepp in the summer of 1880.

    In mentioning Salem Wales's "expostulating" demonstration of the persistence of mismanagement of the landscape of Central Park, Olmsted may be referring to the letter by Wales in the *New York World* of December 18, 1881, from which he took the quotation at the beginning of Section I of *The Spoils of the Park*. In that letter, Wales also asserted that "A conspicuous example of the failure of a commission to render earnest and effective service where the best possible service is required is the past and present Park Commission. It fails absolutely–as it has failed for some years past–to meet the reasonable and just expectations of the people . . ." By his reference to the new tools being used to harm the scenery of the park Olmsted may be referring to the fact that the problem in 1879 was neglect of thinning of vegetation, while under the regime of superintendent Jones in 1881 it was instead too-thorough cutting and clearing (*New-York Daily Tribune*, May 1879, p. ; DPP, *Minutes*, May 21, 1879, p. 28; Calvert Vaux, "A Plea for the Artistic Unity of Central Park," *New-York Times*, Aug. 27, 1879, p. 5; S. B. Parsons, "Central Park Neglected," ibid., Sept. 7, 1879, p. 7; "The Mismanagement of the Park," ibid., Sept. 8, 1879, p. 8; "Central Park's Condition," ibid., Sept. 18, 1878, p. 8; "The Legislature and Municipal Reform," *New York World*, Dec. 18, 1881, p. 6; DPP, *Minutes*, July 22, 1880, p. 191; ibid., Aug. 14, 1880, p. 244).

19. In a long journal article discussing ornamental and landscape gardening, Sir Walter Scott declared of landscape gardening that "The importance of this art, in its more elegant branches, ranks so high in our opinion, that we would willingly see its profession (and certainly it contains persons worthy of such honour) more closely united with the fine arts than it can now be esteemed" (*The Quarterly Review*, 37 [March 1828]: 319; Edward Wagenknecht, *Sir Walter Scott* [New York, 1991], p. 136).

20. Olmsted here draws from, respectively: Francis Bacon's essay, "Of Gardens" (1625); James Russel Lowell's "Preliminary Note to the Second Edition" of *A Fable for Critics* (1848); Ralph Waldo Emerson's essay "Love" published in *Essays, First Series* (1844); and Henry Wadsworth Longfellow's poem "Sunrise on the Hills." Olmsted used these quotations—and in the case of Longfellow, a different passage from the same poem—at the beginning of his report *Mount Royal. Montreal* that he published in 1881 (*Papers of FLO*, SSI: 350, 411).

21. Olmsted's friend and office clerk, Howard A. Martin, saved newspaper articles about his ouster. Among the papers which reported on the matter extensively were the *New York World*, *New-York Daily Tribune*, *New York Herald*, and the *New-York Times* (See Patronage Journal, p. 706, n. 18, below; DPP, *Minutes*, Jan. 23, 1878, pp. 557).

22. The editors have found no references to a "Park Defence Organization" in contemporary newspaper accounts of Olmsted's dismissal nor is it mentioned in the published minutes of the board. On January 12, 1878, the West Side Association, a group of developers and property owners interested in the upper West Side since the mid-1860s, passed resolutions that called for Olmsted's retention. The board received copies of the resolutions and filed them without comment (DPP, *Minutes*, Jan. 16, 1878, p. 527; *New York World*, Jan. 18, 1878, p. 2).

23. In 1875, Andrew H. Green charged that the Department of Public Works had appointed a blind sewer inspector (George Alexander Mazaraki, "The Public Career of Andrew Haswell Green," [Ph.D. diss., New York University, 1966], p. 245).

24. In the letter to the *New York World* that Olmsted quoted as a headnote for this pamphlet, Wales had testified concerning his experience on the park board in 1873–74, that ". . .I well remember what agony wrung the soul of the late Colonel Stebbins at the miserable intrigues which environed his administration and which finally led to his resignation of the office of President. I became his successor and my official life was made miserable by reason of the same intrigues, so that finally, as no relief appeared possible to me, I resigned my office and went to Europe for a few months of comfort." Olmsted recounted in his patronage journal the circumstances preceding Wales's resignation from the board in June 1874 (*New York World*, Dec. 18, 1881, p. 6; FLO, Patronage Journal, May 9, 1874, above; DPP, *Minutes*, June 3, 1874, p. 67).

THE SPOILS OF THE PARK (1882)

25. Olmsted was in Europe by the time the board formally abolished the Bureau of Design and Superintendence.
26. In 1862 George Opdyke, Republican mayor of New York, offered Olmsted the position of street commissioner but was unable to secure the necessary approval of the Board of Aldermen (*Papers of FLO*, 4: 289).
27. Mayor A. Oakey Hall named Olmsted to the board in May 1872 to fill the seat temporarily vacated by Henry G. Stebbins. The other board members immediately elected him president and treasurer, positions that he held until he resigned them upon Stebbins's return in late October 1872 (*Papers of FLO*, 6: 40–41, passim).
28. That is, Tammany Hall, whose partisans had controlled patronage on the park the previous year.
29. That is, the pending proposal, publicly endorsed by Wales, to reduce the board to one commissioner.
30. Possibly a reference to the *Sunday Mercury*, a Democratic weekly whose editor, William Cauldwell, was a Tammany member of the state assembly (William C. Gover, *The Tammany Hall Democracy of the City of New York* [New York, 1875], p. 120).
31. John W. Manning, dismissed by the board in June 1876, apparently ran for the state assembly shortly afterwards (DPP, *Minutes*, June 21, 1876, p. 145; FLO to *New York Herald*, Feb. 2, 1881, ms. letter in Olmsted Papers, LOC).
32. In February 1858 Olmsted had assumed the duties of training and administering a force of keepers to maintain order on Central Park and to provide information and assistance to its visitors. He implemented policies to ensure the highest decorum and discipline of the force, which remained under his management until 1861. In 1872, when he assumed the presidency of the park board, Olmsted found the force rife with patronage appointees and barely meeting its duties. Pursuant to a resolution of the board that autumn, Olmsted presented a report that called for a reorganization of the keepers. In late November the board authorized him to reduce the number of men on the force and to organize an auxiliary force composed of park workmen, to be called to special keeping duty as occasions warranted (*Papers of FLO*, 3: 219–21; ibid., 6: 574–83, 610–19).
33. Surgeon R. D. Nesmith examined the park keepers in December 1872. The printed *Minutes* of the board do not indicate precisely when it dismissed him, but it appears that he had been replaced by July 1873 (*Papers of FLO*, 6: 43; DPP, *Minutes*, July 16, 1873, pp. 116–17; R. D. Nesmith to FLO, Aug. 9, 1873).
34. Olmsted relates substantially these same events in his patronage journal dating them to early 1875. Similar instances of keepers abandoning their duty to rest in secluded parts of the park apparently were common before Olmsted's reforms of 1873 (FLO, Patronage Journal, March 26, 1875 and May 21, 1875, both above; *Papers of FLO*, 6: 620–21).
35. In late March 1873 the board adopted Olmsted's "General Order for the Organization and Routine of Duty of the Keepers' Service of the Central Park." This order reorganized the keepers into three branches: the patrol keepers, the post (or gate) keepers, and extra keepers (the latter were uniformed maintenance workers to be called to keeping duties as circumstances warranted). The patrol keepers were divided into two groups, one assigned to specific "beats" or areas of the park and the other to make "rounds" of the park drives at designated intervals and at a brisk pace (*Papers of FLO*, SS1: 281–307; ibid., 619–26).
36. In late May 1873 the *New-York Daily Tribune* published two articles by "Jan Vier," apparently a pseudonym that attacked the new park keepers' organization as a "Chain-Gang System." The writer alleged that the changes had introduced a reign of lawlessness and indecency in the park. The name of the writer, those who retained him, or

APPENDIX II

the Sunday papers where his writings first appeared, have not been identified (*Papers of FLO*, 6: 43–44, 604–10).

37. Olmsted met Sir Richard Mayne (1796–1868), commissioner of the Metropolitan Police of London, during his ten-week visit to the public grounds of England and the Continent in the fall of 1859. Sent by the commissioners of Central Park to study design and management considerations, Olmsted also investigated numerous parks and suburban improvements in Paris and Dublin (*Papers of FLO*: 3: 234–42).

38. Olmsted recalled incorrectly that the series of southern travel letters he had published in the *New-York Daily Tribune* in the 1850s was "A Tour in the Southwest," which formed part of his book *A Journey Through Texas*. At least three editions of this volume were published in Leipzig in German. Olmsted had in fact published the "Southwest" series in the *New-York Daily Times* in 1854, after the completion of his first, longer series of letters entitled "The South." The series of letters he did publish in the *Tribune*, in 1857, was "The Southerners at Home," which he incorporated into *A Journey in the Back Country* (see *Papers of FLO*, 2: 459–61).

39. Olmsted's reply, published in the *New-York Daily Tribune*, June 3, 1873, pointed out that the new system had been in effect barely a month before Jan Vier's letters appeared. Since its implementation the health of the keepers had never been better, they were more effectively deployed at all hours than under the previous system, and none had made complaints to Olmsted or the commissioners about the new arrangement. He stressed that the park's success depended upon a disciplined, specially instructed keepers' force, hired and retained to assist visitors in the proper enjoyment of its peculiar attractions — not to act as ordinary street police or to enjoy the post as patronage appointees. The new system did not cause but was intended to reverse the very demoralization in the force that Jan Vier described, a condition reached over the previous five years. The *Tribune* commended Olmsted's reply the next day and agreed that political patronage had caused the "destruction of discipline and lowering of the standard of character among the force" (*Papers of FLO*, 6: 604–10).

40. On September 25, 1873, the board rescinded Olmsted's organization of the park keepers' force and ordered "that he be relieved of all duties of superintendence" — the park keepers included — "until further orders" (DPP, *Minutes*, Sept. 25, 1873, pp. 296–97; ibid., Oct. 1, 1873, pp. 308–9; see also, FLO to DPP, c. Jan.–Feb., 1875, above).

41. The board assigned oversight of the police force to its executive committee, composed at the time of Henry G. Stebbins, Phillip Bissinger, and Salem H. Wales, the latter two who had sat on the board for only a few months. Lieutenant Robert P. Scofield and sergeant Thomas Beaty were likely the two members of the keepers' force dismissed at this time whom Olmsted mentions here (DPP, *Minutes*, Sept. 10, 1873, p. 262; ibid., Sept. 25, 1873, p. 297; FLO, Patronage Journal, March 25, 1875, above).

42. Olmsted presented his resignation to the board on September 17, 1873, after having failed in July to persuade its members to give his office superintendence of the plantations and keepers' force. Revised bylaws approved by the board in late August had granted his office supervisory powers in name only. His resignation letter stipulated that should the board desire him to continue with "duties of design" he would do so, provided that he "be relieved of responsibilities under which present circumstance I can not satisfactorily meet." The only "modified arrangement" of his duties apparent from the printed *Minutes* of the board took place the following week, when it approved the motion of President Salem H. Wales and "relieved" him of "all duties of superintendence until further order." At the same time it directed him to proceed with the preparation of plans for Riverside and Morningside Parks. Perhaps Olmsted felt that this move shielded him from any opprobrium henceforth to fall on the gardening and keeping forces — while his reputation as a landscape architect would be associated exclusively with the accomplishment of new landscape projects (FLO to S. H. Wales,

Sept. 17, 1873; FLO to Philip Bissinger, July 15, 1873; *Papers of FLO*, 6: 44–46, 595, 610–30, 633–45; DPP, *Minutes*, Aug. 29, 1873, pp. 239–45; ibid., Sept. 17, 1873, p. 282; ibid., Sept. 25, 1873, p. 297).
43. That is, the "Revised and Additional Rules for the Conduct of Patrol and Post Keepers" and the "Conditions of Holding Appointments" that were part of Olmsted's 1873 "General Order" of the Central Park keepers' force but were not specifically rescinded by the board when it abandoned the round system, dispensed with the extra keepers, and authorized the remaining keepers to carry clubs.
44. On January 4, 1882, the board approved the resolution of commissioner Charles MacLean that no person should gain appointment to the police force of the department without presenting a certificate that they had successfully completed the fourth grade of grammar school in the city of New York or passed an equivalent examination before the principal of such a school (DPP, *Minutes*, Jan. 2, 1882, pp. 466–67).
45. Olmsted's information on the devastation being carried out in the park by superintendent Jones came from William E. Fischer, who had directed the original planting of the park in the years 1858–1870, and whom Olmsted had brought back as superintending gardener in 1875. A typical and revealing description written to Olmsted by Fischer is as follows:

> Jones is continuing his sanitary measures in thinning out shrubbery, though it seems he is no longer allowed to grub out any shrubs, but they are mutilating the masses of young healthy shrubbery in the lower park, . . . and they cut mercilessly through it for the free circulation of the air. In the upper park they clean the dense masses of natural growth carefully from the dry branches inside, which nobody can see, as Jones alleges the dry wood poisons the air . . . . If the Commissioners visit the Park it is just as when you bring deaf and dumbs in a concert.

(W. E. Fischer to FLO, Nov. 7, 1881).
46. See FLO to DPP Board, [March 1, 1875], above.
47. The board passed an order banning the cutting of all trees without its approval on August 20, 1873 (DPP, *Minutes*, Aug. 20, 1873, pp. 217–18; ibid., Feb. 19, 1873, p. 684).
48. Olmsted quotes from William Robinson, *Alpine Flowers for English Gardens*, 2d ed., (London, 1875) (See FLO to William Robinson, March 20, 1875, above).
49. Olmsted and Vaux presented their resignation to the Board of Commissioners of the Central Park on May 14, 1863. The board accepted it and the landscape office remained unfilled until the board reappointed them on July 19, 1865. On November 22, 1870, the park board under the Tweed Ring dismissed Olmsted and Vaux as its landscape architects and for the next year assigned design work to its chief engineer and to its landscape gardener. Upon the downfall of the Tweed Ring, the new members of the park board on November 23, 1871, reappointed Olmsted and Vaux as its landscape architects (*Papers of FLO*, 4: 623–24; ibid., 5: 405–6; ibid., 6: 392–94, 493–94, 535, 658–59).
50. Olmsted refers to problems in the drainage system of Central Park that came to light in the summer of 1875. Engineer John Bogart, who had worked on the system when it was installed in 1858, began an examination of it in October 1875 but was dismissed three months later because of a budget shortfall (FLO to George W. Jones, Nov. 19, 1875, above; FLO to William R. Martin, Aug. 9, 1876, n. 23, above; *Papers of FLO*, 3: 27).
51. Olmsted may be referring here to the request of the Caledonian Club and New York Athletic Society in early 1873 to set aside a large portion of the lawn at the lower end of Central Park for a running course (John Knox to FLO, Feb. 24, 1873).
52. Olmsted recounts these incidents, from 1857 and 1876, in his essay "Influence" (above, p. 541), and in his patronage journal entry of September 1, 1876 (below, p. 700).

APPENDIX II

53. Olmsted here refers to developments in the summer of 1877.
54. The two commissioners were presumably the Tammany Hall Democrats William Wetmore and James Wenman.
55. Possibly a reference to the *Sunday Mercury* article entitled "Cornering a City Leech," printed in early December 1877, that reported Olmsted was under investigation by comptroller John Kelly because, with Central Park complete, his job had become a sinecure, and that he was absent from his office for weeks on end but still drew a salary. William R. Martin, near the end of his tenure as president of the department, addressed the charges at the board's meeting of December 12, 1877 (*Sunday Mercury*, Dec. 9, 1877, p. 1; DPP, *Minutes*, Dec. 12, 1877, pp. 433–434).
56. Section 28 of the New York charter of 1873 provided that no clerk or head of a city bureau could be removed until formally notified of charges against him nor until he had had the opportunity of answering them (New York [State], *Laws of the State of New York, Passed at the Ninety-Sixth Session of the Legislature* [Albany, N.Y., 1873], chap. 335).
57. John Kelly notified the department of this action in early December 1877 (John Kelly to William R. Martin, December 4, 1877; DPP, *Minutes*, Dec. 12, 1877, pp. 433–34).
58. On December 26, 1877, the board granted Olmsted's leave of absence; it abolished his office on January 5, 1878 (see [FLO,] "Review of New York City Park Department Polices in 1878," notes 2–4, above).
59. Commissioner Samuel Conover accused Olmsted of profiting from sales of trees to the park department (*New York World*, Jan. 18, 1878, p. 2).
60. One element of the Tweed Ring board's cleaning up of the park involved painting objects white: this included the statue that Olmsted mentions and the skeleton of a whale donated by Peter Cooper (Alexander Callow, Jr., *The Tweed Ring* [New York, 1966], p. 127).
61. When on January 23, 1878, the park board had removed Olmsted as Landscape Architect to the department, they passed laudatory commendations of him and appointed him "Consulting Landscape Architect," his services to be paid for "from time to time, as they are availed of." Thereafter, commissioners made occasional mention of his new position according to their interests. In August 1879, for instance, commissioner Smith Lane proposed to invite Olmsted, as consulting landscape architect, to prepare a general report on management of vegetation in the park so as to realize the original design intent. In October 1881 commissioner Charles MacLean, not wishing to appoint Olmsted to a salaried position, pointed out that the board could at any time secure his advice under the current arrangement. He said this despite the fact that the board had not asked Olmsted for any advice during the period of nearly four years that he had been their unsalaried consulting landscape architect (DPP, *Minutes*, Jan. 23, 1878, pp. 556–57; ibid., Aug. 20, 1879, pp. 166–67; "Harmony, But Not Agreement. Fruitless Meeting of the Park Board," *New-York Daily Tribune*, Oct. 27, 1881, p. 8).
62. Olmsted is referring to the mismanagement of Central Park since his dismissal under superintendents Columbus Ryan, John F. Dawson, and the carpenter Aneurin Jones–men with no standing in the profession of landscape architecture, or indeed in any field. They had treated the park in ways antithetical to the plans he had drawn up over the years with extended discussion and approval of the commissioners. He is also referring to the failure of these superintendents to secure construction of Riverside Park and Avenue according to the plans and specifications drawn up by Olmsted and his staff (see above, pp. 377–81).
63. This quotation is not by Victor Hugo: it is from Alexandre Dumas, *The Count of Monte Cristo*, chapter 12.

64. See, for instance, "The Maintenance of the Park," *New-York Daily Tribune*, Oct. 3, 1881, p. 4; "Save the Park," ibid., Oct. 26, 1881, p. 5; and "The Spoliation of Central Park," ibid., Oct 31, 1881, p. 5.
65. A reference to Calvert Vaux's work as architectural partner with Andrew Jackson Downing from 1850 until Downing's death in 1852, and his involvement with Downing's planning of a public park between the Capitol and White House in Washington, D.C. In 1882, during his own work on the U.S. Capitol grounds, Olmsted described Downing's design for the Smithsonian Institution grounds as "the only essay, strictly speaking, yet made by our government in landscape gardening" (*Papers of FLO*, 1: 74–77; Francis R. Kowsky, *Country, Park & City, The Architecture and Life of Calvert Vaux* [New York, 1998], pp. 45–48).
66. In referring to his early reading of English works of the eighteenth century on scenery and landscape gardening, Olmsted made special mention of the writings of Uvedale Price, William Gilpin, William Shenstone, and William Marshall. His most important instructor in appreciation of scenery in his childhood was his father, who took the family on annual "tours in search of the picturesque" and amassed a significant collection of prints of landscape scenes. (*Papers of FLO*, 1: 115–17).
67. Olmsted refers here to his six-month tour of the British Isles and the Continent in 1850, and his travels in 1856 while a partner in the publishing firm of Dix, Edwards, and Co., which included a two-month residence in London. The travels in America to which he refers included his two journeys through the South in the 1850s as well as childhood "tours in search of the Picturesque" that he took with his family in the Connecticut Valley, the White Mountains, and upper New York State (*Papers of FLO*, 1: 99–100, 116–17).
68. Olmsted studied with Frederick Barton, a survey and engineer, from 1838 to 1840; he studied farming with his uncle Erastus Brooks in 1840 and with the prize-winning scientific farmer George Geddes in Camillus, New York, in 1846. He also took scientific courses at Yale College in 1845, an arrangement that he later viewed as a precursor of the Sheffield Scientific School (Reminiscense of Charles Loring Brace, private collection).
69. Olmsted had managed his own farm at Sachem's Head in Guilford, Connecticut, 1847, and his farm on Staten Island from 1848 to the fall of 1857, at which point he became superintendent of Central Park. He had developed a detailed system for managing the laborers on his Staten Island farm, and had written on the subject primarily in his book *Walks and Talks of an American Farmer in England*, published in 1852. He had been corresponding secretary of the Richmond County Agricultural Society and had written articles for A. J. Downing's journal the *Horticulturist*.
70. Olmsted lists here some of the signers of petitions supporting his application in 1857 for the position of superintendent of Central Park (Petition, September 1857; "To the President of the Board of Commissioners of the Central Park," August 28, 1857; "Names on Petition to Park Comrs –185[7]").
71. In an article in *The Garden* in 1871, William Robinson had written that ". . . the Central Park of New York is magnificent, as many already know. There is not much fine gardening in it, rightly, as I think; but, in point of design, it certainly is much better than any park we have in London. There are, in many places, nice quiet breadths of open grass, and I have never anywhere seen so many great breaks of picturesque, natural rock crop up; fortunately these have been preserved, and now offer the finest positions I know of for planting with rock-shrubs and alpine plants" ("Parks and Public Gardens in America," *The Garden*, Dec. 9, 1871, p. 45).
72. A reference to the suggestion made by his friend Charles W. Elliott, a commissioner of Central Park, in the summer of 1857, that he apply for the position of superintendent.

73. A reference to the architects, gardeners, and engineers on Central Park in the early years. The group included the architects Calvert Vaux (who was Olmsted's subordinate once he became architect-in-chief) and Jacob Wrey Mould; the gardeners Ignaz Pilat and William L. Fischer, and the engineers William H. Grant, John Bogart, John Y. Culyer, John Henry Pieper, and George E. Waring, Jr. Several of these men were Olmsted's collaborators and assistants in later years.
74. That is, his appointment in May 1858 as architect-in-chief of Central Park, following the selection of his and Calvert Vaux's plan "Greensward" as the winner of the design competition for the park.
75. A reference to the rage for raising tulips that swept Holland in the seventeenth century and the enthusiasm in the United States from 1826 to 1844 for growing the mulberry tree species *Morus multicaulis*, introduced from the Philippines, as food for silkworms (Ulysses P. Hedrick, *A History of Horticulture in America to 1860* [New York, 1950], pp. 216–18).
76. Olmsted here describes his response to visiting the estate of Eaton Hall in Cheshire during his first visit to England in 1850 (*Walks and Talks*, 1: 133).
77. Olmsted visited the Parc des Buttes Chaumont in Paris with Édouard André in 1878. The two-year absence from the park to which André refers came during the German siege and occupation of Paris in the Franco-Prussian War of 1870–71.
78. A reference to the four sunken transverse roads and thirty-two arches designed by Olmsted and Vaux for separation of ways in the park. These constructions, with the dense planting that concealed them, created a series of distinct passages of scenery instead of the open, undifferentiated landscape and display of architectural features favored by superintendent Aneurin Jones.
79. In addition to the landscape architects mentioned elsewhere in this volume, Olmsted was suggesting the following men, all from the Boston area: Henry Winthrop Sargent (1810–1882), horticulturist and landscape gardener, a Boston-born banker who retired in 1841 to his estate "Wodenethe" near Fishkill, N.Y., where he practiced his art and prepared important supplements for A. J. Downing's *A Treatise on the Theory and Practice of Landscape Gardening*; Col. Francis L. Lee (1823–1886), of Boston, a wealthy man who devoted himself to botany, horticulture and landscape gardening. The competition plan that he and Joseph H. Curtis submitted for the Back Bay park in Boston in 1878 had received high praise from the *American Architect and Building News*. He lived for some time in Albany, N. Y.; John Robinson, curator of the herbarium of the Arnold Arboretum; Ernest William Bowditch (1850–1918), a landscape gardener and civil engineer of Brookline, Mass. He and his partner Robert Morris Copeland also submitted plans for the Back Bay park competition of 1878. He had a long and distinguished career in both of his fields of expertise; and John Hubbard Sturgis (1834–1888), an architect living in Brookline who was engaged in commissions for several of Olmsted's friends and acquaintances (*DAB*; *ANB*; "Obituary. Francis L. Lee," *Boston Post*, Sept. 3, 1886, p. 4; FLO to [Frederick Knapp], Aug. 5, 1880; *NCAB*, 29: 157; *American Architect and Building News*, June 8, 1878, p. 202; S. B. Sutton, *Charles Sprague Sargent and the Arnold Arboretum* [Cambridge, Mass., 1970], pp. 64–65).
80. The *New York Evening Post* in October 1881 published two articles ridiculing the clearing of vegetation that was taking place under the regime of superintendent Aneurin Jones. Typical of the critique offered was the following passage:

> Everywhere you will find the undergrowth and the shrubbery coming out, the trees cut, and hacked, the wild vines destroyed. The next step will probably be the appearance of old women with pails and scrubbing brushes ready to work at cleaning the rocks of moss, lichens and vines. By clearing out all the underbrush and cutting down trees judiciously it will be possible to see half a mile in any direction from any spot in the park.

THE SPOILS OF THE PARK (1882)

According to the Central Park gardener William E. Fischer, the author of the articles was a reporter for the *Evening Post* named Hubert ("Central Park," *New York Evening Post*, Oct. 22, 1881, p. 6; ibid., Oct. 29, 1881, p. 6; Fischer to FLO, Nov. 22, 1881).

81. A reference to the management of Central Park by the Tweed Ring. The park board cut down trees on the boundary of the park, asserting that "The right to an unobstructed view from his residence opposite the Park is one of the benefits and advantages for which the avenue owner has been assessed." They also directed their staff to clear out dense plantings of shrubbery that Olmsted had established, while clearing elsewhere to "provide extensive views wherever desirable . . . and permit the circulation of air and growth of grass." In doing so, the Tweed Ring board destroyed the indefiniteness of boundary and uncertainty of extent of space that were an essential quality of the landscape that Olmsted and Vaux had sought to create in the park. They also lessened the contrast between different passages of scenery that was a major intent of the designers (DPP, *First Annual Report* [New York, 1871], pp. 20, 26–27, 296–97; for the commentary of Olmsted and Vaux on the Tweed Ring's policies, see *Papers of FLO*, SS1: 250–52, 265–68).
82. The noted English authority on landscape gardening William Robinson (see note 71 above).
83. Jean-Pierre Barillet-Deschamps (1824–1873), who became gardener in chief of the Bois de Boulogne in Paris in 1855 and thereafter played an important role in the planting of small parks and squares in Paris. He also participated in the management of the larger parks, such as the bois de Boulogne and bois de Vincennes — which Olmsted appears to mean by "much more important works" and where he felt that the tropical and decorative plantings favored by Barillet-Deschamps were distinctly out of place (Luisa Limido, *L'Art des Jardins sous le Second Empire: Jean-Pierre Barillet-Deschamps, 1824–1873* [Seyssel, France, 2002], pp. 276–79).
84. A reference to the "fancy dress breakfast" of Mrs. Leo Hunter described in the *Pickwick Papers* by Charles Dickens, chapter 15.
85. Olmsted is translating a passage on page 118 in chapter 5, "Du Sentiment de la Nature" in the work by Édouard André, *L'Art des Jardins: Traité Général de la Composition des Parcs et Jardins* (Paris, 1879).
86. That is, a city square of limited extent and unsuited by size, use, and position for the broad landscape effects that Olmsted and Vaux had made the primary feature of Central Park.
87. Olmsted is referring to the fact that only the design for Central Park submitted in 1858 by himself and Calvert Vaux proposed to sink below the surface the four roads for crosstown traffic required by the rules of the competition. After their "Greensward" plan won first prize, the *New York Herald* claimed that "many competent engineers" said that the quality of rock on the park site would not permit construction of the proposed transverse roads. An article in the *Atlantic Monthly* reported that some engineers had expressed the same reservations ("The Central Park Job," *New York Herald*, May 31, 1858, p. 4; "Cities and Parks: With Special Reference to the New York Central Park," *Atlantic Monthly*, 7: 42 [April 1861], p. 423).
88. That is, the four sunken transverse roads.
89. James E. Cooley (*New-York Times*, May 1, 1857, p. 1).
90. See, for instance, the discussion of changes in the Greensward plan proposed during the summer of 1858 by commissioners August Belmont and Robert J. Dillon ("The Central Park," *New-York Times*, June 7, 1858, p. 5; *Papers of FLO*, 3: 24–26, 194–97).
91. A reference to Peter B. Sweeny and Thomas C. Fields (A. B. Callow, Jr., *Tweed Ring*, pp. 218, 283).
92. In an address to the Board of Alderman on the day of James Garfield's death, mayor William R. Grace (1832–1904), an international businessman and anti-Tammany

APPENDIX II

Democrat, declared that the president's assassination was the "necessary logical result" of uncontrolled patronage politics: "the American political idea lies prostrate before that other idea which sees in the State only an inexhaustible treasury of spoils." Vengeance should not be directed at the assassin, who would stand before the law, but against the "incipient political caste" of the spoils system that threatened the nation's free institutions. The Board of Aldermen read Grace's message and put it on file (*DAB*; *New York World*, Sept. 21, 1881, p. 4).

93. The National Academy of Design was incorporated in New York City in 1826, having as its object "the cultivation and extension of the arts of design." Its membership was to consist of fifty "Academicians," who were chosen from professional artists resident in the city; "Associates," who were resident professional or amateur artists; and Honorary Members, who were non-resident professional artists and "lovers of the arts" (*Constitution and By-Laws of the National Academy of Design* [New York, 1839], pp. 7–9).

94. On or about February 13, 1882, a bill was introduced in the state Assembly to replace the park board of New York City with a single Superintendent of Parks, who would be appointed by the mayor with no provision for confirmation by the Board of Aldermen: a similar bill was introduced in the Senate on February 15 (*New-York Times*, Feb. 11, 1882, p. 1; ibid., Feb. 16, 1882, p. 2).

III

PATRONAGE JOURNAL

[32: 283–87]   Dec. 30th 1873.

  This afternoon I said to the President:[1] "Early in the work on the Central Park a man was employed named Jos Mollard,[2] who soon showed himself so uncannily expert in heavy rock work of all kinds, quarrying and moving, that he was put in general supervision of all such work. He was a Cornish man regularly brought up from childhood in the business and proved competent and faithful in the managmnt of a large number of subordinates scattered over all parts of the work. He held the position for several years and left the park only when work of that class ceased. When we started the Brooklyn Park work we hunted him up and he was placed in general charge of the heavy team work there. When Mr Martin the Chief Engineer left the Brooklyn Park to take charge of the construction of the East River bridge,[3] he had formed so high an estimate of Mr Mollard that he asked the President, as a matter of public interest to transfer him to the bridge work. He has since been there in a responsible position which he has filled satisfactorily but with the stoppage of that work for the winter he is free. The Superintendent of the Park has requested me to obtain from you his appointmnt[4] to fill a vacancy among his foremen until spring in order that he may if possible be secured for his old office of general foreman in starting the new work next spring on the Riverside Park. He is willing to accept the place of foreman and I strongly advise and request that it may be offered him."

  The President having explained to me in detail why he did not think Mr Mollard could be appointed, I said "Had you not better relieve yourself of the responsibility of rejecting him by repeating what I have said to the Board, and by saying that you have seen him and, if you please, that you think it desirable he should be appointed"? The President assenting to this I brought in & introduced Mr. Mollard. What the President said to him, there being three other persons present, one of them not connected with the Department, I do not consider confidential — "I should be very glad to appoint you as requested by Mr Olmsted and Mr Ryan but I can't do everything I would like to do and I can't do this. I have given Mr Olmsted the reasons in detail;

it is sufficient to tell you that political necessities are stronger than I wish they were or than they ought to be. Let me ask you — I confess I feel humiliated that I must do so. Have you any political friends? — You know that in these matters, as the old saying is, kisses go by favor — If you could bring any influence to bear on the members of the Board possibly there might be a better chance for you."

"No Sir," said Mr M. "I can do nothing in that way. I never did, Sir, It is not in my line — Mr Olmsted knows me and Mr Ryan. They can tell you what I am good for on your work — "

"Tisn't that," interrupted the President, "Mr Olmsted has already done so and I perfectly understand but I should be glad if you could be fortified with something that would weigh more, just now, with our Board."

[32: 454–66] February 5th 1874.

An act of the last legislature was so ambiguously drawn as to leave room for doubt whether a certain piece of work was to be done under the Department of Public Works or the Department of Parks. On this ground an order of the Common Council that the Departmnt of Works should proceed with it was vetoed by the Mayor. Early in the session of this year a bill was introduced giving the settlement of the question to the Common Council, the effect of which it is presumed would be to give it to the Departmnt of Works. In the public discussions of the matter nothing appears but a wish to get a highway made as soon and as economically as possible and that in making it some of the great number of laborers lately thrown out of work may be soon employed.[5]

The Bill had rapidly passed to a third reading in the Assembly, a large majority favoring it, when during the period of a Sunday adjournmnt I met one of its members in the Park Commissioners' Office. His business was to procure appointmnts for a few men. After accomplishing it he was asked why the Assembly was so ready to pass the bill. He replied: "It's because the members think that the Commissioner of Works[6] will treat them better than your departmnt in the matter of appointments." As he went out another member came in on the same business. The question was soon put to him and he answered in almost the same words. Meeting a third, I explained to him that the passage of the bill without some amendment would incidentally prevent a most desirable improvement. "Oh! I see", he said, "but the fact is nobody's thought of anything but the patronage." At the request of the President I called on the Commission of Works and urged him in the interest of the city to have a slight amendment made in the bill before its passage. In reply he said, "Mr Olmsted you know very well that this is a fight for patronage." Two days afterwards the Comptroller[7] spoke with me about going to Albany to oppose the bill. In doing so, he used the identical words of the Commissioner of Works. "This is a fight for patronage."

Feby 6th

The lobby of the Park Board Room is every morning filled with men, mostly mechanics, armed with letters from legislators and politicians, seeking employment; in an inner room there are always some of their patrons waiting their turn to see one of the Commissioners; I seldom enter the Commissioners' room that I do not find one or two engaged in pleading the duty of the Department to provide employment for those who are out of work. It is claimed that there were never so many men out of work before in the city; never so much distress for want of employment. At the same time there are two trades on strike, one for higher wages and one to prevent anyone in it from working over eight hours a day. The latter (the Stair builders threaten (says the Times of this morning) not to handle any stone that has been dressed out of the city by men working 10 hours day).[8]

Albany
Feb. 17th 1874.

Coming here on the cars this P.M. President Wales said (to Mr Bacon),[9] "The constant pressure of politicians for employment urged as it is now on the ground that men are starving for want of work, forces us to do a good many things that I can't think right and that trouble me a good deal. I'm strongly tempted sometimes to resign. We are getting stone now for filling at a cost of a dollar a load, when we might get it I've no doubt by contract at 50 cts. The only reason we don't is because of the pressure upon us to give employment to the owners of the carts."

Albany Feby. 18th 1874

I was dining with a friend on a Sunday evening ten days ago when a messenger came to say that the President of the Dept had been to my house and wished to see me at once on business of importance. Calling on him I found that Col ——, a leading republican member of the Assembly,[10] had been to see him and had represented that a certain bill affecting the interests of the Dept of Parks was likely to pass the Assembly the following night and he wanted that I should go with him on the train to Albany the next morning in order that I might supply him with argumnts which he could use to defeat it. I agreed to call on the Colonel early the next morning, prepared if he thought it necessary, to go with him — and did so. Our interview was had in a public room of a hotel. I gave him at once the key to the only argumnt that he was at all likely to use effectively but said that it appeared to me that the bill having passed to a third reading it was too late to prevent its passage in the Assembly. He acknowledged this and that it was not necessary that I should go with him but assured me that he would defeat it in the Senate and even if by any arts and combinations he should not be able to do so the influence he had with the Governor[11] would secure its veto. This assurance he gave me so loudly, vehemently and oratorically as to attract general attention which was evidently gratifying to him, so that when I rose to leave, he also stood up and in still louder and more vigorous language than before assured me of his confidence that he would be able to defeat the upholders of the measure in the Senate. "We'll whip 'em Sir, yet; Rely upon it Sir; They stole a march upon me in the Assembly but I'll whip 'em in the Senate, Sir, I'll whip 'em out of their boots; out of their boots, Sir!"

Today the Senate Committee on Cities met to hear argumnts in regard to the bill. It was to be apprehended that if it passed without amendment, Riverside Avenue would have to be constructed according to a plan on which it had originally been laid out and which I had satisfied the Departmnt of Parks was most objectionable. I was present, therefore, under their instructions to show by plans, diagrams, sections & comparative tables the great advantages which a change of plans such as was not contemplated in the bill would secure to the city.

The first to address the Committee was the same Colonel —— who had with so much warmth & eloquence made himself the champion of the Park Dept at the hotel. He first stated that a delegation of working men was present, one of whom would represent their views and wishes. For himself he had opposed the bill when it was before his house as he had then thought it better that the jurisdiction of the Avenue should be with the Department of Parks, but he found the working men thought differently. He had listened to their arguments and was converted by them to the opposite conclusion. He came before the Committee therefore to urge the immediate passage of the bill. I was very curious to know what argumnt had effected so rapid & complete a change. The Commissioner of Works, the President of the Park Commissioners, a gentleman representing an association of Taxpayers and two gentlemen representing the property holders near the line of the Avenue successively addressed the Committee and I laid the plans before them and explained them.

The Workingmen's spokesman then came forward and began his speech by arguing that none of those who had before spoken had any claims to be heard. Who were the taxpayers whom the gentleman said that he represented? In the end all taxes came out of the earnings of the working man. As for the owners of property on the Avenue whom another gentleman spoke for; it was, he believed, three miles long and if they owned all the property on it they must be rich enough. If they wanted an Avenue there, they might have put their hands in their pockets and got it made long ago and not waited for the legislature to do anything. A lot of plans had been shown to the Committee. The people did not want plans; they wanted work; the men who had been making all their plans might have been better employed at something else and the money they had cost, would have been better spent if it had been paid to working men. The question was how were the people to be provided with work; who would give them the most and who would give it to them the quickest. Now he had had an experience which settled that question. He had been with a delegation of his Association to the President of the Park Commissioners and asked him to put ten men at work. The President gave him tickets for five and said he could not put more on without the consent of the other Commissioners of the Department. The same day they went to the Commission of Works and he put on ten men for them right off without consulting anybody. It was evident then that the Park Commissioners had to get together and consult before they could put men on, but the Commissioner of Works could go right ahead and put on men as fast as they came. All that the Commissioner of Works needed was that the legislature should give him the work to do. Therefore the people demanded of the legislature to let him have it without wasting any more time about plans or about what taxpayers or property holders wanted.

{*This be it noted was the argument by which a legislator — a leading republican — had been led to change his views.*}

Albany
Feb. 19th 1874.

Mr. Hawkins[12] when about to address the Commission on Cities yesterday, was asked whom he represented. He replied that he represented an association of 50 gentlemen who were among the largest taxpayers of New York. He told me that he represented the Council of Political Reform. He is engaged to serve the Dept of Parks by its Committee on Legislation, but the Dept. not being authorized by law to employ a legislative agent; it is stipulated that he shall demand no payment for his services. So he told me.

Tonight we spent three hours (Hawkins & I) with Senator Wood,[13] my business being to give him as complete a knowledge as possible of the topographical conditions affecting the question of a plan, and as complete an understanding as possible of the two plans of Riverside Park and Avenue, and Mr Hawkins's business being to ground him strongly in other respects with a view to his speaking in the Senate for the Park Dept. In the course of conversation he said, "The difference between the two departments is this: If a man who is running for the legislature thinks that to make his election sure he must obtain employment for fifty men he goes to Dept of Works and says so; 'Certainly'—would be the reply—'very happy to accommodate you', and the men would be put on—of course with the understanding that the favor was to be reciprocated. That's what makes that Dept so strong here. The same man would go to the Depart^t of Parks and make the same request. What would be the answer? 'No, Sir! this Department never has gained its ends by such prostitution and it never will. It will be governed in its appointmnts by no considerations except those of the strictest economy.'"

A friend of the Commissioner of Works said to me: "Hawkins is here for Green.[14] Green wants to be Mayor of New York and he wants the Park Dept to get this work because he thinks he can use its patronage to help him." Tonight, Hawkins, talking to Senator Wood, said: "Van Nort has got it into his head that he can be mayor of New York and he thinks that if he can get control of this work it will give him a chance at some critical time to give employment to a thousand men more or less, which may be enough to turn the scale in his favor."

Wood

Feb. [19,] 1874

At Albany —
A bill was before a Committee of the Senate which it was desired to defeat. A senator of the highest standing was consulted about it when I was present. He took up the list of the Committee and reading the names said without lifting his eyes.
"A. can be bought with patronage
B. can be bought with patronage
C. will vote as —— says.
D. well; possibly, an argumnt on the merits would get him.
E. He is close — you can't tell what he will do."

Feb. 24th 1874

A friend [Mr Wales] remarked to me today that one of the Commissioners [Williamson][15] had said to him: "The Riverside matter is not of so much consequence in itself as it is in the effect it may have on the disposition of patronage."

Feb. 25th.

Bogart tells me that a Sunday paper [Mercury] says that Green regards it as possible that he may be so hard pressed to retain himself in the Comptrollership that it will be better that he makes a compromise and giving up his present office take the head of the Park Dept.[16] Hence he is using every means to increase & hold patronage with that Dpt. B. says he several times heard this alledged by members of the legislature, while in Albany.

PATRONAGE JOURNAL (1873–1877)

Febry 1874.

President Wales having returned from Albany said—"Assemblyman ⸻ was on the car and I had quite a talk with him. I tried to stir him up to look at the matter from a higher plane but he could see nothing but the patronage. He asked why we could not give him a few more men. I said 'well now you ought to take a different view of this matter. It's a question of the interests of the city—' 'I don't know that, said he, 'I guess the interests of the city are about as safe one way as another. What I look at is how the poor men are going to be taken care of.'"

[47: 347] Dr W. De F. Hay, Sanitary Superintendent of Board of Health, examined by Committee of Investigation of Legislature reg^d to Street cleaning, testified that he did not think the business of removing ashes & garbage could be done worse.—have always had the impression that the men employ^d in street cleaning were not proper men as a class; that they were taking a little gentle exercise for their health when at work; generally aged & infirm & their actions very deliberate. Should not employ such men to do my private work unless as an act of charity. Times. March 3^d 1874[17]

[32: 512–22]   March 10th 1874.

At this time, as I am informed by the President (D.P.P.) an eminent politician [Green] and one upon whom this Dept. is much dependent for success in its purposes, is laboring with the Commissioners to induce them to remove a man who first became my assistant more than ten years ago.[18] He has been with me in three different works and has always occupied positions of trust & confidence. He has been in his first position under the D.P.P. two years and there is not another man in its employment who has been more efficient in the duties assigned him; who has worked harder, more faithfully more discreetly or by whose discretion and skill the Department has more directly profited. There is not another whose loss it would be more difficult to make good. The President some months since expressed the opinion to me that his pay was less proportionately to the value of services rendered than that of any other man and said that he would propose an increase of it. He failed to do so however.

The only reason assigned by the politician for his demand is that he is a near relative of a man who has publicly criticized both himself and the Department.[19] The President told me that this demand was urged so frequently & so strongly upon members of the Board that he thought it very probable that they would yield to it.

Later

Later (same day) Another member of the Board spoke to me on the same matter. He said that he was informed that the relative above referred to was employed as the attorney of another department the interests of which were opposed to those of the D.P.P.[20]

I could not see any reason in this circumstance why the Park dept should deprive itself of the services of a very valuable servant—"Suppose then" said the Commissioner, "that you were told that the attorney obtained information through him which he might use to our disadvantage, what would you say?"

"Has anyone told you so?"

"Never mind that. What would you say if told so?"

"I should say I did not believe it."

"Why not?"

"Because aside from any question of good faith on his part I don't see how he could know anything which is not public property or which could be used to your disadvantage."

"But suppose you were assured that such information had gone from here and could have gone only through him what would you do about it?"

"You mean, if I were you would I not dismiss him? No, I would not. I would tell him the facts, say that he might have been indiscreet and that I hoped he would be cautious how he answered inquiries about the business of the Dept."

"But suppose his dismissal were asked for by a politician who could give us a great deal of trouble?"

"Asked for on the ground that he was suspected of giving information that he should not?"

"Yes."

"I can only say that there are some things which can be bought at too high a price."

"That is true."

March 19th 1874

A contracting mason whom I lately employed to do some work on my own house today told me that since January he had estimated on over $300,000 worth of work, which had been given up because it could not be done at lower rates than he offered. He said that there were thousands of mechanics now idle in the city because capitalists would not build at present rates of cost of building, and he complained that a chief cause of these excessive rates was the course pursued by the city in supporting a large number of lazy men at high wages who were the chief cause of the refusal of their trades societies to work more than eight hours a day or at moderate wages. He said that the President of two of the Trades Societies were employd as foremen on the park; giving me the name of one [John Tuomy [Tuamy] foreman of Masons & President of Stone Masons Society].[21] The Park Dept were now paying $4.24 per day of eight hours. He could engage men at $3, and as many as he might want of the best class at $3.50. But even at the higher wages he added, "your men don't do half a fair day's work. I met with three other builders who like myself have now almost nothing to do and spent three hours on your work a few days since, watching the men with watches in our hands. We saw a man stand with a pointed trowel set holding it by his left hand and doing nothing. It was 23 minutes by the watch before he put his right hand to it. We saw {men} in a place where they were pretty well hidden who were talking together for two hours without doing a stroke of work. There were many men who did not in three hours do more than 5 percent of the work that should have been required of them. I am sure that your Departmnt although it is paying more than a fair day's wages can not on an average get 50 percent of a fair day's work."

[32: 453]   [c. March 19, 1874]

     On the 26th Jan. 1874, it appears by the Minutes that the Board: "Resolved that a Committee of three be appointed by the chair, with power to make such statemnts and explanations as may be found necessary in all cases where legislation is meditated by the legislature and having reference to this Dept."[22]
     Since then the bill has been every week under discussion & some representatives of the Department have been almost constantly in Albany to influence legislation — as follows — [23]
     The President — 3 times
     Commissioner Williamsn
     Commissioner Hall.
     the Secretary
     the Assistant Secretary
     The chief clerk
     The Disbursing Clerk
     The Landscape Architect twice
     The Chief Engineer — 4 times
     to March 19th
     Green has had his private clerk, Morrison, and John Kelly, President of Tammany has been on the floor of the Senate during the discussion — also a contractor Tracey. Tracey denies that he went for Green[24] —

APPENDIX III

[32: 571–72] March 31st 1874.

Among the men who have visited Albany for the D.P.P. has been one Tracy. He had a paper on which the Senators were named in classes. Those sure for the Bill; those sure against it, & those to be influenced. With the latter he talked as he had opportunity in the character of a (taxpayer) and (property holder). He also canvassed property holders for signatures to a petition against the Bill. The bill was withdrawn last week and it is since announced that Van Nort recognizing his defeat & considering that he has been treacherously dealt with is about to resign.[25] Today I heard one say to another in the Department office. "Tracey don't have to wait long for his pay," and presently found that our order had been given him to supply 900 yards of embankment material at $1 a yard on the park at a point near the property which he owned and the value of which would be favorably affected by the work to which this filling would contribute.[26] The law forbids contracts to be made for amounts exceeding $1000 except by advertised competition & to the lowest bidder.

The Departmnt is now getting filling from other contractors at the same price; the President not long since told me that he felt that it was not right, having no doubt that by advertized competition contracts could be made at considerably lower rates.

[32: 564–70] March 31st 1874

The Board of Aldermen have passed an ordinance intended to make it illegal for any person employed by the city to reside out of it — (afterwards vetoed by Mayor).[27]

Several employees of Board have been to me to ask advice saying that they are now in Brooklyn, to move to NY would add 20% to their household expenses.

The Engineer on behalf of two valued assistants called on the President. The President said all who lived out must be expectd to be removed.

It was pointed out to him that this was equivalent to saying that if they remained it must be at reduced pay and we might lose men impossible to replace. Reply: no man that we can't replace. Not a place we couldn't fill tomorrow, lots of men glad to get it. Experience counts for nothing.

March 1874.

Mr J. W. Gelray — introduced to me by Mr. F. G. Shaw — entered army at 20 yrs {of} age — Col. Shaw's Regiment 22(?) Massachusetts;[28] promoted for gallantry; lost an arm; At close of war, Brevet Lieutenant Colonel, Captain Regular U.S.A. Resigned after 2 yrs service — Friends obtained him appointment in Permit Bureau of Mayor's Office — Found he had nothing to do, that the business of the office was swindling and petty tyranny and that it supplied berths for men whose real value was in their service at primary meetings. Several times told the mayor so and offered his resignation. Mayor at length, as he thinks to get rid of him, gave him letter to one of the Park Commissioners — (Dr Hall). Was offerd position of Assistant Superintendent. Saw the Superintendent & learned what the duties were; said he feared he was not qualified, never having been engaged in gardening or the like & declined — Said that he evidently gained much in respect of Superintendent, & of President & Commissioner Hall[29] by doing so. Would be glad if any other place could be found which he could honestly take. Would be content with moderate compensation.

Suggested Captain {of} Keepers which he thought just in his way.[30]

Thought he could not get any sincere assistance from Havmyer.[31] Havmyer did not like his objecting to his former place & would in fact put obstacles in his way if he could.

Made the suggestion to the President who thought it an excellent one & said he wished it were possible to make such an exchange as he was disgusted with Koster.

[32: 580]   April 6th 1874

Ryan at Board Office, wanted me to try again to get Burns appointed foreman — says he is the best foreman at shaping ground we have ever had & he'd like him in place of some of the sticks[32] we have — men just good enough not to be dischargd — "I'd report 'em for discharge in a minute if I did not suppose they'd send me up just the same sort of sticks in their place. Now there is a vacancy but I don't report it. I just make one of the carpenters I can depend on acting foreman, I know I shan't get as good a one if I report it. He's a good carpenter & a good foreman."

[32:576b]   6th April —

I went to the park stables at 20 minutes before 5 and found the foreman of the Division and several of the cartmen already come in from their work.[33] On inquiry of the foreman I found that to comply with the 8 hour law he allows his men to knock off work at 4:30. They can then get to the stable, untackle and clean off their horses before 5. The horses are fed by a watchman but the men are expected to clean & tackle them before the hour for beginning work, so that (one hour being allowed for nooning) they are at work about 8 h. 20 m.

[32: 585–86]   April 15th /74.

Visiting the Buffalo park,[34] I found yesterday that the laborers employed were working 10 hours a day at wages of $1¼ a day=12½ cts an hour. The Park Dept of New York is paying (as it has been through the winter & for

several years past) 25 cts an hour (8 hours a day at $2) just twice as much. The Buffalo Superintendent[35] early in the winter spent a day or two in the study of the New York work and observed that he had much better men & that they worked harder; he felt sure that his men did half as much again work every hour as those at N. York. That is to say the laborers in New York earn a dollar in four hours in which time they move say 8 yards of material. In Buffalo the laborers earn a dollar in 8 hours in which time they move 24 yards of similar material. Cost in
Buffalo — per yard — 4 1/6 cts.
New York "   "   12 1/2 cts.

[32: 562–63] April 16th

Yesterday the President said to me that there was one thing he could not do — give contracts to men in consideration of political services — "There's Tracey", he said, "I gave him an order for filling at a dollar — it was not because he had been at Albany for us, though he probably thought it was,[36] but because we wanted the filling & I thought a dollar was a fair price for it — but since then another man has offered to supply it at 90 cts; and I took him up and gave him an order for 900 yards. So Tracey comes down complaining. He says the other man has done nothing for us, while he has been working as hard as he could for us and been several times to Albany. I told him that I should allow no such consideration to affect me in the least and if I had had this offer before I gave him his order I should have accepted it all the same and should have refused to deal with him unless he was ready to take the same price. Of course [I] would rather deal with our friends but not at any expense to the interests of the city."

[32: 587–92] April 16th 74

President observed that Mr Van Nort had concluded not to resign but seemed to have started on a new policy. He was going to discharge all the Tammany Hall men in his employ. Callahan (a Tammany H. member of legislature)[37] had been in to get employmnt for some of his men whom Van Nort had just discharged — he had discharged 29 of his men last week, and as he had taken the side of the Park Dept in its fight with Van Nort he claimed that we should take care of them.

April 1874

W. McMillan, Superintendent Buffalo Park writes to me April 20th 1874:
Since 6th December, I have been paying laborers 12 1/2 and foremen 20 cts per hour. On the City & County Hall[38] the *present* wages are, Laborers

12½, Formen 20 c., Carpenters 25, Stone Masons (Setters & Bricklayers) 25 cts, Stone cutters 35 c. per hour.

On contract work, deepening the canal,[39] laborers wages are 15 c. an hour since 1st April.

April 28th

Owing to certain technical difficulties the city is in arrears of payment to engineers who have been employed under the Park Department in surveying & laying out the north end and Westchester districts of the city over 40,000. A Bill to provide for the paymnt and for continuing the work has been for some time before the legislature. Among other duties of the Dept referred to in the Bill is that of placing surveyor's "monuments" at the angles of streets. The sum to be provided by the Bill for all purposes was $100.000. When discussed in Committee it was considered as a Bill for ornamenting the suburbs with "monuments and statues" and on general grounds of economy was about to be thrown out, when the fact was stated that nearly half the amount was for payment of wages already due, whereupon the sum was reduced to $50,000 and the bill reported. The President hearing of this went immediately to Albany and after explaining what the monuments were, the original sum was restored.[40]

(on authority of Commissioner Williamson)

April 29—

Ten urinals (brick walls open at top (— x — ft & — ft high.) were years ago placed on the C park. Neither Mr Vaux nor I were consulted in regard to their plan or position — They were designed to be covered with vines. When I returned to the park in 1871, no vines had grown upon them, I found them in some cases badly placed, conspicuous, the metal work corroded and much out of order. They were cleaned at irregular intervals during the day, were often used improperly & the brick being soft & absorbant, so loaded with ammonia that immediately after they had been scrubbed out I have smelt the odor when passing at a distance of fifty feet on a thronged main walk. When President I succeeded in substituting better arrangements in several cases. In other cases I had ordered the removal of the brick structures & the substitution of the scotch iron, of which several had been imported by the Ring & were lying in store unused.[41] At this time I was often called on by gentlemen who wished to secure an order for a certain urinal patented by a German.[42] It resembled a summer house in appearance & occupied —— times as much ground as those we had on hand. We had one specemin of it in use. I thought it would be unnecessarily expensive and conspicuous & avoided it. "Pressure" continued to be brought on the Board in its favor.

APPENDIX III

Soon after the reorganization of the Board, Commissioner Bissinger[43] told me that friends were urging this upon him. I told him it was unnecessary while we had the scotch urinals still on hand.

On the 7th April, without consulting me or any subordinate, he informed the Board as the President tells me, that he had promised Mr Bacharach that the Commission would take 10 of them at $1000 each. As the Board can contract for not more than $1000 except by advertized competition to the lowest bidder, he asked it to so far meet his promise as to order one at $1000 but with the understanding that the other nine should be subsequently ordered. He wanted them to replace the brick urinals on the C. Park. After some expressed reluctance the Board passed the vote desired — Mr B. immediately afterwards sent for the Engineer & directed him to have one placed immediately. The Engineer came to me for advice & I to the President. I asked among other things how is the work to be charged: to construction or maintenance — It is replacing complete work — of course {it} is maintenance. "But we can't put it to maintenance for we have no money to spare for that — It must go to construction."

"But in our estimates for the year we have allowed but $500 for urinals. And you have now but $20,000 left not already appropriated."

"It was very wrong."

I had shortly before reported on the subject — Report printed, maps prepared — Evident from remarks that no member of Board understood the question[44] —

('75) The urinals have cost *set* according to Engineer's estimate $1600 each.

1875. 21st May.

The matter being referred to on the Board,[45] by Commissioner Martin, as an apparent evasion of the law, the President (Stebbins) stated that the Landscape Architect had recommended the adoption of the urinal. He repeated this statemnt & turned to me as wishing me to support it. I was obliged to say that he was mistaken. I had not recommended it & had not been consulted — but had privately told the President Wales that they were over large & excessively costly.

May 9th [1874]

By act of legislature the Board of the Dept was last week reduced from 5 to 4 members. Dr Hall's term expiring.[46] President Wales has been assuring me that from the manner of the two Democrats he was assured that they were content with the organization & that he should remain President & no further changes be made in the staff offices. This afternoon Col. Stebbins wished to speak with me confidentially. He said "suppose at the meeting this evening it should be determined to hold an annual election, & there should be a wish to get rid of Mr Wales; suppose I should vote for Mr Wales & he, out of delicacy & courtesy should vote for me, & that the others calculating on his doing so should also vote for me. You see he would be no longer President. He ought to have his attention called to this but I can't do it." —

"It will be easy for me to do so if you wish."

"If you could do so without its coming from me."

"I can & will" —

I did so. Finding what I said made little apparent impression on Mr Wales's mind, he repeating that he felt no danger — that there was no desire to get rid of him — I put the case as Col Stebbins had done, and again, making sure that he saw it and he thanked me & said if it came to a vote he would vote blank.

Sunday. Mr Wales came to my house early in the morning & asked what I had said to him. I repeated it word for word — "That is precisely what occurred last night. I foolishly voted for Col. Stebbins feeling sure that the three other votes would be for me, and in consequence I am no longer President & Col. Stebbins is."

Col Stebbins afterwards admitted to me that he had had an intimation of what might occur & he was divided between his duty to his informant & to Mr Wales.

(Wales soon resigned Commissionership)[47]

[32: 640–48] June 2^d 1874.

Yesterday came information that "Tom Stewart"[48] was to be appointed Park Commissioner in place of Mr Wales. A friend of the mayor's who had been told by him that Stewart would be the man said (D^r —— to Ryan) "Tom Stewart is a right good clever fellow; he is a politician of course and will let nothing stand in the way of serving his party interests but aside from that you will find him a pleasant man to get along with." President Stebbins in the afternoon read me a note he had just received from a friend at the City Hall informing him that the appointmnt had been made. The note said that Stewart was chairman of the Liberal Repub. Central Committee and was appointed as an act of grace to that faction. There was nothing else to commend him but that he was a pipe laying politician[49] whom the mayor wished to conciliate.

The papers this morning all take the same view, the Tribune, organ of the Liberal Republicans, only observing that the mayor has made worse appointments.[50]

APPENDIX III

At the Board room I met and was introduced to Mr Stewart, the President & Commissioner Williamson being present. In conversation he presently said something of applications for employmnt & while he was talking a card was brought in — "I suppose," said he, "this is some man who wants to get an appointmnt. I have had several at me already." (His own appointment had not yet been officially notified to the Department.) The President promptly took the occasion to say that in this Department no political appointments were made. The Department had always been managed independently of parties and so on. "Yes", said Mr Stewart slightly frowning. "I suppose that is so; The chief good I expect to get out of it is in the advantage it will give me in dealing with other Departments."

"But" said Col S. "you can only have such advantage by reciprocity in some form and that is very difficult. For that reason I have never allowed myself in the fifteen years since I entered the Department, to ask a favor in respect to appointments of any other Departmnt."

"I did so", said Commissioner Williamson "once, when I first came here; I asked a very petty place for a man who was fit for nothing here and got it and I have had abundant reason to regret it ever since, for I have been asked repeatedly to return the favor by securing the appointmnt here of men to positions for which they are totally unqualified."

The pay-rolls for officers and engineers and for the keepers were brought in by the Secretary. Learning what they were, Mr Stewart immediately took a seat and asked the Secretary to sit with him that he might examine the rolls, putting his finger on each name, the designation of office or duty, and the rate of pay of each man. He asked the number of keepers, of gate keepers and of men in other petty employmnts not laborers. When he had gone out, his character was discussed. "I am told" said Commissioner W. that he is a thorough politician. ——— says he was a politician before he was born: he takes to intrigue as naturally as a duck to water." And it was agreed that he would come into the Dept with but one interest, namely to make use of the parks to bring about appointmnts and secure patronage and that he would be greatly disappointed at the small business to which he would be confined. Col S. also told me that a friend who knew Stewart well advised him to resign as he would "sneakingly" give him no end of trouble in his pursuit of patronage and it would be impossible with the means Stewart would command to maintain the reputation of his Department. To which I replied — "There are two of us; & Mr Stewart is but one."

June 2^d

Entering the President's room at his request one day last week, I found a young man with him who at the moment was saying in a confident pleased way as if he {were} uttering a pleasantry. "I simply repeat that if after having voted for your bills every time through the whole session of the legislature I have not the right to the appointmnt of a foreman from you when I want it, I just want to understand it, that's all?"

"Did you vote for the bills because you thought it would give you such rights here?" asked President S.

"It's no matter whether I did or not. I voted for them and you know as well as I do that it is always perfectly well understood that when a member of the legislature supports the bills of any Departmnt of the city governmnt he is entitled to a share in its patronage. You can't tell me that that is not so and you know very well that what I ask for in the appointmnt of this man as a foreman is no more than my right. If I can't have my rights in this Department I want to know it."

"How long have you been in public life, Mr ———?"

"Not very long; I am a young man as you may see." (a boy in appearance)

"Well Sir, I have been in public life more or less during the last thirty years; I have occupied this seat before now five years consecutively and I tell you Sir, that I never acknowledged such a right; I never went to Albany to ask votes for the Bills prepared in this Department, I never made a bargain expressed or implied with any gentleman for his vote and I never acknowledgd that any member of the legislature had gained a right to dictate to me whom I should appoint for any duty under this Department — I never did & I never will — But when a member of the legislature evinces an intelligent interest in the affairs of this Department as you have done and from an intelligent conviction that such bills as proceed from this Departmnt are calculated to further the best interests of the city, gives his votes and his influence for them as you have done, I naturally feel a respect and regard for him and common courtesy prompts me to do all in my power to meet his wishes in respect to the business of the Department. I am sure that you would not wish a man appointed whom you did not know to be one who would serve the best interests of the city in the office for which you proposed him.

You are convinced that the man you name would be a good foreman — I am bound to respect such a conviction on your part and you may be sure that I will give him the appointment as soon as it is possible for me to do so, but you know that at this time we have been obliged to suspend the larger part of our work for want of appropriations and we have now a number of our best foremen suspended.[51] Under these circumstances you will see that it would not do for us to be making many new appointmnts. In fact we cannot just now make any, but as soon as we can you may be sure that we will do the best for you that we can, not as a matter of right which you can claim of us but as a proper courtesy and mark of respect to a gentleman who seems to have understood the requiremnts of the Departmnt much better than the majority of his colleagues in the legislature."

[32: 642b] 1874

In December 1874, I visited Buffalo. The Superintendent of Parks said that it had occurred several times in succession that from 50 to 200 men had been standing at his door when he first went out in the morning. They were there to seek employmnt and as they must have started from home before daylight and walked three miles, he inferred that he must be paying higher wages than could be got elsewhere, and had therefore reduced to $1 a day. I asked if he felt free to do that without special orders from the Park Commission. He would not to increase wages he said but he did not think that they could object to his doing anything by which the cost of work would be reduced — Wages are thus fixed at Buffalo at $1 a day, for 9 hours. The Park & other Departments in N. York, continue to pay $2 for 8 hours.

[33: 31] 17th March 1875.

D.P.P.

The Board being in session Alderman Gillon(?) sent in his card & was admitted. He wanted certain appointments. He was asked whether the report was true that the Tammany Committee had agreed to divide the patronage of the Dep. P. Works on the basis of 1.50 for every vote for Tilden.[52] "We thought", he replied, "that as there must be some kind of agreement about it that that would be a fair business arrangmnt."

"And when are you going to divide up our departmnt?" —

"All I want now is just these men I have asked for."

Under the same circumstances with Alderman Gillon came in a Member of Congress. After salutations and introductions, seeing that the regular business of the Board was interrupted he said: "Well now I will not take up your time. I'll tell you what I want. I just want three little offices." —

"Three what?" asked the President, not hearing the word.

"Three little offices. I don't know what you have and I don't much care. I have three men I must take care. These are not of much account — most anything you have will answer for them. But I want something somewhere. If you have not any just now, you have only to tell me so and I won't keep you." He was told so (seriously & with full explanations) and went so good naturedly that I think he was willing to see the humorous side of the conversation but he had no other business.

[33: 44–57] D.P.P.
25th March 1875.

The Board is now equally divided, one party urging the removal of certain officers, the other which includes the President resisting the movemnt. It is avowed by the first that those they wish to discharge are all friends of (Green), that they wish to remove all who distinctly owe their appointment or retention to him. In the more important cases no other reason is given.[53] In 1873 removals were made for the reason that G. had not confidence in the men. One such removal was that of the book-keeper. His place was supplied by a gentleman, not a professed book keeper, who had failed in business & whom Mr G. favored.[54]

Day before yesterday this gentleman reported the discovery of an error of $70,000 in his accounts, which leaves the Department with nothing to its credit for construction account. The President immediately gave me a written order[55] (copy appended (B)) suspending all forces on construction. By an established fiction (originally adopted from a motive of political convenience & absurdly sustained for consistency against my repeated protests) the whole engineers & architectural force has been paid, however employed, solely from construction funds. The order of yesterday has the effect of disbanding all these officers, and of reducing the pay of all executive officers one half, by striking us off the construction roll. When informed of the President's order, one of the Commissioners laughed and avowed himself much pleased, for now he said the President has done just what we wanted, suspended a lot of G's men and (A) (under the recent order of the Board) he will not be able to get them back.[56]

Yesterday morning, the Board in session, I stated that the duties of the Dept could not be met without engineers' & architects' services. That one important work—(repairs of Battery sea wall) was in progress under contract, chargeable to maintenance fund—must be superintended by an engineer. There were contracts for construction in progress requiring engineering & architectural certficates of inspection &c. I recommended that the first engineer should be invited to remain on half pay & volunteer to give what superintendence on construction was essential without pay until legislation could be obtained, & that one man in each office should be kept if found practicable on the same terms. One of the Commissioners immediately proposed to retain—(Calkins) on full pay from maintenance fund. "Why"! I said "he knows nothing of the Battery business & would be less valuable in the emergency than any other. He could only be used with advantage on certain works, now suspended, of construction."

"Never mind," was the answer, "we must take care of him. Don't you know his brother is Clerk of the Assembly?"—I did not. The Board adopted this motion, and then my suggestion with an addition of a clerk whom I had not asked for and could have easily dispensed with. Why? In order as I was told by one of them not to offend (Hugh Hastings), an editor of great influence at Albany who had asked to have the clerk's salary increased.[57]

Commissioner Martin goes today to Albany to urge appropriation for our Dept—He told me that he was advised that Green (comptroller) had 3 men there to lobby against it.[58]

It was stated by one of the Democratic Commissioners today on the

APPENDIX III

Board that he understood that all the working force of the Dept of Works was now being discharged to make room for new under the new dispensation of patronage. confirmed

As the catastrophe of yesterday will have the effect of greatly increasing the expenses which must be paid out of our limited appropriations for maintenance, and will thus lead to many uneconomical and improvident shifts, I took the opportunity to again urge a reduction of wages — repeating that we were paying more than twice as much as was necessary for nearly all our common labor. No one denied this & it was conceded to be most desirable that a reduction should be made, but it would not do to be in advance of other departments in reducing.

The order above referred to ((A) p. 2) is a repeal of a rule first made by me in 1868, that a man absent from work more than 2 days, was to be suspended, but would be restored on coming to the Office of Superintendence with a note from the foreman certifying to good character & that his absence was caused by illness.[59] The Commissioner who moved that no restorations should be made except by order of the Board, stated that he was constantly beset by aldermen & other politicians who wanted laborers appointed & that to gain more opportunity to meet these demands this rule must be discontinued.

Today the President stated that the Superintendent reported that owing to reductions, six laborers were wanted. As this number could not be divided between the four Commissioners, it was agreed to make it 8 — and each Commissioner was to have the appointmnt of 2.

Speaking of a certain piece of work, one of the Commissioners (Stewart) expressed a unfavorable opinion first of the engineer, afterwards of the inspector — they were incompetent he feared. I asked the Superintending Engineer what he supposed gave the Commissioner this opinion. "As to the Engineer, all I know is that a few days ago the Commissioner sent a young man to see me who filed an application for appointmnt as an assistant engineer. I suppose he wants to take ———'s place. As to the inspector, he ranks as a detailed laborer. He was appointed by the President at the request of ——— who is a friend of Green's. (Van Valkenberg). Both are perfectly competent" The inspector was removed by order of the Board. (Subsequently, the engineer also)[60]

A few hours after the order suspending work of construction, by which 127 men were thrown out of employmnt, was known on the park, the Alderman from the Yorkville district, in which most of them live called on the President and denounced him for issuing it, (as the President said to me) in the most offensive way. He refused to receive the President's explanation, assumed that it was because the construction funds had been dishonestly misappropriated and a few hours later made this charge publicly before the Board of Aldermen, who then at his suggestion ordered an examination.[61] Two days afterwards this same alderman sent in a list of 60 names of men, demanding their employment.

PATRONAGE JOURNAL (1873–1877)

Of the members of the Commission in 1873 when Scofield, (Lieut of Keepers) was removed, Hall and Wales both told me shortly after that they considered him to be a much better man to command the force than Koster, who was retained as Captain, a few days since.[62] Stebbins said the same thing—that he always found him perfect in his duties, could trust him entirely, had similar confidance with no other commander, and was now ready & would be glad to get him back in place of Koster. He also said that Williamson would vote for him. He could be elected at once but for the two new Commissioners[63] who have never seen him. Hall, Wales & Stebbins each declared or admitted that Scofield was removed to gratify Green.

There has been in 18 years no act of legislation of the State, County or City by which the affairs of the Central Park Commission & the Departmnt of Parks was to be directly affected that has not been made the occasion of attempts and generally of successful attempts to obtain money from the public treasury through "the dispensation of patronage."

26th March, 1875. (5th May)

The Board some time since suspended Captain Koster, leaving the recently appointed lieutenant[64] in command. (I have spoken with him, being commissiond by the President to give him some instructions, for the 1st time on the 5th May, when he gave me the following particulars.) He had several times made a visit to the park at night without finding any keepers on duty but had let it pass. On the evening of the 24th March between 8 & 10 he did so, but on the next, 25th, entering the park at 8 o'ck he spent more than {an} hour on one beat finding no keeper. At 9:30 he met a sergeant, and asked if he had found the keeper on duty on either of two beats which he had visited. The sergeant said that he had seen them both. He was then required to go back with the captain and find them. It was a bright moon light night. After searching some time in vain as they were passing near the cottage on Hern's Head,[65] the Captain thought he saw a movemnt of a window blind in it. Going to the cottage he called and recvd no answer. After trying the door, he found a small window loose and obliged the sergeant to go in at it and open the door. In the door was found a false key. Then drawing a match he found three keepers in the room, all with their coats and one with his boots off. They had each rolled up his coat to serve as a pillow and had evidently been lying each on a settee, with his feet to the stove in which they had made a warm fire. Each had a pipe in his hand and had been smoking. The captain after sending these men to their beats, went on with the sergeant to another beat and without wasting time in looking for the man on duty, went at once to a cottage, (the childrens cottage near the Kinderberg).[66] In this two keepers were found and evidence that they were lodged for the night as in the other case. Going to the 3 other beats, the men were found on duty but the captain said, and Commissioner Stewart who examined those reported told me that he had no doubt that they had been housed in the same way as the others but had been roused and warned by the three men first found. The next day I was in the Board room when Commissioner Stewart, who had special charge of the police for the time,[67] came in and spoke of it to the President. He said unless some explanation could be made it would be necessary to dismiss these men. The President thought this would be hard — a first offence should be dealt with leniently — he thought it was the first offence of these men, their record was good he believed, he was sure that neither of them had been reported against for a long time back and he turned to me, asking if he was not right? I was obliged to say that so far as I knew, no man had been reported against for a long time past. The President, however, said that he would send an order, immediately.

The President had written an order [32: 838–39] suspending the men until they could be examined. Commissioner Stewart begged him not to do so, for that would frighten the men and start them all at work to get political influence to prevent the Board from doing anything. "The Board meets Monday morning, I will have them here tomorrow, Saturday evening, and examine them and report Monday and the Board can then take what action is right before any movemnt can be organized to prevent it." — This was done and on Monday they were all dismissed[68] and though they have made some effort, none have succeeded (May 5th) in getting back. Commissioner Stewart has said to me, that he was much surprised that {they} were able to give the commissioners no more trouble than they had. At their trial, and afterwards in conversation, all admitted the truth of the Captain's report, 4 of the 5 made the usual explanations — water closet, something in his boot, wanted a drink of water — (this from one who had walked near half a mile from his beat on which there was plenty of water.) Donaldson[69] one of the oldest and of the best of the old men, alone, made no pretence of this kind — but said simply "We are all human." All admitted, and pleaded in excuse, that it was a customary thing to do on the force, they were no worse than the rest. Every man did it; the officers all knew it and all allowed it. The very sergeant who gave testimony against them — (who accompanied the lieutenant) had often come into the cottages when the men were off post and sat and taken a pipe with them. So had the others. The lieutenant said he had no doubt it was so — he believed that the sergeant knew the men were in the cottage at the time. He added — if we had the best men who could be picked out of the whole population of New York these sergeants would demoralize them in a month so they would be good for nothing. The sergeants are afraid of offending the men and they think of nothing but to make it as easy for them as they can. There are four sergeants and each of them sits in the station house 6 hours a day, then makes an inspection — that is to say he goes out on the park and does not return to the station that day; He is supposed to make a round of the park and see that each man is on his post or beat. There is no sergeant for the upper station & the men go there, get their clothes & go on and come off duty, no officer observing them. The captain has been accustomed to make his own inspection by driving over the roads in a buggy. Except at the unveiling of a statue and at some of the concerts, I have never, in 3 years, seen him on his feet in the park. I have never seen him in the Ramble or anywhere off the drive, even on the above occasions never 100 yards from the drive; I have never seen him but once, (a ceremony at the Muster Ground where he stood with the reviewing officers & allowed his men to take care of themselves) in any of the small parks.

The above occurrence was on a clear, mild night (following rain) and before the hour for closing the park to visitors. Both Commissioner Stewart & the lieutenant told me that they were satisfied it was and long had been the rule that the men going on duty at night went directly to a cottage and passed most of the period of duty asleep.

[33: 57–58]   26th March (1) 1875.

Two or three weeks since, the President had an interview with the new Commissioner of Public Works[70] and it was agreed that a reduction of laborers' wages should be made simultaneously in both Departmnts. Their conclusion was reported to the mayor who said, "Wait a bit and let me feel the way." The President yesterday, apprehending that with the special charges which would now come on our maintenance fund, we should not be able to keep our expenses low enough, I said "if you make a reduction of wages to anywhere near the market rate, you will gain more than enough over the necessary additions. Why should you not make a reduction at once?."

"I'm afraid," he replied, "that we cannot do it. You know that the mayor stopped us in order that he might consult about it. He has said nothing more about it but yesterday Mr Hewitt, (M.C.)[71] who is in his confidence & whom he probably has consulted, spoke of the proposition to me & said it would not do — he said the mere suggestion of it, if it should get out in his district, would make a revolution."

31st March 1875.

The President said to me this morning that in all his experience the pressure for removal and appointments had never been as great or made in such peremptory and intolerable forms as at present.

As I was entering his room a man who looked like a prize fighter was passing out, who saluted me as an acquaintance. I asked who he was. "Oh he is an agent of the President of the Board of Aldermen;[72] comes here often to get appointments for him."

Commissioner Williamson told me that the respectable members of the Democratic party were many of them not pleased that all the laborers of the Dept of Works were discharged in order to gain a new distribution of patronage — a large part of those discharged were democrats and the course would breed dissatisfaction.

Tierney.[73]

[32: 576] 3ᵈ April 75.

There was a debate in the Board this evening in which it was evident that each party was desirous to draw from the other a report that could be quoted publicly, to its injury, favoring a reduction of wages. "Oh, you know very well," said Commissioner W. "that if we should pass a resolution now for a reduction of wages, there's not a member of the Legislature from this city who would dare vote to give the Department a dollar." There is a bill before the L. appropriating $817.000 to the Dept.

[47: 330]

The Times. 8ᵗʰ Ap. 1875. says that during the whole 13 years existence of the Old Park Commission the ward politicians were ignored in the appointment of laborers and to the selection of foremen & heads of bureaux. "To that policy we owe the fact that the C.P. was practically completed without a taint of jobbery." The Tribune of same date reports interview with John Kelly in which he observed of Mr Green that "he had always stood ready at any time to grant favors to Republican politicians if they would assist him in procuring such legislation as he might need."[74]

[33: 129–51] 27ᵗʰ April 1875

I reported to the Board that for the time actually at work in the field — i.e. making due allowance for time used in traveling after & before roll-calls — the Depart^t was paying at least 27 ᶜᵗˢ an hour for wages of laborers of an inferior class.[75]

The Superintendent confirmed this calculation, and the President said he did not doubt it.

Contractors are paying for 1ˢᵗ class laborers 12½ cts an hour — in the suburbs less, (see Culyer's letter).[76]

27ᵗʰ April 1875

The Herald of today states that the present President of the Department of Parks has "on occasions denounced," Comptroller Green's interference with the Department of Parks "'as a system of interference and espionage inconsistent with the interests of the city and injurious to the Department'" — (these words being quoted)[77]

28th April 1875.

The Board of the Dept has for some time passed (since Jany 1st) been equally divided between two parties — the friends of the Mayor Wickham and the friends of the Comptroller Green.[78] Of late the antagonism has been very marked and at times somewhat heated.

P.S. Shortly afterwards Martin offered resolutions in the absence of Williamson. The President fearing they would pass became much agitated. Martin began to read another and the President to remonstrate. "Oh!" said Martin, "don't you be alarmed — wait till I get through." Whereupon the President rose & said I'll tell you what I think of you, Sir, You are a contemptible puppy." — At this I left. The next time I saw the President & Martin together, they were conversing amicably.

The Times of this morning has a leader in which it is assured that the Green party is fighting simply to keep it out of the hands of political jobbers; the other simply to capture it in the interest of Tammany politicians. On the supposition that something has been gained by the latter, the Times asserts that the property (of the parks) is not being as well looked after as it was, and that if the Mayor is successful the park will be utterly ruined, and Mr Green is called upon to give his friends in the Dept such encouragment and assistance as he can in their resistance.[79]

The fact is that the Park has not for many years been as efficiently and economically managed as during the last month, and that the struggle is in no sense as to whether the patronage of the Dept shall be used or shall be prevented from being used for the benefit of the politicians, but whether the Mayor or the comptroller shall have the benefit of it.

28th April 1875.

In the Times article of today headed "Another raid on the Central Park" it is said:
"The great work [of constructing C. Park] was carried out without robbery or jobbery chiefly because politicians were not allowed to meddle with it", and the whole article assumes that up to 1st Jany 1875, when Martin was appointed a Commissioner, the park had been completely free from the pernicious influence of political patronage.

29th April — 1875

Under the direction of the Commissioner of Accounts, 3 or 4 men have been engaged daily for some weeks and are still engaged in examining all the accounts and vouchers of the business of the Departmnt for several years past.⁸⁰ The Committee room of the Board has been given up to them for the purpose, the labor is great, the cost to the city considerable and the irritations caused by the proceedings very wearing to the President, Treasurer and Officers chiefly interested. A few days since the President referring to it said to me. "This is all done to make a place for a book keeper. See note of 25th—I knew it from the first. If I had consented to turn out Mr L———. all this trouble would have been saved."⁸¹

29th April 1875.

The President today expressed to me the conviction that the Comptroller would not allow a single bill to pass the legislature favorable to the work of the Departmnt. I asked why—"Why?—Why should he when he is attacked in the way he is, here? Have you seen this letter of Mr Martin's published this morning"?

"No."

"Well then, read it!"

"Is this from the Times?"

"No, it was written for the Times but they would not publish it & he sent it to the World."

The letter is a proper reply to an "attack" of the Times on Martin in which facts are mistated and base motives attributed to him.⁸²

April 29th 1875

There are two ways in which the value of "a place" may be increased, either, that is to say the emoluments may be increased or the obligations made lighter. There is a constant tendency in both directions and men in office are striving to have their duties made easier and more agreeable and the pay, commonly in some indirect form made greater. Both processes can be carried far without attracting the smallest degree of public attention.

An officer who is eager to get more and better work from his subordinates or who is disposed to require duties of his subordinates demanding more intelligence, skill, method or industry will be unpopular with them & this unpopularity will act through a circuit upon those upon whom he must depend for means to enforce his wishes.

The manner in which my efforts to secure good service of the Keepers is the most marked illustration of this of my personal experience. (For outline see letter to the President July 30—1873.)⁸³ Less marked but not less weighty to me—the whole organization of management—of C.P. (see also above letter which gives outline to that date.) Since then till this spring 1875 have kept systematically aloof. The removal of Ryan and appointment of Muncwitz led me to ask to have a distinct responsiblity in the management again. By laws revised accordingly.[84] At this time the Dept is more closely run than ever before and I can ask for no increase in any division of force. The total force employed on C. Park is about 400, of which but 10 rank as working gardeners (omitting those for hothouse & nursery). Efforts to secure wild character in rocks ineffective hitherto. Demand of foreman for 500 yards of soil for lower division of park. I object & ask for what. To fill up and round out surfaces on declivities and among rocks where soil washed out — done every year — the rocks (N.W. of) Copcot (near VI) pointed to.[85] Examination showed that peaty soil and ferns set in there year ago by me all last year overlaid and the surface rounded and smoothed out with soil and turf. Gave orders that no more should be done and showed what was desirable — on the 27th April, going to the place with the gardener[86] to instruct him about new attempt to wilden it, found 5 men, laborers, engaged clearing the ground & rocks, raking out all loose and matted vegetation, patting round & smooth the surface with back of shovel and sweeping the crevices and faces of the rocks with a (carpet) corn broom. Asked who was in charge — no one. Had been told by the foreman to clean out and fix up the place and were doing it in the usual way. The Superintendent came as I was standing, puzzled to know what to do with them. He said he had been over all the division and had not seen the foreman, might look two hours without finding him. The men finally ordered to go to a gardener and dig holes for trees under direction of Superintending Gardener who was with me. — An hour afterwards the Superintendent found the men back again & at the same work. The following (3d) day he found the foreman who said he meant no disrespect but thought there must be some mistake as he knew the rocks needed some cleaning. Therefore when he found the men at other work and heard their report he sent them back with orders not to do any more at the particular place where I had interrupted them but to finish the work on the other side. He knew that Mr Olmsted could not wish the rocks to be left with heaps of rotting leaves packed among them — but the men were again allowed to go to work with no one in charge & under general orders to clean up the rocks only not so carefully & completely as usual.

Going over the ground afterwards with the foreman, he saw a place which his men had happened to neglect. It was a mat chiefly of Chinese honey-suckle growing over a flat piece between and below two bold blocks of rock. On and in this mat were a few russet and yellow dead leaves, adding greatly to its beauty. The foreman pointed it out to me and said "Now, there, Mr Olmsted, I know you would like to have them leaves left there." And he could evidently hardly believe me sincere when I said that I certainly would. While he professes his intention of obeying orders; it is evidently, with a certain degree of contempt for my taste and no good will, that he receives instructions under which the smugness will be lessened, which for many — years it has been his chief business to gain and preserve as far as possible.

APPENDIX III

1st May—1875.

The President soon after the appointmnt of Commissioner Martin in Jany began to say of every actual proposition of Martin's or which was sustained by him, and which favored a change either in the personnel or the methods of the Departmnt, that the Comptroller would regard it as moved by personal hostility toward himself on the part of Martin; that just so far as the Board allowed itself to go with Martin, under whatever good argumnts, it would lose the confidence, favor and support of the Comptroller, and that only through the support of the Comptroller could it hope to succeed in anything.

Apprehension that the report of the Commissioner of Accounts[87] would condemn the system of accounts, for which he considers the Comptroller responsible, and that fault would be found with the old Commission in which Green was allowed to order everything to suit himself has made him feel more and more that his own reputation is bound up with Green and that he must depend for defence and support on Green. That anything reflecting on one is a reflection on the other. That an admission that anything could be better than it has been before Martin came in, is an admission of weakness. The prolonged and silent investigation of the Commissioner of Accounts and the constant urging of improvements by Martin has gradually brought him to a condition of the most painful and excited apprehension, and for a week or two past it has been difficult for me or for the Superintendent of Parks to make the simplest suggestion without drawing from him manifestations of this state of angry jealousy. He once said to me "Martin is the worst man I ever knew. He is a worse man than Tom Fields."[88] He has repeatedly said that unless Green was conciliated he would allow nothing to pass the legislature favorable to the Dept and he could not be conciliated as long as Martin continued his course. That Green was the strongest man in N York and would get the better of all who opposed him.

I had not been aware how completely he had been driven to identify himself with Green and Green with the Departmnt when I made my first general report after assuming supervision of Superintendence under the new By Law. In this report I showed that the fund remaining for maintenance for the rest of the year was smaller than for the similar period of any previous year— relatively to the price of labor and work to be done smaller than under Green, and sought to suggest means by which the park could be properly kept with less labor than usual. To do so I pointed out various matters in which I thought savings could be made and stated how they might be bettered.[89] I had intended to read the report privately to the President and get his approval before presenting it to the Board, but not finding him in and obliged to leave town to attend a funeral, I left it for him to read. He failed to read it until the Board met. When it was then read, as one of the Commissioners told me the President said that it appeared to him an attempt to gain credit for myself at his expense and asked to have it laid over.[90] On reading it over with him afterwards he questioned many of the statements and one incident of no consequence as affecting the conclusions, quoted from a statement to me of the Superintendent I found not to be strictly accurate. To remove all grounds of apprehension that the report would be used against him or Mr Green, I offered to ask leave to withdraw it & did so — on the ground of its containing an inaccuracy. The Board consenting, I then revised it, omitting all the passages which he disliked but making my recommendations more distinctly. I then read the revision to him & offered to strike out anything else, omitting any suggestion of which he did not approve, but he found none. When it came up in the Board, however, at an adjourned session (for the purpose of considering it) he moved it be laid on the table without reading, because he wished to examine the suggestions more carefully. They were important & he did not know that he had any objections to them but at this time when there seemed to be a disposition to revolutionize the business of the Dept, he was disposed to receive every suggestion for change with caution and should not be prepared to act — The Board consented — At the same meeting (1st May, 75)[91] he offered a resolution to restore Captn Koster, but after hot debate on a point of order, withdrew it.

5th May —

My report was again called up and again the President advised that its reading be postponed & the Board assented.[92]

5th May 1875.

Meeting of Board, Annual election postponed — motion of Martin seconded by the new Commissioner ODonohoe[93] who takes the place of Stewart. President afterwards sent for me to talk about it — Considers it evidence that Donohoe means to join Martin in resisting Green's party in the Depart^t — Then told me that he expected the Commissioner of Accounts would make a report intended to give the Mayor ground for removing him & Williamson (Treasurer),[94] that he should have to reply to it & would want my assistance in preparing his defence. "This is all done only because the Tammany politicians have not been able to get as much from me as they wanted. Alderman McCarthy[95] threatened me a long time ago. Then he came in again, after insulting me before the public in the Board of Aldermen. I was astonished at his impudence. He came in without sending in his name, or knocking at the door. Came right in and drew a chair close up to me, where I was writing at my desk, put his face close up to me, stooping and looking up to me with the most brutal expression I ever saw on a man. He said a man in

APPENDIX III

whom he was interested had been suspended by the Superintendent and he wanted him immediately restored. I answered, that will be a question for the Board to settle sir, I cannot restore him but will refer the question to the Board; then he looked so wickedly at me, I added, 'if it depends on my vote, I do not think he will get back.' He drew back at that & threatened me in very coarse language and after he had got out of the door and closed it he reopened it and putting in his head, 'You'll find there's a day of reckoning coming for you. Your time is short'—or something like that. This is what he meant. If I wouldn't do just what such fellows as he want, they'd find some way to drive me out and disgrace me."

The Treasurer, said there was no doubt of it. "And they are after me because I won't turn out every republican. They want every republican turned out and to put in their own men without any regard to fitness. I won't aid them in that, and so they mean to turn me out."

5th May 1875

The President asked me to instruct the lieutenant commanding how to proceed in carrying out the orders of the Board providing for night watchmen and a special class of invalided men[96]—"Why," said the lieutenant reading the list, "there are men on the force much more disabled than any of them. There's old —— for instance, he's hardly able to walk. (I had this man dismissed 3 years ago on surgeon's certificate that he was unfit for duty) he's not on it, and why did they put Loeffel[97] on it? He is all right so far as I know." In the evening Loeffel came to me and said he had seen the list in a newspaper and I might explain what it meant. "The doctor told me he found me perfectly sound and I never had a sick day in my life. I have a father & a wife & 6 children to support and I want to make all I can. I went to Mr Conklin[98] as soon as I saw it, and he advised me to come & see you." I promised to ask for the surgeon's report[99] & see if there had been a mistake.

13th May.

The Board today adopted the propositions of my report (see note of 1st May) with a preamble setting forth the special necessity of reducing the cost of labor in all possible ways—(See Minutes).[100] In the course of the debate on the proposition to exact full 8 hours work the President said that he had no doubt that the Department might within a week put a force of 5000 men at work at $1—or $1 & a shilling (1.12½) for 10 full hours. Nor did any Commissioner express a doubt about it, i.e. we have been paying (as I reported with the assent of the President) 27 cts an hour when we could readily get better men at 11¼ cts an hour. In a special emergency and for special reasons, set forth in the preamble & in a circular (poster) addressed to the men by the President, we are taking courage to screw our wages down to 25 cts. an hour.

PATRONAGE JOURNAL (1873–1877)

[33: 158–81] 21ˢᵗ May 1875

    The night after the carpenter began to set the punch boxes, (a device of mine by which it could be determined whether the night watch went their rounds) one was smashed and another wrenched off and removed. A day or two afterwards the Board of Aldermen adopted a resolution, directing an investigation to be made as to the expenses of the Landscape Architect.[101] At a meeting of the Park Board today I urged a resolution (adopted) offering a reward for the detection of the man who removed the punch boxes. One of the Commissioners said he supposed it was one of our own men. "No doubt it was", replied another; "I am told that it was some of our men who don't like Mr Olmsted's ideas about these things that got the Aldermen to pass that resolution yesterday that he should be investigated."

    The Commissioners also agreed on believing, or in accepting Mr Conklin's opinion that the stealing of eggs & plants & breaking off of nests was the work of our own men.

22ᵈ May 1875.

    I have made repeated efforts since last winter to get the Commissioners to come with me to the park that I might point out to them the evidence of the results of ignorance and blundering in its managmnt; the need of reforms and the falsity of statements, reports & complaints by which they have been more or less affected. I have invariably failed. After reading a long circumstantial report on the ruin of the turf of the park at their meeting yesterday[102] in which I begged them to see the facts for themselves — I verbally pressed upon them the need of their doing so. After discussion it was found that today at 4 o'clock all were free and it was agreed that they should meet me at that time on the park. At 5 two arrived, the others failed. It was agreed by these two, Martin and ODonohoe, that my estimate of the destruction of the turf was much within the fact — at least one half the turf of the Mall being absolutely dead & the ground bare.

22ᵈ May 75 continued.

    In the morning, having invited the newspapers to send representatives to see the statue of the Falconer, the setting of which is just finished,[103] I took them over the ground & they came to the same conclusion. The reporter of the Tribune, who a few days since stated that he found the turf never in better condition, acknowledged that more than half of it had been tramped to death.

APPENDIX III

24th May.

The Tribune reporter promised me to see the City editor and deliver him a message from me requesting that he would do me the favor to simply state the fact as the reporter might bear witness to it, or as he might observe it for himself. But the Tribune, though it has a paragraph on park affairs, has no word on this subject.[104]

The Times has a report about the park in which it says that the grass in all the broad sweeps is beautiful. "There are however numberless places where the turf suffered terribly during the winter and where patches of dull brown stand out. These the authorities are commencing to cover with fresh sods [not a sod is being laid or has been except perhaps a little edging] and no doubt by the middle of June all will be perfect."[105]

There were reporters from the Herald (Macdonna), Tribune (McCarthy), Times, World, & Post, all but the last of whom went over the ground with me and saw and acquiesced in my statemnt that on the Mall, the Ball Ground & the East Green, the larger part of the turf was dead & the ground bare and that there was evidence that it was the result of foot wear — points protected from foot wear being in good condition, the turf though not very even, being thick and luxurient, while points most open and tempting to trespassers were completely worn down — no trace of turf being left.

The Tribune of this morning has the following —

"It is so much more agreeable to praise than to criticise that we thank the Park Commissioners for allowing us to congratulate the city on the completion of three or four fountains in our small parks, before the first hundred years of our national existence are over. We hear rumors that some time during the next century the fountain in City Hall Park will again be permitted to moisten its parched lips of marble, and that within the lifetime of babies now playing in Madison square the fountain in that public nursery may be expected to gush — if gushing has not been driven out of fashion by recent frightful examples."[106]

Not a stroke of work has been done on the fountains for 6 months past, and the Dept has not had and yet has not a dollar that it could legally apply to the purpose.

Previous delays in constructing fountains has been due to the failure of contractors — specially in a contract made under the Tweed ring in 1871.[107]

23d May 1875.

When the error of accounts was discovered in March (See Note of 25th March) and the Engineers force put on half pay to be defrayed from Maintenance Account — an exception was made in favor of Calkins — who has all the time recvd full pay though having no other responsibility & doing no more work than others.[108]

Today Bogart (Superintending Engineer) when I asked about some work with which Calkins was charged & which should have been completed, said in explanation, Calkins has not been worth much lately. He has been too much interested in getting his pay raised. He says Stewart (Commissioner) promised his brother that it should be advanced and he has been worrying because it was not done. (Stewart has retired.) Calkin's brother is Clerk of the Assembly (?) and at the close of the session was complimented by the gift of a valuable gold watch from members of the assembly — (See newspaper reports of closing proceedings).[109]

Commissioner ——— told me that Calkins gave him valuable assistance in carrying through a bill not concerning the Departmnt, in which he had an interest.

May 1875

In spite of the Mayor's injunction (see his Annual Message 1875. Jan.) and the professed and formal acquiescence of the Board (it will be found in a letter to him of the President) in his view that the Departments should not attempt to influence legislation or have any business at Albany except through him,[110] 3 out of 4 members of the Commission have each this winter been more than once to Albany avowedly to influence legislation — One in favor of proposed legislation to which the Mayor is warmly opposed.

23ᵈ May.

Legislature adjourned. During the last week Commissioners Martin & ODonohoe (new) have been at Albany & by their influence the Senate abandoned an amendmnt reducing the appropriation to the D.P.P. from 575– to $250.000 — and granted all asked.[111]

28th May 1875.

At a meeting of the heads of Departments it was agreed to reduce wages from $2 for a day of 8 hours to 20 cts an hour.[112] The Times (2ᵈ June) states that it is the intention to work two sets of men 5 hours each daily and the motive to thus get opportunity to employ a larger number of those who are pressed as candidates — but probably the fact that the money which can be commanded for the remainder of the year is insufficient to give steady employment to those now engaged has had more influence. I reported at the last meeting that our force was inadequate for the work to be done in every class of workmen and that nonetheless a considerable further reduction was necessary {because} of the rate of expenditure.

In a report of the Dock Commission (published Tribune 3ᵈ June) in which the intended reduction is announced with other retrenchments, some-

APPENDIX III

thing *"approaching"*—*"more nearly* corresponding" to the economy of private undertakings is claimed to be aspired to. It is stated that the amount saved by the reduction of wages alone will be $50.000 a year.[113]

The Departᵗ of Works was the 1ˢᵗ to act on the agreement. The laborers at first declined to work on the reduced wages and came to the City Hall to protest & plead but on the 2ᵈ day went to work—(Times of June 2ᵈ).

On the 3ᵈ the Board, D.P.P. met & the President reported what had been agreed to at the meeting at the City Hall. The proposition to carry it out was made. Commissioner ODonohoe asked that its consideration might be postponed—said he could not vote for it—Explained that he was Chairman of the Tammany Committee of his Senatorial District in which were many laboring men. If the Dept made this reduction he would never be able to explain it to them. He thought it a great mistake. He wanted to see the Mayor & Genl Porter—(Commissioner Public Works) and remonstrate with them.[114]

Rates of wages D.P.P. May 1875 for 8 hours:
- Carpenters 3.75 to 4–
- Plumbers 3.50
- Painters 3– to 3.75
- Masons 4.25
- Carts 3.60
- Double Teams 5.60

May 1875

As I pass over the Park now with Mr Fischer, pointing out to him places on which I am most anxious to have something planted, he often says to me, "Yes, this is one of these places where we did not get through. We began planting in the fall and could not get in time all we wanted to complete the group from the nurseries and put off completing it till Spring, then Mr Green would say that it looked well enough and he considered all this part of the park finished and we must do all we could on new ground where what we spent would have more effect at once."[115]

At others, he says, "I remember planting this ground, and at one time it looked very well here. But afterwards they wanted large shrubs somewhere else and came and took them out."

There are still many points especially about the pond and in the South East part of the park where in the first construction I had the surface approximately shaped by common foremen and laborers, leaving it smooth and rounded like a dish cover, directing the Gardener that when the planting season came he should have its formality broken by the planting men while working under his own eye. Mr Fischer now points out several of these places, which have remained unplanted and unmodified from that day to this.

PATRONAGE JOURNAL (1873–1877)

May 1875

When the Dairy was built,[116] it was designed to have it look out upon a nice little croft upon which a cow or two and calves were to be kept for a part of the day, simply to help make out a pleasant and appropriate picture. The croft was prepared and was very pretty — a fine close turf & the ground being moist very green & mountain like. The Ring of course misused it — a little stable was built for the cows — it was used as a paint shop. On the change of administration in 1872 I had some rows of ugly formal trees which had been planted taken out, directed some more harmonious planting on the borders which has not yet been done, and begged Ryan to put a couple of nice gentle little cows that would not hurt children if they should stray near them, in the croft. I fully explained the idea to him — or as fully as I well could. He said he understood and would attend to it, which in time he did but in his way, by tethering an old Kerry bull upon it, who amused himself by pawing and digging up the turf. When he had completely destroyed it in one circle he was moved to another, and this process has been repeated. The ground has been reseeded and I hope this summer to take some pleasure in it.

[43: 519]1875   21 June.

(Illustrations of careless newspaper reports). The Tribune had a Monday morning report of the park — describing the turf as never in finer condition — I found the writer of the report on the park the following week and on looking at the turf he acknowledged that not more than half of it was alive.[117]

Today the Times has a similar Monday morning review — in which the Camera obscura is described — The camera was closed last autumn and the house containing it was torn down more than a month ago.[118] (Reporter asking me to assist him in obeying orders to find fault with something.) Reporter coming to me in town for material of a report of observation on the park had never seen the park & did not know how to go to it. In conversation I used some slightly technical word — "Stop," said he, "what was that word? That was a good word, how do you spell it? What does it mean?"

[33: 190–95]   8th July 1875.

Just at the close of the session the legislature passed the Bill providing the Dept with construction funds. As to the means by which they were led to do it, in a recent discussion of what work should be undertaken under it, one of the Commissioners in urging a measure said that it was desired by ——— a member of the legislature, who had done much to carry the Bill, who expected it and had a right to it. Another said that the object of this legislator was to make employmnt by starting the work in question for the laboring men in his district—($30,000 was on these grounds transferred from other work on the list I had prepared to this—in the schedule of work for the year).

The Bill having passed was held the full time allowed by law by the Governor,[119] and when I last asked no official copy of it had been recvd by the Departmnt. On the newspaper statement that it was a law, however, the Board has been making preparations for starting the year's work. (All the planting intended to be done last spring necessarily goes over a year). I have arranged and reported a scheme of works which to carry out would require an average force of 300 men from 1st July to January. It will be past midsummer before we can put 100 men at work. Now that we have the means and everything is settled as to what shall be undertaken, all business is delayed and embarrassed by the difficulty which the Commission is in as to whom it shall employ. There are not to my knowledge half a dozen men in its whole force of administrative agents from myself down to foremen and messengers whose further employment is not a matter of doubt. The engineer is threatened. The Engineer & a clerk and draughtsmen of the old staff remain as yet on half pay. There are no rod men, and although work is ordered there is no force for laying it out, setting stakes etc.

I reported this to the President a week ago and asked immediate action. There has since been no meeting. One was called for yesterday but Commissioner ODonohoe was at Long Branch,[120] and it was not thought courteous to proceed in any matter of appointmnt in his absence. Urging the necessity, I was privately consulted as to the political standing of the men whom I wanted restored (suspended assistant engineer & rod men) whether Tammany or anti Tammany. I knew nothing of this. After due consideration I was authorized to employ them for one week—leaving the question of their appointmnt open.

With regard to labor—

The placards, one at the outer door & one in the lobby of the Board room ("No Labor Tickets Given out") remain displayed as they have for two years or more. Understanding this, since it has been known that the Bill is signed, there has been a constant body of men applying for employmnt and of politicians waiting to urge their claims on Commissioners occupying the sidewalk, stairways and outer and inner lobbies of the Board room. There are men in the crowd whom I have seen almost daily for six months or more in the same place with many new ones.

Two weeks ago, urging a resolution directing the immediate employ^t of 100 men, one of the Commissioners said, "That would give us 25 a piece. Now I've no doubt that every Commissioner would find it a great relief to him to be able to dispose of that number of the applicants who are more urgently pressed upon him. I know that for my part there are half a dozen men whom I have been importuned about since last Christmas almost every day. Someone is trying to see me about them almost every hour. They come to my house and to my office and they are now outside the door there waiting to get at me as I go out. They follow me in the street and get into the cars omnibus with me. I've no doubt its the same with all the rest of you, and if we could each put on but half a dozen of the most pressing of these cases it would be a great relief and then we could afford to wait if necessary a few weeks for the rest." Yesterday the same Commissioner said, I find that its no use trying to select 25 men out of the whole number who are pressed upon me; to do so would make more trouble than to put on none. I think that we had better authorize 300 men at once, and get them all on and have done with it. Then we can answer that no more are to be employed."

That the other Commissioners have had the same difficulty and have not dared to discriminate against the whole number of applicants by selecting only 25 each, is evident from the fact that as yet, in a fortnight but 16 men have been appointed. The Superintendent yesterday said to me, Commissioner (Williamson) has sent me only 4 men. Each one of them is over 60 years old & one I judge to be over 70. There is not one that could do a quarter of a fair day's work; and the Commissioner knows it, for he saw them himself & they came to me directly from him.

(This morning a woman came to my house before I had breakfasted to ask me to aid her in getting employment for a son. Another Commissioner had promised it a long time since but she had waited so long she feared that he might be overlooked. She urged my assistance on the ground that her son was unfit for hard work. He had a weak back and if he had to stoop at his work it sometimes made him sick & he was laid up for several days).

I went twice yesterday into the Board room, on each occasion there were from 4 to 6 members of the late legislature and of the Board of Aldermen present, and each of 3 Commissioners was engaged in a whispered conversation apart with one of them. There were others waiting their turn outside besides the mob of candidates, the larger part of whom were of the dirty, ruffianly and loafish sort. The large room with all the windows open was filled with a sickening odor from them.

[33: 198]   8th July. 75. Wages.

Crosby, contractor on the 4th Avenue Improvemnt,[121] told me that when their bid for the work was made they calculated on a basis of $2– a day. They had been able last year to get their men at $1.50 and retaining the same men and feeling that {they} had been fortunate they were disposed to be liberal and therefore maintained their wages this Summer at the same rate — But, said he, "if a man were about starting some extensive new work in the city at this time and were to advertize that he wanted men but none need apply who were not willing to work 10 hours for $1– he would have all he wanted at that price. They would come by thousands. I am troubled by men who come to me now every day & who say they will work at any price; they have been so long idle & earning nothing. I know I could get thousands at $1– a day."

APPENDIX III

The Dept now pays 3.60 per day of 8 h. for carts — Crosby says that he can hire carts at $3. for 10 h. and paying by the yard there would {be} many who would be glad of a chance to earn 2.60 a day.

[33: 200]   8th July 1875.

Since the 28th May (q.v.) the subject of a reduction of wages has not been mentioned in the Board. The other departments of the city are all working smoothly on the reduced wages. Meanwhile the parks are suffering greatly for want of labor which cannot be afforded them. I shall report today on two complaints of citizens of the neglected condition of small parks that I find the statements true but that the Departmnt has not men enough to apply the remedy.[122] On the Central Park a considerable part of the enrolled force is worked half time. Numerous duties are neglected and the Superintending Gardener and foremen all answer when asked why, that they have not force enough.

From this to May, statements in the minutes will show that the outlay is constantly outrunning the rate of the allowance for the year & that the Board is unable to find a satisfactory remedy.

[33: 159]   To July 19th

    10 boxes broken
    6   ″   stolen
    3 punches ″
    1 keeper refused to use p. & suspended —
    various keys broken & lost.

[33: 215–17]   21st July 1875.

The D.P.P. Board being about to go in session and a knot of half a dozen Aldermen sitting together in the inner lobby; one of the Commissioners came and took a seat among them, saying in a hearty way, "Why don't you fellows give us what we want?" (referring to a negative vote at the last session of the Aldermen on a proposition by which the Park Dept would have been able to proceed with work on the Riverside Park).[123] "We never get what we want out of you when we do;" one replied.

"Make your bargains before hand then. Make your bargains before hand," returned the Commissioner. "You can depend on any arrangement you make with me. You can rely on that."

"Thats right, that's what we want." All this was in loud voices, in the presence of several strangers and four of the Departmnt's officers and clerks, and within hearing of the outer lobby which was crowded with applicants for employment. The voices then fell. I went out & shortly afterwards returning, asked the Secretary whom I met if the Board had yet gone in session — it being a full hour after the time appointed for its meeting. No, he said, there's a lot of Aldermen and members of the Legislature in there. I went & found 12 of them — each member of the Park Board stood in a seperate corner of the room, engaged in an "aside" conversation with one of them.

[33: 199] The city Engineer of Providence told me (Aug 1875) that certain work which I advised on the park could be done in the winter cheaply as all needed laborers could then be hired by the city at $1– a day (10 h.)[124]

[33: 231–37]   Gardening C.P.
6th September 1875.

    I have today, after nearly four years effort, succeeded in inducing the Board to return to the system which I originally devised for the gardening care of the Central Park and had in operation in 1860.[125] Soon after I left in 1861 it was abandoned and except during the Sweeny Hilton period of 1870–71, when a more elaborate organization was formed, there has been no gardener with any distinct responsibility for the gardening work on the park, while there have been foremen trained only in common labor, as of sewer and canal digging, in command of all the working gardeners and often directing gardening work, even the removal and setting out of trees and plants, without consultation with the head gardener or myself.[126] There have been constant difficulties in consequence of the ambiguous position of the head gardeners and of the efforts of the foremen to control the gardening business. Knowing that the motive of this bad arrangmnt was at bottom a political one, I have limited my requests to but two simple points; that every part of the park should have a capable gardener responsible for the ordinary care of the trees, shrubs & plants (not turf) upon it, and that all work on trees, shrubs & plants, should be under the direction of the Superintending Gardener — the foremen neither giving orders to his limited force, nor being allowed to direct their own force to work on trees, shrubs & plants.

    On the 4th June last I addressed a report to the Board on the subject, which was laid on the table — and has since slept. On the 8th July I read another report on the subject, which was also laid on the table.[127]

    Soon afterwards one of the repeated quarrels growing out of the bad organization having been brought before the President and he consulting me, I illustrated its defects and begged him to give more consideration to my proposition for improvement. He admitted the need of a reform — of changes in the organization — but said that he thought there were greater defects in mine & greater evils would arise out of it. He would not state what they were but promised to give the matter more consideration & me the opportunity of arguing it. Shortly afterwards, grave charges were made against Wolf — who occupied an anomalous position of "foreman of gardeners"; his business being to keep the time, independently of the regular maintenance foremen, of a small special gardening force (from 4 to 8 men) chiefly employed about the restaurant at Mt St Vincent and in the propagating dept.[128] Wolf was not himself a gardener—or had not been before he came on the park, but had been made one by order of Green & through his influence had been advanced in this position in which his pay was considerably above any of the skilled & trained gardeners of the Department, the Supertending Gardener—a salaried officer—excepted. The President was much excited about these charges against Wolf; sent for me & for the Superintendent; and was very angry with the Superintendent, for not at once dismissing the men who made the charges—regarding them as insubordinate. The Superintendent was induced to drop the matter. Some of the complainants however came to Commissioner O'Donohoe, who insisted on an investigation, made it himself and was satisfied that Wolf had made false returns of time and had been grossly neglectful of his duty. He recommended his dismissal, Martin voted with him, and, Williamson, who is supposed to be now trying to find a way back to good fellowship with the Tammany men, at length did so also, greatly to the chagrin of the President. Williamson did not regard the charges of fraud & neglect as proven but said that he was informed that Wolf's wife kept a Beer Shop, and that being so he did not think he was a proper man to be a foreman.[129] The President told me this, & I saw at once from the tone of his remarks that a large part of his interest in maintaining the old vice of organization, was based on the conviction that Wolf held a better position under it than he was likely to if any change occurred. I accordingly took an early opportunity to ask him to review my report. I took it up & read it to him, and he had no objection to make to any part of it. Today, the Board being in session, I requested that it might be taken from the table and this being done the President asked Williamson to state his objections. He said that he could consent to nothing which would prevent the foremen from returning the time of the gardeners the same as of other men, nor to anything which would prevent the Superintending Gardener from directing and controlling the working gardeners. His objection to my proposition was only that it did prevent these things. On the contrary, I said, the cardinal points of my proposition are that it provides that the time of all gardeners shall be returned alike by the ordinary foremen—thus securing simplicity and uniformity of the accounts—but that these foremen shall have nothing more to do with them, they receiving their orders solely from the Superintending Gardener. "Oh! is that so?" he said, "then I will vote for it." The vote was immediately taken and my proposition carried unanimously (See Minutes).[130] Three years of argument, entreating and practical illustration have done nothing—But it happens at this moment that no Commissioner sees any private or political interest dependant on maintaining the old abuse, it is abandoned without the least difficulty. Had it been done when I first urged it, the park would now be greatly more valuable and the force much less demoralized. Had Wolf's wife not kept a beer shop, the opportunity would have been deferred, at least.

PATRONAGE JOURNAL (1873–1877)

[43: 521] September 1875

A man who had been employed (I think as watchman—a "soft place") last year and discharged on a general reduction of force has since been assiduously trying to obtain reemploymnt and finally in the general enlargement of work preparatory to the fall election, obtained a "ticket" as stone cutter. The superintendent when he presented {it} said: "Why I know you very well & you are no stone cutter." The man insisted that he was & the Superintendent assigned him to a gang. In course of the day the foreman of the gang reported that he found him unqualified—he knew nothing of stone cutting, and he was discharged.

[47: 354]

He left threatening the foreman; went again to the President to obtain restoration; the Superintendent met him before the President and prevented his success. He then went immediately to the Park; demanded of the foreman that he should take him back and on his refusal shot him. The foreman's life was saved by some metallic object in his pocket from which it glanced passing through his body. (Minutes will show pay ordered him for time lost while under surgeon's care.)[131]

[33: 196] 10th Oct.

A similar crowd has been before the Office at every meeting since (8th Oct)—Of late a policeman has been employed to keep them from crowding into the building. Of late much of the work planned and arranged to be done this summer & some in addition has been ordered, and several hundred men taken on. At the last meeting the Superintendent stated that of those supplied with tickets not more than 60 to 70 pr cent were to be relied upon for a week—30 to 40 perct dropping off from discontent with the exactions of the foremen. Yet I have never seen men walking more slowly than the new gangs. On this ground 100 additional men were authorized.[132]

[33: 238–39] 10th Oct.

I have not been able to work through the necessary blanks and changes of form of accounts for fully carrying out the reorganization of gardeners but have carried the order of the Board mainly into effect.[133] A few days after the changes were made, Commissioner Williamson told me that there was one of the gardeners in whom he was interested and he was surprised to find that under this order he had been put down, and asked me to see that he was restored as soon as possible. The fact was simply that he had not been chosen for one of the more responsible positions being unfit for it, & was engaged & trying to get some one of the better qualified men removed & the place given to him by influence. Next I recved the accompanying letter from a member of the legislature in regard to another in similar position:[134]

[33:252] Sept. 28, 1875.

Dear Sir

The bearer Mr. McManus, one of your gardeners, is a constituent and friend of mine.

It appears that he has been overlooked in promotions made within the past week, I am interested in his success, and any favor you may do him will be gratefully appreciated by
        Yours respectfully,
        James Daly

[33: 159] 10th Oct.

Several boxes having been repaired & new ones set—during the last week 3 have been forced open & punches stolen.

In cleaning the lake the following autumn most of the boxes were found in it. Two night watchmen discharged came voluntarily to me and assured me that the boxes were destroyed & removed by the keepers for the purpose of bringing discredit on the system, & which they feared tended to a reduction of wages.

[33: 254] Nov. 1st 1875.

Throughout the canvass now about closing the republican & anti Tammany speakers have been seeking to fasten upon the Tammany party the odium of the attempted reduction of wages, the Tammany party to repudiate responsibility for it. Not one so far as I have seen, has attempted to defend it. No one appears to have benefitted by it politically & the Tammany party has evidently suffered.

[33: 281–82] 19th Nov. 1875.

During the last fortnight the Herald has repeatedly & for several days successively published sensational attacks on the Park Departmnt beginning with a statemt from General Viele implying that the Central Park had never been under drained and was in a pestilential condition. After some days the Times took up the matter in an editorial hereto annexed.[135] This was for some days followed by others of similar import.

The matter occasioned some excitement among the officers of the

Departmnt and one and all believed the attacks were in the nature of a punishmnt of the Commissioners who had prevented Green from using the patronage of the Dept against Tammany during the late election canvass and was premonitory of an intention to obtain legislation abolishing or reorganizing the Departmnt. The President & one of the Commissioners expressed the same idea to me, the President saying that he knew it was so from other circumstances, and it was what he had all the time believed would be the result of the folly of the Tammany Commissioners.—Commissioner Martin addressed a note to Mr Bennett of the Herald[136] suggesting that he should take some pains to ascertain the facts before going further. Two days afterwards I was requested by the President to see a reporter from the Herald who wanted to make inquiry about the sanitary condition of the park. I found him a perfectly competent man, a physician with some training as an engineer. I took him to the park and spent most of a day in exhibiting the drainage, sewerage, lakes etc. At the end he voluntarily remarked that the Herald reports were greatly exaggerated and that he suspected Gen'l Viele, whom he had seen, was something of a quack in Sanitary matters. He expressed a doubt whether the Herald would publish his report. Today the Herald has an article (I am told) in which it says in effect that the Park Commissioners have acted promptly on its suggestions and the park is now all right.[137] There have been no new orders during the month & no work is being done not ordered before the publications.

I have made a report to the Board showing the falsity of most of the reports and have addressed a letter to Mr Jones, the publisher of the Times from the following draught.[138]

[43: 520]   1875.

A plan for the summer work of 1875 was made by me and adopted by the Board in January (I think), sanctioned by the Legislature at the close of the session, by the Governor at the last moment the law allowed. Soon afterwards mainly readopted by the Board, but it was not till after the first frosts of autumn and the heat of the election canvass that the necessary force was taken on and the larger number of the works specifically authorized to be proceeded with. See minutes.[139]
See dated notes 8th July & 10th Oct 1875

[33: 330–31]   26th April. 1876.

Yesterday it was generally understood in the Departmnt that a bargain had been made by which Mr Green would again obtain entire control of the Department, and that on Sunday last he was engaged with Col. Stebbins, Ryan, Manning and others of his adherants in determining who should take the offices to be made vacant by the removal of those who had not been of his

faction. From inquiries made by the President and the change in his manner and that of other of "Green's men", it was clear to me that there was some foundation for these reports. This morning the pendulum swings back as indicated below:[140]
(The bill passed the Senate on the 2^d May, passage in the house prevented by filibustering to the close of the session. (3^d)

[33: 338–49]   5th May 1876.

     The Legislature adjourned on the 3^d. For some weeks past the question whether a Bill introduced in the interest of Mr Green, to reduce the Commission to one, (Col Stebbins), was or was not to become a law has been one of intense interest.[141] The President stated in the Board and afterwards repeated to me, nearly two months ago, that he did not believe that there was a man in the Departmnt who was not ranged on one side or the other or who was not demoralized by his partisanship. Almost every man has been of the opinion that according as the legislature acted he was to hold, or lose, his place. At the very least that his place was to be a much more or less comfortable & profitable one. When the chances of the passage of the bill have appeared very good the Superintendent, who is classed as anti Green has told me that some of his assistants — foremen — as well as of the administrative clerks — have been recklessly exultant, defiant and insolent in manner, studiously careless and ostentatiously forgetful in regard to his orders and requests. It has so happened that the movemnts in Committee and otherwise have been alternately indicative of opposite conclusions, and the foremen, clerks and police officers have been advised by private direct telegraphic dispatches as often as anything occurred of marked significance. A large part of the force has consequently been under a state of extreme excitement — one day of depression the next of exultation and triumph, for weeks. It is impossible to overstate the degree of uncertainty which has existed to the last moment. On the morning of the 2^d I was assured by a manager (Warren in Buffalo)[142] of the Democratic party that whatever might be done in the House, Green could not carry his bill in the Senate. At the moment he said so, Green's bill was passing the Senate by one majority. It was then considered by all certain that it would pass the House but the leading opponents of it assumed confidence that it would be vetoed. Green's men were so exultant that the Superintendent told me that they stood in all but open defiance of his authority and were plainly laughing at him. He said, "if the Bill passes the House today as I suppose it will, there will be no use in my going to the park tomorrow for they will give no attention to anything I say." Commissioner Martin told the Superintendent that he must encourage his loyal subordinates, & especially the Police Captain, not to lose his command, with the assurance of a veto, and said the more the Green men were carried off their feet and into open mutiny, the better he should like for the better reason there would be for dismissing them. The conclusion is indicated in the following published dispatches.[143]

It is to be observed that nearly every other Departmnt was in similar condition.

6th May

Commissioner Wetmore sworn in yesterday & immediately afterwards meeting held at which Martin, (Tammany) was elected President of the board, vice {president} Stebbins (Green).[144]

It is already rumored that the law reducing the Commission to one may pass in an extra session — Hopes being had by Green men that it will be called chiefly to pass an Apportionmnt Bill required by the Constitution but failing in the regular session.[145]

6th May 1876.

During the session of the Legislature which closed on the 3d, three of the Commissioners visited Albany and two appeared before Committees.[146] Most of the lobby work was, however, done in New York, during the Sunday recesses of the session.

At one time for a week or more there were six employees and recently dischargd employees of the Department in Albany, all with the recognized purpose of working for "Green's Bill", for reducing the Commission to one. They there met the Commissioners against whom the Bill was directed.

The Minutes show that a Superintendent of the Departmnt was engaged in getting signatures to a petition favoring the passage of the Bill.[147]

14th May 1876

The Herald is now again having a series of sensational articles on the park turf abounding in statemnts & reports wholly false.[148]

30th May 1876

Commissioner Martin when elected President D.P.P. told me that he meant to be independent of the politicians, to remove no good men & appoint no bad ones, under whatever pressure. I believe that he was sincere. Today going on the park with the Superintendent I found one of the Division foremen 18 years on the park, thoroughly conversant with the work of his division & with whom I have had less occasion to find fault than any other, had been suddenly dismissed & a new man appointed, whom I saw & conversed with. An Irishman 60 years old apparently (gray headed) corpulent, slow, good natured, easy going. The Superintendent said the change came without warning. He found the new man waiting instructions & utterly helpless, needing to be advised in everything. He believed he had failed in the grocery trade—probably dram shop—and had obtained the appointment as a charity. He had had no experience in any of the various kinds of work to be done, had never managed men—in fact was utterly unqualified.—The President said of this—"I know—but there were special reasons which at this time made his appointment absolutely necessary." The Superintendent told me a fortnight later that it took about half his time to follow him up and that he knew much less of his out door business & was less capable of managing it than his men. He did not know what grass ought to be cut, had set four men to mowing who never had a sythe in their hands before and had started them in with the right hand man in advance.[149]

7th June.

President Martin said yesterday that it was impossible not to employ men in most positions and all laborers & mechanics as politicians demanded, but he meant to keep all important & controlling offices in his own hands & to have only good trusty efficient men in them & oblige them to do the best that was possible with what they had to employ of a lower grade.

[33: 356] 8th June. 1876.

Soon after President Martin's election, as he was talking with me at his desk, a card was handed to him. "Ask him to take a seat outside and wait till I am through with Mr Olmsted" he said, then to me, "I am going to attend to one thing at a time and not let the politicians over run me."—Today he sent word that he wished to see me about 5 o'clock which is the close of office hours. I went to his room, and found the Superintendent there and several politicians. Others called & were admitted, one going another coming until after six; when, as the last one went out, he said, "Well now I hope we shall {be} able to begin the business of the day. There's no use trying to do anything while these politicians keep coming." He was then occupied till after seven with the Superintendent & me—The dinner of each of us had been ordered at six.

[33: 377–84]   11th June 1876.

    The Superintendent said to me. "Whatever I propose that does not call for more men and a distribution of patronage I find Mr O'Donoho opposed to. Whatever I propose that calls for more men, I find him ready to advocate without inquiry. If I want to repair a building he asks "would that make a place for a plasterer or a painter or a joiner" and if it would he is eager for it, but if I say that it is something to be bought outright and can be put up with our own force, he frowns upon it."

                                                                           11th June, 1876.

    Contractors could readily get all classes of the work of the Dept done at considerably less than half the price which the Dept is obliged to pay — doing the same work by the day. I have made all my estimates for work on Riverside & Morningside Park on the expressed condition that the work was to be contracted. President Martin is strongly interested to have the work on Riverside done as soon as possible and also as cheaply as possible. It has been a prominent object with him since he entered the Departmnt a year & a half ago. By one means or another he has been thwarted. Perfectly realizing that the cost of the work will be doubled if done by day's work, he yesterday told me that he was satisfied there was no alternative. The patronage of a day's work policy would enable us to override all opposition. We can overcome it in no other way.

                                                                           22d June 1876.

    Am informed today that contractors are now paying but 90 {cents} for 10 hours sewer work at Manhattanville.[150]

                                                                           2d Aug. 1876.

    A deputation of working men came to see the Park Commission this morning to urge employmnt (See papers for some days back showing the movement)[151] at the same time that they were receiving a deputation of property owners urging uptown improvmnts. Having made their set speeches, the question of contract and day's work came up and property holders described what they had seen of laborers employed under the city loafing and getting pay for the baldest pretence of work. One of the laboring men then said "we know that that is so Sir, we know that men are put on your pay rolls by politicans and that when they go on the work and the foreman tries to make them work they tell him to go to a hot place and ask him if he supposes that they expect to work, and they tell him that if he don't mind his business & let them alone they have influence enough to get him out of his place."

APPENDIX III

7th Aug. 1876.

Not a day passes that some move intended to influence the public is not made in the quarrel between Green & Martin.[152]

Sep 1st 1876.

Recently (in August) the Board of Aldermen adopted a resolution authorizing the Departmnt to go on with the suspended work at Tompkins Square,[153] on the condition that it should be completed by the 1st Sep^r—an absurd condition wholly impossible to be realized if for no other reason because the work includes the planting of trees.

The day following this action I was in the Board room when it was announced that a deputation from the Board of Aldermen were in waiting. "What is their business I wonder?" said one.

"Why! don't you know", answered another. "They are coming to see what appointmnts they can get as the price for extending the time for the work in Tompkins Square." I remained only long enough to hear their first question which was as to the number of men the Departmnt could employ on the Square.

The crowd of men, working men and politicians, which now gathers about the Commission office whenever a meeting has been called is larger than it has been before for years. A short time ago a meeting of the Board had been called at 9 o'clock but there was no quorum and no meeting & the Commissioners that came, except the President, left early. Nevertheless a good many men held on hoping to be able to importune the President. At two o'clock he asked me to go out to lunch with him at a hotel one block below. The policeman attending at the outer door during meetings had been withdrawn and as soon as the President came to the head of the stairs there was a rush toward {him} from below and we were several minutes getting to the street. As soon as we reached the sidewalk the applicants pressed upon him so closely that he found it very difficult to move. After struggling for half a block he said to me. "I can't have this mob go with me into a hotel, try and get me clear of them." I worked out & brought a carriage near, into which he made a leap and we drove off rapidly going to a hotel a mile away.

[33: 390–98]   26th Sept 1876

After the meeting of the Board this morning Commissioner Donelly[154] stood surrounded by a circle of politicians who were demanding appointment of him—"The republicans claim that {they} have gained 400 votes in my district"—said one. "Do you know how they do it? Why it's by giving them appointmnts—you know it is. How the hell do you suppose we are ever going to carry the district, if we can't give any appointmnts?"

"Well, you know," replied the Commissioner, "I have given all my appointments to the Committee, I don't keep nothing back, why should I? I don't want no office."

"I don't know about that, Mr Commissioner," called out another, "I think I've heard your name mentioned a few times lately for Mayor."

"I don't care if you have, I have not asked for it. I tell you if you want more men appointed you must go to the Aldermen & get them to vote us more work. I've given you all the appointmnts I can get, until they let us put more men on. You go to the Aldermen."

Nov 22^d 1876.

On one occasion I was urged to have a plan and report ready for presentation to the Board as soon as possible. I promised to present it in a fortnight. In order to do so and to feel safe in doing so I worked during the intermediate time to the utmost of my strength, taking not half my required ration of sleep and passing two nights without sleep. At the meeting of the Board at which the report was to be made there was no quorum and it was adjourned for a week. At the adjourned meeting there was a full Board. In due time the President called up my report. "How long it goin' to take?" asked one. (O'Donohoe).

"I shall be perhaps 10 minutes in reading it," I replied.

"I ain't got no ten minutes to spare to hear no readin,'" said the Commissioner, looking up at the clock, "and before I go I want some other business attended to." The matter was then dropped and a two hours' wrangle began on matters of which the interest all lay in patronage, the Commissioner remaining to the end.

7th Dec. 1876.

One of the clerks asked me this morning, "Do you know, Mr Olmsted, if Commissioner ODonohoe is going to resign? It has been reported that he was but his men here say that he told them this morning that he had no thought of it."

In the afternoon while drawing at the Engineer's Office on the Park a clerk whom I did not know by name, opened the door and said, "Mr Olmsted, Commissioner Donohoe has resigned." As I was going home my driver said, "Its all over the park that Commissioner O'D. has resigned. His men are all very down in the mouth about it Sir. I suppose it's true Sir."—The evening papers reported it & it was true.[155]

APPENDIX III

Dec. 1876.

Nearly a year ago the Superintending Engineer (Bogart) was notified that he would be no longer paid for his services but allowed to serve the Department gratuitously.[156] During the year he has done much important work for the Department, especially in preparing the working plans & specification of the Riverside Avenue, (which has been let at 530.000). Supporting himself however, by work outside the Dept — (Various young men of the Engineer corps have been at work without being sure of their pay & irregularly without discipline). On the 22^d (?) Nov. the President informed the Board that the contractors had begun their work, having 300 men employed, that he had made temporary arrangements for engineering but they were insufficient & unauthorized. He thought it possible to get on without employing Mr Bogart & proposed to place the Superintendence of the work with our assistant, (Mr Aldrich) & offered a scheme for a staff.[157] It included 6 men. Mr. Aldrich had said that 9 were necessary but he thought he could get along with 6. 4 of the 6 were new men and most of them were experienced engineers, who were willing for the winter to take the rank & pay of chain men & axe men. "Whose men are these any how"? asked a Commissioner (ODonohoe).

"I had all the applicants who came here sent to [Mr Aldrich] [the engineer to be in charge]," said the President, "and asked him to examine them and report to me as to their qualifications. These four are those that he has found to stand highest among all those who were willing to take the respective places. He knew none of them before the examination and he did not know by whom they had been sent to us." No commissioner knew or was particularly interested in any of the applicants, "so I thought that was the best way."

"I don't believe in havin' no man whom we employ comin' here and dictatin' to us what appointmnts we shall make and I ain't a going to vote for no such men" rejoined the Commissioner. The President explained that the pay of the Engineer force for the work was to be paid (a fixed sum for all) by the contractor & it would cost the city nothing, but the Commissioner was inexorable. Finally a temporary arrangement was made.

1876 December.

Contractors for Riverside Avenue have 300 men employed, laborers 90 cts a day, 9 hours or more according to light, laborers furnishing shovels.

Dept still pays $2 per day but men volunteer to work 9 hours.[158]

PATRONAGE JOURNAL (1873–1877)

10th Jan. 1877.

Wages reduced today to $1.60 per day of 8 hours, with priviledge of working 10 at $2. vote unanimous.[159]

[1876]

Wages. at Montreal, laborers constructing the road up the mountain 65 cts for 10 hours; extremely hard work; men sometimes frost bitten & driven from the ground by wind when mercury 20° below 0.
 65c=74 paper
 U.S currency — wages
 Park Dept being $2 for 8.

Changes — Not only changes of men filling offices but changes of functions of office. A certain kind of duty belongs first to one office then to another. I have known a single continuous process of duty transferred from one man to another five times in a year, there being no dismissals or appointmnts but simply so many shifts of responsibilities.

[33: 418–20]   March 1877.

On a certain day this winter a member of the legislature called on the Secretary of the Commission (D.P.P.) and stated that he had sometime before asked for an appointmnt from him. "I want you now to tell {the president} that if the appointment is not made at once — at once — I will make him trouble." He then wrote to the President "I have left a message for you with your Secretary to which I recommend your immediate attention." (or to that effect). The President made no reply. He could make no appointmnt. The second day following the same member of the legislature introduced a bill to transfer to another Departmnt an important division of the Park business and a part in which it was known that the President took much personal pride & interest.[160]

(March 1877)

Another member of the legislature who introduced a bill of the same character spoke to me about it. I told him that {I} thought he was mistaken in certain statements he made on the subject. Thereupon he began speaking of the President in insulting terms. I interrupted and said "You will please remember that I am his subordinate."

APPENDIX III

"Yes, I know, but he has no heart. I heard him say that he was glad when the snow came and he could not put any men to work."

This member afterwards endeavored to make a provision for carrying on the New Capitol building that would force me to retire from the partnership of E. R. & Cº. and gave privately as his reason that I stood by Martin, the President.

[39: 187–89]   1877.

I have been 11 years in the Service of the Park Commissions of New York and five in that of the Park Commissions of Brooklyn. I have been at the request of one and the other at least sixteen times to Albany to aid in obtaining legislation desired by these Commissions or to aid preventing legislation deprecated by them. The duty required of me has been almost solely that of a witness either as to facts or as an expert but I have necessarily been present at numerous conferences upon the matters in question and have been more or less in the confidence of the Commissioners & those managing for them. It is my impression that not in a single case has the object sought been accomplished, whether in obtaining or preventing legislation, that the good will of legislators has not been cultivated by holding out prospects of patronage. In numerous cases patronage has been promised. In some it has distinctly and in plain terms been made a matter of bargain — a compensation for votes and influence as much so as if dollars had been counted out. After every session of the legislature in which Acts have passed or Bills failed in accordance with the wishes of the Commissions, legislators aiding these results have asked or demanded appointmnts from them distinctly on the ground that they had rendered such service and were entitled to special consideration in consequence. The most respectable & worthy members of the legislature have been as ready to do this as any others. They have only made their demand more euphemistically and civilly than the ruder and baser sort.

In the conversation of those interested of all classes the fact that the good will of legislators was to be purchased, was expected by them to be purchased, or that it had been purchased, was generally assumed.

I have had confirmatory experiences in my connection with the State Survey & the Capitol Commissions.[161]

The same is true, but much more distinctly in regard to all dealings with the Common Council of every large town in which I have been consulted as to any public works employing a working force. All most every year there have been proceedings in Common Council apparently unfriendly to the Heads of Departments with which I have directly dealt, which by these heads & their subordinates have been commonly assured in conversation and in debate as the managemnt of their affairs have been assumed to be in the nature of black mailing operations — threats to be appesed by patronage.

PATRONAGE JOURNAL (1873–1877)

The editors have compiled this document from draft memoirs written by Olmsted in which he noted his experience of patronage politics, primarily in the New York City parks, and primarily during 1874 and 1875. Olmsted dated the entries, and they are arranged for the most part in chronological order in the Frederick Law Olmsted Papers collection in the Library of Congress, from which we have drawn. We give microfilm reel and frame numbers of that collection for each entry.

1. Salem H. Wales.
2. This was Joseph Mollard, born in Staffordshire, England c. 1819 (U.S., Census Office, 8th Census, *8th Census 1860. New York* [Washington, D.C., 1860], Schedule 1, Johnstown, p. 34).
3. Charles Cyril Martin (1831–1903), a civil engineer, was chief engineer of Prospect Park during the late 1860s. In 1870 he left the park to become first assistant engineer on the Brooklyn Bridge and succeeded Washington A. Roebling as chief engineer and superintendent of the bridge in 1883 (*Papers of FLO*, 6: 271; NCAB, 14: 49).
4. Columbus Ryan had not been able to make such appointments since the adoption of new bylaws in late August 1873, which gave to the board the power to make all but minor appointments. For a period of ten months before then Ryan had been able to hire foremen, mechanics, and laborers, which allowed him considerable influence in dispensing patronage (DPP, *Minutes*, Oct. 24, 1872, p. 545; ibid., Aug. 29, 1873, p. 243; *Sunday Mercury*, Feb. 2, 1873, p. 4).
5. In June 1873 the New York state legislature granted the Department of Public Parks authority to determine the lines and grades of Riverside Avenue within Riverside Park but did not specify whether that department or the Department of Public Works had the power to build the avenue. In December 1873 Mayor William F. Havemeyer vetoed an ordinance of the Common Council that ordered the Department of Public Works to proceed with the work. He warned that without firm legal authority to conduct the work, tax assessments to pay for it could be vacated in court, a process that recently had added millions to the city's debt in other cases. Within two weeks of his veto, Democrat state assemblyman James Daly introduced the bill Olmsted mentions here. Besides allowing the Common Council to decide which department would construct the avenue, the bill set aside Olmsted's plan, approved by the Department of Public Parks and the legislature, to treat the park and avenue as a whole, and reinstated the original plan that kept them separate. In urging passage of his bill, Daly pointed to growing public pressure to provide immediate employment for the thousands without work since the financial panic of late 1873 had nearly stopped manufacturing and the building trades in New York and the city government had curtailed expenditures on public works. The assembly read the bill for the third time on January 30, 1874, and forwarded it to the senate (*Papers of FLO*, 6: 596–600; *The City Record*, Jan. 17, 1874, p. 54; *New-York Times*, Jan. 16, 1874, p. 2; ibid., Jan. 27, 1874, p. 4; ibid., Jan. 31, 1874, p. 1; New York [State], *Journal of the Assembly of the State of New York . . . Ninety-Seventh Session*, 2 vols. [Albany, N.Y., 1874], 1: 47, 174–75; *Sunday Mercury*, Nov. 23, 1873, p. 4; ibid., Dec. 14, 1873, p. 4; *New-York Daily Tribune*, Jan. 31, 1874, p. 4).
6. George M. Van Nort.
7. Andrew H. Green.
8. Capmakers struck on February 5, 1874, and demanded that their wages be more than doubled. The stairmakers intended their boycott of stone cut outside of New York City to promote the eight-hour workday, which municipal workers in the city had kept by state law since 1870 (*Papers of FLO*, 6: 628; *New-York Times*, Feb. 6, 1874, p. 4; *New-York Daily Tribune*, Feb. 10, 1874, p. 8).

APPENDIX III

9. Probably broker Hackley B. Bacon, the treasurer, executive board member, and chairman of the committee on improvements of the West Side Association in New York City (see n. 19 below).
10. Probably Waters W. Braman (b. 1840), Republican assemblyman from West Troy and brevet major of the 93rd regiment, New York Volunteers, who had opposed the bill in question in the state Assembly (W. H. McElroy and Alex McBride, *Life Sketches of Government Officers and Members of the Legislature of the State of New York for 1874* [Albany, N.Y., 1874], pp. 161–63).
11. John Adams Dix (1798–1879), soldier and lawyer, served as Democratic governor of New York from 1873 to 1875 (*DAB*).
12. Dexter Arnoll Hawkins (1825–1886), educator, lawyer, and publicist, was an early critic of the Tweed Ring. Between 1872 and 1874 he occasionally lobbied the legislature on behalf of Andrew H. Green and the Department of Public Parks about municipal finances and park matters and apparently collected payment for his services in violation of the charter of 1873. On other occasions, such as that Olmsted describes here, he pleaded the same causes as a spokesman for the Council of Political Reform, a loosely organized group of anti-Tammany Democrats (David McAdam et al., eds., *History of the Bench and Bar of New York*, 2 vols. [New York, 1897], 1: 356; *New York Herald*, Feb. 19, 1874, p. 7; ibid., March 4, 1872, p. 10; DPP, *Minutes*, June 27, 1873, pp. 75–76; *Sunday Mercury*, Oct. 19, 1873, p. 4; ibid., Feb. 22, 1874, p. 4; Seymour J. Mandelbaum, *Boss Tweed's New York* [New York, 1965], pp. 89, 112–13).
13. Daniel P. Wood was among the Republicans in the senate opposed to the Daly bill (*Sunday Mercury*, March 8, 1874, p.4).
14. Andrew H. Green.
15. David B. Williamson was appointed to the park commission in June 1873, apparently at the suggestion of Andrew H. Green, and held the position of treasurer (*Papers of FLO*, 6: 44, 609).
16. John Bogart, engineer for the Department of Public Parks, paraphrased the report in the *Sunday Mercury*, edited by Tammany Hall Democrat William D. Cauldwell. On February 22, 1874, the paper alleged that Mayor Havemeyer had promised Green a seat on the park commission if he was removed as city comptroller. Green was said to have put lobbyists, including Dexter A. Hawkins, at work to increase the department's patronage in preparation for this move (*Sunday Mercury*, Feb. 22, 1874, p. 4; William C. Gover, *The Tammany Hall Democracy* [New York, 1875], p. 120).
17. Olmsted paraphrased the testimony of Dr. Walter De F. Day, superintendent of the sanitary bureau of the Health Department, before a state assembly committee investigating corruption and malfeasance in the city's Bureau of Street Cleaning (*New-York Times*, March 3, 1874, p. 2).
18. Andrew H. Green was pressing for the dismissal of Howard A. Martin (1835–1889), Olmsted's clerk in the Bureau of Design and Superintendence since August 1872. Martin had served him as chief clerk on Central Park before the Civil War, as an accountant for the U.S. Sanitary Commission in 1862 and 1863, and as chief clerk of the Mariposa Estate in California from 1863 to 1865. Olmsted told Wales the day after this entry that "no man in your employment is more zealous, faithful and discrete in all his duties and no one is paid less relative to the value of his work" (*Papers of FLO*, 5: 84, 142; DPP, *Minutes*, Aug. 7, 1872, p. 484; *Sunday Mercury*, Jan. 3, 1875, p. 4; FLO to Salem H. Wales, March 11, 1874; *New-York Times*, Jan. 22, 1889, p. 5; see also FLO to DPP, [c. Jan. 5, 1878]).
19. Howard Martin's brother was the prominent West Side booster and lawyer William R. Martin. He had promoted the development of the area since the mid-1860s and conferred with Olmsted about Riverside Park and Avenue periodically since then. He was

PATRONAGE JOURNAL (1873–1877)

president of the West Side Association, a group of property owners who lobbied for uptown development and denounced Andrew H. Green for thwarting park department projects crucial to them. In the association's *Proceedings* and in letters published in the *New York World* and the *New-York Times*, he applauded commissioner of public works George M. Van Nort for a department run with economy and dispatch, and urged that it undertake the Riverside project. In 1872 William Martin had represented the *New York World* in an unsuccessful legal action against Green, apparently the start of a bitter feud between the two men that continued through the Riverside controversy and grew worse when Martin joined the park commission in 1875 (West Side Association, *Proceedings of a Public Meeting Held at Lyric Hall . . . on the 22d of January, 1873* [New York, 1873], pp. 65–71, 95–100; *New-York Times*, March 8, 1874, pp. 3–4; ibid., March 19, 1874, p. 4; *New-York Daily Tribune*, March 9, 1874, p. 8; ibid., March 19, 1874, p. 2; *Sunday Mercury*, Jan. 3, 1875, p. 1; George T. McJimsey, *Genteel Partisan: Manton Marble, 1834–1917* [Ames, Iowa, 1971], pp. 167–68).

20. Olmsted is referring to rumors that William Martin held a salaried position with the Department of Public Works, a view stated publicly by the *New-York Times* shortly after this entry. Martin denied the charge but admitted holding positions on two street-opening commissions in the city (*New-York Times*, March 19, 1874, p. 4; ibid., March 21, 1874, p. 6).
21. John Tuomey (1813–1898), foreman of masons and president of Stone Masons Society (*New-York Times*, June 9, 1898, p. 7).
22. The "Committee on Legislation," comprised of commissioners Philip Bissinger, David B. Williamson, and Henry G. Stebbins, was organized specifically to lobby against legislation to authorize the Department of Public Works to construct Riverside Avenue. On February 17, 1874, it sent a memorial to the legislature advocating that the Department of Public Parks retain its authority to plan, construct, and manage all streets and avenues bounding the parks north of 58th Street (DPP, *Minutes*, Jan. 26, 1874, pp. 540, 544–45; ibid., Feb. 17, 1874, pp. 568–70; *New-York Times*, Feb. 18, 1874, p. 2).
23. Olmsted here lists department members, himself included, who had lobbied against the bill to give the Riverside Avenue project to the Department of Public Works: Salem H. Wales, David B. Williamson, Samuel Hall, department secretary William Irwin, assistant secretary Issac Evans, chief clerk David P. Lord, disbursing clerk William Van Valkenburgh, and chief engineer John Bogart (*City Record*, Jan. 23, 1874, p. 78).
24. R. J. Morrison was Andrew H. Green's private clerk. John Kelly (1821–1886), first Irish leader of the New York Democrats, was strongly affiliated with Tammany Hall as county sheriff during the 1860s. Absent from New York between 1868 and late 1871, he was untainted by the corruption that brought down the Tweed Ring. He led the reconstruction of the organization along "reform" lines and enlisted the assistance of such former Committee of Seventy members as Samuel J. Tilden and Green. This alliance shifted in the spring of 1874 when he broke with Mayor Havemeyer and Green for cutting back the public works that his Irish constituents depended upon for employment. The *Sunday Mercury* identified Daniel "Boulevard" Tracy as a lobbyist for Green (*Sunday Mercury*, Nov. 15, 1874, p. 4; ibid., March 15, 1874, p. 4; S. Mandelbaum, *Boss Tweed's New York*, pp. 92–93, 110–12; Gustavus Myers, *The History of Tammany Hall* [1917; rpt. ed., New York, 1971], pp. 218–19, 250–57).
25. On March 23, 1874, the state senate voted to recommit the bill to the Committee on Cities, which took no action on it before the session ended. Shortly afterward, George Van Nort announced his intention to resign as a commissioner of the New York City

APPENDIX III

Department of Public Works effective May 1, 1874, but decided in mid-April not to do so (*New-York Times*, March 24, 1874, p. 4; ibid., March 31, 1874, pp. 4, 8; ibid., April 15, 1874, p. 4).

26. Within several weeks of this entry, the park board voted unanimously to pay Daniel Tracy $900 for fill he had deposited on the 110th Street side of Central Park (DPP, *Minutes*, April 17, 1874, p. 647).
27. The ordinance, approved by the Board of Aldermen on March 19, 1874, was vetoed by the mayor on April 2, 1874 (New York (City). Board of Aldermen, *Proceedings of the Board of Aldermen of the City of New York* [New York, 1874], 133: 449–50; ibid., vol. 134, pp. 17–22).
28. Joseph Wiley Gelray (d. 1900) served in the 2nd Massachusetts Infantry regiment from May 1861 to July 1864, much of the time under Robert Gould Shaw. Shaw, who shortly thereafter took command of the famous black regiment, the 54th Massachusetts, was the son of Francis George Shaw, a wealthy philanthropist and abolitionist. Olmsted had known the elder Shaw since 1857, when he had assumed the debts of a failed publishing firm in which Olmsted was partner with his son-in-law, George W. Curtis. During the war, Shaw urged Olmsted's appointment to head several relief and humanitarian organizations (Francis Bernard Heitman, *Historical Register and Dictionary of the United States Army . . .*, 2 vols. [Washington, D.C., 1903], 1: 451; NCAB, 8: 142; *Papers of FLO*, 2: 55–56; ibid., 4: 23, 25, 287–88, 306).
29. Superintendent Columbus Ryan, park board president Salem Wales and commissioner Samuel Hall (1820–1911). On Hall's motion, Gelray was hired temporarily as foreman, but he declined the appointment (American Medical Association, *Directory of Deceased American Physicians, 1804–1929*, 2 vols. [Chicago, 1993], 1: 639; DPP, *Minutes*, Jan. 7, 1874, p. 502; ibid., Jan. 21, 1874, p. 535).
30. That is, Olmsted suggested that Gelray take over the position held by Henry Koster, whose command of the Central Park keepers Olmsted frequently criticized. Koster remained Captain of the force until he was suspended on March 5, 1875 (*Papers of FLO*, 6: 583, 617–21; FLO to Henry G. Stebbins, Aug. 27, 1874, and FLO to DPP, c. March 1875, above; DPP, *Minutes*, Dec. 13, 1870, p. 310).
31. Mayor William F. Havemeyer.
32. That is, those who lacked the capacity for work (*OED*).
33. The foreman of the stables was responsible also for the supervision of laborers in the third of four territorial divisions of Central Park. In April 1872 the board had created the divisions and designated foremen, gardeners, and laborers for duties in each (FLO to Henry G. Stebbins, April 12, 1875; FLO to Henry G. Stebbins, May 25, 1872, and July 30, 1873 [*Papers of FLO*, 6: 556–59, 633–41]).
34. That is, Delaware Park.
35. The park superintendent was William McMillan (see FLO to William McMillan, Sept. 10, 1876, above).
36. In late March 1875, Olmsted returned to this entry and added this note: "Tracy being [*referred to*] the following year as one who had the previous year visited Albany in the interest of the Dept. published a card (in the Times) loftily denying it—It was solely in interest of property owners & taxpayers." Tracy's notice appeared in the *New-York Times* on March 9, 1875, page 10.
37. Thomas H. O'Callaghan (1828–1893) represented the nineteenth assembly district in Manhattan (*Trow's New York City Directory for the Year Ending July 1, 1894* [New York, 1894], p. 1051; William H. McElroy and Alex McBride, *Life Sketches of Government Offices and Members of the Legislature of the State of New York for 1874* [Albany, N. Y., 1874], p. 258).
38. Presently known as Old County Hall, this building had been under construction since 1871. Olmsted provided plans for its grounds and approaches in 1875–76, the

708

PATRONAGE JOURNAL (1873–1877)

planting of which McMillan superintended (see FLO to Dennis Bowen, Jan. 1, 1876, above).
39. That is, the routine work of dredging and repairing the Erie Canal, overseen by a state board of commissioners (New York [State], *Laws of the State of New York, Passed at the Ninety-Seventh Session of the Legislature*. . . [Albany, N.Y., 1874], chap. 399).
40. The bill, passed by the legislature on June 5, 1874, appropriated the money needed to pay the engineers and continue the work through the year. It also codified the authority of the department to survey and establish street, sewage, and drainage systems in the districts recently annexed to the city (ibid., chap. 604; *New-York Times*, April 8, 1874, p. 1; ibid., April 9, 1874, p. 5).
41. In 1870, shortly before it dismissed Olmsted and Vaux as its advisory landscape architects, the Tweed Ring park board ordered the placement of numerous urinals on Central Park. During Olmsted's tenure as board president between May and October 1872, the board ordered that all brick urinals be removed from the park. Scotch iron was a type of pig iron made in Scotland for light or ornamental castings (DPP, *Minutes*, Sept. 13, 1870, p. 148; ibid., Nov. 22, 1870, p. 272; ibid., June 12, 1872, p. 424; W. K. V. Gale, *The Iron and Steel Industry: a Dictionary of Terms* [London, 1971], p. 180).
42. Olmsted is referring to a street urinal patented by Mortiz Bacharach of New York City on January 18, 1870. In June 1871 the Sweeny park board ordered that one be placed on Central Park (U.S. Patent No. 98,905, Record Group 241, Records of the U.S. Patent and Trademark Office, NARA, Washington, D.C.; DPP, *Minutes*, June 10, 1871, pp. 127–28).
43. Philip Bissinger was among three commissioners William F. Havemeyer appointed in June 1873 when the park board was reorganized under the terms of a new city charter (*Papers of FLO*, 6: 44; *New-York Times*, May 20, 1873, p. 1).
44. In January 1874 Olmsted recommended that the brick urinals be replaced with small iron ones instead of the Bacharach structures. Placed near the park gates, they could "be arranged so as to be perfectly convenient without being obtrusive or injuring the rural character of the park." Bissinger's motion to purchase the Bacharach urinals passed unanimously, and by late September 1874, nine had been authorized and three installed ("Document No. 55," in DPP, *Minutes*, Jan. 7, 1874, p. 13; DPP, *Minutes*, April 7, 1874, p. 632; *City Record*, Nov. 18, 1874, p. 1365).
45. The discussion Olmsted relates here is not reflected in the printed minutes of the park board.
46. With the expiration of Dr. Samuel Hall's term on May 1, 1874, the legislature reduced the park board to four members. Those who remained split evenly between Democrats and Republicans. Salem H. Wales and Philip Bissinger were Republicans, and Henry G. Stebbins and David B. Williamson were "reform" Democrats (New York [State], *Laws Passed at the Ninety-Seventh Session*, chap. 300; *Papers of FLO*, 6: 44, 67; *Forty Years*, 2: 108).
47. Wales lost the park board presidency to Stebbins on May 9, 1874, and he resigned his commissionership three weeks later (DPP, *Minutes*, May 9, 1874, pp. 20–21; ibid., May 29, 1874, p. 65; *Sunday Mercury*, May 31, 1874, p. 4).
48. Thomas Elliott Stewart (1824–1904), lawyer and politician, had served a term in Congress between 1867 and 1869 as a Republican, and in 1872 was chairman of the Liberal Republican general committee of New York City. He attended his first park board meeting as commissioner on June 3, 1874 (*BDAC*; DPP, *Minutes*, June 3, 1874, p. 67).
49. That is, a politician who either brought in voters not legally qualified as such, or who openly dealt in patronage (Mitford M. Mathews, ed., *A Dictionary of Americanisms on Historical Principles*, 2 vols. [Chicago, 1951], 2: 1251).

709

APPENDIX III

50. The *New-York Daily Tribune* stated that Stewart's affiliation with the Liberal Republicans qualified him for the mayor's appointment more than expertise in park matters. Still, the paper considered it "a selection far superior to some of his recent ones." The *Sunday Mercury* claimed that Havemeyer hoped to win the support of Liberal Republicans in a bid for reelection that autumn (*New-York Daily Tribune*, June 2, 1874, p. 4; *Sunday Mercury*, May 31, 1874, p. 4).
51. Because of a shortfall in its construction budget, the board on May 20, 1874, reorganized and reduced department personnel engaged in surveying, engineering, architecture, and landscape architecture. The board reduced the number of positions in the last three areas by approximately two-thirds (*City Record*, Jan. 23, 1874, p. 78; DPP, *Minutes*, May 6, 1874, p. 8; ibid., May 20, 1874, pp. 42–43; *New York World*, May 23, 1874, p. 4).
52. In November 1874, a resurgent Tammany Hall had put William H. Wickham in the mayor's office, and helped Samuel J. Tilden become governor. Its committee on patronage announced that the patronage positions it controlled in the Department of Public Works would go to the city's assembly districts in proportion to the vote each had delivered for Tilden. Based on the value of salaries and payroll to be rewarded, it calculated that each vote was worth $1.50. Edward Gilon, Tammany alderman from the city's Ninth Ward, here confirmed accounts of the division of spoils that had reached Olmsted (G. Meyers, *History of Tammany Hall*, pp. 255–56; *New-York Times*, March 15, 1875, pp. 1, 4; S. Mandelbaum, *Boss Tweed's New York*, pp. 112, 131–33; *Sunday Mercury*, Sept. 13, 1874, p. 4).
53. The division of the park board into two camps emerged in January 1875, after Mayor Wickham appointed William R. Martin to the position made vacant when Philip Bissinger resigned. Martin, a Tammany Hall Democrat, joined Thomas E. Stewart on the board's executive committee. Within weeks the two took sides against the board's "reform" Democrats, Henry G. Stebbins and David B. Williamson, in a fight over the positions and influence of Andrew H. Green's favorites in the department. They soon removed three major staff members that had been appointed through Green's influence. By January 31 they succeeded in forcing longtime park superintendent Columbus Ryan to resign. In early March they removed Henry Koster, captain of the park keepers, by suspending him without pay, and later that month took steps to force out the disbursing clerk, William Van Valkenburgh. They also pushed through revisions in the bylaws that restored to Olmsted powers of superintendence and design that he had not enjoyed since the board was reorganized under Green's influence in July-September 1873 (DPP, *Minutes*, Jan. 12, 1875, p. 452; ibid., Jan. 20, 1875, pp. 465–69; ibid., Feb. 1, 1875, pp. 496–97; ibid., Feb. 23, 1875, p. 536; ibid., March 5, 1875, pp. 559–60; ibid., March 27, 1875, pp. 611–12; ibid., March 30, 1875, p. 619; *Sunday Mercury*, Feb. 7, 1875, p. 1).
54. Andrew H. Green, who had last attended a meeting of the park board as a member on December 21, 1872, nominally retained his position through May 1873. Nevertheless, he still wielded considerable influence through 1874. Two of his close associates, David B. Williamson and Columbus Ryan, the board's treasurer and superintendent of parks, controlled appointments and dismissals in the clerical and laboring forces through August 1873. Furthermore, as city comptroller and member of the Board of Estimate and Apportionment, he helped determine a large part of the department's budget. According to his critics, Green routinely used these connections and powers to control how the park board dispensed patronage. On May 20, 1874, the board dismissed Samuel T. Houghton from the book-keeping position he had held for four years. According to the *Sunday Mercury*, the action was taken "to make room for 'Green' men." The board apparently hired his replacement shortly thereafter, but the

printed minutes of the board record neither the action nor the identity of the new book-keeper ("Document No. 30," in DPP, *Minutes*, Nov. 28, 1871, p. 9; ibid., May 20, 1874, p. 43; ibid., March 27, 1875, p. 610; *New York World*, May 23, 1874, p. 4; ibid., May 30, 1874, p. 4; *Sunday Mercury*, May 24, 1874, p. 4; see also, *New-York Daily Tribune*, May 21, 1873, p. 8; *New-York Times*, May 29, 1874, p. 4).

55. Stebbins's March 23 order read:

> On examination of the books, it is found that all our construction fund is exhausted. You will therefore suspend all construction works of every kind to-day, until further order.
>
> All clerical force solely employed on construction works is suspended without pay until further order.
>
> All clerical force employed partly on construction and partly on maintenance works, will be employed from to-day only on maintenance and their time so returned.

(DPP, *Minutes*, March 24, 1875, p. 598).

56. At its meeting of March 24, 1875, the board approved these actions. In October 1874 it had adopted Thomas E. Stewart's motion that the superintendent not restore men dropped from the payroll without the board's approval. No copy of either document "A" or document "B" referred to in this section has survived (DPP, *Minutes*, March 4, 1875, pp. 598–99; ibid., Oct. 21, 1874, p. 309).

57. The board kept Superintending Engineer John Bogart and several other employees on half pay drawn from the maintenance fund, while it retained assistant engineer Frank A. Calkins with full pay. Hugh J. Hastings, a prominent Republican lobbyist in Albany for decades, had edited the *Commercial Advertiser* since 1868. A member of the Stalwart faction of the party, Hastings opposed civil service reform and, according to the *New-York Times*, "not only advocated the spoils system, but justified it as a proper political expedient" (DPP, *Minutes*, March 24, 1875, pp. 599–600; *New-York Times*, Sept. 13, 1883, p. 5; Alexander B. Callow, Jr., *The Tweed Ring* [New York, 1966], p. 215).

58. Olmsted is referring to the park department's request for an appropriation of $575,000 in construction money, contained in a bill then being considered by the assembly's Committee on Cities. On March 26, 1875, the committee approved the bill. The full assembly concurred a month later, and forwarded it to the senate, where Green's lobbying effort against it and the Riverside Avenue bill carried more weight (*New York World*, March 25, 1875, pp. 4, 8; New York (State), *Journal of the Assembly of the State of New York: at their Ninety-Eighth Session*, 2 vols. [Albany, N.Y., 1875], 1: 430, 577, 963, 1030; FLO to William R. Martin, Aug. 9, 1876, n. 14, above).

59. See page 671, above.

60. Olmsted apparently is referring to another episode in the campaign of Thomas E. Stewart and William R. Martin to rid the department of those appointed through Andrew H. Green's influence. His appointees had controlled the Civil and Topographical Corps since May 1874 and had responsibility for laying out streets in the Twenty-third and Twenty-fourth wards. With the support of Henry G. Stebbins one of their number, Eugene C. Morrison, quickly rose from the position of assistant division engineer for Morrisania to engineer-in-charge of both wards. Shortly after the present entry, Martin tried unsuccessfully to convince the board to reorganize the engineers corps. Instead it moved Morrison from the corps to a supervisory position. A year later, after Martin took over as its president, the board fired Morrison (*City Record*, July 24, 1874, p. 798; ibid., Sept. 11, 1874, pp. 1013–14; DPP, *Minutes*, June 3, 1874, p. 69; ibid., June 14, 1876, pp. 125–26).

APPENDIX III

61. The Board of Aldermen unanimously adopted William H. McCarthy's resolution that the commissioners of accounts, the city's auditing body, investigate the fiscal condition of the parks department (*New York World*, March 26, 1875, p. 2).
62. Robert P. Schofield, who as lieutenant since December 1870 was the second highest ranking officer of the Central Park keepers, was among those dismissed by the board in October 1873 when it rescinded Olmsted's system of beat patrols. At that time the board kept Henry Koster on as captain of the keepers. In early March 1875 the board nearly fired Koster for poor performance but instead suspended him without pay (*Papers of FLO*, 6: 629; DPP, *Minutes*, Sept. 24, 1873, p. 291; ibid., Oct. 1, 1873, p. 317; FLO to DPP, c. Jan.–Feb. 1875, above).
63. Thomas E. Stewart and William R. Martin, appointed in June 1874 and January 1875, respectively.
64. Phillip Corcoran, a gate and park keeper on Central Park for over a decade, who was appointed lieutenant on February 3, 1875 (R. D. Nesmith, "Special Report of the Surgeon of Police upon the Physical Condition of Park-Keepers and Gatekeepers in the Employ of the Department of Public Parks," Dec. 15, 1872, Olmsted Papers; DPP, *Minutes*, Feb. 3, 1875, p. 507).
65. Hern's Head, an outcrop of land on the west shore of the Lake, was the site of a cottage for ladies' conveniences.
66. Erected in 1866, the Kinderberg was a large rustic shelter southwest of the Mall, reserved for children, mothers, and nurses. The Children's Cottage was located just south of the Dairy (BCCP, *Tenth Annual Report* [1867], pp. 37–39).
67. Thomas E. Stewart, who as a member of the board's executive committee had been formally investigating the park keepers' force since December 1874 and took over its supervision in February 1875 (DPP, *Minutes*, Dec. 19, 1874, p. 417; ibid., Feb. 23, 1875, p. 536).
68. At the same special meeting where the board dismissed dozens of employees because of the construction fund shortfall, it adopted Stewart's recommendation that five park keepers be fired for neglect of duty (DPP, *Minutes*, March 27, 1875, p. 613).
69. Julius A. Donaldson.
70. Fitz-John Porter (1822–1901), former Union army general, was named commissioner of public works in early March 1875 by Mayor Wickham. Reflecting in 1863 on Porter's conviction by a courts martial for misconduct in the face of the enemy and disobedience to a superior officer's orders, Olmsted concluded that he deserved "hanging as much as any other criminal who remains unhung. . . ." (*Papers of FLO*, 4: 640, 644; *Sunday Mercury*, March 7, 1875, p. 4).
71. Abram S. Hewitt (1822–1903), iron manufacturer and philanthropist. Prominent among the Democrats who struck down the Tweed Ring and then rebuilt Tammany Hall along "reform" lines, Hewitt had just begun a term as congressman from the tenth district in New York City (*DAB*; *BDAC*; *Congressional Directory* [Washington, D.C., 1876], p. 43).
72. Samuel A. Lewis.
73. Olmsted apparently intended to recount another story at this point, possibly involving Thomas Tierny, a foreman for the parks department (*City Record*, Feb. 5, 1875, p. 232).
74. That is, the *New-York Times* and the *New-York Daily Tribune* (*New-York Times*, April 8, 1875, p. 6; *New-York Daily Tribune*, April 8, 1875, p. 2).
75. Olmsted's observations on park wages were included in a report he had prepared to reduce department expenses (see n. 88 below).
76. John Yapp Culyer (1839–1924), Olmsted's former colleague on Central Park and Prospect Park. In 1875 Culyer, as chief engineer of Prospect Park, reported that the Brooklyn park commission was paying laborers fifteen cents per hour and that

PATRONAGE JOURNAL (1873–1877)

"we can get as many as wanted for that or a less price" (*Papers of FLO*, 6: 162; John Y. Culyer to John Bogart, April 6, 1875).
77. Olmsted is quoting from an editorial in the *New York Herald* that accused Green of hampering the business of the park department because of his antipathy toward William R. Martin (*New York Herald*, April 27, 1875, p. 6).
78. See note 46 above.
79. Olmsted is paraphrasing from a *New-York Times* editorial entitled "Another Raid on Central Park" (*New-York Times*, April 28, 1875, p. 4).
80. Commissioner of Accounts Lindsay I. Howe and his assistants were conducting an investigation ordered by the Common Council in late March 1875 (see note 57 above).
81. Olmsted's reference is to his note of March 25, 1875, above, which details the budget consequences of a $70,000 bookkeeping error by a Green appointee. Stebbins was probably referring to the board's chief clerk, David P. Lord, another Green appointee, whom commissioners William R. Martin and Thomas Stewart apparently had tried to fire. The Common Council ordered the Commissioner of Accounts to investigate the department's books, ostensibly because of the late March budget crisis (*Sunday Mercury*, Jan. 17, 1875, pp. 1, 4; ibid., Feb. 7, 1875, p. 1; *New-York Times*, March 26, 1875, p. 12).
82. Two days before the editorial "Another Raid on Central Park" appeared, the *Times* charged that "obstructive and disorganizing efforts" by William R. Martin and his political cronies had left the parks in their worst condition in years. Martin agreed that the parks needed more attention but argued that abuses begun by Green as a park commissioner and sustained by him as comptroller were the root of the problem. Martin cited the ousting of Columbus Ryan and Henry Koster as first steps in the department's reform. Changes had to follow, he said, in the administration of financial accounts, street openings, and laying out the Twenty-third and Twenty-fourth wards. Until the legislature acted on the department's appropriation, however, most work on the parks would remain suspended (*New-York Times*, April 26, 1875, p. 4; *New York World*, April 29, 1875, p. 5).
83. Olmsted is referring to a letter he wrote on that date to Henry G. Stebbins, in which he described how a campaign of published attacks and word-of-mouth innuendo undermined public confidence in his organization of the park keepers. The letter also contained his critique of proposed changes in the bylaws that assigned to others his responsibilities for the park keepers and the supervision of laborers, and that created an independent office of landscape gardening. Despite Olmsted's protests, the board revised the bylaws in a manner which turned these functions over to others and significantly reduced his powers (FLO to Henry G. Stebbins, July 30, 1873; *Papers of FLO*, 6: 633–41; see FLO to DPP, [March 1, 1875], above).
84. In February 1875 Julius F. Munckwitz took over the superintendent of parks position vacated the month before by Columbus Ryan. In February and March 1875 the board revised the bylaws to restore Olmsted's authority over the landscape work of the department. Olmsted, as head of the Bureau of Design and Superintendence, henceforth was to issue all orders for park maintenance and to supervise their execution through officers made subordinate to his office: the superintending architect, superintending engineer, superintending gardener, and superintendent of parks (DPP, *Minutes*, Feb. 23, 1875, pp. 533–34; ibid., March 19, 1875, pp. 594–95).
85. The Copcot, a rustic structure built in the early 1860s, overlooked the Pond from the west, near the Sixth Avenue entrance to the Park.
86. That is, superintending gardener William L. Fischer.
87. A reference to the examination of the books of the Department of Public Parks that was ordered by the Common Council following the discovery on March 23, 1875, of

APPENDIX III

a $70,000 error by a book-keeper who had been appointed through the influence of Andrew H. Green (see pages 671 and 711, n. 55 above).

88. A reference to Thomas C. Fields (1825–1885), who as a member of the old Central Park commission from its inception in 1857 through 1870 had opposed Olmsted at every turn. He served as a commissioner until May 1870, when he joined fellow Tammany Hall Democrats Peter B. Sweeny and Henry Hilton on the board of the new Department of Public Parks. He was among those indicted during the investigation of the Tweed Ring scandals and at the time of this entry was a fugitive in Canada (*Papers of FLO*, 3: 93, 324–25; *New-York Times*, Jan. 26, 1885, p. 1).

89. Olmsted's report, a draft of which is dated April 12, 1875, focused on Central Park and identified maintenance work (on drives, rides, walks, buildings, and turf) that could be deferred without lasting damage to the park. It proposed that some hourly positions at the menagerie and arsenal museum be changed into salaried ones to reduce the department's outlays for overtime, and that workers be paid only for time actually at the work site (and not time spent gathering tools and walking to the site). It also advocated a return to one element of Olmsted's controversial and short-lived 1873 organization of the park keepers — the replacement of a full shift of park keepers on duty at night with ten night watchmen. The savings could be used to place more park keepers on daytime duty, especially at times when the number of visitors was greatest during afternoons and weekends (FLO to Henry G. Stebbins, April 12, 1875; see FLO to William L. Fischer, March 14, 1875, n. 4, above; FLO to Henry G. Stebbins, May 18, 1875, n. 8, above).

90. Stebbins read the report at the board meeting of April 14, 1875. The board adopted his motion that the report be received and laid over (DPP, *Minutes*, April 14, 1875, p. 648).

91. The board returned the report to Olmsted for revision on April 21, and voted to table the revised report on motion of the board's president, Henry Stebbins, on April 30. Henry Koster, who had been appointed captain of the park keepers through the influence of Andrew H. Green, had been suspended without pay in March (ibid., April 21, 1875, p. 664; ibid., April 30, 1875, p. 694; see note 53, above).

92. See DPP, *Minutes*, May 5, 1875, page 12.

93. Joseph John O'Donohue, a wealthy merchant and Tammany Hall Democrat since 1869, quit that organization in 1871 and joined the Committee of Seventy that helped depose it. He rejoined the "reformed" Tammany Hall in 1874 as a member of its General Committee from the Nineteenth Ward. He contributed generously to its campaign coffers and was friends with Mayor Wickham (*New-York Times*, May 2, 1875, p. 5; *The Irish-American*, May 8, 1875, p. 4).

94. David B. Williamson.

95. William H. McCarthy, Democratic alderman from the city's Yorkville district (see n. 57 above).

96. On April 30, 1875, the board ordered that the park keepers be differentiated between patrolmen, fit for the severest active duty and post-keepers, those who as patrolmen had become "physically disqualified for such duty, but are still fitted for duty requiring less activity, strength and endurance." Both classes of park keepers, Olmsted told Lieutenant Corcoran, were to aid visitors in enjoying the park to the best advantage and to protect the park itself from misuse and damage. The board provided also for ten night watchmen who were employed solely for that duty between 11:00 P.M. and 6:00 A.M., when the park was closed to visitors (DPP, *Minutes*, April 30, 1875, pp. 689–90; FLO to Philip Corcoran, May 18, 1875).

97. Probably Philip Loeffel, a park patrolman first hired in 1858, whom the board ordered be demoted to post-keeper (*City Record*, Sept. 10, 1875, p. 1484; R. D. Nesmith, "Special Report of Surgeon of Police," Dec. 15, 1872).

PATRONAGE JOURNAL (1873–1877)

98. William A. Conklin, director of the Central Park menagerie.
99. The report of park department surgeon George Z. Hunter on the physical fitness of the park keepers.
100. The park board unanimously approved a series of resolutions embodying proposals in Olmsted's report of April 14, 1875, that reduced maintenance and salary costs. The preamble to the resolutions cited a deep cut in the city's appropriation to the department's maintenance fund and the state legislature's apparent intention to cut the department's construction fund (DPP, *Minutes*, May 14, 1875, pp. 26–29).
101. The Board of Aldermen adopted the resolution of William H. McCarthy that the Commissioner of Accounts add an investigation of Olmsted's salary to its ongoing investigation of the department (*New-York Times*, May 21, 1875, p. 5).
102. See FLO to Henry G. Stebbins, May 18, 1875, above.
103. A monumental bronze figure by George Simonds, located south of the Lake (Henry Hope Reed, *Central Park: a History and Guide* [New York, 1967], p. 153).
104. The paragraph in the *Tribune* that Olmsted refers to was apparently the one he quotes three paragraphs further along in this section, praising progress in providing fountains in the parks. However, on the following day the *Tribune* contained the following brief article on turf in Central Park:

> Mr. Olmsted, the Landscape Architect of the Department of Public Works, calls attention to the condition of the turf in those portions of Central Park which are most frequented by the people, especially the Ball and Croquet Grounds, and the tracts on either side of the Mall. About one-third of the turf on these grounds is worn away, and the grass generally in a very poor condition. The climate is very trying, and turf will not stand the usage that it bears in England. It is stated that the only means of protecting the turf in the playgrounds and in the portions of the Park which are most frequented, is to restrict their use for a year or two to allow the turf some time to recover and the Park Commissioners time to patch it up, fill in the bare places, and plant seed where necessary.

("The Turf in the City's Pleasure Ground," *New-York Daily Tribune*, May 25, 1875, p. 9).
105. Olmsted is quoting from the article, "Warm Days in Central Park," *New-York Times*, May 24, 1875, p. 8.
106. See the *New-York Daily Tribune*, May 24, 1875, p. 6.
107. In June 1871 the park board had empowered treasurer Henry Hilton to let contracts for the construction of fountains in Madison Square and other city parks (DPP, *Minutes*, June 10, 1871, pp. 132–34).
108. The park board voted unanimously to retain assistant engineer Frank A. Calkins on full pay (DPP, *Minutes*, March 24, 1875, p. 599; see above, p. 671).
109. Calkins' brother, Hiram Calkins, retired as clerk of the New York state assembly on May 18, 1875 (W. H. McElroy, *Life Sketches of . . . and Members of the Legislature . . . for 1875* [New York, 1875], p. 323; *New York World*, May 20, 1875, p. 1).
110. On January 4, 1875, Wickham, in his annual message to the Common Council, denounced the lobbying of the state legislature by city department officers. The park board unanimously adopted a resolution that the president inform the mayor that all its requests to the legislature would be submitted to him for review and approval (*Proceedings of the Board of Aldermen of the City of New York* [New York, 1874], 137: 56–57; DPP, *Minutes*, Jan. 6, 1875, pp. 428–29).
111. See FLO to William R. Martin, Aug. 9, 1876, note 14, above.
112. Mayor Wickham and the heads of the parks, police, and public works departments agreed to the wage reduction in late May 1875 (*New-York Times*, June 2, 1875, p. 7).

113. The Dock Commission, headed by former park board president Salem H. Wales, was responsible for the repair, improvement, and expansion of city-owned wharves, piers, and slips (*New-York Daily Tribune*, June 3, 1875, p. 9; Isaac Newton Phelps Stokes, *The Iconography of Manhattan Island, 1498–1909*, 6 vols. [New York, 1915–28], 5: 1938).
114. Commmissioners Henry Stebbins and David Williamson supported implementation of the wage reduction while commissioners William R. Martin and Joseph O'Donohue opposed it. With no majority vote either way, the board failed to approve it, which left the old wage structure in place. Commissioner O'Donohue wished to consult with Mayor Wickham and Commissioner of the Department of Public Works Fitz-John Porter (DPP, *Minutes*, June 4, 1875, pp. 73–75).
115. William Fischer was recalling the period 1859–60, when Andrew H. Green, as treasurer and comptroller of the Central Park commission, constantly criticized what he saw as extravagant expenditures on plantings, much to Olmsted's frustration (*Papers of FLO*, 3: 57–58).
116. Designed by Calvert Vaux, the Dairy was under construction when he and Olmsted were dismissed by the Sweeny park board in late 1870. The Ring board completed it the next year but did not put it to its designed use as a retreat for mothers and children ("Document No. 10," in DPP, *Minutes*, May 31, 1870, p. 3; "A Review of Recent Changes, and Changes which have been Projected, in the Plans of the Central Park," Jan. and Feb. 1872 [*Papers of FLO*, SS1: 244, 246, 275]; ibid., 6: 39).
117. See his journal entry of May 22, 1875, above.
118. See the *New-York Times*, June 21, 1875, page 8.
119. Governor Samuel J. Tilden did not sign the department's appropriation into law until mid-June 1875, approximately one month after the legislature had approved it (*New-York Daily Tribune*, June 1, 1875, p. 2; DPP, *Minutes*, June 16, 1875, p. 87; ibid., June 23, 1875, p. 99).
120. That is, the seaside resort at Long Branch, New Jersey.
121. Olmsted apparently is referring to a contractor with the Department of Public Works.
122. The park board did not reach a quorum on July 8, 1875, and Olmsted made his report at the next board meeting two weeks later (DPP, *Minutes*, July 21, 1875, pp. 142–43).
123. On July 8, 1875, the Board of Aldermen laid over a report by its committee on law that recommended a commencement of work on Riverside Park by the Department of Public Parks (*New-York Times*, July 9, 1875, p. 2).
124. In August 1875 Olmsted visited Providence, Rhode Island, and consulted with city officials about the development of a park there (FLO to Thomas A. Doyle, Aug. 6, 1875, above).
125. That is, to give the superintending gardener and each of the division gardeners responsible for specific areas of Central Park the laborers, supplies, and authority necessary to properly develop its landscape qualities. Since the spring of 1872, Olmsted had urged the park board to implement such an organization, derived from the arrangement he had in place between late 1858 and 1861, when he was architect-in-chief of Central Park (*Papers of FLO*, 6: 541; FLO to Henry G. Stebbins, May 25, 1872 [ibid., 6: 556–59]).
126. Although the Sweeny park board's Bureau of Landscape Gardening had long since vanished as an organization, its influence persisted into early 1875 through Robert Demcker and the projects he undertook as landscape gardener, along with the superintendent's control of laborers and supplies. Although Olmsted regained some of his power in these areas with the revision of bylaws in February-March 1875, it remained for him to strengthen the organization of gardeners (FLO to DPP, March 1, 1875, and FLO, Patronage Journal, p. 679, both above).

127. In his letter of June 1875, Olmsted pointed out that while the engineering and artisanal work on the park was carried out under the direction of foremen trained and experienced in those classes of work, the same had not been true of the horticulture, "the park work upon which the value of all the rest depends. . ." This work had been done primarily "by men enrolled with the common laborers and under the direction of the common foremen uneducated in and indifferent to the craft of the gardener." He then stated the changes needed in organization of the horticultural branch of the park, as he had summarized them in the previous paragraph of this section of the Patronage Journal. On July 8 he submitted a more detailed report, proposing that Central Park be divided into six gardening districts, each under the authority of a division gardener, each of whom was to have two gardeners and two garden laborers available to him at all times. This entire force was to be under the exclusive control of the superintending gardener "and nothing to be done on ground occupied by trees, shrubs or plants except under his orders or with his approval" (See *Forty Years*, 2: 358–60).
128. John Wolf, who had been employed by one of the gardening departments the board had abolished in February 1875. The restaurant at Mount St. Vincent, in the upper northeast corner of the park, was operated under a concession by former park superintendent Columbus Ryan, who had resigned that position in January 1875 under pressure from the board (*City Record*, Feb. 5, 1875, p. 232; *Papers of FLO*, 6: 524).
129. The board's vote to fire Wolf took place at its meeting of August 25, 1875. The Wolf "beer shop" was located at 578 Hudson Street in lower Manhattan (DPP, *Minutes*, Aug. 25, 1875, p. 229; *Trow's New York City Directory for the Year ending 1875* [New York, 1875], p. 1419).
130. See DPP, *Minutes*, Sept. 6, 1875, page 261.
131. See ibid., Sept. 27, 1875, pages 293–94.
132. In late September the board authorized the employment of some 200 laborers, and over a dozen rockmen, bricklayers, and masons. It hired 100 additional laborers at its meeting of October 8 (DPP, *Minutes*, Sept. 27, 1875, p. 291; ibid., Oct. 8, 1875, pp. 324–25).
133. In late September 1875 Olmsted had issued instructions to the park superintendent about how his responsibilities related to those of the division gardeners and garden laborers, and the board had named men to the new positions created by the reorganization (FLO to Julius Munckwitz, Sept. 25, 1875; DPP, *Minutes*, Sept. 29, 1875, p. 306).
134. The author of the letter was Democratic assemblyman James Daly, who in late 1873 had attempted to remove the design and construction of Riverside Avenue and Park from the department (see n. 5 above).
135. Seven articles critical of the design of Central Park, its drainage and that of surrounding areas, its policing, and its provisions for carriages and pedestrians, appeared in the *New York Herald* in the first half of November 1875. Egbert L. Viele had long accused Olmsted and Vaux of stealing his original design of 1856 for the park, which had been formally adopted by the first Central Park Commission. That commission, appointed by Mayor Fernando Wood in 1856, had been superceded by the commission created in 1857 by the state legislature that hired Olmsted as superintendent and held the design competition that he and Calvert Vaux won in 1858. In the first *Herald* article of 1875, Viele stated that if his plans for the underdrainage of the park and nearby streets had been followed, these areas would not be spreading malaria and disease throughout the city. The *New-York Times*, in an editorial published on November 15, 1875, made similar charges about the park and its management (*New York Herald*, Nov. 6, 1875, p. 4; ibid., Nov. 7, 1875, p. 8; ibid., Nov. 12, 1875, p. 6; ibid., Nov. 13, 1875, p. 6; ibid., Nov. 14, 1875, p. 8; ibid., Nov. 16, 1875, p. 6; FLO to George Jones, Nov. 19, 1875, above).

APPENDIX III

136. That is, James Gordon Bennett (1841–1918), editor of the *New York Herald* since 1866 (*DAB*).
137. See "Good News for Pedestrians," *New York Herald*, Nov. 19, 1875, page 6.
138. Olmsted reported on the park's drainage and sewerage at the board's meeting of November 17, 1875, and two days later recapitulated his main points in a private letter to George Jones, the publisher of the *New-York Times*, printed above (DPP, *Minutes*, Nov. 17, 1875, p. 393; FLO to Henry G. Stebbins, Nov. 16, 1875; FLO to George Jones, Nov. 19, 1875, above).
139. In late January 1875 Olmsted presented his plan of work for the year to the board, which ordered that it be printed and sent to the mayor. The plan formed the basis of the department's appropriation from the state legislature but was not signed by Governor Tilden until mid-June. The board reaffirmed its approval later that month but delayed ordering the work to begin and laborers to be hired until late September ("Document No. 63," in DPP, *Minutes*, Jan. 29, 1875, p. 482; ibid., Sept. 23, 1875, p. 286; see nn. 118 and 131 above).
140. Olmsted is discussing Andrew H. Green's attempt in the spring of 1875 to gain control of the parks department through passage of a bill in the state legislature that made the current president of the department—Green's ally Henry Stebbins—the sole commissioner, and abolished the positions of the other commissioners. The bill appeared to have good prospects in both houses, but the *New-York Times* of April 26 carried the report, which Olmsted affixed to his draft manuscript, that on the previous day, following the decision of the legislature to end its current session on May 3, the park bill was passed over in the Senate and sent to the bottom of the calendar, "thus killing it effectually." Considerable confusion surrounded this action, however, and the bill was in fact passed by the Senate on May 2. However, it still needed to pass the Assembly, where, in the short session of the final day, the Democrats succeeded in preventing a vote on that and several other major bills affecting New York City (*New-York Times*, March 7, 1876, p. 6; ibid., April 26, 1876, p. 4; ibid., May 3, 1876, p. 1; ibid., May 4, 1876, p.1).
141. See "The State Legislature," *New-York Times*, March 10, 1876, p. 5.
142. That is, Joseph Warren (1829–1876), publisher of the *Buffalo Courier* and member of the Buffalo park commission, whom Olmsted had come to know in the early 1870s while at work on the city's park system and the Buffalo State Hospital for the Insane (*New-York Times*, Oct. 2, 1876, p. 7; *Appleton's Cyc. Am. Biog.*; *Papers of FLO*, 6: 455).
143. Olmsted here appended articles from editions of May 3, 1876, of the New York *Telegram* and *Evening Post* describing the atmosphere in the legislature during the final days of the session and the successful filibustering by Democrats that prevented passage of several important bills relating to New York City.
144. William Courtney Wetmore (1797–1880), a well-known real estate lawyer and former vice president of the New-York and Harlem Railroad, lived in Fordham Heights and owned considerable properties in the Twenty-third and Twenty-fourth wards. As a Tammany Democrat, he formed a new majority with commissioners William R. Martin and Joseph O'Donohue against Henry Stebbins. The new coalition promptly elected Martin president of the board. "Tammany Hall now holds undisputed possession of the Park Board," was the assessment of the *New-York Times*, "a fact which the public will probably discover to their cost before long" (DPP, *Minutes*, May 6, 1876, pp. 3–5; *Sunday Mercury*, May 21, 1876, p. 4; *New-York Times*, May 9, 1876, p. 6; ibid., March 24, 1880, p. 8).
145. No extra session of the state legislature was held in 1876.
146. On December 20, 1875, Henry G. Stebbins appeared before a committee chaired by state senator James W. Booth that was investigating New York City government. Steb-

PATRONAGE JOURNAL (1873–1877)

bins opposed retention of an even number of park commissioners because votes often ended in stalemates. He preferred a board of three or five members, provided they were committed to the park as a work of art and architecture, were unconnected with political organizations, and were left alone to exercise their own judgment in its management. In his testimony, he did not express opposition to a single commissioner. No other park commissioner appeared before this committee, but William R. Martin criticized Stebbins for appearing before it without informing the board in advance. Martin and Joseph O'Donohue attempted without success to place a rebuttal in the board's printed minutes and have the board send it to the senate committee. Failing in this, they had it published as a pamphlet. Among other statements, they opposed placing the park department under a single commissioner. The printed minutes of the park board in early 1876 show also that Martin lobbied the state assembly for money to improve small parks along Fourth Avenue ("Report of the Committee of the Senate of the State of New York, Appointed to Investigate the Several Departments of the Government in the City and County of New York," in "Document no. 79," in New York [State], *Documents of the Senate of the State of New York, Ninety-Ninth Session...* [Albany, N.Y., 1876], pp. 883–99; DPP, *Minutes,* Jan. 7, 1876, p. 502; ibid., Jan. 13, 1876, p. 528; ibid., Jan. 18, 1876, p. 542; ibid., March 29, 1876, pp. 710–11; ibid., April 5, 1876, p. 734; "Statement in Reference to the operations of the Department during the year 1875, presented to the Board by Commissioners Martin and O'Donohue, and published by them," printed pamphlet, IRH p.v. 10, No. 14, New York Public Library, The Irma and Paul Milstein Division of United States History, Local History and Genealogy, Astor, Lenox and Tilden Foundations, New York City).

147. The printed minutes of the park board do not refer to a superintendent gathering signatures in support of the Green bill.
148. The *Herald* claimed that all of the turf in Central Park was healthy and thick and objected to any restrictions on access to it. It cited the more open use of turf in London parks and in Prospect Park as proof that it could withstand unlimited use by the public. It called the Central Park restrictions unseemly in a free society and criticized overzealous enforcement of the regulations by the park keepers (*New York Herald,* May 10, 1876, p. 6; ibid., May 11, 1876, p. 10; ibid., May 12, 1876, p. 6; ibid., May 13, 1876, p. 4; ibid., May 14, 1876, p. 7).
149. That is, the grass cut by the right hand man would be deposited in the path of the mower to his left. The correct arrangement for right-handed mowers was to start the left one first, with each succeeding one several feet behind and to the right (Henry Stephens, *The Farmer's Guide to Scientific and Practical Agriculture,* 2 vols. [New York, 1852], 2: 340–41).
150. That is, the old village located on the bluff overlooking the Hudson River at 120th Street, adjacent to Riverside Park.
151. Unemployment remained high in New York and laborers and politicians impatient with continued delays of work on Riverside Park and Tompkins Square pressured the park commissioners to expand hiring. Their calls for employment and resolutions critical of the department passed by Democratic aldermen in late July 1876 were widely reported in city newspapers (DPP, *Minutes,* March 3, 1876, pp. 655–56; ibid., July 26, 1876, pp. 185–89; *New-York Daily Tribune,* July 21, 1876, p. 2; ibid., Aug. 3, 1876, p. 2; *Sunday Mercury,* July 23, 1876, p. 5; *The Irish American,* July 15, 1876, p. 4; ibid., July 29, 1876, p. 4).
152. A reference to a series of letters and interviews published in the *New York Herald* in which William R. Martin and Green traded charges of official misconduct, political jobbery, and obstructionism. Their fights over payrolls, contract versus day's work, and personnel, especially in regard to Riverside Park, Tompkins Square, and the parade ground, had intensified since May 1876, when the new Tammany majority in

APPENDIX III

the park board elected William R. Martin president (*New York Herald*, Aug. 6, 1876, p. 5; ibid., Aug. 7, 1876, p. 7).
153. The Tompkins Square resolution, adopted by the aldermen on July 22, 1876, was approved by Mayor Wickham on August 1, 1876 (*Irish American*, July 29, 1876, p. 4; DPP, *Minutes*, August 4, 1876, p. 215).
154. Olmsted apparently meant commissioner Joseph J. O'Donohue.
155. Joseph O'Donohue's resignation occurred after it became known that he had held the office of a state elector in the late presidential election, in violation of the New York City charter that prohibited simultaneous tenure in city and state or federal offices (DPP, *Minutes*, Dec. 12, 1876, p. 461; *New-York Times*, Dec. 12, 1876, p. 5).
156. On January 31, 1876, the park board unanimously approved a motion by William R. Martin to suspend John Bogart's pay until further notice. The commissioners believed that engineering services were unnecessary since little construction work was scheduled, a notion to which Olmsted strongly objected. Assistant engineer Frank A. Calkins remained on the payroll. In late December 1876 the commissioners, except for Henry Stebbins, who abstained, voted to pay Bogart back pay for the first half of the year (DPP, *Minutes*, Jan. 31, 1876, p. 566; ibid., Dec. 20, 1876, p. 486; FLO to Henry G. Stebbins, Jan. 28, 1876).
157. On November 22, 1876, President William R. Martin introduced his resolution naming James C. Aldrich and others to engineering positions on the Riverside work. The board, after the debate detailed below, approved the positions (DPP, *Minutes*, Nov. 22, 1876, pp. 422–23; see [FLO,] "Review of New York City Park Department Polices in 1878," above).
158. Olmsted made these entries as commissioners William R. Martin and Joseph O'Donohue appeared before the mayor to answer charges brought by a citizens' group led by Col. Rush C. Hawkins and Dorman B. Eaton that park laborers were paid too much. The commissioners cited their authority to set departmental wages and defended the policy of providing relief to the laboring classes through public works. These charges and others that they had fired employees without cause emanated, they said, from Comptroller Green, whose followers had lost the most positions. The mayor, who had the power to recommend their removal by the governor, declined later in the month to do so (*Irish American*, Dec. 2, 1876, p. 4; ibid., Dec. 9, 1876, p. 4; George A. Mazaraki, "The Public Career of Andrew Haswell Green," Ph.D. diss. [New York University, 1966], pp. 256–57).
159. In January 1877 the park board faced a reduced maintenance appropriation from the Board of Estimate and Apportionment for the third year in a row, and acted to reduce wages throughout the department. On January 10 the new commissioner and treasurer James F. Wenman proposed to reduce laborers' wages to $1.60 a day. William R. Martin introduced an amendment that allowed $2.00 to those who volunteered to work ten hours and the proposal was adopted unanimously. The salaries of officers, clerks, and other employees, including Olmsted's, were cut later in the month (DPP, *Minutes*, Jan. 10, 1877, pp. 534–35; ibid., Jan. 24, 1877, pp. 564–67).
160. Olmsted is referring to Ambrose H. Purdy (1842–1919), a Democrat in the assembly, who on February 27, 1877, introduced a bill to transfer to the Department of Public Works the power to lay out and build streets in the Twenty-third and Twenty-fourth wards, an undertaking closely associated with William R. Martin (*New-York Times*, Aug. 13, 1919, p. 11; *New York World* Feb. 28, 1877, p. 5).
161. That is, his work with the Niagara scenic reservation and the New York state capitol.

IV

LIST OF TEXTUAL ALTERATIONS

Each entry in the list gives the page and line number of the altered text, followed by the original form of the text. For documents beginning after the first line of a page, lines are counted from the addressee line or from the first line of the title of the document. Alterations of text in the endnotes of a document are identified by page, note, and line number.

INTRODUCTION

CHAPTER I

To Justin Smith Morrill, January 22, 1874
36: 14   afterwards more   39: 5   West owing
36: 26   is the   39: 5   trees there
37: 16   gained the   40: 17   relieved being

To William Hammond Hall, March 28, 1874
53: 11   square" the

To Seymour Ainsworth, Hiram Tompkins & John L. Perry, April 21, 1874
55: 4   Ainsworth Tompkins   58: 21   moticed
58: 16   could except   58: 23   permant
58: 16   fountain under   58: 23   sufficitly
58: 16   superintendence could be

To Montgomery Cunningham Meigs, May 14, 1874
62: 4   desired annual

To Justin Smith Morrill and James Henry Platt, Jr., June 9, 1874
64: 36   large umbrageous   66: 29   trees but

To Justin Smith Morrill, August 16, 1874
69: 10   Ground I   71: 8   Partridge was
69: 14   duties neglected   71: 18   grading sewer
70: 2   c. yd.

721

APPENDIX IV

CHAPTER II

To Albert Gallatin Browne, November 12, 1874
82: 5   Depart
82: 6   Apportmt
82: 11   Apportmt
82: 15   Apportmnt
82: 18   Appt
83: 1   acct
83: 9–10   opinion but
83: 19   particularly
83: 26   Apportmnt

To the Commissioners of Mount Royal Park, November 21, 1874
87: 11-12   Montreal but
87: 44   Reservoir another

To the Buffalo Park Commission, December 15, 1874
101: 8   Square New

To Montgomery Cunningham Meigs, January 15, 1875
106: 11   Capitol I
106: 14   assistant Mr
106: 15   Wisedell I

To Frederick William Poppey, January 21, 1875
115: 10   sands the
116: 3   shrubs vines
116: 20   one

To the Board of Commissioners of the Department of Public Parks, c. January–February 1875
118: 9   poetical sentimental
118: 24   refers. and
118: 32   Koster
119: 21   that, they
120: 14   this that
120: 17–18   conscious uneasy

CHAPTER III

To the Board of Commissioners of the Department of Public Parks, March 1, 1875
124: 13   Comssrs
124: 17   and but
124: 17   detail in
124: 29   growing the
124: 34   it even
124: 35   soil would
125: 3   refce
125: 8   referce
125: 12   boldly;
125: 26   arrangmnt which
125: 30   refence
125: 36   done the
126: 25–26   abandoned: the
126: 32   and so
126: 35   it that
126: 40   believe or
127: 3   it's

To Thomas Pynchon, c. March 10, 1875
129: 5   convntly
129: 25–26   view the
131: 33   yourself your

To William L. Fischer, March 14, 1875
133: 26–27   Garden and
133: 31   Hedera, as

To William Robinson, March 20–30, 1875
135: 5   wh.
135: 19   them each
136: 27   seen, and
136: 38   thoroughly sometimes

To Henry G. Stebbins, May 18, 1875
139: 9   gained but
140: 4   be and
140: 5   was a
140: 12   will if
140: 12–13   summer extend
141: 1   rejected partly
141: 7   first on
141: 19   illegally without
141: 26   cluster
141: 30–31   day especially the

LIST OF TEXTUAL ALTERATIONS

141: 39 First by
141: 41 turf shrubs
142: 6   laws of
142: 38 goats some

To Montgomery Cunningham Meigs, June 1, 1875
145: 24 commission unless
145: 25 instructed to

To Walter L. Sessions, October 9, 1875
152: 1–2 character hoping
152: 40 felt but
153: 15 summer the
153: 20 arragmt
153: 21 disease not
153: 21 health and
153: 26 studied substantial
153: 29 permant
153: 30 be
155: 3   worthy industrious
155: 14–15 summer transported

To Horatio Admiral Nelson, October 11, 1875
156: 15 steepness and are

To George Jones, November 19, 1875
161: 25 climate) of

To Dennis Bowen, January 1, 1876
170: 11 attempted. but
170: 32 pressure no

To Henry G. Stebbins, February 1, 1876
177: 18 photographed drawn
177: 38 growth constitution
177: 40 climate exposure,
177: 42 transplanted grown
177: 43 irrigated lopped,
178: 11 Suptg
178: 14 forestry arboriculture

To J. H. Miller, February 28, 1876
179: 12 for of roads
179: 26 quantity 320,000
179: 31 wish
179: 31 Clost
179: 32 recomnd
179: 32–33 Engineer Newport R.I

CHAPTER IV

To Charles Eliot Norton, April 2, 1876
188: 32 introduction

To Horatio Admiral Nelson, April 4, 1876
191: 14 use. it
191: 18 &c. the

To Charles Henry Dalton, April 8. 1876
193: 35 advantges
193: 41 imprmnts
195: 1   imprmnt
195: 12 costiness

To Horatio Admiral Nelson, June 6, 1876
202: 18 exemplify a
202: 26 done not
202: 33 man however
202: 34 it who
202: 37–38 motives but

To Charles Eliot Norton, June 7, 1876
204: 24 imprvmnts

To Horatio Admiral Nelson, July 26, 1876
206: 20 an

To William Runyon Martin, August 9, 1876
217: 11 &c.,

To William McMillan, September 10, 1876
229: 30 frame all

723

APPENDIX IV

To Dennis Bowen, September 10, 1876
231: 10   repeated
231: 13   season fall
231: 13   spring had
231: 31   lacking to for
231: 39   ammnt
233: 11   stream as

To William McMillan, September 11, 1876
233: 5   6ᵗʰ I
234: 12   fall if
234: 13   landscape less
234: 16   amnt
234: 27   soft natural,

To Horatio Admiral Nelson, September 28, 1876
235: 27   engineer the
236: 5–6   safe conservative economical
236: 12   public but
236: 17   admitted the

To Frederick Law Olmsted, Jr., October 1, 1876
238: 17   Grinner "and
239: 29   When
239: 32   John
241: 39   say?
242: 1   There
242: 6   him.
242: 7   Good night.
242: 8   Good night.

"Report of the Landscape Architect and the Civil and Topographical Engineer, Accompanying a Plan for Laying Out that Part of the Twenty-Fourth Ward Lying West of the Riverdale Road," November 21, 1876
259: 16   horizontally will
259: 29   properties will
259: 35   streets remains
260: 33   cost as

To J. M. Lanahan, December 23, 1876
269: 12   felt but

To Charles Eliot Norton, December 27, 1876
277: 8   states the
277: 14   riots and
277: 19–20   feeling that
277: 20   say that
277: 26   reformer even
278: 42   writing the

CHAPTER V

Memorandum on New York Capitol Patronage 1877
283: 10   Cap Comsn
283: 10–11   said There
283: 13   administration for
283: 29   were if
283: 20   offered to
283: 22   patriotism a
283: 25–26   legislature nevertheless
283: 29   "Well said

To Whitelaw Reid, March 2, 1877
287: 18   park, of

New York State Capitol Testimony, March 2, 1877
288: 3   Chamn
289: 1   idea and
289: 2   idea that
289: 25   recognized more
289: 29   fair legitimate
289: 40   principles none
290: 2   dissolute malicious
291: 42   for
292: 9   rich deep warm
292: 18   strikes
292: 25   used be
292: 34   compromises combinations
292: 34   rivals. Such
293: 6   rumor gossip slander
293: 21   business can
293: 31   Commsn
294: 17   amnt
294: 35   good prudent,
295: 8   might if
295: 8   so better
295: 9   like if
295: 9   interest to
295: 10–11   know but
296: 22   duty that
296: 22   another that
296: 23   court I

724

LIST OF TEXTUAL ALTERATIONS

296: 23   added but
296: 26   if
296: 31   architect.
298: 17   knowledge training,
298: 33   building. and
300: 11   dignity repose
300: 18   that
300: 19   a
300: 21   schools their
301: 38   room but
302: 7   much. but

To William McMillan, March 16, 1877
305: 2   bay the
305: 13   gate Southmead

To Horatio Admiral Nelson, March 26, 1877
314: 5   point whichever
314: 5–6 taken the
314: 16   planting a
314: 20   embankments. between
314: 28   done but
314: 28   before it

To the Public, March 26, 1877
315: 5   heat haste
315: 9   matter a
315: 12   achiture
315: 14   fancy these
316: 1   building not
316: 5–6 construction uncalled
316: 9   produced the
316: 22   down one
316: 29   done bringing
316: 31   *good not*
316: 38   inappropriate insignificant,
316: 39–40 construction that

To the Mount Royal Park Commission, April 28, 1877
318: 14   tedious much

To William Runyon Martin, May 16, 1877
319: 39   park streams

To Horatio Admiral Nelson, July 24, 1877
328: 32   Scrubs
328: 33   Sett
328: 33   asside

To Mary Perkins Olmsted, August 10, 1877
332: 11   writing, as
332: 17   asked—What
332: 17   it? No
332: 24   but

To John Charles Olmsted, October 7, 1877
333: 17   &c. bid
334: 28   Gard^n I
335: 14   kindergarten. &

CHAPTER VI

To William Runyon Martin, October 31, 1877
344: 5   avenue and

To Charles Henry Dalton, May 13, 1878
363: 36   competion
364: 11–12 intended like
365: 5   invita-
365: 8   signed)

To Robert Garrett, June 5, 1878
366: 5   Bal°
366: 8–9 unnoticed all
366: 31   will I
366: 31   remember I
367: 32   Balto
367: 35   purpose even
367: 35–36 good and
367: 39   judge but
367: 43   recivd

Notice to Watchmen for the Capitol Grounds, July 7, 1878
370: 5   that the all
370: 12   carless
370: 20   temper to
370: 22   civility quietness
370: 26   govt

CHAPTER VII

REVIEW OF NEW YORK CITY PARK DEPARTMENT POLICIES, JANUARY 8, 1879
376: 14–15   removal the
383: 7   long frequent,

TO CHARLES SPRAGUE SARGENT, JANUARY 27, 1879
388: 17–18   water and
388: 21   face will

TO CHARLES SPRAGUE SARGENT, JANUARY 29, 1879
389: 3   picturesque natural,
389: 24   them but
389: 14–15   formed the
389: 35   variety including

TO EDOUARD FRANÇOIS ANDRÉ, JUNE 6, 1879
394: 35–36   America if
395: 3   Gds

TO H. Y. ATTRILL AND B. E. SMITH, JULY 30, 1879
400: 1   strengthing
406: 17   York not
401: 12–13   York Brooklyn
406: 18   designed but
402: 6   smooth soft,
406: 24   exist the
404: 24   establishment Aunt
407: 34   competion
404: 26   these yet
409: 12–13   house to occupy
404: 36   verandas they
409: 21   them their
406: 13   cousins their
410: 1   festivals fireworks,

TO H. Y. ATTRILL, SEPTEMBER 23, 1879
418: 3   cannon
418: 32   theory with
418: 20–21   them. *given*
418: 32–33   problem. I

TO JAMES TERRY GARDNER, OCTOBER 2, 1879
420: 28   reservations the

TO JAMES TERRY GARDNER, OCTOBER 3, 1879
422: 17–18   capacious well

TO CHARLES ELIOT NORTON, OCTOBER 10, 1879
425: 7   (not
425: 13   shld.
425: 9   interest.

CHAPTER VIII

TO CHARLES HENRY DALTON, DECEMBER 9, 1879
428: 12   puff for
428: 20   (Tuileries) Long
428: 19   Gate. Brick
428: 20   Bridge. Dobb's

TO TIFFANY & COMPANY, DECEMBER 9, 1879
431: 23   time. rising
432: 2   aftwds

TO HENRY WHITNEY BELLOWS, DECEMBER 24, 1879
434: 13   sharp excited,

TO JOSEPH P. DAVIS, JANUARY 24, 1880
447: 11   railroad of
448: 1   others)
447: 21   believe,

TO CHARLES HENRY DALTON, JANUARY 24, 1880
450: 15   so. but

TO THE BOARD OF COMMISSIONERS OF THE DEPARTMENT OF PARKS OF THE CITY OF BOSTON, JANUARY 26, 1880
455: 8–9   inconvenience relief

TO BARTHOLD SCHLESINGER, FEBRUARY 9, 1880
466: 35   elswhere
467: 32   standards that

LIST OF TEXTUAL ALTERATIONS

To Charles Henry Dalton, May 5, 1880
484: 4   Prst
488: 5   ock

To Charles Eliot Norton, May 7, 1880
488: 7–8   arboretum which
489: 12–13   museums lecture
489: 3   parcels one

CHAPTER IX

To John C. Phillips, May 11, 1880
492: 7   lake whatever
494: 1   coffee reading
494: 1   room. large

To the Earl of Derby, June 11, 1880
497: 2   Honble
497: 13   favor the

To Thomas Wisedell, June 13, 1880
499: 25   you, to
500: 35–36   regularly systematically
499: 27   denial that
501: 4   me to
499: 30   unconsciously I
501: 7   Office,
500: 15–16   injudicious embarrassing

To W. O. Buchanan, June 15, 1880
503: 16   dont

To J. C. Phillips, August 23, 1880
506: 15   drawings if

To Edward Clark, June 1879–1880
508: 7   walks the
508: 21   provided looked

To Sylvester Baxter, November 9, 1880
510: 11–12   purpose various
511: 17   absoluting
510: 21–22   managmnt extravagance
512: 5   order everything
511: 10   effcts
512: 5–6   sensational bustling

To Edward Clark, November 18, 1880
513: 33   roads there

CHAPTER X

To Charles Eliot Norton, May 30, 1881
533: 12   you you
533: 15   can please

To Berthold Schlesinger, June 17, 1881
536: 10–11   chimneys It
536: 24   ground the
536: 11   terrace veranda,
536: 25   knoll at
536: 13–14   building barrack office jail hospital
536: 25   swell Under
536: 39   plants it
536: 20   station the

Influence, c. 1881–1882
539: 11   govermt
542: 43   instructed custom
540: 2   Respy.
543: 2   details but
540: 9   made the
543: 5   subordinates was
540: 42   sources it
543: 10   people was
540: 42   govmt
543: 33   visitors men
541: 34   rail-cars. The
543: 33   men women
542: 20   large shifting
543: 41   me these
542: 32   disatrously
544: 12–13   off but
542: 42   that as
544: 15   condition disabled

APPENDIX IV

544: 25   vigilant bold
544: 28   ill-judged tasteless
544: 32   work revisions
544: 33   arising. The
544: 39   Ring many
544: 40   exhorbitant yet
544: 43   had in
544: 44   trust laid
545: 19–20   recruiting in
545: 42   seem some
546: 8   that needing
546: 8   recruits every
546: 25   That
546: 25   me when
546: 30   I
546: 31   strength.
547: 13–14   Shop-keepers our
547: 18   trade trade
547: 20   efforts but
547: 23–24   ministers elders
547: 25–26   it is to

To John C. Phillips, September 27, 1881
549: 17   surface anything
549: 38   lawn trees
550: 2   completely but
550: 13   it the
550: 16   hickories sumachs
550: 21   no
550: 38   beets rye
553: 3   not the

To Cornelius Rea Agnew, c. June–October 1881
555: 12   bleak incongruous
555: 32   apparnt
555: 34–35   shrubbery trellises
555: 38   upon it
556: 4   that made
556: 5   stone you

To Edward Clark, October 1, 1881
558: 3   prospective

To Charles Eliot Norton, November 2, 1881
563: 9   matter and
563: 10   Nov) he
563: 11   wd
564: 7   wd

CHAPTER XI

Central Park Circular, c. February 1882
584: 2   purposes.) in
584: 8   divesified
584: 17   covered material
584: 23   ft. the
585: 5 $15000.000
585: 14–15   fashions manners,
585: 28   open. and
586: 13–14   false reputable
586: 20–21   objects principles

To George Kessler, March 5, 1882
588: 5   West been
588: 8   me I
589: 10   Loudon Gilpin above
589: 11   Picturesque) All
589: 17   you you

To John C. Phillips, March 6, 1882
590: 12   house-garden lawn,
590: 16   terrace and
590: 21   sythe broom
590: 22   forlorn would
590: 23   bushes vines
591: 6   woodland stable
591: 12   exits
591: 20   forest) I
591: 20   detaild
591: 22   E. North
591: 24   dogwood white
591: 25   Kohlreuteria sassafras,

To Charles Loring Brace, March 7, 1882
593: 16   generous sympathetic

APPENDIX II: SPOILS OF THE PARK

The Spoils of the Park, February 1882
629: 27   Raymond Mr.

APPENDIX III: PATRONAGE JOURNAL

Patronage Journal
653: 3   President. "Early
653: 5   uncanly
653: 17   Supdet
653: 22   him.
653: 26   Board and
653: 29   present one
654: 6   you.
654: 9   work—
654: 10   that,
654: 10   Mr
654: 12   Board.
654: 15–16   Dpt
655: 5–6   men mostly
655: 13   strike one
655: 14   day.
655: 19   Prest.
655: 19–20   Bacon) The
655: 26   carts.
656: 7   Govenor
656: 26   present one
657: 25   Com
658: 1   That whats
658: 4–5   cosiderations
658: 5   economy."
658: 6   Com^r
658: 33   at
659: 6   diffrt
659: 9   of.'
659: 10   Hay Sanitary
659: 11   Com.
659: 22   ago, He
659: 25   employt
659: 27   Depment
659: 34   himsf
660: 8   Pk
660: 10   Com'r. that
660: 12   say?
660: 21   it?
660: 25   Dept.
660: 28   ground, that
660: 29   not?
661: 5   Prst
661: 5   Soc.]
661: 8   added your
661: 18   work.
661: 20   B^d.
661: 26   Dep
661: 28   Prest
661: 29   Com^r
661: 30   Com^r
661: 32   Asst Secy

661: 35   Arct
661: 38   Prest
662: 17   Presd^t
662: 21   Aldm
662: 22   aftds
662: 26   exps.
662: 27   assists.
662: 27–28   Pres^t.
662: 28   Prest
662: 31   Reply no
662: 31–32   tomorrow lots
662: 35   Reg.
662: 35–36   Mass. promoted
662: 36   gallantry lost
662: 36–37   war Brev. Lt Col. Capt Reg.
663: 3   Asst Supdt
663: 4   Supdt
663: 6   Supdt,
663: 7   Com^r
663: 14   Prst.
663: 18   Bd
663: 18   Office. wanted
663: 18   apptd
663: 19   foreman. says
663: 21   I'd
663: 23   it I
663: 25   foreman.
663: 30   4.30
664: 2   Supt
664: 4   evy
664: 14   I
664: 16   was. but
664: 17   offrd
664: 25   city.
664: 34   Supdt
664: 35   1874;
665: 1   12½ Foremen
665: 1   20 c. Carpenters
665: 1–2   25 cts Stone
665: 7   emplyd
665: 16   amnt
665: 20   Com^r
665: 31   arragmnts
665: 36   German It
666: 1   Com
666: 5   Prest
666: 9   understandg
666: 12   aftds
666: 13   placd
666: 13–14   Pres^t.
666: 14   charged to

729

APPENDIX IV

666: 17   that — "It
666: 21   reprted
666: 21   printed maps
666: 24   accdg
666: 27   refd
666: 27   Com^r
666: 29   Landsc Archt
666: 32   Presd^t
666: 36   Prest
667: 4   eving
667: 23   aftwds
667: 26   Commisship
667: 29   Com^r
668: 2   Com
668: 8   manged
668: 8–9   independentally
668: 16   Com
668: 18   since for
668: 22   were Mr
668: 23   Secrety
668: 25   no.
668: 27   Com
668: 28   politician ——
668: 30   interest namely
669: 9   patronage." You
669: 13   How
669: 13   ——?
669: 16   Well
669: 26   city gives
669: 43   legislature. In
670: 15   Ald^m
670: 17   Comttee
670: 23   Ald^m
670: 37   divided one
670: 38   includs
671: 8   Departmt, with
671: 13   archtec^l
671: 17   order one
671: 17   Commirs
671: 21   mrng,
671: 25–26 archtc^l
671: 27   shd
671: 27–28 supertndnce
671: 30   Coms
671: 34   construction.
671: 35   mind,
671: 41   Com^r
671: 44   Coms
672: 10   shd
672: 12   refd
672: 16   Com^r
672: 17   shd
672: 21   no.

672: 22   Comm^r
672: 24   Commsns
672: 25   engineer afterwds
672: 26   Suptg
672: 27   Com
672: 27   opinion. As
672: 29   assist
672: 32–33 competent. The
672: 38   Prst
673: 1   Commsn
673: 5   duties could
673: 22   eving
673: 23   next 25th entering
673: 25   at 9.30
673: 26   srget
673: 39   Kinderberg) In
673: 42   Com^r
674: 3   Com^r
674: 7   lieniently
674: 14   Com^{r}s
674: 17   tomorrow Saturday eving
674: 21   The President on the 1st May
           (see note of that date) proposed
           & urged the restoration of
           Koster & denounced the lieu-
           tenant as a failure.
674: 21   Com
674: 24   conversation all
674: 30   every
674: 33   were, off post, and
674: 44   duty no
675: 10   Com^r
675: 11   liet^t
675: 15   since the
675: 16   Com^r
675: 19   Prest
675: 19   yesterday apprehending
675: 23   additions".
675: 24   afraid he
675: 24   replied that
675: 28   it if
675: 38   Com^r
676: 8   Com^r
676: 10   dollar.
676: 14   Commsn
676: 15   appntmt
676: 20   need.
676: 26   Supdt
677: 6   aftds.
677: 10   Your
677: 12   amicably. The
677: 24   politicians but
677: 28   said

LIST OF TEXTUAL ALTERATIONS

677: 29	constrctg		681: 19	or
677: 32	appted		681: 20	it,
677: 35	Comms		681: 26	Comm^r
677: 35	Accts,		681: 27	aftwds
678: 5	This		681: 29	Comm^r
678: 13	morng		681: 29	Accts
678: 14	No.		681: 32	This
678: 15	it!		681: 34	Ald^m
678: 16	Is		681: 35	Aldrm
678: 16	Times?		682: 4	if
678: 17	No,		682: 5	back."
678: 18	World.		682: 7	"You'll
678: 23	emolumnts		682: 16	lieut^t
678: 26	made lighter		682: 18	Why,
678: 30	skill method		682: 18	said, the
678: 36	mangmt		682: 18	lieut^t
679: 1	appt		682: 19	list there
679: 2	magmt		682: 23	eving
679: 7	demand		682: 34	Departt
679: 10	year the		682: 35	nor
679: 12	roundd		682: 35–36	Comm^r
679: 13	shd		682: 36	it. i.e.
679: 15	it. found		682: 37	Prst
679: 16	vegation,		683: 5	aftwds
679: 18	one had		683: 7	offring
679: 20	Supt		683: 20	statements reports
679: 23	Suptg		683: 25	ock
679: 24	aftds		683: 26	arrived the
679: 24	Supt		683: 30	contind.
680: 2	Comm^r		684: 5	Tribune though
680: 11	Comr		684: 5	affairs has
680: 11	Accnts		684: 8	There
680: 19	Coms		684: 9	suffd
680: 22	it is has		684: 13–14	Tribune, (McCarthy) Times,
680: 22	Supdt		684: 16	Green the
680: 39	rept		684: 37	accts
680: 39	Pres^t		684: 39	Acct
680: 40	prstg		685: 1	Suptg
680: 40	Board. but		685: 4	Comm^r
680: 40	oblgd		685: 10	Com^r
680: 42	Commrs		685: 22	Comm's
680: 42	Prst		686: 2	amt
681: 2	aftwds		686: 7	Prst
681: 4–5	Supdt		686: 8	C.
681: 5	grnds		686: 9	Comm^r
681: 7	grnd		686: 14	Comm P.
681: 8	consenting I		686: 26	me. Yes,
681: 10	revise		686: 31	once.
681: 10	else omitting		686: 32	I
681: 11	approve but		686: 34	out.
681: 12	considg		687: 6	it a
681: 17	shud		687: 20	mring
681: 19	offd		687: 21	rprt

731

APPENDIX IV

687: 27–28   reporter
687: 28–29   park. had
687: 30   "Stop,
687: 30   what
687: 35   it one
687: 36   Comms^{r}s
688: 4   Govenor,
688: 9   be the past
688: 19   Prst
688: 20   meeting one
688: 21   Com^r
688: 24   asst
688: 31   this since
688: 32   signed there
688: 33   Commiss^{r}s
688: 33–34   sidewalk stairways
688: 38   Comms
689: 5   Commsnr
689: 10   Commssrs
689: 11   discrimate
689: 13   Supt
689: 13   Comm^r
689: 16   Com^r
689: 19   Commssnr
689: 21   grnd
689: 26   Commns
689: 28   dirty ruffianly
689: 32   Crosby contractor
689: 37   if
689: 42   day.
690: 31   make
690: 32   hand,
690: 37   aftwds
690: 38   Secy
691: 13–14   1870–71 when
691: 14   formed there
691: 16–17   digging in
691: 32   aftwds
691: 41   independtly
691: 41   maintence
692: 5   Departmt the
692: 8   Supdt,
692: 10   Supdt
692: 11–12   Comm^r
692: 35   Suptg
692: 37   argumnt entreating
693: 6   supt
693: 6   said. Why
693: 7   cutter.
693: 7–8   Supdt
693: 13   Supd^t
693: 24   Supdt
693: 33   Com

694: 3   accomping
694: 32   Villi
695: 5   Commissns
695: 8   Comm^r
695: 12   sanity
695: 13   man a
695: 16   Ville,
696: 5   May. passage
696: 10   Comsn
696: 11   afterwrds
696: 15   hold or
696: 29   mrng
696: 30–31   House Green
696: 36   if
696: 38   Comm^r
696: 39   Supt
697: 6   Com^r
697: 6–7   afterwds
697: 8   board vice
697: 14   3^d three
697: 19   Albany all
697: 28   Com^r
697: 30   sincere Today
697: 31   Supt
697: 32   park thoroughly
697: 33   other had
698: 3   Supt
698: 7   done had
698: 10   Supdt
698: 12   manging
698: 17   Prest
698: 25   me. "I
698: 27   °ck
698: 28   Supdt
698: 30   said Well
698: 33   Supdt
699: 2   Supdt
699: 4   men I
699: 14   Prest
699: 26   Commssin
699: 27   morng
699: 28   recing
699: 32   we
699: 36   work and
700: 12   one; "Why!
700: 13   They
700: 21   °ck
700: 22   came except
700: 22   President left
700: 24   o'ck
700: 31   them.
700: 31   near into
700: 34   Brd

LIST OF TEXTUAL ALTERATIONS

700: 34   Commss^r
701: 1   "do
701: 7   I
701: 8   Mayor", "I
701: 21   How
701: 21   take?
701: 30   I
701: 30   morng Do
701: 30   know Mr
701: 30–31 Olmsted if
701: 31   Com
701: 35   said. "Mr
701: 36   Comms^r
701: 36–37 said. "Its
701: 37   Com^r
701: 37   resigned, His
701: 38   its
702: 2   Suptg
702: 11   arragmts
702: 19   I
702: 20   charge] said
702: 20   President and
702: 22   among them all

702: 24   us.
702: 30   Comm^r
702: 31   arrangmt
703: 6   hours extremely
703: 7   grnd
703: 18   Secy
703: 19   I
703: 21   trouble.
703: 21   Presidnt
703: 22   Secry
703: 22   reccomnd
703: 23   Presidnt
704: 3   aftds
704: 5   Martin. the
705: 8   Coms
705: 9   Coms
705: 12   an
705: 16–17 accomplished whether
705: 17   legislation that
705: 28   ephemistically
705: 31   purchased was

733

INDEX OF PLANT MATERIALS

Current Latin and English names are given in brackets. Entries are presented in alphabetical order in the form that Olmsted wrote them.

Alpine plants, 649
Apple, 64
Aralia, 510
Arborvitae [*Thuja*], 354
Ash, 260
Ash, weeping [*Fraxinus excelsior* var. *pendula*], 58
Aster, 260, 354, 389, 457

Barberry [*Berberis*], 158, 457
Barley, 117
Basswood [*Tilia*], 591
Beach-plum [*Prunus maritima*], 457
Beech, 353
Bindweed [*Convolvulus*], 354
Birch, 550, 591
Blackberry, 64
Blue-grass, Kentucky [*Poa pratensis*], 61
Brake [*Pteridium*], 354
Bramble (*Rubus*), 133, 260, 354
Buckthorn [*Rhamnus*], 591
Bullrush [*Typha*], 390
Bushes, 133, 354, 478, 550
Buttercups, 158, 354

Camelia, 51
Candleberry [*Myrica pensylvanica*], 457

Catalpa, golden [*C. bignonioides* cv. 'Aurea'], 510
Catnip, 354
Cedrela, 510
Chestnut, 64
Chickweed, 354
Cinquefoil [*Potentilla*], 354
Clematis, 133, 354
Clover, 148, 158
Cockscomb (*Celosia cristata*), 354
Coleus, 19
Creepers, 556
Crocus, 354
Currant, 64
Cydonia [Quince], 457
Cydonia Japonica, 591

Daffodil, 354
Dog-rose [*Rosa canina*], 354
Dogwood [*Cornus*], 352, 354, 494, 591

Elder [*Sambucus*], 354
Elm, 260, 591
Elm, American [*Ulmus americana*], 61
Elm, English [*Ulmus procera*], 61
Elm, European [*Ulmus carpinifolia*, *U. procera*], 515

INDEX OF PLANT MATERIALS

Evergreens, 135, 155, 354, 513
"Exotics," 158, 461, 508

Ferns, 260, 494, 508, 510, 679
Flowering plants, annual, 61
Flowers, 96, 136, 155, 272, 350, 409, 460, 497, 506
Forget-me-not, 354
Fuschia, 51

Gentian, 260, 354
Geranium, 19
Goldenrod [*Solidago*], 260, 354, 457
Gooseberry, 64
Grape, wild, 527
Grass (turf), 61, 140–41, 146–48, 210
Grass, beach [*Ammophila*], 117
Grass, black [*Juncus gerardi*], 389
Grass, salt hay, 388, 457

Hazel [*Corylus*], 354
Hedera [Ivy], 133
Hemlock, 134, 569
Hepatica [Liverleaf], 354
Herbaceous plants, 116, 569
Hickory, 64, 550
Honeysuckle, 354
Honeysuckle, Chinese [*Lonicera standishii*], 679
Honeysuckle, evergreen, 510
Hop-hornbeam [*Ostrya virginiana*], 591
Hornbeam [*Carpinus*], 591

Iris, 354
Ivy, 270, 508, 510, 533, 582
Ivy, Dahurican [*Parthenocissus tricuspidata* (?)], 510
Ivy, Irish [*Hedera helix* var. *Hibernica*], 510

Juniper, prostrate [*Juniperus communis* var. *nana*], 354

Kohlreuteria, 591

Laburnum, 591
Larch [*Larix*], 550
Laurel, 582
Lichens, 495, 621, 650
Lily-of-the-valley, 354
Lime, American [*Tilia americana*], 61
Linden, European, *Alba pendula* [*Tilia petiolaris*], 351

Lonicera (Honeysuckle), 133
Loosestrife, 353
Liverwort, 353
Lupine, 117

Magnolia, Chinese [*Magnolia sinensis*], 582
Maple, 260
Maple, Norway [*Acer platinoides*], 61
Maple, scarlet [*Acer rubrum*], 61
Maple, sugar [*Acer saccharum*], 61
Maple, Sycamore [*Acer pseudoplatanus*], 61
Marigold, 354
Moosewood [*Acer pensylvanicum*], 591
Moss, 510, 536, 621, 622, 650
Mountain ash [*Sorbus*], 591
Mountain plants, flowering, 508
Mouse-wort, 510
Mulberry, white [*Morus alba*], 352
Myrtle [*Myrtus communis*], 51, 582

Nannyberry [*Viburnum lentago*], 354

Oak, 260
Oak, willow [*Quercus phellus*], 510
Oleaster [*Elaeagnus*], 510

Pansy, 354
Papaw [*Asimina triloba*], 64
Peach, 64
Pear, 64
Pecan, 64
Perennials, 61, 457, 494, 506, 507, 569, 622
Periwinkle [*Vinca*], 510
Persimmon, 64
Pine, 550, 569
Pine, mountain [*Pinus mugo*], 354, 494
Pinks [*Dianthus*], 354
Plane tree [*Platanus*], 68
Plantain, 353
Plants, in containers, 8, 561, 579
Poppy, 354
Prickly Pear cactus [*Opuntia*], 510, 533
Privet [*Ligustrum*], 591

Raspberry, 64
Red-top [*Agrostis alba* var. *vulgaris*; *Poa nemoralis*], 61
Reeds, 388
Rhododendron, 582
Rock-plants, 556, 622, 649

INDEX OF PLANT MATERIALS

Rose, 62
Rushes, 388, 569
Rye grass (*Lolium*), 148

Sassafras, 352, 591
Savin (*Juniperus horizontalis*), 354
Sea Buckthorn [*Hippophae*], 457
Sedge [*Carex*], 388, 389, 460
Sedge, salt [*Carex pendula*], 457
Sempervivum (Houseleek), 510, 533
Shadbush [*Amelanchier*], 354
Shrubs (bushes), 116, 234, 314, 492, 651, 686
Solidago [goldenrod], 389
Sorrel [*Rumex*], 353
Spruce [*Picea*], 136, 354
Spruce, Norway [*Picea abies*], 134, 467
Strawberry, wild, 354
Subtropical plants, 367
Sumach, 494, 550

Tamarisk, 457
Thorn tree [*Crataegus*], 354
Thuja [*Arborvitae*], 136

Trees, 44, 47, 65, 67, 79, 124, 125, 133, 230, 260, 263, 265, 314, 352–53, 390–93, 478, 510, 515–16, 549, 550, 569, 590, 621, 651
Trees, fruit, 59
Trees, nut-bearing, 59
Trees, Siberian, 314
Trumpet creeper (*Campsis radicans*), 158, 159, 527
Tulip tree [*Liriodendron tulipifera*], 61
Turf (lawn), 51, 58, 353, 582, 461, 557, 591, 683–84

Vinca [Periwinkle], 133
Vines, 58, 116, 155, 494, 495, 525, 536, 556, 622, 650
Violets, dogtooth, 353
Virginia creeper [*Parthenocissus quinquefolia*], 159, 527

Walnut, English [*Juglans regia*], 65
Wistaria, 527

Yucca, 510

GENERAL INDEX

Italic numbers indicate illustrations.

Academic campus design, 129–32. *See also* names of individual colleges and universities
Adams, Charles Francis, 566
Agnew, Cornelius Rea, 556–57
Ainsworth, Seymour, 58
Aldrich, James Colwell, 72, 113, 378, 379, 383, 386, 702, 720; removal by DPP, 375–76, 381, 385, 386
Allen, Sir Hugh, 91
Alphand, Jean-Charles-Adolphe, 265, 332–33
American Architect and Building News, 188, 205, 326, 327, 483
American Institute of Architects, 294, 303, 324, 326; and the New York State Capitol Remonstrance, 184, 185–86, 186, 188, 197, 205–6, 300–301, 302, 317
American Museum of Natural History (N.Y.C.), 359, 361–62, 443
American Public Health Association, 265
American Social Science Association, 250, 524
American Zoological and Botanical Society, 361, 362
André, Édouard François (1840–1911), 230, 327, 335, 395, 633–34, 650; on decorative gardening, 633; *L'Art des Jardins*, 393–95, 634; on Parc des Buttes-Chaumont, 631
Architects, on design competitions, 296, 297–98, 303, 363–65
Architectural competitions, 296, 297–98, 303, 363–65
Architectural Iron Works, 59
Architecture, essence of, 315–16
Architektonisches Skizzen-buch, 528
Arnold Arboretum (Boston, Mass.), 334, 395, 496; arrangement between Harvard College and City of Boston for, 484–89; description of site, 484–88, 489; FLO's role in, 12, 69, 334, 395, 450, 484–85, 488, 488–89; plan for, 486–87, 570
Asylum design: Buffalo Asylum (State hospital), 174, 327, 424, 479; McLean Asylum, 10, 197
Attrill, Henry Y., 415, 417–18, 419
Auchmuty, Richard T., 303

Babcock, Orville E. (General), 42, 54; Olmsted on, 42
Bacharach, Mortiz, 666, 707
Back Bay (Boston, Mass.), 517–21, 568–69; drainage of (basin for), 517–18; neighborhoods of, 520–21

739

GENERAL INDEX

Back Bay Fens (Boston, Mass.), 428, 430, 482, 571; beaches in, 460, 463; boats in, 459; circulation system of, 459–62, 463; collection of water-birds and fish in, 459, 463; Commonwealth Avenue, extension of, 461, 463; control of flood waters in, 456–57; criticism of FLO's plan for, 483–84; design competition for, 10–11, 363, 365, 462, 650; FLO's plan for, 11–12, 452–53, 454–56, 462; landscape effect for, 454–58; marshland scenery of, 387–88, 483; name for, 428, 430; plan for, *194*, 570; plants for, 457, 461; promenade in, 456, 459–60; purchase of lands for, 454, 462; purpose of, 451; sanitary condition of, 457, 481–82; site of, 451, 454, 462; Stony Brook diversion, 454, 455; structures of, 460–61; treatment of, 388–90, 454–58, 481–82
——— bridges, 447–49, 450; Boylston Street Bridge, 447–48, 450, 460–61; Commonwealth Avenue bridge, 449; Railroad bridge, 447, 459–60
——— Muddy River, diversion of, 454, 456, 462
Back Bay Park (of 1876), 193, 197, 454; approaches to, 195; location of, 193, 198; park-way of, 194, 195, *196*, 198; plans for, *429*, *448*
Bacon, Francis, 225, 228, 644
Bacon, Hackley B., 706
Baltimore, Maryland, 268; squares in, 273
——— Washington Monument, squares for, 266–72, 276, 366–37, 368; cost, 273; FLO's compensation and, 369; FLO visits to, 368; fountains in, 269, 270, 272; management of, 367–69; plans for, 270, *271*, *272*, *274*, *275*; seasonal gardens for, 269–70, 272, 276
Barillet-Deschamps, Jean-Pierre, 633, 651
Barnard, Frederick A. P., 357–58
Barras, Charles M., *The Black Crook*, 416
Barret, Mary, 331, 335
Barrett, Addison, 63
Barton, Frederick, 649
Bath, England, 264
Baxter, Sylvester, 512
Belle Isle (Detroit, Mich.), plan for, 592; park commission of, 572–73
Bellows, Henry Whitney (1814–1882), 384, 433–34, 439, 441, 444; on Calvert Vaux, 434; on FLO and Central Park, 434–35; *Historical Sketch of the Union Club . . . of New York*, 433–34; relations with FLO, 433–34
Bennett, James Gordon, 718
Berry, W. M., 527
Bickmore, Albert Smith, 337
Bissinger, Philip, 122, 128, 129, 646, 707, 709, 710
Blackwood, Frederick Temple (Lord Dufferin), 471, 472
Blatchford, Richard M., 377
Bloor, Alfred J., 184, 186, 302, 326; relations with Vaux, 326, 327; on Vaux's role in CP design, 324–26, 327
Board of Commissioners of the Central Park (N.Y.C.) (1857–1870), 80, 143–44, 349, 358, 361, 632–33; and creation of Central Park, 636–37; and early relations with FLO, 640; FLO and Vaux resign, 647; and FLO's positions on CP, 640–41, 642–43, 647; membership of, 640, 642; patronage pressures on, 615–16; and plans of Central Park, 632–33; political affiliation's of, 636, 637; and street plans in 1867, 249
Board of Commissioners of the Department of Public Parks (N.Y.C.) (1870–), 80, 143, 349, 361, 383, 607–9, 627–28, 629, 654, 664, 720; abolishes Exotic and Propagating Department, 82; and alteration of original CP plan, 633–35; appropriations and, 685–86, 687–88, 711, 720; and architects, 608; and Battery sea wall, 671; and Bureau of Design and Superintendence, 373, 384, 642–43, 713; and charges against FLO for official misdemeanors, 624–25; construction funds for 1875, 687–88; and contractors, 375, 379, 381, 383, 661, 664, 684, 699, 702; and debate over control of Riverside Avenue, 656–57; and eight-hour work day, 84, 663–64, 682; and FLO as Landscape Architect Advisory, 611, 642–43; FLO as President and Treasurer of, 80, 544, 548, 613, 640, 645; FLO's leave of absence from, 359, 362, 373, 384, 648; and FLO's opinion of commissioners, 606–7, 612; FLO's salary with, 373, 384; and fountains, 684, 715; journalistic criticism of, 160–62, 607, 610, 611, 617, 625, 627, 632–33, 641, 650, 676, 694–95, 713; laborers

GENERAL INDEX

for, 661; lobbying by, 661, 685, 697; management practices of, 605–6, 626, 631–32; membership of, 609–10, 641–42, 670–71, 676, 710; and office of landscape gardening, 125, 128, 610, 622, 626; and organization of gardeners for CP, 691–92, 716; and "Park Defense Organisation," 611, 644; patronage pressures on, 6, 613–17, 654–55, 657–64, 668–95, 697–702, 703–4, 706, 709–11, 715; and plan for the Twenty-third and Twenty-fourth wards, 242–28, 249, 251–63, 265; policies of, 606–7; and "practical" management, 612; and public concern over landscape art of the Park, 610–11; and reduction of FLO's authority, 713; reinstates FLO's pay, 625; relations of Board with Vaux, 606, 643; relations with FLO, 606–7, 624–25, 643, 646; relations with Tammany Hall, 162; remonstrance against, for removal of FLO, 373–74, 384, 435–36, 642; and reorganization of the park keepers, 618; and Riverdale plan, 251, 256, 263–64, 265; and Riverside Park and Avenue, 114, 705; and the Tweed Ring, 122, 544–45; Calvert Vaux and, 593–94; and wages, 660–61, 663–64, 672, 675, 684–86, 689–90, 702–3, 715, 720; withholds FLO's salary, 382, 387, 624–25; and work stoppages, 671–72, 684, 711. *See also* Twenty-third and Twenty-fourth wards

—— appointments and dismissals by: appointments of FLO or Vaux and, 640–41, 643, 647; appoints Aldrich superintending engineer of Riverside Ave, 378, 386; appoints Aneurin Jones superintendent, 587; appoints FLO Consulting Landscape Architect, 384, 626, 648; appoints Vaux Superintending Architect, 641; dismisses FLO and Vaux as landscape architects (1870), 3, 647; dismisses FLO as Landscape Architect, 5, 625; dismisses J. J. R. Croes, 374, 385; dismisses William L. Fischer, 374, 385; reappoints FLO and Vaux landscape architects, 4, 647; relieves FLO from supervising park maintenance, 127; removes FLO from Bureau of Design and Superintendence, 373–74, 381–82, 384, 435–36

—— Reorganization of the Park Board: abolition of park board for single head, 639, 652, 695–97, 718–19; and plan for two-member park board, 640–41; 1873 reorganization, 4; reorganization from 5 to 4 members, 666–67

Bogart, John, 82, 223, 276, 385, 647, 685, 702, 706, 711, 720

Bois de Boulogne (Paris), 140, 195, 256

Boston, Mass., 246, 561–62; Brighton Park, 1876 proposal for, 568, 571; and Charles River Embankment, 193, 195, 197–98, 569; comprehensive park system for, 567–69; FLO's involvement with 1876 proposal, 10, 192–98; Jamaica Pond, 193, 569, 570; Parker Hill Reservoir, 193, 194, 198; parks and public spaces in, 9–13, 570; parochial allegiances in, 567; pleasure drive in, 456; Public Garden, 454, 569

—— Muddy River, 569; diversion of, 454, 456, 462; improvement of, 517–20, 571; plans for improvement of, *519*, 570

—— park commission of: and arrangement for Arnold Arboretum, 489; and Elm Hill property, 193, 195, 198; FLO's relations with, 192–93; 1876 park system proposal, 10, 13, 195–97, 337, 567, 571; and sites for parks, 567–71

—— streets of: West Chester Park Avenue, 456, 462. *See* Commonwealth Avenue

—— West Roxbury Park, (Franklin Park), 198, 529, 531, 567–69; and Elm Hill property, 193, 195; land to be deaccessioned, 530; plans for, *529*, *531*, 570; site of, 193, 195, 528–31. *See also* Arnold Arboretum; Back Bay Fens; Back Bay Park

Boston Common, 569
Boston Public Garden, 454, 463, 569
Bowditch, Ernest William, 650
Bowen, Dennis, 174, 231–33
Brace, Charles Loring, 593
Brace, Letitia Neill, 594
Brackenridge, William D., 54
Bradley, William Hammatt, 483
Braman, Waters W., 706
Brighton (England), 264
Brighton Beach, N.Y., hotels at, 403, 405–6
Brookline, Mass., 458, 520; Aspinwall Hill Land Company, 20; FLO's plan for

741

GENERAL INDEX

Brookline, Mass. (cont.)
  Barthold Schlesinger's estate, 469, 538, 602; FLO's residence in, 523, 601, 602, 603; Holm Lea estate, 470; parkway of, 198, 520–21; railroad embankment in, 518
  —— Muddy River, 462; improvement of, 517–22; plans for improvement of, 519, 570
Brooklyn, N.Y., 443; access to Rockaway beaches from, 401, 403, 410, 419, 444; Board of Commissioners of Prospect Park, turf usage and, 161, 163; East River Bridge, 653; FLO's relations with park commission of, 67, 161, 704; Green-Wood Cemetery, 137. See also Prospect Park
Brooks, Erastus, 649
Brown, Lancelot "Capability," 337
Browne, Albert Gallatin, 83
Brush, Alexander, 504
Bryant, John, 593
Bryant, Owen, 593
Bryant, William Cullen, 323
Buchanan, William Oliver, 503–4
Buckinghamshire (England), 337
Buffalo, N.Y.: City and County Hall in, 170–71, 172–73, 708–9; Delaware Street (Avenue), 101, 103; and Ladies Union Monument Association, 103; parkways of, 103; State Asylum in, 174, 327, 424, 479; war memorial in, 101–2, 103
  —— Buffalo Park Commission: creation of, 103; and Fillmore Avenue, 229, 231, 333; laborers' pay and, 229–30, 663–64, 670
  —— Delaware Park (The Park), 103, 229–30, 231–33; Gala Water (lake), 230; lakeshore plantings of, 234; names of features in, 304–5; seasonal work on the plantations of, 229–30, 231–32, 234; Spirehead area in, 234; work force in, 229–30, 231
  —— parks and public spaces in, 101–2, 303; late additions to plan for, 232; Niagara Square, 99–101, 103; Niagara Square, plan, 100; public meetings on, 328–29; Soldiers Place, 102, 103; visits to, 663, 670
Bulfinch, Charles, 42
Bullard, Oliver Crosby, 4, 67, 82, 134, 369, 502, 514

Burges, William, 131, 132
Burnham, Gordon, 49, 50

Cady, J. C., 641
Calhoun, John S., 42
Calkins, Frank A., 671, 684–85, 711, 720
Calkins, Hiram, 715
Campbell, George Douglas, 480–81
Campbell, J. L. (Dr.), 331–32, 384
Campbell, John Douglass Sutherland (Marquis of Lorne), 425, 481
Cape May, N.J., 403
Carlyle, Thomas, 421, 425, 426, 471, 472
Cemetery design, 135–36, 137, 149–50; "lawn system," 137, 150; monuments and, 138; and notable cemeteries, 149–51. See also individual cemeteries
Central Park (N.Y.C.), 44–47, 322–23, 649; athletics in, 141, 143–44, 647; carriages in, 86–87, 164, 627; circulation system of, 584, 635, 642; condition of, 82–83, 139–41, 166–67, 562; and contract work (day's work), 699; cost of, 322, 325, 585, 607, 632, 633; cows in, 687; creation of, 636–37; crime in, 76–77, 121, 141–42, 620; damage to, by crowds, 321–22, 324; "damn the landscape," 623, 624; description of, 583–85; design competition for, 325, 364–65, 650, 651, 717; deterioration of, 139–41; drainage in, 160, 162–63, 622, 647, 695, 717; drives of, 86–87, 167; and eight-hour law, 663–64; and "entente" between Vaux, Parsons, Green & Tilden, 593–94; exotic and floral gardening in, 125, 358–59, 630, 650; FLO and trees for, 625; FLO's positions at, 4, 124, 125, 127, 626, 642–43, 647; goats in, 142; grading of, 113, 127; Greensward plan of, 48, 325–26, 361, 365, 626, 650, 651, 717; health benefits of, 76, 81, 85; journalistic criticism of, 650–51, 694–95, 717, 719; journalistic reports on, 684; key points in design of, 44, 48; labor force in, 82, 678, 687–88, 689–90, 716–17; landscape gardening office, 125; malaria and, 160–61, 162, 163, 622, 717; Menagerie, 80, 358, 361; and office of landscape gardening, 128; and organization of gardeners force, 691–94, 716; parade ground in, 213, 221, 286–87, 288, 323, 417; pastoral landscape in,

742

586; patronage issues, 541–44; place names in, 304–5; plan of, 45; planting of, 686; promenade in, 164–67; prostitutes and tramps in, 620–21; public appreciation of, 611; purpose of, 76, 143–44, 607–8; role of CV in design of, 324–36, 384, 433–36; running course in, 647; sanitary conditions in, 160–61, 162, 695; skating in, 75, 82–83; stables in, 663; taxes and bonds for, 77–78, 81; transverse roads in, 635, 650, 651; tree cutting in (by FLO), 621; trees, record of (proposed), 175; urinals in, 665–66; vandalism in, 620, 683; visitors to, 320–21, 714; water features of, 160, 162–63; Zoological and Botanic garden for, 359–60. *See also* New York (City) Board of Commissioners of the Central Park; New York (City) Board of Commissioners of the Department of Public Parks; New York (City) Board of Estimate and Apportionment; New York (City) patronage pressures on

—— architectural structures in, 127, 134, 712; arches, 136, 608, 642, 650; arches, William Robinson on, 138; Arsenal, 361; Belvedere, 44, 49; camera obscura, 687; fountain for, 49–50; restaurant at Mount St. Vincent, 717; urinals, 665–66, 709

—— areas in: Ball Ground, 141, 143; Dairy, 687, 716; The Green (Sheep Meadow), 140–41, 287; Mall, 44–46; North Meadows, 143; North Park, 166; The Ramble, 133; South Park, 139–40, 143, 166; Vista Rock, 44, 49

—— Keepers force, 75, 76, 126, 620, 663, 672–73, 681–83, 712, 713, 714; discipline of, 118, 119–20, 618, 673–74, 675; enlargement of, 76, 77, 120, 142; expense for, 75; FLO relieved from superintending duties of, 81, 118–19, 122, 127, 129, 619, 646; FLO's plan for organization of, 143, 618–19, 645–46, 678–79, 682–83, 690, 694, 714; FLO superintends, 617–18, 645; and guarding of turf, 139–43, 144; and Halleck statue celebration, 319, 321–22; and journalistic criticism of organization of, 645–46; "practical" management of, 619–21; surgeon's survey of, 617–18, 682. *See also* Henry Koster

—— landscape, treatment of: hardy native and exotic specimens in, 134; plantations, 124–25, 128–29, 175, 178, 374, 686; planting to obscure bridges and roads, 133, 635; "smugness" of, 679–80; trees in, 47, 175–78; tree thinning, 47, 49, 79, 81–82, 124–26, 128–29, 133, 134

—— maintenance of, 127; cleaning out of plants, 621; construction suspended on, 80–1; expenditures, 74–75, 77–78, 81, 139, 144; expense estimates 1873–1875, 74–75, 81; FLO's report on funds for, 680–81, 682, 714, 715; FLO's system for gardeners, restoration of, 691–92, 693; irrigation in, 143

—— management of, 6, 124–26, 583–86, 587, 593–94, 621–22, 630, 631–32, 637–40; district gardener system of, 716, 717; "practical" management of, 622, 626–27, 631, 632; undesirable management practices in, 620–23, 626–28, 636, 637, 640, 643–44, 647, 648, 650–51, 678–80, 683–84, 686–87, 691–93, 716–17

—— statuary in, 648, 683; colossal statues in, 46–48, 50; Daniel Webster statue, 43–50; Fitz-Greene Halleck statue, 49, 318–23, 324; Robert Burns statue, 49; Shakespeare statue, 46, 49; Sir Walter Scott statue, 49

—— turf, 139–43, 161, 687, 697; destruction of, 139–43, 683, 687, 715; regulations concerning, 163, 719; repair of, 140, 142; use of, 139–43, 161, 163
Chandler, Zachariah, 277, 279, 281
Chautauqua Institution. *See* Fair Point Camp
Child, Francis J., 416
Church, Frederic Edwin, 48, 128, 377, 472; concerning statues in Central Park, 48–49; and the Niagara Reservation, 471, 472, 474, 479
Cicero (Roman orator), 287
Cities, development of, 437–38, 566
Civil-Service Reform Association, 540, 548
Clancy, John, 548
Clark, Edward (1822–1902), 43, 67, 68, 69–71, 72, 98, 99, 106, 107, 327, 370–71, 392, 393, 432, 501, 509, 514, 560, 575, 582
Cleveland, Henry Russell, 525

Cleveland, Horace William Shaler (1814–1900), 34–35, 36, 154–55, 156, 524–25, 632; *Landscape Architecture, as Applied to the Wants of the West* . . . , Olmsted on, 34–35
Cleveland, Sarah Paine Perkins, 524
Cobb, Frederick H., 337, 370–71, 432, 501, 509, 512–14, 561, 576, 582, 583
Cogan, William, 501, 513–14, 576
Columbia College (N.Y.C.), 245
Commonwealth Avenue, Boston, Mass., 12–13, 521, 569; drives and walks in, 455, 460–61; extension of, 461, 463; plantings of, 515–16, 602; preparation of soil for plantings, 516; tree planting along, 515–16, 517
Commonwealth Avenue Bridge, Boston, Mass., 449
Coney Island, N.Y.: comparison to Rockaway Point, 397–407, 417–18; hotels at, 415, 416; water supply and, 400, 415
Conklin, William A., 80, 682, 683
Conservation of forests, 174–75
Cook, Clarence, 436
Copeland, Robert Morris, 650
Copperheads, 277
Corcoran, Phillip, 712, 714
Cornell, Alonzo B., 9, 473, 533, 535, 564
Cornell, Paul, 527
Cornell, Thomas C., 263
Crafts, Nathaniel Henry, 483
Crawford Notch, N.H., 158, 159
Croes, J. James R. (1834–1906), 1, 248–49, 250–51, 264, 282, 313, 348, 349, 374, 379, 381, 385, 386; plans by Croes and FLO, *261, 309, 341*
Culyer, John Yapp, 650, 712–13
Curtis, George W., 6, 525, 547, 708
Curtis, Joseph H., 10, 650

Dalton, Charles Henry (1826–1908), 197, 365, 489; FLO relations with, 10, 192–93
Daly, James, 705, 717
Darwin, Charles, 426, 497–98
Darwin, Sara (Sedgwick), 426, 481
Davis, Joseph Phineas, 1, 449, 483
Dawson, John F., 648
Dawson, Sir John William, 336
Day, Walter De F., 706
DeGrauw, Aaron A., Jr., 417
Demcker, Robert, 81, 82, 127, 128, 361, 716

Democratic Party, and Election of 1876, 278
Detroit, Mich., Belle Isle, plan for, 572–73
Dickens, Charles, 386, 387, 651
Dillon, Robert J., 361, 377, 651
Dix, John Adams, 706
Dobbs Ferry, N.Y., 428, 431
Doherty, Charles W., 333
Donn, John W., 415
Dorsheimer, William Edward (1832–1888), 7, 9, 186, 188, 189, 201, 205, 278, 281, 286, 295, 296, 303; and Niagara Reservation, 471–72, 479, 533
Downing, Andrew Jackson (1815–1852), 41, 42–43, 54, 156, 324–25, 327, 433, 434, 554, 588, 649; *Treatise on the Theory and Practice of Landscape Gardening* . . . , 394, 395, 588, 620
Dudley, Henry, 302

Earth closets, 179, 182
East River Bridge (Brooklyn, N.Y.), 653
East River Park (Carl Schurz Park), N.Y., 4
Eaton, Dorman Bridgman, 54, 71, 73, 720
Eaton, James W., 281, 423
Edinburgh, Scotland, "New Town," 255, 265
Eidlitz, Leopold (1823–1908), 112, 115, 289, 297, 304, 327, 387; and criticism of construction of Riverside Avenue, 385; and the New Capitol (N.Y.), 8, 183, 184, 186, 199, 200, 205, 278, 283, 297, 317
Eidlitz, Richardson & Co. (Architects), 7, 278, 280, 284, 299, 302, 704
Eliot, Ellsworth (Dr.), 329–30
Eliot, Ellsworth, Jr., 329–30
Ellicott, Joseph, 103
Elliott, Charles W., 649
Emerson, Ralph Waldo, 421, 472, 611, 644
Errington, Harriet, 335, 337
Europe: city plans in, 244, 245; decorative gardening in, 630; palaces of, 38, 42, 184, *185*, 187
Evarts, William Maxwell, 305
Everglade, use of term, 428
Expositions, 410, 417, 444

Fair Point Camp (Chautauqua Institution) (Chautauqua Lake, N.Y.), 151–55; Palestine Park at, 151, 155
Far Rockaway, N.Y., 416
Fay, Joseph Story, 550, 554

GENERAL INDEX

Field, Alfred T., 264, 333, 334, 335, 593, 594
Field, Charlotte Errington, 337, 594
Field, Rosa, 593, 594
Fields, Thomas C., 168, 548, 680, 714
Fischer, William L. (1819–1899), 4, 82, 133–34, 305, 374, 379–80, 385, 593–94, 647, 650, 686, 716; attempted replacement by Parsons, 593–94, 642, 643; removal of by DPP, 374, 379–80, 381, 385, 643; and study of trees, 175, 176
Flagg, Thomas Wilson, 35, 512; *Woods and By-ways of New England*, Olmsted on, 34–35
Florence (Italy), Ponte Santa Trinita at, 449
Folsom, Charles Follen, 457, 463
Forbes, John Murray, 554
Forests, conservation of, 174–75
Franconia Notch, N.H., "Profile" in, 159
Franklin, Thomas, 385, 386
Fuller, Thomas (1822–1898), 186, 188, 278, 284, 286, 292–94, 295–96, 298–99, 303; Advisory Board's opinion of, 293, 294, 297–99; descriptions of the design of the New Capitol by, 184, 188, 189, 199–200, 205, 284–85; dismissal of, 200, 201, 205, 206, 299, 302; as head of Albany Society of Architects, 294; remonstrance of, 204, 205, 281, 302–3

The Garden (journal), 223, 227, 326
Gardening: decorative, 18–19, 630, 633–34; decorative, André on, 633–34; parterre and specimen, 351
Gardens, botanical and zoological, 334, 336–37
Gardner (Gardiner), James Terry (1842–1912), 8–9, 421, 423, 445, 479, 503
Garfield, James, 547, 638, 651–52
Garrett, Robert, 273, 276, 368
Geddes, George, 424, 426, 649
Gelray, Joseph Wiley, 663, 708
Gibbs, Oliver Wolcott, 434
Gilman, Arthur D., 303
Gilman, Daniel Coit, 52
Gilman, Emily Perkins, 338
Gilman, Katherine Beecher Perkins, 338
Gilman, William Charles, 338
Gilpin, William, 588, 589, 649
Godkin, Edwin L., 279, 384, 435–36, 472
Golden Gate Park (San Francisco, Calif.), 51, 117

Grace, William R., 651–52
Grace Church (N.Y.C.), 245
Grant, Ullysses S., 278
Grant, William H., 250, 263–64, 650
Gray, Asa, 334, 336, 394, 477, 480
Green, Andrew Haswell (1820–1903), 3, 4–5, 9, 80, 84, 161, 223, 280, 287, 361, 435, 548, 641, 710–11; and DPP patronage, 658–59, 661, 670–71, 673, 676–77, 680, 681, 686, 692, 695–97, 700, 706, 707, 714, 716, 720; opposition to Riverside Park work, 114; and planting in CP, 686; and relations with William Martin, 700, 706–7, 713, 719–20; and reorganization of the DPP commission, 695–97, 718–19; and Riverside Park and Avenue, 114; and support of Vaux, 593–94
Greene, George S., 250, 264
Green-Wood Cemetery (Brooklyn, N.Y.), 137
Grundel, Hermann, 11, 365
Guiteau, Charles J., 539, 547–48

Hall, Samuel, 708, 709
Hall, William Hammond, 51, 117; University of California (Berkeley), 50, 51
Halleck, Fitz-Greene, statue of in CP, 49, 318–23, 324
Hamilton, W. T., 592
Harney, George E., 470, 535, 537–38
Harper & Brothers publishers, 394
Harris, Elisha, 393
Harris, Hamilton, 190, 285–86, 302
Harrison, Jonathan Baxter, 564
Hartford, Connecticut, 16–17, 129–31
Harvard College, Arnold Arboretum and, 484–85, 488–89
Haskell, J. H., 507
Hastings, Hugh J., 671, 711
Haussmann, Georges Eugène, 249, 256, 265
Havemeyer, William F., 115, 705, 706, 707, 710
Hawkins, Dexter Arnoll, 657, 706
Hawkins, Rush C., 720
Hayes, Rutherford B., 279, 305; visit to Central Park, 318, 320–21, 323–24
Hepp, August, 643
Hewitt, Abram S., 281, 712
Hill, Rowland, 504
Hill, Thomas, 159; on exotics, 159
Hoffman, John T., 287

745

Holley, George W., *Niagara: Its History and Geology* . . . , 424
Holly Manufacturing Company, Lockport, N.Y., 182
Holmes, Oliver Wendell, 421
Hooker, Sir Joseph Dalton, 334, 336, 477, 480
Horticulture, branches of, 350
Hosack, Dr. David, 590
Hoskins, George G., 302
Hotels (resorts), 402–7, 416; Coney Island hotels, 415, 416, 417; Far Rockaway, N.Y., 376; Saratoga Springs, N.Y., 55–58
Houghton, Lord. *See* Milnes, Richard Monckton
Howe, Timothy O., 107
Hugo, Victor, 626
Hunnewell, Horatio Hollis, 550, 554, 589, 590
Hunt, Richard Morris, 186, 204, 205–6, 284, 285, 302, 443–44
Husted, James W., 206, 286, 419

Ingalls, Rufus (Colonel), 146
Institute of Architects. *See* American Institute of Architects
International Workingmen's Association, 72

Jeffersonville Dépôt, Indiana, 59–63; planting map, 60
Jennings, Louis J., 162
Jones, Aneurin, 6, 587, 640, 641, 642, 643, 644, 647, 648, 650
Jones, Chilion, 186
Jones, George, 162
Jowett, Benjamin, 472–73

Kane, Sir Robert John, *Elements of Chemistry* . . . , 445, 446
Kearny, John Watts, 20
Kelly, John, 5, 385, 387, 593, 648, 661, 676, 707
Kent, William, 228
Kerr, Robert, 560
Kessler, George, 589; advice from FLO, 588–89
Kimball, Francis H., 132, 502
King, Clarence, 421, 563, 565
Knapp, Frederick, 159
Koster, Henry (Captain, Central Park Keepers), 80, 119, 127, 663, 673, 681, 712; criticizes FLO's management policies, 117–18, 120, 121; suspension of, 121, 122, 708, 710, 713, 714

La Farge, John (1835–1910), 201, 303, 447; and aesthetic sensibility, 446
Lanahan, Thomas M., 273, 367–68, 369, 376
Landscape, charm of, 355
Landscape, poetic beauty of, 355
Landscape and music, 355
Landscape Architecture
—— characteristics of, 223–24, 227, 351; as an art, 524, 562, 627–28, 629; design principles governing, 584–86, 640; and the Imagination, 355; origin of the term, 228; profession of, 380, 628; scale of, 43. *See also* Landscape Gardening
—— practice of: architectural elements in, 68, 223–24, 559–60; cemetery design, 135–36, 137, 150; "clerk of the works" and, 131; definition of, 350–52; and earth closets, 179, 182; "exotics" in, 158, 159; fences in, 555; floral bedding-out, 136, 137–38; flower gardens in, 506, 507; formal gardens and, 583; grading in, 39–40, 43; grounds, preparation of, 147–48; irrigation and, 143; McAdam road construction in, 235, 237; ornament in, 34, 559–60; parks, character and purpose of, 43–44, 48; process of creating plans, 572–73; promenades, 164–66; residential design, 18–19, 34–35, 350–57; role of architects in, 223–27, 228, 325–26; in semiarid regions, 50–51, 52, 115–16, 117; and setting for residences, 555; social value and the idea of civilization, 34–35, 195; statuary and, 43–48, 267, 317–18; in tidal marsh lands, 387–88; trees, planting and transplanting of, 67, 147; trees, thinning of, 42–43, 128; trends in, 630, 650; turf, treatment of, 61–62, 140–41; water features and, 182; winter gardens, 582. *See also* Cemetery design
Landscape design styles: forest scenery and, 549–50; natural scenery and, 355–56, 395, 511–12, 528, 549, 563, 630, 631, 638; pastoral scenery, 137, 528–30, 586, 630; picturesque scenery, 228, 389, 394, 395, 492, 621–22; wild sylvan scenery, 511

Landscape gardening, 350–57, 584–86; as an art, 585, 610–11; fences in, 352; gateways in, 352; and landscape painting, 356; mowing of turf, 352; and nature, 355–56; origin of, 226–27, 228; ornaments in, 352; paths in, 352; plants in, 352; and poetic beauty, 355–56; in small areas, 351; treatment of grounds of modest homes, 350–57; turf, near trees, 352
Lane, Smith E., 385, 648
Latrobe, Benjamin H., 42
Lauder, Sir Thomas Dick, 394, 395
Laver, Augustus, 303
Lee, Francis L., 650
Lee, James Grafton Carleton, 62–63
L'Enfant, Pierre Charles, 41–42
Lesage, Louis, 206, 210
Lienau, Detlef, 286, 302
Littré, Maximilien Paul Émile, 446
London, England, 249–50, 255, 263; Courts of Law buildings in, 296, 303; museums in, 334, 336; Westminster Abbey in, 184
Long, Samuel P. *Art: Its Laws* . . . , 445–46
Long Branch, N.J., 155, 402, 403, 416
Longfellow, Henry Wadsworth, 421, 472, 611, 644
Longfellow, William Pitt Preble, 190, 327, 483
Loudon, John Claudius, 128, 224, 336–37, 588, 589
Low, James, 504
Lowell, James Russell, 351, 358, 484, 611, 644
Loyal Publication Society, 197

Maclean, Charles, 648
MacQuisten, Patrick, 90, 91
Maher, James, 42
Manning, John W., 144, 645
Martin, Charles Cyril, 705
Martin, Howard A., 706
Martin, William Runyon (1825–1897), 5, 21, 114, 128, 143, 220, 222–23, 323, 377, 640, 648, 653–54, 666, 671, 677, 680–81, 697–98, 706–7, 710, 711; pressure on, for hiring laborers, 700–701; relations with Andrew H. Green, 678, 700, 706–7, 713, 719–20; relations with Henry G. Stebbins, 4, 677; and Riverside Park, 699; and Twenty-third and Twenty-fourth wards, 264, 265, 312–13, 349–50
Mayne, Sir Richard, 619, 646
McCarthy, William H., 714
McCloskey, John, Cardinal, 472
McDowell, Irvin, 277, 280
McGibbon, William, 90, 91, 204
McKim, Mead & White (Architects), 556
McLean Asylum (Belmont, Mass.), 10, 197
McMillan, William, 174, 230, 232–33
Meigs, Montgomery C., 42, 62–63, 107
Merry-Mount park (Quincy, Mass.), FLO on, 566
Metropolitan Board of Works (London), 249
Metropolitan Museum of Art, (N.Y.C.), 49, 359, 361–62, 443
Mexicanization, 278, 280
Mexico, 280
Michler, Nathaniel, 41, 54
Middlesex Fells, Massachusetts, 510–12; name for, 510, 512
Milan, Duomo in, 184, 187
Military installations, treatment of grounds of. *See* Jeffersonville Dépôt, Indiana; Schuylkill Arsenal, Philadelphia
Miller, J. H. (Rev.), 155, 182
Milnes, Richard Monckton (Lord Houghton), 421, 471, 472
Mollard, Joseph, 653
Montauk Association, 556
Montauk Point, Long Island, 555, 556; summer community at, 555–56
Montreal (Quebec, Canada), benefit of a park to, 86
Morningside Park (N.Y.C.), 4, 114, 127, 361, 386, 699
Morrill, Justin Smith (1810–1898), 14, 15, 40, 43, 53, 54, 67, 71, 72, 98, 106, 107; relationship with FLO, 33, 40; and Summer House on Capitol grounds, 509; U.S. Capitol watchmen and, 370–71
Morrill, Ruth Barrell Swan, 73
Morris, Gouverneur, 344, 349
Morrisey, John, 277, 280
Morrison, Eugene C., 711
Morrison, R. J., 707
Mould, Jacob Wrey, 50, 222, 327, 641, 650
Mountain View Cemetery (Oakland, Cal.), 151
Mount Auburn Cemetery (Cambridge, Mass.), 137

Mount Royal (Montreal, Quebec, Canada), park on: accessibility of, 85–87, 89; carriages and, 86–87; design map, 88; FLO's design work at, 13; FLO's two lectures about, 328, 333, 335–36; FLO visits, 334; H. B. Smith property and, 91, 206, 208; and Hotel-Dieu Hospital, 87, 91, 313; J. Tompkins property and, 91, 209–10; laborers wages and, 703; landscape features of, 313–14; McTavish monument, 86, 90; park commission of, 91, 237; pastoral scenery in, 89, 91, 206, 209–10; plan for, *207*, *209*; planting of, 314; promenade drives for, 208, 209; proposed monument on, 317–18; proposed rules for, 328; refectory for, 191–92; relation of, to Saint Jean Baptiste, 313–14; scenery of, 89; and Sir Hugh Allan's estate, 87, 91; as site for small-pox hospital, 313–14, 315; site of, 84–85, 89–90, 333, 336; small-pox hospital in, 313–14; trees in, sanitary value of, 263, 265; use of, by invalids, 85, 86; Victoria Square and, 87, 91; views from, 206, 208; visitors to, 235, 237; water works for, 206
———— areas in: "Crown of the Mountain," 210; McTavish Reservoir, 91; reservoir in, 206, 208, 235, 237; Upperfell section, 191–92
———— circulation system of, 86; approach road to top of the mountain, 85, 86–87, 90, 156–58, 201–3, 208, 235–36, 237, 314; sub-routes of approach, 89
———— entrances: Côte des Neiges Road, 89, 91, 208; foot approaches, 89; inclined lift, 89; sub-routes of approach, 89
———— exterior streets, 87, 89; Bleury Street, 90, 157, 208, 210, 315; McTavish Street, 87, 90, 157–58; Peel Street, 87, 90, 157–58; pleasure drives and, 86, 156, 235; Sherbrooke Street, 91
Mowatt, Sir Oliver, 424, 425, 426
Muddy River (Boston and Brookline, Mass.), 458, 569; diversion of, 454, 456, 462; improvement of, 517–20, 571; plans for improvement of, *519*, *570*
Munckwitz, Julius F., 49, 77, 81, 162, 222, 324, 327, 641, 713
Museum of Natural History (N.Y.C.), 361
Muskau, Silesia, 588

Nation (journal), 277, 278–79, 280, 281
National Academy of Design (N.Y.C.), 652
National Board of Health, 576
Nelson, Horatio Admiral, 157, 192, 237, 314–15
New Orleans, yellow fever in, 444
New York (City): arboretum for, 359; Battery Park in, 82, 671; Board of Commissioners of the Central Park [*see* Board of Commissioners of the Central Park (N.Y.C.) (1857–1870)]; Board of Commissioners of the Department of Public Parks [*see* Board of Commissioners of the Department of Public Parks (N.Y.C.) (1870–)]; Bowling Green, 216, 222; City Hall Park, 80, 82, 684; Claremont Park, 349; commercial position of, 438–39; Dock Commission, 685–86, 716; draft riots in, 277, 279–80; early development of, 442–43; and eight hour work day in, 705; FLO on future of, 436–44; growth of, 248, 255–56; housing in, 245, 250, 439–42, 444; malaria and, 253, 263, 265; Manhattan Square, 361; as a metropolis, 438–39; Plan of 1811, 243–47, 249, *440*, 444; rapid transit in, 343; Riverdale (*see* Twenty-third and Twenty-fourth wards); rowhouses in, 439–41, 444; sanitary condition of, 439, 442; street cleaning of, 659; street plan of, 114, 439, 441, 442; suburban residential areas in, 443; Twenty-third and Twenty-fourth wards [*see* Twenty-third and Twenty-fourth wards (N.Y.C.)]; unemployment in, 660–61, 719; Union Square, 101, 634
———— Board of Aldermen: and investigation of FLO, 683; and patronage, 541–42, 613, 672, 690; residency bill and, 662; and Tompkins Square, 700
———— Board of Apportionment, FLO as member of, 548; Board of Audit, FLO as member of, 548
———— Board of Commissioners of the Central Park (1857–1870). *See* Board of Commissioners of the Central Park (N.Y.C.) (1857–1870)
———— Board of Commissioners of the Department of Public Parks (1870–). *See* Board of Commissioners of the

Department of Public Parks (N.Y.C.) (1870–)
—— Board of Estimate and Apportionment, estimates for public parks, 80–81; reduction in park department's budget, 81, 82, 83–84, 178
—— Department of Public Works, 115, 156, 653–55, 675; and controversy over control of Riverside Avenue, 656–57, 705; patronage pressures on, 654, 657–58, 664, 670, 671–72, 675–76
—— Twenty-third and Twenty-fourth wards. *See* Twenty-third and Twenty-fourth wards (N.Y.C.)
New York (State): city government of, 304, 305; and rapid transit commissions, 312–13
New York (State) Legislature: and patronage, 704; anti-Tilden Democrats in, 205; Senate Committee on Cities of, on Riverside Avenue construction, 656–57, 707
New York State New Capitol, 7–8, *190*, 290, 704; Advisory Board of, 186, 187, 204, 278, 280, 284, 289, 291–93, 295–97; AIA chapter, Remonstrance concerning, 186–87, 188, 197, 205–6, 286, 300–301, 302, 315–17; Assembly Chamber of, 284–85; attacks on the administration of, 283; Commissioners of, 286; controversy concerning architectural styles of, 184–85, 186, 187, 188–89, 199–201, 204, 283–86, 291, 299–301, 302–3, 317; design competition of, 292, 303; Eidlitz, Richardson & Co. and, 278, 280, 284, 299, 302, 704; FLO on mixture of architectural styles of, 184–85, 278, 316; FLO's compensation for, 296–97, 302; FLO's response to remonstrances, 315–16, 317; FLO's role in design of, 8, 188, 189, 204–5, 278, 280, 283, 284, 288; FLO's testimony at hearings, 288–302, 304; FLO's visits to Albany for, 278, 283, 284; Fuller's design for, *189*; Land Office and, 205; patronage and, 283, 285; remonstrance against report of Advisory Board, 184, 186, 187, 188, 197, 204, 205–6, 285–86, 300–301, 302, 315–17; roof of, 204; Senate Finance Committee and, 188. *See also* Fuller, Thomas

New York State Survey, 421, 424–25, 704; Commissioners of, 421, 424, 473, 474–79, 497
New-York Times and attacks on DPP, 160–62
New York World, 277, 278–79
Niagara Falls, 416; FLO visits, 419; literary descriptions of, 475–77, 478–79, 480–81; rapids above, 475–77, 476, 478–79, 480, 481; vegetation at, 477–78, 480; visitors to, 474–75, 479–80
Niagara Reservation (N.Y.), 9, 395, 422, 504; and admission, 423; bill to purchase lands for, 503, 504; campaign for, 8–9, 420–21, 424–25, 445, 446, 471–72, 473, 480–81, 503, 533, 535, 563–64; circulars (petitions) concerning, 9, 395, 420–21, 424–25, 445, 471–72, 473, 497–98, 503; and damage to scenery, 474; foreign interest in, 497; funding for, 421; Goat Island in, 423, 477–78; governor's opposition to, 533; natural scenery of, 422–23, 477–79; "Notes by Mr. Olmsted," on, 474–79; Olmsted named to commission to choose lands, 504; origin of idea for, 479; and proposed military encampment on, 422–23; "Prospect Park" in, 422; purpose of, 422–23; Tugby building (bazaar) on, 422. *See also* New York State Survey; Charles Eliot Norton
Norman, Henry, 535, 563–64, 565
Norton, Charles Eliot (1827–1908), 185, 187, 188, 189, 334, 632; and the 1876 presidential election, 277; and the New York State New Capitol, 185, 200, 300–301, 304; role in Niagara Reservation campaign, 424–25, 426, 445, 446, 471–72, 563, 564–65

O'Brien, James, 277, 280
O'Callaghan, Thomas H., 708
O'Conor, Charles, 277, 280
O'Donohue, Joseph John, 681, 683, 685–86, 688, 692, 701–2, 714, 720
Olmstead, B. S., 227, 228
Olmsted, Charlotte (Chatty), 337
Olmsted, Frederick Law (1822–1903): as an "unpractical man," 640; as "Architect" for New York State New Capitol, 290; and Bureau of Design and Superinten-

Olmsted, Frederick Law (*cont.*)
dence, 384, 435–36, 643, 713; and charges of official misdemeanors, 624–25; club membership of, 472, 473; cranberry-growing venture, 159; dismissal by DPP, 5, 373, 381–83, 384, 625; furor over, 434–36; early career/training of, 628–30, 631, 649; early instruction in scenery of, 649; on education for architects and landscape gardeners, 224–26, 628–30; education of, 628–29, 649; preparation for landscape gardening, 588–89; on engineers, 450; Greensward plan and, 48, 325–26, 361, 365, 626, 650, 651, 717; journalistic attacks on, 387, 617, 619, 624, 625, 629–30, 648; journalistic criticism of ("as The Great Leech"), 382; lobbying work in Albany, 704; and Loyal Publication Society, 197; nominated for Street Commissioner, 613; and origin of the term "landscape architect," 228; as partner in Vaux, Withers & Co., 1, 303; partnership with Vaux ends, 1; patronage pressures on, 6, 539–46, 613–15, 617–18, 623, 636, 688–89; and preparation of report to DPP commission, 701; professional practice of, 1874–82, 2–3; as reporter for *New-York Times*, 160, 162; residences of, 280, 330, 369, 523; salary withheld by DPP, 382, 387; urges reduction of wages on CP, 143, 672, 676, 682, 686; and U.S. Sanitary Commission, 433–34. *See also* Board of Commissioners of the Central Park (N.Y.C.) (1857–1870); Board of Commissioners of the Department of Public Parks (N.Y.C.); Central Park (N.Y.C); Central Park (N.Y.C.) Keepers Force

——health of, 5, 499, 592, 624–25, 641; crisis in 1877, 624–25; eye ailment, 41, 556; and leave of absence from CP, 359, 362, 373, 624–25

——architectural features in landscape designs: arbors (pergolas), 55–56, 217–18, 494–95, 525–27, 555; fountains, 100–101, 103, 270, 272, 276, 411, 432, 508, 533; grottoes, 218–19, 270, 508

——landscape design projects; Arnold Arboretum (Boston, Mass.), Aspinwall Hill Land Company (Brookline, Mass.), 20; "Bellegrove," N.J., 20; Belle Isle (Detroit, Mich.), 592; G. Nixon Black estate (Manchester, Mass.), 18; John Bryant estate (Cohasset, Mass.), 20; Buffalo Asylum (State hospital), 174, 327, 424, 479; cemetery design and, 135–36; College of California (Berkeley), 50–51, 52; Charles A. Dana estate (Oyster Bay, N.Y.), 20; W. T. Hamilton estate (Syracuse, N.Y.), 592; Henry B. Heyde estate (Suffolk County, N.Y.), 20; Industrial Home School (Washington, D.C.), 20; Jeffersonville Dépôt (Indiana), 59–63; McLean Asylum (Belmont, Mass.), 10, 197; Morningside Park (N.Y.C.), 4, 114, 127, 361, 386, 699; Parkside (Buffalo, N.Y.), 17; railroad in White Mountains, N.H., 158, 159; Schuylkill Arsenal (Philadelphia, Pa.), 1, 20, 144–46; South Park (Chicago, Ill.), 525–27; Thomas Circle (Washington, D.C.), 20; Thomas Crane Public Library (Quincy, Mass.), 566; University of California (Berkeley), 52; Barthold Schlesinger estate (Brookline, Mass.), 19, 464–71, 535–37, 538; William Windom residence. *See also* Arnold Arboretum; Back Bay Fens; Baltimore, Md., Washington Monument, squares for; Buffalo, N.Y., Delaware Park (The Park); Central Park (N.Y.C.); Commonwealth Avenue (Boston, Mass.); Delaware Park (The Park) (Buffalo, N.Y.); Mount Royal (Montreal, Quebec, Canada); Muddy River Improvement (Boston and Brookline, Mass.); New York State (New) Capitol; Niagara Reservation (N.Y.); Point Chautauqua community (Lake Chautauqua, N.Y.); Riverside Park and Avenue (N.Y.C.); Rockaway Point, N.Y.; Tompkins Square (N.Y.C.); Twenty-third and Twenty-fourth wards (N.Y.C.); U.S. Capitol grounds; University of California; West Roxbury Park (Franklin Park) (Boston, Mass.)

——landscape design theory; on design competitions, 296, 297–98, 303, 363–65; on mixture of architectural styles, 316; on prevention of malaria, 263, 265, 575; on pursuit of single leading purpose, 510–11; on residential community design, 555–56; and scale, 46; in semiarid regions, 50–51, 52; on urban streams, 520

——political views and activities: Civil Service reform, 638–40; political activities of, 160; on Presidential election of 1876, 276, 279

——relations of, with: Édouard André, 327, 393–95, 650; Henry Attrill, 397, 418–19; Henry W. Bellows, 433–35; Boston Park commissioners, 192–93; Central Park commissioners, 640; Edward Clark, 69–70, 106, 370–71, 392, 512–13; clients, 469, 471; Charles H. Dalton, 10, 192–93, 197, 365, 489; DPP commissioners, 606–7, 624–25, 643, 646; Leopold Eidlitz, 184, 200, 204–5, 280, 289; Thomas C. Fields, 714; Thomas Fuller, 200, 284, 293, 298; Howard A. Martin, 706; William R. Martin, 5, 21, 677, 697; Justin S. Morrill, 33, 40, 54, 72; Charles Eliot Norton, 185, 188, 284, 300–301; Frederick Law Olmsted, Jr., 138–39, 237–42; John C. Olmsted, 1, 332, 333–35; Mary Perkins Olmsted, 5, 330–32, 535; Owen Olmsted, 565; Prospect Park commissioners, 67, 161, 704; Henry Hobson Richardson, 9–10, 184, 200, 204–5, 280, 289; Benjamin Smith, 417–18; Henry G. Stebbins, 5, 680–81; Calvert Vaux, 1, 324–27, 382, 384, 433–36, 626–27, 629; Egbert Viele, 640; Thomas Wisedell, 498–501, 502

——social values and the idea of civilization: art education, 445–46; national character, 547; residential suburbs, 254–58, 265; rowhouses, 17, 18, 439–41, 444

——travels of, 479, 480, 548, 592, 628–29, 649, 650; 1856 and 1859 trips to Europe, 42, 265, 417, 548; 1850 tour, 42, 264–65, 594; 1878 trip to Europe, 335, 362, 365, 367, 373, 384, 417, 625

——writings, 619, 629, 646, 649; "A Consideration of the Justifying Value of a Public Park," 524; "A Healthy Change in the Tone of the Human Heart," 566; "Country Living," 34–35; "Influence," 523–24, 539–47, 547; "Landscape Gardening," *American Encyclopedia*, 137; "Landscape Gardening," *Johnson's New Universal Cyclopaedia*, 350–57; *Mount Royal, Montreal*, 13, 336, 563, 644; "Notes by Mr. Olmsted," *in Special Report of the New York State Survey*, 474–79; "Patronage Journal," 6, 644, 645, 653–704, 705; *Public Parks and the Enlargement of Towns*, 10; "The National Capitol. Mr. Fred. Law Olmsted on the Improvements in Progress" (*New-York Daily Tribune*), 93–97; *The Spoils of the Park*, 6, 372, 586–87, 592, 605–40; *Walks and Talks of an American Farmer in England*, 631

Olmsted, Frederick Law, Jr. (1870–1957) (Henry Perkins Olmsted) (son), 139, 242, 281, 335, 337; and pet dog Quiz, 138–39; relations with FLO, 138–39, 237–42

Olmsted, Henry Perkins. *See* Olmsted, Frederick Law, Jr.

Olmsted, John Charles (1852–1920) (nephew, stepson), 329, 331, 471, 501, 507, 562–63, 564; relations with FLO, 1, 332, 333–35

Olmsted, Marion (1861–1968) (daughter), 332, 335, 337

Olmsted, Mary Perkins (Mrs. Frederick Law) (1830–1921) (sister-in-law, wife), 5, 335, 436; relations with, 330–32, 335

Olmsted, Owen (1857–1881) (stepson), 281, 329–31, 384, 435–36, 562–63, 564, 565

Olmsted, Vaux & Company, 1, 3, 116, 155, 416, 423, 444

Ontario, Canada, 420–21; Council of, 421, 424–25

Paris, France, 249, 256, 263, 265; Avenue de L'Imperatrice in, 199; Exposition Universelle, 417

Park Defence Association (N.Y.C.), 611

Parkman, Francis, 446

Parks and Public spaces: approaches to, 195; attractions of, 221; carriages in, 86; chief elements of, 84–85; choice of place names in, 304–5; early designs of, 221; impact of neglect in, 631–32; management of, 236, 237, 304, 585–86, 587, 626–27, 637–40; park commissions for, 13; process of planning of, 572–73; promenades in, 164–67; purpose of, 44, 76, 322–23; regulations for use of, 322–23; sites for, 84, 567–68; and use by

Parks and Public spaces (*cont.*)
invalids, 85, 216; value of, 236, 322–23. *See also names of individual parks and public spaces*
—— in the British Isles, 334, 337; Birmingham Botanic Garden, 334; Burnham Beeches (Buckinghamshire), 336; Derby Arboretum, 337; Glasnevin Horticultural Garden (Ireland), 334, 336; Hyde Park (London), 255, 265, 620, 630; Phoenix Park (Dublin), 334, 336; Regent's Park (London), 195; St. James's Park (London), 484
—— in Europe: Parc des Buttes-Chaumont (Paris), 631; Parc Monceau (Paris), 484
Parsons, Samuel, Jr. (1844–1923), 593–94, 641–42, 643
Parsons, Samuel, Sr. (d. 1907), 594
Partridge, John A., 71, 72, 148, 576
Pavia, Certosa di, 184, 187
Peabody, George, 276
Peabody, Robert Swain, 496
Pendleton, George Hunt, 548
Perry, John L., 58
Philadelphia, Pa., 145; Centennial Exposition in, 417. *See also* Schuykill Arsenal (Philadelphia, Pa.)
Phillips, Anna Tucker, 507
Phillips, John Charles (1838–1885), 496, 591
—— estate of, 492–96, 504–6, 506, 549–53, *551*, 552, 554, 590–91, 592; FLO visit to property, 496, 549, 553; forest on, 590–91, 592; garden at, 506; lawn area of, 592; pavilion at, 492, 494, 506; plans for, *493*, *494*, *495*, *505*; plantings on, 591; terrace of, 492–95, 504, 552, 554; "wild garden" at, 494
Phipps, Frederick A., 419
Picton, W. J., 204, 206, 208
Platt, James Henry, 66
Poggi, Giuseppe, 250
Point Chautauqua (community) (Lake Chautauqua, N.Y.), plan for, 18, 156, 179, *180–81*, 182
Poppey, Frederick William, 116, 117
Porter, Fitz-John, 712
Post, George B., 8
Potter, Edward T., 250
Potter, Howard (1826–1897), 416, 444, 563–64, 565, 593

Potter, William A., 560
Price, Uvedale, 394, 559–60, 588; on the Picturesque, 589
Promenades, planning of, 165
Prospect Park (Brooklyn, N.Y.), 87, 116, 417, 712–13; Long Meadow, drainage of, 163; Board of Commissioners of Prospect Park, turf usage and, 161, 163
Providence, R.I., 691
Public buildings, grounds of, 357; City Hall, Buffalo, N.Y., 170–71, 174; on Mall, Washington, D.C., 36–40. *See also* U.S. Capitol Grounds
Pückler-Muskau, Hermann Ludwig Heinrich von, 589
Pulsifer, Royal Macintosh, 490
Purdy, Ambrose H., 720
Pynchon, Thomas Ruggles, 131–32

Radford, George Kent, 1, 20, 71, 72, 131, 132, 146, 148, 203, 502
Railroad Strikes of 1877, 329–30
Raymond, Henry, 162
Rayner, Dr. Henry, 594
Reid, Whitelaw, 92, 99, 288, 384
Renwick, James, Jr. (1818–1895), 284–85, 444
Repton, Humphry, 332, 337, 588, 589
Residential crescent housing: in Europe, 254–55; in NYC, 264
Residential grounds, 34–35, 350–57
Residential grounds, and health, 357
Resorts (England), 255, 264
Rhode Island (resorts of), 403, 416
Richardson, Henry Hobson (1838–1886), 11, 289, 296–97, 303–4, 327, 331, 387, 424, 479, 566; and Boston parks, 365; and Boylston Street Bridge, 449, 450; and New York State New Capitol, 1, 115, 184, 186, 199–200, 201, 204–5, 281, 299, 302, 317; and Niagara Square, Buffalo, 103, 303; relations with FLO, 9–10; and Trinity Church, Boston, 279, 285, 303
Riverside Park and Avenue (N.Y.C.), 108–9, 112, 361, 383, 648, 690, 699, 702, 707, 719; 1867 act for, 112; Common Council and, 114; DPP adopts plan for, 114; FLO's plan for, *110–11*, *169*, 657; grades of, 108, 113; location of, 114; patronage and, 113–14, 658; 1868 plan for, 114; plan to combine park and

752

avenue, 112, 114; pleasure drive in, 109; ravine in, 112, 115
—— Riverside Avenue (N.Y.C.), 108, 167, 377–84; Aldrich's removal from supervision of, 375–76, 385, 386; bill for construction of, 656–58, 662; campaign in state legislature, 377; construction of, 375, 385; contractors and, 378–79, 381, 386; DPP granted authority over, 705; 1873 plan for, 109; FLO's work on, 377; independent engineers investigation of, 375, 380, 381, 385–86; payments to contractors suspended, 375, 385; tunnels of, 376, 385–86
—— Riverside Park (N.Y.C.), 4, 113–14, 127, 220, 386; promenade in, 114, 168
Robinson, John, 650
Robinson, Lucius, 205, 281, 421
Robinson, William (1838–1935), 137, 227, 332–33, 649; *Alpine Flowers for English Gardens*, 475–76, 480, 621–22; on Central Park, 138; *God's Acre Beautiful; or the Cemeteries of the Future*, 137, 150; *Queen Anne's Flowers*, 137–38; *The Wild Garden*, 133, 134, 496
Rockaway Point, N.Y. (resort for): comparison with Coney Island, 397–407, 471–18; description of plans for, 397, 402, 407–12, 419; failure of, 419; Far Rockaway and, 402–3, 416; FLO visits, 397, 415, 419; FLO withdraws from project, 419; hotel for, 417–19; issues of drainage and sewerage, 397–400; plans for, 408, 413, 414; preparation of grounds, 398–400; provision for day visitors to, 405–7; as a refuge from "malarial conditions," 400; unfavorable circumstances of, 397–98
Rockwell, Alfred Perkins, 449
Rodgers, John F., 146
Rogers, William Findlay, 423–24
Roger Williams Park (Providence, R.I.), 524
Rollins, Edward Henry, 576
Ruskin, John, 421, 471, 472
Ryan, Columbus, 80, 127, 128, 648, 653, 663, 679, 687, 695, 705, 708, 717; resignation of, 710, 713, 717

San Francisco, Calif., 115, 117, 416, 582; Park commission of, 117; plan by William Hammond Hall, 117; proposed rural cemetery association in, 150

The Sanitarian (journal), 250
Saratoga Springs, N.Y., 406, 416; Congress Park, 59; United States Hotel, 56–57, 58
Sargent, Charles Sprague (1841–1927), 69, 334, 335, 394, 395, 489, 496, 507, 517, 592
Sargent, Henry Winthrop, 650
Satsuma (Japan), 354
Schlesinger, Barthold S. (1828–1900), 469; estate of, 464–71, 535–37, 537; plan of, 468, 538; terraces for, 536–37, 538–39
Schlesinger, Mary McBurney, 469, 470
Schoenborn, August, 16
Schofield, Robert P., 712
Schurz, Carl, 4, 305
Schuylkill Arsenal (Philadelphia, Pa.), improvement of, 1, 20, 144–46
Scott, Frank Jessup, 156, 632
Scott, Sir Walter, 49, 559, 561, 610, 644
Sedgwick, Maria Theodora, 285
Sessions, Walter L., 155
Seymour, Horatio, 471, 473
Shaler, Alexander, 222, 287
Shaw, Francis George, 662, 708
Smith, Benjamin E., 415; relations with FLO, 417–18
Smith, H. B., 90, 91
Smith, William R., 54, 148
South Park (Chicago, Ill.), 90, 156, 159, 463, 525–27
Spring Grove Cemetery (Cincinnati, Ohio), 135, 136, 137
Staehlen, W., Jr., 369
Stanley, Edward Henry (Earl of Derby), 498
Staten Island Improvement Commission, 393
St. Botolph Club (Boston, Mass.), 473
Stearns, John Goddard, Jr., 496
Stebbins, Henry G. (1811–1881), 5, 80, 83, 115, 121, 168, 220, 377, 386, 548, 640, 644, 681; concerning statues in Central Park, 48–49; and patronage, 668–70, 672–73, 711; relations with Andrew H. Green, 680–81; relations with William R. Martin, 4, 677–678; and reorganization of the park board, 666–67, 709, 718–19; and Riverdale plan, 266
Stephen, Sir James Fitzjames, 422
Stephens, Benjamin F., 415

Stewart, Thomas Elliott, 114, 121, 128, 667–68, 672, 673–74, 685, 709, 710, 711, 712
Stoneleigh Abbey (Warwickshire), 334
Stout, Francis A., 445, 446
Strauch, Adolph (1822–1883), 135, 136, 137, 138, 149, 150, 632
Street systems:
—— curvilinear, 345–46; advantages of, 260
—— rectilinear, 345–46; disadvantages of, 258, 259–60
Sturgis, John Hubbard, 650
Sturgis, Russell, 278, 280
Stuyvesant Park (N.Y.C.), 222
"Succotash" (railroad engine), 237–42
Sumner, Charles, 98
Sweeny, Peter B., 49, 168, 714

Tammany Hall, 677, 681–82, 694–95, 707; and presidential campaign, 670, 710
Thornton, William, 42
Thurber, George, 394, 395, 609
Tiffany & Co., 431, 432
Tilden, Samuel, 277–78, 279, 280, 593–94, 710, 716, 718
Tompkins, Hiram, 58
Tompkins Square (N.Y.C.), 214; abuse of trees and turf in, 212; arbor in, 210, 217–18, 219, 276; architectural features in, 212, 213, 217–18, 222; cost of, 215, 219–20; early condition of, 211–12; improvements of, 210–11, 212, 221–22; and invalids, 217; mothers' plea for park, 213; parade ground in, 212–13, 215–16, 221, 287, 417; site of, 211, 220; turf of, 211–12; uses of, 215–16; water features of, 218–19; work stoppage on, 223, 700, 719
Tracy (Tracey), Daniel, 662, 664, 708
Trees: monoculture street planting of, 515; planting and transplanting of, 67, 147; sanitary value of, 263, 265, 390, 392, 393, 396, 575
Trinity Church (Boston, Mass.), 279, 281
Trinity College (Hartford, Conn.), 16–17, 129–31, 132; positioning of the campus, 131; residential lots and, 132
Troup, George, 233
Tweed Ring (N.Y.C.), 3–4, 80, 81, 361, 544, 642, 647, 651, 714
Twenty-third and Twenty-fourth wards,

(N.Y.C.), 17, 242–48, 342, 362, 374, 720; Bronx park in, 362; part of Westchester County annexed to N.Y.C. for, 83; plans by J. J. R. Croes and FLO for, 247–48, 249, 261, 309, 341; Railroad avenue in, 344–45; rapid transit system of, 306–12, 309; as site for arboretum, 360; as site for permanent residential quarter, 17; street arrangement of, 247, 251, 257–62, 340, 342–43, 345–46, 348, 385; surveyors' monuments in, 665; topography of, 247–48; Village of Morrisania in, 344, 345–47, 349
—— Central District of, 248, 340–47; business sections of, 340, 342; parks for, 346–47, 348–49; parkways for, 349–50; rapid transit system for, 343–44, 349; rapid transit system for, grade separation in, 306–7, 312; residences of, 342–43; sidewalks of, 342, 348; street system of, 340, 342–43, 345–46, 348, 385
—— Riverdale, 266; by-roads in, 266; housing in, 253, 258; as a permanent residential suburban quarter, 254–63, 265; pleasure drive in, 256; previous plans for, 251–53, 263–64; roadside planting, 262–63; street system for, 251, 257–62; terrace (crescent) housing in, 264; topography of, 252–53, 255, 260

University of California (Berkeley, Calif.): comparison of Olmsted and Hall plans for, site of, 50–51, 52; Olmsted declines to submit plans for, 52
Upjohn, Richard Michell (1828–1903), 204, 250, 302
Urbino, Ducal Palace in, 185, 187
U.S. Botanical Garden (Washington, D.C.), 53, 54, 392
U.S. Capitol grounds, 14–16, 53, 54, 62, 66, 67, 72, 370, 507–8, 557, 575; approaches to, 64, 66, 67, 68, 93, 96, 148; architectural features of, 66, 67–68, 97, 99; circulation system of, 99; Congress approves FLO's plan, 107; esplanade stonework of, 99; FLO's description of, 93–97; FLO's position at, 500–501, 502; FLO visits to Washington for, 54, 69–70, 92, 106, 107, 199, 335, 368, 371, 397, 514; funding for, 40, 67, 72, 108; grading of, 40, 43, 69–70, 72, 94, 96; improvement of, 36–40, 40–43, 54, 64,

96–97, 99; and labor force, wages of, 70–71, 72; malaria and, 576; management of, 38, 53; map of proposed belt of woods, *391*; *New-York Times* account of, 92; plan of, *65*, *95*; policing of, 369–71, 512–13, 514; protection of, from malaria, 390, 392–93, 575; purpose of design of, 96; role of, in shaping taste of the nation, 92; sidewalks of, 15, 276; site of, 93, 98; subordination to the building, 15, 96–97; terraces of, polychrome pavement for, 15; theft of plants on, 371, 513; tree planting on, to prevent malaria, 575; vandalism to, 370–71; watchmen and, 369–70; work begun on, 94. *See also* U.S. Capitol; terraces
—— landscape features of; grounds, treatment of, 15, 94, 96, 146–48; trees, before improvement, 93–94; tree thinning and removal on, 67, 98
—— Summer House on, 16, 222, 431, 432, 507–8, 509, 533, 534; carillon for, 431, 432; misuse of, 513; opposition to, 509; purpose of, 507–8; as "subterranean grotto," 533

U.S. Capitol (Washington, D.C.), 39, 97, *104*, *105*, 578; construction of, 42, 560; East Front extension of, 106, 107; fronts of, 38–39, 43, 64; West Front extension of, 106, 107
—— terraces of, 39, 39–40, 42, 66, 67–68, 99, 103, *104*, *105*, 106, 557–59, 578, *581*; appropriations for, 583; basement floor plan of, *580*; cost of, 107, 561; FLO's proposals for, 14–15, 16, 106, 107, 509, 557–59, 560, 577–79, *582*; plantings on, 579, 583; two-level arrangement of, 577–79; for West Front, 67–68, 106; winter garden in, 577, 583

U.S. Sanitary Commission, history of, 433–34

U.S. Senate Committee on Public Buildings and Grounds, 40, 43, 62, 576; approves FLO's terrace plan, 107; revised proposal to, 99, 106–7

Van Nort, George M., 84, 115, 658, 662, 664, 707–8
Vaux, C. Bowyer, 436
Vaux, Calvert (1824–1895), 9, 51, 54, 90, 113, 128, 156, 161, 186, 228, 230, 264, 416, 628; American Museum of Natural History and, 443; assists FLO on designs for Riverside and Morningside parks, 49; attempt to regain position with DPP, 6, 593–94, 641, 643; and Buffalo park system, 103, 186, 230; and Buffalo State Asylum, 174; Central Park and, 49, 81, 161, 163, 166, 361, 433–36, 643, 647, 648; and Chicago South Park, 463, 527–28; collaboration with Frederic Church, 128; and colossal statue proposal for Central Park, 48–49; commissions of, 21; and CP design competition, 364–65, 717; and "entente" concerning CP, 593–94; and Greensward plan, 49, 325, 626, 650, 651, 717; journalistic criticism of, 629–30; and Metropolitan Museum of Art, 48–49, 443; and Niagara Reservation, 479; and Olmsted's dismissal from N.Y. Parks Department, 434–35; position with DPP, 641–42; and promenade designs for Central and Riverside parks, 166, 168; and Prospect Park, 423, 449; and relations with A. J. Downing, 649; and relations with the DPP board, 605–6; and Riverside Park and Avenue design, 113–14, 168, 386; and role in partnership with FLO, 1, 324–27, 382, 384, 433–36, 626–27, 629; and statuary, 48–49
Vaux, Withers & Company, 116, 303, 326, 327, 501
Viele, Egbert, 640, 694, 717
Vienna, Austria, 249
Villa suburbs, in Europe, 255–56

Wales, Salem (1825–1902), 49, 80, 128, 377, 606, 609, 610, 631–32, 634, 641, 642, 643–45, 646, 658, 673; and criticism of DPP, 612–13, 621, 641; and reorganization of DPP board, 615, 666–67; and resignation from DPP, 644, 709
Walter, Thomas U. (1804–1887), 42, 106–7, 392, 560
Ward, J. Q. A., 303–4
Waring, George E., Jr., 1, 182, 470, 650
Warner, Andrew Jackson, 174
Warren, Joseph, 718
Washington, D.C.: Board of Public Works in, 42; canal district of, 37, 42; Capitol Hill and, 98; House of Delegates, 72; Lafayette Square in, 41; malaria and, 576; Parking Commission, 40, 42, 576;

Washington, D.C. (*cont.*)
  public grounds improvement of, 36–40, 40–43; Reservation 17 in, 392, 393, 396, 576; Reservation 17, street plan for, 396; Smithsonian Institution, grounds of, 649; "Swamppoodle" area in, 41; tobacco plantations in, 98; treatment of buildings on, 36–39, 41. *See also* U.S. Capitol grounds
  —— Mall in, 38, 41–42; botanical gardens on, 54–66; grounds of governmental institutions on, 53–54; Olmsted's proposals for, 53
  —— public buildings in, 36–37, 41, 53, 54; need for "federal bond" between, 37–38
Washington Square (N.Y.C.), 211, 212, 221
Waterer, Anthony, Sr., 334, 336
Watson, John H., 497, 554
Weidenmann, Jacob (1829–1893), 1, 58–59, 146, 150, 182, 266, 594, 632
Welch, Thomas V., 479
West Roxbury Park (Franklin Park) (Boston, Mass.), 198, 529, 531, 567–69; and Elm Hill property, 193, 195; land to be de-accessioned, 530; plans for, 529, 531, 570; site of, 193, 195, 528–31

West Side Association (N.Y.C.), 644, 706–7
Wetmore, William Courtney, 220, 344, 697, 718
Whitney, Solon Miron Napoleon, 504
Whittier, John Greenleaf, 421
Wickham, William H., 114, 220, 710, 715
Williamson, David B., 121, 128, 668, 706, 710
Wilson, James Grant, 323
Wisedell, Thomas (1846–1884), 68, 71, 72–73, 192, 327, 335, 436, 499, 502; and Buffalo City Hall, 174; and New York State New Capitol, 8; relations with FLO, 498–501, 502; and Schuylkill Arsenal, 145–46; and U.S. Capitol Grounds, 68, 106, 107, 222, 335, 337, 392, 432, 501–2, 509, 582; and Washington Monument squares, Baltimore, 276, 367–68
Wolf, John, 691–92, 717
Wood, Daniel P., 657
Woodlawn Cemetery (N.Y.C.), 348
Worcester (England), 334, 336
Wren, Sir Christopher, 184, 186